Blackstone's

Handbook for Policing Students

Blackstone's

Handbook for Policing Students

Eighteenth Edition

Edited by

Dr Dominic Wood,
Professor Sarah Bradshaw,
Dr Tara Dickens,
and
Dr Julian Parker-McLeod,
with
Christina Davis

Contributors:

Jessica Bombasaro-Brady, Dr Erika Brady, Paula Bradbury, Professor Robin Bryant, Scott Clarke, Professor Karen Duke, Stewart Frost, Dr Paul Gilbert, Dr Sofia Graca, Dr Katja Hallenberg, Barbara Hillier, Richard Honess, Graham Hooper, Anjali Howard, Gary Jones, Dina Kapardis, Dr Susanne Knabe-Nicol, Kevin Lawton-Barrett, Dr Vincent Leonard, Dr David Lydon, Dr Elena Martellozzo, Susanna Mitchell, Jack Moss, Dr Katarina Mozova, Jennifer Norman, Paul Norman, Dr James Nunn, Dr Martin O'Neill, Claire Smith, Dr Paul Stephens, Vince Straine-Francis, Dr Paul Swallow, Helen Sykes, and Steve Woliter

Great Clarendon Street, Oxford, OX2 6DP,
United Kingdom

Oxford University Press is a department of the University of Oxford.
It furthers the University's objective of excellence in research, scholarship,
and education by publishing worldwide. Oxford is a registered trade mark of
Oxford University Press in the UK and in certain other countries

First Edition published in 2006
Eighteenth Edition published in 2024

Published in the United States of America by Oxford University Press
198 Madison Avenue, New York, NY 10016, United States of America

British Library Cataloguing in Publication Data
Data available

Library of Congress Control Number: 2023948495

ISBN 978–0–19–889493–3

DOI: 10.1093/law/9780198894933.001.0001

Printed in the UK by
Bell & Bain Ltd., Glasgow

Contents

Part II Core Policing Values and Behaviours

Part III Core Aspects of Police Work

About the Authors

Jessica Bombasaro-Brady

Jessica Bombasaro-Brady is Senior Lecturer and Course Director of BSc Policing and Applied Security Studies at Canterbury Christ Church University.

Paula Bradbury

Paula Bradbury is a Senior Researcher at the Centre for Abuse and Trauma Studies (CATS) and a Criminology lecturer at Middlesex University.

Dr Erika Brady

Dr Erika Brady is a Senior Lecturer at Canterbury Christ Church University.

Professor Robin Bryant

Professor Robin Bryant is at Canterbury Christ Church University.

Scott Clarke

Scott Clarke is the Policing Education Qualification Framework Deputy Director at Canterbury Christ Church University and the Police Education Consortium.

Professor Karen Duke

Professor Karen Duke is Professor of Criminology at Middlesex University.

Stewart Frost

Stewart Frost is Senior Lecturer in Policing Practice within the Policing Team at Middlesex University.

Dr Paul Gilbert

Dr Paul Gilbert is a lecturer within the policing team at Canterbury Christ Church University and also works at Queen's University, Belfast.

Dr Sofia Graca

Dr Sofia Graca is a Principal Lecturer within the School of Law, Policing and Social Sciences at Canterbury Christ Church University.

Dr Katja Hallenberg

Dr Katja Hallenberg is a Principal Lecturer and Deputy Director of Policing at Canterbury Christ Church University.

Barbara Hillier

Barbara Hillier is a Teaching Fellow in Policing at the University of Portsmouth.

Richard Honess

Richard Honess is a Senior Lecturer in Policing on the PCDA and DHEP programmes at Canterbury Christ Church University.

Graham Hooper

Graham Hooper is the Head of Innovation at Kent Police.

Anjali Howard

Anjali Howard is a Detective Inspector with Kent Police working in Central Safeguarding.

Gary Jones

Gary Jones is a Senior Lecturer on the PCDA programme at Canterbury Christ Church University.

Dina Kapardis

Dina Kapardis is a lecturer in Law & Criminal Justice at the University of Portsmouth.

Dr Susanne Knabe-Nicol

Dr Susanne Knabe-Nicol is a lecturer at the School of Law, and programme leader for the BSc Criminology (Policing & Investigations) at the University of Middlesex.

Kevin Lawton-Barrett

Kevin Lawton-Barrett is Senior Lecturer in Forensic Investigation at Canterbury Christ Church University.

Dr Vince Leonard

Dr Vince Leonard is a Training Consultant at Zoodart Consultancy.

Dr David Lydon

Dr David Lydon is Senior Lecturer in Professional Policing and Course Director—PhD by Portfolio at Canterbury Christ Church University.

Dr Elena Martellozzo

Dr Elena Martellozzo is an Associate Professor in Criminology and Associate Director of the Centre for Abuse and Trauma Studies (CATS) at Middlesex University.

Susanna Mitchell

Susanna Mitchell is a Senior Crown Prosecutor for the Crown Prosecution Service and lectures at Canterbury Christ Church University.

Jack Moss

Jack Moss is an Associate Lecturer in Policing at the University of Middlesex.

Dr Katarina Mozova

Dr Katarina Mozova is Senior Lecturer in Policing at Canterbury Christ Church University.

Jennifer Norman

Jennifer Norman is the Head of Policing at the Open University.

Paul Norman

Paul Norman is a Specialist Crime Trainer with Kent Police.

Dr James Nunn

Dr James Nunn is a Senior Lecturer in Police Practice at Brunel University.

Dr Martin O'Neill

Dr Martin O'Neill is Director of the Canterbury Centre for Policing Research at Canterbury Christ Church University.

Claire Smith

Claire Smith is a Teaching Fellow in Policing at the University of Portsmouth.

Dr Paul Stephens

Dr Paul Stephens is the Director of Academic Studies in Law, Policing & Social Sciences, and Principal Lecturer in Cybercrime & Digital Policing at Canterbury Christ Church University.

Vince Straine-Francis

Vince Straine-Francis is a lecturer in Policing at Anglia Ruskin and Christ Church Canterbury University.

Dr Paul Swallow

Dr Paul Swallow is Senior Lecturer in International Policing and Counter Terrorism at Canterbury Christ Church University.

Helen Sykes

Helen Sykes is a lecturer in Policing at Canterbury Christ Church University.

Steve Woliter

Steve Woliter is Senior Lecturer and Course Leader for the PCDA at the University of Portsmouth.

Table of Cases

Table of Legislation

United Kingdom

EU Legislation

Directives

Regulations

Table of International Instruments

Table of Secondary Legislation

Table of Statutory Instruments

Table of Codes of Practice

Table of Circulars

Introduction

This is the eighteenth edition of *Blackstone's Handbook for Policing Students* and much has happened since the last edition. The UK has a new monarch, with King Charles III replacing Queen Elizabeth II who had reigned for 70 years. The monarch is an important figure in British Policing and the loss of Her Majesty Queen Elizabeth II will have been felt deeply across the policing communities. The scale of the police operation for King Charles III's coronation on 6 May 2023, *Operation Golden Orb*, demonstrated the capacity of the British police to support such grand, large scale public events, with the ceremony attended by over 100 heads of state from around the world. However, the controversy surrounding the security operations, in particular what has been seen as inappropriate use of measures introduced in the Public Order Act 2023, which itself only came into force on 2 May 2023, demonstrates the complexities surrounding contemporary policing and the challenges police face in ensuring policing continues to be legitimate and consensual.

The authors of the Handbook have taken care to ensure the accuracy of the information contained within. However, neither the authors nor the publisher can accept any responsibility for any actions taken, or not taken, as a consequence of the information it contains. We would be grateful for feedback on the new Handbook, and for the identification of errors. Please email police.uk@OUP.com with your comments or queries.

Please note that references in the Handbook to College of Policing materials (including Authorised Professional Practice and other forms of guidance) have not been reviewed or endorsed by the College of Policing.

1 Introducing the Handbook

1.1 Introduction

In this chapter we provide you with guidance about how to use the Handbook, and some background information and advice on studying policing. We are familiar with the wide range of experiences that learners (either on pre-join programmes at a college, university, or private training provider, or as trainee police officers) bring to their education and training, and the Handbook has been written and set out to be both accessible and of value to all our readers.

We also provide a glossary in 1.3, which is likely to be useful to learners on 'pre-join' policing programmes and during initial training as a student police officer. Policing, like most areas of professional life, is full of acronyms and jargon. There will be times when you feel that the people around you are speaking a different language; you will not want to ask what this or that means, and the glossary will hopefully provide an answer.

1.2 The Handbook as a Survival Guide

The Handbook is designed to support people new to policing, who are studying on a policing degree and/or undertaking initial police training. For example, to help you to learn more effectively, we have omitted some of the more detailed aspects of the law and police procedure, and instead provided a simplified version that shows the key points. Of course, this does not mean that the detail is not important; it is just that learning is usually easier when moving from the simple to the complex, so we start you off with the simple. In the case of the law, the full complexity will normally be introduced and explained to you by your tutors and trainers using a variety of teaching and learning methods.

Importantly, you will also need to look beyond the Handbook at times. There are constant changes in society that you need to be aware of. These may be subtle changes in societal sensibilities; for example, the #MeToo and #BlackLivesMatter movements have both had a profound influence on how people see the world and provide important contexts to contemporary policing in the UK. They are dynamic movements and this requires police officers to keep abreast of issues that change people's perceptions in nuanced ways. The legitimacy of the police is largely driven by perceptions.

There are a number of notable changes since the last edition of this Handbook. Firstly, Her Majesty Queen Elizabeth II passed away and her 70 year reign came to an end shortly after the Platinum Jubilee celebrations in 2022. The coronation of the new monarch, King Charles III, took place on 6 May 2023. These events were not only highly emotional for many across the UK and beyond, but also have more mundane consequences regarding royal insignia and other monarchical references in policing and related areas. For example, the attestation is amended accordingly.

There are also two pieces of legislation that have been introduced since the last edition of the Handbook worthy of note here. Firstly, the Police, Crime, Sentencing and Courts Act 2022 came into force on 8 November 2022, with amendments affecting legislation and an array of criminal justice aspects. The second is the Public Order Act 2023, which came into force on 2 May 2023, just days before the King's Coronation. Both Acts are cited in and across various chapters in this edition of the Handbook.

Finally, by way of introduction, it is important to note the publication of Baroness Casey's Final Report in March 2023, following the independent review that she led into the standards of behaviour and internal culture of the Metropolitan Police Service (Casey, 2023). The Report is highly critical of the MPS and it has provided a spotlight on the shortcomings of that particular police service, the largest by some margin in the UK. However, the Report will also no doubt have significant ramifications for policing more generally over the coming years. The integrity of the MPS is questioned in the Report, which also found 'systemic and fundamental problems in how the Met is run'. Baroness Casey also highlighted examples of 'institutional racism, misogyny and homophobia' and stressed ways in which women and children are being let down by the MPS. She sums up the attitude in the MPS as excessively hubristic and lacking humility.

The recommendations in the Report focus on measures to clean up the MPS and to rebuild trust in the communities served by the MPS, with a particular focus on the service to woman and children, and also to Black, ethnic minority and LGBT+ communities. The sense of urgency and significance of the Report's findings are demonstrated by the consideration of structural reforms to the MPS if substantial improvements are not evident in subsequent, follow-up reviews.

The police have always needed to be dynamic and responsive to changes, and to be able to adapt to significant societal challenges, and in the wake of the Casey Report, this has never been more apparent and necessary.

The style of the Handbook represents a judgement concerning the best ways of introducing and describing a subject area. For many aspects of the law we have adopted a bite-size approach for legislation and police practice. We have simplified and condensed the topics into relatively short sections of text and diagrams, each dealing with a particular topic.

We have also made some changes to the structure in this edition and introduced new chapters to better reflect and complement the College of Policing's Curriculum. The contents page should help you navigate your way around the book, and if there is something specific that you are looking for, try the index at the end of the Handbook, which alphabetically lists topics/subjects/aspects of policing etc.

We have deliberately kept the volume of referencing in this Handbook to a minimum, generally restricting it to where the source of the ideas and information might be useful. Referencing sources is a common courtesy to those authors whose work we have utilized, and respects the intellectual property rights of others, but we have minimized it to make the Handbook more accessible to a wider range of readers: in this way, the flow is not disturbed by frequent references to other material.

We also indicate where further reading might be useful. You will find more detail and further explanation in your university library, including electronic resources, and in your College of Policing notes, if you are on an approved pre-join programme, the PCDA, or DHEP.

The College of Policing website also has links to learning materials and best practice that will be of use during your studies and professional development (see in particular the College's Authorised Professional Practice (APP) and *What Works* web pages). We frequently state that further information, or the source of the underpinning material we have utilized, is available 'online'. The usual search techniques, using web-based search engines such as Google, should provide the relevant hypertext links.

1.2.1 Extracts from legislation, circulars, and codes

Throughout the Handbook, there are numerous extracts from primary legislation or codes—often from Acts of Parliament. These are quoted in their original form but sometimes with minor changes to make the meaning clearer. Often an explanation in everyday language is also given, normally in a text box to the right of the original legislation. Quotations are signified by the use of a different font (or quotation marks), while explanations and comments are in ordinary text, like this:

if when not at their place of abode.

The term 'place of abode' means the place or site where someone lives. It normally includes the garage and garden of a house and should be given its normal meaning, but it will be a question of fact for the court to decide. If a homeless person sleeps in their car, the car counts as an abode while they are asleep. However, when the same car is being driven by the same person, it is not considered as a place of abode for the purposes of the offence of going equipped (see *R v Bundy* 1977).

When changes have been made to the original, this is usually because legislation tends to use the word 'he' to cover 'all persons'. However, in some legislation, eg for some sexual offences, 'he' really does mean just 'he'. We have de-gendered pronouns where appropriate so 'he' will become, for example, 'they' and 'his' becomes 'their', and so on. We have also occasionally changed a particular word if it helps the sentence make more sense when quoted alone. Minor changes to the wording of legislation or codes in the Handbook are shown in square brackets, as in the following example.

The original, from s 74 of the Sexual Offences Act 2003, states:

> For the purposes of this Part, a person consents if he agrees by choice, and has the freedom and capacity to make that choice.

Our revised version reads:

> For the purposes of this [offence], a person consents if [they] agree by choice, and has the freedom and capacity to make that choice.

As you can see we have changed 'Part' to '[offence]' and 'he' to '[they]'. You will also find the detail of legislation covered in other publications. Most recent legislation is available from the government website <https://www.legislation.gov.uk>. Legislation can be confusing as it may have been subject to amendment and changed by subsequent legislation, for example the definition of a religiously aggravated offence in the Crime and Disorder Act 1998 was subsequently added to by the Anti-terrorism, Crime and Security Act 2001. This added a new subsection 28(5) to the four subsections of the 1998 legislation. The government website at <https://www.legislation.gov.uk> provides 'updated' versions of much (but not all) original legislation.

Further explanation of legislation can be found in sources such as:

- Oxford University Press publications such as *Blackstone's Police Operational Handbook 2022: Law* and the Blackstone's Police Manuals;
- the PNLD website at <https://www.pnld.co.uk/> (note that this is a subscription service unless you have a police.uk email address);
- prosecution guidance from the CPS at <https://www.cps.gov.uk/prosecution-guidance>;
- the 'official' home of UK legislation at <https://www.legislation.gov.uk> (turning on the 'explanatory notes' can be helpful);
- the online legal databases Westlaw (<https://legalresearch.westlaw.co.uk)> and Lawtel (<https://www.lawtel.com)> if you are studying at university or college; and
- subscription policing publications such as *Police Professional*.

1.2.2 Structure of the Handbook

As you might have already discovered through reading the Contents, the Handbook is divided into five parts as follows:

- **Professional Policing in England and Wales**—this section establishes the parameters of professional policing in England and Wales, highlighting key aspects of the police role.
- **Core Policing Values and Behaviours**—this section includes new chapters that address the values and behaviours underpinning the police services today.
- **Core Aspects of Police Work**—this section outlines the seven major areas of police work: response, community policing, intelligence, investigation, digital policing, counter-terrorism, and policing the roads.

- **Processing Policing**—this section outlines different aspects of the processes through which policing is manifested.
- **Specific Aspects of Police Work**—this section outlines a number of different examples of police work.

1.3 Glossary of Terms Used in Policing

You will encounter many acronyms and forms of jargon during your training and thereafter in your police career. The following glossary of terms covers a wide range of the often bewildering words and phrases used within policing. Note that many police services also publish their own glossary of terms.

3 × 5 × 2 A 'three by five by two' intelligence form. The numbers refer to 'qualities' of the intelligence, measured in three categories, using the scales 1 to 5 and A to E, and the letters P or C.

5 × 5 × 5 A 'five by five by five' intelligence report. The numbers refer to a scale that is used to attempt to measure the reliability of, access to, and other factors about the source providing the intelligence.

16 \+ 1 Reference to the system used to record self-defined (as distinct from officer-defined (see IC1)) ethnicity: eg A1 is used for Indians.

ABC (1) Acceptable Behaviour Contract; (2) Activity-Based Costing, a finance/budgeting methodology that enables costs of an activity to be calculated (as opposed to a value which can only be assessed).

ABE ('A-B-E') Achieving Best Evidence, guidance on interviewing victims and witnesses, and using 'special measures' (qv), usually employed in more serious crimes such as rape.

ABH Assault resulting in actual bodily harm.

ACC Assistant chief constable; a senior police officer command rank (see 3.2.2).

ACE Adverse Childhood Experience

Active defence A proactive approach to defence which involves a rigorous examination of police investigation procedures and the prosecution case; the title of an influential book by Roger Ede and Eric Shepherd.

Ad hoc A Latin phrase meaning 'for this special purpose', which has come to mean 'off the cuff' or 'unrehearsed'.

ADVOKATE ('advokate') Mnemonic used in police training to assist the recollection of the so-called 'Turnbull' rules for witness recall.

AFO ('A-F-O') Authorized Firearms Officer.

Airwave The digital national police radio communication system.

AirwaveSpeak A standardized form of communication when using Airwave (qv).

Alpha/Bravo, etc The phonetic alphabet used in police communication

AMHP Approved mental health professional.

ANPR Automatic Number Plate Recognition system.

APCC Association of Police and Crime Commissioners

APACS ('aippax') Association of Payments and Clearing Services.

APEL ('A-P-E-L' or sometimes 'aipell') Accreditation of Prior Experiential Learning.

APL ('A-P-L' or sometimes 'aipull') Accreditation of Prior Learning.

APP ('A-P-P') Authorised Professional Practice.

ARU ('A-R-U') Armed Response Unit.

ARV ('A-R-V') Armed Response Vehicle.

ASB ('A-S-B') Anti-social Behaviour.

ASP ('asp') An informal term for an extendable metal baton (a reference to the US company Armament Systems and Procedures Inc).

Assistant commissioner Senior police rank in the Metropolitan Police, generally considered to be equivalent to a chief constable.

ASU ('A-S-U') Air Support Unit, usually in the form of police helicopters.

Attestation The formal point at which the powers and responsibilities of the office of constable are assumed, accompanied by the swearing of an oath.

AVLS Automatic (or Automated) Vehicle Location System.

Baton A side-handled self-protection weapon carried by uniformed police officers.

Baton round The formal term for a rubber or plastic bullet.

BAWP ('B-A-W-P') British Association for Women in Policing.

BCE Bad-character evidence.

BCS British Crime Survey (now replaced by the Crime Survey for England and Wales).

BCU Basic Command Unit (Area, Division) or sometimes Borough Command Unit (particularly amongst MPS officers).

Biometrics The use of unique human physical characteristics (such as the iris of the eye) as identifiers.

BLS Basic Life Support (part of First Aid training).

BLM Black Lives Matter

BAME Black and Minority Ethnic (groups).

Border Force The UK's law enforcement body responsible for immigration and customs control.

BPA Black Police Association.

BTP British Transport Police.

BWC Body-Worn Camera (qv BWV).

BWV Body-Worn Video.

Byford Report A review by Sir Lawrence Byford on the police investigation into the 'Yorkshire Ripper' (Peter Sutcliffe) murders between 1975 and 1981; the report was instrumental in the establishment of HOLMES (qv).

CAP ('C-A-P' or 'cap') Common Approach Path.

CAR (often 'car') Cumulative Assessment Record.

Cat A/B/C murders ('Cat A', etc) Categories of homicide.

CBO Criminal Behaviour Order.

CBRN Chemical, Biological, Radiological, or Nuclear (hazard, etc).

CCR Contact and Control Room.

CCTV Closed-Circuit Television.

CCU Computer Crime Unit.

CDI Crime data integrity, a general term referring to the accuracy of a police service's crime recording, according to national (crime) counting rules set by the Home Office.

CDRP Crime and Disorder Reduction Partnership.

CEOP ('see-op') Child Exploitation and Online Protection Centre.

CEPOL ('seepol') European Police College.

Cf Latin for 'compare'.

Chief officer A police officer with the rank of assistant chief constable and above: command rank.

CHIS ('chiss') Covert Human Intelligence Source (informant).

Child sexual abuse The collective term used to describe any form of sexual abuse of children and young persons both historically and in the present day. CSA is now a major priority for police services.

CI ('C-I') (1) Cognitive Interview; (2) Cell Intervention.

CIAPOAR ('see-a-poor') Mnemonic for factors to remember when making decisions within the NDM (qv); Code of ethics, Information, Assessment, Powers and policy, Options, Actions, and Review.

CID ('C-I-D') Criminal Investigation(s) Department, now replaced in many police services by Specialist Crime Investigations, SCI, or similar.

Civil Nuclear Constabulary A non-Home Office police service that provides security and protection to civil (non-military) nuclear sites in the UK.

CJPOA Criminal Justice and Public Order Act 1994.

CJ(S) A process or unit concerned with Criminal Justice (Systems).

CKP Certificate in Knowledge of Policing (qv).

CLDP Core Leadership Development Programme.

CLO ('C-L-O') Community Liaison Officer.

CLUE2 ('klue-too') A case-tracking data system.

CNC Civil Nuclear Constabulary.

CnC Command and Control system used by a number of police services and other agencies.

College of Policing CoP. The professional body for policing (successor to the NPIA, qv).

Commander Metropolitan and City of London chief police officer rank, equivalent to assistant chief constable in all other forces.

Commissioner Top rank (head of service) in the MPS and the City of London police. The commissioner of the Metropolitan Police is considered to be the most senior police officer in the UK.

Confirmation The final stage of successful initial training, when a student police officer/ trainee is confirmed as a police constable.

Continuity (of evidence); an audited and continuous trail for evidential items from crime scene or suspect to court, to prevent interference or contamination.

CPA (1) Crime Pattern Analysis; (2) Child Protection Agency.

CPIA Criminal Procedure and Investigations Act 1996.

CPN Community Protection Notice.

CPO Crime Prevention Officer.

CPOSA Chief Police Officers' Staff Association.

CPP Crime Prevention Panels.

CPR Cardio-pulmonary resuscitation.

CPS Crown Prosecution Service, the governmental body of qualified lawyers who prosecute criminal cases before the courts.

CRaSH/CRASH Collision recording and data sharing digital system.

Crimelink Crime analysis software used by some analysts, developed by the company 'Precision' Computing Intelligence.

CRO ('C-R-O') (1) Criminal Records Office; (2) Criminal (vernacular).

CROPS ('crops') Covert Rural Observation Posts (or Points).

CSAI Child Sex Abuse Images.

CSI Crime Scene Investigator.

CSM Crime Scene Manager.

CSODS Child Sex Offender Disclosure Scheme.

CSP (1) Communications Service Provider; (2) Community Safety Partnership.

CSU Community Safety Unit.

CT Counter Terrorism.

CT Units Regional (outside London) counter-terrorism units where constabularies collaborate to create additional capability and capacity to tackle terrorism and extremism.

CTM Contact Trace Material.

Custody or custody suite A designated area in a police station (usually close to the cells), where arrested persons are logged and processed.

CW Cannabis Warning.

Cybercrime An all-embracing and somewhat ambiguous term for crimes committed using computers and/or digital networks, or against computer systems.

Dabs Colloquial term for fingerprints.

DC Detective Constable.

DCC Deputy Chief Constable.

DCI Detective Chief Inspector.

DCS Detective Chief Superintendent; command rank.

DDA Disability Discrimination Act 1995.

Deputy assistant commissioner Senior police officer rank in the Metropolitan and City of London police services. Equivalent to deputy chief constable in other police services.

DFU Digital Forensics Unit.

DHEP Degree Holder Entry Programme: a short programme for graduates (in any subject) to fully qualify as a police constable.

DHRs Domestic Homicide Reviews.

DI Detective Inspector.

DIC Drunk in charge (of a person or object).

Diploma in Policing The minimum national qualification for trainee police officers, soon to be replaced.

Disclosure The police and the prosecution provide the defence with certain information and documents which might be pertinent evidence in a criminal case.

DNA Deoxyribonucleic Acid, the genetic material from cells (can be used to obtain a 'genetic fingerprint').

DNA-17 A DNA profiling technique (uses all the DNA areas for SGM\+ and six additional areas).

Doctrine A body of knowledge and procedure concerned with police practice, notably criminal investigation—eg as expressed in the MIM (qv) and the NCPE Volume Crime Investigation Manuals.

DPP Director of Public Prosecutions (also head of the Crown Prosecution Service).

DS Detective Sergeant.

DVCVA Domestic Violence, Crime and Victims Act 2004.

DVLA Driver and Vehicle Licensing Agency.

DVPN Domestic Violence Protection Notice.

DVPO Domestic Violence Protection Order.

EAW European Arrest Warrant.

EBP Evidence-based policing.

ECHR European Convention on Human Rights.

EEK Early Evidence Kit for use after a sexual assault.

EHRC Equality and Human Rights Commission.

Element (within a unit of an NOS (qv)). NOS units are usually divided into two or more elements which describe more precisely a skill or competence.

EPO Emergency Protection Order, used for protecting children from imminent harm.

ERO ('E-R-O') Evidence Review Officer.

ESDA ('ezzder') Electrostatic Detection Apparatus.

ETA ('E-T-A') Estimated time of arrival.

et al Latin for 'and others'.

Europol The European Union law enforcement organization.

FA ('F-A') Forensic Alliance (an independent forensic science laboratory and service).

FAO or FOAS ('F-A-O' or 'F-O-A-S') First Attending Officer/First Officer Attending the Scene/first responder.

FBO Football Banning Order.

FCA Forensic Computer Analyst.

FCC Force Communications (or Control) Centre.

FCP Forward Control Point.

FDR Firearm Discharge Residue.

'Federation' The Police Federation of England and Wales (qv).

Fence Vernacular for a person who buys or exchanges stolen goods.

FERRT Fingerprint Evidence Recovery and Recording Techniques.

FGM Female Genital Mutilation.

FIO Field Intelligence Officer or Financial Intelligence Officer.

FLA Family Law Act 1996.

FLINTS Forensic Linked Intelligence System: a database and comparative analysis system developed by West Midlands Police.

FLO (1) Family Liaison Officer; (2) Forensic Laboratory Officer.

FME Forensic medical examiner.

FMPO Forced Marriage Protection Order.

FMS Force Management Statement. An annual document required of each constabulary by HMICFRS (qv) detailing likely demand over the next four years.

FOI ('F-O-I') Freedom of Information, as in a request under the Freedom of Information Act 2000.

Foundation degree/FD A qualification at higher education level. Foundation degrees in policing often incorporate the NOS (qv) and the Diploma in Policing (qv) units for initial policing.

FPN Fixed Penalty Notice.

FSU (1) Family Support Unit; (2) Firearms Support Unit.

FTS Forensic Telecommunications Services.

Garda Síochána The police service of the Republic of Ireland.

GBH Grievous Bodily Harm; a category of assault.

GMP Greater Manchester Police.

GPA Gay Police Association.

H2H House-to-house (as in conducting enquiries).

Handler Vernacular term for police officer responsible for liaising with and tasking a CHIS (qv).

Handling Taking illegal ownership of stolen or otherwise illegally obtained goods.

HATOS ('hay-toes') Informal term for highways authority traffic officers.

Hearsay A reference to information that is not given directly (orally) to the court, but is somehow second-hand.

HMCPSI His Majesty's Crown Prosecution Service Inspectorate.

HMICFRS His Majesty's Inspectorate of Constabulary Fire & Rescue Services (replaces HMIC). It inspects at BCU (qv) and force levels, and carries out thematic inspections (eg into police training). It also inspects fire and rescue services throughout England & Wales.

HMPS His Majesty's Prison Service.

HMRC His Majesty's Revenue and Customs.

HOLMES, HOLMES2 Home Office Large Major Enquiry System: an information system designed to support large-scale police investigations (eg homicide).

Home Office A government department responsible for policy relating to policing and crime.

Home Secretary The senior government minister responsible for policing and security in England and Wales, including police reform (the Welsh Assembly has some devolved powers for policing in Wales).

HORTies ('hortiz') Police vernacular for the HORT/1 and HORT/2 forms for requiring the production of driving documents.

HOSDB Home Office Scientific Development Branch, was part of NPIA (qv).

Hot spot A geographical location with a high incidence of crime and criminality.

HPDS High Potential Development Scheme for police promotions.

HQ Headquarters.

HRA Human Rights Act 1998.

HSE Health and Safety Executive.

Ibid Latin for 'in the same place'.

IC1, IC2 to IC9 (eg 'I-C-2') A reference to Identity Codes used by police officers to record ethnicity (eg IC1 is White European).

ICIDP Initial Crime Investigators' Development Programme.

ICO Information Commissioner's Office, the regulatory office for data protection and electronic privacy.

ICV Incident Command Vehicle used in situations where public order might be a problem.

IDENT1 ('ident-wun') The national database of fingerprints.

Idents Identifications (vernacular).

IDIOM Information Database for IOM (qv); for tracking and monitoring prolific offenders.

IED ('I-E-D') Improvised Explosive Device (a 'bomb').

IIMARCH ('eye-eye-march') Mnemonic for content of briefings: Information, Intention, Method, Administration, Risk assessment, Communications, Human rights compliance.

IL4SP Initial Learning for the Special Constabulary.

ILP/ILPM ('I-L-P') Intelligence-Led Policing and hence Intelligence-Led Policing Model; sometimes referred to as Intelligence-Based Policing. Also related to Information-Based Policing or Information-Led Policing.

IMPACT A College of Policing (qv) programme to improve police information access and sharing.

IMSC Initial Management of Serious Crime course.

Independent Patrol The ability of a trainee police officer to conduct a police patrol without the constant supervision of a qualified police officer.

Informant A person (often a criminal) who passes intelligence to a source handler: a CHIS (qv).

Institutional racism The idea that institutions can behave in a manner prejudicial to ethnic minorities, through their written and unwritten policies and procedures.

Inter-agency Approaches that involve partnership between several agencies: for example, collaboration with the Probation Service and Social Services. See also CDRP (qv).

Inter alia Latin for 'among other things'.

Interpol International policing organization.

IO Investigating Officer.

IOM Integrated offender management.

IOPC The 'Independent Office for Police Conduct'; deals with serious complaints against the police, and investigates all instances where police officers have used firearms in the course of their duties.

IP ('I-P') Injured Person or Party (often literally the person injured in a crime involving personal violence).

IPLDP (1) Initial Police Learning and Development Programme: the programme for initial police training since 2006; (2) Central Authority Responsible for the implementation and policy direction of IPLDP training programme.

ISA Information Sharing Agreement (between the police and other agencies).

ISO ('I-S-O') Individual Support Order, for a young person aged 10–17 years.

ISVAs Independent Sexual Violence Advisors.

JAPAN *J*ustification, *A*uthorization, *P*roportionality, *A*uditable, and *N*ecessary; a checklist for policing actions.

JBB Joint Branch Board of the Police Federation of England and Wales (qv).

JRFT Job-Related Fitness Test.

KCPO Knife Crime Prevention Orders

KSB *K*nowledge, *S*kills and *B*ehaviours, for trainee police officers.

Latent prints/marks These are invisible until revealed by dusting or other techniques.

Lawrence, Stephen/the Lawrence Inquiry/the Macpherson Inquiry Refers to the death of the Black teenager Stephen Lawrence in 1993, the subsequent investigation conducted by the MPS (qv), and the reports that followed (eg as conducted by Lord Macpherson, 1999).

LCN Low Copy Number; a tiny amount of DNA recovered through advanced scientific processes.

LEA Law Enforcement Agency.

Learning Diary Sometimes kept by trainee police officers as part of the process of reflective learning.

Learning Requirement A set of learning requirements that underpin the IPLDP (qv) curriculum.

Level 1 Local crime signifier (used within NIM (qv)). Illegal possession of a controlled drug is a Level 1 crime.

Level 2 Cross-BCU or cross-service crime signifier (used within NIM (qv)). Dealing in illegal drugs is a Level 2 crime.

Level 3 National or international crime signifier (used within NIM (qv)). Organizing the importing or distribution of illegal drugs is a Level 3 crime.

LGC Laboratory of Government Chemists (service provider for scientific analysis).

LIVESCAN Commercial computerized database and digital system for taking fingerprints.

LOCARD Forensic database system.

Loc cit Latin for 'at the place quoted'.

LPG Legislation, Policy, and Guidelines modules, part of the IPLDP curriculum (qv).

MAPPA ('mapper') Multi-Agency Public Protection Arrangements (part of the joint agency approach to managing violent and sex offenders).

MARAC Multi-agency Risk Assessment Conference.

MASH Multi-agency sharing hub.

MG forms The forms for recording information from investigations; sent to the CPS (qv) for an initial charging decision.

MG11 Witness statement form.

MIM ('mim') Murder Investigation Manual (sometimes called the 'Murder Manual').

Ministry of Justice Government department responsible for probation, criminal law and sentencing.

Minutiae Latin for 'of small parts'; the individuality of a fingerprint or mark through examination of its ridge (qv) characteristics (up to 150 characteristics in a single finger print).

Misper Missing person, or the forms used during an investigation about a missing person.

MO ('M-O') Modus operandi is Latin for a characteristic way of doing something. Often used to refer to a particular way of committing a crime.

MoDP Ministry of Defence Police.

MOPAC Mayor's Office for Policing and Crime (London's equivalent of a police and crime commissioner).

MoPI ('moppy') Management of Police Information.

MOU ('M-O-U') Memorandum of Understanding.

MPS Metropolitan Police Service: London's police service.

MSF Most Similar Force (for comparing police services).

Multi-agency Approaches to crime investigation and reduction that involve partnership between the police and non-police agencies.

NABIS ('nay-biss') National Ballistics Intelligence Service.

NACRO ('nak-roh') National Association for the Care and Resettlement of Offenders.

NB Latin for 'take especial note of'.

NBPA National Black Police Association.

NCA The National Crime Agency, the national law enforcement agency (takes responsibility for some of the work previously undertaken by the NPIA (qv), SOCA (qv), and the CEOP (qv)).

NCDV National Centre for Domestic Violence.

NCLCC National County Lines Coordination Centre.

NCSP National Community Safety Plan.

NDM National Decision Model.

NDNAD National DNA (qv) Database.

NDORS National Driver Offender Re-training Scheme.

NEFPN Non-endorsable Fixed Penalty Notice.

NFA (1) No Further (police or CPS) Action; (2) No Fixed Abode.

NFD National Footwear Database (replaces the NFRC).

NFFID National Firearms Forensic Intelligence Database.

NFIB National Fraud Intelligence Bureau, a central access point for individuals and organizations for suspected cybercrime, overseen by the City of London police.

NFIU National Football Intelligence Unit.

NFLMS National Firearms Licensing Management System: a database containing details of all firearm or shotgun certificate holders (and those in the process of applying for certificates).

NID National Injuries Database. A searchable national database of wounds (mainly victims'), enabling comparisons.

NIE ('N-I-E') National Investigators' Examination.

NIM ('nim' or 'N-I-M') National Intelligence Model, sometimes described as a business model for policing. All police services are required to follow the NIM.

NMAT ('en-mat') National Mutual Aid Telephony, a national call-handling system for use in emergencies.

NMPR National Mobile Phone Register/National Mobile Property Register.

Nominals Vernacular police term for those perceived to be active and often recidivist, high-volume criminals.

Non-Home Office forces Police services that are not one of the 43 county or city-based 'territorial' ones, eg BTP (qv).

NOS National Occupational Standards for policing, developed by Skills for Justice (qv).

NPAS National Police Air Service.

NPB National Policing Board.

NPC National Policing Curriculum.

NPCC National Police Chiefs' Council, established in 2015 with the objective of coordinating operational policing at national levels, replaces ACPO (qv).

NPPF The National Police Promotion Framework, for promotions to sergeant and inspector ranks.

NPT Neighbourhood Policing Team.

NPTC National Police Technology Council.

NSPIS National Strategy for Police Information Systems: a suite of databases and software to support case preparation, command and control, and custody processes.

NSY New Scotland Yard.

NTSU National Technical Services Unit.

NVQ National Vocational Qualification. There are NVQs at Levels 3 and 4 in policing and other law enforcement roles, incorporating the relevant NOS (qv).

OCC Operations and Communications Centre.

OCD Out-of-court disposal (OOCD is also used).

OIC ('O-I-C') Officer in Charge.

OP ('O-P') Observation point for carrying out surveillance.

Op Operation, usually refers to a targeted police operation against a criminal problem, eg 'Op Damocles'. The name does not reflect the nature of the operation.

Op cit Latin for 'see the work cited'.

ORC ('O-R-C' or 'ork') Operational Response Commander.

OST Officer Safety Training.

PAC ('P-A-C' or 'pack') Police Action Checklist. In many forces the satisfactory completion of the PAC is one of the criteria for Independent Patrol Status (qv).

PACE ('pace') Police and Criminal Evidence Act 1984.

PAS ('P-A-S') Police Advisers' (or Advisory) Service.

Passim Latin for 'everywhere', but used in the sense of 'throughout'.

PBE Pocket book entry.

PC or Pc Police constable.

PCC Police and Crime Commissioner.

PCDA Police Constable Degree Apprenticeship.

PCeU Police Central e-Crime Unit, a national resource based at the MPS (qv). It is partly funded by the Home Office (qv).

PCP (1) Police and Crime Panel; (2) Police and Crime Plan.

PCR Postal Charge and Requisition, a formal charge and direction to attend court is issued by post.

PCSCA Police, Crime, Sentencing and Courts Act 2022.

PCSO Police Community Support Officer.

PDP The Professional Development Portfolio is a tool for recording an individual police officer's professional development.

PDPP Pre-join Degree in Professional Policing, see PJDPP.

PDS Police Digital Service.

PDU Professional Development Unit for police employees, including trainee officers.

PEACE ('peace') Mnemonic for an interviewing model used by all UK police: *P*lanning and preparation; *E*ngage and explain; *A*ccount, clarification and challenge; *C*losure; and *E*valuation.

PEEL The acronym for describing the three areas ('pillars') used when inspecting police services: P (police), E (effectiveness), E (efficiency), and L (legitimacy).

PentiP The Penalty Notice Processing system.

PEQF Police Education Qualifications Framework, encompasses all professional qualifications in policing from 2020 onwards.

Phonetic alphabet The system commonly used by the police to communicate letters of the alphabet.

PI ('P-I') Performance Indicator; a type of quantitative measure, used by the Home Office to assess the police service.

PIMS ('pimz') Performance Indicator Management System.

PIP ('pip') 'Professionalising Investigation Programme' at levels 1–4. Level 1 is embedded in the initial police officer training (mapped to the NOS (qv) 2G2, 2H1, and 2H2).

PIRA ('peer-rah') Provisional Irish Republican Army, a proscribed terrorist group.

PJDPP Pre-join Degree in Professional Policing: a policing degree after which the student is eligible to apply to a constabulary for a police officer post (also known as PDPP).

PLO ('P-L-O') Prison Liaison Officer (a police officer).

PM Post mortem examination.

PNAC (sometimes 'p-nack') Police National Assessment Centre for superintendents and chief superintendents who aspire to chief officer (qv) ranks (also called 'Senior PNAC').

PNB (1) Pocket notebook; (2) Police Negotiation Board.

PNC Police National Computer.

PND (1) Penalty Notice for Disorder; (2) Police National Database.

PNLD Police National Legal Database.

POCA Proceeds of Crime Act 2002.

Police and Crime Panels Set up by the Police Reform & Social Responsibility Act 2011 to act as a 'check and a balance' on a PCC's performance.

Police Degree Apprenticeships A new entry route into policing via an apprenticeship programme (from 2020). Officers will have to undergo police training and complete a degree in policing to be confirmed in the rank.

Police Federation of England and Wales The national staff association for the federated ranks of constable, sergeant, inspector, and chief inspector, resembling a trade union.

Police Memorial Trust Charitable organization for police officers killed in the line of duty (has a national memorial in London).

Police Now An initiative where graduates are trained as police officers for a two-year period, with particular emphasis on developing 'leadership skills'.

Police Scotland The single police service in Scotland, created in 2013 (eight regional constabularies were merged).

Police Staff Official designation of support (civilian) staff, some of whom are operational but do not have the police officer warranted powers. Includes PCSOs (qv).

Policing Protocol Order 2011 A statute-based description of the legal responsibilities of chief constables, police and crime commissioners, the Home Secretary, and police and crime panels.

PolSA/POLSA ('polsah') Police Search Advisor.

POP/BritPOP ('pop') Problem-Oriented Policing and its UK derivative.

PPF Policing Professional Framework, soon to be discontinued and replaced by the PPP (qv).

PPP Policing Professional Profiles.

Predictive policing Uses software based on mathematical algorithms to predict crime patterns, to decide how to deploy police resources.

Pre-entry course/programme See pre-join programme.

Pre-join programme A course of study leading to entry to the police service as a trainee officer.

Probationer An older informal term for a police officer in initial training. The terms apprentice police constable, student police officer, or trainee police officer are now more commonly used.

Profiler An informal term for a behavioural analyst or behavioural adviser, who carries out 'profiling' (qv).

Profiling An informal and imprecise term, as in 'offender profiling' and 'geographical profiling'. Often predicts the psychological traits of an unknown offender.

PRRB Police Remuneration Review Body.

PS or Ps Police sergeant.

PSAEW Police Superintendents' Association of England and Wales**,** the national staff association for the ranks of superintendent and chief superintendent.

PSB or PSBM The basic personal safety course often included by constabularies as part of IPLDP (qv).

PSD Professional Standards Department.

PSNI Police Service of Northern Ireland (previously called the RUC, Royal Ulster Constabulary).

PSO Prohibited Steps Order (for protecting children).

PSPO Public Spaces Protection Order.

PWITS ('pee-wits') Possession (of drugs) with intent to supply.

QPM Queen's Police Medal.

qv Latin for 'for which, see . . .'. It refers the reader to another item or word.

R&D Research and Development Unit (usually for intelligence analysis and tasking at BCU (qv) level).

RCT Randomised Control Trial, a research method often employed to support Evidence-based policing (qv).

Re-coursing/back-coursing An informal term for trainee police officers having to repeat elements of initial training, normally as a result of failure or for personal reasons.

Redcap Vernacular term for an officer of the RMP (qv).

Reflex Nationally funded project to deal with organized immigration crime.

Ridge and furrow Identifying features in fingerprints.

RIPA ('ripper') Regulation of Investigatory Powers Act 2000. It regulates undercover police work and the use of informants, but is now partly subsumed by the Investigatory Powers Act 2016.

RIRA ('real I-R-A') Real Irish Republican Army, a proscribed terrorist organization.

RMP Royal Military Police.

ROLE ('role') Recognition of Life Extinct. A statement from a medical professional confirming a person is dead.

ROTI ('roh-tee') A written summary of an audio recorded interview (previously taped).

ROVI ('roh-vee') A written summary of an audio-visually recorded interview.

RTA (1) Road Traffic Act; (2) Road Traffic Accident—now largely replaced by RTC (qv) or RTI (qv).

RTC Road Traffic Collision. The term 'collision' is preferred to 'accident' as most collisions on roads are due to human error, negligence, or a criminal act, rather than a chance event. However, the term 'accident' is still present in legislation.

RTI Road Traffic Incident.

RUC Royal Ulster Constabulary—the former police force for Northern Ireland, replaced by the Police Service of Northern Ireland (PSNI) in 2001.

RV(P) Rendezvous (point) at a crime scene or major incident.

SAB Safeguarding Adult Board.

Safeguarding A term used to describe policies to address vulnerable adults and children/young persons, who may be at risk of harm through exploitation by criminals.

Sanitized The term for describing intelligence from which the identifying features and origins have been omitted.

SARA ('sarr-rer' or 'S-A-R-A') *S*can, *A*nalyse, *R*espond, and *A*ssess.

SARC ('sark') Sexual Assault Referral Centre.

SB Special Branch: the part of every police service that specializes in matters of national security. SB officers do not wear uniforms.

SCAIDP Specialist Child Abuse Investigation Development Programme.

Scarman Inquiry (Scarman Report) An official inquiry into the rioting in the Brixton area of London in 1981. It recommended reforming the law, changing police training and practice, and improving community relations.

SCAS ('Scaz') Serious Crime Analysis Section. A database of homicides and stranger rapes maintained by the NCA (qv).

SDE Self-defined Ethnicity.

SDN Short Descriptive Note (part of a case file, such as a reference to a transcription of an interview with a suspect).

SDPO Serious Disruption Prevention Order introduced as part of the Public Order Act 2023 and designed to minimize disruption to the public by individual protesters.

SFO Serious Fraud Office.

SGM Second Generation Multiplex: a DNA-profiling system using seven areas for discriminating between people.

SGM\+ A DNA-profiling system similar to SGM, but more accurate as it uses 11 areas for discrimination.

Sgt Abbreviation for 'sergeant', a policing rank sometimes also referred to as 'skipper'.

Shoe marks Informal term for footwear prints which can match a suspect to a crime scene.

SHPO Sexual Harm Prevention Order.

SIA ('S-I-A') Security Industry Association.

Sic Latin for 'just as it is written'.

SIO ('S-I-O') Senior Investigating Officer (usually a detective officer) investigating a serious or major crime, such as a Category A or B murder (qv), or a rape.

SIODP Senior Investigating Officers' Development Programme.

SIU ('S-I-U') Special Investigation Unit (for child abuse and child protection investigations).

Skills for Justice/SfJ/S4J The Sector Skills Council (SSC) for Criminal Justice, including Policing. Skills for Justice is responsible for the National Occupational Standards (qv) for Policing, and other justice-related bodies and organizations (such as the Probation Service).

Skillsmark Quality assurance scheme introduced by Skills for Justice (qv).

SLA Service Level Agreement.

SLDP Senior Leadership Development Programmes (SLDP1 and SLDP2) for chief inspector roles or above.

SLP Senior Leadership Programme.

SMART(ER) Used in reference to objectives: *S*pecific, *M*easurable, *A*chievable, *R*ealistic, *T*imely (and *E*valuated and *R*eviewed).

SMT Senior Management Team (on a BCU (qv), usually the commander, a superintendent (or a chief superintendent on large BCUs), together with one or more chief inspectors (Crime and Operations) and a business manager).

SNT Safer Neighbourhood Teams (an alternative name for Neighbourhood Policing Teams).

SO19 Firearms unit in the MPS (qv).

SOCO ('sockoh') Scenes of Crime Officer; older term replaced in many police services by CSI (qv).

SOCPA ('sockper') The Serious Organised Crime and Police Act 2005.

SOIT ('S-O-I-T') Sexual Offences Investigative Trained (officer), an MPS role.

SOLAP ('soh-lap') Student Officer Learning Assessment Portfolio, now replaced by an electronic assessment portfolio in many services.

SOLO ('solo') Sex Offender Liaison Officer.

SOP ('S-O-P') Standard Operating Procedure.

Special measures Used in investigations and courts to provide support and protection for witnesses of more serious crimes.

Spit hood A shroud to cover a detained person's face and head, to protect police officers and others from spitting or biting.

SPoC/SPOC/spoc ('spock') Single Point of Contact.

SPP Strategic Policing Priorities.

SPR Strategic Policing Requirement (qv).

SRO Sexual Risk Order.

Stinger Pronged device for stopping cars by puncturing their tyres.

STO ('S-T-O') Specially trained officer.

STR Short Tandem Repeat: a section of DNA that can be used in profiling methodologies such as SGM\+ and DNA-17 (qv).

Strategic Policing Requirement A statement by the Home Secretary outlining national risks and threats to England and Wales. It also states the government's expectations of police services in terms of capacity and capability to collectively address such threats. The SPR is regularly updated.

Superintendents' Association The Police Superintendents' Association of England and Wales.

Supervised Patrol Undertaken by trainee police officers under the supervision of a qualified police officer or officers.

SVRO Serious Violence Reduction Order. Introduced as part of the Police, Crime, Sentencing and Courts Act 2022.

T&CG Tasking and Coordinating Group.

Tac/TAC team (1) Tactical Support Team—eg used to serve a warrant; (2) Terrorism and Crime Team (MPS (qv)).

TDA or TADA Taking and Driving Away: a reference to a form of vehicle crime. Also known as TWOC (qv).

Tenprint A fingerprinting process whereby prints of all ten fingers are recorded.

Test purchase The authorized purchase of drugs, alcohol, or other items by an undercover police officer or another person, to provide evidence of illegal activity.

TFU Tactical Firearms Unit.

TIC ('T-I-C') Acronym for offences 'taken into consideration' by a court.

TIE (sometimes 'ty') *T*race, *I*mplicate, and/or *E*liminate (in investigations).

TNA Training Needs Analysis.

TOS ('T-O-S') Traffic Officers Service (part of Highways England Traffic Officers Service). Such officers are often still known as HATOs (qv).

TWOC ('twok') Taken Without (Owner's) Consent—normally used in reference to a motor vehicle: see also TDA or TADA.

UC (or UC officer) Abbreviation for an undercover officer.

Undercover Policing Inquiry Judge-led public inquiry into all undercover policing since 1968.

UVP Ultra-Violet (Light) Photography.

VCMM Volume Crime Management Model (Practice Advice on the Management of Priority and Volume Crime).

VCSE Volume Crime Scene Examiner (forensic).

VDRS Vehicle Defect Rectification Scheme.

VEM ('V-E-M') Visible Ethnic Minority: refers to both individuals and communities.

ViCLAS ('vy-class') Violent Crime Linkage Analysis System—a database used by SCAS (qv) in the UK, originally devised by the Royal Canadian Mounted Police (RCMP).

VIPER ('viper') Video Identification Parade Electronic Recording.

ViSOR ('vy-zor') Violent and Sex Offender Register: a database of individuals considered a potential danger to the public because of their history of violence and/or sex offending.

VOO Violent Offender Order.

VPS Victim Personal Statement.

Vulnerability An overarching term used in policing to describe people who are especially vulnerable by reasons of age (a child or young person), their relationship to the suspect or offender, or the mental health of the victim.

WBA Work-based Assessment.

Whorl Characteristic pattern seen in fingerprints.

Winsor Review(s) Two reports (2011 and 2012) by Tom Winsor on pay, conditions, entry routes, and career pathways for police staff.

WPLDP Wider Police Learning and Development Programme.

YOT ('yot') Youth Offending Team.

YPVA Young People's Violence Advisor.

2 Maintaining Professional Standards

2.1 Introduction

Throughout this book, across the various chapters, you will see many references to different aspects regarding the professional expectations in policing. The purpose of this chapter is primarily to appeal to your own intuitive sense of what it means to be professional. We trust that you are joining the police for the right reasons and the chapter accordingly seeks to set the tone and to give you a flavour of what we think it means to be a police officer in the UK today. We recognize that it is easy to be overwhelmed by the sheer volume of legislation thrown at you in the early stages of your policing career, and by the extent to which, at the same time, you will be subjected routinely to behaviours and incidents that most people rarely, if ever, see in their lifetimes.

The title of this chapter is 'professional standards', and this has a very specific, technical and legislative meaning in the police world. It captures a threshold expectation for police officers and as such, it can never be more than a minimal approach to setting professional standards, ie it sets the minimal requirements (Waddington, 2013). There is a College of Policing Authorised Professional Practice (APP) on professional standards that captures this minimal meaning and we will outline the key parameters of this APP later in this chapter (2.3). However, there is an alternative, more general sense in which we refer to professional standards, and this relates to what Waddington (2013, p 12) calls the 'nobility' of an officer's 'calling'. It is an aspirational approach to professional standards and therefore seeks to establish a maximal understanding of what it means to be professional. It is here that we start the chapter.

2.2 Why Do People Join the Police?

Let us start by acknowledging that some people, perhaps too many people, will join the police for the wrong reasons. For the moment, we will ignore these people as they will be dealt with later in the chapter when we look at how *minimal* standards of professional behaviour are maintained through institutionalized processes within and across the professional standards policing infrastructure.

Instead, we wish to start by thinking about the many people who join the police for the right reasons; the people who want to make our communities safer, protect the vulnerable, ensure that justice prevails, and that we can live in a fairer society. These are all laudable qualities that represent the noble calling referred to by Waddington (2013). They are aspirational values and it is important that we do all we can to preserve this sense of purpose within those joining the police.

There will be times during your career when these values that have motivated you to join the police are lost, hopefully only temporarily, as you face traumas and tragedies, injustices, violence, and heart breaking situations. It is easy to become desensitized to suffering and to lose perspective. So you need to find ways of reminding yourself of why you joined the police in the first place; to seek help when you need it, and to offer support to colleagues when you see signs of them losing sight of these values. Above all else, you need to remember that it is these aspirational values and this sense of noble calling that set the *maximum* professional standards that should be sought and fought for. This approach and understanding of professional standards means that you are always striving to be better and to learn more, so that you can fulfil the motivational aspirations that inspired you to become a police officer in the first place.

2.2.1 What is expected of police officers?

There is an idea of British policing that states police officers are ordinary citizens in uniform. This idea is intended to remind police officers that they are part of the communities they police and it establishes a clear distinction away from colonial models of policing, in which the police are an outside force imposing themselves on the communities they police. However, beyond this important distinction, the reality is that police officers are not, and never have been, ordinary citizens. Police officers are people who are willing to go above and beyond what ordinary people are willing to do, and whilst being paid for doing this is an important incentive, payment alone will not sustain a person's commitment to do what is expected of police officers for 35 years.

Police officers, as we have noted, are motivated by aspirational values and they are willing to endure a whole range of limits and restrictions that most ordinary people would not tolerate. There are, for example, restrictions on an officer's private life and business interests. These are set out in Sch 1 to the Police Regulations 2003 which states that 'The restrictions on private life ... shall apply to all members of a police force' (reg 6(1)) and that:

> A member of a police force shall at all times abstain from any activity which is likely to interfere with the impartial discharge of [their] duties or which is likely to give rise to the impression amongst members of the public that it may so interfere; and in particular a member of a police force shall not take any active part in politics. (Sch 1, para 1.)

So police officers are not permitted to do things that ordinary people take for granted as basic human rights. In addition, a police officer 'shall not wilfully refuse or neglect to discharge any lawful debt' (Sch 1, para 4). This does not mean a police officer cannot obtain a mortgage or a car loan, as these are lawful, but any debt which could place the officer in danger of being coerced is unacceptable. What an ordinary citizen might perceive as a private matter of no interest or concern to others, especially their employers, needs to be so much more transparent and visible for police officers.

The Police (Amendment No 3) Regulations 2012 state in reg 8 that:

> If a member of a police force has or proposes to have a business interest which has not previously been disclosed, or, is or becomes aware that a relative has or proposes to have a business interest which, in the opinion of the member, interferes or could be seen as interfering with the impartial discharge of the member's duties and has not previously been disclosed the member shall immediately give written notice of that business interest to the chief officer.

For the purposes of their integrity and credibility, police officers must disclose business interests in order that they may be checked for compatibility with the role of a constable.

Police officers will be regularly confronted by individuals who will challenge the authority of the police on civil liberty grounds, but police officers themselves are subject to intrusions that many ordinary citizens would find unacceptable. For example, in relation to personal records, reg 15 of the Police Regulations 2003 states that the chief officer of a police service 'shall cause a personal record of each member of the police force to be kept' throughout a police officer's service, which will contain details of the officer *and their relatives*, alongside a history of courses attended, expertise gained, promotions achieved, and the outcomes of any disciplinary investigations. Regulation 18 of the Police Regulations 2003 concerns taking and recording a police officer's fingerprints and reg 19 of the Police Regulations 2003 obliges an officer to supply a sample such as a mouth swab for DNA analysis. These are understandable and necessary for the purposes of eliminating officers from any forensic investigation, but they are a reminder that the expectations of a police officer go beyond what ordinary citizens experience. In addition, any officer can be selected for random drug testing (Police Regulations 2003 and Police (Amendment No 2) Regulations 2012), and for students on the PCDA and DHEP (see chapter 5) programmes, failing an assignment can have much more serious consequences than would befall most ordinary students: a student officer can be dismissed under reg 13 of the Police Regulations 2003, or at least have their probationary period extended under reg 12.

As a police officer you will also need to get used to how people perceive you when they see you in a uniform. People expect police officers to know things and to be able to help in all circumstances. Expectations of police officers go way beyond what one might expect of an ordinary person.

2.2.2 The police officer's uniform

There was much thought given to the uniform worn by police officers at the outset of the modern police in 1829. In the spirit of police being ordinary citizens in uniform, the challenge was to make it clear and obvious that a person was a police officer, without making them look too militaristic or alien from the ordinary population. This becomes ever more challenging as the safety and well-being of police officers, and the increasing complexities of policing, means that police officers are required to routinely carry a range of equipment and technology when on patrol. Various items are used for personal protection, for controlling violent or potentially violent people, and for communication with other police staff. The more specialized and extensive the police uniform becomes, the greater the distance between the police officer and the ordinary citizen, and this is something that you will need to be mindful of when encountering citizens in the course of carrying out your duties. The uniform is representative of legitimate authority in society and the far from ordinary powers that an officer wields. This sets expectations amongst the public that are far from ordinary and it is important not only for your own professional standing, but for the police service as a whole, that you retain the highest of professional standards to ensure the public's expectations are met.

2.3 Maintaining Professional Standards in Policing

Perhaps the most challenging aspect of being a new recruit in the police is balancing this sense of aspirational purpose and enthusiasm against the harsh realities of operating as a police officer in the most difficult of circumstances. At times the tension between your sense of moral conviction and the pragmatics of getting through a shift will test your resolve.

Police organizations are also hierarchical and disciplined with a rigid rank structure and clear chain of command. Conditions of service for police constables are regulated by law under various Police Regulations contained in Statutory Instruments. Full details may be found in other textbooks such as *Blackstone's Police Manual: Volume 3 General Police Duties* and online. From the moment of attestation, a student police officer becomes subject to Police Regulations.

This includes the need to follow orders. Regulation 20 of the Police Regulations 2003 states that every member of a police force:

> shall carry out all lawful orders and shall at all times punctually and promptly perform all appointed duties and attend to all matters within the scope of [their] office as a constable.

Police supervisors and managers may require certain actions to be carried out. Police officers are expected to carry out these orders if they are lawful. However, police officers are confronted routinely with difficult decisions to make in time restricted contexts, without having the luxury to check with supervisors and managers on what is the best course of actions.

At the same time, police officers are afforded a significant amount of autonomy and the office of constable requires individual officers to take responsibility for the decisions they take. So officers are at the same time both (1) autonomous moral agents with discrete responsibilities and original authority to make decisions, and also, (2) individuals situated within a defined rank structure in which there is a clear expectation for orders to be followed without the need for further explanation or clarification.

2.3.1 Professional standards procedures

To some extent, the tensions described above are managed by and through various bodies and procedures. The College of Policing APP identifies four aspects of the professional standards operations in policing. These relate to:

- dealing with and countering corruption;
- vetting;
- complaints and misconduct (see 3.7);
- police standards governance.

Each police service will have its own Professional Standards Department (PSD) responsible for dealing with routine complaints and misconduct charges internally. More serious cases of police wrong doing might be dealt with by the National Crime Agency (NCA) or the Independent Office for Police Conduct (IOPC) (see 3.7.3); other bodies play an important role in maintaining and enhancing standards across policing, such as the His Majesty's Inspectorate of Constabulary and Fire & Rescue Services (HMICFRS).

The College's APP also makes reference to the Code of Ethics (see 3.5) as a guide for officers considering what is appropriate behaviour, and to the National Decision Model (NDM) (see 4.2.1) in supporting decisions officers make.

Clearly issues to do with corruption, and likewise examples of misconduct and upheld complaints, are illustrative of policing falling below minimum, threshold standards. It is important to stress here that these aspects of professional standards are minimal, indeed Waddington (2013) emphasizes this point, that a discussion about police performance through the language of professional standards will always land at the minimum expectations, the very least we should expect from officers. This is because there needs to be a threshold and if this is set too high, too many officers will fall short of the target expectations. Casey (2023) is critical of the extent to which discrimination is tolerated within the MPS, and it might be the case that minimum standards are set too low. The problem here is that meeting the minimum threshold does little to reassure the public that the police service is doing a good job. As Wood (2020) notes, the absence of unethical policing does not mean that ethical policing has been achieved.

The professional standards governance is clearly needed to deal with police wrong doing and disciplining officers falling short of minimum threshold standards is an important part of maintaining the trust and support of the general public. However, alone this is not enough, and in light of Baroness Casey's (2023) Report, much more needs to be done to ensure the professional standards in policing are continually raised. This should be at least in line with public expectations, but as Delattre (2004) argues, the preference is for the police to be driving public expectations up, rather than simply meeting them.

The issue of vetting is an important starting point for raising police professional standards. It is identified as a recommendation in the Casey Report 2023. The College of Policing (2017a) *Vetting Code of Practice* sets out the principles and parameters of vetting, and more detail is provided in the subsequent *APP on Vetting* (College of Policing, 2021a). Vetting is important to make sure that inappropriate people are not allowed to join the police. This is easier to say than it is to achieve. In order to drive forward the professional standards of policing we need to make sure that we are continually reducing the number of wrong people joining a police service but we need to recognize that some people who should not be police officers will make it through the vetting process. So, we also need to utilize the professional standards governance structures to make sure that when the wrong people manage to slip through the vetting processes, and are able to join the police, we ensure that appropriate measures are taken as swiftly as possible to ensure that they are removed, following due process, to maintain the integrity of the police service.

More also needs to done at the point of selection to ensure not only that the wrong people are rejected, but also that the right people are allowed to join the police. This brings us back to where we started the chapter. We need to keep in mind the sense of purpose that brings the right people to join the police. In order to raise and sustain professional standards in policing, the police need to recruit more individuals who have the motivation and sense of purpose to continually improve and develop their own capacity to be better at making the right decisions in difficult, challenging, and complex contexts; to take responsibility for not only their own actions but to also support colleagues and to challenge them when necessary to ensure the integrity of the service as a whole is preserved and enhanced.

Delattre (2011) makes an important observation, that only someone with a disposition to do the right thing, a person who is motivated to pursue the good, can demonstrate the required level of moral agency to be a good police officer.

Hopefully, you are that kind of person and as you read through this Handbook, and as you progress through your career, you will be able to maintain a spirit of purpose and continually develop your capacity to raise your own professional standards as a police officer, and to contribute to the ongoing enhancement of the professionalism of the policing organization for which you work, and the police service as a whole.

3 Understanding the Police Constable Role

3.1 Introduction

This chapter will explain the purpose of the police service and the responsibilities of those charged with delivering this professional service. To achieve this, the chapter has been structured to firstly discuss the history of modern policing in the UK, together with the purpose and role of the police service and its members. In addition, the chapter will discuss the other law enforcement agencies in the UK, together with how a police constable can support these agencies to keep the community safe. The structure and functions of the police service together with the roles of the members of the organization will be explained along with the concept and principles of policing by consent which is a central tenant of the British Policing Model. How police acquire their powers and guidance given on their use will be discussed together with the concept of police legitimacy. The chapter also discusses national policing strategies before concluding by explaining what is meant by the term *profession* and what *professional policing* entails.

3.1.1 The UK's policing and law enforcement agencies

Policing in England and Wales has rarely been simply the province of the police alone. Many responsibilities for law enforcement, public order, and policing continue to be shared amongst a large number of agencies, as shown in the table.

Type	Description	Examples	Comments
The 'territorial' or 'Home Office' police services	The 43 county or metropolitan police services in England and Wales, and the single Police Services of Scotland and of Northern Ireland	Essex Police, MPS, Derbyshire Constabulary, PSNI	What most people mean when they refer to the 'police'
Sector-specific police services	Police services for specific sectors or industries (eg transport, nuclear power)	BTP, CNC	Powers are at least equal to those of the territorial police forces
'Heritage' constabularies and police services	Individual constabularies established previously under Acts of Parliament, restricted to small geographical areas	Port of Dover Police, Royal Parks Constabulary, Cambridge University Constabulary	Powers are the same as those for territorial police but the forces are smaller
Armed services police	Organizations responsible for policing the armed forces (eg the Navy)	MoD Police, Royal Military Police	Some armed services police are civilians (ie not members of the armed forces)
Agencies	Home Office or non-statutory bodies with extensive powers of search, detention, arrest, and investigation	NCA for England and Wales	The NCA has now subsumed many former agencies such as SOCA
National police units or sections	Normally NPCC or College of Policing-supported units offering specialist support to police forces	National Wildlife Crime Unit (NWCU), SCAS	Normally made up of seconded police officers, but not exclusively

Type	Description	Examples	Comments
Other organizations with investigatory powers	Non-police organizations with limited powers of investigation (but might have surveillance powers)	Local authorities, HM Revenue and Customs, IOPC	Some powers are governed by RIPA 2000 and IPA 2016
Other organizations with enforcement and/or regulatory powers	Regulatory bodies with responsibility for enforcing regulations	Trading Standards, HSE	Powers normally fall short of arrest, although they can usually prosecute
Other emergency services	Services, other than the police, usually involved in the case of fire, vehicle collisions, and apparent accidents etc	Fire and Rescue Services	Some emergency services have powers for stopping people and vehicles, entry, investigation, and prosecution
Private security or investigatory services	Companies and individuals from the private security industry	Security guards, 'private detectives', debt collectors	In some cases licensing is required or forms of self-regulation
Informal policing	Social control and enforcement as a secondary occupational responsibility	Teachers, park rangers, bus drivers	Normally no powers beyond those of any civilian

Informal policing activities are also undertaken at the secondary and tertiary levels of social control, for example by teachers and security staff, and even through institutions such as the church and trade union organizations. These informal policing mechanisms are not underpinned by particular powers, beyond those of every citizen, and such activities are better understood as secondary occupational responsibilities, or even as less tangible societal responsibilities.

Despite the increased sharing of policing powers, the public police still retain unique and profound powers. The formal status of the police is also demonstrated in more symbolic ways—for example, the use of the royal crown as a mark of authority, which is protected under law.

3.2 The Origins of Modern Policing

The public police are a relatively modern phenomenon. One key date in modern-day policing is 1829, when Sir Robert Peel, then Home Secretary, had secured a Bill through Parliament for the establishment of a Metropolitan Police Service (MPS) for London. So, the police service as we recognize it today is not even 200 years old. However, the formation of the MPS is often referred to by police historians as the beginning of the *new* police, to clearly delineate the police we know today from the previous ad hoc local policing bodies and watch systems.

3.2.1 Chronology of law enforcement and policing

A chronology provides a list of important historical moments in date order. However, it does more than that; it also provides insights to what was happening at different times, and helps us to understand why changes to practice occurred, or how a particular event informed police reforms. An understanding of the past is an important precursor to understanding the present. Current practice and the reasons for it are sometimes easier to appreciate if we consider the historical context.

So, for example, we might highlight the following events from the most recent period:

2022	An Independent Office for Police Conduct (IOPC) report into the behaviour of officers at Charing Cross police station from 2016 to 2018 found the existence of misogynistic, racist, and homophobic communications between officers. The Commissioner of the MPS, Dame Cressida Dick, announced her resignation in February.
2023	An independent review into the standards of behaviour and internal culture of the Metropolitan Police Service, the Baroness Casey Review, was published in March 2023. The Review found that there were systematic and fundamental problems in how the MPS was run, it lacked accountability and transparency, it was not successfully managing the integrity of its officers, and there was institutional racism, misogyny, and homophobia (Casey, 2023).

These are both damning and challenging reports that require urgent and drastic action in response, particularly from the MPS, but across all police services more generally. The findings in these reports will no doubt feature in your learning and training, and will probably remain significant milestones throughout your policing careers.

TASK 1 Take some time to look back at other significant moments throughout the history of the new police. Start from now and work your way backwards and see how many key events, reports, legislative changes, reforms, and policy developments you can find.

3.2.2 Police organization and ranks

You may sometimes hear the police referred to as a 'disciplined organization'. This refers not only to the need for self-discipline and restraint but also to the fact that police officers are organized into ranks in a hierarchical fashion, involving the issuing and receiving of orders. The diagram shows a typical structure for a police service with 6,000-plus staff.

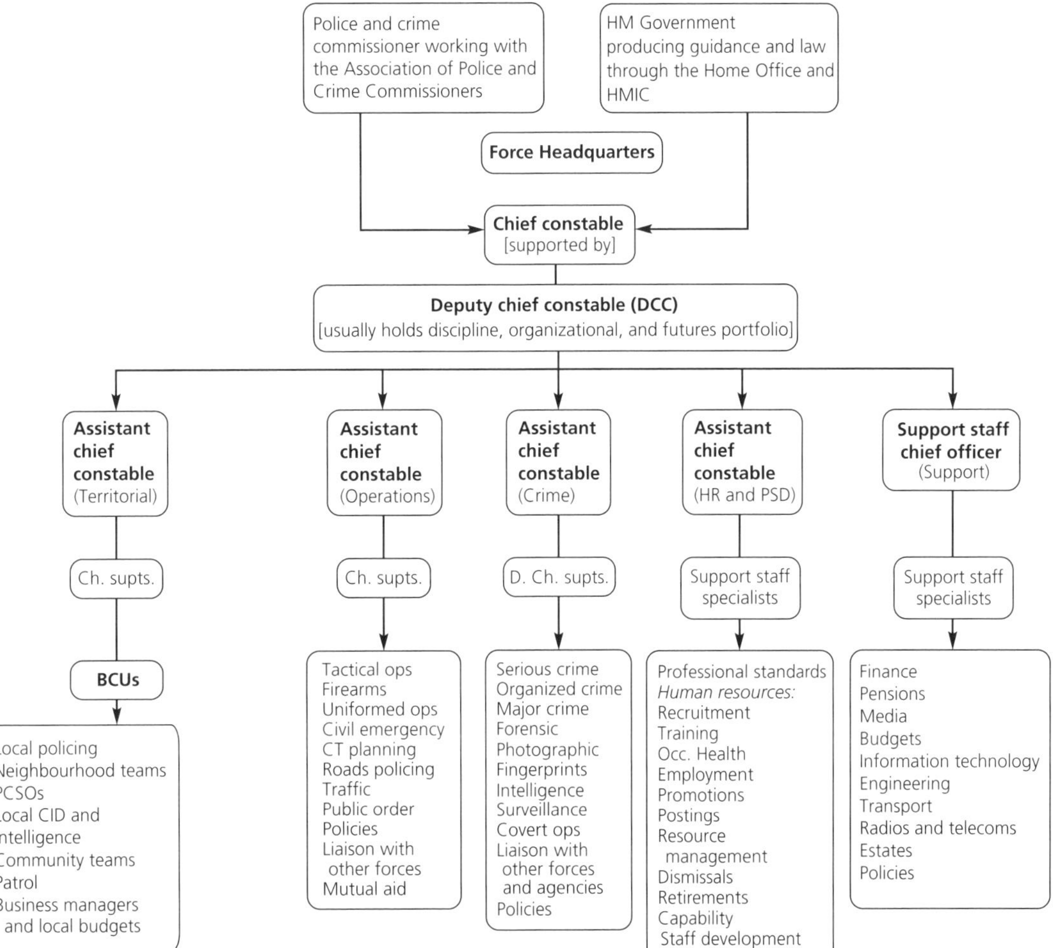

3.2.2.1 Police ranks

Apart from the MPS and one or two other police services such as the City of London, the rank structure and the associated badges on the epaulettes of uniforms are as follows in order of decreasing superiority:

- chief constable;
- deputy chief constable;
- assistant chief constable;
- chief superintendent;
- superintendent;
- chief inspector;
- inspector;
- sergeant; and
- constable.

In the non-uniformed equivalents, 'detective' often precedes the rank, for example detective chief inspector. This does not signify a higher or more senior police rank—it simply defines the officer's *role*.

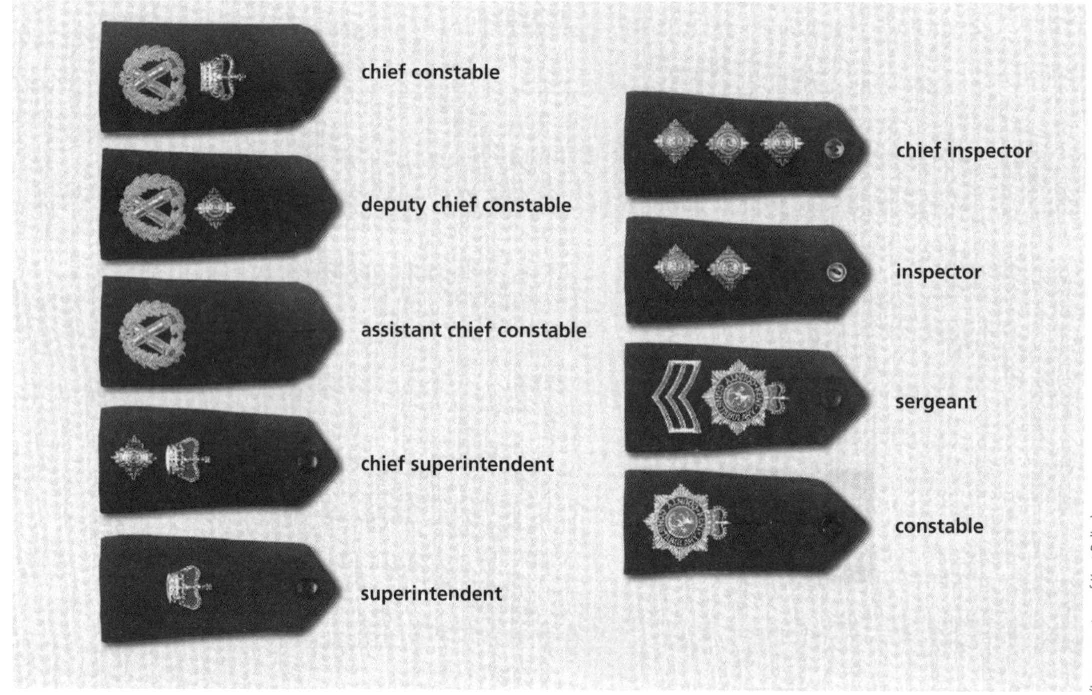

(Image courtesy of Kent Police)

In the MPS and the City of London Police, the rank structure is different for the higher ranks:

- commissioner;
- deputy commissioner;
- assistant commissioner;
- deputy assistant commissioner (MPS only);
- commander;

The ranks from chief superintendent down to constable are the same as in other police services.

The insignia of the ranks may vary from service to service. You should also take the time to familiarize yourself with the insignia of uniformed members of the extended police family, such as special constables and PCSOs.

3.2.3 The College of Policing

The College of Policing was established in 2012 as the official professional body for policing. Its focus is on:

- knowledge and sharing good practice ie the development of research and evidence of What Works;
- professional development of individual members of the profession; and
- standards for police services and individuals.

Initially, the College of Policing aspired to achieve charter status as The Royal College of Policing and be independent of government. However, the College remains a company limited by guarantee legally owned by the Home Secretary.

A key requirement for professionalization appears to be specialist knowledge and expertise. The 2011 Neyroud Review into police leadership and training made proposals on how to align policing more fully with other professions, including the establishment of a new professional body. The College of Policing has developed a Code of Ethics for policing, Authorised Professional Practice (APP), a Knowledge Hub to share ideas, and the Police Education and Qualifications Framework (PEQF), its qualifications framework for policing, including the Police Constable Degree Apprenticeship which underpins initial training.

The College also offers bursaries to individual police officers as a contribution to higher education course fees, including for research-based programmes such as Masters and PhDs.

Finally, as part of its role as a professional body, the College offers training, increasingly via digital platforms, and often in response to a particular need. For example, in 2018–19 in excess of 75,000 individuals undertook the College's training on disclosure (CoP, 2020a, p 2).

In 2021 the new chair of the College of Policing, a former policing minister, Lord Herbert, launched what he called a fundamental review of the work of the College—in essence, a consultation using a survey, focus groups etc, with the police service and other interested parties. A number of challenges were identified, including a lack of awareness in policing of the College's existence, the overly bureaucratic and risk-averse nature of the organization, a perception that the College is not sufficiently responsive to the demands made on policing, and the low quality of some of its training and learning products, particularly the online provision (CoP, 2022a, pp 13–17).

The College of Policing has taken on the responsibility of regulating and maintaining standards across the police service. There is now also a *National SIO Register* for senior investigating officers (SIOs) and it is envisaged that it will eventually contain the details of all investigators accredited through the Senior Investigating Officer Development Programme (SIODP), or through other means of demonstrating competence, although progress on this appears slow. Nonetheless, it appears that to remain on the register an SIO will be required to provide appropriate and relevant details of CPD activity. A similar system applies for doctors—to retain their place on a professional register they have to provide evidence to show they have kept up to date and are fit to practise (GMC, 2012). In early 2020, the College announced in its annual report for the year ending 31 March 2019, a Licence to Practice (LtP) initiative 'to help bring about national consistency and support, increasing professionalization of high-risk roles' (CoP, 2020a, p 58) particularly in regard to public protection and safeguarding. However, progress with this initiative will probably have been affected by the College's response to the Covid-19 pandemic and in late 2021 the College was still 'exploring whether ... LtP can contribute to improving standards' (CoP, 2021a, p 38). In 2022 the Police Foundation, an independent think tank, called on the Home Office to introduce a Licence to Practise for all police officers, renewable every five years subject to an officer demonstrating CPD or equivalent (Police Foundation, 2022, p 112).

Establishing and maintaining policing as a full profession is important for the following reasons:

- to develop the body of knowledge, doctrines, and skills required for modern-day policing;
- to protect the right of the police, in certain key respects, to regulate themselves;
- to improve public confidence in the work of the police by providing a full professional register implying the need for its members to regularly demonstrate that they have met the requirement to maintain their skills and knowledge; and
- to distinguish the work and the professional standing of the police officer from others, including members of the extended policing family (see 3.3) and other law enforcers.

3.2.4 Police representative organizations

There are a number of different bodies representing police officers. Some are referred to below. However, perhaps the most significant, especially for new recruits into the police, is the Police Federation.

3.2.4.1 The Police Federation of England and Wales

The Police Federations are the staff associations for police constables, sergeants, inspectors, and chief inspectors. England and Wales have a single Police Federation (s 64(1) of the Police Act 1996, Membership of Trade Unions), as do Northern Ireland and Scotland. This section describes the Police Federation of England and Wales (PFEW), but many of the observations also apply to Scotland and Northern Ireland.

Until April 2015, all trainees automatically joined the Police Federation on entry into the police. However, in 2015 the law changed so that police officers would not simply become members by default (Home Office, 2014b). To that effect, the Police Federation (Amendment) Regulations 2015 was introduced, with a clause added to the 1969 Regulations. These changes mean that when a student officer joins the police service now, they can decide whether to join the Police Federation. Also, in 2016 the Home Office decided that special constables should not be represented by the Police Federation.

The PFEW has eight regions, with each region electing representatives to form the national Joint Central Committee. The Joint Central Committee is responsible for the national policy of the Federation.

The PFEW is not a trade union, and indeed, police officers are forbidden from joining a trade union (s 64(1) of the Police Act 1996, Membership of Trade Unions). The PFEW, therefore, does not have the right to call for any kind of industrial action such as a strike and cannot affiliate itself to any political party or organization. However, in many other respects the PFEW was established to represent the views of its members on local, regional, and national levels in much the same way as any other staff association.

Each of the police services in England and Wales has a Joint Branch Board (JBB). Within the JBB there are separate boards, representing the interests of constables, sergeants, and inspectors. These boards each have separate agendas and meetings but also combine to form the force JBB. The JBB represents the views of police officers to the chief constable or commissioner and to others in positions of responsibility.

On behalf of its members, the PFEW negotiates aspects of pay, pensions, and allowances through the Police Remuneration Review Body (PRRB). This body consists of representatives from the Police Federations (England and Wales, and Northern Ireland), the Superintendents' Association, and the National Police Chiefs' Council (NPCC); the PRRB was established through the Anti-social Behaviour, Crime and Policing Act 2014. The members of the body meet with representatives of the government ministers responsible for the police (the Home Secretary, the Northern Ireland Secretary) and representatives of the local authorities and magistrates. The PRRB has an independent chair and deputy chair (appointed by the Prime Minister). Scotland was not included in the remit of the PRRB and continues to use its own Police Negotiating Board.

The Police Federation is also represented at Police Advisory Board meetings (chaired by the Home Secretary), which consider professional subjects such as training, promotion, and discipline. After taking these discussions into account, the Home Secretary may then make proposals to amend the Police Regulations.

One of the primary functions of the Federation is to give advice and assistance to its members who are the subject of a formal complaint or internal investigation. In such circumstances, the Police Federation's advice to an officer is to contact their local Federation representative if unsure of what to do next. The Independent Office for Police Conduct (IOPC) has a web page containing information for police officers and staff, available on the IOPC website (IOPC, 2017). The PFEW also offers advice and assistance to police officers (including student officers) who sustain injuries whilst on duty and who wish to claim compensation from the Criminal Injuries Compensation Authority (CICA). It also offers advice and assistance to police officers (including student officers) on matters arising from the conditions of service set out in the various Acts and Regulations governing the police service.

3.2.4.2 Other police representative organizations

There are other organizations that represent different groups and interests, and some have links with the Police Federation. For example, the British Association for Women in Policing (BAWP) is represented on the Equality Subcommittee of the Police Federation. The BAWP seeks to address women's issues in policing and not simply to represent women; membership is open to both men and women. Further information is available on its website.

The National Black Police Association UK (NBPA) is an independent charitable organization which seeks to further the position of all police officers of 'African, African-Caribbean, Middle-Eastern, Asian or Asian sub-continent origin'. A student officer may join the NBPA through membership of their local Black Police Association (BPA), of which there are about 40 in the UK, covering nine regions. Further information is available on its website.

The National LGBT + Police Network UK promotes inclusiveness and equality for LGBT people who work in the police service and other crime agencies.

The Disabled Police Association (DPA) was founded in 2012 to help provide a co-ordinated response to national police matters that could affect disabled police officers and staff in the UK (see the DPA website for further information).

The Police Superintendents' Association (PSA) represents the ranks of superintendents and chief superintendents (there are similar organizations for Scotland and Northern Ireland). As with the Police Federation, the PSA represents its members at the national Police Negotiating Board.

The National Police Chiefs' Council (NPCC) represents the interests of chief officers in England, Wales, and Northern Ireland. Chief officers are defined as police officers of the rank of ACC or above (commander in the MPS), and senior police staff equivalents. The NPCC states that its remit is to enable independent chief constables and their constabularies to work together to improve policing for the public, and that every police service is represented in the work of the NPCC through attendance at Chief Constables' Council. While all chief officers have the opportunity to be involved in, and shape the work of the NPCC, it is not a membership body in the traditional sense (NPCC, no date).

3.2.5 Police and crime commissioners (PCC) and police and crime panels

Each police service now has a PCC who is responsible for holding chief officers to account and managing the funding of the force from a precept, a type of local tax. PCCs are directly elected by the public every four years and most are affiliated to a political party. The PCC is answerable to the local police and crime panel (PCP).

The police and crime panel members are appointed, with at least ten panel members being elected local authority councillors. The other members are appointed and they are usually individuals with specific skills or knowledge within their police locality. The panel has only limited powers and functions mainly as a check and a balance on the PCC's actions. The panel can review a PCC's draft crime and police plan and make recommendations about it but cannot reject it outright. Similarly, the panel can veto the PCC's recommended precept the first time it is submitted but cannot block a resubmitted precept.

There are three important differences between the PCC system and the previous local police authority in that:

- the PCC is a single person as opposed to typically 17 individuals from different backgrounds, as was the case with the police authorities;
- the PCC is directly elected rather than appointed, as was the case with local police authority members—some have said this makes policing democratically accountable; and
- the panel and the PCC have a broader remit, as other local crime-related agencies can be held to account compared with the much narrower scope of the local police authorities.

The introduction of PCCs has arguably made the political dimensions of police work more explicit and transparent, although critics remain concerned that this new system could undermine police independence and lead to political interference.

The Policing and Crime Act 2017 places a duty on police, fire, and ambulance services to work together. PCCs can take on responsibility for fire and rescue services where a local case is made to support this.

The Home Office conducted a two part review of the role of PCCs; the first part was published in 2021 and made recommendations on the accountability, visibility, and transparency of PCCs as well as considering the role of PCCs in fire service governance (Home Office, 2021a). The second stage of the review was published in 2022 and made recommendations around offender management, partnership working, and increasing public confidence (Patel, 2022).

3.2.5.1 Police and crime plans

Every PCC in England and Wales is required by the Police Reform and Social Responsibility Act 2011 to produce a police and crime plan setting out a strategy for policing and crime reduction. The plan is devised in consultation with the chief constable and other community safety partners, eg health, local authorities, fire and rescue services. Other criminal justice agencies are also involved in setting priorities. Each plan covers a four-year period but can be revised annually.

The plans are likely to contain specific priorities, for example one priority in the PCP for the county of Kent for April 2022 to March 2025 is to 'tackle violence against women and girls' (Kent PCC, 2022). Undoubtedly, these police and crime plans have at least an indirect effect on the work of police service staff and in many cases the effects will be relatively easy to see, in terms of changing priorities in operational policing.

3.2.5.2 Other police service strategies, plans, and corporate statements

In addition to the formal, statutory plans they are required to hold, almost all police services have their own statements of how they wish to operate and what they expect of their staff. These are sometimes referred to as the Mission, Vision, Values, and Priorities (MVVP). Such pledges and aspirations will be very important to a police service, and will guide actions and behaviours. MVVPs are often revised when a new chief constable takes charge of a constabulary.

3.2.5.3 The Policing Protocol Order 2011

The Police Reform and Social Responsibility Act 2011 also sought to redefine and clarify the constitutional/governance positions of the key actors in policing in England and Wales—the Home Secretary, the chief constables, and the police authorities, now replaced by a PCC in each service. This was achieved in a document called the Policing Protocol Order 2011, and perhaps the most sensitive area the Protocol touches upon is police operational independence. The Order sought to reaffirm that operational control would remain solely in the hands of chief constables, and this has largely been achieved.

In 2022 the Home Office announced a consultation with targeted stakeholders on how to refresh the Policing Protocol Order 2011. This consultation ran from March to May 2022 and sought views on whether the protocol should be amended to:

- specifically clarify that the remit of police and crime panels to scrutinize mayors with PCC functions extends only to their PCC functions and not their wider mayoral functions.
- further clarify the panel's role and remit in respect of operational policing matters, that it would be only in exceptional circumstances that a chief constable would appear before a panel.

(Newson, 2023)

3.2.6 Policing by consent

The concept of policing by consent is one of the central philosophies of British policing. It is based around what is known as Sir Robert Peel's Nine Principles of Policing which were published in 1829 following his establishment of the Metropolitan Police. It is not clear that the principles were actually written by Peel; it is more likely that they were written by the first joint Commissioners of the Metropolitan Police, Charles Rowan and Richard Mayne (Home Office, 2012a). Indeed, Lentz and Chaires (2007) suggest that Peel's nine principles were actually created by Charles Reith in 1956. Nonetheless, what are commonly referred to as the 'Peelian Principles' show that the power of the police comes from the common consent of the public to be policed, rather than from the power of the state to impose its will on the public.

The Peelian Policing Principles

1. To prevent crime and disorder, as an alternative to their repression by military force and severity of legal punishment.
2. To recognise always that the power of the police to fulfil their functions and duties is dependent on public approval of their existence, actions and behaviour and on their ability to secure and maintain public respect.
3. To recognise always that to secure and maintain the respect and approval of the public means also the securing of the willing co-operation of the public in the task of securing observance of laws.
4. To recognise always that the extent to which the co-operation of the public can be secured diminishes proportionately the necessity of the use of physical force and compulsion for achieving police objectives.
5. To seek and preserve public favour, not by pandering to public opinion; but by constantly demonstrating absolutely impartial service to law, in complete independence of policy, and without regard to the justice or injustice of the substance of individual laws, by ready offering of individual service and friendship to all members of the public without regard to their wealth or social standing, by ready exercise of courtesy and friendly good humour; and by ready offering of individual sacrifice in protecting and preserving life.

6. To use physical force only when the exercise of persuasion, advice and warning is found to be insufficient to obtain public co-operation to an extent necessary to secure observance of law or to restore order, and to use only the minimum degree of physical force which is necessary on any particular occasion for achieving a police objective.
7. To maintain at all times a relationship with the public that gives reality to the historic tradition that the police are the public and that the public are the police, the police being only members of the public who are paid to give full time attention to duties which are incumbent on every citizen in the interests of community welfare and existence.
8. To recognise always the need for strict adherence to police-executive functions, and to refrain from even seeming to usurp the powers of the judiciary of avenging individuals or the State, and of authoritatively judging guilt and punishing the guilty.
9. To recognise always that the test of police efficiency is the absence of crime and disorder, and not the visible evidence of police action in dealing with them.
(Home Office, 2012a)

Irrespective of when these principles were written, they are considered to be relevant for today's modern police organizations. Prevention is placed first in this list, because it was seen as one of the prime functions of the new police, and despite being difficult to measure, prevention remains a policing priority.

3.2.7 Police legitimacy

The issue of legitimacy is central to debates about the police role in democratic societies and has been elevated as a concern in recent years through the growing body of literature on procedural justice (Tyler, 1990; Bradford *et al*, 2009; Bottoms and Tankebe, 2012). When we speak of police legitimacy we are referring to a sense in which the police are considered to be on the side of the people and a police officer's right to enforce the law, protect the vulnerable, and use reasonable force when necessary goes largely unchallenged. In recent times we have witnessed a number of events where that legitimacy has been called into question.

The existence of police authority requires individuals to willingly sacrifice a degree of personal freedom and liberty in order to secure a greater degree of collective freedom and liberty. The logic behind this way of thinking is made explicit in the writings of the seventeenth-century English philosopher Thomas Hobbes: without authority in society there would exist 'a war of all against all'. For Hobbes, therefore, the existence of any authority is preferable to none at all and the necessity *for* authority must be considered before questioning the legitimacy *of* authority.

The difficulty in justifying police authority is illustrated by the fact that it took six attempts from 1785 onwards to pass a Police Bill through the Houses of Parliament to create the new police in 1829. Clearly, there was opposition at the time to the very existence of a professional standing body of police in England and Wales.

Today, we largely take the existence of the police for granted and relatively few people have questioned whether we would be better off without any police, although this is changing. There have been growing calls to de-fund the police and even abolish police services in the wake of Black Lives Matter (BLM) campaigning in the USA. These campaigns are also influencing discussion in the UK, and in the wake of Baroness Casey's Report (2023) there were suggestions that the MPS should be abolished and the whole of policing reconsidered (Jones, 2023). The benefits of having a police presence need to be balanced against the loss of civil liberties arising from policing activities, and the societal deficit of institutionalized discrimination.

The continuing importance of legitimacy in policing is clear; it is one of the areas assessed in HMICFRS in its annual integrated PEEL inspection. There are two distinct means through which legitimacy can be established: consensual and moral legitimacy.

3.2.7.1 Consensual and moral legitimacy of the police

The police are quite rightly governed by the law, but the issue of legitimacy is central to debates about the police role in liberal democratic societies in other ways too. Consensual legitimacy is gained through the support of the people and communities who are being policed. It reflects the democratic aspect of policing within a liberal democracy, the notion of *policing by consent*.

From the perspective of those advocating consensual legitimacy, the police are legitimate to the extent that the public consent to policing. Of course, there are differing degrees to which we might say the public consents to the police. One view is to say that the public consents passively by not opposing what the police do. On the other hand, we might insist on the public having an ongoing engagement with the police in order for consent to be given actively.

In practice, the kind of consent gained will be dependent upon the type of police response and the particular problem addressed. For example, if the police are required to deal with a serious threat of terrorism, then the consent will have to be passive in order to allow the police to be effective. The more the public know about how the police intend to counter the terrorists, the more the terrorists would also know, and the police intervention might fail as a consequence.

Conversely, when the police are required to resolve low-level but persistent offending, there is a greater need for the police to communicate with the local community, to establish and agree the best way to address the problem. In this latter case, the consent must be active and ongoing. The police need to negotiate their response to the problem and ensure that the community supports, as much as is possible, any police interventions. In this respect, to ensure consensual legitimacy of the police there must be appropriate public involvement in negotiating police responses and the response must deal effectively with the particular problem.

There are, however, limits to consensual legitimacy; for example the police could theoretically be too responsive to the views of the communities being policed. As Waddington (1999) has noted, the police are required to deal with conflicts in society and in the exercise of this function they may be perceived to police against some sections of the community. A real concern exists that the police might be overly responsive to one section of the community against another. This could lead to the exclusion and/or targeting of groups of individuals who are seen to be on the periphery of a community. A key message from the Casey Report (2023) is that 30 years on from the murder of Stephen Lawrence in 1993, Black minority communities in London continue to be over-policed and under-protected.

The popularity of the police is no guarantee that the police are acting in a morally legitimate way. Procedural justice measures the extent to which the public deem policing to be legitimate. But as Bottoms and Tankebe (2012) note, procedural justice captures the perspective of the audience (public), rather than what the actors (police) themselves do.

Consent is a *necessary*, but not *sufficient*, aspect of police legitimacy. In liberal democratic terms, consent reflects democratic, but not liberal concerns (Wood, 2016). The liberal concerns within liberal democratic contexts are expressed more through the moral legitimacy of the police rather than consensual legitimacy. It is becoming increasingly important for the police to do the right thing from a moral perspective. The course of action that would be supported by a local community is not always the moral one, and the community might not support all morally correct policing actions. For example, the police will not always be able to gain consensual support for protecting a known paedophile living within a residential area or allowing a racist organization to march through the town centre. However, the reason why the police do what they do is often a matter of moral legitimacy rather than consensual legitimacy. The Human Rights Act 1998 gives legislative support to this point of view. Increasingly, police officers must take into account a number of often different or contradictory moral considerations in order to make professional judgements. Policing by consent remains an important part of police legitimacy but the police must operate primarily within moral boundaries if they are to be truly legitimate.

3.3 Police Officer and Staff Roles

Policing involves an array of providers which together form an extended policing family which includes special constables, police support staff and police community support officers, police volunteers, and private security firms. This is not an exhaustive list, but it does provide an indication of the various kinds of policing arrangements, including voluntary, regulatory, and private policing providers. Many members of the extended policing family are important in policing communities.

On 30 September 2022 there were 227,649 full-time equivalent staff working for the police services of England and Wales of which 142,145 were police officers, 77,242 were police staff and designated officers and 8,263 were PCSOs (Home Office, 2023a). In addition, there were 7,840 special constables serving with police forces in the UK on 30 September 2022 (Home Office, 2023a).

3.3.1 Police officers

After attestation, a student police officer holds the office of constable, with the position being confirmed normally after successful completion of a probationary period. The origins of the office of constable in the UK can be traced back hundreds of years, and it was appealed to, and reaffirmed, as the starting point for the new police in 1829.

In recent years, constables have become just one of many members of the extended police family and they no longer have a monopoly on certain traditional policing powers. They nonetheless continue to hold a special position within policing and the role of the police constable is clearly defined in terms of its significant responsibilities, and the high standards required regarding attitudes, values, and professional knowledge.

In March 2023 a police constable from the Metropolitan Police was dismissed for making discriminatory comments against some of their colleagues (Jacques, 2023a). Between 2019 and 2021 the officer used language and acted in a manner that 'belittled, mocked and humiliated officers', they also asked a colleague 'Why don't you go back to your own country?' (BBC, 2023). Following a hearing for gross misconduct, the officer was found to have breached the police standards for professional behaviour in respect of equality and diversity, authority, respect, and courtesy, and that the conduct had been discreditable. They were dismissed from the MPS and their details were added to the Barred List held by the College of Policing. This list contains details of all officers, special constables, and police staff members who have been dismissed from the police under the Police (Conduct) Regulations 2020 or the Police (Performance) Regulations 2020 (CoP, 2023a).

3.3.1.1 Attestation of police constables

Attestation is the stage at which a student police officer is formally given the powers of a police constable, which enables them to arrest someone according to the law and Codes of Practice. The legal detail is set out in s 29 of and Sch 4 to the Police Act 1996, as amended by s 83 of the Police Reform Act 2002. Parallel legislation covers the non-Home Office police services, eg in s 24 of the Railways and Transport Safety Act 2003, for the British Transport Police (BTP).

In many services, attestation occurs early on in a trainee officer's career; on initial appointment or within the first few weeks. The warrant card can also be issued at attestation although some police services issue a student police officer identity card. There is often a formal attestation ceremony to which family and friends may be invited. The declaration is usually taken by a Justice of the Peace. The student officer will make a formal oath, which should be learnt by heart, as follows:

> I . . . of . . . do solemnly and sincerely declare and affirm that I will well and truly serve the King in the office of constable, with fairness, integrity, diligence, and impartiality, upholding fundamental human rights and according equal respect to all people; and that I will, to the best of my power, cause the peace to be kept and preserved and prevent all offences against people and property; and that while I continue to hold the said office I will, to the best of my skill and knowledge, discharge all the duties thereof faithfully according to law.

An alternative Welsh-language version can be used in Wales and there are alternative versions for police officers in Scotland and Northern Ireland and in the BTP.

The making of a declaration or oath may seem somewhat old-fashioned. However, it is worth bearing in mind that the declaration police officers make has a statutory basis in law and its symbolic importance remains strong, both within police culture and in the wider political and social world.

3.3.1.2 Special constables

Special constables, known as specials, are volunteers who are sworn officers with full powers. They undertake police duties on a part-time basis, a minimum number of hours is normally required eg 16 hours per month. Most specials are not paid employees of a police constabulary but they are reimbursed expenses. However, a number of measures have been introduced by some police services or local authorities to reward specials for their service such as an allowance, eg for extra winter duties, or a council tax discount. They must be over the age of 18 and be a national of a country within the European Economic Area (EEA) or a national of a country outside the EEA with the right to reside in the UK without restrictions.

Most special constables undertake paid employment elsewhere, the system functions very much in the same way as the Territorial Army, RAF, or Naval volunteer reserve forces. In most police services they work alongside regular officers, go out on patrol, and deal with the range of activities which a patrol constable would encounter during an ordinary shift. Specials are subject to the same Code of Ethics as other police officers, which means, for example, that they must not take any active part in politics.

Some police services now require future applicants to the police service to serve as special constables before applying for full-time employment, so there are a growing number of specials who are in full- or part-time education. The training for specials in many police services is the College of Policing Special Constable Learning Programme (SCLP), aligned with the PEQF (in particular the first year of the PCDA) and utilizes both workplace assessments and the assessment of knowledge and understanding. Successful completion of the programme leads to the status of a 'Qualified special constable' (QSC).

Whilst such initiatives are currently welcomed, primarily on economic grounds, there might be issues further down the line with respect to the status of specials as more focus is placed on what a police officer needs to know before being issued with a warrant card. For example, consider the implications if a special constable applies to become a paid full-time police officer through the national SEARCH© assessment process, or online alternatives but is rejected, perhaps on the grounds of respect for diversity. This could raise concerns over whether this individual should retain the status of a warranted special constable.

3.3.1.3 Police Community Support Officers

The PCSO role was specifically designed to provide presence and to be accessible to the community, and also to enable local people to contribute to Neighbourhood Policing Teams. PCSOs work alongside police constables to help to reduce crime and anti-social behaviour in local neighbourhoods and to provide reassurance to the public. In some police services, PCSOs now undertake specialist roles such as victim liaison.

PCSOs engage with the public, identifying their concerns and supporting people who are affected by anti-social behaviour, crime, or the fear of crime. They patrol a limited beat where they can be seen and spoken to and there is an emphasis on meeting and talking to young people. PCSO uniforms are approved by police services but are usually similar to those of warranted police officers, but their badges and epaulettes clearly identify them as PCSOs. For example, PCSO epaulettes and ties are usually blue in colour. PCSOs do not have a power of arrest but do have many other powers. All PCSO officers carry documentation detailing the powers they have been granted. There are 20 potentially available standard PCSO powers (Home Office, 2012c), which include the power to:

- enter and search any premises for the purposes of saving life and limb or preventing serious damage to property;
- require the name and address of a person in specified circumstances, eg for anti-social behaviour, for road traffic offences, or if the suspect is believed to have committed certain offences such as causing injury, alarm, or distress to another;
- control traffic under certain circumstances;
- issue certain fixed penalty notices, eg for cycling on a footpath, or littering;
- require surrender of certain items, eg alcohol from people under 18, or from people drinking in a designated place;
- seize certain items, eg tobacco from a person aged under 16, and vehicles which have been used to cause alarm; and
- remove abandoned vehicles.

Another 43 discretionary additional powers can be granted by chief officers, such as the power to:

- issue fixed penalty notices, eg for disorder, truancy, dog fouling, graffiti, fly posting, driving the wrong way along a one-way street, and unlicensed street vending;

- deal with begging;
- detain a person for up to 30 minutes, using reasonable force to prevent them from escaping;
- search detained persons for dangerous items, and use reasonable force to prevent escape;
- require a person claiming to be a charity collector to provide appropriate certification, name, address, and signature.

In some police services, training follows the College of Policing PCSO initial learning programme. This is an adaptation of the first year of the PCDA, but with a greater emphasis on community policing (CoP, 2021b). A College of Policing National Policing Police Community Support Officer: Operational Handbook is available online.

3.3.2 Police support staff and volunteers

There were 77,242 police support staff and designated officers in England and Wales on 30 September 2022 (Home Office, 2023a). In many police services, support staff can make up to one-third of total numbers, and they undertake a wide range of tasks. For some areas in policing, it may be more appropriate to employ specialist support staff, cybercrime and fraud being two obvious examples, than to rely on omnicompetent officers. This issue touches on a wider debate about the purpose of sworn officers and the responsibilities and tasks assigned to this role.

Police support volunteers (PSVs) are unpaid volunteers who assist the police in various administrative tasks including manning the front counters of police stations but also more specialist activities such as monitoring CCTV cameras or using specialist skills from their own workplace to assist the police. In September 2022 there were 8,077 PSVs in England and Wales (Home Office, 2023a).

Police volunteers are individuals who work for the police in a variety of non-enforcement roles—these include helping with front desk responsibilities, Neighbourhood Watch support, and assisting neighbourhood policing teams with community initiatives. Typically, a non-metropolitan police service will have between 100 and 200 volunteers. Police volunteers are security checked but do not hold any police powers. The police are now exploring the recruitment of volunteers to specialist roles such as computing and cybersecurity.

3.3.3 Neighbourhood Watch

The Neighbourhood Watch (NhW) scheme involves bringing groups of residents together and has a mission to 'support and enable individuals and communities to be connected, active and safe, which increases wellbeing and minimises crime' (Neighbourhood Watch, 2020). It was established in 1982 and there are now approximately 90,000 volunteers in the UK covering some 2–3 million households. NhW is usually organized by volunteers and led by a co-ordinator who is supported by a liaison officer linked to the local police station. These local networks are part of a larger national structure supported by the National Police Chiefs' Council and the Home Office, and need to be registered with the police. NhW groups collect information about local concerns, eg criminal damage, anti-social behaviour, bogus callers, child sexual exploitation, elder abuse, and provide the police with any information regarding crimes or suspects (see more at www.ourwatch.org.uk).

The police can also share information about crimes committed in the NhW area and offer advice on how community members can protect themselves. Police officers can encourage communities or individuals to start new schemes or join established schemes by directing people to liaison officers or established co-ordinators. Police services throughout the country are now engaged in a whole range of watch-type schemes, including Hospital Watch, Boat Watch, Business Watch, National Pubwatch, Shed Watch, Church Watch, Forecourt Watch, Bicycle Watch, Country Eye, Horse Watch, Farm Watch, School Watch, and Shop Watch. These schemes are very important in the policing of our local communities (see Chapter 11).

3.4 The Origins of Police Powers

The main duty of the police service is to protect the public by detecting and preventing crime. This is established in Common Law, precedents set by decisions of the courts, and the police have common law and legislative powers given to them to enable them to perform this duty. The powers of the police in the UK are largely defined by statute law, also known as an Act of Parliament, which is a law made by the UK Parliament. All Acts initially begin as bills introduced in either the House of Commons or the House of Lords. Once a bill has been agreed by both of Houses of Parliament and it has been given Royal Assent by the Monarch, it becomes an Act.

The Acts of Parliament are what give the police the powers necessary to carry out their role. New pieces of legislation are constantly being passed, or existing legislation is being amended by the UK Parliament. However, there are some key pieces of legislation that provide police with many of the powers they use, for example the Police Act 1996 which covers the attestation of officers, the Police and Criminal Evidence Act 1984 regarding police powers of arrest, and the Police Reform Act 2002 which extended some policing powers to PCSOs.

Police powers can basically be grouped into three categories:

- Powers to investigate crime: This includes a range of powers to collect the evidence needed to identify suspects and support their fair and effective trial.
- Powers to prevent crime: This includes a range of powers to maintain public order, prevent anti-social behaviour, and manage known offenders/suspects.
- Powers to 'dispose' of criminal cases: These powers allow police officers to dispose of criminal cases out of the court or charge suspects so that they can be prosecuted.
  (Brown, 2021)

All police personnel are individually responsible for using their powers, which must be done in accordance with the law and the use of these powers should be: necessary, proportionate, and comply with human rights and equality legislation. All police officers and staff receive training and guidance on the effective and lawful use of their powers and authority, but they are allowed at times to use their own discretion concerning the application of their powers.

Police officers and staff are provided with guidance on the use of the powers they are given. This comes from three sources. Firstly there is statutory guidance which is issued by the College of Policing, which is the body responsible for professional standards in policing. They are responsible for issuing the Codes of Practice to chief police officers. These codes are issued under section 39A of the Police Act 1996. One example of these would be the Code of Ethics which complements the policing standards of professional behaviour. However, some legislation requires the government to provide guidance on the powers contained within the act; an example of this would be Part IV of the Police and Criminal Evidence Act 1984, which requires the government to publish and maintain the Codes of Practice for the Act itself.

The second source of guidance is the Authorised Professional Practice (APP) which is published by the College of Policing. These guides are based around different aspects of policing for example, roads policing, public order policing, critical incident management, and so on. These reports are to show police officers and staff how to use their powers lawfully and effectively; in so doing they support the training and development of police personnel.

Finally the police themselves issue operational guidance. The National Police Chiefs' Council (NPCC), the co-ordinating body of all of the UK police services, publishes this guidance which has been endorsed by all police services and consequently applies at a national level. Each constabulary also issues their own internal operational policies and practices.

3.5 The Code of Ethics

The Code of Ethics was introduced by the College of Policing in July 2014 and is available from the College of Policing website. It was issued as a Code of Practice under s 39A(5) of the Police Act 1996, as amended by s 124 of the Anti-social Behaviour, Crime and Policing Act 2014 (CoP, 2014a). The Code of Ethics is central to the professionalization of the police service and police practices. All police officers and staff must observe the Code and ensure it is applied for all police officers, staff, and volunteers engaged in policing within the service.

The College drafted a revised Code of Ethics for consultation in 2023, which promoted the idea of policing being guided by three primary principles: prioritizing public service; leading with professional courage; and responding with respect and empathy. The revised Code is also supported by a Code of Practice for ethical policing, requiring chief officers to support colleagues and provide an environment in which the ethical principles set out in the revised Code can be realized and put into practice. Details of the consultation are provided on the College's website at https://www.college.police.uk/consultation-code-ethics.

3.6 National Policing Strategies

The major police reforms around 2011 also included the creation of the Strategic Policing Requirement (SPR). This was a bold attempt by the Home Office to outline the commitments and priorities that would require a co-ordinated and joint response from the police service and, where a number of police services could act in unison, to tackle a serious national threat or risk.

The first SPR was issued by the Home Secretary in 2012 and required both PCCs and chief constables to be ready to respond anywhere with trained, equipped, and deployable resources to address incidents of terrorism, serious public disorder, or civil disaster. In 2015, the SPR was reviewed and revised. Child sexual abuse was added to the list of national threats to which police services may have to respond in a collective and co-ordinated manner.

A further review has just been completed in February 2023 and from this Violence against Women and Girls (VAWG) was also included in the national threat list. The latest list is as follows:

Violence Against Women and Girls
Terrorism
Serious and Organised Crime
National Cyber Event
Child Sexual Abuse
Public Disorder
Civil Emergencies
(Home Office, 2023b)

A number of regional collaborations have since been established between police services to deal with crime and policing issues that some found difficult to address alone, and the SPR remains one of the most important statements about how constabularies are expected to work together—in effect as a national police service.

3.6.1 Policing Vision 2025

The Association of Police and Crime Commissioners (APCC) and the National Police Chiefs' Council (NPCC) produced a report entitled Policing Vision 2025 in 2016, this set out the plan for how these two key organizations saw policing adapting and developing nationally to ensure that the police service as a whole could continue to meet the needs of the communities whilst ensuring that the service continues to adapt to the challenges that exist in today's modern policing environment.

3.7 Misconduct and Complaints Procedures

Police misconduct and complaint procedures are primarily governed by three pieces of legislation, namely: Police (Complaints and Misconduct) Regulations 2020, Police (Conduct) Regulations 2020, and Police (Performance) Regulations 2020. These regulations are outlined in *Home Office Guidance: Conduct, Efficiency and Effectiveness: Statutory Guidance on Professional Standards, Performance and Integrity in Policing* (Home Office, 2020a) and replace the Police (Conduct) Regulations 2012 with the aim of creating a culture of learning and development rather than sanction and punishment.

'Misconduct', under the Police (Conduct) Regulations 2020 (PCR 2020), is defined as 'a breach of the Standards of Professional Behaviour that is so serious as to justify disciplinary action' (reg 2 of the PCR 2020). 'Gross misconduct' is a more serious failure to meet the standards (so serious that it could lead to dismissal) (reg 3(1) of the PCR 2020). Allegations concerning the conduct of a police officer fall into one of two categories:

- 'conduct matters'—which concern allegations made against a police officer by a colleague; and
- 'complaints'—which are allegations made by a member of the public about the conduct of a police officer.

The process of making such allegations, the investigation, and subsequent methods of disposal are together known as the Police Complaints System.

Complaints and conduct matters can be handled by a line manager or supervisor, or if more serious by the 'appropriate authority' or the Independent Office for Police Conduct (IOPC). The appropriate authority would be a chief officer (chief constable or commissioner) but they can delegate this function to a police officer of at least the rank of chief inspector or another police staff member of at least a similar level of seniority. This will frequently be an officer within a Professional Standards Department.

3.7.1 Conduct matters

Police officers are required to abide by the standards of professional behaviour set out in the Code of Ethics. This includes the requirement of a police officer to report, challenge, or take action against the conduct of any colleague whose behaviour has fallen below any of the standards. Failure to report such instances would render the officer liable for claims of misconduct. Normally, an officer should report any concerns to their supervisor or the Professional Standards Department, but concerns can also be raised confidentially with the IOPC as it is designated as an official body for the purposes of public interest disclosure.

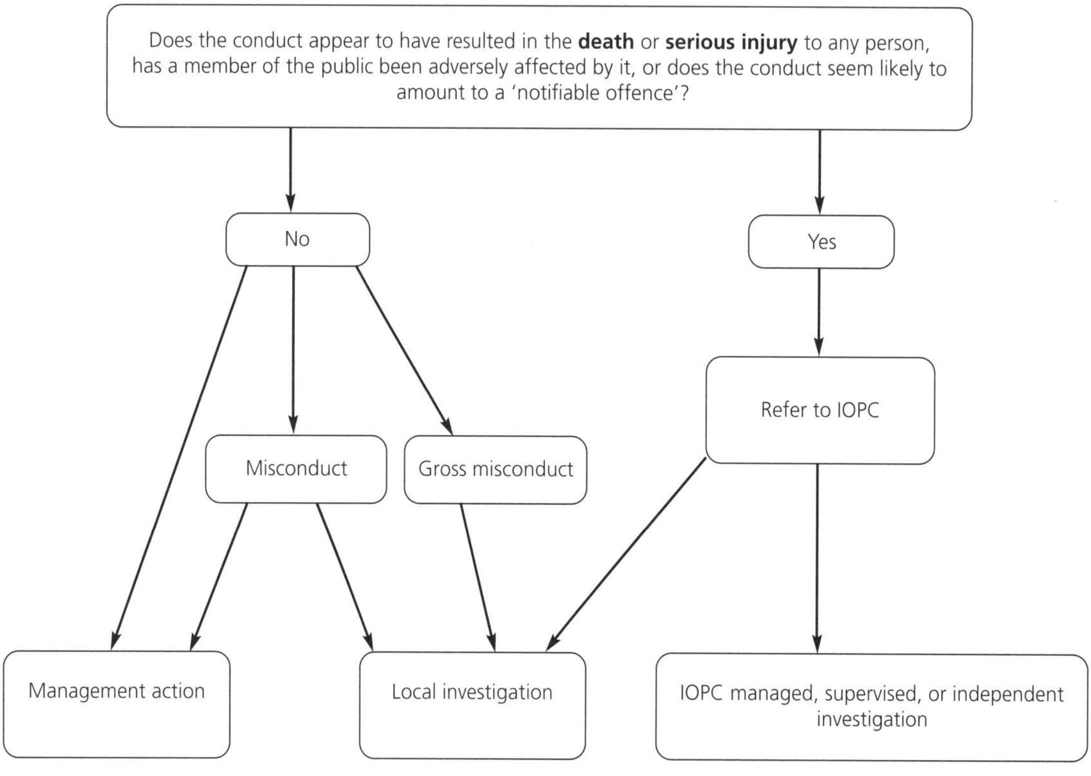

3.7.2 Complaints

Allegations made by members of the public concerning the conduct or behaviour of a police officer (student officer or confirmed) are called complaints. Examples might include complaints of rudeness, the use of excessive force, or unjustified arrest. Allegations can only be made by a member of the public who:

- claims to be the victim of the conduct;
- claims to have been adversely affected by the conduct (but is not the victim);
- claims to have witnessed the conduct; or
- is a person who is representing any of the above.

The appropriate course of action will be decided by the appropriate authority.

Statutory guidance on the handling of complaints is available on the IOPC website, as are policy updates regarding all matters regarding the complaints and investigation processes https://www.policeconduct.gov.uk. The flowchart summarizes the current process for managing complaints.

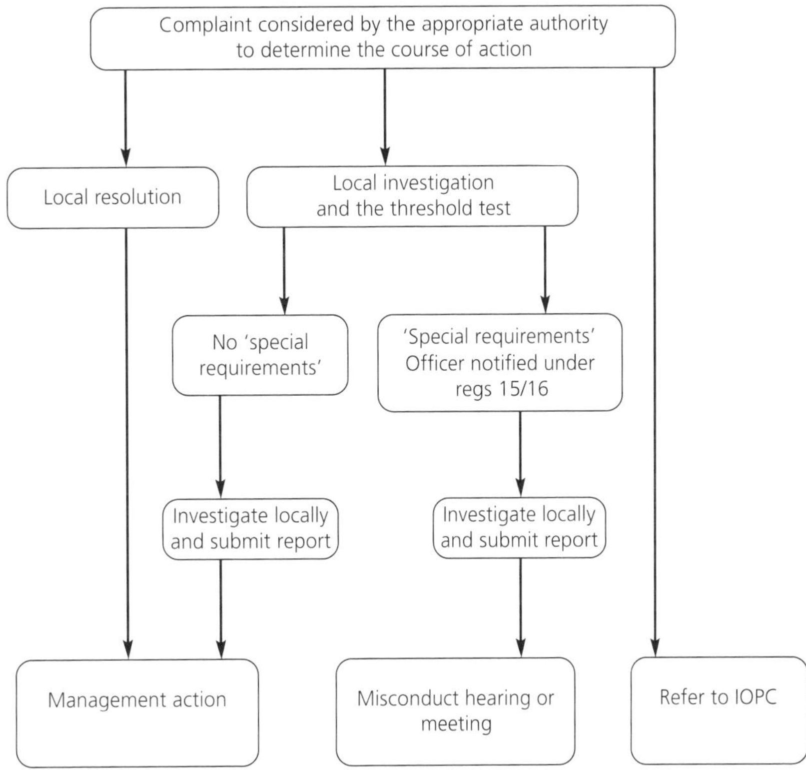

The threshold test establishes whether it appears likely that the officer who is the subject of the complaint has committed a criminal offence or behaved in such a way that disciplinary proceedings are likely to be required. If this applies, the investigation will be subject to 'special requirements' and the officer must be formally notified about the investigation.

3.7.3 The Independent Office for Police Conduct (IOPC)

The IOPC replaced the Independent Police Complaints Commission (IPCC) in 2018, reflecting an enduring feature of debates regarding police complaints in the UK, which have centred on the lack of independence from the police, of those investigating complaints against the police. The Director General was Michael Lockwood, but he resigned in December 2022 after it emerged that he was the subject of a police investigation. An independent review, led by Sir David Calvert Smith is expected to report on the matter later in 2023. The Interim Director General of the IOPC is Tom Whiting, formerly the IOPC's Deputy Director General Strategy and Corporate Services before taking on his current responsibilities in December 2022.

The IOPC will not only investigate allegations involving the police but will also deal with serious complaints and conduct matters relating to staff at the NCA, GLAA, Home Office, HMRC, Mayor's Office for Policing and Crime (MOPAC), and Police and Crime Commissioners.

When the IOPC receives a referral from a police service, the IOPC assessment unit reviews the information it has received. The IOPC then decides if the matter requires an investigation, and if so of what type. There are three different types of investigation: local, directed, and independent. There are fewer high-level investigations, and as you might expect, the more serious the matter, the higher the level of the investigation and the greater the level of direct IOPC involvement.

3.7.3.1 Local police investigations and local resolution

A local investigation is carried out for less serious matters and the IOPC will not be involved. It would usually be carried out by the constabulary's Professional Standards Department and be similar to any other police inquiry, including, for example, the collection of evidence through interviews from witnesses and suspects. The investigator is appointed by the appropriate authority and the officer under investigation must be notified (under reg 15 of the Police (Conduct) Regulations 2012, or reg 16 of the Police (Complaints and Misconduct) Regulations 2012).

Local (or informal) resolution may be possible, in which case reg 15/16 notices are not required, no blame is attached, nor is there any need to involve disciplinary procedures. The process will not affect a trainee officer's personal development plan, staff appraisal, or any subsequent misconduct hearing. Note that a police service cannot make an apology to the complainant unless this is authorized by the officer against whom the complaint was made.

3.7.3.2 Investigations involving the IOPC

Investigations into more serious matters will involve the IOPC. An IOPC-**directed** investigation is used for complaints or allegations of misconduct which are of considerable significance and probable public concern. The IOPC will direct and control the investigation using police resources. The complainant has the right of appeal to the IOPC. An **independent** IOPC investigation is used for incidents that cause the greatest level of public concern, have the greatest potential to impact on communities, or have serious implications for the reputation of the police service (for deaths in custody). These require a wholly independent investigation conducted only by IOPC staff.

3.7.3.3 Notification

The officer in question must be notified for all investigations that are:

- referred to the IOPC;
- into a complaint where special requirements apply; or
- into conduct matters where it seems likely there has been misconduct or gross misconduct, a notifiable offence, a death, or serious injury.

The notice must be served in writing and as soon as practicable. It will be served under reg 15 of the Police (Conduct) Regulations 2012 or reg 16 of the Police (Complaints and Misconduct) Regulations 2012, as amended by the PCR 2020. The same form is used for both conduct matters and complaints. The notice may be referred to in police circles as a 'reg 15'. A notice may also be given for less serious investigations.

The notice will include a description of the conduct, the outcome of the severity or threshold test, and a reminder that the officer can seek advice from the Police Federation. The Police Federation advises any officer receiving a reg 15/16 notice not to say anything before seeking advice from a Federation representative. If the officer is to be interviewed, once again the advice is to contact a Federation representative who will arrange to attend the interview or, in some circumstances, help to arrange for legal representation.

3.7.4 Outcomes and sanctions

After the evidence has been collected in an investigation, the appropriate authority decides if the officer's behaviour amounted to misconduct or gross misconduct.

A misconduct meeting may be held for an officer falling slightly short of the standards of professional behaviour, and a misconduct hearing will be held for more serious failures or when the officer already has a final written warning. The only outcomes available at a misconduct meeting, following the changes brought in by the new PCR 2020, are a **written warning** and a **final written warning**. The length of time that written warnings and final written warnings remain in force has also been extended—from 12 to 18 months for written warnings and from 18 months to two years for final written warnings.

At the misconduct **hearing**, the disciplinary actions available when the conclusion is misconduct are:

- written warning;
- final written warning;
- reduction in rank;
- dismissal without notice.

A panel at a **misconduct hearing** can find that the case against the officer, on the balance of probabilities, amounts to misconduct or gross misconduct or neither. If the panel decides that the conduct amounts to neither, the panel may direct the matter to be referred under the

Reflective Practice Review Process or determine that no further action is taken. This is set out in reg 42(1)(b) of the PCR 2020.

If the panel find the case against the officer proven as to misconduct, disciplinary action will follow, and it must decide to impose one of the following disciplinary actions:

(a) written warning;
(b) final written warning;
(c) reduction in rank (re-introduced in the PCR 2020 where misconduct or gross misconduct is proven);
(d) dismissal without notice.

If a panel finds the case against the officer proven as to gross misconduct, actions (b), (c), and (d) are available; that is, final written warning, reduction in rank, or dismissal without notice. Where a **written warning** is imposed as the disciplinary action, this will be fixed at 18 months. Where a **final written warning** is imposed, the panel will decide on the length that this warning will remain on the officer's record, at a minimum of two years to a maximum of five years. The warning remains live on the officer's file for the period stipulated. Should an officer transfer constabulary during the live period, the warning transfers with the officer.

In the recent past, there was a public perception that some officers under investigation for gross misconduct were resigning to avoid being held to account for their alleged failings. This loophole was closed by the Police (Conduct, Complaints and Misconduct and Appeal Tribunal) (Amendment) Regulations 2017 which came into force in December 2017. These regulations allow for an investigation into a retired officer to continue in certain circumstances, even if the officer has left the police service.

3.7.5 Unsatisfactory performance or attendance

Unsatisfactory performance or attendance is an 'inability or failure of a police officer to perform the duties of the role or rank [they are] currently undertaking to a satisfactory standard or level' (Police (Performance) Regulations 2012). The 2017 Home Office Guidance Document *Police Officer Misconduct, Unsatisfactory Performance and Attendance Management Procedures* (Home Office, 2018a) suggests that early interventions by a manager ('management action') should be sufficient to improve and maintain a police officer's performance or attendance. It also states that formal action should not be taken unless the police officer has earlier been offered supportive action but had declined or failed to cooperate, resulting in no improvement.

The Unsatisfactory Performance Procedures (UPP) can also be invoked for officers who are on long-term sick leave and supported by management action if a return to work within a reasonable time frame is unrealistic. Note that the UPP do not apply to officers during their probationary period; reg 13 of the Police Regulations 2003 would be used instead.

There are three stages in the UPP with 3–12 months between each. During this time, there must be improvement, and the satisfactory performance must be maintained for a year in order to avoid moving on to the next stage. For a full explanation of how this process works, see Home Office (2018a).

3.8 Protest, Disorder, and Anti-social Behaviour

This section of the chapter deals with a number of disparate aspects of policing that deal with, in one way or another, mostly groups of people gathering together across a range of activities in different circumstances. The intentions of those gathering, and the reasons for them being together, also vary significantly but include sporting and other recreational events, protests, trespassing, and different forms of anti-social behaviour. There is not space here to cover each aspect in detail; instead we provide brief summaries for awareness and we identify key legislation, guidance, and policing priorities.

3.8.1 Anti-social behaviour

The definition of anti-social behaviour (ASB) is behaviour which has 'caused or is likely to cause harassment, alarm or distress to any person' (s 2(1)(a) of the Anti-social Behaviour,

Crime and Policing Act 2014 (ASBCPA)). ASBCPA 2014 provides powers and injunctions to help the police and local authorities address ASB and also disorder, which can become more serious, involving harassment, violence, and criminality. Note also that the Police, Crime, Sentencing and Courts Act 2022 abolished the common law offence of public nuisance and replaced it with a new offence of intentional or reckless causing of a public nuisance. This is triable either way and carries a maximum sentence of ten years' imprisonment on indictment.

The Home Office guidance *Anti-social Behaviour, Crime and Policing Act 2014: Reform of anti-social behaviour powers: Statutory guidance for frontline professionals* (Home Office, 2014a) was revised in March 2023, with an emphasis on two priorities areas:

- 'putting victims at the heart of the response to anti-social behaviour' (p 4), with a focus on the importance of the formal Anti-social Behaviour Case Review, previously referred to as the Community Trigger. The revised guidance also stresses the importance of the Community Remedy in this regard;
- 'the use of powers provided by the 2014 Act', with a focus on ensuring that powers are used flexibly, proportionately and appropriately in recognition of the 'different forms of anti-social behaviour' (p 5).

ASB can have a significant detrimental impact on individuals, communities, and businesses, and this is both recognized and emphasized in the March 2023 updated guidance. It is recognized that the persistent and repeated nature of ASB has a cumulative impact and therefore the emphasis is on putting the victim first. The focus on victims in this way requires the police, working with other agencies, to rethink what are appropriate and proportionate measures, and this should guide your approach to ASB. Preventative measures should also be considered in line with this focus.

As part of the revised guidance, attention is drawn to the five principles of ASB:

1. Victims should be encouraged to report ASB and expect to be taken seriously. They should have clear ways to report, have access to help and support to recover, and be given the opportunity to choose restorative approaches to tackling ASB.
2. Agencies will have clear and transparent processes to ensure that victims can report ASB concerns, can understand how the matter will be investigated and are kept well informed of progress once a report is made. Anti-social behaviour powers—Statutory guidance for frontline professionals.
3. Agencies and practitioners will work across boundaries to identify, assess and tackle ASB and its underlying causes. Referral pathways should be clearly set out between services and published locally. This includes pathways for the ASB Case Review and health services.
4. The public's ASB concerns should always be considered both nationally and locally in strategic needs assessments for community safety. Best practice should be shared through a network of ASB experts within each community safety partnership, each policing area and nationally.
5. Adults and children who exhibit ASB should have the opportunity to take responsibility for their behaviour and repair the harm caused by it. Agencies should deliver appropriate interventions, which may include criminal justice options, based on the seriousness, risks and vulnerabilities of the case.
   (Source: https://www.gov.uk/government/publications/anti-social-behaviour-principles/anti-social-behaviour-principles)

These principles are intended to support agencies in providing a consistent approach to dealing with ASB with a focus on the victim. They are also intended to guide the approach to two mechanisms that help centre responses around community needs:

- ASB Case Review—this was formerly referred to as the Community Trigger and provides victims a process through which a formal case review can be established;
- Community Remedy—allows victims a voice with regards to community resolutions and (youth) conditional cautions.

3.8.1.1 Powers to deal with ASB

Details of the various measures available to the police are included in the March 2023 updated guidance. Here we note some of these measures with a brief summary.

Civil Injunctions are covered by ss 1 to 21 of the Anti-social Behaviour, Crime and Policing Act 2014 and are primarily used to prevent ASB or to stop it quickly before it becomes more serious. Note the distinction between housing related and non-housing related contexts and youth offending teams should be consulted when applying for injunctions against under 18 year olds.

Criminal Behaviour Orders (CBOs) can be used to deal with the most persistently anti-social individuals who engage in criminal activity. CBOs are issued by a criminal court on conviction for any criminal offence, but the ASB does not need to be part of the offence. The court must be satisfied beyond reasonable doubt that the offender had already engaged in behaviour that caused or was likely to cause harassment, alarm, or distress to any person, and that making the order would help to prevent the offender from engaging in further similar behaviour (s 22 of the ASBCPA).

Dispersal powers allows a police officer in uniform to direct any person committing or likely to commit ASB, crime, or disorder to leave an area for up to 48 hours. These powers are covered in ss 34 to 42 of the Anti-social Behaviour, Crime and Policing Act 2014 and there is a focus on the impact the powers may have on the most vulnerable members of society.

Community Protection Notice is designed to address ASB caused by an individual aged over 16, or by businesses and other organizations. The ASB needs to be having a detrimental effect on the quality of life for people in the locality and to be unreasonable and persistent/continuing. This is covered by ss 43 to 58 of the Anti-social Behaviour, Crime and Policing Act 2014 and again there is an emphasis on considering the likely impact on the vulnerable.

Public Spaces Protection Order (PSPO) is issued by a council and designed to manage a specific problem which is caused by individuals or groups in a particular public place and is injurious to the local community. The restrictions imposed by the order must be proportionate and justified, eg keeping dogs on a lead or prohibiting the consumption of alcohol in a particular area. A PSPO takes precedence over any by-law which already prohibits an activity in the restricted area and are covered in ss 59 to 75 of the Anti-social Behaviour, Crime and Policing Act 2014. Again, protecting the vulnerable is stressed with consideration given to risks associated with displacement.

Expedited Public Spaces Protection Order (E-PSPO) deal with the specific challenges caused by the ASB of individuals targeting people who work in or use schools, vaccination sites, NHS Test and Trace/Test, Trace, Protect sites. E-PSPO is covered by ss 59A to 74 of the Anti-social Behaviour, Crime and Policing Act 2014 as amended by ss 82 of, and Schedule 7 to, the Police, Crime, Sentencing and Courts Act 2022 (s 82 of the 2022 Act inserted new ss 59A, 60A, 72A and 72B into the 2014 Act). Consideration of the vulnerable is stressed with specific mention of an individual's rights under the European Convention on Human Rights and risks associated with displacement.

Absolute Ground for Possession (AGP) can be used by landlords to evict tenants where ASB or criminality has already been proven by another court. The police should not be directly involved in any AGP-related action as it is a civil matter, but they should be aware of its existence in providing advice to landlords, etc. This is covered by ss 94 to 100 of the Anti-social Behaviour, Crime and Policing Act 2014.

3.8.1.2 Dangerous dogs and anti-social behaviour

Dogs must be kept under control and prevented from injuring people or other dogs. The owner of a dog, or the person in charge of it at the time (A), commits an offence under s 3(1) of the Dangerous Dogs Act 1991 if the dog is dangerously out of control in any place. The offence is aggravated if the dog causes injury to a person (B) or an assistance dog. However, these offences do not apply if the dog is in a dwelling or forces accommodation (in the building, or partly in it, or in part of it) and B was in (or entering) as a trespasser or if A was present and believed B to be trespassing.

Guidance for dealing with owners or breeders of dangerous dogs (defined in s 1 of the Dangerous Dogs Act 1991) can be found in *Dangerous Dogs Law Guidance for Enforcers*.

3.8.2 Breach of the peace

Breach of the peace is not a criminal offence or part of statute law, but is instead part of common law. Case law has set a precedent in defining its meaning. Some police constabularies discourage their officers from the use of police powers in relation to a breach of the peace, whereas others continue to view it as an important means of reducing the likelihood of harm taking place. In all cases, the police use of breach of the peace should be consistent with Article 5 (the right to liberty and security), Article 10 (the right to freedom of expression), and Article 11 (the right to freedom of assembly and association) of the European Convention on Human Rights (as set out in the Human Rights Act 1998).

The case of *R v Howell* [1981] 3 All ER 383 defines the meaning of breach of the peace:

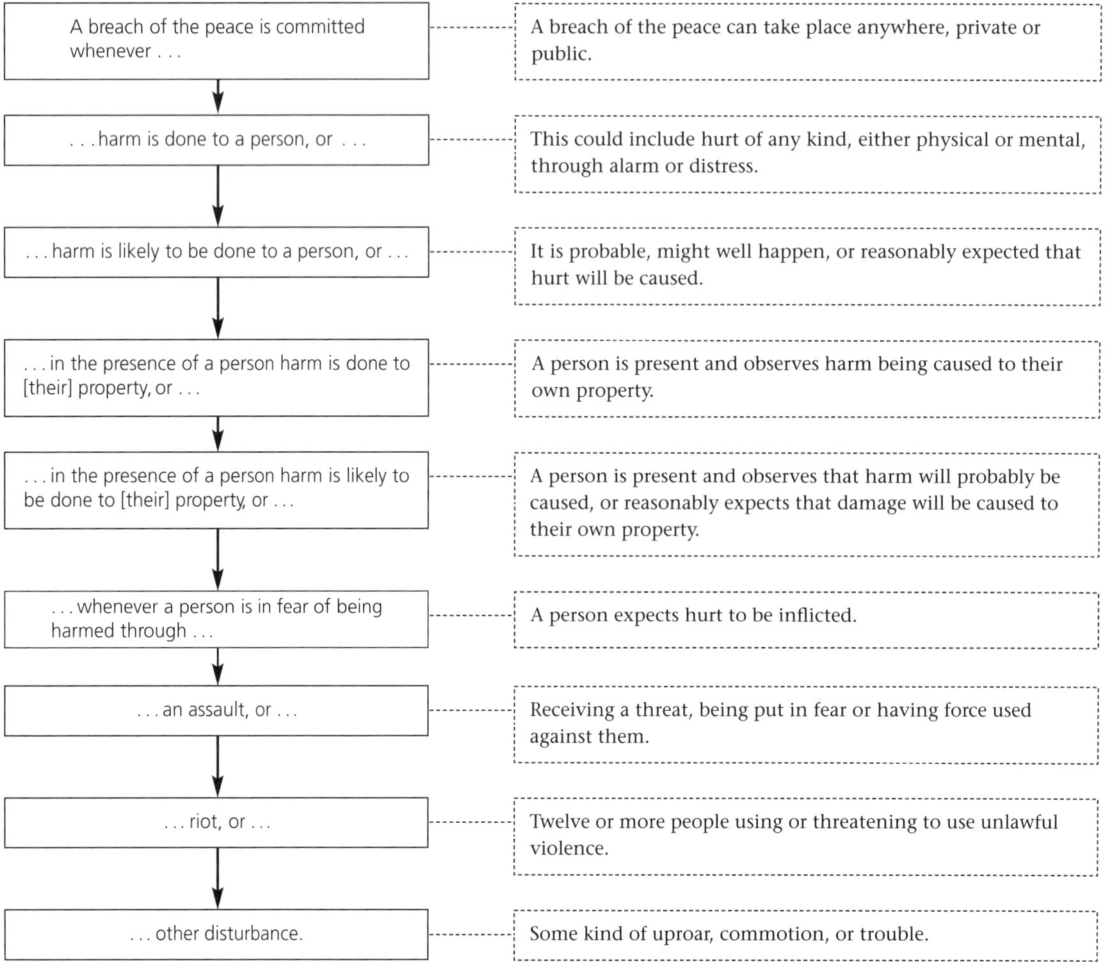

A breach of the peace is committed whenever . . .
A breach of the peace can take place anywhere, private or public.
. . . harm is done to a person, or . . .
This could include hurt of any kind, either physical or mental, through alarm or distress.
. . . harm is likely to be done to a person, or . . .
It is probable, might well happen, or reasonably expected that hurt will be caused.
. . . in the presence of a person harm is done to [their] property, or . . .
A person is present and observes harm being caused to their own property.
. . . in the presence of a person harm is likely to be done to [their] property, or . . .
A person is present and observes that harm will probably be caused, or reasonably expects that damage will be caused to their own property.
. . . whenever a person is in fear of being harmed through . . .
A person expects hurt to be inflicted.
. . . an assault, or . . .
Receiving a threat, being put in fear or having force used against them.
. . . riot, or . . .
Twelve or more people using or threatening to use unlawful violence.
. . . other disturbance.
Some kind of uproar, commotion, or trouble.

The powers of arrest for breach of the peace are unique. It can take place in many different ways, but must satisfy the elements set out in the case *R v Howell*.

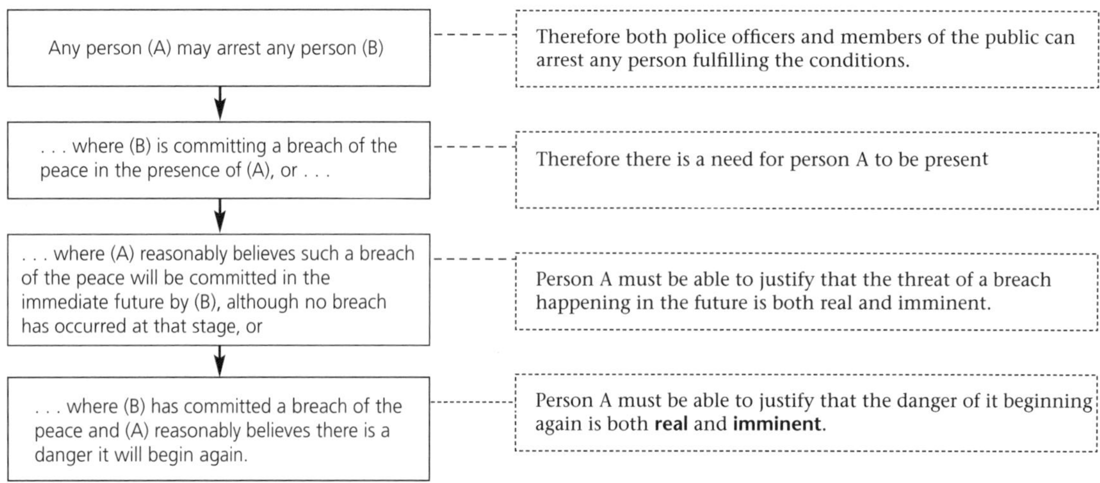

Any person (A) may arrest any person (B)
Therefore both police officers and members of the public can arrest any person fulfilling the conditions.
. . . where (B) is committing a breach of the peace in the presence of (A), or . . .
Therefore there is a need for person A to be present
. . . where (A) reasonably believes such a breach of the peace will be committed in the immediate future by (B), although no breach has occurred at that stage, or
Person A must be able to justify that the threat of a breach happening in the future is both real and imminent.
. . . where (B) has committed a breach of the peace and (A) reasonably believes there is a danger it will begin again.
Person A must be able to justify that the danger of it beginning again is both **real** and **imminent**.

Under common law, an officer is entitled to enter either private or public premises in order to make an arrest for a breach of the peace or to prevent such a breach. Once the breach has come to an end, the officer should not remain on private premises and should leave within a 'reasonable time'. If they are assaulted during that reasonable time, this could be regarded as an assault on a police officer in the lawful execution of their duty. However, if the officer has not left within a reasonable time, their presence may be unlawful and therefore they might not be protected under criminal law (*Robson v Hallett* [1967] 2 QB 939).

3.8.2.1 Binding-over after an arrest for breach of the peace

After arrest for breach of the peace, the police can release the person without further action when it is deemed that a risk of a breach no longer exists. However, in other circumstances the CPS may decide (s 3(2)(c) of the Prosecution of Offences Act 1985) that further action is needed to reduce the risk of another breach. A magistrates' court can issue a binding-over order which can refer to general terms of protection or it can be more specific by naming people. The order can also require the recipient to keep the peace for a specified time and/or enter into a recognizance for a specified sum.

3.8.2.2 Containment

Containment, also known as *kettling*, is used by the police to maintain public order and safety. It involves putting a cordon around a large number of people and confining them to a relatively small, easily managed public area, and police officers decide who remains inside the cordon and for how long. The police argue that the likelihood of an imminent breach of the peace provides them with common law powers to confine people in this way, but this has been challenged in the courts.

In *R (on the application of Hannah McClure and Joshua Moos) v Commissioner of Police of the Metropolis* [2012] EWCA Civ 12, the containment was justified by the reasonable apprehension of imminent and serious breaches of the peace likely to be caused by another substantial crowd of protesters arriving at an airbase. The justification was not the violent and unruly behaviour of the main crowd.

Containment is only lawful if the police actions are proportionate, reasonable, and necessary. The police must not use containment until they have taken all other possible steps to prevent the breach or imminent breach of the peace and protect the rights of third parties (*Austin v Commissioner of Police of the Metropolis* [2009] 1 AC 564). The containment of children is lawful if s 11 of the Children Act 2004 is followed regarding the welfare of the children (*R (on the application of Castle and others) v Commissioner of Police of the Metropolis* [2011] EWHC 2317 (Admin)). It is accepted that police actions may affect people who are not actively involved in the breach of the peace.

Further case law on containment can be found in *Laporte v Chief Constable of Gloucestershire Constabulary* [2007] 2 AC 105 (see also *Moss v McLachlan* [1985] 1 RLR 76 in relation to the policing of the 1984 miners' strike).

It should be noted that people released from containment have no obligation to provide personal information nor is it acceptable for them to be photographed (*Susannah Mengesha v Commissioner of Police of the Metropolis* [2013] EWHC 1695 (Admin)).

3.8.3 Public Order legislation

The Public Order Act 2023 came into effect on 2 May 2023 and introduces a number of new offences, with a particular focus on responding to the changing nature of protests. Environmental groups, such as *Extinction Rebellion* and *Just Stop Oil* have had significant impact in disrupting people's lives in order to get their messages across. These disruptions have included particular tactics to close roads and other modes of transport, including the rail network. The Act introduces new offences related specifically to the tactics used by protesters, such as locking on (s 1) and being equipped for locking on (s 2), along with causing serious disruption through tunnelling (s 3), causing serious disruption by being present in a tunnel (s 4), and being equipped for tunnelling etc. (s 5). Other offences relating to the environmental protest groups include obstructing major transport works (s 6) and interfering with key national infrastructure (s 7).

Other developments in the contemporary nature of protest are also reflected in the Public Order Act 2023. There is an offence relating specifically to those who target abortion clinics (s 9) and the impact of one-person demonstrations are dealt with (ss 15–16). The Act also provides more scope for stop and search powers (ss 10–14), and police powers in relation to journalists are qualified (s 17).

In Part 2 of the Public Order Act 2023, there is the introduction of a new measure, Serious Disruption Prevention Orders (SDPO), which clearly target individuals who are repeatedly engaged in protest activities that have a major impact on other people's lives.

The Public Order Act 1986 deals with a wide range of behaviours and offences, in descending order of seriousness: riot (s 1), violent disorder (s 2), affray (s 3), fear or provocation of violence (s 4), intentional harassment, alarm, or distress (s 4A), and non-intentional harassment, alarm, or distress (s 5). As you might expect, the least serious offences are the most commonly committed. Note that intoxication is not a defence in public order offences unless the intoxication was due to prescribed drugs as part of a medical plan or was not self-induced, eg spiked drinks.

Offences under ss 4, 4A, and 5 of the Public Order Act 1986 are for the most part only committed in a public place, but in certain circumstances they can also be committed within the confines of a private place, for example a communal area such as a shared laundry in a block of flats (see *Le Vine v DPP* (2010) DC (unreported, 6 May)). These offences can also apply when the conduct occurs in the confines of a private place but it causes a person who is in a public place to be harassed, alarmed, or distressed. The more serious public order offences (riot, violent disorder, and affray) can take place in private as well as in public places.

Sections 5 and 4A of the Public Order Act 1986 are used for relatively minor forms of public disorder such as persistent swearing and shouting. Section 4 is used for more serious public disorder involving fear or provocation of violence. The distinctions between offences under ss 5, 4A, and 4 require careful consideration and still cause some debate in legal and police circles. The intentions of the suspect and the nature of the conduct differentiate the offences. Note that the Police, Crime, Sentencing and Courts Act 2022 introduced new elements into the 1986 Act regarding one-person protests (s 79).

3.8.3.1 Section 5 of the Public Order Act 1986

Section 5 of the Public Order Act 1986 states that a person is guilty of this offence if they use threatening or abusive words or behaviour, or disorderly behaviour, or if they display any writing, sign, or other visible representation which is threatening or abusive and this is done within the hearing or sight of a person likely to be caused harassment, alarm, or distress thereby. The offence is also referred to as causing non-intentional harassment, alarm, or distress; or disorderly behaviour/conduct. Note that police officers are expected to be accustomed to higher levels of abuse than the general public (*DPP v Orum* [1989] Crim LR 848), so in most circumstances police officers will not usually be considered to be a person likely to be harassed, alarmed, or distressed.

The offence is triable summarily and the penalty is a fine but can also be dealt with by way of a community resolution or a penalty notice for disorder. This offence can also be racially or religiously aggravated.

3.8.3.2 Section 4A of the Public Order Act 1986

A s 4A offence is often referred to as causing intentional harassment, alarm, or distress. A person is guilty of this offence if they use threatening, abusive, or insulting words or behaviour, or commit disorderly behaviour, or display any writing, sign, or other visible representation which is threatening, abusive, or insulting with intent to cause a person harassment, alarm, or distress thereby causing that or another person harassment, alarm, or distress.

This piece of legislation is aimed at supporting the most vulnerable members of the community who may be specifically targeted because of their inability to respond appropriately to intentionally directed acts which cause them harassment, alarm, or distress. These victims may feel particularly uncomfortable as witnesses so every opportunity should be taken to support them throughout any police or legal process.

This offence is triable summarily and the penalty is six months' imprisonment and/or a fine. This offence can be racially or religiously aggravated.

3.8.3.3 Section 4 of the Public Order Act 1986

A s 4 offence is also referred to as fear or provocation of violence. A person is guilty of this offence if they use towards another person threatening, abusive, or insulting words or behaviour or if they distribute or display to another person any writing, sign, or other visible representation which is threatening, abusive, or insulting. The intent must be to:

- cause that person to believe that immediate unlawful violence will be used (against them or another) by any person; or
- provoke the immediate use of unlawful violence (by that person or another);
- cause that person to believe it is likely either that such violence will be used or be provoked.

For this offence, the intentions of the suspect are the key issue; the actual effect of the behaviour on other people is not relevant. The intention must be to make the recipient feel fear or to provoke other people or another person to be violent. For the suspect's intentions to be held as genuine, their conduct must be directed towards a recipient who is present when the words or behaviour are used. The recipient must be able to see or hear the conduct (or the suspect must at least believe that the recipient is able to see or hear the conduct (see *Atkin v DPP* [1989] Crim LR 581)).

If the suspect's intentions are to cause fear of violence, they must intend the recipient to fear that violence will be used. However, the threatened violent acts do not need to involve the suspect or the recipient directly: the violence could be threatened against another person or be carried out by a person other than the suspect.

A police officer may enter any premises to arrest any person reasonably suspected of committing an offence under s 4 of the Public Order Act 1986 (s 17 of the PACE Act 1984). The offence is triable summarily and the penalty is six months' imprisonment and/or a fine. This offence can be racially aggravated.

3.8.3.4 Serious public order offences

These offences under the Public Order Act 1986, in increasing order of seriousness, are affray (s 3), violent disorder (s 2), and riot (s 1). These offences all involve unlawful violence and can be committed in private as well as in public. Violence is essentially aggressive or hostile conduct towards property or persons and includes acts capable of causing injury even if no injury or damage is caused, for example throwing a full can of beer towards a person even if it falls short (see s 8 of the Public Order Act).

The legislation describing offences under ss 1–3 also uses the term a 'person of reasonable firmness', sometimes referred to as the 'hypothetical bystander'. This is not defined under law but can be taken to mean an average person in terms of their reaction to violent incidents around them.

Affray

For an affray (s 3 of the Public Order Act 1986), the threat of violence needs to be capable of upsetting others. The primary objective of the law is to protect the general public around the affray and therefore the court will consider how a hypothetical person of reasonable firmness who witnessed the incident would feel (*R v Sanchez* (1996) The Times, 6 March).

Therefore, there are in effect three parties involved in an affray:

- the individual making the threats;
- the person subject to the threats; and
- one or more bystanders or sufficient likelihood of one or more bystanders arriving at the scene.

In drawing a conclusion about the conduct of the suspects and the person of reasonable firmness, the court can consider evidence from witnesses at the incident, the extent of any injuries, and recordings such as from CCTV or the media.

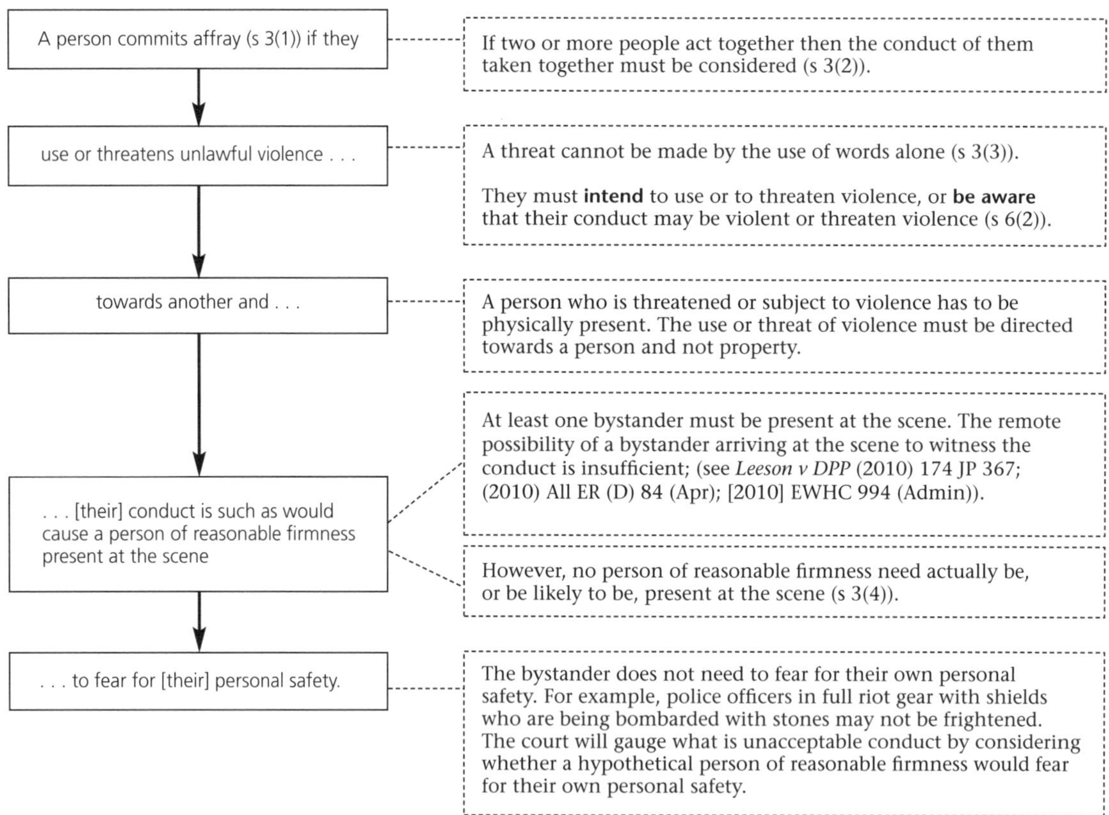

A person commits affray (s 3(1)) if they
If two or more people act together then the conduct of them taken together must be considered (s 3(2)).
use or threatens unlawful violence . . .
A threat cannot be made by the use of words alone (s 3(3)).
They must **intend** to use or to threaten violence, or **be aware** that their conduct may be violent or threaten violence (s 6(2)).
towards another and . . .
A person who is threatened or subject to violence has to be physically present. The use or threat of violence must be directed towards a person and not property.
. . . [their] conduct is such as would cause a person of reasonable firmness present at the scene
At least one bystander must be present at the scene. The remote possibility of a bystander arriving at the scene to witness the conduct is insufficient; (see *Leeson v DPP* (2010) 174 JP 367; (2010) All ER (D) 84 (Apr); [2010] EWHC 994 (Admin)).
However, no person of reasonable firmness need actually be, or be likely to be, present at the scene (s 3(4)).
. . . to fear for [their] personal safety.
The bystander does not need to fear for their own personal safety. For example, police officers in full riot gear with shields who are being bombarded with stones may not be frightened. The court will gauge what is unacceptable conduct by considering whether a hypothetical person of reasonable firmness would fear for their own personal safety.

This offence is triable either way. The penalty if tried summarily is six months' imprisonment and/or a fine and on indictment three years' imprisonment.

Violent disorder and riot

For the offence of violent disorder (s 2 of the Public Order Act 1986), three or more persons must be present together and use (or threaten to use) unlawful violence. There must be an intention to use or threaten violence or an awareness that the conduct may be violent or may threaten violence.

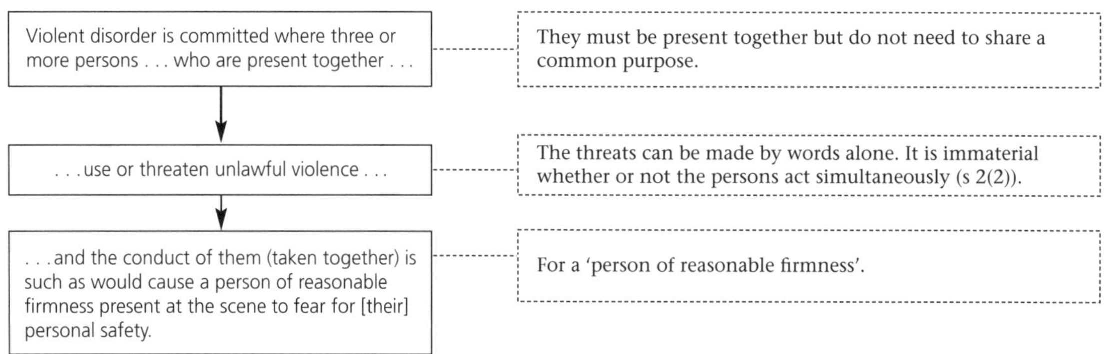

Violent disorder is committed where three or more persons . . . who are present together . . .
They must be present together but do not need to share a common purpose.
. . .use or threaten unlawful violence . . .
The threats can be made by words alone. It is immaterial whether or not the persons act simultaneously (s 2(2)).
. . .and the conduct of them (taken together) is such as would cause a person of reasonable firmness present at the scene to fear for [their] personal safety.
For a 'person of reasonable firmness'.

If it is only possible to arrest and investigate one person out of such a group, then they can still be charged with this offence, but it must still be proved that at least two other people using or threatening violence were present and they must be mentioned in the charge. However, there is no requirement for a common purpose to be held by those using or threatening violence (see *R v NW* [2010] EWCA Crim 404). This offence is triable either way. The penalty if tried summarily is six months' imprisonment and/or a fine, on indictment five years' imprisonment.

The offence of riot (s 1(1) of the Public Order Act 1986) is similar to that of violent disorder but 12 or more people must be present. Charges of riot are very rare. A riot offence is triable on indictment only and the maximum penalty is ten years' imprisonment.

3.8.4 Preventing harassment and the Criminal Justice and Police Act 2001

Harassing or intimidating behaviour by individuals towards a person in their home is an offence under the Criminal Justice and Police Act 2001. This legislation should not be seen as a way of stopping people from carrying out their lawful rights to protest peacefully or express strong opinions. Nor is it intended to prevent a fan from standing outside the home of their favourite television celebrity or to stop media commentators from trying to record first-hand comments from people in the news. Rather, this legislation aims to provide a balance between the right to carry out such activities with the rights of residents to be protected from harassment, alarm, or distress in their own homes.

The legislation referred to here provides more than one tool to deal with this type of situation. The direction to leave is useful but, of course, it does not prevent the same protesters from returning and continuing with the same type of behaviour. Charging a person with an offence, however, is a more serious matter. Therefore, you will need to consider carefully which of the powers to use and this will depend on factors such as the number of people in the vicinity of the person's home, their behaviour and purpose, and the impact of their presence on the resident(s) and people in the surrounding area.

As well as causing distress to a resident inside their dwelling, other people can also be affected such as friends of the resident inside the dwelling or people living nearby. Courts will use the 'reasonable person' test to decide if the relevant activities should be regarded as significantly disturbing.

Under s 42(1) of the Criminal Justice and Police Act 2001, a police officer has the power to give 'directions' to a person (or a group) in order to prevent them from causing harassment, alarm, or distress to residents (or other people in the vicinity). The wording of a direction (s 42(2)) might be 'You have caused harassment and distress to people living in this area. I therefore require you to leave immediately.'

The direction can be given orally or in writing and will instruct the person(s) to leave the vicinity and for a specified period (not exceeding three months) and conditions may be attached. An officer of any rank can give the direction (s 42(6)) but it will usually be given by the most senior officer present. An offence is committed under s 7A if a person who has received a direction to leave then fails to leave or leaves but then returns within the specified time period to try to persuade a resident to follow a particular course of action. This offence is triable summarily and the penalty is six months' imprisonment and/or a fine.

3.8.5 Policing football

Trainee officers might be involved in policing football matches, particularly in constabularies covering large towns and cities. The offences described in this section are covered under the Sporting Events (Control of Alcohol etc) Act 1985 and the Football (Offences) Act 1991. Currently, football is the only sport considered necessary to control.

Policing football matches became a significant challenge during the 1970s and 1980s as violence at football matches became increasingly problematic. There are growing concerns that violent behaviour at football matches is on the increase, and in particular the issues of flares, throwing projectiles on to the field of play, and pitch invasions by supporters have attracted attention.

The Football (Offences) Act 1991 deals with problem behaviour at football matches. It covers throwing objects, racist chanting, and pitch invasions. Section 2A of the Sporting Events (Control of Alcohol etc) Act 1985 also covers the possession of fireworks and similar objects at designated sporting events. The prohibited objects (s 2A(3) and (4)) include fireworks, rockets, distress flares, fog signals, pellets, and fumigator capsules, and any other item which is for 'the emission of a flare for purposes of illuminating or signalling, or the emission of smoke or a visible gas'.

Throwing objects at a designated football match is an offence under s 2 of the Football (Offences) Act 1991. Indecent or racist chanting at a designated football match is an offence under s 3(1) of the Football (Offences) Act 1991. The offence is triable summarily and the penalty is a fine. Spectators going onto the playing area at a designated football match commit an offence under s 4 of the Football (Offences) Act 1991. This includes 'any area adjacent to the playing area to which spectators are not generally admitted, without lawful authority or lawful excuse (which shall be for [the suspect] to prove)'. This offence is triable summarily and the penalty is a fine.

At present there is not the suggestion to introduce new legislation to deal with problems at football matches, but rather to make prosecutions the 'default response' (BBC, 2022).

Policing football also includes the travelling to and from games. Supporters will often travel to sports events by train, coach, or minibus. Drivers, owners, and passengers of some types of vehicle used for the principal purpose of carrying passengers to or from a designated sporting event are subject to legislation under s 1 of the Sporting Events (Control of Alcohol etc) Act 1985. Public service vehicles covered by this legislation include buses and coaches, passenger trains, and minibuses. It is an offence under s 1(2) to knowingly cause or permit intoxicating liquor to be carried on such a vehicle.

It is also a summary offence for a person to be drunk inside the ground or to be drunk while entering or trying to enter a ground at any time during the period of a designated sporting event at that ground (s 2(2)). The penalty is a fine.

3.8.5.1 Powers of entry and search for sports grounds

Section 7 of the Sporting Events (Control of Alcohol etc) Act 1985 allows a police officer to enter and search any part of the ground if they have reasonable grounds to suspect that an offence under the same Act is being/about to be committed, or to enforce the provisions of the Act. This relates to the possession of alcohol, fireworks, and similar articles and applies during the period of a designated sporting event at any designated sports ground. There is a power to search a person (s 7(2)) or a vehicle (s 7(3)) if there are reasonable grounds to suspect that an offence under this Act has been/is about to be committed.

3.8.6 Criminal trespass and outdoor gatherings

New legislation was introduced in 2022 to deal with what is perceived as a growing trespassing problem despite the fact that 'the number of authorised traveller pitches had increased by 41 per cent from January 2010 to January 2020' (Home Office 2022a). The legislation in question is Part 4 (ss 83–85) of the Police, Crime, Sentencing and Courts Act (PCSC) 2022. Travelling people with no fixed abode sometimes find a temporary place to live on privately owned land. This may cause anxiety and distress for the owners of the land or for local residents.

The PCSC Act 2022 amends s 60 in Part 5 of the Criminal Justice and Public Order Act 1994 by inserting a new offence *relating to residing on land without consent in or with a vehicle* (s 60C as amended by PCSC Act 2022 s 83). Section 85 of the PCSC Act 2022 requires the Secretary of State to provide guidance on the exercise of police powers in respect of trespassers on land etc. in light of the PCSC Act 2022. This was published at the same time as the legislation went live (Home Office 2022b) and provides detail of the new offence and the amendments to ss 60–62 of the Criminal Justice and Public Order Act 1994. The new legislation is designed to make it easier for trespassers to be moved on, with enhanced powers for the police, and tougher sentences being imposed.

3.8.6.1 Open-air gatherings with music at night

Sections 63, 64, and 65 of the Criminal Justice and Public Order Act 1994 can be used to deal with complaints about larger gatherings in the open air. The type of gathering is defined in s 63; more than 20 people must be present out of doors at night with amplified music with repetitive beats. The music must be loud or go on for a long time and be 'likely to cause serious distress to local residents'. The Act includes the power for police officers to give directions to people present at/travelling to such gatherings. Predictable exemptions are listed in the legislation.

A power is available to disperse ten or more people who are at a gathering with music at night (s 63(2)). It also applies for two or more people who are making preparations for such an event. The direction must be made by an officer of at least superintendent rank and, if not communicated by an officer at this rank, may be communicated by any constable at the scene (s 63(3)). A person will be regarded as having received the direction if reasonable steps have been taken to bring it to their attention (s 63(4)). It is an offence (s 63(6)) if a person fails to leave the land as soon as reasonably practicable or leaves and re-enters within seven days. A person who has been directed to leave a gathering who then moves on to another similar gathering within 24 hours commits an offence under s 63(7A). The offences are triable summarily and the penalty is three months' imprisonment and/or a fine.

A power of entry for the police when dealing with night-time open-air musical events is provided under s 64 of the Criminal Justice and Public Order Act 1994; police officers may need to be deployed to determine whether the gathering is covered under s 63, ie is a rave. If a police officer of at least the rank of superintendent reasonably believes that the relevant circumstances exist, then they may authorize any constable to enter the land (s 64(1)). A warrant is not required (s 64(3)). If the s 63 conditions are met, then s 63 directions can be given.

3.8.7 Fireworks offences

Under the law, a firework is any device which burns and/or explodes to produce a visual and/or audible effect and is intended for use as a form of entertainment. Some fireworks offences relate to misuse that could cause danger or annoyance, some relate to the time of year, and some relate to the age of the person buying fireworks. Of particular concern in recent years has been the use of powerful fireworks such as 'aerial shells, aerial maroons, shells-in-mortar and maroons-in-mortar', which can register sound levels above 120 dB—about the noise level of a jet aircraft 100 metres away, and could also be used to damage or even destroy large objects such as cars. The sale of these products to the public in the UK is banned but people can purchase them abroad and bring them back to the UK.

Relevant legislation includes the Explosives Act 1875, the Fireworks Act 2003, the Fireworks Regulations 2004, and the Fireworks (Safety) Regulations 1997. It is an offence for any person:

- to throw, cast, or fire any firework in or into any highway, street, thoroughfare, or public place (s 80 of the Explosives Act 1875);
- to wantonly (deliberately) throw or set fire to a firework in the street to the obstruction, annoyance, or danger of residents or passengers (s 28 of the Town Police Clauses Act 1847).

It is also an offence for anyone under the age of 18 years to possess fireworks in a public place, except for indoor fireworks (reg 4 of the Fireworks Regulations 2004). Indoor fireworks include caps, sparklers, and throwdowns. These offences are triable summarily. Alternatively, a PND can be used, apart from an offence under s 28 of the Town Police Clauses Act 1847.

3.8.7.1 Selling fireworks

A special licence is required for a trader to sell fireworks to the public throughout the year. Traders without a special licence can only sell fireworks to members of the public during the following periods:

- first day of Chinese New Year and three days prior to this;
- Diwali and three days prior to this;
- between 15 October and 10 November; and
- between 26 and 31 December.

Under s 12(1) of the Consumer Protection Act 1987, it is an offence to supply fireworks (including sparklers but excluding all other indoor fireworks) to persons under the age of 18 years. This offence is triable summarily and the penalty is a fine.

3.8.7.2 Firework curfews

A 'firework curfew' is a period of time where the general use of fireworks is not permitted. Under reg 7(1) of the Fireworks Regulations 2004 it is a summary offence for a person to use an 'adult firework' (essentially all fireworks other than indoor fireworks) between 2300 and 0700 hours the next day except for during the periods shown in the table. Other exemptions apply for local authority employees using a firework during a local authority display or national commemorative event.

The penalty for this offence is six months' imprisonment and/or a fine, or a PND can be used.

3.8.7.3 Restrictions on large fireworks for public displays

Public displays frequently use large fireworks, known as category 4 fireworks. They may only be used by an appropriately qualified person (reg 5 of the Fireworks Regulations 2004). Members of the general public are prohibited from possessing such fireworks, except for any person who is employed by a local authority or who is involved in public or commercial firework displays. A breach of reg 4 or 5 is a criminal offence under s 11 of the Fireworks Act 2003. The offence is triable summarily and the penalty is a fine.

3.8.8 Gangs

Under s 34(5) of the Policing and Crime Act 2009, a gang is defined as a group that consists of at least three people; uses a name, emblem, or colour or any other identifiable characteristic; and is associated with a particular area. The members of the group may also identify with or lay claim over territory, have some form of 'identifying structural feature', and/or be in conflict with other similar gangs (Home Office, 2012b).

Recently, it has become evident that gang members may be both perpetrators of crime and victims of crime, as they have been coerced, exploited, or groomed into criminal activity (Rigg *et al*, 2018). Some police services are now utilizing modern slavery legislation to target certain gang members who are trafficking and exploiting victims.

Many measures have been introduced to tackle problems associated with gangs. The Anti-social Behaviour, Crime and Policing Act 2014 created new offences such as threatening with a knife in a public place or school and possessing illegal firearms with intent to supply (s 2(A) of the Firearms Act 1968), the latter carrying a maximum penalty of life imprisonment. The maximum penalty for importation of firearms has also been increased to life imprisonment (ss 50 and 5(A) of the Customs and Excise Management Act 1979).

In 2017, the Home Office provided further funding to tackle knife crime, which is often a key feature of gang culture. The Criminal Justice Act 1988 has also been amended to ban the sale, manufacture, rental, or importation of a certain type of long knife often referred to as a 'zombie knife' or similar. These knives can have serrated-edge blades over 60 cm long and are held in high esteem by some gang members as they glamorize violence. Also in 2017, a number of UK constabularies made a co-ordinated response to focus on persistent knife carriers and the people who sell them. The use of amnesty bins has resulted in thousands of weapons being taken off the streets (Newton, 2017).

For investigations into gang-related crime, the police can apply for an 'Investigation Anonymity Order' for any person who gives information to the police. This can help to persuade witnesses to cooperate as it reduces the risk of reprisals from other gang members.

Councils and police chief officers can apply for a 'gang injunction' under s 34(3) of the Policing and Crime Act 2009 to forbid a person from being involved in gang-related violence or gang-related drug-dealing activity. The application for over 18s is made to a High Court or County Court. It must be shown that the person has engaged in, encouraged or assisted, or needs to be protected from being drawn into more serious activity involving violence or drugs. The 2015 Home Office document *Injunctions to Prevent Gang-Related Violence and Gang-Related Drug Dealing* provides more detailed guidance.

For 14–17-year-olds, the application for an injunction is made to a youth court. Local partners can also apply and be involved as they have a responsibility to protect and improve the well-being of a child (s 10 of the Children Act 2004). Although a breach of a gang injunction is a civil matter, the prohibition is likely to include a power of arrest for any breach. Adults breaching the injunction could be remanded in custody or on bail with conditions. For 14–17-year-olds, supervision orders (attending regular appointments with a mentor or supervisor), activities orders (attending rehabilitative programmes), or curfews can be used (Home Office, 2015a).

3.9 Answer to Task

TASK 1 There are numerous moments in police history that you should have identified, but here are a few moments that you might wish to explore further: Royal Commission 1962 and the Police Act 1964; The Scarman Report 1981; The Macpherson Report 1999; Police Reform Act 2002; The O'Connor Report 2005 and the Flanagan Report 2008; Neyroud Report 2011; the introduction of PCCs in 2012; IOPC introduced in 2018.

4 Decision-making and Professional Judgement

4.1 Introduction

The topics covered in this chapter are likely to contribute to the learning required for the National Policing Curriculum subject areas of 'Decision-Making and Discretion' and those parts of 'Response Policing' that are concerned with stop and search.

Police officers are expected to make many decisions during each shift that can have a profound impact on people's lives. These decisions must be made quickly and ethically, and are often scrutinized by others after the fact. Decision-making in policing is not always easy and requires training and practice. The chapter emphasizes the importance of respecting human rights and using ethical principles in decision-making, particularly when interacting with members of the public. We look in particular at the National Decision Model (NDM), a decision-making tool used by police officers to structure their decision-making process during policing activities. The College of Policing Authorised Professional Practice provides further guidance on the NDM, risk assessment, and management, as well as addressing potential barriers to effective decision-making.

Chapter 4 also examines and describes the police procedures of stop, search, and entry. It outlines police officers' power to search individuals, premises, and vehicles, and their powers and policies when entering premises. The purpose of stop and search powers is to allow officers to confirm or allay their suspicions about individuals without arresting them. The College of Policing has produced guidance for the police use of stop and search. Despite its usefulness, stop and search has been criticized for alleged discrimination against visible ethnic minorities and for lack of effectiveness or incompetent use.

4.2 Decision-making in Policing

Imagine the following scenario. You are an MPS trainee police officer on Independent Patrol at about 1530 within a pedestrianized shopping area in the London Borough of Lewisham. You pass a group of school children and young people waiting for buses and notice the pungent smell of what you suspect is 'skunk', a particularly potent form of cannabis. What action, if any, should you take?

It is likely that in this scenario a criminal offence is being committed. Whilst it is possible that the smell is not that of cannabis, but of something else, such as a legal herbal cigarette, this seems unlikely. Cannabis is a Class B drug, carrying up to five years in prison, an unlimited fine, or both, for anyone caught in possession. One possibility is that you decide to stop and search the person that you suspect of being in possession of cannabis. After all, your duty is to maintain law and order and there could also be welfare issues concerned given the mix of children and young people that you observed in the crowd.

However, the situation clearly requires more thought than the application of a simple decision. To start, there is the practical problem of accurately identifying a suspect or suspects in the crowd. You might also cause more harm than good; for example, a serious public order incident could arise as a result. So, would a stop and search be proportionate in the circumstances? Are there *reasonable* grounds? The IOPC (2022a, p 15) recommended that 'the NPCC takes steps to support forces to reduce their officers' reliance on the smell of cannabis alone when deciding to stop and search someone and instead use grounds based upon multiple objective factors'. Are there 'multiple objective factors' present in this situation that might justify stop and search, beyond the apparent smell of cannabis? As is often the case in policing, you will need to be guided by local police policy concerning the smell of cannabis. This scenario takes place in Lewisham, a Borough in Greater London, and 'Metropolitan Police policy has been clear since 2013 that the smell of cannabis alone is insufficient to provide reasonable grounds for a search' (Mayor of London, 2023).

One appropriate course of action to consider, is to talk with the group. Just talk, and assess the group and the responses you receive. This might help you make a decision, whether you wish to withdraw and possibly make a '3 by 5 by 2' intel report, or stop and search an individual, or some other course of action.

Consider a second scenario. You are a police officer on the Safer Neighbourhood Team and are emailed by a concerned parent who believes that their 15-year-old child may have been involved in sexting at their secondary school. What action would you take in response to the alleged incident in this email?

Sexting is potentially an offence under the Protection of Children Act 1978 and Criminal Justice Act 1988 as it is a criminal offence to create and/or share explicit images of a child, even if the person doing so is a child. You will therefore need to gather further information, from the parent and the child's school, but also from your police systems, including the PNC, PND, and police intelligence databases to provide background checks on the alleged victims, perpetrators, and the school locations. You might also need to view and record the alleged sexting imagery, but avoid the need to seize phones unless absolutely necessary. This information and intelligence gathering will enable you to assess the risks and develop a working strategy. Your police service is also likely to have its own policy on sexting amongst children and young people, which will provide you with a basis for decision-making but it might also be worthwhile consulting with a supervisor if this is your first experience of dealing with the issue. The school is also likely to have a policy on sexting, possibly as part of a more overarching safeguarding and child protection policy. However, the following questions are likely to guide your subsequent decisions and actions:

- Is there any evidence of 'exploitation, coercion, a profit motive or adults as perpetrators' (CoP, 2016a, p.2)? For example, have threats of violence been used in an attempt by one child to gain sexualised imagery from another? Have images been used by one child or young person to 'blackmail' another for sexual or other purposes?
- Have background checks thrown up concerns about the alleged victims, perpetrators, or the school? For example, is there intelligence to suggest a link with child sexual exploitation (CSE)?
- As far as can be ascertained, was the sharing of imagery consensual in nature? For example, between boy/girlfriends? Or were images created without the consent of another and then sent to third parties with malicious intent?
- Have images been uploaded and shared online?

Answering these questions will help you decide on your next decisions and actions. In our case you discover that there are no complicating or aggravating factors—all the information and intelligence you have gathered suggests that the sharing of imagery was consensual in nature and was restricted to pupils of the school. Hence you decide not to take the investigation further, instead you decide that the most appropriate action is to give advice to the parties concerned, eg sources of support and guidance for both the pupils involved and the school. However, you will still need to make a crime report made but using 'Outcome 21', namely that 'further investigation, resulting from the crime report, which could provide evidence sufficient to support formal action being taken against the suspect is not in the public interest—police decision'.

Your police decision should be clearly explained to those involved, particularly the school and parent who first alerted you to the problem. Reassurance should be given that the children concerned have not been convicted or cautioned for any offence, but you should also make it clear that a record has been made. The school should be asked to ensure that all inappropriate images have been deleted from both pupil's phones and the organization's own IT systems. Understandably some children or young people may be fearful that images have found their way into the public domain via social networking. If this is the case the school should be encouraged to seek specialist advice, eg from the Internet Watch Foundation.

Although there could well have been clear indications to you that crimes have been committed, the decisions taken are justified here as:

- There were no apparent exacerbating features such as 'exploitation, grooming, profit motive, malicious intent, eg extensive or inappropriate sharing such as uploading onto a pornographic website, or it being persistent behaviour' (gov.uk, 2016).
- It is not in the public interest to criminalize any of the children or young people involved: a prolonged investigation followed by a prosecution would not be necessary and proportionate.
- The decision meets the policing Code of Ethics in that you have used your authority in a way that is 'proportionate, lawful, accountable, necessary and ethical'; you have considered the needs of a 'protected group', in this case children, and you 'have used your training, skills and knowledge', you have considered 'what you are trying to achieve and the potential effects of your decisions' and you have taken relevant policing codes, guidance, and policies into consideration.

As a police officer you will be required to make dozens of these types of decisions during every shift. Moreover, many of the decisions you will be expected to make as a police officer will make a difference to other people's lives, in some cases a very profound difference. Far-reaching decisions will need to be made on a frequent basis, in many cases very quickly and sometimes on your own. As well as applying good general judgement you will also be expected to adopt an ethical approach to decision-making as well as being completely familiar with the powers you have to intervene in people's lives. Some of the decisions you make will be very carefully scrutinized by others, but after the event and they will have the benefit of hindsight that was denied you in the heat of the moment. We should therefore acknowledge at the outset that decision-making in policing is often not easy or straightforward. Nor will it come naturally to you: it needs training and practice and not simply the application of 'common sense'. It will be hard to master, but the legitimacy, authority, and effectiveness of the police depends on the exercise of sound and ethical decision-making.

There is an expectation on the police, from the public and others, that the police make decisions rationally and based on a set of ethical principles and not in an arbitrary manner or according to emotional response or prejudice. In particular, where decision-making involves members of the public such as with stop and search, the human rights of the individuals concerned must be respected.

4.2.1 The National Decision Model (NDM)

The National Decision Model (NDM) seeks to provide the decision-making basis and ethical underpinning to structure a rationale of what police officers do, or do not do, during policing activities such as attending an incident.

The model consists of a number of stages which police officers work through to aid decision-making, with the policing Code of Ethics being central. The wording of the NDM is mainly drawn from operational police culture, but the intention is that anyone making decisions in the police service (both operational and non-operational) should use it.

The NDM, introduced in 2012, appears to have been developed in part from the Conflict Management Model (CMM) which was employed for decision-making in the context of public order and firearms incidents. The models are similar, although the NDM is focused around the Code of Ethics and includes 'review' as one of the essential elements. In more general terms one of the major drivers for the development and introduction of the NDM was the need for more consistent and transparent police decision-making, helping decisions to be made in a more systematic way and in keeping with the more complex (and 'risky') situations that police officers were increasingly facing.

The NDM has six main components (note that the College of Policing group together 'action and review' as a single component) and the mnemonic CIAPOAR can be used as an aide-memoire:

C Code of Ethics is in the process of being revised but will remain at the centre of the NDM and is cross-referenced throughout.
I Information—gather information and intelligence.
A Assessment—assess threat and risk, and develop a working strategy.
P Powers and policy—consider powers and policy.
O Options—identify the options and contingencies.
A Action—take action, and then
R Review.

(adapted from CoP, 2023b).

According to the College of Policing, the NDM is 'suitable for all decisions' and can be applied to 'spontaneous incidents or planned operations'. However, there are clearly some situations, of a dynamic and potentially dangerous nature, where you simply won't have the time to methodically work your way through all the stages of the NDM to determine what decision(s) to make. However, even in these cases the NDM might still prove useful in terms of a structure for the subsequent writing up of notes and statements.

In some circumstances, there will be an organizational or even legal requirement to document decisions whereas in others it may be left to your discretion—as with some other aspects of police procedure, you need to be guided by local police service policy on this. The College of Policing does recognize however, that professional judgement is often used to decide whether or not to record the rationale for a particular decision, and that when records are made these should be in keeping with the seriousness of the situation. When records are made, for example, in your pocket notebook (PNB), then the College of Policing suggests that they are made against the mnemonic CIAPOAR.

Other mnemonics might be taught, such as PLANE (Proportionality, Legality, Accountability, Necessity, and Ethical) to emphasize key priorities when making a decision. Likewise, the College of Policing Authorised Professional Practice (APP) includes a set of risk principles that provide guidance on how to assess and manage various situations where threats, harms, and risks are associated with your decision making, as in the sexting example earlier in the chapter.

There are many challenges associated with good decision making and you need to be mindful of these when considering the legislation and policies underpinning police work. Later in this chapter we look in some detail at the legislation surrounding stop and search, a highly contentious tool utilized by police officers. You need to know and understand the legislation and policies regarding stop and search, but this alone will be insufficient. Why? Because no matter how detailed and precise the legislation is; no matter how thoughtful and considerate policy-makers and legislators have been; it is impossible to capture the nuances and variabilities of each and every policing instance in legislative form. The circumstances you encounter will not necessarily correspond neatly in a precise way with the framing of the legislation, or at least there will be gaps in what you know about an incident that make it difficult to know what you need to know in order to follow the legislative approach.

When it comes to making decisions, you will commonly lack relevant and/or reliable information that might only become available after you have made a decision. You will probably always want more time than you have to make a decision and the priorities within a given situation might not be clear. You will also need to be aware of your own emotional state, to avoid prejudicial or discriminatory decisions; likewise, you need to prevent any cognitive biases, your gut feelings, from skewing your judgments. Finally, it is important to be aware of *group think*, a tendancy to be unduly swayed by those around you.

You will be taught in training what strategies are available to help you overcome some of the obstacles to effective decision-making, including the application of the NDM where appropriate. In general these might include: clarifying your goals, objectives, and priorities; gathering as much pertinent information as you can; considering the range of decisions available to you; assessing the pros and cons of each; evaluating the impact of each possible decision;

assessing the risks and benefits of each decision; talking to other officers that are more experienced, and finally, reflecting on, and then evaluating the outcome of your decisions.

4.2.2 Ethical decision-making and discretion in policing

One of the key skills police officers have to develop during training and over their careers is the ability to apply discretion through their decision-making. For example, imagine a student officer on Supervised Patrol and their tutor is called to deal with a theft at a supermarket, with instructions to investigate the matter and determine a course of action. The offender is a confused 94-year-old, who has apparently picked up a bag of apples and walked out of the store, pursued by store detectives. They have committed a crime but there are mitigating circumstances: age and frailty must be taken into account, and proving 'intention permanently to deprive' (the basis of the Theft Act 1968) would be somewhat difficult. Enforcing the law might not be the most appropriate response but police officers must be prepared to justify the reasons for any decision.

4.2.2.1 Police discretion

Police discretion has been a contentious issue and over time it has been curbed through legislation and various policies. The reasons for this are that discretion came to be seen as opportunity for officers to act in discriminatory ways according to their own prejudices and biases. Communities lost trust in the police and the consequences were to be more directive and prescriptive in dictating how officers should deal with ever more situations.

The arguments against discretion over recent years has been understandable given the arguments around institutionalized discrimination in the police, as recorded most recently concerning the MPS in Baroness Casey's (2023) Report. However, there are a number of reasons why discretion is an unavoidable, inevitable, and desirable aspect of policing.

It is unavoidable and inevitable because policing in the British tradition is first and foremost about maintaining order and keeping the peace. This is enshrined in the very concept of the office of constable, and Lord Scarman was at pains to remind the police of this in the aftermath of the 1981 Brixton Riots (Scarman, 1981). Enforcing the law is a tool used by the police to achieve these ends, but only when it is appropriate to do so. As we saw in the scenarios earlier in this chapter, enforcing the law is not the only option available to the police officer, and it is often not the most appropriate option available.

This is why discretion is desirable; understood properly it is not discretion that allows discrimination; it is rather a means of redressing discrimination. Discretion is a form of practical wisdom borne out of knowledge, understanding, and experience; it is not something that can be achieved in a classroom, but rather requires practice and reflection over time. Discretion is the art of making the most appropriate decision in each and every circumstance, a form of professional judgement that can be explained, justified, and legitimized as required. It needs to be open and accountable and in this way it challenges all forms of discrimination, at the level of the corrupt officer, but also in institutional forms.

This understanding of discretion is recognized in the College's revised Code of Ethics, which promotes an ethical approach to policing that is guided by the following three principles:

- prioritizing public service;
- leading with professional courage;
- responding with respect and empathy.

(Source: https://www.college.police.uk/consultation-code-ethics/ethical-policing-principles)

These principles emphasize the need for police officers to be mindful of the public they serve, to be brave within the parameters of their professional responsibilities, and to be understanding of the emotional impact their actions have on individuals. You need to keep these principles at the forefront of your thinking when considering the legislative and policy dimensions of stop and search outlined in the remainder of this chapter. Moreover, these principles need to shape your thinking and actions as police officers, to ensure you develop the practical wisdom required for good, discretionary, and ethical reasoning and decision-making throughout your career.

4.3 Stop and Search

In this section of Chapter 4 we outline the police procedures around stop, search, and entry, including searching people, premises, and vehicles, and the powers and policies around entering premises. The decision to stop a person and to carry out a search clearly involves police officers exercising their professional judgement and using the NDM. Stop and search can be a very useful tool for police officers, particularly in terms of tackling drug and knife crime, but there remains opposition to its use; as the IOPC (2022a, p 5) state, 'stop and search is a legitimate policing tactic', but is nonetheless, 'one of the most contentious policing powers'.

The main purpose of stop and search powers is to 'enable officers to allay or confirm suspicions about individuals without exercising their power of arrest' (PACE Code of Practice A, para 1.4). Carrying out a stop and search is where a police officer detains a person in order to search them and their belongings. In order to do this, an officer must have reasonable grounds to believe the person they are stopping and detaining has been involved in a criminal activity, is about to be involved in criminality, or is in possession of a prohibited article. There are some situations where reasonable grounds are not required and these will be discussed throughout the remaining sections of this chapter.

The College of Policing has produced extensive Authorised Professional Practice (APP) for the police use of stop and search and, if you are undertaking initial police training, then you may be expected to familiarize yourself with the guidance. For example, police officers are expected to adopt a 'procedural justice' approach to stop and search as this can have a 'positive influence on people's attitudes' (CoP, 2017b).

Despite its usefulness, police use of stop and search has often been criticized, usually on the grounds of alleged discrimination against visible ethnic minorities, but also (some claim) on the basis of lack of effectiveness or incompetent use. For example, in 2021 HMICFRS published an inspection report that indicated the police disproportionately used police power on stop and search and that no constabulary fully understands the impact of the use of these powers (HMICFRS, 2021). For some, particularly Black, Asian, and minority ethnic people, stop and search can reinforce the perception that there is a culture of discrimination within the police (HMICFRS, 2021), particularly when viewed alongside statistics which show that in the period ending March 2021 individuals from a Black or Black British background were searched at a rate seven times higher than those from a White ethnic group, across England and Wales. Individuals identifying as Asian or Asian British were searched at a rate 2.4 times that of those from a White ethnic group (Home Office, 2021b). A full discussion of the rights and wrongs of stop and search is beyond the scope of this Handbook.

Stop and search can be used under many different powers; for example, s 1 of the PACE Act 1984 and s 23 of the Misuse of Drugs Act 1971. Every search must conform to the guidelines set out in PACE Code of Practice A and must be recorded. The data collected from these records show which areas and ethnicities are involved, and what types of criminal activity are being encountered by officers. It is also used as one of the quantitative measurements of police performance. Any person who has been searched can access a copy of their search. Members of the public could want a copy for various reasons, for example to establish whether the search complied with the Codes of Practice. A failure to comply can result in the search being deemed unlawful and could lead to a police misconduct investigation.

Police powers in searching properties and entering premises will be covered in this chapter, along with the practicalities regarding searching premises, open spaces, and vehicles. Post arrest searches, under s 32 of the PACE Act 1984 will be covered, as will s 18 of the PACE Act 1984, and the differences between the two. We will also cover searches of properties under a warrant issued by a court (s 8 of the PACE Act 1984).

In February 2019, the government decided to introduce a stop and search power to cover the use of corrosive substances as weapons. However, s 1 of the PACE Act 1984 can still be used for these substances although it does not cover certain situations, eg when the corrosive substance is in its original packaging.

As a result of the increase in knife crime and stabbings in some parts of the UK, in March 2019 the Home Secretary enhanced s 60 search powers and allowed the authority to be granted by a police inspector rather than an assistant chief constable.

There are currently over 19 different stop and search powers available to police officers. The powers permit officers to search people, vehicles, and/or premises for drugs, weapons, stolen items, fireworks, and even animals. Each stop and search power varies slightly in terms of the grounds necessary to carry out the search and the location in which it can take place.

The most commonly used stop and search powers are s 1 of the PACE Act 1984 and, to a lesser extent, s 23 of the Misuse of Drugs Act 1971. Section 1 of the PACE Act 1984 allows officers to search for stolen items and prohibited articles.

Section 1 of the PACE Act 1984 requires officers to have reasonable grounds to search individuals, but s 60 of the Criminal Justice and Public Order Act 1994 does not. The Public Order Act 2023 introduces new stop and search powers under the headings emphasizing 'on suspicion' (s 10) and 'without suspicion' (s 11). These are both primarily aimed at new forms of protest by groups such as *Extinction Rebellion* and *Just Stop Oil*, and relate to new offences introduced in the Public Order Act 2023 relating to locking on (s 1), and causing serious disruption through tunnelling (s 3). So the need for reasonable grounds and the extent to which suspicion is required might vary according to each power, but in all cases there must be some justification for the search. The reasons should be based on objective criteria and an honest appraisal of an ongoing situation, and failure in this respect would render the stop and search unlawful. It might even amount to the officer having committed common assault.

Stop and search is governed by the PACE Codes of Practice and the precise meanings of the wording for stop and search legislation are set out clearly in PACE Code A. The Code governs the use of searching prior to arrest, including the beliefs officers should have, the protocol they should follow, and the time frame for recording the search.

The Best Use of Stop and Search (BUSS) was introduced in 2014 to support a more intelligence-led approach and to achieve greater transparency and community involvement with regard to the use of stop and search (Home Office, 2014c). The BUSS involves recording the powers and laws used for each stop and search, the ethnicity of the person stopped, and the outcome of every stop. HMICFRS inspections check for compliance with the scheme's requirements and any police service that fails to comply can be suspended (Home Office, 2014b, p 7). However, in contrast, the then Home Secretary Priti Patel in October 2021 announced the permanent removal of the voluntary safeguards relating to the use of 'section 60' (suspicionless) stop and search powers from the BUSS scheme, as part of the government's 'Beating crime plan' (Home Office, 2021c).

In summary, any decision to carry out a stop and/or search must be fair and the reasons must be lawful and be able to withstand legal scrutiny. The conduct of the search must follow the proper procedures and a record must be made to that effect. In addition, the interactions with the public during the whole encounter must be professional; it is vital that stop and search powers are used in a manner that is transparent and accountable. According to PACE Code A, para 3.1 and the Terrorism Act 2000 Code of Practice, para 5.1.1, 'all stops and searches should be carried out with courtesy, consideration and respect for the person concerned. This has a significant impact on public confidence in the police.'

It should be noted that 'stop and account' is different from stop and search. An officer in uniform or in plain clothes can speak to any person during the course of their duty; this could include a 'stop and account'. The interaction could be in order to prevent crime or carry out investigations to locate suspects. There is no requirement for a police officer to make a record of every person they speak to during the course of a shift. Should a person provide information about a crime they have witnessed, that person's details should be recorded in line with the required crime report. Or if the individual provides some intelligence, again, this information should be recorded and their details noted. Some police services have systems in place for officers to record stop and accounts, but others do not. It is advisable to record an interaction if the officer was considering carrying out a search but then decided against it, or if the individual was not happy about being approached by the police. In the course of such a conversation, the officer may become suspicious and grounds to search may emerge, and the stop and account may become a stop and search. As soon as this happens, Code A applies and the search will need to be recorded. As with searching, or reporting crime, or any interaction with the public, if a person is dissatisfied with how they are treated and requests the officer's details, the officer should provide the information.

4.3.1 General procedures for stop and search

PACE Code A, para 1.1 states that police officers must use their powers to stop and search 'fairly, responsibly, with respect for people being searched, and without unlawful discrimination'. In addition, 'any misuse of the powers is likely to be harmful to policing and lead to mistrust of the police' (Code A, para 1.4). The police also have a responsibility to safeguard and promote the welfare of all persons under the age of 18 (s 11 of the Children Act 2004), and stop and search can sometimes help to protect young people from harm.

For each stop and search, it is the officer's responsibility to conduct a risk assessment. If it seems necessary to handcuff the individual before or during the search, the officer must be able to provide justification. This could relate to the individual's behaviour, eg verbal and/or physical aggression, or to the item the officer is looking for, such as a knife. Almost all officers now wear a body-worn camera and this should most certainly be used during a search as it records all actions of the officer and the individual. Such information could prove useful at a later point, for example as evidence of an offence or to defend against complaints about police officer conduct.

4.3.1.1 Locations for searches

The location in which a person can be legally searched varies with each stop and search power. Various categories of locations that apply to searching are referred to and defined in different pieces of legislation. In order for a search to be legal, it must comply with the location in which a person is stopped; for example, a search conducted under s 1 of the PACE Act 1984 must be in a public place, whereas a search conducted under s 23 of the Misuse of Drugs Act 1971 can be carried out in any place.

A **public place** is anywhere 'the public or any section of the public has access, on payment or otherwise, as of right or by virtue of express or implied permission' (s 1(1)(a) of the PACE Act 1984).

Some locations are only public areas at certain times, for example a park that closes and is locked between 10 pm and 8 am each day; during these hours it would not be a public place. Similarly, the public have express permission to enter cinemas, theatres, or football grounds having paid an entrance fee, and they can remain there until that particular entertainment is over, when permission to be there ends. Again, following this, it could be argued that a location is **not** a public place, unless a person has a reasonable excuse for continuing to be within that area. There is an implied permission for persons to enter any privately owned building to carry out business transactions with the owner and to use a footpath to the front door of a house to pay a lawful call on the householder. That implied permission remains until withdrawn by the householder or the owner of the business premises.

Private places to which the public has ready access are also regarded as public places, for example a private field (if it is regularly used, even by trespassers) or a garden (if it is accessible by jumping over a low wall). Ultimately, it would be a question of fact for the court to consider whether members of the general public can gain ready access to the place, and whether a landowner has given permission for the public to use a privately-owned place.

A **private place** is land or premises that are privately owned, and to which the general public does **not** have ready access, for example a private residence or a private office block. Privately owned lands or premises that are used by the general public during opening hours, reverts to being a private place during closing times.

Premises is a very general term and under s 23 of the PACE Act 1984 includes vehicles, vessels, aircraft, hovercraft, offshore installations, renewable energy installations, and tents and other moveable structures.

A **place of residence** is not defined in law so would be a question of fact for the court to decide.

4.3.1.2 Reasonable grounds

For a search to be lawful, an officer must be able to justify why the search is necessary. This justification is referred to as 'reasonable grounds' and is required in most searches. Under PACE Code A, para 2, the grounds for reasonable suspicion have two parts:

1. a genuine suspicion in the mind of the officer that the object for which the power of search is being used will be found; and
2. the suspicion must be reasonable, formed on an objective basis from facts, information, and/or intelligence which help to make it likely that the object will be found, and that a reasonable person would also draw the same conclusions.

The grounds must be a true representation of the situation and can be derived from many different factors such as the individual's general behaviour, the location, and the time of day. The grounds can also stem from intelligence about the area, that particular person, or the vehicle being driven, or from speaking to members of the public. The grounds make up part of 'GO WISELY' (see 4.3.1.3); the information that must be provided to the individual before the search and recorded after the search.

Descriptions from witnesses that refer to personal factors about a suspect, eg age, clothing, hair colour, and height, can contribute to reasonable grounds as these would help to pinpoint a particular person (Code A, para 2.4). But the reason for stopping and searching a suspect cannot be based upon physical appearance alone, particularly with regard to 'the protected characteristics', such as age, sex, race, religion, or belief. Generalizing, ie stereotyping, groups of people as being more likely to take part in criminal activity must be avoided (Code A, para 2.2B(a) and (b)). Sufficient grounds for carrying out a stop and/or search require more specific information, for example intelligence giving a specific description of a suspect or reports from a member of the public that the person was carrying a weapon.

Some police services use the mnemonic SHACKS (CoP, 2014b, p 11) to help police officers remember what should be considered when deciding whether there are sufficient grounds to stop and search:

Seen	What did you actually see, for example in terms of a person's behaviour?
Heard	What did you actually hear, for example in terms of what somebody said? Or an alarm sounding nearby?
Actions	How did the person respond to you (in terms of their actions) and did this response confirm or challenge your proposed grounds for a search? For example, did they appear to hide an item on their person?
Conversation	What did they say in reply to you, or of their own accord, and did their words confirm or challenge your proposed grounds for a search?
Knowledge	What is known about the person, for example is there specific information or intelligence that describes the person, or item they may be carrying, in sufficient detail and that links them with criminal offences?
Smell	Can you smell illegal drugs, dangerous substances? (Although note that in some forces the smell of cannabis is not, in the absence of any other factors, sufficient reasonable grounds.)

Factors to consider for establishing the 'reasonable grounds' for a stop & search (adapted from CoP, 2014b, pp 11–12)

Note that the College of Policing state that one of these six factors may be enough but that 'you will often need a combination to provide reasonable grounds' (CoP, 2014b, p 11). Remembering our hypothetical scenario at the start of the chapter, smell in particular would likely be insufficient on its own.

An example of a situation providing grounds for reasonable suspicion

A police constable is informed during a daily briefing that a male who often carries a large knife for protection has been dealing drugs to school children by the chicken shop. He rides a moped which is described as black in colour, and the year reference on the number plate is 67. The male has been described as White, about 16–20 years old, he carries a small man bag, and always wears a puffer jacket.

At about 4.45 pm, officers see a young White male loitering by the chicken shop. He is about 17 years old, has a man bag, and is wearing a cap, grey tracksuit, and a black puffer jacket with a fur hood. As police slow down, he goes to a black moped with the registration MK67JPW and makes to get on it. On questioning, he would not give a reasonable explanation about what he is doing or where he has been and refuses to give his details.

Refusing to answer any questions, on its own, can never be used to provide reasonable grounds for suspicion (Code A, para 2.9), nor can grounds be established retrospectively through questioning (Code A, para 2.11).

The requirements for reasonable grounds are different for certain categories of people, eg gangs and protest groups, and in certain situations. For example, a police officer may have reasonable grounds to stop and search a person who is believed to be a member of a gang if there is reliable and relevant information or intelligence to that effect and the person may be in possession of certain prohibited items (PACE Code A, para 2.6 and Note 9A). The same applies for protest groups, where unlawful objects could have been brought to a demonstration (Code A, para 2.6A). In such circumstances, it is not always necessary for the searching officer to have reasonable suspicion that each and every member of the group is in possession of a prohibited article before carrying out a search of an individual from the group (*Howarth v Commissioner of Police of the Metropolis* [2011] EWHC 2818 (QB)).

4.3.1.3 Information to provide before conducting a search

Prior to searching a person, the officer must provide certain information to make the search legal (s 2 of the PACE Act 1984, and PACE Code A). The required information is summarized by the mnemonic 'GO WISELY' as shown here:

G Grounds of the suspicion for the search
O Object/purpose of search
W Warrant card (if the officer is in plain clothes or if requested by the person)
I Identity of the officer performing the search
S Station to which the officer is attached
E Entitlement to a copy of the search record
L Legal power used
Y You are detained for the purposes of a search

GO WISELY does not need to be given in a particular order, but should be given prior to the search. However, it is more natural for you to want to give your name and station first and for this reason some forces prefer the mnemonic ISOGELWY.

Consider the following example:

A police constable is informed during a routine briefing that there has been a spate of burglaries in a particular area, occurring between 2 am and 3 am. CCTV has captured images of a male getting into a large white van near the location of one of the burglaries. Whilst on mobile patrol at 2.30 am, the officer sees a male, who appears to be carrying something, run out from a side gate. The male gets into a white van which moves off at speed. The officer stops the van and speaks with the driver, who is impatient, aggressive, and evasive. He says he is visiting a friend but does not provide a name or address for the friend when asked. The police officer says the following:

> I am PC JONES from COLINDALE police station and you are detained for the purposes of a search. I am going to search you under section 1 of PACE. Here is my warrant card. I am searching you for stolen items, as I have seen you run from a gate down the side of a house, in an area which is being targeted for burglaries. You cannot give me a good reason to be in the area at this time of day and you are driving a vehicle which is similar to that seen in recent burglaries. You are entitled to a copy of this search.

TASK 1 Consider what PC Jones says in the example above. Identify where the officer covers each aspect of GO WISELY (or ISOGELWY if you prefer).

It is not always possible to provide GO WISELY in full before searching, for example when dealing with an aggressive shoplifter. However, the officer should at least state their name and station, the power of search, and that the person is being detained in order to conduct the search.

There have been several cases where failing to provide the GO WISELY information prior to the search made the search unlawful. In the case of *O (a juvenile) v DPP* (1999) 163 JP 725, it was decided that a breach of s 2 of the PACE Act 1984 renders a search, and probably any later arrest and detention, unlawful. In another case (*R v Bristol* [2007] EWCA Crim 3214), a search had been carried out under s 23 of the Misuse of Drugs Act 1971. The defendant was convicted of obstructing a police officer but the conviction was overturned on appeal because s 2 of the PACE Act 1984 had not been followed. A search was also deemed unlawful in another case (*Browne v Commissioner of Police of the Metropolis* [2014] EWHC 3999 (QB)), as the searching officer failed to abide by s 2 of the PACE Act 1984 and used excessive force; damages were also awarded for assault.

4.3.1.4 Conducting the search

The search must be conducted thoroughly but in a reasonable period of time. The person should be detained for as short a period as possible. The officer should seek cooperation from the person and should take extra care and be patient if the person could be considered vulnerable, eg due to age, mental or physical illness, or any disabilities.

The extent of the search must relate to the object the officer is looking for, for example if you stop someone and tell them you can smell cannabis and describe your search grounds are linked to drugs, you should not then search them under s 1 of the PACE Act 1984. However, should an officer be searching for drugs and then find a weapon for example, they should still act upon this.

Under s 117 of the PACE Act 1984, reasonable force may be used as a last resort, but only after attempts to search have been met with resistance (PACE Code A, para 3.2).

When conducting a search on the street or in public view, an officer can do the following:

- place their hands inside the pockets of outer clothing;
- feel round the inside of collars, socks, and shoes (para 3.5);
- search a person's hair, if this does not require the removal of headgear (para 3.5);
- require the person to remove their outer coat, jacket, and gloves.

The person cannot be required to remove any further clothing in public but can be asked to remove more clothing voluntarily. If the person refuses, an officer has no grounds to insist. It should be noted that for this type of search the sex of the officer is irrelevant; for example, there is no legal requirement that only female officers can search female members of the public.

Officers should methodically cover all areas thoroughly but in a reasonable time. Items from pockets should be removed and placed in a safe place, such as on a table or in a bag, until the search is concluded. Officers should be aware of a person wearing multiple layers, and be aware of pockets inside tracksuit bottoms worn underneath jeans; such places can be used to conceal smaller items.

A more thorough search, eg requiring the removal of a T-shirt, can be conducted but this must be out of public view, for example at a nearby police station (see para 3.6). If anything beyond an outer coat, jacket, gloves, headgear, or footwear is removed, the searching officer and any other officers present must be the same sex as the person being searched, that is unless the person specifically requests otherwise. A search that exposes intimate parts of the body can be carried out if necessary, but not as a routine extension of a less intrusive search where nothing has been found.

Whilst conducting a search, you must act in accordance with the Codes of Ethics, abide by PACE Code A,,adhere to the Policing Principles, and comply with the Standards of Professional Behaviour. A search which does not abide by these outlines would be one that is dishonest, disrespectful, uses excessive use of force, is unfair, and not based on the law under which it is being conducted. You must also ensure that all persons present (you as the searching officer, the individual, and your colleagues) are safe.

- The search must be conducted thoroughly, but in a reasonable period of time; the detention time for a search should be as short as possible.
- The search must also be relevant in that the extent of the search must relate to the object the officer is looking for. However, should an officer be searching a person for weapons under s 1 of the PACE Act 1984, and find drugs (for example), the officer should still act upon this.
- The officer should seek cooperation from the person. Under s 117 of the PACE Act 1984 reasonable force may be used as a last resort, but only after attempts to search have been met with resistance (para 3.2).

Extra care and patience should be taken when dealing with people who are considered vulnerable (eg due to age, mental or physical illness, or any disabilities).

4.3.1.5 Recording the search

A record of the search needs to be made as soon as possible, and in any case within 24 hours of the search. It must include the following information:

- the date, time, and location of the search;
- the officer's name and those of any other officers present;
- the name, age, self-defined ethnicity, and address of the person who has been searched; and
- the grounds or authorization for the search.

Should the individual refuse to provide their details, a record of the search containing the available information will still need to be made.

If the search required intimate parts of the body to be exposed, the search record should explain the reasons for this, where it took place, which supervisor was contacted, and what time the authorization was given. The search is recorded on an electronic database, each created with a unique reference number.

Any objects found also need to be recorded on the search record, and described or photographed. If a vehicle has been searched, its registration, make, and model should be recorded. After searching an unattended vehicle, or anything in or on it, a record of the search must be left, preferably inside the vehicle. If the vehicle is locked, the record should be attached to the outside (see Code A, para 4.8, and s 2(7) of the PACE Act 1984).

Almost all police officers in England and Wales have body-worn cameras and these should be used to record all stop and searches. The footage should be attached to any electronic record. This can help to ensure that professional standards are met and prevent or counter unjustified formal complaints from the public. For video-recorded searches, the links or access to video content should be noted in writing.

The individual being searched might request a copy of the search at the time and this should be provided on the spot. Some police services issue officers with a portable tablet or laptop, so the search can be recorded and the unique reference number given immediately. Failing that, a paper record can be given straight away. Alternatively, the officer could explain how to obtain a full copy of the search, possibly as an electronic record, or at least provide the reference number. Any request for a copy of the search record must be made within three months of the search (Code A, para 3.8(e)).

You might also wish to consider completing an entry in your PNB about the search, and in particular your decision for doing so, using the NDM as a framework.

4.3.1.6 Intimate searches

An intimate search is a search that requires an individual to remove their clothing and expose intimate body parts. The officer must have reasonable grounds to suspect that the person has concealed something inside their clothes below the clothesline, for example drugs hidden inside underwear.

The sensitivities of such searches are clear and guidance is provided by Nickolls and Allen (2022). For example, before conducting this level of search an officer is required to contact a supervising officer to explore the appropriateness and necessity for the search. The final decision rests with the officer at the scene unless given a lawful order not to proceed by the supervisor, but there are things the officer **must** do in these circumstances, and other things that they **should** do. For example, an intimate search **must** be done to maximize the privacy of the person being searched, ie it must be 'out of public view' and it **must** be performed 'by an officer of the same sex' as the person being searched (Nickolls and Allen, 2022, p 4). The person being searched cannot be asked to travel far for the intimate search; it '*must* be conducted at a nearby police station' and the supervisor **should** be consulted by the officer before the person is taken to the police station to be searched (Nickolls and Allen, 2022, p 4). The search **should** be conducted by at least two officers of the same sex as the individual being searched and the individual **should** also be completely out of sight from anyone of the opposite sex other than when an appropriate adult of the opposite sex is present.

The search should be conducted as quickly as possible and at no point should the individual be completely undressed. The person should be asked to remove one half of their clothing first (eg from the top part of the body), and the exposed areas will then be searched. This clothing should then be replaced before the other clothing is removed for the rest of the search. Examinations of the genital area must be only visual with no touching.

4.4 Searches under s 1 of the PACE Act 1984

Searches under s 1 of the PACE Act 1984 can be conducted by any officer, in uniform or in plain clothes, and must be conducted in a public place. Any items located during the search can be seized as evidence and the individual dealt with accordingly.

4.4.1 What items are included in s 1?

A search under s 1 of the PACE Act 1984 must be for a stolen or prohibited article, and this covers a wide range of offences and items. A stolen article is one that an officer suspects or knows to have been stolen, and there must be reasonable grounds to suspect this such as intelligence, the officer's own personal knowledge of the person/item, the time of day, and the location.

Prohibited articles include bladed or sharply pointed items, fireworks, offensive weapons including acid or corrosive substances, or items which could be used to commit a criminal offence.

4.4.2 The location of a search under s 1

A search under s 1 of the PACE Act 1984 must occur in a location considered a public place such as on the street, in a park, in a car park, or on the forecourt of a petrol station. Under no circumstances can a s 1 search be conducted within a dwelling. This applies even if the person in the dwelling is an intruder and does not have the resident's permission to be there; in such circumstances, the person would probably be immediately arrested on suspicion of burglary and searched under s 32 of the PACE Act 1984. A person can be searched under s 1 in the garden attached to a dwelling, eg the front garden of a house, but only if the person:

- does not live in the dwelling; or
- does not have the resident's permission to be on the property.

If the person lives in the attached dwelling or has the resident's permission to be there, the person cannot be searched under s 1.

4.4.2.1 Vehicles and searches under s 1

When an officer sees a vehicle in a public place and believes there are reasonable grounds to search it or anyone in the vehicle for prohibited or stolen items, the vehicle and any person in it can be searched under s 1. The flowchart provides further details.

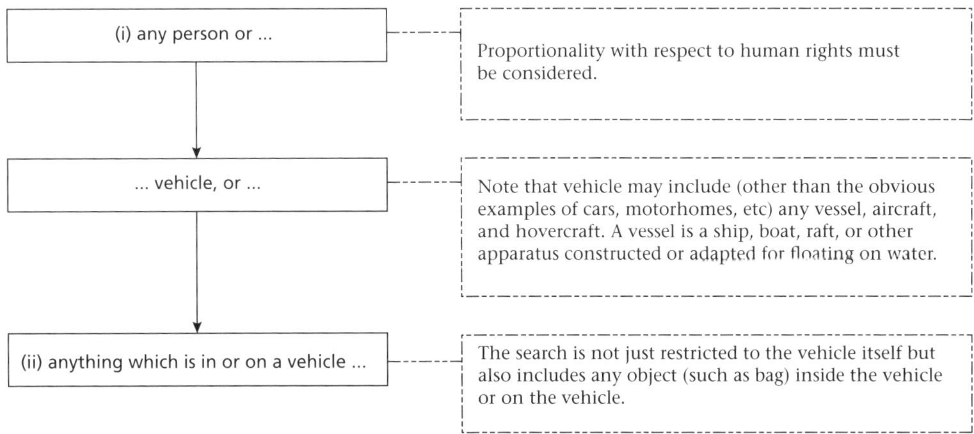

If a vehicle is on land attached to a dwelling (such as a driveway or garden) and the resident of the dwelling owns the vehicle or has given permission for it to be there, the vehicle would be considered as part of the dwelling. It could not therefore be searched under s 1 of the PACE Act 1984.

4.5 Other Stop and Search Powers

In addition to s 1 of the PACE Act 1984, there are many other pieces of legislation that include search powers. These include:

- the Misuse of Drugs Act 1971;
- the Psychoactive Substances Act 2016;
- the Criminal Justice and Public Order Act 1994;
- the Terrorism Act 2000;
- the Proceeds of Crime Act 2002;
- the Animal Welfare Act 2006; and
- the Firearms Act 1968.

We cover some of the more frequently used and important powers here.

4.5.1 Searches for controlled drugs

Section 23 of the Misuse of Drugs Act 1971 (MDA 1971) provides a police officer (in uniform or plain clothes) with the power to search any person, place, or vehicle for controlled drugs. The officer must have reasonable grounds for suspecting that the person is in possession of illegal drugs or is involved in manufacturing or supplying a controlled substance. The flowchart outlines some key points.

If a person smells of cannabis, has dilated pupils, is evasive to police questions, and appears nervous and agitated, this would be more than enough grounds to consider detaining them for the purpose of a search. The reasonable grounds could also be derived from intelligence, personal knowledge, or local knowledge, ie the person displaying these behaviours is in a known drug-dealing hotspot.

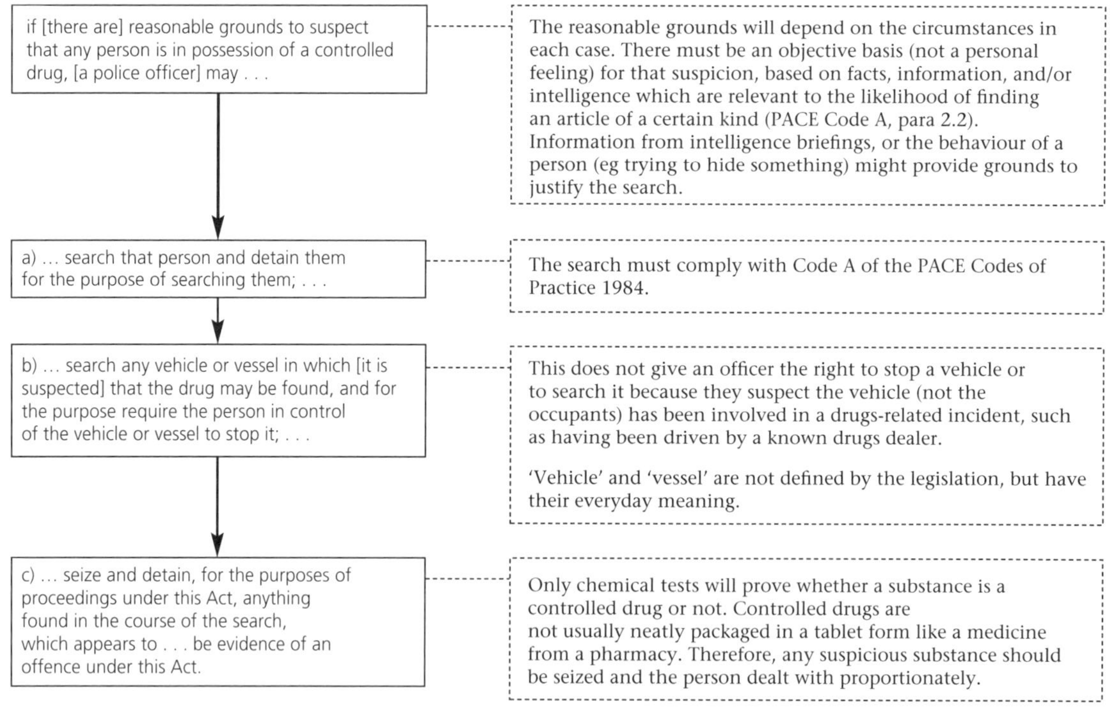

if [there are] reasonable grounds to suspect that any person is in possession of a controlled drug, [a police officer] may . . .
The reasonable grounds will depend on the circumstances in each case. There must be an objective basis (not a personal feeling) for that suspicion, based on facts, information, and/or intelligence which are relevant to the likelihood of finding an article of a certain kind (PACE Code A, para 2.2). Information from intelligence briefings, or the behaviour of a person (eg trying to hide something) might provide grounds to justify the search.
a) . . . search that person and detain them for the purpose of searching them; . . .
The search must comply with Code A of the PACE Codes of Practice 1984.
b) . . . search any vehicle or vessel in which [it is suspected] that the drug may be found, and for the purpose require the person in control of the vehicle or vessel to stop it; . . .
This does not give an officer the right to stop a vehicle or to search it because they suspect the vehicle (not the occupants) has been involved in a drugs-related incident, such as having been driven by a known drugs dealer.
'Vehicle' and 'vessel' are not defined by the legislation, but have their everyday meaning.
c) . . . seize and detain, for the purposes of proceedings under this Act, anything found in the course of the search, which appears to . . . be evidence of an offence under this Act.
Only chemical tests will prove whether a substance is a controlled drug or not. Controlled drugs are not usually neatly packaged in a tablet form like a medicine from a pharmacy. Therefore, any suspicious substance should be seized and the person dealt with proportionately.

In contrast to searches under s 1 of the PACE Act 1984, a s 23 search can be conducted in any place, public or private. However, to search a person under s 23 within a dwelling, the officer must have been invited or allowed on the premises by the resident. Alternatively, a search warrant could be used under which any person in the property can be searched.

The person's mouth can be searched as this is not considered to be part of an intimate search, but such searches should be exercised with caution—a suspect died after swallowing drugs in similar circumstances in an incident in East London in 2017. Should an intimate search be required, the authority of a senior officer must be obtained.

An individual who attempts to obstruct a drug search commits an offence under s 23(4) of the MDA 1971. The officer must have provided their name and station to the person, and stated that the detention is for the purposes of a search under the power of s 23. Should the person then continue to obstruct the search, the offence is complete.

4.5.2 Searches for psychoactive substances

In 2016, the Psychoactive Substances Act 2016 (PSA) was introduced to tackle the supply and production of psychoactive substances, often referred to as *legal highs*. The PSA includes its own power (under s 36) to detain and search people for psychoactive substances. The officer must have reasonable grounds to suspect that the person is committing or has committed an offence under the PSA. Such an offence would need to relate to the supply or production of psychoactive substances as personal possession is not an offence, unless in a custodial institution.

A s 36 PSA search can be conducted in any place to which the officer has lawful access, whether or not it is a public place. Any relevant items found during the search should be seized and then exhibited and submitted for forensic examination under ss 36–38 and s 43. Small amounts of suspected psychoactive substances can only be seized if they are deemed to be for more than just personal use, because possession of psychoactive substances is generally not an offence.

4.5.3 Searches related to public order incidents

Section 60 of the Criminal Justice and Public Order Act 1994 (CJPOA 1994) provides additional search powers for the police if there is a belief that an incident of serious violence is likely to occur, or has already occurred. Authorization is required under s 60 of the CJPOA 1994 (often referred to as a 'section 60').

4.5.3.1 Authorization

A 'section 60' must be authorized as shown in the flowchart, and the authorizing officer must have a reasonable belief that there has been or is likely to be a serious breakdown in public order. The authorization provides police officers with the power to conduct 'no suspicion' stop and searches of any pedestrian or vehicle, or anything being carried in that vehicle or by that person, for dangerous instruments or offensive weapons for a limited time in a specified area. Where possible, an officer of at least inspector rank should be consulted. A section 60 will be authorized for a specific geographical area and the area should be relevant to where the violence has already occurred, is believed to have occurred, or might occur.

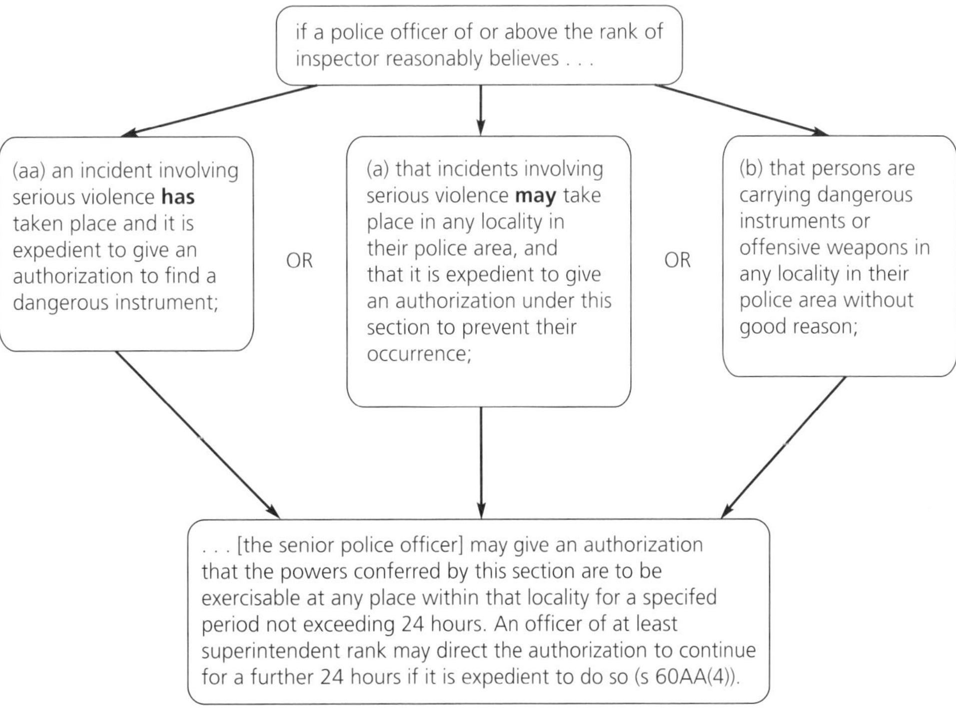

The authorization must be in writing (as soon as this is practicable) and the public should be made aware that it is in place by means of local posters, leaflets, or social media such as

Twitter and Facebook. A map of the area it covers is usually included. The initial period is for a maximum of 24 hours but it can be extended for a further 24 hours if required.

4.5.3.2 Powers provided by a s 60 authorization

A section 60 power, once authorized, allows officers in uniform to conduct stop and searches without reasonable grounds (in the relevant locality). The search must be for:

- a dangerous instrument; or
- an offensive weapon, which includes 'any article used in the incident to cause or threaten injury to any person, or otherwise to cause intimidation'. This could include a firearm (Code A, Note 23).

The person to be searched must have the item in their actual possession, and vehicles can also be searched.

The authorization also provides officers in uniform with a power to require any individual to remove clothing, such as a mask or scarf, if it seems that a person may be using it to conceal their identity. The officer should have reasonable grounds for believing that the item is being worn for that purpose. It is an offence to fail to remove such items when required to do so, and the individual could be arrested for not complying (s 60AA of the CJPOA 1994). Note that this is not a power to stop and search a person for items that could be used to conceal their identity; it is only a power to stop a person and make the requirement to remove the item.

When making the decision on who to target within the geographical area, officers must take care not to discriminate. There have been concerns about the potential for racial discrimination in such a situation, but in *R (on the application of Roberts) v Commissioner of Police of the Metropolis* [2012] EWHC 1977 (Admin), it was agreed that although there was potential for discrimination in such situations, searches under s 60 remain compatible with the European Convention on Human Rights.

4.5.4 Searches under the Terrorism Act 2000

The Terrorism Act 2000 provides search powers under ss 43, 43A, and 47A. Section 43 allows police officers to stop, detain, and search any person who they suspect to be a terrorist, or any person who may be in possession of an item which may constitute evidence of being involved in terrorist activity. As with previous search powers, an officer would be required to give GO WISELY prior to conducting the search, and give reasonable grounds for believing that the individual is involved in terrorist activity. These searches can be conducted by police officers in uniform or in plain clothes.

The s 43A power is similar but relates to vehicles. The search should be for evidence of terrorist activity and applies to everything in or on the car, for example bags inside the car or in a roof box. The owner of the vehicle does not need to be present for the search. If any relevant items are found, they should be seized as evidence. Any information gleaned should be written up as an intelligence report.

Section 47A of the Terrorism Act 2000 relates to authorizations which are in some ways similar to those made under s 60 of the CJPOA 1994. A s 47A authorization allows any officer within a specified area and time period to search any person or vehicle. The search can only be for evidence of terror activity but there is no need for the officer to have reasonable suspicion that the particular individual or vehicle is connected to terrorist activity. The search includes searching anything a person is carrying, or has with them in or on the vehicle. The officer carrying out such a search must be in uniform. The s 47A power needs to be authorized by a senior officer who, in most forces, would be at least an assistant chief constable. This officer would have to suspect with good reason that a terrorist act would be forthcoming and that the authorization would allow police actions that could prevent the act of terrorism.

4.5.5 Searches for proceeds of crime

Section 289 of the Proceeds of Crime Act 2002 provides officers with the power to search people, vehicles, and properties for cash. The power can only be exercised when the officer is lawfully within the property, for example having been let into the property by the occupier or if exercising another power, eg searching for drugs under a warrant.

The officer should have reasonable grounds to suspect that at least £1,000 cash is present and that it is either proceeds of criminal activity or is intended for use in unlawful conduct. Where possible, a senior or supervising officer should be contacted before the search.

4.5.6 Searches in relation to animal welfare

Under s 54 of the Animal Welfare Act 2006, officers in uniform have the power to stop and detain any vehicle in order to search it for animals that are believed to be suffering or are likely to be suffering or are likely to suffer should the circumstances not change (s 19 of the Animal Welfare Act 2006). The officer must have reasonable grounds for such a belief. An animal suspected to be involved in animal fighting can be seized under s 22 of the Act. Officers also have the power to enter a property with a warrant to search for evidence that may support the commission of an offence.

Further powers to stop, search, and seize in relation to animal protection are also provided under:

- the Wildlife and Countryside Act 1981 (s 19(1)), to help prevent the taking and killing of wild birds and other animals;
- the Wild Mammals (Protection) Act 1996 (s 4), which relates to vehicles as well as to persons; and
- the Police, Crime, Sentencing and Courts Act 2022 (s 67), which relates to seizing the dogs used in hare coursing.

4.5.7 Searches for firearms

Under s 47 of the Firearms Act 1968, any person or vehicle can be searched by an officer if the officer has reasonable cause to suspect that the person is in possession of a firearm, with or without ammunition, in a public place and is committing (or is about to commit) a serious firearms offence such as an armed robbery or a shooting. This power can be used instead of searching for an offensive weapon under s 1 of the PACE Act 1984 if the search is specifically for a firearm. It should be noted that possession of a firearm is often an offence in itself, with a few exceptions.

4.6 Searching Premises, Vehicles, and Open Land

Police officers often need to search premises and places for evidence, for example after searching a person who has been at the location. During a search of a vehicle or premises, you may uncover evidence of other illegal activities. For example, in the course of a search in relation to card fraud or drug sales, the officers may also find documents supporting terrorist ideologies. Indeed, the proceeds of the fraud could be funding terrorist activities. If such searches uncover evidence that provides grounds for further suspicion, the information should be passed to the appropriate authority.

The flowchart shows which powers can be used to search a property or place. Note that a 'no' answer to questions can require you to seek further advice as they sometimes lead to dead ends in the flowchart as seen below.

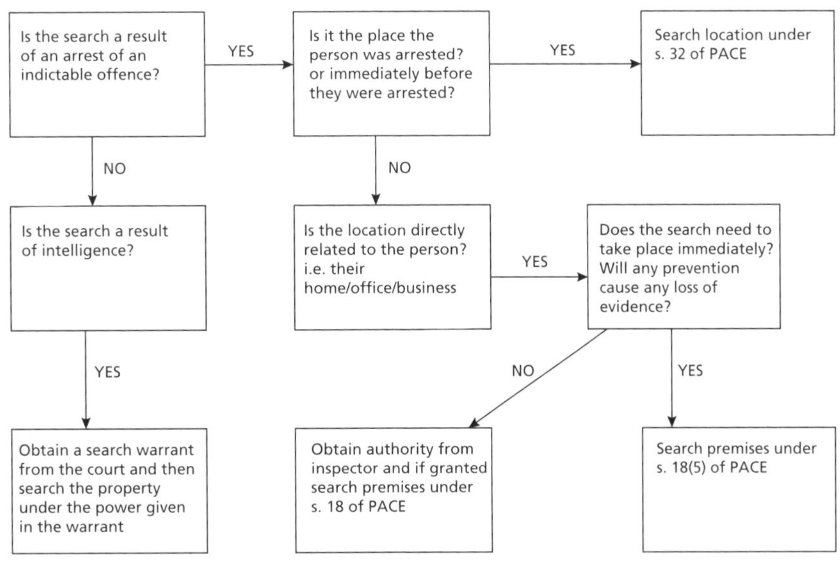

4.6.1 Search powers for premises

It will often be necessary to search premises in relation to a suspected offence. Most of these searches will be under s 32 or 18 of the PACE Act 1984, and will follow an arrest. Search warrants can also be used.

4.6.1.1 Searching the premises where a person has been arrested

A search under s 32 of the PACE Act 1984 is conducted following the arrest of an individual for an indictable offence. It allows an officer to search the location where the person was actually arrested, and their location immediately before the arrest (see the flowchart). The arrested person will also almost certainly be searched on arrest.

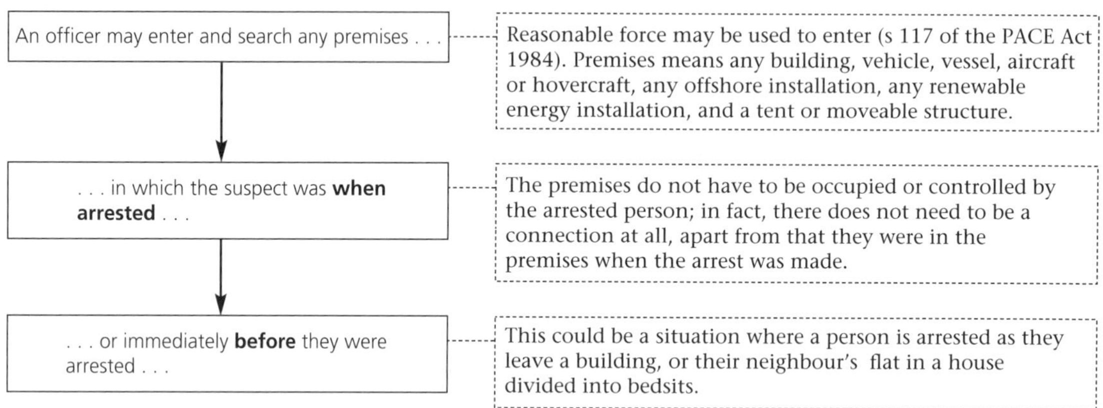

An officer may enter and search any premises . . .
Reasonable force may be used to enter (s 117 of the PACE Act 1984). Premises means any building, vehicle, vessel, aircraft or hovercraft, any offshore installation, any renewable energy installation, and a tent or moveable structure.
. . . in which the suspect was when arrested . . .
The premises do not have to be occupied or controlled by the arrested person; in fact, there does not need to be a connection at all, apart from that they were in the premises when the arrest was made.
. . . or immediately before they were arrested . . .
This could be a situation where a person is arrested as they leave a building, or their neighbour's flat in a house divided into bedsits.

If a person was stopped and arrested outside the block of flats where they lived, their flat could be searched, as could the communal area. Other flats in the block could not be searched unless there was evidence that the person had been in a different flat just before they were arrested. The search must be for evidence of the offence.

It should be noted that if the arrest was found to be unlawful, a search conducted under s 32 would also be considered unlawful, as ruled in *Lord Hanningfield of Chelmsford v Chief Constable of Essex Police* [2013] EWHC 243 (QB).

4.6.1.2 Searching other premises after a person has been arrested

After an arrest for an indictable offence, other locations relating to the arrested person, such as their home address or workplace, may need to be searched for evidence. This type of search is conducted under s 18 of the PACE Act 1984. The search must be for evidence of the indictable offence for which a person has been arrested. This power is particularly useful because the s 32 power of search only applies to the location of the arrest and the investigation may be concerned with other locations.

Written authority from an inspector is needed for a search under s 18, except when the presence of the person is necessary, and officers should record the time and date the authority is given. There must be reasonable grounds for suspecting that:

- the person has access to and has used the location; and
- there is evidence on the premises that relates to the offence in question, a similar offence, or to another related indictable offence.

If possible, the authority should be recorded on the Notice of Powers and Rights, and signed. Details of the grounds and the evidence sought should be recorded on the notice, on the custody record, in the search record, and in the officer's PNB.

Anything found during such a search can be seized and retained (s 18(2)) for long as necessary (s 22 of the PACE Act 1984). As for s 32 searches, officers should be aware that evidence relating to other offences could be found whilst conducting the search. The flowchart provides additional information.

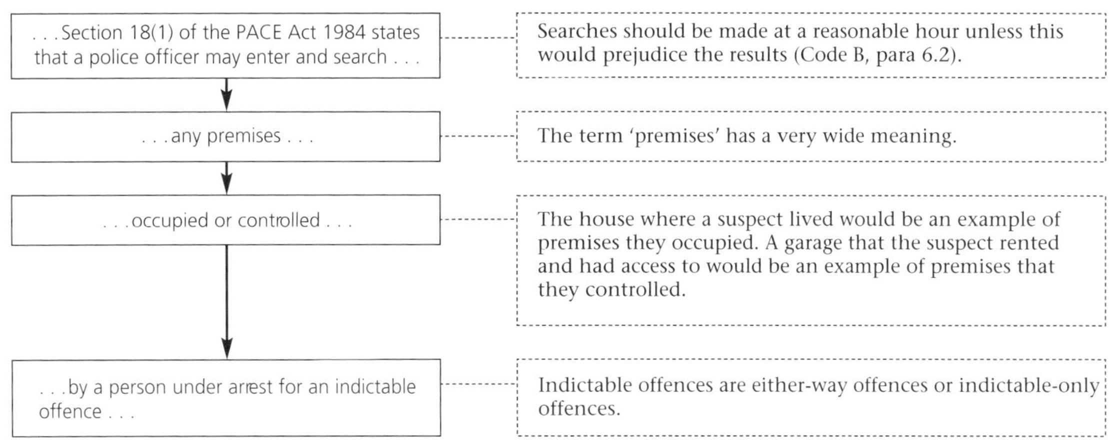

. . . Section 18(1) of the PACE Act 1984 states that a police officer may enter and search . . .
Searches should be made at a reasonable hour unless this would prejudice the results (Code B, para 6.2).
. . . any premises . . .
The term 'premises' has a very wide meaning.
. . . occupied or controlled . . .
The house where a suspect lived would be an example of premises they occupied. A garage that the suspect rented and had access to would be an example of premises that they controlled.
. . . by a person under arrest for an indictable offence . . .
Indictable offences are either-way offences or indictable-only offences.

The suspect's home address may need to be searched promptly to prevent evidence being removed. For example, imagine that two burglars are seen to run away from a burglary and one is stopped and arrested while the other gets away. The suspect who is still at large could go to their accomplice's flat and quickly remove any incriminating evidence. In such relatively urgent circumstances, a search can be carried out under s 18(5) of the PACE Act 1984. This differs from a s 18 search as it can be carried out without prior authorization and therefore without delay. An inspector should be made aware of it as soon as possible but advance authority is not required.

4.6.1.3 Search warrants

Not all premises searches take place after an arrest. Police intelligence could suggest a person is involved in an illegal activity or officers may even come across such activity by chance. If the activity seems to amount to an indictable offence, the police can obtain a search warrant which allows officers to enter and search a particular premises, vehicles, or land for evidence of this criminal activity. The grounds and procedures for applying and carrying out a warrant can be found under s 8 of the PACE Act 1984. Additionally, the Police Crime Sentencing and Courts Act 2022 (ss 55–57) build on the existing law and widen the circumstances in which a search warrant or production order can be applied for in relation to material relating to the location of human remains.

A warrant is issued by a Justice of the Peace (magistrate) and the application can be made at a court of law or via an appointment booked with the magistrate and conducted over the phone. An on-call magistrate can be contacted if an 'out of hours' warrant is needed. There must be reasonable grounds for believing that an indictable offence has been committed and that the object of the search is likely to be of substantial value to the investigation (but is not subject to legal privilege, excluded material, or special procedure material). In addition, at least one of the following conditions must apply:

- it is not practicable to communicate with a person who is entitled to grant entry to the premises or to the evidence;
- entry to the premises will not be granted without a warrant; and/or
- the purpose of a search may be frustrated or seriously prejudiced unless a constable arriving at the premises can secure immediate entry.

The warrant would be granted under the legislation that provides the relevant search power, for example s 23 of the MDA 1971. Other statutes provide particular powers for the police to enter and search premises in certain circumstances, such as the Theft Act 1968 (for stolen property), and in such cases the police will be able to obtain a search warrant under the relevant Act. Any search warrant application, as well as the subsequent search, must comply with ss 15 and 16 of the PACE Act 1984.

There are two main categories of warrant. A 'specific premises warrant' applies for just one premises and an 'all premises warrant' applies to any premises occupied or controlled by the person specified in the application. For an 'all premises' warrant, the Justice of the Peace must be satisfied that it is really necessary, for example due to the particulars of the offence, or because it is not reasonably practicable to specify each and every premises which might need to be searched. Premises may be entered and searched on more than one occasion under the same application, but this must be separately authorized by an officer of the rank of inspector or above and there must be an extremely good reason for returning.

When conducting a warrant, assistance from a specialist unit may be needed, for example a dog unit with dogs that have been trained to detect money or drugs, or a crime scene investigator (CSI) who is able to 'make safe' firearms. The specialist units can be organized prior to conducting the warrant or, for quick time events, contacted to attend immediately. The s 8 PACE power also allows police to seize any relevant evidence found during the search.

4.6.2 General considerations for searching premises, vehicles, and open land

Officers conducting a search should keep an open mind and consider all material at the location as possible evidence for the offence in question, and for other offences. They should also remember that some items or materials might have health and safety implications, such as chemicals for producing drugs. For major and serious crimes, the senior investigating officer may require that a forensic examination is carried out before a search for intelligence materials to ensure preservation of all the available forensic evidence.

The officer in charge of the search should oversee and closely control the whole process, and keep a record of all decisions made and all items found. All objects that have been moved should be returned to their original positions when first found, and any damage recorded in the search log. Failing to do this could lead to complaints and disciplinary procedures.

4.6.2.1 Planning a search

Proper planning is essential for the success of a search. The size of the area and the objects that are sought are key factors. The number of officers required will vary, for example searching a bedsit for evidence during a s 18 search or under a warrant could require just two officers, but in a large or complex search up to ten officers might be needed. Clearly, searching a wheelie bin would require fewer officers than searching a cluttered bedroom.

Officers with special skills—such as trained entry officers, taser-use officers, or a dog handler—may also be needed. Search dogs are an invaluable tool for specialist targets such as people, drugs, cash, blood, and firearms although dogs can damage fragile forensic evidence. A CSI may be useful for photographic recording and advising on specialist packaging. When searching for a person out of doors, a police helicopter with heat sensors may be required. In searches related to cybercrime, or involving digital materials, a member of the Digital Forensics Unit may be required. Police Search Advisers (PolSA) are officers specially trained to help plan and oversee searches of vast or particularly difficult areas, or in searches for tiny or very significant pieces of evidence. When conducting searches in the open air, further considerations apply, such as the weather, terrain, and any surface vegetation. Small items can be easily missed in heavy vegetation or in wet conditions. The search officers can obviously be more widely spaced when searching for a larger object on short grass but may need to work more closely when searching woodland for small items. All these factors must be taken into account during the planning phase.

Personal safety equipment such as helmets, gloves, and knee protectors may be required, as well as tools to access hides, dismantle equipment, or dig in gardens. If it is likely that several items will be seized, it is best practice to allocate an exhibits officer who will record and exhibit all pieces of evidence at the scene. The exhibits officer can help to ensure that police protocols regarding the handling, exhibiting, and storage of exhibits are closely followed. It is important that sufficient packaging material, transport, and storage facilities are available for the anticipated quantity of evidence. The evidence must be correctly packaged to avoid items being destroyed or damaged in storage or becoming forensically contaminated.

The IIMARCH mnemonic can be used when planning a search, as a reminder to consider all of the following:

- Information—why the search is needed, intelligence, local issues.
- Intention—the aim or reason for the search, the target material.
- Method—how the search and management of it will be conducted.

- Administration—maps, plans, transport, equipment.
- Risk assessment.
- Communications—such as which channel to use, mobile and landline numbers, and code words.
- Human rights compliance.

(Source: https://www.college.police.uk/app/operations/briefing-and-debriefing)

A senior officer, such as a sergeant or inspector, usually conducts a risk assessment of the venue prior to the search. This will take into account the physical risks, such as the safety of buildings and their contents, as well as the likelihood of resistance from occupants. Force intelligence systems and local knowledge could provide information on any contingency plans already in place for particular premises, and any warnings regarding possible occupants. The assessment will inform decisions regarding the number of officers and whether a PolSA and/or a specialist search team are required.

4.6.2.2 After the search

If any items are located during the search, the officer who found the item should complete a statement describing it and stating where it was found and whether they exhibited it personally or handed it to another person.

When the search is complete, officers should ensure they remove all of their equipment. Appropriate paperwork should be completed, including a record of the search. For locations with an identifiable owner or occupier, a copy of the record should be provided or left in a place where it is easily found. If any damage has been caused, this should be reported to the officer in charge, recorded in notes, and photographed. The occupier should be shown the condition of the property if present. The property must be left secure if force was used to secure entry.

In some searches, intelligence-related items might be found. The intelligence might be relevant for the safety of officers who attend later or it might suggest that some illegal activity could be occurring at the location. In both cases, an intelligence report must be completed.

4.6.3 Procedures for searching buildings

A search of a building should be logical and systematic. For houses and flats, the space is already divided into zones by the walls and floors which can help to ensure that all areas are covered but larger structures can be more complex. It is essential that every effort is made to ensure all areas are searched effectively—there are likely to be voids behind drawers and under cupboards and any access panels must be removed. Remember that many enterprising criminals attempt to hide evidence, for example beneath floorboards, behind sliding panels, or in a freezer.

Upon arrival at the premises, or if any person arrives during the search, the officer in charge should identify themselves and state the purpose and grounds of the search. Any other officers involved should also be identified and introduced (Code B, para 6.5). This does not apply if there are reasonable grounds for believing that alerting the occupier would frustrate the object of the search or put officers in danger (Code B, para 6.4). No consent is required for unoccupied premises or if the people present or available are not entitled to grant access. In a lodging house, a search should not be made solely on the basis of the landlord's consent; every reasonable effort should be made to obtain the consent of the tenant, lodger, or occupier (Code B, para 5.2). If practicable, the consent must be given in writing on the Notice of Powers and Rights before the search (Code B, para 5.1).

If any items are found during the search, a police officer who is lawfully on any premises has a general power under s 19 of the PACE Act 1984 to seize anything where they have reasonable grounds for believing that it:

- has been obtained in consequence of the commission of an offence;
- is evidence that relates to an offence which they are investigating, or to any other offence; and
- it is necessary to seize it to prevent it being concealed, lost, damaged, altered, or destroyed.

The seized items can be retained for only as long as necessary (s 22 of the PACE Act 1984).

4.6.4 Procedures for searching open spaces

Searching open spaces can be very difficult but is often required, for example in missing persons investigations. The weather, drains, and outbuildings can all present additional challenges and make such searches even more difficult. The best way to search will depend on the location, the size of the area, and the officers present; there are a number of different search patterns to choose from such as spiral, zone, grid, or strip search patterns.

Planning is critical and local knowledge can assist in locating any dangerous points. Copies of plans and maps of the search area and any relevant intelligence should be provided to each officer. Police helicopters and drones can also be used to assist outdoor searches for missing people, suspects who have recently made off from incidents, or vehicles in ongoing situations. The offender, any accomplices, the public, and the media may also have access to the search area, especially when cordoning is impractical. This can cause further difficulties, especially when utilizing dog handlers or a police helicopter.

On open and featureless ground, police tape is normally used to divide the area into strips, grids, or zones. If a line search with a return 'sweep' is used, the boundary of the previous sweep is always covered again. The whole line stops when an object such as a ditch or hedge bars the way, and the object is normally searched immediately.

A search of remote areas and woodland can sometimes reveal caches of weapons or explosives, or hides containing stolen materials. It is common to find a wide variety of material that is unrelated to the offence under investigation. Obviously, any item such as a timer, knives, or a mobile phone found in a surprising, suspicious, or unexpected place should be treated with caution.

4.6.5 Procedures for searching vehicles

When searching vehicles, they can be regarded as comprising five main areas: the engine bay, the passenger cabin, the boot, the exterior, and the underside. These should be searched systematically in turn. Vehicles contain a significant number of possible voids that could be used for concealing things, and indeed commercial vehicles intended for illegal drugs importations, may have specially constructed voids built into their structure. Officers should be aware of any loose panels and be sure to check the gear stick casing, air vents, and radio/CD player/multimedia areas.

All officers must keep their own personal safety at the forefront of their minds whilst conducting the search. At a roadside search, safety with regard to traffic should be considered and it may be necessary to install traffic control systems. Searches should certainly not be carried out on blind bends or adjacent to fast-moving traffic. Officers should also be aware of all the moving and electrical parts within the vehicle. They should ensure the key is always removed from the ignition prior to commencing the search, and ideally held in police possession to prevent suspects from attempting to get back into the vehicle and drive away.

4.7 Answer to Task

TASK 1

I am PC SMITH from HACKNEY police station	I S
and you are detained for the purposes of a search.	Y
I am going to search you under section 23 of the Misuse of Drugs Act	L
Here is my warrant card (if not in uniform).	W
I am searching you for drugs,	O
as I have seen you driving erratically and at speed, and when speaking to you I can smell cannabis coming from within your vehicle. You appear anxious; your pupils are dilated, and you look dazed. I can also see drug paraphernalia within your vehicle.	G
You are entitled to a copy of this search	E

5 Evidence-based Policing and Problem Solving

5.1 Introduction

The main focus of this chapter is Evidence-based Policing (EBP). Since the 1980s, several public policy arenas in England and Wales, such as education, social work, and medicine, have applied the notion of evidence-based practice. It is characterized using the 'best available evidence' to inform policy and practice (Nutley, Davis, and Walter, 2002). Originating from the medical profession, the principles of evidence-based practice are to systematically use scientific knowledge as 'evidence' to enhance operational, strategic, and/or policy decision-making. The approach recognizes the value of conducting robust research and ensures that research evidence informs practice. This way decision-making is based on the most current understandings of a particular problem or issue, offering insights into what works best for future action.

In 2012, the professional body for policing, the College of Policing was set up in England and Wales. The role of the College is to set professional standards in policing. They have developed several workstreams to professionalize policing. These workstreams have involved establishing a code of ethics, developing leadership, standardizing training to incorporate more formal accredited learning through university education, and advocating for evidence-based practice, known as evidence-based policing (EBP). For policing to achieve EBP, it requires practitioners and organizations to understand EBP, the role of research knowledge, and the skills needed to conduct ethical, systematic, and thorough research. Therefore, this chapter will cover two important aspects of evidence-based practice used in policing. The first will present some of the origins and definitions of evidence-based policing and how it links with professional practice in policing. The second will cover some of the basic research skills involved in developing EBP, relevant for policing students or other practitioners in policing. The focus of these areas should help police practitioners consider the role as EBP, and how EBP might be used either as students on their learning programme or as established officers/members of staff when dealing with a particular issue or problem at work.

However, before looking at EBP in more detail, it is worth noting the evolving educational framework that places learning at the heart of policing and informs the entry routes into policing.

5.2 Learning in a Policing Environment

People learn in different ways (Kolb, 1984). Over time, researchers have differentiated four main learning styles: activist, theorist, pragmatist, and reflective. Most people employ one or two of these styles. The **activist** learning style involves being actively involved with a task; this might involve taking part in simulations or role-plays; setting tasks or writing questions or case studies; taking part in computer-based learning; and/or using pre-formed questions before sessions so that learning can be continually checked. The **theorist** learning style involves having a logical outlook and developing underlying theories; the desire to read about a subject and drawing independent conclusions; challenging the underlying assumptions; and/or designing logical diagrams to summarize the subject matter as a sequence of points to be learned. The **pragmatist** learning style involves thinking or dealing with the problem in a practical way, rather than using theory or abstract principles; finding the use of theory and discussion frustrating; and/or looking for the practical applications for learning. The **reflective** learning style involves learning in a slow, deliberate way; taking a step back and looking at a subject from all angles before drawing a conclusion; discussing issues.

You will be encouraged to think about how you learn best and doing this might help you find ways to maximize your learning experience. But there are also basic study skills that will help you meet learning requirements, complete assignments, and develop your understanding of policing.

5.2.1 Studying and study skills

There are numerous guides, books, and websites which can be used to help develop your study skills. For example, if you are undertaking a higher education award as part of your education and training, then you may find it useful to work through Dr Stella Cottrell's *Study Skills Handbook* (Cottrell, 2019). Students based at an HEI on a degree in professional policing, studying on the DHEP, or as a PCDA student will almost certainly find that support for study skills is available. The following skills are normally required:

- reading skills;
- note-taking and writing skills;
- memorizing and revising for assessments;
- using libraries, learning centres, and e-learning resources;
- researching and using internet search engines; and
- time management.

If you feel you have concerns around your learning which may be impacting on your ability to study, it is important to speak to your tutor, coach, or lecturer. HEIs often offer screening for students as they first join. There may be a specific department within the HEI to help support any diagnosed needs, so the support is there should you need it.

5.2.2 Reflective practice in policing

Reflective practice has its origins in the educational theories of John Dewey in the 1930s. He saw the merits in learning through doing, and learning outside of formal classroom settings. He introduced the concept of 'reflective action', based on the idea that people try to develop and improve their performance and, in order to learn, they think about their actions by asking:

- What went well?
- What did not go well?
- What would I do differently next time?

Schön (1983) developed the concept of reflective practice and importantly identifies this at the level of the practitioner, the level of the practice in which practitioners operate, and at the societal level, which involves a practice and its practitioners negotiating and legitimizing professional norms and expectations. Wood (2020) has linked this aspect of Schön's (1983) to Alisdair MacIntyre's (1985) concept of practice as it relates to virtue ethics. The police are often subject to intense scrutiny especially after tragic incidents. Enquiries into tragedies will often include questions about the training and experience of the officers involved, how and why they made certain decisions, and whether other officers would have acted in the same way in the same circumstances. These enquiries are generally focused upon learning lessons to improve future practice.

You may be expected to undertake reflective practice as part of the PCDA or DHEP. As Norman and Williams (2017) argue, the complexity of policing and the changing nature of crime mean that police officers need to be more reflective in their approach to problem solving in order to meet these new challenges.

There are different models of reflection; the reflective model currently encouraged by the College of Policing is Gibbs' (1988) Reflective Cycle (CoP, 2020b). This is a popular model of reflection that has been traditionally used in police training.

5.2.3 Forms of reasoning and arguments

For both student police constables and experienced police officers alike, a logical and structured approach to problem solving is important. This is not to deny the use of intuition as a problem-solving approach: in some cases, it can be very effective (Bryant, 2019). However, it is important to develop an awareness of when using intuition is appropriate, and when it is not.

Logical ways of thinking are skills that need to be nurtured and developed. Logic underpins the development of sound arguments and the ability to identify fallacious lines of argument. A fallacy is a statement that is incorrect, often because of flawed logic. On occasions, these have contributed to miscarriages of justice and to innocent people enduring long prison sentences.

5.2.3.1 Inductive reasoning

Inductive reasoning involves generalizing from a number of previous examples to establish a rule or theory. This form of reasoning is very commonly employed in everyday life and, indeed, was the basis for much scientific discovery in the past. Despite induction being a widespread technique for reasoning, it has an inherent weakness. Sometimes there is no logical reason why the generalization should follow from an observation. Additionally, you may have incomplete information and therefore might draw false conclusions; this can be the case even with accurate observations. The danger for student police constables of using inductive methods resides in the problem of generalizing from a limited number of experiences, especially as the experiences new officers encounter might be significantly different from what they have experienced prior to joining the police. As such, these experiences will have an undue impact on the officer and seem therefore to be more significant than they actually are. This special characteristic of police officer experiences becomes contextualized over time and officers will accordingly draw more nuanced conclusions. Likewise, police officers tend to experience individuals and incidents that will become routine and common to themselves, but will nonetheless be far from what is normal in society. The police deal with people who are often on the margins of society doing things that most people do not do. So a police officer's every day experience is unrepresentative of what a normal day is like for most people.

5.2.3.2 Deductive reasoning

Deductive reasoning is the form of reasoning where a conclusion or *deduction* must necessarily follow if the assumptions or *premises* are true. One of the most well-known forms of deduction is that of the *syllogism*. A famous example is:

- 'All men are mortal' (premise 1),
- 'Socrates is a man' (premise 2), therefore
- 'Socrates is mortal' (conclusion).

A more everyday example of deduction at work would be: 'if a person is in one place then they cannot be in another at the same time'. We can express this as a syllogism in the following way:

- a person cannot be in two places at the same time;
- the suspect is captured on CCTV at 0100 on 5 May 2023 at London St Pancras station; therefore,
- the suspect could not have been in Cardiff at 0100 on 5 May 2023.

The strength of using deductive reasoning flows from its watertight nature. However, the flaw with deduction is that we can only be completely certain about the truth of a conclusion if both the assumptions are correct and the deductive reasoning has been correctly applied. For example, the time stamp on the CCTV footage might be wrong or the image could have been tampered with.

5.2.3.3 Abductive reasoning

Abductive reasoning is 'reasoning to the best available explanation' or deriving the most likely explanation that fits the observed facts, observations, or assumptions. We often employ abduction when we observe effects and infer causes. For example, if during Supervised Patrol, a trainee police officer observes members of the public running away from a particular location, they are likely to infer that something dramatic and probably dangerous has caused them to flee.

5.2.3.4 Reasoning and arguments

Reasoning becomes important when formulating arguments, whether within your practice or in assignments as part of your learning and development. In practice, the three forms of reasoning we have outlined here, induction, deduction, and abduction, are often combined. For example, reasoning during a police critical incident might involve employing abduction as starting point, which is then tested using induction (gathering more information and evidence) and deduction (thinking about explanations that follow from the evidence). The circumstances we are in, and the available evidence at hand, will determine whether we use induction, deduction, or abduction. Abduction is appropriate for formulating initial thoughts and narrowing down our focus, but is less helpful in getting to the details of a matter. Deduction is necessary when we have little evidence to go on and we need to think laterally about possibilities and most likely scenarios in the absence of details. Induction is appropriate when there is a large amount of evidence that needs to be gathered, documented, and sorted, but in some circumstances that might be disproportionately time consuming and expensive.

There are a number of common fallacies that were identified by the Ancient Greek philosopher Aristotle, who referred to them as the informal fallacies. In each example, the informal fallacy is a form of distraction away from the logic of an argument. The person committing an informal fallacy focuses on one feature related to the topic to the exclusion of all other factors. Informal fallacies include:

Attacking the person (*'argumentum ad hominem'*). This is a fallacious argument that seeks to undermine the position of an opposing view by highlighting characteristics of the person or people presenting an argument, rather than the reasoning and evidence they have presented, eg:

> Of course they support paying police officers more money; they work for the Police Federation.

The fact that an argument to increase officers' pay has been presented by Police Federation representatives is not entirely insignificant, but if a well-reasoned case has been presented, with an exhaustive and thorough review, detailed information, and due consideration to counter points, then it becomes little more than a minor detail. Moreover, focusing on the Police Federation angle implies that there is little of substance to object to in the case presented by the Police Federation representative.

Argument from ignorance (*'argumentum ad ignorantiam'*). This fallacy argues that since something has not been proven false it must be true, or conversely, that since something has not been proven true, it is therefore false, eg:

Q: Do you think the suspect is guilty?
A: Well they don't have an alibi (so they must be guilty)
or,
Q: Do you think the suspect is guilty?
A: Well they don't have a clear motive (so they could not have committed the crime).

In both cases the answer provided exaggerates the significance of what is otherwise an important piece of information. The absence of an alibi keeps an investigation live, but little more than that; it is not enough on its own to suggest guilt. Likewise, motive is important in many crime scenarios and it helps frame an investigation, but the absence of motive should not close an investigation; it might be that we have just not found the motive, or it might be a motiveless crime.

Appealing to the people (*'argumentum ad populum'*). This is the fallacy of claiming that a proposition is true because it is subscribed to by popular opinion. An example would be:

> The most appropriate penalty for child murder committed by paedophiles is the death sentence. Opinion poll after opinion poll demonstrates that the British people believe this to be the case.

The right thing to do is not always what is popular, but the weight of public opinion can be persuasive. It becomes more challenging to hold a position if you know that everyone else thinks the position is wrong. Of course sometimes we find ourselves in a minority of one because we are wrong; we should not let our convictions blind us to this possibility. But there will be times when the minority of one is correct and the overwhelming majority are wrong. Using the popular argument though is at best lazy reasoning and it is always best to provide reasons than simply stating that this is what everyone thinks.

5.2.4 Entry routes into policing, the National Policing Curriculum (NPC), and the Policing Education Qualifications Framework (PEQF)

There are currently four entry routes listed by the College of Policing for people wishing to join a police service as a constable. These are:

- the Police Constable Degree Apprenticeship (PCDA) route, which requires recruits to gain an undergraduate degree over three years whilst training as a police constable and receiving a salary at the level of an 'apprentice police officer'—The achievement of key milestones in the early career of police officers, eg Independent Patrol Status (IPS) and Full Operational Competence (FOC) are embedded within the design of this route;
- the Degree Holder Entry Programme (DHEP) route, designed for graduates from non-policing disciplines, this route requires recruits to undertake a level 6 Graduate Diploma over two years whilst training as a police constable and receiving a salary. There is a generic DHEP route and also a specific Detective Constable DHEP route—again, IPS and FOC are embedded in the DHEP routes;
- a College of Policing-approved pre-join professional policing degree route, which requires recruits to complete a self-funded degree prior to applying to join a police service—on being accepted, recruits are required to complete a two-year probationary period, in which time IPS and FOC need to be achieved.

All three of the above routes are offered by Higher Education Institutions (HEI) working in collaboration with police services and are modelled on the College of Policing's National Policing Curriculum (NPC).

The fourth route listed by the College of Policing is:

- the initial police learning and development programme (IPLDP) route, described by the College as the 'traditional' route on its website; it was established in 2006 and is being phased out. It is a non-degree route and the College have stated that they do not see it as fit for purpose moving forwards. However, the option of joining via this route was further extended in 2023 by 12 months until 31 March 2024.

There has been some resistance to the idea of making policing an all graduate profession and this was expressed by the Home Secretary, the Rt Hon Suella Braverman in a speech made on 9 November 2022 at the Association of Police and Crime Commissioners and National Police Chiefs' Council Partnership Summit 2022. The Chief Constables' Council supported the idea of developing a new level 5, fourth route into policing in March 2023, to be available to police services as soon as possible but by no later than 1 April 2024. The details of how this will work alongside the degree entry routes will need to be addressed and the Police Federation has voiced its concern and objection to the new fourth route.

The three degree entry routes into policing are part of the College's Policing Education Qualifications Framework (PEQF). The PEQF was introduced in 2016 and it is this that led to the major change in 2020, for all new police constables to be required to already have a degree-level qualification or to be working towards a degree-level qualification through the PCDA programme.

Notwithstanding the politics surrounding the proposed fourth entry route, and the extent to which this will impact upon the three degree entry routes into policing, the College of Policing's PEQF agenda has firmly established the idea that knowledge plays an important role in the development of police officers and professional police practice more widely. At the heart of the promotion of professional knowledge in police practice we find the idea of evidence-based policing (EBP).

5.3 The Origins and Definitions of EBP

The College of Policing and academics promote EBP as a means of using the best available evidence to inform and challenge policing policies, practices, and decisions. EBP has been inspired by the success of evidence-based practice in other professions, and is concerned with what works best. This means that changes made to existing practices, or new initiatives are based on research evidence, and changes can be measured through research to explore whether they are effective. The aim is to use research to aid decision-making and enhance policy-making by the police and partnership organizations, following the same principles of evidence-based practice.

Professor Lawrence Sherman originally introduced the concept of EBP in a presentation to the American Police Foundation in 1998 (Sherman, 1998). Sherman based his ideas on what was then a recent development in 'evidence-based medicine'. He used the term 'experimental criminology' and promoted the used of scientific research methods as an essential part in police decision-making, which led to the EBP movement in the United States (US). Sherman believed that EBP leads to more professional decision-making as it provides a more comprehensive understanding of police problems. The experimental nature of research approach advocated by Sherman meant that measuring the police responses to problems was more objective, and could inform future action more effectively. Providing evidence to the decision-makers reduces the likelihood of ill-informed, knee-jerk decisions being made.

5.3.1 The development of EBP in England and Wales

Using evidence, research, and analysis to inform policing is not new, but EBP marks a shift in the extent to which this is made explicit and supported institutionally as a feature of routine practice. The shift is expressed by Sherman (2013, pp 2–3) as a move from less effective approaches of policing from the past: the so-called 'three Rs' of random patrol, rapid response, and reactive investigations; towards an EBP approach that emphasizes the 'three Ts' of targeting, testing, and tracking.

This does not mean that policing before the formal advent of EBP was never evidence based; there are numerous examples of 'experimental' approaches dating back to at least the 1970s. Moreover, Intelligence Led Policing (ILP) emerged in the early 1990s and the National Intelligence Model (NIM) has been a central feature used in police services for tactical decision making throughout England and Wales since 2000. The aim of ILP and the NIM is to provide actionable intelligence based on systematic analysis and research (Tilley, 2008a; Seidler & Adderley, 2013). Another popular model used since the early 1990s within problem oriented policing is Scanning, Analysis, Response, and Assessment (SARA).

So in some respects, policing has been *doing* EBP for some time, although it is not until the College is introduced with a responsibility to set professional standards and an ethos to encourage professionalization, that EBP is developed and promoted as a core aspect of policing. Sherman remains a key player in EBP and in late 2022 it was announced that he was to become the MPS's first Chief Scientific Officer. But the College of Policing has broadened its definition of EBP to also include non-experimental forms of research.

A broader definition of EBP was an important change. Sherman favoured the use of experiments or randomized control trials (RCTs) as the 'gold standard' of research given their quantitative and experimental design. RCTs are useful given their random nature of the sampling, as this removes bias and the variables used within the experiment are controlled, so comparisons can be made between the treatment group and control groups. The idea of control is important. In medical research, researchers can accurately measure the impact of treatment to variables given the controlled nature of a laboratory environment. However, within social science research, control is much harder to achieve. Human nature is not predicable and not easy to replicate in a controlled way, so other forms of research methods are necessary to use when capturing the context and complexity of social life. Therefore, the new EBP definition means that the research conducted to understand what works in policing is not limited to quantitative experiments, and qualitative approaches are also valid ways to capture insights into policing. Wood (2020) has also argued that philosophical enquiry can contribute to understanding policing better and this is supported in the College's recent rapid evidence assessment on ethical decision-making in policing (Bruce-Smith *et al*, 2023).

Quantitative research is concerned with systematically understanding an issue through **numbers** and **statistics** (Given, 2008). The analysis is based on **quantity** where data is split into parts or **variables** to **measure** the effects on each other, to answer a research question (Mishra, 2017). Quantitative research is usually **deductive** to **test** ideas or **hypotheses** and to **model theories**.

Qualitative research explores human **behaviour**, **motivations**, attitudes, and **experiences** through understanding **quality**, **context**, and a **holistic** view (Mishra, 2017; Ary *et al*, 2010). Qualitative research is **inductive**, where the collected data is used to **establish theories**.

The College's latest EBP definition also indicates that there is an onus on police officers and staff to undertake EBP as part of their role. Incorporating EBP as a standard function of police work ensures that policing develops using high-quality evidence that can be used to inform policing and a professional response to the public. However, conducting EBP requires a specific skill set, which means that learning and education provision for new recruits and serving officers/staff should develop these skills to enable officers to undertake EBP.

As policing students and practitioners, gleaning an understanding of research methodologies is essential for you to undertake EBP as part of your role. The PEQF programmes for new recruits involve EBP as a core element included in the curricula of all three entry routes into policing. It is one of the subject areas in the NPC and trainees on the PEQF programmes are required to conduct their own EBP projects in their final year. Some subjects within the NPC develop students' research methods knowledge and skills, which also cover EBP principles.

Further information on EBP is available on the College of Policing website, from other organizations such as the Center for Evidence-Based Crime Policy (CEBCP) and the Society of Evidence-based Policing (SEBP). The CEBP and SEBP both have public access websites.

5.4 Research Methods—Skills Required for EBP

EBP research is a relatively recent innovation in England and Wales, in terms of its introduction into initial police training and its day-to-day use in the police service. There are several different models emerging on how to undertake EBP research, in terms of addressing particular issues, testing interventions, and/or evaluating policing initiatives. The College advocates the use of a 'logic model' for evaluating policing initiatives, based on a sequence of 'Problem', 'Response', 'Outputs', and 'Outcomes' (see the College of Policing website). Another useful way of thinking systematically about exploring a police problem in an evidence-based way is to use the research process. Police practitioners need to be aware of the basic principles of social research methods and how to design and conduct projects on their practice. This section of the chapter covers the research process and the systematic approach that is useful to take when conducting EBP research. Whether quantitative or qualitative approaches are applied in the research or when exploring a police intervention through EBP, there are common features to exploring data in the research process, which when followed, can provide new insights, conclusions, and recommendations to inform police interventions.

5.4.1 Social research and the research process

Social research provides a 'comprehensive understanding of social life' (Khan *et al*, 2022). Social research helps uncover new insights into social problems, which can be complex and involve different social groups, their environments, cultures, institutions, organizations, and social systems, which are interconnected and multi-layered. Given the social nature of the police as a public agency in dealing with crime, the application of social research methods is helpful when describing EBP. Following a process to understanding the connections between the problems, groups, and systems through research can help provide a picture of what works in terms of interventions and what can be recommended in policy and practice for future action.

Khan *et al* (2022) adapted Neuman and Robson's (2018) model of the social research process and present the following (see diagram below) as core characteristics in social research.

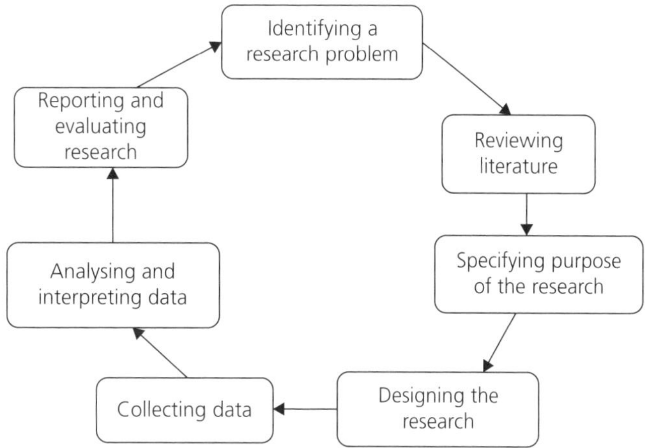

Source: Khan *et al* (2022) adapted from Neuman and Robson's (2018) model of the research process.

5.4.2 Identifying a research problem

The first step of conducting a research/EBP project involves outlining the problem or question that requires exploration. This can include increasing our understanding of a policing challenge or crime problem, and how national/international research might apply to a particular local force or community. The question should be defined as precisely as possible and, importantly, be such that it can be answered. Questions which relate to the specifics of the circumstances are often more useful. For example, what recent interventions have been found to reliably reduce the theft of mobile phones from people in an urban location? A well-formulated question helps police practitioners or researchers to devise the best ways to explore the problem and gather the evidence through research.

5.4.3 Reviewing the literature or existing evidence

The next consideration is to explore what literature or evidence might help to answer the question. University-based readers should note that this is more than simply drawing up an academic 'literature review'; some of the evidence might be exclusively professional. For some questions such as a crime prevention technique, the answer might already be available through methodically reviewing secondary data or non-empirical research, or indeed reviewing the existing literature may help define the research question further. A secondary data analysis might consist of the following information:

- *Secondary data*—information on a database of research, academic publications, or a policing professional body website, published statistics, for example: data published on the Office for National Statistics website. It is important to question or seek the necessary approval if police databases are being used and that the information being explored is appropriate for research use. Or there are alternative resources that can be explored. The *What Works Centre for Crime Reduction*, part of the College of Policing, provides a range of useful sources. The Centre reviews, collates, and shares the best available evidence for crime reduction. The College also has a repository of its own research publications which are 'peer reviewed to ensure that government standards are met' (CoP, 2018a). These include the categories of 'Community Engagement and Crime Prevention' and 'Crime and Investigation' (ibid). In America, there is the Center for Evidence-Based Crime Policy (CEBCP), based at George Mason University, which has an 'Evidence-Based Policing Matrix' including all EBP studies that it deems meet threshold standards to 'qualify' (CEBCP, 2018a). In 2019, there were 165 studies on the Matrix, most US-based and carried out between 1970 and 2016 (CEBCP, 2018b).
- Systematic reviews (SR) are an example of secondary research. SR involve an in-depth and methodical exploration of existing evidence available. These are particularly important but should be carefully scrutinized. In terms of EBP, the 'Campbell Collaboration' (see <https://www.campbellcollaboration.org/>) is often recommended, but in 2022 the Campbell Library listed only 57 reviews for 'Crime and Justice', not all of which are relevant to EBP in the UK, and those that are can be of variable quality. Fortunately, there is also a growing number of 'Rapid Evidence Assessments' to inform EBP, for example *What Works in Supporting Victims of Crime* (Wedlock and Tapley, 2016).

Of course, when undertaking the review, questioning *what didn't work* is also important to capture. In all cases, you will need to critically examine the methodology used, whether the publication was peer-reviewed, and if any conclusions are justified, particularly if only a few studies have been published. Such critical examination requires considerable skill and knowledge on behalf of the researcher.

5.4.4 Skills and considerations needed to conduct non-empirical (or 'desk-based') research

Locating the evidence requires good searching and sifting skills, and access to a wide number of databases, some of which may not be available on the open web such as subscription-only databases.

Searching and sifting

While undertaking desk-based research, researchers use inclusion/exclusion criteria, using a range of keywords to locate relevant studies and findings, while excluding others. The available databases include the results of one-off studies, case studies, cohort studies, the outcomes of randomized trials and randomized control trials, other types of experiment, 'trial and error' approaches, and many other forms of evidence, including findings from qualitative research.

Assessing the existing evidence

Assessing the existing evidence that is being reviewed needs to be done by establishing how good the evidence is, and what relevance it might have to the EBP research question; this can often be challenging. We can never be certain about any conclusions derived from EBP evidence, even if the evidence is considered to be good. Many types of error occur and researchers need to be particularly mindful of false positives (wrongly believing something is present) and false negatives (wrongly believing something is absent).

The criteria for assessing the quality of evidence focuses on the following:

- its validity, robustness, and reliability; and
- its 'relevance' or how far the evidence pertains to the specific circumstances under study, for example any research about the police use of firearms in the US, where police carry guns on a routine basis, might not be relevant to the UK.

Rating and ranking the evidence

The 'EMMIE' framework system (Effect, Mechanism, Moderators, Implementation, Economic cost) can be used to help EBP practitioners 'rate and rank' evidence. The origins and justification for using EMMIE are covered in a 2016 academic paper by Nick Tilley (Tilley, 2016, p 307). The system was originally developed by the College of Policing in conjunction with University College London. Other forms of assessing evidence are also available. The 'Maryland Scientific Methods Scale' can be used for evaluating crime prevention evidence (the 'randomized control trials' score at the higher end of the scale).

Summarizing the findings

Undertaking a thorough review of the existing literature means that you will have a good understanding of all the available evidence about what works and what may be less effective. Next you should summarize your findings, offering some recommendations from your review. This is useful for a report at work, informing a problem-solving profile or if you are studying, this could form part of an academic literature review. Desk-top research would conclude at this stage. However, the findings from the review of existing evidence can inform the rationale for primary or empirical research. Conducting primary research involves developing research skills, the next section takes you through some of the basic ideas when conducting empirical research.

5.4.5 Specifying the purpose of the research

The review of the existing literature and relevant information provides the foundation of what you are striving to achieve through the research. The process undertaken in the review will mean that a systematic understanding of what works in addressing the research question, and what gaps in the literature exist. This helps identify the problem and the next steps for the research project design.

5.4.6 Designing the research

There are many types of research that can be used in a research project or EBP. In many instances, for a police student, a secondary or non-empirical research design (previously discussed) is sufficient. However, it might be necessary to conduct a primary or empirical research study.

- *Primary or empirical research*—primary or empirical research can be undertaken using quantitative approaches for example, an RCT or conducting surveys, qualitative approaches such as conducting observations, focus groups, and interviews or designing research that uses a blend of both approaches, known as a mixed methodological approach.
- For all primary or empirical research undertaken it is vital to follow an ethical framework to ensure informed consent is sought from participants and that the area of research conducted is ethically sound to explore. Seeking ethical approval is important to protect the subjects involved in the research and to protect you as a researcher.

Check with your constabulary and/or HEI provider to ensure you complete appropriate forms to ensure ethical approval is gained before conducting empirical research.

There are different types of primary research that can be useful to undertake to research a question at work, or indeed use to test an intervention applied to address a policing problem that forms an EBP project. See the table below on the various types of social research.

Type	Description
Basic research	Characterized as being pure research, providing new knowledge from scientific exploration of the world (Sarantakos, 2013)
Applied research	Characterized through the specific approach to understanding an existing problem to uncover causes and identify solutions (Sarantakos, 2013; Neuman and Robson, 2018)
Descriptive research	Characterized by the descriptive approach to understanding the connections within society (systems and people). It provides a holistic profile as opposed to an individual account (Robson, 2011)
Exploratory research	The exploratory nature of this approach means that it provides the opportunity to uncover different ideas to seek new understandings of the world (Robson, 2011), and to identify problems (Saunders *et al*, 2019)
Exploratory research	Can also be defined as causal research, where the research aims to understand the causal relationships between different variables to consider the effects (Creswell, 2018; Neuman and Robson, 2018)
Longitudinal research	Characterized by data collected over time about social issues across time periods to identify changes and influences on populations (Creswell, 2018; Neuman and Robson, 2018)
Comparative research	Characterized by examining the changes of different events from a variety of perspectives (Khan *et al*, 2022)
Action research	Characterized through collecting data related to the research question as an iterative and dynamic process to help define, inform or evaluate subsequent actions for the study. Typically the researcher works with practitioners to develop the work and embed in practice (Sarantakos, 2013)
Participatory action research	Characterized by the collaboration between the researcher/s and participants, or a community in the development of the research (Kemmis and McTaggart, 2005; Sarantakos, 2013)
Evaluation research	Characterized through the exploration of impact and effects of policies or programmes (Bryman, 2016). Limitations, implications, and future recommendations for practice will be identified to improve the programme or policy.
Feminist research	Characterized by the examination of women, culture, and empowerment to explore practices and gender inequality (Creswell, 2018)

Source data from: Khan *et al* (2022, pp 32–36)

There are several aspects involved in designing a research project. Once the research problem has been identified, and the type of research design has been decided, the sample of participants need to be defined, the data collection methods need to be chosen, along with the timescales and a plan to collect the data. Once these aspects have been determined the approach to the data analysis needs to be outlined to ensure there is robust scrutiny of the data to ensure the interpretation is accurate.

5.4.7 Collecting the data

Secondary research can be collated in a form, such as a database or spreadsheet, which can be used to help review and analyse the data methodically, and to interpret the data accurately.

For primary research, quantitative, qualitative, or a mix of the two can be applied and the approach to collecting the data is different but uses the same principles of using a systematic approach so that robust analysis can be undertaken.

Collecting and collating quantitative research data

A simple survey with closed questions is a good example of a quantitative approach to collecting data. The questions in such a survey might capture, for example, responses from participants that indicate their views on an attitude scale. The closed answer format means that the data captured is consistent and easy to collate—it will normally equate to a numerical value. Nowadays, researchers commonly use online survey tools, which means the data from the survey responses are automatically generated, in the form of a dataset for analysis.

Collecting and collating qualitative research data

Qualitative research involves collecting data directly from participants. This can be done through conducting observations, undertaking interviews whether semi-structured or unstructured, or bringing a people together to conduct a focus group. For observations, the researcher writes field notes, these notes form the data for analysis. The interviews are usually recorded on a Dictaphone, requiring informed consent from participants, and these recordings are transcribed. The collated transcripts formulate the data for analysis. The questions asked in interviews and focus groups are *open*, providing the participant with the opportunity to answer the question using their own words, as opposed to a survey which has closed questions with pre-determined answers provided from which the participant selects. Qualitative data can also come from a survey, if it includes open questions that require an unprompted written response from the participant using their own words.

Collecting and collating the data for qualitative research is more time consuming and costly to the researcher. However, the open nature of the data means that context can be explored and deeper insights into the problem can be derived from the analysis. The qualitative approach can be most useful in providing insights into *why* something happens. This is helpful when researchers are exploring social life and complex problems.

5.4.8 Analysing and interpreting data

This section explores some of the difference between quantitative and qualitative strategies that are applied in data analysis. The skills involved can take some practice, but it is important the right approach is undertaken otherwise the wrong conclusion from the data will be made.

Quantitative data analysis

Quantitative research usually follows a deductive approach. Using a process of deduction means that there is a theory or hypothesis that is being tested. The data is organized into different categories or variables. The variables are analysed to describe the data or population. Different variables are used to compare against each other to look for causes and correlations. This means that the researcher directly interrogates the data through asking specific questions within the analysis.

Statistics are routinely used for this analytical process in quantitative analysis. Descriptive statistics are used to understand the proportions of different variables within the data, for example, calculating the average age of participants, or the percentage breakdown of the sample population by gender or ethnicity. Once a researcher understands who is in the data, they can start to test the relationships between different variables to gather a picture of the relationships between, for example, a particular type of crime and the age, gender, or ethnicity of the sample population. We can explore if one variable is correlated to another, or through more sophisticated statistical testing, whether one variable can predict another. This requires advanced levels of statistical knowledge and large sample sizes to draw accurate conclusions from the data.

You can access data from <https://data.police.uk/> and this allows you to search by police service over different time periods. Note that in order to undertake to make sense of the data, you will need to understand and be able to use some basic statistical techniques provided as part of your programme of study.

Qualitative data analysis

There are several ways to analyse qualitative data. The approach should be applied to the type of data you have collected and the research questions you are exploring. Examples of qualitative approaches to analysis are: analytic induction, grounded theory, narrative analysis, or thematic analysis. The type of qualitative data that might be used to analyse are: field notes from an observation, interview notes, or transcripts from individual or group interviews. Qualitative analysis is usually inductive where the data analysis drives new discoveries or theories that are uncovered through establishing codes, patterns, and themes from the data. Using the example of thematic analysis, the table at the end of the chapter outlines Braun and Clarke's (2006) phases of thematic analysis.

When you are analysing data in this way, it is important to read and re-read each data source carefully (*familiarizing yourself with the data*). Then you can begin to apply codes to the data consistently across the data (*generating initial codes*). You can do this using a software package (for example: NVivo or MAXQDA) or you can do this by hand using a highlighter pen. The codes can be categorized into different areas where there are commonalities or differences (*searching for themes*). Next you can start to analyse these themes to explore the relationships between them (*reviewing the themes*) and order them according to where they link together. Once you have done this across all of the data sources you can identify the story through the connections between the themes (*defining and naming the themes*). The narrative provides the basis of what you will write up as your findings (*producing the report*).

5.4.9 Reporting and evaluating research

When you are reporting your findings from your research or EBP project this needs to be done in a way that is applicable to the audience who are reading your report. For policing students undertaking a university project, this might be in the form of a dissertation or an Evidence-based Research Project (EBRP). In any case, having a structure to reporting the findings is sensible so that your audience can digest what you have done and found in an easy way. The following components are often involved in a research report:

- An executive summary (or an abstract in academic writing);
- Introduction;
- Literature/existing information;
- Aims;
- Methods;
- Findings;
- Discussion;
- Conclusions and recommendations.

It is important to demonstrate critical thinking in your research and it is translatable to practice. Criticality can be characterized by having a logical approach to the work, which is justified and informed by the literature and a range of existing sources. An in-depth analysis is presented where the findings have been robustly analysed, challenged by existing literature presenting strong arguments and new 'knowledge' of policing. Key debates should be discussed and drawn together in the conclusions and any implications for practice.

5.4.10 Evaluating the implementation

A full-blown EBP initiative would include deciding whether to implement a change of practice based on the findings of the review. Student police officers are unlikely to be involved in this decision, or in evaluating the results of any implementation, but a supervisor may implement a new initiative to address a problem as a result of a review.

Evaluating the implementation of the findings to establish what was successful and how this led to the desired change in outcomes is a crucial aspect in terms of determining the evidence base for future action. These might appear to be relatively straightforward questions but providing accurate answers can be challenging. For example, we might correctly discern an improvement immediately after an EBP implementation, but subsequent testing might find that the effect fades away. A further complication is that the circumstances in which a change is made might also be shifting, which could be confounding any effects.

It is important to be mindful of counter-intuitive results in research. In 1978, an award-winning documentary called *Scared Straight!* was shown on US television. It featured *juvenile delinquents*, young people convicted in most cases of relatively minor offences visiting a high security prison and interacting with prisoners serving life imprisonment. Watch the documentary (or at least the first 20 minutes or so) on YouTube at <https://www.youtube.com/watch?v=gXRIR_Svgq4>. Note that offensive language is used throughout so avoid watching the video in a public place.

Intuitively, we might expect a project like this to reduce the likelihood of the juvenile delinquents from further offending. Indeed, after the documentary was shown, similar initiatives and other deterrence programmes employing a similar philosophy were adopted across different states and countries on the belief that such programmes would have the intended deterrence impact. However, some people were sceptical about the efficacy of *Scared Straight!* (Kilby, 2015), and consequently, a number of 'randomised control trials' were conducted on initiatives such as *Scared Straight!* Perhaps surprisingly, many trials found that the programmes did not succeed in dissuading young offenders from committing further crimes. Indeed, it was found that some of the programmes seemed to make young people **more likely** to commit further crime. For further details and explanation, you might want to look at <https://www.college.police.uk/research/crime-reduction-toolkit/scared-straight>.

5.5 Undertaking an Evidence-based Research Project (EBRP)

So far this chapter has outlined the developing emphasis of EBP as part of the College's professionalization agenda and covers some basic considerations when undertaking research.

This section of the chapter considers the EBP agenda in the context of the evidence-based research project (EBRP), a requirement for students studying the PEQF programmes. The premise of the EBRP is that it encourages officers from the outset to engage with EBP. Gander (2023, p 53) summarizes how the EBRP can be used to:

- *'Develop a better understanding of the issue—by describing the nature, extent and possible causes of a problem or looking at how a change was implemented*
- *Assess the effect of a policing intervention—by testing the impact of a new initiative in a specific context or exploring the possible consequences of a change in policing.'*

Having discussed the definitions of the EBP and the role of research in the earlier sections in this chapter, we can see how this particular requirement of the PEQF programmes enables officers to think and use research in their practice and offers a justification as to the wider benefits this knowledge can bring to policing as profession.

5.5.1 The End Point Assessment as part of the PCDA

If you are a student studying on the PCDA you will have to complete the 'End-Point Assessment' (EPA). The EPA starts when minimum standards set out by the Education Skills and Funding Agency (ESFA) have been evidenced and verified by the employer and the learning provider. This is known as the *gateway* and students will need to demonstrate they are fully operationally competent (FOC), have functional skills in English and maths, completed mandatory operational training, and successfully attained the required standard throughout the duration on the PCDA. Once achieving the gateway, the EPA can begin. There are three components of the EPA:

1. A *professional discussion* with an independent assessor reviewing progress and reflections on the individual portfolios that evidence operational competence.
2. *EBRP*—an evidence-based research project which is set and marked through the university. However, police services will be involved in identifying areas that require research in the organization, this formulates a list of projects suitable for students to research and maximizes the chances for the findings to be relevant at an operational level.

3. *Assessment*—presentation to a panel involving police, university representatives, and the independent assessors justifying the rationale of the EBRP and the presenting the findings.

These three elements of the EPA are challenging but can often be empowering for students. Students have some freedom to undertake in-depth research in an area they are interested in and have the opportunity to use the research and analytical skills they have been taught on their programme. The panel discussions involved in the process are undertaken with police colleagues, academics, the independent assessor, and the students to reflect on the research findings. This is a way of bringing knowledge and research into policing practice. When we remind ourselves of the wider EBP principles to use evidence to understand policing problems and to enhance future decisions on police action, we can see how the EPA in itself contributes to the EBP ethos.

The EPA is a distinct part of an apprenticeship, and students studying on the other degree entry routes will have different arrangements in their final year, but the EBRP is a requirement on all programmes.

5.5.2 Undertaking an EBRP

Before undertaking your EBRP, you may need to agree the project with your sponsoring police service. In the case of empirical research as part of an evidence-based project, ethics approval will be required from your HEI and/or police service. Your constabulary may be involved in setting some areas requiring research around their own strategic and operational priorities. This means you should have a question or problem that is pre-defined for you to explore in your EBRP. It will be derived from one of the five specialist learning policing areas (response, community, intelligence, investigation, or roads/transport) and will also articulate with the needs of your local communities and police service.

Your project might only involve secondary, non-empirical, desk-based research, and it is almost certainly the case that you will not conduct a full-blown RCT as part of your project, not least because of the lack of time, the expense, and the technical assistance that would be needed. However, it is possible that you may undertake a more limited form of primary or empirical research as part of your project, for example, a survey. This will complement the desk-based research carried out for the project but will not replace it.

You will need to demonstrate the rationale of whatever approach you take, whether it is empirical/non-empirical, quantitative/qualitative. There is no right or wrong answer here but your decision will need to be justified and this might come from your engagement with the literature and what is already known. Presenting your research findings according to the assessment rules is vital. It is also useful to think about any key messages from your findings and where these link to police practice. Consider who needs to know about your research and the best way of disseminating your work to them. Your EBRP provides context to a force area priority and forms part of the available evidence for future decision making.

5.5.3 Disseminating EBRP findings—bringing knowledge to practice

Once your EBRP has been formally assessed and confirmed by the university, there are several ways you can disseminate your findings from your project. You might want to write up key points in an executive summary or in some presentation slides and send these to police leaders in your constabulary who have responsibility for the area you have researched. Making your work digestible is important to a practice audience, so summarize your research neatly and concisely. Consider the following points when you are doing this:

- clearly describe the rationale of your work, ie what problem you were addressing and why it is operationally important;
- briefly cover how you have conducted your research outlining the methods, demonstrating to the audience how robust your work is and the contribution it makes to understanding the problem;
- then summarize your findings and think about how these can be applied in recommendations for practice, which means you are linking your work to the organizational world, bringing knowledge or evidence into practice to aid decision-making.

There are other ways you can disseminate your EBRP findings externally. Prior to doing so, complying with ethics is important. Make sure you have the approval to do this from your police service. It is useful to look at how others present their work and where it is published.

You could also write your work up in a blog form and explore whether it could be published on a policing blog site such as Policing Insights, or your police service or university might have a blogsite that you could use. Academics and/or researchers also routinely write up their studies for publication in academic journals, such as, the *Cambridge Journal of Evidence Based Policing*, *Crime and Criminal Justice*, *Criminal Justice Matters*, *Policing and Society*, and *Policing: A Journal of Policy and Practice*. However, a more practitioner-based journal might be more comfortable to share your findings. Check with your local police service to see if there are opportunities to publish internally. In addition, *Going Equipped* was launched in 2020 by the College of Policing providing a journal publication to share research and ideas from police officers and staff.

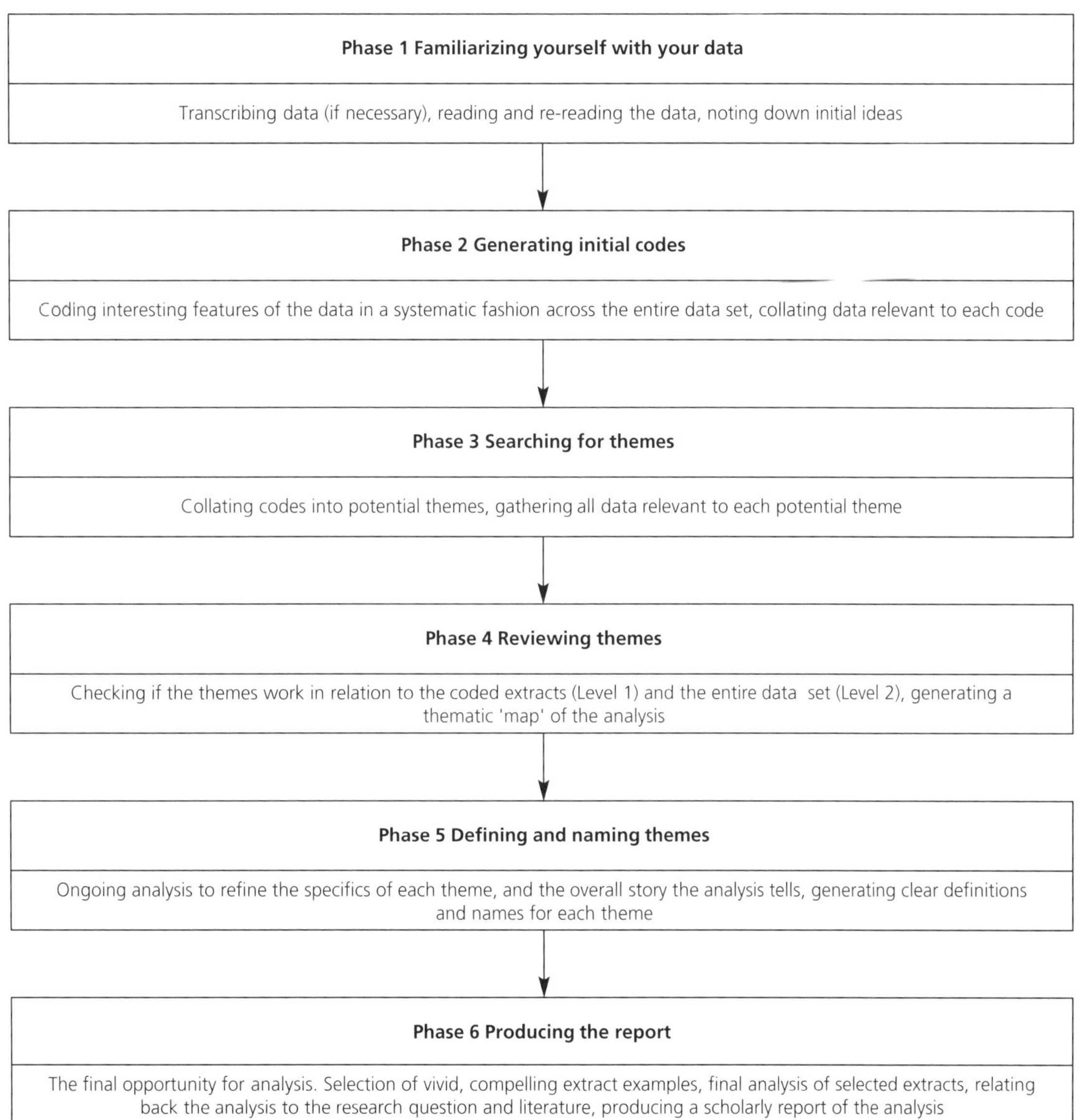

Phase 1 Familiarizing yourself with your data
Transcribing data (if necessary), reading and re-reading the data, noting down initial ideas
Phase 2 Generating initial codes
Coding interesting features of the data in a systematic fashion across the entire data set, collating data relevant to each code
Phase 3 Searching for themes
Collating codes into potential themes, gathering all data relevant to each potential theme
Phase 4 Reviewing themes
Checking if the themes work in relation to the coded extracts (Level 1) and the entire data set (Level 2), generating a thematic 'map' of the analysis
Phase 5 Defining and naming themes
Ongoing analysis to refine the specifics of each theme, and the overall story the analysis tells, generating clear definitions and names for each theme
Phase 6 Producing the report
The final opportunity for analysis. Selection of vivid, compelling extract examples, final analysis of selected extracts, relating back the analysis to the research question and literature, producing a scholarly report of the analysis

Source: Adapted from Braun and Clarke (2006, p 87)

6 Wellbeing and Resilience

6.1 Introduction

This chapter focuses on matters concerning the wellbeing and resilience of officers, acknowledging the challenges faced by officers and identifying strategies to maintain personal welfare. The landscape of policing is recognized as ever more complex, creating unprecedented demands on officers and presenting progressively broader challenges. Officers will need to possess a corresponding range of skills and knowledge to meet those challenges. Police services are therefore becoming more aware of the importance of, and the impact, mental wellbeing can have on individuals, teams, and police organizations. Officers deal with members of the public who are often at their lowest point. It is widely acknowledged that dealing with trauma and high stress situations on a daily basis can have a cumulative effect. Cartright and Roach (2020) found absences caused by 'psychological ill health, trauma, and stress had nearly doubled in the past 10 years' when analysing data from just over half of the police workforce. The College of Policing (2022b) recognizes both the rewards as well as the challenges of a career in policing and states that 'we must look after our people so they are best able to look after the public'.

Within this chapter policing related stressors will be identified, and strategies for maintaining personal wellbeing discussed. All professional work has the potential to create stress, but policing presents its own unique challenges. Police work involves not only the usual sources of stress when employed by a large organization but also sees officers coping with individuals at times of personal crises, emergencies, and the aftermath of crime including serious and violent offences.

The chapter will discuss the professional expectation on all officers to reflect on, and maintain, not only their wellbeing but also that of peers, and will provide an introduction to available support. The topics covered will contribute to the areas of learning within the 'Wellbeing and resilience' requirements set out within the National Policing Curriculum, and this chapter will conclude with a section providing guidance and support for neurodivergent officers and their colleagues.

6.2 Mental, Physical, and Spiritual Wellbeing

To provide an effective service officers need to be mentally and physically able to carry out their duties, while seeking support should they experience any difficulties that impact on their physical or mental wellbeing. Wellness covers aspects of mental, physical, and spiritual health, which are outlined below, as well as social and financial wellbeing, while resilience can be described as an individual's ability to combat and recover quickly from life's difficulties. Aked *et al* (no date) identified five ways to wellbeing; connecting with people, being active, taking notice, continuous learning or trying something new, and acts of kindness, which draw many parallels with a police officer's role, while emphasizing the importance of these actions to maintaining the continued health and wellbeing of officers. Positive wellbeing and resilience can link to professional and personal success and development. However, officers are frequently exposed to trauma, and historically officers felt they should be impervious to its effects, instead protecting and supporting those in need. However a culture shift has seen a welcome rise in support and interventions to maintain officer wellbeing.

6.2.1 Physical wellbeing

To meet the physical demands of the role officers are expected to achieve and maintain a level of fitness. The job related fitness test (JRFT), as well as being part of the recruitment process, will be completed from the outset of a career in policing, and each year thereafter as part of personal safety training (CoP, 2021d). The JRFT comprises a bleep test, made up of 35, 15 metre shuttles between two points, with the time allowed for each shuttle gradually decreasing across levels. While the standard test requires officers to achieve level 5.4, if moving to a specialist role such as Authorised Firearms Officer (AFO) or Air Support there may be different requirements, or the requirement for a larger number of shuttles to be completed. Where an officer has an injury or disability, they can be offered an adapted test.

6.2.2 Mental wellbeing

Mental wellbeing is about both how well we feel and how well we function (Ruggeri *et al*, 2020) and everyone experiences good or poor mental health throughout life, while understanding mental health leads to seeking appropriate support. As part of a Trauma Informed Policing response, Goodall (2022) suggests that having a better appreciation of your own mental health will also lead to a better understanding of complex issues affecting victims, witnesses, and suspects, such as Adverse Childhood Experiences (ACEs). Childhood or adult trauma can be a motivation for joining a service such as the police, where protecting the public has significant appeal. However exposure to traumatic and distressing incidents can have a cumulative negative impact on mental health, which this chapter will discuss, setting out strategies to mitigate these impacts.

6.2.3 Spiritual wellbeing

Spiritual wellbeing refers to the need for purpose and meaning, while encompassing an individual's beliefs and values. Where there are personal challenges such as change or disruption to plans, or where a person's values or beliefs are challenged, spiritual wellbeing can be eroded. This can have consequences for mental wellbeing and physical health. Spiritual practices such as prayer, meditation, and mindfulness can help individuals manage stress more effectively, and spiritual wellbeing can contribute to mental wellbeing by promoting coping skills, providing a sense of purpose, offering social support, and fostering compassion.

Each of these areas of wellbeing interlink, influence, and impact the others, therefore understanding and recognizing stressors in policing, and other impacts on health and wellbeing will support the maintenance of wellbeing and resilience.

6.3 Identifying Stress and Trauma in Policing

As a police officer, many skills are learned in relation to operational policing, the law, and policy and procedure. However, it is important to also learn how to identify and recognize stress and trauma, not only in yourself, but in others. Policing is fast paced and dynamic with the potential to have to deal with many multi-faceted situations. A lot of the time this includes dealing with other people's issues, worries, stress, and trauma, therefore it is imperative your own wellbeing is looked after with as much care as that of those you serve.

6.3.1 Causes of stress

Stress can be caused by many things in life including personal health, relationships, work, homelife, and financial difficulties. For many people the list could go on, therefore dealing with stress is an important part of everyone's lives. As noted above, policing can have a significant impact on stressors but overall the following could lead to stress:

- Going through periods of uncertainty
- Facing big life changes
- Feeling under lots of pressure
- Lacking control over situations
- Having responsibilities that are overwhelming
- Experiencing discrimination, hate, or abuse

Everyone experiences stressful events in their lives and in isolation these may seem insignificant, however combining a number of these together can have serious impacts on someone's life and also their ability to deal with it.

A question to ask then is how might you recognize stress within yourself and others? As humans, this can be very challenging as it is not always possible to identify the signs of stress before the symptoms start to manifest themselves. Being aware of what to look for will help to recognize them as early as possible.

Mind (2022) provide a plethora of information around how to recognize signs and symptoms of stress, not only linking to what these are but also how they may manifest themselves in how you may feel yourself, but also how others may respond. The following table will help you identify how stress can make you feel, the physical effects of stress, and also how it can make you behave.

How stress makes you feel	How stress affects you physically	How stress makes you behave
• Neglected or lonely • A sense of dread • Uninterested in life • Unable to enjoy yourself • Anxious, nervous, or afraid • Irritable, angry, impatient, or wound up • Over burdened or overwhelmed • Depressed • Worried or tense	• Panic attacks or difficulty in breathing • Fatigue and sleep problems • Muscle aches • Chest pains and high blood pressure • Indigestion and heartburn • Change in weight both gain or loss • Sweating • Blurred eyesight or sore eyes • Constipation or diarrhoea • Change in menstrual cycle	• Difficulty making decisions • Lack of concentration • Snapping at people • Grinding your teeth or clenching your jaw • Eat too much or too little • Smoke, drink, or use drugs • Restless • Cry or feel tearful • Withdraw from people around you • Experience sexual problems • Loss of memory

Source: Table adapted from Mind (2022)

6.3.2 The Stress Bucket

Making links to what might affect someone and what might not, is important. Everyone is different and everyone copes with stress and trauma in their own way. Recognizing personal vulnerabilities is important so that officers can develop positive coping strategies to deal with this, thus improving personal wellbeing and resilience.

The principles of the Stress Bucket could help answer some questions around how different people may deal in varying ways with their own vulnerabilities. For example, an officer may have experienced something very similar to a colleague, but they may have reacted in a very different way. This may be because people have varying degrees of vulnerability, or just that some are more resilient than others, but either way the Stress Bucket principle, which has been adapted from ideas by Brabban and Turkington (2002), can go a long way to explaining this.

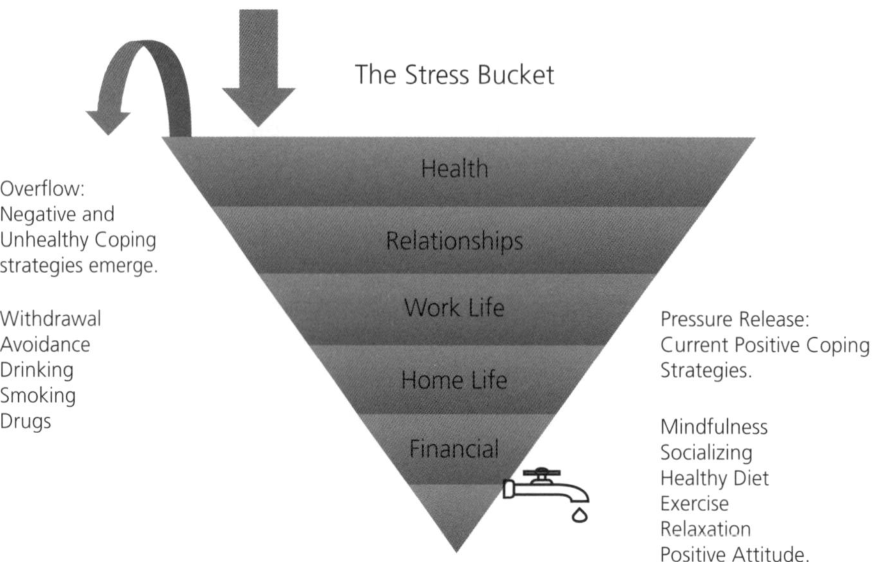

Source: Image adapted from principles by Brabban and Turkington (2002)

The Stress Bucket here depicts numerous things that can affect stress throughout life, not simply work related; issues outside of work may also affect how an individual reacts to things that happen within work, and keeping a healthy balance is important for personal wellbeing and resilience. Everyday stressors can continue to fill up this bucket and sometimes it may not be obvious this is happening until the bucket overflows. This is why it is important to use positive coping strategies on a regular basis to allow the bucket to drain, thus avoiding an overflow.

Humans are very adaptable, however there are limits to this and it is now being recognized that stress, trauma, and mental health are significant issues within the police service. Sometimes stress might become too much, and putting it back to the Stress Bucket idea, the bucket fills more quickly than the pressure can be released, coping strategies might stop working. If this becomes the case, it is important to recognize this, or recognize this in others, so that referrals can be made to Police National Wellbeing services.

6.4 Recognizing Trauma

The UK Trauma Council (no date) defines trauma as 'the way that some distressing events are so extreme or intense that they overwhelm a person's ability to cope, resulting in lasting negative impact'. Trauma can be caused by many things and often it is caused by things that are out of a person's control. This could include things such as sexual abuse, physical abuse, war, natural disasters, terrorist attacks, serious car accidents, the list could go on. Police officers are sometimes put into positions where they themselves will experience traumatic events such as being first to the scene of a fatal car accident, or being involved with a person who commits suicide. The witnessing of traumatic events can be just as impactive as being involved in the traumatic event.

6.4.1 Secondary trauma

As already identified, police officers may not often find themselves experiencing or witnessing a traumatic event first hand, however an area that is far more prevalent and can happen on a daily basis is experiencing Secondary Trauma, or sometimes known as Vicarious Trauma. This is an indirect experience of, or exposure to a traumatic event. Police officers attend incidents on a daily basis where a person may have called the police due to a traumatic experience they have had, and thus as they are providing details of the event as a witness or a victim, officers may experience some indirect trauma from empathetic engagement. The British Medical Association (2022a) provides details of common signs of secondary trauma to look out for:

- Experiencing lingering feelings of anger, rage, and sadness about the person's victimization
- Becoming overly involved emotionally with the victim or witness
- Experiencing bystander guilt, shame, and feelings of self-doubt
- Being preoccupied with thoughts for the person outside of work
- Over identification with the victim or witness
- Becoming distanced, detached, or numb to other people when describing traumatic experiences
- Difficulty in maintaining professional boundaries

6.4.2 Post Traumatic Stress Disorder (PTSD)

PTSD is used to describe a particular profile of symptoms that is sometimes developed after someone has experienced or witnessed a traumatic event. There are many reactions a person can have, and PTSD may not describe the full range of reactions to traumatic events, therefore sometimes people can react to traumatizing events without being diagnosed with PTSD. But how do you recognize someone who may be suffering from PTSD, and how could you recognize this in yourself?

The UK Trauma Council (no date) describes three groups of symptoms that are sometimes considered to be the core symptoms of PTSD:

- Re-experiencing of the event, such as intrusive memories, flashbacks, nightmares, repetitive play of certain aspects of the event and distress triggered by reminders of the event.
- Avoidance, such as avoiding people, places, or conversations associated with the event, or avoiding feelings, thoughts, and memories of the event.

- Arousal and reactivity or sense of current threat, such as being over vigilant, irritability, being easily startled, and experiencing concentration and sleep problems.

There may be other symptoms that fall under these areas and a broader range of symptoms may increase the overlap into other mental health difficulties. If you are experiencing some of these symptoms, or if a friend or colleague is, there are interventions that are recommended including Trauma-Focused Cognitive Behaviour Therapy (TF-CBT) and Eye Movement Desensitisation and Reprocessing (EMDR).

6.5 Compassion Fatigue

So far this section has spoken about stress that police officers may experience within work, and also outside of work. It has looked at trauma, secondary trauma, and PTSD. The terms 'Compassion Fatigue' and 'Burnout' are often associated with emergency services and more increasingly within policing.

Compassion Fatigue is described as a detached state felt when a person is constantly and routinely dealing with distressed individuals and is sometimes referred to as the 'cost of caring' (Davies *et al*, 2022). From looking at the earlier discussion in relation to secondary trauma, some strong links could be made to this that compassion fatigue could be a result of experiencing secondary trauma on a regular basis. When it comes to recognizing compassion fatigue, there are strong similarities to the symptoms of PTSD detailed previously. Police officers, therefore, who are unaware of, or ignore the presence of the symptoms and continue to perform their duties as normal without seeking help, are highly likely to suffer from Compassion Fatigue (Papazoglou *et al*, 2020). The impact that this can have on a person's personal life and work life is significant and if not successfully managed can result in cumulative burnout. Burnout is a term used in many professions and is described as 'Prolonged Occupational Stress' (World Health Organization, 2020) and again if unmanaged will result in high sickness levels in staff.

However, studies do indicate that many police officers also experience 'Compassion Satisfaction' which describes feelings of increased satisfaction and motivation from helping people who have experienced traumatic events. This in turn can go on to improve performance and quality of life (Davies *et al*, 2022), and it is this Compassion Satisfaction that is the drive for, not only police officers, but all those who work in the emergency services, to do their jobs effectively.

6.6 Fostering Personal Resilience

With everything that has been so far discussed, it is clear that being a police officer can have some effects in relation to stress and trauma. That is why it is very important to continue to foster resilience.

Resilience refers to maintaining psychological well-being in the face of adversity by having the ability to adapt to stressors successfully (Hesketh *et al*, 2019). Everyone is born with a level of inbuilt resilience but it can be built on through time and experience, and on a personal level characteristics such as adaptability, flexibility, effective problem solving skills, and independence assist in building resilience (McEwen, 2011). However, there are ways that this can be improved through maintaining positive coping strategies. As detailed in the Stress Bucket, positive strategies are essential in relieving that stress. Hesketh *et al* (2019) state that resilient individuals are better equipped to deal with the stressful nature of both policing and uncertain working environments. Through research conducted, they explain that a combination of effective leadership and a harmonious working environment that supports employee wellbeing, enhances subsequent organizational performance.

6.6.1 Developing effective coping strategies

Building effective coping strategies is the best way of relieving stress or dealing with trauma, compassion fatigue, or even PTSD. Different people will have very different coping strategies and it can be as simple as doing regular exercise or enjoying a regular hobby outside of work. Below are some easy go-to suggestions for coping with stress and building resilience.

Being Active	Exercise can help reduce some of the emotional intensity that you may be feeling and can help clear your thoughts allowing you to problem solve more effectively.
Connecting with people	Have a good support network of colleagues or friends and family. These can ease your troubles and help you see things in a different way. Activities with friends and family can also help you to relax and relieve stress.
Have some personal time	Having time to yourself is important. Time away from the things that cause you stress can help, this could be socializing, taking exercise, or enjoying a hobby which is away from work and possibly home.
Challenge yourself	Setting yourself goals and challenges whether in or outside of work, can help build confidence and also may help deal with stress. An example could be something as simple as learning a new language, or learning to play an instrument.
Help other people	Evidence has shown that helping other people either as a volunteer or through community work can often help build resilience. If volunteering is not something that is accessible, maybe try helping someone with something each day, like a simple task in the workplace, or helping someone with their bags in the supermarket.
Try to be positive	Try to look for positives in life, or look around you and find the beauty in other things. Think of what makes you grateful in life. A simple exercise for this is writing down three things at the end of each day that made you feel good.

Source: Table adapted from NHS.uk (2022a)

However, there are some coping strategies that people turn to which could have a very detrimental impact on their lives, such as alcohol or drugs. Some may say that popping out for a drink and socializing helps to relieve stress and often this is the case, however alcohol, if overused, can have extremely negative effects on individuals and can often lead to more problems over time.

Unhealthy coping strategies can lead to further problems with mental health and where possible officers should avoid unhealthy habits as coping strategies. Alcohol, smoking, and caffeine are the most common negative coping strategies. Even though they may provide temporary relief, they will not provide relief in the long term and will likely become crutches that will not solve your problems, only create new ones. Below are further unhealthy coping strategies that should be avoided.

Avoiding issues	Avoiding an issue may feel like the easiest way to deal with current problems, however pushing back the problems will ultimately find a way of reaching the surface, possibly with some kind of trigger.
Over sleeping	This is similar to avoiding issues. The body may need sleep and rest but it also needs physical activity as well to remain fit and healthy.
Excessive drug or alcohol use	Alcohol, in small doses, can often be seen as a way of relieving stress, however substance misuse is a slippery slope. Stimulants and depressants may numb feelings, pain, and negative thoughts in the short term, however long term excessive use will only lead to severe health complications, addiction, overdose, and possibly death.
Impulsive spending	Many people find retail therapy a way to relieve stress, however, again this could very quickly lead to overspending and then on to severe financial problems. By relieving some stress, you will be replacing this with other problems.
Over or under eating	Food is important for your body and provides nutrition and fuel to function throughout the day, however many people, when feeling anxious, have a tendency to either over or under eat, sometimes to extremes. This will go on to cause major health issues or sickness.

Source: Table adapted from centerstone.org (no date)

6.6.2 Available support

There are numerous articles, books, and websites with advice on coping with stress, some of which have been detailed in this chapter so far. Police services also have counselling facilities as well as occupational health support (through the Occupational Support Unit). The advice typically centres on dealing with both the symptoms (which may require specialist medical help) and the causes of stress. The College of Policing provides a wide range of support through its Authorised Professional Practice for those in need of mental and emotional support, and the Samaritans provide 24-hour, 7-day-a-week support helplines.

This section will detail what support services are available to officers, and their families, to help maintain positive wellbeing and keep physically and mentally prepared for the role of police officer as set out with the Police (Conduct) Regulations 2020.

6.6.2.1 Occupational health—Oscar Kilo

Oscar Kilo is the Police Occupational Health practitioner network which is committed to improving the provision of occupational health in policing. The network aims to act as the voice of occupational health professionals in policing to help communicate, influence, and inform national developments, and is home of the National Police Wellbeing Service. Sources are provided for wellbeing at work, individual resilience, mental health, and peer support.

Individual police services' Occupation Health Support teams are there to provide support around health and wellbeing, which can be as a result of self-referral, or through a third party referral.

6.6.2.2 TRIM

Trauma Risk Incident Management (TRIM) is a welfare led process which is intended to assess the response of a member of staff exposed to a potentially traumatic incident. This can be done on an individual basis or within a whole team and acts as a form of debrief of a situation. The aim is to assist officers or the team to discuss the incident, understand the impact of this, and explore the next steps within a safe environment. TRIM should be offered by constabularies after any potentially traumatic incident that their officers attend.

6.6.2.3 Police Care UK

Police Care UK is a charity for veterans, serving police officers, staff, volunteers, and their families who may have suffered physical or psychological harm as a result of policing. Services include the following:

- Counselling
- Ill health retirement peer support
- Assistance grants
- Support around working with indecent or extreme material
- Self support techniques after traumatic incidents

6.6.2.4 Mind Blue Light

Blue Light Together and the Mind Blue Light Programme provide support and advice to all members of the emergency services such as tips and advice for looking after your mental health as an emergency responder.

6.6.2.5 Employee Assistance Programme

The Employee Assistance Programme provides around-the-clock mental health support to officers and their immediate family. The service provides:

- 24/7 confidential helpline
- up to six sessions of structured counselling
- 24/7 crisis assistance and manager support
- in-house legal and financial information
- access to a healthy advantage wellbeing app

6.7 Neurodiversity (neurodivergence) in Policing

A diverse workforce is an essential component of policing in order to reflect the communities they serve, and forces acknowledge the variety of skills that neurodiversity brings to policing. As many as one in five of the population are estimated to be neurodivergent, a term which recognizes hundreds of conditions. Working with diverse communities and understanding concerns is a core aspect of policing (this is covered in 11.5.1), and policing aims to reflect those communities through a diverse workforce. This section does not set out to discuss all conditions but acknowledges that many officers will be neurodivergent and therefore looks at support available to maintain wellbeing.

In their Discovery Report into Workplace Adjustments, the College of Policing (2021e) advocates a social model of disability, or a way of viewing the world which says that people are disabled by barriers in society, not by their impairment, and approaches to support for the wellbeing of neurodiverse officers is often shaped by this approach.

6.7.1 Neurological differences and terminology

Neurodiversity, although referring to the diversity of all people, has become a widely acknowledged term that includes conditions and differences, associated with cognitive function, seen as 'divergent' from the typical. The Brain Charity (no date) explains that the term *neurodivergent* is frequently used to denote the opposite of neurotypicals, or those who may *not* receive diagnoses of conditions, including:

- Learning difficulties such as dyspraxia, dyslexia
- Autism spectrum condition
- Attention deficit disorder
- Tourette's syndrome

As research progresses, there are a broadening range of identified differences that sit within the neurodivergence umbrella, and it has been found that if an individual has one neurodiverse condition, they are more likely to have at least one other. Therefore individuals can present differently despite the same diagnosis, and the ability to think differently can bring with it real advantages. The College of Policing (2021e, p 6) acknowledges that 'safe and inclusive workplaces allow us to benefit from the widest pool of talent available', and there are a number of support groups and mechanisms available for police employees to develop working practices that harness the benefits those individuals bring to the role.

6.7.2 Support for neurodivergent officers

Police services have policies to support neurodivergent officers and officers with Specific Learning Difficulties, with some offering screening which can provide indicators of dyslexia. The Equality Act 2010 protects employees with disabilities of health conditions, including a legal obligation to make reasonable adjustments in the workplace, and not to treat these individuals less favourably. This duty is 'anticipatory', which requires employers to explore reasonable changes to remove or reduce a disadvantage in advance. New officers are often attracted to the role because of the variety it offers, opportunities for engagement with the public, and to make a difference, then find that other aspects of the role such as the paperwork can present challenges. By applying a social rather than medical model, which recognizes that difficulties arise 'due to environmental and attitudinal barriers' (Macdonald & Cosgrove, 2019) work based adjustments can provide neurodivergent officers with a supportive and accessible working environment.

The discovery report into workplace adjustment (CoP, 2021e, p 16) identified that 'Employee networks are the key to driving local engagement' and sets out some benchmark organizations providing good practice and guidance to constabularies adopting additional support for neurodiverse officers and staff such as disability passports. The document signposts readers to PurpleSpace, a forum for networking and the professional development of disabled employees, and where employers and disability networks can come together to share best practice.

It should be noted that police services take an enabling approach to neurodivergent officers and staff, with support being offered both within constabularies and through national groups, which notably includes the National Police Autism Association. The Association provides support and guidance to police officers and staff affected by autism and other neurodivergent conditions including dyslexia, dyspraxia, and ADHD. They host the Police Neurodiversity Forum, described as 'a safe online space for peer support, discussion and information-sharing' (National Police Autism Association, no date). Their first national Neurodiversity in Policing Conference, was held in 2019, with these forums signifying the groundswell of interest and support for neurodiverse officers.

The Disabled Police Association (DPA) raises awareness of issues and provides a 'coordinated response to national policing matters affecting disabled officers and staff within the police services of the United Kingdom' (DPA, no date). The group supports police services in their approaches to disability related employment issues, and shares good practice, while providing a range of resources and links to support improved mental health.

Support provision for neurodivergent officers is expanding, and following a review of workplace adjustments the College of Policing launched the Workplace Adjustments Toolkit, which provides resources for police services to ensure they offer a supportive environment for officers and staff with neurodivergences and disabilities. Within their remit is advice for constabularies on legal frameworks and case studies.

It is also important to support diverse colleagues and obtain an understanding of any differences while remembering that with neurodiversity there can often be comorbidity, or the presence of more than one neurodivergence. There also can therefore be variances between individuals with the same diagnosis, bringing with them a host of strengths.

TASK 1

Look at the neurodiversity champions and support groups within your own organization and write a brief description of each and the services and support they offer.

6.8 Answer to Task

TASK 1 You will have no doubt found that as well as nationally available support, the range of force specific support covers a number of differences and needs. You may also have noted the opportunities to get involved in championing and developing groups. Other sources of support can come from online forums such as Twitter or Instagram where you will find interest-based blogs for sharing ideas and to keep informed, such as The Dyslexic Cop @dyslexic_cop.

7 Valuing Diversity and Inclusion

DISCOMFORT AHEAD!

The human species has evolved to quickly spot similarities and differences, to separate the familiar and unfamiliar. It is how we make sense of the world. Observing something unfamiliar can evoke a lot of different responses: curiosity, astonishment, appreciation, fear, suspicion. Whatever the response, there is often a sense of discomfort to encountering something new. This is good. It alerts us to a learning opportunity: we need to make a conscious effort to learn and to understand. One key question to ask is whether it is simply something different or whether it is actually harmful in some way. The two are rarely the same.

This chapter challenges you to accept your discomfort and to use it. Some of the questions and the tasks here may make you feel uncomfortable. They will definitely make you think. The chapter asks you to consider not just policing, but life experiences more broadly, from perspectives different to your own. Both uncritical acceptance and immediate rejection of different beliefs and values can be equally problematic, so we ask you to keep an open mind and be honest in your reflections. Take responsibility for your learning, accept that it will be difficult at times but very much worth the effort. Just like policing.

7.1 Introduction

By this point you've probably been asked 'why did you want to join the police?'. Think back to your answer. 'Helping people' probably featured somewhere in it. This is very common and obviously positive. Many people who want to work in policing, healthcare, social care, and other public service professions, value the service aspect of it greatly and want to make a positive difference in the lives of others.

But how do we know what help people need or want? Hopefully your answer is 'you ask them'. Imagine that you're meeting a friend around lunch time. Do you just assume that they must be hungry and march them to the nearest café? Do you assume that they want a cheese sandwich because that's what you like? Hopefully not. It's far more likely that you ask if your friend actually *is* hungry and if so, what food they want to get. As a police officer you will encounter individuals from a wide variety of backgrounds, with diverse characteristics and values. This is why it's important to do your research beforehand when possible and always, always ask rather than assume. One of the criticisms of policing, including community policing, is that it has sometimes been done *to* individuals or communities without much input from them on what kind of help they would like.

Another key consideration for providing a policing *service* to the public is how police *treat* people they interact with as members of the public, victims, witnesses, suspects, colleagues. The attestation oath (see 3.3.1.1) invites officers to serve with '*fairness, integrity, diligence, and impartiality, upholding fundamental human rights and according equal respect to all people*'. These themes are then formalized in the Professional Standards and the Code of Ethics (see Chapter 3 and 7.3) including *fairness* and *respect* as some of the core principles of policing. But what does

GLOSSARY OF KEY TERMS	
Age	A specific age (eg, 55-year-olds), an age range (eg, 35–49-year-olds) or a general group (eg, young person)
Bias	A person's tendency to prefer one thing over another in a way that is not objective
Direct Discrimination	Treating someone less favourably because of their identity
Disability	A physical or mental impairment that has a substantial and long-term effect on someone's ability to carry out daily tasks
Diversity	Understanding people are unique and recognizing individual differences
Culture	Way of life including beliefs, values, traditions, systems, and institutions. Operates at many levels such as nationally or organizationally
Equality	Not treating everybody the same, but ensuring everyone has equal opportunities to achieve
Equality Act 2010	Legislation prohibiting employers and service providers from discriminating
Equity	Recognizing people's differences and allocating resources appropriately so that everyone can achieve an equal outcome
Ethics	An impartial set of rules that demands certain types of behaviour and prohibits others
Gender identity	Someone's internal sense of their gender, often discussed when their gender differs from their assigned sex at birth
Harassment	Unwanted conduct related to a protected characteristic
Human Rights Act 1998	Legislation that sets out fundamental rights and freedoms that everyone in the UK is entitled to
Indirect discrimination	Practices or rules which apply to everyone but disadvantage a particular group
Institutionalized racism/sexism/ homophobia or other type of discrimination	Institutional systems, policies, and practices that result in discriminatory outcomes, because of either structural social inequalities or inherent but irrelevant differences between different groups
Misogyny	Dislike, contempt and/or prejudice against women
Prejudice	A negative feeling or negative attitude towards the members of a group based on incorrect information
Race	Race relates to a group of people who share the same physical traits and includes skin colour, nationality, national origin, and ethnic origin
Racism	Racism is prejudice or discrimination because of a person's membership of a racial or ethnic group
Religion	Under the Equality Act 2010, religion refers to any religion, both mainstream and less well known
Sexual orientation	Sexual orientation relates to the gender or genders that a person is sexually attracted to
Stereotypes	Generalizations about social groups that are rigidly held, illogically derived, and erroneous in content
Unconscious bias	An unconscious bias is when someone is unaware that they tend to prefer one thing over another in a way that is not objective
Values	The standards we use to judge the merit of ideas, situations, or people
Victimization	Treating someone badly after they report experiencing discrimination

that mean? Two simplistic answers are often offered: treating everyone the same, and treating others how you would like to be treated. A decent starting point but the world is more complicated than that and treating everyone exactly the same is not the same as treating everyone fairly. If a shop has one entrance, accessible by a set of steps then everyone has to enter using that. Fair? Not for people with mobility issues. Tying promotion prospects to the amount of work experience a candidate has assumes everyone has an equal opportunity to accumulate it. Similarly, the golden rule of 'treat others the way you want to be treated' is useful when considering the broad principles of respect, dignity, and fairness, but it glosses over the details. An everyday example—think about how you like to be treated when you are ill. Perhaps you like to be fussed over or maybe you just like to sleep. Think about how a friend, your partner, or child wants to be treated when ill. Is it the same?

We view the world through our subjective experience but often forget that our experience is not a universal default. To put it in other words: *different people experience the same environment differently*. Consider the shopping experience a person has if they are considered beautiful versus someone considered unattractive. Both individuals may experience some staring and comments, but they are probably rather different in tone. So when a white person says 'I don't see any racist behaviour' or a heterosexual person says 'I've never witnessed homophobic discrimination' they are probably telling the truth. But that does not mean it does not exist. Indeed, the high number of hate incidents (see Chapter 19) provides us with a stark reminder that many people's lived reality is negatively impacted by how others react to their actual or perceived difference.

We live in a highly diverse society. The latest 2021 Census results presented in the table below provide some useful insights on this. By now you have probably heard the saying 'the police are the public and the public are the police' reflecting the ideal that British police are representative of the British public, and that it is this that gives them the legitimacy they need to do their work. Comparing the diversity statistics from Census 2021 and from the latest (at the time of writing) Police Workforce data highlights that the police are not as representative as we might hope.

Category	Census 2021	Police Workforce, England and Wales, March 2022 (ONS, 2022d)
Sex	**England and Wales:** Female 51% Male 49%	**Police officers, England and Wales:** Female 33.5% Male 66.5%
Ethnicity	**England:** Asian or Asian British 9.6% Black, Black British, Caribbean or African 4.2% White 81.0% Mixed of Multiple ethnic groups 3.0% Other ethnic groups 2.2% **Wales:** Asian or Asian British 2.9% Black, Black British, Caribbean or African 0.9% Mixed of Multiple ethnic groups 1.6% White 93.8% Other ethnic groups 0.9%	**Police officers England and Wales:** Asian or Asian British 3.7% Black or Black British 1.3% Mixed 2.5% White 91.9% Other ethnic group 0.7%
Sexual orientation	England and Wales, of population aged 16 or over: Heterosexual 89.4% Gay or Lesbian, Bisexual or Other sexual orientation 3.2% Did not answer the question 7.5% Note that there are stark generational differences here, with the recent research (Stonewall, 2022) reporting that in Gen Z (currently aged 16–26) only 71% report as being heterosexual, the percentage being even lower (53%) when we look beyond the label, to patterns of attraction.	Note that recent changes to HR systems mean that large proportions of police officers have not yet entered this information. For sexual orientation, 41.7% of police officers had not yet declared any status, and 5.8% have chosen 'Prefer not to say'. Of the 52.4% of who had provided information: Heterosexual 92.5% Gay or Lesbian 4.7% Bisexual 2.5% Prefer to Self-Describe 0.2%
Religion	England and Wales: Christian 46.2% No religion 37.2% Muslim 6.5% Hindu 1.7% Sikh 0.9% Buddhist 0.5% Jewish 0.5% Other religion 0.6% Did not answer the question 6.0%	Note that recent changes to HR systems mean that large proportions of police officers have not yet entered this information. For religious beliefs, 39.3% of police officers had not yet declared any status, and 5.2% have chosen 'Prefer not to say'. Of the 55.5% of who provided information: Christian 48.3% No religion 42.4% Muslim 2.1% Hindu 0.5% Sikh 0.7% Buddhist 0.4% Jewish 0.3% Any other religion or belief 5.3%

Source: Equality and Diversity Data, Census 2021 (ONS, 2022c) and Police Workforce Data (ONS, 2022d)

TASK 1 What are the challenges these differences in the representation pose to policing?

This chapter is divided into four main parts. First it introduces you to some key concepts that help you situate your own experience and that of others, and understand for example how attitudes, stereotypes, prejudices, and discrimination develop. The next sections address the main question 'why should the police value diversity and inclusion?' Interestingly, the three answers offered correspond with a well-established theory of moral development by Lawrence Kohlberg (1969). Kohlberg's model (below) explains how we move from very egocentric perspective of the world as children to gradually taking other perspectives into account as we mature.

Why should the police value diversity and inclusion?	Kohlberg's Theory of Moral Development
It is the lawful thing to do: Legal and regulatory framework relating to equality and diversity (7.3)	Pre-conventional level: Morality is defined by external rules, which are obeyed to avoid punishment.
It is the smart thing to do: Valuing diversity and inclusion is essential to securing legitimacy and public cooperation, without which the police cannot do their job (7.4)	Conventional level: Morality is about maintaining good relationships with others and the social order.
It is the right thing to do: Ethics of policing, respect for people's differences, fair treatment, and equality of opportunity are at the very heart of ethical policing (7.5)	Post-conventional level: Morality is about common good and universal ethical principles and values. What is right and justified transcends laws or social norms.

Source: (Kohlberg, 1969). Stage and sequence: The cognitive-development approach to socialization

7.2 Situating Your Own Experience

There is real benefit in respecting and accepting the many differences between us all. When we feel accepted for who we are, we are more comfortable and more effective in our lives and our job roles. You will work with people whose lives and experiences are different to your own, and valuing these differences can inspire greater collaboration and forge stronger relationships within communities. This, along with inclusion and mutual respect, will allow the police to better represent the communities they serve.

7.2.1 Values, attitudes, and beliefs

Differences between people are often in the form of the values and beliefs. Values are the criteria or standards we use to judge the value or merit of ideas, situations or people (MacVean and Neyroud, 2012). First it is helpful to recognize how you have come to hold the values and beliefs that you do.

TASK 2

Think of some of the values that are important to you. Now consider the following points:

- Can you identify an individual or any circumstances that have helped you form these values?
- Are your values the 'right' ones to have? If so, how do you view those with very different values to yours?
- How would you feel if you had to live by a set of values that were different to yours and had been imposed on you?

Massey (1979) suggested that as children develop into adults, they create their own values systems based on influences from family, teachers, friends, peer groups, as well as outside influences from the media. Massey went on to propose that an individual's values system is set by the age of 21 unless that person experiences a significant emotional event that causes them to reconsider their beliefs about people. As a police officer, you are likely to encounter situations that you would have not previously experienced—people living lifestyles you cannot relate to or aggression directed at you and your colleagues. Indeed, after a few years or possibly only months of service, you may hear friends tell you that you have changed.

Your coach, your peers, and other colleagues can all influence the direction of that change through the information they give you to help you explore and make sense of situations you experience (Taylor, 1986). Because of this, you should seek to debrief incidents and discuss situations with colleagues who show professional and appropriate values and beliefs; a colleague who has become cynical about the job they do is more likely to guide your thinking to match their own.

7.2.1.1 Stereotyping and unconscious bias

Stereotyping and bias are familiar terms for most of us. Stereotypes can be defined as 'beliefs about the characteristics of groups of individuals' and stereotyping is 'the application of these stereotypes when we interact with people from a given social group' (Stangor, 2000, p 1). Stereotypes can be thought of as the mental picture we have when we think of a person from a particular group and this includes not just how they look, but how we think 'they' behave. Lipmann (1922, as cited by Judd and Park, 1993, p 109) defined stereotypes as 'generalizations about social groups that are rigidly held, illogically derived, and erroneous in content'.

A bias is a person's tendency to prefer one thing over another in a way that is not objective. Allowing your biases to guide your decision making could mean that you miss out on many experiences and relationships due to closed thinking and, more importantly, make unfair decisions about others.

Our brains subconsciously turn to stereotypes to shortcut the effort required when sifting through large amounts of information (Allport, 1954). The term 'unconscious bias' describes how a person uses their previous experiences and stereotypes to make decisions daily about the people they meet and the choices they make (Noon, 2018). Yet as these decisions are made based on partial and/or false information, they will often result in unfair consequences for others.

We all hold unconscious biases, and accepting this means we all have to actively act to counter this in our own decision-making. Identifying where you have knowledge gaps about people from other communities and recognizing your own biases are the first steps in challenging the biases you hold.

7.2.1.2 Sense of belonging and prejudice

It is natural to feel a sense of belonging with some people more than others. When you were growing up, it is likely that you felt closest to the people who lived with you. This group would have been your first 'in-group'—the people about whom you could say 'we' with significance (Allport, 1954). As you grew up, you would have belonged to other in-groups such as your circle of friends. Later in life, other in-groups could include those you work with. The group that you identified as being your in-group at the time would often be decided by who you would call 'them' at that time. For example, during a school competition, you might be competing against another class, in which case your in-group would be your own class, yet if the competition was against another school, your in-group would expand to include all your fellow school pupils. If asked, you are most likely to think that those in your in-group are better than those who aren't (Allport, 1954). It is this feeling of being allied to those that are most like you that can lead you to prejudicial thoughts.

Prejudice is a 'negative feeling or negative attitude towards the members of a group' (Stangor, 2000, p 1) or when incorrect information is used to make a judgement about a person or social group (Allport, 1954). Prejudice is more than a misconception that is corrected when new information is received—it is a solid belief that is unchanged even when new information suggests that the original belief is wrong. Stangor (2000) suggested that stereotyping comes about due to thinking of others as belonging to different groups rather than as being individuals, perhaps due to their skin colour, age, sex, or occupation. If we exclude someone or deny them an equal access to a service due to prejudiced beliefs about them purely due to their membership or perceived membership of a particular group, this would be classed as discrimination under the Equality Act 2010 (see 7.3.1) and unacceptable under the Code of Ethics (see 7.3.2).

Stereotyping, unconscious bias, and prejudice all stem from judging others without full information about their individuality. As suggested at the very beginning of this chapter, you will need to be open to challenging your own attitudes and adopt an objective, investigative mindset when you look for evidence to test your understanding. In order to explore your beliefs, it can be useful to put yourself in others' shoes.

TASK 3

Take a moment to think about the following questions and use them to learn more about other communities and the challenges they may face:

- How would I feel if a close relative was in an intimate relationship with someone from a different racial background?
- How might my life be different if I were born as the opposite sex?
- How much did my family influence my political beliefs?

7.2.2 Microaggressions

If you were to see an advert that said 'Friendly, caring woman required for customer service role' you would identify this as unlawful discrimination. Yet while overt discrimination such as this is unlawful and therefore less frequently seen, this does not mean discrimination no longer occurs. Discriminatory acts can be subtle and are often less visible to those who are not affected by them. The term *microaggression* describes 'brief and commonplace daily verbal, behavioural or environmental indignities, whether intentional or unintentional, that communicate hostile, derogatory, or negative slights toward people who are not classified within the "normative" standard' (Johnson and Johnson, 2019, p 1).

TASK 4 Consider these following conversations and think about how someone could be affected if comments of this nature were directed at them on a regular basis.

- A group of friends are competing in a fun driving competition, and a woman beats her male friend in a race. A second male turns to the first and says, 'You got beaten by a girl!'. *The inference here is that all women are likely to be worse drivers than men and being beaten by a woman is shameful.*
- You work on a team that has just recruited a new employee aged in their 60s. You hear a colleague say to the new employee, 'There's a computer system we'll train you on. Don't worry if it's too difficult for you, we can always get one of the younger ones to help you out.' *The inference here is that someone in their 60s could not possibly be knowledgeable about computers due to their age, but a younger person is likely to have natural skills in this area.*

7.2.3 Discretion and decision making

You will often hear the term 'discretion' used to describe the choice of actions a police officer can make in their daily duties (see 4.2.2.1). For a community to consider that police discretion is being applied appropriately, the use of the discretion must reflect the norms, standards, and customs of the community it is being applied to (Fielding, 1999). In this section, you will be encouraged to think about how your use of discretion and your decision making can be influenced by the values, attitudes, and beliefs you hold. You have already identified how your upbringing and life experiences, as well as the people around you, have formed the values, attitudes, and beliefs that you hold. As everyone will have experienced life in different ways, the values, attitudes, and beliefs will also differ, and so may their ideas on how a situation is best dealt with.

As an officer, you can use your discretion in many ways. Discretionary decisions include the areas you choose to patrol, the vehicles you stop, the people you target, and the offences you prioritize, as well as how you decide to deal with any offences that are disclosed. The Code of Ethics sits at the heart of any decision-making process (see 4.2.1 on the National Decision Model) and within the Code of Ethics is the need to treat people fairly and objectively (CoP, 2014a). This, therefore, requires an officer to take account of how they view the world and strive to remove their personal biases and prejudices about others from their discretionary decisions.

7.3 Legal and Regulatory Case for Equality, Diversity, and Inclusion

For a fair and functioning society, every person needs to be valued and given equal access to employment, goods, and services regardless of their abilities, their background or their lifestyle. Legislation has been introduced to protect the rights of those who can experience lesser treatment because of their inherent characteristics, such as the way they look or the people they choose to have a relationship with. As a police officer, you are expected to not only abide by this legislation but also to adhere to the Code of Ethics and other guidance that outlines acceptable behaviour in relation to equality and diversity.

7.3.1 The Equality Act 2010

Over time, there have been groups of people who have suffered significant discrimination and so different pieces of legislation, such as the Sex Discrimination Act 1975 and the Race Relations Act 1976, were put in place to protect these groups from unfair treatment. The Equality Act 2010 (gov.uk, 2010) brought together all previous anti-discrimination laws and, in doing so, simplified the legislative framework and covered a wider range of characteristics. The Equality Act 2010 protects everyone from being treated unfairly because of who they are. It applies to employers, businesses, health care providers, education providers, transport services, public bodies, and organizations that provide goods and services.

7.3.1.1 Protected characteristics

Under the Equality Act 2010, it is unlawful to discriminate on the grounds of the 'protected characteristics' identified in the legislation. These characteristics are:

Age

Disability—a physical or mental impairment (or both) that has a substantial and long-term effect on the ability to carry out day-to-day tasks. This includes non-visible disabilities, such as neurodiversity.

Gender reassignment—protects someone who was born in one biological sex but identifies as the opposite sex. This includes if they are planning to undergo, are undergoing, or have already undergone a process to reassign their sex. The individual does not need to have a medical diagnosis, to be receiving any medical treatment or to have obtained any legal documentation to be protected.

Marriage and civil partnership—This category does not include single people or those engaged to be married, living together as a couple, or those who are now divorced.

Pregnancy and maternity—extends from when a person becomes pregnant to 26 weeks after giving birth.

Race—relates to groups of people defined by their race, colour, nationality, national origin, or ethnic origin. Racial groups can also be made up of two or more distinct racial groups, such as British Asians and Irish Travellers. Nationality refers to where someone holds the right to apply for a passport, whereas national and ethnic origins may be different. For example, someone who has British citizenship may have national origins in India.

Religion or belief—this includes having no particular religious belief. A belief is considered as having significant influence on how someone chooses to live their life or perceive the world. Protected beliefs include humanism, vegetarianism, and the belief that humans are responsible for climate change.

Sex—protected characteristics are male and female. At present, there is no protection offered through the Equality Act 2010 for someone who identifies as non-binary.

Sexual orientation—relates to the gender or genders that a person is sexually attracted to. A person is protected if they are heterosexual (attracted to the opposite gender), gay (male attracted to male), lesbian (female attracted to female), or bisexual (someone attracted to both sexes).

For many people more than one protected characteristic applies eg being a Black woman, and the notion of *intersectionality* captures this and the fact they will have a specific experience of discrimination (Crenshaw, 1989). While the rights of most people are protected in relation to one or more of the protected characteristics, some people also suffer poor treatment due to characteristics they have that are not legally protected. This could include hair colour or weight. As a police officer, it is important to recognize that you must not discriminate against anyone based on either protected or non-protected characteristics—this would be considered as unfair discrimination.

7.3.1.2 Prohibited conduct

The Equality Act 2010 sets out situations where conduct that is less favourable because of an individual's personal characteristics is prohibited.

- Direct discrimination—where someone suffers detrimental treatment purely because of their personal characteristics. For example, stopping and searching a person purely because they are Black.
- Indirect discrimination—this type of discrimination is embedded in societies and policies. For example, a company introduces regular training during evenings and weekends to help those seeking promotion. This is open to all but women who are more likely to have caring responsibilities are less likely to be able to attend.
- Discrimination by association—this is discrimination because of who an individual associates with. For example, not giving a promotion to a parent who has a child with a disability because you think that they will be less available.
- Discrimination by perception—this discrimination is when someone incorrectly believes a person has a certain characteristic and treats them less favourably as a result. For example, someone is turned down for a job interview because their name (gained through marriage) is predominantly used in a Muslim country. While they are not Muslim, they are perceived as one and suffer discrimination.

There are two other forms of prohibited conduct outlined in the Equality Act 2010, which are harassment and victimization:

- **Harassment**: This is when someone engages in behaviour related to a protected characteristic that violates another person's dignity or creates an environment that is hostile, degrading, or offensive. For example, a transwoman is regularly referred to using male pronouns at work by her colleagues despite asking them to use the pronouns she and her (this is called misgendering).
- **Victimization:** If someone were to make a complaint, either formally or informally, about the unfair treatment they have received in relation to a protected characteristic and then suffer additional unfair treatment, this would be victimization. For example, an employee in their twenties is always passed over for promotion in favour of older but less qualified colleagues. The employee makes a complaint of direct discrimination and afterwards they are moved to a different team against their will.

Consider how you would feel if you were assumed to be a liar, rapist, or murderer because of the publicized criminal actions of other police officers. It is understandable that those who experience discrimination are angry and upset about assumptions made about them that are completely unfounded and unfair.

7.3.1.3 Public Sector Equality Duty

Public authorities, including the police, have additional responsibility under the Equality Act 2010 known as the Public Sector Equality Duty. This duty requires police officers and staff, in their daily activities, to always consider if their actions are working to eliminate discrimination, advance the equality of opportunity of those who experience disadvantage because of a protected characteristic and foster good relations between people who share a protected characteristic and those who do not. An officer can do this by, for example, ensuring that the decisions they make in relation to patrol activities and investigations can be objectively justified so that a community is not under- or over-policed based purely on their protected characteristics.

7.3.2 The Code of Ethics and supporting guidance

The Code of Ethics, first issued by the College of Policing in 2014 and being reviewed at the time of writing, sets guidelines for the ethical and professional behaviour of police officers. The Code of Ethics (see Chapter 3) outlines the qualities that the public rightly expects to see displayed by all those working in policing and reflects the attestation that all officers made at the beginning of their service. In their Diversity, Equality and Inclusion Strategy 2018—2025, the National Police Chiefs' Council (NPCC, 2018a) has set out their vision to create a more representative police force that can meet the needs of increasingly diverse communities and respond to policing demands with ethical and fair application of the law. The Independent Office for Police Conduct (IOPC) Statutory Guidance on the Police Complaints System highlights the need for a strong learning culture within police services.

Given the powerful positions police officers hold in society, it is important for all officers to ensure their own prejudices do not lead to discrimination or unfair treatment due to another's personal characteristics. As the Institute for Apprenticeships (2018b) explains, police constables 'exercise wide-ranging powers to maintain the peace and uphold the law across complex and diverse communities. They must justify and personally account for their actions through differing legal frameworks including courts, while also under the scrutiny of the public.'

Alongside this, the Institute for Apprenticeship's standard for those undertaking the PCDA is for trainees to exhibit professional integrity, which the Institute (2018b) explains means to 'maintain the highest standards of professionalism and trustworthiness, making sure that values, moral codes and ethical standards are always upheld, including challenging others where appropriate'.

When starting a new job or joining a new team, it can be tempting to ignore any unethical behaviour within that job or team. While most police teams pride themselves on being professional and efficient, you could experience a team that uses unprofessional terms to talk about others. You may find yourself tempted to express opinions that go against the Code of Ethics and even ones that you do not agree with to fit in. Not only can this make you feel uncomfortable, but you can be putting yourself in a position where you breach the Code of Ethics and the Equality Act 2010. There are a few choices you can make in this situation. You could acquiesce in the behaviour of the team and act unprofessionally or you could leave the room whenever there are conversations that make you uncomfortable. Both of these choices will mean that the behaviour will continue unchanged. The expectation of the police service and the public is that you always take the third option and resist any inappropriate behaviour by challenging it directly or reporting it to a supervisor or the Professional Standards Department. In this way, you maintain your integrity as a professional police officer and prevent the escalation of inappropriate behaviour into significant incidents.

7.4 Business Case for Diversity and Inclusion

Understanding the impact of our behaviour on others, as individual officers and as a police service, is necessary for *changing* it to ensure that impact is positive rather than harmful. Valuing diversity and inclusion is *essential* for policing by consent. A starting point is seeking to understand people's experiences of being different, in society, in interactions with the police, and within the police service itself—the idea of being able to 'walk in someone else's shoes'.

7.4.1 Being 'different'

Research into diverse life experience is vast and varied but brief snapshots offer valuable insight into the inequalities that still persist. These include various socio-economic disadvantages, lack of social support, and policies and practices developed without understanding of or consultation with the groups affected by them.

The latest figures for the UK indicate a gender pay gap of 8.3 per cent for full-time employees (with women earning less on average) (ONS, 2022e). The ethnicity pay gap is varied with some groups (Pakistani, Bangladeshi, White, and Black African/Caribbean) earning considerably less and others (Indian, Chinese, White Irish) more in comparison with the 'White British' group (ONS, 2020a). This may reflect disparities in educational achievement. Whilst pupils from most ethnic minority backgrounds outperform White British students at GCSE level, the reverse is true at A-levels and higher education (The Centre for Social Justice, 2020). Almost a fifth of people in England and Wales report a disability in the latest census (ONS, 2023a). Being disabled comes with several 'hidden' costs of goods and services such as insurance, heating, travel, or help with everyday activities like cooking or cleaning. The difference in earnings between disabled and non-disabled is 13.8 per cent (ONS, 2022f).

Health inequalities are also rife. The life expectancy in the most affluent areas is 19 years higher than in the most deprived neighbourhoods (Office for Health Improvement and Disparities, 2022b). The Covid-19 pandemic exposed multiple disadvantages in society, with higher mortality rates apparent among ethnic minority groups and those already affected by economic deprivation. This reflects the higher rates of people from ethnic minority backgrounds working in frontline roles and living in multi-occupancy and multigenerational households (Race Disparity Unit, 2021; Scientific Advisory Group for Emergencies, 2022). LGBT+ people experience mental health problems, self-harm, and suicidal thoughts at high rates. For example, over half report experiencing depression due to rejection by the community, harassment, discrimination, and hate crime (Stonewall, 2018a). As a consequence, only 46 per cent of lesbian, gay, and bi people, and 47 per cent of trans people, are open about their sexuality or gender identity to everyone in their family (Stonewall, 2018b). In the workplace, 35 per cent of LGBT+ people hide or disguise this aspect of their identity for fear of discrimination (Stonewall, 2018c).

7.4.2 Being different in interactions with the police

Police and minority populations typically have a history that is fraught with ignorance and mistrust at best and outright prejudice and persecution at worst. Unfortunately, these issues are not just historic as two recent reports into police conduct demonstrate (Operation Hotton Learning Report and the Casey Review, see 7.4.4). This section provides a brief overview of how being different can affect both the quantity and quality of one's interactions with the police.

The murder of a Black teenager Stephen Lawrence in 1993, the poor handling of the investigation, and the consequent inquiry by Sir William Macpherson (1999) remains a watershed moment for policing in terms of equality and diversity. It found the police service to have displayed '*professional incompetence, institutional racism, and a failure of leadership by senior officers*' (Macpherson, 1999: 46.1). Whilst the focus of the inquiry was on race, the 'post-Macpherson era' of policing highlighted the need to repair relationships between the police and *all* marginalized groups (Jones & Williams, 2013; Williams, 2015). This, coupled with the change in legislation such as possibility of sentence uplifts for crimes motivated by hate or prejudice, and the clear articulation of protected characteristics in the Equality Act 2010, brought about a gradual reframing of many persecuted groups to groups that now needed protection (Pickles, 2020).

Who we are increases our vulnerability to victimization. Chapter 20 discuss the concept of vulnerability in much greater detail but the picture of being different in society would not be complete without considering the topic here too. For example, certain offences are strongly 'gendered', meaning one's gender can drastically increase the risk of victimization. Domestic violence, as well as female genital mutilation, forced marriage, and modern-day slavery (see Chapter 20) are highly gendered with women making up the majority of victims. Despite this, the recent Casey Review on the Metropolitan Police (Casey, 2023) reported that child protection, rape, and sexual offences, and domestic abuse were not prioritized as officers lack the necessary time, resources, and specialist knowledge to deal with them effectively.

Being victimized because of who you are hurts more and inflicts more psychological and emotional damage than being a victim of a crime in general does (Iganski & Lagou, 2015). Police-recorded hate crime increased by 26 per cent between March 2021 and March 2022, reflecting likely both improved recording and increased victim reporting (Home Office, 2022c). The majority (110,000) of them were motivated by race, followed by sexual orientation (26,000) and disability (14,000). The highest percentage increases were for transgender (56 per cent increase), disability (46 per cent increase), and sexual orientation (41 per cent increase) hate crime. And yet, research suggests that hate crime remains substantially underreported for a variety of reasons, including fear of consequences, regarding the incident too trivial to bother, and notably lack of confidence that the police would or could do anything about it often stemming from previous experiences (eg Wong & Christmann, 2016). When hate crime victims do report to the police, they tend to be less satisfied with the way the matter is handled (Home Office, 2020b) and the response they receive can be inconsistent. The 2018 HMICFRS inspection found several examples of good policing practice but also noted a number of issues, including inaccurate flagging of hate crime, insufficient information collection, lack of victim risk assessment, and hate crime victims not being prioritized despite College of Policing operational guidance to do so (HMICFRS, 2018a).

Black and other ethnic minority groups are overrepresented at all stages of the criminal justice system, including prisons and young offenders' institutions (Lammy, 2017). Racial discrimination is a significant explanation for the disparity in, for example, stop and search (Equality and Human Rights Commission, 2010 see also 4.3) and simplistic explanations that ethnic minority individuals are more involved in crime or more represented among 'available' populations on the streets, lack evidence. When asked, young people from ethnic minority groups describe their interactions with the police in terms of hostility, confrontation and perception of racist attitudes, discrimination, and abuse of power (Sharp & Atherton, 2007). There is a reluctance to report crime due to a lack of confidence in anything being done (ibid).

Political, media, and public discourse can stigmatize certain groups as 'suspect communities' due to the involvement of *some* group members in criminal activity (Hillyard, 1993). Examples of this include the Irish people in the UK during the conflict in Northern Ireland, and Muslims in the global 'war on terror'. In an illustrative study, Minhas and Walsh (2018) demonstrated how stereotypes influence investigative decision-making. They provided police officers with a written scenario of a suspect in possession of a Class A drug. The officers were asked whether they would proceed to interview the person with an aim of charging them for possession only or for possession with an intent to supply. What varied was the suspect's name. 'Muhammad Ali' was more likely than 'Richard Fisher' to be charged with the more serious offence of intent to supply.

In England and Wales, male same-sex sexual activity was first formally criminalized under the Buggery Act 1553 and remained so for four centuries. Following the recommendations of the Wolfenden Report (1957), the Sexual Offences Act 1967 legalized it for men over 21. Female same-sex sexual activity has never been formally criminalized although there is no doubt that lesbian relationships were subject to social censure. Police raids of clubs, bars, pubs, restaurants, bathhouses, and other spaces catering for the LGBT+ community were commonplace during the latter half of the twentieth century.

Unsurprisingly, members of the community were reluctant to come forward as victims for fear of facing discrimination and harassment by the police (Jones, 2015). The historic 'baggage' is still there, and its influence must be understood. Older members of the community especially will often equate the police with a source of persecution, which in turn hinders reporting of hate crime, which some research puts as low as 4 per cent of incidents being reported (Pickles, 2020). Police service of this community requires consideration of unique sensitivities, such as understanding that not all LGBT+ individuals are out to their friends, family, colleagues.

7.4.3 Being different in the police

As the previous table demonstrates, we are still a good way from a representative police service. Moreover, increasing numerical representation alone is not enough because whilst policing practices have changed, the culture within the workplace is often still described as 'white, straight, male, and machismo' (Pickles, 2020, p 753).

Research on female officer experiences in the 1980s and 1990s (Holdaway & Parker, 1998) highlighted experiences of discrimination, sexual harassment, differential deployment and access to opportunities, devaluing of work with female or child victims typically undertaken by female officers. Female officers are still overrepresented in roles relating to domestic violence and child protection, and underrepresented in areas of work such as traffic and firearms units (Sebire, 2020). A recent survey (Boag-Munroe, 2019) indicated that in England and Wales, female officers had lower expectations and aspirations for career progression. This is a reflection of perceptions about how realistic and achievable progression is and stems from a lack of role-models, incompatibility with family life, and emphasis on time served (Silvestri, 2006). Gendered assumptions of the qualities needed for leadership roles also play a part (Silvestri, 2006).

The story for other groups in policing is depressingly similar. Experiences of racism and reluctance to report it due to fear of further isolation and lack of operational support are themes that emerge from research. Such aspects of occupational culture have shown remarkable resilience and continued to undermine equality and diversity reforms (Holdaway, 1996; 2013).

An example of internal differential experience is ethnic minority officers' disproportional involvement in misconduct proceedings. This includes formal referrals to professional standards boards and experiences of 'revenge complaints' (perceived to have been made as a backlash from complaints first made by ethnic minority officer) (Smith *et al*, 2012; 2015). In the Metropolitan Police, Black officers are 81 per cent more likely to be involved in misconduct proceedings compared to White officers (Casey, 2023). In interviews with Asian officers from the Greater Manchester Police, Smith and colleagues (2015) describe how the police service's lack of cultural understanding, such as the tradition of lending money interest-free to family, had led to suspicions of criminality on the basis of officers withdrawing large sums of money from their bank accounts. Socializing that centres around alcohol is still an important part of police culture, but for officers who do not drink such as Muslim officers, this becomes another area of exclusion (Smith *et al*, 2015).

Thirty years ago, LGBT+ officers were viewed as 'deviant' and as a 'threat to the integrity of the service' by their colleagues, routinely facing refusals to work together, professional discreditation, derogatory language, violations of privacy, and leading most to hide this aspect of their lives at work (Burke, 1994). Post-Macpherson and Equality Act 2010, LGBT+ officers were actively recruited and the service has undoubtedly made a visible effort to be more inclusive, eg participation in Pride events and celebration of the LGBT+ history month. Indeed, more recent research (Jones, 2015) found a much-improved working environment, with the majority of LGBT+ officers feeling supported by their constabulary (75 per cent) and never having experienced discrimination in the workplace (82 per cent). For the 17 per cent reporting discriminatory treatment, this typically occurred in areas with high level supervisory discretion such as deployment, training, promotion, or recruitment. Whilst the headline figure of 79 per cent of LGBT+ officers participating in the study (Jones, 2015) being 'out' to their colleagues is positive, it also hides complexities of managing one's sexual orientation in a professional setting. For example, 17 per cent had been involuntarily outed by a colleague, while only 40.5 per cent had disclosed their sexual orientation from the very start of their career, the majority choosing to do so after some risk assessment of the potential costs to career and professional setting. And for 21 per cent of the LGBT+ officers, the perceived risks were such that they continue to hide their sexual orientation at work. Experiences of overt homophobia within the police still persist (Casey, 2023) although some research (Pickles, 2020) reports more positive findings.

> **TASK 5** There are a number of staff networks that support officers from underrepresented backgrounds. The below provides a short summary so do explore these to find out how you can support their work.

The British Association of Women Police (BAWP) was founded in 1987 and works to ensure women's voices are heard in the police.

The Black Police Association was created in the Metropolitan Police in 1994, with the National Black Police Association (NBPA) established in 1998 with the mission to improve the working conditions for Black and other ethnic minority officers and staff.

National Association of Muslim Police, established in 2007, supports welfare and religious needs of Muslim officers and staff, understanding of Islam and works to improve recruitment and progression initiatives.

National LGBT+ Police Network, started in 1990 to represent LGBT+ staff in the police. It acts as a point of reference and resources on LGBT+ issues in policing, offering guidance to support inclusivity within the service and operational knowledge necessary for serving the LGBT+ community.

Disabled Police Association, founded in 2012, works to ensure the fair treatment of police officers and staff who are disabled, injured, or ill, and enhance the relationship between the police and disabled people in society.

7.4.4 Trust and legitimacy

The common law tradition of this country emphasizes that justice must be served by people representing the community, familiar with and sharing its norms, with understanding that those norms change over time and the law and those enforcing it must accommodate that.

Sometimes the police's solutions to community problems are brought in without understanding what the community wants, without expertise in the issue, and when the uptake is less than enthusiastic the community in question may end up with a label of uncooperative.

The concept of police legitimacy and its sources is discussed elsewhere (see 3.2.7) but it is worth returning to here in the context of diversity and inclusion. There is a connection between people's perception of procedural justice (see 17.6.6) and the level of legitimacy granted for the law enforcement (Jackson *et al*, 2012). In other words, people comply with the law and the agencies enforcing it if they view both as fair and equal. The lack of diversity is a key impediment for securing community confidence in the police (HMICFRS, 2019, see 11.5.1).

Unfortunately, levels of trust in the police are currently very low, especially among ethnic minority groups and women. Likewise confidence in the Independent Office of Police Complaints has reduced noticeably, particularly among women and Black respondents, and currently only 36 per cent overall agree that the IOPC does a good job (IOPC, 2022c). Positive attitudes toward the police have also declined overall and particularly among Black and Asian respondents, with 49 per cent, 38 per cent, and 40 per cent respectively reporting feeling positive toward the police (IOPC, 2022c). Perhaps most damningly, half of the respondents report not being confident that the police will deal fairly with complaints made against them (IOPC, 2022c).

Two recent reports have scrutinized the structural and cultural issues that contribute to equality and diversity not being valued by the police or in the police as they should be. Whilst both pertain to the Metropolitan Police, the issues are likely to be of concern to policing more widely and must trigger serious self-reflection, review, and meaningful change nationally.

Operation Hotton, an investigation/report into the behaviour of officers based predominantly at Charing Cross Police Station found evidence of 'discrimination, misogyny, harassment and bullying' (IOPC, 2022b, p 2). This included numerous examples of violent, discriminatory and highly sexualized messages such as references to raping people, comments that were clearly racist, homophobic, derogatory of people with disabilities or those from non-Christian religions, which were typically dismissed as banter. Other types of misconduct included demeaning actions toward probationers, threats, sexual harassment of female officers, and evidence of domestic violence by serving officers against their partners. There was also a noted reluctance to challenge or report inappropriate behaviour due to fear of repercussions, lack of support, and being ostracized. The report cites both cultural and structural factors that meant this behaviour was able to continue unchecked such as isolation of specific shifts or teams from the wider station, the stressful nature of the work facilitating 'us vs them' thinking, and a lack of adequate supervision.

A similar picture emerges from the Casey Review (2023) in relation to the whole of the Metropolitan Police. 22 per cent of staff and officers surveyed reported experiencing bullying, the figures being higher for those with protected characteristics; for example, 33 per cent of those with a disability, long-standing illness or other infirmity, 30 per cent of LGBT+ respondents, 36 per cent of Asian respondents, 35 per cent of Black respondents, and 25 per cent of female respondents reporting experiences of bullying. Poor management, especially of people, lack of clear systems and strategies around needs and skills assessment, recruitment and vetting, support, and wellbeing exacerbate the cultural issues identified. Baroness Casey makes it very clear that the below do *not* characterize *everyone* in the organization but the following are nonetheless representative of the prevailing 'the way we do things' culture.

As you read the descriptions below (Casey, 2023, pp 13–14), consider whether you have seen examples of these kinds of behaviours and attitudes in your constabulary, or examples to the contrary.

- **Too much hubris and too little humility** (dismissal of external views and criticism, an attitude that no one outside the profession can understand)
- **Defensiveness and denial** (not accepting criticism or owning up to mistakes including focusing on the flaws in the criticism rather than addressing the problems identified)

- **Speaking up is not welcome** (including the attitude of ignoring problems and negative consequences for raising concerns)
- **Optimism bias** (including always looking for a positive spin on events, blaming 'bad apples' instead of considering deeper systemic issues)
- **'Initiative-itis'** (focus on short-term campaigns and projects instead of long-term strategic changes that would address the deeper issues and provide clear direction)
- **Elitism** (imbalance between well-resourced specialist units at the cost of under-resourced and demoralized frontline)

It is appropriate to conclude this section with a thought-provoking quote from Baroness Casey. In the foreword of her stark and uncompromising review, she writes:

> Policing attracts the best of humanity. I have met many shining examples during this Review – those who uphold the highest of standards and who put themselves at risk in order to protect the rest of us. [...] I accept that so many police officers go to work for the right reasons. They are committed to public service, and I thank them for that. But policing needs to accept that the job can also attract predators and bullies – those who want power over their fellow citizens, and to use those powers to cause harm and discriminate. All of British policing needs to be alive to this very serious risk. It needs to keep them out when they try to get in, to root them out where they exist, and to guard against the corrosive effects that their actions have on trust, confidence and the fundamental Peelian principles of policing by consent. (Casey, 2023, pp 6–7)

The blunt conclusion of the Casey Review (2023) is that institutional racism, sexism, and homophobia persist and as a result the consent with the communities the Metropolitan Police serves is broken. This is a reminder for every police service, every police officer and staff member in the country: the police must not be complacent about consent. Consent is not passive, it is not the default, and it is not something the police are somehow entitled to. The police do not secure the consent of the people simply through *who* they are but through *what they do and how they do it.* Every encounter, every interaction, every decision presents an opportunity to actively build trust and confidence with members of the public. Without demonstrable and genuine valuing of diversity and inclusion at every level of policing, securing consent becomes impossible.

7.5 Ethical Case for Diversity and Inclusion

So far in this chapter, you have looked at the legal requirement to value difference and promote equality. You have read about how treating people with dignity and respect can promote public trust and confidence in the police. We hope that you appreciate that these are not the only reasons why you should treat everyone you interact with fairly. Respecting people's differences and providing fair and equitable treatment to all is at the very heart of ethical policing.

7.5.1 Theories and concepts of ethical behaviour

Ethical systems outline the basis for decision making by shaping what it means to be good. Bruce-Smith *et al* (2023) identify three main approaches to ethical reasoning in their review underpinning the revision of the College's Code of Ethics. These are *consequentialism,* which focuses ethical reasoning on outcomes, *deontological* reasoning, which focuses on what we are duty bound to do through reason, and *virtue* ethics, which requires interpreting the specifics of a context as it relates to established values. Wood (2020) argues that consequential reasoning dominated policing historically but deontological reasoning has come to dominate ethical thinking in most aspects of public life, including policing. However, Wood (2020) favours virtue ethics and notes that there is growing interest in this approach to ethical reasoning.

The Code of Ethics as established by the College of Policing in 2014 reflects mostly the deontological approach, which is most closely associated with the German philosopher, Immanuel Kant (1724–1804), who outlined an ethical system that was concerned with the ethics behind an individual's chosen actions rather than the result of what they did. He believed that an *act* was ethical if the person's *intent* when carrying it out was ethical and moral. This aligns with the Code of Ethics, where officers are urged to do the right thing for the right reasons. For this reason, the ACPO Risk Principles (CoP, 2013a) state 'Risk decisions should, therefore, be judged by the quality of the decision making, not by the outcome.'

Importantly, Kant felt that no one should ever be treated as a means to an end. For example, when investigating a crime, it could be tempting to tell a witness that they would not need to give evidence if they provided a witness statement, despite this not being your decision to make. It could be argued that securing the conviction of an offender through coercing a witness to give evidence could prevent further victims, but lying in this way is not only legally prohibited, it is also ethically forbidden for a police officer.

It is worth remembering, however, that even the most carefully considered and appropriate actions can have unintended consequences, and this is a weakness in deontological reasoning. For example, you may save someone from trying to take their own life, only for them to later commit a crime that injures many others. Being duty bound to act in a pre-determined way because it is the right thing to do can be limiting and lead to suffering and this is where virtue ethics has appeal. Kant's deontology can lead to ethical rule following whereas virtue ethics requires you to think ethically in each and every encounter (Wood, 2020).

To help you apply ethical concepts in decision making, Davis (2014) suggested the use of ethical 'tests' and the tests below are adapted from his suggestions:

- Harm test—Does this option do less harm than any alternative?
- Rights test—Would this option violate anyone's rights, especially a human right?
- Colleague test—What might my colleagues say when I describe my problem?
- Defensibility test—How would I defend my choice of this option before a local council meeting, a committee of my peers, or my parents?
- Professional test—How would the Professional Standards Department view my decision?
- Organizational test—How might the Chief Constable view my decision?
- Virtue test—What would I become if I chose this option often?
- Publicity test—Would I want my choice of this option published in the newspaper?

7.5.2 The categorization of victims

In the introduction to this chapter, you reflected on why you had joined the police. The reason many people give is because they want to help others. This is an admirable reason to have yet also deserving of scrutiny. Early in your career, you may have thought that the people you wanted to help were the 'good' people—the innocent ones who had done nothing wrong and had suffered at the hands of a 'bad' person. This may mean while you identify some victims as innocent and deserving of full police support and others are seen as somewhat contributory to their situation and therefore less deserving. There have been rape cases in the past where police interest was visibly heightened when an offender offended against what society viewed as 'respectable' women rather than preying on sex workers (Zvi, 2022). Understanding some as 'undeserving victims' is just too simplistic an approach (Charman, 2020).

In the case of County Line drug dealing, for example, children are often groomed and exploited into becoming involved, but then go on to groom and exploit others in their turn. Looked After Children were once considered to be streetwise and able to manage their own safety yet are at a higher risk of being introduced to County Lines (Caluori, Corlett, and Stott, 2020) and are some of the most vulnerable children in society (Public Health England, 2020). Many of these children can be considered both victims and offenders at the same time.

7.5.3 Adapting your approach

Complex situations in policing can create ethical challenges for officers, yet it is important to always ask yourself this question, 'Am I here to help everyone, or just the people I deem worthy of my help?' We hope that, without hesitation, you commit to helping *all* people. In doing so, you may experience situations where the person you want to help is not interested in the help you have to offer or even grateful of the time you spend with them. We are confident that of all the things you have heard about policing, not one person has told you that it is an easy job to do. You will often experience people at their lowest and most vulnerable, perhaps because they have been a victim, perhaps because they have committed a crime. Remember that your service should be offered equitably to all, regardless of background, appearance or other personal characteristics. Taking the time to understand the other person may give you insight into why they are behaving the way they are. Ask yourself the following questions:

- Have they had poor experience(s) with the police or other forms of authority?
- Have they experienced prejudice or discrimination?
- Do they feel that they will not be treated fairly or believed?

Once you begin to show empathy and understanding, you may find that not only do you have a more professional attitude, but you will also have a more open mindset. When you understand the person you are dealing with, you will then be able to provide a service that meets their actual needs rather than the needs you thought they had. This links back to the very beginning of this chapter—instead of treating people the way you would want to be treated, treat them the way *they* want to be treated.

While no-one can ever fully understand the lived experiences of others, you can and should take the time to listen, ask questions, and try to see things from their perspective.

If you accept that bias and prejudice stem from lack of knowledge and understanding, no effort made to understand others will be wasted.

7.6 Conclusions

This chapter has provided a number of answers to the question of why the police should and must value diversity and inclusion. Doing so ensures that the police are acting lawfully and within the Code of Ethics of the profession. Doing so ensures that the police provide effective and good quality service to the communities, and treat staff with dignity and respect, creating a working environment that gets the best out of people. And finally, valuing diversity and inclusion is simply the right, the ethical thing to do. That does not mean that it is easy. In fact, the complexities of policing mean that ethical dilemmas are everyday occurrences.

Sometimes, things are not clear-cut and the difference between right and wrong can be difficult to see. The important thing to remember is that you are not alone. Your colleagues and supervisors, and indeed the communities that you serve are there as sources of support, information, and choices that you on your own may not have been able to see.

Meeting the needs of and inspiring trust in the diverse communities both within the police, and outside it is challenging. It is not enough to seek guidance only when things go wrong. It is the responsibility of each officer and police employee to proactively make themselves aware of the needs of their different communities and take steps to meet them. Open-mindedness, curiosity, and a willingness to understand different perspectives and to have one's existing views and decisions challenged are qualities of a professional police officer. They are also necessary to delivering a fair and unbiased experience of the police service.

8 Leadership, Communication, and Teamwork

8.1 Introduction

National discussions on the issue of leadership in policing have sought to articulate and define the concept of a police leader. Pearson-Goff and Harrington (2014) proposed that effective leadership was critical at all ranks, and in an extensive literature review of empirical research identified seven key leadership characteristics which determined an effective police leader. Specifically, someone who was ethical (exhibiting integrity and honesty), trustworthy (within and external to the organization), legitimate (considered a good copper), a good role model (lead by example), a good communicator (within and external to the organization), a capable decision maker (seen as competent), and had sound thinking ability (critical, strategic, and creative). These characteristics are not just required at senior ranks, but highly applicable to any role within policing and to you, the student officer.

In the UK, there is general agreement that investment in leadership is imperative to support an effective and cost-efficient police service. The College of Policing (2015a, p 6) Leadership Review articulates leadership as 'the quality which connects an understanding of what must be done with the capability to achieve it'. This, it could be argued, is an over simplified version of describing leadership but at its core is a concept applicable to all ranks and potentially, this sets the tone for the policing mission and provides a platform of understanding for all police professionals. The Policing Vision 2025 suggests leadership is about valuing difference and empowerment, supported by reflective and innovative practices, which offers a positive contribution to recognizing the diverse communities both internal and external to police organizations (NPCC, 2016; Roberts *et al*, 2016). This chapter will outline different theories of leadership, because the differing demands on a police officer require flexibility in both approach and style.

Leadership is closely interlinked with the need for good teamwork and excellent communication. The need to work effectively as a member of a team is reflected in the Policing Professional Profiles from the College of Policing and linked to their Competency and Values Framework (CVF). One of the CVF competencies emphasizes the need to work collaboratively and therefore includes team working (CoP, 2023c). Effective teams communicate well, and this skill is critical for a police officer to be successful in their responsibilities to colleagues and external partners. The term communication includes verbal, non-verbal, visual, and written communication and is evidenced in the day-to-day responsibilities of a police officer. For example, explaining the caution on arrest (verbal), calming an anxious victim with appropriate body language (non-verbal), using signage/pictures (visual), and completing legal documentation (written).

A national crisis of confidence in policing was recently highlighted in the Independent Strategic Policing Requirement (Home Office, 2023b) and a key competency to promote positive interaction, trust, and understanding between the public and police, is effective communication (Antrobus, 2019). Better communication between communities and the police helps

(a) restore trust and confidence and (b) create opportunities to increase public participation in policing strategies. The Police Reform and Social Responsibility Act (2011) places legal requirements for the police to remain accountable to the public (eg to consult with the public and provide information about crime and policing). As a student officer your every interaction with the public contributes to this overall framework of public accountability and its subsequent right to 'police by consent'.

Effective policing requires effective communication and when dealing in person with members of the public this requires you to be cognisant of differing and diverse needs within a community (see Chapter 7). For example, there may be different cultural or religious factors that may influence who can attend public meetings, meaning that they may not be truly representative of male and female views, and language barriers may prevent full engagement in some communities. A detailed understanding of community needs and concerns should influence the approach taken toward engaging with community groups. As an operational police officer effective communication is a critical and essential skill frequently utilized to gather evidence, to seek the cooperation of witnesses, or when dealing with people at a time of trauma and vulnerability. To do this police officers need to be able to gather public respect in the face of its decline (Casey, 2023).

To be an effective communicator will involve a variety of techniques, often used at the same time, which are often referred to as 'soft skills' (Vasanthakumari, 2019). Soft skills in a policing context include active listening, empathy, building rapport, negotiation, conflict management, and emotional intelligence (Pepper and McGrath, 2020; Hall and Knapp, 2013; CoP, 2020c; Majid *et al*, 2012; Millar *et al*, 2018). Police officers need to be able to listen carefully and explain things well by focusing on the key points, and talking to people using language they understand. This applies in all circumstances, many of which can seem ordinary to a police officer but can be extremely emotive for survivors, victims, or witnesses.

This chapter will explore approaches to effective communication. Work by Majid *et al* (2012) identified that the two barriers to good communication skills were nervousness and a lack of confidence, traits that a trainee police officer would need to address. It will help you to understand how different communication skills can be used interchangeably, and what soft skills should be used in given situations. For example, failing to show empathy and talking over a vulnerable victim is an example of unacceptable and ineffective communication, conversely, this approach may be necessary when dealing with a violent and aggressive group. The key component for successful communication is to understand the styles and methods that are effective in differing situations.

8.1.1 Defining leadership

The College of Policing (2021f) declared that everyone in policing is a leader. 'Everyone in policing has a leadership role. Whether you're taking the lead when responding to an incident, supervising a recruit, delivering a project or managing a large team or department.'

All police professionals are leaders, practical examples include the importance of the tutor constables who perform coaching and mentoring roles daily, often supporting peers to achieve personal and organizational goals. Externally, police professionals engage the general public 24/7, often in the most difficult of circumstances. These encounters require dynamic leadership and decisive decision making (see 4.2). For example, a police officer managing a road traffic collision (RTC) is likely to be presented with a challenging and stressful environment that requires a professional and sensitive investigation. They must be able to calmly address multiple competing complexities that may include human fatalities and/or serious injuries to people, ongoing health and safety risks, traumatized witnesses, road traffic problems, and so on.

8.1.2 The policing hierarchy

Grint (2010) defines hierarchical leadership as being 'activity undertaken by someone whose position on a vertical, and usually formal, hierarchy provides them with the resources to lead'. Within the policing hierarchical structures (see 3.2.2) team leaders, sergeants, or police staff equivalents, are responsible for leading policing teams, often managed and supported by an Inspector or police staff manager. Within a policing team there will be a diverse range of skills and abilities; how colleagues support each other is a measurement of both the leadership and teamwork.

Coaching and mentoring is a recognized leadership trait and in certain circumstances it will be provided by tutor constables who are trained to facilitate work-based learning, development, and assessment of trainees (CoP, 2023d; 2023e). The role of the tutor within policing is an opportunity for police professionals to demonstrate high levels of leadership competence and skill, akin to those used by team leaders. The leadership qualities required to be a good tutor include good communication techniques, a problem-solving mindset, and an ability to make ethical decisions. These developed skills are transferrable and are essential competencies for police professionals routinely engaging with the public in times of crisis. The developed skills will be relied upon within encounters such as the de-escalation of a large public disorder incident, the sensitive response to a mental health concern, or the management of a complex domestic abuse incident.

8.2 HMICFRS Police Leadership Reviews

His Majesty's Inspectorate of Constabulary and Fire and Rescue Services (HMICFRS, 2018b) routinely conduct PEEL inspections across all the 43 police services in England and Wales. Policing leadership is investigated by the Inspectorate as part of a legitimacy inspection criteria. The inspection findings provide a sense of the value placed upon high-quality leadership and how it contributes to the policing mission and further reading here is recommended. The College of Policing (2015a) leadership review identifies ethical and professional leadership as being one of the core tenets required to deliver a diverse and legitimate service that meets the needs of a globalized society.

Baroness Casey's (2023) review into the professional standards and cultural behaviours within the Metropolitan Police Service (MPS) identified significant leadership failings that suggest there is an organizational disconnect. The review findings have contributed to an assessment that the MPS is, in fact, institutionally racist, sexist, and homophobic. Importantly, Baroness Casey has also commented on the potential for professional failings to extend beyond the MPS boundaries. This has served as a timely reminder to all about the need for high quality leadership within policing to support the ongoing ambition to police by consent. In response to the Casey report the Home Secretary Suella Braverman remarked 'It is clear that there have been serious failures of culture and leadership in the Metropolitan Police' (Jacques, 2023b).

8.2.1 Professional standards

Kotter (2012) remarked that hierarchal organizations, such as the police, are defined by leadership strategies that develop professional skills and abilities. This suggests that ethical leadership values will promote workforce harmony and professional policing confidence. In the case of policing this sense of empowerment encourages police professionals to confidently perform policing duties to the highest possible standards, based upon the development of core role knowledge, skills, and behaviours (see Chapter 2 for professional standards).

Police professionals have a responsibility to publicly demonstrate corporate values. This means that everyone must be able to understand what is expected of them and be able to discharge their duties in a way that promotes the policing values, in effect set a good example for others to follow. On 22 June 2021, the MPS conducted a Gross Misconduct hearing and dismissed a police officer for the use of racist language within a WhatsApp group chat. The hearing outcome was linked to the inappropriate taking of photographs at a crime scene by several police officers employed on a murder crime scene in Wembley (IOPC, 2021). The use of social media platforms must be conducted in a responsible and professional manner to avoid undermining the policing reputation and adversely impacting public confidence levels (CoP, 2014a).

8.3 Effective Leadership

Effective police leadership often aligns to both individual and organizational performance, providing the sense that everyone is a leader and working to a single set of goals (Dobby,

Anscombe, and Tuffin, 2004). The policing goals are defined by the Code of Ethics, a set of behavioural principles and standards (CoP, 2014a). As guardians of the law, police constables are required to maintain the highest levels of professionalism. The College of Policing (2023e) reinforce the sense that police constables are active members of the community who hold public leadership roles. As a pillar of society and a committed leader, a police professional will work with influential community stakeholders, such as local councillors, and groups such as Neighbourhood Watch to address local problems. Statutory partners will often look to the police for leadership and direction. To discharge these duties effectively a police leader needs to understand how a local issue may directly relate to a bigger problem, such as the impact that a County Lines incursion may have locally and how this fits into the regional and national problem profile (NCA, 2021) (see 21.7 for more on county lines).

8.3.1 Leadership impact on well-being

The Strategic Review of Policing in England and Wales showed that leadership styles can impact directly upon the well-being of policing professionals, this being particularly pertinent when police services undergo significant change programmes. Change programmes are a constant within policing, due to a need to adapt and meet societal needs. Muir *et al* (2022) warn that 'top down' leadership styles that impose organizational changes upon a workforce without due consultation, can negatively impact upon the workforce's well-being. To counter this approach the College of Policing (2023g) has undertaken a public consultation exercise that sought to gather opinions about the proposed changes to the Code of Ethics, and its legitimacy to support community needs (Jacques, 2023c). This transformational approach is a good example of leaders listening to a broad range of views and ideas, a process designed to positively impact upon the proposed Code of Ethics final presentation.

8.4 Leadership Theories

Theories of leadership have evolved considerably during the twentieth century and in the most part they tend to focus on the traits and behaviours of leaders (Horner, 1997). Below you will see a summary of some key leadership theories that have emerged during this time. In your police organization you may be able to identify differing styles and approaches to leadership, either directly in your team or within the wider police organization. Take time to reflect on your leadership style and those you work with or report to and consider what style you feel is the most effective.

- **Trait Theory**
  Thomas Carlyle (1795–1881) and Francis Galton's (1822–1911) systematic trait leadership was popular within policing during the period of the 1920s and 1930s (Zaccaro *et al*, 2004; Antonakis, 2011). Trait theory fundamentally believes that people are born with leadership qualities such as intelligence and physical attributes. Trait theories are predominately focused upon individual personas, rather than the impact upon others.
- **Behavioural theory**
  This theory suggests that leaders are not born with leadership qualities, rather there is an emphasis upon how leaders perform their roles with leadership skills developed and learnt. These developed qualities enable leaders to operate flexibly and adapt to changing circumstances. Behavioural leadership qualities include an emphasis upon demonstrating skills that can be replicated by colleagues. Tutor constables and team leaders are often viewed as peer role models.
- **Situational theory**
  Ken Blanchard and Paul Hersey's 1969 situational leadership is based upon four core relational themes: delegating, supporting, coaching, and directing. The four foundational cornerstones are considered theoretical strengths within any values-based organization, such as policing. Situational leadership holds a prominent position within contemporary policing practices, often demonstrated by leaders who modify their behaviours to meet the diverse challenges of others. The movement of policing professionals within the organization is commonplace, situational leaders are therefore able to routinely cope with the personnel changes. Policing teams are adept at coping with changes brought on by external factors, such as a requirement to police large sporting events and public gatherings. These incidents require resources to be removed from core policing responsibilities, thereby creating a capacity challenge as the service seeks to meet demands.

- **Transformational theory**
  Transformational leaders are people who inspire colleagues to work together and achieve shared organizational aims. This sharing approach provides everyone in the team with a voice. The leader is then able to make a decision based upon a range of thoughts and opinions, the inclusive style provides the workforce with a sense of organizational ownership. Transformational leaders often feel confident to empower motivated colleagues who share organizational goals enabling them to continually develop and improve. Steve Jobs has been described as a transformational leader, this is demonstrated by his vision to challenge others to develop and achieve outcomes way beyond their basic capabilities. Transformational leaders work closely with others and listen to their needs; a policing team leader may adopt this approach during a staff 1:2:1 designed to support development and performance.
- **Transactional theory**
  Transactional leadership is a much-maligned approach within contemporary policing. It is viewed as an inflexible, authoritarian approach that can be directive and a change inhibiter, due to the absence of consultation and idea sharing. However, within policing there is a place for this style, particular where decisive directional action is needed to achieve an operational objective. A police constable directing congested road traffic or protecting life at the cordon for a suspicious package may need to use a transactional approach when communicating with members of the public to maintain public safety.

8.5 Characteristics of Good Leadership

The College of Policing's leadership expectations document (CoP, 2023c) sets out what good leadership in policing should look like. Stage one sets out the expectations for all policing professionals:

- An ability to demonstrate core values and inspire others to actively participate in organizational change proposals;
- Positively negotiate and influence community stakeholders to set and deliver local strategic plans (such as a town centre violence reduction ambition);
- Take responsibility for personal development and actively value people, this includes coaching and mentoring;
- Actively support the creation of an inclusive working environment, one that represents the communities served;
- Demonstrate collaborative partnership working skills, both within policing and externally such as with Social Care and National Health Service providers (see 11.4 on partnership working);
- Support service improvements through the use of innovative evidence-based thinking skills (eg problem solving using creative and affordable techniques);
- Create a safe environment for individuals and the organization to benefit from learning opportunities;
- Demonstrate high levels of emotional intelligence that include a clear sense of self-awareness and empathy for others;
- Use reflective and evaluation techniques to explore and understand practical experiences that lead to performance improvement opportunities.

8.6 Leadership Conclusions

In conclusion, diverse and inclusive police leadership is pivotal in achieving public representation and legitimacy to operate, in other words policing by consent. The HMICFRS (2018b) report into police leadership suggests that procedural justice will be delivered by policing role models who make good evidence-based decisions and treat the public fairly. The report also declared that policing leadership should be underpinned by a willingness to be accountable. These are all core tenets of the Code of Ethics (CoP, 2014a). Everyone in the police service has a responsibility to contribute to the overarching policing vision leadership jigsaw and this will only be achieved through collective ambitions to achieve a common policing purpose.

8.7 The Nature of Effective Team Working

A team is small number of people with complementary skills who are committed to a common purpose, performance goals, and approach for which they hold themselves mutually accountable (Katzenbach, 1992). As police officers, team working will be a constant part of daily life and to be able to work effectively with others is paramount to your work. Whether you are conscious of it or not the whole police service works as a team in everyday life.

You will not only need to be part of a team with your police colleagues but also be able to work in partnership with different agencies, such as the Fire and Ambulance Service, Coast Guard, teachers, healthcare professionals, etc. Without the support of others around you, building and working as an effective team would not be possible.

Occasionally, there can be disagreements between team members or with a supervisor. It is important to resolve disagreement diplomatically to avoid undermining police responses, as this might otherwise result in poor performance. Unless conflicts are resolved, a sense of distrust is likely to develop between team members and supervisors, and they will no longer be able to work together effectively. Individual interpersonal skills are important here to avoid conflict as they can help people to understand the views and opinions of others and to respond in an appropriate manner. (See Chapter 9 for methods to overcome conflict.)

Core Policing Values and Behaviours

8.7.1 Five stages of team development

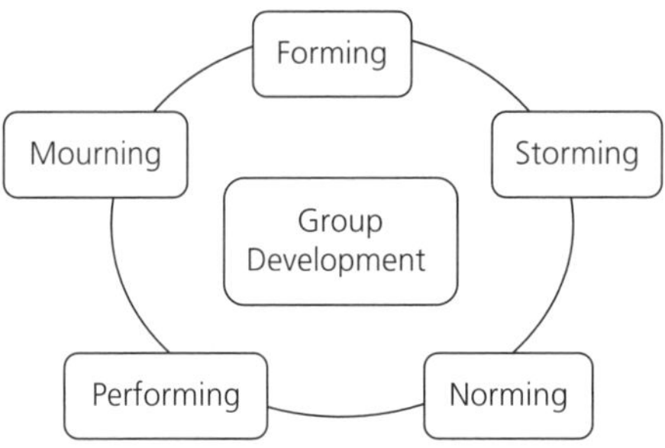

Source: Adapted from the Bruce Tuckman Development Model

The model above was originally created by Tuckman (1964). He identified that it was too much to expect a new team to come together and work seamlessly straight away. He originally suggested that new teams go through a set of stages as they develop: forming; storming; norming; performing. He later updated his original model adding a further stage—adjourning or mourning (Tuckman and Jenson, 1977). Rickards and Moger (2000) went on to rework this model and ask two further questions, 'What mechanisms are at play when a team fails to achieve expected performance?' and 'What mechanisms lead to outstanding performance?' To attempt to answer these questions they developed a 'two-barrier model to creative performance in teams'. It is important to keep in mind from this model that an effective team needs to work through the barriers. A team will fail if it gets stuck behind the first barrier and remains in the 'Forming' and 'Storming' stages.

Trust is another key component of teamwork, regulating the ability of people in the team to interact with other team members and influencing the information flow between parties. Trust is deeply connected to successful team performance and has been declared a key component of effective teams, because without proper communication and collaboration, both of which are influenced by trust, teams cannot function properly (Morita & Burns, 2014). Having a lack of trust between team members, and between team members and their supervisors, can be one of the biggest barriers to effective team working. Consider how you would tackle trust issues. How would you feel having to address such issues? Who might you turn to for support?

Doyle (2008) completed a study looking at both the barriers and facilitators of a multidisciplinary team working within nursing which can also be related to policing. These include:

- Poor working relationships
- Lack of awareness and appreciation of roles and responsibilities of others
- Limited time and resources
- Overlapping of roles and duplication of service
- Poor communication

- Lack of collaboration
- Lack of trust and confidence in the abilities of others
- Increased workload
- Constant reorganization

8.7.2 Strategies to maintain or improve relations within a team

The best way to promote team success is not to focus on individual efforts but on overall team performance (Katzenbach & Smith, 1992). Group morale is an effective way of maintaining and improving relationships within a team.

Think about strategies you may be able to employ to improve working relationships within your team. Think about the teams you have been in before joining the police and whether you can identify something that worked for you then. You will see that there are a number of factors that can influence how teams perform and that it is the individuals that make the teamwork. Throughout your learning and your careers, you will be part of many teams from your whole constabulary and its partners to the shift members you work with and the officer you are crewed with. Being aware of the barriers and what makes an effective team will help you flourish.

8.8 Effective Communication Skills

8.8.1 Verbal communication

Research conducted by Mehrabian *et al* (1967) suggested that only 7 per cent of the communication message is verbal, whilst 55 per cent is visual and 38 per cent is vocal (tone, inflections, etc); this became widely known as the 3 V's of communication. This myth still prevails today but has since been discredited by Mehrabian himself and others.

> Suppose I want to tell you that the eraser you are looking for is in the second right-hand drawer of my desk in my third-floor office. How could anyone contend that the verbal part of this message is only 7% of the message?
>
> (Mehrabian (1995), as cited in Lapakko (1997), p 65)

Language is of course hugely important when communicating with others, this includes the correct use of spoken English rather than using slang, together with other factors such as the pitch, tone, volume, and terminology used as these can all have an impact on the message being conveyed (Rocci and De Saussure, 2016). For police professionals this varies based on the situation, for example, it is common within different professional environments for occupation-specific terms to be used. Policing is no different and language is often adapted that may be understood by other officers, but not by the public or other partner agencies. The following Airwave update will mean more to the control room than it will to the partner subject to abuse: 'Misper, appears to have gone AWOL, ASNT so far, is NPAS free? They've TWOC'ed neighbour's car, index Yankee Delta 60 X-ray, Charlie Zulu, disappeared after a DA incident, likely DiC....'. It's vital that the victim is updated in language they will understand.

Language should be inclusive and appropriately tailored to the audience, for example, you may speak in softer tones and simpler terms to a child victim, and more procedurally when dealing with a regular offender who may be very familiar with detention and custody processes. Differences in language use may also vary when dealing with our diverse communities (eg with non-English speaking people requiring an interpreter). There will also be differences in language and terminology when dealing with our partners, such as those in education, health, local authorities, who will also have their own occupation-specific terms and phrases; it is important that we do not assume that they understand our occupation-specific language, just as we will probably not understand theirs.

Adapting your verbal skills to the audience demonstrates professionalism and excellent communication abilities.

8.8.2 Active listening

Good police leadership requires active listening and this is a fundamental skill for student police officers to develop. Active listening skills can be difficult for some people, even those well versed in it may find it difficult in certain policing situations such as a violent arrest, but it is important to try to always engage these skills to understand what is being said.

Hoppe (2014) suggests that effective active listening skills can be developed using a 6 stage cyclical process, specifically, this technique involves taking time to **listen carefully**. This means giving the person you are talking to your full attention; put down any distractions such as your phone, radio, or paperwork and look them in the eye so it shows that you are ready to listen to what is being said (Anderson, 2008). Listen with an **open mind**, this means approaching a conversation without any preconceived biases, being receptive to new ideas, and suspending judgement, so even if you think you are dealing with a burglary victim, listen with an open mind as they may go on to disclose more serious offences (Teng *et al*, 2020). Once the message has been passed do not **respond** immediately, this will allow you to process their message, and importantly it shows respect, meaning that you are taking what they have said seriously. This is particularly useful when dealing with vulnerable victims as, although you may have heard similar disclosures from others in the past, you are listening to their message sincerely and helping to build a relationship (Teng *et al*, 2020). At this point in the conversation, you will undoubtedly have many questions that you would like them to **clarify**, it is important that you have not interrupted before now as it can demonstrate disrespect and inadvertently distract the person, so that full disclosure is not achieved. However, it is appropriate to use encouragers when they are speaking such as nods, looking them in the eye and minimal encouragers such as 'mmmh' as these show that you remain engaged in the conversation (Drollinger & Comer, 2013). Then it should be **summarized** and **shared** to check understanding, this is a process whereby you take the key themes or main points and condense them down into a shorter version, removing irrelevant information. For example, a witness describing events '*so from what I saw, a man I know called Martin, ran into the middle of the road shouting "it bit me" he was being followed by a big black dog who was barking, I think that the dog belongs to Mrs Jones*', summarized by you as '*You saw Martin run into the road, followed by Mrs Jones's black dog barking, he shouted "it bit me"*'. Sharing avoids misunderstandings and ensures that you have fully grasped the speaker's message while allowing the other party to correct any errors in the summary (McNaughton *et al*, 2007; Hoppe, 2014).

Consider this active listening scenario. When dealing with a household that frequently reports domestic assaults, you can see that one party has a bloody nose and they state, 'Andi did it'. A poor active listening example would be not to acknowledge what has been said and using your radio to arrange for the partner to be arrested. This would not only demonstrate poor listening skills but would show a lack of empathy or ability to gather information. Conversely, active listening could be demonstrated in the same situation by making eye contact with the victim, devoting time to accurately hearing their account, asking clarification questions, and not jumping to any conclusions before condensing the account down to key points. By doing this you are able to establish a connection, gather information, question assumptions, and accurately recount events, and you discover that the bloody nose was caused by tripping over Andi's shoes, not by being assaulted.

8.8.3 Non-verbal communication

Findings suggest that non-verbal cues represent two-thirds of communication (Brook and Servatka, 2016). Police officers often find themselves in situations where they need to quickly interpret and understand situations they are faced with. The way you present and display your own body language is as important as trying to interpret that of others. Body language is described as communication using gestures, posture, positions, and distance, either consciously or subconsciously (Lewis, 2012). In simple terms, it is communication through movements and gestures of our head, face, eyes, hands, legs, arms, etc. Most of us pick up on the body language of others, but we are less perceptive about how we display our own. For example, if an officer is speaking to a witness and they start to yawn and rub their eyes most officers would associate that with tiredness and may ask if they needed to take a break from giving their statement, conversely, think of your witness's perception of you if you display similar expressions, these could be construed as you appearing disinterested and lacking empathy.

The tone of voice, together with pitch and inflection are all extensions of body language and when joined with other physical movements of the body can create a strong message used to convey one's innermost thoughts, feelings, and emotions (Brook and Servatka, 2016). As part of your officer safety training, you will have learned that body language can exhibit important warning signs of impending danger. Fridin *et al* (2009) demonstrated that when perceiving angry and fearful body postures, participants mainly gazed at the hands and the arms, whereas with happy body postures, they focused on the head. Body language can also reflect a person's vulnerability. Imagine visiting an address where you see that a child is sitting quietly in a crouched position and notice how they flinch when the adult you are engaging with goes near them. This would be a significant warning sign that needs to be explored more fully as a safeguarding risk.

It has been observed that adopting similar body postures and mannerisms communicates a positive attitude, often described as mirroring (Lewis, 2012). This is the concept whereby the listener physically and behaviourally mirrors the other's body language, a technique seen as being able to build trust with other people (Leonardo, 2020). A student police officer could use such techniques (in a discreet manner) when communicating with witnesses, suspects, victims, or other members of the public. For example, imagine a resident is trying to explain that a group of youths is regularly causing antisocial problems, the witness is calm and has their arms down by their side occasionally pointing down the road to the local youth club. You may find yourself mirroring some aspect of this body language to show that you are listening—you might have your arms relaxed too and not folded in a defensive position—so remember to monitor your own body language, which needs to be appropriate in the circumstances.

8.8.4 Empathy

Cuff *et al* (2016, p 145) describe empathy as 'understanding another's emotions through perspective taking', distinguishing it from sympathy as 'intentionally reacting emotionally'. The difference is that in certain situations a police officer should show empathy for those who are vulnerable or in crisis by trying to understand it from their perspective; the term 'walking in their shoes' aptly captures empathy. By contrast, sympathy is displaying feelings of pity for a victim who may be experiencing trauma by matching their emotion, such as crying, which would be inappropriate for a police officer.

Perceiving events from the point of view of another person (Abanonu, 2018) is vital for police officers as the incidents they deal with can impact significantly on witnesses and victims and can lead to lasting trauma; lack of police empathy can compound this trauma (Skogan, 2006). A police officer should try to grasp how a victim feels after an incident but at the same time have the capacity to regulate their own perceptions in order to act professionally, recognizing that this is likely to be the first time this victim has been subject to crime. In contrast, as a police officer, you may have seen this type of event many times before and may not feel personally affected (Inzunza, 2022) (see Chapter 6 for mental wellbeing). Imagine dealing with a range of different incidents and reflect on the levels of empathy required. For example, a member of the public is involved in a minor damage-only road traffic accident. Your first consideration will be for their safety, recording any necessary evidence, and moving vehicles to allow the road to reopen, so what empathy do you need to show? Even though you may perceive this as a minor event it may prove to be highly emotive for those involved; the car may be written off, how will they get their children to and from school and how can they now get to work, do they face losing their job, will they experience flashbacks? Reflect on how you would like your family member to be professionally dealt with if it were them involved. Whilst it is not your responsibility to resolve these issues, it still means that you need to be empathetic with those involved as the impact may be wider than initially thought. A second example might be dealing with a first-account from a rape victim, this will be a very emotive, sensitive, and distressing time for this person, probably the worst time of their lives and perhaps their first experience of crime, so how can you try to perceive their point of view and feelings at this time? You could imagine how you would like to be professionally dealt with at this time, and what would be your key considerations. Most of us would like to be dealt with compassionately and empathetically and not just as another victim.

The Competency and Values Framework (CVF) (CoP, 2023h) sets out nationally recognized behaviours for police officers describing empathy as a vital skill, particularly when dealing with those who are vulnerable. Empathy is a key skill for promoting and fostering relationships with victims, witnesses, suspects, communities, partners, and other agencies and is critical across policing for core responsibilities such as gathering information and intelligence, securing evidence, and suspect cooperation. For further areas relating to empathy see Chapter 18 Criminal Justice, Chapter 19 Victims and Witnesses, and Chapter 20 Vulnerability and Risk.

8.8.5 Building rapport

Establishing rapport is useful in developing and fostering communication with victims, witnesses, partners, and team members. Defining rapport Vallano and Schreiber-Compo (2015) suggest that it involves positive engagement that results in mutual respect and a productive relationship. Alison and Alison (2020) argue that a solid and adaptable set of interpersonal skills, as well as the capacity to empathize and change, are necessary for rapport, with the most difficult of all being that it requires you to focus on listening to and understanding other people rather than your own agenda.

There are a number of key factors that are essential to building rapport, the first few require you as a police officer to be genuine, trustworthy, personable, and professional. Police officers often define rapport as the way they interact with a victim or witness to forge a connection or bond that makes them feel at ease (Kim *et al,* 2020). We all know people who make us feel at ease in their company for a variety of reasons such as previous dealings, the kindness of their manner, their positive and professional approach. These are the type of rapport skills that foster good relationships.

Building rapport is considered a principle component of the PEACE investigative interviewing process (Milne and Bull, 1999). For further reading on PEACE see Chapter 13.

8.8.6 Negotiation

The FBI (Dalfonzo and Deitrick, 2015) developed a mnemonic to remind hostage and crisis negotiators of the key steps to negotiation. These considerations can be useful in other aspects of policing such as dealing with those who are aggressive, in crisis, and otherwise unable to think clearly. The steps below give structure and thinking time for both you and the other person and have subsequently been adopted by the College of Policing (2020d).

Minimal Encouragers—using verbal and non-verbal communication: use single or double words to show you have heard what has been said (not 'okay' as this could be construed as you agreeing to something) and a nod of the head.
Open questions—those that elicit a reply other than 'no' or 'yes', such as why, when, how, etc.
Reflection—echo phrases used by the person; it demonstrates that you have listened to what they have said.
Effective pauses—this is hugely important, as it allows the person to disclose more or vent their anger, it also gives you thinking time and makes you appear confident.
Paraphrase—condense what has been said but in your own words to show that you have not only listened but understood what they have said. This allows them to challenge or correct you.
'I' messages—start your sentence with 'I' to make the message more personal and to build rapport.
Emotional labelling—'You appear to be angry' shows empathy.
Summary—conclude the negotiation by summarizing what has been said and agreed upon to cement the negotiation.

8.8.7 Conflict management

During the early part of your training, you will cover practical conflict management skills as part of your scenario learning. As part of this you will also be taught key models that will assist you. These will include the Code of Ethics (CoP 2014a), National Decision Model (NDM) (CoP, 2023b), Five-Step Appeal, LEAPS (CoP, 2020d), and Betari's Box (CoP, 2016b), all of which are designed to help you practise as an operational police officer. See Chapter 9 Managing Conflict for more details.

8.8.8 Emotional intelligence

Emotional intelligence (EI) is considered to be a combination of self-awareness, self-management, social awareness, and relationship management (Goleman, 1995; Wicks *et al*, 2023).

- **Self-awareness**; recognizing your own emotions and understanding how they affect thoughts and behaviours.
- **Self-management**; regulating and managing your own thoughts, emotions, and behaviours in a positive way.

- **Motivation**; motivated for internal reasons rather than external factors such as wealth or recognition.
- **Empathy**; how others feel and how you would feel in their position.
- **Relationship management**; teamwork, good communication skills, maintaining strong relationships, inspiring others.

Research has demonstrated that police officers with a high EI have improved decision-making abilities if they understand themselves, are able to weigh up the options using the NDM (CoP, 2023b), keep an open mind, and remove all irrelevant emotions from their decision (Abdel-Fattah, 2020). For example, a police officer with high emotional intelligence is more likely to calm a distressed person in a potentially critical situation to ensure everyone's safety. Imagine you respond to a call about a person who is threatening to kill or seriously harm themselves, using the NDM, you would consider your options which could include the use of force to control the distressed person or taking time to build rapport with them. Instead of initially using force, you can apply your emotional intelligence and approach the situation calmly and empathetically. For example, you might start by giving them your first name, asking theirs, and attempt to understand what is causing them distress. Then listen actively, show genuine concern and empathy (creating a relationship), and use effective communication to reassure them that you are there to help and support them. It can help the victim to talk about their future to remove the focus on the here and now and to demonstrate that they can overcome this obstacle. By using your emotional intelligence in this way, you can help prevent a potentially harmful situation from escalating, build trust and rapport with the individual, and ensure that everyone involved remains safe and supported. Further support can be requested from crisis negotiators and mental health professionals who can offer more specialist advice and longer-term care.

The College of Policing (2023d) highlights EI as a key policing skill as it demonstrates that officers are culturally sensitive and able to understand different perspectives with compassion and warmth. The history of policing has demonstrated that it has not always been as culturally sensitive as it should; the Brixton Riots in 1981 (Scarman, 1982) were a result of poor police training and lack of cultural awareness, the Macpherson Report (1999) after the murder of Stephen Lawrence, described the Metropolitan Police as 'institutionally racist' and yet despite the introduction of the Equality Act (2010) and the Code of Ethics (CoP 2014a), a report by Baroness Casey (2023) found 'institutional racism, misogyny, and homophobia' in the Metropolitan Police Service. Critics may say that police cultural sensitivities are getting worse, not better; analysis of the Casey review in The Times (Hamilton, 2023) refers to the organization as 'rotten'.

The College of Policing (2023d) believes that cultural awareness is important because it helps create and maintain public trust and confidence in policing. Being culturally aware requires police officers to act with sensitivity and compassion, recognizing that people have different needs, values, and beliefs, based on their cultural background and that we should strive to embrace those differences rather than oppose them (Pepper and McGrath, 2020). Examples of cultural difference include different religions and beliefs, the way people choose to dress, differing races and genders, and even the way people choose to prepare and eat food. For further reading see Chapter 7 on Valuing Diversity and Inclusion.

8.8.9 Getting it wrong

It is important to understand that there are also risks associated with getting your communication style wrong, such risks could include:

- Misunderstandings—This could stem from a lack of communication and could lead to some serious issues further down the line. In one case a member of the public reported someone walking along a dual carriageway at night, the dispatcher incorrectly recorded the location on the dual carriageway and attending officers were unable to find the individual. Subsequently, another member of the public reported a second sighting of them on the dual carriageway, however, incorrect information was again passed to officers who ended their search before the correct junction and the male was subsequently killed by a passing vehicle. The Independent Office for Police Conduct (IOPC, 2023a) investigated the police response to the incident and determined that mistakes had been made due to misunderstandings and incorrect recording.

- Missed Opportunities—Victims or witnesses may not provide certain details due to either misunderstandings or lack of trust, and police may miss opportunities to engage with vulnerable people. A serious case review (Lock, 2013) identified missed opportunities in the case of Daniel Pelka who was subsequently murdered by his mother and her partner. The review identified significant occasions when police, social workers, and teachers failed to act on the recognizable abuse and neglect Daniel suffered before his death.
- Mistrust—Withholding important information or communicating inaccurate information, or over-aggressive behaviour or body language inappropriate to the situation would give rise to mistrust. In one case a suspect had their clothing removed for a search in custody, during which time they alleged they were sexually assaulted. The IOPC (2023b) investigation noted that the case papers failed to record who conducted the search which increased mistrust in policing with a sense that there was something to hide.
- Unnecessary Conflict—A lack of understanding of what is happening or what is expected of somebody due to poor communication is likely to cause unnecessary conflict. Within policing this could also result in people being harmed if things were to escalate unnecessarily—an example could include the arrest of a suspect where the arresting officer needs to clearly explain instructions the suspect should follow so that the handcuffs can be applied. If the officer fails to give clear instruction this could quickly escalate if the suspect were confused and scared by what was taking place and ultimately resisted arrest.

To help mitigate some of these risks you need to remain aware of your communication style and be ready to adapt it where necessary. If a style you have adopted is not working, then try something else. A style that may have been effective with one person, or group of people, may not be as effective with others.

In the long-term, if people feel their interactions with the police are negative, this can damage their confidence in the service and make them reluctant to come forward with information and intelligence or make them less likely to cooperate with the police in the future. To minimize any risks, you should always be aware of how your communication style is being received by the people around you and be prepared to be flexible. Be mindful of your personal safety if you feel a situation is escalating and consider the powers and options available to you, but always try to ensure that you prevent an incident from reaching this point if possible. This is why developing effective communication skills and being able to read the body language of those around you is an essential skill for a police officer.

8.9 Barriers to Communication

A barrier or enabler to effective communication can be the attitude and behaviour of a person and is demonstrated in the Betari's Box model (discussed in 9.2.2). This outlines how a circular pattern can occur between the attitude and behaviour of two individuals that may influence either positive or negative outcomes. For example, this may be evidenced by the signals individuals send, such as emotional expression, voice tone, use of particular words, and actions towards others. Importantly, Betari's Box demonstrates how your attitude will influence and inform your behaviours when communicating with another person. These circular behavioural patterns can cause people to get stuck in subconscious loops. Recognizing it is the first step to addressing it. To change the behaviour of others, first, be aware of your own attitude and how it affects your behaviour. Then notice how your behaviour affects other people. You can break the unconscious loop by spotting how the behaviour of others makes you feel and refusing to let it affect your attitude without first censoring this process (Ishoy, 2016).

The following areas can block or seriously undermine effective communication:

a. **Unconscious bias**—refers to the attitudes, stereotypes, or prejudices that people hold at a subconscious level, which can affect their behaviour and decisions without their awareness (Oberai and Anand, 2018). In policing this could include associating certain neighbourhoods or communities with crime and disorder. This can lead to over-policing of these areas and a focus on punitive measures rather than community-oriented policing strategies. Alternatively, it can lead to under-policing or avoiding an area because 'they never tell us anything so why should we bother!'

b. **Prejudice**—a feeling of resentment without substance or experience (Brown, 2010), for example, if an officer believes that all individuals who wear hoodies are potential criminals, they may stop and search individuals who are wearing hoodies, even if there is no evidence of criminal activity. But what does it mean to be racist or sexist, for example, or to be prejudiced against a particular demographic group? Munton (2021) suggests it necessitates three aspects, firstly, a particular cognitive attitude that the group in question is in some way inferior, secondly, a negative feeling of hostility or disgust toward the group, and finally, negative conduct towards that group (the three components are often used interchangeably).
c. **Direct discrimination**—is where someone is treated less favourably than others because of a protected characteristic such as age, disability, race, marriage/civil partnership, and sex (Equality Act, 2010). For further information see Chapter 7 Valuing Diversity and Inclusion.
d. **Indirect discrimination**—refers to a situation where a policy, practice, or rule that appears neutral or fair on the surface has a disproportionate and negative impact on a particular group of people. This can occur when a policy or practice is applied uniformly to everyone but unintentionally puts certain individuals or groups at a disadvantage (Equality Act, 2010). For further information see Chapter 7 Valuing Diversity and Inclusion.
e. **Stereotyping**—Stereotyping is the process of making assumptions or generalizations about a person or group based on limited or incomplete information, such as their appearance, gender, race, ethnicity, religion, or other characteristics. Stereotypes are often reinforced as a result of socialization between like-minded groups, through the media and social media, and language (Dovidio, 2010).

8.10 Communication to Control Situations

As a police officer you will be expected to lead and control many different situations, some you may feel comfortable dealing with and others that may be new to you. These situations will often involve you taking assertively control to bring order or engaging in a difficult conversation. A typical example of combining all three skills is dealing with a suspected drink/drug driver. Suspecting the driver is impaired you will need to stop the vehicle, prevent the driver from escaping, and complete the drink/drug process; taking control. If the test is positive you will need to arrest the driver, this often prompts emotive outpourings about losing livelihoods, family, and friends; difficult conversations. Suppose the driver refuses to cooperate with your requests to leave their vehicle, this will require you to be assertive, if this does not work you will move to the physical control stage; assertive and taking control.

8.10.1 Taking control of a situation

Police officers have many skills which combined to good effect will allow them to take control of most situations; however, often the key skill behind the implementation is communication. The public expects professional police services to be able to control chaotic situations like public order incidents where order needs to be restored to allow the public to return to a state of normality. Cases where control is less clear can include domestic abuse incidents; often officers are faced with a couple screaming at each other. The police cannot simply walk away but need to take positive action to control the situation and bring the incident to a close.

8.10.2 Difficult conversations: with the public

In your professional policing practice you will have many difficult conversations—sometimes you may experience many of these during a single shift, which can be exhausting. Do remember to keep a check on your own physical and mental wellbeing as it can be easily overlooked, particularly when caring for others. The College of Policing (2023f) has produced an excellent guide to wellbeing (search 'College of Policing Wellbeing') which draws together some useful information on the National Police Wellbeing Service and Oscar Kilo as well as guidance on responding to trauma in policing, see also Chapter 6 of this book on Wellbeing and Resilience.

So, what is a difficult conversation with the public? Suppose you inform a parent that their child has been arrested for a sexual offence, this will potentially elicit many different types of responses, which may include anger aimed at you—'how dare you arrest them, they cannot possibly have done anything wrong!', to feelings of despair, embarrassment, and thoughts of recrimination toward the family and its standing, to the feeling of public humiliation and ruined future career prospects for their child. Think about how you would go about delivering this message.

Or suppose you attend the scene of a road traffic collision and see the body of a teenager with fatal injuries. With the arrival of other services, you are dispatched to deliver the death message to parents. You recognize that you have just experienced a traumatic incident but you need to deliver a professional message. Below is a process you could use to structure your conversation.

- **Plan** how you intend to deliver the message and think about how you will structure it. You may place yourself in the position of the other party, how would you like this message to be delivered?
- **Be professional**, empathetic, and compassionate when dealing with emotive messages, remember empathy, not sympathy.
- **Slow the delivery**—try not to speak too fast, breathe, and leave pauses to allow your message to be heard and processed.
- **Listen carefully** to what is being said back and answer any questions before moving on.
- **Handle reactions** carefully and sensitively. Reactions will vary from person to person so do not try to second guess how someone may react to receiving a death message.
- **Anticipate difficult questions**—Who did they sexually assault, what type of sexual assault, will they go to prison? What fatal injuries did they have, can I see the body, can I go to the scene? Think of the type of questions you would ask if you had the same message delivered to you, speak to a supervisor beforehand to seek advice on how to answer them.
- **Stay on message**—make sure that you have said what you need to before you leave.

8.10.3 Difficult conversations: internal

Handling difficult internal conversations with fellow team members can also be challenging so it's important to employ the same strategies, particularly displaying your professionalism and listening skills. Knight (2015) suggests that when engaging with colleagues a slightly different mindset should be applied. Rather than thinking of it as a difficult conversation think of it more as a positive and constructive professional discussion. The other factors highlighted above, however, are equally important when speaking with colleagues.

The Casey Review (2023) has exposed significant internal concerns in policing (Metropolitan Police), often as a result of internal conversations not taking place, for example, supervisors and colleagues are known to have failed to challenge racist, misogynistic, and homophobic language in the workplace, when there is both a moral, ethical, and professional requirement to do so (CoP, 2014a). The report also highlights instances where initial internal conversations have taken place but have not been followed up, reports of bullying not being investigated with the accuser ostracized by colleagues, creating a toxic environment where others are fearful of speaking out.

Research has shown that constructive work conversations generate positive well-being, feelings of closeness, shared effort, and productivity when professionals engage collaboratively to explore new ideas and solutions (Reis, 2017). This is particularly true in policing where there are new and complex challenges to resolve each day. Difficult conversations where people disagree with one another or introduce something controversial can also foster good feelings in the workplace (Grimshaw, 1990; Zhang *et al*, 2018) and deliver positive results if dealt with in a supportive way (Stone *et al*, 2010; Tjosvold *et al*, 2014). This can often be useful when there are opposite views on something as working together it may be possible to arrive at a mutually agreeable third option which you may even find is a better way of dealing with it in future.

8.10.4 Assertiveness and taking control

The public expects that when required to do so, the police will be assertive and take control, this however must be lawful, proportionate, and necessary. When the police attend almost any incident, they will be subject to community observation, often being recorded on mobile phones, so it is professionally important to get the balance right.

Being assertive and taking control can often be misinterpreted, for example, edited video clips are often posted to social media depicting police violence during an arrest. However, most omit the initial stages of the interaction where police officers are perhaps trying to be balanced and fair, before needing to escalate the situation; clipped footage of a suspect being batoned or tasered can be labelled as police 'losing control' but as long as the tactic is lawful, proportionate, and necessary then it is the right thing to do to bring the situation under control. If the police do not employ assertive tactics, when necessary, then they run the risk of being viewed as being ineffective. It's a difficult balance to strike.

The majority of police interactions with the public are reactive calls for assistance, calls where society requires the police to intervene with a view that they should remain present until it is resolved. So how does society view proactive police action such as stop and search or a routine vehicle stop? In these instances, police are assertive and taking control but it can be viewed by that individual and wider community as a citizen being 'picked on' by the state, often eliciting more defensive responses, and perceived as the police being aggressive, discriminatory, and discourteous (Quinton, 2019). These police tactics should still be employed if they are proportionate, legal, and necessary—noting that responses may be more emotive.

9 Managing Conflict

9.1 Introduction

This chapter outlines the police constable's role in managing conflict. Conflict is an inevitable part of human interaction, but how an officer deals with conflict, particularly with members of the public and colleagues, will affect the officer's operational effectiveness and decision-making. In this chapter, conflict is understood as a process of disagreement.

Managing conflict appropriately and effectively is an essential skill in a police officer's arsenal and can literally save a person's life, including your own. Beyond being operationally effective, 'Managing Conflict in a Professional Policing Context' is also a named Area of Operational Competence required to achieve Full Operational Competence (FOC). As discussed in previous chapters (see 3.2.6), one of the founding principles of policing in Britain is 'policing by consent' (Reiner, 2000).

The topics covered in this chapter contribute to learning required for the National Policing Curriculum particularly in the subject areas of 'Understanding the Police Constable Role', 'Valuing Diversity and Inclusion', 'Maintaining Professional Standards', 'Problem Solving', 'Decision-Making and Discretion', 'Vulnerability and Risk', 'Policing Communities', 'Communication Skills', and 'Managing Conflict'.

There are two steps to resolving conflict (Furlong, 2020):

1. Understand the origins of the conflict.
2. Considering the conflict's origins, take action to manage the conflict.

This chapter provides you the knowledge and understanding to complete these steps *deliberately* rather than relying on your unconscious reactions (Furlong, 2020). To complete step one, you must understand the theoretical frameworks that underpin conflict management, origins of conflict, and responses to conflict. Completing step two requires, in the context of policing, an understanding of the relationship between conflict and personal safety training. Finally, the chapter will reinforce previous learning of reflective practice and the importance of accurately recording decisions and actions.

It is important to remember that conflict is not inherently bad. Appropriately managed conflict may reveal an outcome that suits everyone's needs, lead to more nuanced and holistic approaches to problem solving and decision-making, and improve relationships between individuals.

Conflict occurs in daily life—it may be external, between police officers, a police officer and member of the public, members of the public; or it may be internal, as in between different thoughts or beliefs in one individual. In this chapter, the concept of conflict will largely be explained in terms of conflict between individuals, however, it is important to remember that conflict can also include an inanimate item. For example, an officer may decide to use discretion (see 4.2.2) in dealing with a particular issue or individual even though the issue or individual's behaviour or actions *conflict* with policy or practice. In these situations, the officer must be able to accurately explain and record their decision-making. Managing conflict is an essential part of decision-making and may inform discretion as well as outcomes drawn from the National Decision Model (see 4.2.1).

9.2 Theoretical Frameworks of Conflict

Theoretical frameworks help illustrate the relationship between conflict management and policing principles, the types and cycles of conflict and how these might inflame or diffuse situations, and the critical role self-awareness plays in navigating conflict.

9.2.1 Conflict management and policing principles

Appropriate and effective conflict management is a vital part of achieving the public's consent to exercise policing authority, and ensure procedural justice. For example, a member of the public who witnesses a police officer see red in a conflict and use force inappropriately, or even get into a screaming-match with another person, will likely have a different and probably negative view of police officers generally because of how that police officer mismanaged the conflict. This experience may make it less likely that that member of public reports a crime in the future or assists police in their enquiries in future, creating a ripple effect from that one negative experience.

9.2.2 Types and cycles of conflict

As discussed in 9.1, conflict can be internal, as in within one person (intra-personal), or external, as in between people (inter-personal). These dynamics can also be applied to groups of individuals, whereby conflict within a group of people (intra-group conflict) contrasts with conflict between groups of people (inter-group conflict).

The College of Policing created the model of Betari's Box to explain how individuals may enter and become stuck in a cycle of reacting and responding to another person's behaviours and attitudes rather than taking a step back from the situation and observing the situational dynamics and forming a considered response.

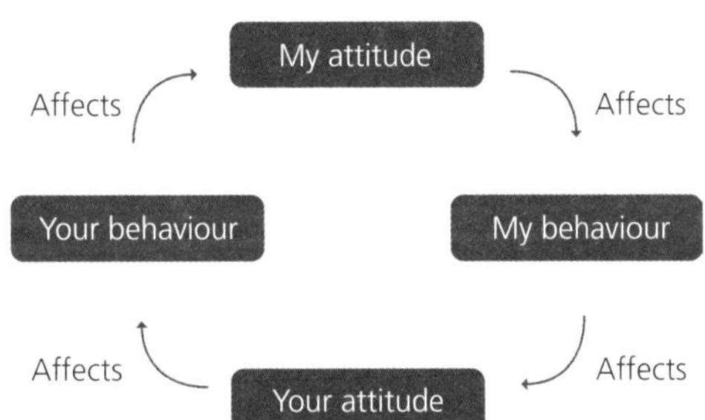

Source: Conflict Management Skills (CoP, 2020c). © College of Policing Limited (UK). Reproduced with permission under licence SF00300.

In this chapter, two models will be used to explain how individuals approach conflict: the Drama Triangle and the Thomas-Kilmann Conflict Mode Instrument (TKI). The Drama Triangle is discussed first because it presents three types of negative behaviours that may compound or prolong conflict without appropriate intervention. In the Drama Triangle, someone needs to interrupt the cycle and provide an escape for the victim, rescuer, and persecutor. The 'victim' feels or acts like a victim and may use blame (of the persecutor) to get their way. A victim seeks a 'rescuer' to resolve the issue or at least obtain sympathy, but the rescuer's involvement embeds the victim's identity as the 'victim', incapable of independence. The persecutor is resentful of the victim and the problems they bring to the conflict (Wright *et al*, 2018).

Some police officers might feel co--mpelled to embody the role of the 'rescuer' when they attend an incident. But, this could have negative consequences for the victim, persecutor, the individual police officer, the policing organization, and the community.

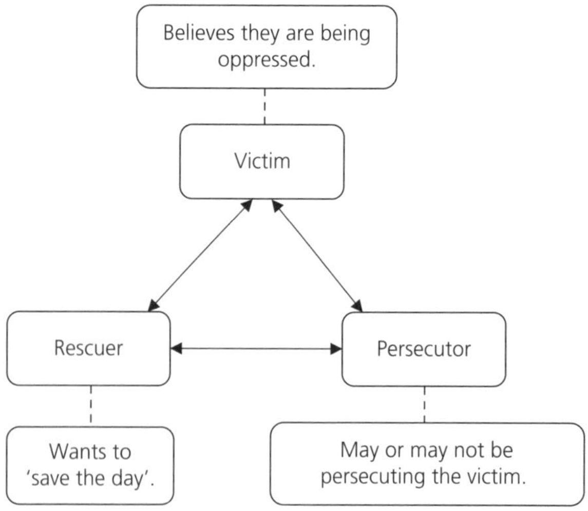

Source: Adapted from Wright, Etchells, and Watson (2018) 'Meeting in the Middle: Eight Strategies for Conflict Mediation in Your Classroom', Kappa Delta Pi Record, 54(1), pp 30–35.

The second model, and one of the most widely used in understanding conflict management styles, is the Thomas-Kilmann Conflict Mode Instrument (TKI). The TKI includes both positive and negative conflict management types, totalling five: competing, collaborating, compromising, avoiding, and accommodating. According to TKI, an individual's behaviour in a conflict is measured according to two dimensions: assertiveness and cooperativeness, whereby assertiveness focuses on 'attempting to satisfy one's own concerns', and cooperativeness is driven by 'attempting to satisfy the other person's concerns' (Thomas and Kilmann, 1977). A *competing* mode is one in which an individual tries to fulfil their own objective at the expense of another person. A *collaborating* approach tries to find a win-win or a positive outcome for all parties of the conflict. A *compromising* method tries to find a satisfactory result that achieves at least a part of all parties' issues. A person using an *avoiding* tactic would circumnavigate the conflict and not address any of the issues. An *accommodating* approach, the opposite of the *competing* mode, would prioritize another person's concerns over their own. The TKI asks respondents 30 questions and scenarios to determine the respondent's conflict management style (Schaubhut, 2007).

TASK 1 Use the graphic below to match the conflict management type with the dimensions. While you're doing this, consider which conflict management type describes how you handle conflict.

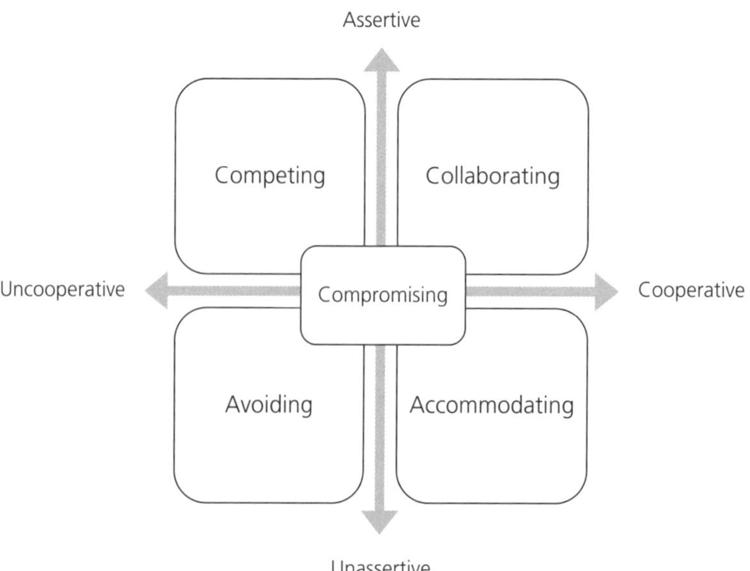

Source: Adapted from Schaubhut, 2007. Thomas-Kilmann conflict mode instrument. CPP Research Department. Adapted from 'Conflict and Conflict Management' by Kenneth Thomas in The Handbook of Industrial and Organizational Psychology, edited by Marvin Dunnette (Chicago: Rand McNally, 1976).

9.2.3 Self-awareness

Self-awareness is the knowledge that you experience as an individual and your thoughts, or reactions are specific to you and may be different from another person. Emotional awareness, self-regulation, active listening, and communication skills are key in determining success in a conflict situation (see Chapter 8). Decision-making relies upon both your emotional and rational brain. For example, if you were attending a family home to deliver a death message, you would probably ensure that you did not laugh while you were speaking to the family out of respect for their anticipated sadness, even though it is not *your* loss. This decision, though seemingly unconscious, is a self-regulation that you have made because of your self-awareness and desire to avoid an unnecessary conflict.

9.3 Origins of Conflict and Responses to Conflict

Anything can cause or spark a conflict—whether it's parking, an assault, winning a sports match, or even something as simple as whether you unloaded the dishwasher—however, these sparks are not necessarily the actual origin of the conflict, they may just be the proverbial 'straw that broke the camel's back'.

9.3.1 Origins of conflict

The officer's initial goal in responding to a conflict is to understand what is causing the conflict in the first place (Filley, 1982). In some situations, the spark of a conflict is irrelevant or appears trivial because the conflict is about a wider, perhaps less immediately apparent, issue. For example, if a shop-keeper attacked and seriously injured an individual who had stolen a packet of crisps, it might seem like the shop-keeper had an exaggerated response. However, if during the police interview, the shop-keeper said that the petty thief came into the shop every week and made derogatory comments to the shop-keeper before stealing a packet of crisps, the interviewing officer (and indeed, the CPS and eventually, the jury) may feel differently about the shop-keeper's assault. The origins of conflict are important to understand because they may change the course of the conflict or the effectiveness of the outcome from the conflict.

Social, cultural, personal, and medical issues may cause or contribute to origins of a conflict. In the example above, were the shop-keeper described as a Muslim woman who wore a hijab and the petty thief as a White male, but no mention was made about the White male making derogatory comments, an astute officer would follow lines of enquiry to investigate whether race, ethnicity, religion, or gender were factors in the conflict and offence (see 11.5.2 and Chapter 19). In making these enquiries, the investigating officer in the example above would need to be sure to employ appropriate and effective interpersonal communication with all parties (victim, suspect, and witnesses), by observing non-verbal communication and engaging in active listening. See Chapter 8 for more on communication skills in policing.

The officer's enquiries would likely examine whether race, ethnicity, religion, or gender were *causal* or *contributing* factors of the conflict and offence. A causal factor means that an event occurred because of something else, whereas a contributing factor means that a combination of factors led to the event. Differences, predispositions, and influences may also be factors (either as causal or contributory) in a conflict, these may be particularly relevant in group-related conflict. For example, a group from one neighbourhood may be predisposed to be hostile, and therefore more likely to engage in conflict, towards another neighbourhood group. As a police officer engaging with residents in these communities and taking the partnership approach (see 11.4), it would be important to be aware of these predispositions so that you can assess risk appropriately, pre-empt potential conflict, and avoid an escalation of the conflict, while protecting vulnerable people.

9.3.2 Responses to conflict

Responding to conflict is a central part of policing, therefore mastering methods of de-escalating conflict are vital to ensuring your safety and the safety of those around you. The image below depicts the nine stages of conflict identified by Glasl (Glasl, 1982). Importantly, a conflict can start at any stage, it does not necessarily start with 'tension', and a conflict may end at any stage, hopefully avoiding the 'abyss'. Officers may rely on non-verbal communication (see 8.8.3), negotiation, and active listening (see 8.8.2) to de-escalate the situation and avoid a 'forcible intervention'.

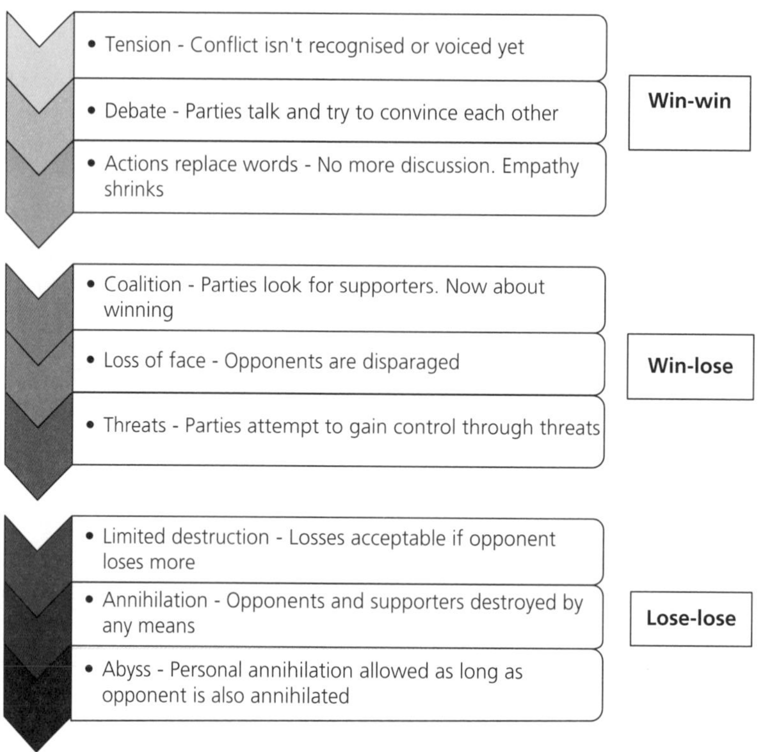

• Tension - Conflict isn't recognised or voiced yet
• Debate - Parties talk and try to convince each other
• Actions replace words - No more discussion. Empathy shrinks
Win-win
• Coalition - Parties look for supporters. Now about winning
• Loss of face - Opponents are disparaged
• Threats - Parties attempt to gain control through threats
Win-lose
• Limited destruction - Losses acceptable if opponent loses more
• Annihilation - Opponents and supporters destroyed by any means
• Abyss - Personal annihilation allowed as long as opponent is also annihilated
Lose-lose

Source: Adapted from Wall-Skills.com (2017) Glasl's Stages of Conflict Escalation, Wall-Skills.

Officers may find that they need to rely on legislation to de-escalate the conflict. Policing powers and laws that are particularly relevant to de-escalating conflict include:

- Articles 2 and 3 of the Human Rights Act 1998
- Section 117 of the Police and Criminal Evidence Act 1984 (22.5.1)
- Section 3 of the Criminal Law Act 1967 (see 10.13.3)
- Common Law
- Section 76 of the Criminal Justice and Immigration Act 2008

Of course, as with all use of force, officers must ensure the force is proportionate, legal, accountable, necessary, and ethical (PLANE).

9.4 Dealing with Conflict and Personal Safety Training

Police officers and police staff, in public facing roles, at some point in their career will be required to deal with conflict in violent or potentially violent situations. The police service recognizes the need to meet its obligations under health and safety legislation to protect its personnel whilst achieving its wider duties to protect the public and fight crime.

The College of Policing, on behalf of the National Police Chiefs' Council, has produced comprehensive guidance and Authorised Professional Practice (APP) relating to the use of force in the more specialized areas of Public Order Policing and Armed Policing.

The police service provides detailed Personal Safety Training to its police officers and staff that helps individuals develop and maintain the skills needed to resolve situations safely and effectively, and if necessary, when and how to use force appropriately in conflict situations.

9.5 Assessing Threat and Risk in Conflict Situations

Maintaining situational awareness in any conflict situation is important. Situational awareness is about understanding what is happening around you and thinking about why it might be happening. It gives you the chance to identify any threats to the safety of the persons involved in the conflict, to the police officers and staff attending the incident, and to any bystanders who are watching what is happening.

> **TASK 2** Imagine that you are a police officer who has been called to a report of a large group of people fighting in a busy pedestrian precinct at midnight on a Friday. What factors do you think need to be considered and what dangers may be present?

Building situational awareness is about gathering information and intelligence and can start before you arrive at the scene of an incident. Information and intelligence will normally come from your constabulary's control room, from colleagues, or directly from members of the public. It will include what a caller said and, depending on the incident, may include information from police intelligence databases, previous calls to the same address, or 'live' CCTV feeds from the scene. It will also include the evidence you gather from what you see at the scene or reports by witnesses.

Based on this information, you can develop your risk assessment, which will consider three aspects:

- **Person**—What they are saying? What they are doing? Are they behaving violently? Are they under the influence of drink or drugs or is it an indication of an underlying physical or mental health condition? The impact factors, if a physical confrontation resulted, namely the differences between the subject and police officer in gender, age, size, strength, and skills levels.
- **Object**—Do they have access to a weapon or items that could be used as a weapon, such as a knife, screwdriver, or a pool cue?
- **Place**—Are there any dangers present because of the location of the incident? For example, the search for a person in dense woodland at night in an area unfamiliar to the police officer, or a fight on the pavement outside a pub on a busy road or the presence of a large hostile crowd.

The College of Policing (2017c) uses six categories of Profiled Subject Behaviour in their Personal Safety Training programmes:

- **Compliance**—the subject readily follows police requests
- **Passive Resistance**—the subject stands still or sits down but does not move if asked
- **Verbal Resistance and Gestures**—the subject says they will not comply
- **Active Resistance**—the subject pulls away or pushes the police officer
- **Aggressive Resistance**—the subject attacks the police officer
- **Serious or Aggravated Resistance**—the subject attacks the police officer with a weapon or in a way that could cause death or serious injury

Having considered all the factors, the incident would be graded as High Risk if there was an obvious risk such as the presence of a weapon, or Unknown Risk for all other incidents.

9.6 Using Tactical Communication to Resolve Conflict

Police officers and police staff will need to be able to communicate effectively with a wide variety of people, from many different cultural backgrounds, in many different circumstances throughout their career. Effective communication can resolve conflict without the need to use force, and this will always be the preferred option. There are a number of different models of communication but two key approaches are LEAPS and the Five-Step Model.

The LEAPS model of communication sets out the phases:

- **Listen**—actively listen to what is being said, not just the words but also the person's tone of voice and patterns of speech along with any gestures to try to understand the whole

message. Do not interrupt and do not jump to conclusions about what has happened. Non-verbal cues can often be as important as the actual words used
- **Empathise**—understand the other person's views and feelings as they see it. Empathy is not sympathy which is about feeling sorry that someone has a problem
- **Ask**—establish the facts and get further information using open, probing, or closed questions. You will learn these effective questioning techniques as part of your initial police training
- **Paraphrase**—Check your understanding of what has been said by re-stating the key aspects. This helps to generate a rapport with the person who you have been talking to
- **Summarize**—provide a succinct summary of the conversation you have had including the actions you will take to resolve the situation

It will not always be possible to negotiate a mutually agreed outcome in conflict situations, in which case the Five-Step Model may be more appropriate to resolve the incident and will normally be used if it is likely that force will be used to resolve the conflict:

- **Simple appeal**—the police officer simply asks the subject to comply with their request
- **Reasoned appeal**—the police officer gives a more detailed reason, often including what behaviour has been witnessed, in what way that breaks a specific law, and what the officers wants the subject to do
- **Personal appeal**—the police officer attempts to persuade the subject to comply by presenting negative outcomes that the person may experience if they do not comply, such as getting a criminal record
- **Final appeal**—the subject has not complied with the previous approaches and remains unwilling to comply with the police officer's request so they are told again what is required and this is followed by the phrase 'Is there anything I can reasonably say or do which will make you comply with my request?'
- **Action**—at this point reasonable force may be the only way to get the subject to comply. The most appropriate technique from the Personal Safety Training Programme would be selected

9.7 Using Personal Safety Techniques to Resolve Conflict

The guidance on conflict management is supported by learning resources in the Personal Safety Training Programme (CoP, 2017c). The Personal Safety Training Programme consists of a number of modules that offer a menu of tactics and techniques that enable forces to design training programmes to meet their local operational policing needs or respond to specific policing problems. The training will be delivered in a combination of online learning and face-to-face sessions.

The tactics and techniques, all of which have been subject to legal and medical review, support a consistent national standard for training delivery. The content and duration of initial and refresher training is based on the role of the individual being taught and the level of knowledge and skills required to develop and maintain competence in the use of conflict management skills for that role.

If you join the police service, you will complete Personal Safety Training during your initial phase of training, which is often known as Foundation Training. You will not necessarily be taught all the techniques available during initial training, but your programme will normally cover:

- Tactical Communication
- Unarmed Skills
- Handcuffing
- Irritants
- Batons
- Searching

Throughout your policing career you will receive regular refresher training to remain competent in the use of the techniques.

When using many of the techniques in the Personal Safety Training Programme, the subject may be controlled using the Ground-Pin. This involves the subject being held face down for the shortest possible period of time. On some occasions, the restrainer may need to use their knee or body weight to control the person, but the pressure used should be no more than the absolute minimum required to achieve control.

The improper use of restraint by police officers can result in serious injury to the person or even death. Leaving aside the possibility of a cardiac arrest, one of the more serious risks is positional asphyxia (PA), also referred to as postural asphyxia. This can occur when a person's body position reduces their ability to breathe. It may occur through poorly executed or incorrect restraint techniques or be consequent to some form of accident, such as fainting onto a chair or other raised surface. Asphyxiation can also be caused by keeping a person seated with their chest close to their knees, particularly if they are overweight.

The risk of PA is increased for a person who:

- is under the influence of alcohol or drugs or is unconscious
- is overweight
- has a particularly light frame
- has engaged in a violent struggle or heavy exercise
- is under extreme stress

Prevention is relatively simple: pressure should not be applied to the chest area or the back, and a seated person should not be forced to lean or be left leaning forwards. A detained person should be made to stand or sit upright as soon as possible, for example after handcuffs have been applied.

Most of the warning signs of impending PA are relatively obvious and include:

- suddenly becoming quiet, limp, or agitated—any change in consciousness should be considered
- complaining of not being able to breathe—any such complaint should be taken seriously even if the detainee has an aggressive demeanour
- noisy breathing, gurgling, or choking, foaming saliva, convulsions
- signs of cyanosis (blue lips, eyelids, or gums—although the latter is often difficult to spot)
- signs of force or stress in the face and neck, such as raised blood vessels or bleeding

The risk of in-custody deaths from PA is reduced by exercising caution and common sense. Officers should pay close attention if there is a particular risk and, in the event of asphyxiation, any hold or position potentially affecting the subject should be immediately removed and their clothing loosened. If this does not improve the person's condition, then CPR should be performed but it should be noted that resuscitation in such circumstances often fails.

9.8 Explain and Record Conflict

When you are recording your experience and actions later, you may refer to some of your considerations as part of your ongoing reflective practice. Individuals deal with and manage conflict differently (Sternberg and Soriano, 1984). There will be times where your decisions or actions in response to a situation *conflict* with a colleague's decisions or actions. It is important that police officers understand their own conflict management style and spend time observing their colleagues' approaches. In these instances, consider how your perspectives may be different and what skills or assets each of you brought to resolving the situation. Reflective practice can help you identify actions and behaviours that are more (or less) successful in achieving your desired result and prepare you better for the next conflict. Use your skills in reflective practice (see Gibbs, 1988) to understand which types of management styles lead to the best outcomes.

TASK 3 Think about a conflict that you recently encountered or observed—this could be at work or at home. Use the Gibbs model of reflective practice to understand the conflict more deeply. In the description phase, what are the participants in conflict about and what do they want? In the feelings phase, consider if there are any non-articulated issues that may be contributing to the conflict? In the evaluation phase, consider which type(s) of conflict management style did each of the conflict participants adopt? In the analysis phase, consider how effective each participant was in achieving the outcome? In the conclusion phase, consider which conflict management style would have led to a better result? In the action plan phase, consider how the participants could have behaved differently to lead to this improved result?

9.9 Answers to Tasks

TASK 1 Competing is assertive and uncooperative. Collaborating is both assertive and cooperative. Compromising is in the middle of both assertiveness and cooperativeness. Avoiding is both unassertive and uncooperative. Accommodating is both unassertive and cooperative.

TASK 2 You may have thought about:

- Can the control room see the fight on CCTV?
- Exact location of the incident?
- The number of people involved in the fight?
- Is anyone injured?
- Are there any weapons visible?
- Who has been sent to the incident?

10 Response Policing

10.1 Introduction

This chapter is primarily concerned with the general procedures to be followed when working on a response policing team. This includes principles when attending incidents, including setting up and managing crime scenes and the law surrounding detention and arrest, and collecting evidence—both from a crime scene and from people. It is of course vital that police officers know the law and how to apply it in relation to detaining a person, carrying out an arrest, and taking a suspect into custody.

Throughout we link the subject matter to police officer initial training, undertaken through the PCDA or DHEP, but the content will also be useful to those undertaking a pre-join programme. We also examine attending and dealing with incidents involving loss of life, often untimely deaths, although not necessarily of a suspicious nature. Moreover, in all situations officers should use the National Decision Model (see 4.2.1) to ensure that all decisions are made lawfully in accordance with the Code of Ethics, national and local policies, and procedures. Further details on investigation, interviewing, and forensic procedures are covered in detail in Chapter 13.

The police have a responsibility to respond and deal with many types of incidents, but the majority of police everyday activities can be described as Steady State policing. There are also major incidents which are unexpected and cannot be planned for. Examples include large-scale rail, road, air, and sporting disasters or acts of terrorism. They may be classed as emergency, major, or critical incidents. Planned Operations are where the police have had advanced warning of a situation, eg a large demonstration and will have contingency plans in place (see 10.8).

The police clearly attend volume crime scenes and minor incidents more often than major crime scenes, but in a number of key respects, the principles of attending a volume crime scene are no different to those employed when attending the scene of a serious crime: the differences might simply be those of scale. However, as we note in 10.5, emergencies, major, and critical incidents may give rise to crime scenes of significant geographical size and complexity, eg the Manchester Arena bombing in 2017 or the Salisbury Novichok 2018 poisonings, and might require multi-agency emergency responses, adding to the demands of crime-scene management.

Much of the information in this chapter relates to crime scenes, but response officers very frequently attend non-crime incidents as well and as first responders, are clearly expected to provide various forms of public protection and general support to the community whatever they are called to. It could be anything from taking control of lost property and other items members of the public wish to hand over to someone in authority to dealing with someone behaving 'erratically' in the street—an increasingly frequent incident. It is very important to ascertain in this latter case whether someone may in fact be unwell or have been the victim of a crime in some way. Officers should always check to see if the person is carrying medical documentation or wearing MedicAlert jewellery or identity discs relating to a medical condition.

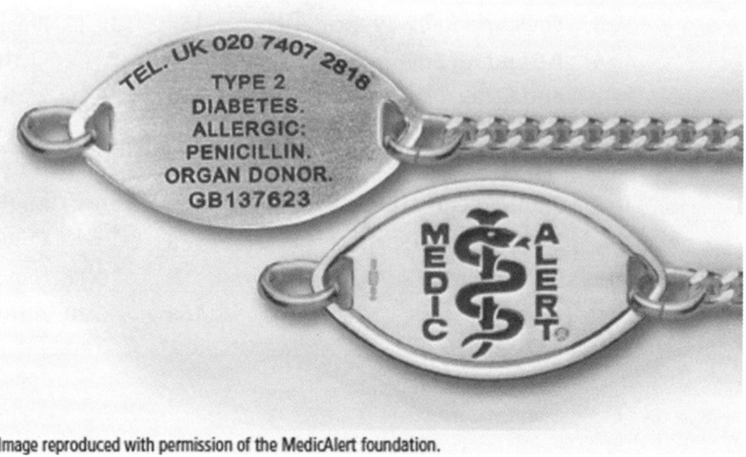

Image reproduced with permission of the MedicAlert foundation.

It would also be the responsibility of the response officer to safeguard any belongings that person may have.

A recent UK legal case needs mentioning here as it is of especial relevance to response officers. *Robinson v Chief Constable of West Yorkshire Police* [2018] UKSC 4 overturned previous rulings that police officers were not liable to prosecution for any harm caused during the course of their duties. The successful case was brought by an elderly woman knocked over by police officers as they tried to arrest a suspect on the street. In the light of this decision it is imperative that officers constantly risk assess the incidents they respond to.

The topics covered in this chapter are likely to contribute to the learning required for the National Policing Curriculum subject areas of 'Response Policing', 'Conducting Investigations', 'Public Protection', and 'Counter Terrorism'.

If you are undertaking the PCDA or DHEP, then you will need to know and understand how to effectively respond to incidents, preserving scenes and evidence when necessary and to manage health and safety for self and for others. For qualification as a police constable, you will need to be able to safely and lawfully:

> manage dynamic conflict situations in policing through leadership, and by dealing with a wide range of behaviours and incidents, taking personal accountability for the use of proportionate and justifiable responses and actions.

Further, you will be expected to safely and lawfully provide an initial, autonomous, and ongoing response to incidents, which can be complex, confrontational, and life-threatening, to bring about the best possible outcomes and to provide an initial, autonomous response to crime scenes, where encountered, that require the management and preservation of evidence and exhibits.

10.2 Police Notes and Records

Police officers need to keep accurate notes and records of their work, particularly if there has been an interaction with a member of the public. The usual place for such records is the pocket notebook (PNB). However, a PNB entry is not normally necessary if other relevant official police documents have been used, such as 'stop and search' forms, 'evidence and action' books (EAB) following an arrest, or a 'collision/accident report book' for road traffic collisions (C/ARB).

Most constabularies now equip officers with mobile data devices, including body-worn video (BWV) which can be used for some tasks instead of the handwritten PNB. The software is designed to provide secure access to databases such as the PNC and electoral roll. These devices have a facility to complete standard pro forma documents that can then be uploaded to a force network and which are increasingly used to record other information, for example statements made by suspects and witnesses.

In the longer term, the Emergency Services Network (ESN) should allow for a more standardized approach and avoid the need for officers to carry two hand-held devices. The programme has been described as 'one of the most technologically advanced systems worldwide' but also as 'inherently high risk' (National Audit Office, 2016). Implementation of the ESN has been delayed a number of times. However, in 2019 the government reiterated that the ESN 'will transform emergency services' mobile working, especially in remote areas and at times of network congestion' (gov.uk, 2019).

Home Office regulations and all police services place obligations upon officers to record certain matters (Home Office, 2018b), and the courts can examine any record used by an officer while giving evidence, eg the officer's PNB). Therefore, certain rules apply, and if these are not followed then the accuracy or even the authenticity of the entries could be questioned. The National Policing Curriculum (as part of the Policing Education Qualifications Framework, PEQF) refers to the need to keep accurate, legible, and complete records.

10.2.1 The pocket notebook

The PNB has been historically used to make a written record of the details of incidents and other pertinent information, particularly whilst on patrol, for example a statement made by a suspect or a description given by a witness. Increasingly, though, PNB also refers to the recording of information, such as statements, through the use of electronic devices which are becoming the norm.

The main functions of the PNB are to:

- note the start and finish time of each period of duty;
- keep a record of significant information collected during an incident in order to comply with the Criminal Procedure and Investigations Act 1996;
- make a contemporaneous account (as the events unfold) or, if this is impossible, as soon as reasonably practicable afterwards;
- state clearly where another police officer (eg your assessor whilst on Supervised Patrol) has been consulted when writing an entry; and
- increase the extent and accuracy of recall in court (see Chapter 18).

Officers are usually issued with a PNB soon after joining a police service. The local policy will be explained on how to complete a PNB, where it should be stored, its surrender, the issuing of new PNBs, and so on (in accordance with the Management of Police Information procedures: see 12.7). Note that the rules of disclosure apply to PNB entries (see 13.4.3). The language used in PNB entries must be clear, factually based, and avoid the use of exclusionary terms. Police officers must keep their PNB in a safe place whilst on and off duty and inform their supervisor straight away if it is lost.

It is not normally necessary to complete a PNB entry if other relevant official police documents have been used (such as 'stop and search' forms) but local policy should be followed. In most constabularies, officers use mobile data devices instead of a paper notebook, but in some police services trainee officers will still use the traditional police pocket notebook.

10.2.1.1 How to use the pocket notebook

The importance of the PNB and its proper use cannot be overemphasized. Police officers are obliged to record certain matters within it, and the courts can examine an officer's PNB if they refer to it when giving evidence in court (see 18.7.6.4).

The following depicts some pages from a PNB outlining the general rules that police officers should apply for making PNB entries. These rules must be followed so that the accuracy and authenticity of the entries cannot be put in doubt.

01

Write the day, date, and year at the beginning of entries for each day and underline them

	DO NOT LEAVE SPACES
	If spaces are left then — draw — a — line, to — indicate nothing further can be added. —
	Always make the pocket book entries in, black, ink. —
	Make all entries legible. —
WRITE THE TIME IN THIS COLUMN	Entries should be made in the pocket book as the event happens. If the circumstances make it impossible to do so at the time, then the entry should be made as soon as practicable after the event, and the reason for the delay should also be noted eg: 'Whilst using officer safety techniques, I was unable to make any entries'. —
USING THE	Each entry should include the time and name the location where the notes were made. —
24 HR CLOCK	Entries must only be written in single lines of writing on the lines of the pages of the book (except when drawings are made, in which case, draw across the page). —
	Use every line and page of the pocket notebook and do not write anywhere else in the book such as inside the cover. —
	Do NOT overwrite errors. —
	Do NOT erase or obliterate errors. —
	Any mistake should be crossed out with a single line (~~so it can be read~~) and initialled beside the deletion. Any correction should then be written straight after the initials. —
	If two pages are turned over by mistake a diagonal line should be drawn across the blank pages and 'omitted in error' written across the page. —
	Do NOT tear out or remove any of the pages or parts of the pages. Write all SURNAMES in BLOCK CAPITALS. —
	Write down the names and addresses of victims, suspects, and witnesses. —
	Write down all identifying features such as serial numbers of property, including vehicles or documents, e.g. the registration numbers of vehicles. —
	What a person says should be 'written down in direct speech!' and the conversation recorded verbatim or word for word. —

10.2.1.2 Example of a PNB entry

The following shows how the rules are applied in a PNB entry.

	01 *Wednesday 16th January (0000)*
	Duty 0600–1600 —— Patrol ZZ 10
	Refreshment time 0900 and 1400
0545	*Briefing at ZZ*
0550	*Collected keys for ZZ 10 patrol vehicle index number ZZ 00 ZZZ*
0600	*Checked vehicle seats and feet areas for property—no trace of any property*
0605	*Commenced patrol*
0610	*At the time stated on the date above, I was alone on mobile patrol in uniform*
	travelling in an easterly direction along Sheerbury Road, Ramstone,
	approximately 50 metres east of the junction with Applebreaux Road, when I saw
	a Fordover motor vehicle, index number YY 00 ZZZ being driven in the same
	direction approximately 20 metres in front of me. There was a clear unobstructed
	view of this vehicle. I caused the vehicle to stop in Sheerbury Road, 20 metres
	West of the junction with Applebreaux Road and spoke to the driver who was the
	sole occupant of the car. The driver identified him/herself to me as First Middle
	LASTNAME, born 00/00/00 address 101 Hernegate Road, Ramstone, Kentshire.
Q	*'May I see your driving licence and insurance for this vehicle please?'*
R	*'Haven't got my insurance with me because I have only just bought the car*
	yesterday, but here's my driving licence'. Driving licence details
	LASTN000022FM9ZZ
Q	*'As you are unable to produce your insurance to me right now and as I need to*
	ask you some more questions relating to your insurance, I would like to take the
	opportunity to inform you of your rights at this point'. I cautioned Mr LASTNAME
	and told him was not under arrest.
Q	*Where is your insurance certificate right now?'*
R	*'I guess it's on its way in the post, I rang them yesterday'*
Q	*'What is the name of your insurance company?'*
R	*'I'm not sure—can't remember.'*
Q	*'How much did you pay for the insurance?'*
R	*'Again, sorry, I can't remember.'*
Q	*'How long have you owned this vehicle?'*
R	*'One day, I bought it yesterday.'*
	PNC check no trace LASTNAME. PNC vehicle check LASTNAME RO at address
	given. Voter's register check confirmed LASTNAME living at address I completed
	an HO/RT/1 form.

Q	'As you haven't been able to produce your insurance to me now, please produce your certificate of insurance and this form at a police station within 7 days. Have you got any questions, and do you understand what you have to do?' LASTNAME gave no reply.
Q	'I have been making a record of our conversation, would you please read these notes I have made, and if you agree they are a true record of what we have said, and then sign my notes to that effect?'
	This is a true record. FM Lastname
Q	'As you have been unable to produce your certificate of insurance to me here, I am going to report you for the offence of failing to produce or not having a certificate of insurance for this vehicle.' I cautioned LASTNAME and there was no reply. These notes were made at the time between 0610 and 0630.
	CL Underwood PC 118118:
0630	Resumed patrol.
0900	Refs ZZ
0945	Resumed patrol.
C	No insurance—unacceptable because of possible consequences for passengers in the vehicle, pedestrians and property owners if vehicle was involved in a collision.
I	PNC check showed vehicle had no insurance.
A	Vehicle was stopped safely , driver spoken to on the footpath beside car.
P	S 136 RTA 1988 to stop vehicle, no insurance covered by s143 RTA 1988.
O	Could have used verbal warning, but due to the serious offence and possible outcome, prosecution is in public interest.
A	20 minutes for questioning and reporting the driver was proportionate here.
R	Driver remained calm. Safe environment throughout.

The reasons for making a particular decision need to be clear. The National Decision Model (see 4.2.1) provides an 'official' framework for making decisions, and the mnemonic CIAPOAR can be used to ensure that a PNB entry includes all the aspects that need to be taken into account, that is the Code of Ethics, Information, Assessment, Powers and policy, Options, Action and Review. Further information is available on the College of Policing APP website.

Top Ten Hints for Using a PNB

1. It should be carried at all times on duty.
2. It should be used to record evidence (not opinion, except in cases of drunkenness).
3. It is a supervisor's responsibility to issue a new one when needed.
4. The general rules (see ELBOWS(S)) should always be applied.
5. Make use of the useful information it contains (such as an aide memoire for the caution).
6. It may be referred to while giving evidence.
7. It remains police property.
8. Diagrams should be included (where appropriate) as part of the written notes.
9. On duty, additional pieces of paper should not be used to supplement the PNB, or as an alternative.
10. Don't lose it!

The rules concerning PNB entries can be summarized by the mnemonic 'no ELBOWS(S)', commonly used in police training.

E no Erasures
L no Leaves torn out/Lines missed
B no Blank spaces
O no Overwriting
W no Writing between lines
S no Spare pages
(S) but Statements should be recorded in 'direct speech'

10.2.1.3 PNB entries and conferring with others

To comply with the Code of Ethics, it is important that an individual officer's account is an honest and accurate account of what they actually saw, heard, and did. If an officer did not see or hear see something, it should not appear in their notes even if another conferring officer did.

The College of Policing APP is clear that as a general principle, a police officer should not confer with others prior to recording their personal account of an incident (CoP, 2013b). However, if other police officers have been involved in the same incident, then there may be occasions when it is necessary for them to consult with each other so that the notes can be as full and comprehensive as possible, but a record to the effect that consultation has taken place (including names, dates, times, locations, and the reasons for consultation) must be made. Police officers who are involved in an incident are legally permitted to confer with each other about their involvement together, before they give their first account in a PNB or statement (*R (on the application of Saunders & Anor) v The Association of Chief Police Officers & Ors* [2008] EWHC 2372 (Admin)).

Firearms officers have come under particular scrutiny in recent years with regard to conferring. In 2005, Jean-Charles de Menezes was shot and killed by MPS firearms officers in the mistaken belief that he was a suicide bomber. In the subsequent inquest, the coroner criticized the practice of MPS firearms officers having 'conferred' when writing their notes some 36 hours after the fatal shooting. The same practice was criticized after Mark Saunders was shot and killed by MPS firearms officers in 2008 (*R (on the application of Saunders & Anor) v The Association of Chief Police Officers & Ors* [2008] EWHC 2372 (Admin)). MPS firearms officers were also challenged over conferring after they shot and killed Mark Duggan in 2011 (*R (Delezuch) v Chief Constable and R (Duggan) v ACPO* [2014] EWCA Civ 1635). As a result, the following guidance was issued for firearms officers: officers should not as general practice confer with others before writing their accounts, although there may of course be a need to converse in order to resolve an ongoing safety or operational matter. Most importantly, each officer's honestly held recollection of the incident should be recorded individually, as there should be no reason why an officer should need to confer about what was in their mind at the time force was used. However, if discussion must take place on other issues, then a record must be made of the time, the date, and place of the conferring, the content of the discussion, who was involved, and the reasons why it took place.

Consideration as to the separation of officers in these circumstances is contained in the College of Policing APP on Key Police Witnesses. Where practicable, this should only be done in consultation with a Post Incident Manager (PIM). Officers or staff need not be separated as a matter of routine.

10.3 General Procedures at Crime Scenes

Deployment to any incident has the potential to generate numerous challenges, for example unlawful violence against persons and premises, and public disorder. Victims and witnesses may also need support, including first aid, and in the case of more serious injuries, an ambulance or paramedic may be required. As such, an officer may need to make difficult decisions on how to respond and which actions to take first. The rationale for the decision(s) should be recorded, unless the officer's professional judgement regards it as obvious.

A crime scene is frequently the most important component of any criminal investigation because it is very likely to contain physical and electronic evidence which could identify suspects, corroborate or refute statements made by witnesses, and demonstrate guilt or innocence. Early and effective protection of the crime scene ensures that the greatest amount of potential evidence is available for recovery and, therefore, maximizes its value to the investigation.

Crime scenes are not purely geographical locations to which we can apply an address or map reference; a victim or suspect in a crime such as a sexual assault is also a crime scene. Treating a person, especially a victim, as a crime scene may be distressing and potentially offensive to the person and to their family or friends, but it is vital that we consider people as sources of evidence and intelligence. This is to ensure that we effectively 'protect and preserve' them and recover the evidence or intelligence we need. Anything that could be a source of evidence or intelligence is also part of a crime scene, including articles related to the offence, such as weapons and vehicles, computer hard drives, digital storage media, as well as the intangible, such as networked environments.

Some of the biggest 'offenders' in relation to poor scene preservation are victims of crime, so any opportunity to encourage good scene management is vital and will pay dividends. Call centre staff should be trained to explain what the victims or informants could do to help to preserve evidence, and the FAO (First Attending Officer) can instruct victims and the public on simple issues such as staying clear of the crime scene and not handling evidence. Victims are often vital sources of physical evidence (especially in offences against the person and sexual assault) and preventing their contamination by others (such as supportive family members) is important. Sexual assault victims should be forensically examined before they smoke, eat, drink, wash, or go to the toilet (unless absolutely necessary) because such activities can destroy evidence. This is sometimes very difficult to explain and may be a source of considerable conflict, yet the problem can often be solved with a diplomatic and respectful approach.

Nearly all officers carry a personal mobile phone with a camera, and it might be tempting to use it to photograph a crime scene. This may occasionally assist an investigation in the early stages, eg when a wet shoe mark is evaporating. However, generally, it is better not to use the camera on a personal mobile phone at a possible crime scene because the phone would then become a source of evidence and would normally be retained for analysis of the image in its original state. It is important to note that officers should at no time share photographs taken at a crime scene or take personal photographs at a crime scene; this would be considered misconduct.

10.3.1 Early priorities at crime scenes: the FAO

The overriding principle at any incident is that all attending officers rigorously ensure the safety of the public, their colleagues, and themselves. Some of the people present at a scene of a criminal offence may be emotional, aggressive, or confused and might represent a danger. In addition, damage to premises, such as by fire, may weaken the structure of a building, resulting in further hazards.

Prior to responding to an incident, officers should ensure that they have the basic information they need to ensure they are prepared and safe. This includes a meaningful address or location, an idea of the incident type, and the location of any rendezvous points (RVPs). While travelling to the scene of an incident, a 'dynamic' risk assessment should be made based on the information gathered from the initial report (see 13.5.1). The assessment should be based upon:

- what is known (objective fact/information) or believed (subjective fact/information) to have happened;
- the number of people likely to be present;
- any information on the PNC and local intelligence databases about the individuals involved (eg that a suspect has been violent in the past);
- if any weapons are present at the scene;
- any risks associated with the location and local community sensitivities.

10.3.1.1 Arriving at a crime scene

The first police officer who attends the scene, possibly as the result of an emergency call, is known variously as the FAO, the First Officer at the Scene (FOAS), or sometimes the Initial Responder; different police services use different terms. We use FAO in the remainder of this chapter. The FAO may be of any rank and position within the organization—indeed, it could be a trainee police officer undertaking the PCDA or DHEP—this will entirely depend on who happens to arrive first.

The first few minutes after arriving at the scene of a major crime may be confusing. The FAO should first control any person in the vicinity, including colleagues, and direct them to carry out urgent tasks where appropriate. Many members of the public who were close to the location at the time of the incident could be valuable witnesses and must be identified swiftly. The FAO may also have to arrest a suspect.

It should be remembered that all physical evidence is expendable when balanced against human life. Hence, the FAO should not preserve a crime scene to the extent that it causes delays which aggravate a victim's injuries or increase any risks to life and limb. This is not to say that physical evidence can be disregarded during the life-saving process; the FAO can advise the ambulance crew where not to tread and can carefully move furniture away from the victim to facilitate medical aid when **necessary**. However, if items are moved, they should be left in their new position and not moved again in an attempt to recreate the original crime scene, because moving furniture, switching on lights, and even opening doors removes items from their original context and is likely to cause 'contamination' (see 10.3.5.1). All these actions must be reported to the crime scene investigator (CSI) early on in the investigation and should also be recorded as PNB entries.

It is good practice in these instances for the officer to also note the decision-making process and the rationale for the action, as both may be useful when writing a statement or appearing in court. For example, imagine that an officer moves a piece of furniture to allow paramedics to access an injured person. The officer would need to note the original location of the furniture, time and date of the move, the reason for deciding to move it, and how they came to that decision. The decision-making process in this instance would refer to the National Decision Model (see 4.2.1) and the Code of Ethics.

As soon as the initial response and emergency treatment of any casualties have been completed, all police officers, including the FAO and other personnel attending crime scenes, should withdraw. They should only re-enter if approved, and protective clothing must be worn for their own safety and to avoid adding more misleading material to the scene. Chapter 13 provides further details on forensics and investigative actions at crime scenes more generally.

10.3.1.2 The 'golden hour'

The first period of any incident, particularly in major crime and critical incidents, is often described as the 'golden hour'. This is a shorthand reference to the need to identify witnesses and preserve a scene quickly so that evidence can be protected or gathered while it is still fresh and undisturbed. For example, bloodstains should be sampled or protected before they are diluted by rain, shoe impressions (shoe marks) may need to be covered in poor weather, and the body of a deceased person could be initially examined before rigor mortis sets in.

It is also advantageous to identify and interview witnesses whilst their recollections are still clear. Suspects, however, should only be questioned or interviewed once a caution has been given and the suspect's rights have been fully protected (see 13.8.2). A police officer should always listen carefully to witnesses and evaluate what they say in the light of what is already known. Officers will, of course, record what is said as a PNB entry and may also make a note of further questions to ask or other lines of enquiry.

10.3.1.3 Cordons

Cordons are erected as a visible barrier to identify the parameters of crime scenes or other incidents. The cordon tape that is most often used is clearly not a physical barrier: it is more of a 'statement' to help to limit and control access for relevant personnel. In criminal investigations, cordons are generally only used for more serious offences such as major crimes and fatalities.

Cordons should be set up promptly to completely prevent public access, and the cordoned area should be a larger area than might seem immediately necessary. The tape should be securely attached to carefully chosen fixed objects, but any objects that might be a source of evidence should not be used as the evidence might be at risk. For example, if the tape was attached to a parked car any movement of the tape due to gusts of wind could erase bloodstains and finger marks.

The size of the cordon should not be determined by the location of convenient fixed objects: if necessary, the tape can be affixed further out until poles are available. Whilst installing the tape, the officer must also control witnesses and keep them out of the freshly cordoned area, and this is sometimes difficult. Further information about cordoning bomb scenes is provided in 10.7.4. A single cordon (or the inner or first cordon) must encompass:

- the venue of any incident or suspected offence;
- all possible routes into or out of the venue;
- any location where physical evidence could possibly be found: for example, communal bins, under cars in the street, nearby gardens; and
- any location identified as significant by witnesses.

A secondary cordon (the outer cordon) can also be installed to restrict public access and viewing. As a guide, if the public can see significant evidence, then the cordon is almost certainly too small. It also makes sense to position the outer cordon, so the movement of traffic is not affected, to minimize local congestion.

Once the inner cordon is in place, nothing may leave or enter it until sanctioned by a CSI, unless it is required to save life—for example, an ambulance or fire appliance. Vehicles moving through a cordoned area may damage vital evidence, for example at a bomb scene components of the device may be picked up by the tyres of emergency vehicles which are then driven out of the scene, and the evidence is likely to be lost. Or an offender might have leant against a vehicle outside the venue of the offence when they made off, so CSIs may need to examine every vehicle within the cordon or, on occasions, every vehicle in the street.

The powers available to the police to secure crime scenes were considered in the case of *DPP v Morrison* [2003] EWHC 683 (Admin). In a serious incident in a shopping centre involving groups of young people, the police had sought to cordon off four areas in the shopping centre to secure and preserve evidence. Morrison was arrested for obstruction of a police officer in the lawful execution of his duty and for an offence under the Public Order Act 1986. He had walked into one of the cordoned areas, despite being told not to do so by police. He was initially convicted but appealed and the Crown Court allowed the appeal, stating that there was no lawful authority to erect the cordon and therefore the police were not acting in the lawful execution of their duty. The prosecution in turn appealed to the High Court. The High Court considered case law and existing legislation and decided that it was unlikely that anyone would have a right to stop police installing a cordon in a public area, and that on private property the police were entitled to assume that the owner would consent to cordoning. The shopping area in the *Morrison* case was privately owned but had a public right of way so the cordoned areas were in a public place (see 4.3.1.1), and the police were therefore entitled to install a cordon. The appeal was successful. On a practical level, this decision makes it clear that in certain circumstances police officers might need to obtain search warrants (under perhaps s 8 of the PACE Act 1984) in order to remain on private premises for the purposes of a crime-scene search.

10.3.2 The rendezvous point and the common approach path

The rendezvous point (RV point or RVP) is vital to the smooth running of the investigations at the scene and should be carefully chosen at an early stage. It may have to accommodate several vehicles, rest stations, major incident vehicles, and even a command tent. RVPs should always be in a roadway or on land with good access, which is unconnected to the investigation, and should never be placed in a narrow street with restricted access. When attending the scene of a suspicious explosion, care must be taken to search the selected RVP for secondary devices. In incidents involving firearms officers, the forensic personnel and other emergency services will normally attend the RVP rather than the crime scene as a matter of safety.

The 'common approach path' (CAP) is a designated route from the edge of the cordon into the crime scene proper. It should not be the route likely to have been taken by victim or offender, nor should it necessarily be the route taken by the FAO who was acting early on without full knowledge of the facts. If the scene is 'empty' (ie there are no living victims), there will be more time to choose the most suitable route. The selected route should minimize damage to potential evidence, particularly material which is small or almost two-dimensional—such as shoe marks and blood. Wherever possible, the CAP should be laid on solid ground as this will help to prevent evidence being accidentally concealed (eg if personnel walked on a CAP over soft soil). Ideally, the CAP should be marked with tape but, in the early stages, this may not be possible. If tape is used, it should not be anchored with rocks and other debris found in the vicinity since one of these may have been a weapon.

Some of the other problems associated with CAPs include:

- having no choice of route when a building has only one entrance;

- having too much choice when selecting the route for a CAP in a flat, featureless field—how do you decide?;
- establishing a CAP through the rear of the premises—entering the premises via a back door and searching for a key may destroy vital evidence; and
- having no immediate available means to mark the CAP.

One of the early tasks of the CSI is to search the CAP for evidence; this may involve rerouting the CAP if any evidence is found, or at least recording and removing potentially valuable material. The CAP should be guarded by a scene control officer.

10.3.3 The crime scene log and attending personnel

Perhaps the most important document at the crime scene is the log, a booklet or paper form for recording the details of all attending personnel. In essence, it records any event that could have led to contamination of evidence. The log should contain a description of the CAP so that every person attending the scene can familiarize themselves with it prior to entry. It must also record details of:

- every person already at the scene when the FAO arrived;
- every person who subsequently attended the scene and the time of attendance; and
- every person who entered the crime scene or inner cordon, with the time of attendance and the reason.

Whilst the scene control officer should be on hand and easy to find, it is the responsibility of all attending personnel (including trainee police officers on Supervised or Independent Patrol) to seek them out. Note that logging or resourcing databases which manage deployments and information at incidents (such as STORM and the older systems like CAD and OIS) do not record officer deployments in sufficient detail and should not be relied upon.

The scene control officer and every individual must ensure the log is completed correctly. It will be copied and probably be disclosed to the defence (see 13.4.3), which will study it and compare it to statements, PNBs, and other scene logs. If it has not been properly maintained, then some (or even all) of the evidence from the scene could be deemed inadmissible.

10.3.3.1 Non-police personnel at crime scenes

Ambulance crews should be allowed controlled access in order to save life. They are generally aware of how to behave in a crime scene but may have to be reminded not to touch anything needlessly and to show caution where they walk. The FAO could accompany the crew and point out apparently significant evidence so they can avoid it and should also take their names in case they need to be contacted for later elimination (particularly for evidence relating to shoes, clothing, and finger marks). Clearly, ambulance personnel should wear gloves, as should the FAO. Efforts to resuscitate by ambulance staff can generate very considerable quantities of debris, such as wrappers and used medical equipment. This material should be left at the scene for the attending CSI.

If a death has occurred, a doctor is not always required to establish this since ambulance crews can make a 'recognition of life extinct' (ROLE). In such circumstances, the attending officer should take any forms completed by ambulance crew or doctors and ensure they are returned to the police station. Attending doctors should wear protective clothing, disturbing the body as little as possible. The use of oral, rectal, or deep-tissue thermometers is not generally permitted because this can interfere with biological evidence, such as DNA. If there is any concern that the death may be suspicious the doctor or ambulance crew should be requested not to turn the body or search through clothing to view hypostasis or injuries until a CSI is in attendance. The attending personnel could be asked for an opinion as to the cause of death, particularly if the deceased has apparently suffered a sudden death and is known to the doctor. Certification of death is carried out by a doctor afterwards. There is no requirement for a senior officer to enter the scene once a death has been confirmed or to confirm that a death is suspicious. Every additional person in the crime scene can potentially destroy or contaminate evidence.

Other police colleagues (including senior officers) should not enter the inner cordon unless:

- the offender is likely to be within and must be apprehended;
- they are saving life;
- they can assist in urgent and immediate acts to prevent loss of the scene (eg putting out a small and manageable fire); and/or

- a dog is required to pick up a track from within the cordon.

The CSI will attend at the RVP and will liaise with the FAO and other personnel to decide how to proceed. In general terms, the CSI's initial role is to gather information, start with photography where appropriate, and advise detectives and uniformed police on the arrangements for any arrested persons. Once this has been achieved, the CSI will examine the CAP, record and recover vulnerable evidence from it, and occasionally move the CAP to another location. It is common for the CSI to enter the scene with the doctor to certify death or examine a deceased person.

A **crime scene manager** (CSM) is appointed in a major crime enquiry to manage the scene and deal with scientific resources. Typically, the CSM will be hands-on, but will also be flexible enough to attend strategy meetings and deal with other issues. In a more serious or complex case, there may be several CSMs and a **crime scene co-ordinator** (CSC).

A variety of **emergency personnel** may attend a scene and will be recorded in the log if they enter the crime scene, unless it is a serious incident and is impractical. The following groups will also keep their own records of attendance:

- the Fire and Rescue Service (FRS);
- Explosives Ordnance Disposal (EOD) in the case of explosions or suspected explosive devices;
- HM Coastguard and RNLI;
- mountain rescue and lowland search organizations (with dogs).

Other personnel who may attend as required include forensic scientists, borough or district surveyors and structural engineers (to assess the safety of damaged buildings), National Grid (for gas leaks), and scaffolding contractors (to support damaged structures in order to prevent collapse). However, once cordons are in place, no one should enter the crime scene until sanctioned and briefed by a CSI unless the safety of the public or attending personnel is at risk.

The following powers of entry apply:

- police officers have a power of entry in relation to a person who is under arrest for an indictable offence (s 18 of the PACE Act 1984);
- a civilian designated as an 'investigating officer' has a power of entry in relation to a person who is under arrest for an indictable offence (s 38 of the Police Reform Act 2002);
- a civilian designated as a 'designated person' (see PACE Code B, para 2.11) can attend with the police when executing a warrant to search and seize evidence (s 16 of the PACE Act 1984).

In many cases, however, formal permissions are not required because the occupier will invite the police and other investigators to attend and enter the property.

10.3.4 Fast-track actions

In every major crime, the senior investigating officer (SIO) will consider fast-track actions which might rapidly resolve the investigation. These decisions are taken after careful thought and are noted in the decision log or policy file (which records the decision-making process of the senior officer). However, in the very early minutes of an investigation, some actions may be necessary to prevent the loss of evidence or facilitate the apprehension of a suspect. These can include the following:

- using a dog to track the offender, particularly if the scent is not contaminated—the dog may have to enter the inner cordon;
- collecting evidence which is in danger of being lost immediately, such as wadding and cartridge cases being blown away by the wind, photographing the image on a computer screen, or powering off a smartphone (which might otherwise be remotely 'wiped');
- switching off a cooker if it might start a fire;
- covering shoe marks and tyre marks in poor weather (boxes or bin lids taken from an area well away from the crime scene could be used);
- conducting an urgent search of the street (sometimes called a 'flash search') for evidence which has been discarded, especially when the area is busy; and
- controlling large groups of people in confined situations (eg a pub) which might cause the loss (or gain) of fibres which could be used as evidence.

In these circumstances, care must be taken to make the right decision. Protective clothing (at the least, clean medical-style gloves) might be needed to prevent contamination of the evidence. Police officers (including supervised trainees) should be prepared to justify their actions (or lack of them) to the senior investigating officer.

10.3.5 Forensic considerations at volume crime scenes

The attending police officer may need to take a crime report, assess the likely modus operandi of the offender, record losses, identify potential witnesses, and assess the scene for the potential attendance of a CSI. Overall, fewer actions will be taken by CSIs and police officers at a volume crime scene (compared with a major crime scene). The police will also try to minimize disruption to normal life in the immediate vicinity of the crime. If the CSI is delayed, a police officer may need to:

- close doors to control children and pets (instead of using cordon tape);
- close windows and consider boarding up in inclement weather (if windows are to be boarded-up, ensure the contractor leaves the original window in place);
- cover shoe marks inside premises with a chair (not a piece of paper which is more likely to be moved or trodden on);
- bring broken glass and property inside (as moisture makes fingerprinting difficult), handling it by the edges and wearing gloves;
- cover shoe and tyre marks outside with bin lids, trays, or boxes, even in sunny weather;
- on a bed, use the blanket or quilt to funnel any material to a corner; and
- allow the victims to make drinks and food, unless it would damage good evidence or cause a health risk.

In the presence of DNA-rich material, a mask should be worn (if available) to prevent contamination from the officer. Protect any articles that have to be moved by wearing gloves, and handle the material carefully: **gloves do not protect finger marks from being destroyed.** Continuity must be considered as the police officer who moves articles of interest should—technically—exhibit them. Local protocols should be followed on this issue. Details of investigative forensic procedures are covered in Chapter 13.

10.3.5.1 Preventing contamination

Contamination is the transfer of trace evidence by any means other than direct or indirect involvement with the crime, be it accidental or deliberate. The term is also broadly used to describe damage to evidence or altering its state in some way that is not required for its preservation. Contamination could occur, for example, if a police officer is tasked to deal with a suspect and has previously been to the crime scene; the officer could potentially contaminate the suspect with material from the scene. This may reduce the value of evidence that links the suspect with the crime scene.

Certain forms of forensic evidence are, in all practical senses, incontrovertible (eg DNA evidence), but are at risk of contamination. Such evidence will be scrutinized by the defence in a criminal case to try to cast doubt on the integrity of an exhibit and to have it disallowed by the judge. An effective defence team will look for errors in continuity, packaging, and handling and for any possible source of contamination. The following general advice applies to reduce the risk of contamination:

- wear new surgical-type gloves and a face mask as a minimum when dealing with exhibits or whilst inside a crime scene (in the absence of a face mask, at the very least, all persons present should avoid coughing or talking over exhibits);
- store exhibits properly to prevent decay and damage. Property stores should be cool and dry. Electronic exhibits should not be stored on plastic shelving or near a magnetic field (from motors or speakers, for example);
- never deal with exhibits from two facets of the same offence, such as from the victim and the suspect;
- do not deal with clothing from one person in an offence (eg take it out of packaging) in a room that has previously been used for sampling another person;
- do not place a prisoner in a cell until it has been cleaned.

In relation to vehicles, two people from the same offence (such as victim and suspect) should never be conveyed in the same vehicle, even at separate times, until all parties have been forensically examined. Police vehicles which could contain blood in any form should be cleaned or washed down once any forensic examination has been completed, and all patrol cars should be regularly and fastidiously valeted.

10.3.6 Exhibits and exhibiting

According to common law, 'it is within the power of, and is the duty of, constables to retain for use in court things which may be evidence of crime' (*R v Lushington, ex p Otto* [1894] 1 QB 420). The 'things' can include physical objects (eg a knife) and are often referred to as exhibits (as they may be exhibited to a court or 'shown to a witness [at interview] and referred to by [the constable] in [their] evidence' (ibid)). The 1894 ruling in *Lushington* later formed the basis of important sections of the PACE Act 1984 (s 19 on the seizure of material, s 20 in relation to computers and digital evidence, and s 22 on police powers to retain seized material). Under a Code of Practice within the Criminal Procedure and Investigations Act 1996, any police officer investigating alleged crimes 'has a duty to record and retain material which may be relevant to the investigation' (see 13.4.2 on recording and retaining).

A police officer or a member of the public who finds an article which could be used as evidence should 'exhibit' it. This involves formally recording certain details about the object. If the item was originally found by a member of the public, a police officer will complete the process, but the finder's initials and name will be recorded on the exhibit label and used as part of the exhibit number. The officer will also be responsible for taking a statement from the person about how and where it was found. The items will be packaged and labelled by the officer who found or received the item from a member of the public. Police officers and CSIs are advised not to accept an unpackaged exhibit from anyone other than a member of the public as this is a potential cause of contamination.

The item must be properly packaged to preserve the evidence and labelled. The basic information required on the label is:

- the **name** of the person exhibiting (ie the person who first found the item);
- an **exhibit number**: normally the initials of the person exhibiting the item and a sequential number;
- a **description**, which should be brief and to the point—to prevent other people shortening the description for convenience (any index or serial numbers should be included for clarity); and
- the **date, time, and place** the exhibit was found.

It is the mark of a professional to make detailed notes about the exhibit to assist other investigators. If the records on the contents of a package are not sufficiently detailed, then another person might open it to check the contents, which could cause contamination. The notes should record the precise location and orientation of the exhibit at the scene, any identifying marks, the size of clothing, any damage or stains, any logos or identifying features, and serial numbers. The procedures for storing items as they come into police possession are described in 10.14.

10.3.6.1 Signing exhibit labels

The exhibit label records the continuity (or chain of custody) of the exhibit. Ideally, the chain should be unbroken from its seizure until it arrives at court, so unless local protocols dictate otherwise, every person who takes control of the exhibit should sign the label (and later write a statement). The movement of bulk quantities of exhibits is often recorded on a pro forma by the driver, and major crime exhibits officers do not normally write a statement for every receipt of every exhibit. If, however, police officer X temporarily passes a packaged exhibit to officer Y for comment, but it remains in X's custody, then Y need not sign the label. An example might be where X asks Y for a casual opinion, for example 'Is this a ball-peen hammer?' However, if Y gave a professional opinion or transported the exhibit to another place, then they should sign the label and write a statement describing their actions.

10.3.6.2 Firearms as exhibits

Safety must always be considered when dealing with firearms as exhibits. That said, firearms are excellent sources of evidence. They provide ballistics evidence, their smooth surfaces are good sources of finger marks, and DNA can be collected from their rough control surfaces such as the grip, slide, and trigger (and from the muzzle if it has been in contact with skin or saliva). We will look at the different types of firearm, their component parts, and the associated law in Chapter 25.

All police services will have strict protocols in place for accepting weapons from members of the public and seizing them during searches. For health and safety reasons, all personnel at a crime scene should treat every weapon as if it is loaded and call for a firearms officer to make it safe. For weapons suspected of being involved in crimes, it is normal practice for a photographer or CSI to be present during the making-safe process. Whilst making it safe, a firearm should not be pointed at the floor or wall if people could be below or on the other side of the wall. None of the controls should be tampered with apart from those necessary to make it safe, nor should it be 'dry-fired'.

In addition, no one should:

- handle or move a firearm unnecessarily or place another article on top of a firearm;
- move a firearm by poking a pen, or any other object, into the barrel or trigger guard;
- stand in front of a firearm or point a firearm at any person, even when it has been 'made safe'.

Every person who handles a firearm, for example when passing it to or receiving it from another person, should clearly demonstrate that it is safe. In terms of labelling, there may be police service policies for firearms at scenes or in storage (often a red label means it has not been made safe, and a green label that it has). Loaded firearms should not be conveyed to the police station or laboratory unless this is necessary and suitable safety measures are in place.

Above all: presume every firearm is loaded and ready to fire.

10.3.7 Attending major crime scenes

Many of the actions that should be taken by the first attending officer at a major crime scene are common to any crime scene (see 10.3.1 onwards). The FAO should attempt to:

- provide first aid and get assistance from an ambulance crew when necessary;
- cordon off the scene (as wide as practicable) and prevent unauthorized entry, except to preserve life or prevent further damage; and
- create a CAP and begin a 'scene attendance log'.

If deaths have occurred, the bodies should not be covered, but if they are in public view the public should be removed or screening should be installed until the first attending CSI arrives with a small tent.

Evidence collection can also commence, such as recording witness details and any comments they make and recording if anything is disturbed or moved. Assistance may be needed to preserve the scene. It is vital to maintain communication with the force control centre and keep them informed. The FAO should also, of course, remain calm, be positive, and manage the situation until help arrives.

Most police services have specialist (often centrally based) departments or units which deal with major crime investigations. Chapter 13 provides more details on the process of criminal investigation.

10.4 Incidents Involving Deaths

Police officers will certainly encounter fatalities that have occurred during criminal offences but will also deal with incidents where a death seems to be due to natural causes such as illness and old age. For example, the local police station might be called by the neighbour of an elderly person who has not been seen for some time or there are other circumstances which give cause for concern.

Any death which occurs outside the hospital environment and is in some way unexpected is referred to in police circles as an 'untimely death'. All such deaths will be subject to some form of investigation but, of course, this does not mean that the death is associated with criminal activity. A police officer in early attendance at a scene of a fatality could reflect on the following:

- For an apparent suicide, were the means available to the victim?
- Are any of the injuries puzzling?

- Would the victim have been physically capable of the act?
- Is there any sign of a struggle?
- Is anything apparently missing?
- Is there evidence of a possible forced entry?
- Does the position or state of the body fit logically with the information received?

In relation to suicides, there are some commonly held misconceptions but investigators should rely on observation and experience rather than generalization. The chief issues with suicide are that the person must have had access to the object which caused their death and must have been physically capable of committing the act. If there is any uncertainty, the scene can be treated as 'suspicious' until proven otherwise.

10.4.1 Police actions for incidents with deaths

The general procedure to follow for untimely deaths will vary from area to area, although all subscribe to certain basic principles (and relate to the procedures for attendance at a crime scene). A police officer should:

1. ensure their own safety before approaching, as the scene of a death can be dangerous (particularly if there have been multiple deaths);
2. decide whether there is a chance the person is still alive: could first aid be administered—is an ambulance required?
3. establish and use a CAP to preserve the scene;
4. touch nothing until a visual inspection has been made, and beware of bodies in contact with live electrical systems, as well as toxic fumes, poisons, firearms, needles, and body fluids;
5. consider that any death might be the result of crime if it is in any way suspicious.

The officer should make a PNB entry which records the location, position, and general description of the body, including any visible injuries. Any potential evidence should also be noted, such as physical evidence in the immediate area, or from witnesses. The officer should also note any disturbance made to the scene by their presence, including the time and nature. Details of any person (such as member of the emergency services or a witness) already within the scene or subsequently allowed into the crime scene should be recorded. If it seems that evidence could have been compromised in any way, the officer should record this and the decision-making process for taking any actions. Obviously, if the identity of the deceased is known this should be included—any relatives or friends who are present can be asked.

There are also administrative considerations. The attending officer should arrange for the death to be certified by a doctor, nurse, or paramedic, and take any paperwork they produce. For any unexpected death (such as unexplained, apparent suicide, accident, fire, decomposed remains, etc), a supervisory CID officer and a CSI should be contacted as appropriate. If the victim is under the age of 18, then this must be reported clearly to the control room because an investigative policy regarding the death of a child will be activated. If the deceased is a visiting serviceman/woman (on or off duty), the Visiting Forces Act 1952 may be relevant and the investigation could be taken over by a foreign authority, such as the US Air Force, but the police should meanwhile maintain control of the investigation.

The officer should take control of the scene and anything within it or near it which may be associated with the death (a weapon, drugs, alcohol bottles, suicide note). If the death is not suspicious, then local policy may require the officer to search the deceased for signs of injury and to take from them any valuables—these should be packaged and stored securely according to local protocols. However, any sudden death could be the result of a crime so an investigative mindset should be employed throughout because the scene could have been staged to delay or avoid a murder investigation.

After the examination at the scene, the body will be removed. If relatives need to be informed, this must be done as soon as possible by a police officer (in person, unless the conditions are exceptional). Police forces across the UK carry out this task for each other when distance makes it difficult. A family liaison officer can be used in cases of murder, road fatalities, and other incidents.

Some police officers will suffer psychologically after dealing with a sudden death, ranging from being generally upset to severe changes in behaviour. Every police service has structures in place to provide support and assistance: getting help is not a sign of weakness. (See Chapter 6 on Wellbeing and Resilience.)

10.4.2 Certifying death

If there is the slightest chance a victim is alive, medical assistance should be obtained. A medical professional (a doctor, nurse, or ambulance crew) is required to attend the scene to certify that death has occurred or to make a ROLE ('recognition of life extinct'). There are some exceptions to this rule based upon the notion that a person is 'obviously dead' but, for the trainee officer, it is better to err on the side of caution and seek advice.

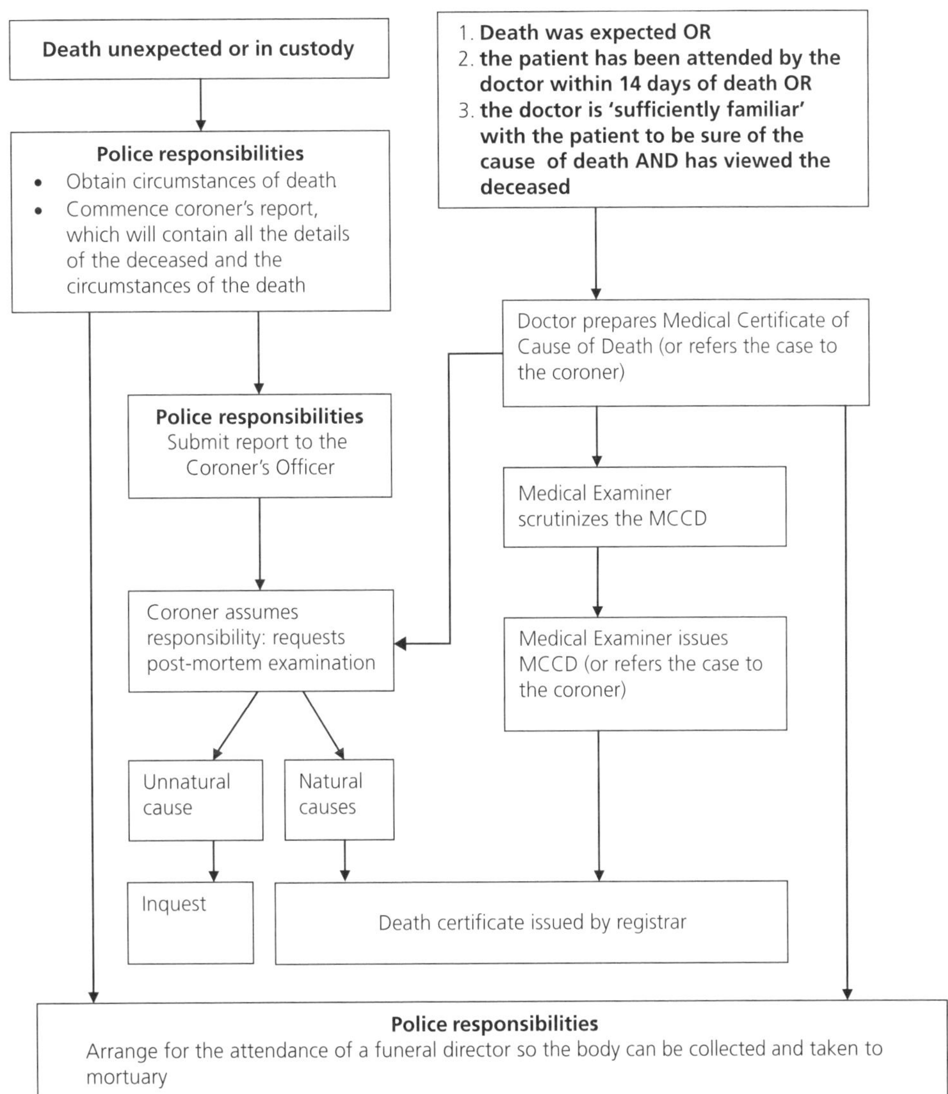

The procedure for certifying death depends on whether the death was expected or unexpected, as shown in the diagram.

The role of 'Medical Examiner' was created in 2012 as a second check on the findings in the MCCD, consequent to the offences committed by Dr Harold Shipman.

10.4.3 Changes to the body after death

A body changes quite quickly and predictably after death, so this can assist investigations. The most immediate change is the colour of the skin, which can appear lifeless and wax-like within a few seconds of losing its blood flow.

Hypostasis occurs when the blood settles to the lowest parts due to gravity and enters parts of the skin creating a port-wine colour (dark red) stain. This is also known as post-mortem lividity or *livor mortis*. Where a body is upright, the blood drains to the lower parts of the limbs, cheeks, and ears. After three to four hours, the blood clots and can no longer flow, so if the body is subsequently moved, the dark areas will no longer be on the lower or underside parts of the body. Pressure can cause distortion to the pattern of hypostasis, for example any areas of skin that have been under pressure will be pale because they are uncoloured by blood. These effects can be produced by the weight of the body on textured fabrics and clothing seams, and even by floor tiles.

Rigor mortis occurs when chemical changes in the muscles gradually cause them to stiffen. The process normally begins in the head and works down the body. In very general terms, it might start after four hours and disappear after 24 hours (when the body begins to break down biologically). However, the process is dependent upon a number of factors, particularly the ambient temperature (the process is quicker at higher temperatures). Crucially, immediately after death the body becomes limp and will flop to rest on adjacent structures and, if left for a number of hours, rigor mortis will stiffen it in that position. If subsequently moved, the body will be rigid and fixed in that initial posture—it will not flop until the rigor mortis fades.

The core temperature of the deceased will gradually equalize with the ambient temperature after death, so it will usually fall in the UK climate. The relationship between the rate of fall in the core temperature and the ambient temperature is well documented but cannot provide an estimated time of death to the nearest few minutes. The ambient conditions (eg air flow), the amount of clothing, and the previous general health of the victim may all affect how fast the temperature falls. Later, decay and insect activity can cause the body temperature to increase.

Other changes to the body will depend on the conditions. If the weather is not too cold, it will begin to break down quite rapidly which may attract a variety of animals which will feed upon it. Blowflies are the most mobile carrion feeders and will appear first, followed by successive waves of insects and other animals. The results include putrefaction and even dispersal of bones over time. In hot or dry environments, the body may become mummified. The process of change in a body after death is covered by a specialist field: forensic taphonomy.

10.4.4 Murder investigations

The level of resources put into a murder investigation depends on the classification of the murder. Murders are classified as Category (Cat) A, B, or C within a more general system of categorizing major crime. Cat A and Cat B murder investigations will be led by an SIO who will probably be centrally based, while a Cat C murder could be investigated by detectives in a local BCU. However, there are variations on these basic categories, and a Cat C murder can often turn out to be more complicated than first thought, requiring more than just a local response.

The 'Murder Investigation Manual' (the 'MIM') and the 'Practice Advice on Core Investigative Doctrine' (ACPO, 2006 and ACPO Centrex, 2005, respectively) provide a five-stage investigative model which is used by most police services as the template for major violent crime enquiries. The five stages are fast track, theoretical process, planned method of investigation, suspect enquiries, and disposal.

10.5 Fires and Railway Incidents

Any scene involving fire, and railway property present particular risks. The policing of most railways and the London Underground is the responsibility of British Transport Police (BTP), but other constabularies will sometimes be involved, for example pursuing suspects, searching railway property for missing persons or property related to crime or providing cover when BTP are not immediately available. BTP officers' training is augmented by Personal Track Safety (PTS) courses: most other police services do not offer this certification.

10.5.1 Attending a fire

Fires are caused by the oxidation of fuel which creates heat. In order for a fire to occur, three elements are required: a fuel source (such as furniture or petrol), oxygen, and an external heat source to cause ignition. Once a fire has started, the heat generated can speed up the rate of burning so yet more heat energy is liberated, causing a chain reaction effect. A fire can be extinguished by removing one of the three elements; removing the fuel, starving the fire of oxygen, or reducing the temperature with water. Fires in buildings will often self-extinguish once most of the available fuel or oxygen has been consumed. However, in such a situation opening a door or window will introduce fresh air (containing oxygen) to any remaining hot fuel, and the fire can suddenly explode into an inferno within seconds.

The heat from fires spreads by convection (hot air rises), conduction (heat travels through solid objects), and radiation (glowing heat that crosses empty space). Fires can grow very fast and the chain reaction effect means that small fires, which appear to be insignificant, can spread quite rapidly. During a drought, the fuel load in outdoor environments such as grasslands, forests, and gardens, is so dry that the fire spreads far faster than would normally be expected.

Fires are emotional scenes and there may be irrational or angry outbursts levelled at anyone which might include physical assault. A number of agencies are available to assist such victims, for example the local authority can provide temporary accommodation, and practical assistance may be sought from the Salvation Army or Citizens' Advice. If a family member or colleague has died or been injured as a result, then more specialist support can be arranged through Victim Support, the NHS, a Family Liaison Officer (FLO), and charities such as Cruse Bereavement Care.

10.5.1.1 The role of the police at fires

The overriding principle at fire scenes is to prevent the loss of human life. The critical issue of your own safety as a police officer extends to fighting fires: police officers should not attempt to take action against anything but the smallest of fires. Police officers have powers under s 17 of the PACE Act 1984 to enter a premises to save life or prevent damage, and PCSOs have powers under the Police Reform Act 2002, Sch 4, Part 1, but no unnecessary risks should be taken to save lives, protect property, or rescue animals.

Putting out the fire and saving lives is the role of the Fire and Rescue Service (FRS), but police officers can assist by controlling the public (s 37 of the Road Traffic Act 1988), assisting with evacuations, and closing roads (ss 35 and 163) as appropriate. If the cause of the fire is unknown or suspicious, then local policy will almost certainly require the attendance of a patrol supervisor or inspector, CID, and a CSI. An incident may be deemed to be 'serious' if injury or significant loss occurs, and an appropriate police response and investigation will take place. If the FRS is at the scene, the FAO should make contact with the senior fire officer and provide localized information as required.

If the FRS is not in attendance, police officers should employ the JESIP M/ETHANE mnemonic (see 10.6.1). During the early phase of an incident, a fire may be small enough to tackle with available fire-fighting equipment or imaginative use of a hose or towel. The attending police officers will need to make a judgement and keep the control room informed, particularly if it seems the fire could spread. The control room will contact the FRS which will decide whether or not to attend and will also contact relevant security companies, homeowners, and key holders of houses or businesses so that they can take appropriate action. If there is any conceivable risk to people in nearby properties, the street, or in passing vehicles then decisive action must be taken: evacuate all nearby properties and keep everybody clear. Follow the old adage: GET OUT and STAY OUT.

People in or near a fire may have burning clothes or hair, and these can also 'spontaneously combust' at a distance due to the radiant heat. Such victims may well panic and be unable to follow advice. They should be pushed into a lying position on the ground and the flames smothered with a coat or blanket. A horizontal position is particularly important to prevent convected heat rising from burning clothes and damaging the eyes and mouth.

Any large fire will inevitably attract onlookers, many of whom will merely wish to watch, but some may be intent on stealing rescued property or may even try to enter the property to steal. Scene security, management of the public, and a continuing eye on traffic problems need to be maintained. Some arsonists will return to observe the activity at the scene and a few may even obstruct attempts to extinguish the fire.

10.5.1.2 Fire and Rescue Service powers and obstruction offences

The Fire and Rescue Services Act 2004 confers a number of powers on the FRS and its members in relation to emergencies, particularly for incidents which are likely to cause death or serious illness or injury, or serious harm to the environment and any plants or animals in it. This applies for emergencies such as fires (or situations where there is a major risk of a fire) and road traffic incidents. It also covers actions required to prevent consequent damage to property (s 44(1)). Authorized FRS staff can enter premises by force, move or break into vehicles, close roads, control the traffic, and restrict access in order to achieve these aims (s 44(2)).

A person interfering with or obstructing firefighters in the course of their work could be charged with an offence, for example:

- obstructing or hindering personnel engaged in emergency operations when extinguishing a fire or protecting life and property in relation to a fire (or going anywhere to deal with it or prepare for it) (s 1 of the Emergency Workers (Obstruction) Act 2006);
- obstructing a person who is assisting a firefighter (s 2 of the Emergency Workers (Obstruction) Act 2006);
- obstructing or interfering with an employee of a fire authority who is entering a property or vehicle by force, or carrying out other emergency work (s 44 of the Fire and Rescue Services Act 2004).

10.5.1.3 Health and Safety

By its very nature, policing has always been and will continue to be a potentially hazardous occupation and while risks are present in all work activities, response officers are more frequently exposed. Health and safety duties are covered by ss 2–7 of the Health and Safety at Work etc Act 1974, and became applicable to police officers, special constabulary officers, and cadets by virtue of the Police (Health and Safety) Act 1997.

Section 2(2) of the Health and Safety at Work etc Act (HSWA) 1974 sets out the employer's role for health and safety while legislation also places general duties on employees to take reasonable care for their own health and safety (s 7(a) of the HSWA) such as using work items in accordance with training and instructions received (reg 14(1) of the Management of Health and Safety at Work Regulations 1999).

Given the potentially traumatic nature of police work it is also imperative that officers get the right support with their mental health (see Chapter 6 on Wellbeing and Resilience).

Core Aspects of Police Work

10.5.1.4 Risk and control measures

The formal levels of classification for hazard levels are:

- high—death, major injury, or serious illness may result;
- medium—serious injuries or ill health, off work for more than three days; and
- low—less serious illness or injury, off work for less than three days.

The levels of classification for risk levels are:

- high if the event is very likely or near certain to occur;
- medium if the event is likely to occur; and
- low if the event is very unlikely to occur.

The overall threat level for any given activity is the combination of these two factors and control measures are steps that officers can take to lower the risk and reduce the threat level.

THREAT LEVEL ↘		HAZARD		
		High	Medium	Low
RISK	High	INTOLERABLE **high** threat level	SUBSTANTIAL **high** threat level	MODERATE **medium** threat level
	Medium	SUBSTANTIAL **high** threat level	MODERATE **medium** threat level	ACCEPTABLE **low** threat level
	Low	MODERATE **medium** threat level	ACCEPTABLE **low** threat level	TRIVIAL **low** threat level

(Adapted from Home Office, 1997)

For example in relation to the road network, officers can: adopt the correct procedures learnt during training; wear the correct personal fluorescent equipment; keep the control room updated with your location; and be aware of the limitations of communications equipment.

Bearing in mind the risks inherent in policing, Personal Safety Training for officers is seen as an important part of initial training and successful completion is a requisite before Independent Patrol Status can be achieved.

Likewise, as first responders there is a responsibility on response officers to be trained in basic first aid which is also likely to be a necessary condition for Independent Patrol Status. Training will probably cover the following:

- Managing scenes and casualties
- Basic Life Support for Adults and separately Infants and Children
- Choking
- Sprains and strains
- Scalds and burns
- Heatstroke and hypothermia

10.5.2 Incidents and offences on railway property

Railways and their associated infrastructure are exceptionally dangerous places. The electrical conductors which carry the power for trains are either a third rail or overhead, suspended between gantries. It should always be assumed they are 'live' because the power runs continuously. Given that they carry so much power, death is almost certain if a person (or anything they are touching) comes into contact with railway power conductors. Overhead power lines can also arc, transmitting electricity through the air to nearby objects. If a person has fallen onto the third rail, there is nothing which can realistically be done until the power is turned off, so police officers should be absolutely certain that this has been done before acting in such circumstances; **there is no room for ambiguity.**

Further dangers are posed by 'rolling stock' (engines and carriages), particularly as modern trains are fast and relatively silent in operation. Railway apparatus (ie railway equipment other than rolling stock) is also dangerous: electrical components, moving parts, and trip hazards are universal. Therefore, police officers engaged on foot pursuits or assisting on railway property, for example at a station, should continuously consider their safety and that of colleagues and the public. **Essentially: there is no reward worth the risk of stepping onto a railway line**. Most local policies will require the abandonment of foot pursuits if the suspect enters railway property, unless there is an immediate risk to life and the officer feels that the situation warrants entry to the track area (after a dynamic risk assessment).

For searches, special measures called 'Safe Systems of Work' (eg stopping trains and cutting the power) should be arranged before carrying out **any** search on operating railway lines or associated property, and it is wise to post a lookout for any carriages or engines that are still moving, however slowly. When searches of railway property are required, close negotiation with Network Rail and train-operating companies is essential to reduce the risk of accidents and—where practicable—minimize disturbance to the network. Under the Railway Safety Accreditation Scheme, BTP can accredit organizations and selected personnel with powers to deal with anti-social behaviour by issuing Fixed Penalty Notices and enforcing by-laws. Such staff can act as a visible deterrent and provide reassurance, and free up BTP officers for more frontline duties.

Apart from the common offences which might be committed on railways (thefts, assaults and criminal damage), specific legislation applies for crime and trespass on the railway network.

10.5.2.1 Trespass and authorized crossing point offences

Under s 16 of the Railway Regulation Act 1840 it is an offence to wilfully trespass on any railway or railway premises, and to refuse to leave when asked to do so by any officer or agent of the railway company. Another piece of Victorian legislation is the Regulation of Railways Act 1868, which prohibits a person from crossing a railway line other than in an authorized place (eg level crossings). Under s 23, a person commits an offence if crossing at an unauthorized place after being warned to desist by a servant or agent of the railway company.

Nearly a century later, the British Transport Commission Act 1949 added legislation on trespass to cover trespass along 'railway lines, embankments, tunnels and sidings or any "works" (equipment) and electrical installations' (s 55). The section raises the issue of being in 'dangerous proximity' of lines and electrical installations. It is important to note that the investigating officer must produce evidence of a notice exhibited at the station nearest the place of the offence providing a clear public warning not to trespass on a railway. These signs are most obviously seen at the ends of platforms and at pedestrian and level crossings. Such trespass is a summary offence and can be dealt with by a £60 PND.

10.5.2.2 Throwing objects and causing damage to railway property

Section 56 of the British Transport Commission Act 1949 makes it an offence to throw, or cause to fall, any object (likely to cause damage) into or upon any rolling stock or static equipment on any railway or siding or any 'works', or which is likely to cause injury. It is immaterial whether the train or equipment is in motion or is static. This is a summary offence and can be dealt with by a £60 PND (see 10.18.2.2).

The Offences Against the Person Act 1861 is a more complex but overarching piece of legislation which discusses 'unlawfully and maliciously' throwing or causing objects to fall. If an intent to injure or endanger any person on a train can be proved, then an offence has been committed (ss 32 and 33). Drunkenness and failing to follow by-laws are covered in s 34, and other acts of misconduct by railway employees are covered in s 17 of the Railway Regulation Act 1842.

The Malicious Damage Act 1861 (s 35) covers placing items (eg a railway sleeper) on a railway, and also covers the removal of rails, turning (or switching) points, and showing or hiding signals. There must be intent to obstruct, overthrow, damage, or destroy an engine, carriage, or truck. This offence is triable on indictment only and the maximum penalty is life imprisonment. Section 36 deals specifically with obstructing engines, or carriages, or railways. The offence is triable either way and it is not necessary to prove intent.

10.6 Attending Emergency, Major, and Critical Incidents

Initial police training is likely to cover the police role in handling emergencies, major incidents, and critical incidents, and emergencies. These categories of incident are all similar in terms of their scale and significance, and it is for this reason that we have grouped them together here. Of all of these types of incident, trainee officers are most likely to attend emergency scenes.

An **emergency** is defined by s 1 of the Civil Contingencies Act 2004 as 'an event or situation which threatens serious damage to human welfare in a place in the United Kingdom', and will include one or more of the following:

- human illness, injury, or loss of life;
- homelessness or damage to property;
- disruption of a supply of money, food, water, energy, or fuel;
- disruption of transport, communication, or health systems and services;
- serious environmental damage (eg radioactive contamination);
- war or terrorism which threatens serious damage to the security of the UK.

(Note that the College of Policing subdivides emergencies into 'rapid onset emergencies' and 'rising tide emergencies' (see CoP, 2017d for further details).)

A **major incident** is an emergency that requires the implementation of special arrangements by one or more of the emergency services, the NHS, or local authority. It is likely to involve serious harm, damage, security risk, disruption, or risk to human life or welfare, such as floods or widespread illness.

A **critical incident** can be defined as 'any incident where the effectiveness of the police response is likely to have a significant impact on the confidence of the victim, their family and/or the community' (NPIA, 2011). This definition was subsequently adopted by the College of Policing. Any incident can escalate to being critical, while other incidents are obviously significant from the very start such as a train crash or a large fire.

Police officers in training will practise and rehearse effective ways to intervene to resolve a problem such as a domestic dispute, dealing with a shoplifter, or calming people down who have been involved in a minor road collision. They will learn to defuse, control, restrain, or manage a wide range of such incidents. But for more serious incidents—those with the potential to 'go major' and get out of hand—there are far fewer opportunities for practice.

Every constabulary and every emergency service will have contingency plans to deal with a whole variety of emergencies and incidents, and for some types of incident this will be a legal requirement under the Civil Contingencies Act 2004.

The Joint Emergency Services Interoperability Programme (JESIP) was set up for co-ordinating major incidents requiring a multi-agency response. It developed procedures which allow for joint working between police, fire and rescue, and ambulance services, enabling each organization to work with others but still maintain autonomy and follow their own procedures. These guidelines facilitate co-ordinated and coherent decision-making in situations that can be very fluid and demanding. The JESIP procedures also permit a shared assessment of risk to be made, and take into account that each organization will have its own operational focus during an incident. Trainee officers are unlikely to be involved in the management of a major incident but should be aware that the JESIP procedures will be used.

Large-scale incidents of any type are not simply 'dealt with' and then closed: after the incident there will be serious issues to consider concerning the impact upon the community at large, such as a fear of further crime or where the public's expectations of the police have not been met. Liaison with victims, their families, and the community at large is important for several reasons, not least of which is to restore public confidence.

10.6.1 JESIP 'M/ETHANE' emergency procedures

The JESIP M/ETHANE mnemonic (JESIP, 2021) can be used to guide decisions during the early stages of managing a major, or multi-agency, incident (with 'ETHANE' being used for incidents that would not be classified as 'major'). Any police officer may find themselves as the first responder at an incident and, if the control room has not already decided whether a multi-agency response is required, the first responder may need to make that decision.

The mnemonic for the standard JESIP procedure for incidents (full details available from the JESIP website) is M/ETHANE as follows:

- Major incident declared?
- Exact location;
- Type of incident;
- Hazards, present or suspected;
- Access—routes that are safe to use;
- Number, type, severity of casualties; and
- Emergency services—those present and those required.

When a major or multi-agency incident has been declared, it can take time to implement the appropriate strategic and tactical response, so it is vital to ensure that incidents are identified and declared as soon as possible. Accurate information is essential. A number of 'apps' are available for smartphones and tablet devices which claim to help with recording and conveying the information associated with 'M/ETHANE', but you should only use these if instructed to do so by your constabulary.

Out of all the services that may attend such an incident, only the police will be constantly alert to the possibility that a crime has been committed and that the emergency, major, or critical incident could also be a crime scene (see 10.3). For example, after a road traffic collision, consideration must be given as to whether the driver was under the influence of drink or drugs; and after a fall from a height, did the woman fall or was she pushed; is this a natural or a suspicious death? Police officers should be suspicious and be alert to any characteristic signs that there is something wrong. Given the recent prevalence of marauding terrorist incidents, this awareness is increasingly important as a scene may not be what the FAO initially believes it to be; further lives may be at risk. Additional information and problem-solving skills can help to illuminate the incident beyond the initial assessment.

The actions of the FAO are crucial to the proper and managed outcome of the incident, and relying on instinct is not sufficient in such situations. For example, a trainee officer may be tempted to act heroically at a house fire but, without the proper apparatus or an understanding of how fires develop and the risk of structural collapse of the building, the officer may become a victim rather than a rescuer. A police officer needs to follow proper procedures and to think and act calmly and rationally in order to:

- assess the situation and work out what is going on;
- communicate as quickly as possible; and
- prioritize actions.

10.6.2 Control and responsibility

The FAO is in control of the incident as Silver, the forward Commander until relieved by someone of superior rank. The incident may include a crime scene, so preservation of evidence and keeping the scene clear and untouched is very important. In an emergency involving firearms or the risk of violence, current practice is that the FAO would not let other emergency services go forward into the line of fire either. Currently, most ambulance trusts will also not permit their personnel to enter ongoing firearms-related crime or terror-related scenes as a matter of safety: in 2019, the London Ambulance Service explained to the media that its response to an incident in Streatham, where two people were stabbed by an assailant later shot dead by armed police, involved waiting at a 'rendezvous point until the police confirmed it was safe for them to approach patients' (*London Evening Standard*, 2020). However, policy evolves and, as with all matters concerning attending incidents, ensure that you are familiar with local police policy.

In scenes where additional risk is present, such as a firearms incident, terrorist attack, or CBRN attack, areas will be designated as 'hot', 'warm', and 'cold' depending on the risks within those areas. 'Hot' zones contain the most risk with the risk reducing through the 'warm' and 'cold' zones. Changes following the Kerslake Report (Kerslake, 2017) now allow for emergency personnel to be sent into a 'hot' zone. Remember to always follow local guidance on attending high-risk scenes.

In practice, it is unlikely that an FAO would be alone for that long, unless the incident is in a really remote and inaccessible place, or there are corollary problems such as a natural disaster of some kind and access roads are blocked. A senior officer may arrive quite quickly but, if not, the golden hour is the responsibility of the officers present. All this sounds complicated and difficult to remember; however, training and experience enable police officers to maintain clear priorities and to follow procedures properly, acting calmly, positively, purposefully, and promptly.

10.6.2.1 Levels of command

The standard command sequence in use in all police forces across the UK is Gold, Silver, Bronze (GSB). The levels refer to the function of the command level and not necessarily to the rank of the officers concerned (see the College of Policing APP *Operations and Command Structures* for further information). The Home Office guidance document *Critical incident management, Version 11.0* provides the role descriptions shown in the table.

Gold	Strategic command of the incident, usually at police headquarters or at a designated strategic police command centre
Silver	Tactical police command at a forward point closer to the scene of immediate crisis
Bronze	Operational local response at the crisis point itself, eg cordons or firearms, often carried out by a number of people (Operational Response Commanders or ORC) rather than one designated commander

When available, the more senior officer assumes the command level. Therefore, a trainee officer on Independent or Supervised Patrol may be Silver for a short period of time, but only until a more senior or more experienced officer arrives on the scene. This tiered structure is considered by many in the police service to work effectively, and has been exhaustively tested at all levels.

10.6.2.2 Responding to marauding terrorist attacks

There have been an increasing number of such attacks in recent years, such as the Manchester Arena attack and the London Bridge attacks in 2017 and 2019. The response to the Manchester Arena attack was evaluated in the Kerslake Report and the system by which areas were designated as 'hot', 'warm', or 'cold' to direct emergency services support was judged as insufficient in the context of responding to a marauding terrorist attack.

The Joint Operating Principles (JOP) for emergency services response to a marauding terrorist attack were changed in 2019, and unarmed police officers can now be required to enter areas of high risk, to preserve life and provide first aid. In addition, emergency services staff may now be directed to 'hot' or 'warm' zones without an armed police escort. This was highlighted as being good practice in the inquests into both the Manchester and the London Bridge terrorist attacks.

10.6.3 Risk assessment and deployment decisions

A risk assessment must be carried out to facilitate a proportionate response in the right sequence. The senior officer carrying out the assessment will ask the person who is 'Silver' at the time for information about the situation.

Resources should not be committed too early unless there is a clear picture of what is happening on the ground and filling a site with armed officers, dog teams, and underwater search personnel may turn out not to be necessary.

In the case of missing persons and especially when there may be other factors, possibly criminal, there are many components to the response: search teams are called out, assessments of transport needs are made, command and control, strategic, and tactical responses are all set up, and the control room will alert other emergency services.

For larger incidents, the military might be required and military aid to the civil authority (MACA) will be invoked. Specialists such as explosives ordnance otherwise known as bomb disposal, helicopters, search and rescue, engineers, nuclear, chemical, and radiological detection and containment units may be called upon. Note that deployment of armed officers is usually a top-level Gold command decision, made by a chief superintendent or chief officer.

10.6.4 Information management at incidents

At some incidents there may be bystanders; they may be a help or a hindrance so will need to be controlled, even at a relatively limited incident. Well-intentioned people may offer to help, and in some circumstances volunteers can be used effectively until more help arrives, for example to instruct and contain people, to direct traffic, and conduct evacuation. However, bystanders may not always be so helpful; police and other emergency service support can be delayed because of passers-by who want to see what is going on. Police officers should always be prepared to move such onlookers away. There is another and very important reason why the area itself must be controlled: it could be a crime scene and controlling access and the preservation of evidence is vital.

Newspapers, internet sites, social network sites, radio, and television have apparently inexhaustible appetites for crime stories, and this quest has produced an edgy, sometimes fraught, relationship between the media and the police. The media can be rather superficial and sensationalist in an endless quest for headlines (see Leishman and Mason (2003) for more detail), and the unfair presentation of witnesses, victims, or suspects by the media can undermine their credibility before due process has taken place. However, there is no doubt that the media can help with appeals for information to help to solve complex crimes, raise awareness of danger, alert the public to emergencies or major disruption, or appeal for help with searches for missing people. The media can very quickly engage with large numbers of people over a large geographical area, and this can help, for example, locate suspects or witnesses who have left the local area.

Communications from the police to the media must be carefully managed. Too much information could put informants at risk, limit the range of questions that could be asked of a potential suspect, or encourage them to dispose of items that could provide crucial evidence. An individual police officer should never be tempted to communicate with the media; each police service will have a specialist unit for these functions and some BCUs have their own media relations staff too. An officer's comments might inadvertently be misleading—they might not have the full picture and are unlikely to have much experience in communicating through the media. In major incidents, the police will hold a press conference to brief the press and provide up-to-date and appropriate information.

10.7 Attending Scenes with Suspect Devices

Suspect devices include bombs, incendiary devices designed to start or sustain a fire, and CBRN devices containing chemical, biological, radiological, and/or nuclear material. In 2006, a former Russian KGB officer Alexander Litvinenko, who had taken asylum in Britain, was poisoned with radioactive polonium whilst at a central London hotel, and died a few weeks later in hospital. And in 2018 Sergei Skripal, a former Russian army officer, and his daughter suffered the effects of a nerve agent whilst in Salisbury city centre. The first Wiltshire police officers on the scene also required hospital treatment.

Terrorist incidents can be regarded as those incidents that involve the use or threat of violence (often extreme violence) to attempt to instil fear in order to further or to publicize a political or extremist belief. The Terrorism Act 2000 provides both an 'official' definition of the meaning of 'terrorism' and the particular powers for situations which might involve terrorism. Similar powers are available under other primary legislation or procedure, but the Terrorism Act 2000 provides wider powers to stop and search and to arrest.

The precise nature of any suspect device cannot be determined by visual means alone. **The cardinal rule is: do not touch it.** At such an incident, the FAO should create a very wide space around the device (as wide as is practicable) and get people out of the area. The preservation of evidence is a high priority, but at all times is secondary to public safety.

10.7.1 Cordons and the Terrorism Act 2000

An area can be designated as a cordoned area under s 34 of the Terrorism Act 2000. The designating officer will usually be at least superintendent rank but could be any rank if the matter is considered urgent under s 34(2). Police officers have certain additional powers in a designated cordoned area (s 34(1)). Once an area has been cordoned, under s 36(1) a police officer can:

- order a person to immediately leave a cordoned area or any adjacent premises, and to move a vehicle from a cordoned area (if the driver or in charge of the vehicle);
- arrange for the removal of a vehicle from a cordoned area or for it to be moved within a cordoned area; or
- prohibit or restrict pedestrian or vehicular access to a cordoned area.

(Note that slightly different legislation applies for BTP and MOD police officers.)

Failing to comply with any of these requests (without reasonable excuse) is a summary offence (s 36(2) of the Terrorism Act 2000), and the penalty is three months' imprisonment and/or a fine.

10.7.2 Suspected explosive devices

Alerts for suspected explosive devices present major demands on police and other emergency service resources. However, it must be assumed that every suspect device has the potential to kill and injure. The National Counter Terrorism Security Office (NCTSO) provides extensive advice, updated in 2017, on what to do in the event of a suspected explosive device which is available on the gov.uk website. The advice was written for the public and employees such as shop staff, but much of it is also relevant to police officers in training.

The advice in this context can change on a frequent basis, partly in response to emerging terrorist threats and tactics. For example, the NCTSO advice states that in some circumstances complete evacuation is not the ideal action (eg if a suspect device has not been found or the presence of multiple devices is suspected (see *Recognising the Terrorist Threat* available on the gov.uk website)). They suggest instead a partial evacuation or no evacuation at all; officers should seek advice from the emergency co-ordinator and senior officers and follow local constabulary procedures.

For cordoning at the scene of a suspect device, many police services adopt the practices shown in the table but as in all matters involving critical incidents, be guided by local police policy.

Size of object (approximate)	Distance between cordon and device
Briefcase	100m
Car or small van	200m
Van or larger vehicle	400m

The initial cordons may be installed by the fire or ambulance services during the rescue phase, using red and white tape. The outer cordon will generally be installed by the police using blue and white tape, and will be managed by scene control officers who permit authorized entry as required, and record activity in their crime-scene log.

In an urban area, streets lined with buildings create a potential blast corridor for any explosion so personnel are safer behind hard cover such as concrete buildings with no line of sight of the suspected device. No person should be located behind or beneath windows or other glass panels, however far away from the device.

The CAP to the object should be marked out if practicable (see 10.3.2), consistent with the overriding priority of personal and public safety. The control room should be informed of the precise location of the device, especially if a wider evacuation is taking place outside the immediate cordon, but note that hand-held radios or mobile phones must not be used within 10 metres of the suspect object, and vehicle-based radios must not be used to transmit within 50 metres.

10.7.3 CBRN incidents

A CBRN incident has the potential to cause very widespread loss of life. Fortunately, this type of incident is rare and all police services will have detailed contingency plans—the considerations and procedures are the same as for any other type of suspect device. Some CBRN attacks can be hard to recognize such as those involving nuclear radiation, but any reports of groups of people suddenly collapsing or feeling unwell, or of a strong or noxious smell, could indicate the presence of chemicals.

In a suspected CBRN incident, the Steps procedure should be followed (Home Office, 2015b). Here, the step number corresponds with the observed number of casualties. For a Step 3 incident, a JESIP M/ETHANE assessment should be made if at all possible but police safety must not be compromised.

Step	Number of casualties	Procedure
Step 1	One	Approach the site using the usual procedures.
Step 2	Two	Approach with caution and do not discount any possibility. Report arrival and do not touch any object. Report updates continually.
Step 3	Three or more	Do not enter the scene. Create an RV point outside the area, identify safe arrival routes, and await instructions.

10.7.4 Attending the scene of a bomb explosion

After a bomb explosion, there is likely to be wreckage, smoke, flames, badly injured people, dead bodies, and confusion. The role of the FAO is the same in principle as for a train crash or major road traffic accident: take charge, clear those who can walk out of the area, close off the area with a cordon, attend to the injured if possible, and treat the area as a crime scene.

As well as complying with the JESIP M/ETHANE guidelines (see 10.6.1), all officers should ensure they continue with their duties at a major incident as defined by their constabulary procedures. Every attempt should be made to preserve the scene for further investigation, but the first priority is always the preservation of life.

The control room must be kept informed of the situation so that appropriate support can be dispatched to the incident and the commanders have all the information they require. Overall, an officer will usually find that their duties will be centred on three main priorities: preserving life, organizing the response to the incident, and maintaining order at the scene.

Nothing can really prepare a trainee police officer for the emotional impact of witnessing such scenes. However, it has been said, and in our view rightly, that what distinguishes a police officer from the general public is not their exercise of powers, or uniform, or knowledge of the law, but knowing what to do in an emergency. That knowledge can only come from training and experience.

10.8 Planned Operations

Planned Operations are where the police have had advanced warning of a situation or event and therefore will have developed suitable contingency plans and strategies. Examples include disruption at sea and airports due to strikes, pre-planned demonstrations, and large music festivals. As soon as the necessity for such an operation has been identified, it is given an operational name to distinguish it from other incidents. The operation covers the period from instigation, through planning, execution, and debrief. We provide a summary here, but more details are available on the College of Policing website.

10.8.1 Planning an operation

All police organizations have contingency plans for identified risks in their own areas, with a degree of flexibility to cover all eventualities. A range of tactical options can be used for planned operations. Some are also employed in 'steady state' policing (see 10.1) such as using police dogs and batons and entering buildings, but others are more specialized, for example armed response personnel who can fire attenuating energy projectiles and CS smoke. Other tactical options include shield tactics, air support, barricade/obstacle removal, cordons and intercepts, water cannon, containment, and evidence-gathering teams.

The GSB hierarchy of command is nationally recognized by the police, partner agencies, and other emergency services. At each level of command, tactical advisers from the police and external organizations provide knowledge, understanding, and skills for the planning phase and for responding to changing circumstances throughout the duration of the operation. For example, Gold Command could elect to convene a strategic co-ordinating group or Silver Command could assemble a tactical planning group to develop a strategy.

Commanders and co-ordinating groups require specific, accurate, and relevant information at each stage of the operation so a dedicated intelligence function will be required (see Chapter 13). This could be located at the GSB incident room or elsewhere, for example at the Force Intelligence Bureau. A Community Impact Assessment (CIA) will be conducted to assess the extent to which businesses, community groups, families, and individuals may be affected by the proposed police response; all vital information for planning a successful operation. Personnel from within the police family, eg neighbourhood teams, and external representatives from the third sector such as charitable, non-profit-making organizations and community bodies can all provide input for the CIA.

Gold Command determines the strategy and will plan the police response accordingly. All the relevant information is recorded in a single document, the *operational order*. The personnel participating in the operation are briefed as required, following the categories set out in the JESIP IIMARCH model as shown in the table.

Heading	Key features
Information	Such as evaluated intelligence, results of the community impact assessment, length, duration, and location of the operation
Intention	Objectives of GSB strategies, tactics, policies, powers, and procedures
Method	Process by which the tactics, policies, powers, and procedures will be used
Administration	Logistics pertaining to start times, location, and lengths of duty and periods of refreshment
Risk assessment	Based on gathered information from intelligence sources
Communications	Including media broadcasts and inter-operability between personnel
Human rights and other legalities	Preserving the rights of individuals and groups and adhering to codes of practice in the use of legislation

Source: Derived in part from JESIP (2017) and Home Office (2014d) but authors' interpretation and description.

The police information generated by an operation must be collected, recorded, shared, and retained in accordance with local police and national guidelines. These specify the use of the Government Security Classifications Policy (GSCP), under which information is classified as either Official, Secret, or Top Secret.

10.8.2 Participating in a planned operation

During a planned operation, police officers will of course follow the tactics outlined in the operational order, but within these limits individual officers will probably need to decide what specific actions to take. They should use the College of Policing National Decision Model as a framework for taking a decision. Records of any decisions made, and actions carried out should be made in accordance with the PACE Codes of Practice (see 18.6.1) and the rules of disclosure (see 13.4.3). The decisions and actions should be recorded as a PNB entry, although this might not be possible at the time, depending on the circumstances.

The operational order may specify the use of personal protective and operational equipment particularly if the use of force is likely to be required. The use of force to challenge unacceptable behaviour will be covered under personal safety training and limited by legislation such as the Human Rights Act 1998 and common law. Each individual officer must remember that their own health and safety is just as important as maintaining the health and safety of others.

10.8.3 Effective communication for planned operations

Effective communication with partners, communities, and other stakeholders helps to build trust and confidence, and ensure that the appropriate strategy is adopted. Openness and transparency can help to identify potential problems and make it less likely that the situation will escalate and result in the use of unplanned, and less suitable, police response tactics. All officers participating in an operation have an individual responsibility to maintain effective interpersonal communication (see Chapter 8). Various communication channels are available to GSB during planning and during the operation itself, such as:

- face-to-face, for example public meetings, under-represented groups, independent advisory groups, partnership working, and information sharing;

- digital and social media platforms such as Facebook, Twitter, YouTube and digitally enabled meetings;
- corporate communication via traditional media, for example press releases and statements, television, radio, and newspaper interviews.

After a planned operation, there will be a debriefing process to identify examples of good practice and opportunities for improvement. This could help to streamline procedures and reduce demands for frontline staff in the future. The information from the debrief should be recorded and retained for revelation and disclosure (see 13.4.3). Further information on debriefing can be found on the College of Policing APP website.

10.9 Dealing with Suspects

On occasion you will be called to, or come across, an incident where not only do you suspect a crime has been committed, but the suspect for the crime is also present. Alternatively during the course of your duties you may come across suspects for other crimes. This section will outline how you would deal with that suspect from the initial caution through to their arrest and the disposal of their case.

10.9.1 Cautions

From the moment a police officer suspects a person of committing an offence, the suspect has the right to certain information. A caution or warning is given to protect the suspect's rights and keep them informed of the possible consequences of what they say, or don't say, during an investigation. PACE Code of Practice C, para 10, outlines when a warning or caution must be used during the investigative process. Case law states that a caution is required 'when, on an objective test, there are grounds for suspicion, falling short of evidence which would support a *prima facie* case of guilt, not simply that an offence has been committed, but committed by the person who is being questioned' (*R v Nelson and Rose* [1998] 2 Cr App R 399). The type of caution described here should not be confused with the cautions used in out-of-court disposals (see 10.18).

There are three different cautions for use during investigations and each is used at a different stage. The *when questioned* caution is used at arrest and interview, the *now* caution is used just before a person is charged with an offence, and the *restricted* caution is used only for interviews after charge. In all cases, the suspect is being warned about how their words can be used as evidence and that whatever they say, or don't say, can be used in evidence.

There is no need to provide a caution:

- when asking for a person's identity or the identity of the owner of a vehicle;
- when asking for a driver's name and date of birth under the Road Traffic Act 1988 (see Code C, para 10.9, and 16.4.2.2);
- when asking a suspect to read and sign records of interviews and other comments (see Code C, para 11 and Note 11E, and 'unsolicited comments' in 10.9.7); or
- before conducting a search (see Chapter 4).

A police officer using a caution must have a thorough understanding of the *when questioned*, *now*, and *restricted* variations of the caution, so that the meaning can be passed on to the suspect. Minor deviations in the wording of cautions are acceptable, but any clear breach of the Codes could mean that any evidence obtained will be inadmissible, ie rejected by the court. Police officers must always record when a caution has been given either via a PNB entry or on a record of the interview, including the type of caution used (see Code C, para 10.13).

10.9.2 The importance of the proper use of a caution

The correct version of the caution must be used or the evidence obtained might be rejected by the court. For example, in *Charles v Crown Prosecution Service* [2009] EWHC 3521 (Admin) the defendant was arrested for being drunk in charge of a motor vehicle (s 5(1)(b) of the Road Traffic Act 1988). He provided a positive specimen in a breath test and was informed that he would be charged with a s 5(1)(b) offence. Later he was interviewed about the incident and given the wrong type of caution. During the interview, the suspect admitted to actually driving the vehicle and the charge was therefore changed to the more serious offence of driving a vehicle on a road above the prescribed limit. The conviction was quashed, however, due to the incorrect procedures.

Some people, particularly those who do not have English as their first language, may not understand the formal wording of a caution. Police officers must ensure that the detained person understands the caution (Code C, para 10.7 and Note 10D). This may not be possible at the time of arrest: a full explanation of the caution might only be possible at interview, once an interpreter is present. When in doubt, an interpreter who is fluent in the suspect's own first language should attend the custody area, and may be needed during the interview process as well (see 13.8). The caution can be given in the Welsh language where appropriate.

10.9.3 The three parts to a caution

There are three parts to a caution (Code C, para 10.5), as shown in the diagram:

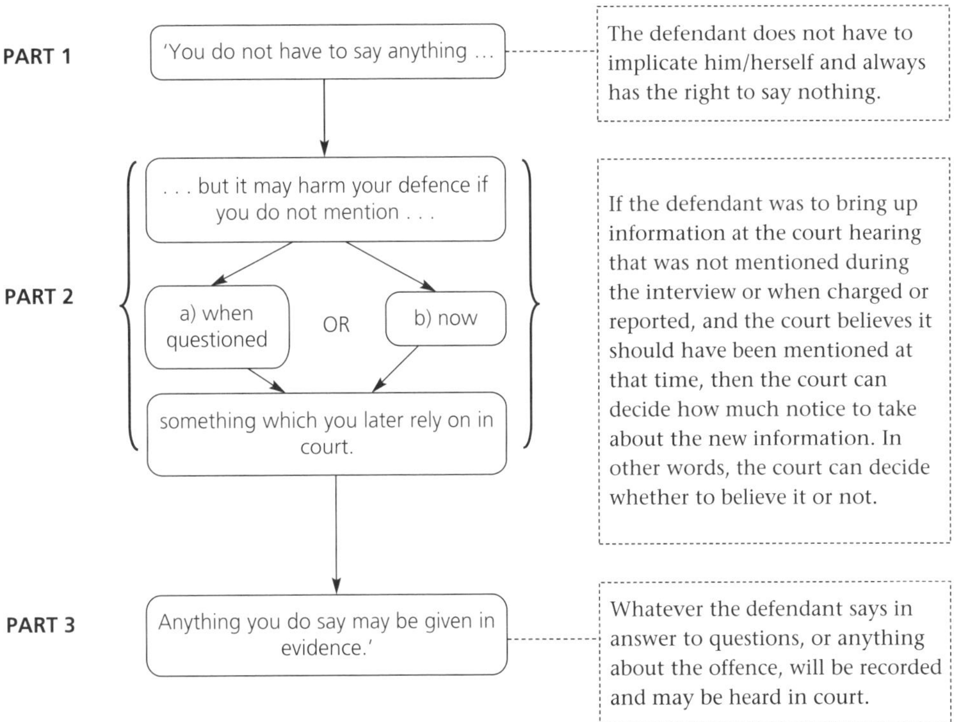

PART 1
'You do not have to say anything ...
The defendant does not have to implicate him/herself and always has the right to say nothing.
PART 2
. . . but it may harm your defence if you do not mention . . .
a) when questioned
OR
b) now
something which you later rely on in court.
If the defendant was to bring up information at the court hearing that was not mentioned during the interview or when charged or reported, and the court believes it should have been mentioned at that time, then the court can decide how much notice to take about the new information. In other words, the court can decide whether to believe it or not.
PART 3
Anything you do say may be given in evidence.'
Whatever the defendant says in answer to questions, or anything about the offence, will be recorded and may be heard in court.

10.9.4 Use of the *when questioned* caution

The *when questioned* caution is given to a suspect at the time of arrest, unless:

- it is impossible, for example if the person is very intoxicated or was violent and needed to be restrained (Code C, para 10.4 and Code G, para 3.4); or
- the caution has been given earlier (eg when a person who is suspected of committing an offence has attended a police station voluntarily to be interviewed (see 10.11 and Code C, para 3.21)).

The *when questioned* caution is also used at the start of an interview and when continuing with an interview after a break (see also Chapter 13 on interviewing).

At the same time as being cautioned, certain additional information must be provided, depending on the circumstances. For example, a suspect who has been arrested must also be reminded of the entitlement to free legal advice, and a suspect who has not been arrested must be clearly told that they are not under arrest.

10.9.5 The use of the *now* caution

This caution is the suspect's last chance to have anything recorded about the offence (see Code C, para 16.2). It is used at the end of an investigation, for instance when charging a detained person with an offence, or at the end of reporting a person for an offence.

Some suspects who are to be prosecuted may not need to be arrested (see 10.11). When informing such a suspect of the impending prosecution, there is no requirement under the

Codes of Practice to use the *now* caution, but it can still be used. If it is not used, this may help the defendant's case if they provide new information at the hearing; they could simply claim that there had been no earlier opportunity. This could be seen as a fair point and the court might be more likely to believe the new information (see Code C, Note 10G). Therefore, it is advisable to always use the *now* caution after informing a person that they may be prosecuted.

10.9.6 The use of the *restricted* caution

If a suspect is interviewed after being charged, although this is unusual (see Code C, para 16.5), then the *restricted* caution is used. It is referred to as such because it is shorter than the other cautions. The following words could be used: 'You do not have to say anything unless you wish to do so, but anything you do say may be given in evidence.' The interviewer should also remind the detainee about their right to legal advice.

TASK 1 Imagine an officer arrests a young person. First decide which caution they should use. Then imagine that they use the standard wording but it seems the youngster does not understand. Write down simplified wording.

10.9.7 Unsolicited comments by suspects

A suspect who has been arrested must be taken to the nearest designated police station (see 10.13.6) before being interviewed or questioned in any way about the relevant offences (Code C, para 11.1). Asking any sort of questions about their involvement in a criminal offence is regarded as 'an interview' and particular rules apply (see Chapter 13 on interviewing). However, before the interview an arrested suspect may spontaneously say something that is relevant to the offence, and which could be used in evidence. Such utterances are referred to as unsolicited or voluntary comments and are of two types: relevant comments and significant statements.

A **relevant comment** includes anything which might be relevant to the offence (Code C, para 11.13 and Note 11E), for example 'That other person you've arrested, they did it. You'll see, just ask them, they'll back me up, you'll see!'

A **significant statement** includes anything which could be used in evidence against the suspect (Code C, para 11.4A). The term derives from Part III of the Criminal Justice and Public Order Act 1994 and must have been made in the presence and hearing of a police officer or other police staff member. It could be a direct admission of guilt, for example.

All unsolicited comments made by suspects should be recorded in a PNB entry, noting when the comment was made and signed by the police officer. When practicable, the suspect should be asked to read it, and if they agree that it is a true record they should endorse the record with the words 'I agree that this is a correct record of what was said' and then sign (Code C, Note 11E). If the suspect does not agree with the record, the officer should add the details of any disagreement to the PNB recording, for the suspect to read and sign as an accurate account of the disagreement. Any refusal to sign should also be recorded (Code C, Note 11E).

10.10 Identification of Suspects by Witnesses

Some criminal offences are witnessed by members of the public who may feel able to recognize and identify the perpetrator(s). Obviously, this could provide useful evidence. (Here, identify means that the witness can point out the suspect; it is not about providing the suspect's name.) The Codes of Practice must be followed in order to safeguard the rights of a possible suspect. If the witness is successful in pointing out a person, the circumstances under which the identification was made must be recorded. Such an identification process by a witness is only permitted when the police do not have enough information to justify arresting anyone, ie the identity of the suspect is 'not known' (Code D, para 3.2). (The identity of a suspect who has been arrested is regarded as 'known' (Code D, para 3.4) even if the police are not certain of their name. When investigating a suspect who has been arrested, different identification procedures are used, such as VIPER video identification parades, see <http://www.viper.police.uk/>.)

10.10.1 The identification process

Before asking a witness to pick out a particular person, the witness should be asked to describe the suspect and a record should be made of this 'first description' (Code D, para 3.2a). The record is ideally made as a PNB entry, although some report books have a specific section for recording first descriptions. Then the witness can be asked to identify the suspect. The witness's attention must not be directed to any individual (Code D, para 3.2b) as this might compromise the identification (see Note 3F). However, a witness can be asked to look carefully at the people around or in a particular direction. This might be necessary to ensure they do not overlook a possible suspect or to encourage comparisons between several people. If there is more than one witness, they must be taken separately to attempt an identification (Code D, para 3.2c); additional officers are likely to be required. The police officer accompanying the witness must make a full PNB record of the action taken as soon as possible (Code D, para 3.2e).

The witness will have had two opportunities to see the suspect: first, around the time the offence was committed and, second, when taken to make an identification. The visual evidence from the first sighting may be disputed in court but this is less likely if the '*Turnbull*' guidelines have been followed.

10.10.2 ADVOKATE

The guidelines for identifications were set by case law in *R v Turnbull* (1976) 63 Cr App R 132. The mnemonic ADVOKATE is a useful way to remember the main points:

A Amount of time the suspect was under observation
D Distance between the witness and the suspect
V Visibility, eg what was the lighting like, what were the weather conditions?
O Obstructions between the witness and the suspect
K Known or seen before ie do they know the suspect and, if so, how?
A Any reason for remembering the suspect
T Time lapse between the first and any subsequent identification to the police
E Errors between the first recorded description and the suspect's actual appearance

In terms of the **Amount** of time the suspect was under observation, for how long was the witness looking at the suspect, and from what positions as it is very unlikely that the suspect was in exactly the same position for the whole period, and from what distances? It should also be noted if were there any breaks, however brief, in the observation and whether it was a frontal, rear, or profile view. In terms of the **Distance** between the witness and the suspect, how far away was the witness from the suspect when the incident took place? The distance is likely to vary during the course of the observation and will rarely be one measurement, so the longest and the shortest distance and the timings should all be recorded. In a street, the kerbstones can serve as a guide as they are usually one metre long.

In terms of the **Visibility**, consider the light levels; was it day or night, and if at night were the streetlamps on? The weather conditions must be included in detail—it is not sufficient to simply say 'It was raining'. The effect of sunlight should be considered; where was the sun in relation to the suspect and the witness, and were any shadows cast? If possible, state the distance of available visibility. It is important to record whether the witness was wearing glasses or contact lenses, or if they need corrective lenses.

In terms of **Obstructions** to their view of the suspect, any obstruction between the witness and the suspect should be described in detail. It is insufficient to say, for example, that the view was obstructed by a hedge—how tall, how wide, how dense was it? A glass obstruction should be described as clean/dirty, frosted/clear/double-glazed, and whether there was any glare or reflection from the sun or other sources. The extent of the obstruction as perceived by the witness must be ascertained. Record the distance between the witness and any obstructions.

In terms of whether the suspect is **Known** to the witness, is the suspect a friend, relation, or a work colleague? If so, how long have they known the suspect and how well? When did they last see the suspect? Has the suspect's description changed in the interim period, eg a change of hair style?

In terms of the existence of **Any** reason why the witness should remember the suspect, consider any distinguishing feature or peculiarity of the person or the very nature of the incident itself that made the person memorable. This can also relate to previous sightings. What, if anything, first attracted the witness's attention?

In terms of **Time**, how much time elapsed between the witness seeing the suspect at the incident and obtaining a first description? And how much time elapsed between the first description and the subsequent identification?

In terms of **Errors**, how similar is the first description to the appearance of the person identified as the suspect? Any differences must be noted to show integrity of the evidence, eg the identified suspect is wearing a black sweatshirt and the first description recorded a black jacket.

One of the most important issues to consider when using this process of identification is whether it is actually required. If there is sufficient evidence to justify an arrest, the suspect should be arrested instead.

10.11 Arrest Without Warrant

A police officer may need to arrest a person whom they suspect of committing a criminal offence. This would usually be 'arrest without warrant', a general power derived from s 24 of the PACE Act 1984 and governed by PACE Code G. There are other powers of arrest without warrant, for example for when a person has breached bail conditions. Warrants for arrest are covered in 10.12.

In the year ending 31 March 2019, 671,126 arrests were made by police in England and Wales, a fall of 5,000 arrests on the previous year (Home Office, 2020c). This continues a downward trend in recent years and compares to 1,462,139 arrests in 2008/9. The reasons for this decrease are not certain but it could be related to the increased use of voluntary attendance at a police station for interview and the greater use of other outcomes such as community resolutions (ibid). The right to liberty is an important principle under Article 5 of the European Convention on Human Rights (see 18.5.1) and the power to arrest and detain a person clearly challenges that right (Code G, para 1.2). It is therefore obvious that the power to arrest and detain should only be used for the right reason and at the right time.

Arrest can be used as a means to arrange for a suspect to be interviewed but it has become more common in recent years to invite the suspect to attend a police station voluntarily for interview. Investigative interviews with suspects are covered in detail in Chapter 13. It should be noted that if the rights of such an individual in a police station are not observed (such as being allowed to leave at any time), the investigation will be discredited at best, and at worst discontinued. There could also be claims for damages for an unlawful arrest and false imprisonment (Code G, para 1.3).

Police officers must use the power of arrest fairly, responsibly, with respect for the suspect, and without unlawful discrimination (Code G, para 1.1). Indeed, the Equality Act 2010 makes it unlawful for police officers to discriminate against, harass, or victimize any person on the grounds of the 'protected characteristics' of age, disability, gender reassignment, race, religion or belief, sex and sexual orientation, marriage and civil partnership, pregnancy and maternity (see Chapter 7).

The information provided here will contribute towards the knowledge evidence to meet assessment criteria requirements of the National Policing Curriculum units on 'Understanding the Police Constable Role' and 'Criminal Justice'.

10.11.1 The two elements for a s 24 PACE arrest to be lawful

Under PACE Code G, para 2.1, two elements must both be satisfied for a s 24 arrest to be lawful:

1. the person has been involved, has attempted to be involved or is suspected of involvement in the commission of a criminal offence; and

2. there are reasonable grounds for believing that the person's arrest is 'necessary' (see *Shields v Merseyside Police* [2010] EWCA Civ 1281).

10.11.2 Reasonable grounds for suspicion

For an arrest to be lawful under s 24 of the PACE Act 1984, the arresting officer must have a 'reasonable suspicion', relating to both the likelihood that the offence has been committed and that the suspect is the person who committed that offence (Code G, para 2.3A). Although words such as suspicion, grounds, and belief are in common usage, they have particular meanings within the context of policing and the law. In a law enforcement context, the following meanings apply:

- A **reasonable** conclusion is one that one or more people would agree on as a result of the same personal experience or understanding. It is a practical, level-headed, and logical result.
- **Grounds** for something include a reason or argument for a thought to exist.
- To **suspect** something is to think that it is probably true, although you are not certain.
- To **believe** something is a stronger and more concrete conclusion.

Therefore, in order to decide whether there are reasonable grounds to suspect, the component parts of that offence must be considered, and whether or not a like-minded person who was party to the same facts would draw the same conclusions about the suspect and the offence. The opportunity, motive, presence of mind, means, and incentive for committing the offence should all be considered. Alternatively, certain facts might be known about the suspect, so a person who fits the same profile in terms of employment, description, name, or clothes, or has previous convictions for similar offences and lives near the crime scene could be considered. Any of these could contribute to grounds for suspecting (see *Chief Constable of West Yorkshire v Armstrong* [2008] EWCA Civ 1582). However, taken individually they may not be enough so, for example, simply having previous convictions would be insufficient grounds for suspicion (see also Code A, para 2.2B(a)).

Information that might dispel suspicion, such as claims of innocence, should also be taken into account (Code G, Note 2). For example, common and statute law provide defences to assault for school staff in relation to the use of reasonable force (see 22.5.1) against pupils in their care, so these defences should be taken into account (Code G, Note 2A). An arresting officer as an investigator must pursue all lines of enquiry under para 3.5 of the Criminal Procedure and Investigations Act 1996 Code of Practice (PACE Code G, Note 2B.

The officer must form their own opinion before arresting a person; an arrest can never be justified simply on the basis of obeying the orders of a supervisor or manager. If information that appears to be reliable is given to a police officer, then they can use that information as reasonable grounds for making an arrest (*R (Rawlinson & Hunter Trustees) v Central Criminal Court; R (Tchenguiz and R20 Ltd) v Director of the Serious Fraud Office* [2012] EWHC 2254 (Admin)). If the supervisors or managers have information that could justify arrest, they must provide it to the arresting officer so they can generate their own reasonable grounds for suspicion. If the information is too sensitive to be passed to a more junior officer, then the supervisor or manager would have to make the arrest themselves. Relevant case law on this matter includes *O'Hara (AP) v CC of the RUC* [1997] 1 Cr App R 447; *Commissioner of Police of the Metropolis v Mohamed Raissi* [2008] EWCA Civ 1237; and *(1) Sonia Raissi (2) Mohamed Raissi v Commissioner of Police of the Metropolis* [2007] EWHC 2842 (QB).

10.11.3 Involvement in the commission of a criminal offence

The first element of a lawful arrest under s 24 of the PACE Act 1984 is a person's involvement, suspected involvement, or attempted involvement in the commission of a criminal offence (Code G, para 2.1). The guidance in para 2.3 provides more detail on the circumstances in which this might apply. The table provides summaries and illustrative scenarios set in an electrical goods shop, with a police officer who is on duty but not in uniform. (Remember, however, that before arresting the person the officer must be certain that it is *necessary* to arrest the suspect.)

Level of involvement	Example
A person is about to commit an offence (s 24(1)(a))	The officer sees someone, who is obviously not a member of the shop staff, select a pack of batteries, and put it under their coat. They then walk towards the exit of the shop, making no attempt to pay for it. The officer stops them as they are about to leave the shop.
A person is in the act of committing an offence (s 24(1)(b))	The officer sees a person walk up to a display of DAB radios, cut a security link, pick up a radio, and walk towards the door of the shop past the check-outs, without paying for the radio. The store alarm is activated, and the person continues to walk out of the shop. The officer concludes that the person is stealing the radio and stops them just outside the shop.
There are reasonable grounds for suspecting a person to be about to commit an offence (s 24(1)(c))	The officer sees a youngster walk up to a display of mobile phones, take a metal cutter out of their pocket and reach out with the tool towards the security chain of the mobile to cut it. But then the youngster is disturbed and puts the tool back in the pocket and walk away. A few seconds later, the same youngster returns to the display of mobiles, takes out the same tool, places the tool around the security chain, and sets off the alarm. At this moment, the officer decides they have reasonable grounds for suspecting that they are about to commit an offence.
There are reasonable grounds for suspecting a person to be committing an offence (s 24(1)(d))	The officer is just outside the shop and notices an individual standing just inside, near the doorway. They appear nervous and are holding an unpacked, brand-new set of hair straighteners under an arm with the lead hanging down. The officer sees the individual put the straighteners into their bag. They then walk towards the door as if to leave the shop. The officer notes the obvious facts: the straighteners should be in their packaging; the individual is anxious to leave the shop quickly; and they should not have put the straighteners in the bag. This all forms reasonable grounds for the officer to suspect that the person is in the process of committing an offence of theft.
There are reasonable grounds for suspecting an offence has been committed and that a particular person is guilty of the offence (s 24(2))	The officer is just outside the shop and notices someone run out of the shop clutching an apparently unpackaged white and chrome-coloured object. The store alarm is activated. The officer runs after them but loses sight in the crowd. A short while later, they spot a person who looks the same as the suspected shoplifter; the officer believes it is them. They decide that they have reasonable grounds for suspecting this person had stolen something from the shop.

Section 24 of the PACE Act 1984 also caters for situations in which it will be clear that an offence has definitely been committed. For example, a camera shop owner who deals with every sale in his shop sees a person walk up to a display of cameras, pick one up, and walk towards the door of the shop without paying for it. The store alarm is activated. The shop owner decides that they have stolen the camera and runs out and stops them, and then calls the police. In such circumstances, the officer could arrest any person:

- **who is guilty of the offence** (s 24(3)(a)). For example, the shop owner describes the suspect's actions to the officer in the presence and hearing of the suspect and the suspect does not refute the allegations;
- **concerning whom there are reasonable grounds for suspicion of guilt** (s 24(1)(b)). Imagine that the camera shop owner in the example had run after the suspect but could not catch up with them. The owner calls the police and supplies a first description of the person. The description is passed to an officer who the next day sees a person fitting the description. They decide therefore that they have reasonable grounds for suspecting them of the theft.

The officer must also believe the arrest is necessary.

10.11.4 Reasons that make an arrest 'necessary'

In 10.11.1 we explained that there are two elements for a lawful arrest under s 24 of the PACE Act 1984: involvement in the commission of an offence and that the arrest is 'necessary' (Code G, para 2.4). An arrest is deemed to be necessary if one or more of the following reasons (s 24(5)) apply:

1. to ascertain a person's name;
2. to ascertain a person's address;
3. to prevent injury, damage, indecency, or obstruction;
4. to protect a vulnerable person;
5. to ensure prompt investigation; or
6. to prevent a suspect disappearing.

There must be reasonable grounds for believing that the arrest is necessary (*Richardson v The Chief Constable of West Midlands Police* [2011] 2 Cr App R 1, [2011] EWHC 773 (QB)). The officer's belief must be objectively reasonable (*Hayes v Chief Constable of Merseyside Police* [2012] 1 WLR 517), the implication being that any other officer in the same position would be likely to have the same belief. The necessity to arrest an individual using these reasons should be proportionately justified, carefully balanced, and accompanied by substantive grounds. Note that a suspect who attends a police station voluntarily could be arrested on arrival if new information has come to light and it was not practicable to make the arrest any earlier (PACE Code G, Note 2G).

These six reasons are set out in full in s 24(5) of the PACE Act 1984 and Code G, para 2.9, available online. The table lists the six reasons and the mnemonic ID COP PLAN.

I	Investigation	To allow the prompt and effective investigation of the offence or the person's conduct.
D	Disappearance	To prevent the person disappearing as this could hinder any prosecution for the offence.
C	Child	To protect a child or other vulnerable person from the person.
O	Obstruction	To prevent the person causing an unlawful obstruction of the highway.
P	Physical injury	To prevent the person causing physical injury (to him/herself or any other person).
P	Public decency	To prevent the person committing an offence against public decency.
L	Loss or damage	To prevent the person causing loss of, or damage to, property.
A	Address	To enable the person's address to be ascertained.
N	Name	To enable the person's name to be ascertained.

10.11.4.1 To ascertain a person's name or address

It should be made clear to the suspect that their name and address is required in relation to an offence, so the investigation can proceed. If the suspect refuses, the officer must always explain that it may lead to arrest. The officer should ask the person in an assertive manner, and it may be necessary to ask more than just once. Remember, this is not a power to arrest any person who simply refuses to give their name or address; the officer must suspect that an actual substantive offence has been committed.

An officer may also arrest a suspect where there are reasonable grounds for doubting that the name or address provided is correct (Code G, para 2.9(b)). There must be a logical reason for believing the information is not correct, for example:

- the person cannot provide any identifying documents (eg a driving licence with a photograph);
- there is no record of the name or address in the voters' register or telephone directory;
- the officer suspects the person is using the name or address of a close relative with the same details; or
- the officer suspects the name or address is fictitious because it is the name or address of a famous person or character.

Code D of the Codes of Practice provides guidance on the definition of an unsatisfactory address. It would include an address where the location does not exist. Other examples of unsatisfactory addresses include where the person's name does not appear at the address on the voters' register or if the person is very soon to leave the UK never to return or is of 'no fixed abode' and cannot supply a permanent address. However, an address can be regarded as satisfactory if someone else at the address, eg an employer or relative, will accept service of the written charge and requisition on the person's behalf. This procedure could be used for a person whose home address is not in the UK.

10.11.4.2 To prevent injury, damage, indecency, or obstruction

A reason for arresting someone could be to prevent the person:

- **causing physical injury to any other person (Code G, para 2.9 (c)(i))**: for example, if investigating an offence of throwing fireworks in a street or public place (s 80 of the Explosives Act 1875), the officer might conclude that the suspect may harm somebody else;
- **suffering physical injury (Code G, para 2.9 (c)(ii))**: for example, if investigating the offence of being a pedestrian on the carriageway of a motorway (s 17(4) of the Road Traffic Regulation Act 1984), the officer might conclude that the suspect may suffer physical injury from a passing vehicle veering off the main carriageway;

- **causing loss of or damage to property (Code G, para 2.9 (c)(iii))**: for example, if the offence of interference with a motor vehicle or trailer (s 9 of the Criminal Attempts Act 1981), the officer might conclude that the suspect's actions could cause damage to the vehicle;
- **committing an offence against public decency (Code G, para 2.9 (c)(iv))**: for example, if investigating for the offence of using profane or obscene language (Town Police Clauses Act 1847), an officer might conclude that the suspect was committing an offence against public decency; or
- **causing unlawful obstruction of the highway (Code G, para 2.9 (c)(v))**: for example, if investigating for an offence of wilful obstruction of the highway (s 137 of the Highways Act 1980) and the suspect was stopping or slowing vehicles on a road, the officer might conclude that the person needed to be removed.

10.11.4.3 To protect a child or other vulnerable person

It might be necessary to arrest a suspect if they are risking the health and safety of a vulnerable person or child (Code G, para 2.9(d)). For example, a parent is suspected of abusing their children at home and so the arrest is necessary to protect the children.

10.11.4.4 To allow prompt and effective investigation

An investigation might be hindered or delayed if the suspect is not arrested. PACE Code G, para 2.9(e) sets out the circumstances for the reason for arrest being 'to allow prompt and effective investigation of the offence or conduct'. For example, it might be necessary to arrest a suspect who is unlikely to attend the police station voluntarily to be questioned (para 2.9(e)(i), Note 2F). There might also be a need to take fingerprints, footwear impressions, samples, or photographs of the suspect (Code G, Note 2H). All these actions would not be possible unless the person had either consented or been arrested. Code G, para 2.9(e) suggests other circumstances where this reason would apply. These include where there are reasonable grounds to believe that the person:

- has made false statements such as date of birth or presented false evidence like a forged driving licence;
- may steal or destroy evidence, eg disposing of stolen property from a burglary;
- may alert co-suspects or conspirators who could then arrange to go into hiding; or
- may intimidate or threaten witnesses.

10.11.4.5 To prevent the disappearance of the person in question

Arrest can be necessary if there are reasonable grounds for believing that the suspect will otherwise fail to attend court. Such grounds could include a proven track record of failing to appear at court or to answer bail at a police station. If an arrest is not necessary, then alternatives will be considered, for example the suspect can be reported for summons or later issued with a postal charge requisition (PCR). Under the ECHR, these alternatives should be considered as they would have less impact on an individual's rights and freedoms. Arrest may also be the best solution if a person is homeless and cannot provide a suitable contact address for issuing a written charge and postal requisition. This is explained in more detail in PACE Code G, para 2.9(f).

10.11.4.6 Using the NDM when considering an arrest

The College of Policing NDM (see 4.2.1) should be considered in any situation where arrest is envisaged. Here we provide an example where the police have been called to a local supermarket. The security staff have stopped a person walking out of the store with two large bottles of whisky without making any attempt to pay. The police use the NDM to determine the best course of action.

NDM Stage 1—Gather Information

- Who is the person? Can we confirm their ID?
- Do they have an address? Can we confirm this?
- Are there any health/drug abuse issues?
- What is the value of the property stolen?
- Was the property recovered intact?
- Who witnessed the offence? Will they give formal statements?
- Will the store (victim) support a prosecution? Do they wish to proceed with civil recovery?

NDM Stage 2—Determine the Threat and Risks

- Any officer safety issues with regards to the suspect?
- Any threat to other members of the public?
- Any child or vulnerable person involved?
- Is the suspect a repeat offender?
- Is the store a repeat victim?

NDM Stage 3—What Powers Do the Police Have? What is local police Policy?

- Is a search necessary?
- What is the police service policy with regards to shoplifting?
- Is there a reason to arrest present (ID COP PLAN)?

NDM Stage 4—Draw Up List of Options

- Confirm suspect details for the store to institute civil recovery?
- Confirm suspect details for the store to ban them from premises?
- No further action necessary?
- Invite suspect for a voluntary interview?
- Arrest suspect for theft?

NDM Stage 5—Take Action and Review what has happened

- Consult the Code of Ethics before making decision to arrest, and only do so if powers allow.
- What might you do differently next time?

10.11.5 Arrest without warrant by other persons

Any person may arrest another person, but only in certain limited circumstances, as shown in the diagram.

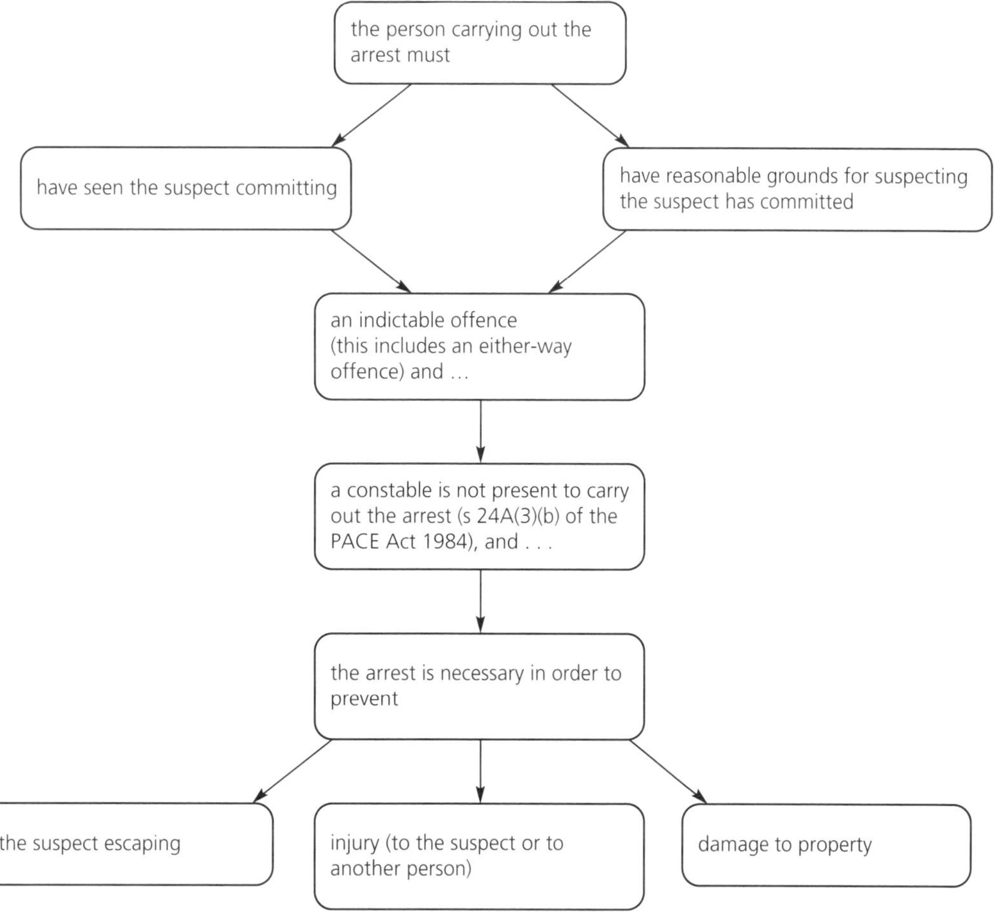

An example of reasonable grounds for suspecting an offence had been committed could be that a person suspects a burglary is being committed because they have seen someone they do not recognize climbing into their neighbour's house through a window.

The arrest could also be carried out later (s 24A(2)). For example, a store detective sees someone commit a theft and is unable to apprehend them at the time but sees them soon afterwards and arrests them.

A person who is not a constable has no right to arrest another person if the offence is a summary-only offence.

10.11.6 Persons wanted for an offence circulated on the PNC

If the identity of a suspect is known and all local lines of enquiry to trace and arrest them have failed, or if they have not answered bail to a police station or court, a police officer can circulate the person's details on the PNC. This will need authorization from a supervisor or manager, who will assess the seriousness of the situation. Most volume, priority, and major crime offences will be judged as serious enough for a person to be placed as wanted on the PNC. The wanted marker on the PNC should specify the offence, the circumstances (reason), and the necessary criteria for arrest in order to satisfy the legal conditions under PACE for the arresting officer (see 10.11.1). A person who has absconded from prison could also be placed on the wanted list on the PNC.

10.11.7 Arrest in other circumstances

A police officer also has powers to arrest in circumstances that are unrelated to a suspected offence (see PACE Code G, Note 1A). These include arresting a person who:

- fails to answer police bail to attend police station (s 46A of the PACE Act 1984, see 10.18.3);
- has been bailed to attend court and who is suspected of breaching, or is believed likely to breach, any condition of bail (s 7(3) of the Bail Act 1976);
- is suffering from mental disorder, to remove them to place of safety for assessment (s 136 of the Mental Health Act 1983, see 20.5.2);
- is unlawfully at large, to return them to prison (s 49 of the Prison Act 1952);
- is a young person who has absconded from the place where they are required to reside, and to return them there (s 32(1A) of the Children and Young Persons Act 1969);
- might not have the right to remain in the UK, so examination is required (Sch 2, Immigration Act 1971); or
- is causing or may cause a breach of the peace (a common law power, see 3.8.2).

10.12 Warrants of Arrest

A warrant is a formal written document issued by a magistrate or judge that authorizes the arrest of a named individual or a group of people. It is normally addressed to the police and directs them to carry out an action on behalf of the court. A police officer can execute a warrant without having physical possession of the warrant at the time (s 125 of the Magistrates' Courts Act 1980). A warrant of arrest is often used in relation to a failure to:

- pay fines (s 76(1) or (2) of the Magistrates' Courts Act 1980);
- appear at court (s 55(2) of the Magistrates' Courts Act 1980);
- answer bail (s 7(1) of the Bail Act 1976).

A warrant may also be issued for the arrest of a witness required in a court if they have not attended despite having been summoned. For non-appearance at court, the warrant will be issued under s 97 of the Magistrates' Courts Act 1980 (for a magistrates' court) and under s 4 of the Criminal Procedure (Attendance of Witnesses) Act 1965 for a Crown Court.

There is a power of entry under s 17(1)(a) of the PACE Act 1984 to search a premises to execute an arrest warrant issued 'in connection with or arising out of criminal proceedings' (subsection (i)). The wording 'is deliberately widely drawn' (Home Office Circular 88/1985, para 8) so, for example, a constable can enter and search premises to arrest a person for non-appearance in court or failing to pay fines in relation to a criminal offence.

TASK 2 Find out how a police officer should execute a warrant to arrest a person.

10.13 Making an Arrest

Here we deal with the process of making an arrest and a police officer's responsibility to protect the suspect's rights. Making an arrest is an important milestone to achieve within the National Policing Curriculum and is a key activity required to achieve Independent Patrol Status. It also features within the PCDA/DHEP requirements for student officers.

The relevant National Policing Curriculum assessed units are 'Understanding the Role of a Police Constable' and 'Criminal Justice'. The evidence for the achievement will come from successfully conducting arrests whilst under supervision on at least three different occasions.

10.13.1 Preparing to make an arrest

When an arrest is planned or imminent, a police officer must plan in advance where possible. The circumstances might be difficult, for example the precise location and circumstances of the suspect are unlikely to be known. Note that unless it is unavoidable, a young person should not be arrested at their place of education, but if this is necessary the principal (or their nominee) must be informed of the arrest (Code G, Note 1B).

10.13.1.1 Risk assessment and arrest

A police officer should make a risk assessment about a planned arrest, guided by the National Decision Model (see 4.2.1). Inevitably, there are risks when force is used to enter and search in unplanned situations: it is impossible to predict who or what the officer(s) might encounter. Consideration should be given to whether it is really necessary to immediately enter the premises. It might be better to stay outside, watch the front and back, and secure the area until colleagues with appropriate equipment and resources arrive.

The risk assessment could be made in advance on the way to an incident or it may need to be done at the incident itself. The assessment will be ongoing and may need to be modified when approaching a suspect to make the arrest. An officer should consider how their demeanour, presence, and attitude could influence how the suspect reacts. If they become agitated or aggressive, the officer could issue a verbal warning outlining the behaviour of the individual and the consequences of their actions but there is no legal obligation to do this.

10.13.1.2 Power of entry to arrest

There is a power of entry under s 17(1) of the PACE Act 1984 to enter and search premises in order to arrest a person on warrant (see 10.12) or a person suspected of committing an offence (arrest without warrant, see 10.11). It applies for any indictable offence and for certain summary offences, as listed in the table.

Summary offence with a power of entry in order to arrest	Legislation
Prohibition of uniforms in connection with political objectives	s 1 of the Public Order Act 1986
Causing fear or provocation of violence	s 4 of the Public Order Act (see 3.8.3)
Failing to stop when driving a vehicle or cycle when requested	s 163 of the Road Traffic Act 1988 (see 16.4.1)
Driving or being in charge of a vehicle when unfit through drink or drugs	s 4 of the Road Traffic Act 1988 (see 16.9.2)
Being under the influence of drink or drugs when operating railways and trams, etc	s 27 of the Transport and Works Act 1992
Using violence to secure entry	s 6 of the Criminal Law Act 1977 (see 22.7)
Trespassing on premises whilst an interim possession order is in place	s 76 of the Criminal Justice and Public Order Act 1994
Trespassing with a weapon of offence	s 8 of the Criminal Law Act 1977 (see 23.4.3)
'Squatting' on premises	s 7 of the Criminal Law Act 1977
Squatting in a residential building	s 144 of the Legal Aid, Sentencing and Punishment of Offenders Act 2012
Causing harm or distress to animals	ss 4, 5, 6(1) and (2), 7, 8(1) and (2) of the Animal Welfare Act 2006
Bringing animals into the UK (risk of rabies)	s 61 of the Animal Health Act 1981

Core Aspects of Police Work

Section 17(2) of the PACE Act 1984 explains the factors that must be taken into account before entering, for example whether there are reasonable grounds for believing that the person is on the premises—can the officer see them through a window?

This power of search is limited to the extent that is reasonably required to achieve the objective (s 17(4)). For example, if the entry and search was to find and arrest a certain person, there is no justification for looking in a teapot. If a police officer has made an unlawful entry, any evidence of criminality (such as the seizure of controlled drugs) may be excluded by the court under s 78 of the PACE Act 1984 (see *R v Veneroso* [2002] Crim LR 306 (Crown Ct)).

When searching a flat or bedsit, the communal areas such as hallways, stairs, and shared kitchens and bathrooms can also be searched. A neighbouring flat cannot be searched 'just in case', but of course any of the flats could be searched if there was reason to believe that the person was in that particular dwelling.

For arrests that are not related to investigating an offence, other powers of entry are available under s 17(1) of the PACE Act 1984. This could include the arrest of a person who has escaped after being arrested, escaped from involuntary custody at a psychiatric unit, this only under circumstances of 'hot pursuit' and not after a period of days or weeks, or escaped from a prison, remand centre, young offenders' institution, or secure training centre. It would also include the arrest of a child or young person who is absent from local authority care or who has escaped from detention for having committed 'grave crimes'.

10.13.1.3 Entering property to save life or limb

Importantly for response officers, the police have the legal power to enter and search premises to save life or limb (s 17(1)(e) of the PACE Act 1984). In the case of *Baker v Crown Prosecution Service* [2009] EWHC 299 (Admin), it was further decided that entry and search under subsection (e) can be carried out:

- without seeking the permission of the occupant (this might be self-defeating);
- without giving the occupant a reason if it is impossible, impracticable, or undesirable to do so;
- to save someone from themselves as well as from a third party; but
- only to the extent that is reasonably required to satisfy the objective for using the power of entry (s 17(4) of the PACE Act 1984).

These powers should only be used if 'something serious' seems to have occurred (or is likely to occur) within the property and not 'simply on the basis of concern for the welfare' of someone in the premises, as shown in *Syed v DPP* [2010] EWHC 81 (Admin).

Reasonable force may be used to secure entry (s 117 of the PACE Act 1984) where any part of the PACE Act 1984 grants a power of entry. If met with force, an officer might have to use equal force to negate it, and then use even more force to take control. This is covered as part of personal safety training. In a prosecution, the court has to determine whether an officer honestly believed that the force they used was reasonable and proportionate in the circumstances. The principles are similar to the use of force during an arrest (s 3 of the Criminal Law Act 1967).

10.13.2 Information to be given on arrest

Under s 28(1) of the PACE Act 1984 and Code G, para 2.2, when a person is arrested the officer must tell the person at the time of the arrest:

- that they are under arrest (even if it seems obvious);
- the reasons for the arrest; and
- the necessity for the arrest.

The actual words 'I am arresting you' are recommended although this is not essential. It is definitely not sufficient for the officer to simply place a hand on the suspect's shoulder; they must be clearly informed in words (s 28(2)) and provided with sufficient information to understand what has happened and why (Code C Note 10B). An arrest is not lawful unless the suspect is fully informed of the arrest and reasons at the time or as soon as practicable (Code C, para 10.3), unless this is not possible because, for example, the suspect is acting in an aggressive manner and needs to be physically restrained. In addition, for an arrest to be lawful, the reason given must be correct.

To fulfil the requirements of both s 28 and Code G, para 2.2, an officer might say to the suspect:

> I have just seen you run out of the shop with a joint of meat under your arm. I heard the store alarm sound at the same time and I therefore suspect that you have stolen the meat. I am arresting you on suspicion of theft of that meat as the arrest is necessary to allow the prompt and effective investigation of the offence by interviewing you at the police station and by searching premises occupied or controlled by you for evidence relating to similar offences.

Here the suspect has been clearly informed that they have been arrested, and the reasons for the suspicion and necessity of arrest are also covered.

10.13.3 Using force during an arrest

During an arrest, the use of force may be required but this must be 'reasonable' (eg see s 117 of the PACE Act 1984). The arresting officer must have an honest belief that the force used was reasonable and appropriate in the circumstances. The force would be 'reasonable' if the arresting officer met with force and had to use equal force to negate it, and then use more force to take control. Such procedures are covered in personal safety training.

Section 3 of the Criminal Law Act 1967 (see the flowchart) provides a defence for the use of force for law enforcement activities.

Note that if a police officer restrains a person but does not at that time intend or seem to intend to arrest them, the officer is committing an assault even if an arrest would have been justified (see *Fraser Wood v DPP* [2008] EWHC 1056 (Admin)).

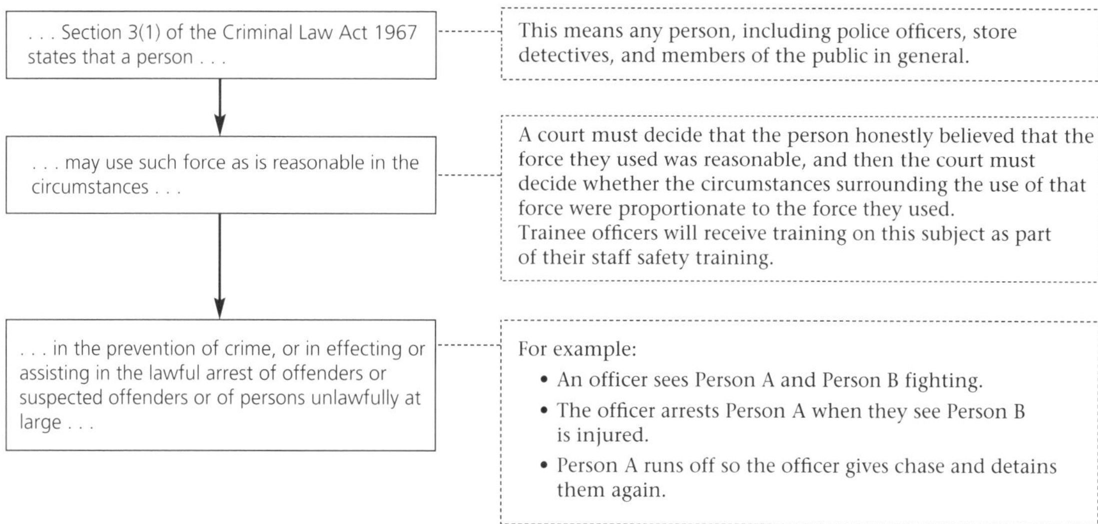

. . . Section 3(1) of the Criminal Law Act 1967 states that a person . . .
This means any person, including police officers, store detectives, and members of the public in general.
. . . may use such force as is reasonable in the circumstances . . .
A court must decide that the person honestly believed that the force they used was reasonable, and then the court must decide whether the circumstances surrounding the use of that force were proportionate to the force they used.
Trainee officers will receive training on this subject as part of their staff safety training.
. . . in the prevention of crime, or in effecting or assisting in the lawful arrest of offenders or suspected offenders or of persons unlawfully at large . . .
For example:
• An officer sees Person A and Person B fighting.
• The officer arrests Person A when they see Person B is injured.
• Person A runs off so the officer gives chase and detains them again.

10.13.4 What to do after an arrest

The suspect must be cautioned (see 10.9.1) and the officer must make a PNB record (unless it is impracticable to do so) about:

- the nature and circumstances of the offence leading to the arrest;
- the reason or reasons why the arrest was necessary;
- that a 'when questioned' caution was given; and
- anything said by the person at the time of arrest.

If the arrest took place in a location other than in a police station, the suspect can be searched by a police officer (s 32 of the PACE Act 1984) if there are reasonable grounds for believing that they may present a danger to any person or are in possession of anything which could be used to escape from custody or which could be evidence relating to an offence. The search must only be to the extent required to find the particular item—for example, if the search is for a hacksaw, there is no reason for looking in a person's mouth (s 32(3)). In public, a person cannot be required to remove any clothing other than an outer coat, jacket, or gloves, but their mouth may be searched (s 32(4)).

A person who has been arrested can be photographed on the street (s 64A(1A) of the PACE Act 1984) and consent is not required. In order to take the photograph, the person can be required to remove anything covering part of the head or face (out of public view if the covering is a religious garment). If a person refuses to remove a covering garment, a police officer has the right to remove it (s 64A(2)).

10.13.5 Searching premises after an arrest

After a person has been arrested for an indictable offence, the premises they were in immediately prior to the arrest can be searched (s 32(2)(b) of the PACE Act 1984). In addition, any other premises associated with that person can also be searched under s 18 of the PACE Act 1984, with authorization. Further details of these types of searches are given in 4.6 and the practical procedures for searching premises are covered in 4.6.1.1.

10.13.6 Taking the suspect to a police station

A person who has been arrested must be taken without delay to a designated police station (s 30(1) of the PACE Act 1984 and Code C, para 11.1A). (A 'designated police station' is any of the 'police stations in the area that are to be used for the purpose of detaining arrested persons' (s 35 of the PACE Act 1984).)

The only reasons for delaying (s 30(10), and see diagram) are that taking the person to a police station could:

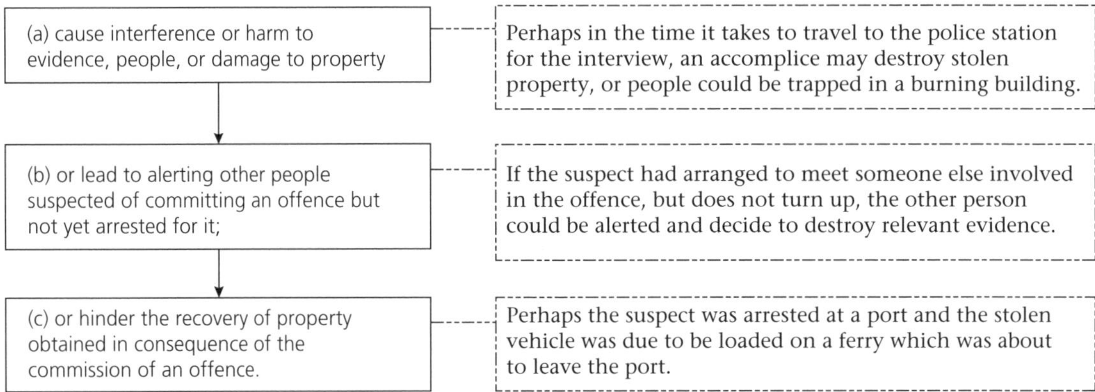

(a) cause interference or harm to evidence, people, or damage to property
Perhaps in the time it takes to travel to the police station for the interview, an accomplice may destroy stolen property, or people could be trapped in a burning building.
(b) or lead to alerting other people suspected of committing an offence but not yet arrested for it;
If the suspect had arranged to meet someone else involved in the offence, but does not turn up, the other person could be alerted and decide to destroy relevant evidence.
(c) or hinder the recovery of property obtained in consequence of the commission of an offence.
Perhaps the suspect was arrested at a port and the stolen vehicle was due to be loaded on a ferry which was about to leave the port.

Before placing the detainee in the police vehicle it is advisable to:

- search the suspect for possible weapons;
- use restraints such as handcuffs (whilst considering human rights and the limitations of reasonable force);
- search the area in the vehicle where the suspect will sit to locate any unexpected items, and remove police equipment such as items of clothing, stationery, and bags;
- check that rear-door 'child' locks are activated and that electric windows are deactivated;
- position another officer (rather than the suspect) behind the driver, if the vehicle has no barrier between the front and rear seats;
- accompany the suspect in the rear of a van, or in its cage, and be able to communicate with the driver at all times; and
- search the vehicle on arrival at the police station (in the presence of the suspect).

Any discussion of the alleged offence on the way to the police station should be avoided. This is because any questioning of a person regarding their involvement or suspected involvement in a criminal offence is considered to be an interview, and interviews must be carried out under caution in a suitable place (Code C, para 11.1A). However, if a suspect freely provides information, then follow the guidelines in relation to significant statements and relevant comments (see 13.7.2 on how this can be used during interviewing).

10.13.7 'De-arresting' a suspect

Any person arrested in a place other than at a police station must be released if there are no longer any grounds for keeping them under arrest (s 30(7) of the PACE Act 1984). For example, a suspect might initially refuse to provide their name but then provide it on the way to the police station. A PNB record must be made of such a release, explaining the circumstances and why the reasons for the arrest no longer exist.

10.13.8 The suspect has committed further offences

After the arrest and taking the suspect to the police station, it might become apparent that they have committed further offences. The police officer has to decide whether to arrest the suspect again for the further offence(s). The officer will need to reflect as follows: if the suspect had committed only the further offences and was not at a police station, would there be a need to arrest? If the answer is 'yes', then they should be arrested for the further offences (s 31 of the PACE Act 1984). All the procedures that apply for any arrest must be carried out in full for this second arrest (such as stating why the arrest is necessary (see 10.11.4) and cautioning the suspect appropriately (see 10.9.1)).

10.14 Retaining Items in Relation to an Offence

Certain items found on a suspect or at a crime scene may be required as evidence during a subsequent investigation and prosecution. These items are often referred to as 'seized property'. The use of the word 'property' in a policing context means any article, object, or item which comes into the possession of the police, whether ownership details are known or not, and includes 'found property' ie lost items handed to the police.

Property can be seized directly from the suspect after arrest. The item(s) may either be directly linked to the crime, such as objects suspected to have been stolen, or be other items which need to be sent for forensic examination, such as a suspected illegal substance. Any other items can also be seized at or near the scene of the crime, such as a crowbar found in a front garden, even if those items cannot immediately be linked to the suspect. Such items are likely to require forensic examination to establish if there is a link between the suspect and the offence.

10.14.1 Retention and storage of seized property

The main guidance regarding retention of seized property is found in s 22 of the PACE Act 1984, although detailed guidance will also be given during training with a police service. Note that s 22(4) states that 'nothing may be retained if a photograph or copy would be sufficient'.

The legislation describes two main reasons for retaining items:

(a) for the purposes of a criminal investigation, for use as evidence at a trial for an offence, or for forensic examination or for investigation in connection with an offence;
(b) in order to establish its lawful owner ... where there are reasonable grounds for believing that it has been obtained in consequence of the commission of an offence.

Contamination must be minimized when seizing and retaining items, and a record of continuity must be kept. Seized items 'may be retained so long as is necessary in all the circumstances' (s 22) but common respect for the property rights of others (as described, for example, in the Human Rights Act 1998) would suggest that any item that is no longer relevant to an investigation should be returned to its owner as soon as possible. Each police service is likely to have a Property Management Policy that sets out the protocols for return. For mobile phones, each phone has a unique serial number which may be listed on the National Mobile Property Register (NMPR), available online. This can be used to identify the registered owner and establish whether the phone has been stolen.

10.15 Presentation of Suspects to Custody Officers

For most suspects, being arrested is a highly charged emotional event, and police officers must maintain a professional approach throughout. An arrest is the start of a long process and all staff involved have a responsibility to preserve the suspect's rights throughout their detention. The information provided here is relevant to the curriculum area of 'Understand and apply the processes for detaining and escorting a suspect to custody' and is an area of occupational competence you will be expected to perform thoroughly.

10.15.1 Arrival at the police station with an arrested person

Once at the police station, the person should be taken before a custody officer as soon as practicable (Code C, para 2.1A). The police officer who brings in the suspect should note the arrival time (the 'relevant time' (s 41(2) of the PACE Act 1984)) in their PNB. This is to provide continuity of evidence between time of arrest and of arrival at the police station, and any subsequent authorization of detention by the custody officer. A suspect cannot normally be detained for more than 24 hours from the relevant time without being charged.

10.15.2 The custody officer

The custody officer is usually a police officer of at least the rank of sergeant, but in some constabularies a police support employee is designated as a 'staff custody officer'. The custody officer's main duty is to ensure that any person in police detention is treated according to the PACE Act 1984 and the Codes of Practice, and that certain events are recorded on the custody system. The entered information will automatically update the Police National Computer (see 12.8.1.1) and will also be available for officers to use when preparing case files (see 18.7.5).

When an arrested suspect is taken to the custody suite, the custody officer must be informed of the relevant circumstances of the arrest; ie the suspect's involvement in the commission of a criminal offence and the reason(s) why the arrest was necessary. This is obligatory under s 24 of the PACE Act 1984 and Code G, para 2.2. The arresting officer would say for example:

> At 11.00 hours today I was on duty outside an electrical shop in the High Street when I saw this person run out of the shop with a brand-new digital radio under his arm. I heard the store alarm sound at the same time and I therefore suspected that they had stolen the radio. I arrested them on suspicion of theft of the radio to allow the prompt and effective investigation of the offence by interviewing them here at the police station, and also to obtain authority from an inspector to search any premises occupied or controlled by the suspect for evidence relating to similar offences of theft.

The officer should stay with the suspect during the initial stages of the custody process.

If there is insufficient evidence to charge a detainee but the investigating officer still has further enquiries to complete, then the person may be 'released under investigation' or bail could be used. But it may become clear that there is neither sufficient evidence or further lines of enquiry to pursue. In such circumstances, and if the investigating officer agrees, the custody officer will release the person without charge (Code C, para 1.1). This process is called 'refused charge' and it will usually be the end of the matter unless fresh evidence is found.

The custody officer will also assess whether the detainee will be a risk to themselves or to others, for example are they dependent on drugs or alcohol, do they have any welfare concerns, is there a risk of self-harm, or is vulnerability an issue? This will include checking the PNC and consulting with the arresting officer and appropriate health-care professionals, for example the custody nurse (Code C, para 3.6).

10.15.3 Charging and detaining a suspect

The custody officer must decide if there is already enough evidence to charge the arrested person at this point (s 37(2) of the PACE Act 1984). If there is not, the suspect can be detained if the custody officer has reasonable grounds for believing that the detention is necessary to secure or preserve evidence relating to the offence (eg to carry out searches for evidence) or to obtain such evidence by questioning the suspect.

The precise time that the custody officer authorizes the detention is called the 'authorised time' (s 41(2) of the PACE Act 1984). (This is different from the 'relevant time' referred to in 10.15.1.) The need for continued detention will be reviewed not more than six hours after the 'authorised time' and further reviews will be conducted at nine-hourly intervals after that. The reviews are carried out by an inspector and the timings are sometimes referred to as the 'custody clock' (see 10.18.3). Section 40A(2) of the PACE Act 1984 permits a review of a detention by telephone but only when it is not reasonably practicable to use video-conferencing (s 45A).

10.15.4 The detainee's rights after arrest

If the custody officer decides to detain the person, they must inform the detainee of the grounds and record the grounds for detention in their presence (Code C, para 3.4). If the detainee cannot be informed because they are incapable of understanding, is violent, or is in need of medical attention, the grounds must be given as soon as practicable (para 1.8). The custody officer must also make sure the detainee is clearly informed about certain rights that apply throughout the whole period of detention (Code C, para 3.1). The rights are:

1. to have someone informed of their arrest;
2. to consult privately with a solicitor and receive free legal advice; and
3. to consult the PACE Act 1984 Codes of Practice.

The detainee must be given two written notices explaining the rights and other arrangements (Code C, para 3.2). Detainees who need an interpreter must be given appropriately translated notices (Code C, para 13.1). The first notice sets out the three rights noted above and also the arrangements for obtaining legal advice, the right to a copy of the custody record, and an explanation of the caution. The second notice sets out the detainee's entitlements while in custody, for example the provision of food and drink and access to toilets (see Code C, Notes 3A and 3B).

The custody officer (or other custody staff as directed) must ask the detainee whether they would like legal advice and for someone to be informed of the arrest. The detainee will be asked to sign the custody record to confirm their decision (Code C, para 3.5). The custody officer must also note on the custody record whether the detainee requires:

- medical attention, for example as a result of an injury or lack of medication;
- an appropriate adult, for example the parent or guardian for a juvenile, or a relative or guardian for a mentally vulnerable person;
- help with checking documentation, for example providing clarification of any of the rights; or
- an interpreter, for example for a detainee with a speech or hearing impairment or who cannot speak English well enough.

10.15.4.1 The detainee's right to have someone informed of the arrest

The detainee may have one friend, relative, or interested person informed of their whereabouts as soon as practicable (s 56 of the PACE Act 1984 and Code C, para 5.1). If the first attempt fails, the detainee can suggest two other people to be contacted. Any number of further attempts can be made, at the discretion of the custody officer or the officer in charge of the investigation, to contact other people until the information has been conveyed to one person. For a young person in detention who is under 18 years, the person responsible for their welfare must be informed.

The detainee should be allowed to telephone one person in addition to the person informed above and speak for a reasonable time. Writing materials should be provided if requested.

10.15.4.2 Delaying the detainee's right to contact

The right to contact people and to legal advice can be delayed if the offence is an indictable offence or if it seems that the communication is likely to lead to:

- interference with or harm to evidence or other people;
- alerting other people who are suspected of committing an indictable offence, but not yet arrested; or
- hindrance to the recovery of property.

Delaying a detainee's right to legal advice (s 58 of the PACE Act 1984 and Code C, Annex B) is very rare and must be authorized by an officer of the rank of superintendent or above. With regard to trying to inform another person of the detainee's whereabouts (under s 56), any decision to delay must be authorized by an officer of at least the rank of inspector and the delay must not exceed 36 hours (s 56 of the PACE Act 1984 and Code C, Annex B).

10.15.4.3 Receiving visits

At the custody officer's discretion, the detainee can receive visits from friends, family, or others who are likely to take an interest in their welfare, or from a person in whose welfare the detainee has an interest (Code C, para 5.4). Such visits are subject to the availability of supervising staff and any possible hindrance to the investigation will also need to be considered (Code C, Note 5B).

10.15.5 Searching the detainee

The custody officer has the power to search the detainee or can ask another officer to carry out a search. The searching officer must be of the same sex as the detainee (see s 54(9) of the PACE

Act 1984 but also refer to your police service's policy on how to accommodate individuals who wish to be treated according to their preferred gender). The custody officer will decide the extent of the search but it must not be intimate without further authorization (s 54(6) and (7). The forensic examination of suspects is covered in 13.3.4.

A record of all of the items found during a search must be made. This could be on the custody record or elsewhere (in which case the location must be noted on the custody record (Code C, para 4.4)). Clothes and effects can only be seized if there are reasonable grounds for believing they may provide evidence relating to an offence or if the custody officer believes the detainee would use the items to harm themselves, to damage property, to interfere with evidence, or to try to escape (s 54(3) and (4)). It has been held that taking away clothing under s 54 to avoid its use as a ligature is not a breach of Article 8 of the ECHR (see 18.5.1) as long as the requirements of the Codes of Practice are followed (*Davies (by her mother and litigation friend) v Chief Constable of Merseyside Police* [2015] EWCA Civ 114).

The custody officer is responsible for any of the detainee's possessions that are unrelated to the offence and not to be used as evidence (Code C, para 4.1), and must arrange their safekeeping.

10.15.5.1 Strip searches and intimate searches

A strip search involves removal of clothing and the detainee can be required to lift their arms and stand with their legs apart. It requires authorization from the custody officer, who must reasonably consider that the detainee has concealed an article which they would not be allowed to keep and that a strip search is necessary to find the article (Code C, Annex A, para 10). The search must be conducted in accordance with Code C, Annex A, para 11. For example, it must be carried out by an officer of the same sex with at least two people present (other than the detainee), or in line with police service policy regarding individuals wishing to be treated according to their preferred gender, but away from other people in general and in a safe place. The search should be conducted with regard to sensitivity and as quickly as reasonably possible. In relation to establishing the gender of persons for the purposes of searching, see Code A, Annex F.

An intimate search is more detailed than a strip search and involves the examination (including touching) of any part of the body, including orifices (see Code C, Annex A, para 1 and the College of Policing APP). Such a search must be authorized by an officer of at least the rank of inspector, who must have reasonable grounds for believing that at the time of the arrest the detainee had concealed on their person:

- anything which could be used to cause physical injury to themselves or others; or
- a Class A drug with the appropriate criminal intent (s 55(1)). (The criminal intent must relate to a further criminal offence such as an intent to supply (see 21.6.2) or exportation with intent to evade a prohibition or restriction (s 68(2) of the Customs and Excise Management Act 1979).)

10.16 Statements from Witnesses and Victims

An important part of any investigation is supporting witnesses (who may also be victims) through the process of making a witness statement. This is recorded on an MG11 form, which will be included in the case file. Victim personal statements are also recorded on an MG11 form, either following on from the first part of a witness statement or on a separate form. Detailed and accurate accounts are required and no abbreviations and jargon should be used.

The MG11 form is available as a paper or an electronic version. The paper version has a front sheet and continuation sheets if required (use paper clips rather than staples). On handwritten copies, black ink should be used and any written mistakes crossed out with a single line and initialled in the margin—do not overwrite or use correction fluid. The back of the form (once completed) is for police and prosecution use only in order to protect witnesses.

Some of the guidance provided here is adapted from the unpublished document 'A Guide to Form MG11, General Completion' by Kent Police, as interpreted by the authors.

10.16.1 Witness statements

Witness statements are generally compiled by the interviewing officer after they have interviewed the witness (see 13.8.3) and they have together agreed the facts that are to be recorded. The officer should outline the consequences of the witness stating anything they know to be false or do not believe to be true and draw attention to the need for the witness to sign a declaration that they believe everything in the statement is true.

The witness's name should be written out in full at the top of the form, using capitals for the family name only. If capitals are used throughout, then the family name should be underlined. Any people named in a witness statement should be referred to by the name the witness used. For all descriptions of a person, object, or incident, *R v Turnbull* guidelines (ADVOKATE) must be adhered to in full (see 10.10.2). Descriptions should be recorded in detail and any uncertainties fully recorded.

Enter your rank and force number.

Sign with your rank and number.

Use the 24 hour clock and use 'at' not 'at approximately'.

Always begin with the time, day, date, location, and other persons present. Do not include your name, title, number, or station in the main body of the text.

This is hearsay evidence (she said that he said), and should be recorded in direct speech; see 24.2.5.1

Arrests must be recorded in direct speech, but the caution does not have to be. Any response from the suspect must be accurately recorded.

Sign and date after the last word of the statement, and include your rank and number.

For a duty statement, the signature does not need to be witnessed.

Sign at the foot of every page, and include your rank and number.

MG 11 (T)

RESTRICTED (when complete)

WITNESS STATEMENT

(CJ Act 1967, s.9; MC Act 1980, ss.5A(3) (a) and SB; MC Rules 1981, r.70)

URN

Statement of: *Charlotte UNDERWOOD*

Age if under 18: *over 18* (if over 18 insert 'over 18') Occupation: *Police Constable 118118*

This statement (consisting of *one* page(s) each signed by me) is true to the best of my knowledge and belief and I make it knowing that, if it is tendered in evidence, I shall be liable to prosecution if I have wilfully stated anything in it, which I know to be false, or do not believe to be true.

Signature: *C. Underwood PC 118118* Date: *01.03.00*

Tick if witness evidence is visually recorded ☐ *(supply witness details on rear)*

At 1600 hours on Wednesday 1st March0000 I was on uniformed patrol in a marked police vehicle with PC 69900 HODDIM. At this time we attended Kerrie's Corner shop,98 High Street, Maidbury, Kentshire. As we arrived I saw a man who I now know to be Nathan JONAH born 09.09.1973 sitting on the pavement holding a plastic carrier bag approximately 1 metre from the front door of the shop on the pavement outside. I got out of the car and walked towards JONAH. I would describe JONAH as... The plastic carrier bag JONAH was holding looked as if it contained something lumpy. I heard JONAH shout 'That's it, you're all for it now!' and he tried to stand up, but stumbled and fell. As I approached him I could smell intoxicating liquor on his breath, his speech was slurred, and his eyes were glazed. He tried to stand up again but could not. He was drunk or otherwise intoxicated. He was groaning and looking downwards with his eyes shut sometimes.

A woman came up to me and introduced herself as Mrs STONER. She said in the presence and hearing of the suspect 'I heard him say "what's it to you if some of us 'ain't got nothing to eat" and then I heard a long bang—I think he pushed the shop assistant against the wall behind the door and ran out'. PC HODDIM came over with a shop assistant from the store, a person I now know to be Janis DEE. In the presence and hearing of the suspect I said to Mrs DEE 'Can you please tell me what happened?' Mrs DEE replied 'I was filling the refrigerator with packets of bacon when this bloke here took a pack from out of the box on the floor. He walked around the store for a little while, well staggered really. I tried to stop him and then he just walked out without paying for it.' At 1635 hours the same day I said to the suspect JONAH 'As a result of what this person has told me I am arresting you on suspicion of theft of a pack of meat from the shop. Your arrest is necessary for the prompt and effective investigation of the offence and because you are drunk you may suffer physical injury to yourself'. I then cautioned him to which he replied 'It wasn't me, you've got the wrong person ... why me?' ... As JONAH was drunk I believed that he may present a danger to himself or others if he had possession of a weapon. I also believed he may have other articles from the store which he had not paid for. Therefore I searched him before placing him into the police vehicle. I looked inside the bag he was carrying and it contained a large packet of meat which I seized (exhibit labelled and marked CU/1). JONAH was placed in a police vehicle and conveyed to Maidbury Police Station arriving at 1645 hours the same day where he was introduced to the custody officer PS BENN.

C. Underwood PC 118118, 01.03.00

Signature: *C. Underwood PC 118118* Signature witnessed by: *n/a*

PTO

Use capital letters for all this part.

For example, if previously married.

If no MG 10 form is available, then record the relevant information here.

Remember to get the witness to sign here.

The time and date the statement was made should be recorded in your PNB.

MG 11 (T)

RESTRICTED—FOR POLICE AND PROSECUTION ONLY (when complete)

Witness contact details

Home address: 31 JENNER ROAD, MAIDBURY, KENT

Postcode: MA99 1XX

Home telephone No: 1234567 Work telephone No: 123456789

Mobile/Pager No: 1234567 E-mail address: N/A

Preferred means of contact: HOME PHONE

~~Male~~/Female (delete as applicable) Date and place of birth: 12.00.65 BIG CITY

Former Name: N/A Height: 163cm Ethnicity Code: W1

Dates of witness non-availability: see MG 10

Witness care

(a) Is the witness willing and likely to attend court? ~~Yes~~/No. If 'No', include reason(s) on form MG6. What can be done to ensure attendance?

(b) Does the witness require 'special measures' as a vulnerable or intimidated witness? ~~Yes~~/No. If 'Yes' submit MG2 with file.

(c) Does the witness have any specific care needs? ~~Yes~~/No. If 'Yes' what are they? (Healthcare, childcare, transport, disability, language difficulties, visually impaired, restricted mobility or other concerns?)

Witness Consent (for witness completion)

a) The criminal justice process and Victim Personal Statement scheme (victims only) has been explained to me: Yes/~~No~~

b) I have been given the leaflet 'Giving a witness statement to the police—what happens next?' Yes/~~No~~

c) I consent to police having access to my medical record(s) in relation to this matter: Yes☐ No☐ N/A☑

d) I consent to my medical record in relation to this matter being disclosed to the defence: Yes☐ No☐ N/A☑

e) I consent to the statement being disclosed for the purposes of civil proceedings e.g. child care proceedings (if applicable): Yes☐ No☐ N/A☑

f) The information recorded above will be disclosed to the Witness Service so that they can offer help and support, unless you ask them not to. Tick this box to decline their services: ☑

Signature of witness: AMStoner

Statement taken by (print name): PC 118118 UNDERWOOD Station: Maidbury Police Station

Time and place statement taken: 17.50 01.03.00 MAIDBURY POLICE STATION

Witness statements must record only what the witness has experienced directly through their own senses. The statement though written by a police officer should be in the witness's own words and avoid police jargon. Opinion should not be included unless the witness is a relevant expert providing an expert opinion or a competent witness stating whether another person was drunk.

Exhibits, any items that could be used as evidence in court, must be given a reference number that includes the initials of the person who handed the item to the police officer. So, for example, the bag of shopping Alice Stoner gave to PC Hoddim will have the reference number AMS/1. The other bag (the orange bag held by the man on the pavement) will have the reference number CU/1 because it was the first item of evidence collected by PC Underwood in this incident (see 10.3.6 for more on numbering of exhibits).

10.16.2 Victim personal statements

The victim will provide a statement as a witness but can also make a further statement as a victim. Such a victim personal statement (VPS) provides extra information on how the crime has affected the victim and what support may be needed. A VPS can also be made by the relatives and partners of homicide victims or the parents and carers of children or adults with learning difficulties. It will form part of the case file and is used during the court process, particularly in sentencing and applications for bail.

A VPS is normally made immediately after a witness statement, on the same MG11 form. This is known as a Stage 1 VPS. A caption should be inserted between the evidential part of the statement and the VPS to emphasize this separation, for example:

> I have been given the Victim Personal Statement leaflet and the VPS scheme has been explained to me. What follows is what I wish to say in connection with this matter. I understand that what I say may be used in various ways and that it may be disclosed to the defence.

A separate or an additional VPS (a Stage 2 VPS) can be made at a later date. The same caption should be used to emphasize it is a VPS and not an evidential witness statement. If a previous VPS has been made, the caption should include the phrase 'This statement adds to what I said in my previous victim personal statement'.

The officer should explain that the victim can express anything they choose, including:

- whether they want to be told about the progress of the case;
- whether they would like extra support, particularly if appearing as a witness at a trial;
- whether they feel vulnerable or intimidated;
- whether they are worried about the suspect being given bail, eg if the suspect and victim know each other;
- if racial hostility is felt to be part of the crime or if they feel victimized because of their faith, cultural background, or disability;
- whether they are considering trying to claim compensation from the offender for any injury, loss, or damage suffered; and
- whether the crime has caused, or made worse, any medical or social problems such as marital difficulties.

Victims can choose whether the VPS will be heard in court, either read out by the victim or the CPS or from a recording. There may be consequences for a victim's privacy if the statement is heard in open sessions, particularly if reported by the media. If it is not heard and the defendant is found guilty, the contents of the VPS will still be considered as part of the evidence prior to sentencing. All this must be clearly explained to the victim.

The completed statement should be sent to the CPS with information on any arrangements made, and the victim's preferences. Further guidance on victim personal statements is available on the Ministry of Justice website.

10.17 Duty Statements

A duty statement is a witness statement made by a police officer as a witness to events. The general guidance for completing MG11 forms still applies but there are additional considerations. On the back of the MG11, for the home contact details asked for at the top a police officer should use their work address, email, and telephone number. The Witness Care and Witness Consent sections do not need to be filled in for a duty statement: simply put 'N/A' where appropriate.

When referring to other police officers, for the first mention the family name should be in capitals, with the officer's rank and number. If the same officer is mentioned again, only the rank and name is needed. Witnesses should be referred to using either both names or Mr/Ms and the family name in capitals. The first time a suspect is named in a duty statement, the full name should be used with the family name in capitals, but in the rest of the statement only the family name is used.

10.18 Methods of Disposal of Criminal Suspects

Here we describe the various methods of *disposing* of a criminal suspect. By disposal we mean the result of an investigation and its outcome for the suspect. We have split these into three main categories: directing to court, out-of-court disposals, and bail.

The disposal can be final, leading to a *positive disposal* such as a charge, caution, or penalty notice, or a *No Further Action* when no crime can be confirmed or there is not enough evidence to support a prosecution. These disposals usually signify the end of the investigation, although if further evidence comes to light, they can be reopened. However, some disposals, such as release under investigation or police bail, can be *interim* if further investigation is to be undertaken.

10.18.1 Directing to court

Once an investigation has been concluded and a decision to prosecute has been made by the police or the Crown Prosecution Service (see 18.7.3), the defendant will be formally accused of committing a criminal offence. In less serious cases, the defendant will receive a formal accusation by way of a written charge and postal requisition by a public prosecutor. In more serious cases, the charge will be read out to the suspect in a police station.

10.18.1.1 Written charge and postal requisition by a public prosecutor

Criminal proceedings can be instituted by a written postal charge and requisition (PCR) (s 29(1) and (2) of the Criminal Justice Act 2003), after a police officer reports a suspect at the roadside for a road traffic offence or a suspect attends a police station voluntarily at an officer's request (reporting for an offence). This has largely replaced the former practice of issuing a summons to attend court.

To report a person for the purposes of issuing a written charge, the officer must:

1. state the offence(s) involved;
2. gather evidence in the usual way, ie using the senses, for example what was seen or heard;
3. point out the offence(s) to the suspect;
4. caution the suspect using the 'when questioned' caution (follow PACE Code C, para 10. 2) and also inform the suspect that they are not under arrest, but that any failure to co-operate or to answer particular questions may affect their immediate treatment;
5. make a PNB record of the questions and answers about the offence(s), including points to prove and negations to available defences;
6. offer the PNB to the suspect to read and sign that the notes are a true record of the interview (see Code C, para 11.11);
7. tell the suspect 'I am reporting you for the offence(s) of …';
8. caution the suspect (using the 'now' caution: see 10.9.1).

The evidence is used to form a case file (see 18.7.5) which is then submitted by the officer in the case for review. If the decision is to prosecute, the public prosecutor will issue a written charge to the suspect. This will describe the relevant offence and state the Act under which the offence was created. The public prosecutor will also issue a requisition which requires the suspect to appear before a magistrates' court. The documents will be served by post, with copies sent to the court named in the requisition.

10.18.1.2 Charging at a police station

For less serious offences, the Evidential Review Officer (the ERO, usually a sergeant) will decide whether a suspect should be charged or released without charge. This applies for summary-only offences or either-way offences with an anticipated guilty plea. For either-way offences with anticipated not guilty pleas, and for all indictable-only offences, the ERO will refer the matter to the CPS for a decision. For a juvenile or a vulnerable adult, any action taken should be taken in the presence of an appropriate adult (Code C, para 16.1 and Note 16C).

The suspect to be charged (or the appropriate adult) is given a written notice (an MG4 form, see 18.7.5.2) which includes the following details:

- reference number of the case and custody record number;
- time and date the charge is made;
- the suspect's details, including name, address, and date of birth;
- the name of the police officer who charged the suspect and the name of the custody officer who 'accepted the charge'; and
- any reply from the suspect in response to charge.

The charge will always include the 'now' caution and is likely to be worded as follows. In this example the charge is for an assault:

> You are charged with the offence(s) shown below. You do not have to say anything. But it may harm your defence if you do not mention now something which you later rely on in court. Anything you say may be given in evidence. On (date) at (town) in the county of (name of county) you assaulted (name of victim) contrary to Section 39 of the Criminal Justice Act 1988.

After a suspect has been charged or informed that they may be prosecuted for an offence, no further interviews should be conducted unless it is necessary for the following reasons (listed in Code C, para 16.5):

- to prevent or minimize harm or loss to some other person or the public;
- to clear up an ambiguity in a previous answer or statement; or
- to put new information (relevant to the offence) to the detainee in the interests of justice.

A 'restricted' caution must be given at the start of such an interview (see 10.9.6).

After being charged, the suspect will usually be released, with or without bail. The custody officer may, however, decide that the suspect should be kept in custody if, for example, they have no current abode, their name is not known, or if the charge is for a serious offence (see s 38(1) of the PACE Act 1984 and s 25 of the Criminal Justice and Public Order Act 1994 for a full list). A suspect who has been charged and kept in custody will be brought before a magistrates' court at the next sitting.

10.18.2 Out-of-court disposals

Custody officers and other decision-makers have a duty to consider whether an out-of-court disposal (OOCD) would be more appropriate for the offender than prosecution. Prosecution can have serious consequences for the offender and OOCDs are an attempt to avoid disproportionate criminalization of citizens. The seriousness of the offence and the proportionality of the outcome will both be taken into consideration. The National Decision Model can help to ensure consistent and effective decision-making when considering an OOCD. The College of Policing APP provides further information in the *Possible Justice Outcomes Following Investigation* (CoP, 2015b).

10.18.2.1 Restorative justice

Restorative justice (RJ) is a form of OOCD which has been successfully used over a number of years for some offences and some offenders and can take a variety of forms. At its simplest, police officers can deal with minor crimes and incidents on the spot with a 'community resolution'. Acceptable Behaviour Contracts and Parenting Contracts are other disposal methods aimed specifically at young people. Community resolutions can also be used after investigations into low-level crime and anti-social behaviour. They have the advantage of not criminalizing suspects but still deal with the incident to the victim's satisfaction, and also amount to a documented clear-up for the police. The NDM can be used when making decisions on whether to use RJ in a particular situation.

A more formal RJ procedure may also be used if the victim and offender agree, in which they are brought together in a restorative meeting facilitated by an appointed police officer or volunteer. For more serious or persistent matters which cannot be dealt with immediately, a series of meetings with additional participants may be needed to seek longer term reparative solutions. Research suggests that RJ conferencing can reduce reoffending rates particularly for violent crimes (What Works, 2015).

Using the NDM—Example

An officer is called to the scene of a group of young people who are committing acts of ASB outside a local resident's home. They have been repeatedly kicking a football against the resident's wall. The resident came out to remonstrate with them, and they verbally abused them.

NDM Stage 1—Gather information

- Who are the young people involved? Do you have their names/addresses?
- Why have they chosen this location to play football? Are there any alternative locations?
- How does the resident confront the young people? Are they aggressive?

- What form does the verbal abuse take? Language, aggression, swearing? Does any of it amount to a substantive offence?
- Are the young people aware of the impact they are making?

NDM Stage 2—Determine the threat

- Is this a one-off or ongoing problem?
- Does the officer need to act straight away?
- What is the likely outcome/implication if the officer does/does not act straight away?
- Are the police the most appropriate people to deal with the problem? Local authority?

NDM Stage 3—What powers do the police have to deal with the problem?

- Arrest? Dispersal? Warnings?

NDM Stage 4—Draw up list of options

- High visibility patrols as deterrence?
- Arrest for Breach of the Peace (if immediate) or Public Order?
- Penalty Notice for Disorder?
- Speak to the young people in question and verbally warn them of their behaviour (and complete a community resolution form)?
- Report the ASB to the local authority?
- Invite young people, parents, and resident to a sit-down Restorative Justice Conference?

NDM Stage 5—Take action

- Based on all the information, options, and referring to the Code of Ethics to ensure proportionality, officers can take one or more of the options. On completion, officers should return to NDM Stage 1 to determine if intervention(s) were successful.

10.18.2.2 Penalty notices

A Penalty Notice for Disorder (PND) allows perpetrators aged 18 or over to pay a fine without going to court. The scheme was introduced in 2001 under ss 1–11 of the Criminal Justice and Police Act 2001 and its key aims and objectives are:

- to reduce the amount of time that law enforcement officers spend completing paperwork and attending court;
- to increase the amount of time law enforcement officers spend on the street;
- to reduce the burden on the courts; and
- to deliver swift, simple, and effective justice that carries a deterrent effect.

The term 'Fixed Penalty Notice' is used in a number of different circumstances but the common factor is that the recipient has to pay a fixed penalty or charge. The first penalty notices were introduced over 50 years ago for motoring and road traffic offences. The Anti-Social Behaviour Act 2003 also provided for local authority personnel and PCSOs to issue penalty notices, also sometimes referred to as fixed penalty notices, for graffiti and other minor offences such as littering or dog control offences. The Anti-social Behaviour, Crime and Policing Act 2014 enabled police officers, PCSOs, and council officers to issue fixed penalty notices for failing to comply with a community protection notice and for public spaces protection offences (see 3.8.1.1) Civil Enforcement Officers issue penalty charge notices (PCNs) for decriminalized parking/waiting offences in most parts of the UK. PCNs are also used in London for some moving traffic offences related to bus lanes, no-entry signs, restricted turns, red routes, and yellow box junctions.

A police officer who has reason to believe that a person aged 18 or over has committed a relevant offence can issue a penalty notice (s 2(1) of the Criminal Justice and Police Act 2001).

The offences for which a PND can be used are shown in the tables.

PND offence with a fine of £90	Legislation
Wasting police time/giving false report	Criminal Law Act 1967, s 5(2)
Using public electronic communications network in order to cause annoyance, inconvenience, or needless anxiety	Communications Act 2003, s 127(2)
Knowingly giving a false alarm to a person acting on behalf of a fire and rescue authority	Fire and Rescue Services Act 2004, s 49 (England only)
	Fire Services Act 1947, s 31 (Wales only)
Causing harassment, alarm, or distress	Public Order Act 1986, s 5
Throwing fireworks	Explosives Act 1875, s 80
Drunk and disorderly	Criminal Justice Act 1967, s 91
Selling alcohol to person under 18 (anywhere)	Licensing Act 2003, s 146(1)
Supply of alcohol by or on behalf of a club to a person aged under 18	Licensing Act 2003, s 146(3)
Selling alcohol to a drunken person	Licensing Act 2003, s 141
Purchasing or attempting to purchase alcohol on behalf of a person under 18 (includes licensed premises and off-licences)	Licensing Act 2003, s 149(3)
Purchase of alcohol for consumption in licensed premises by person under 18	Licensing Act 2003, s 149(4)
Delivery of alcohol to person under 18 or allowing such delivery	Licensing Act 2003, s 151
Destroying or damaging property worth £300 or less	Criminal Damage Act 1971, s 1(1)
Unlawful possession of cannabis and its derivatives	Misuse of Drugs Act 1971, s 5(2)
Theft (retail) of property worth £100 or less (but see* at the end of this table)	Theft Act 1968, s 1
Breach of fireworks curfew (2300–0700 hrs)	Firework Regulations 2004, reg 7 (Fireworks Act 2003, s 11)
Possession of a category 4 firework	Firework Regulations 2004, reg 5 (Fireworks Act 2003, s 11)

* For 'theft from a shop' (other than by an employee) only one such PND should ever be issued to an individual, and only for incidents where the value of the goods is £100 or less and the property has been recovered (consuming the stolen property may be an exception).

PND offence with a fine of £60	Legislation
Dropping or leaving litter or refuse except in a receptacle provided for the purpose in a Royal Park or other open space	Royal Parks and Other Open Spaces Regulations 1997, reg 3(3)–(5), and the Parks Regulation (Amendment) Act 1926, s 2(1)
Using a pedal cycle, a roller blade, etc except on a Park road or in a designated area	
Failing to remove immediately any faeces deposited by an animal of which that person is in charge	
Depositing and leaving litter	Environmental Protection Act 1990, ss 87(1) and 87(5)
Throwing stones at a train	British Transport Commission Act 1949, s 56
Trespassing on a railway	British Transport Commission Act 1949, s 55
Drunk in the highway	Licensing Act 1872, s 12
Consumption of alcohol by a person under 18 in a bar	Licensing Act 2003, s 150(1)
Allowing consumption of alcohol by a young person (aged under 18) in a bar	Licensing Act 2003, s 150(2)
Unlawful possession of khat and its derivatives	Misuse of Drugs Act 1971, s 5(2)

A PND can be issued on the spot by an officer in uniform, known as a street issue, or at a police station by an authorized officer, usually the custody officer. In many forces, PNDs can be issued using mini digital printers instead of handwritten PND tickets; officers will need to be familiar with the type of PND forms used locally. The national data-sharing system for recording PNDs (PentiP (Penalty Notice Processing)) can be used to check for unpaid penalties from previous incidents.

A person who accepts a PND is not admitting to a crime; they are simply supporting a suspicion by a police officer that an offence has been committed and recognizing that there will be no further proceedings. It would not affect a person's 'good character' and *R v Hamer* [2010]

WLR (D) 235). The recipient has 21 days to either pay the penalty or request a court hearing. In some areas, an education option is available as an alternative; the recipient must pay for the course and complete it. Failure to take any of these options may result in a fine which is one and a half times the penalty amount, or court proceedings.

If after receiving a PND it comes to light that the person may have committed a more serious and non-penalty offence during the same incident, the further offence can be investigated and prosecuted separately (see *R v Gore; R v Maker* [2009] EWCA Crim 1424, WLR (D) 240). The flowchart shows the process model for issuing a PND (adapted from the current Home Office operational guidance (Home Office, 2013a).

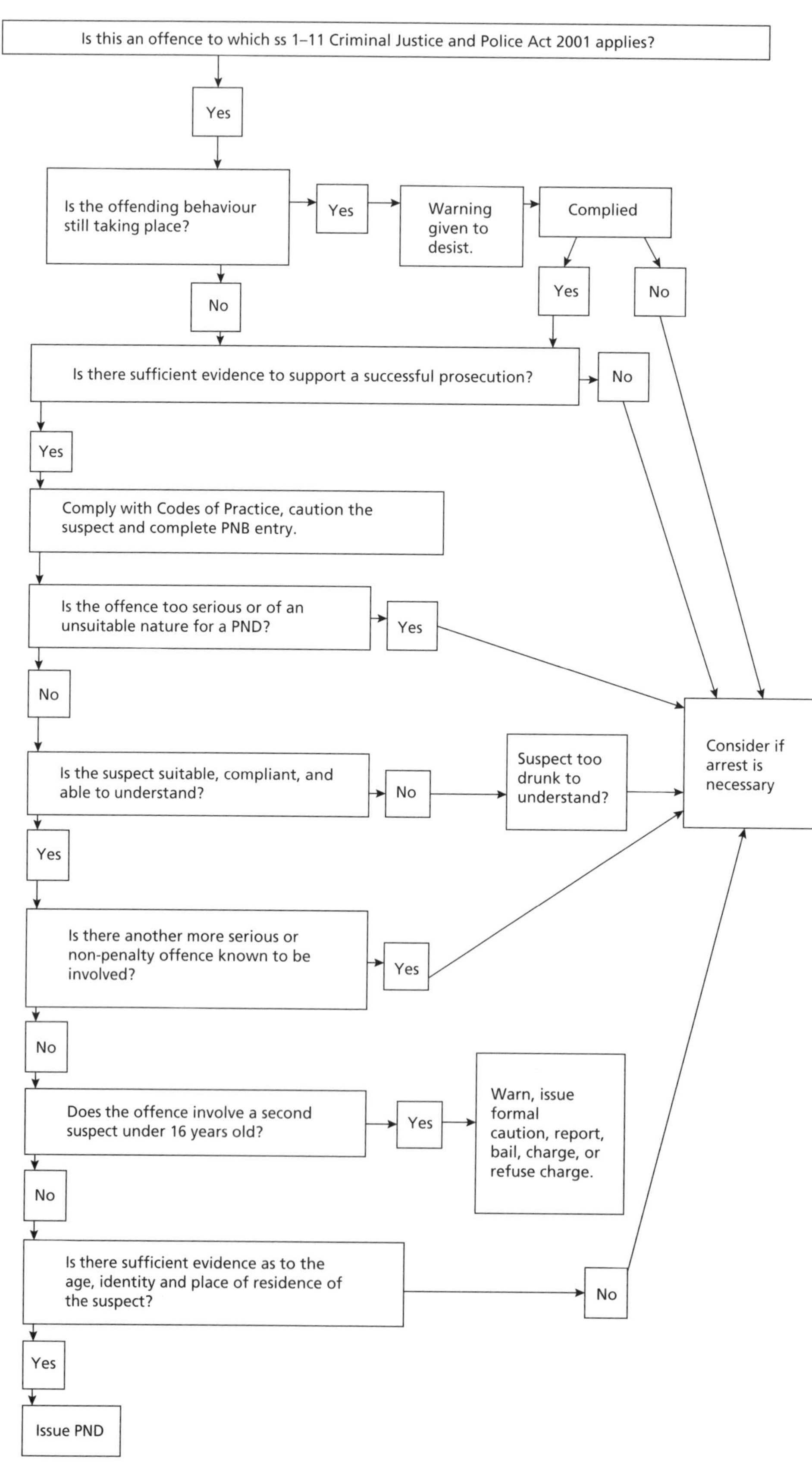

A person who has been given a PND may be photographed on the street (s 64A(1A) of the PACE Act 1984). This can be without consent (either withheld or if it is not practicable to obtain it). Before the photo is taken the person can be required to remove anything worn on or over any part of the head or face and an officer can remove it the person refuses (s 64A(2)). However, for a religious garment the person should be taken out of public view before removing the garment and being photographed.

10.18.2.3 Adult cautions

There are two types of caution for adults aged 18 years and over, the *simple caution* and the *conditional caution* (ss 22–27 of the Criminal Justice Act 2003). They both involve a formal warning given by a senior police officer or by a more junior officer on the instructions of a senior police officer. Note that the cautions covered here are a method of disposal, and must not be confused with the other forms of cautions used in investigations (see 10.9.1).

A simple caution can be given to a person who has admitted guilt for certain summary or either-way offences. They cannot be used for the offences listed in the Criminal Justice and Courts Act 2015 (Simple Cautions) (Specification of Either-Way Offences) Order 2015 (s 17(3) of the Criminal Justice and Courts Act 2015). To use a simple caution, all of the elements of the offence must be proved (*R (on the application of W) v Chief Constable of Hampshire Constabulary* [2006] EWHC 1904 (Admin)). The caution is recorded on the PNC and, if the recipient is later convicted and sentenced for a further offence, the court can take the caution into consideration. Further details are provided in Home Office Circular 016/2008 and in the Ministry of Justice guide *Simple Cautions for Adult Offenders*, available online.

A conditional caution is similar to a simple caution but has rehabilitative or reparative conditions attached. It can be used to address the offender's behaviour and to make reparation for the effects of the offence on the victim and others. The conditions must be appropriate, proportionate, and achievable (see the Code of Practice for adult conditional cautions). For example, a condition for a person who has been involved with low-level alcohol-related crime and/or disorder could be 'no possessing an open container of alcohol in a public place for six months'. Conditional cautions can be given by a police constable, an investigating officer, or any other person authorized by the prosecutor. Five requirements must be met:

1. The police officer has sufficient evidence that the person has committed an offence.
2. The police officer or relevant prosecutor (or other authorized person) decides that there is sufficient evidence to charge the person with the offence and that a conditional caution should be given.
3. The offender admits the offence to a police officer (or other authorized person).
4. The effect of a caution and the consequences of failing to observe a condition must be explained to the offender.
5. The offender signs a document that sets out details of the offence, and that they admit guilt and consent to the caution and the attached conditions.

Failing to comply with the conditions will result in criminal proceedings and the caution will be cancelled. If there are reasonable grounds for believing that an offender has failed (without reasonable excuse) to comply with a condition, they can be arrested without warrant (s 24A of the Criminal Justice Act 2003). Further details are provided in the CPS Conditional Cautioning Code of Practice, available on the CPS website.

10.18.2.4 Youth cautions

The Crime and Disorder Act 1998 provides for the youth caution (s 66Z(1)) and the youth conditional caution (s 66A) for young people aged between 10 and 17 years. They can be used even if the recipient has previous convictions for any offence. The suspect must admit the current offence and must also be referred to the Youth Offending Team (YOT, see 11.4.3) as soon as practicable. Further information can be obtained from the *Youth Out-of-Court Disposals Guide* (MoJ and the Youth Justice Board, 2015).

For a youth caution, the officer must have sufficient evidence to charge for the offence and must also believe it is not in the public interest to prosecute or give a youth conditional caution. An appropriate adult must be present when the caution is given. For a young person receiving a second youth caution, the YOT will be expected to make an assessment and, if appropriate, arrange a voluntary rehabilitation programme.

Youth conditional cautions are the next level up from a youth caution and involve conditions being placed on the perpetrator. The five requirements listed in 10.18.2.3 must all be met, and both the views of the victim and the behavioural needs of the young person should be taken into consideration.

10.18.2.5 Foreign national offender conditional cautions

Some offenders will be foreign nationals who have entered the country illegally and have no right to remain in the UK. It may be in the public interest if such a person simply receives a caution and leaves the UK, rather than being prosecuted. The primary conditions for these cautions are that the offender must cooperate with the authorities and then leave the UK and not return for five years. Secondary rehabilitative conditions can be imposed, including attending a treatment course, for drug addiction, for example, prior to departure. Reparative conditions can also be imposed such as paying compensation, repairing damage, and apologizing to the victim.

10.18.3 Police bail

Bail is a process of attempting to ensure that a person appears at a specified time at a specified place, such as a police station (police bail) or a court (court bail). Bail had been used much less frequently in recent years and under the terms of the Policing and Crime Act 2017 there was a general presumption of release without bail (Release Under Investigation (RUI)), unless the need for bail met very strict criteria for necessity and proportionality. However, the Police, Crime, Sentencing and Courts Act 2022 has now introduced Kay's Law following the death of a woman at the hands of her partner who was Released Under Investigation rather than bailed and this act seeks to reverse the presumption against pre-charge bail (Home Office, 2021d).

Bail is used during investigations to allow more time for further enquiries, as there is a time limit on how long a suspect can be held without being charged (see 10.15.3). The 'custody clock' is stopped when a suspect is released on bail but restarts when they return to the police station on the specified date, carrying on from the time it was stopped. Bail can also be used to bind a defendant who has been charged to appear in court.

Any initial police bail must be authorized by an officer of at least the rank of inspector and may only be for a maximum period of 28 days. An extension of up to three months can be authorized by an officer of at least superintendent rank. Any longer extensions must be authorized by a magistrates' court (ss 62 and 63 of the Policing and Crime Act 2017).

10.18.3.1 'Street bail'

Street bail allows police officers to release a suspect on bail without going to a police station. The suspect must then attend a specified police station on a specified date (ss 30A–30D of the PACE Act 1984). Street bail is also subject to the new more stringent conditions in relation to authorization and time limits, and most officers now proceed by inviting the suspect to a police station for a voluntary attendance interview unless there are pressing reasons to arrest, for example if the offender is drunk and likely to become violent.

The following questions must be considered when deciding whether to grant street bail.

1. What type of offence has been committed and is it too serious for street bail to be used?
2. What has been the impact of the offence?
3. Would the delay caused by using street bail result in loss of vital forensic evidence?
4. Is the person fit to be released back onto the streets?
5. Does the person understand what is happening? Are they vulnerable?
6. If released on bail, is the person likely to commit a further offence?
7. Has the person provided a correct name and address? This is needed for street bail.

Note that statements concerning guilt are not relevant to the decision to grant bail—interview and examination of evidence will take place later.

A decision to grant street bail should be explained to the offender and a notice issued covering points 1–7 above. The person must understand the requirement to attend a police station on a specified date and that they are not being legally discharged and may be subject to court proceedings or other disposal actions. The notice will list any conditions imposed and name the police station at which the conditions can be varied. There is a power to arrest without warrant if there are reasonable grounds for suspecting any of the conditions have been broken or for failing to answer bail at the specified time (s 30D of the PACE Act 1984).

10.18.3.2 Bail from a police station

The overarching power for the police to grant bail and to require individuals to report back to the police station is contained in s 47(3) of the PACE Act 1984. There are five main circumstances for granting bail:

Circumstances for granting bail	PACE subsection	Return location	Conditions can apply?
Further investigation and evidence gathering is planned as there is insufficient evidence to support a charge at present	s 34(5)	police station	No
Insufficient evidence to support a charge and no further investigation planned, but review is required	s 37(2)	police station	Yes
Sufficient evidence to support a charge but consultation with the CPS is required to agree charges	s 37(7)(a)	police station	Yes
Sufficient evidence to support a charge but consultation with the CPS is required to agree on an alternative form of disposal, such as a caution (see 10.18.2.3)	s 37(7)(b)	police station	Yes
After a person has been charged with an offence	s 37(7)(d)	Court	Yes

A person who fails to attend the police station or court at the appointed time, or breaks attached conditions, can be arrested without warrant under s 46A(1) of the PACE Act 1984 (see 10.11.4.5).

> **TASK 3** What offence, if any, is committed by a person who fails to return on bail to a police station or fails to surrender to custody at a court after having been bailed?

10.19 Handover Procedures

After initial enquiries into a suspected crime, eg taking statements, collecting potential evidence, the arrest of a suspect, the arresting officer may hand over responsibility for the subsequent investigation to another colleague, for example a volume crime investigator (see Chapter 13). In some police services, the case files are handed over to a Criminal Justice Unit or Department where case-builders obtain further statements and evidence, and, if appropriate, prepare files for submission to the CPS. Practice varies; in some constabularies the arresting officer may be expected to see the process through to a more advanced stage.

The key principle for handovers is that the information provided will enable the receiving colleague to become as familiar with the circumstances of the alleged offence as the arresting officer. The 'handover package' will include documents and references to artefacts, for example forensic evidence and special property. It will also include a general checklist (the 'single source document') which will be likely to list the following:

Checklist entry	Examples/notes
Names of the alleged offender(s)	Provide names, DoB, and custody numbers
The arresting officer's account of the circumstances leading up to arrest	Remember to avoid offering opinion in this section
Investigation checklist	• A series of tick-box lists addressing the arrest (including a copy of PNB entries); • searches; • exhibits; • scene and forensic evidence; • detainee and custody considerations; and • PNC/force intelligence database checks
Witness details and statements	• names, addresses, and contact numbers of witnesses; and • a summary of witness statements
Other officers involved	• details of those who also attended; and • copies of their PNB entries and statements

Note that the single source document could be 'relevant material' so it must be included on the MG6C form.

10.20 Answers to Tasks

TASK 1 There are many examples but you might have considered the following: The caution means that you have the right to silence and you do not have to say anything or reply to any question you are asked. Anything that you say now or during the rest of the investigation can be given to the court for consideration. However, if you choose not to say anything now or during the investigation, but decide to say something in court, they can ignore it.

TASK 2 They should:

- locate the person through the use of intelligence, a stop check, the PNC, or their local police database;
- identify themselves, then confirm their identity, and then arrest and caution them;
- endorse the back of the warrant (also known as 'backing up');
- record the event in their PNB;
- send the 'backed-up' warrant to the appropriate court, following local procedures.

If they are not in possession of the warrant at the time of the arrest and the suspect asks to see it, they must show it to them as soon as is practicable.

TASK 3 Section 66(1) of the Bail Act 1976 states that it is an offence for a person who has been released on bail in criminal proceedings to fail without reasonable cause to surrender to custody. This is a summary offence, and the penalty is three months' imprisonment and/or a fine.

11 Policing Communities

11.1 Introduction

This chapter is concerned with policing in communities, focusing on practices in England and Wales. It explores the concept of community policing and the function and impact of neighbourhood policing as a strategy. It considers the police role in maintaining public trust and confidence and outlines future challenges for community policing.

The topics covered in the chapter contribute to the learning requirements of the National Policing Curriculum, inter alia: 'Understanding the Police Constable Role', 'Response Policing', 'Policing Communities', 'Problem Solving', 'Crime Prevention', and 'Valuing Difference and Inclusion'. If you are undertaking the PCDA or DHEP, the content will also be relevant to the knowledge and skills requirements.

The National Police Chiefs' Council (NPCC) considers the relationship between the police and the communities they serve, as the bedrock of British policing (NPCC, 2016). It sees public security and protection as driven by local priorities and evidence-based demand analysis. In 2018, the College of Policing produced evidence-based guidelines on implementing the strategy of neighbourhood policing (CoP, 2018b) to support and guide chief constables and police and crime commissioners. The *Final Report of the Strategic Review of Policing in England and Wales* (Police Foundation, 2022) made recommendations that seek to reinvigorate neighbourhood policing at the heart of British policing. The neighbourhood policing guidelines can be found on the College of Policing website.

The terms 'community' and 'neighbourhood' policing are often used interchangeably, yet definitional criteria are not unanimously agreed. There is clearly a distinction to be made between *policing of* communities and *community* policing. As Rowe (2018) explains, community-focused policing is a meaningful way for the police to gain public support in dealing with crime and disorder. We might consider community policing to be a *philosophy* of policing that seeks to engage and work with the public on local problems of crime, fear of crime, and quality-of-life issues. Ideally, community policing rests on a democratic model of policing and is community-centric, rather than the authoritarian exercise of state power, providing a broadening of the police mission to incorporate 'creative, community driven solutions for a host of social problems' (Kappeler, 2017, p 435). This means that community policing elevates the public and their concerns above those of the police organization and beyond a narrow crime control purview. Skogan (2006) highlights that community policing is a *process* rather than defined products of police activity. In contrast, neighbourhood policing is a strategy and the means of delivering such things.

As a strategy, neighbourhood policing has its focus on reducing crime and the fear of crime and attempts to improve perceptions of police legitimacy, by creating and maintaining public trust and confidence in the police. Several studies and reports have identified effective elements of neighbourhood policing: Skogan and Steiner (2004), Tuffin *et al* (2006), and Connell *et al* (2008) have all highlighted the value of targeted foot patrol, community engagement, and problem-solving approaches to solving community problems. A systematic review undertaken by Gill *et al* (2014) demonstrates the role of neighbourhood policing in increasing trust and confidence in the police. In his review of policing, Flanagan (2008) identified key characteristics of effective neighbourhood policing:

- strong Community Safety Partnerships (CSPs);
- an understanding of local neighbourhoods;
- strong community engagement;
- dedicated, multi-agency teams;
- provision of information to the public;
- jointly shared performance measures, monitoring, and management;
- financial planning and shared budgeting to support outcomes.

The demands on police resources have dramatically changed over the years, due in part to budgetary constraints, reduced police numbers, and the emergence of modern technologies and threats; this demand is forecast to expand further in the future operating environment of policing (CoP, 2020f). The Home Office, College of Policing, HMICFRS, and Police Foundation are all active in reviewing, promoting, and supporting neighbourhood policing as a strategy in England and Wales. The *Final Report of the Strategic Review of Policing in England and Wales* (Police Foundation, 2022) makes recommendations to reinvigorate neighbourhood policing, calling for greater investment in frontline resources, particularly in geographic areas where public trust and confidence are least.

11.2 Neighbourhood Policing in Context

Government policies and media have consistently focused on the policing of communities and neighbourhoods. Often perceived as the 'softer' side of policing, community-oriented approaches provide critical opportunities for public engagement, proactively combatting crime through crime prevention strategies, and addressing community safety concerns. There is a demonstrable link between public confidence, neighbourhood policing staffing levels, and police visibility (Police Foundation, 2022).

11.2.1 Defining neighbourhood policing

As Rowe (2018, p 93) highlights, community policing is something of a 'nebulous concept' and is most often associated with the *practice* of neighbourhood policing that began with the National Reassurance Policing Programme (NRPP), which ran between 2003 and 2005. Its focus was on providing a visible and accessible policing presence, engaging communities in identifying local problems, dealing with them in partnership with other agencies and the local community through a problem-solving approach (Higgins, 2018). However, many of the ideas associated with it derive from Alderson's (1998) notion of principled policing: identifying a philosophy of policing; developing innovative ideas about the policing function; and formulating policies and practices through consultation and performing and measuring the outcomes. In short, Alderson's desire was to transform the way that policing was done by viewing the local level as the foundation for all policing (Alderson, 1998; Higgins, 2018). Moreover, principled policing draws together both the *process* and *outcome* features of the 'community' and 'neighbourhood' policing definitions.

Following the NRPP 2003/2005 pilot, neighbourhood policing was implemented nationally between 2005 and 2008, comprising a strategy of:

- accessibility (having accountable, named police officers and police community support officers (PCSOs));
- communication between the police and public through greater dialogue;
- working together with agencies and communities to identify joint priorities;
- collaboration in developing solutions.

Her Majesty's Inspectorate of Constabulary reported limited success, in that all constabularies had met the minimum requirement to have neighbourhood policing teams (NPTs) as a key element of operational policing (Higgins, 2018). However, concern has been consistently expressed since about the erosion of neighbourhood policing and the way that the police engage with communities at local levels (Higgins, 2018; HMIC, 2017a, 2017b; Police Foundation, 2022).

The key aims of a neighbourhood policing approach are intended to prevent and control crime, and to reduce the fear of crime. It should be noted that the fear of crime and nuisance behaviour, the role of intelligence gathering, and effective communication between the police and public have much wider implications. As HMIC (2017b, p 27) explains:

> Neighbourhood policing can be a powerful force for protecting the vulnerable and tackling petty crime and anti-social behaviour that blights people's lives. But it can also be the eyes and ears in communities and can therefore help with gathering intelligence for disrupting serious and organized crime and terrorism.

11.2.2 Neighbourhood policing: a brief history

Even before the creation of what we now know as the new police in 1829, there is long-standing evidence of community participation in policing (Rawlings, 2002). The notion of local policing and community involvement can be traced back before the 1800s when community representatives served as petty constables and local 'watchmen' (Emsley, 1991). The significance of community-based policing has been widely recognized since the 1960s and its absence is seen as a factor in disturbances such as the Notting Hill disorders in 1958, the Brixton riots in 1981, and the August 2011 riots. After such disturbances, the inevitable examination of the causes predictably resulted in recommendations to improve dialogue and engagement between local communities and the police. Various reforms in policing have been introduced over the years to support the building of partnerships in an attempt to secure greater public support and community engagement. There was public demand for a more accessible and visible police service, and the emphasis in policing began to shift from a focus on crime-fighting to a recognition of the types of activity that impact on people's quality of life and their fear of crime.

These influences provided impetus for some changes in policing: the Police Reform Act 2002 introduced PCSOs as an increased visible presence and the promotion of the 'big society' (Herbert, 2011). These changes represented attempts to develop more local approaches to policing. In addition, the Police Reform and Social Responsibility Act 2011 set out a legal requirement for the police to consult with the public in local areas.

In a review conducted in 2008 (*Engaging Communities in Fighting Crime*), the UK government put forward proposals aimed at reducing crime, creating safer communities, and increasing public confidence. The focus was on the public as an important means of tackling crime, and one of the central roles for the police was engagement with communities. The proposals called for greater consistency in posting police officers to local communities.

In 2010, the Home Office produced the consultation document *Policing in the 21st Century: Reconnecting police and the people* (Home Office, 2010). This set out the government's vision of cutting crime and protecting the public and a directly accountable police service offering 'value for money'. It also made proposals to empower communities and provide greater visibility and availability. These measures have had limited impact, with public trust and confidence in the police remaining in decline, leading to renewed calls for urgent action in specific areas where it is most problematic (Police Foundation, 2022). Regrettably, with numerous scandals and reports of wrongdoing, there currently exists something of a crisis in the perceived legitimacy of British policing.

11.2.3 Community and neighbourhood policing today

There is evidence of continued support for this type of policing model in England and Wales, demonstrated in the strategic plans published on individual police service websites, its presence as a central theme of government and official bodies such as the College of Policing, HMICFRS, NPCC, and police and crime commissioners (PCCs), and through recommendations for a local policing 'reset' (Police Foundation, 2022). However, concerns endure that neighbourhood policing has been seriously eroded (HMICFRS, 2017a; Police Foundation, 2022). In response to earlier concerns and the intentions outlined by the NPCC in the Policing Vision 2025 (NPCC, 2016), the College of Policing produced new guidelines to promote a revised neighbourhood policing strategy (CoP, 2018b). The College of Policing states that its guidelines were developed through the 'What Works' process and by independent committees working collaboratively. The participants included specialist and generalist practitioners, subject-matter experts from academia and partner agencies, and the third sector. The guidelines claim to be evidence-based and supported by practical case studies (CoP, 2018b). The three key areas include:

- delivering neighbourhood policing;
- supporting neighbourhood policing;
- identifying evidence gaps.

The *Final Report of the Strategic Review of Policing in England and Wales* (Police Foundation, 2022) is the latest in the catalogue of reviews and reports to seek to place neighbourhood policing at the heart of the policing function in society.

> **TASK 1** Is neighbourhood policing a strategy applied in your area? How does it work? What partners are involved?

11.3 Delivering Local Policing

A feature of the neighbourhood policing approach is its emphasis on communication and joint problem-solving between the police and the community. The community can contribute to the setting of priorities and engage through a process of consultation. NPTs typically involve dedicated PCSOs and police constables using proactive, intelligence-led and evidence-based approaches to tackle issues of crime and anti-social behaviour. NPTs engage with the public to understand their concerns and are tasked with providing solutions in conjunction with the community to 'co-produce' safer neighbourhoods. Several models and approaches have been employed including problem analysis and solving, problem-oriented policing (POP), hot-spots, and zero-tolerance policing. It is worth noting that theoretically these share an environmental and experimental criminological base and are underpinned by rational actor, routine-activity, situational, and crime prevention through environmental design (CPTED) theories and methods which will be discussed in more detail later.

11.3.1 Community engagement

A dialogue between the public and police is essential if the police are to gain a better understanding of community needs and the risks affecting them. Legally, s 34 of the Police Reform and Social Responsibility Act 2011 provides a requirement for chief officers to plan to consult with the public in each neighbourhood, to provide local information about crime and policing, and hold regular public meetings. All national police services publish details of local community initiatives and consultations on their web pages and social media. PCCs are responsible for engaging with communities to inform them of planned reforms and changes to local policing, and seeking their views on policing priorities. The Policing Vision 2025 (NPCC, 2016) stresses that PCCs continue to be at the heart of engaging communities and through the system of local Police and Crime Panels (PCPs), comprised of local councillors, a degree of democratic oversight is provided.

Community engagement takes different forms, ranging from structured meetings and consultations to more informal contacts such as meeting PCSOs and officers during their regular patrol duties. Research indicates that informal contact can be as beneficial as formal but that it is the *quality* of the contact is significant, ie negative encounters can have a 'much greater impact on public and victim satisfaction and confidence than positive ones' (Police Foundation, 2015, p 38). The idea of 'procedural justice' has gained prominence in policing, whereby respectful treatment at the hands of the police plays an influential role in maintaining positive and effective community relations, public cooperation, and compliance with the law (Tyler, 1990, 2003).

Social media platforms are also key communication channels for the police to gather and share information, providing a simple and effective method of engaging with the public in a more direct way. The use of social media is now firmly embedded in all police service communication strategies throughout England and Wales, supported by robust guidelines to ensure that it is used positively. However, we might consider the extent to which this can be fully engaged in by sections of the community not connected with the digital world.

It is also important to consider a long-established engagement method and one which has formed the basis of local policing in the past—visible foot patrol. Lamentably, it has been in decline, with the move to technology-enhanced policing and focus on evidence-based patrol strategies, however, it remains strongly supported and appreciated by the public (Police Foundation, 2015, 2022). Although it would be difficult to show that foot patrol is an effective means of *reducing* crime, evidence suggests that it can improve community relations, reduce the fear of crime, and increase public trust and confidence (Police Foundation, 2022).

PCSOs were an important addition to visible presence in communities. The first were employed across England and Wales in 2005, their main purpose being to tackle low-level disorder, gather intelligence, and interact with the public. PCSOs have become an effective means of enabling community engagement, interacting with the public, acquiring local knowledge, addressing local problems, and gathering intelligence. Effective use of PCSOs can facilitate dialogue between the police and the public, and enable the police to develop a greater understanding of risks and threats to social cohesion. However, PCSO numbers have declined over recent years from a high of 17,198 in 2010 to an all-time low in 2018 of 9,547 (Home Office, 2019a). Those in neighbourhood policing roles (both PCSOs and officers) have diminished from 62 per cent in 2015 to 45 per cent in 2020, in tandem with a fall in public trust and confidence levels (Police Foundation, 2022).

The key ingredients of successful community engagement can be summarized as a commitment and interest in the community's views and concerns, actively seeking ways to engage with hard-to-reach groups, ensuring continued informal contact, as well as structured, relevant, and measurable approaches to local policing problems.

11.3.2 Collaborative problem solving

Overall, there is evidence to support the idea that collaboration with the public can reduce disorder and increase the perceived legitimacy of the police (CoP, 2018c). Collaborative problem solving also ensures that police resources are used in the most efficient manner and enables areas of greatest public concern to be addressed using effective interventions. Problem solving can be based upon the cognitive agency of the professional practitioner, informed by the law, organizational values, the code of ethics, and appropriate research evidence. In support, are models of problem solving that may be useful, for example the Problem Analysis Triangle (PAT) and the Scanning, Analysis, Response, and Assessment process (SARA).

11.3.2.1 Problem Analysis Triangle

The PAT approach is associated with routine-activity theory (Cohen and Felson, 1979) and problem-oriented approaches (Tilley, 2008a). In its simplest form, the model contains three main points of analysis: a target/victim, the location, and offender. Crime is said to occur when each converge in time and place. Solutions are found through identifying practical measures to address one or more of these points, for example:

- protection of the *victim* through crime prevention or target-hardening measures;
- providing surveillance or additional patrols in the *location* concerned; and
- targeting or persuading *offenders* to cease their activities.

While some might consider this to be a simplistic model, it does provide a rationale for responding to problems and collecting information needed to find solutions. Although the approach is aimed at the problem of crime, there is scope for it to be used more widely.

The SARA model takes the process a step further through to assessment and review. It involves continual evaluation of decisions with the intention of improving practice and tackling the root causes of problems (Weisburd *et al*, 2010). The key stages are:

- **scanning:** identifying a problem or a crime;
- **analysis:** assessment of available information surrounding the circumstances;
- **response:** appropriate strategy chosen to deal with event;
- **assessment:** review and evaluation of impact or effectiveness.

Although this model may seem mechanistic, it provides a framework in which to confront problems and inform decisions (Bullock and Tilley, 2003). There are other problem-solving models which focus on distinct aspects of decision-making or problem-solving processes. The professional practitioner needs to apply their own cognitive agency in identifying a method of working that suits the policing problem and the context (see Wood *et al*, 2017).

11.3.2.2 Problem-oriented policing

Herman Goldstein originally developed the concept of problem-oriented policing (POP) (Goldstein, 1990). He defined POP as follows:

> In its broadest context, problem-oriented policing is a comprehensive plan for improving policing in which the high priority attached to addressing substantive problems shapes the police agency, influencing all changes in personnel, organisation, and procedures. Thus problem-oriented policing not only pushes policing beyond current improvement efforts, it calls for a major change in the direction of those efforts. (Goldstein, 1990, p 32)

This view was particularly important in the context of the police repeatedly responding to crimes or calls for service in a reactive manner. This responsive approach or 'fire brigade policing' (Rowe, 2008, p 165) would not necessarily address underlying problems in the community and could stretch police resources without improving public safety. Goldstein (1990) suggested that the police should analyse calls from the public and examine the underlying factors causing the need for police assistance. Thereby, particular attention could be given to cases where repeat calls and minor cases might escalate to more serious problems (Rowe, 2008). The emphasis of POP encourages a move from reactive to proactive policing. One criticism is that POP is a strategy that seeks to apply 'scientific methods to social problems' without any community control of the policing agenda (Kappeler, 2017, p 437); it therefore retains a top-down approach and offers less equitable power-sharing between the police and public on matters of local concern.

POP's systematic way of dealing with community problems presents certain challenges including 'crude performance management regimes, staff turnover, lack of trained analysts and interagency hostilities' (Tilley, 2008b, p 226). In addressing community problems, Goldstein (1990) argues that the police frequently need to engage with other private, public, and voluntary organizations. Such partnership approaches may create tension due to differing organizational cultures and operational objectives (Tong, 2008). Thus, although POP appears to be a sound proposition in principle (and has had some success), we need to consider the potential barriers to its implementation and impact on communities. The College of Policing (2018b) has found that to implement effective problem-solving within neighbourhood policing, certain key issues need to be considered:

- **defining the problem**—a detailed specification needs to be formulated;
- **assessing the impact**—ensuring ongoing monitoring of actions and outcomes;
- **working with partners**—to ensure capacity and reduce duplication;
- **ensuring strong governance and accountability**—a commitment to finding solutions and recognizing the good work of staff.

11.3.3 Targeting policing activity in a community setting

The police have historically focused on ensuring that their resources are aligned with targeting the highest risk neighbourhoods and offenders. This section explores hot-spot and zero-tolerance policing in the local community context. Other models of policing that may be relevant to policing communities include intelligence-led policing and predictive policing. Note that members of the public (and policing students) can view crime patterns and statistics for their local postcode area at <http://www.police.uk>.

11.3.3.1 Hot-spot policing

Research by Sherman and others in the US drew attention in the late 1980s to areas of concentration of calls for service and response (Mitchell, 2022; Sherman *et al*, 1989). This highlighted that crime appeared clustered in small areas, which came to be known as 'hot spots' and 'small worlds' (Weisburd, 2015). Hot-spot policing aims to identify the locations where crime is most common and to take targeted action in those areas. It has been shown to be an effective model when combined with initiatives designed to reduce opportunities for crime. There is some evidence which suggests that hot-spot policing works to reduce a broad spectrum of crime types such as drug, disorder, property, and serious violence offences (Braga *et al*, 2019).

Some people, premises, or organizations are repeat victims of certain crimes, such as burglary, and the reasons for this are not always apparent. From an offender's perspective, it may be that it worked once so it will work again (this would include a burglar allowing enough time for a resident to claim on their insurance for property, before returning to steal the replacement (Bowers *et al*, 2004)). It should be emphasized that data strongly suggests that victims of crime who fail to take precautions *post hoc* may be targeted again and that the phenomenon of repeat victimization (RV) should be considered in police responses to crime (see 17.5.3). We also know that those who repeatedly victimize the same target tend to be established career criminals. This suggests that intelligence about the nature of a crime and its repetition should help police to predict where, when, and by whom the next attempt will be made.

A regular police presence may help to reduce the level of crime in a particular area, but it may not be sustainable. Other crime prevention initiatives (such as installing CCTV or improved street lighting) can demonstrate longer term positive outcomes for some types of crime, and the local knowledge of patrol officers can contribute to devising such initiatives. More information about the hot-spot policing model can be found in 17.5.2.

11.3.3.2 Zero-tolerance policing

Early intervention in low-level crime and disorder matters has been viewed as significant in preventing escalation. For example, intervening in anti-social behaviours in the community has been suggested to prevent youths from embarking on a life of crime. These ideas stem from Wilson and Kelling's (1982) 'Broken Windows' thesis and the zero-tolerance policing (ZTP) strategy of Bill Bratton in New York City. This approach argued that the need to 'nip bad behaviour in the bud' was linked with a systematic process of police managerial accountability using crime data, known as 'CompStat'. While there appeared to be a reduction in crime following the introduction of ZTP in New York, critics later pointed out that similar reductions had occurred in other parts of the US which had not adopted it. The overzealous approach adopted by New York City officers, after crime rates had fallen, also began to attract criticism from local citizens. However, ZTP made Bratton a 'global policing celebrity' (Bowling and Sheptycki, 2012) and many other countries imported it as a policing strategy (Rowe, 2018). In the UK, it was adopted in the late 1990s in Cleveland under the direction of Detective Superintendent Ray Mallon. However, controversy led to his suspension and retirement from policing. Nonetheless, the notion of ZTP regularly comes to the fore. Variations on it have been developed and implemented by several police services in England and Wales, particularly where anti-social behaviour is associated with young people or identifiable groups in the community (Squires, 2017).

TASK 2 How would a) problem-oriented policing and b) community-based or neighbourhood policing approaches address ASB issues?

11.4 The Partnership Approach

Working in partnership and engaging with communities is a defining feature of effective neighbourhood policing. The police are required and encouraged to collaborate with several agencies in reducing crime, and on issues concerning public protection. A multi-agency approach to crime and disorder is officially endorsed by the Home Office and contained in various College of Policing Authorised Professional Practice (APP) guidelines. In addition, some aspects of the partnership approach are legislated. Police service policies and procedures set out how multi-agency cooperation should operate. Multi-agency collaboration is evident in areas such as:

- Vulnerability and protection: this is likely to involve cooperation between the police, health, social, and education services. For example, if you are a student police officer who has attained Independent Patrol Status, you might attend an incident and notice that a child or vulnerable person in the care of the suspect appears at risk. You will report this to your service using the appropriate channels. Other services may then become involved, and the circumstances investigated further.
- Domestic abuse: similarly, the police response to domestic abuse is likely to include working with specialist charities, housing, education, social and health services, and other voluntary organizations. A multi-agency approach is recommended to provide protection and

support to the victim and any dependents. Note, however, that none of this detracts from the presumption that the police will take positive action against the alleged offender where possible.

- Crime and disorder reduction: the Crime and Disorder Act 1998 imposed a duty on key public sector organizations to work together to make communities safer. The legislation created Crime and Disorder Reduction Partnerships (CDRPs) or Community Safety Partnerships as they are now known, which brought together the police and local authority, fire and rescue services, the police authority (now PCCs), health, and probation to design strategies for crime reduction. These arrangements are now supplemented by specific responsibilities contained in the Police, Crime, Sentencing and Courts Act 2022 (PCSCA, 2022). This legislation requires specified authorities in a local government area to collaborate in plans to prevent and reduce serious violence. Violence in this context refers to domestic abuse (under the Domestic Abuse Act 2021), sexual offences, violence against property, and threats of violence.
- Partnerships with local councils or authorities over penalty notices (see 10.18.2.2): penalty notices are often issued for parking infringements or driving offences. The partnership is likely to include close cooperation with local authority CCTV-monitoring teams, especially in city centres and popular club or pub venues.
- Multi-agency public protection arrangements (MAPPA), provided under the Criminal Justice Act 2003, are designed to protect the public from serious harm by sexual and violent offenders (these are covered in 19.3.1).

11.4.1 Community safety partnerships

The Crime and Disorder Act 1998 (as amended by the Police Reform Act 2002) established community safety partnerships (CSPs) and made partnership working a statutory requirement for the police, local authorities, fire and rescue services, primary care trusts, the Probation Service, and Drug and Alcohol Action Teams. Their key objectives are to:

- establish the level and extent of crime and disorder within the area;
- consult widely with the local population;
- develop a strategy aimed at tackling problems, with a clear action plan of organizational responsibilities;
- periodically review the strategy; and
- work closely with the local PCC.

This promotes the sharing of information and working with other public, voluntary, and private organizations. There are five areas associated with mandated partnership working. Firstly, PCCs and CSPs must heed each other's priorities within their plans ensuring that the PCC's objectives are acted upon at the local level, and the CSP priorities are recognized and resourced. Secondly, the PCC holds accountability over CSPs; and can call representatives of CSPs to account for its strategies; thirdly, the PCC can obtain a written report from a CSP. Fourthly, PCCs have the power to approve mergers between CSPs in their local areas; and, finally, PCCs can grant funding for crime and disorder-reduction activities.

Student officers are most likely to encounter CSPs in terms of their local service priorities and the introduction of measures directed by the PCSCA (2022).

TASK 3 In order to develop your local knowledge further, search for information on your local CSP arrangements.

11.4.2 Community safety units

Community safety units (CSUs) coordinate the work of the police locally, in collaboration with other local agencies. Police services contribute resources to their local CSU. CSUs implement CSP strategic decisions and respond to local needs through a multi-disciplinary community safety team. Given the local focus of CSUs, there will be different priorities in different areas, but there are several common roles and functions. For example, they have an obligation under the Crime and Disorder Act 1998 to audit the crime and disorder problems in their respective areas and to devise suitable strategies (every three years) to prevent and reduce crime. This includes addressing quality-of-life issues and the fear of crime. Chief officers must consult with the public in each neighbourhood, provide local information about crime and policing, and hold regular public meetings (s 34 of the Police Reform and Social Responsibility Act 2011). Broadly speaking, CSUs operate to reduce offending and reoffending and safeguard vulnerability (of adults and vulnerable persons at risk of abuse and exploitation, and those affected by mental health and substance misuse).

11.4.3 Youth offending teams

Youth offending teams (YOTs) deal with young people who are at risk of offending or reoffending, and offer support through education, work placements, psychological support, and mentoring. They were introduced through the Crime and Disorder Act 1998 as a multidisciplinary team run by local authorities. They comprise representatives from agencies such as the police, social services, probation, health, education, and drug and alcohol professionals. YOTs also provide support and decision-making for cases involving young people, making recommendations about the use of pre-court interventions such as reprimands and final warnings.

11.5 Community Cohesion in Local Policing

The police can do much to develop social harmony and reduce tension in communities. The College of Policing highlights that 'police officers should identify potential "susceptible" communities and proactively make efforts to build relationships with those communities and relevant partners' (CoP, 2020e). This has gained further traction in the latest recommendations for the future of policing set out in the *Final Report of the Strategic Review of Policing for England and Wales* (Police Foundation, 2022).

It is clearly beneficial for the police to understand their own communities, who lives there, and the problems faced. There is much that can be done by the police and partners to understand and work to reduce community tensions within their areas:

- Find out the tensions or divides that may exist.
- Which people or streets are a problem—and why?
- Are the police engaging with the community effectively ie via social media?
- What could be done to bring groups together?
- Are there local businesses that might have an impact?
- Is there a Neighbourhood Policing Plan in place?
- Is there a Neighbourhood Watch?
- Does the area need regeneration?

Indicators of community tension can include incidents of disorder, hate crime, gang disputes, repeated anti-social behaviour, political unrest, and a noticeable increase in critical incidents.

There are many communities with complex needs and within these communities there may be minority groups forming their own communities. If the police are to identify and respond to community problems, then they must know and understand the communities they serve, be representative of them, respect differences, adapt the policing style when necessary, and act ethically with integrity (see Alderson, 1998; Wood, 2020).

11.5.1 Diversity, equality, and inclusion

For a local policing strategy to work effectively, it is crucial that the public are treated with fairness, respect, and equitably (see the Equality Act 2010 and 'protected characteristics'). Lister *et al* (2015) have highlighted the importance of community engagement involving minority and marginalized groups.

Involving the diverse communities in decision-making, and working towards understanding their local issues and concerns, helps to provide reassurance and improves public confidence. Building trust and confidence will result in greater public involvement and engagement with crime detection and prevention activities (Jackson *et al*, 2013; Tyler, 2003). Respecting diversity and equality and applying discretion are crucial in neighbourhood policing, therefore police staff and officers must receive suitable development and training to meet these demands. The complex issue of police discretion is covered in 4.2.2.

Communities are becoming increasingly diverse and, more importantly, we have become more conscious of such differences and more determined to afford inclusivity to individuals from diverse backgrounds. Many people believe that the coming together of differing values, beliefs, cultures, and perspectives makes life more interesting, dynamic, and enriches society in several ways.

It is important to note that diversity is not just about the differences between people; it is also about *perceptions* of such differences. People who are identifiable or perceived as minorities in society can find themselves victimized by members of majority groups, for example when individuals from minority ethnic groups are targeted by racists. Sometimes the victimization can be more subtle, and student police officers need to think carefully about how their actions are perceived, and to what extent their own values and prejudices might influence their actions. Some actions could be deemed offensive by others even though this was not the intention. As a professional, a police officer has a responsibility to do everything possible to resolve problems and this includes seeking to ensure that police actions are not misunderstood or misinterpreted. The Code of Ethics (CoP, 2014a) and police misconduct regulations (Home Office, 2018a) set out standards that are expected by the public and your organization.

TASK 4 We have already referred to ethnicity as part of diversity and inclusion. Consider some other differences that may contribute to diversity and inclusion matters.

11.5.2 Diversity and vulnerability

One important way in which diversity informs policing is in relation to the responsibility the police have towards vulnerable people (see Chapter 20). A police officer needs to ensure that any judgement about a particular person as vulnerable is based as far as possible on the facts about the person and the context, rather than on the officer's own social conditioning. It would also be a mistake to assume that every individual from a minority group will necessarily feel vulnerable. Indeed, in relation to all aspects of diversity, police officers need to tread a fine path that recognizes diversity without imposing preconceptions on the situation. Cosgrove and Ramshaw (2015) recognize that some vulnerable people may lack trust in the police and that this can dissuade them from wanting to engage. Officers can often reassure people through procedurally just practices and by demonstrating understanding of the needs of diverse groups in their communities.

Matters of mental health and neurodiversity are particularly useful in illustrating the complicated nature of diversity. Mental health issues exist to varying degrees in the general population but many people have preconceived ideas of what is healthy and unhealthy, which makes recognizing diversity and difference in relation to mental health particularly difficult. Police actions in relation to people with a mental illness are covered in more detail in 20.5. More recently, neurodiversity has gained attention, but progress is slow—there is a growing recognition that the police should be better trained and equipped to understand and respond to those with neurodiverse conditions. In a UK context, there appears to be no dependable, consistent, or systematic data collection about levels of neurodiversity in the CJS, nor a common tool used for the screening of individuals encountering it (HMIP, 2021).

11.5.3 Diversity and discrimination

Police services have been under scrutiny for discrimination on the grounds of race and ethnicity for several decades. Both the Scarman Report, published in 1981, and the Macpherson Report, published in 1999 following the murder of Stephen Lawrence, refer to racial discrimination by the police and a failure to address it. In 2009, a Home Affairs Committee published an evaluation of the impact of the Macpherson Report on tackling 'institutional racism' in the police. It concluded that there were clear positive changes in the way that the police dealt with ethnic minorities and in the investigation of homicides where the victims were from ethnic minorities. There are, however, still concerns regarding the disproportionate number of stop and searches being conducted on individuals from ethnic minorities as well as a disproportionate number of individuals from African-Caribbean backgrounds featuring on the National DNA Database, and in the wider CJS. More recently, there have been shocking revelations concerning the attitudes and behaviours of some officers and staff in specific police areas, which damage the image and tradition of British policing (see HMICFRS, 2022; IOPC, 2022b). These are clearly critical issues for policing in communities.

11.6 The Future of Community Policing

The future operating environment (FOE) of policing is described in a 'futures' report by the College of Policing (CoP, 2020f). It highlights challenges and issues, providing information and resources which the police may use to develop their plans and capabilities. Features of the FOE that directly impact community policing include: growing inequality and social fragmentation leading to deprivation and increased potential for violence; unregulated online (mis)information polarizing society; technology-related civil unrest; dependence on artificial intelligence (AI); a growing vulnerability to crime in an elderly population, a fragile global economy, and climate change leading to greater local competition for resources.

The intersection of all these is likely to create uncertainty in local policing organization and service delivery (CoP, 2020f). To respond to this changed landscape, it is anticipated that new policing skills, structures, and resource deployment on a scale not seen before will be required. Many of the responses will involve reliance on data analytics and AI, which carry a risk of creating a physical gap between the police and community. The challenges for community policing will be in continuing to engage and respond meaningfully on a local level to these demands and threats while maintaining collaboration to secure public trust and confidence.

11.7 Answers to Tasks

TASK 1 You will be able to find out what neighbourhood policing strategy applies in your local police service by looking on its website. The Community Safety Plans and Partnership details can also be found through local authority websites.

TASK 2 Start by speaking with those who can really help us: members of the local community and the patrol officers who collaborate with them. How can we mobilize parents and others in the community to address both the anti-social behaviour and its underlying causes? In summary, do not simply view this as a matter of law enforcement; it is likely to be part of a wider issue concerning the stability of the local community.

TASK 3 Community safety partnerships all have their own internet sites and social media platforms to follow. Many also provide a newsletter to which you can subscribe.

TASK 4 Did you list sexual orientation, age, belief, marital status, gender identity, neurodiversity, and disability? Also check 'protected characteristics' contained in relevant legislation.

12 Information and Intelligence

12.1 Introduction

This chapter examines how criminal intelligence is used to support policing objectives. We will also consider some of the components of intelligence gathering: sources, source handling, surveillance, research and development, the intelligence 'target package', and some of the laws and rules about what can and cannot be done with intelligence. Many of the serious and organized-crime investigations which result in a successful prosecution have their origins in good intelligence, and the UK's strategy for counter terrorism heavily depends on the UK intelligence community.

Criminals will usually go to some lengths to prevent knowledge about their activities leaking out. Covert surveillance can be used to help to establish such information. For example, after the 2015 Hatton Garden burglary, police were able to video-record some of the people responsible for the crime while they were in a cafe discussing their involvement. Without such covert evidence, it would sometimes be difficult to prosecute all the individuals involved in similar cases. Such covert work often impinges upon the private lives of members of the public so this type of activity is carefully controlled under the Regulation of Investigatory Powers Act 2000 (RIPA), and officers would need to seek authority for surveillance.

As a student police officer, you will come into contact with the public for much of your working time. You may therefore be in a better position to gather intelligence that could impact upon criminality in your locality. You need to be alert to intelligence gathering opportunities, understand how you should record it, how you can input it into the intelligence system, how it is assessed, and how it is ultimately utilized. Some of the methods for obtaining intelligence, information, and evidence (and how they are managed) are explained in the remainder of this chapter.

An understanding of the National Intelligence Model (NIM) is an important requirement for student police officers. Your geographical policing area is likely to have an intelligence collection plan (ICP) formulated by the constabulary's strategic 'Tasking and Coordinating Group' (T&CG) process. This will consider local crime trends and particular crime patterns and then identify what particular information needs to be collected at a particular time (see 12.6.1 for more detail). However, this does not prevent any officer putting other information into the system. The intelligence can be assessed later by other more experienced colleagues (see 12.5.2 on submission procedures). Finally this chapter will examine the police's national intelligence databases and information sharing facilities and explain the ways to properly convey police intelligence into those networks.

As with many aspects of operational policing, extensive APP guidance on this subject is available from the College of Policing (under the Intelligence Management heading).

The topics covered in this chapter are likely to contribute to the learning required for the National Policing Curriculum subject areas of 'Information and Intelligence' and 'Conducting Investigations'.

If you are undertaking the PCDA or DHEP, you will be expected to demonstrate that you can 'systematically gather, submit and share information and intelligence to further policing-related outcomes'. You will also need to develop an 'in-depth knowledge, understanding and expertise relevant to organisational/local needs, including the ... operational policing context [of] intelligence'.

12.2 Information and Intelligence

Information can be obtained in many ways, for example, by a call from the public advising the police of an incident. Intelligence is more difficult to define but is generally considered to be information derived from many sources (some confidential) that has been recorded, graded, and evaluated. If information is received concerning an increase in the number of thefts of radios from cars in a particular area, and this information is linked to a change in payment policy by a local drug dealer (who is now accepting goods in lieu of money in payment for drugs), intelligence can begin to be derived from that information.

12.2.1 Obtaining intelligence

Sources of intelligence range from conversations with a member of the public to specialist covert surveillance operations. A police officer can let colleagues know that they are interested in an individual and would welcome any useful information gleaned during interviews. The same applies, of course, to police patrols who often spend some part of their duty deployment on open observation and interaction with the public. Information can also be obtained from prisons via the force Prison Intelligence Officer (PIO). Formal intelligence gathering in prisons is subject to strict protocols and risk assessments but plenty of open information about criminal targets is available from prison visits, interviews, preparations for release, and so on (see CoP, 2013c for further details).

Some types of information, particularly financial, can be obtained under the provisions of the Proceeds of Crime Act 2002. This places obligations on certain occupational groups, such as bank managers and solicitors, who must report the handling of sums of money for which there is little or no apparent justification, as this may indicate criminal activity (see 23.5.2). Useful information could be obtained through Action Fraud, the national centre for reporting fraud and cybercrime (see 14.3.2). Certain offences such as cybercrime and fraud are often linked to serious and organized crime or terrorism so all fraud and online crime should be reported through Action Fraud so that intelligence can be gathered.

Many different intelligence-gathering techniques are used in counter terrorism to detect the facilitation of an attack or the act itself. At its simplest, information about the facilitation of an actual terrorist attack could be volunteered by members of the public, from the police on routine calls, or when conducting stop and searches. The intelligence gathered will be shared between UK police services working closely with security and intelligence agencies as part of counter-terrorism policing to prevent, deter, and investigate terrorist activity.

Police services routinely share information with other constabularies, particularly through the Police National Database. Even if it seems trivial or incomplete, police should always communicate information as it might have a bearing on the activities of someone in another police service area (Bichard, 2004).

12.2.2 Open sources of information and intelligence

The first and most obvious source of 'open' intelligence about crime and criminality is likely to come from the general public. Criminals live within communities, they have to go shopping and socialize, and of course they are very likely to have families or interests which have nothing to do with crime. A profile can be built up of a criminal's daily habits: where they shop or go for a drink, what car they drive. Neighbours, garage mechanics, newsagents, parking attendants and the like may all have information that could be useful in an investigation.

There will be specific policies regarding open-source searches in the area where you work so as a trainee officer make sure you find out about these before you do anything on your own initiative. Some sources can be more straightforward, for example gleaning information from a local newspaper.

12.2.2.1 Online sources of information

The internet is a valuable source of open intelligence through social networking sites and online forums. If you decide to use open online sources within your work, however, it is not as simple as it sounds. Much of the information lacks provenance and could be inaccurate, unreliable, or even false. It might also be impossible to use such information as evidence in a court of law because the authors may be untraceable.

There are, however, several ways in which open-source material might assist a police investigator, for instance by identifying a suspect's associates or corroborating information that is already suspected. Remember, though that without careful planning you may inadvertently leave a digital (police) footprint. You may, for instance, have searched from a computer with a police IP address. Many criminals might well be knowledgeable about such matters and will be able to find the IP address of anyone who has searched for them. (The IP address allocated to a police service is permanent and can be easily identified.) Once a suspect realizes they have been the subject of an online police search, they will be alerted and may change tack.

In summary, open-source searches can be of value in gathering further intelligence but must be done properly. The NPCC has issued guidance to police officers regarding open-source investigation, and it provides minimum standards for officers and staff to obey before engaging in such activities and is derived from a report from the Royal United Services Institute (RUSI, 2015). Before engaging in any such activities, you are urged to seek advice from your supervisor and line manager.

12.3 Covert Human Intelligence Sources

The police term for an informant or source is 'CHIS', which stands for Covert Human Intelligence Source. Criminals use other terms (all unflattering), such as 'grass', 'snout', and 'nark'. Many intelligence sources are criminals themselves, as non-criminals are unlikely to have real access to criminals and their plans. That said, there can be non-criminals who have close family or social ties and may be in a position to obtain important information that could assist the authorities.

It is interesting to note that many government agencies are permitted to use sources to gain intelligence (provided for in the Home Office Codes of Practice under RIPA). Such agencies and departments include HM Revenue and Customs, the Ministry of Defence and the Department of Health. Any agency using a CHIS must have a responsible authorizing officer and observe the other RIPA requirements. Local authorities must obtain judicial approval for using a CHIS and for other surveillance activities (ss 37 and 38 of the Protection of Freedoms Act 2012).

12.3.1 The definition of a CHIS

A member of the public who simply volunteers information about criminals or crimes is not generally defined as a 'source'. A person is regarded as a source (s 26(8) of RIPA) if they establish or maintain a personal or other relationship with a person for the covert purpose of:

- obtaining information or providing access to information to another person; or
- disclosing information obtained by the use of such a relationship or as the consequence of the existence of such a relationship.

The Covert Human Intelligence Sources Revised Code of Practice (Home Office, 2022d) describes public volunteers, those with a statutory duty to disclose to authorities, and those who may, for instance, be tasked to record car numbers arriving and leaving an address as examples where no CHIS authorization is required. Thus, solicitors or bank officials who pass details of suspicious activity to the police are not sources because they are working in an open relationship with the police and not acting covertly. None of the examples involve a covert relationship being established or maintained to gain information.

In essence, a CHIS is therefore someone who covertly cultivates another person to obtain information, or who provides access to information, or who discloses information. Notice that the words 'criminal' and 'unlawful' are not used here. This is because the information need not necessarily be crime-related, at least to start with.

In general terms, the term 'covert' usually means hidden but RIPA provides a precise legal definition (s 26(9)(b)–(c)):

> a purpose is covert in . . . a relationship if it is conducted in a manner which is calculated to ensure that only one of the parties to the relationship is unaware of the purpose [and] . . . [a] relationship is used covertly, and information obtained is used or disclosed in a manner that is calculated to ensure that one of the parties to the relationship is unaware of the use or disclosure in question.

What this means is that the person being cultivated by the CHIS (or from whom information is obtained because of that relationship) does not know that the CHIS is informing the police.

Under RIPA, any use of a CHIS by the police will always require authorization granted by the police's authorizing officer who is answerable to a surveillance commissioner with a national remit. The authorization (or 'authority') will normally last 12 months.

The use and management of a CHIS under the age of 17 (identified as JCHIS) presents additional challenges and the Regulation of Investigatory Powers (Juveniles) Order 2000 and Regulation of Investigatory Powers (Juveniles) (Amendment) Order 2018 currently apply. In 2019, a UK charity, Just for Kids Law, challenged the legal basis of the current scheme for using a JCHIS. The court heard that at the time of the application there were 17 JCHIS nationwide, 16 between 16 and 17 years of age and one aged 15. The court denied the application and decided that under the scheme there was no unacceptable risk of a juvenile's rights under Article 8 of the European Convention on Human Rights (ECHR) being breached. The response of the court also suggested that the safeguards regarding the welfare of children were adequate (*R (on the application of Just for Kids Law) v Secretary of State for the Home Department* [2019] EWHC 1772 (Admin)). The charity mounted an appeal but dropped this after the government agreed to update the CHIS Code of Practice with enhanced safeguards for JCHIS deployment. These have been drafted to take into account new legislation such as the Covert Human Intelligence Sources (Criminal Conduct) Act 2021, as well as other proposed amendments. The Draft Code is still awaiting parliamentary approval at the time of writing (Home Office, 2022d).

12.3.2 Handling sources

Handlers are usually detectives who have undergone an intensive training programme during which they learn how to keep control when tasking informants, arranging secure meetings, and handling sources who may be dishonest and manipulative. A source-management unit is staffed by a CHIS controller, CHIS handlers, and support staff. The CHIS controller is responsible for the supervision, management, and control of all the staff in the unit. The CHIS handlers are responsible for the day-to-day management and recruitment of CHISs.

TASK 1 What qualities do you think are needed for a person to make a good source handler? Make a list of the attributes, skills, and competencies necessary to handle a covert source who has access to criminal information.

Most police services use a qualified and experienced detective constable as a source handler, probably paired with another (perhaps less experienced) handler. It is good practice to have two handlers so that a CHIS has less chance of exerting control over the handlers. A further advantage is that two can share the responsibility of handling, welfare issues, and recording of meetings with a CHIS. To ensure that relationships between handlers and the CHIS remain appropriate and objective, some police services rotate handlers after a period of time (meaning a new one takes over from the old one). This approach may have much to commend it due to previous experiences involving inappropriate, unprofessional, or corrupt practices, but it may inevitably mean the loss of a small amount of CHISs who will not wish to maintain a relationship with another officer.

A handler submits a report with details of the intelligence they have obtained from the CHIS and writes a separate note to their controller detailing the meeting itself. The intelligence is passed in its raw state to the Research and Development unit or Force Intelligence Bureau, where it is assessed against what is already known, considered in the wider context, and then sanitized (see 12.5.1).

12.3.3 Restrictions on the use of sources

We have already noted that RIPA provides the definitions of a source and what is meant by covert, but the Act also determines the legal and practical parameters for handling a CHIS. There is a regular audit of authorizations by a surveillance commissioner (appointed nationally under a chief surveillance commissioner).

Attention is also drawn throughout RIPA to proportionality and to Articles in the Human Rights Act 1998 (HRA 1998) legislation, particularly with respect to the right to a private life. In terms of proportionality, a CHIS with excellent access to the upper echelons of criminality would not be used to establish the identity of a local graffitist. RIPA provides the necessary framework for the ethical and legal use of a CHIS by properly trained source handlers who are aware of the full extent of their powers (but will not abuse them), as well as ensuring that the risks are proportionate to the expected gain.

> **TASK 2** We noted earlier that a CHIS is often also a criminal themselves. What problems might arise for a police service when recruiting and using an active criminal as a CHIS? Aside from the ethical and moral considerations, what practical difficulties might there be?

12.3.4 The consequences for the CHIS

A CHIS may provide the police with information about a planned crime in which the CHIS will participate. The Covert Human Intelligence Sources (Criminal Conduct) Act 2021 now places authorizations of such conduct on a statutory footing. It creates provision for a 'Criminal Conduct Authorisation' (CCA). CCAs will allow authorizations in the interests of national security, for the purposes of preventing or crime or disorder or detecting crime, or in the interests of the economic well-being of the UK.

Authorizations will need to demonstrate proportionality and demonstrate that consideration has been given to whether the activities sought are part of efforts to prevent more serious criminality and that no other reasonably practicable means are available to achieve the same outcome. Revised Codes of Practice have been produced to include these amendments (Home Office, 2022d).

A CHIS who is not a participating informant may also be able to take advantage of the 'assisting prosecutions' legislation in the Serious Organised Crime and Police Act 2005 (SOCPA), under which a formal agreement can be made with an offender in order to secure evidence for the prosecution of other offenders. In most cases outside the SOCPA legislation, the police and the CPS will try to keep the identity of a CHIS confidential and will adopt what they see as a pragmatic approach: if there is a risk to the CHIS, the prosecution is very likely to be withdrawn and charges dropped. An added advantage is that the CHIS can be used again. No one can pretend that these are easy judgements; you may like to read further on this matter—see Harfield & Harfield (2005 and 2008).

As a trainee police officer, you need to be aware of the risks a source may face by talking to you. You should keep the information to yourself at all times, even after you are able to input it into the intelligence system. For instance, just because a person has given you information about a local crime, does not automatically mean that all their family and friends know about it too. It might be useful to see yourself as a sponge, sucking up information and keeping it in, rather than giving information away! It is important to faithfully record the information provided and avoid prejudging whether it is true or not; the issues of truthfulness will be considered later, when the information is investigated.

12.3.4.1 Motivation of informants

The handler should identify a potential source's primary motive or motives because this will affect whether the CHIS should be recruited and how they should be handled. The source's primary motivation must be sufficient to sustain them throughout the long period of gathering intelligence. This is a very under-researched area and hence what follows should be treated with some caution.

TASK 3 Consider for a moment why someone might decide to become a source for the police. Why would you betray your criminal colleagues? How would you keep it up, week after week, month after month?

Many sources will suggest that money is a key motivator, but a potential CHIS might well be able to make more money from the criminal enterprise they are reporting on so we must look a little deeper; motivation is psychologically complex. For example, an experienced and 'lifestyle' criminal might inform on other criminals who are threatening their dominance. Other sources may be motivated by distaste for the crimes committed by the target criminal. In one case, a person with two young children informed on their sibling, a prominent local criminal, because they had seen the sibling downloading child abuse images on a computer and suspected that they were an active paedophile.

It is easy to overlook the human needs of sources: like most people, they want affection, praise, encouragement, and a sense of being valued. Handlers can provide all these things for a source but overdependence on the handler can lead to problems. Other ethical dilemmas may also arise: for example, imagine a CHIS drug-user overdoses on drugs purchased with the money he received from the police. To what extent would the police be ethically, morally, or legally responsible?

Police handlers are acutely aware of safety issues surrounding any human sources and will make complex arrangements to protect a source's identity, particularly from other criminals. Police officers have a legal duty of care and confidentiality towards sources so they must take reasonable steps to protect their identities (see *Swinney v Chief Constable of Northumbria* [1996] EWCA Civ 1322). Sometimes the right of the prosecution to keep these details confidential overrides other rights (ie press freedom). In a recent case the BBC wanted to expose a potential CHIS in an upcoming TV programme. The Attorney General sought to prevent this from happening. The court found in favour of confidentiality but gave serious consideration to competing rights (*Attorney General v BBC* [2022] EWHC 826 (QB)).

12.3.5 Undercover officers and 'test purchase' operations

A highly trained police officer can work to penetrate a group of criminals, for example by posing as a drugs importer or as a document supplier. However, the risk must be proportionate to the outcome so an undercover officer would only be used in relation to very serious crimes, such as high-profile robberies, conspiracy to murder, child grooming, or terrorism. Undercover police officers (and those employed by other organizations such as the National Crime Agency and the military) are a form of CHIS called a 'relevant source'. All operations using a 'relevant source' require authorization and the risk assessment must be very thorough (see the Regulation of Investigatory Powers (Covert Human Intelligence Sources: Relevant Sources) Order 2013 for further information (Home Office, 2013c)).

Officers cannot sustain undercover roles for long and need to be reintegrated into police services before they are compromised or exhausted by the continuous strain ('turned or burned'). Recent problems with undercover police activities have led to calls for more stringent supervision of such police practices. For example, an HMIC report criticized an undercover police officer for defying management instructions when working undercover with a group of environmental campaigners (HMIC, 2012); the trial against the activists subsequently collapsed. Other revelations relating to the misuse of undercover operatives have turned the spotlight on police decision-making, particularly the decisions to deploy such tactics, for example see the *Stephen Lawrence Independent Review: Possible corruption and the role of undercover policing in the Stephen Lawrence case*, available online. Presumably because of these high-profile disclosures, the Codes of Practice on CHIS were amended in 2014 to ensure deployment of relevant sources is authorized by a minimum of assistant chief constable rank, deployment beyond 12 months can only be authorized by a chief constable, and an additional requirement mandated that operatives must comply with the College of Policing Code of Ethics (see Home Office, 2022d). A public inquiry into undercover policing was convened in 2015. The inquiry is ongoing, and proceedings are regularly updated at <https://www.ucpi.org.uk/about-the-inquiry/>. An interim report is expected, but no date of publication has been announced. In a recent judgment, the Investigatory Powers Tribunal found that the police operation to gain intelligence about political activists and public disorder violated several human rights (Articles 3, 8, 10, 11, and 14). This involved deception of a woman by an undercover police officer who then engaged in a long-term sexual relationship with her and continued to gain intelligence against the activists. The tribunal found that the actions were not just those of a rogue undercover police officer and argued that there was a lack of oversight of the police officer's activities and flawed authorizations under RIPA (*Wilson (Kate) v (1) The Commissioner of Police of the Metropolis, (2) National Police Chiefs' Council* [2021] 9 WLUK 354).

Test purchase operations are used relatively frequently, for example a police officer can pose as a potential buyer for an illegally acquired firearm. The whole transaction is monitored carefully (with surveillance teams deployed and uniformed officers on hand) and, when the moment is right, the dealer or seller is arrested and charged. The advantage for the police of such 'sting' operations is that an officer only needs to appear once in one location, thereby reducing the risk. The advantage in terms of criminal justice is that the criminal is caught in the act and is therefore more likely to plead guilty.

Officers planning and undertaking such operations must be sure that the proposed operation is proportionate and does not entrap individuals into committing offences they would not normally commit. If there is a lack of proportionality, or obvious entrapment, the defence could apply under s 78 of the PACE Act 1984 to have the evidence obtained ruled inadmissible or will put forward an abuse of process argument to stop the proceedings (ie a court will not allow a prosecution to continue as the trial would be unfair or it would be 'unfair' to have a trial at all).

12.4 Surveillance

In a police and legal sense surveillance generally means that the subject of the surveillance is unaware that they are being monitored and the monitoring is planned in advance. The use of covert surveillance is tightly controlled by RIPA (see 12.4.2). However, other types of monitoring, such as the use of CCTV by local authorities, generally do not involve the planned observation of a particular person and are not regulated so closely.

Principles of liberty and freedom must be respected; the surveillance might risk infringing the 'right to privacy and family life' (see 18.5.2). For obvious reasons, we only provide a general description of what is involved here.

12.4.1 CCTV

The simplest and most obvious form of open surveillance is the ubiquitous CCTV camera overlooking public and private premises. The benefit of CCTV is that it can provide 24-hour coverage of a location and its images are retrievable within a certain period; the disadvantage is that the location of the cameras is fixed. In addition, CCTV cameras are usually easy to spot so an astute criminal will note the locations of cameras and avoid them.

CCTV cameras are usually operated by local authorities or shop security officers. If an operator spots a person behaving suspiciously and decides to observe them using the CCTV for a while, this is not covert surveillance as it is not part of a planned operation; the observation is spontaneous as it is in response to immediate circumstances. The police can arrange to have access to recordings from a particular CCTV camera. Furthermore, some constabularies have live access to CCTV coverage and can therefore respond immediately to any incidents unfolding on the screens. The procedures for arranging to view CCTV footage are covered in 13.5.1.3.

Some local authorities and other organizations (see Sch 1 to RIPA for a full list) carry out directed surveillance using CCTV for their own enforcement activities, for example to monitor criminal behavior such as fly-tipping.

Sections 29–35 of the Protection of Freedoms Act 2012 introduced powers for the Secretary of State to issue codes of practice for surveillance camera systems, as well as a system for regulating such activities, spearheaded by a Surveillance Camera Commissioner (Home Office,

2013b). In recent years, the Information Commissioner's Office has revised the Codes that regulate the use of surveillance cameras and personal information by businesses and organizations other than public authorities (ICO, 2017).

The use of automatic number plate recognition systems (ANPR) by a range of organizations has increased in recent years. The surveillance commissioners have concluded that ANPR cameras are sometimes utilized for covert purposes without proper authorization (see 12.4.2.2). The ANPR Independent Advisory Group is responsible for ensuring that use of ANPR is underpinned by respect for privacy.

Recently, a member of the public challenged a South Wales Police pilot scheme that involved Automated Facial Recognition. He suggested that it was unlawful and was likely to infringe his right to privacy under Article 8 of the ECHR (see 18.5). The Divisional Court refused the application, finding that the current regime provided sufficient legal safeguards with regard to data protection, human rights, and equality. However, the Court of Appeal recently upheld part of the appeal by the member of the public and made declarations that: (a) the police's use of the technology between December 2017 and March 2018 and ongoing breached Article 8(2) of the ECHR; (b) as a consequence of that decision, its Data Protection Impact Assessment (DPIA), required by law, did not comply with the Data Protection Act 2018; and (c) they did not comply with s 149 of the Equality Act 2010 by failing to take account of research suggesting potential racial or gender bias in this kind of technology and breaching their obligations of continual review (*R (Bridges) v Chief Constable of South Wales Police* [2020] EWCA Civ 1058).

12.4.2 Covert surveillance

Covert surveillance is surveillance that is planned in advance and is covert:

> if, and only if, it is carried out in a manner that is calculated to ensure that the persons who are subject to surveillance are unaware that it is or may be taking place. (s 26(9) of RIPA)

The Act divides covert surveillance into two types; directed and intrusive. The type depends on the location of the target and hence the level of intrusion. Directed surveillance is when the person is anywhere apart from residential premises or a vehicle, and intrusive surveillance is when the person is in residential premises or in a vehicle.

Directed surveillance is defined in s 26(2) of RIPA, as shown in the flowchart.

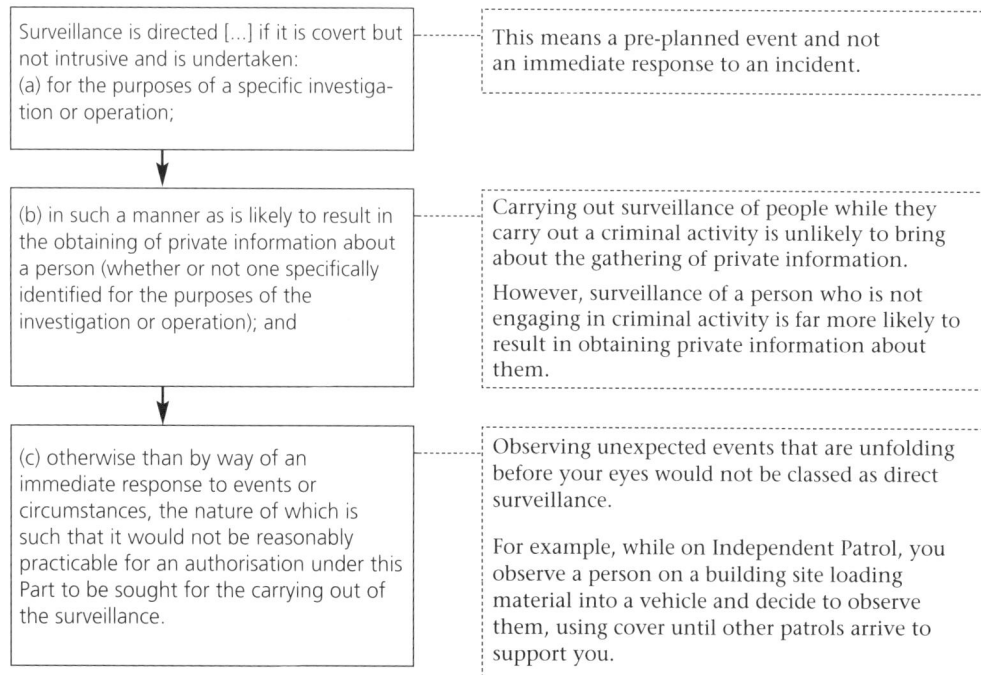

Surveillance is directed [...] if it is covert but not intrusive and is undertaken: (a) for the purposes of a specific investigation or operation;	This means a pre-planned event and not an immediate response to an incident.
(b) in such a manner as is likely to result in the obtaining of private information about a person (whether or not one specifically identified for the purposes of the investigation or operation); and	Carrying out surveillance of people while they carry out a criminal activity is unlikely to bring about the gathering of private information. However, surveillance of a person who is not engaging in criminal activity is far more likely to result in obtaining private information about them.
(c) otherwise than by way of an immediate response to events or circumstances, the nature of which is such that it would not be reasonably practicable for an authorisation under this Part to be sought for the carrying out of the surveillance.	Observing unexpected events that are unfolding before your eyes would not be classed as direct surveillance. For example, while on Independent Patrol, you observe a person on a building site loading material into a vehicle and decide to observe them, using cover until other patrols arrive to support you.

The provisions in RIPA are intended to ensure that police actions are proportionate and justified; the police often use the mnemonic PLAN—*P*roportionate, *L*awful, *A*uditable, *N*ecessary (and some have added the letter E for *E*thical). The JAPAN mnemonic has also been used in the past: *J*ustification, *A*uthorization, *P*roportionality, *A*uditable, and *N*ecessary.

An example of directed surveillance might be the installation of a concealed camera in a tree opposite a suspect's residence so that a surveillance team can see when the suspect is about to leave. If the camera captured a neighbour's house and the neighbour's activities, this would amount to 'collateral intrusion' and authority could be withheld until the risk of intrusion was minimized or avoided. If CCTV is to be used for a covert pre-planned investigation, then authority should be sought.

Intrusive surveillance (s 26(3) of RIPA) is described in the second flowchart.

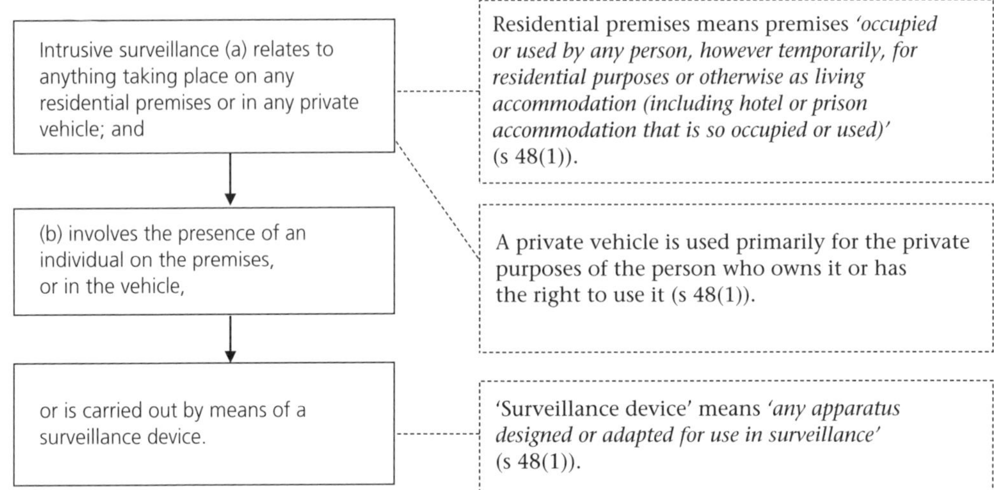

Intrusive surveillance (a) relates to anything taking place on any residential premises or in any private vehicle; and
(b) involves the presence of an individual on the premises, or in the vehicle,
or is carried out by means of a surveillance device.
Residential premises means premises 'occupied or used by any person, however temporarily, for residential purposes or otherwise as living accommodation (including hotel or prison accommodation that is so occupied or used)' (s 48(1)).
A private vehicle is used primarily for the private purposes of the person who owns it or has the right to use it (s 48(1)).
'Surveillance device' means 'any apparatus designed or adapted for use in surveillance' (s 48(1)).

An example of intrusive surveillance would be using a hidden listening device in a hotel room (or outside the room if it consistently provided information of the same quality and detail as if it were inside the room (s 28(5)). Surveillance is not intrusive if it only provides information about the location of a vehicle or if it is a one-sided consensual interception (eg of a telecommunication system) with no intercept warrant (s 28(4)(a) and (b) respectively).

In a landmark case, the House of Lords (now the Supreme Court) concluded that covert surveillance of communications between lawyers and their clients is allowed under Part II of RIPA. This was somewhat surprising as those communications might well be covered by legal professional privilege, and a person in custody has enshrined rights to consult privately with their legal representative (*In re McE (Northern Ireland) & In re M (Northern Ireland) & In re C (AP) and another (AP) (Northern Ireland)* [2009] UKHL 15).

More recently, the Court of Appeal was asked to deliberate on police use of covert surveillance. During the course of an investigation for violent robbery and burglary, the police had 'bugged' the prison van used for transporting the suspects and overheard incriminating remarks. The trial had allowed the evidence to be heard and the men were convicted. They subsequently appealed against conviction, arguing that the prison van should have been regarded as akin to a prison cell which, in their view, made it a private residential premises within the context of intrusive surveillance. (If this were the case, then the authority for the surveillance should have been provided by a chief officer of police not the superintendent.) They also argued that the surveillance was not necessary or proportionate and that their convictions should be quashed because the surveillance evidence should have been ruled inadmissible at trial under s 78 of the PACE Act 1984. The Court of Appeal did not agree that the prison van was private or residential, and accepted that the police action had been both necessary and proportionate as another suspect had yet to be found. The appeal was dismissed (*R v Plunkett and Plunkett* [2013] EWCA Crim 261). The case is a good illustration of the importance of clear decision-making by investigators to demonstrate both reasonableness and good faith.

12.4.2.1 Covert surveillance methods

Surveillance work involves a variety of approaches depending on the information required.

Static observations can be carried out from a fixed vantage point (Observation Point or OP), for example from a park bench or an unmarked parked police vehicle. If the OP is on private property, the identity and safety of the owner or user must not be compromised. The surveillance could be either directed or intrusive depending on the location of the subject under observation.

Mobile conventional surveillance involves officers following the subject on foot or in a vehicle. If the location of the subject is the only information recorded, then this is directed surveillance. Two key factors to consider are the location and the awareness of the subject. A rural community would be a difficult location as strangers and unknown cars will 'stand out' in a small village or a quiet residential street. Different problems occur in busy high streets where it is difficult to keep the target in sight. Some criminals use sophisticated counter-surveillance techniques to shake off such surveillance.

Mobile technical surveillance involves attaching tracking devices to vehicles, packages, or other items. If the device is used to simply identify the position of an object, then this is directed surveillance. Tracking by GPS is commonly used by the police and private sector organizations.

Audio and visual surveillance employs devices such as binoculars, cameras, or recording equipment. These can be used when following a subject or observing and recording them from an OP. Microphones and sound-recording equipment can be used to record a subject's speech when an undercover officer engages them in conversation in order to obtain evidence or intelligence. The use of audio-visual equipment for surveillance is tightly regulated and the authorization must relate to the specific methods to be used.

12.4.2.2 Authorization for covert surveillance

Authorization for covert surveillance must be given in writing and is valid for three months. It will be scrutinized (usually monthly in the case of intrusive surveillance) by a surveillance commissioner. The authorization can be withdrawn and the operation cancelled if they are not satisfied that the grounds were reasonable and the justification proportionate and any intelligence already obtained would probably be destroyed.

For directed surveillance, the authorization should be given in writing by a police officer not below the rank of superintendent. In urgent cases, a superintendent can provide a verbal authorization for 72 hours but written authority should be provided within the 72-hour period.

Intrusive surveillance is a highly specialized area of police work and will only be authorized if it involves serious crime. All such operations must be authorized by a person holding the rank of chief officer (ie assistant chief constable rank and above) and the authorization must be approved by a surveillance commissioner.

Some operations involve the use of a CHIS, OPs, and mobile surveillance so multiple applications for authority will be required. These complex procedures ensure that the police (and other agencies) operate in a system which is open to both scrutiny and monitoring, and in compliance with the HRA 1998.

12.4.3 Communications data

Communications data (CD) is the 'who', 'when', 'where', and 'how' of a communication but not its content (the 'what'). It can provide valuable intelligence to the police and other agencies, particularly when investigating organized crime and terrorism, and has two main components:

- 'entity data' (about a person or organization making the communication); and
- 'events data' about the existence and timing of the communication.

The Investigatory Powers Act 2016 (IPA) governs the use of CD and how it is obtained.

12.4.3.1 Entity data and events data

CD consists of entity data (about a person or organization) and events data (the timing of telecommunications events) (s 261(5) of the IPA).

Entity data identifies the person or organization making the communication or the location of the communication equipment being used and/or the network through which the data are transmitted. Examples include the 'header' of an email which identifies the IP address of a sender or the postal address on a letter.

Events data is concerned with data about how a communication service has been used, such as a list of numbers called by a particular mobile phone or a list showing when letters have been delivered to a particular address.

12.4.3.2 Communications data and investigation

CD can be obtained by the authorities from telecommunications providers for specific investigations or operations (listed in s 61 of the IPA), but the necessity and proportionality criteria defined under the IPA must be met. The public authority must consider (s 2(2) of the IPA):

- whether there are other less intrusive means to obtain the information;
- the sensitivity of the material;
- the public interest in the integrity and security of the telecommunications systems; and
- protecting privacy.

Many police officers use the PLANE mnemonic to assess their approach; it must be Proportionate, Lawful, Auditable, Necessary, and Ethical. The data gathering must be authorized by a designated senior officer who is independent of the specific investigation or operation (unless there are exceptional circumstances (s 63(2) of the IPA)). An authorization to obtain under s 61 usually lasts for one month although extensions are available. The material sought can also be material that does not yet exist (eg ongoing communications by a potential suspect). Communications service providers must comply with requests under this section unless it is not practicable for them to do so (s 66 of the IPA).

12.4.3.3 The Investigatory Powers Act 2016

The IPA received Royal Assent in November 2016 and was created to:

- consolidate and clarify existing police and intelligence services powers in relation to obtaining CD;
- create independent oversight of certain warrants (judicial sanction will be required);
- create an office of Investigatory Powers Commissioner; and
- make provision for the retention of internet records.

Whilst extensions are available for some of the powers, the government suggests that built-in safeguards will ensure that they are only used in appropriate circumstances. Many of the investigative powers in the Act were already in place (eg under statute law, case law, and EU Directives) and were merely consolidated. The IPA consists of:

- Part 1: describes responsibilities in relation to privacy and provides offences relating to unlawful interception of communications and the unlawful obtaining of CD;
- Part 2: describes the circumstances in which communications interception is lawful and how any obtained material should be managed;
- Part 3: sets out the procedures for obtaining CD, including authorization and management of the material;
- Part 4: concerns the authorizations for retention notices served upon telecommunications operators and the resulting obligations;
- Parts 5 and 6: describe the powers and warrants in relation to equipment interference.

Other parts of the Act deal with bulk personal dataset warrants and other miscellaneous provisions. Note that some Parts of the Act are still not yet in force (see the legislation.gov.uk website for updates and more details). The Investigatory Powers Commissioners Office (IPCO) was also created in 2017, combining the Office of Surveillance Commissioners (OSC), the Interception of Communications Commissioner's Office (IOCCO), and the Intelligence Service Commissioner's Office (ISComm).

The IPA 2016 was amended following a case in the European courts (Judgment in Joined Cases C-203/15 *Tele2 Sverige AB v Post-och telestyrelsen* and C-698/15 *Secretary of State for the Home Department v Tom Watson and Others*) other UK court decisions, and subsequent government consultations. The amendments to the IPA (Smith, 2018) include:

- restricting access to events data so it will only be permitted for serious crime; and
- creating the Office of Communications Data Authorisations (OCDA), an independent body to authorize relevant CD requests, to be overseen by the Investigatory Powers Commissioner and Investigatory Powers Commissioner's Office.

Mckay (2017) provides a more detailed overview of the Act, and the more recent amendments can be found in various regulations and updated codes of practice issued in 2018 (Data Retention and Acquisition Regulations, 2018 (Home Office, 2018c) and the Communications Data Code of Practice, 2018 (Home Office, 2018d)).

12.5 Managing, Processing, and Using Intelligence

Intelligence should be managed, processed, and analysed so that it can be effectively and legally used by the police and other agencies. For level 3 crimes, the national intelligence agencies link closely with the police and other agencies. For example, the NCA works with police forces, the Serious Fraud Office, HM Revenue and Customs, and other law enforcement agencies to curtail serious and organized criminality. The Security Service (MI5) also uses intelligence from police sources to counter threats to national security.

12.5.1 Data protection and intelligence

The police collect information every day, some of which is personal. Personal data is held on systems such as the police national computer, computer-aided dispatch, Police National Database, ANPR, and intelligence and crime reporting systems.

Such data must only be accessed for a legitimate purpose. Everyone who uses personal data (including the police) has to follow strict rules called 'data protection principles'. They must make sure the information is:

- used fairly, lawfully, and transparently;
- used for specified, explicit purposes;
- used in a way that is adequate, relevant, and limited to only what is necessary;
- accurate and, where necessary, kept up to date;
- kept for no longer than is necessary; and
- handled in a way that ensures appropriate security, including protection against unlawful or unauthorized processing, access, loss, destruction, or damage.

When the stored information is about a vulnerable person (eg a missing person suffering from dementia or a child), it may in some circumstances be shared with other agencies but police officers should check local police service policies.

As a trainee police officer, you should ensure that you do not leave your PNB insecure or leave any electronic devices 'unlocked'. You should also have a legitimate policing purpose for any search for information on police databases or other systems, and the purpose must be recorded in your PNB.

There are several pieces of legislation associated with the management and holding of information, such as:

- Article 8 of the HRA 1998, which gives individuals a right to respect for private and family life that may not be interfered with;
- the Data Protection Act 2018;
- the General Data Protection Regulation 2016 (implemented in 2018) which includes how the police manage information; and
- the Freedom of Information Act 2000 that allows an individual to request what information is being kept about them.

The key point is that information should only be collected if it is deemed relevant for a policing purpose, such as the preservation of life, maintaining order, and investigating and detecting crimes. This provides the legal basis for the police to deal with that information, for instance by recording it, sharing it with other agencies, or simply retaining it for future use. Information is collected (sometimes because of strategic direction, see 12.6) and then collated, evaluated, and disseminated. This is the 'intelligence cycle'.

12.5.2 Intelligence reports

Intelligence is usually reported by police officers on a 3 × 5 × 2 form ('three by five by two'). The numbers refer to 'qualities' of the intelligence, measured in three categories. For example, for a CHIS the scales refer to their reliability, the reliability of the intelligence, and the level of security to be implemented.

A summary of the 3 × 5 × 2 approach is given in the table (note that headings might vary from constabulary to constabulary).

Reliability of source (Do we trust them or it?)	Reliability of intelligence (Do we believe the specific intelligence?)	Distribution (Who can see it?)
1. Reliable 2. Untested 3. Not reliable (ie intelligence has normally turned out to be incorrect in the past)	A. Known directly (eg direct observation by CCTV) B. Known indirectly but corroborated C. Known indirectly D. Not known E. Suspected to be false	P. Lawful sharing is permitted C. Lawful sharing permitted but with conditions

A piece of intelligence may be graded for example as '2 by B by P' (all combinations of scales are possible). A police officer will complete the main body of the form with the intelligence and the service's Intelligence Unit provides the grades concerned with its distribution (sometimes referred to as the 'Handling Code'). The College of Policing has developed further codes to identify the best means for implementing this 'exploitation of the intelligence' (CoP, 2018d).

Reports dealing with a common theme may be collated from several sources and be circulated as a single composite intelligence item (further protecting each source). The information may be 'sanitized'—this is the removal of any features of the intelligence that could identify the source or the circumstances in which the intelligence was obtained. The 'need to know' principle applies to protecting sources because the police want the source to continue their covert relationship with the target. R&D staff may return to the handler(s) with requests for directions to pursue and more targets; a productive source will be heavily tasked.

These 3 × 5 × 2 forms are a major part of the intelligence in-flow into a police service 'Research & Development' unit. They ensure that reports are circulated to those who need to know, for example the Tasking & Coordination Group (see 12.6.1). The importance of accuracy and objectivity in reporting cannot be overstated—this raw information still has to go through a process of collation, evaluation, and analysis in order to assess its reliability. It is also essential that information is input into the system promptly on the day it is received.

12.5.3 Analysing intelligence

At some point in the distribution chain, analysts will analyse the intelligence, for example to establish and identify the MO (the *modus operandi*). The MO is how the criminal has carried out the offence—how did the burglar gain access to the property, what type of items were taken, etc? The next stage will be to try to match a particular event with what is already known about other similar crimes. In some constabularies, this happens with the raw intelligence, in others with the sanitized version.

The NIM suggests that intelligence analysis should be undertaken within four main areas.

- Problem profiling—for example, the identification of crime hot spots (see 17.5.2).
- Subject profiling—analysing the actions of suspected criminals and their associates, and of victims.
- Tactical assessment—essentially a management-support function undertaken by the analyst which involves recommendation of the deployment of resources based on the intelligence available.
- Strategic assessment—involves likely future developments in criminal activity Strategic assessment is normally undertaken by a senior or principal analyst.

Many different techniques can be employed by analysts, such as 'crime pattern analysis', 'network analysis', 'case analysis', and 'crime trend analysis'. There are up to ten different analytical techniques although research shows that in practice often significantly fewer than ten are used (Cope *et al*, 2005).

Crime analysis can be used in many ways, for example crime trend analysis can help to identify patterns in crimes or incidents in a locality (as described in the College of Policing APP). It could also help to find out whether the number of a particular crime is increasing, decreasing, or remaining steady which is important for deciding how to allocate resources. Crime trend analysis would also be able to identify whether particular crimes or incidents are happening within specific time frames. Some crimes, for instance, are frequent in particular seasons, such as burglaries at Christmas. Such analysis might also be able to identify where crime has been displaced, for instance a successful drive to remove street crime from a particular location may only serve to move it to another nearby location.

The theoretical and empirical methods that underpin the ten techniques include formulating and testing hypotheses and drawing inferences. Analysts also use various software packages, for example the 'Analyst's Notebook' from the i2 company. The R&D unit will, in turn, try to gather enough intelligence to construct a 'targeting package' for the Tasking and Coordination Groups to consider (see 12.6.2).

12.5.4 Intelligence packages

An intelligence package is a number of items of intelligence with related content. They are fundamental to police operational planning at the T&CG level and above. Intelligence packages are not just put together as a response to crime, but may also be used to support other objectives, such as planning appropriate levels of policing for a demonstration.

An ideal package would provide a highly accurate picture of how particular crimes are carried out in a given locality, by whom, with what success, how the acquisitions from the crime are fenced, how money is laundered and by whom, the likelihood of repeat victimization, and how the crime series is likely to develop. However, many lack such detail and are much more likely to combine hard intelligence and reasoned hypothesis-testing.

12.5.5 Dissemination

As discussed, intelligence may be disseminated to others within the extended policing family, such as others in your constabulary or police services or agencies elsewhere. Disseminated intelligence is likely to be sanitized to protect sources. However, police services also have sharing agreements or arrangements with other agencies and various other considerations apply, for example the sharing agreement might be a legal requirement made by a judge in court (eg in family proceedings). Secondly, and more usually, the police will enter into information-sharing agreements with partner agencies to ensure a professional and 'joined up' approach, as, for example, it would obviously be difficult if social services and police could not share relevant information in a child neglect investigation. Despite any agreements, police must give due consideration to issues of proportionality, risk, data protection, and freedom of information, as well as the human rights of those affected by any sharing of information. In some restricted circumstances, dissemination could involve the provision of information under statute or common law so that a parent could protect their child from a potential abuser (eg the Child Sex Offender Disclosure Scheme, see 24.8.3). Even in these cases, however, particular care needs to be demonstrated to ensure lawful disclosure. For further information, see the Information Management section of the College of Policing APP, under the heading 'sharing'.

12.6 The National Intelligence Model

The NIM is concerned with using intelligence to determine key priorities for policing. The Home Office described the NIM as 'a validated model of policing ... representing best practice in the use of intelligence to fight crime' (Home Office, 2001, p 45). All police services in England and Wales are required to implement the NIM and it is also used by the NCA and local Community Safety Partnerships (see 11.4.1).

The NIM is not the same as Intelligence-led Policing (ILP); the NIM is more concerned with using intelligence to determine priorities for policing, while ILP is essentially concerned with using intelligence to counter crime. Further information on the NIM and its associated Codes of Practice (2005), can be found in the College of Policing APP *Intelligence management*.

12.6.1 Key features of the NIM

The key part of the NIM process is shown in the centre of the diagram: the Tasking and Coordinating Process, overseen by Tasking and Coordination Groups (T&CG). This determines the operational responses to crime and disorder and prioritizes intelligence requirements (eg identifying car-crime hot spots or obtaining information about a series of burglaries). The arrows on the diagram show how intelligence and other factors influence decision-making.

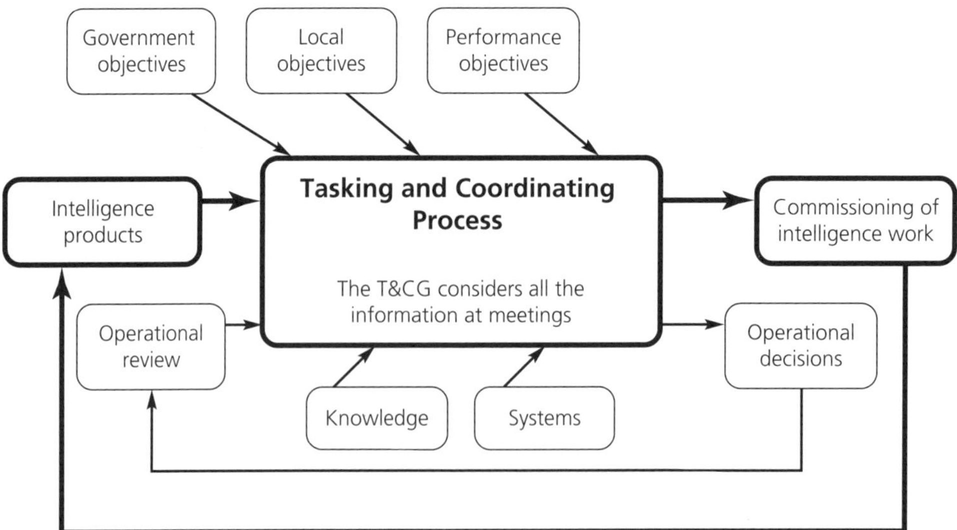

The bold lines indicate the key aspects of the process and emphasize the use of intelligence products to determine what further intelligence work needs to be commissioned. It is a continual cycle of policy development, implementation, and review (and thus bears some resemblance to Kolb's learning cycle).

The Tasking and Co-ordinating Process is conducted at three levels to correspond with the specified levels of crime:

- level 1 (local BCU level) in relation to local crime capable of being managed by local resources (which may include the most serious crime) and anti-social behaviour;
- level 2 (local and regional) in relation to constabulary, inter-constabulary, and regional criminal activity, usually requiring additional resources; and
- level 3 (national) in relation to the most serious and organized crime.

The classification of the crime is significant for resourcing. A single BCU does not have the resources to cope with, say, a group of criminal associates carrying out thefts from ATMs (cash machines) across the police service area. A force-level response (level 2) would be needed and this would usually be centrally co-ordinated and directed. Level 3 crime is dealt with by linking with national agencies such as the NCA and its international counterparts if required.

Whether on a national, regional, or local scale, assessed intelligence informs operational decision-making following the same principles as set out in the NIM. Care must be taken to avoid isolating the work at one level from the work at other levels.

12.6.2 The tasking and co-ordinating process

At the heart of the business process are the Strategic Tasking and Coordination Group (Strategic T&CG) meetings. Most police services will have a strategic-level T&CG dealing with serious level 2 crime. The purpose of the meetings is to initiate a Control Strategy which will establish the intelligence requirement and set the agenda for prevention, intelligence, and enforcement priorities. The Strategic T&CG do not routinely determine the operational tactics to be deployed but instead maintain an overview of priorities. So, for example, if the Strategic T&CG required that countering ATM raids was to be made a priority, then specialist operations such as surveillance and CHIS recruitment would be tasked to challenge that criminal network. Strategic issues are considered every six months at police service-level Strategic T&CG meetings. Members of a Strategic T&CG include the police service-wide senior management team, intelligence specialists, crime analysts, and other senior staff as required.

A second category of T&CG meetings also takes place: the Tactical Tasking and Coordination Group meetings. At a BCU level (level 1), the Tactical T&CG meets at least every two weeks. The group comprises the senior supervisory officers and support staff from the local area, and they apply the planned response to the Control Strategy, review progress, and make changes to plans if judged appropriate. They can call on other agencies to assist in tactical decisions but compared with Strategic T&CG meetings there is generally not such a wide range of senior staff present at Tactical T&CG meetings.

12.6.2.1 Inputs to the tasking and co-ordinating process

The T&CGs are informed by intelligence products which have been researched and written by analysts working with police officers. Both the strategic planning at police service level and the local-tasking operational planning at BCU level are guided by these intelligence products and other forms of analysis.

Strategic Assessments are long-term strategy documents, usually produced every six months. Tactical Assessments review the progress of current operations and approaches. The T&CGs also commission, and are subsequently informed by, intelligence products. These include target/subject profiles about named offenders, victims, or networks and problem profiles about issues of concern such as a hot spot or the increased availability of a particular street drug.

The decisions taken by the T&CG will be influenced by a number of other factors such as:

- Government objectives: for example, to raise the priority level of thefts from cars or deal with public order issues.
- Local objectives: including police objectives, such as dealing with so-called 'problem families', 'problem estates', and local disorder. These objectives will have arisen through canvassing both the police (eg through community liaison officers) and local government councillors, local authority officials, and other parts of local government. Their views will be conveyed to the area or BCU commander (usually a superintendent) through routine meetings and consultations and will be converted into local objectives.
- Performance objectives: the long-term (yearly) objectives for the BCU will also be taken into account. These may be to develop strategies to reduce all crime locally (and might include reducing burglaries by a specific percentage, for example), to deal with anti-social behaviour, to improve arrest rates, or 'brought to justice' data. These determine the BCU Commander's strategic approach.
- Knowledge: the professional knowledge required by staff in order to contribute fully to the NIM and other aspects of police work. It includes knowledge of legislation, codes of practice, and police service policies.
- Systems: the IT systems and associated procedures for the storage, retrieval, analysis, and dissemination of intelligence information.

12.6.2.2 Outputs from the tasking and co-ordinating process

The Control Strategy will be implemented, for example commissioning of new intelligence work (the intelligence requirement) and making operational decisions to improve the management of crime and the local community. Teams may be assembled to tackle particular issues, and budgets will be set; the overtime budget is frequently of particular significance.

As well as the weekly or fortnightly Tactical T&CG meetings at BCU level, there are likely to be daily meetings to monitor and direct the daily aspects of police work. The daily meetings (sometimes known as 'Intelligence Daily Briefing' meetings, or more colloquially in some police services as 'Morning Prayers') are part of the process of ensuring that the T&CG strategy is implemented and kept on track.

12.6.3 Links with the wider policing role

The NIM is intended to be the engine room that drives the policing machine. Police officers undertake much of their non-reactive work at the direction of the T&CG, to help policing in their area to be co-ordinated, specific, and focused. For example, it would not be appropriate for the T&CG to recommend an operation targeting thefts from cars when local priorities were largely focused on reducing alcohol-related violence. (However, the BCU Commander may still judge that disrupting car thefts is a temporary but urgent priority.)

12.6.4 The NIM in practice

To illustrate the way in which the NIM is used in policing we will track through a crime from start to finish.

Suppose we receive several reports of an 'artifice burglary' (see the start of 23.4). The reports will enter the process as information and a key early requirement will be for analysts to assess the criminal's MO, such as the type and location of targeted property. The findings may be incorporated into a subject profile (if the offender is known) or a problem profile (if their identity has not yet been established).

The T&CG may then task the police staff who are responsible for gathering intelligence to find out whether there is access to information about criminals known to undertake this type of crime (perhaps through a regular 'fence') and whether there is local knowledge of such individuals. The T&CG will assign a priority to the investigation and will commission further work, such as checking the police databases and trying to match other spree. Analysts might note, for example, that the offences have all taken place within half a mile of a railway station, in which case the police may approach British Transport Police for help, and look at relevant CCTV footage.

Suppose the frequency of artifice burglaries increases and one of the victims becomes seriously ill as an indirect consequence of the theft. At the next T&CG meeting, the priority level for artifice burglary will be raised and the operational plans will be revised and developed. The BCU Commander will take into account government objectives, local feelings about the nature of the crime, media pressures, and the chances of apprehending the offender(s). Now suppose that a CHIS (see 12.3) provides useful information to their handler and a report is submitted. It is assessed by the R&D unit and compared with other intelligence, and provides a name, a likely location for offences in the near future, and a clear idea of the MO. An operation is mounted, two people are arrested, and a case is prepared. The final outcome for the offender(s) could be a prison sentence, a caution, a fine, seizure of assets, or community service. Other outcomes might include displacing the activity of artifice burglars and the development and implementation of a crime-reduction (prevention or disruption) strategy (see 17.6), and probably some useful media coverage.

The NIM process has led to an assessment of the nature of the crime, to tasking the intelligence-gathering parts of the police, and giving the crime a higher priority level in the midst of competing claims for attention. The newly acquired intelligence was assessed and used to develop a package of operational measures through the T&CG and the subsequent police action disrupted that type of crime and probably helped to reassure the local community. This is a simple example of the business-process model of policing, and the same principles will operate whether the issue is the vandalizing of cars or a more serious crime enquiry, such as systematic violent assaults on young people near a sports centre.

12.7 Managing Police Information

This section examines the need for police officers to protect the confidentiality of information and data under the Data Protection Act 2018 (DPA, gov.uk, 2018a). The section also considers the procedures around the sharing of information under the requirements of the Freedom of Information Act 2000.

Sections 35–40 of the DPA require that personal data must be:

- processed lawfully and fairly;
- collected for specified and legitimate purposes;
- adequate and relevant and not excessive;
- accurate and kept up to date;
- kept no longer than is necessary;
- processed in a secure manner.

Police data gathering must be accurate, relevant, and timely. Once information is collected, it is important that the police adhere to legal requirements. In addition, the recording of information and confidentiality policies should be explained to victims and witnesses.

12.7.1 Confidentiality

Police officers (including student officers and special constables) will frequently encounter information of a sensitive and confidential nature. It is probably obvious, but confidentiality must be maintained, particularly in relation to witnesses, victims, and intelligence. The DPA, the General Data Protection Regulations 2018 (GDPR), and the Human Rights Act 1998 (HRA) were enacted partly as a response to European legislation for protecting individual rights.

The collection, storage, and disclosure of police information is subject to controls under the DPA and the Management of Police Information (MoPI). Each constabulary has a 'data controller' who considers applications for information and decides whether the information requested can be disclosed. The DPA also provides certain rights to individuals (including witnesses and victims) for information. It is an offence under the DPA to disclose personal information without the consent of the data controller, except for the purposes of crime prevention or detection.

12.7.2 Management of Police Information (MoPI)

The means by which the police collect, record, share, and retain information has been the subject of some controversy over the years, most notably as a result of the inquiry into the circumstances preceding the Soham murders in 2002 where a school caretaker killed two pupils and the subsequent police investigations (see Bichard, 2004). The College of Policing (2019) sets out the basic principles that police organizations should adopt for the collection, recording, sharing, and retaining of information. At the level of the individual police officer, the information may take the form of intelligence and evidence gathering, details concerning domestic crime, search form completion, and pocket notebook (PNB) entries.

The HRA requires all UK legislation to correspond with the European Convention on Human Rights (ECHR). This means that any act by a public authority (such as the police) that contravenes the ECHR will be unlawful. An individual's rights to privacy and family life (Article 8) can be 'interfered' with by the collection of personal information, and this interference is only permitted under certain circumstances.

The DPA places additional constraints on those holding 'personal data' (defined in the Act as any information which can identify a living person). However, exemptions are permitted when such data is used for the prevention or detection of crime, or the apprehension or prosecution of offenders.

The Code of Ethics, the HRA, the GDPR, and College of Policing information all set out obligations to manage police information in ways that are both effective and meet certain ethical and professional standards. Many of these obligations are made manifest through standing orders and policies such as the local policing 'Information Management Strategy'. However, the same principles also apply for all levels of police staff, regardless of rank or role.

12.7.3 Freedom of information

The Freedom of Information Act 2000 (FoI) provides a general right of access to all types of recorded information held by public authorities, such as police services. Each constabulary will publish (normally online) details concerning the public's right under the FoI to access information kept by it, the procedures for accessing it, and have a publication scheme listing what information is available as a matter of routine, thereby reducing the number of requests for the same information. Not all requests for information will be successful—some of these are obvious, for example requests relating to the identity of a Covert Human Intelligence Source (see 12.3 on the use of a CHIS), but the right to information is the norm rather than the exception. Requests can be made, and are made, on all kinds of topics.

There are two main ways that the FoI might directly affect a student police officer. First, they may personally receive a request for information under the FoI, perhaps in the form of a letter or by email. The officer should not normally respond in person but should promptly pass the request to the person responsible for handling FoI requests. Secondly, all student officers and officers should always be aware when recording information as a police officer, that someone may apply to view that record and, as this will normally be permitted, it is very important to choose words accurately and carefully.

12.8 Operating IT and Communication Systems

Student police officers will use IT systems on a general level and will also learn how to use specific police-related systems such as the Police National Computer and the Airwave radio communication system. Police services may also have their own information systems which officers will need to be able to use. The ability to use 'force information management systems' is one of the requirements under the Police Action Checklists (PAC) 'Information Management' heading.

12.8.1 Police information systems and databases

There are two large national databases of information for police use in the UK: the Police National Computer (PNC) and the more recently established Police National Database (PND). The PNC tends to be used by officers for 'street level' checks on a suspect, while the PND is more often employed within the context of an investigation and is likely to contain much more detailed intelligence on individuals (both convicted and suspected). The police in the UK did have access to the Schengen Information System II (SIS II) which operates across Europe and provides alerts concerning people and property. However, since leaving the European Union at the end of 2020 this has been replaced by the use of Interpol red notices.

Apart from these national and international systems, each local police service is likely to have its own databases, and you will learn about these when you enter training.

12.8.1.1 The PNC

The PNC is a large database containing information on people (eg those with criminal records), vehicles (including registered keepers), driving licences, and property, and other records pertinent to policing. It is also used by other agencies such as the Crown Court (for checking potential jurors), the Environment Agency, the Gangmasters and Labour Abuse Authority, and the United Kingdom Border Force.

A police officer could use the PNC to establish, for example, whether a driver is disqualified or to assess the potential for a particular suspect to respond with violence. However, the PNC can do more than perform these relatively simple checks. For example, the Driver and Vehicle Licensing Agency (DVLA) database is linked to the PNC, so a police officer is able to check the expiry date of an MoT and other details (such as 'advisory notices'). The linked DVLA database will reveal information relating to tests, endorsements, and so on. The PNC can also be used to search for information such as nicknames used by offenders, tattoos, scars, hair colour, and similar distinguishing features.

The PNC is normally accessed by radio and speaking to an operator based at the Force Control Room. This is a routine to be mastered; a particular sequence of requests is made to the operator, first specifying the nature of the request (eg a vehicle check). The officer then provides their name and service number before stating the reason for the check. The phonetic alphabet is used to spell out words to ensure there is no mistake in transmitting the information (see 12.8.4.1). Officers must make a PNB record (see Chapter 10) of the details of the checks carried out so that their work is auditable. Student officers undertaking the PCDA or DHEP will be instructed on using the PNC and demonstrating the ability to use the PNC effectively is required before Independent Patrol Status is achieved.

It will certainly be emphasized during police training that there is a requirement to access the PNC in a responsible and professional manner. Inappropriate use of the PNC is viewed by the police service as a serious matter and could lead to dismissal of a student police officer. It is not only a contravention of the PNC Code of Practice, but it is also against the law. Alleged misuse of the PNC can lead to an IOPC inquiry and subsequent prosecution.

Examples of inappropriate use of the PNC are easy to find. In 2018, a Staffordshire Police officer was dismissed and given a six-month community order for conducting checks for personal reasons on neighbours, an ex-partner, and the family of their new partner (Ross, 2018). Police constabularies and other non-police organizations such as the Environment Agency are subject to HMICFRS inspections for PNC-compliance.

12.8.1.2 The PND

The PND enables information and intelligence to be shared between police areas. It was set up in 2011 and replaced the IMPACT Nominal Index. The PND contains 'POLE' data, which is information about:

- *P*eople (eg offenders and suspects) or organizations (companies);

- *O*bjects (eg stolen vehicles);
- *L*ocations (eg addresses of offenders); and
- *E*vents (eg crime reports).

The data is located within five discrete but interconnected sets of records: custody, intelligence, crime, domestic abuse, and child abuse. Police can check what information or intelligence is held on an individual (a 'nominal') by any other police service. Much of the information to be found on the PNC will also be present in the PND and vice versa.

12.8.2 Emergency Services Network (ESN)

Several years ago the government signalled its intention to replace the existing police TETRA communication network Airwaves, with a new network called the Emergency Services Network. At the beginning of 2023 the Home Office announced that it would be delivering ESN in an incremental way so it can be tested and used as it becomes available, rather than having to wait until every element is finished. At the time of writing EE is upgrading its existing network of masts while working with the Home Office to deploy new 4G masts to ensure full national coverage. Airwaves will remain in place until 2026.

12.8.2.1 ICCS

Radio communication in policing operates within the Integrated Command and Control System (ICCS). This links telephony, radio, and other digital technologies, and allows police services to communicate internally with one another and with other emergency services. In 'trunked mode operation' (TMO), several Airwave users can communicate as a 'talk group'. (A talk group could comprise, for example, all the police officers involved with a particular enquiry or staff from a variety of agencies when responding to a major incident.) Direct Mode Operation (DMO) provides voice communication between two or more hand-held or mobile terminals without using Airwave. It can be used in areas with little or no coverage but is usually limited to line of sight so has a more limited range than TETRA and uses more battery power than TMO.

Capacity, congestion, and coverage are important factors for ICCS; for example, 'telephony' and 'point-to-point' occupy a lot of capacity and their use should therefore be limited. The most efficient use of Airwave is through an open talk group (this uses the same capacity as a single point-to-point Airwave communication). Mobile terminals should be set to the correct talk groups and unnecessary monitoring or usage avoided.

All users must also consider data security when using ICCS. Information that may be sensitive or operationally significant can be sanitized or an alternative means of communication could be used. In the event of an Airwave system failure, emergency services control staff will revert to using mobile phones or the Airwave mobile phone facility, while others could use status and text message with certain limitations.

For further information on ICCS and the various functions and capabilities, the following sources are available online: Standard Operating Procedure Guide on Multi-Agency Airwave interoperability and Standard Operating Procedure Guide on Police to Police and Inter-Agency Airwave interoperability (both published by the NPIA in 2010).

12.8.3 Mobile data devices

Most police services allocate mobile data devices such as smartphones, tablets, and laptops to their officers, with the intention of reducing the amount of paperwork. A mobile data device provides an electronic means of:

- entering and sharing data (eg a witness statement collected in electronic format at the scene of an incident);
- recording and sharing location data (eg using GPS); and
- printing some types of completed forms on a 'mini-printer' connected by Bluetooth or similar methods.

This allocation process certainly increased across the board during the Covid-19 pandemic with many constabularies introducing innovative ways of using mobile data devices. The devices allow a police officer to access the PNC, local force tasking and briefing bulletins, missing person reports, police intelligence systems, other information systems (eg the PNLD), and information relating to an individual's name and address (eg the electoral roll, the Quick Address System), and to send emails. In addition, mobile data devices normally incorporate a digital camera which (in some constabularies) a police officer can use to record potential evidence. The exact functions and applications used on the mobile data devices are specific to each area and normally kept confidential, but it is assumed that all data is securely encrypted.

Trainee police officers issued with a mobile data device will be informed of the relevant protocols and rules. For example, when a police-issued mobile data device is switched on it is likely to become 'visible' to the control room, therefore many police services forbid their use whilst off duty. Concerns have also been expressed over both the cost of the devices and of ongoing data usage, but it seems inevitable that the police use of mobile data devices will increase.

12.8.4 Conveying information

If you have ever attempted to spell out a word on the phone to another person you have probably experienced the difficulty of clarifying the difference between 'm' and 'n', 's' and 'f', and so on. Mistakes made in the context of ordinary phone calls are seldom life-threatening, but if these same mistakes were made during a police communication it could prove costly, both in time and in terms of safety. This is the reason the 'phonetic alphabet' (sometimes referred to as the 'radio alphabet') and conventions for communicating numbers, time of day, and dates were developed and subsequently adopted by police services throughout the UK.

12.8.4.1 The phonetic alphabet

With the phonetic alphabet, each letter is given a phonetic equivalent. This is to avoid confusion over letters which sound the same, such as 'p', 'b', and 'd'; instead of saying 'd', the police officer will say 'delta'. The following is a list of the phonetic alphabet as normally employed by police in the UK (and beyond).

The phonetic alphabet

A	Alpha	J	Juliet	S	Sierra
B	Bravo	K	Kilo	T	Tango
C	Charlie	L	Lima	U	Uniform
D	Delta	M	Mike	V	Victor
E	Echo	N	November	W	Whisky
F	Foxtrot	O	Oscar	X	X-ray
G	Golf	P	Papa	Y	Yankee
H	Hotel	Q	Quebec	Z	Zulu
I	India	R	Romeo		

You may well be asked to memorize and use it after you join the police.

12.8.4.2 Numbers

When communicating a number (eg the age of a person), each digit of the number is said individually. There is a further convention that zero is referred to as 'zero' and not 'nought' (nor as the letter 'O'). Hence the number 2,306 (two thousand, three hundred, and six) is communicated as 'two-three-zero-six'. A less common rule is to give large numbers in pairs, for example 245,671 being conveyed as 'two-four, five-six, seven-one'. However, practice does vary in this respect (particularly with phone numbers).

12.8.4.3 Time and date

Police services use the 24-hour clock for conveying the time of day. For example, 7.26 pm is written as 19.26 hrs and said as 'one-nine, two-six hours'. Dates are given as the day-month-year, in the UK style.

12.8.4.4 IC and SDE codes

There are several different situations in which a police officer might need to communicate or record a person's ethnicity, based upon an individual's appearance. The system used by some constabularies to communicate the perceived ethnicity of a person is known variously as 'IC codes', 'IC 1 to 6 codes', 'PNC Codes', and 'ID codes'. An officer could use this to describe a suspect's ethnicity when searching for a record on the PNC (or the PND) as shown in the table. (Note that ethnicity and nationality are not the same, and that the examples shown here are for illustration only.)

'IC' Code	Ethnicity	Example of a nationality
IC 0 (sometimes IC 7 or IC 9)	Unknown	N/A
IC 1	White North European	Swedish
IC 2	White South European (sometimes 'Dark European' or 'Mediterranean')	Greek
IC 3	Black (sometimes 'African-Caribbean')	Nigerian
IC 4	Asian (sometimes 'South Asian')	Pakistani
IC 5	Chinese/Japanese/SE Asian (sometimes 'Oriental' or 'East Asian')	Chinese
IC 6	Middle Eastern (sometimes 'Arab')	Egyptian

Note that IC 0/IC 7 are not always used, and some police services may use a different system.

A person can also be asked to define their own ethnicity, for example when a police officer is completing a form. The Self-defined Ethnicity (SDE) codes have 18 different options plus the option of 'not stated' (also known as '18\+ 1'), as shown in the following table.

General ethnic group	Self-defined ethnicity	SDE Code
White	British	W1
	Irish	W2
	Gypsy or Irish Traveller	W3
	Any other white background	W9
Mixed	White and black Caribbean	M1
	White and black African	M2
	White and Asian	M3
	Any other mixed background	M9
Asian or Asian British	Indian	A1
	Pakistani	A2
	Bangladeshi	A3
	Chinese	A4
	Any other Asian background	A9
Black or black British	Caribbean	B1
	African	B2
	Any other black background	B9
Other ethnic group	Arab	02
	Other ethnic group	09
Not stated	Not stated	NS

12.9 Answers to Tasks

TASK 1 You may have come up with the following:

Integrity and honesty; patience and attention to detail; strong-minded and not easily diverted; adaptable and flexible; firm sense of duty but objective. A good source handler can be trained to a high level but there must be strong pre-existing character traits upon which the training can build. You can see that it takes someone with considerable investigative experience and 'life skills' to succeed in this role.

TASK 2 The first consideration for the police is whether the identity of the informant will be revealed and, if so, whether they would be at risk of serious harm. In such circumstances, their identity would never be revealed. If the informant was the main source of evidence, the prosecution of the case in open court would probably be abandoned.

You might also have referred to the difficulty of using an active criminal as a source. If a CHIS takes part in an organized crime or is involved in criminal planning, they could be charged and brought before a court. A further difficulty is deciding whether, in order to obtain the intelligence, the crime should be allowed to go ahead with the source taking part.

TASK 3 As Canter and Alison (2000) noted, the motivation a person may provide is not necessarily the most useful for understanding their actions and will be only one of a number of possible explanations. Money is unlikely as the amounts paid out to informants are normally quite small, usually less than £100. (The total amount paid out yearly by police services in England and Wales to all their informants in 2017 was approximately £80,000—figure derived from BBC, 2017.)

13 Conducting Investigations

13.1 Introduction

The topics covered in this chapter are likely to contribute to the learning required for the National Policing Curriculum subject area of Conducting Investigations. The chapter covers different aspects of the criminal investigative processes including those relating to evidential matters, including the role of forensic investigation, and investigative interviewing.

It is important to note that trainee police officers may be directly involved in criminal investigations, and this will provide many opportunities for collecting evidence to demonstrate operational competence as required. Trainee officers will be expected to attain PIP Level 1 status, which will allow them to 'own' investigations into priority and volume crime offences. They would not take charge of investigations into more serious crimes, but could be present as a first attending officer (FAO). If you are undertaking the PCDA or the DHEP, you will also be expected to demonstrate that you can 'manage and conduct effective and efficient priority and high volume investigations' and 'use initiative to diligently progress investigations, identifying, evaluating, and following lines of enquiry to inform the possible initiation of criminal proceeding' and are able to 'apply an investigative mind-set when decision-making' (Institute for Apprenticeships, 2018b).

13.2 Key Principles for Investigations

Central to the investigative process is the collection, collation, and evaluation of many differing categories of information. This is a complex process, as O'Neill (2018, p xix) explains, 'like trying to complete a jigsaw puzzle without a picture, without all the pieces and without any parameters'. There are however a number of documents that help shape investigative processes, such as the *Volume Crime Management Model* (VCMM) (2009), the *Murder Investigation Manual* (MIM) (2006), and the *Major Crime Investigation Manual* (MCIM) (2021). Guiding investigative principles are also provided by the College of Policing APP and these include honesty, integrity, confidentiality, and conducting effective investigations proportionately, within the law, and in a transparent fashion. These core principles are echoed in the Code of Ethics for police officers, and the Code of Practice for Victims of Crime also provides important standards regarding updating victims on the progress of investigations, the treatment victims should expect from the police, and referrals to victim support.

Criminal investigations are also directed through legislation, most importantly:

- the Police and Criminal Evidence Act 1984 (PACE) and its Codes of Practice 2004;
- the Criminal Justice and Public Order Act 1994 (CJPOA);
- the Criminal Procedure and Investigations Act 1996 (CPIA);
- the Human Rights Act 1998 (HRA);
- the Regulation of Investigatory Powers Act 2000 (RIPA);
- the Serious Organised Crime and Police Act 2005 (SOCPA); and
- the Investigatory Powers Act 2016.

Finally, by way of introduction, it is important to recognize the need for officers to develop and maintain an *investigative mindset*. The mnemonic UPERE is used to provide five principles that help guide an investigative mindset:

- Understanding the source that produces evidence, eg a witness, CCTV footage;
- Planning and preparation of materials, scheduling interviews etc;
- Examination of the account provided by a witness or the material evidence;
- Recording and collation of materials and statements;
- Evaluation of evidence and identification of further actions required.

(adapted from ACPO Centrex, 2005, pp 60–3)

An investigative mindset helps to maximize the amount of information gathered and encourages officers to be thorough and thoughtful about the material they have obtained. It ensures that the material is tested, appropriate actions are initiated, proper records are kept, and that material is appropriately stored. Investigators must examine material with a critical eye, assuming nothing, believing no one, and checking everything. With forensic evidence especially, officers should consider speaking to the attending Crime Scene Investigator to ensure there are no misunderstandings. Inevitably, the more serious and complex a case, the more onerous this task becomes.

The College of Policing APP suggests that it is sometimes useful to generate a number of hypotheses based upon all available facts once all the material evidence has been gathered. It cautions against trying to find material that fits the hypotheses; the hypotheses should be made to fit the material. Investigators are also encouraged to use the National Decision Model (NDM) when making decisions within a criminal investigation.

Conducting investigations in these ways makes for a more ethical and effective approach, thereby improving public confidence in police investigations.

13.2.1 Resources for investigations

The investigation of a crime will often depend on whether the crime is a volume, priority, or major crime. Volume crime is 'any type of crime which, through its sheer volume, has a significant impact on the community and the workload of the local police' (NPIA and ACPO, 2009, p 8). It usually includes street robbery, burglary of dwelling-houses and other premises, theft (including shoplifting), theft of vehicles and from vehicles, criminal damage, common assault, and illegal possession of controlled drugs. Priority crimes for many basic/borough command units (BCUs) in recent years have included street robbery, burglary, and car crime. Hence, a priority crime might also be a volume crime and vice versa, but the terms are not synonymous. It is important to ensure that volume crime is accorded sufficient attention and the VCMM sets out the minimum standards of response to volume crimes identified by the TCG planning process at BCU level.

13.2.1.1 Resources for the investigation of more serious crimes

Some crimes are more complex and require significant local resources, for example the deployment of a team of specially trained detectives. The following might also be required:

- the intelligence department could task a covert human intelligence source (CHIS) to find information on a particular crime;
- an analyst could be asked to build a picture of the suspect's associates or understand an offending pattern of behaviour;
- the financial department could look into the sources of a suspect's income;
- an investigator in communications data and open-source intelligence could be asked to fill in gaps about a suspect's communications and private life;
- deploying a number of CSIs to different crime scenes and appointing a forensic lead (which would normally be a Senior CSI or equivalent).

The investigation of major crimes also requires significant resources. A 'major crime' would be any crime that includes serious violence (eg murder, manslaughter, and rape) or the potential for serious violence, and a crime that requires resources beyond those of a single BCU. Any crime of grave public concern or the threat of terrorism is also likely to come under the umbrella of major crime. Major crimes are classified as shown in the table (ACPO, 2006).

Category	Definition
A+	Public concern and the associated response to media intervention are such that 'normal' staffing levels are not adequate to keep pace with the investigation
A	An incident of grave concern or where vulnerable members of the public are at risk; where the identity of the offender(s) is not apparent or the investigation and the securing of evidence requires significant resource-allocation
B	The identity of the offender(s) is not apparent, the continued risk to the public is low, and the investigation or securing of evidence can be achieved within normal resourcing arrangements
C	The identity of the offender(s) is apparent from the outset and the investigation and/or securing of evidence can easily be achieved

In each constabulary, there will be a Major Crime Unit headed by a senior detective officer (eg a superintendent) who can designate any crime as a major crime in order that the appropriate resources can be made available for its subsequent investigation.

The Serious Crime Analysis Section (SCAS), part of the National Crime Agency, can help to identify evidence that could indicate that the same offender has committed a number of similar serious offences. Serious 'live' offences are added to the SCAS database where they can be compared to old cases that remain unsolved. Physical and behavioural aspects of the offender can be used in 'domain searches' to try to find links to other crimes. If potential offenders are identified, the relevant police service would then be notified.

13.2.2 Managing and recording investigations

Effective communication is a key component in case management as the investigating officer (IO) will interact with other officers, members of the police family, and members of the public. It provides clarity between all of the 'players' within a particular investigation.

Risk-management is also important and must be borne in mind throughout an investigation in relation to colleagues, victims, witnesses, and the public. There are several examples where police failed to appreciate the real risks posed to victims of crime (for instance, the investigation into the death of Alice Ruggles in 2016). The police have been criticized for their failure to recognize risk, particularly in relation to their poor response to domestic abuse cases (HMIC, 2014a) and more recently Evidence Led Domestic Abuse Prosecutions (HMCPSI and HMCFRS, 2020) and stalking (HMCPSI, 2017) which are prosecutions where a victim is not giving evidence. This is important, especially where the police become aware of a threat to life as they have a legal duty to protect life where there is a real and immediate risk. This derives from Article 2 of the European Convention on Human Rights (ECHR) and is outlined in an ECHR ruling (*Osman v UK* (2000) 29 EHRR 245).

Consideration should also be given to colleagues for example, a family liaison officer (FLO) will provide support to families and become an investigative asset but is also likely to absorb some of the distress felt by the family. Welfare and TRiM (Trauma Risk Management) can be used to identify colleagues within an investigation team who may be particularly vulnerable.

Records of the investigation must be kept so that investigations are auditable and transparent. As such, the decisions, actions, and strategies will be recorded in a variety of media by investigating officers. For example, in a volume crime investigation and for routine priority crimes, the investigation is likely to be recorded within the electronic crime report. However, the investigation of a serious or major crime will be recorded on a decision log or policy file which will set out the key strategic decisions (for further information, see ACPO Crime Committee (1999) *Revised Guidelines For the use of Policy Files*). The policy file could be vital if an investigation is transferred to another officer, which is not uncommon, so it is crucial to have an accurate record of what has been done. Poor policy file completion was mentioned in the Macpherson Report (1999) which considered the failings of the Stephen Lawrence murder investigation in 1993.

The early decisions made when initially attending a crime scene become very important at a handover (eg crime scene management, forensic opportunities, CCTV, and house-to-house enquiries). The new investigating officer needs to understand what has been done already and what still needs to be done. It also allows the new IO to form their own opinion on the sufficiency of those decisions.

13.2.3 Witnesses in investigations

The evidence of a witness (including victim(s)) may be vital in obtaining a conviction. Many, if not all, witnesses will cooperate if officers provide reassurance and information about what to expect.

13.2.3.1 Types of witness

There are various categories of witness and the dialogue between the witness and the police officer, and the means by which evidence is obtained, will vary accordingly.

A **defence** witness is a person who the accused is going to call to give evidence at the trial in relation to an alibi or to other matters. The name, address, and date of birth of any such witness must be disclosed in advance to the prosecution (s 6 of the CPIA) as the police may wish to interview them. A defence witness may be reluctant to assist, fearing, for example, police coercion to change their account. In these circumstances, consultation with the CPS is advised. Any interview with a defence witness has to comply with the relevant Code of Practice (under s 21A of the CPIA).

A **significant** or key witness is someone who can provide evidence that is particularly important to a case. They are designated as such by the SIO, usually in a serious or major crime enquiry involving an indictable offence such as murder, rape, or kidnap. The witness may have witnessed the offence (or part of it) or may stand in a particular relationship to the victim, or have other evidence or intelligence to offer. An interview with a significant witness may be visually recorded if it seems that this will contribute significantly to the investigation.

A **vulnerable** witness (s 16, Part II of the Youth Justice and Criminal Evidence Act 1999) is any person:

- under the age of 18 (as amended in s 98 of the Coroners and Justice Act 2009);
- with a 'mental disorder' (this is the phrase used in the Act);
- with significant impairment of intelligence and social functioning; or
- with a physical disability or a physical disorder.

An **intimidated** witness (s 17, Part II of the Youth Justice and Criminal Evidence Act 1999) is:

- any elderly and frail person;
- a witness experiencing fear or distress about testifying in the case;
- any witness who self-neglects or self-harms;
- any complainant in a sexual assault case;
- a victim of a domestic violence, a racially motivated crime, or repeat victimization; or
- a relative of the victim in a homicide case.

A **reluctant witness** is a witness who declines to cooperate or who makes a statement but then refuses to attend court; they might fear repercussions or might simply not want to assist the police. If the police can establish that a reluctant witness has important evidence to offer, a witness summons can be issued to compel attendance in court (see Home Office Circular 35/2005). Some witnesses can offer opposing evidence against the party that called them, these are called hostile or adverse witnesses.

13.2.3.2 Support for witnesses during investigations

Witnesses are likely to be unfamiliar with the procedures employed during investigations and some may also be a victim in the case. Victim Support and the Victim Communication and Liaison (VCL) scheme can provide support for victims and witnesses. The VCL reflects the CPS approach to directing services towards victims in greatest need, and takes account of the revised Code of Practice for Victims of Crime (MoJ, 2020). The witness service will also offer support at court for witnesses and victims.

Witnesses under 18 years of age and complainants in sexual cases always require special measures. Other vulnerable or intimidated witnesses may require special measures but further assessment will be required through the use of an MG2 form. More information on special measures can be found on the CPS website.

A witness may be granted anonymity in the interests of justice. Certain conditions must be met for a 'witness anonymity order' to be issued by a court. For example, the order (issued under the Coroners and Justice Act 2009) must be necessary to protect the safety of the witness or another person, to prevent any serious damage to property, or to prevent real harm to the public interest—and the court must take the witness's feelings into account on these matters. The order must also be seen as necessary for the defendant to receive a fair trial (and without the order either the witness would not testify or the public interest would be harmed if the witness were to testify without anonymity). The police must obtain as much corroborative evidence as possible in any case where witness anonymity might be involved. An important case involving witness anonymity is *R v Mayers (Jordan)* [2008] EWCA Crim 2989. It dealt with several separate investigations into murder and drug-dealing, and anonymous witnesses were allowed to provide evidence at the trials of several defendants. Appeals were made on the grounds that the witness anonymity orders should not have been allowed but the Court of Appeal upheld the decision.

13.2.3.3 Offenders as witnesses for the prosecution

Under the Serious Organised Crime and Police Act 2005 (SOCPA), agreements can be made with offenders who offer to assist with the prosecution of offences committed by others. The agreement must be in writing and could state, for example, that the person will not be prosecuted (an immunity notice under s 71) or that certain pieces of evidence will not be used (a 'restricted use undertaking' under s 72).

In order to benefit from the agreement, the person must fully admit their own criminality, agree to cooperate in full, provide all the information they have regarding the matters under investigation, and give evidence in court if required. A witness against the accused may also be a co-accused, as in the Rhys Jones murder investigation in 2007. In that case, the CPS originally planned to charge a co-accused with firearms offences but instead offered him immunity from prosecution provided he met certain conditions, including attending court and giving a truthful account. He accepted these terms and the CPS was able to use the new evidence to charge a suspect with murder.

13.2.4 Evidence in investigations

Evidence comes in many different forms and can be categorized in many different ways. The nature and types of evidence are covered during initial police training, for example modules within the 'Conducting Investigations' subject area of the National Policing Curriculum. We focus here on a number of important features and aspects of evidence as it relates to criminal investigations. In section 13.3 we focus specifically on the forensic aspects of evidence, where importance is placed on what is commonly referred to as the *continuity of evidence* or the *chain of evidence*. The reporting or arresting police officer is responsible for ensuring the secure retention of evidence. There must be an auditable trail for evidence, from the moment it was discovered or recovered until it is produced in court. A failure to properly package and record evidence can lead to later problems with its appearance as a court exhibit. For instance, Weir (2007) criticized the police for the 'cavalier disregard for ... integrity' in the case of *R v Hoey* (NICC 49) regarding evidence recovered and stored in relation to the Omagh bombing. In complex cases, an exhibits officer will be appointed and in some police services a designated specialist is responsible for safeguarding certain materials, such as forensic items or CCTV footage.

Before turning to the forensic aspects of evidence, there are two important types of evidence that a police officer needs to be aware of: *hearsay*, and *bad character*.

13.2.4.1 Hearsay evidence

We refer to evidence as hearsay when it is a second-hand account of events. A general principle in legal proceedings is that it should be possible to cross-examine and challenge a person providing a statement as evidence within court. This is clearly not possible if a second person is reporting in court on what another person has said, seen, or written outside court. The person in court, in such instances, does not have a first-hand account to offer, but is rather reporting on behalf of someone else. The hearsay rule therefore prohibits such second-hand accounts that cannot be adequately cross-examined.

However, there are many good reasons why the person who has witnessed something first-hand is unable to present in court and to be cross-examined. The person may be out of the country at the time of the court proceedings, or might have died.

The Criminal Justice Act 2003 therefore changed the law relating to the admissibility of hearsay evidence in criminal proceedings and can be seen as a major shift in attitude towards this type of evidence. The 2003 law was predicated upon the assertion that juries in particular could be trusted with more evidence than before, including hearsay evidence and the net effect of the 2003 changes was to increase the amount of evidence potentially admissible at trial. The old law was criticized (Spencer, 2016) for being too complicated, difficult to find (because it was in different Acts of Parliament or case law), and too inflexible. In an infamous trial for indecent assault (*R v Sparks* (1964)), the court would not allow a defendant to use hearsay evidence and he was convicted even though that evidence might have exonerated him. He subsequently appealed and was successful but on other grounds. In the 2003 Act there is a specific clause allowing for flexibility and admissibility of evidence if it would be in the interests of justice for a court to hear it.

A trainee officer does not have to learn all the details of all the provisions for hearsay, but a basic understanding serves to underline why it is vital for all officers to make a PNB record of exactly what was said, and to ensure that body-worn cameras are switched on.

13.2.4.2 Bad character evidence

Bad character evidence (BCE) can sometimes be used in criminal cases and officers should always consider whether relevant BCE exists. Bad character is defined by s 98 of the Criminal Justice Act 2003 as evidence of:

- misconduct (including previous convictions, cautions, and offences for which a person has been charged but the charge has not been heard or the person was acquitted (s 112)); or
- a disposition towards misconduct, for example 'other reprehensible behaviour' (s 112), which, for instance, could include anti-social behaviour, persistent lying, and racist behaviour.

Thus, the law makes it clear that reprehensible behaviour falling short of a conviction counts as bad character, as well as obvious instances such as previous convictions. For instance, a person may have a propensity to be violent when drunk and this may become relevant in a case of assault against a family member, irrespective of whether the accused has been previously convicted in relation to similar behaviour. The evidence for BCE cannot come from the offence currently under investigation nor can it be related to the process of the current proceeding, eg the defendant not attending court when required. Therefore, police officers should record matters that might relate to BCE contemporaneously and provide such intelligence to the relevant department. This information could be crucial to a subsequent criminal investigation.

Here we have provided a simple overview of BCE to the extent it is relevant to the trainee officer. The CPS website provides information on BCE and the College of Policing APP website also contains further information (under the heading *Prosecution and case management*).

13.3 Forensic Investigation

This section is concerned with the use of forensic investigation and the role it plays in investigations. It does not seek to explain forensic science in depth, and will concentrate on the aspects of forensic investigation that are most relevant to providing leads and supporting investigations carried out by the police and other agencies.

13.3.1 Introduction to Forensic Investigation

Forensic investigation is a tripartite arrangement, which involves forensic science, the investigator, and the criminal justice system (CJS). For the most part forensic science is taken to be any science whose application to the legal system can support notions of guilt or innocence and potentially have a role in the investigation of an offence. To reduce it to its simplest: Forensic Investigation is about answering investigative questions, solving investigative problems, or filling gaps in knowledge using science.

Some key principles underpin the application of forensic science to criminal investigation, for example that:

- when two or more objects come into contact, they exchange material because all matter divides;
- all things are unique and can be individualized;

- the interpretation of forensic evidence is context-sensitive, which means that it is given meaning when its place or role within the investigation is understood.

13.3.1.1 Locard's Principle of Exchange and Divisibility

Edmond Locard (1877–1966) is credited with the development of his 'Principle of Exchange' where he asserted that material from the crime scene would be found on the suspect and vice versa. The original work has been reduced to the simpler expression that 'every contact leaves a trace'. For example, an offender could leave fingermarks, blood, and shoe marks at the crime scene and might take away fibres from fabrics such as curtains and carpets or glass fragments on their clothing; the contacts have left a trace. Importantly, the use of 'trace' implies that tiny quantities of physical material have been transferred, but the traces can be any size and can extend to impressions left by teeth, weapons, tyres, tools, and even digital traces. The transfers can be one-way, two-way, or more.

Locard's Principle is important principally because all matter is divisible if enough force is applied (Inman and Rudin, 2002); that is, objects break down during contact and, potentially, most things ultimately erode into smaller parts which can transfer to other objects.

Locard studied the work of Hans Gross (1904) which was later solidified by Kirk (1953) and both asserted that failures by investigators to find or understand physical evidence were the only real problems with forensic evidence, rather than the veracity of the evidence itself.

After finding this transferred material or impressions, we then need to show that it came from the source in question, such as a person or something associated with them.

13.3.1.2 Uniqueness and individualization

According to Kirk (1963, p 236) 'all objects in the universe are unique'. If true, then every material object that concerns forensic science should be considered as unique.

Many apparently identical objects become visibly or measurably unique during use because they develop 'individual characteristics'. A standard 'slot' screwdriver, for example, will be made on a production line, and every screwdriver will appear identical even though, theoretically, they are all unique. During subsequent use each screwdriver will develop clearer unique characteristics, which provide the means for a forensic scientist to tell them apart and, possibly, show that an object is associated with its source, whether screwdriver, fingerprint, blood, or bullet. In this case it has been 'individualized'. Typical examples include demonstrating that a specific sample of blood discovered on a weapon is shown to have come from a specific person.

Forensic science describes three levels of classification of evidence. To understand this, consider several unused, apparently identical, screwdrivers of the same brand. These will have:

- class characteristics, which are qualities produced by a controlled process, for instance, a 10 mm slot screwdriver;
- sub-class characteristics, which are the features on a batch of screwdrivers—these features may be imparted by poor quality control or minute changes in machine settings. One batch of screwdrivers may be almost imperceptibly different to other batches;
- individual characteristics, that are unique to a particular screwdriver. Kirk's statement tells us that screwdrivers are modified by use and acquire obvious 'accidental' damage. They are demonstrably different. In this case, the unique screwdriver can be 'matched' to the damage it caused.

The principle can be applied to all types of physical evidence, even naturally occurring material such as soil.

13.3.1.3 Applying theory to criminal investigation

Although any police officer may be involved in searching a crime scene, most scenes are examined by specially trained CSIs. Together, the CSI and investigator will use evidence of transfer to demonstrate that contact has *previously* occurred. Transfer can be demonstrated by the traces that comprise debris found at scenes of crime or on people and objects, or impressions which include prints made by fingers, shoes, tools, tyres, and so on. We must also remember the transfer of digital data held by computers, servers, mobile phones and emails etc.

Locard's Principle is primarily used to create physical links between the differing parts of an investigation by forensic scientists comparing a 'questioned sample' from the crime scene with a 'control' or 'exemplar' of known origin. This is set out in its simplest form in the following diagram for an offence against a person.

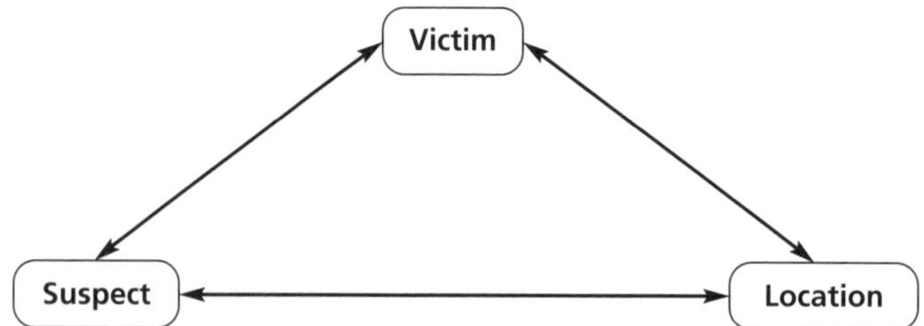

Locard's Principle states that transfers occur because all things erode or break down, so evidence will continue to change: fibres on the guilty party will be lost, shoes continue to wear out, screwdrivers are modified, and DNA decays. One key objective for the police, therefore, is to intervene as quickly as possible to recover the potential evidence from scene and suspect to prevent any further changes.

13.3.2 The role of the Crime Scene Investigator

The most visible example of a forensic investigator is the Crime Scene Investigator (CSI) who is normally attached to a Basic Command Unit. CSIs are responsible for examining crime scenes to harvest forensic evidence which is later used by forensic scientists. Indeed, they have been described as the 'scientist's hands' and their chief roles are to:

- photograph crime scenes, articles, or people associated with crime, such as weapons, injuries, victims, and suspects (but not so-called 'mug shots');
- locate, assess, and package physical or biological evidence (including fingermarks) from crime scenes;
- attend post-mortem examinations for suspicious deaths;
- provide advice to investigators on matters related to physical evidence, photography, prisoner sampling, and laboratory submissions, and;
- gather intelligence (from utterances, personal observations, or physical material) to support the National Intelligence Model (NIM) and for use in databases.

CSIs are also involved with non-crime incidents such as sudden deaths, suicides, and fatal industrial accidents on behalf of HM Coroners and in support of Health and Safety Executive investigations. They may also be involved in the recording of loss through fire prior to arson being ruled out, especially at high-value scenes and those of significant public interest.

Most CSIs in the UK police are police support staff attached to a constabulary's scientific support department, which might include departments responsible for photographic services, a laboratory for enhancing fingermark evidence and computer forensic investigators.

Investigators can capitalize upon forensic evidence by reading scene reports and statements made by attending personnel and forensic scientists, but the best understanding of the crime scene, the evidence, and its dynamics in the early stages of an investigation, particularly prior to interview, is achieved by speaking to the CSI who attended. The CSI might be able to reconstruct the incident tentatively, explaining how an incident occurred, the meaning of the evidence, which has been found, and what any laboratory results represent.

13.3.2.1 Applying forensic science to investigations

Forensic science is often concerned with two main forms of mainly physical evidence:

- corroborative evidence (material that will confirm or refute a hypothesis about the crime, for instance that a powder is, or is not, heroin) and
- inceptive evidence, which identifies an unknown, for example a person.

Forensic experts analyse and interpret evidence for the investigator to support the initial investigative phase or help build a case against a suspect in an evidential phase (Barclay, 2009, p 344) in an attempt to fill the investigator's identified knowledge gaps.

While the evidence from an expert witness may be pivotal in establishing the guilt or innocence of a suspect their role is actually to provide objective opinion: it is for others to establish the relevance and/or significance of this evidence as it relates to the innocence or guilt of the accused.

13.3.2.2 Working with forensic scientists

Efficient communication with forensic scientists is vital to the investigative process. In volume crime, this is normally carried out by the CSI but in major crime it will be a senior CSI and sometimes one or more investigators comprising a Forensic Management Team (FMT). In order to provide an efficient and effective service to the police, the forensic scientist expects unbroken continuity of evidence, excellent quality packaging to preserve the evidence, and clear communication about the investigative needs (referred to as 'points to prove' on lab forms). Communication with forensic laboratories, but not fingerprint bureaus, is conducted using the MG21 form and investigators are encouraged to seek guidance on it, and the best use of physical evidence, from CSIs.

Importantly, forensic evidence is context sensitive: the significance of physical evidence depends on its location and orientation within the scene and the time it was left there. For example, fingermarks found in a property may appear to be valuable, yet they may be rendered useless if the suspect was invited to a party in the premises before the incident occurred. A second string to contextual value relates to the relative rarity of a substance which has been encountered. For instance, polypropylene baler twine and wheat pollen are common in rural areas, yet rare in cities, and stained-glass windows are common in churches.

13.3.3 Types of forensic evidence

Forensic evidence is classified in a number of different ways, but here we have chosen a range of common evidential sources found at crime scenes and/or on people. This includes:

- *Fingerprints and fingermarks*
  Fingerprints are a useful and non-invasive form of evidence. The regulations governing their use by the police are provided in Code D, paras 4.1–4.8. Police officers receive training on how to fingerprint suspects using Livescan (in all main police stations), portable devices for use on patrol, and sometimes on ink systems. Livescan and portable scanners have the advantage of being digitally linked to IDENT1 through a 'Biometric Services Gateway', so they are quick and accurate. Ink systems include traditional copper plate and printers' ink, and peel-apart pre-inked strips. The latter have the advantage of being portable and they are mainly used to take elimination fingerprints from, for example, victims of crime.
- *DNA*
  Every cell in the human body—with a few exceptions—has a nucleus, which typically contains 23 pairs of chromosomes, and these are made up of genes. The genes are made of DNA and the nucleus of nearly every cell contains a complete copy of the DNA for the entire organism, so a cell from a person's cheek contains the same genetic material as a white cell from their blood. As with fingerprints, DNA can be taken from arrested people in custody and searched against crime scene material—because the CJS accepts that the type of DNA (called Short Tandem Repeats, or STRs) used in most forensic analyses is unique to the individual, the only exception being identical siblings.
- *Toxicology samples*
  This is a specialist field engaged in the analysis of poisons and drugs and may be crucial to an investigation, to calculate whether a person is over the drink-drive limit, or to establish if alcohol or drugs have influenced behaviour, such as violence or drowsiness, or to establish the presence of drugs such as those used in 'date-rape' offences, or to establish the causes of illness and death.
  Roadside breath tests are the most common forms of toxicological measurement carried out by the police, but these are normally used as screening tests prior to more stringent evidential tests. A variety of field-test kits can be employed to screen for drugs but the opinion of an expert toxicologist should be sought to provide evidence suitable for a prosecution, unless local policy allows the suspect to make a guilty plea prior to caution or if there is an intervention model in place at the time. Commonly, blood or urine is sent for analysis for toxins but other samples from the body tissue of deceased victims (including from the eyes) may also be used, depending upon the circumstances. Toxicology samples must always be treated as a potential health hazard.

- *Physical fits*
  A physical fit (sometimes called a mechanical fit or jigsaw fit) between two or more fragments of an object is an extended application of the theory that all things are unique and can be individualized. In its simplest form, imagine an object breaks into several parts. If those parts are later found separately then it is a reasonable presumption that they originate from the same source. This would provide exceptionally powerful evidence in a police investigation. For example, small fragments of a blade were found in the chin of a deceased person and a suspect was found in possession of a damaged craft knife. The blade of the craft knife and the metal fragments were reconstructed successfully to rebuild the blade in its original form.
- *Trace evidence—typically very small quantities of material*
  Trace material can be any material transferred from the suspect to the crime scene and/or victim and vice versa. It ranges from common materials such as fibres, glass fragments, and paint flakes transferred during property crimes to the more exotic, such as pollens, soils, and even insects or their fragments. Imagination is important here and consideration should not be limited to any specific groups: creativity is a vital element in forensic investigation.
- *Impressions or marks*
  Marks left by fingers, shoes, tools, tyres, stamping machines, printers, and typewriters can be a direct 'stamped' effect, but are sometimes made up of irregular scrapes and smudges and even cutting or drilling marks. All forms of impression can be easily destroyed: be cautious about what is touched and where people walk. All forms of impression evidence are capable of providing intelligence and can be readily compared to the object suspected to have left the mark. Common examples of impressions come from footwear, tyres, and bite marks.
- *Documents*
  This includes typically all letters, paperwork, invoices, cheques, application forms, and any other written material, whether handwritten or printed by typewriter, computer printer, or other device. The writing on a document, eg a hate-mail letter, can be compared with material obtained during the investigation, including handwriting samples provided by a suspect. A document can also be analysed for 'impressed' handwriting, typically found when a pad of paper is used and an impression of writing on one page is transferred to the pages below. This can be enhanced using Electrostatic Detection Apparatus (ESDA). Printers and typewriters can also be analysed and compared with a specimen document. The presence of printer-head faults or damage to paper caused by rollers may be reproduced under laboratory conditions and compared with the suspect document. The physical features of paper can also be examined, such as tear marks, staple holes, and batch faults in envelopes. Other features such as watermarks, obliterations, paper type, security inks, and 'reactive fibres' can be analysed in a number of ways, for example by microscopy and by using a Video Spectral Comparator (VSC) which employs different wavelengths of light and can identify handwritten additions to cheques and payment forms, and reveal obliterated text.
- *Firearms*
  The National Ballistics Intelligence Service (NABIS) can examine used bullets and cartridge cases for intelligence purposes at their hub laboratories. The examiners will look for marks and use their database to establish links between crime scenes where bullets and cartridges have previously been found. Recovered firearms are also test-fired at the hub laboratory to generate spent bullets and cartridges for comparison with evidence already in the database. The functionality of the NABIS database is like that of IDENT1 and the NDNAD; as links can be generated, so crime series can potentially be identified and detected. Clearly, one firearm can be used at several crime scenes so the intelligence provided by NABIS can be very useful.
- *Digital devices*
  The quantity of digital data stored in computers, servers, mobile phones, and a wide array of storage devices make digital evidence problematic for CSIs and other personnel attending crime scenes. Computer forensic investigators are employed by all police services and are routinely required to examine digital devices because our daily activities, movements, and communications are logged and stored by them—even after the data has been assiduously deleted. The sheer amount of usable data from any form of device that processes data is staggering. The Golden Rule with all forms of digital data is: do not interfere with it without either following strict local protocols or garnering clear advice from an expert. (See Chapter 14.)

- *Security marking systems*
  Unique markers or *taggants* are used on products for identification purposes. These increasingly employ a fluorescent dye which glows under ultraviolet (UV) light and may contain a range of techniques, such as microdots and chemical traces (including synthetic DNA) that form a code which is unique to a specific object or place. Some types of microdots are virtually indestructible and can even withstand the very high temperatures required to smelt (stolen) metals. Such high-tech security markers can be applied to individual at-risk assets, eg jewellery, and to larger surfaces such as sheets of lead on church roofs. They can also be incorporated into metals or into pastes and sprays, which activate in burglaries.
  It is good practice to scan recovered property and burglary suspects with a UV light and any fluorescence should be seen as suspicious and reported to a CSI, who will take samples from suspects and scenes as necessary, and can arrange for further analysis.
- *CCTV*
  At some crime scenes, CCTV or dashcam footage might provide vital information. Even digital storage systems are likely to be overwritten at some stage, so any delay in obtaining recordings should be kept to a minimum. Copies of CCTV recordings can be obtained with appropriate authorization and a forensic analyst can conduct a more thorough analysis. CCTV and dashcam footage should not be ignored or deleted if the activity which concerns the investigator is not seen on the recording. A great deal of evidence can be recovered from crime scenes, victims, suspects, prisoners, and witnesses, and this can be compared to data stored in a variety of databases, such as IDENT1 (the national fingerprint database), the National DNA Database (NDNAD), and footwear collections. The information taken even from a crime scene with limited evidence can be valuable when it is compared to other crime scenes, including the MO, the size of tool marks, types of shoes worn, and even the behaviour of the suspect. This information can be stored in crime systems (such as Athena) or forensic management databases and may be capable of linking offences.

It is also worth considering that many types of physical evidence can be derived from digital devices too, for example fingermarks, DNA, and fibres. There may be a conflict of priorities when considering the seizure of a digital device so advice should be sought from a CSI and computer forensic investigator.

13.3.3.1 Fingerprint database *IDENT1*

The IDENT1 database is a national system that contains records of the fingerprints ('tenprints') and palm prints of arrested persons, and crime-scene marks recovered by CSIs and other personnel. It also contains records from vulnerable people at risk from exploitation. The Biometric Commissioner routinely reports that IDENT1 contains about 8.45 million individuals' tenprints taken under the PACE Act 1984 and more than 2 million unidentified crime-scene marks.

The IDENT1 database carries out three processes:

- **mark to mark**—new crime-scene marks are compared with other crime-scene marks to search for links between offences;
- **print to mark**—new tenprints and palm prints are compared to crime-scene marks (and vice versa) whenever a new person's prints are taken by a scanner in custody, or when a new crime scene mark is uploaded; and
- **print to print**—new tenprints are compared to those already on file to confirm identity or establish that an arrested person is not using a pseudonym. This takes about ten minutes.

13.3.3.2 The UK National DNA Database

Just like IDENT1, the NDNAD contains material taken from people in custody and crime scenes.

The NDNAD carries out three processes:

- **crime scene to crime scene**—new crime-scene samples are compared with other crime-scene samples to search for links between offences;
- **CJ sample to scene**—newly taken DNA is compared to crime scene samples (and vice versa) whenever a new person's DNA is taken in custody, or when new crime scene DNA is uploaded; and

- **CJ sample to CJ sample**—new DNA samples are compared with those already existing in the database. This is really just good housekeeping and assists data managers in identifying double sampling.

Approximately 531,000 new subject samples are added annually. Separate sections of the database also contain records of the DNA from many missing and vulnerable people. The database also stores records of DNA recovered from crime scenes, which may have been found as blood, saliva on cigarette ends, bite marks, and so on. The Biometric Commissioner typically reports that the database contains approximately 6.7 million subject profiles and 660,000 crime-scene samples. Most of the retained samples (approximately 80 per cent) are from males (Sampson, 2021). Currently, it matches over 30,000 crime scenes to subjects annually.

Potentially, its greatest strength lies in making 'cold hits' which is when a sample from a crime scene or victim identifies a suspect, often in older cases where the crime has never been solved. For instance, in 1988 a man sexually assaulted two young girls in Canterbury, Kent, and was not identified at the time. In 2001, he was arrested in Derbyshire for shoplifting and the arresting PC took his DNA sample. It was matched to DNA found at the Kent crime scene and he later admitted the offences and was sentenced to 15 years in prison.

13.3.4 What samples should be taken?

Upon delivery to a custody area, all arrested persons are subject to mandatory sampling where their fingerprints, DNA, and a photograph are taken. Constabulary policy may also require the scanning of shoe patterns. DNA will not be required if a successful profile has been created previously. Sampling of suspects for evidence to link them to recent crimes is carried out as soon after arrest as possible to recover the maximum available material. Remember that in major crimes and sexual offences there may be an operational order in place for the suspect so you should consult it and almost certainly contact a CSI for advice if you wish to carry out Livescan fingerprinting or DNA swabbing prior to the arrival of the medical practitioner, because trace evidence can be lost during these processes.

The person being sampled should stand on a paper sheet, which will catch any debris which falls from them.

Typically, the sampling is conducted from the top downwards and might include:

- Swabs of hands and face for blood or security taggants.
- Nails may have skin or other debris beneath them. They are cut or scraped by using a 'nail module' which typically contains cocktail sticks, A4 paper, bags, and clippers. The samples from each hand form separate exhibits.
- Mouths are of interest because forensic odontologists can compare the teeth to bite marks, the mouth may contain some form of residue, such as DNA from another person, and the interior linings of the cheeks are a good source of DNA for the DNA database.
- Hats and religious head coverings, such as turbans—be especially sensitive and respectful when dealing with religious garments.
- Hair (including head hair and beard hair) could contain trace evidence such as blood, glass, plant material, foreign hairs, and other particulates and should be dealt with before clothing is removed. The hair may be combed, cut to remove matted material like blood, or pulled. Pulled hair is also an alternative DNA sample.
- Upper clothing is a rich source of trace evidence, particularly the blood of the wearer and other people after an assault. Clothing may attract evidence and, of course, shed fibres and even leave impressions on suitable surfaces. It is best practice to record colours, makes, sizes, stains, and damage in order to prevent another person having to open the bag to view logos etc which tie-in with CCTV footage and witness statements.
- Lower clothing is best taken after upper clothing but, typically, the shoes prevent the easy removal of trousers. Treat as for upper clothing and, in particular, trousers should be searched, and any objects removed and exhibited separately.
- Footwear is incredibly valuable as a source of blood in assaults, footwear marks are left in many scenes and other traces like mud and glass might be found in the tread. Shoes should always be packaged separately.
- Underwear, while consideration to proportionality should be made, is especially valuable after sexual assaults. It is not normally taken in property crimes and minor assaults.

The types of sample taken from victims and suspects will depend on the nature of the offence. The following table describes the **minimum** samples for consideration (represented by a tick in the table). Note that PACE Code D requires that the suspect be informed about the reason for sampling (including speculative searches) and that an inspector has given authority. The Human Rights Act 1998 must be complied with, and the reasons for taking a particular sample must be noted in each case.

	Cheque or other fraud. Hate mail	Burglary or other property crime	Sexual assault or rape	Theft from motor vehicle with damage caused	ABH and other assaults	Homicide victims and suspects
Blood and/or urine for toxicology			✓		✓	✓
Clothing (inner)			✓		✓	✓
Clothing (outer)		✓	✓	✓	✓	✓
DNA	✓	✓	✓	✓	✓	✓
Fingerprints	✓	✓	✓	✓	✓	✓
Hair (combing)		✓	✓	✓	✓	✓
Hair (pulled/cut)		✓	✓	✓	✓	✓
Handwriting sample	✓					
Photographs of injuries		When relevant	When relevant	When relevant	When relevant	Effectively mandatory
Sexual offence kit			Mandatory			Normally used
Shoes	✓	✓	✓	✓	✓	✓

Evidence sometimes needs to be collected at hospitals. It is important to note that hospital priorities are about life saving, not evidence, but medical personnel will do their best to help police officers and CSIs on condition that recovering evidence will not interfere with the health or treatment of individuals. It is **critically important** that officers attending hospitals do their utmost to dissuade medical personnel from cutting clothes off patients in such a way that tears or cut marks in clothing are 'cut through'.

- Patients may be given large quantities of donated blood or plasma which affects toxicology results if blood is drawn later. If possible, it is best practice to track down any pre-transfusion samples that have been sent to the pathology lab and ask for them to be retained.

Brand-new, unused packaging equipment must be used to prevent contamination of the evidential material and specific kits are available, for example for the sampling of hair or urine, and these should be used where accessible.

13.3.4.1 Sampling from crime scenes

This is a complex area so CSI trainers provide specific training for new police officers and many of those on refresher or CID courses. The material in this Handbook provides a mere flavour and can be used as a guide, but local CSIs are best able to provide the most up-to-date information on local force protocols, especially in light of ISO requirements.

A police officer may seize exhibits in the course of their duty at crime scenes, for example when part of a search team or if it seems there are only one or two items to seize and they can be safely recovered without a CSI, such as documents, or a single moveable shoe mark, but note that local policies on CSI deployment and evidence seizure must be followed. There may also be situations where the CSI is unable to attend or where evidence could be lost if not recovered immediately, eg a shotgun cartridge on a windy day.

13.3.4.2 Quality standards

It is important to understand that quality is critically important in the crime-scene examination arena, and this extends to laboratory analyses. The chief objectives of quality mechanisms are to ensure that rigorous standards and integrity are maintained in the crime scene to court process, and of no lesser importance, that the public can have confidence in the processes involved. The collection and recording of crime-scene evidence is covered by ISO 17020 and laboratory processes are covered by ISO 17025 with adherence to other standards, such as

ILAC G19. Both sets of ISO standards are administered by UKAS in the UK and are required by the Forensic Regulator as described in their Codes of Practice and Conduct (Forensic Science Regulator, 2021).

13.4 The Criminal Procedure and Investigations Act 1996

The CPIA relates to the conduct of all aspects of an investigation but is considered here more specifically as of particular importance in relation to disclosure. The Act makes an important distinction between revelation and disclosure; the former relates to material revealed to the prosecutor by the police on the relevant forms (MG6 series), whilst disclosure relates to material disclosed to the defence by the prosecutor. Much of the recent legislation relating to investigation was enacted to combat fears that the police had historically withheld important information, ignored exonerating facts, and constructed cases against individuals who were sometimes innocent. High-profile miscarriages of justice often demonstrated these failings in abundance (such as the 'Guildford Four' and the 'Maguire Seven', the 'Birmingham Six', the case of the Taylor sisters, and Stefan Kiszko). For more information on these and other miscarriage of justice cases, see Eddlestone (2012).

The codes also set out the key roles in an investigation as follows:

- the investigator(s), defined as any police officer or employee who plays an active part in an investigation;
- the OIC who directs an investigation;
- a disclosure officer (more serious investigations may have more than one, eg there may be a separate disclosure officer for sensitive intelligence-based material); and
- the prosecutor who takes responsibility for the conduct of the criminal proceedings.

The definition of a criminal investigation in s 22 of the CPIA (and honed by the Code of Practice) makes it clear that investigators have certain responsibilities and duties, and that these apply right from the very start of a criminal investigation. Relevant material (any evidence that might be pertinent) must be recorded and retained and lines of enquiry that might exonerate a suspect must also be pursued. Subtly, the Act and Codes promoted a shift towards truth-seeking in investigations rather than trying to prove the guilt of a suspect. The CPIA should be seen as a set of legal responsibilities that run through an investigation from the moment it begins. In an investigation into a major crime, a disclosure officer and other staff will often be appointed at the earliest stage to ensure that all relevant material is dealt with in the correct fashion.

The CPIA requires investigators to provide a list of unused material to the prosecutor, who will then consider what material might need to be disclosed to the defence out of fairness. Seen from this perspective, it might seem that the disclosure procedures do not need to be considered until the very end of an investigation. But, in fact, the CPIA and its associated codes require exactly the opposite, and this is by no means fully appreciated, even today.

Material that is not used as evidence for the prosecution case will be revealed to the CPS which then decides which parts of it should be disclosed to the defence. You should note that *revealing to the CPS* and *disclosing to the defence*, are both often referred to as the *disclosure test*, and this can cause confusion. The information presented here is drawn from the CPIA and its associated Code of Practice, and the Disclosure Manual (CPS, 2018a).

To illustrate the importance of this issue, imagine a case in a local magistrates' court. The prosecution counsel opens the case by outlining the circumstances of a major public disturbance in a town centre, witnessed by a number of people. Officers from the nearby police station and surrounding areas had attended and a woman was arrested. Statements from the arresting officer and witnesses provided strong evidence of an assault by the defendant. In court, one of the witnesses gives evidence for the prosecution and is then cross-examined by the defence counsel. Next, the arresting officer (AO) takes the witness stand and the prosecution asks them to outline the evidence of the arrest. After this has been done, the defence counsel rises, and says:

> **Defence:** Officer, we will hear shortly from my client that there were several other police officers at the scene of the alleged assault. Who were these other officers and why are they not giving evidence today?

AO: There were approximately ten officers at the scene; I do not know their names as they came from a neighbouring police area.

Defence: Officer, the last witness has told this court that when you arrived at the location you had a conversation with him about what actually happened. Where are your notes of that conversation?

AO: I have no record of the conversation; I remembered the name and address and then a statement was taken later.

The defendant now takes the stand and tells the court the reason for the assault was self-defence and that the arresting officer was completely wrong about how drunk she was. The defence counsel asks his client if there is anyone who can corroborate this, and she replies that if the other police officers and witnesses had been at court they would be able to confirm her account. The focus of the defence lawyer has now switched from what his client actually did at the scene, which may seem the most important issue, to examining whether the police officer had kept proper records of the events, including whether the identity of the other police officers present had been noted. The defence applies to stay the proceedings on the basis that his client is being deprived of the right to a fair trial under Sch 1, Art 6 to the Human Rights Act 1998, stating that the prosecution has effectively prevented the defence from accessing a number of witnesses who are crucial to their client's defence.

Whether the application would have been successful or not in this imaginary case is irrelevant here: the point we wish to make is that a lot of time and effort can be wasted if certain information is not recorded, and that cases can be lost as a consequence.

Investigations need to be conducted as a search for the truth and police investigators are obliged to search for evidence that will not only point to guilt but also to innocence. It could be said that disclosure helps to create a 'level playing field' because the prosecution has access to significant professional services and capabilities for producing evidence for the prosecution, while the defence case is sometimes constructed by only one person, the defence solicitor.

13.4.1 Relevant material

Material is said to be relevant when it has a bearing on any offence under investigation or any person being investigated, or on the surrounding circumstances of the case. 'Material' is any information and objects of any kind obtained in the course of a criminal investigation and includes written materials, moving or still images, mobile data, software, and information given orally.

In general terms, all relevant material obtained or generated during the course of an investigation must be recorded and retained, even if it is not subsequently used by the prosecution. If it is not recorded correctly, or is not retained, then it is 'lost' to the defence and hence has not been properly shared with them through the CPS. This could be a serious loophole that can be exploited by the defence. The responsibility to record and retain relevant material does not relate just to prosecution material but also to material that might assist the defence. As an example, imagine that CCTV recordings of an incident involving assault at a nightclub in the centre of a town have been collected. If the recording showed the suspect talking to a security guard outside the club, this could be an alibi for the suspect and the material would be relevant. However, it can be difficult to decide whether materials are or will be relevant because the defence strategy cannot be predicted in advance. CCTV and dashcam footage should not be ignored if the activity which concerns the investigator is not seen on the recording. Such actions may be challenged at appeal: in *R (Ebrahim) v Feltham Magistrates' Court* [2001] 1 All ER 831, the investigating officer did not seize a CCTV tape because he saw nothing of significance on it, but this was challenged on the ground that a fair trial would not be received as a result. Recordings are disclosable material under the CPIA.

It is sometimes necessary to liaise with other organizations or individuals when building a case file. This should take into account the circumstances under which the information is shared. There are instances where there is a statutory obligation to share information (eg under a freedom of information request). In other situations, there may be a statutory power to share information but not an obligation. Any statutory purpose for sharing the information must be identified and, if there is none, the risk of sharing it must be assessed. This will take into account the source of the information and the possibility of its further dissemination, the common law duty of confidentiality, and possible breaches of the Human

Rights Act 1998 and the General Data Protection Regulation 2018. Police services often have Information Sharing Agreements (ISAs) that help to streamline the exchange of information. Any sharing of personal information, eg medical information or religious or political beliefs, must be necessary for the particular purpose; it must not be shared out of mere curiosity or interest. The information must be accurate, judged on its own merits, and decided on a case-by-case basis, and its relevance should be clearly explained. The College of Policing document *Information management: Sharing police information* (available online) provides further details and explanations.

13.4.2 Record, retain, review, and reveal

The officer in charge of the investigation is responsible for ensuring that relevant material is recorded in a durable or retrievable form, for example in writing, on tape, or on a computer drive. The record should be made when the material is received or as soon as possible afterwards. The contents of any material (eg a recording) deemed not relevant should be summarized before discarding the material.

The following materials are routinely recorded and retained (para 5.4 of the CPIA Code of Practice):

- crime reports (including crime report forms, relevant parts of incident report books, and officers' PNBs);
- custody records;
- records derived from recordings of telephone messages (eg 999 calls) containing descriptions of an alleged offence or offender;
- final versions of witness statements (and draft versions where their content differs from the final version);
- any exhibits mentioned in witness statements (unless they have been returned to their owner on the understanding that they will be produced in court if required);
- interview records (written, audio, or video records of interviews with actual or potential witnesses or suspects);
- CSI crime scenes worksheets (which might be electronic), evidence submission forms, and photographs;
- communications between the police and experts such as forensic scientists (but not the prosecutor), reports of work carried out by experts, and schedules of scientific material prepared by the expert for the investigator for the purposes of criminal proceedings;
- records of the first description of a suspect by each potential witness who purports to identify or describe the suspect, whether or not the description differs from subsequent descriptions by that or other witnesses; and
- any material casting doubt on the reliability of a witness.

There is a particularly important point concerning potential witnesses who the police know about but have not interviewed. In the case of *R v Heggart and Heggart* (November 2000 (CA)), it was determined that the courts should automatically assume that any evidence from uninterviewed witnesses would either undermine the prosecution case or assist the defence case. Therefore, a record should be made of any witness details and what they observed in relation to the incident at the scene. There is, however, a notion of proportionality here: there would be no expectation to record the details of all spectators at a football match.

Material relevant to an investigation must be retained for a certain period of time. The length of time varies, depending on whether the case continues to court, the outcome, and the length of sentence following a conviction (see para 5.8 of the CPIA Code for more detail). If the case goes to court, some of the relevant material will be exhibited as part of the prosecution case, but some will not. This 'unused material' will be 'revealed' to the CPS which will then decide whether it should be disclosed to the defence. This makes reviewing of material from the start of the investigation through to trial essential.

13.4.3 Disclosure

Disclosure is providing the defence with access to any material, which has not previously been disclosed, and which could possibly be used to undermine the prosecution case against the accused or otherwise assist their case. The CPS decides which material should be disclosed, and the police are usually responsible for implementing any subsequent disclosure. In routine and minor cases, the arresting officer or the case officer will also be the disclosure officer. In more serious cases, the disclosure officer is a specific and dedicated specialist and not necessarily a police officer.

The forms used for disclosure are MG6 B, C, D, and E. The Streamline Disclosure Certificate (SDC) can be used for a summary case at a magistrates' court where a not guilty plea is anticipated; the SDC will then replace the MG6C. The disclosure officer ensures that copies of these forms are provided to the CPS. The CPS reviews the forms and decides what else should be disclosed and when. Some of the more sensitive information revealed to the CPS will not be disclosed, such as personal details of a CHIS. The police will then disclose the selected items to the defence.

TASK 1

1. Reference was made earlier to material that is relevant but will not be used as evidence. In relation to the disclosure process, what is the term for this material?
2. Who is responsible for examining the records created during the investigation with a view to revealing the material to the prosecutor?
3. Who makes the decision regarding what unused material is actually disclosed to the defence?

The failure to disclose certain information led to 20 convictions being quashed in the high-profile case of *R v Barkshire and others* [2011] EWCA Crim 1885. The appellants had been convicted of conspiracy to commit aggravated trespass in preparation for climate change protests at a power station. The prosecution had failed to disclose the actions of an undercover police officer who had infiltrated the group and could have been seen to be inciting the events. The convictions of a further 29 appellants involving the same police officer were also quashed (see *R v Bard (Theo)* [2014] EWCA Crim 463). A number of other high-profile cases have also highlighted the prosecution's failure to provide the defence with potentially exonerating material. The majority of cases coming to light were rape cases where material was only discovered after trials had commenced (Dodd, 2017; Bowcott, 2018). The MPS undertook urgent reviews of 600 similar cases to establish the extent of the problem.

13.4.3.1 Pre-Charge Engagement, Investigation Management Document, and the Disclosure Management Document

The nature of Pre-Charge Engagement (PCE) as set out in the Attorney-General's Guidelines on Disclosure 2020 (AGG) is to ensure that there is a clear system in place to promote early and effective communication between the investigator and prosecutor on the approach to take. If using PCE Information, it should be provided to the suspect or their representative before or after the interview and an explanation given as to the process in a way that is easily understood. PCE can take place at any time after the first PACE interview and up until the commencement of Charge, so this can include periods whilst on bail pending decision to charge. It is a voluntary process that may be terminated at any time but it can be initiated by the investigator, prosecutor, the suspect, or the suspect's representative by joint agreement. Primarily it allows:

- The suspect to comment on any proposed further lines of inquiry they might identify.
- The suspect to provide access to known digital material that has a bearing on the allegation and reveal passwords or encryption keys linked to evidence.
- Agreeing any key word searches of digital material that the suspect would like carried out.
- Obtaining a suspect's consent to access medical records.
- The suspect identifying and providing contact details of any potential witnesses.
- Clarifying whether any expert or forensic evidence is agreed and, if not, whether the suspect's representatives intend to instruct their own expert, including timescales for this.

Any PCE can be undertaken face to face or via correspondence, but a written record should always be made and retained. It is important in the interest of fairness that disclosure of material must be considered as part of the PCE process to prevent suspects being misled as to the strength of the prosecution case.

In some cases where PCE is being considered, the investigator and prosecutor will need to consult so that the details of the PCE can be considered and agreed regarding areas such as further lines of enquiry in relation to examination of digital material, identifying other lines of enquiry, and discussions around expert and forensic evidence.

The Investigation Management Document (IMD) was introduced in December 2020. Central to the National Disclosure Improvement Plan it encourages a 'thinking' approach to disclosure. This means that CPIA considerations must be integral to investigators' identification and execution of reasonable lines of enquiry (RLE) from report to court (CPS, 2022a). The IMD will see that reasonable lines of enquiry are documented and explained by investigators at the outset of the investigation. The CPS will then use the IMD to inform the Disclosure Management Document (DMD). The IMD will be used when there is a need for the DMD to be completed.

The Disclosure Management Document (DMD) sets out how all seized electronic media and data are managed. The prosecution must explain to the defence and the court what has been done (or will be done) and why. The DMD should be provided to the defence and the court before the plea and case management hearing. The defence are invited to identify any additional lines of enquiry that they consider to be reasonable. The judge can then manage the case robustly from the outset.

The use of the DMD was extended in November 2019 and it is now used in the following instances:

- all cases where social media/phone evidence is crucial;
- GBH and wounding, and GBH with intent;
- murder and attempted murder;
- drug trafficking and supply offences; and
- rape and other serious sexual offences cases.

The DMD was introduced in response to problems around the sheer quantity of digital evidence. In the case of *R v R and others* [2015] EWCA Crim 1941, the police seized 85 computers and other devices between 2007 and 2011, and the subsequent review of the material took several years. This was felt to be far too long and The Hon Sir Vivian Ramsey gave specific advice on how police should manage digital material henceforth. The first recommendation was to put the prosecution 'in the driving seat' at the initial disclosure stage. It was also felt that there should be a more considered approach when deciding between seizing electronic devices or downloading data *in situ*. Other considerations included selecting the appropriate equipment and software for reviewing data, how to choose the words or phrases to find relevant material, and material that might be considered legally privileged.

Since 2015, a number of judges have also expressed a lack of confidence in the prosecution's ability to manage the disclosure process (HMICFRS, 2017b), and the collapse of the Liam Allen case (see CPS, 2018b) drew yet more attention to the problems around reviewing and disclosing digital media. It is hoped that the broader introduction and use of the DMD in 2018 will help to avoid such problems in the future.

13.5 The Investigation Stage by Stage

The response to priority and volume crimes involves many different police staff, from call-handlers to trained investigators. Most incidents are dealt with by the FAO who will often be the only investigator for the case.

The quality of an investigation and the chances of a successful prosecution are enhanced by actions taken early on in the investigation. These actions include locating, gathering, and retaining material, and making an initial report. Call-handlers, frontline support staff, and police officers are all obliged to record, retain, and reveal information to the investigating officer or disclosure officer, and must follow the specified procedures described for the 'Management of Police Information' as set out in the CPIA and its associated Code of Practice. If other investigators are subsequently involved, they may benefit from questioning and gathering evidence from the person who originally reported the crime and from the person who received and wrote the initial report.

Some of what follows is an interpretation of the VCMM (*Practice Advice on the Management of Priority and Volume Crime (The Volume Crime Management Model)*, 2nd edn (NPIA and ACPO, 2009)). This document and the College of Policing APP provide further detail relating to investigations. Here we have attempted to outline the procedures adopted in a 'typical' police service, with the investigation of priority and volume crime presented as a series of separate activities for clarity. In practice, however, they are more likely to overlap and merge into a single process, and may not all necessarily feature in any particular investigation nor in the precise order implied.

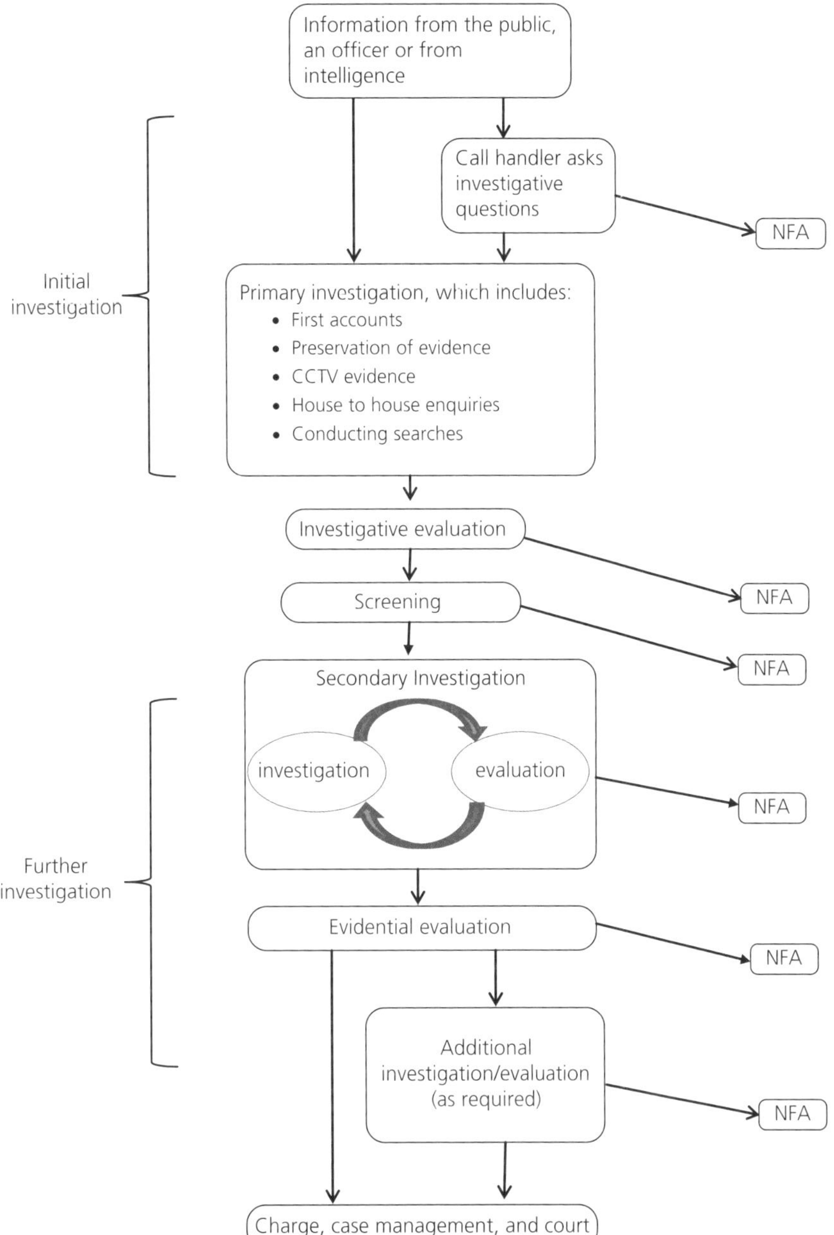

At any stage of the investigation it might become clear that no further action is required (NFA) or that certain actions are necessary, for example to arrest the suspect. When the decision is NFA, intelligence systems may be updated and the case will be filed as undetected. If further evidence or information comes to light, the case can be reopened.

Trainee police officers will be involved in both the primary and secondary investigations into priority and volume crimes during their second year of initial training. The actions outlined here could provide evidence of competence at PIP Level 1, perhaps as part of the PCDA or DHEP.

An investigation has a starting point, and this is referred to as an Instigation. There are two routes this can happen, it might be a member of the public calling the police or police coming across an incident. The second route is a pro-active approach to a problem in the community such as drug dealing; this may require an intelligence and evidence building strategy that leads to an eventual prosecution. There can be other methods such as third-party referrals from agencies such as social services.

During any investigation there will be activities that take place to allow the gathering of material to understand what happened, who did what and how, where they went and with whom etc.

During an investigation an investigator will make lines of enquiry (LOE) to gather material. Those LOE will fall into two categories that will allow the more important material to be prioritized. When enquiries can locate and preserve evidence such as CCTV, answer important questions such as a person's alibi, or bring a conclusion to an investigation, they will be fast track actions. The less prioritized actions are known as other actions and are listed sequentially below.

Some parts of an investigation may require a more considered approach due to complexities such as interviewing a suspect or interrogating a mobile device. So, a plan of action to achieve defined objectives is required, such as identifying necessary actions, identifying the required resources, and recording key decisions to allow the investigation to progress effectively and efficiently.

Priority Lines of Enquiries (PLOE)

During the course of a more serious investigation, it may become evident there are parts of an investigation of which little is known. Perhaps a vehicle comes into an enquiry that may be linked to a suspect leaving the scene of a crime. As this vehicle may identify the offender or secure evidence, it may form a key part of the investigation. As little is known, a significant number of actions may help filling in large gaps of knowledge. Often strategies and lots of actions will fall out of PLOE.

Hypothesis

Investigators use hypotheses as a tool to gain focus in an investigation such as when lines of enquiry are hard to find. An investigator should consider all explanations based on material gathered during an investigation. As each hypothesis is created and deleted an investigator records their justification. All hypotheses created must be tested by creating lines of enquiry to prove/disprove. A hypothesis is generally used in more serious and complex crimes when sufficient material is available and all actions completed early in an investigation.

13.5.1 Initial investigation

Initial investigation covers a wide range of activities involving police officers and other policing staff. It begins at the very moment a police officer arrives at an incident or a call-handler answers a call from a member of the public. Some investigations are instigated proactively, for example as a consequence of research and development of intelligence gathering, others reactively, when new information becomes available from sources such as:

- the general public;
- partnership agency reports;
- intelligence derived from other crimes or new information received about an old crime;
- police actions, for example discovering a cannabis factory.

13.5.1.1 Call handling as initial investigation

Many investigations start when a member of the public calls the police or emergency services. Call-handlers play a key role in the initial investigation and screening, for example their guidance to a caller may help to preserve forensic material at a scene. Their questions are part of an initial investigation and they will then help to determine what needs to be done next. Call-handlers collect a large amount of information and may use scripts or computer dropdown menus to help to ensure all relevant information is gathered. They will use some of the information to conduct a risk assessment, probably using the 'THRIVE' risk management tool, an acronym that stands for 'Threat, Harm, Risk, Investigation, Vulnerability, Engagement' (but to which we can also add 'Prevention and Intervention'). These are the key considerations when evaluating any given situation. The THRIVE tool articulates with both the Code of Ethics and NDM and helps a police service react with the appropriate level of response. In summary, a call-handler will make an assessment regarding:

- whether a **Threat** exists, or is implied, to harm a person or property;

- where the **Harm** could be either physical or psychological;
- how likely the **Risk** of action leading to harm is of being carried out;
- what **Investigative** actions are required regarding the scene, people, and evidence and whether attendance is required to find out more about the problem or crime;
- the **Vulnerability** of a person, in the circumstances described (which may impact on them not being able to protect either themselves or other people, or their own property or the property of another).

In addition, the call-handler is likely to end the call with:

- **Engagement**—consideration of further engagement (particularly if the caller is one of a 'hard to reach' group); signposting to other sources of police information or other agencies.

Any incident that has given rise to the call will be graded according to the level of police response required (typically as 'immediate', 'priority', 'scheduled' (eg a later phone call)). Depending on the BCU deployment policy, officers may be dispatched to a location (there may be a dedicated team of officers for attending volume crime scenes). If immediate attendance is not required, the caller will probably be transferred to a 'crime bureau' where details of the incident will be considered and recorded. This may be the end of the investigation for that incident unless any further relevant information comes to light.

13.5.1.2 Primary investigation

Police officers may be deployed to a location based upon the decisions of the call-handlers or may encounter an incident whilst on patrol. An officer's initial appraisal of the situation and a few preliminary questions will often be sufficient to determine whether any persons present could reasonably be suspected to have been involved in a criminal offence. The answers to these questions comprise the first or initial account, and would aim to establish:

- the type of alleged offence;
- the approximate time of the alleged offence;
- the scene of the alleged offence—only sufficient detail to understand what might be said in an interview; and
- how the alleged offence came to the notice of the police.

A police officer who is trying to discover whether, or by whom, an offence has been committed can question any person from whom useful information might be obtained (PACE Code A, Note 1). If there are reasonable grounds for suspecting that the person has been involved in a criminal offence, then a caution must be given before asking any further questions. Any conversation that takes place with a suspect before a caution is given should be summarized in a EPNB entry as it could be used in court. Once arrested, a suspect cannot be interviewed about the offence except at a police station (Code C, para 11.1) unless the delay would irretrievably hinder the investigation.

In the majority of cases, you may well have both suspect and victim or witness at the scene of the crime. If so, the most beneficial way of using witness evidence is to ask the witness to explain what they saw or heard in the presence and hearing of the suspect(s). Care must be taken in cases of domestic abuse or sexual offences where the victim might be reluctant to speak in front of the suspected abuser. This will be a judgement call by the officer based upon the circumstances of the case, a risk assessment regarding their own safety, and consideration of the safety of the witness and victim. The answers given by a witness should be recorded word for word in a EPNB entry or equivalent. The record could later be used as evidence in court as part of an officer's duty statement.

First accounts from witnesses can also provide the information required for planning an interview with the suspect or for constructing a 'handover package' for other officers to conduct the interviews. A first account can also be compared with an account given under oath verbally at court, and any inconsistencies between the two accounts would require an explanation from the witness.

Information about all the witnesses and any actions, statements, comments, or other relevant material must be recorded, ensuring compliance with the CPIA. A case could be undermined in court if the defence asked a police officer about something a witness had said and the officer has no record of it. If for some reason a EPNB record cannot be made, the record should be made separately.

Written police records of early accounts from victims and witnesses may be admissible as hearsay evidence if a witness or a victim cannot appear in court in person because they are seriously ill or unwilling to give evidence through fear. The police records of such witness accounts must be recorded verbatim. The names and addresses of any other people the victim has told about the incident should also be noted so these can be followed up.

In addition to obtaining first accounts, other actions are required as shown in the table.

Taking a report of a crime	All actions taken to trace witnesses and suspects should be recorded. A list should be made of any other enquiries that have been made, or could be made
The crime scene	The scene should be preserved for the CSI to avoid contamination. This might require a cordon for a large or serious crime scene
CCTV evidence	The location of cameras that could have recorded the incident should be recorded (for CPIA purposes and evidence recovery). The CCTV hard copy should be preserved, recovered, and exhibited where possible
Managing witnesses	First accounts must be recorded, including full names and addresses. These accounts might suggest further potential witnesses and these should be recorded in full
House-to-house enquiries	These are likely to concern witnesses or potential witnesses. A record should be made of all persons spoken to and of any absent potential witnesses (for a future visit). The content of the discussions should be carefully noted including any refusal to reply
Other evidence	Photographs, plans, and maps might suggest opportunities for obtaining forensic evidence. All documents, captured texts, images, or sequences from electronic devices should be retained
Taking statements	Statements should be obtained as a matter of urgency where violence has occurred (or been threatened), where a suspect has been detained, or if witness contamination must be avoided (eg where a description of a person is relevant)
Recording actions taken	Before going off duty, full details of all actions taken must be recorded as handwritten PNB entries or electronic entries (depending on the circumstances)

Source: Adapted from *Practice Advice on the Management of Priority and Volume Crime (The Volume Crime Management Model)*, 2nd edn (NPIA and ACPO, 2009).

These would generally be taken during the 'golden hour' or as 'fast-track actions' and a trainee police officer could well be involved. The official recommendation is that the NDM should be used to take any decisions but this may be of limited use in this context. It is usually necessary to prioritize certain early actions and take into account, which can be realistically pursued at the time. All decisions made by officers when gathering evidence should be both legal and ethical to ensure the process, procedure, and source is not criticized later in court. A particular decision may be well motivated but if it steps outside the law then the evidence gathered could be rendered inadmissible, for example the interviews and confessions in the Christopher Halliwell case.

With regard to possible witnesses, any people in the vicinity who were not involved or did not see what happened should be eliminated from the enquiry. Careful judgement is needed to establish who was a material witness to the event and who was not. This is not as easy as it sounds because some people become over-excited when they think they have witnessed a crime and will be keen to provide their account. Note, however, that an effective response to supporting survivors, victims, and witnesses will improve the quality of investigation by maximizing the availability of evidence, and it will also help to increase public confidence in the police.

All the actions listed in the table should be completed so that the information can be pieced together. It is important to realize that a primary investigation is not simply a collection of information concerning an alleged crime; it is an integral part of the whole investigation, eg as a precursor to an evidential evaluation and possible secondary investigation, which may lead to prosecution.

The primary investigator produces a crime report, which is sent to the principal screener or links directly with the crime bureau to provide information for the crime report. The FAO must be thorough regarding these initial actions to achieve a professional product. The report will be handed to an investigator who may take the investigation further or it may be filed with no further investigation necessary.

13.5.1.3 Obtaining CCTV evidence

CCTV evidence can also form part of a primary investigation. It can be used to establish the sequence of events and to provide evidence, including supporting the defence case. Relevant material would include footage that showed the suspects were near to the relevant vicinity around the time the crime was committed. The ACPO document *Practice Advice on the use of CCTV in Criminal Investigations* is still available online; we have summarized the key points here.

In an investigation, CCTV footage should ideally be obtained during the 'golden hour' to avoid it being lost, but this may be difficult if specialist services are required. In theory, any officer could seize and exhibit CCTV evidence but when and who depends on the circumstances. A trainee officer undertaking the PCDA or DHEP could at least ensure that the recording system is safe and secure before referring the matter to a supervisor.

The storage format and technical requirements for recovering recordings should be established before accessing the equipment. Often the images are stored on a disc, and taking away the machine or its hard drive is not always possible. If the footage is likely to be relevant, it can be dealt with in one of two ways. Either it can be viewed *in situ* and a decision made about its relevance or it can be seized without viewing, following the rules on the preservation of evidence. Working copies must be made for any further viewings, following ACPO's four principles. In either case, a record would be made of what was viewed in accordance with PACE Code D. The record will also contain any initial reactions to any viewings so that it can be scrutinized at a later date to assess the reliability of any assertion. Seized hard drives should be placed in anti-static bags, tough paper bags, tamper evident cardboard packaging, or wrapped in paper and placed in aerated plastic bags.

13.5.2 Investigative evaluation and screening

As part of a first formal investigative evaluation the crime will be screened to decide if it should be classed as mandatory, priority, or non-priority. This process will also assess the quality of the initial and primary investigation and ensure that all evidence-gathering opportunities have been exploited for the current incident and for other related incidents. A principal screener will normally be an experienced police officer with investigative skills at PIP Level 2 or above. The exact role title can vary and Crime Management Unit staff may also undertake this role.

Non-volume serious crimes such as homicide and rape will be classed as mandatory and will certainly be assigned for secondary investigation. The likelihood of solving priority and/or non-priority crimes will also be assessed. A secondary investigation will be allocated for any crimes which are part of a series, involve a named suspect, or for which there is good evidence or credible intelligence linked to a named offender. To determine the future direction of the investigation, the College of Policing APP suggests four key questions for an investigative evaluation:

- What is known?
- What is not known? Identify gaps in knowledge through gap analysis.
- What are the consistencies between the findings so far?
- What are the contradictions?

These questions provide the focus to create lines of enquiry to fill gaps in knowledge.

The results of the evaluation will lead to a range of outcomes, for example that the investigation is filed with no further action because no leads exist and little else can be done or that it should be handed on for further investigation because there are further lines of enquiry and/or suspects might be known.

In a complicated or lengthy investigation, several staged investigative evaluations will be needed to maintain focus. These will form part of an ongoing secondary investigation and will be conducted by the officer leading the investigation. Repeated cycles of further investigation and investigative evaluation will continue until the case is ready for evidential evaluation, assuming a suspect has been arrested at this stage. If a suspect has not been found despite lengthy enquiries, the investigation may be filed as NFA. Each evaluation should be recorded so that decisions can be reviewed throughout the investigation. The VCMM makes it clear that, as a minimum, an investigation plan should be prepared for any secondary investigation.

If the decision is not to investigate any further then the crime report is filed ('finalized') as NFA and the reasons for the decision are recorded. This process has been criticized as there are indications that many cases are screened out at an early stage and therefore receive little investigative attention.

The principal screener can allocate secondary investigations to several investigators, each with a different role. The investigators could be patrol officers, neighbourhood officers, volume crime investigators working as part of a volume crime investigation team, or officers on specialist squads, eg a burglary squad. Depending on local protocols, a trainee officer might be allocated certain volume crimes to investigate as lead investigator; these might include domestic abuse, hate crime, and public order offences.

13.5.3 Further investigation

The investigation plan from the principal screener will help to direct any secondary investigation and identify relevant lines of enquiry. These may be, for instance, to trace witnesses, identify a victim, or protect scenes. The plan will set out the minimum enquiries expected but for other investigative strategies the investigator will use their discretion.

In serious cases, the police might, for example, decide to employ a media strategy to ask the public for assistance with a challenging investigation. For some less serious cases where a person is 'caught on camera' committing minor crime but has not yet been caught by police, the police might publish the images to try to find out who the suspect is. Other strategies include house-to-house enquiries, searching, forensic retrieval, e-fit circulation, statements from witnesses with full descriptions, capturing text or other electronically generated data, and interviewing. Each strategy employed must be carefully planned and executed.

The guidance in the College of Policing APP distinguishes between investigative activities that have a specific aim in mind, eg to trace a suspect, and activities that are part of a general trawl for information, eg house-to-house enquiries. Each investigator will apply discretion to decide which strategies to use in a particular context, and record the reasons for each decision.

As more evidence is gathered, the investigator will need to conduct further investigative evaluations. This might lead to further lines of enquiry, the employment of other investigative strategies, a decision to arrest, or a decision to proceed no further with the investigation. Once a potential suspect is identified, the investigation will move into the suspect management phase.

13.5.3.1 Management of suspects

Once a suspect has been identified, a range of options will need to be explored. If the suspect has not already been arrested, consideration would need to be given to arrest, search, and seizure of evidence and the appropriate timings for each action. Both the VCMM and the College of Policing APP contain detailed information on strategies for making arrests, searching, and interviewing. Trainee officers should also seek advice from peers and supervisors if in any doubt about to how to progress the suspect management phase.

Any arrest must be lawful and necessary. In terms of making the arrest, this must be carefully planned. First, consideration needs to be given to what is known about the suspect and their criminal history, for example have they been violent to police officers in the past? If so, meticulous planning would be needed on how to safely carry out the arrest. Another issue is if the officers attend but the suspect is not at home. The suspect might now be alerted to the fact that the police have called and might decide to go into hiding or to dispose of possible evidence. An alternative approach would be to obtain a search warrant from a magistrates' court providing a power to enter for the police even if the suspect is absent; any potential evidence could be secured in the suspect's absence. Whether this is necessary, proportionate, and legal is a significant issue for the investigator and requires careful thought and planning. The investigator will also need to plan which police station(s) the suspect(s) will be taken to following arrest, particularly if a number of suspects are to be arrested at the same time.

Once a suspect is in custody, key considerations include the suspect's medical condition, whether there is any 'bad character' evidence, whether any identification procedures are applicable, further searches of premises, when to interview, who is to conduct the interviews, the exact nature of the interview strategy, and the potential to recover forensic evidence from his clothing, shoes, hair, and body.

The outcome of an investigation could be NFA but there are many other methods of disposal, for example charging with an offence, giving a formal caution, and fixed penalty notices. Once a suspect is charged, the investigation then moves into the case management phase.

13.5.3.2 Evidential evaluation

If the investigation has progressed through secondary investigation, then a further evaluation is necessary—an 'evidential evaluation'. Again, this is likely to be undertaken by the officer in charge of the investigation. The evaluation considers whether there is sufficient evidence to allow for a criminal justice disposal or whether no further action can be taken because all 'leads' have yielded no further evidence. The strengths and weaknesses of the case will be taken into account and whether there is sufficient evidence to charge. The evidential evaluation stage never takes place in a vacuum—investigators will liaise with peers, supervisors, case review officers, and evidence review officers (EROs). If it seems there is sufficient relevant evidential material, the investigators will send an advice file (an MG3 form, all key statements, and an outline of the available evidence) to the CPS for a charging decision. The CPS will sometimes provide advice about evidential gaps that would need to be addressed before deciding whether to charge a suspect.

13.5.4 Gap analysis

Allied to the concept of the investigative mindset, and particularly to the principle of investigative and 'evidential evaluation', is the notion of a 'gap analysis'. This is the periodic examination of material gathered during an investigation in order to identify and then fill any gaps in investigative and evidential knowledge. It often employs the '5WH' approach; the 'Who?, What?, When?, Where?, Why?, and How?'

Gap in knowledge	Explanation
Who?	The identities of witnesses, suspects, victims, etc
What?	The sequence of events leading up to, during, and after an alleged offence
When?	The time(s) of events linked with the alleged offence
Where?	The locations linked with the alleged offences
Why?	Motivation—why this place, this time, this alleged victim?
How?	The means of conducting the alleged offence

Investigators are frequently advised to use such an approach when considering the progress of enquiries as it is believed that it helps to ensure a more methodical and thorough investigation.

13.6 Investigative Interviewing

Interviewing witnesses, victims, and suspects is a key part of the police investigation process and a frontline police officer will carry out an interview nearly every day. There are a number of definitions of an interview; the one most often used by trainee officers is provided in PACE Code C, para 11.1A. This states that an interview is 'The questioning of a person regarding their involvement or suspected involvement in a criminal offence or offences which, under Code C paragraph 10.1, must be carried out under caution.' However, this definition does not include interviews with witnesses nor does it provide us with any real focus to the process. To maximize the information gathered, we also need to recognize the importance of the key component of an interview, namely the two-way conversational process.

The common element in all investigative interviews with a witness, victim, or suspect is face-to-face communication between two persons. The interviewer must therefore be aware that the conversational process is central to the success of the encounter and that social skill and appropriate conversational behaviour will affect the outcomes of the interview. Shepherd's

(2008) SE3R ('Survey, Extract, Read, Review, Respond') approach is also widely used to help the interviewer gain a fuller and more detailed understanding of the relevant events.

The modern approach to police interviewing in the UK is to see the interview as a means of seeking to establish the truth. This sounds obvious but it does in fact represent a marked change in emphasis from the past: it is no longer simply a case of working through a list of 'points to prove'. Instead, interviewing is now much more of an information-gathering 'inquisitorial approach'. The term **investigative** is key here as the interview is a central part of any investigation and can significantly affect the outcomes. In the past (particularly in the 1970s and 1980s), the police were sometimes accused of using oppressive techniques for obtaining a confession and there were a number of notorious miscarriages of justice where innocent people were wrongly convicted or the guilty were acquitted.

The advent of the PACE Act 1984 represented a major step forward, as for the first time the police were obliged to routinely audio-record interviews of suspects. There were many benefits to this (both legally and ethically) but the interviews also provided a rich source of data to be examined by researchers, particularly psychologists and criminologists. They found there were a number of areas of poor practice in interviewing. An influential report (Baldwin, 1992, p 34) notes that when interviewing suspects, the main weaknesses were 'a lack of preparation, a general ineptitude, poor technique, an assumption of guilt, unduly repetitive, persistent or laboured questioning, a failure to establish the relevant facts and the exertion of too much pressure'. This and other reports led to the development of a common approach to interviewing and increased standardization of interview training across the whole of England and Wales. The PEACE model (see 13.7) was an important step forward in reaction to the perceived shortcomings in police interviewing.

In this part of the chapter we will examine investigative interviewing processes and procedures in depth, and the recommended methods for conducting interviews. Trainee officers will also practice interviewing procedures and techniques, including how to follow the relevant codes and legislation. If you are on a professional policing degree at a university, or undertaking the PCDA or the DHEP, you might have the opportunity to explore some more of the underpinning theory and research involved in police interviewing—for example, in relation to memory enhancement, lying and deception, and false confessions. The College of Policing has published APP covering investigative interviewing and further information can be found on its website. The topics covered in this chapter are likely to contribute to the learning required for the National Policing Curriculum subject area of 'Conducting Investigations'.

13.6.1 Key principles for interviewing

In order to establish an ethical framework for police interviewing, some general principles have been adopted by the police service. These principles apply to all interviews and assist with effective planning and implementation. Home Office Circular 2/1992 on investigative interviewing initially outlined seven principles. These were updated in 2007 and formed part of the National Investigative Interviewing Strategy (NPIA, 2009). The NPIA Strategy was further developed as part of the College of Policing's APP website in 2013 and most recently updated in March 2019—<https://www.app.college.police.uk/app-content/investigations/investigative-interviewing>. The seven principles are as follows:

1. 'The aim of investigative interviewing is to obtain accurate and reliable accounts from victims, witnesses or suspects about matters under police investigation.'
2. 'Investigators must act fairly when questioning victims, witnesses or suspects.' 'People with clear or perceived vulnerabilities should be treated with particular care, and extra safeguards should be put in place.'
3. 'Investigative interviewing should be approached with an investigative mindset. Accounts obtained from the person who is being interviewed should always be tested against what the interviewer already knows or what can reasonably be established.'
4. 'When conducting an interview, investigators are free to ask a wide range of questions in order to obtain material which may assist an investigation.'
5. 'Investigators should recognise the positive impact of an early admission in the context of the criminal justice system.'
6. 'Investigators are not bound to accept the first answer given. Questioning is not unfair merely because it is persistent.'

7. 'Even when the right of silence is exercised by a suspect, investigators have a responsibility to put questions to them.'

The UK's rapport-based ethical standards on Investigative Interviewing are inspiring investigators internationally. In May 2021, the former United Nations Special Rapporteur on Torture, Juan E Mendez, published the Principles on Effective Interviewing for Investigations and Information Gathering (Anti-Torture Initiative, 2021), known more commonly as the Mendez Principles. In it, he identified six fundamental principles, many of which draw significant parallels to our own principles dating from 1992. These state that effective interviewing:

1. 'is instructed by science, law and ethics';
2. 'is a comprehensive process for gathering accurate and reliable information while implementing associated legal safeguards';
3. 'requires identifying and addressing the needs of interviewees in situations of vulnerability';
4. 'is a professional undertaking that requires specific training';
5. 'requires transparent and accountable institutions';
6. 'requires robust national measures in its implementation'.

Putting both of these sets of principles together, it is clear that an investigative interview should, first and foremost, be lawful, in that the information should be obtained in accordance with statute so that it may be usefully admitted in evidence if required. The information should be obtained in an ethical manner and should respect the individual's rights, such as freedom and dignity. The investigative interview should maximize the opportunity to establish detailed information which can be used to establish the reliability and truthfulness of the interviewee's account. It should also meet and extend the aims and objectives of the overall investigation. The outcomes of the interview must stand up to judicial review and challenge by the criminal justice system.

The legislation around police interviewing is complex and here we cover the basics. The following legislation (all available on the www.legislation.gov.uk website) is also important for interviewing:

- ss 76 and 78 of the PACE Act 1984, including provisions under Codes C, E, and F;
- Part III and ss 34, 36, and 37 of the Criminal Justice and Public Order Act 1994 (CJPOA), including 'special warnings';
- the criminal law relating to the offence(s) for which suspects are charged;
- the Human Rights Act 1998;
- the Criminal Procedure and Investigations Act 1996 (CPIA); and
- the Youth Justice and Criminal Evidence Act 1999 (especially on 'vulnerable', 'intimidated', and child witnesses).

Other legislation covers specific provisions which we will refer to later, but those noted here set out the key principles governing what an interviewer can say and do during an interview. Legislation such as the PACE Act 1984 and its Codes of Practice have certainly helped to reassure the public, lawyers, academics, and the police themselves, that interviewing is now more tightly controlled, more ethical, and often more effective. Of course, simply knowing the law is not enough, the law must also be followed and applied and that is the key role for a police officer. If mistakes are made through incompetence, poor practice, or acting in 'bad faith' during the interview process, parts of the evidence may be rendered void or inadmissible. This could mean that a guilty person might avoid prosecution and be free to offend again or an innocent person might be wrongly charged and convicted.

13.6.2 Strategic oversight

Investigative interviewing is now seen as a crucial part of the criminal investigation process and, in line with a professionalization agenda, the development of both witness and suspect interviewing is overseen by the National Strategic Steering Group on Investigative Interviewing (NSSGII). It aims to develop policies, practices, and procedures that are appropriate for modern investigative activity. Working in conjunction with the NSSGII, each police service now has a local lead on investigative interviewing and coordinators at both regional and national levels provide advice and guidance to practitioners on current best professional practice. In addition, at the tactical level, trained and qualified interview advisers are available to support colleagues in formulating both suspect and witness strategies. All of this is a far cry from the pre-1990s, when officers conducted interviews with little guidance, mainly to obtain a confession. This was to the detriment of major investigations as poor and illegal tactics were sometimes exposed at court (see for instance, the IRA cases in the 1970s and 1980s and the George Heron case in the early 1990s).

13.6.3 The investigative interview as a professional conversation

An investigative interview is a professional conversation with a purpose. A police interviewer cannot approach it in quite the same manner as a social conversation, but can utilize some aspects of everyday experience to help. Investigators manage the 'conversation' in accordance with predefined investigative objectives and overall aims.

Everyday conversation often takes the form of a verbal exchange between two people, with each person taking turns to meet the desired social outcome, for example:

P¹: Good morning, how are you?
P²: Very well thank you, and you?
P¹: Couldn't be better ... (next topic of conversation)

We have all assimilated the norms of conversation through our everyday lives. Consider a recent conversation you have had. It is highly likely to have started with a greeting that is appropriate to your relationship (a handshake, fist bump, or hug). After that you will have generally chatted, taking conversational turns, exchanging news. When the conversation started to come to an end, you will have used language to indicate this to the other person by saying something like 'It's been really nice talking ...' to see if you are both ready to disengage and depart. If so, you will go through a process of saying goodbye and this will be in a manner appropriate to your relationship. Milne and Bull (1999) and Shepherd and Griffiths (2021) have described a form of professional conversation management that echoes this as the 'GEMAC' model: that is, 'Greeting, Explanation, Mutual Activity and Closure'. GEMAC is used by some investigative interviewers as a framework for 'decoding' the underlying conversational process.

13.6.4 Questioning in interviews

Questioning is a skill that needs to be practised. With experience, each interviewer will develop a questioning style that suits their persona and working context, but there are a few basic pointers that will help all interviewers, for example to:

- listen intently;
- indicate interest in what the interviewee is saying using verbal and non-verbal encouragement;
- pause for a moment after each response to process what has been said;
- frame the next question as far as possible on the previous answer as this will help to develop detail and progress beyond the superficial; and
- make a link to your next objective once the current questioning 'thread' has been exhausted.

When developing an account from an interviewee, the 'narrative' and 'context' are both important. As a rule, if you initially focus on the narrative and develop this in detail, the contextual elements will gradually emerge. The narrative can be thought of as the outline of a drawing, and context being the shading and colours. To develop the narrative, it is often quite productive to limit the questioning in the early stages to questions that start with:

- 'Tell me ...'
- 'Explain ...'
- 'Describe ...'
- 'What happened next ...'

Remember to focus on your objectives. Once you have developed the full narrative using productive questioning sequences, the contextual detail can be developed by a similar process, starting with more open-ended questions. You will then be able to progress to more specific detail by using five 'Wh' questions: the 'Who?, What?, When?, Where?, Why?', and one 'H' question: How?' (see 13.5.4). This will be followed by closed confirmatory questions. The type of question therefore changes as the interviewer progresses down the basic questioning hierarchy shown in the diagram.

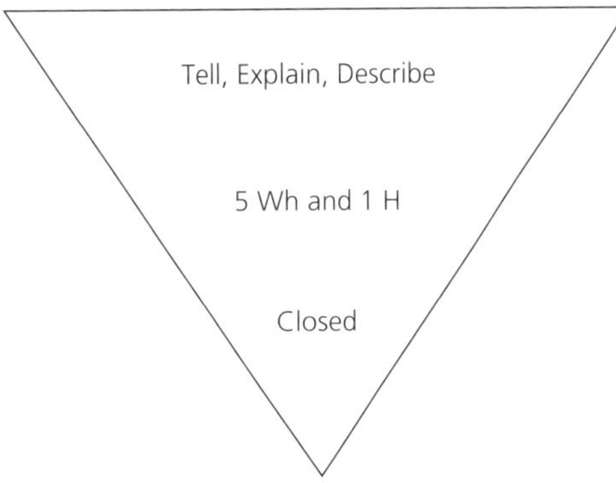

By using questions in a structured sequence, you will develop a systematic and detailed approach to information gathering.

Social scientists have offered numerous theoretical definitions of question types but generally classify questions as either *open* or *closed* in their wording. Open questions are ones that invite the person being questioned to provide answers in their own terms without restriction, as opposed to closed questions which constrain the person answering to a limited selection of acceptable responses. For example, some closed questions are used to confirm what a person has said. The most extreme example of a closed question is one that can only be answered with a simple yes or no.

Open questions seek to capture the perspective of the person answering; to hear their voice and their narrative. Leading questions, on the other hand, constrain and influence the respondent by imposing the interviewer's assumptions that frame the respondent's answers.

Shepherd and Griffiths (2021) offer a more pragmatic classification of questioning that places more emphasis on thinking about the type of answer to expect from a particular kind of question. This focus on outcome leads them to see questions as being productive, counterproductive, and/or risky dependent on the most likely answer to the question posed. From this pragmatic perspective, open questions are generally preferable because they are more likely to be productive as they invite a fuller, richer response. The interviewer should ensure that the interviewee provides as much detail as possible in their own words as this makes any potential evidence more powerful. Leading questions are, in this respect, likely to be counterproductive as they can direct or influence a person to overstate or understate a point, and closed questions are likely to be counterproductive if they fail to elicit the required level of detail to support the investigative and/or prosecution processes.

The skill of a good interviewer is to ask the right question at the right time in the right way. So, an open question, whilst generally preferable, could be unhelpful if asked at the wrong time, for example when a closed confirmatory question would be more appropriate and therefore more productive in terms of making sense of a person's testimony. For much of the time, it will be fairly obvious when to ask open questions and when to ask closed questions but this will not always be the case. This is where we have the category of risky questions which could be either productive or counterproductive depending on a variety of factors. A question is categorized as risky not in terms of whether it is open, closed, or leading but in terms of not being clear as to whether the likely answer will be productive or counterproductive.

In a suspect interview, to prove the *mens rea* the interviewer might ask an open question, for instance starting with 'Explain how you were feeling when you ...?' or 'Tell me what you were thinking when you were ...?' Open questions such as 'Explain in detail what happened to you last night?' can be very productive as they can initiate a lengthy narrative. Closed questions can be equally productive too, for example 'Did you assault them?' could lead the suspect to replying 'Yes, I did, they were asking for it ...', and providing a detailed explanation of why.

13.7 PEACE

Police services in England and Wales use the 'PEACE' approach to interviewing: Planning and Preparation; Engage and Explain; Account, Clarification, and Challenge; Closure and Evaluation (CoP, 2013f). Each of these elements will be considered in turn but the detail will depend on whether the interview is with a suspect or a witness. The key points to consider are as follows:

- **the objectives** (what is to be achieved and how: remember, the emphasis is on establishing the truth);
- **the relevant law** (eg recent stated cases, intention, effect of drink/drugs on intention, recklessness, etc);
- possible **defences** (eg statutory defences, reasonableness, mistake, coercion, self-defence);
- possible **mitigating and aggravating factors**; and
- **the pre-interview briefing** (to solicitors or legal representatives).

We devote considerable time to looking at the preliminaries because establishing an appropriate tone, mood, and format for an interview from the very start is beneficial to the overall process. Most interviewees will not know what is happening and may need reassurance.

Evaluations of the use of PEACE by police services in England and Wales have been provided by Clarke and Milne (2001) and Walsh and Milne (2008). In the latter case, the two researchers found particular concerns with rapport building and the lack of summarizing during the interview. Clarke, Milne, and Bull looked at PEACE interviewing again in 2011 and found that further improvement in training was required, particularly in terms of the communication skills of interviewers (Clarke *et al*, 2011). It might be worth thinking about this as you read through the rest of this chapter.

The change from interrogation to investigative interviewing and the context underpinning the development of the PEACE model is described in more detail in Shepherd and Griffiths (2021).

13.7.1 PEACE: planning and preparation

Many aspects of an interview appear to be merely practical issues, but on closer inspection several of these factors could also influence its outcome so careful planning is essential. For example, the number of interviewers present is likely to affect the approach. Every interview is different and every witness, victim, or suspect will behave differently so interviewers must be prepared for these differences and plan accordingly. The plan should be in writing.

Practical aspects to be covered in the plan include:

- the order of interview if more than one person is to be interviewed;
- who will be present and the seating plan (how will this affect communication?);
- the time and location;
- the timing of breaks; and
- how it will be recorded and how the recording will be later used.

For interviews with suspects there are also statutory considerations, such as recording the interview and the PACE requirements for rest and review times (see PACE Codes of Practice C, E, and F).

As well as covering the practical aspects, the plan should take into account all the topics that need to be covered; these will be the interview objectives, one of which will be selected as the key objective. The College of Policing APP suggests that a properly conducted 'wants analysis' will help an investigator to formulate objectives. There is a saying in interviewing, the meaning of which is often overlooked: 'If I know what I want to know, I will know when I have been told it.' At face value this appears obvious, but it can be challenging to actually define what you need to know in order to be able to accept or reject an investigative hypothesis. This always requires careful thought and must be completed prior to the interview.

An interview plan helps an interviewer to keep track of what has been covered and what remains to be explored. SE3R can be used as an aide-memoire during the interview and will also help you to see if the accounts from different interviewees contradict each other or vary significantly from what seem to be the facts. The plan may contain a series of prompts, thereby enhancing topic selection and thoroughness, but these should be used with care to ensure the interviewer appears professional and in control of the interview. Remember also that whatever sort of plan is used, the plan will be 'relevant material' (as set out in the CPIA) and must therefore be retained as a document to be revealed.

Certain information is required about the interviewee in advance as part of the preparation process, for example:

- Has the interviewee's identity been confirmed? A Livescan and IDENT1 check could be used.
- How old are they? (Establishing the age of a person is not necessarily a simple process. Some adults will claim to be younger in an attempt to avoid prosecution.)
- Is the interviewee on the police's intelligence database? Are they suspected of other crimes elsewhere or flagged as active or of interest to other police or agencies (for instance on the PNC or PND)?
- Does the interviewee have any medical or mental health conditions to take into consideration?

Normally the same interview team would conduct all the interviews relating to one incident. However, once the arrest and detention procedures are complete, the responsibility for an interview is sometimes handed over to another investigator (perhaps from a dedicated unit for prisoner handling). In such circumstances, the new investigator will need to be fully briefed so that they can prepare properly for the interview. In these situations, SE3R can be used as a tool to assess and become fully conversant with every detail of a case.

In terms of the general approach, the qualities of an interviewee can be considered in terms of two variables:

- the 'ability' to tell, ie what they know that is important and relevant to the investigation;
- the 'willingness' to tell, ie the motivation to cooperate.

This can be illustrated as follows:

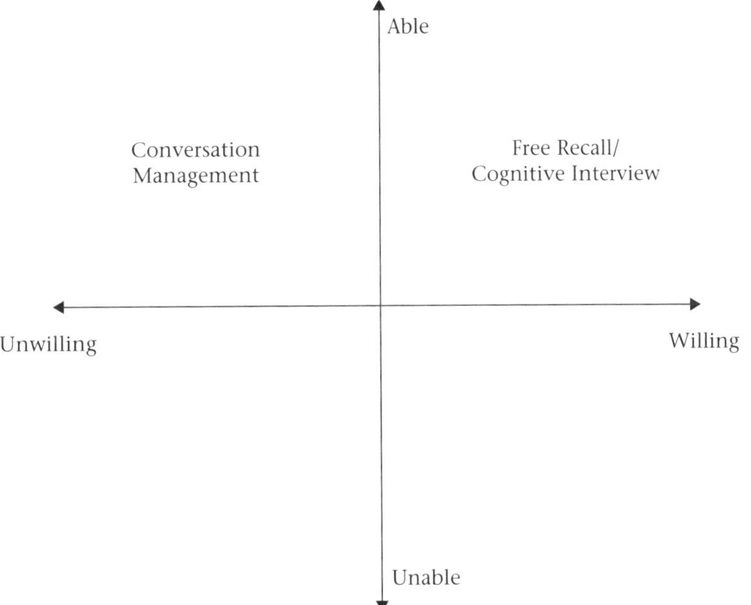

These two variables, *willingness* and *ability*, can each vary across their ranges and may change during an interview. If the interviewee has information and is willing to cooperate, then a free recall or cognitive style of interview would be most appropriate. If the person is less willing to cooperate, then a more directed, conversation-managed approach should be considered. Both approaches will follow the GEMAC principles.

13.7.1.1 Establishing the aims and objectives of the interview

The aim of the investigative interview is to establish a detailed explanation (an account) and to compare it to the material facts that have been established from witness(es) or other evidential sources such as CCTV or forensics. For this, we will need interview objectives and one of these should be identified as the key objective. The key objective will provide a useful focus for the interviewer.

When we formulate objectives, we are defining the parameters of the account to be obtained from an interviewee and we are seeking to obtain detailed information that can be used to test the reliability and truthfulness of the account given and of other accounts and evidence. For example, we may have physical evidence from the scene of a road traffic collision in the form of a skid mark left by a motorcycle; this indicates the motorcycle is likely to have been moving at a high speed and that the wheel locked. If we obtain witness testimony from the driver of a vehicle overtaken by the motorcycle, this would put the physical evidence into context and would also help to corroborate it. All this information in turn could be used to deconstruct the motorcyclist's account; they stated that they were adhering to the rules of the Highway Code. This illustrates how one interview, in this case with a witness, can inform an interview with another person, in this case with the suspect.

13.7.1.2 Planning the questions

Questions are arguably the principal tool of the interviewer. The opening questions of the interview are very important as these tend to set the agenda and tone for the rest of the interview and, to a certain extent, dictate interviewing tactics. The first questions should reflect the key objective(s) for the interview. For example, imagine that the interview concerns a case where a person is accused of stealing a chocolate bar from a shop. They are observed entering the shop, walking to the confectionery display, and looking furtively over each shoulder before selecting a chocolate bar and placing it into their pocket. They then walk calmly from the store and are challenged and detained by a member of staff outside, where a chocolate bar is recovered from their pocket.

From this we can identify many key material facts:

- they were inside the shop;
- they carried out various actions inside the shop;
- they walked from the shop;
- they had a chocolate bar in their possession when stopped.

The aim of the interview will be to establish their account in detail so our interview objectives here could be:

- Explain (in detail) their reason for going to the shop.
- Explain (in detail) their actions inside the shop prior to approaching the confectionery display.
- Explain (in detail) their actions at the confectionery display.
- Explain (in detail) their route after leaving the confectionery display.
- Explain (in detail) their possession of the chocolate bar.
- Explain (in detail) what they were thinking at each of the above points in the chronology.

Note that these are not specific questions but are instead 'questioning areas' that can be developed conversationally by the interviewer who now 'knows what they want to know … '.

The key objective here would probably be 'Explain (in detail) the person's possession of the chocolate bar.' This provides a starting point for the conversation and can be used to formulate an opening question such as 'Tell me in detail how the chocolate bar came to be in your pocket?' or 'Explain in detail how the chocolate came to be in your pocket when you were stopped outside the shop?' Both of these questions are open-ended and both address the key objective. By starting with the correctly selected key objective, the interviewee is drawn towards focusing on the most important issues, which in turn can be used to develop the other objectives. Once all the objectives have been met (in detail), the interviewer has established an account that can be tested against other evidence to determine the reliability and truthfulness of the interviewee's account, which was the overall aim of the interview.

13.7.1.3 Using bad character evidence

Interviewers must carefully assess at the planning stage whether any relevant bad character evidence will be raised. The previous behaviour would have to be relevant to issues in the current investigation. For example, having many theft convictions would add very little to an assault case where the key issue was whether the suspect intended to commit GBH. BCE can be used by interviewers to rebut an innocent explanation, to suggest untruthfulness, or even to demonstrate that the suspect committed the crime on the basis of 'unlikelihood of coincidence'. (For example, a person's offending history might make it seem more likely that they are the offender for the current offence (*R v McAllister* [2009] 1 Cr App R 129).) This type of bad character evidence was used in the conviction of Levi Bellfield for the murder of Amanda ('Milly') Dowler (*R v Bellfield* (2011)).

There are no hard-and-fast rules as to when to raise such issues in interview, but it does make sense to include them in the plan as a separate objective to explore once other objectives have been fully covered. Then each previous conviction or incidence of behaviour can be explored in fine-grain detail until all relevant areas have been discussed. Any similarities or other reasons for raising the material should be discussed within the interview.

13.7.2 PEACE: engage and explain

The aim of this phase of the interview is to create an environment that encourages the interviewee to cooperate with the interview process. It builds upon the 'greeting' phase and seeks to establish a productive social and conversational dynamic for the encounter. This is known as 'set induction' and has two important aspects.

1. Orientation of the interviewee regarding the context of the encounter and orientation towards the task in hand and the expected outcomes.
2. Behaviours required by both parties to undertake the agreed mutual activity.

The interviewer should explain what is going to happen and how things will proceed as this will help to reassure and relax the interviewee and provide the correct conversational dynamic for the encounter. If the interviewee understands exactly what the interviewer is trying to achieve, and what is expected from them in terms of content and detail (and why), then it is more likely that this will be achieved. It will also help to reduce anxiety in the interviewee and they will probably be more likely to provide the information the interviewer requires. Adopting a consultative and non-threatening manner will improve the chances of the interviewee cooperating; this is vital as encouraging the person to talk is a primary aim of the interview process. The interviewer should definitely not read from a plan as this does not help to build a rapport and is likely to convey a general lack of competence and professionalism.

In this stage of a PEACE interview, the interviewer should:

- **establish a rapport** by including introductions, concerns, considerations, and by using appropriate humour. This will help to establish common ground and hopefully create a cooperative atmosphere;
- **explain the reasons for the interview** (for a suspect, this should include an explanation of the alleged offence, the grounds for arrest, and that the interview provides an opportunity for the suspect to provide their account of what happened, and for the police to seek the truth);
- **set out the route map**—what happens during and after the interview process and the general (not the specific) line of questioning;
- **describe the routines**—depending on the nature of the interview, this might include explaining why certain persons are present, the recording procedures, the need for interviewers to refer to their notes and make further notes, the production of exhibits, etc;
- **state the expectations**—ground rules such as no over-talking or interruptions, politeness, time to think, and the need to seek clarification of questions and answers; and
- **explain the interviewee's legal rights**—especially for suspects, including the role of the solicitor and legal advisers.

For suspect interviews, any significant statements or silences must be put to them at the start of the interview in compliance with the PACE Codes of Practice (Code C, para 11.4).

Setting the right tone is very important: not all interviewees and suspects are guilty. The rule of thumb would be to treat people as you would wish to be treated yourself. For each interviewee, any cultural or behavioural factors should be noted and taken into account. For example, asking directly how they wish to be addressed might provide an easy ice-breaker at the beginning of the interview. An interviewer could also offer the interviewee a cup of tea or other refreshment.

13.7.3 PEACE: account, clarifications, and challenge

This is the main part of the interview. The interviewer should first seek a 'free' account, without any interruption if possible, focusing on the key objective(s). The account should then be developed by conversational probing of what has been said, moving systematically from one objective to another, clarifying or seeking greater detail. *Turnbull* and the ADVOKATE checklist could be used here if appropriate. Each objective should be explored in fine-grain detail, thus exhausting relevant questions on that objective before moving on to another.

A good strategy to develop is using the interview objective as a conversational opener and to let a free narrative develop. The ongoing narrative can then be used to formulate the next question. This will create a continuous sequence where each question will seem to flow from what the person has already said. The interview will feel more like a natural conversation where the interviewer is really listening to what the interviewee says. This is almost always more productive than a disjointed series of questions and answers. It requires great concentration on the part of the interviewer and needs practice and, as you might expect, appropriate training from a skilled practitioner.

The account should then be summarized before selecting the topics that are relevant, in dispute, and checkable. These will then be examined in greater detail. To clarify the account the interviewer may need to seek new/additional information before summarizing again, with commitment and agreement if possible. The account should make chronological sense. The account and 'topic phase' of the interview should establish the interviewee's full and detailed account.

13.7.3.1 Challenging

Once the complete account is established, it can be compared with the evidence and any inconsistencies can be challenged. Challenging should be restricted to inconsistencies and facts that can be checked and proved, and are also admissible. The interviewer should take care not to criticize or accuse, but should instead ask for an explanation where discrepancies emerge. The challenge phase should not be a confrontation; even hard-to-answer questions can be asked in a conversational manner. The interviewer must also consider whether a special warning is needed.

One effective conversational method of challenging is to:

1. Confirm the detail given by the interviewee in the account.
2. Reveal the detail that contradicts or is inconsistent with any aspect of other details.
3. Ask an open-ended question.

This approach can be illustrated in a suspect interview as follows (where I is the interviewer, S is the suspect, and detail X is contradicted by information Y):

I: In your earlier account you said X (detail), do you agree? [Point 1 above]

S: Yes.

I: The evidence shows Y. How do you explain that? [Points 2 and 3 above]

The suspect then needs to account for the inconsistency and this can then be further probed. The interviewer should listen carefully because the suspect may now start changing their account (which should have been fully developed, summarized, and agreed in the topic phase of the interview). An interviewer can be robust and persistent in line with the seven principles without being confrontational and oppressive.

13.7.3.2 The importance of breaks

Breaks are useful for making arrangements and gathering thoughts, particularly if the interview has taken an unexpected turn; the plan may need to be revised. It may be useful to plan breaks as follows:

- Account Phase—use the key objective and develop a detailed account.
- Break—analyse information, review plan, undertake relevant fast-track actions.
- Topic Phase—develop topics that are relevant, checkable, and in dispute.
- Break—analyse information, review plan, undertake relevant fast-track actions, plan challenges.
- Challenge Phase.

After a break it is good practice to summarize what has been said and to invite the interviewee to comment on the accuracy of the summary. This demonstrates that the interviewer has been listening carefully and has realized the significance of what has been said and that the interviewee is being taken seriously.

13.7.4 PEACE: closure

The interviewer should aim to maintain the good rapport built up during an interview as it might be necessary to interview the same person again. Closure is one of the stages in the GEMAC conversation model. Before finishing the interview, the interviewer should:

- review the interviewee's account in full;
- allow the interviewee the chance to correct, confirm, deny, alter, or add to their account;
- ensure that all the planned objectives and topics have been covered;
- check whether the interviewee (or the solicitor, if present) wants to ask any questions; and
- explain what will happen in the future.

The interview can then be formally closed. This is likely to include recording the time when the interview finishes. For interviews with suspects, there are additional requirements relating to recording the interview.

13.7.5 PEACE: evaluation

The evaluation stage includes what has been achieved and how well the interviewer's aims and objectives were met. The interviewer should refer to their plan and reflect on what went well, what might have gone better, and (for next time) which areas they would try to develop or improve. The following questions might be relevant.

- Have other reasonable lines of enquiry (such as an alibi) been discovered?
- Are other forensic opportunities now apparent?
- Have all the points to prove from the offence under investigation been covered?
- Have the statutory defences, mitigation, or explanation, perhaps pointing to innocence, been considered?
- Have the objectives been achieved?
- Does the interview add to the investigation as a whole?
- Have the requirements of the CPIA been satisfied?
- How have I performed, and what can I learn from this interview to develop my skills?

Trainee police officers should assess their personal level of skills and knowledge about interviewing and use this in their assessment portfolios. All interviewers should regularly evaluate their performance to ensure continuing professional development.

13.8 Other Interviewing Considerations

There are further, different considerations worthy of note in relation to interviewing as they relate to investigations.

13.8.1 The needs of the interviewee

Many suspects will be anxious and want to know what is going to happen next and in the longer term. The common questions are 'Will I be released?', 'Will I get bail?', and 'How long will I be here?' If the suspect asks such questions, the interviewer should explain that they cannot determine the decisions of the custody officer or the CPS reviewing lawyer. Obviously, there should be no attempt to gain a confession through promise of favours such as early release or bail, as this could render any subsequent confession inadmissible at court.

The Police, Crime, Sentencing and Courts Act 2022 created a presumption that the suspect will be released on pre-charge bail, if necessary and proportionate, for an initial period of three months. Certain conditions can also be applied to this bail, which aims to safeguard victims and witnesses, preserve evidence, and prevent re-offending. These imposed safeguards must be balanced against the rights and freedoms of the suspect.

13.8.1.1 Meeting the needs of all interviewees

The interviewer and the custody officer should be alert to the special circumstances involved in interviewing a person with a physical impairment, a mental health condition, a mental disorder, or other possible vulnerability. They should always try to ascertain the nature and extent of the vulnerability although the individual may or may not be willing to divulge it.

There were major changes to PACE Code C in 2018, partly as a result of police failures in identifying suspects as vulnerable. It is now insufficient to rely on the suspect's opinion regarding their own vulnerability when determining whether an 'appropriate adult' is required. Code C, para 1.4 makes it clear that reasonable enquiries should be made to ascertain what information is available. Furthermore, if at any time an officer has any reason to suspect that a person may be vulnerable, in the absence of clear evidence to dispel that suspicion, that person shall be treated as such. In the case of *R v Aspinall (Paul James)* [1999] MHLR 12, the failure to follow the requirements to have an appropriate adult in the interview of a mentally disordered suspect meant that, despite his apparent lucidity in interview, it was unfair to admit material from the interview as evidence.

For a profoundly deaf individual, a 'signer' may be required. A partially deaf person will find it easier if they can see the interviewer's face in order to lip-read, and people should speak one at a time. A deaf person's attention could be attracted by lightly touching their sleeve. The local police Diversity and Inclusion Team may be able to provide Braille texts that explain, for example, a suspect's rights, the caution, and the management of the disks after interview (note, however, that not all visually impaired people can read Braille).

Other impairments, such as speech impediments, may be more difficult to deal with but interviewers should always be sensitive to the individual's needs and requirements and should try to satisfy these needs. The simple question is: 'Have I done all I can to ensure that this person is not disadvantaged in any way because of a vulnerability or impairment?' If this is the case, then all reasonable steps have been taken. No one should be placed at a disadvantage in a police interview because of physical or mental vulnerability.

13.8.2 Interviews with suspects

A suspect interview is defined as 'the questioning of a person regarding their involvement or suspected involvement in a criminal offence or offences which must be carried out under caution' (PACE Code C, para 11.1A). This applies to *any* conversation once a caution has been given and it is irrelevant whether or not the suspect has been arrested. Not all suspects are arrested, for example a suspect on the street being reported for a road traffic offence or a suspect who volunteers to be interviewed to assist with the investigation of an offence.

Suspects who have been arrested must always be interviewed at a police station (Code C, para 11.1) unless the requirements for an 'urgent interview' are met. Suspects who have not been arrested and who volunteer to be interviewed to assist with an investigation are normally interviewed at a police station but could be interviewed at another suitable location. Suspects being reported for a minor road traffic offence are usually interviewed at the roadside under caution, with the suspect's full rights and entitlements fully set out.

13.8.2.1 General rights of the suspect

The suspect has the normal rights of being treated with dignity, fairness, and objectivity, and the right to free independent legal advice (FILA) during interview, and for a vulnerable person, an 'appropriate adult' should also be present. A number of laws and associated codes regulate the process of police interviews in order to protect the interviewee. The suspect should be assessed as 'fit for interview'. If a suspect appears to be ill, hurt, or suffering from a psychological condition, a doctor or custody nurse will make this decision but it can be decided on the person's own say so, supported by the custody officer's independent observations.

Unquestionably, there have been many instances in the past of the police abusing their powers to question suspects. This could range from using oppressive behaviour to obtain confessions under duress, to a lack of safety provisions when interviewing a vulnerable person. The custody officer and the suspect's legal adviser both have a responsibility to monitor the suspect's rights and the process of interviewing, and there are now far fewer opportunities for foul play. The rights should be fully explained to the suspect and reinforced with a written explanation.

The EU Directive 2012/13/EU enhances the rights of suspects at police stations and covers the right to information in criminal proceedings. It enshrines the right of a suspect to:

- information concerning procedural rights, eg to free legal advice and to remain silent;
- information relating to the reason for arrest and the suspected offence; and
- access to case file material that relates to the legality of the arrest (Cape, 2015).

So, as soon as the custody officer becomes aware of the existence of material relevant to the legality or otherwise of the arrest, they must communicate this information to the suspect. This will allow the defence to make submissions to the custody officer (and beyond) regarding the suspect's continued detention.

Cape (2015) suggests that decisions about how much information is provided to a suspect and/or their solicitor prior to interview can be problematic. PACE Code C, para 11.1A states:

> Before a person is interviewed, they and, if they are represented, their solicitor must be given sufficient information to enable them to understand the nature of any such offence, and why they are suspected of committing it, in order to allow for the effective exercise of the rights of the defence.

R v Roble [1997] Crim LR 449 states that a legal adviser must be in a position to 'usefully advise [their] client'. Interviewers have discretion when deciding which material will be disclosed to the legal adviser prior to interview and will need to consider the matter carefully at the planning stage. This area has produced some interesting case law (see *R v Howell* [2003] EWCA Crim 01 and *R v Knight* [2003] EWCA Crim 1977).

13.8.2.2 The presence of an 'appropriate adult'

PACE Code C, para 3.15 states that an 'appropriate adult' must be provided for any suspect who is a juvenile (under 18) or who is vulnerable. The definition of vulnerable has been significantly widened to also include any suspect who, because of a mental health condition or mental disorder, may, among other things, have difficulty in understanding the full implications for them in relation to their arrest, detention, or questioning or be prone to becoming confused or unclear about the situation. PACE Code C, para 1.13d provides a full definition of vulnerable, but see also Chapter 20.

The role of the appropriate adult is to safeguard the rights, entitlements, and welfare of a suspect (Code C, para 1.7A). They will support, advise, and assist the suspect when:

- the suspect is given or is asked to provide information or participate in any procedure;
- observe whether the police are acting properly and fairly;
- assist the suspect to communicate with the police whilst respecting the suspect's right to choose to say nothing; and
- help the suspect to understand their rights and ensure that those rights are protected and respected.

PACE Code C, para 1.7 sets out the categories of person who can be an appropriate adult. In the case of a juvenile, it would generally be the parent or guardian. If the juvenile is in the care of a local authority or voluntary organization, it would be a person representing that authority or organization. A social worker may stand *in loco parentis* (in the place of a parent). As a last resort, any responsible person aged 18 or over who is not a police officer or employed by the police may act as the appropriate adult.

For a person who is vulnerable, an appropriate adult should be a relative, guardian, or other person responsible for their care and custody. Alternatively, it could be someone experienced in dealing with vulnerable persons, such as an approved mental health professional (AMHP) or a specialist social worker. Any appropriate adult needs to be truly appropriate in order to perform the role. Therefore, for a vulnerable adult, the last resort cannot merely be any responsible person aged 18 or over who is not a police officer or police employee but also has to be one who is appropriate to deal with that vulnerability.

Some categories of people cannot be the appropriate adult. PACE Code C, Note 1B states:

> A person, including a parent or guardian, should not be an appropriate adult if they are: suspected of involvement in the offence; the victim; a witness; involved in the investigation, or have received admissions prior to attending to act as the appropriate adult.

The interviewer should check that the appropriate adult is invited to sign the custody record to show that they understand the responsibilities involved before the interview begins. An interview involving an appropriate adult may take longer, especially if it also involves interpretation. Translation from one language to another generally doubles the time taken for an interview so allowances should be made for this. An extended timeframe can have advantages, however, in that the interviewee has more time to consider their replies. The interviewer will also have more time to observe and consider the suspect's non-verbal communication (NVC) and demeanour, although, of course, any interpretations must always allow for cultural and linguistic diversity.

13.8.2.3 Confessions, oppression, and unfairness

Any statement that is in any way adverse to a person, eg admitting to a crime or even to being present at the scene of a crime, can amount to a confession under s 82 of the PACE Act 1984. The statement can be made to any person not just a police officer, and can include written or spoken words, actions, or even silence. However, even if a person confesses in one of these recognized ways, the evidence might not be admissible in court. The defence can argue that a confession should be rendered inadmissible because:

- it was, or may have been, obtained by oppression (s 76 PACE);
- the manner in which the evidence was obtained means it is unfair to admit it (s 78 PACE); or
- it is too prejudicial to admit it (eg if the offender has previously confessed to a similar but more serious offence, the bench or the jury might not fully consider the evidence in the current case) (s 82 PACE).

Many of the unfair practices that were adopted in the past by the police to secure a 'confession' from a suspect in custody have been made less likely, if not impossible, by legislation and practice guidelines.

Oppression usually means behaviour akin to breaching a person's human rights under Article 3 of the ECHR, which refers to torture, inhumane or degrading treatment, or the use or threat of violence. Case law has widened the definition of oppression to include 'exercise of authority in a burdensome, harsh or wrongful manner' (*R v Fulling* [1987] 2 All ER 65), as well as:

> questioning which by its very nature, duration or other circumstances (including the fact of custody) excites hope (such as the hope of release) or fears, or so affects the mind of the subject that his will crumbles and he speaks when otherwise he would have stayed silent. (*R v Prager* [1972] 1 WLR 260, 266, adopted by the House of Lords in *R v Mushtaq* [2005] UKHL 25).

This latter definition can encompass many situations and is often used by defence solicitors. If the court or the defence raise the issue of oppression, the prosecution must prove beyond reasonable doubt that it was not used to obtain the confession.

Inducements to confess could include offers to grant bail or for the police to refrain from arresting family members. Threats could be suggesting that bail will not be granted or that family members might be arrested.

Section 78 of the PACE Act 1984 underpins many strategies used by defence solicitors. It allows for any potential prosecution evidence to be rendered inadmissible, not just confessions (see *R v Mason* [1987] 3 All ER 481). To use s 78, the defence has to show that the manner in which the evidence was obtained means it should not be admitted as it would be unfair to the proceedings. The defence might argue, for instance, that DNA evidence should not be admissible because the prosecution has not proven continuity of the evidence from the moment it was found to the moment it was examined at the laboratory. Note, therefore, that if a s 76 argument does not succeed, the defence could argue that a confession should be rendered inadmissible under s 78 instead.

The Halliwell case is a notable example of where the suspect's rights were denied (Cox, 2012). A superintendent was judged to have breached PACE by interviewing the suspect in circumstances that were oppressive and that deliberately denied him his rights (both ss 76 and 78 PACE arguments were employed by the defence). Halliwell was arrested for the abduction of Sian O'Callaghan but some of the interviews were conducted prior to arrival at a police station under the guise of an urgent interview. However, no caution was given and he was questioned without a solicitor and without Halliwell's agreement. He confessed to the murder of O'Callaghan and another woman, Becky Godden, and was subsequently charged with both murders. After lengthy legal arguments at the start of the trial, all of Halliwell's confessions were ruled inadmissible and the second murder case failed. The O'Callaghan case continued based upon other evidence and Halliwell was convicted. There was extensive media coverage and an IPCC investigation ensued. The superintendent was found guilty of gross misconduct for the breaches and was given a final written warning.

13.8.2.4 Planning suspect interviews

As well as the general PEACE considerations for planning interviews, other factors apply for suspect interviews, such as:

- the legal framework for interviews with suspects;
- the suspect's right to a free independent legal adviser and for the adviser to be present throughout the interview; and
- the arrangements for recording the interview.

These requirements need to be covered in the interview plan. The interviewer also needs to consider what defences the suspect might employ and how these might be countered.

One of the first things to consider for a suspect interview is what potential offence or offences are being investigated. Remember that if an offence has actually occurred, the following must be proved.

1. **Criminal intent** (*mens rea*): What was in the suspect's mind at the time? Why did they commit the offence?
2. **Criminal action** (*actus reus*): What did they actually do? How did they do it?

For each offence, the following will be required: the points to prove, the evidence that the suspect committed the offence, case law, and the specific parts of the criminal law under which the suspect may be charged. The relevant legislation should be consulted and the key points established. Information such as witness accounts or statements should be considered as they will help to clarify what is required from the interview.

Core Aspects of Police Work

13.8.2.5 Defence solicitors

The defence solicitor is the defendant's legal adviser. They are obliged to prevent the defendant from further assisting the police by way of self-incrimination if that is not in the defendant's interest (Code C, Note 6D). The solicitor's only role in the police station is to protect and advance the legal rights of their client (Code C, Note 6D).

A 'duty solicitor' is drawn from a retained panel of solicitors who are available to advise an arrested person who does not have a solicitor of their own available for the interview. They provide 'free and independent legal advice' (FILA) and are there to advise their clients at any time. They are, of course, independent of the police and the CPS. The custody officer will make the initial contact with the solicitor, following a request from the detained suspect, and the interviewer will then become the point of contact for the defence solicitor. Note that confidential handover documents or witness statements should not be attached to the custody record.

If the evidence looks weak or merely circumstantial, the solicitor will probably advise the suspect to remain silent or to submit a jointly prepared statement. It is sometimes difficult for a trainee officer to accept that a solicitor can advise a suspect against providing details about a crime or admitting guilt. It is important to recognize that these are emotional reactions and should be set aside. It is essential to remain objective and focused on the real evidence. There may be sound reasons for a legal adviser to advise the suspect to remain silent or reply 'no comment', for example there may have been very little disclosed during the pre-interview briefing. The decision to make 'no comment' and the possible reasons could be examined by the court (see eg *R v Howell* [2003] EWCA Crim 01) and the jury may be suspicious about a suspect's silence at interview.

Sometimes an admission of guilt is better for the client, especially if there is strong or irrefutable evidence, and/or a reason for what has been done. A solicitor might adopt an 'active defence' approach (Ede and Shepherd, 2000) and try to dominate an interview, particularly if the interviewer seems to lack experience. If a solicitor is disruptive, there is a risk of 'losing the interview' and the interviewer may therefore need to take control; a good command of the relevant areas of Code C, Notes 6D and 6E will be needed. However, it is very rare for a police interviewer to have to stop the interview and seek to have the solicitor excluded under Code C, para 6.9. In any case, the whole interview is recorded; the court will undoubtedly take a negative view of a disruptive solicitor and this might even prejudice the suspect's defence.

13.8.2.6 Briefing a solicitor before an interview

Before the interview begins the solicitor must be briefed (provided with the relevant information) so that their client may be usefully advised (see *R v Roble* [1997] Crim LR 449). The interviewer must plan what to disclose, considering:

- What is the evidence?
- What evidence should be disclosed or withheld?
- At what stage of the interview will evidence be disclosed?
- Can the withholding of any evidence be justified, see *R v Imran & Hussain* (1997)?

PACE Code C, para 11.1 and Note 11ZA cover the legal minimum that should be included in the pre-interview briefing. The solicitor must be told about the nature of the offence(s) that the suspect is alleged to have committed, including the time and place in question and why their client is suspected of committing it. Exactly how much needs to be provided to cover the latter point is not defined and a decision as to what is enough lies with the interviewer. PACE Code G, Note 3 clarifies that material may be withheld from the legal advisor, and therefore from the suspect, when prior disclosure of such details might give the suspect an opportunity to fabricate an innocent explanation or to otherwise conceal lies from the interviewer.

However, the pre-interview briefing should not be approached from a bottom-up perspective. Just because the interviewer thinks that they have provided enough to satisfy the requirements in PACE and the relevant case law mentioned above, does not mean that this is appropriate. It would be wrong not to include evidence simply on the basis that the minimum legal requirement had been met and it limits the opportunity for tactical benefit that might be gained by revealing specific additional information determined on a case-by-case basis. The risk in sharing more than the minimum information with a solicitor is the increased likelihood of the suspect being made aware of information they would not have known and using it to construct a false defence. Difficulties can occur if the solicitor believes the amount of information that has been revealed is not sufficient for them to usefully advise their client and the interviewer does not believe it appropriate to provide further information. If this occurs, it may result in the suspect providing a 'no comment' interview and limit the prospect of arguing adverse inference at court. The solicitor's tactics during interview may also be more proactive and when further evidence is revealed they may request the interview is stopped for a private consultation with their client, disrupting the interview flow.

Therefore, pre-interview briefing should be viewed from a top-down approach, specifically that everything will be revealed to the solicitor unless there is a good reason not to. Any evidence derived solely from intelligence should not be included as the protection of sources and sensitive tactics are important considerations; evidence that the suspect would not already be aware of should also be withheld if possible; and any material that would be a breach of data protection against a potential witness should be withheld. The interviewer can seek advice and guidance about what to hold back from a supervisory officer. So, for example, if you are investigating an assault, you might consider revealing all the information that the victim provides about the events before and during the assault as the offender was there and would know what led up to it and what occurred during it. However, if the offender left the scene immediately after the assault they might not know what happened afterwards or the specific nature of the injury sustained. In this case, you might also reveal the existence of a witness who saw the events and identified the suspect by name as this strengthens the case against the suspect, but withhold the identity of the witness (under data protection) and exactly what the witness saw (the suspect might not have known there was someone else there). In some situations, a fuller briefing might also facilitate a frank and productive interaction between the suspect and the police and should increase the amount of positive non-court disposals, eg cautions, or early guilty pleas at court providing a more beneficial outcome for the victim.

When delivering the briefing, the interviewer and the solicitor will ideally meet in a quiet room, ensuring that there will be no interruptions. At the start of the briefing, the interviewer should explain that they will read the briefing out and then invite the solicitor to ask any questions once it is complete. During this, sufficient time should be allowed for the solicitor to take notes or the interviewer can choose to provide a photocopy of the briefing. The solicitor should then be invited to ask questions, which may be reduced if a risk-free, top-down approach was adopted during preparation rather than a bottom-up approach. At this stage, it is unlikely that any additional evidence or information will be revealed by the interviewer in response to those questions. Rather than simply refusing to answer them, an explanation should be provided as to why. For example, 'I have revealed all that I am prepared to do so about [this]. I need to be able to test the truthfulness of any admissions your client makes' or 'I have revealed all that I am prepared to do so about [this]. I do not want to further unduly influence your client's account.' A solicitor may try different tactics, such as switching abruptly from questions about evidence to questions about other aspects of the case in order to disrupt the interviewer's resolve. The interviewer needs to remain calm and self-possessed and will, of course, be able to deal more confidently with such situations if they know all the details of the case and have a thorough understanding of the relevant law.

A written record must be kept of the details that have been disclosed, including the additional questions asked by the solicitor and any responses provided, so that the CPS can be informed of the contents of the briefing on the MG6A form. The briefing process can also be video-recorded, and a copy given to the solicitor, which may also cause the more disruptive solicitors to moderate their behaviour.

13.8.2.7 The start of a suspect interview

The time spent on engaging and building rapport with the suspect and following the procedures properly may all prove productive later. In addition, no irregularities will have been provided for the solicitor to use in the defence of their client.

There is a legal requirement for certain information to be mentioned at the start of the interview (see PACE Code E, paras 3.4–3.7), for example the time, date, and location of the interview. Before asking any questions about the offence, and after any break, the interviewer must caution the suspect (see Code C, paras 10.8 and 11.4) and check their understanding of the caution. It is important that the interviewer is satisfied that the suspect understands the implications of the caution before asking them any questions (PACE Code C, Note 10D). To that end, the interviewer might say to the suspect, for example:

> You have an absolute right to remain silent if you wish, you do not have to speak to me or answer any of my questions. However, if this matter goes to court and at court you rely on a fact in your defence that the court think you could have reasonably given me here today, then the court are entitled to ask themselves 'why did you not reveal this fact at the time of the interview?' They might think that the facts you give in defence in court are untrue or have been made up since the interview, and they may be less likely to believe you. And remember, everything being said here today is being recorded and could be played in court.

The solicitor should not be asked to explain the caution or to acknowledge that their client understands it—this is the responsibility of the interviewer. The suspect's understanding of the caution should be checked by asking them three simple questions, such as:

1. Do you have to answer any of my questions?
2. What might the court think if you tell them something in your defence that you have not told me during interview and the court reasonably believes that you could have done so?
3. Where can this recording be played as proof of what has been said in this interview?

Further information must be provided to the suspect, depending on the circumstances and location of the interview. For example, a suspect who has been arrested and who is being interviewed at a police station must also be reminded that they are entitled to free legal advice in person or on the phone, and that the interview can be delayed until it is obtained. Such reminders and the suspect's response should be recorded in the interview record (Code C, para 11.2).

Other information that must be provided to a suspect who has not been arrested is shown in the table.

Circumstances and location of interview with a suspect who has not been arrested	Additional information to be provided to the suspect
Suspect is on the street being reported for an offence	That a failure to cooperate (eg by not providing a name and address when being reported for an offence) could amount to committing a further offence or lead to arrest (Code C, para 10.9)
Suspect has volunteered to assist with the investigation of an offence and is being interviewed	That they can leave at any time and can also obtain free and independent legal advice if they agree to remain (Code C, para 3.21)

Core Aspects of Police Work

Any significant statement should also be discussed. The suspect must be given the opportunity to clarify, confirm, deny, or add to an earlier statement. Sometimes it may be difficult to distinguish between a significant statement and a 'relevant comment', but if there is any doubt, the statement or comment should be put to the suspect at the beginning of the interview, after caution and before questioning.

13.8.2.8 Tactics during interviews

The interviewer should be polite, professional, and proceed with the interview as planned. However, interviewees may be hostile and refuse to cooperate. A common temptation for an interviewer in such circumstances is to confront the solicitor or to start rushing the questions, but this must be avoided. The interviewer must not be drawn into asking closed questions (requiring a yes or no reply) or into speeding up and thus allowing little time for answers (as if a 'no' answer is expected). Nor should the suspect be asked why they are not answering the questions. The simple advice in this situation is to adhere to the PEACE model of interviewing and not to be thrown. Skilful and persistent questioning may slip under a hostile suspect's defences. For example, they could be unnerved by a new line of questioning and forget to 'brazen it out' with a repeated 'no comment', and suddenly provide vital evidence or information.

Most defence solicitors, particularly duty solicitors, will have a good understanding and plenty of experience of the PEACE interview model and the approaches that an interviewer is likely to adopt. For example, the solicitor will know that the interviewer will try to build a rapport with the interviewee but it is very unlikely that they will assist with the process. If the interviewer starts with a few informal words such as whether the suspect would like a drink, to encourage the suspect to open up, the solicitor is likely to challenge its relevance unless it relates directly to the suspect's welfare. Therefore, all opportunities to build a rapport before the interview should be recognized and utilized to the full.

The PACE Codes of Practice provide some guidance on what is acceptable behaviour by the solicitor in an interview. A legal adviser is permitted to seek clarification, offer the client their advice, including to refrain from answering a question, and can also challenge an improper question or the manner in which it is put. A legal adviser may not, however, answer questions on the client's behalf or provide them with written responses to quote (see Code C, Notes 6D and 6E).

The solicitor will also closely monitor the interview process itself. This is because, however overwhelming the evidence, any flaw in police procedure can lead to charges against the suspect being dismissed or evidence being ruled inadmissible. A solicitor has no obligation to immediately point out any police failing or non-adherence to the appropriate Codes and may only mention it later when it is of particular advantage to the client, for instance in court. This is one of the reasons why the interviewer needs to know the law and the associated police procedures very well indeed. Asking leading questions, adopting a threatening or bullying manner, or seeking to offer the suspect a lighter sentence in exchange for giving more evidence will all prompt the solicitor to intervene (and rightly so). If, however, the interviewer is acting fairly, proportionately, and properly, then the solicitor's grounds for intervention are much reduced.

13.8.2.9 Prepared statements

The solicitor may present the interviewer with a written 'prepared statement'. This is often written by the solicitor and the suspect, and signed by the suspect. The suspect might then not want to say anything more about the matter and may make this clear at the start of the interview, after the caution. The most appropriate response in such a situation is to temporarily suspend the interview and consider the contents of the statement. It can then be included in a revised interview plan, and the interview restarted. The receipt of a prepared statement does not mean the interview process is over. As an interviewer, you still have the right to ask relevant questions relating to the investigation.

The case of *R v Knight* [2003] EWCA Crim 1977 should be studied by all interviewers as it provides useful guidance on what to do when presented with a prepared statement. If the factual defence is stated in the prepared statement in writing, and the suspect gives oral evidence at court which is wholly in line with the statement, then no adverse inference can be drawn. The case makes it clear that the purpose of s 34 of the Criminal Justice and Public Order Act

1994 is to encourage the early disclosure of a suspect's account. However, *R v Knight* recognizes that a prepared statement does not give automatic immunity to adverse inference as the prepared statement might be lacking in detail or deficient in another manner.

All prepared statements should be carefully analysed (eg using SE3R) and any omissions noted. The case of *R v Lewis* [2003] EWCA Crim 223 is particularly relevant in this context. If the prepared statement lacks detail, including explanatory detail, this gives the interviewer the opportunity to ask questions about what is not contained in the statement. In *R v Lewis*, it was observed that 'a fact supporting a fact, is also a fact that can reasonably be expected to be mentioned'. The careful analysis of the content then gives rise to new interview objectives, based on information that is not included in the prepared statement. These objectives can then be developed during a further interview, being mindful that it is highly likely this will be a 'no comment' interview.

13.8.2.10 Recording suspect interviews

The principle of PACE Code E (para 2.1) is that an audio-recording should be made of any interviews under caution with suspects for any offence, but there are some exemptions to this. Most interviews are now supplemented with a simultaneous visual recording, so Code F will also apply.

The information provided to a suspect in order to arrange a voluntary interview is on a par with that provided to an arrested suspect (see Code C, paras 3.21(b) to 3.22). This information and the subsequent consent to the interview must be thoroughly recorded. On arrival for the voluntary interview, a sergeant must conduct a risk assessment on the suspect (similar to the way a custody officer would for an arrested person).

At the start of the interview, the suspect's consent to be interviewed must be confirmed. However, they can withdraw consent and are free to leave at any time (subject to any necessity to then arrest the suspect if that were to be the case under PACE Code G).

PACE Code E, para 2.3 details the circumstances under which a suspect interview would not be audio-recorded as a minimum standard. These include:

- an authorized recording device in working order is not available; or
- such a device is available but a location suitable for using that device to make the audio-recording of the matter in question is not available; and
- the 'relevant officer' (described in para 2.4) considers, on reasonable grounds, that the proposed interview should not be delayed until an authorized recording device in working order and a suitable interview room or other location become available and decides that a written record shall be made.

It is also possible for the interview to be recorded solely in written form if the suspect, or the appropriate adult on their behalf, objects to the interview being audio-recorded. The decision to continue recording the interview against the wishes of the suspect may be commented upon in court as this could be seen as being oppressive (Code E, Note 3D). The evidence could then be rendered inadmissible under s 76 or 78.

If the interview takes place other than at a police station, for example at the roadside in relation to a motoring offence, the PNB is the most appropriate place to record such an interview in writing, complying with Code C, para 11.7.

13.8.2.11 Procedures for recording interviews

Audio-recordings of interviews are made using DVDs or secure digital networks, depending on the facilities available. PACE Code E makes various provisions for the use of these different types of media.

For DVD recordings, the sealed disks must be shown to the suspect at the start of the interview to show they are sealed and have not been tampered with. The following information must be recorded as a PNB entry or on the paper seals wrapped around the disks at the end of the interview (see Code C, para 11.7):

- the time, day, date, and location of the interview;
- the name, rank, and role of the interviewer;
- the name, address, and date of birth of the interviewee; and

- the persons present.

When a DVD recorder is first switched on there will be a continuous sound while it is formatting the disks, and this must be explained to the suspect. Two recordings are made simultaneously (sometimes three, depending on the equipment). At the end of the interview, one of them will be sealed as the 'master recording'. The other(s) will remain with the case file; these are known as the 'working' copy/copies. A further copy will also be provided for the solicitor on request. The master recording is filed by the designated responsible person and will not be opened unless it is needed in exceptional circumstances or is to be examined on the direction of a judge or a senior member of the CPS.

TASK 2 Find out what happens to the working copy of the recording.

At the end of the interview and before switching off the machine, the interviewer must record the time when the interview finishes. For DVDs, the labels must be signed by everyone present and the master recording must be sealed in the presence of the suspect. If a suspect or the solicitor refuses to sign the labels, this is recorded. No signing is required for a recording made on a secure digital network. The suspect should be told what happens to the recordings and this is reinforced by handing them a pre-written explanation.

Where the interview is recorded onto a secure digital network, Code E makes separate provisions for the start of the interview. In brief, the recording device would need to be switched on as soon as the interviewer enters the room with the suspect; the interviewer must log directly into the secure digital network and commence the recording. The interviewee must be told that the interview is being recorded onto a secure network, that the recording has begun, and of their rights of access to it should a prosecution ensue. At the end of the interview (as with all interviews), they will be provided with a notice about the rights of access to the recording. The interviewer should also make a PNB note of the date and time, together with the identification number of the recording.

Interviews are normally visually as well as audio-recorded. There is no statutory requirement to do this but Code F suggests circumstances where it should be considered, for example where the suspect is deaf and uses sign language to communicate, where there is a need for an appropriate adult, and where the interviewer wants to invite the suspect to demonstrate their actions (Code F, para 2.2).

At the start of a video-recording, the interviewer must explain that a visual recording is going to be made and then unwrap the DVDs in the presence of the interviewee, load the equipment, and start recording. Similar legal necessities apply to video interviews as for audio interviews, ie cautions and significant statements or silences, etc. The suspect has the right to object to the visual recording at this point; if accepted, the interviewer will explain that the visual recording cannot be completed and then stop the disks (see Code F). The interview will then be recorded using audio-only equipment. Once a video interview is complete, the DVDs must be sealed in the presence of the interviewee, and the audio-only recording procedures followed.

PACE Code E, para 1.6 extends the range of audio and audio-visual devices that may be used to record suspect interviews. It established the term 'authorised' recording device, which means any device authorized by the chief officer of a police service as long as the interviewer has been trained to use it. This would include the use of body-worn-video (BWV) to record a suspect interview as long as it meets the above criteria. Even if BWV cannot be used as an authorized device, it is an ideal back-up to a written-only interview record. The contemporaneous written record would be the evidential product but the video would add transparency to the interview process.

Further details concerning recorded interviews may be found in the 'investigation' area of APP on the College of Policing website. Note that under the PACE Act 1984 there is no requirement to record the suspect's NVC, apart from the interviewer making references to actions.

13.8.2.12 Taking offences into consideration

Admissions of other offences can sometimes be treated as TICs (taken into consideration). These assist police to solve crimes and enable the police to gather essential intelligence relating to criminal activity. For victims, they promote 'closure' and allow them to claim compensation. A suspect may wish to tell the police about other offending behaviour fearing for instance that further evidence could emerge over time, leading to repeated arrests.

TICs should be discussed with suspects. However, no admissions to crimes should be obtained by inducements or favour. Safeguards have been put in place to prevent abuse of the TIC system; in the past, some criminals undoubtedly 'assisted' the police by admitting to offences they had not committed, hoping for more lenient treatment. However, the opposite applies—the Sentencing Council (2012a) makes it clear that where a defendant has admitted TICs, the sentence should reflect the totality of the offending. It is legitimate for an interviewer to ask a suspect if they wish for any further offences to be taken into consideration, as long as the interviewer adheres to these considerations.

Where a suspect discusses another crime that they have committed, the interviewer should obtain sufficient detail of the crime to be able to satisfy the points to prove, as if the case were going to court as a charge. This includes seeking out any evidential material that may already exist, for example forensic evidence. Each subsequent admission should be dealt with in the same manner, providing a thorough and professional response to the investigation of the relevant crime. Interviewers will also need to check whether the admitted crimes have already been reported and recorded or whether they are new crimes that should be recorded. The MG18 form must be completed so that the prosecutor and the court are made aware of any relevant factors, as well as the MG19 form, which relates to possible compensation for victims. If the suspect refuses to accept the TICs in court at a later stage, they will already have been warned that the offences concerned could be investigated separately.

Sentencing guidelines issued in 2012 made it clear that TICs are unlikely to be accepted for sexual or violent offences or for offences more serious than the main charge. If there is any doubt about the appropriateness of certain charges or TICs, advice is available from the CPS, custody officers, and PIP Level 2 investigators. Further information is provided on the CPS website.

13.8.2.13 Special warnings and adverse inference

Special warnings are used when the suspect fails, or refuses, to answer questions satisfactorily after due warning. If they present a 'no comment' interview when asked questions or fail to respond to questions based on special warnings, then at trial a judge may advise the jury that they are entitled to draw an 'adverse inference'.

Special warnings

The use of a special warning (ss 36 and 37 of the CJPOA 1994) is a further caution to the suspect and their legal adviser. A special warning may be needed for a suspect who has been caught directly in the commission of a crime (*in flagrante* or 'red-handed').

Section 36 warnings relate to a suspect's refusal to account for objects, marks, or substances or marks on such objects. Further details are shown in the flowchart.

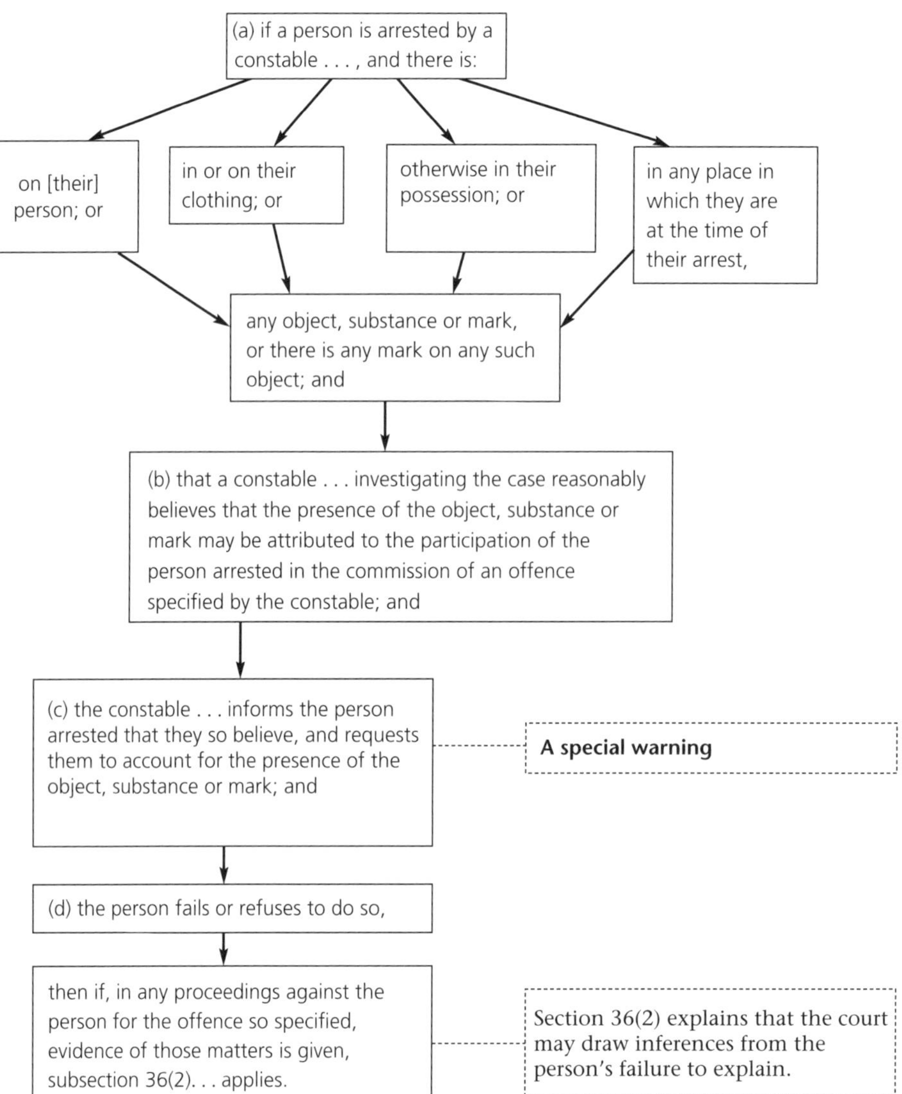

(a) if a person is arrested by a constable . . . , and there is:
on [their] person; or
in or on their clothing; or
otherwise in their possession; or
in any place in which they are at the time of their arrest,
any object, substance or mark, or there is any mark on any such object; and
(b) that a constable . . . investigating the case reasonably believes that the presence of the object, substance or mark may be attributed to the participation of the person arrested in the commission of an offence specified by the constable; and
(c) the constable . . . informs the person arrested that they so believe, and requests them to account for the presence of the object, substance or mark; and
A special warning
(d) the person fails or refuses to do so,
then if, in any proceedings against the person for the offence so specified, evidence of those matters is given, subsection 36(2). . . applies.
Section 36(2) explains that the court may draw inferences from the person's failure to explain.

Section 37 warnings relate to the failure of a person to account for their presence at a place at or about the time of an alleged offence. If an interviewer believes that the suspect's presence is linked to their participation in the offence, then the suspect must be warned that an 'adverse inference' could be drawn if no explanation is provided. If a suspect has given a reasonable account of the fact in question, a special warning should not be used as it could be interpreted as oppressive behaviour and the suspect's legal adviser would almost certainly intervene.

The special warning should include the following points, put in language which the suspect will understand:

1. the nature of the offence being investigated;
2. the particular fact the suspect needs to account for;
3. that the interviewer believes that the fact arose because the suspect was involved in the offence;
4. that an inference may be properly drawn if the suspect fails to account for that specific fact; and
5. that a record of the interview is being made.

Once the warning has been given, the interviewer must immediately ask the suspect to account for that specific fact. Suggested wording and more guidance on special warnings may be found in the 'investigation' area of APP on the College of Policing website. It may be necessary to give several special warnings if a number of separate material facts have been identified under s 36 or 37.

Once any particular special warning topic has been probed in detail, it is important that interviewees are made aware when the special warning no longer applies. Special warnings indicate that they need to explain something, so if they do not, an adverse inference can later be drawn at court. When a special warning no longer applies, the interviewee should no longer feel compelled to answer: the normal right to silence would apply.

Adverse inference

'Adverse inferences' under ss 34–37 of the CJPOA 1994 can be drawn in court if the defendant presents new significant information. It must be information concerning a fact in their defence that the court would reasonably expect to have been divulged earlier. The information could have been provided at interview following a caution (s 34), after a special warning (ss 36 and 37), or before the person is charged or reported. The jury would be entitled to ask 'Why didn't they mention this earlier?' and may conclude that the defendant had recently fabricated the fact. Therefore, during a police interview the suspect **must** be asked all the relevant questions to cover possible defences. If the crucial grounds for defence were not covered during the interview, then the defence might be able to argue in court that the defendant would have provided the information at interview 'if only they had been given the opportunity'. Where an investigator feels that adverse inferences could be drawn as a result of silence or failure to answer questions, the College of Policing APP suggests that an adverse inference package is compiled for the CPS, to highlight where this might be the case. Always seek advice from peers, supervisors, and consult APP guidance before undertaking this work.

TASK 3 When should the special warning be used—before caution, during the main questioning phase, or at the end of the interview as things are being brought to a close?

13.8.2.14 Urgent interviews

We have covered the standard rights and entitlements afforded to people being questioned about involvement or suspected involvement in criminal offences. However, in some very limited circumstances these rights can be withheld during urgent interviews.

Normally, this type of interview will involve asking no more than a couple of questions but is only permitted for indictable-only offences and where there are reasonable grounds for believing that the consequent delay might lead to:

- interference with, or harm to, evidence connected with an offence;
- interference with, or physical harm to, other people;
- serious loss of, or damage to, property;
- alerting other people suspected of having committed an offence but not yet arrested for it; or
- hindering the recovery of property obtained in consequence of the commission of an offence.

The interview must cease once the relevant risk has been averted or the necessary questions have been asked (in order to attempt to avert that risk).

Column one of the table lists the circumstances of the interview where some normal rights are withheld.

Circumstances of the interview	PACE Code C	Authorization
Prior to arrival at the police station, after arrest	para 11.1	None required but must be recorded on the custody record
Before suspect has received legal advice, having requested it	para 6.6	Authorization required by an officer of at least the rank of superintendent
No appropriate adult or interpreter (when one is required)	para 11.18	Only authorized by a superintendent in exceptional cases and only if satisfied that the suspect's physical or mental state would not be significantly harmed.

13.8.3 Interviews with witnesses

The PEACE process applies to all interviews but interviews with witnesses are not governed by the PACE Codes of Practice so there is more flexibility. Different approaches and techniques for gathering witness testimony can be adopted, eg video- or audio-recording, depending on the category of the witness and the nature of the interview in prospect.

Ideally, interviewers should only know a little about the alleged offence(s) before the interview. Too much knowledge might result in the interviewer contaminating the interview by introducing information not already mentioned by the witness. Another pitfall can be the interviewer failing to ask all the questions needed to fill any gaps in a witness's account. This can happen when the interviewer subconsciously supplements the account with their own knowledge of the offence.

APP suggests that a witness interview strategy should be developed in the early stages of an investigation. Any strategy should consider such issues as:

- appropriate level of interviewer required;
- how the evidence is to be captured (ie audio, video, statement);
- location of interview (ie police station, home address, sexual assault referral centre); and
- any vulnerabilities or particular needs of the witness or victim.

The correct strategy is particularly important in complex investigations where there may be a number of victims and witnesses, but can still apply in volume crime cases.

13.8.3.1 Recording witness interviews

The account from a witness is usually written up on an MG11 as a witness statement. Some categories of witnesses and victims such as intimidated witnesses, are interviewed away from a police station at designated facilities with suitable recording facilities.

In a serious crime, the interview with a significant witness is often video-recorded to capture their detailed oral account of events. This has numerous advantages for the investigator; it is less obtrusive and more fluent than the stop/start approach required for a written statement, so the witness may be more forthcoming. In addition, the witness's own words and intonation are recorded, reducing the risk of the statement-taker unintentionally influencing the content. A video-recording can also help to assess the witness's ability to provide convincing oral evidence from the witness box; some witnesses may not be able to perform reliably in court due to nervousness or forgetfulness. After the interview, a ROVI (record of a video interview) document may be prepared by the police to help to inform decisions on criminal charges or a full witness statement (MG11) can be prepared. The existence of the video-recording must be revealed to the CPS. Vulnerable witnesses can be supported by an intermediary, which may alleviate communication problems and allow better evidence to be obtained.

13.8.3.2 Achieving best evidence

Interviews conducted in compliance with Achieving Best Evidence (ABE) guidelines are used for a witness assessed as having a particular vulnerability or characteristics that will require special measures. Each witness must be assessed prior to formal interview in order to identify whether ABE procedures are required. Interviewers should use the special measures available so that they can offer reassurance in the face of questions from a witness such as 'Will I have to face them in court?' or 'Will everyone be able to hear all this?'

Interviews that are likely to be more difficult will be conducted by specialist interviewers qualified to at least PIP Level 2, and will follow ABE guidelines. The College of Policing APP makes clear the similarities between the PEACE model of interviewing and ABE. The phases identified in an ABE interview are establishing rapport, initiating and supporting a free narrative account, questioning, and closure (MoJ, 2022a). Guidance is also available regarding the structure of visually recorded interviews with witnesses (NPCC, 2015a) and this should be read in conjunction with the ABE guidance.

Trainee officers may engage with such witnesses in obtaining vital first accounts or might attend a full interview to brief and assist the interviewers. Where a first account is being obtained, it cannot be stressed enough that it is imperative to ask open, non-leading questions and to record what the person says verbatim in contemporaneous notes (usually in your PNB).

13.8.4 Interviews and criminal intelligence

An often overlooked by-product of a formal police interview is the 'intelligence interview'. These are used to gather criminal intelligence on the activities and lifestyle of the interviewee and others. It is a separate process from an investigative interview and must be undertaken by specialist intelligence officers. A trainee officer is unlikely to be involved in these but it helps to know that it happens.

All interviewers should carefully consider whether an interviewee would have access to information about criminals whose criminality comes within the service's strategic intelligence requirement. Such access should be noted and reported to the BCU Intelligence Unit which will arrange for an intelligence interview. This is often carried out by a fully trained intelligence analyst who does not work 'in the field', so that other criminals who may be in the vicinity will not recognize them. Any interview conducted whilst the subject is in custody, which is often the only opportunity for a secure approach, must be recorded on the custody record, but there must be no specific reference to the purpose of the interview. The record will simply show the transfer of custody from one investigator to another. In order to enhance confidentiality, intelligence interviews should not be recorded on disk or the secure digital network and no other people should be present. Any information obtained will be recorded on a 3 × 5 × 2.

An Investigation Anonymity Order (IAO) can be used when a person, other than a witness, can assist the police with relevant information or intelligence but they want to remain anonymous. It applies for cases involving murder or manslaughter with a firearm or knife, and the suspect must be between 11 and 30 years of age and belong to a group of people of a similar age (Coroners and Justice Act 2009). The group should also be identifiable by the types of criminal activity undertaken by its members and also be likely to use intimidation against a member who provides the police with relevant information about the offence. The legislation is primarily intended to tackle 'gang culture' crime but may in time be extended to cover a wider range of criminal acts. An IAO prohibits the disclosure of information that identifies the person or might lead to their identification.

13.9 Answers to Tasks

TASK 1

1. Unused material.
2. A disclosure officer is responsible for examining the records created during the investigation (and any criminal proceedings arising from the investigation). They will also complete the appropriate forms (MG6 series) to reveal relevant material to the prosecutor.
3. The prosecutor.

TASK 2 A shortened version of the interview will be prepared as a transcript for the reviewing lawyer on an MG15 form (a Short Descriptive Note (SDN)). It is not usual practice for a full transcript (Record of Taped Interview or ROTI) to be made as this is very time-consuming and therefore costly.

TASK 3 Many police practitioners argue that the best place to use a special warning is after the suspect has had a full opportunity to account for what happened but has not done so. This would normally be immediately following the 'challenge' phase of the PEACE interview.

14 Digital Policing

14.1 Introduction

Cybercrime is an umbrella term used to describe two distinct but closely related criminal activities: cyber-dependent and cyber-enabled crimes (CPS, 2019a).

The government's National Cyber Security Strategy 2022 glossary (Cabinet Office, 2022) defines these as:

- **Cyber-dependent crimes**—crimes that can only be committed through the use of information communications technology (ICT) devices, where the devices are both the tool for committing the crime and the target of the crime.
- **Cyber-enabled crimes**—crimes that may be committed without ICT devices, such as financial fraud, but are changed significantly by the use of ICT in terms of scale and reach.

The term cybercrime has been more widely used since the creation of the Council of Europe (2001) Cybercrime Convention (commonly known as the Budapest Convention on Cybercrime) and is now the common term for a whole range of criminal activities.

Although the terminology may seem confusing, there are, in effect, five main ways that digital technology can impact on crime:

- **Technology as the target of crime**—often referred to in the UK as 'cyber-dependent' or 'pure' cybercrime, these are offences that can only be committed using a computer, computer networks, or other form of ICT. These acts include the spread of viruses or other malware, hacking, and distributed denial of service (DDoS) attacks (McGuire and Dowling, 2013).

  Hacking is a form of trespass; it is the unauthorized use of, or access into, computers or network resources which exploit identified security vulnerabilities in networks (ibid). The hacker may simply wish to show that they have the skills to hack into a security-protected computer system, but there are other more sinister reasons for hacking, such as stealing data or restricting access to damage a business. This type of crime is usually investigated by highly trained staff from specialized cybercrime or computer crime units at national or local level.
- **Technology as an aid to crime**—this is where a traditional crime is committed, and digital technology is used to support the commission of the act. In the UK, this is called 'cyber-enabled' crime. Cyber-enabled crimes are traditional crimes which can be increased in their scale or reach by use of computers, computer networks, or other forms of ICT (McGuire and Dowling, 2013).

  An example would be a blackmail demand (a traditional crime) made by email or other electronic communication. The blackmail offence could be committed without the use of digital technology, but it is easier for the criminal to use digital resources to issue demands and instructions for payment of ransom. The internet can also be used to commit crimes such as stalking, harassment, fraud, identity theft, hate crimes, as well as the sharing of images of child sexual abuse and exploitation (sometimes, inaccurately and inappropriately referred to as child pornography or kiddie porn—however, law enforcement should not refer to it as such as it trivializes a serious crime (ECPAT International, 2016), and insinuates a consensual sexual exchange, which it is not). A vast range of crimes can be aided by using digital technology, indeed to the point that digital devices are now intermeshed into almost all criminal offences (Horsman, 2017, p 1).

- **Technology as a communications tool to plan or enact crime**—this could be, for example, where a group of criminals use digital technology to communicate with each other about their plans about a proposed crime. The criminals presume that their communications are not being monitored and, in any case, will often use anonymous services and encryption (this is often built in to popular instant messaging smartphone applications such as WhatsApp). Law enforcement agencies may find it difficult to even establish that any communication took place. An example would be for County Lines offences, whereby organizational groups extensively use digital devices to communicate with drugs runners across county borders (McClean, Robinson, and Densley, 2019).
- **Technology as a witness to crime**—this is an increasingly important tool in combatting criminal activities and other types of behaviour investigated by the police. While passive data generators such as CCTV and ANPR are extremely valuable tools for law enforcement, the police are still required to make other enquiries to support or counter the evidence available in digital form. One way in which technology is being used by police officers in the UK is through body-worn cameras. Such devices can provide a wealth of important evidence when dealing with incidents such as public order offences, assaults against officers, and disclosures made during and after an arrest (Wright and Headley, 2021). It can also provide a greater degree of transparency and accountability in policing practices that will lead to an increased level of trust and confidence in the police (Chapman, 2019)
- **Technology as a storage medium**—this includes the deliberate or inadvertent storage of data on any device which could then be used as evidence in an investigation. It is extremely important that the data and the devices are handled correctly from the very first contact with the police, and throughout the whole investigation or legal process. If the 'first officer at the scene' does not preserve the data correctly, its evidential value may be lost. In some situations, specialist support will be required, although for more straightforward cases all police personnel should have the requisite skills and knowledge to deal with such devices (see 14.4).

Cybercrime (sometimes called digital crime) and the police response (digital policing) is covered on policing degrees. This might include an overview of the internet (including some basic knowledge on identification and addressing of devices using Internet Protocol (IP) addresses and more advanced topics such as social media including Facebook, Instagram, YouTube, TikTok, Snapchat, WhatsApp, Discord, and Omegle, the rapidity of technological development, Deep Web platforms, and the Dark Web (the part of the internet that is not indexed by search engines and is intentionally hidden requiring a specific browser, known as Tor, for access. It provides an extensive degree of encryption by bouncing IP addresses across multiple hidden servers to provide its users with complete anonymity). It is important to note that Deep Web and Dark Web platforms are not solely used by people for criminal means. They can be used by government agencies targeting criminal activity, journalistic investigators, and researchers (Mirea, Wang, and Jung, 2019).

A police officer must be able to recognize new forms of crime in new environments and take appropriate and timely actions. Technological change is likely to continue at an ever-increasing pace and this will inevitably place additional demands on the police who will have to keep abreast of the impacts of technology on criminal behaviour.

Police officers are also expected to know what to do in cases involving digital technology, as well as what not to do. Some officers will be very familiar with day-to-day use of digital technology, but all officers will be required to deal with the technology in an appropriate way to ensure the integrity of any evidence from digital devices. The *National Policing Digital Strategy 2020–2030* (PDS and NPTC, 2020) has been produced to support police officers at all ranks with their digital policing knowledge, with the aim of developing a digitally literate workforce and leadership.

The temptation to 'take a quick look' at a computer or mobile phone must be avoided. In fact, unless there is a specific power to seize and search through a mobile phone, such a 'quick look' could constitute an offence under s 48(1) of the Wireless Telegraphy Act 2006.

The vast majority of technology-related crimes can be treated as offences under traditional legislation; specific legislation such as the Computer Misuse Act 1990 is only needed for particular types of crime. Many offences committed online are able to be prosecuted under legislation that exists to counter and prosecute more traditional crime. For example, internet-facilitated grooming (see 24.7.6) is covered by the Protection of Children Act 1978. This same Act is now also a key piece of legislation in combatting the presence and distribution of indecent images of children on the internet but was initially used to tackle distribution of non-digital photographs.

The main complication when dealing with cybercrime is often the international nature of evidence gathering. For many cybercrimes, eg if someone 'breaks into' a UK resident's Instagram account and deletes valuable photos, the victim will be local but the offence may well have been committed by someone in a different country, and the digital forensic evidence, such as data held on cloud storage, is likely to be in yet another country. Jurisdictional issues and access to international cooperation may prove difficult, costly, and time-consuming, if not impossible. The Council of Europe is one of the organizations attempting to address this (the UK's membership of the Council is unaffected by Brexit) and the UK is a signatory to the Budapest Convention (Council of Europe, 2001) and a second additional protocol (Council of Europe, 2022) that should enhance cooperation and disclosure of electronic evidence.

14.1.1 The extent of cybercrime

The extent of cyber-enabled and cyber-dependent crimes is the subject of some debate and estimates regarding the economic consequences of these crimes for the UK vary widely. Cybercrime and fraud involving the internet are becoming more prominent. For example, in the period between March 2017 and September 2020, the number of 'traditional' crimes went down by 6.4 per cent yet the number of fraud and Computer Misuse Act offences rose by 17.8 per cent (ONS, 2021a). The estimated annual cost to the UK of cybercrime runs into billions of pounds. Indeed, UK residents are now more likely to be victims of fraud than any other type of crime (see 23.9 for offences related to fraud). Malware and phishing emails are used to obtain customers' details and are key drivers of fraud. Such data can be used to commit fraud directly or to add authenticity to any other fraudulent approach (NCA, 2017, p 21).

The assumption is that many organized crime groups have moved their activities online as the potential rewards are greater and detection less likely. In addition, an attack on a computer system can appear to be an in-house malfunction and the initial response of information security professionals is to try to restore normal services as soon as possible. Therefore, some attacks may not even be recognized and reported as such. The extent of the crime can also be difficult to determine, such as whether an attempted fraud or an attack is a stand-alone incident or part of a wider series. However, if an attack involves personally identifiable information being exposed and obtained, the breach must be reported within 72 hours **of becoming aware of the breach**, where feasible under the Data Protection Act 2018.

Online criminals often use automated means to target a huge number of victims at the same time, each for fairly small amounts of money. Victims will sometimes not even notice, or feel less inclined to report, thefts of £10 or less to Action Fraud (the UK's national reporting centre for fraud and cybercrime) or their bank given the small amounts involved. Researchers have identified that this leaves criminals escaping with millions of pounds which is going unnoticed (Dawda, Janjeva, and Moiseienko, 2021). Victims of such crime should always be advised to report low-value online fraud to Action Fraud (see 14.3.2) as the activity might form part of a broader picture.

14.2 Examples of Cybercrime

The Home Office has been working with a number of police services on collecting information concerning the scale and nature of cyber-enabled crime. This involves flagging crimes where the reporting officer determines that the offence was committed in full, or in part, using a digital device such as a computer, computing network, or another digital device. Examples include a crime involving the use of a social media site or other site such as eBay to commit fraud. However, crimes where a mobile phone has been used to make phone calls or send text messages would not be flagged, nor would crimes where a PC and printer have been used to produce a counterfeit ticket for an event. Inevitably, as we have already noted, there are likely to be numerous cases where the decision on whether to flag falls in a grey area.

Here we outline some of the main types of cybercrime and provide some examples.

14.2.1 Abuse of network activities

Abuse of network activities are cyber-dependent crimes. Computers are often linked by networks within and between organizations and individuals and this can be exploited by criminals or people who want to cause disruption. For example, a Distributed Denial of Services (DDoS) attack involves sending multiple requests or messages to the target network. The intention is to overload the processing systems and impede normal functions. The table shows some examples of abuse of network activities.

Activity	Example
DDoS attacks	ICMP flood, peer-to-peer forms of attack
PBX hacking ('phreaking')	Hacking into a business phone network to generate a profit from international calls, at the expense of the business
Spamming	Emotet trojan (taken down in 2021, see Europol (2021)), contained in a malicious attachment to a phishing email, intended to steal financial information stored on the network.
Botnets	MyKings botnet controlling your computer to mine cryptocurrency

The term spam is frequently used for unwanted and unsolicited emails. Huge numbers of such communications can be sent out to sell a product or to distribute malware—this is known as spamming. The malware could have a variety of functions, such as sending out another wave of electronic communications to cause disruption, for example as part of a DDoS. Spamming can also be used to help set up botnet networks that are formed by machines compromised by malware (Silva *et al*, 2013, p 378). The affected computers can be linked to form a network and remotely assigned to a variety of tasks. Each user will not know this is happening but may notice that their computer seems to be working rather slowly.

14.2.2 Hacking: digital trespass, illegal access, or interception

Hacking is when a person intentionally accesses an online account, network, computer, or other digital device, without the permission of the legitimate user. It has inevitably been put to criminal use, for example stealing personal and business data and selling to organized crime groups. It also includes the interception of VoIP calls eg Skype services. Simple hacking is a criminal act, but it is often used to facilitate other criminal activity and then becomes a more serious matter.

Such unauthorized access to digital devices is required to manually install stalkerware apps. These track and monitor the victim's movements and communications and are increasingly used as part of coercive and controlling behaviours and domestic abuse offending. Globally, the reported number of victims with such apps covertly installed on their devices increased by 35 per cent in 2018/19 and the UK was the eighth worst affected country (Kaspersky, 2019). Kaspersky (2021) gives more current information including how to deal with the threat.

14.2.3 Malware

Malware is software that has been created to be used with a malicious intent to cause harm through disrupting digital devices and networks. It can operate in many ways and there are a number of different types, some of which are listed and explained in the table.

Name/type of malware	How it operates	Examples
Virus	Part of the coding helps it to spread and replicate by inserting a copy of itself in another program.	'Drive-by' websites, ransomware (eg Citadel malware) and Humming Whale virus (Android operating system).
Trojan	A form of malware which is 'smuggled' into a computer or network and which then performs unauthorized actions such as deleting data or secretly providing a 'backdoor' to enable another person to take over an infected computer.	'Man-in-the-Browser' (and 'Boy-in-the-Browser') Trojans secretly re-route web traffic from a victim's browser through an offender's own system, allowing the offender to capture passwords and other sensitive information (eg banking details).

Name/type of malware	How it operates	Examples
Spyware	Logs a person's activities on the internet, collecting and collating information that is used to target them.	Spyware that is used for (often unwanted) 'pop up' advertising in web browsers. Also includes 'key loggers' to secretly and remotely record a user's logon and password details.
Worm	A stand-alone program that replicates itself over a computer network (without the need for a host program).	They sometimes are delivered by an email that then looks at a person's address book and sends a copy of itself, often along with a message that purports to come from the sender.

14.2.4 Offensive material and illegal services

The anonymity afforded to internet users is exploited by people who wish to share and obtain offensive images and material, whether for personal satisfaction or commercial gain. Such material includes images of sexual abuse, grooming, and exploitation of children (see 24.4.2), and internet hate crime (see 19.8 on hate crime). A current phenomenon is the use of sexually explicit images by individuals wishing to humiliate or harm ex-partners known as Revenge Porn (see 24.4.3). The table shows some of the different ways the internet is used as a means of committing hate crime and providing illegal services.

Activity	Description	Example
Internet hate crime	Distributing material electronically intending to stir up hatred	Extremist political webpages glorifying violence against ethnic minority groups
'Cybersex'	Sharing sexual images without the permission of the person portrayed	Sexting via smartphones
Pharmaceuticals, controlled substances, and alcohol	Selling prescription-only and other restricted drugs through the internet	Illegal online pharmacies
Weapons and firearms	Selling weapons and firearms over the internet to people with no legal right to ownership	Alleged market in weapons through the 'Dark Net'
'Revenge porn'	The publication of explicit material portraying someone who has not consented for the image or video to be shared	An ex-partner publishing intimate photographs of a former partner on social media without their permission, with the intention of causing them distress

The Dark Net (or Dark Web) is increasingly used to commit crimes. This part of the World Wide Web is not visible to the normal user and can only be accessed with dedicated software. An example of this software is 'The Onion Router' (Tor), which is advertised as 'free software that helps you defend against traffic analysis, a form of network surveillance that threatens personal freedom and privacy, confidential business activities and relationships, and state security' (Tor, 2016). As with many ideas and developments created for lawful purposes, criminals exploit these new technologies for their own unlawful purposes. Criminal activity in this arena is typically more difficult to investigate due to the anonymity it provides and the nature in which certain criminal groups permit access to their platforms (eg, Child Sexual Abuse groups may require original submissions of child abuse material in order to be granted access). There are legitimate uses of Tor and the Dark Web, such as protecting privacy, but it is also a way of accessing information under oppressive regimes, for example the BBC (2019a) and *New York Times* (2022) both have Dark Web versions of their websites.

14.2.5 Cyber aggression

This can be on an interpersonal level such as cyber-harassment and cyber-bullying through social media sites (see the table for examples), but would also include conflict and espionage conducted through the internet. Despite anxiety in the media, there have as yet been few documented cases of cyber-terrorism. That said, the Center for Strategic & International Studies (CSIS) maintains a list of impactful cyber aggression over the past few years. Many of these are examples of state-sponsored cyber aggression (such as the Stuxnet attack on the Iranian nuclear programme, believed to have been perpetrated by the UK and Israel), but several are linked to terrorist and hacktivist groups (CSIS, 2022).

Activity	Description	Example
Cyber-harassment	Using digital means to harass, threaten, or unreasonably embarrass a person	Repeated sending of bullying SMS texts
Cyber-stalking	Constant monitoring, contacting, and spying by digital means	Stalking an ex-partner using GPS tracking systems on a smartphone
Libel	Libelling of a person online	Allegations made through a Twitter account

14.2.6 Theft, fraud, and extortion

The cyber-enabled crimes of theft and fraud are particularly common and ransomware is a clear example of extortion. There are numerous ways of conducting theft, fraud, and extortion through the internet, as shown in the table.

Activity	Description	Example
Re-chipping, unblocking telecommunication devices	Changing a SIM card; reprogramming a mobile telephone	Unblocking services (via software or hardware)
Advanced fee fraud	Requesting by digital means an upfront payment for non-existent goods or services	Scams such as the West African '419' fraud
Identity theft/identity fraud	Obtaining another person's personal and/or official information online, normally to commit an offence	Creating a false profile on a social networking site using someone else's name and details
Online auction fraud	Offering items which are then not delivered, or are misrepresented in some way	Using digital images to portray a non-existent item for auction
User account theft	Using various means to collect information about a person's computer or network account	User-accounts (eg on websites and forums, and Xbox live accounts) are hacked
Phishing	Trying to steal login, password, and personal identification numbers using electronic means	Emails that seem to be from a tax office, requesting details to be completed online
Spear phishing	Phishing which is personalized and individualized, which makes it seem more credible	An email with authentic details harvested from a social network site, seeming to be from a person's employer, but which contains malware
Phone-based scams	Trying to persuade a person to provide information, which can then be used to conduct theft	Phone call (vishing) purporting to be from recipient's bank, or a message (smishing) stating the person has won a prize; 'SIM-jacking' where fraudsters obtain the code from a person's service provider and take control of the victim's number
Cyber-squatting, domain name piracy	Registering domain names that are similar to well-known brands, intending to gain or profit	A confusingly similar company domain name is chosen to make a profit from unwary consumers
Ransomware	A form of malware that allows a criminal to lock a computer from a remote location, and then display a pop-up window informing the owner that the computer will not be unlocked until a sum of money, a ransom, is paid	Examples in 2017 included Wannacry and Not Petya. Some ransomware demands are accompanied by an accusation of illegal activity, or a pornographic image appears on the locked screen. This makes it more difficult to seek help so the recipient is more likely to simply pay the ransom
Sextortion, webcam blackmail	Blackmail in which sexual information or images are used to extort sexual favours and/or money from the victim	An online relationship develops into performing sexual acts via a webcam, but the blackmailer then threatens to publicly release the recordings if payment is not made
Business Email Compromise (BEC) (also referred to as CEO fraud)	The attacker gains access to a corporate email account and spoofs the owner's identity to defraud the company or its employees, customers, or partners	A bogus invoice is sent from a compromised email account requesting a change in payee information, to transfer payments to the perpetrator's account

Virtual currencies such as Bitcoin are frequently the currency of choice for criminals committing crimes of extortion, for example using ransomware. Although Bitcoin transactions are in the public domain, tracing the individuals involved is more difficult than tracing traditional bank transactions because the participants use anonymous servers. As law enforcement has had some success investigating cases involving Bitcoin, criminals are now turning to other types of crypto-currency, such as Ethereum, Monero, and Litecoin.

14.2.7 Intellectual property rights (IPR) crime

IPR crime is frequently cyber-enabled. This includes intellectual property theft where images and designs are taken and used without consent, for example downloading music or text without authority from the owner or composer.

Activity	Description	Example
Intellectual property theft	Stealing intellectual property, such as images and designs	Hacking a company's computer systems to steal software for computer chip design
Copyright infringement	Making unauthorized copies of digital content	Music and video shared with torrents, 'warez' software, commercial DVD copying, android boxes for accessing streamed films and sport without payment
Trademark infringement	Unauthorized use of a registered trademark	Selling goods online, using the logo from another company
Counterfeiting	Producing an imitation version	Using digital means to make forged banknotes
Circumventing conditional access systems	Bypassing the access systems to paid products or services	Satellite TV card-sharing using customized Linux firmware

14.3 Responding to Cybercrime

Cybercrime has impacted on UK policing since the 1980s. The first national response was created in 2001 as the National High Tech Crime Unit. 'Prevention is better than cure' remains a sensible piece of advice and this certainly applies to cyber-enabled and cyber-dependent crime. As a policing student, you will no doubt receive advice on safeguarding your digital information and remaining safe online so you should be familiar with such information. Police officers are increasingly likely to be asked by members of the public for advice on computer security.

14.3.1 Local level police responses to cybercrime

Each police service in the UK has its own locally based resources to investigate cyber-dependent crime. The units have often evolved from former fraud squads and tend to be relatively small, but their capabilities are increasing with the development of digital forensic technology. They also provide additional support to other investigations, for example into child sexual exploitation and abuse.

A number of police services (eg Sussex and Surrey, and Kent and Essex) have combined their resources and formed joint units for investigating cyber-dependent crime.

Many cyber-enabled and some cyber-dependent crimes are effectively screened to decide whether further investigation is appropriate. For example, local police-based units are likely to be responsible for investigating plastic-card crimes in the first instance; however, constabularies do not have the resources to investigate all reported incidents (particularly credit- and debit-card offences such as 'card not present' fraud where payments are made over the internet or by phone).

Although the investigation of cyber-dependent crime will invariably involve collecting traditional forms of evidence (eg in written form), there might also be digitally based evidence such as a deleted file recovered from a PC hard drive, or the address book from a mobile phone SIM card. Police officers at crime scenes must ensure the correct actions are taken to ensure that digital evidence is not destroyed or contaminated (see 14.4). The ACPO good practice guidelines recommend that digital evidence strategies should form part of the wider investigative process (ACPO, 2012a; Horsman, 2020). The Police, Crime, Sentencing and Courts Act 2022 and associated Home Office Circular 005/2022 has been created to standardize how and when the police can extract information from a digital device that has been provided voluntarily. The Home Office (2022e) has also produced a Code of Practice on extraction of data from digital devices.

The forensic techniques from initial data recovery to analysis are a specialist field within investigation (see 14.4). Once a device is seized and submitted to your Digital Forensics Unit, they will follow the ISO/IEC 17025:2017 standards (ISO/IEC 17025 is the international standard that sets out the general requirements for the competent, impartial, and consistent operation of laboratories) to ensure the integrity and admissibility of the forensic evidence. Police services may choose to 'outsource' some digital forensic analysis to non-police contractors who are also expected to meet the ISO 17025:2017 standards and follow the good practice guidelines.

14.3.1.1 Cybercrime prevention advice

If you are a police officer, you might well be expected to offer some form of 'cybercrime prevention' advice, especially for people who have been victims of small-scale online fraud. The National Cyber Security Centre's Information for Individuals & Families is an invaluable resource and is available here: <https://www.ncsc.gov.uk/section/information-for/individuals-families>.

Most emails sent out by financial and other organizations now include specific information such as part of a postcode and address the recipient personally. Many such organizations also provide guidance for customers to prevent internet-related crime, and it is good practice to remind members of the public to use such information.

In advance of any transaction, banks will often send a One Time Password (OTP) to the customer's mobile phone. Any customer receiving such a message unexpectedly should contact the bank immediately. Before travelling abroad, customers should also consider informing their bank which countries will be visited and about any foreseen transactions in those countries. Two-factor authentication (2FA) may also be used by banks and other businesses, especially those in the finance sector. Online purchasing systems will generally employ 'user authentication' methods to help to counter potential fraud. 2FA is now also a key security setting on most online accounts. This is probably the single-most important additional security feature that someone can apply to their accounts, dramatically reducing their chances of being hacked. For example, following a relationship break-up, an ex-partner may well be blocked on Instagram by their previous partner so that they can no longer see what is being posted. However, chances are the previous partner has not changed their password, so if this is known by the ex-partner then they can easily log into the profile and passively watch what is happening. Access to the profile would have been prevented if the victim activated 2FA, as a verification code would have been sent to the victim's mobile phone. Therefore, 2FA requires a person to not only know something (a username and password) but also have something in their immediate possession (their mobile phone for the authentication code).

Some people may be more vulnerable to certain crime types, such as widowed or single people. Middle-aged people may become victims of 'romance fraud' and young people may receive sextortion threats. However, criminals often target a wide and non-specific audience to try to locate potential victims. They only expect a tiny proportion to respond but this could still amount to thousands of victims.

There are many online resources with further information and guidance such as ThinkUKnow run by CEOP, the National Crime Agency's Child Exploitation and Online Protection commend (CEOP, 2013); GetSafeOnline.org and InternetMatters.org for instructions on personal and home technology security settings. More specific victim support is available from TheCyberHelpline.com, SuzyLamplugh.org, VictimSupport.org, and IWF.org.uk for issues around child sexual abuse and exploitation.

Police officers can use these sources to obtain up to date, accurate, and appropriate cybercrime prevention guidance and will then be able to provide bespoke cyber-security advice to individuals within local communities as required.

14.3.2 National measures to counter cybercrime

The National Cyber Crime Unit (NCCU) is responsible for investigations into 'high end' cyber-dependent crime, for example investigating large-scale DDoS and other hacking attacks and significant cyber-enabled frauds. It is part of the National Crime Agency and also works closely with the Child Exploitation and Online Protection (CEOP) Centre, and is actively engaged in countering the development of malware. The NCCU works with business and industry to counter cyber-dependent crime and historically has close links with the European Cybercrime Centre (EC3) based within Europol in The Hague.

Action Fraud is the national fraud and cybercrime reporting centre for the UK. Complainants for these crime types should be advised to report the crime online via the Action Fraud website. Action Fraud is responsible for collating all reports of cyber-dependent crime and fraud, including cyber-enabled fraud, and can use the information to identify patterns of criminal activity and thus facilitate investigations.

The banking industry supplements the police resources available to investigate plastic-card crime. For example, the industry body UK Finance sponsors the work of the Dedicated Cheque and Plastic Crime Unit (DCPCU).

14.3.3 International measures to counter cybercrime

In 2011, the UK acceded to the Budapest Convention on Cybercrime, a major international treaty designed to harmonize legislation and facilitate the effective investigation of cybercrime (Council of Europe, 2001). It improves international cooperation between nations, including the rapid transfer of electronic evidence across international borders where required.

From the perspective of the police officer, the importance of this Convention lies in its procedural provisions. It sets out procedures for processes such as:

- the preservation of stored data;
- the preservation and partial disclosure of event data;
- the legal means available to produce evidence;
- the search and seizure of computer data;
- the real-time collection of event data; and
- the interception of content data.

The Convention also facilitates some types of transborder access to stored computer data and helped to set up a 24/7 network to help ensure speedy assistance among the signatory parties. While police officers are unlikely to make use of such procedures daily, it is nonetheless important to know that they exist—there may be vital digital evidence in any investigation and this, by its very nature, is often transient. In such investigations, it is therefore important to respond as quickly as possible to preserve the maximum amount of evidence. The UK has also recently signed the Second Additional Protocol to the Convention on Cybercrime (Budapest Convention) which seeks to further enhance cooperation and disclosure of electronic evidence.

The number of law enforcement requests for data has reached such a level that companies such as Facebook, Apple, Microsoft, and Google now have their own dedicated procedures for handling such requests.

They can choose to provide some types of communications data (see 12.4.3) if the request is lawful, without the need to invoke complex formal legal assistance provisions. Any requests for communications data will have to be made through the 'Single Point of Contacts' within your local Communications Intelligence Unit. The most sought information in investigations is the identity of the subscriber of a communications service ('entity information').

14.3.3.1 The 24/7 system

The 24/7 network makes it easier and faster for signatory countries to seek assistance from one another in cybercrime and electronic evidence cases. The UK point of contact is housed by the National Crime Agency and, as a party to the Convention, the UK can use the Convention provisions during an investigation. For example, vital data could be preserved in another signatory country pending an application for legal assistance (which may take many months during which the requested data may otherwise be deleted by normal business processes).

If information is required from a country that is not a party to the Budapest Convention, there are other options to preserve and obtain data, although these requests are sometimes refused by the host country.

14.4 Seizure and Packaging of Digital Devices

At many police incidents there will be digital evidence. When such evidence is encountered and dealt with by the police, certain procedures must be followed. The importance of this cannot be overstated! The way in which the evidence is handled at this initial stage of an enquiry will impact on its admissibility in any subsequent criminal proceedings. Your actions may mean the difference between evidence being allowed or not allowed at trial. This type of evidence is inconstant (ie the data held on digital devices can be transient and easily altered) so special considerations apply for seizure and packaging of digital devices at crime scenes.

If a computer needs to be seized, the Digital Forensics Unit (DFU) (or Computer Crime Unit, CCU) should be contacted in advance for advice and may also attend the scene if they think it is necessary. Reasons for DFU involvement may include the suspect's use of encryption, network connections, or to preserve data only in the memory of the computer (which would be lost if standard procedure was followed without DFU involvement). DFU personnel are specially trained to recover data and present it in an evidential form acceptable to the courts. In doing so, they will be mindful of ss 19 and 20 of the PACE Act 1984 (which provide the legal basis for the seizure of data) and the ACPO *Good Practice Guide for Digital Evidence* (ACPO, 2012a). This is included within the Investigations APP under the Forensics section. The Good Practice Guide outlines (p 6) the four principles of digital evidence which must be adhered to. The first principle is relevant for all police officers and the remaining three are more relevant to specialists but are included here for completeness:

- Principle 1: *No action taken by law enforcement agencies, persons employed within those agencies or their agents should change data, which may subsequently be relied upon in court.* For the trainee police officer, this means, for example, that they should not turn on a PC that is turned off or have a quick look at the contents of a smartphone or other device.
- Principle 2: *In circumstances where a person finds it necessary to access original data, that person must be competent to do so and be able to give evidence explaining the relevance and the implications of their actions.*
- Principle 3: *An audit trail or other record of all processes applied to digital evidence should be created and preserved. An independent third party should be able to examine those processes and achieve the same result.*
- Principle 4: *The person in charge of the investigation has overall responsibility for ensuring that the law and these principles are adhered to.*

Apart from data and programs that may be stored, the plastic, metal, and glass surfaces of a digital device may also provide useful evidence. The outer skin of most computers is usually slightly textured and will therefore not yield latent finger marks. However, the smooth screen can provide latent finger marks as can areas which are not normally seen such as inside the case, under the support foot, and at the rear.

Local policy must be followed for all seizures and storage of computers and associated equipment, particularly relating to packaging. In serious or major crimes, great care must be taken as DNA and finger mark analysis may be required for whole devices. There may be a conflict of priorities between the physical and digital evidence retrieval—this must be resolved prior to any activity.

A key point is that a computer which is to be seized as part of an investigation that is currently powered 'on' should never be turned 'off' by following a standard shutdown procedure but should instead have its power supply removed (see 14.4.1 and 14.4.3). It is just as important that a digital device that is 'off' when found must not be turned 'on'.

Computers that are attached to networks present particular problems. If you encounter a network during an unplanned seizure and you need to seize one or more of the computers, you should contact your DFU or equivalent for advice. Further information may be found in Bryant and Bryant (2014).

The *Electronic evidence guide—a basic guide for police officers, prosecutors and judges* produced by the Council of Europe (COE) provides additional guidance. This is a restricted document but is available to police officers and investigators by visiting <https://www.coe.int/en/web/octopus/home>. This site is in itself an excellent resource for cybercrime-related matters. The guide provides advice on how to handle traditional computer-based evidence and deals with

Live Data Forensics (see 14.4.2). It also covers the procedures for obtaining evidential materials during online investigations; it is not as simple as just going online and downloading the data. The guide has easy-to-use flowcharts for using in search and seizure exercises and these may be printed off and used (in conjunction with local policy) when attending crime scenes with electronic evidence.

Digital forensics scientists are subject to the same codes of practice as other forensic science providers, such as the *Codes of Practice and Conduct for forensic science providers and practitioners in the Criminal Justice System*. The codes deal with laboratory-based activity but the level of scrutiny for those collecting digital evidence will no doubt increase—the correct procedures must be followed. The Forensic Science Regulator (appointed by the Home Office) developed the codes and ensures that all forensic science providers meet certain standards.

14.4.1 Unplanned seizures of digital equipment

Where a seizure is unplanned, the DFU or equivalent should be contacted for advice. The scene should be secured and people moved away from the equipment and any power supplies. If a printer is still printing, then it should be allowed to complete its run. The display of any active screen should be photographed or captured on body-worn video.

In the meantime:

- do not power-on any device;
- do not touch any key or the mouse;
- do not interfere with any other device on a network;
- do not use the telephone system; and
- treat any 'advice' from the owner or user with caution.

The layout of the devices and associated cabling should be photographed or sketched where practicable. Separate photographs should be taken of the computer from the front, sides, and back, and of any cables and devices such as portable drives that may be connected to the computer. For small portable devices, such as smartphones and tablets, local policy should be followed, but they should not be browsed through prior to being seized as this will be a breach of Principle 1 of the ACPO guidance.

If the devices are unconnected to other devices, then the DFU may suggest a simple seizure. If a device is powered on, unless advised to the contrary, the best course of action would be to turn off the device to prevent the loss of evidence (see 14.4.3.1).

However, care is needed as some devices may be part of a network and be able to communicate with other systems and devices through wi-fi, Bluetooth, NFC, and infrared. The contents of some networked connected devices (eg smartphones, tablets, and similar) can be deleted remotely and a suspect may want to do this to try to destroy potential evidence. These 'kill commands' can only be effective if the device is switched on and connected to a network. If a device needs to remain powered-on because live data forensics is required, then a 'Faraday bag' can be used to prevent such wireless communications being received by the device.

Seized hard drives should be placed in anti-static bags, tough paper bags, tamper-evident cardboard packaging, or wrapped in paper and placed in aerated plastic bags.

Given the growth in internet-connected devices and the increased use of the 'Internet of Things' (IoT), the number of devices that could hold vital evidence in an investigation has increased dramatically. Virtual assistants, such as the Amazon Alexa, smart TVs, smart watches, games consoles, routers, and even some doorbells and fridges could all be significant. Car infotainment systems and vehicle telematics could equally be valuable sources of evidence. Hence, police officers now need to look beyond smartphones, tablets, and computers, but this inevitably creates additional considerations. Always seek advice from your DFU before seizing any non-standard digital devices.

An understanding of where the data is stored, and therefore where the evidence is to be obtained, is essential. For example, an Amazon Echo smart assistant speaker does not store activity data on the device itself. This is held in cloud storage so the device that is used to access that account, such as the person's smartphone, should be sought for seizure so that the data can be accessed and downloaded.

14.4.2 Live data forensics

Live data forensics (LDF) procedures allow data to be recovered from a device that is found powered-on and is becoming increasingly important and necessary as a significant amount of data on devices is held in temporary memory. Such data would be lost if someone turned off the device when seizing it as evidence. Specially trained and equipped staff have the requisite knowledge and skills to recover the data while at the same time minimizing any changes to the data.

The increasing need for LDF in daily police work reinforces the advantages of contacting your DFU in advance of any search and seizure activity where digital evidence is likely to be encountered.

14.4.3 Procedures for computers and mobile devices that are powered-on

For all powered-on devices, and once any LDF has been completed, the following actions should be taken in this order to preserve as much evidence and data as possible:

1. photograph the device (particularly the screen);
2. make a PNB record of any on-screen text and imagery that might be visible, and the current activity of the device (eg loading a web page);
3. put the device into 'flight mode' or 'airplane mode' if possible; and then
4. turn it off by doing a 'hard shutdown' or remove the power supply (unless local policy determines that under the specific circumstances it should be left powered-on).

Removing the power supply to a computer prevents automated routines from being activated or drives being formatted—these might otherwise destroy vital evidence on the hard drive.

Every effort should be made to obtain the Personal Identification Number (PIN) password, or other decryption code that is used to unlock the device. Without this, it may not be possible for DFU to recover the stored data and evidence on the device.

14.4.3.1 How to turn off computers and other devices

To turn off a computer the power lead should be removed from the back of the PC base unit. (Unplugging it from the mains would not necessarily cut the power supply as the computer might have an uninterruptible power supply (UPS).) Care must be taken when removing the power lead as there is a low of risk of electrocution to the person doing this. This risk will be very much reduced by not holding the very end of the power lead where it connects to the computer.

Laptops generally have a battery so removing the power lead will not turn them off: this can be a particular problem in unplanned seizures. It would therefore seem necessary to remove both the battery and the power cable but, as in all matters concerning the seizure of digital equipment, local police policy must be followed. If the battery is removed, it must also be seized. For laptops with a sealed-in non-removable battery and for tablets, the only option would be to perform a 'hard shutdown'. This is done by holding down the on/off button for several seconds until the device turns off completely. For mobile phones and smartphones that are powered-on, similar general advice applies (but check local policy).

14.4.4 Packaging digital equipment

Local police service policy must be followed for 'bagging and tagging' digital equipment. Most policies state that see-through plastic bags should be used. If PC base units or other items of larger digital equipment are seized, then each item should be placed in its own bag. The bag must then be properly sealed and labelled—a cardboard exhibit label should be attached if the bag does not have a pre-printed label. However, care must be taken as finger marks on smooth surfaces will be obliterated if they come into contact with a polythene bag. In serious or major crimes, great care and detailed planning will be required as the entire device may be subject to DNA and finger mark analysis.

For small, portable digital devices the following procedures are likely to apply:

- package each device separately in its own individual bag unless instructed to the contrary;
- where applicable, keep the various media (eg CDs) in their cases;
- check inside all cases at the scene;

- do not place labels directly on any device;
- seize cradles/power packs for tablets, smartphones, and similar equipment; and
- keep packaged devices away from sources of magnetism, including during transport (eg keep devices away from vehicle radios).

Each local police service is likely to have its own policies for seizure and packaging of smartphones and mobile phones. This may include storage in Faraday bags and boxes to prevent the device communicating with the network.

14.5 Legislation and Cybercrime Offences

For most cyber-enabled crime, existing 'non-cybercrime' legislation, such as the Fraud Act 2006, can often be used to address the crime concerned. This also applies for some cyber-dependent crimes. For example, hacking will often be prosecuted as extortion (even though hacking is explicitly covered by the Computer Misuse Act (CMA) 1990). One reason for this is that the penalty for the 'traditional' offence (in this case extortion) will carry the heavier penalty on conviction. Another example of using non-cybercrime legislation to tackle some online offences relates to online harassment. When victims are trolled online, or sent grossly offensive messages, this could constitute an offence under s 1 of the Malicious Communications Act 1988 (see 19.6.2.4) However, the trolling will probably take place more than once and it could therefore be more appropriate to prosecute under the Protection from Harassment Act 1997 (see 19.6.1).

Other legislation can be used to deal with the 'grey' area between cyber-enabled and cyber-dependent crime. For example, a stolen phone with a blocked International Mobile Equipment Identity (IMEI) number will not work on a UK network. A mobile phone is uniquely identified by its IMEI and network service providers can use this to blacklist stolen phones. Therefore, criminals in possession of a stolen phone will often seek to change the IMEI so that it can be used again, possibly in a crime. The phone can be unblocked or otherwise reprogrammed using unofficial hardware and software acquired through the internet. It is a criminal offence to unblock a phone by altering an IMEI, as per s 1 of the Mobile Telephones (Re-programming) Act 2002.

It has, however, been necessary to bring in new legislation to tackle the growing use of digital technology, given that such capabilities were not even imaginable when the older laws were written. This will help to close and clarify the grey areas and loopholes that could otherwise be exploited. For example, several elements of the Regulation of Investigatory Powers Act 2000 have been phased out and replaced by the Investigatory Powers Act 2016. In addition, s 33 of the Criminal Justice and Courts Act 2015 introduced a new offence of disclosing private sexual photographs and films with intent to cause distress, colloquially known as 'revenge porn', and the Voyeurism Act 2019 created the offence of 'up skirting' (see 24.3.2).

A new 'Online Safety Bill' has been proposed (at the time of writing it is still being discussed in parliament) and in the future this will be important in protecting children and adults online (see <https://www.gov.uk/guidance/a-guide-to-the-online-safety-bill>).

14.5.1 The Computer Misuse Act 1990

For cyber-dependent crime, the main legislation in England and Wales is the CMA 1990, together with its various amendments (principally within the Police and Justice Act 2006). The four main offences under the amended CMA 1990 are shown in the table. Offences under ss 1 and 2 relate to unauthorized access whereas the more serious s 3 offence involves unauthorized acts.

Section	The offence	Explanation and examples
1	Unauthorized access to computer material	Prohibits activities such as accessing a person's social media profile using their username and password, without the person's permission. It is simply enough to prove that the suspect knows that the access was unauthorized—there is no need to prove the suspect had any intent to do something malicious after gaining access.
2	Unauthorized access with intent to commit or facilitate commission of further offences	An example of this offence would be hacking the person's social media profile as above and then posting something false about the person from it, thus making it appear that it was a genuine post from the person (here, the further offence would be a malicious communication).
3	Unauthorized acts with intent to impair	This would include spreading viruses, accessing a victim's social media profile (as before) and changing the password, and DDoS attacks. The scope of s 3 was broadened to include 'impair' as the original legislation required that changes be made to the files or programs on the computer, which did not cover DDoS attacks.
3A	Making, supplying, or obtaining articles for use in an offence under s 1 or 3	This would include, eg, supplying a kit to enable a DoS attack in a multi-player online game, thus slowing down the other player's broadband connection, creating lag following the controller inputs.

For the purposes of the CMA 1990, the word 'computer' is defined under case law (*DPP v Jones* [1997] 2 Cr App R 155 (HL)) as a 'device for storing, processing and retrieving information'. This is a wide-ranging definition that would include cloud servers, tablet devices, smartphones, and even an internet-connected fridge-freezer. In terms of the location, the CMA 1990 applies where the perpetrator was in the UK at the time they committed the relevant unauthorized access or acts.

All CMA 1990 offences are triable either way and the penalty for each when tried summarily is a fine or a maximum of 12 months' imprisonment. For convictions on indictment, the penalty is either a fine or imprisonment, a maximum of two years for a s 1 or 3A offence, five years for a s 2 offence, and ten years for a s 3 offence.

15 Counter-Terrorism

15.1 Introduction

Counter-terrorism is a challenging and dynamic phenomenon that defies simple explanation. Different states have created and relied on a range of strategies and sub-strategies to combat the threat from terrorism. It is often framed by political and socio-economic factors which can at times undermine its efficacy while at other times public opinion can make acceptable what would otherwise not be (such as the giving up of freedoms to ensure security). The most notable example of this is perhaps the security process we go through at an airport which has developed as a direct result of terrorist activity.

Because of the complexity of counter-terrorism, this chapter aims first and foremost to provide a solid foundation for understanding the threat from terrorism in the UK, the legislation in place to respond to the threat, the structure of the many and varied agencies involved in counter-terrorism activities in the UK, as well as the UK's counter-terrorism strategy. This is no easy task in a single chapter, but what is provided is a concise starting point from which to explore the topic further. With that in mind, some readings are recommended throughout the chapter and in the bibliography at the back of the book for onward research for those interested in the subject.

15.2 Key Concepts and Terminology

Before looking at counter-terrorism, it is important to understand its *raison d'etre*. Why do we need counter-terrorism strategies in the first place? To be better placed to answer this question, an understanding of some key issues is required.

15.2.1 Terrorism

There is a long-established debate on what the definition of terrorism is. Some consider that only sub-state groups can commit acts of terrorism (this eliminates the possibility of state terrorism and undermines the activities of lone actors) while others hold a broader understanding of the perpetrators. Others believe that only members of the public can be targeted, leaving the military as a more legitimate target. It is widely understood that an element of communication to a broader audience is necessary for an act to be classified as terrorist, often referred to as the 'propaganda of the deed'. And yet how that is done and what it actually means has changed drastically over time with the development of technologies.

Terrorist Murder of a British Soldier

The murder of a British soldier, Fusilier Lee Rigby, took place on 22 May 2013. Fusilier Rigby, a military drummer, was off duty returning to his barracks in Woolwich, South East London. His murderers were two British citizens of Nigerian descent, Michael Adebolajo and Michael Adebowale. Both had been waiting near the barracks in the hope of finding a victim.

Initially they ran Rigby over in a car, and then attacked him with knives and a meat cleaver. They were also armed with a handgun. Adebolajo and Adebowale remained at the scene apparently awaiting the arrival of police officers. When the police arrived, Adebolajo and Adebowale attacked them but were shot and wounded by armed response officers.

Both men were arrested and hospitalized. They were subsequently charged with Fusilier Rigby's murder, found guilty and sentenced to prison, Adebolajo with a whole life order and Adebowale to serve a minimum of 45 years.

Both men had converted to Islam. They claimed their actions were motivated by revenge for the alleged murders of Muslims by British soldiers in Iraq and Afghanistan.

It is not the purpose of this chapter to highlight the debate other than to mention its existence and refer the reader to several interesting publications exploring the subject (see Richards, 2013; Schmid, 2004). For the purpose of understanding counterterrorism activities in the UK, it is appropriate to focus on what has generally been taken as the legal definition in this country. The following is a concise version of the legal definition:

> The Terrorism Act 2000 defines terrorism, both in and outside of the UK, as the use or threat of one or more of the actions listed below, and where they are designed to influence the government, or an international governmental organisation or to intimidate the public. The use or threat must also be for the purpose of advancing a political, religious, racial or ideological cause. (CPS, 2023a)

There are a range of actions which fall under the definition of the crime of terrorism such as 'serious violence against a person; serious damage to property; endangering a person's life (other than that of the person committing the action); creating a serious risk to the health or safety of the public or a section of the public; and action designed to seriously interfere with or seriously to disrupt an electronic system' (CPS, 2023a). The use of firearms or explosives automatically meets the threshold of terrorism, regardless of whether a motive is known (see TACT 2000, s 1(3)).

15.2.2 Extremism

The term 'extremism' is one of the more controversial terms in use today. To enhance our understanding of what is meant by the term, a number of clarifications have been introduced over time. Extremism can be 'violent' or 'non-violent'. It can be motivated by a range of ideologies such as Extreme Right Wing, Left Anarchist, Single Issue, or Islamist. The big challenge is that someone can have extreme views (political, religious, or otherwise) and not break the law. So understanding what extremism is and what types are currently in existence is important.

It is also important to understand the power of labelling. There has been a preponderance of literature referring to 'far right *extremism*' and 'Islamist *terrorism*' without seeming to fully explore the differences. 'Far right terrorism' has traditionally been a rarely used term, as indeed has 'Islamist extremism', although that is now changing. The labelling of groups as one or the other has impacted how actors within each of these ideologies have been viewed by the public and by legislation. It is almost to say that the Far Right is less dangerous than Islamists because one is more involved in 'extremism' and the other is largely involved in 'terrorism'. Clearly this is problematic and has, more recently, been acknowledged as such (Onursal and Kirkpatrick, 2019; Signal AI, 2019).

With this in mind, a number of developments in the UK over the past few years have sought to more appropriately understand these phenomena. Unfortunately, it only expands the threat landscape by acknowledging that the threat from extremism is pervasive across all areas of societies. The publication of the Counter-Extremism Strategy in 2015 (as a separate strategy to the UK's counter-terrorism strategy and the establishment of the Prevent Duty in 2015), the establishment of the Commission for Countering Extremism in 2018, and the process of the Independent Review of Prevent by William Shawcross (2023) all go towards demonstrating the challenging relationships between the pre-crime world of radicalization and the criminal world of terrorism, as well as the range of crimes which arise from activities under these headings and yet do not meet the terrorism threshold (hate crime is one example).

What all of this leads to is a need to understand what extremism is, at what point it breaks the law and at what point it meets the high bar of a terrorist crime.

15.2.2.1 Extreme Right Wing (XRW)

Extreme Right-Wing Terrorism has traditionally been linked with hate crimes (crimes carried out against a minority ethnic group or other groups such as the LGBT+ community) and its inclusion in terrorism data is relatively recent. The UK publishes an annual report on Hate Crime Statistics (see 19.8) and it defines hate crime as 'any criminal offence which is perceived, by the victim or any other person, to be motivated by hostility or prejudice towards someone based on a personal characteristic' (Allen and Zayed, 2022). In the most recent publication of this report, a troubling trend is noted, as can be seen in the graph below.

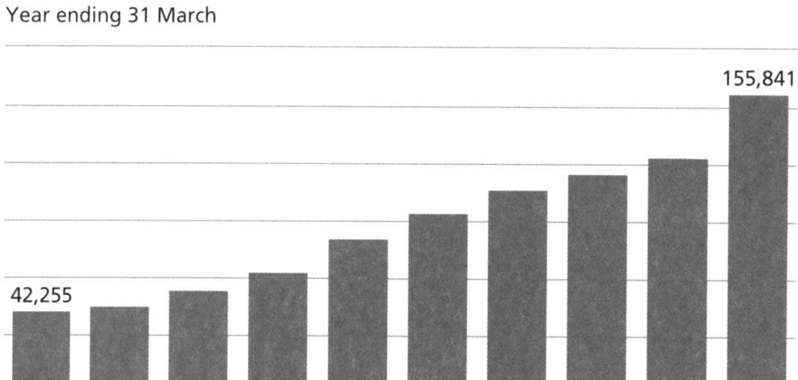

Source: © House of Commons 2023. Reproduced from Allen and Zayed (2022) Hate Crime Statistics, House of Commons Library. 'Police recorded crime figures in 2021/22 show that there were 155,841 offences where one or more of the centrally monitored hate crime strands were deemed to be a motivating factor. This represented a 26% increase on figures for 2020/21'.

The CPS describe XRW actors as those who 'promote messages of hate-filled prejudice which can encourage radicalization among people motivated by race hate'. Because of the interconnection between the two behaviours or actions, extremism and hate crimes are often now perceived, at least in the public sphere, as two sides of the same coin. This is an over-simplification; both police in the UK and the Government still provide statistics on hate crime as an issue in and of itself. Nonetheless, it is important to acknowledge the potential connections between the activities of perpetrators under both crime categories.

Examples of XRW groups which have been active in the UK are National Action, Sonnenkrieg Division, and The Base. In 2016, National Action became the first XRW group to be proscribed (banned) under UK law, demonstrating a new level of threat attributed to such groups. Among several notable events, a firebomb attack on a migration centre in Dover in October 2022 received significant media attention for having been carried out by a 'far right' actor, coupled with controversy over migration as a broader issue.

15.2.2.2 Left, Anarchist, or Single Issue Terrorism (LASIT)

More recently, Left Wing, Anarchist, and Single Issue terrorist activity have been banded together as LASIT. This is largely due to the combined threat that exists from these actors, while acknowledging that individually, activities under these categorizations are not particularly significant in comparative terms. A look through the various open-source reports and datasets provided by the Home Office (available at https://www.gov.uk/government/collections/counter-terrorism-statistics) indicates that the main terrorist threat does not come from these ideologies, although other types of crime may still be attributed to them before the threshold of terrorism is met.

Left Wing actors tend to follow socialist and Marxist ideologies and were particularly prevalent in the 1970s and 1980s. Activities from these groups tend to be protests, although individualized violence can also take place.

Anarchist Ideology has been in existence for a long time. It has taken many guises over the decades but is more recently an international movement resulting from a populist backlash against centrist governments worldwide. Anarchist groups such as Weather Underground, a US-based group active in the 1970, carried out significant acts of violence. Recently, Anarchism has not been responsible for acts of terrorism, although the threat from these groups to move towards violence is growing, as can be seen in the table below.

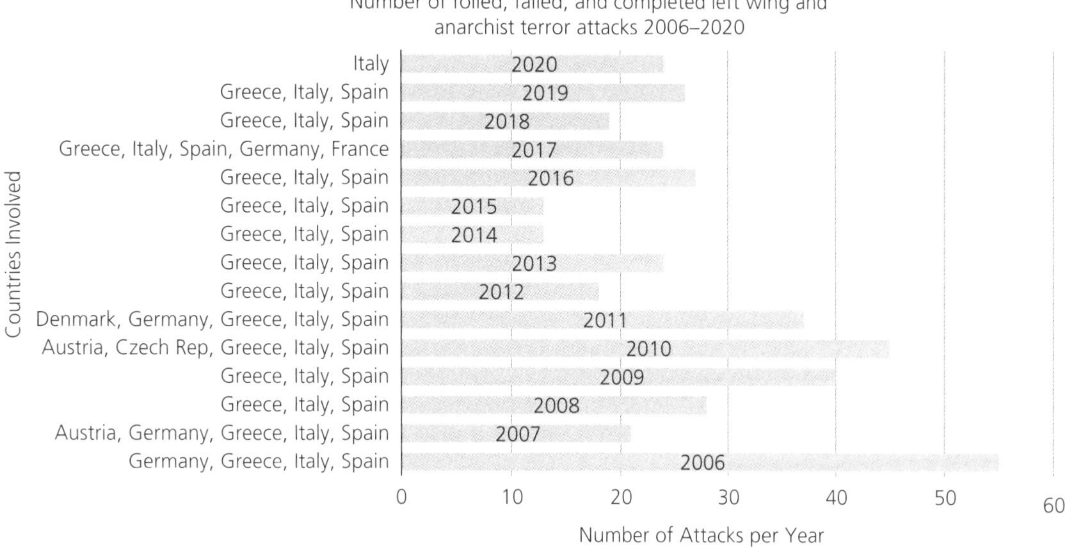

Source: Adapted from Europol TE-SAT reports between 2007 and 2020 and showing left-wing and anarchist terrorist attacks 2006–20.

Finally, Single Issue Terrorism encompasses a range of actors including Pro-Life/Anti-Abortion groups, Animal Rights groups, Environmental groups, and INCEL (Involuntary Celibate) individuals. A complex range of issues motivates these groups and individuals to engage in radicalization, protests and, on occasion, violent activities. Whilst in the main these groups have acted within the law, animal rights and Pro-Life activists in the USA have committed murders (see for example Durkee, 2022). In the UK members of an animal rights group called 'Stop Huntingdon Animal Cruelty' (SHAC) campaigned to close an animal testing facility, engaged in posting hoax bombs and offensive items to homes and offices, physically attacked staff, made threats of violence, and daubed abusive graffiti on property. This resulted in convictions for blackmail in 2010 (Weaver, 2010). In April 2023, 118 Animal Rights activists, from a climate and animal rights group called Animal Rising, were arrested for a range of offences whilst trying to disrupt the Grand National horse race in Aintree. The group was protesting about the use of horses for sport and entertainment.

15.2.2.3 Islamist Extremism

The most well-known extremist actors of the twenty-first century are Islamist groups. More famously considered in terms of terrorism, these groups also engage in extremist activities through the radicalization and recruitment of individuals. The Islamist ideology is complex and well-established and is therefore nefarious and deeply embedded in certain groups' thinking. A brief overview of the issues is provided below.

Islam is a religion which is followed by Muslim people across the world and is one of the three Abrahamic religions along with Judaism and Christianity. Upon founder Mohammad's death, his followers split into two primary streams: Sunnis and Shias. Sunni Muslims are considered the largest of the two groups, holding majority populations in Saudi Arabia, Egypt, Jordan, Syria, Qatar, UAE, Oman, and Yemen. Shias form the majority in Iran and Iraq. Within the Sunni religion, a number of sub-movements have developed, and in terms of terrorist activity, Wahhabism and Salafism have become notorious. These two movements are traditionalist and seek to return to a time where Islam was deemed to be perfect, just after the death of Mohammad. They seek to reinstate the Caliphate, an Islamic state which is ruled through strict Sharia (religious) law. Certain groups within these movements have chosen the path of violence, Osama bin Laden being the most famous of recent times. Therefore, the groups Al Qaeda (more on this group can be found below in 15.3) and Daesh (also known as the Islamic State (IS), the Islamic State of Iraq and Syria (ISIS), and the Islamic State of Iraq and the Levant (ISIL)) catapulted to global attention this small offshoot of a widely celebrated religion which holds no connections to violence at all. This dynamic has resulted in widespread misunderstandings about Muslim people and their religion and feeds into extremist narratives of the XRW.

The modern origin of Islamist ideology stems from the writings of a famous Egyptian called Sayyid Qutb who condemned Western lifestyles and pushed for a return to traditional Islam. As a leading member of the Muslim Brotherhood, he was imprisoned on several occasions by the Egyptian authorities and was ultimately hanged for his supposed role in the attempted assassinations of President Nasser (although he had no direct involvement with those actions). His death gave him the status of martyr and his ideology has inspired some of the most extreme Islamist groups of the twentieth and twenty-first century.

15.2.3 Radicalization

Radicalization is the process whereby someone develops extreme views, potentially to the point of committing acts of violence and terrorism. Significant research has been carried out on the process of radicalization, and some key resources have been provided in the Bibliography section at the back of this book.

There are two primary places where radicalization occurs: in person (also called 'offline') and online. In person radicalization has been taking place for as long as extremism and terrorism has existed, and is more commonly known to occur in domestic locations, religious centres, community centres, prisons, and education centres (for example in universities). Online radicalization is a growing concern and individuals who radicalize in this space have adapted to increased counter-terrorism activities. For example, while social media platforms such as Facebook and Twitter were considered at one time to be the source of most online radicalization, it is now believed that people are being radicalized in the chat rooms of gaming platforms (Kenyon, Binder, and Baker-Beall, 2022), a far more difficult arena to police.

The complexity of the radicalization process has been disseminated over the decades in a number of models (Muro, 2016), the most famous of which is the Pyramid Model (McCauley and Moskalenko, 2017), or Moghaddam's Staircase to Terrorism (see diagram below). It is a useful visual representation of the fact that, while many people can make a first step toward radicalization (the bottom of the staircase) only a very small number will progress through the whole process to carry out an act of terrorism. However, with the understanding that not all terrorism crimes are big and dramatic, and someone can be arrested for being a member of a proscribed organization or for spreading terrorist-related information, the validity of the staircase needs to be viewed cautiously. It nonetheless does provide some basic insights in the radicalization of a person from their first step on the staircase to the most extreme outcome—a terror attack.

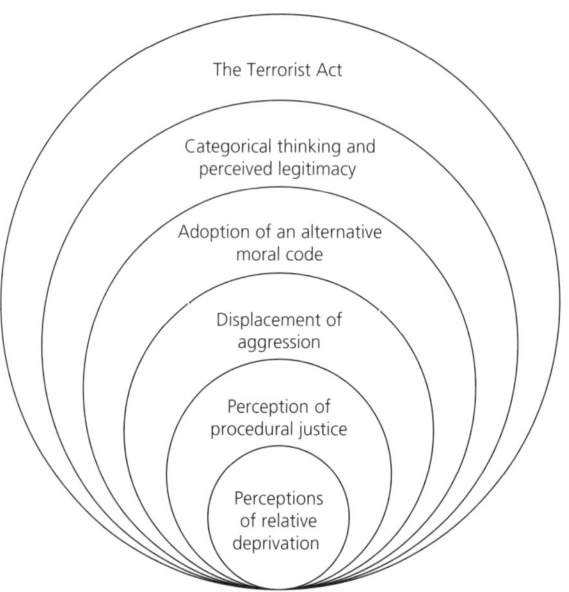

Source: Adapted from Ziemer, 2016. Moghaddam's Staircase to Terrorism.

Core Aspects of Police Work

15.3 A Brief History of Terrorism in the UK

Terrorism has a long history in the United Kingdom, but the word itself is relatively recent, deriving from the Reign of Terror period in the French Revolution. In earlier times people who today would be defined as terrorists might be charged with treason (gov.uk, 1351). The prime example of this is Guy Fawkes whose attempt to blow up the Houses of Parliament in the cause of Catholic emancipation in 1605 resulted in his execution (Nicholls, 1991). Similarly, although many would today consider the violent actions of the Suffragette Movement in the early part of the twentieth century in fighting for votes for women were justified, at the time activists were charged with common law offences. Today their actions could be considered as terrorist (Walker, 2019).

The first time the term 'terrorism' was used in British legislation was the Prevention of Terrorism (Temporary Provisions) Act 1974 introduced at the height of the Troubles in Northern Ireland (gov.uk, 1974). The Act had three sections, allowing the banning of certain terrorist organizations, the exclusion of suspected terrorists, and extending police powers to hold terrorist suspects (Scorer, 1980). This was the first acknowledgment that pre-existing criminal and common law legislation were insufficient to tackle the terrorist threat. This trend for ever more powerful counter-terrorist legislation has continued to this day and has been noted in other countries such as the USA with the implementation of the terrorist-focused Patriot Act (see McCarthy, 2002). The most significant example of terrorism experienced in the UK arose from Ireland's struggle to free itself from colonial domination by the UK. This started with the Norman English invasion of Ireland in 1169. Irish resentment manifested itself regularly over the 800 years of occupation before partial independence was gained in 1922. A significant driver of the independence struggle were the famines caused by the repeated failures of potato crops in the mid-nineteenth century, particularly the Great Hunger of 1845–52. This caused a mass depopulation of Ireland though starvation and mass emigration to escape the famine together representing a reduction of about 25 per cent of the Irish population. The perception that the UK stood by and failed to assist crystallized Irish resistance with uprisings throughout the country.

A leading *terrorist* group at the time fighting for Irish freedom was the Fenian Brotherhood. From the 1860s to the end of the century, the Fenians exported violent activism to Great Britain and parts of the then British Empire, drawing on the support of members of the large Irish refugee community (Whelehan, 2012; Bowman, 2019). Frustration at the failure of various Home Rule bills in the late nineteenth and early twentieth centuries stoked resentment leading to the Easter Uprising in 1916. The Irish Republican Army was formed from other resistance groups in 1917 and led the fight against the British in the subsequent Irish War of Independence (1919–21).

The Irish Free State was established by the Anglo-Irish Agreement in December 1921. Under the agreement, the six northern counties remained part of the United Kingdom with a devolved local government, and the 26 southern counties became self-governing. This division of Ireland caused tensions among the Irish themselves, either supporting or opposing the treaty, resulting in the Irish Civil War from 1922 to 1923. This was won by supporters of the Treaty, with considerable British assistance (Foster, 2015). The end of the Civil War brought in a period of relative political stability in the Free State. However, such stability was less evident in the North where tensions existed between the minority community of Irish Nationalists, often Catholics, wishing to join the South, and the majority community, the Loyalists, often Protestants, intending to remain in the United Kingdom.

This position lasted until the 1960s, when following the example of the Civil Rights Movement in America, Northern Irish Nationalists started protesting for their own civil rights, citing poorer housing and worse education and employment opportunities than the majority population. From this background, and from dissatisfaction with what was perceived as a lack of response of the old IRA, a new armed group aiming to protect the Nationalist community, the Provisional Irish Republican Army (PIRA) emerged in the late 1960s. The existence of PIRA provoked a response from certain loyalists who established Protestant terrorist groups, such as the Ulster Volunteer Force (UVF) or the Ulster Defence

Association (UDA), also known as the Ulster Freedom Fighters (UFF). This was the start of a 30-year period of sectarian violence known as The Troubles, an armed and violent struggle involving PIRA, the British army, Loyalist paramilitary groups, and the Royal Ulster Constabulary (RUC) (Kennedy-Pipe, 2014).

Following complex and delicate negotiations involving leaders from both communities and the governments of Ireland, the UK, and the USA, peace was tentatively established by the signing of the Belfast Agreement, also known as the Good Friday Agreement (GFA), in 1998 (HM Government, 1998). Under the terms of the agreement, the Irish government agreed to renounce its constitutional claims to the territory of Northern Ireland as contained within the 1937 Irish Constitution and the British Government agreed to amend the 1920 Government of Ireland Act, which theoretically retained Ireland as part of the UK. Significantly, there were to be prisoner releases and paramilitary arms decommissioning on both sides. The GFA established the Northern Ireland Assembly and replaced the RUC with the Police Service of Northern Ireland (PSNI). It recognized the birth right of the people of Northern Ireland to hold British or Irish citizenship. Whilst the Agreement was not recognized by all paramilitary groups, notably the splinter Continuity IRA, and although it has not brought a total end to political tensions between the two communities, it is widely considered a success (Fenton, 2018). Despite the overall improvement, small Republican dissident groups such as the New Irish Republican Army (NIRA) rejected the Good Friday Agreement and continue the violent struggle to this day (Hoey, 2019).

More recent terrorism, often referred to as International Terrorism, has its roots in the religious terrorism that arguably started with the establishment of al Qaeda (AQ) in Afghanistan in the late 1980s. Following the occupation of Afghanistan by the Soviet Union in 1979, disparate groups of Afghani resistance fighters, the Mujahideen, trained and armed by the United States and other countries, formed al Qaeda (AQ) initially to provide logistical support to the fighters. With the fall of communism in 1989, Russian forces left Afghanistan, and the Mujahideen regrouped under the leadership of Osama bin Laden to undertake a religious struggle countering Western influence. AQ, and its spin off group Daesh, which developed from al Qaeda's participation in the war in Syria, found a resonance with many disaffected people resentful at what they perceived as Western influence in their affairs. This crystallized around a strict interpretation of the teachings of the Koran and the belief that it was their duty to defend Islam against corrupt influences.

From Al Qaeda's (AQ) first attack in Yemen in 1992, AQ-inspired militants undertook a violent campaign of terrorism targeting either against Western targets or targets in Muslim territories not sharing AQ's interpretation of the Koran. The most symbolic and impactful incident were the four co-ordinated attacks which took place on 11 September 2001 (more commonly referred to as the 9/11 attacks) on the US in 2001, most significantly the plane strikes on the two World Trade Centre buildings in Manhattan (Burke, 2007).

First Al-Qaeda linked attack in the UK

In the UK the first AQ inspired atrocities were the terrorist explosions in London in July 2005, known today as '7/7'. Here four disaffected young men claiming to follow the teachings of Osama bin Laden set off body-worn explosives, three on the London Underground rail system and one on a bus. In total 700 people were injured and 52 people died, including the four attackers themselves.

The attackers, three of whom came from Leeds, were all British people, three of Pakistani decent, and one of West Indian heritage. Two, Mohammad Sidique Khan and Germaine Lindsay, were married with children and one Shehzad Tanweer, lived with his parents, working in a fast-food shop. Hasib Hussain, the youngest attacker at 18 years old, was still at school and played rugby for a local team. All four were well educated leading superficially normal lives with supportive families.

There were no known signs of the radicalization or extremism that led to the attacks.

AQ adherents have undertaken several terrorist attacks in the UK since 7/7. These include the 2017 terrorist bombing at the Ariana Grande concert in Manchester, the gun and stabbing attacks on London Bridge in 2018, and the murder of Mr David Amess MP in his parliamentary surgery in 2021 by an ISIS supporter, Ali Harbi Ali. All these attacks were committed by similarly disaffected, radicalized young men.

Islamic Extremist murders

On 29 November 2019 in Fishmongers' Hall in London, Usman Khan, who had been released the year before on licence from prison for terrorist offences, stabbed two people to death, and injured three others in a terrorist attack.

Khan had been attending an offender rehabilitation programme at the Hall organized by Cambridge University. Wearing a fake explosive suicide vest, and with two knives taped to his wrists, he attacked the other conference attendees before being chased from the building by other participants who at considerable risk, retaliated, arming themselves with items they found in the Hall including a ceremonial pike and a narwhal tusk.

Khan ran from the building onto London Bridge where he attacked passers-by. He was restrained by a passing off-duty police officer and members of the public. Armed police officers soon arrived and took control of the scene. Deciding Khan's suicide belt presented an immediate threat to life, they engaged and shot him. Khan did not survive.

In terms of XRW attacks, the racist and homophobic nail bomb attacks carried out in London by lone activist David Copeland in 1999 is a prime example. Copeland, a former member of several XRW groups and considered a neo-Nazi activist targeted the LGBT+, the Afro-Caribbean, and the Bengali communities in London in three attacks in April 1999 leaving nail-bombs in holdalls concealed in public places. He killed three people and injured 140. Copeland was convicted of murder in 2000 and sentenced to life imprisonment.

Linked to this, the murder of the MP Helen (Jo) Cox in 2016 by an XRW activist, Thomas Alexander Mair, should be included. Mair, a white supremacist, believed that the world's problems had been caused by left wing politicians such as Cox.

Extreme Right-Wing attack

On 30 October 2022, Andrew Leak, a 66 year-old man from Buckinghamshire, drove his car to Dover in Kent and threw three petrol-based firebombs at a Border Force Immigration Centre. The centre was being used to house and process asylum seekers, mainly people who had arrived in the UK in small boats from Northern France. Two members of staff were said to have suffered from minor burns.

Leak immediately escaped in his vehicle following the attack and apparently committed suicide at a local petrol station by tying a ligament around his neck to a fence post and, returning to his seat, driving the car forward.

Leak, who was known to be a supporter of extreme right-wing groups and causes had supported such ideology on social media platforms and said he wanted to end the arrival of the small boats. He had expressed racist views, often targeted at immigrants, especially Muslims and asylum seekers.

The police investigating the scene described Leak's actions as a hate-crime motivated by a terrorist ideology.

Similarly, there have been attacks on mosques by violent members of the extreme right wing, and people claiming to be neo-Nazis have been arrested planning attacks on Jewish targets (see for example Dearden, 2020). The table below provides an outline of terror attacks in the UK which do not relate to Northern Ireland terrorism and demonstrates the prevalence of the threat.

Terror attacks in the UK between 1995 and 2022 which are not attributed to Northern Ireland

Event	Year	Ideology
Nail Bomber	1999	Extreme Right Wing
7/7 Bombings	2005	Islamist
Glasgow Airport Attack	2007	Islamist
Murder of Fusilier Lee Rigby	2013	Islamist
Murder of Jo Cox	2016	Extreme Right Wing
Westminster Bridge Attack	2017	Islamist
Manchester Arena Bombing	2017	Islamist
London Bridge Attack	2017	Islamist
Finsbury Park Mosque Attack	2017	Extreme Right Wing
Parson's Green Attack	2017	Islamist
London Bridge Attack	2019	Islamist
Whitemoor Prison Attack	2020	Islamist
Streatham Stabbing Attack	2020	Islamist
Reading Stabbing Attack	2020	Islamist
Murder of David Amess	2021	Extreme Right Wing
Liverpool Women's Hospital Attack	2021	Unknown
Dover Firebomb Attack	2022	Extreme Right Wing

15.4 Contemporary Terror Threats in the UK

In terms of understanding the most significant terrorist threats to the UK today, it may be appropriate to note that in assessing its priorities, MI5 states that in 2018/2019 its resources were allocated as follows:

- 67 per cent international counter-terrorism
- 20 per cent Northern Ireland-related terrorism
- 13 per cent counterespionage, counter-proliferation, and protective security (MI5, 2023a)

This reflects their assessment of the most significant threats to the UK today, and this can be regarded as a reliable indicator of the threat. As can be seen from this, the most prominent from of terrorism today in the UK is international terrorism, which includes not only AQ/ISIS related terrorism, but any non-domestic political violence unrelated to Northern Ireland such as Sikh and Sri Lankan terrorism.

In 2022, in his Annual Threat Update, the Director General of MI5 stated that since the beginning of 2017, working with the police, they had disrupted 37 late-stage terrorist attacks, eight of which were in 2022. These attacks were planned by both XRW and Islamic terrorists (MI5, 2022).

It should be noted that MI5's activities also relate to dealing with terrorist-related crimes such as raising funds for terrorist activity, radicalizing people to join terrorist groups and also helping such people to travel abroad to carry out terrorist activities.

In this speech, it was noted that the threat from Irish nationalist terrorism was still apparent. For example, a splinter Republican group called the New Irish Republican Army (NIRA) shot and killed a journalist in 2019 in Derry (Carroll, 2022) and is suspected of an attack on an off-duty police officer in 2023 in Omagh (Badshah and Carroll, 2023). Uncertainties around the Northern Irish protocol and loyalist concerns over the possible re-imposition of a border between Northern Ireland and the Republic of Ireland still exist. However, these may have been reduced by the signing of the Windsor Protocol in March 2023 which removed that possibility.

15.4.1 National threat levels and the threat from terrorism

MI5 sets the UK's threat level. There are two categories of threat from terrorism: Northern Ireland-related terrorism and international terrorism. Northern Ireland-related terrorism is further broken down into the threat that Northern Ireland experiences and the threat that the mainland UK experiences.

There are five threat levels in the UK:

- Low—an attack is highly unlikely
- Moderate—an attack is possible, but unlikely
- Substantial—an attack is likely
- Severe—an attack is highly likely
- Critical—an attack is highly likely in the near future.

The National Threat Level has varied between Substantial and Severe since July 2019. The threat level from Northern Irish-related terrorism in Northern Ireland was placed at Severe in July 2019 and has changed twice subsequently, to Substantial in March 2022 and to Severe in March 2023.

National Threat Level

Date	Threat Level
9 February 2022	SUBSTANTIAL
15 November 2021	SEVERE
4 February 2021	SUBSTANTIAL
3 November 2020	SEVERE
4 November 2019	SUBSTANTIAL
23 July 2019	SEVERE

Northern Irish-Related Terrorism in Northern Ireland Threat Level

Date	Threat Level
28 March 2023	SEVERE
22 March 2022	SUBSTANTIAL
23 July 2019	SEVERE

Source: Current Threat Level in Great Britain and Northern Ireland (MI5, 2023c).

MI5 also provides a table showing a historical overview of threat levels prior to 2019 on their website. What is particularly interesting in regard to this table is the Critical threat level. This has only been in place four times since August 2006 when the Threat Level was first openly published. On each of those occasions the level of Critical was left in place for the shortest possible time:

- 10 August 2006–13 August 2006 (three days): Liquid Bomb Plot/Transatlantic Aircraft Plot
- 30 June 2007–4 July 2007 (four days): Glasgow Airport Attack and the failed London Car Bombs
- 23 May 2017–27 May 2017 (four days): Manchester Arena Bombing Attack
- 15 September 2017–17 September 2017 (two days): Parsons Green Attack

15.5 Key Legislation

It is important to note that there can be significant overlap between offences that are terrorism-specific and those which are other forms of criminality. The line between terrorism and non-terrorism activities is becoming more blurred with the increased threat from 'lone actors' or 'self-initiated terrorists', online radicalization, and the increased reach and influence of terrorists across borders.

15.5.1 Terrorism-related offences

It is also important to note that a terrorist crime is not simply the successful enactment of a terrorist attack. A wide range of activities are crimes for which individuals can be prosecuted long before an attack takes place. The table below provides some oversight on the type of offences which fall under terrorism legislation.

A selection of prominent terrorism offences and their legislation.

Offence	Legislation
Preparation of terrorist acts	Section 5, Terrorism Act 2006
Collecting information	Section 58, Terrorism Act 2000
Dissemination of terrorist publications	Section 2, Terrorism Act 2006
Membership of a proscribed organization	Section 11, Terrorism Act 2000
Supporting a proscribed organization	Section 12, Terrorism Act 2000
Finance and money laundering in relation to terrorism acts	Sections 15–17, Terrorism Act 2000
Possession of an article for terrorism purposes	Section 57, Terrorism Act 2000
Encouragement of terrorism	Section 1, Terrorism Act 2006
Dissemination of terrorist publications	Section 2, Terrorism Act 2006
Attendance at a place for terrorist training	Section 8, Terrorism Act 2006

It will be noted that there is an absence of a specific offences relating to committing acts of terrorism. This is because most terrorists who do so are charged with common law offences or statutory criminal offences such as murder and conspiracy to cause explosions. Newly developed terrorism legislation, as well as non-terrorism legislation, is applied pragmatically to prosecutorial cases and more discussion on this can be found below.

15.5.2 Terrorism Act 2000

The Terrorism Act 2000 (TACT 2000) was created in response to the changing nature of the terrorist threat to the UK. There was an increasing concern throughout the 1990s that the global activities of Al Qaeda, would threaten Western interests both abroad and at home. Within this context, the Terrorism Act 2000 was approved in Parliament and became law (gov.uk, 2000).

One of the most important pieces of terrorism legislation, it provides the definition of terrorism under which all policing and security services activity falls (see 15.2.1 and 15.6). Key elements of TACT 2000 include making it an offence to 'collect or make a record of information of a kind likely to be useful to a person committing or preparing an act of terrorism, or to possess a document or record containing information of that kind' (CPS website) and possession of 'an article in circumstances which give rise to a reasonable suspicion that his possession is for a purpose connected with the commission, preparation or instigation of an act of terrorism' (TACT, 2000).

15.5.3 The Anti-Terrorism, Crime and Security Act 2001

Of course, TACT 2000 was introduced before the attacks of 9/11. As per UN Resolution 1368 (United Nations, 2001), published on 12 September 2001, all member states were required to respond to the threat from terrorism through the application of appropriate UN resolutions and the bringing to justice those involved in carrying out or supporting acts of terrorism. The UK's response to this was to enact the Anti-Terrorism, Crime and Security Act 2001. It brought UK terrorism legislation in line with what was perceived as an urgent and existential threat, including the freezing of financial sources believed to be supporting terrorist activity and the extension of disclosure powers. The sense of urgency resulted in the Bill (the precursor to the Act) being moved rapidly through the parliamentary process and this move was heavily criticized. Many considered it to be incompatible with the European Convention on Human Rights, and the House of Lords ruled in December 2004 that at least one element of the legislation, that of detention without trial, which was applied to eight foreign individuals, was unlawful. It nonetheless remained in place until it was replaced by the Prevention of Terrorism Act 2005.

15.5.4 Prevention of Terrorism Act 2005

The key element of the Prevention of Terrorism Act 2005, aside from addressing the concerns of the House of Lords, was to introduce Control Orders. Control Orders allowed for the significant restriction on freedom of those who were suspected to have been involved in terrorist activity. Restrictions were imposed on the use of the internet, access to technology such as mobile phones, interactions with other individuals, and in an effort to break extremist connections, some individuals were forced to live in another location. While the number of Control Orders in place were limited, significant controversy plagued Control Orders and they were ultimately replaced in 2011 with the introduction of Terrorism Prevention and Investigation Measures (TPIMs).

15.5.5 Terrorism Act 2006

The Terrorism Act 2006 is very important in the UK's terrorism legislation history. It was introduced following the coordinated bombings on the London Transport System in July 2005 (commonly known as the 7/7 Terror Attacks) and was highly controversial. In this Act, the encouragement of terrorism, dissemination of terrorist publications, possession of materials intended to be used in an attack, and preparation for carrying out an act of terrorism resulted in a significant increase in what a terrorism offence could be. Further, an amendment to the maximum period a person could be in detention without a charge was increased. Existing legislation, applicable to all forms of crime, allowed for 14 days as the maximum detention period without a charge being brought. The UK Government proposed this should be extended to 90 days in the case of terrorism crimes. This proposal was rejected by a vote in the House of Commons, but an amendment to implement a 28-day maximum, thus doubling the existing term, successfully passed and was enacted.

15.5.6 Terrorist Asset-Freezing etc Act 2010

The next significant piece of legislation was the Terrorist Asset-Freezing etc Act 2010. This Act ensured the compliance with UN Security Resolution 1373. As a very specific but powerful piece of legislation, the Independent Reviewer of Terrorism Legislation (see below for additional information on this role) was tasked with carrying out an annual review and publishing a report based on that review.

15.5.7 Terrorism Prevention and Investigation Measures Act 2011

Terrorism Prevention and Investigation Measures (TPIMs), introduced by this Act, replaced the controversial Control Orders in 2011. In particular, the potential to require an individual to move their residence was removed, addressing one of the more controversial elements of Control Orders. Yet much stayed the same. Focusing on individuals who could not be prosecuted, TPIMs sought to protect the public by imposing significant restrictions on those deemed a terrorist threat. The more nuanced differences were in regard to keeping restrictive measures at a minimum required for the safety of the public, placing the maximum period a TPIM could be imposed for at two years, and full reviews of each case. There were never very many TPIMs in place and they were highly targeted.

15.5.8 Counter-Terrorism and Security Act 2015

As with much of the other counter-terrorism legislation in the UK (and indeed globally) new Bills are usually proposed following terrorist activity and in an attempt to enhance the powers of the police and security services. The CTSA 2015 was put in place in light of the large numbers of UK citizens traveling to Syria to join the so-called Islamic State. It had two primary areas of focus. The first was to disrupt the ability of people to travel abroad to engage in terrorist activity and enhance the security services' ability to monitor individuals who posed a risk to the UK. The second focus was on addressing the underlying ideology that increased the risk of radicalization and extremism. This second element was particularly important as it resulted in the imposition of the Prevent Duty (see 15.9 below) and coincided with the publication of the Counter-Extremism Strategy. Controversy related to the perceived subjectivity involved in decisions to refer individuals to the Channel programme (mentoring system for those identified at risk of radicalization), based on particularly poor training provided to decision makers at the outset. Although significantly improved since 2015, training continues to fall short and the Shawcross Report 2023 indicates a need for continued development in the area of frontline training.

15.5.9 Counter-Terrorism and Border Security Act 2019

The Counter-Terrorism and Border Security Act 2019 (CTBSA, 2019) was passed in parliament in an effort to fill legislative gaps as a result of the several attacks in the UK throughout 2017. In particular, it looked to improve counter-terrorism activities addressing online radicalization. It enhanced s 58 of TACT 2000 to include online materials, and created a new offence in relation to travelling to an international location to join a terrorist group. Impacts on the use of evidence in court obtained from interviews at the border under s 7 of TACT 2000 and the length that DNA and fingerprints could be held on national security grounds were among the other elements of this legislation (gov.uk, 2015).

15.5.10 The Counter-Terrorism and Sentencing Act 2021

The Counter-Terrorism and Sentencing Act 2021 (CTSA, 2021) was implemented as a result of significant flaws in the system which came to light following the London Bridge attack of 2019 as well as the Streatham attack of 2020. It sought to end automatic early release from prison in the case of serious offenders, extended the minimum sentence for serious terrorist offenders to 14 years, and applied tougher monitoring of those who were released from prison on licence.

Overall, terrorism legislation in the UK is extensive. Its detractors have called the legislation at various times draconian or excessive and in breach of human rights. Its supporters consider it to be a necessary response to changing terrorist threats. Following specific terror attacks it certainly seems that legislation is enacted to update the mechanisms in place allowing for increased powers of the police and security services but two issues should be noted. First of all, most legislation goes through a lengthy process of approval which could include public consultation and must receive approval from both the House of Commons and the House of Lords. This should be considered a positive reflection of a robust system of oversight, capped off by the role of the Independent Reviewer of Terrorism Legislation to monitor legislation on an ongoing basis. Secondly, those who have been arrested for terrorism offences are not always prosecuted under terrorism legislation. A wide spread of legislation such as the Criminal Justice and Immigration Act 2008, the Criminal Justice Act 1988, the Public Order Act 1986, as well as Common Law offences such as murder and conspiracy, may also be used in the prosecution of such individuals. The Terrorism Section of the Crown Prosecution Service website provides a link to information on prosecutions and the legislative details from 2016 (see CPS, 2023a).

15.5.11 Police, Crime, Sentencing and Courts Act 2022

The Policing, Crime, Sentencing and Courts Act 2022 (ss 185–187) has given police three new powers involving urgent arrest, premises searches, and personal searches of terrorist and terrorist risk offenders.

TASK 1 Counter-Terrorist legislation provides investigators and courts with greater powers and measures than those available for non-terrorist offences. Is this merited? List five or six of these additional powers and measures.

15.6 Organizational Structure and Lead Agencies

15.6.1 Police

A series of bombing attacks in London in the 1880s by a Fenian affiliate group known as the Irish Republican Brotherhood caused the foundation within the Metropolitan Police of the

'Special Irish Branch' in 1883, shortened to 'Special Branch (SB)' in 1887. This was the first ever police team focused on counter-terrorism. The role of SB was to collect intelligence to protect Queen Victoria and facilitate the arrests and prosecutions of those involved in the campaign (Porter, 1987). Over time, the UK's individual police services set up their own Special Branches, and by the late twentieth century, there was a country-wide network co-ordinated largely by the Metropolitan Police Service from New Scotland Yard. This included the posting of Counter-Terrorism and Extremism Liaison Officers (CTELOs) to about 50 countries, co-ordinated by the Metropolitan Police Special Branch's International Liaison Section (Wilson and Adams, 2015).

The principal role of SB was intelligence gathering and analysis, so in response to a bombing campaign by an extreme left-wing terrorist group known as the Angry Brigade, an investigative wing was set up in 1971, also at New Scotland Yard. Initially it was called the Bomb Squad and later the Anti-Terrorist Branch (ATB). When, during the 1970s, the PIRA bombing campaign extended to Great Britain, the ATB investigated their crimes, and developed considerable expertise, especially in forensic analysis. Although a Metropolitan Police team, the ATB could, if invited by a constabulary Chief Constable, investigate terrorist attacks outside London. In 2006, the ATB and SB in the Metropolitan Police were merged to form the Counter Terrorist Command (CTC) (Wilson and Adams, 2015).

15.6.2 Counter-Terrorism Policing

Although there have been national agencies in the UK dealing with organized crime since 1992, currently the National Crime Agency (NCA), there is as yet no National Counter-Terrorism Agency.

To co-ordinate counter-terrorism policing, in 1996, the National Police Collaboration Agreement Relating to Counter Terrorism Activities was established under s 22(A) of the Police Act 1996. This established, in England and Wales, the Counter Terrorism Policing Network. This consists of nine English and Welsh regional counter-terrorism 'lead' police services, plus Police Scotland and the Police Service of Northern Ireland (PSNI), whose Chief Constables make up the Counter Terrorism Coordination Committee (CTCC) of the National Police Chiefs' Council (NPCC). The CTCC also comprises members of government departments and other agencies including the Home Office and MI5. It is based at the Counter Terrorism Policing Headquarters (CTPHQ) in London. The CTPHQ is housed by the MPS and chaired by their Assistant Commissioner of Specialist Operations (ACSO). This person is also the National Lead for Counter Terrorism Policing. The CTPHQ houses the Counter Terrorism Operations Centre (CTOC) which provides operational support to the Counter Terrorism Policing Network. A Forensic Team is planned to be established to work alongside the CTOC.

Beneath the CTPHQ are five Regional Counter Terrorism Units (CTUs) and six Regional Counter Terrorism Intelligence Units (CTIUs). The CTU's role is to investigate and gather evidence for the prevention, disruption, and prosecution of terrorists. Each CTU has a range of experts including counter-terrorist detectives, financial investigators, intelligence analysts, forensic experts, and skilled IT Investigators. CTUs are resourced by the police services in the area they are responsible for.

The CTIUs are also resourced by the police services in their respective areas and carry out intelligence gathering operations at local, regional, and national levels. This includes developing intelligence by engaging with these communities and fostering community cooperation. It would also include operating surveillance teams, telephone interceptions, and source recruitment and handling. Here they would work closely with MI5, GCHQ, and the CTUs. The CTIUs also have an important role in assisting and training front-line police officers in recognizing vulnerabilities in counter-terrorism, especially in terms of warning signs around radicalization. This forms part of the police's role in the Prevent strategy, discussed in 15.8.

In 2017, the Counter Terrorism Coordination Committee (CTTC) set up the Counter Terrorism Advisory Network (CTAN). This is an independently chaired stakeholder consultation and engagement forum comprising faith group leaders, terrorism survivors, researchers, academics, and community groups. CTAN was established as a non-police group to advise and critique a range of issues linked to strategy and policy.

In support of the CONTEST strategy, there are two Senior National Co-ordinators, one dealing with the Pursue and Prevent strands of the strategy, and the other the Protect and Prepare strands. Additionally, the National Counter Terrorism Security Office (NaCTSO) was established by the NPCC to support the Protect and Prepare strands of CONTEST.

NaCTSO supports a network of about 200 Counter Terrorism Security Advisors (CTSAs) who work within local police services. Their role is to provide help, advice, and guidance on all aspects of counter terrorism protective security to specified industry sectors. In so doing they support the work of the National Protective Security Authority (NPSA), the government's National Technical Authority for protective physical and personnel security of critical infrastructure such as power stations and national banks.

TASK 2 Counter-Terrorism Policing is fragmented with different organizations performing different roles. Would the UK benefit from having a unified National Counter-Terrorist Agency? List some of the arguments against and in favour of the creation of such an agency.

15.6.3 Intelligence agencies

In 1909 the 'Secret Service Bureau' was established by the Home Office. Initially the Bureau had two arms, the Home and Foreign Sections, which evolved into today's domestic Security Service (MI5) and the Secret Intelligence Service (SIS), with its focus on protecting British interests abroad. At the same time, the need to gather and assess enemy signals intelligence (SIGINT) was met with the establishment of what has now developed into the Government Communications Headquarters (GCHQ). MI5, SIS, and GCHQ together now comprise the UK's intelligence community.

The Security Service enjoyed considerable success in its counter-espionage role during both WW1 and WW2. During the post-war period the Communist threat grew, and MI5's role developed in that direction, monitoring and countering Soviet espionage and identifying and expelling foreign agents. With the fall of the Soviet Union in 1989, the role of MI5 changed to include gathering intelligence on both organized crime and terrorism. However, lacking a judicial role, it was tasked with supporting the police in these fields.

In 1989 the Security Services Act (SSA) put MI5 onto a statutory basis (gov.uk, 1989a). This confirmed its role and remit for the first time, authorizing its tasks in supporting both the police and the National Crime Agency.

MI5's headquarters are in central London. Its primary role is 'to keep the country safe' (MI5, 2023b). To do this it will gather, assess, and distribute intelligence and information to disrupt threats to the UK. It focuses on four main areas: counter-terrorism, counter-espionage, counter-proliferation of weapons of mass destruction, and dealing with cyber threats to the UK's infrastructure. MI5 follows the priorities set by the government's Joint Intelligence Committee (JIC).

Its intelligence gathering role uses classified techniques. These include recruiting or introducing Covert Human Intelligence Sources (CHIS), or 'agents', into terrorist or criminal groups, 'intrusive surveillance' by inserting listening devices, covertly accessing computers or other devices, undertaking covert surveillance, intercepting emails, internet traffic, phone calls, or emails, etc. All these activities are undertaken in conformity with relevant legislation, primarily the Regulation of Investigatory Powers Act (RIPA) and are strictly controlled. In undertaking these roles, it works closely with SIS, GCHQ, and the regional CTIUs. For criminal intelligence it has a close relationship with the NCA.

MI5 is responsible for setting the terrorist threat level from Northern Irish Related Terrorism in Northern Ireland, whilst the threat level for the UK from international terrorism is set by the Joint Terrorism Analysis Centre (JTAC). JTAC is based within MI5's London headquarters, and its Head reports directly to the Director General of MI5. Its staff comprises experts in counter-terrorism from agencies involved in this work. Its role is to analyse and assess 'all intelligence relating to international terrorism, at home and overseas. It sets threat levels and issues warnings of threats and other terrorist-related subjects for customers from a wide range of government departments and agencies, as well as producing more in-depth reports on trends, terrorist networks and capabilities' (MI5, 2023d).

In 2007, MI5 took over the lead role in gathering intelligence from the police (HM Government, 2018b), calling on the latter when operational and judicial support was required.

The Secret Intelligence Service's role was put onto a statutory footing in 1994 when the Intelligence Services Act was enacted, which set out its role for the first time (gov.uk, 1994). Newspaper reports from 2016 indicate that it has a total staff of 3,500 people.

Although it is headquartered on the Albert Embankment in Vauxhall, central London, its main role is conducted abroad, where in the words of its website, its operatives work 'secretly' to gather intelligence. Indeed, the Intelligence Services Act 1994 (ISA) only authorizes it to work outside the British Isles.

SIS has three core areas of focus:

- Counter-Terrorism—stopping terrorist attacks in the UK, and overseas.
- Disrupting Hostile State Activity—tackling threats to the UK's prosperity and influencing international affairs.
- Cyber—promoting and defending the UK's cyber realm using cyber expertise to reduce threats.

GCHQ was put onto a statutory footing with the enactment of the ISA. It is based in Cheltenham. Its present role is to monitor and assess electronic communications such as internet and mobile phone traffic (Ferris, 2020).

As with the other intelligence agencies, the Director of GCHQ is advised by a Board, made up of executive and non-executive directors from the government and other agencies. GCHQ has two principal tasks. These are firstly to monitor Signals Intelligence (Sigint) such as internet, radio, and telephone communications channels etc as requested by government agencies and the police and in accordance with the relevant legislation. Secondly, it also undertakes research into new technologies and techniques to ensure it can tackle evolving threats appropriately.

GCHQ also houses the National Cyber Security Centre (NCSC) which is responsible for assisting and advising individuals and businesses to protect themselves from internet risks (Ferris, 2020). It recommends via its website a range of internet security providers which follow the NCSC Cyber Assessment Framework (CAF) principles.

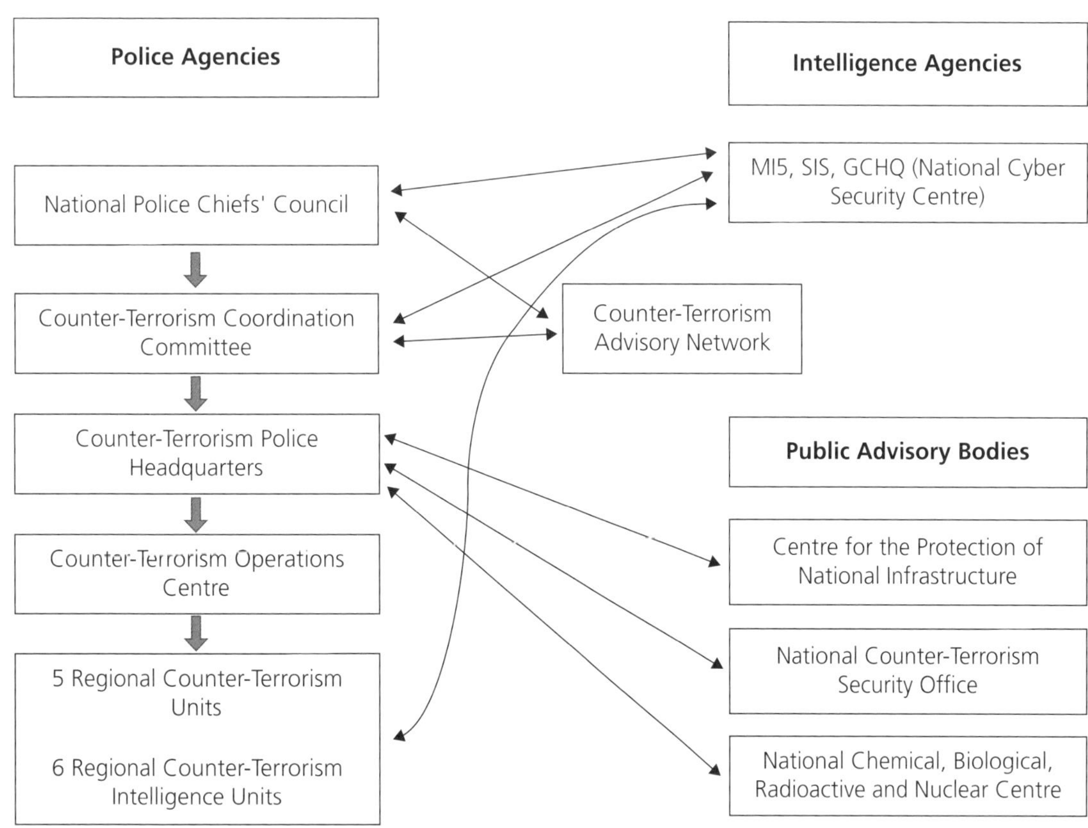

15.7 Counter-Terrorism Strategies

Counter-terrorism is as diverse as any other strategy (Crelinsten, 2009; Van Dongen, 2010). Depending on the threat to the state, the culture of the society, and the history of governance, law, and security, a wide range of options are available. There are two primary types of counter-terrorism strategy: the Criminal Justice Model and the War Model.

The Criminal Justice Model (LaFree and Hendrickson, 2007) is arguably the most prevalent counter-terrorism strategy, certainly in terms of democratic states. It holds that terrorist acts are criminal acts, and need to be dealt with in terms of the existing criminal justice system. The primary actors involved in such strategies are the security services and the police. The military are rarely involved.

The War Model perceives terrorist activity as acts of war and wider conflict and so the military tends to be the dominant response mechanism. There are two main frameworks within which the War Model has applied. The first and most famous would be the War on Terror which was declared by the US following the attacks of 9/11. In the War on Terror, an alliance of countries led by the US invaded Afghanistan and toppled the Taliban regime which had provided safe haven and support to Al Qaeda, the terrorist group responsible for the acts. Iraq was also targeted by the US-led alliance and these two conflicts were the pre-eminent conflicts situated within the 20-year long War on Terror. This was the longest war fought by the US, the most expensive (over $8 trillion tax-payer dollars) and it caused the highest number of war-related deaths globally (about 900,000) in addition to the estimated 38 million displaced persons globally (Brown University, 2021).

However, the War Model (Crelinsten, 2002) does not just have to apply to large-scale conflicts carried out in countries far removed from the state. Throughout history, intrastate conflict has been a more common expression of the War Model. Here, civil discontent and violence motivates a military response from the government, and conflict ensues. There is a significant challenge here in terms of terrorism and its definition, however. For while a government might call an insurgent group terrorist, usually in an attempt to delegitimize the group and their cause or ideology, there may actually be popular support for that group's actions. A range of intra-state conflict harbours elements of terrorism, guerrilla warfare, and other political violence, and lines between terrorism and other violence are complex. The most obvious example of this would be the defeat of the Tamil Tigers (LTTE) in Sri Lanka in 2009, but elements of the War Model could also be said to have framed the early years of the conflict in Northern Ireland with the UK-deployed military personnel there.

Other models include the Intelligence Model (Gill and Phythian, 2012), the Communication Model (Crelinsten and Ozkut, 2000), the Psychosocial Model (Butler, Morland, and Leskin, 2007), and the Environmental Protection Model (Fetzek and Mazo, 2014; Mayer, 2015).

15.8 The UK's CONTEST Strategy—Overview

The UK's Counter-Terrorism Strategy, known as CONTEST and an example of a Criminal Justice Model, was first developed in 2002 and became an active strategy in 2003. Following the London Bombings of 7 July 2005, it was decided to publish the strategy to demonstrate to the public what was being done to combat terrorist activities. Therefore, in 2006, CONTEST was published publicly by the Home Office for the first time. The strategy was updated in 2009, 2011, and 2018, all focusing on contemporaneous and developing threat levels of the time, and all looking to improve on the activities of the past. A new version of the strategy is being developed to build on previous publications and address contemporaneous security threats facing the UK. Nonetheless, much remains consistent, particularly the four component strategies known as the 'Four Ps': Prevent, Pursue, Protect, and Prepare.

15.8.1 Prevent

Prevent aims to 'stop people becoming terrorists or supporting terrorism'. It is primarily focused on individuals who have not committed a crime, but who have been identified as being vulnerable to radicalization. As was seen in Moghaddam's Staircase to Terrorism (see 15.2.3), most people who become radicalized never carry out a terror attack. However, criminality can be present along the various steps and there are a number of objectives that Prevent aspires to meet through a safeguarding process. These include:

- 'Focus our activity and resources in those locations where the threat from terrorism and radicalisation is highest.
- Expand our Desistance and Disengagement Programme with an immediate aim over the next 12 months to more than double the number of individuals receiving rehabilitative interventions.
- Develop a series of multi-agency pilots to trial methods to improve our understanding of those at risk of involvement in terrorism and enable earlier intervention.
- Focus our online activity on preventing the dissemination of terrorist material and building strong counter-terrorist narratives in order to ensure there are no safe places for terrorists online.
- Build stronger partnerships with communities, civil society groups, public sector institutions and industry to improve Prevent delivery.
- Re-enforce safeguarding at the heart of Prevent to ensure our communities and families are not exploited or groomed into following a path of violent extremism.' (gov.uk, 2018b)

These objectives are important in understanding the focus of activities which take place under this strategy. Prevent is a complex and often misunderstood strategy that works across many agencies such as police, local authority, education, social welfare, and health, particularly following the implementation of the Prevent Duty in 2015. Prevent has been in effect since the first iteration of the CONTEST Strategy, and there have been many failings along the way. This has resulted in the alienation of a number of communities throughout the UK and has received significant criticism from a range of civil society actors such as The People's Review of Prevent, CAGE, and Liberty. However, a phenomenal amount of good work is done as well, and more needs to be done to repair the tarnished image of the strategy. William Shawcross was tasked with carrying out an Independent Review of Prevent and his report was published in February 2023. This report, highly controversial itself, outlines 34 recommendations for the improvement of Prevent, and these are being integrated into the next version of CONTEST which is currently in progress.

The main element of Prevent is undoubtedly the Channel programme. This is a multi-agency panel that reviews the cases of individuals who have been referred to it through a range of agencies, including those required to do so through the Prevent Duty. Should an individual's case make it through the referral process to a Channel Panel (see flowchart below), a targeted support system is implemented to assist the individual with the aim of steering them away from the extremist track.

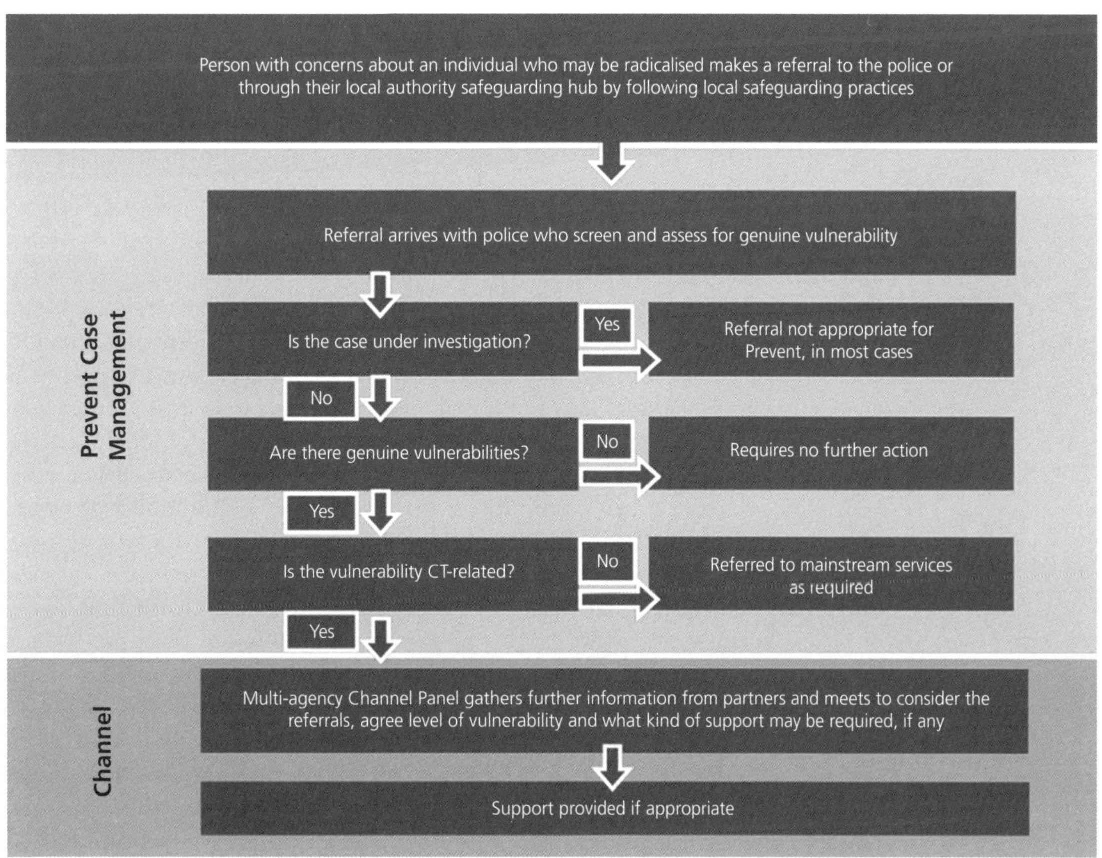

Source: (Gov.UK: Guidance—Making a Referral to Prevent) Referral process to a Channel Panel. Source © crown copyright

This bespoke support system seems logical, but is not perfect, and the media focuses heavily on the negative stories that emerge. In addition, once an individual is referred to Channel itself, they must willingly engage with the process—having done nothing criminal they cannot be coerced to engage with the Channel Panel. This can make it more challenging and, without the support provided by Channel, the chances are higher (but never certain) that the individual will continue along the radicalization path and/or the path toward some form of criminality. Working within the Prevent space is both challenging and important.

15.8.2 Pursue

The aim of Pursue is to 'stop terrorist attacks' (gov.uk, 2018b). There are a wide number of ways that this aim is achieved. In 2018, the UK Government indicated the following steps to achieving this aim, including:

- 'Implement a step-change in our domestic investigative capabilities through implementing the recommendations of MI5 and CT Policing's Operational Improvement Review.
- Introduce new counter-terrorism legislation to disrupt terrorist threats in the UK earlier, taking account of the scale of the threat and the speed at which plots are now developing.
- As set out in the National Security Strategy and Strategic Defence and Security Review 2015, we are recruiting and training over 1,900 additional staff across the security and intelligence agencies.
- Develop a series of multi-agency pilots to trial ways to improve information sharing and enrich our understanding of the threat at the local level, including of closed and closing subjects of interest.
- Bring foreign fighters to justice in accordance with due legal process if there is evidence that crimes have been committed, regardless of their nationality.
- Maintain our use of enhanced legislative tools to target and disrupt terrorist finance.
- Ensure we maintain our global reach to disrupt those that directly threaten the UK or UK interests.
- Ensure strong independent oversight of our counter-terrorism work, including publishing annual reports by the Independent Reviewer of Terrorism Legislation, the Biometrics Commissioner and the Investigatory Powers Commissioner.' (gov.uk, 2018b)

As can be seen here, many agencies are engaged in this category of activity and the success or failure of these activities are played out in the occurrence, or non-occurrence, of terror attacks. Following the successful terror attacks of 2017, MI5 and Counter-Terrorism Policing carried out a number of internal reviews to better understand whether any failings had occurred on their part and what needed to be done to better address any issues going forward.

A large number of recommendations came out of these reviews (Anderson, 2017; Anderson, 2019). One issue of note was in relation to how Subjects of Interest (SOIs) were monitored and dealt with. Anderson concisely describes SOIs as '... persons in respect of whom MI5 has created a Key Information Store record (or in common parlance, a file). There are around 3000 active SOIs, who are either associated with MI5 priority investigations or have come to MI5's attention as part of a lead generated through new intelligence not part of an existing investigation. Each active SOI record is subject to quarterly case review and has an assigned lead investigator responsible for reviewing incoming intelligence and maintaining the record, including by updating it as required' (Anderson, 2017). In addition to SOIs who are actively being monitored, there are a very high number of what are called Closed SOIs. Closed SIOs are '... people who have been part of MI5 Priority Investigations since 2009 but who have been given a holding code which indicates that they are no longer assessed to represent a national security threat. Other closed SOIs have been part of Lead Development investigations or have been transferred from pre-2009 legacy systems. When SOIs are closed they are categorised according to the amount of residual risk, from low to high, that they are likely to pose in the future' (Anderson, 2017). There were, in 2017, about 20,000 Closed SOIs. This perhaps provides some indication of the scale of the job being undertaken by MI5. What is problematic about Closed SOIs in particular, is that one of the primary issues identified was 'the process by which individuals are categorised as closed subjects of interest, and how cases are then reviewed and escalated where indicators of potential re-engagement in terrorist activity are identified' (Anderson, 2017). And yet this issue had been identified by the Intelligence and Security Committee in 2013 following the murder of Fusilier Lee Rigby. Anderson's follow up report in 2019 outlined in detail some of the changes which had been made to address this issue, and was cautiously positive on the changes while also identifying the need for ongoing evaluation of these processes (Anderson, 2019).

15.8.3 Protect

The aim of Protect is to 'strengthen the UK's protection against a terrorist attack' (gov.uk, 2018b). This element of the CONTEST strategy links closely with Pursue, but includes activities such as installing bollards or street furniture at critical infrastructure, protecting crowded spaces, CCTV cameras, and various activities at the borders of the UK.

In order to achieve its goals, Protect's activities include the following:

- 'Collate and analyse greater volumes of high quality data to enhance our ability to target known and previously unknown persons and goods of potential counterterrorism concern.
- Maintain the UK at the forefront of developing world leading screening and detection technologies at the border, including behavioural detection, new detection techniques, data analytics and machine learning.
- Target the insider threat by strengthening information-sharing about those working in sensitive environments in airports, to ensure that persons of concern do not have access to restricted environments.
- Further strengthen security and resilience across the UK's transport network and other parts of our critical national infrastructure that keep our country running and provide essential services.
- Work in partnership with the aviation industry and international partners to deliver robust and sustainable aviation security in the UK and overseas.
- Improve security at crowded places through closer, more effective working with a wider range of local authority and private sector responsible partners.
- Enhance capabilities to detect terrorist activity involving Chemical, Biological, Radiological, Nuclear and Explosives (CBRNE) material and their precursors and to control and safeguard these materials.' (gov.uk, 2018b)

Protect is an incredibly important aspect of the counter-terrorism strategy. While at times, measures taken under this workstream of CONTEST are visible and intrusive to the public, more often than not they are designed to be unnoticed and only become obvious when they fulfil their role of stopping a terror attack.

However, one of the key takeaways from the Manchester Arena Inquiry (all reports are available at https://manchesterarenainquiry.org.uk/) was that poor security processes were in place at the Arena, both in terms of private and public employees. The proposed Martyn's Law (15.9.5) seeks to address this.

Systems, therefore, are always changing, particularly in relation to shifting threats and new technologies. For this reason, it is relevant to point out that London City Airport became the first in the UK to update to a new scanning technology at the security zone which allows passengers to leave liquids and electronics in their bags. This shows that while more often than not there is a perceived ongoing enhancement of restrictions and reluctance to enhance the public experience across the transport sector (and aviation in particular), work is ongoing to reduce restrictions where it is considered safe to do so.

Finally, moving away from technology and more advanced measures which fit within the Protect remit, Project Servator is also worth mentioning. Described as a tactic (see box below) it particularly focuses on increased police presence (both uniformed and non-uniformed) in crowded or busy spaces and the application of behavioural analysis (Gechkova and Kaleeva, 2021). This presence provides a deterrence effect against a range of petty crimes, but also allows the public to approach the police officers if they notice something suspicious. It has proved to be quite effective and while not applied nationally, has been viewed positively in general.

Project Servator is a policing tactic that aims to disrupt a range of criminal activity, including terrorism, while providing a reassuring presence for the public. It is used by a number of UK police forces and New South Wales Police Force in Australia. The approach relies on police working with the community—businesses, partners, and members of the public—to build a network of vigilance and encourage suspicious activity to be reported. Project Servator has been successful in gathering intelligence that has assisted Counter Terrorism Units across the UK in investigating and preventing acts of terror. It has resulted in arrests for a multitude of offences and is responsible for removing firearms, knives, and drugs from the streets.

15.8.4 Prepare

The final element of the UK counter-terrorism strategy, Prepare, does not set out to prevent or stop an attack from happening, but rather to 'mitigate the impact of a terrorist attack' (gov.uk, 2018b). For this reason, it is quite different to the other three workstreams.

The stated objectives of Prepare are to:

- 'Maintain our investment in the capabilities of the emergency services in order to deliver a coordinated and effective response to terrorist attacks.
- Ensure the UK is resilient and ready to respond in a proportionate and effective manner to a wide range of CBRNE threats.
- Fully embed the Joint Emergency Service Interoperability Principles across the emergency services by 2020, to ensure that they can work together effectively in response to a terrorist attack.
- Regularly test and exercise the multi-agency capabilities required to respond to, and recover from, a wide range of terrorist attacks.
- Improve support arrangements for victims of terrorism to ensure a comprehensive and coordinated response.' (gov.uk, 2018b)

Prepare is a complex and multi-dimensional strategy that relies on a wide range of actors and activities leading up to, during, and following a terror attack. On one end of this spectrum is the public, and ACT Campaigns have become common place in public places and around transport networks.

Source: RUN-HIDE-TELL Campaign. © ProtectUK

In addition to these posters Counter-Terrorism Policing also runs campaigns to support people getting in contact with them if they have concerns (see photo below).

Source: (British Transport Police Website). See it. Say it. Sorted. Campaign.

At the other end of the spectrum, should a terror attack take place, various processes are actioned. On 23 April 2023, a test of the new National Alerts system was carried out, resulting in the vast majority of phones in the UK receiving the alert siren. COBR (Cabinet Office Briefing Room) meetings are convened in the case of a crisis, including a declared terrorist incident, and Gold-Silver-Bronze command structure below is implemented.

Source: ACT Campaign. © 2023 ProtectUK

In addition to this command structure, JESIP models and principles are in place. In particular, the JESIP Joint Doctrine and Interoperability Framework is used for every critical

Core Aspects of Police Work

and major incident, and this has been discussed in 10.6.1. It is also discussed in more detail in 15.9 below.

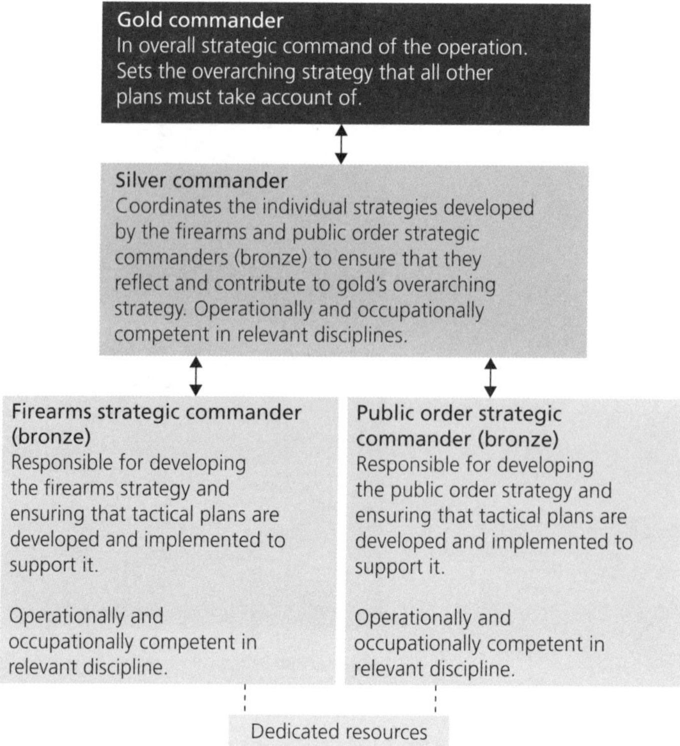

Gold commander
In overall strategic command of the operation. Sets the overarching strategy that all other plans must take account of.
Silver commander
Coordinates the individual strategies developed by the firearms and public order strategic commanders (bronze) to ensure that they reflect and contribute to gold's overarching strategy. Operationally and occupationally competent in relevant disciplines.
Firearms strategic commander (bronze)
Responsible for developing the firearms strategy and ensuring that tactical plans are developed and implemented to support it.
Operationally and occupationally competent in relevant discipline.
Public order strategic commander (bronze)
Responsible for developing the public order strategy and ensuring that tactical plans are developed and implemented to support it.
Operationally and occupationally competent in relevant discipline.
Dedicated resources

Source: (College of Policing). Gold-Silver-Bronze Command Structure. © College of Policing Limited (UK). Reproduced with permission under licence SF00300.

15.9 The Wider Counter-Terrorism Landscape

The CONTEST strategy does not work in isolation, and several connected activities and entities are important to understand in the wider context.

15.9.1 Independent Reviewer of Terrorism Legislation

This role was created in the 1970s, although in a far more limited context within the framework of the Northern Ireland Troubles. By the 1980s, following the publication of the Jellico Report in 1983, it was noted that 'the Independent Reviewer's function would be to look at the use made of the statutory powers relating to terrorism, and to consider, for example, whether any change in the pattern of their use needed to be drawn to the attention of Parliament'. The Independent Reviewer was to have access to all relevant papers, including sensitive security information and ministerial correspondence. They would not be a judge, but 'a person whose reputation would lend authority to his conclusions, because some of the information which led him to his conclusions would not be published' (Independent Reviewer of Terrorism Legislation website). The role evolved over the decades, in the mid-1990s becoming a more permanent position, and following the attacks on the US on 11 September 2001, became even busier and more impactful. Since 2001, four individuals have held the role: Lord Carlile (2001 to 2011); Lord Anderson (2011 to 2017); Max Hill (2017 to 2019); and Jonathan Hall (2019 to present). The position-holder publishes both annual and ad-hoc reports focusing on counter-terrorism legislation and they have continued to provide expert commentary on these and related issues following departure from their role.

15.9.2 Counter-Extremism Strategy

The Counter-Extremism Strategy was published in 2015. The purpose of the strategy is explained as 'to protect people from the harm caused by extremism' (HM Government, 2015). It sets out four main areas through which to deal with the threat from extremism in the UK:

- Countering extremist ideology
- Building a partnership with all those opposed to extremism

- Disrupting extremists
- Building more cohesive communities (HM Government, 2015)

While the emphasis of the Strategy is on Islamist extremism, it does also pay some attention to the rising risk from other forms of extremism, including Extreme Right-Wing groups and Neo-Nazi groups. Since 2015, the extremist landscape has changed considerably, and therefore the Commission for Countering Extremism was established to deal with issues relating to extremism on an ongoing and developing basis.

15.9.3 Commission for Countering Extremism

The Commission for Countering Extremism was established in 2018 with the appointment of Sara Khan as the Commissioner for Countering Extremism. Her selection for the role was controversial, and she was formally replaced by Robin Simcox in summer 2022. 'The Commissioner for Countering Extremism is a non-statutory public appointee of the Home Office who operates independently and at arm's length from government, providing the government with impartial, expert advice and scrutiny on the tools, policies and approaches needed to tackle extremism. The Commissioner is supported by a small secretariat of Civil Servants. The CCE supports the public sector, communities, and civil society to confront extremism wherever it exists; and promotes a positive vision around core, shared values' (Commission for Countering Extremism Website).

15.9.4 Prevent Duty 2015

The Prevent Duty was established in 2015, following the establishment in law of the Counter-Terrorism and Security Act 2015. In this Act, it was set out that there is a duty on specified authorities to 'have due regard to the need to prevent people from being drawn into terrorism' (gov.uk, 2015). These authorities included local authorities, those in the criminal justice framework such as prisons, education sector, health and social care, and the police. Subsequent guidance was also published by the Government to support the authorities' adherence to this duty, but significant early criticism about erroneous referrals and poor training have plagued the Duty, despite some improvements over the years.

15.9.5 Protect Duty (anticipated) (Martyn's Law)

The Protect Duty is currently in the process of being developed. The notion of requiring various agencies to ensure relevant security measures are in place in the case of a major or critical incident was first pushed by Figen Murray, the mother of one of the victims of the Manchester Arena Bombing, Martyn Hett. Her activism in this area has resulted in a public consultation, to which the government responded with a plan for the implementation of what will be known as Martyn's Law. While still in development, it is likely to cover two tiers: small venues of 100+ capacity and large venues of 800+ capacity. The exact timeline of presentation to Parliament and implementation is currently unknown.

15.9.6 Independent Review of Prevent

In February 2023, William Shawcross published his controversial Independent Review of Prevent. The report was plagued by leaks and criticisms prior to its publication. Having been published, Shawcross made 34 recommendations including changes in terminology, updating of objectives in terms of the Prevent strategy itself and also the Prevent Duty for consistency, and to 'reset thresholds to ensure proportionality across Prevent workstreams' (Shawcross, 2023).

15.9.7 Lord Anderson's Reports 2017 and 2019

In the summer of 2017, Lord Anderson was asked in his independent capacity to carry out a review of the review processes of MI5 and CTP following the string of terror attacks in 2017. He published his report in November 2017, and carried out a follow up review one year later, publishing the second report in June 2019. The original 2017 report was the first of its kind, where Anderson was granted unprecedented access to the internal review processes of MI5 and CTP. While the public reports were redacted, for the first time significant insights into the review process were granted to the public. In total, eight reviews were carried out by MI5 and CTP in the summer of 2017 (seven post-attack reviews and one Operational Improvement Review), and a total of 104 recommendations were made.

15.9.8 Lord Harris Reports 2016 and 2022

In 2016, Lord Harris was asked to carry out a review into London's Preparedness to Respond to a Major Terrorist Incident by the London Mayor's Office. His final report eventually had 127 recommendations and he followed up this report with a new review in 2022 titled 'London Prepared: A City-Wide Endeavour'. The new report indicates that much has been done to improve London's response to a major terrorist incident, although areas for improvement are again identified through 294 recommendations. Lord Harris states 'My broad conclusion is that very substantial progress has been made by the emergency services and other agencies in response to my 2016 report and in following up the lessons of the attacks in 2017 and subsequently.' (Harris, 2022).

15.9.9 Post-Terror Event Reports and Inquiries

Follow any terrorist incident that results in deaths, the Coroner's Office carries out an investigation and publishes a report of the findings. As has already been noted, a range of ad-hoc reports are also published by a number of entities, which are requested by a range of bodies including the UK Government and local authorities. The Manchester Arena Bombing of 2017 resulted in a public inquiry which took place between 2019 and 2023 resulting in three reports into the response to the attack. The Intelligence and Security Committee, a select committee of Parliament, also carries out reviews of terrorist attacks, and has published reports on the London Bombings of July 2005, the murder of Fusilier Lee Rigby in 2013, and the attacks which took place throughout 2017. All of these reports provide the public with important insights into the nature of the response, what worked well and what needs improvement, with a view to apply learning and enhance the response of the security services to such events in the future. In particular, the range and depth of the reports, as well as many recommendations which can be found within, highlight the complex and challenging threat landscape within which various bodies need to prevent and respond to the threat from terrorism.

15.9.10 Joint Emergency Service Interoperability Programme (JESIP)

JESIP, developed in 2013, was initially intended to improve the responses of all the Emergency Services to dealing with major incidents. Under the motto 'working together, saving lives, reducing harm' it developed principles and models intended to co-ordinate and harmonize JESIP models and principles which have become the standard for emergency services interoperability in the UK. Whilst not exclusively focused on dealing with terrorist incidents, JESIP has an important role when such attacks take place.

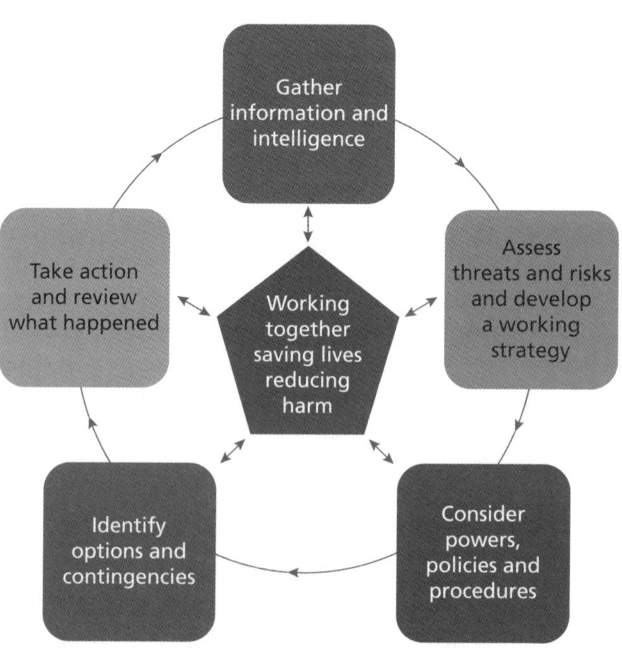

Source: (JESIP website). The JESIP Joint Decision Model.

A Joint Doctrine has been developed setting out the principles for Joint Working. These are the components emergency service commanders are expected to follow when planning a response to a major incident. Secondly the acronym 'M/ETHANE' (see below), establishing a common method for passing incident information between services and their control rooms.

Finally, it sets out a Joint Decision Model (JDM)—a national model to enable commanders to make effective decisions together.

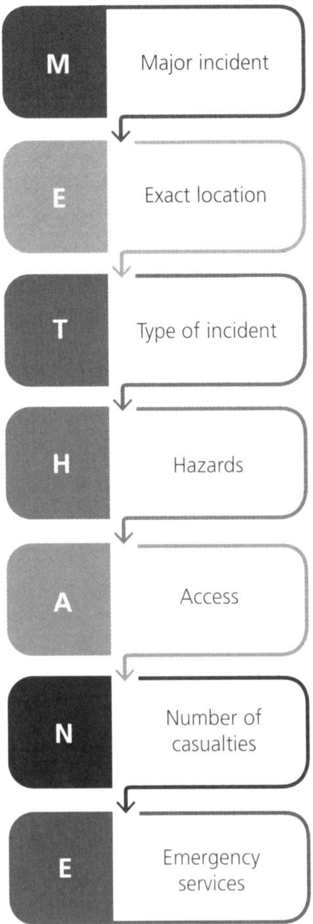

Source (JESIP website). M/ETHANE Model.

15.10 Conclusion

This chapter has demonstrated the many various elements that make up counter-terrorism strategies as well as the context and history of terrorism with a focus on the UK. While most of the population does not consider counter-terrorism on a regular basis, what does stand out is the negative media coverage when things go wrong. This takes shape in two ways: in terms of the Prevent workstream and the concern across a number of areas including human rights impingement, child abuse, and racial bias; and in terms of the post-event analysis of why an event was 'allowed' to take place. In this second scenario, the intelligence leading up to the event as well as the immediate response are usually analysed in great detail.

The counter-terrorism structure in the UK has changed significantly over the years in line with the ever-changing threat from terrorists. However, at its core, the primary goal of CONTEST has never changed: 'to reduce the risk to the UK and its citizens and interests overseas from terrorism, so that our people can go about their lives freely and with confidence' (gov.uk, 2018b). There has never been an expectation that terrorism, as a pernicious crime, can be completely eradicated. However, it should be feasible to reduce the risk of terrorism and minimize the impact of an attack should one take place. This realistic approach clashes with the heightened fear that a single terror attack can inspire, and the imbalanced approach the media takes provides the public with an unrealistic perception of the scale and risk to life of terrorist activities. Therefore, it is very important that the public is made aware of the relevant risks, while understanding that the chances they will be caught up in an attack are very low. Ultimately, the UK has experienced relatively few serious terror attacks, but given the very high level of activity undertaken by the security services and Counter-Terrorism Police, everyone needs to continue to be vigilant.

15.11 Answers to Tasks

TASK 1

a. Terrorist suspects can be held in pre-charge detention under PACE for a longer period than other suspects.
b. Terrorism Prevention and Investigation Measures (TPIMs) allow the authorities to monitor and control people considered terrorists—but who are not facing criminal charges. This only happens to terrorist suspects.
c. There is a minimum of 14 years' imprisonment for most dangerous terrorist offenders.
d. There is no automatic early release from prison for terrorist offenders.
e. Tougher monitoring requirements are imposed for terrorist offenders released on licence from prison at the end of their sentences.
f. The Prevent programme and Channel Panels work to assist, support, and deter people at risk of terrorist radicalization. There is no equivalent scheme for people being drawn into crime.

TASK 2

Against:

a. The present system, despite its complexity, works well.
b. Reorganization would cause disruption, degrading the efficiency of the current system.
c. The present structure is based historically on the traditional organization of 'policing' in the UK.
d. Given their different roles, the separation of the intelligence and judicial services is vital to protect sources and tradecraft.

In Favour:

a. The present system is complex and unwieldy. It would be cost-effective to merge and reduce the number of agencies involved.
b. The risks of intelligence and evidence being lost or overlooked would be reduced.
c. Intelligence links to Organized Crime could be more easily shared with the National Crime Agency.
d. Intelligence officers would be more familiar with judicial requirements and police investigators more acquainted with intelligence gathering and analysis.

16 Policing the Roads

16.1 Introduction

Student and trainee police officers will be expected to demonstrate competence in many areas of roads policing during training as well as Supervised and Independent Patrol, as is reflected in the roads policing content of the police curriculum. This chapter covers the terms commonly used in the legislation, the offences related to circumstance and manner of driving, collisions (the preferred term for accidents), and drink- and drug-driving. It also covers non-driving highways offences such as wilful obstruction and the use of fireworks near highways.

Much of the legislation and regulation surrounds safety and the protection of road users, with pedestrians, motorcyclists, and cyclists being particularly vulnerable (Department for Transport, 2022c). In Great Britain in 2021 there were 1,558 fatalities and a further 25,892 seriously injured casualties (Department for Transport, 2022c), compared to 1,752 road traffic deaths and 25,945 serious injuries on the roads of Great Britain in 2019 (Department for Transport, 2020); however, it should be noted that what appears to be a significant reduction is likely to be a result of the national Covid lockdowns in 2020 and 2021 with a significant reduction in road traffic volumes. Road transport collisions are a common cause of death in the 5–19 years and the 20–34 years age groups in England and Wales, ranking second and third for males in these age groups respectively, and third and fifth for females in both age groups (ONS, 2020b).

Road death and injury are, of course, tragedies for the individuals concerned, as there are often long-term physical and psychological consequences, but they also have a significant financial cost to society as a whole, with estimates for 2021 amounting to around £2.11 million for each fatality (£3.3 billion in total) and £237,000 for each serious injury (£6.2 billion in total); this is compared to the higher figures for 2020 amounting to around £1.93 million for each fatality (£2.8 billion in total) and £217,000 for each serious injury (£4.8 billion in total) (Department for Transport, 2022a). For some reason, there is little public outrage at such high levels of death and injury on the roads compared to homicides and physical assaults (there were 649 homicides over the same period (ONS, 2022b; Scottish Government, 2021)). The importance of roads policing in reducing casualties was recently highlighted by Her Majesty's Inspectorate of Constabulary and Fire and Rescue Services (HMICFRS, 2020a).

Research suggests there is a link between offending on the roads and other forms of criminality. Rose (2000) demonstrated that 79 per cent of disqualified drivers had a criminal record (four times higher than the average for the general population), approximately 50 per cent of dangerous drivers had a previous conviction, and approximately 25 per cent were convicted of an offence within a year (three times the average). Interestingly, drink-drivers were less likely to have a criminal record (40 per cent) than other groups of serious traffic offenders, and 'only' 12 per cent were convicted again within a year. However, these figures are still about twice the average for the general population. Nunn (2018) found that 82 per cent of drug-drivers had previous convictions, of which 82 per cent related to drugs and 53 per cent were for serious motoring offences. Junger *et al* (2001) also identified links between 'risky' traffic behaviour and more general violent crime, and similarly Chenery *et al* (1999) demonstrated in a famous study the links between the relatively minor offence of illegal parking in disabled bays, active criminals, and illegal vehicles. All of this leads us to the notion of 'self-selecting' road and traffic behaviour that police officers could usefully consider as indicators of perhaps more serious criminal predisposition (Roach, 2017).

It has been identified that the following crime types are facilitated by the use of the road network: drug smuggling, human trafficking, child exploitation, counterfeit goods, and organized crime groups, as well as many volume crimes such as shoplifting, burglary, and motor vehicle crime (Roach, 2017). The enforcement of road traffic offences and the imposition of penalties will, of course, deny criminals the use of the roads and hence disrupt their other criminal activities, but the information also provides an invaluable source of up-to-date intelligence on individual criminals. Traffic cameras and automatic number plate readers allow individuals in vehicles to be tracked across the road network and this provides additional information that can be used in crime prevention and detection.

The National Police Chiefs' Council's *National Roads Policing Strategy 2022–2025* (NPCC, 2022) aims to reduce the number of collisions leading to road death and serious injury, and to combat organized crime and terrorism through flexible enforcement based upon intelligence, professional judgement, and discretion. Through working with partners, the aim is to provide a visible and technological presence on our roads and to penalize and educate errant drivers, thereby influencing the behaviour of all road users. Further information is available in the *Roads Policing* section of the College of Policing APP, available online.

'Working in the carriageway' accounts for a significant number of police fatalities and is one of the most dangerous working environments for police officers. The police are governed by the Health and Safety at Work etc Act 1974, and each police service will therefore have risk assessments for this type of work. Trainee constables should be familiar with these assessments and the associated risk mitigation strategies. Working in the carriageway is also governed by the New Roads and Street Works Act 1991 and the Highways Act 1980. These require all individuals (including police officers) to wear suitable high-visibility clothing whilst working in the carriageway (and failing to do so may constitute a criminal offence). For roads with a speed limit over 50 mph, the jacket must comply with the European Standard EN 471 to class 3 (service-issue high-visibility jackets will comply with this).

Trainee police officers will be instructed, shown, and assessed on the police procedures for stopping a vehicle, the actions to be taken when attending the scene of a recent collision, and so on. Officers should also be guided by local policies and the College of Policing *Road Policing* APP, available online.

The topics covered in this chapter contribute to the learning required for the National Policing Curriculum subject areas of 'Roads Policing', 'Understanding the Police Constable Role', and 'Response Policing'.

16.2 Definitions for Vehicles, Roads, and Driving

Road traffic legislation has inevitably developed as times have changed, and new terminology has been introduced to deal with advances in technology. Terms that were valid for the Highways Act 1835 may seem archaic but should be seen in context. It is, however, essential that an officer understands what the terms mean as they often determine the relevant powers and responsibilities.

16.2.1 Definitions of vehicles

Within road traffic legislation various terms are used to describe the different types of vehicle and other wheeled objects, such as carriages, conveyances, and cycles. The following table explains some of these terms but is by no means comprehensive.

Vehicle type	Definition	Examples
'Vehicle'	According to the Vehicle Excise and Registration Act 1994, a vehicle is: 'a mechanically propelled vehicle, or anything (whether or not it is a vehicle) that has been, but has ceased to be, a mechanically propelled vehicle'. The ordinary dictionary meaning can also be used	Milk float, ride-on grass cutter
'Mechanically propelled vehicle'	'Mechanically propelled' means that the vehicle is powered by a motor (driven by electricity, petrol, diesel, or other fuels). The meaning is not defined by any Act of Parliament, so whether a particular vehicle is a mechanically propelled vehicle is therefore a question of fact for a court to decide	Car, van, lorry, go-ped, quad bike, speedway motorcycles, Formula One racing cars, self-balancing personal transporters (Segways, hoverboards, etc), invalid carriages such as powered wheelchairs and scooters
'Motor vehicle'	This is a mechanically propelled vehicle that is intended or adapted for use on roads (s 185 of the Road Traffic Act 1988)	Car, van, lorry, bus, coach, self-balancing personal transporters (Segways, hoverboards, etc)
'Motor bicycle'*	This means a motor vehicle which has two wheels and a maximum design speed exceeding 45 kph. If powered by an internal combustion engine, the cylinder capacity must exceed 50 cc. It includes a combination, such as a motor vehicle and a side-car (s 108 of the Road Traffic Act 1988)	Motorcycle with two wheels, includes those fitted with a sidecar
'Bicycle'	This includes a 'motor bicycle' (ie a motorcycle) for the purposes of vehicle excise duty	
'Moped'*	A moped is a motor vehicle with three or fewer wheels and maximum design speed of 50 kph (note this covers electric-powered two-wheelers). If propelled by an engine, the cylinder capacity must not exceed 50 cc (s 108 of the Road Traffic Act 1988). Older models with an engine (first used before 1 August 1977) can also have pedals for propulsion	
'Pedal cycle'	This must be designed so it can be propelled by pedals, and includes electrically assisted pedal cycles (reg 3 of the Pedal Cycles (Construction and Use) Regulations 1983)	Mountain bike, racing bike, BMX bike
'Carriage'	This means a motor vehicle or trailer (s 191 of the Road Traffic Act 1988). The ordinary dictionary meaning also applies	Any motor vehicle described above, and caravans
'Conveyance'	This is a vehicle constructed or adapted for transporting person(s) by land, water, or air, but not one constructed or adapted for use 'only under the control of a person not carried in or on it' (s 12(7) of the Theft Act 1968)	Motorcycle, bus, boat, and plane

* De-restriction kits are available for mopeds (to allow speeds over 50 kph and/or increase the cylinder capacity), and for 125 cc learner motorcycles, to increase power. If such alterations are made the vehicle becomes a motor bicycle and the rider must conform to the relevant licence requirements.

Some vehicles do not fit within obvious categories. These include mini-motos (small motorcycles designed for use on private land), scooters with a petrol or electric engine but no seat (eg Go-peds and e-scooters), and self-balancing personal transporters such as Segways and hoverboards. All of these have been held to be motor vehicles (carriages) for the purposes of s 185 of the Road Traffic Act 1988. The CPS provides advice on its website in the *Definitions of a motor vehicle* section, including references by case stated (ie the relevant case law) regarding mini-motos, Go-peds, and self-balancing personal transporters. Full details of the legal requirements are also given on the CPS website; see also *Coates v CPS* [2011] EWHC 2032 (Admin). In some circumstances, the use of such vehicles may be an offence against the Highways Act 1835.

Commercial vehicles are either passenger-carrying vehicles (PCVs) or goods vehicles. Some are very large, for example 'large goods vehicles' (LGVs, previously known as heavy goods vehicles and still commonly referred to as HGVs) and can therefore cause immense damage in a collision. The general construction and use regulations for all vehicles also apply to large commercial vehicles, depending on the number of passenger seats or the vehicle weight. However, additional rules apply for commercial vehicles such as:

- driver licensing and operator licensing; and
- restrictions on driver hours.

Note that a commercial vehicle may on occasions be driven for other purposes (eg a vintage lorry at a motor show or a minibus transporting people for a charity on a voluntary basis). In such circumstances, the regulations for commercial purposes may not apply but the individual circumstances will need to be ascertained in each case.

16.2.1.1 Vehicle identification features

Vehicles normally have a number of identifying features unique to each vehicle, and these can be easily recalled by using the police mnemonic VICE, as shown in the table.

V	Vehicle identification number (VIN)	VINs on EU-market vehicles have 17 characters in a unique combination of numbers and letters. A few vehicles have non-standard VINs, usually on imported vehicles that were originally sold outside the EU (often right-hand drive vehicles from Japan). The VIN is displayed on the dashboard (visible through the windscreen) on most vehicles.
I	Index number or registration plate	All mechanically propelled vehicles used on public roads require a registration mark (number).
C	Chassis number (same as VIN)	All vehicles used on or after 1 April 1980 will have their 17-character VIN stamped into the chassis or frame of the car. The location is often described in the vehicle handbook.
E	Engine number	Engine numbers are often tucked away in locations most easily seen when (or if) the engine is taken out of the vehicle. Engines are also sometimes replaced, so the fact that an engine number cannot be found should not in itself be a cause for suspicion.

All vehicles in use on or after 1 April 1980 have the VIN on a metal plate attached to a part of the vehicle not normally subject to replacement and in a conspicuous and accessible position. The VIN will also be stamped on the chassis or frame. The VIN plate will also show the manufacturer and may also show the type approval number (indicating that the vehicle meets EU standards) and the vehicle weight and axle loadings. The VIN plate shown here displays the vehicle weight information but on many vehicles this will be on a separate plate. For UK registered goods vehicles over 3.5t, a separate plating certificate will be issued.

(Image © Kevin Lawton-Barrett)

Example of a VIN on the chassis of a VW camper van.

The four weights in this case (from top to bottom) refer to:

- the total weight of the vehicle, including any people or loads;
- the gross train weight (the vehicle and any trailer attached) including any people or loads;
- the weight limit for the front axle (axle 1) (includes the vehicle and anything (including people) being carried); and
- the weight limit for the second axle (axle 2) (includes the vehicle and anything (including people) being carried).

Vehicles with more than two axles will continue the number sequence.

All the identifying features articulated in the VICE mnemonic are recorded on DVLA databases along with the colour, make, and model of the vehicle. Police control-room personnel have access to databases listing the positions of the stamped-in VIN, the VIN plate, and the engine number for all vehicle makes and models. VIN numbers are also programmed into the electronic control unit of the vehicle and can be checked using a suitable device connected to the onboard diagnostic port of the vehicle.

16.2.2 Roads, highways, and related terms

Legislation relating to road and traffic policing often includes the words 'road', 'highway', and 'public place'. Each term is used in different pieces of legislation, though the term 'road' is used far more frequently, particularly since the introduction of the Road Traffic Act 1988.

- A 'road' is any (length of) highway to which the public has access and includes bridges over which a road passes (s 192 of the Road Traffic Act 1988). The limits of a road are the hedgerows, walls, fences, or building lines on each side so a public footpath alongside a road is part of the road.
- A 'highway' (s 5 of the Highways Act 1835) is a road, bridge, carriageway, cart-way, horseway, bridleway, footway, causeway, church way, or pavement.
- A 'public road' is a road maintained at the public's expense (for the purposes of vehicle excise duty legislation), as defined in s 62 of the Vehicle Excise and Registration Act 1994. Note that just because a road is not gated or blocked, it is not necessarily a public road; if in doubt, consult the Highways Authority for the area.

Note the potentially confusing overlap between a road and a highway: in practice, this does not matter as each relates to individual pieces of legislation.

A number of other terms are also used:

- 'other public place' is a place that any member of the general public has access to without needing specific permission, but it will be for a court to decide. It is likely to include car parks, turning areas, and parks. The term is used in the Road Traffic Act 1988, for example in relation to insurance (s 143(1)(a)), collision reporting (s 170), driving standards (ss 2 and 3), offences surrounding driving-related death (ss 1, 2B, 3ZB, and 3A), and drink- or drug-drive offences (ss 4, 5, and 5A);
- a carriageway is a 'way' that is marked or arranged in a highway over which the public have a right of way for the passage of vehicles but does not include cycle tracks (s 329 of the Highways Act 1980);
- a bridleway is a highway on which the public have a right of way on foot, on horseback, or leading a horse (s 329 of the Highways Act 1980);
- a footpath is a highway that is not adjacent to a road over which the public have a right of way, but only on foot (s 329 of the Highways Act 1980);
- a footway (such as a pavement) is a highway adjacent to a road and to which the public have a right of way on foot only (s 329(1) of the Highways Act 1980);
- a street includes roads, lanes, alleys, subways, squares, and any other similar places open to the public. It also includes doorways, entrances to premises, and any ground adjoining a street (*Smith v Hughes* [1960] 2 All ER 859).

The maintenance of a private road is usually the responsibility of the landowner; the road in the photograph is in a good state of repair. Private roads may or may not be subject to public rights of way.

(Photo by Kevin Lawton-Barrett)

Core Aspects of Police Work

16.2.2.1 Road and road network classifications

As well as the legal definition of a road set out earlier, there are also a number of other terms, such as 'A road' and 'minor road', which are used to describe individual roads and combinations of roads. Many of these will not be used when dealing with offences but are used by police and partner organizations when communicating and when determining responsibility for, and reporting, collisions. Some of the terms are officially recognized and others used anecdotally; an understanding of them is important when dealing with drivers, witnesses, and other agencies. We provide a summary here but for a full explanation see *Guidance on Road Classification and the Primary Route Network* from the Department for Transport.

The Strategic Road Network (SRN) and the Primary Road Network (PRN) form the network of main roads across the country. The Department for Transport is responsible for defining the SRN and the PRN. The SRN includes all the larger roads (eg motorways) that are used for the national distribution of goods and services, and for public travel across the whole country. The roads that form the SRN are also known as trunk roads. The PRN is used for transport on a regional or county level and also feeds into the SRN for longer journeys. The PRN also includes all the SRN in a particular area.

Motorways are subject to particular rules regarding the movement of vehicles, such as direction of travel (see also the table). The Motorways Traffic (England and Wales) Regulations 1982 describe the designation of each part of the motorway (such as 'central reservation' and 'hard shoulder') and the particular rules that apply. Pedestrians and mopeds are prohibited on motorways, as is stopping (apart from on the hard shoulder in emergencies).

The Department for Transport is responsible for classifying roads according to their size and usage as shown in the table. Most UK roads (60 per cent) are unclassified D roads.

DfT road type	Example	Road sign	Key features	Identification in police communications
Motorway	M6	Blue with white text	Each has a unique identifying number Motorways form part of the SRN	By number
A road	A21	Non-PRN: white with black text Part of PRN: green with white and yellow text Road number will be shown	Each has a unique identifying number Some are subject to the motorway regulations and are referred to as A(M), for example the A1(M). May also have a name (often used by local people)	By number
B road	B1231	White with black text Road number will be shown	Each has a unique identifying number May also have a name (often used by local people)	By number
Classified unnumbered road ('C roads')	'Mill Lane'	White with black text (No number will be shown)	Each usually has a name (but may also have a locally designated number)	By name
Unclassified road ('D roads')	'Church Road'	White with black text	Each has a name	By name

For identifying roads when reporting collisions, the Department for Transport guidance (2011) states that the relevant road(s) should be identified as a motorway, A(M), A, B, C, or unclassified (even though C is an unofficial term), including the number of a motorway, A(M), A, or B road.

The Highways Act 1980 includes particular terms for different types of road, although these are not widely used in other contexts, for example:

- a 'special road' is a road where certain types of traffic are prohibited and includes all motorways and some high-grade dual carriageways;
- a principal road is any A road or motorway so includes 'special roads';
- a secondary road is any road that is not a principal road.

Other unofficial terms are also used, for example a 'major road' is generally any A road or motorway and a 'minor road' is generally any classified unnumbered or unclassified road (the unofficial C and D categories in the table).

16.2.2.2 Responsibilities for roads

The highways authorities are responsible for the SRN. English and Welsh traffic officers have some powers related to the control and direction of traffic but they are obliged to follow the direction of a police constable. The authority in England is 'Highways England', staffed by Highways England Traffic Officers Service (TOS) but often still referred to as HATOs (the previous term, derived from the now defunct Highways Agency). In Wales there are two agencies; the North and Mid Wales Trunk Road Agent and the South Wales Trunk Road Agent, staffed by Welsh Government Traffic Officers.

All roads that are not part of the SRN are the responsibility of the relevant local county council, unitary authority, or town council. In London, the City of London is responsible for all roads in its local authority area except those on designated red routes. Red routes (the major road network in London with special stopping, loading, and unloading restrictions indicated by red lines) are administered by Transport for London. If an incident occurs at a boundary between different highway authorities, the relevant authorities will need to work together.

16.2.3 Driving

Legislation relating to road and traffic policing often refers to 'driving' and 'attempting to drive'. The term 'driving' is not defined in any legislative Act but there are precedents which provide guidelines and the final decision rests with the court. The court will consider:

- the degree to which the person had control over the direction and movement of the vehicle;
- the length of time the person had control;
- the point at which the person stopped the driving; and
- the use of the vehicle's controls by the person in order to direct its movement.

Attempting to drive is not defined by statute but the general principles for attempted offences should be applied; an attempt is the last action before the full offence is committed and is more than merely preparatory to the act (see Chapter 27). For example, trying to start a vehicle which will not start because it has a fault could be considered as attempting to drive. The definition of being 'in charge of a vehicle' only relates to drink- and drug-driving.

16.2.4 Using, causing, permitting use of, and keeping a vehicle

Many road traffic offences are committed by the people who use the vehicle, but some offences relate to causing or permitting a vehicle's use. This would apply to vehicle owners and people who hold supervisory responsibilities, for example. You need to have a clear understanding about the meanings of 'using', 'causing', and 'permitting'. We will illustrate the principles in the context of an employer, an employee, and a defective vehicle but it is also important to note that it will be for the courts to decide as a question of fact whether any of these offences have been committed in particular circumstances.

So imagine an employer runs a company van which has a defective tyre, and an employee drives it. Even if that employer is not aware of the defect, then the offence of 'using' would still be committed. If, knowing about the defect, the employer sent the employee out in the vehicle this would be 'causing', and if the employer allows the employee to borrow the van and use it at the weekend for their own purpose, this would be 'permitting'. We provide more details in the following paragraphs.

Using a vehicle is not the same under road traffic law as driving a vehicle; for example, a vehicle can be 'in use' while parked or while being towed. The user of a vehicle can be:

- the driver of a vehicle, including an employee driving a company vehicle for business purposes;
- the employer, if the vehicle is a company vehicle used on company business. The employer can be held responsible for committing an offence (as a user) relating to a vehicle defect even if they are unaware of the defect: in some circumstances, both the employer and the driver (an employee) can be held responsible;

- the owner of a vehicle, if it is being driven by another person with the owner present and for the benefit of the owner; or
- a person steering a vehicle, for example when being towed.

For causing the use of a vehicle, the 'causer' must have the authority to make a subordinate carry out a particular action and must know about the unroadworthy state of the vehicle. In some cases, a company rather than a person can be held responsible for causing the use of an unroadworthy vehicle if the company director knows the vehicle is defective. However, many companies allow employees to use company vehicles for private purposes, and in such circumstances, it is unlikely that the employer could be held responsible for causing the vehicle to be used. Also note that if a person tows a vehicle, then they are causing it to be used on a road.

'Permitting use of a vehicle' is a further legal concept. The 'permitter' must be in a position to either allow or forbid its use and the permission can be given verbally, in writing, or merely implied. The 'permitter' (eg an employer) would commit an offence if they have knowledge of (or 'turn a blind eye' to) the unroadworthy state of the vehicle or its lack of documentation and allow an employee to drive it for business purposes (for relevant case law see the House of Lords' judgment in *Vehicle Inspectorate v Nuttall* [1999] 1 WLR 629, available online). If either of these elements cannot be proved, then offences relating to the 'use' of the vehicle could be considered.

Keeping a vehicle is when a person ('the keeper') has day-to-day responsibility for a vehicle. It is a question of fact for a court to decide who is a 'keeper' as no legislative definition exists. The 'registered keeper', however, is the person to whom a vehicle is registered, ie whose details appear on a national register of vehicles. Consequently, the registered keeper is not necessarily the keeper (see *Mohindra v DPP* [2004] EWHC 490 (Admin)).

The legal owner of a vehicle could be the 'keeper' or the 'registered keeper', although this should not be assumed. It could alternatively be a financial institution which provided a loan for the purchase or an insurance company that has paid out on a claim in relation to the vehicle.

16.3 Vehicle and Driver Documents

The act of driving and the use of vehicles are subject to licensing, statutory requirements, and testing. These regimes create various documents which a police officer needs to understand in order to deal with incidents, and we will explain the key points here. We will also cover some of the offences which may be committed if all is not in order and some of the police powers which may be available in such circumstances.

16.3.1 UK driving licences

In the UK, a driver must have the appropriate licence entitlement for the classes of vehicle that they drive. The licence shows the categories of vehicle that a person is entitled to drive. UK driving licence regulation and design has changed a number of times over recent years, mainly to bring the UK into line with EU regulation, the latest amendments being in July 2015. This section will primarily deal with UK driving licences but also provides some information on licences from other countries. UK driving licences are administered by the Driver and Vehicle Licensing Agency (DVLA).

The DVLA database contains a 'driver record' for each driver which shows their licence and driving history and any Driver and Vehicle Standards Agency (DVSA) test passed. Updates are indicated by a 'marker' on the record, for example 'test passed' or 'licence revoked'. The PNC contains up-to-date copies of all the DVLA driver records as 'driver files' and such a file will have a 'DD' tab if the driver is disqualified.

Offences relating to driving licences under the Road Traffic Act 1988 include:

- driving a motor vehicle on a road otherwise than in accordance with a licence authorizing them to drive a motor vehicle of that class (s 87(1)); this includes drivers on provisional entitlements who fail to comply with licence requirements;

- causing or permitting another person to drive on a road if that person does not have a licence authorizing driving that class of vehicle (s 87(2)); and
- failure to update a change of address on a driving licence (s 99(5)).

When a driver commits a road traffic offence, penalty points can be 'endorsed' on their driving licence or a marker can be added to their licence record. For endorsable offences, the number of penalty points depends on the offence.

16.3.1.1 Vehicle categories and codes on driving licences

There have been several changes to the licence vehicle category designations over time and some older licences will still display some of the discontinued categories. The first table shows the categories that currently apply for vehicles with four or more wheels.

Licence vehicle category	Type of vehicle	Minimum driver age
B1	Light vehicles and quad bikes, 4 wheels up to 400 kg (550 kg if designed to carry goods)	17
B	Cars and light vans	17
B auto	Cars and light vans with an automatic gearbox	
BE***	Cars and light vans with a trailer up to 3,500 kg	
C1	Goods vehicles between 3,500 kg and 7,500 kg (with or without a trailer; 750 kg maximum trailer weight)	18*
C1E**	As for C1 but with a trailer over 750 kg, but combined weight not exceeding 12,000 kg	
C	Any goods vehicles over 3,500 kg, with or without a trailer (750 kg maximum trailer weight)	21*
CE**	As for C, but with a trailer over 750 kg	
D1	Passenger-carrying vehicles max length 8 m, with 9–16 passenger seats (minibuses), and trailer up to 750 kg	21*
D1E**	As for D1 but with a trailer over 750 kg (combined weight not exceeding 12,000 kg)	
D	Bus with more than 8 passenger seats, and trailer up to 750 kg	24*
DE**	As for D but with a trailer over 750 kg	
F	Agricultural tractors	17
G	Road rollers	21
H	Tracked vehicles	
K	Mowing machines or pedestrian-controlled vehicles	16

* These categories can be driven at a younger age in some circumstances, for example if the driver: is a member of the armed forces, a learner driver (only some categories), or received a licence for certain categories prior to 1997.
** A full licence for the towing vehicle category must be obtained before the test can be taken for towing a trailer.
*** Automatically obtained with a B category licence, changed on 16 December 2021 from previous arrangements.

Details can be found on the *Information on Driving Licences* leaflet available from the gov.uk website.

Powered wheelchairs and powered scooters designed for people with disabilities do not require a driver licence.

16.3.1.2 The driver and issue number

Every UK driving licence holder has a driver number. This is the unique reference by which DVLA identifies an individual and is assigned to a single driver record. A foreign licence holder (with no UK licence) can have a UK driver number if they have been dealt with for an offence in the UK and issued with penalty points. It is essential to check the details of a foreign licence holder against the 'driver file' on the PNC because the driver may have UK penalty points or even be disqualified. It should be noted that a person may have more than one driver number if they have been dealt with by the DVLA using slightly different data on different occasions (eg omitting a middle name, giving names in different order, an error in the date of birth). There is a means by which a number of such driver records can be brought together (police service DVLA liaison officers can provide details).

The driver number contains three clusters of information about the driver: family name (five letters); gender and date of birth (six numbers); and a final cluster (five characters). The table shows how to interpret the driver number WILLI 611205 RS9KY for the driver Robert Stuart Williamson.

Cluster	Description	Example
1	The first five letters of the family name. If the name has less than five characters, the remaining spaces are made up using the figure 9 (ie TODD9))	WILLI
2	The first and last digits are derived from the year of birth	611205 shows the year of birth is 1965
	The second and third digits represent the month of birth and the gender. For a female, 5 is added to the second digit, so for a female born in November the cluster would be x61xxx, and for a female born in July, it would be x57xxx	611205 shows he was born in November and is male.
	The fourth and fifth digits show the day of birth:	611205 shows he was born on the 20th of the month
3	The first two characters represent the person's initials	RS9KY (if there is only one initial, 9 is used in place of a second initial, eg R9)
	The third number and the final two letters are computer-generated and are used to avoid duplicate records. If the first 13 digits of the driver number are unique, then the third digit will be a 9, otherwise it will be an 8 (or a 7 in the case of a triplicate, and so on).	RS9KY

The issue number on the driving licence is shown adjacent to the driver number on the front of the licence. A driver's first issue number is randomly generated and is increased by one on their subsequent licences (ie if on first issue the number is 35, the next licence will be 36 and then 37, and so on). Only the current licence is valid as drivers are not allowed to hold more than one licence. The driver file on the PNC shows the issue number of the current valid licence so this should be checked against any licence provided.

16.3.1.3 Motorcycle licensing and training requirements

To legally ride a motorbike on a road, the driver must first obtain a licence with a provisional entitlement for the relevant category, and also complete Compulsory Basic Training (CBT). A CBT certificate is valid for two years and is shown as a marker on the DVLA driver record. It can be retaken if it expires. Once a full motorcycle entitlement has been obtained, a valid CBT is no longer required. A full explanation of the process for obtaining motorcycle licences can be found on the gov.uk website.

The motorcycle categories in the table came into force on 19 January 2013. Note that electrically assisted pedal cycles are classified as pedal cycles so a driving licence is not required.

Licence vehicle category	Type of vehicle	Minimum driver age
Moped AM	2- or 3-wheeled vehicles, top speed 15.5–28 mph (25–45 km/h)	16
	Small 3-wheelers (up to 50 cc and below 4 kW), light quadricycles (under 350 kg, top speed 25–45 km/h)	
Moped p (no longer issued)	2-wheeled, top speed 28–31 mph (45–50 km/h), maximum engine capacity 50 cc if powered by internal combustion.	
Moped q	2- or 3-wheels, top speed 15.5 mph (25 km/h), engine size less than 50 cc if internal combustion, granted with an AM licence entitlement	
A1	Small motorbikes up to 11 kW and 125 cc (power-to-weight ratio not more than 0.1 kW per kg)	17
	Motor tricycles with a power output 15 kW or less	

Licence vehicle category	Type of vehicle	Minimum driver age
A2	Medium motorbikes up to 35 kW (power-to-weight ratio not more than 0.2 kW per kg). If the engine is restricted, its power must be at least half its original (or it will be category A)	19
A	Motorbikes, unlimited size/power, with or without a side-car. Motor tricycles with power output over 15 kW	17 (armed services only) 21 (progressive access*) 24 (direct access**)

* Must hold A2 licence for at least two years before taking the practical test.
** No need to hold the A2 licence for two years before taking the practical test.

16.3.1.4 Additional licensing requirements for commercial vehicles

Drivers of larger vehicles are subject to extra licencing requirements when the vehicles are driven for commercial purposes. This applies for large goods vehicles (classes C1, C1E, C, and CE) and for larger passenger vehicles (classes D1, D1E, D, and DE). The regulations are numerous and complex, for further details see the gov.uk website. Some key features of the regulations for commercial driving are that the driver must:

- be aged at least 18 years (under certain conditions the minimum age is 21 or 24 years;
- hold a full car licence; and
- complete a medical form when first applying (includes a section for their GP and optician to complete) and on each renewal.

As for any driver, the E categories can only be obtained after obtaining a full category for the towing vehicle. For commercial drivers up to the age of 65, the driving licence categories are only valid for five years and need to be renewed (renewal is required every year for drivers older than 65 years).

Drivers of commercial vehicles of classes C, CE, D, and DE must also hold a Driver Certificate of Professional Competence (CPC), obtained by attending a certified training course and passing four tests. They must also complete 35 hours of ongoing training every five years to remain qualified.

16.3.1.5 UK photocard driving licences

A UK licence can be a full or provisional licence, is valid for ten years, and shows the driver's current driving entitlements and personal information. Additional licence information can be accessed online using the driver number and the holder's NI number and postcode. The issue number should be checked on the PNC driver file to confirm it is the driver's most recently issued licence. Penalty points should also be checked on the PNC as these are no longer endorsed on the actual licence. Note that a driver may produce an old-style paper licence which is still valid, usually because they have not recently changed their name or address.

Provisional licences have a green background with a clear pictogram of an L plate on the front. It will show only provisional entitlements, as they are not issued to drivers with a full entitlement in any category. Full licence photocards have a pink background with a Union flag on the front and show all the holder's full entitlements. Full licence photocards do not show any provisional entitlements so these would need to be checked against the driver file on PNC.

The latest version of the full driving licence photocard is shown here.

Both versions have the same information on the front, there has merely been a design change to take account of the UK leaving the EU.

The previous version which will be in circulation until the end of 2030 when they will have expired, is shown here.

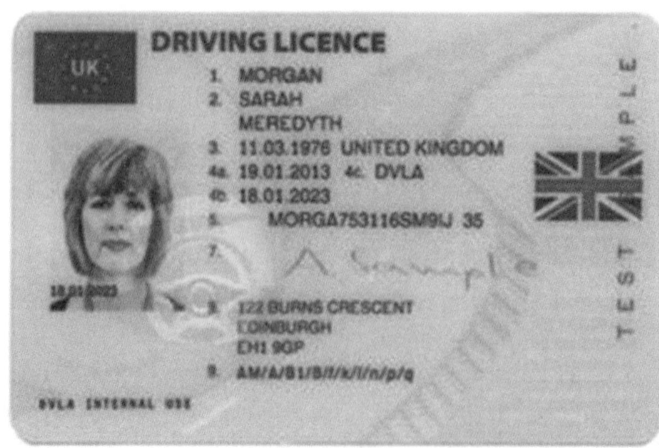

On the front of the card, the issue and expiry dates are shown ((4a) and (4b) respectively). The driver and issue number are shown at (5). The categories of valid vehicle entitlement are shown at (9), with EU directive categories in capitals and UK local categories in lower case.

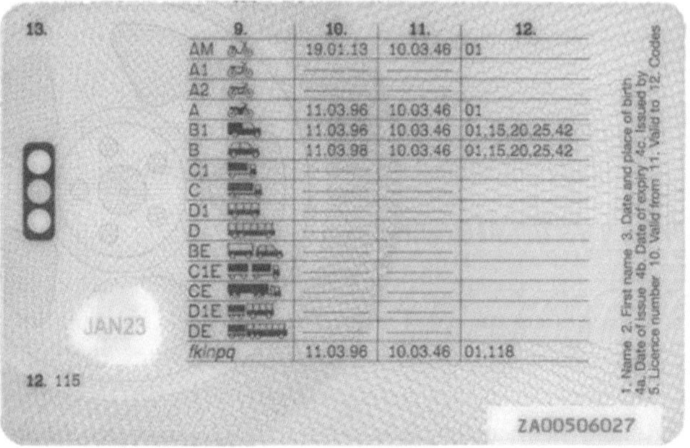

On the back of the card, column 9 shows all the possible entitlements and columns 10 and 11 show the valid entitlements for the licence holder, with start and expiry dates. Column 12 lists the DVLA restriction codes that apply for each entitlement. There are many restriction codes, for example code 01 is 'eyesight correction' for the driver. A breach of the restrictions would amount to driving not in accordance with a licence.

The DVLA leaflet 'Information on Driving Licences' provides further information.

16.3.1.6 Provisional entitlements and learner drivers

All provisional entitlements impose certain requirements on the driver. A breach of any of the requirements will amount to the offence of driving otherwise than in accordance with a driving licence (s 87(1) of the Road Traffic Act 1988). The conditions under which a provisional licence holder can drive a vehicle are set out in reg 16 of the Motor Vehicles (Driving Licences) Regulations 1999.

The main requirement is that L plates must be displayed on the front and back of the vehicle while it is being driven by a provisional licence holder in England. The plates must be clearly visible to other road users within a reasonable distance (reg 16(2)(b)). The correct dimensions for an L plate are shown in the diagram, and it can have rounded corners. D plates can be displayed in Wales but they must be replaced with L plates if driving in England.

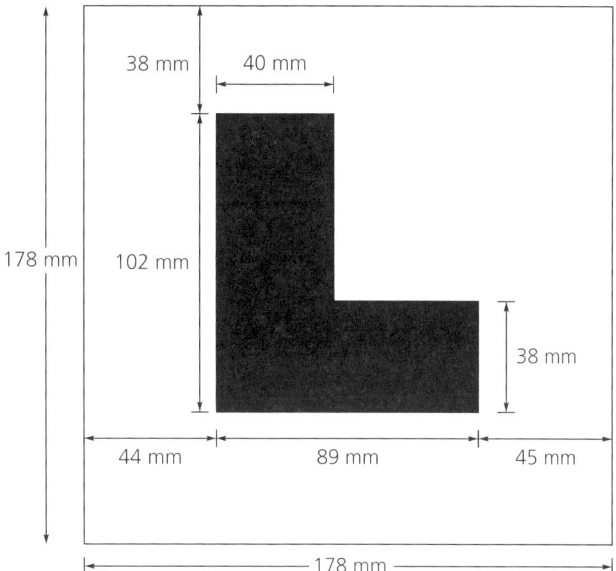

L plates are often 'cut down' for motorcycles (see below) but this is not permitted.

Supervision is required for drivers with a provisional entitlement when driving vehicles with four or more wheels. The supervision must be provided by a 'qualified driver' (reg 16(2)(a)) who must be at least 21 years old, have the relevant driving experience, and have had a full British (including Northern Ireland) or an EU Community licence with the relevant entitlements for at least three years (reg 17(1) and (2)).

There are some situations where a driver with a provisional entitlement can drive without supervision, such as:

- driving certain categories of motor vehicle, for example a three-wheeled vehicle; or
- riding a moped or a motorcycle (with or without a side-car).

Provisional licence holders should not drive a vehicle with a trailer (reg 16(2)(c)) unless learning and being supervised for a vehicle in the E category. Then the towing vehicle should have an L plate on the front and the trailer should have a L plate on the back (reg 16(5)).

16.3.1.7 Disqualification

A driver who has been disqualified cannot legally drive any motor vehicle on a road. When a driver has been disqualified, the DVLA driver record will be marked as such and a Disqualified Driver (DD) tab will appear on the PNC names file and the licence will also be revoked. A person can be disqualified even if absent from court so a driver might not know but this is no defence.

Disqualification can be imposed once 12 penalty points have been recorded ('endorsed') on the driver's DVLA driver record in a three-year period. It is not obligatory to disqualify a driver with 12 points and a driver can present reasons to the court and explain why they should not be disqualified.

Disqualification is also one of the penalty options for certain offences and can be discretionary, for example for 'failing to stop after an accident'. For more serious offences, disqualification is obligatory, such as for driving over the prescribed limit for alcohol or drugs, or dangerous driving. The court will decide the duration of the disqualification, taking into account the offence and the driver's offending history. Permanent disqualification is very rare (*R v Tunde-Olarinde* [1967] 2 All ER 491).

A further option is a DTTP disqualification (Disqualified Till Test Passed). This requires the driver to pass a DVSA test to regain their licence and is often imposed in addition to a conventional disqualification, for example 'disqualified for two years and DTTP'. Once the disqualification has reverted to DTTP-only, the driver will be allowed a provisional licence so that they can practise for retaking the test. All the requirements of the provisional entitlement apply, and if they are not fulfilled the driver is dealt with in the same way as any other disqualified driver, ie under s 103(1)(b).

While disqualified from holding or obtaining a licence, it is an offence to obtain a licence or drive a motor vehicle on a road (s 103(1)(a) and (b) of the Road Traffic Act 1988 respectively). The court will require evidence of the original disqualification (see *Mills v DPP* [2008] EWHC 3304 (Admin)) such as a certificate of conviction under s 73 of the PACE Act 1984, the defendant's admission (at interview or in court), or a statement from a person who was in court when the disqualification was imposed.

These offences are triable summarily and the penalty for obtaining a licence while disqualified is a fine. The penalty for driving a motor vehicle on a road while disqualified is imprisonment for up to six months and/or a fine, discretionary extension of the disqualification, and obligatory endorsement (six penalty points).

16.3.1.8 Revocation

A licence can be revoked, effectively suspended, pending resolution of the circumstances, and the person is no longer authorized to drive under any of the entitlements on the licence. Licences can be revoked by the DVLA for a number of reasons, such as:

- failing to surrender a licence when required, for example when an endorsement is imposed. The DVLA will write to the licence holder requesting surrender of the licence within 28 days and stating that if it is not surrendered it will be revoked. The record will be updated to show the licence as expired;
- disqualification—when a driver is disqualified, the DVLA will mark the licence as revoked on the driver record and add the disqualification. At the end of a fixed-period disqualification, the individual must reapply for a licence and, until it is issued, the DVLA driver record will still show it as revoked;
- medical grounds—the licence holder (or a third party with an obligation to inform) tells the DVLA that the person has a notifiable medical condition (see the gov.uk website for a list).

The circumstances under which a licence can be revoked will often need to be explained to individuals. Depending on the reasons for the revocation, the DVLA driver record will show the licence as revoked or expired. Sometimes the DVLA will alter the expiry date of the licence rather than revoke it in the normal way. Note that a person with a revoked licence is not disqualified from driving; this would need to be imposed by a court. Driving with a revoked licence is 'driving not in accordance with a licence' which is a different offence from driving while disqualified.

New drivers can also have their full entitlement revoked to a provisional entitlement (on one occasion only). This was introduced in the Road Traffic (New Drivers) Act 1995 after research revealed that new drivers were more likely than other road users to be involved in collisions due to poor driving. The full entitlement licence is automatically revoked if the driver receives any obligatory endorsement(s) (s 2(1)(b)) which accumulate to six or more penalty points (s 2(1)(d)).

16.3.1.9 Foreign licences

There are significant numbers of non-UK drivers now residing in the UK and their status with regard to driving and licensing depends on the person's country of origin.

If they hold a licence from an EU country (a 'Community licence') or a country in the European Economic Area, then the holder is treated as if a UK licence is held and can continue to drive on it (until the age of 70). Such a licence can be exchanged for a UK licence at any time but this is not compulsory.

For a driver with a non-EU licence, the licence will remain valid for 12 months after either entering the UK as a visitor or becoming a resident. An individual's status as either a visitor or resident and any change in status will be a matter of fact for a court to decide, but a permanent address, employment, or enrolment of children at a local school may all be indicators of residence. Once the 12-month period has expired, an appropriate UK licence must be obtained.

A person holding a non-EU licence must comply with the above requirement; however, a person from certain designated non-EU countries or territories can exchange their licence for a UK licence within five years of arrival although this is not compulsory. This applies for Australia, Barbados, British Virgin Islands, Canada, Falkland Islands, Faroe Islands, Hong Kong, Japan, Monaco, New Zealand, Republic of Korea, Singapore, South Africa, Switzerland, and Zimbabwe.

A driver with a non-UK licence can still be dealt with for driving matters. If endorsements are imposed, a UK driver number will be allocated and a 'non-licence holder' driver record will be created at the DVLA. See more at: <https://www.gov.uk/driving-nongb-licence>, but officers should also follow local policies.

16.3.2 Insurance

All motor vehicles used on the road or other public place in the UK must have a valid third-party liabilities insurance policy or a 'security' (a financial deposit by a large organization). Third party insurance means the policy will pay out if another person's property is damaged or if someone other than the policy holder is killed or injured (s 145(3)(a)). Insurance cover is usually described as fully comprehensive, third party only, or third-party fire and theft (TPF&T). The cost is based on the risk as assessed from the information provided by the policy holder and any failure to disclose correct or full information may amount to fraud under s 2 or 3 of the Fraud Act 2006. Some vehicles have a black box fitted in the vehicle to record aspects of the driving, which could permit a discount.

The policy will specify the cover in terms of the use of the vehicle and the individuals concerned and if any of the conditions listed on the policy are breached the vehicle will not be insured. The cover will only apply to specific uses such as Social, Domestic and Pleasure (SDP), commuting to a fixed place of work, or business use. The policy can apply to the policy holder only or to the policy holder and named drivers. 'Any driver' policies are sometimes issued (often for company vehicles) and these usually have conditions, for example that all drivers must be over 25 years old or employed by the policy holder.

'Any vehicle' clauses often cause confusion. These allow the policy holder to drive any vehicle with the owner's permission and were previously standard on all comprehensive policies. However, this is no longer the case and some drivers do not realize this. An 'any vehicle' clause cannot be used by an individual who owns more than one vehicle as a way of avoiding insurance payments for all of the cars that they own. So, it does not allow the policy holder to drive another vehicle that they own without insuring each vehicle separately or as part of a multi-car policy. The same restriction applies for any named drivers on a policy. Some any-vehicle clauses require that the vehicle is also insured separately by its owner and may also include a further clause stating that this cover does not extend to recovering vehicles seized by the police for a 'no insurance offence'. It should also be noted that 'any vehicle' clauses only ever provide basic third-party cover.

The policy must be issued by an insurer registered with the Motor Insurers' Bureau (MIB) to be valid in the UK. The policy holder will receive a certificate of insurance (hard copy or electronic) from the company, and this will include at least the following features:

Insurance Company Name and Address:
AAA Insurance Ltd.
The High Street
Registration Number: AA 00 AAA

Certificate number: 000/999/123
Policy holder's name: Orlando SMITH Expiry date: Noon 16th December 2022
Permitted Drivers: Verity SMITH, Noah KAY
Limitations as to use: Use for social, domestic, and pleasure purposes, including travel between the driver's home and place of work.

Note that the existence of an insurance certificate does not prove that a vehicle is currently insured. The MIB maintains a database of all insured vehicles, available via the vehicle file on the PNC, so officers should always refer to this. Short-duration policies are often not shown on the MIB database so further enquiries would be required to establish an accurate picture of the insurance status. The MIB run a help line for police officers who have stopped a vehicle on the street and have enquiries regarding its insurance, although this is not available 24/7. The police control room can provide current telephone numbers for officers to call direct.

16.3.2.1 Driving a vehicle without adequate insurance cover

If a vehicle is not properly insured, any individual who uses, causes, or permits its use on a road or other public place commits an offence contrary to s 143(1) and (2) of the Road Traffic Act 1988. The registered keeper is guilty of an offence (s 144A of the Road Traffic Act 1988) if it is kept without insurance (unless the vehicle has a Statutory Off Road Notification (SORN, see 16.3.5)). A vehicle without adequate insurance can be seized under s 165A of the Road Traffic Act 1988 (see 16.4.3 for details of the procedure).

There are a number of exceptions to the offence of driving without adequate insurance, which must be substantiated. These include vehicles:

- kept by the registered keeper at a location which is not on a road or other public place;
- not kept by the registered keeper at the relevant time, for example whilst lent to another person;
- that have been stolen and not recovered before the relevant time.

If it can be proved that the user did not own the vehicle (or had not hired it), and they were acting in the course of their employment and had no reason to believe that the vehicle was not properly insured, this can be a defence (s 143(3) of the Road Traffic Act 1988).

16.3.2.2 Foreign insurance

A driver visiting the UK with a foreign-registered vehicle will probably have valid insurance from their home country, but it may be time-limited by the policy terms and conditions. Once a visitor becomes a UK resident, a policy with a UK MIB-registered insurance company is required.

16.3.3 Vehicle registration and licensing

A new vehicle is generally first registered in the UK by the motor trade. The DVLA issues a registration document to the keeper and assigns the vehicle a registration mark (also known as a registration number or an index number). The Vehicle Excise and Registration Act 1994 (VERA) provides much of the relevant legislation.

Some older vehicles will need to undergo registration in the UK, for example when the vehicle has only been used on a private estate or has been imported. Vehicles brought into the UK by a visitor must be registered in the UK after six months or when they become a resident, whichever is sooner. Once a vehicle is registered (or becomes subject to registration), it is also subject to the UK insurance and testing criteria.

The registration mark of a particular vehicle can be changed for a number of reasons. These include a 'cherished transfer' (also referred to as a 'private plate', although the DVLA term is 'personalized vehicle registration numbers'). Another reason for a change is that a vehicle was exported and then imported back into the UK. Records are cross-referenced on the PNC vehicle file so any previous registration numbers for a particular vehicle will be shown as will all vehicles that have had a particular registration number.

16.3.3.1 The vehicle registration document and number plates

The vehicle registration document is proof that the vehicle is registered and shows the details recorded on the register. The current version (the V5C with a red front cover) was introduced in 2010 and revised in 2012. The older version (the V5) has a blue front cover and is still valid if the keeper of the vehicle has not changed since 2010.

A vehicle is not properly registered if any of the particulars recorded in the register are incorrect or incomplete. It is an offence to use a vehicle that is not properly registered on a road or in a public place (s 43C(1) of VERA 1994). Other registration documents offences include failure to notify the DVLA about the disposal of a vehicle or a change of vehicle details. Most of these offences are covered under the Road Vehicles (Display of Registration Marks) Regulations 2001 and VERA 1994. Defences for using a vehicle that is not properly registered include that no reasonable opportunity was given to supply the name and address of the registered keeper (eg if the person had only just bought the vehicle) or if there were reasonable grounds for believing that the recorded particulars were correct.

The registration mark or index number is shown on the 'number plate' of a vehicle. The plate should use a standard font and it should not be customized in any way. These and further details on number plates may be found on the DVLA website.

AB51 DVL
(Image reproduced with the permission of the DVLA)
Local memory tag denoting where a vehicle is first registered. AB refers to Peterborough.
Age identifier which changes twice yearly in March and September. The number 51 refers to September 2001.
Random letters which will never include I or Q and which uniquely define the vehicle.

Offences relating to number plates (mostly under the Road Vehicles (Display of Registration Marks) Regulations 2001) include: no number plate or an obscured number plate; forgery of a number plate; incorrect fitting, number, or position of plates; and incorrect style, size, and spacing of characters. These are all summary offences.

16.3.4 Annual testing and 'MOT' test certificates

The majority of vehicles used on roads will be subject to testing. Any motor vehicle registered under the Vehicle Excise and Registration Act 1994 must be tested every year (after a certain period from registration) if it is to be used on a road (s 47 of the Road Traffic Act 1988). This also applies to any vehicle that is subject to registration even if it has not actually been registered (eg a newly imported vehicle). The MOT test system is administered by the Driver and Vehicle Standards Agency (DVSA). Vehicles are grouped into different categories for the purpose of testing and test fees (see the gov.uk website and the DVSA MOT testing manuals for details of each vehicle category).

For most vehicles, the first test is required three years from the date of first registration of the vehicle (s 47(2)). For large goods vehicles, coaches, buses, ambulances, and private hire vehicles the first MOT is required one year from registration (s 47(3)). For vehicles up to 40 years old that are newly registered in the UK, the schedule for MOT testing starts from the date of manufacture. Vehicles built and registered more than 40 years ago and without substantial modifications in the last 30 years are now classed as 'historic' and no longer require an MOT.

It is an offence under s 47 for a person at any time to use (or cause or permit to be used) a motor vehicle on a road without a test certificate apart from:

- driving to a pre-arranged MOT test;
- driving from a failed MOT test to a garage for repairs by previous arrangement (reg 6(2)(a)(i) of the Motor Vehicle (Test) Regulations 1981); or
- being towed from a failed MOT for scrapping (reg 6(2)(a)(iii)(B)).

The results of tests are uploaded immediately and the 'MOT expiry tab' on the PNC vehicle file will be updated. Police officers should cross-reference the information with the MOT data held on the vehicle file of the PNC. The MOT history of any vehicle is available to anyone on the gov.uk website.

16.3.5 Vehicle excise duty

Vehicle excise duty (VED) is payable on any vehicle used or kept on a public road and is covered under s 1 of VERA 1994. The system is also referred to as 'vehicle licensing' and 'road tax'. The registered keeper is responsible for paying VED, and for arranging a Statutory Off Road Notification (SORN). A vehicle with a SORN can be kept off road without paying VED. The PNC vehicle files include an excise licence field and any vehicle's excise duty status can be accessed on the gov.uk website. It has been held that a vehicle is 'kept' on a public road even if it is only there for a very short period (s 62).

The taxation classes include private/light goods vehicles (PLG, such as family cars and light vans), buses, and heavy goods vehicles. (Note that the category 'bicycle' refers to two-wheeled motorcycles rather than bicycles.) Some types of vehicle are exempt from duty, such as vehicles for disabled people, fire engines and most vehicles manufactured before 1 January 1978 (except for LGVs and buses (see s 5(2) of and Sch 2 to VERA 1994)). Exempted vehicles are subject to a 'nil licence' and will appear as such on the vehicle licensing register.

It is an offence for the registered keeper to keep an untaxed vehicle off-road without making a SORN (s 31A(1)) or for any person to use or keep a non-exempted vehicle on a public road if no VED has been paid (s 29(1) of VERA 1994).

16.4 Stopping a Vehicle and Examining Documents

Police officers on foot or mobile patrol will sometimes need to stop vehicles in relation to driving standards or because the vehicle is being used for some other criminal activity.

16.4.1 Police powers to stop a vehicle

All police officers have the legal power to stop any mechanically propelled vehicle on a road (s 163 of the Road Traffic Act 1988) and do not need to have any form of suspicion or authorization. The police officer must be on duty and in full uniform and give a clear direction to the driver to stop. Health and safety considerations are key in relation to where the officer makes the request and to where the vehicle can actually stop. Failing to comply is a summary offence and the penalty is a fine. If the driver flees, the police have a power of entry into premises in order to arrest for this offence (s 17 of the PACE Act 1984 (see Chapter 10)).

16.4.2 Driver and vehicle information checks

Police officers can now check all driver and vehicle documentation electronically by the side of the road and there is now a clear expectation that officers will verify the status of the documentation before allowing a driver to proceed.

Here, a 'driver' is:

- any person driving a motor vehicle on a road;
- any person the officer has reasonable cause to believe had been driving a motor vehicle on a road at the time it was involved in an accident; or
- any person who the officer has reasonable cause to believe has committed an offence in relation to the use of a motor vehicle on a road.

Driving licence checks are carried out on the PNC (including by the person's home post code if there seem to be discrepancies). MOT status can be checked through the PNC vehicle file or over the internet, and insurance details can be accessed on the MIB database (through the vehicle file on the PNC). The MIB help line can also provide useful information.

16.4.2.1 Requiring documents for examination

If it is not possible to make electronic checks at the scene of an incident, a police officer can request production of the following documents:

- the driver's driving licence (s 164(1));
- an appropriate insurance certificate (s 165(1)) (on paper or in electronic format on a suitable device (s 165(2A)));
- the vehicle's MOT test certificate (s 165(1)); and/or
- CBT certificate (only motorcyclists without a full entitlement) (s 164(4A)).

These requirements also apply for supervisors of learner drivers (s 164(1)(d)) in some circumstances (ie when a learner driver on a provisional entitlement is driving a motor vehicle on a road or is believed to have been involved in an accident or to have committed a road traffic offence. A police officer can also request any person driving or otherwise 'using' a registered vehicle to produce the vehicle's registration document (s 28A(1) of VERA 1994).

Under the Road Traffic Act 1988, if the driver cannot produce the insurance or MOT certificate when required, a police officer can require the person to state their name and address and the vehicle owner's name and address (s 165(1)), and in some forces there may still be the option of issuing an HO/RT/1 form for production of documents within seven days.

16.4.2.2 Requesting information from a driver

A police officer may require a 'driver' to state their date of birth (s 164(2)) if they fail to produce their licence, or produces a licence that is unsatisfactory (eg it seems to have been altered or it contains information that seems incorrect). This also applies for a person who is supervising a learner driver at the time of an accident or an offence and there is reason to suspect that they (the supervisor) are under 21 years of age.

16.4.2.3 Failing to produce documents or provide information

Under the Road Traffic Act 1988, it is a summary offence for a person when required to fail to:

- produce their licence or state their date of birth (s 164(6));
- produce their CBT certificate (motorcyclists only) (s 164(6));
- state their name and address and the name and address of the owner of the vehicle (s 165(3));
- produce a certificate of insurance or an MOT certificate (s 165(3)).

Failing to produce the registration document is an offence under s 28A(3) of VERA 1994 (except when the vehicle is subject to a lease or hire agreement). However, a person will not be prosecuted for failing to produce any of these documents if the officer then issues an HO/RT/1 form (not used in all forces) and the driver then produces the documents within a specified time:

- within seven days in person at a police station (specified by the driver at the time of the request);
- as soon as reasonably practicable (a question of fact for a court to decide); or
- at a later time if the driver can prove it was not reasonably practicable to do so before the day on which written charge proceedings were commenced.

For pedal cyclists and drivers of any mechanically propelled vehicle who are suspected of dangerous, careless, or inconsiderate driving or cycling (ss 2, 3, 28, and 29), there is a separate offence of failing to provide their name and address to any person having reasonable grounds for requiring the information (s 168 of the Road Traffic Act 1988). Note that 'a mechanically propelled vehicle' is a very broad category.

16.4.3 Seizing a vehicle

Under s 165A of the Road Traffic Act 1988, a police officer has the power to seize a vehicle if they have reasonable grounds for believing that the driver does not have a suitable licence or that the vehicle is not adequately insured. To seize a vehicle, a police officer must be in uniform and have requested to see the relevant documents. They must also warn the driver that the vehicle will be seized unless the documents are produced immediately. However, if it is impractical to warn the driver then a warning is not required (s 165A(6)). More than two million uninsured vehicles have been seized since the power became available in 2005, with some 137,000 seized in 2019 alone (Motor Insurers' Bureau, 2020).

If the driver has failed to stop or has driven off, the vehicle may be seized at any time in the 24-hour period following the incident. A police officer has the legal power to enter premises to seize a vehicle, including from the driveway or garage associated with a private dwelling-house. The officer must have reasonable grounds for believing the vehicle to be present and reasonable force may be used if necessary.

TASK 1 Imagine you are a police officer and whilst on Independent Patrol you stop a vehicle using your powers under the Road Traffic Act 1988 and a vehicle check on the PNC shows the MOT has expired.

- What are the defences to not having a valid test certificate?
- What questions will you put to the driver to negate any defences?

16.4.4 Police pursuits

Pursuits should be avoided if at all possible. Pre-emptive action such as requesting a vehicle to stop is preferable if suitably trained officers are available, but some drivers and motorcyclists refuse to stop when requested to do so. If a driver's actions or manner of driving suggest that they do not intend to stop and the police driver believes that the driver is aware of the requirement to stop, the police need to decide on the best course of action. Any pursuit must be justified, proportionate, cause the minimum level of risk, and be suitably authorized. Some pursuits will be part of a pre-planned operation if, for example, suspects in a moving vehicle are under surveillance and the police decide that the best tactics are to try to stop the vehicle. It would be obvious that the suspects might not comply and that this could lead to a pursuit.

Pursuits are split into two phases; an initial phase and a tactical phase. The initial phase is the period of a spontaneous pursuit before tactical resolution can be considered and actioned. For any phase of a pursuit, the vehicle must be fitted with audio and visual warning equipment. Certain types of vehicle must not be used for pursuits under any circumstances, for example personnel carriers, vans, hired vehicles, and personal vehicles. Any four-wheel drive vehicle is inherently less stable than other vehicles and only specific vehicles with suitable handling characteristics should be used for pursuits. Drivers involved in pursuits must be suitably qualified and have attended refresher training every two to three years.

For the initial phase of a pursuit, unmarked cars can be used if driven by an advanced driver. Otherwise, suitable marked cars and police response motorcycles can be used, as can any vehicle deemed suitable for the tactical phase. Tyre-deflation systems may also be employed at the initial stage. Pursuit trained standard/response drivers and motorcyclists (with suitable vehicles) may be authorized by an appropriate member of staff from the control/communications room to continue with a pursuit as it moves into the tactical phase. However, their role would be to support the pursuing vehicle and they must not play an active part in tactical resolution.

An appropriate resolution tactic must be selected (such as tyre-deflation devices or implementing tactical pursuit and containment (TPAC) tactics). The pursuit then moves into the tactical phase. The driver must be an advanced driver trained for the tactical phase of pursuits. One of the officers in a pursuing vehicle will be identified as the 'pursuit commander' and will direct the pursuit and the tactics used. Marked or unmarked cars can be used but the vehicle must be deemed fit for use in tactical phase pursuit and any unmarked vehicles should be replaced with marked vehicles at the earliest opportunity (as such vehicles are more visible and therefore safer).

The use of pursuit as a tactic by police is controversial and the reputation of the police can be tarnished if a pursuit-related injury or death occurs. The risk must be assessed against the objective(s), applying the national guidance (see the College of Police APP) and any local policy.

16.4.5 Road checks (s 4 of the PACE Act 1984)

Road checks can be used to determine whether a vehicle is carrying people connected with an indictable offence (a witness or suspect) or who are unlawfully at large (s 4 of the PACE Act 1984). There must be reasonable grounds for suspecting that the person is, or is about to be, in the locality. When directing vehicles to stop, s 163 of the Road Traffic Act 1988 must be followed and the road check must comply with PACE Code A. Road checks cannot be used for road traffic or vehicle excise offences.

The road check must be authorized by a senior officer in writing because the rights of all the individuals stopped must be considered—every vehicle will be stopped in a certain area. The authorizing officer must be a superintendent or above but, if unavailable, an officer of a lower rank can authorize a road check (see s 4(5) of the PACE Act 1984). The authorization must specify the time, place, and reason for the check.

16.5 Construction and Use of Vehicles

Construction and use legislation relates to the maintenance of a vehicle to a roadworthy standard and the circumstances in which it may create a danger to other road users. The legislation is written in the form of regulations, notably the Road Vehicles (Construction and Use) Regulations 1986 (gov.uk, 1986) and the Road Vehicles Lighting Regulations 1989 (gov.uk, 1989b). There are also offences under the Road Traffic Act 1988 (gov.uk, 1988) where no specific regulations apply. Some construction and use offences can be evidenced with a superficial examination of the vehicle, while other more complex matters will require expert training. Conducting a roadside vehicle examination can be dangerous and should not be undertaken if the officer has any doubts concerning safety.

A police-authorized vehicle examiner can test a vehicle (and drawn trailer) on a road to check compliance with construction and use requirements and also to assess the risk of making such checks in particular circumstances. This requires specialist training (s 67 of the Road Traffic Act 1988). If a vehicle examiner is not available, the assistance of a DVSA advanced or forensic vehicle examiner can be sought; in some forces, there are specific arrangements between the DVSA and local police control rooms.

Road Vehicles (Construction and Use) Regulations 1986 and the Road Vehicles Lighting Regulations 1989. These regulations cover a wide range of topics, including:

1. Vehicle dimensions and weight limits
2. Lighting and signalling requirements
3. Braking systems and performance standards
4. Tyre requirements and tread depth limits
5. Exhaust emissions and noise levels
6. Seat belt and child restraint requirements
7. Driver and passenger visibility and safety features
8. Vehicle registration and licensing requirements

The VCU regulations are enforced by the Driver and Vehicle Standards Agency (DVSA) and failure to comply with these regulations can result in fines, penalty points on your driving licence, or even prosecution. It is important for vehicle owners and drivers to be aware of these regulations and ensure that their vehicles are in compliance with them.

16.5.1 Tyres

When dealing with tyre offences it is important to record sufficient information so that the specific tyre on a vehicle can be identified when presenting evidence. This will include a description of the tyre including its size and rating, the dimension and description of any defects, and its location on the vehicle.

The terms used to describe the various parts of a tyre are shown in the diagram. It may also be necessary to specify whether a side wall was the inner (the side you cannot see from beside the vehicle) or the outer (the side to the outside of the vehicle).

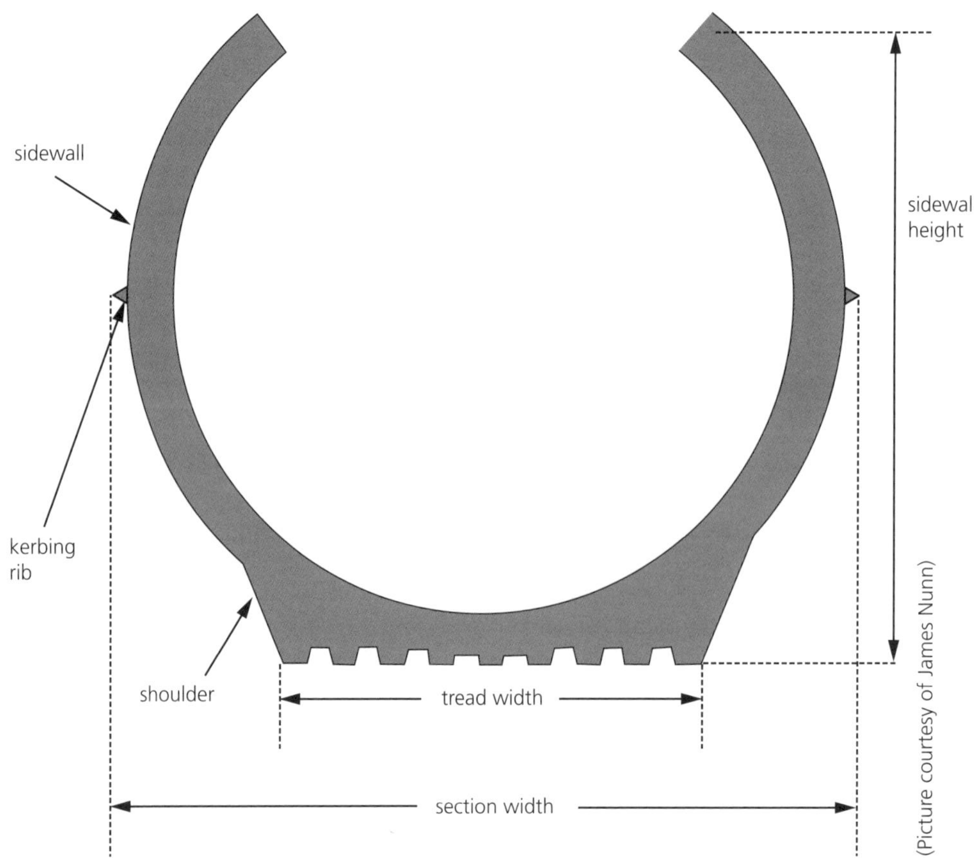

(Picture courtesy of James Nunn)

For use as evidence, all the identifying details, codes, and features on the wall of a tyre should be noted, including serial numbers and characters relating to the type of tyre. This will include the make and model of the tyre, ie Pirelli P6000.

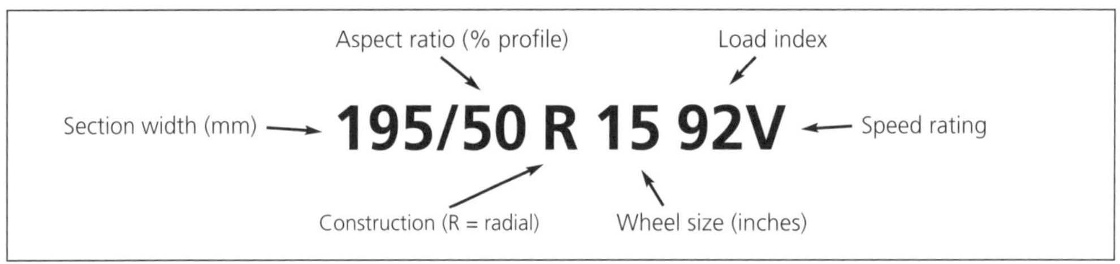

16.5.1.1 Offences relating to tyre condition and maintenance

Tyres on vehicles and trailers must be in good condition and suitable for the purpose for which they are being used. They must also be inflated to the correct pressure. The photograph shows an under-inflated tyre.

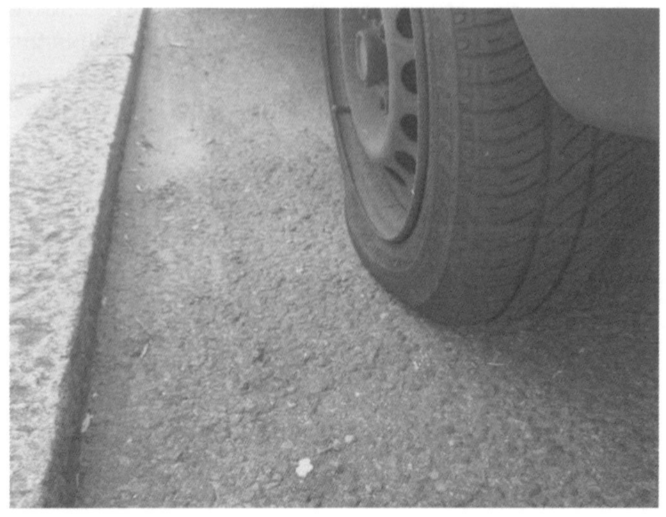
(Photograph courtesy of James Nunn)

Regulation 27 of the Road Vehicle (Construction and Use) Regulations 1986 applies for vehicles and trailers used on roads with pneumatic (inflatable) tyres, and covers a range of problems relating to tyre condition and use. (This regulation does not apply to agricultural motor vehicles with a maximum speed of 20 mph, for vehicles that have broken down or are en route for breaking up, or vehicles being towed at not more than 20 mph.) In all cases, however, tyres should not be in such a condition that they could cause damage to the road surface or persons (reg 27(1)(h)).

Tyres must be the correct type for the vehicle (taking into account the types of tyres fitted to the other wheels) and for the road conditions or purpose. Some wear is permitted, depending on the type of vehicle, but the following types of damage are not allowed:

- cuts anywhere on the surface of the tyre, longer than 25 mm or 10 per cent of the section width of the tyre (whichever is the greater), and also deep enough to reach the ply or cord;
- lumps, bulges, or tears;
- exposed ply or cord.

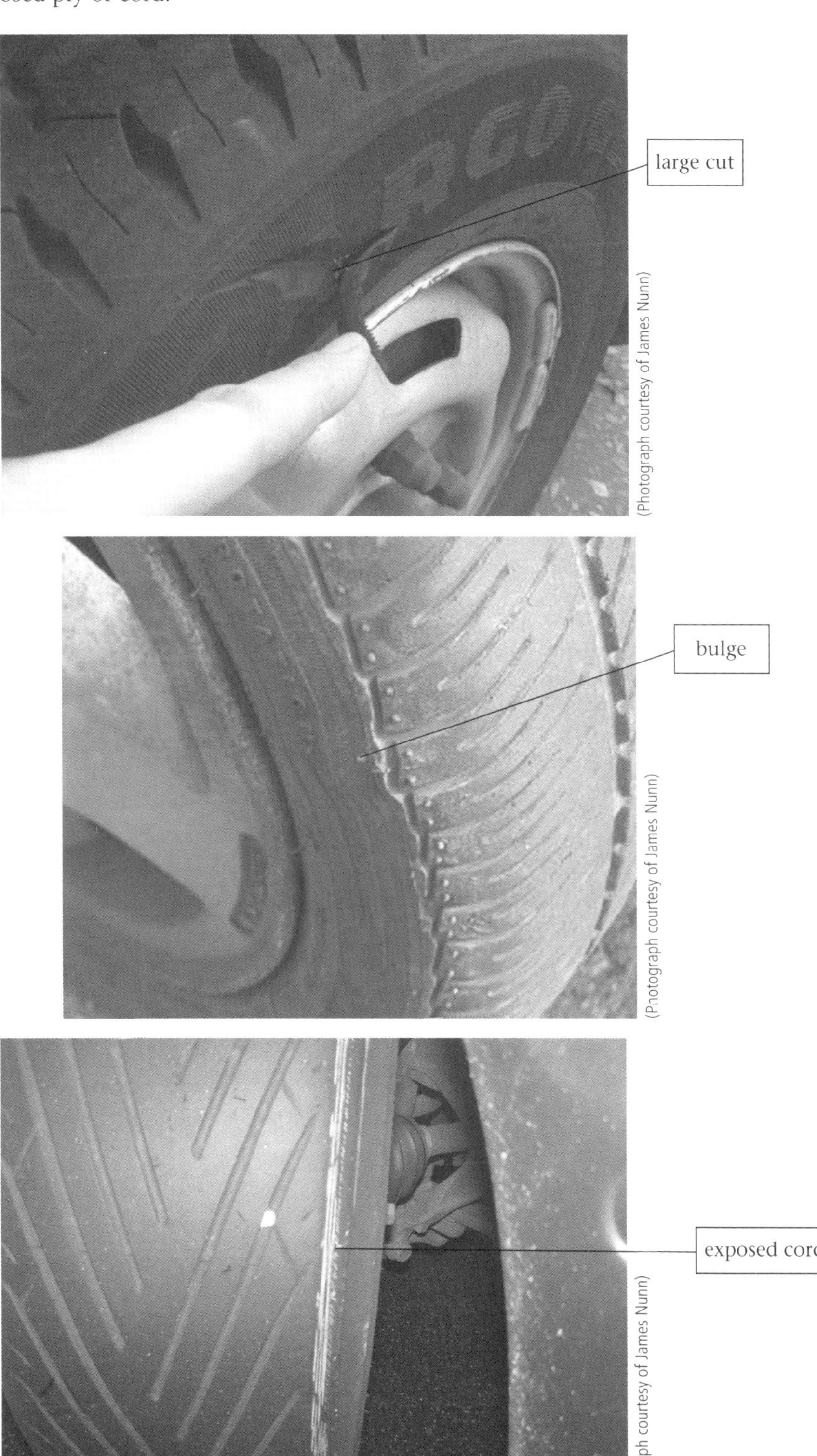

For private cars and vans (driving licence category B and Private Light Goods vehicles) and their trailers, the tread grooves should be at least 1.6 mm deep over the whole central three-quarters of the tread-width. A depth gauge should be used to measure accurately. Areas where there is no visible tread pattern remaining are described as 'devoid of tread'.

16.5.2 Lights on vehicles

The position, style, maintenance, and colour of vehicle lights are important for road safety. Police responsibilities include identifying vehicles with faulty lights, testing and inspecting lights, and bringing the faults to the attention of the owner and/or driver. Drivers should use their vehicle lights with consideration towards other road users.

The following information relates in part to the Road Vehicles Lighting Regulations 1989. There are two main categories of lights: obligatory lights (must be fitted and maintained), and optional lights.

16.5.2.1 Obligatory lights

Here we will examine the obligatory lights required for a car as this is the most common type of vehicle on the road. Other classes of vehicle have different requirements, as described in the regulations.

The obligatory lights on the front of a car are: position lights ('side lights'), dipped, and main-beam headlights, and direction indicators. On the back of the car, the obligatory lights are: position lights, direction indicators, stop lights (brake lights), fog lights, a registration-plate lamp, and a reflector (albeit not strictly a light). A 'hazard warning-signal device' to operate the direction indicator lights on the front and back of the car is also obligatory. These obligatory lights are often clustered together.

16.5.2.2 Optional lamps

Some optional lamps perform the same function as obligatory lights: for example, extra front-position lights (side lights), extra stop lamps, extra direction indicators, and extra dim/dipping (the dipped-beam headlamps operate at less than their normal brightness to replace the need for front position lights (front side lights)) and hazard warning devices. As these all have the same functions as obligatory lights, they must be maintained and in full working order, just like the obligatory lights (which must still be fitted as described earlier).

Other optional lamps include lamps such as reversing lights and front fog lights. They are not obligatory so do not have to be maintained. They must not, however, be in such a condition as to cause danger or be used in such a way that they cause undue dazzle or discomfort to other road users.

16.5.2.3 Vehicle lights when driving at night

The position lights must be used as soon as the sun sets and until the sun rises. Dipped headlights should be used during the 'hours of darkness' which starts half an hour after sunset and ends half an hour before sunrise. The times for sunset and sunrise are available on police databases (via the control room), but these times can also be found in newspapers and on the internet.

Remember:

- hours of darkness for dipped headlights; and
- sunset and sunrise for sidelights.

16.5.2.4 Legitimate use of a vehicle with defective lights

A vehicle with defective lights may be driven in some circumstances without an offence being committed. This is only permitted during the day (between sunrise and sunset), and the lights must have become defective during that journey or arrangements must have already been made to repair the fault (reg 23(3) of the Road Vehicles Lighting Regulations 1989).

There are numerous other exemptions to the lighting regulations in regs 4–9, so unusual circumstances will need to be considered on a case-by-case basis.

16.5.3 Danger of injury from the use or poor maintenance of vehicles or trailers

There are numerous circumstances where the use of a vehicle or trailer may pose a danger or nuisance to other road users. Some of these are specifically addressed in the legislation but many are not. Section 40 of the Road Traffic Act 1988 and reg 100 of the Road Vehicle

(Construction and Use) Regulations 1986 are worded so that they can be used to cover a wide range of situations related to maintenance and incorrect use of a vehicle. The offences relate to using a vehicle, including causing or permitting its use. The vehicle must be on a road.

16.5.3.1 Head and eye protection for motorcyclists

Helmets or other suitable protective headgear must be worn by anyone driving or riding on a motor bicycle. It is an offence under s 16 of the Road Traffic Act 1988 to drive or ride on a road without such protection. The design of the headgear is regulated by the Motor Cycles (Protective Helmets) Regulations 1998. The helmet must bear a mark indicating compliance with the British Standard (BS 6658:1985) or the equivalent EU standard or it must be of a type which seems likely to afford similar protection. A helmet must be securely fastened by straps or other fastenings and an additional strap under the jaw must be used to secure a chin cup (reg 4). Under the regulation, a helmet that is not secured is 'not being worn'. Helmets are not required for some people in some circumstances, such as:

- a person using a ride-on motor mower;
- Sikhs who wear a turban whilst on a two-wheeled motorcycle;
- passengers in a side-car; and
- a person pushing a two-wheeled motorcycle on foot.

Riders or drivers of three-wheeled vehicles do not need to wear a helmet if the distance between any two wheels on the same axle (front or back) is at least 460 mm. The distance between the wheels is measured between the centre of the area of contact with the road for each wheel. Under reg 4, if the two wheels are less than 460 mm apart they are regarded as a single wheel so the vehicle would be classed as a motor bicycle.

Eye protection is not required by law but, if used, it must meet the British Standards EN 1938:1999 or an offence is committed under s 18(3) of the Road Traffic Act 1988.

16.5.3.2 Seat belts

The requirements for the use of seat belts depend on the age of the person and where they are sitting. The requirements are provided in ss 14, 15, 15A, and 15B of the Road Traffic Act 1988, the Motor Vehicles (Wearing of Seat Belts) Regulations 1993, the Motor Vehicles (Wearing of Seat Belts by Children in Front Seats) Regulations 1993, and the Motor Vehicles (Wearing of Seat Belts) (Amendment) Regulations 2006.

A summary of the requirements is shown in the table (based on rules 99–102 of the Highway Code, available online). In addition, some older or classic cars may not have seat belts fitted.

	Front seat	Rear seat	Who is responsible?
Driver	Must be worn if fitted	Not applicable	Driver
Child under 3 years of age	Correct child restraint must be used	Correct child restraint must be used. If unavailable in a taxi, the child may travel unrestrained	Driver
Child from 3rd birthday up to 1.35 m in height or 12th birthday (whichever is reached first)	Correct child restraint must be used	Correct child restraint must be used where seat belts are fitted. Adult belt must be used if correct child restraint is not available in a licensed taxi or private hire vehicle, or for reasons of unexpected necessity over a short distance, or if two occupied restraints prevent fitment of a third	Driver
Child aged 12 or 13 years, OR Child over 1.35m tall (any age under 14 years)	Seat belt must be worn if available	Seat belt must be worn if available	Driver
Passengers aged 14 and over	Seat belt must be worn if available	Seat belt must be worn if available	Passenger

If a child seat or restraint is used, it should be suitable for the weight of the child concerned and fitted in accordance with the manufacturer's specifications.

In some situations a seat belt does not have to be worn, such as:

- a driver engaged in deliveries (eg delivering post or newspapers) or collections if the distance between the stops is less than 50 m;
- a driver reversing a vehicle or supervising a learner driver who is reversing a vehicle (or conducting a manoeuvre which includes reversing);
- an examiner conducting a driving test if wearing the belt would be dangerous;
- people in vehicles being used for police purposes (see local policy; as a general rule the exemption is not used and may vary in relation to people under arrest) and vehicles being used for fire brigade purposes;
- taxi drivers while 'plying for hire', answering calls for hire, or carrying passengers, and private-hire drivers while carrying passengers;
- people taking part in processions organized by, or on behalf of, the Crown;
- people holding a medical certificate providing exemption from wearing a seat belt (provided the certificate is produced at the time or within seven days or includes a relevant letter issued within the EU (in relation to a Community licence holder));
- a disabled person wearing a disabled person's belt;
- the vehicle is driven under a trade excise licence (which allows untaxed vehicles to be driven by the motor trade) for the purposes of investigating or remedying mechanical fault; or
- where the seat belt is an inertia type which is locked as a result of being, or having been, on a steep incline.

16.5.4 Loads

Loads carried by a vehicle must not be a danger or nuisance to any person or property. The weight, packing, distribution, and adjustment of a load must be taken into account (reg 100(1)). An abnormal load is a load which exceeds certain weights or dimensions and special arrangements are required. The load carried by a motor vehicle or trailer must be secured if necessary by physical restraint: for example, the luggage on the roof bars of a car must be tied down (reg 100(2)).

The weight of the load must not cause the total permitted weight of the vehicle to be exceeded. The gross vehicle, gross train (vehicle and trailer), or gross individual axle weight limits are indicated on the vehicle (see the figure in 16.2.1.1 for an example of a VIN plate with weight limits).

16.5.5 'GB rules' for commercial drivers

GB rules apply for goods vehicles under 3.5 tonnes, for passenger vehicles with eight or fewer passenger seats, and for any regular passenger services of less than 50 km (regardless of the number of passenger seats). The daily driving time for each driver must not exceed ten hours (including driving that is not on the public road, ie in a yard or off road). The rules also refer to 'duty time' which must not exceed 11 hours if it includes any driving. The duty time for employed individuals is the whole time at work, and for self-employed individuals is the period driving or otherwise working with the vehicle.

16.6 Pedestrian Crossings and Road Signs

Knowing your pedestrian crossing and road signs is a core part of policing and draws on the Road Traffic Regulation Act 1984 (gov.uk, 1984) and Sch 2 to the Road Traffic Offenders Act 1988 (gov.uk, 1988). A comprehensive explanation of road signs is also provided in the Department for Transport publication *Know your Traffic Signs* available on the gov.uk website.

16.6.1 Pedestrian crossings

The following table shows the key characteristics of the three main types of pedestrian crossing described in the Zebra, Pelican and Puffin Pedestrian Crossings Regulations 1997 (gov.uk, 1997).

Pelican	Pedestrians can push a button to operate traffic lights to bring vehicles to a stop. The traffic light sequence is the same as for normal lights except that, after the red light, the amber light flashes to indicate that vehicles may proceed if the crossing is clear
Puffin	Sensors detect anyone waiting to cross and change the traffic lights accordingly for vehicles to stop. The sequence is the same as for regular traffic lights
Zebra	These are not supported by traffic lights but are indicated by black and white striped poles with yellow flashing beacons on top. Pedestrians walk across a section of road with wide alternate white and black stripes.

16.6.1.1 Layout of crossings

The limits of crossings are marked out by two parallel lines of studs across the carriageway, as shown here.

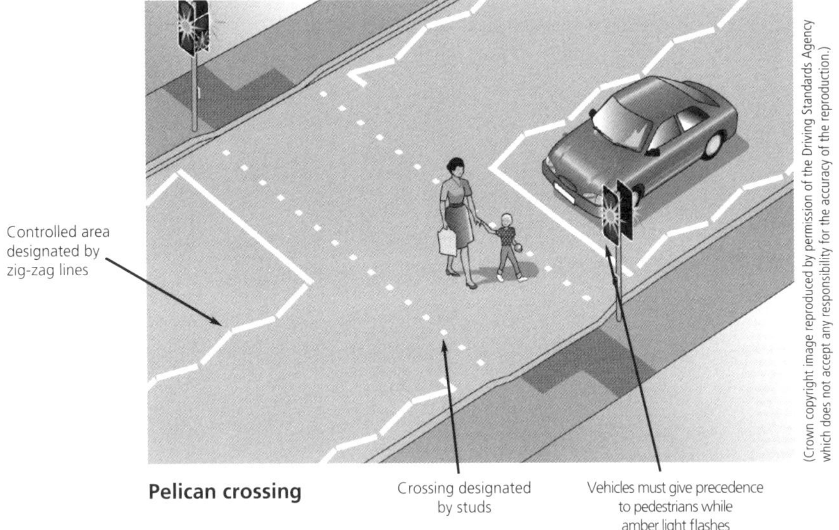
Controlled area designated by zig-zag lines
Crossing designated by studs
Vehicles must give precedence to pedestrians while amber light flashes
(Crown copyright image reproduced by permission of the Driving Standards Agency which does not accept any responsibility for the accuracy of the reproduction.)

Pelican crossing

The stop line for a pelican or puffin crossing is a solid white line across the road, just before the first line of studs. The line at the start of a zebra crossing is a broken white line as the driver has to give way to pedestrians. Drivers and riders must not cross the stop or give-way line if pedestrians are on the crossing (or, of course, if the traffic lights are red for a pelican or puffin crossing).

The controlled area of a crossing is a certain length of road before (entry) and after (exit) a crossing. It is indicated by white zig-zag lines painted along the edge and the middle of the road (between two and 18 zig-zags, depending on the road layout in the immediate vicinity).

Where there is a refuge for pedestrians or a central reservation on a zebra crossing, each part of the crossing is treated as a separate crossing.

16.6.1.2 The correct use of crossings

The regulations for the use of crossings are given in the Zebra, Pelican and Puffin Pedestrian Crossings Regulations 1997 and give rise to several offences which can be committed by drivers or pedestrians. Pedestrians have precedence over vehicles at (or approaching) zebra crossings (reg 25) and at pelican crossings when the amber light is flashing (reg 26). They must not delay on a crossing longer than is necessary to use the crossing in a reasonable time (reg 19).

For vehicles, the following rules apply:

- No overtaking within the controlled area when approaching any crossing (reg 24).
- All vehicles must stop at red/steady amber lights at pelican or puffin crossings (reg 23).
- No stopping in the controlled area of any crossings (reg 20) unless it is to allow pedestrians to cross, to prevent injury or damage, to make a right or left turn, to carry out building work or maintenance of the road or crossing, or to remove obstructions from the road (regs 21 and 22). (This does not apply to pedal cycles or public service vehicles or if the vehicle is beyond the driver's control.)
- No stopping on the actual crossing unless the way is blocked or it is necessary to avoid injury to persons or damage to property (reg 18).

Contraventions of these regulations amount to an offence under s 25(5) of the Road Traffic Regulation Act 1984, and Sch 2 to the Road Traffic Offenders Act 1988.

16.6.2 White lines along the centre of the road

Solid white line systems are used to prohibit overtaking where visibility and vision is limited, or to separate lanes of traffic on roads going up a hill. The lines may be continuous on both sides or continuous on one side and broken on the other. The lines may also be separated by a wider hatched area. The various layouts are set out in reg 26 of the Traffic Signs Regulations and General Directions 2002.

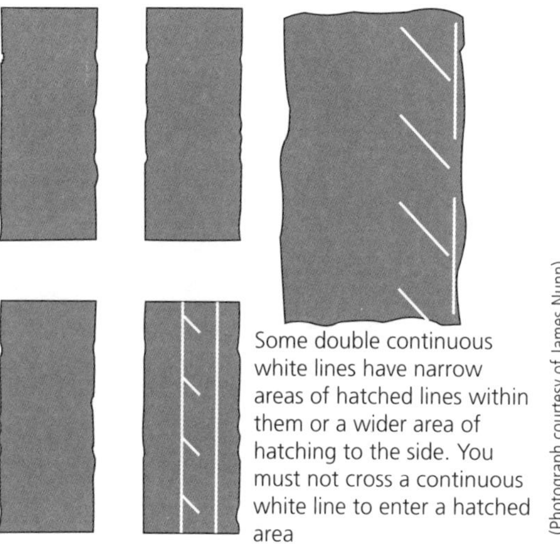

Some double continuous white lines have narrow areas of hatched lines within them or a wider area of hatching to the side. You must not cross a continuous white line to enter a hatched area

(Photograph courtesy of James Nunn)

The presence of at least one continuous central white line means that no vehicle is permitted to stop on either side of the road. Note that this also applies if there is a broken line on one side (reg 26(2)(a)). This regulation does not apply on dual carriageways or to vehicles used for fire and rescue, ambulance, or police purposes. Exceptions also apply for vehicles that have stopped in order to:

- allow passengers to board/alight from a vehicle;
- allow goods to be loaded or unloaded from the vehicle;
- facilitate building or demolition work;
- enable the removal of any obstruction to traffic, road works, or public utility work; or
- avoid an accident.

Exceptions also apply for vehicles that cannot proceed due to circumstances beyond the driver's control (such as stationary traffic) or are required to stop by law or with the permission or direction of a constable in uniform or a traffic warden.

Crossing or straddling a solid white line is also covered by the regulations (reg 26(2)(b)). The solid line must be closest to the driver in the direction of travel and it does not matter whether the other line in the system is broken or continuous. This does not apply when a vehicle is turning right or when the action is unavoidable when passing a stationary vehicle, a pedal cycle, a horse, a road-maintenance vehicle moving at 10 mph or less, or an accident. Nor does it apply when complying with directions from a police officer or a traffic warden in uniform. The offences relating to crossing white lines are committed under s 36(1) of the Road Traffic Act 1988, reg 10 of the Traffic Signs Regulations 2002, and Sch 2 to the Road Traffic Offenders Act 1988.

16.6.3 Disobeying a traffic sign

This is an offence only in relation to signs of the prescribed type (listed under reg 10 of the Traffic Signs Regulations and General Directions 2002) that have been lawfully placed on or near a road (s 36 of the Road Traffic Act 1988). Drivers are therefore under no obligation to heed informal signs erected by members of the public.

Regulation 10 of the Traffic Signs Regulations and General Directions 2002 creates two lists of relevance to s 36 of the Road Traffic Act 1988:

List 1: contravention of a sign on List 1 is an offence under s 36 of the Road Traffic Act 1988.

List 2: these are selected signs from List 1. Contravention of these signs creates a significant danger and may lead to disqualification or endorsement of the driver's licence.

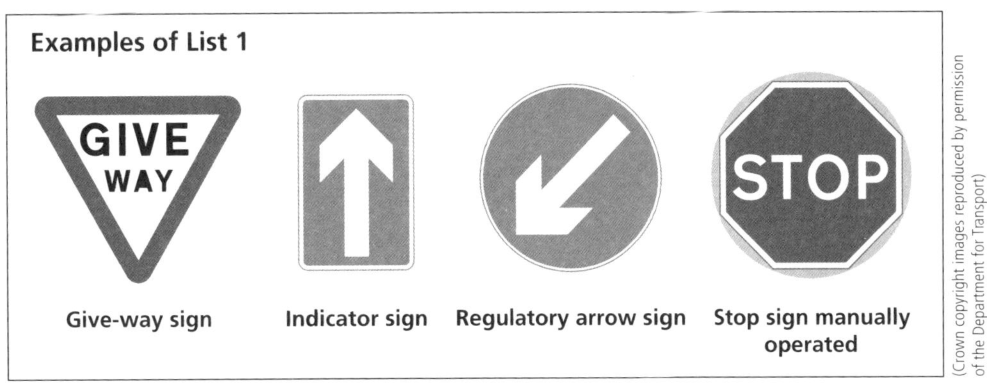

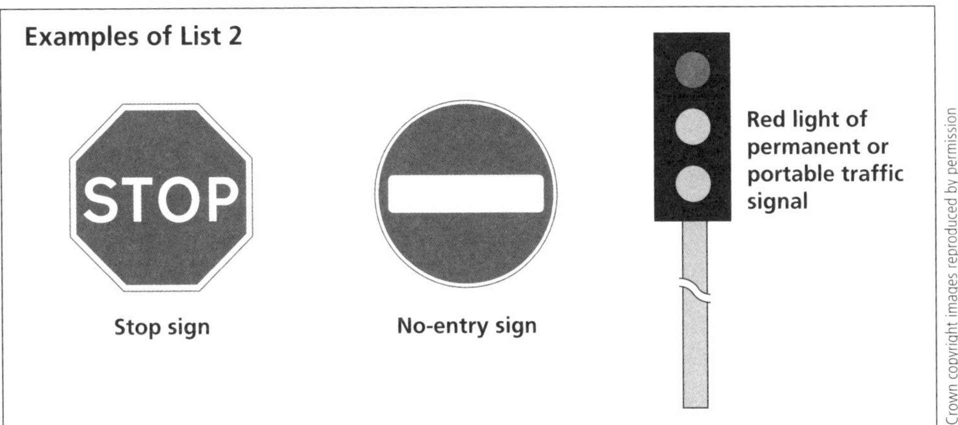

16.7 Road Traffic Collisions

It is common to refer to collisions between vehicles as 'accidents'. However in police circles officers refer to a Road Traffic Collision (RTC) or a 'crash'. This reflects the thinking that incidents of this nature are not random acts of chance but have causes. Most collisions are caused by a combination of factors such as driver error or poor appreciation of a hazard. However, the term 'accident' still features in much of the relevant legislation.

Road traffic collisions are very common and result in a large number of injuries; 128,209 in 2021 (Department for Transport, 2022c) up from 115,584 casualties in 2020 (Department for Transport, 2021a). It is as if the whole population of a town the size of Harrogate in North Yorkshire or the entire district of Wealdon in East Sussex (ONS, 2019a) were to be injured every year, year after year. The number of fatalities has remained around the same since 2010, with the exception created by Covid restrictions, and serious injuries have been rising since 2013.

Collisions are generally categorized as follows:

- Damage Only (where there is only vehicle damage and no injury);
- Non-Reportable Damage Only (NRDO) where there are no grounds for a police report;
- Personal Injury (often referred to as a PI); and
- Killed or Seriously Injured (the term KSI is widely used).

Officers are legally obliged to report certain types of collisions, known as 'reportable accidents' to their police service; these reports will also contain statistical data relating to the circumstances. All police services are then obliged to submit the statistical data regarding collisions to the Department for Transport (referred to as STATS19, see 16.7.2.3).

16.7.1 Management of collision scenes

The police have a number of key responsibilities when responding to collisions and some of these would apply to any potential crime scene. At the scene of a collision, the police must:

- preserve life;
- coordinate the emergency services involved (eg the Fire and Rescue Service);

- secure, protect, and preserve the scene (including any electronic evidence from dashcams or telematics);
- lead and manage the subsequent investigation into the incident; and
- liaise with relatives of the injured or killed.

Incidents with a serious injury or fatality should be treated as a crime scene. Specialist officers will undertake forensic reconstruction and related activities, but all officers need to have a basic understanding of legislation and procedures. In the initial response to a collision on the SRN, the police work very closely with the highways authorities.

Here we provide a summary of the key police responsibilities but for further information see also *CLEAR Keeping Traffic Moving*, available online. CLEAR is a mnemonic for Clear, Lead, Evaluate, Act, and Re-open, and is part of a government initiative for improving incident management and traffic congestion on the strategic road network. It aims to clarify the priorities of the various organizations involved in traffic incident management and promote partnership working. Further detail on the management of emergency incidents on highways is available on the gov.uk website, and police service training will reflect this best practice.

16.7.1.1 Dynamic risk assessments

When attending incidents on roads, police officers should conduct a dynamic risk assessment. This involves continually evaluating the changing circumstances (the location, the vehicles, and the people involved) and adjusting the assessment accordingly.

In relation to the location, the physical layout or position on a road can increase the risk, for example any bends in the road can prevent approaching drivers from seeing the incident. The weather conditions can also reduce the visibility. The speed, volume, and movements of passing traffic should also be considered, as should other problems such as fallen trees or electricity cables. Some locations may suffer poor radio and/or mobile phone coverage.

All the vehicles involved should be identified; as you might expect, multi-vehicle incidents can compound risk factors or create new ones. The contents and the post-impact condition of some vehicles may present additional hazards; high voltages in modern electric vehicles, chemical hazards from vehicles that have caught fire, and body fluids from casualties should all be taken into account. If you are unsure, take advice from fire and rescue units as they are specialists in such hazards. Some of the vehicles or individuals might have been involved in criminal activity (always carry out PNC checks), creating additional complications. Specialist equipment such as lighting or screening is also important and should be available via control rooms, particularly if there has been a fatality or there are special recovery requirements.

All the people at the scene should be accounted for; it is not uncommon for individuals to be thrown some distance from the vehicles. Their demeanour and any need for medical attention should be taken into account and support provided as appropriate.

16.7.1.2 ACE-CARD actions for road traffic incidents

The 'ACE-CARD' mnemonic can be used to help to remember the sequence of considerations and actions required when responding to a road or traffic incident. This approach is summarized in the table. A fuller explanation can be found in the *Roads Policing* section of the College of Policing APP, available online.

Letter:	Abbreviation for:	Meaning:
A	Approach	Before approaching gather as much information as possible. Approach incidents from the rear, where possible.
C	Caution (signs)	Place warning signs and cones correctly. If on a motorway and the matrix speed restrictions need activating, contact 'Control' (or the local highways control room). Establish an appropriate 'exclusion zone' around the incident.
E	Examine (the scene)	Decide whether further assistance is needed. Employ the critical incident procedures if required.
C	Casualties	After protecting the scene, check that all casualties have been found and administer first aid if required. Take details of casualties before they are taken from the scene.

Letter:	Abbreviation for:	Meaning:
A	Ambulance (and Fire and Rescue Service and other support agencies)	Control and manage the scene. Provide a safe working area for the support agencies.
R	Remove (the obstructions)	Recovery services should be contacted promptly (via the control room) but no vehicle should be removed until potential evidence is secured. Breakdown vehicles should be controlled by police or designated highways agency personnel (see 16.2.2.2).
D	Detailed (investigation)	Reporting and subsequent investigation according to local and national policy.

16.7.2 Driver obligations after a collision

The Road Traffic Act 1988 takes a common-sense approach to collisions (referred to as accidents in the Act) and dictates that the drivers involved must stop and be prepared to provide details to anyone who reasonably requires information or report the incident to the police (s 170). The information might be needed for compensation claims for repairs, injuries, or deaths. Police officers need to know what information must be exchanged after a collision and which offences are committed when a person fails to meet their obligations in this regard.

16.7.2.1 Reportable accidents

If an accident meets certain criteria, then the driver has to provide particular information to other people or, failing that, report the incident to the police (s 170(1) of the Road Traffic Act 1988); this is known as a 'reportable accident'. The criteria for a reportable accident concern the location of the accident, the vehicle type, and whether there is any damage or injury apart from to the driver and their vehicle. The definition of an 'accident' is not provided by statute and remains a question of fact for the courts to decide. However, in *R v Morris* [1972] RTR 201 'accident' was held to be 'an unintended occurrence which has an adverse physical result'.

For an accident to be reportable, the location of the vehicle at the moment of the collision is important. It must have been on a road or other public place (which could include hospital grounds, household garage blocks, private roads, or motorway service areas. If the vehicle leaves the road or other public place during or after the accident and comes to rest in a private dwelling, or grounds adjacent to the road or public place, this is still a reportable accident. If a collision takes place at any location other than a road maintained at public expense, evidence will be required to prove that it is a public place (eg concerning the frequency of use, by whom, and under what circumstances).

The vehicle must be mechanically propelled and the collision must be due to its presence on a road or other public place. This includes vehicles intended or adapted for use off-road (eg dumper trucks and off-road motorcycles) and covers a wider range of vehicles than 'motor vehicles'. The phrase 'due to the presence' implies that the incident would not have occurred had the vehicle not been there and does not necessarily mean that the vehicle was directly involved. It may be that the presence of the vehicle purely created the circumstance where other vehicles were involved in an incident. The classic example of this is a legally parked car that creates a slight narrowing of the available space which leads to a collision; had the car not been present, the collision would not have occurred.

The damage must be to another vehicle (a mechanical device, powered or not, for carrying people or goods, such as a cart, trailer, or bicycle; see *R v Parker* (1859) 59 JP 793), or to property such as a road sign, garden wall, or certain animals. Note that lamp posts are the property of the local highways authority or the local council.

(Photograph courtesy of James Nunn)

The damage can be to private property but the vehicle must have been on a road or other public place immediately before the incident. The damage does not have to be permanent or beyond repair but the physical appearance must have been altered in some way. Certain types of animals (horses, cattle, asses, mules, pigs, sheep, goats, and dogs) are classed as property in this context. For injuries, the injury must be to a person other than the driver of the vehicle, for example passengers, pedestrians, or people in other vehicles. The injury can be shock as well as actual bodily harm.

When attending a reportable accident, the police officer must record all the details even if no offence has been committed. A full record of the events should be made because the officer might be called as a witness in a civil court case, for example if a pedestrian had been seriously injured in a collision and is claiming compensation. The format of the record will be subject to local instruction.

16.7.2.2 Information required after a reportable accident

All the driver(s) at a reportable accident must stop and remain at the scene for as long as necessary to provide information to others (s 170(2) of the Road Traffic Act 1988). Failing to stop at any accident is a serious offence and is committed even if the person later reports the accident to the police.

At the scene, a driver must provide particulars to anyone who has reasonable grounds for needing the information; this could include the driver or rider of any other vehicle involved, the passengers in any of the vehicles, property owners, pedestrians, or their representatives. The driver must provide their name and address, the name and address of the vehicle's owner, and the identification marks of the vehicle (eg the vehicle registration number). Failing to stop or report an accident is a summary offence under s 170(4) of the Road Traffic Act 1988. The penalty is six months' imprisonment and/or a fine and the offender may also be disqualified.

If the driver cannot or does not provide the relevant information at the time of the accident, then they must 'report' the accident and provide the relevant information to the police as soon as reasonably practicable, and certainly within 24 hours (s 170(3) and (6) of the Road Traffic Act 1988). They must report in person to a constable or police station; it is not sufficient to telephone or email. It is a matter for a court to decide what is 'reasonably practicable' for the particular circumstances.

A relevant insurance certificate must be produced by the driver where personal injury is caused to another person (an 'injury accident'). The certificate should be shown to a police officer and any person having reasonable grounds for seeing it, for example the injured person (s 170(5)). If this is not possible at the time, the driver must report the accident to the police and produce the insurance as soon as is reasonably practicable and, in any case, within 24 hours (s 170(6)). Failing to produce proof of insurance after an injury accident is a summary offence under s 170(7) of the Road Traffic Act 1988 and the penalty is a fine. When the police attend, many of these arrangements no longer apply as officers are generally able to ascertain insurance status at the scene of the incident using the MIB database through the PNC.

16.7.2.3 STATS19 data

STATS19 data is a statistical record of all reportable accidents. STATS19 data is submitted to the Department for Transport by individual police services. It analyses the data to produce the annual collision statistics, published each September. Some constabularies still record collisions on paper records which are then converted to an electronic format, whilst others record collisions electronically. The Department for Transport is currently reviewing the STATS19 system.

The Collision Reporting and Sharing System (CRaSH) is a Department for Transport electronic system devised for recording collisions and submitting the statistical information and making it available to authorized users such as local authorities. The system has been adopted by over half the police services in England and Wales at the time of writing (the remainder submit paper reports), though more services are scheduled to start using it soon (Department for Transport, 2021b). The use of different reporting systems can affect the way the statistical data is recorded and this is acknowledged in the annual collision statistics report (ibid).

The STATS19 data reports concern the circumstances of the collision, including the police officer's judgement regarding the contributory factors; the most frequent cause in 2021 was 'failing to look properly' (Department for Transport, 2022b). Other information such as the names and full addresses of parties involved and witness details are not included. It is important that the information contained in the STATS19 data is accurate because it provides the evidence base for road safety and casualty reduction strategies. The Department for Transport document *STATS20* provides guidance on completing the STATS19 reports (Department for Transport, 2011).

The analysis of STATS19 data provides insights into the key factors causing collisions and can help to identify strategies to reduce the number of casualties. Previous interventions include national advertising and enforcement campaigns, new locations for speed cameras, setting up community speed-watch initiatives, and the re-engineering of junctions. Casualty reduction policy and activity revolves around the 4Es (enforcement, education, engineering, and evidence); the STATS19 data is fundamental to the success of these processes.

(Photo by Kevin Lawton-Barrett)

16.8 Offences Relating to Standards of Driving

Standards of driving are assessed as sufficient when a driver passes their driving test, but this minimum standard should be maintained. This is defined, for the purposes of the Road Traffic Act 1988, as the standard of a 'competent and careful' driver and it will be for a court to decide based on the facts presented. Offences relating to the standard of driving are listed at the start of the Act. Here we cover the following offences (from the Road Traffic Act 1988 unless otherwise stated):

- causing death by dangerous driving (s 1);
- causing serious injury by dangerous driving (s 1A);
- dangerous driving (s 2);
- causing death by careless or inconsiderate driving (s 2B);
- causing serious injury by careless or inconsiderate driving (s 2C);
- careless and inconsiderate driving (s 3);
- causing death by driving whilst unlicensed or uninsured (s 3ZB);
- causing death by driving whilst disqualified (s 3ZC);
- causing serious injury by driving whilst disqualified (s 3ZD);
- causing the death of another person whilst under the influence of drink or drugs (s 3A);
- careless and inconsiderate cycling (s 29);
- driving elsewhere than on a road (s 34); and
- wanton and furious driving (s 35 of the Offences Against the Person Act 1861).

For ease of explanation, the offences will not be dealt with in the order in which they are presented in the Act. We will examine what we mean by dangerous driving and careless and inconsiderate driving, and then consider the offences that relate to the consequences of such activity.

16.8.1 Dangerous driving

The legislation considers that there are two main causes of dangerous driving: the driver's manner and actions during driving and the condition of the vehicle. These are fully defined in s 2 of the Road Traffic Act 1988.

Section 2A(1) states that a person is regarded as driving dangerously because: (a) the way they drive falls far below what would be expected of a competent and careful driver; and (b) it would be obvious to a competent and careful driver that the driving would be dangerous (a question of fact for the court to decide). The minimum standard of driving applies during the driving test, with knowledge and application of the Highway Code also setting the standard at which a competent and careful person should drive. The Highway Code therefore provides a useful guide when interviewing and gathering evidence for this type of offence. The following are examples of driving activities which may support an allegation of an offence under s 2A(1):

- racing or competitive driving style;
- driving at a speed which is highly inappropriate for the prevailing road or traffic conditions;
- aggressive driving, such as sudden lane changes, cutting into a line of vehicles, or driving much too close to the vehicle in front;
- disregard for traffic lights and other road signs which, on careful analysis, would appear to be deliberate, or disregard for warnings from fellow passengers;
- overtaking in circumstances where it could not have been carried out safely;
- impaired driver ability, such as having an arm or leg in plaster, impaired eyesight, or being too tired to stay awake;
- using a mobile phone (*R v Browning* [2001] EWCA Crim 1831, [2002] 1 Cr App R (S) 88).

The dangerous condition of a vehicle (s 2A(2)) is judged from the perspective of a 'competent and careful driver if it would be obvious ... that driving the vehicle in its current state would be dangerous'. The weight or height of the vehicle, as well as any load carried, should be considered in the context of the location and road conditions. Examples of s 2A(2) circumstances include driving with a load which presents a danger to other road users and driving with knowledge of a dangerous vehicle defect.

When gathering evidence for dangerous driving, the Construction and Use Regulations 1986 and the Highway Code provide useful benchmarks. A wide range of defences are available so, where appropriate, evidence should be collected to negate these. It is for a court to decide whether it would be 'obvious' that the driving was dangerous. The penalty is a fine or imprisonment (six months if tried summarily and two years on indictment).

16.8.2 Careless or inconsiderate driving

Legislation concerning careless or inconsiderate driving is provided in s 3 of the Road Traffic Act 1988. An offence is committed by a person who drives a mechanically propelled vehicle on a road or other public place without due care or attention or without reasonable consideration for other persons using the road or public place. Whether the driving was careless or inconsiderate is a question of fact for the court to decide.

Careless driving (driving without due care and attention) is defined in law as when the standard of driving falls below what would be expected of a competent and careful driver (s 3ZA(2)). (Note the difference between this offence and dangerous driving, where the standard falls *far* below the expected standard.) Examples of careless driving would include a driver who fails to look behind whilst reversing, or using the right-turn direction indicator and then turning left. The driver's knowledge of the circumstances can be taken into account and any factors that they should have been aware of.

For inconsiderate driving, another person must be inconvenienced by the suspect's driving. This would include:

- cutting across the path of another vehicle, for example when turning or changing lanes without prior warning;
- causing traffic problems by failing to conform to directional arrows;
- forcing other drivers to take evasive action by failing to drive correctly;
- deliberately performing skids at high speed or making 'handbrake turns'; or
- driving off-road across grassland with disregard for other users of the space.

A driver can only be charged with careless or inconsiderate driving, not both. They are both summary offences and the penalty is a fine, an endorsement, and discretionary disqualification, or a £100 FPN and three penalty points.

16.8.3 Defences to dangerous, careless, or inconsiderate driving

There are various defences for dangerous or careless or inconsiderate driving summarized in the following table.

Defence	Explanation
Automatism	Automatism is 'the involuntary movement of a person's body or limbs' (*Watmore v Jenkins* [1961] 2 All ER 868), and it must occur very suddenly with little or no warning. This could be due to an epileptic fit (with no prior symptoms) or a wasp sting. Case law has established that falling asleep at the wheel or a hypoglycaemic diabetic coma are not automatism
Unconsciousness or sudden illness	This would include situations where a person suddenly becomes unconscious as a result of circumstances beyond their control, such as being hit on the head by a stone that has smashed through the windscreen. Case law has established that falling asleep at the wheel or a hypoglycaemic diabetic coma are not beyond the driver's control
Assisting in the arrest of offenders	Here, the driver might have a defence if they intentionally shunted a suspect's car off the road in order to help the police arrest the suspect (*R v Renouf* [1986] 2 All ER 449)
Duress by threats	The suspect must be able to show that they drove dangerously due to a threat (that they could not otherwise avoid or escape)
Duress of necessity (of circumstances)	The suspect must be able to show that they had to drive dangerously to avoid death or serious injury (to any person), and that it was not reasonable to act otherwise in the circumstances
Sudden mechanical defect	This does not apply if the driver is already aware of the defect or it could have been easily discovered by superficial examination, for example of tyres (*R v Spurge* [1961] 2 All ER 688)
Authorized motoring event	A person will not be guilty under s 1, 2, or 3 of the Road Traffic Act if they drove in accordance with an authorization for a motoring event given by the Secretary of State (s 13(A) of the Road Traffic Act 1988)

16.8.4 Other offences involving dangerous driving

Section 35 of the Offences Against the Person Act 1861 states that it is an offence for anyone 'having the charge of any carriage or vehicle ... [to cause] or cause to be done bodily harm to any person' by wanton or furious driving, racing, other wilful misconduct, or wilful neglect. This could be used when there has been dangerous driving but the Road Traffic Act 1988 does not cover the circumstances, for example when the driving was not on a road or other public place, the vehicle was not a mechanically propelled vehicle (eg it was a bicycle or horse-drawn vehicle), or the statutory Notice of Intended Prosecution was not given. The offence can only be committed if the driver has a degree of subjective recklessness: they must appreciate that harm was possible or probable as a result of the driving (*R v Okosi* [1996] CLR 666). It is triable by indictment only and the penalty is two years' imprisonment. Disqualification is discretionary although endorsement (three to nine points) is obligatory if the offence was committed in a mechanically propelled vehicle.

Riding a cycle carelessly, inconsiderately, or dangerously on a road is an offence under the Road Traffic Act 1988. This can be riding 'without due care and attention, reasonable consideration for other persons using the road' (s 29) or riding dangerously (s 28(1)). These offences are triable summarily and the penalty is a fine.

16.8.5 Causing death by driving

Road deaths have a devastating effect on families and the community. A family liaison officer (usually referred to as a FLO) can be appointed to provide information, build confidence, and gather any information from the family which could be helpful to the investigation.

The offences are all under the Road Traffic Act 1988 and are categorized by the type of driving that caused the death. It is not relevant whether the person who died was in the suspect's vehicle at the time of the incident. The offences are as follows:

- causing death by dangerous driving (s 1);
- causing death by careless or inconsiderate driving (s 2B);
- causing death by careless or inconsiderate driving whilst under the influence of drink or drugs (s 3A);
- causing death by driving whilst unlicensed or uninsured (s 3ZB); and
- causing death by driving whilst disqualified (s 3ZC).

For a s 3A offence, there must be evidence of careless or inconsiderate driving whilst under the influence of drink or drugs. The driver can be unfit through drink or drugs (s 4), over the prescribed limit (s 5 or 5A), or have refused to provide a specimen (s 7) within 18 hours of the driving, or refused permission for it to be laboratory tested (s 7A(6)). These are explained in more detail in 16.9.

Note that for a s 3ZB or 3ZC offence, the manner of the driving must have contributed to causing the death but it does not have to be the sole reason. It is not necessary to prove careless or inconsiderate driving but the mere presence of a vehicle on a road is insufficient (see *R v Hughes* [2013] UKSC 56). Driver licensing, vehicle insurance, and disqualification are covered earlier in this chapter.

The table compares some key aspect of the various causing death by driving offences and also shows the mode of trial and the penalties.

Section of the Road Traffic Act 1988	s 1	s 2B	s 3A	s 3ZB	s 3ZC
Type of vehicle	any mechanically propelled vehicle		mechanically propelled vehicle if unfit to drive (otherwise motor vehicle)	motor vehicle	
The location	on a road or other public place			on a road	
Mode of trial	indictment only	either way	indictment only	either way	indictment only
Minimum mandatory disqualification	two years	one year	two years	one year	two years
Endorsement	obligatory	obligatory 3–11 points	obligatory	obligatory 3–11 points	obligatory
Retaking driving test	compulsory and extended	discretionary	depends on alcohol/drug level	discretionary	compulsory and extended
Maximum custodial penalty	14 years	six months summarily, five years on indictment	14 years	six months summarily, two years on indictment	ten years

16.8.6 Causing serious injury by driving

Causing serious physical injury to another person by driving can be an offence in certain circumstances. Here, serious injury means physical harm which amounts to grievous bodily harm as set out in the Offences Against the Person Act 1861. There are three specific circumstances, each with its own offence:

- when a mechanically propelled vehicle is driven dangerously on a road or other public place (s 1A of the Road Traffic Act 1988). The penalty is a fine or imprisonment (12 months if tried summarily and five years on indictment);
- when a mechanically propelled vehicle is driven carelessly or without due consideration on a road or other public place (s 2C of the Road Traffic Act 1988). The penalty is a fine or imprisonment (12 months if tried summarily and two years on indictment); and
- when a motor vehicle is driven on a road by a disqualified driver and the driving has contributed in some way to the collision (s 3ZD of the Road Traffic Act 1988). The penalty is a fine or imprisonment (six months if tried summarily and four years on indictment).

All three offences carry an obligatory disqualification and 3–11 penalty point endorsement on conviction. A defendant found not guilty of these offences could still be convicted of dangerous driving or careless or inconsiderate driving.

TASK 2

1. Who would be held to be 'driving' in each of the following scenarios? Use the case suggested as guidance.
   (a) Jerry sits in the driver's seat of a car and lets it freewheel down a sloping road with the steering lock on. See *Burgoyne v Phillips* [1982] RTR 49.
   (b) Maz, a passenger in a car 'driven' by Mel, sees a friend walking along the roadside towards the moving car. To frighten the friend, Maz snatches the steering wheel from Mel's grasp to make the car veer in that direction. Would Maz be held to be 'driving'? See *DPP v Hastings* (1993) 158 JP 118.
   (c) Hari is in the driving seat of the car and 'driving' along the road. Pat leans over from the front passenger seat and steers the car while Hari manipulates the other controls. Hari's view forward is partially obscured by Pat. After some distance, the car runs into a ditch while Pat is steering. Pat had been able to reach both the handbrake and the ignition key and knew the consequences of using the various controls, but did not have access to the foot pedals. See *Tyler v Whatmore* [1975] RTR 83. Who was driving?

16.8.7 Other offences involving standards of driving

Some acts that amount to poor driving may not fall within the scope of the offences of dangerous, careless, or inconsiderate driving but they may still amount to an offence. Combined with other factors, the poor driving could contribute towards one of the more serious offences but would not, in most circumstances, constitute one of the more serious offences per se. Exceeding the speed limit is an important example of poor standards of driving and is covered by s 89(1) of the Road Traffic Regulation Act 1984.

Members of the police service and other emergency services are granted some exemptions from road traffic regulations. However, police officers are expected to drive at least as well as other motorists and should aim to provide a positive role model for other drivers—consider this in relation to personal authority.

The following driving standards offences are derived from the Road Vehicles (Construction and Use) Regulations 1986:

- driving (or causing or permitting any other person to drive) a motor vehicle on a road if the driver is in such a position in the vehicle that they cannot have proper control of the vehicle or have a full view of the road and traffic ahead (reg 104). The penalty is an obligatory endorsement (three points) and a discretionary disqualification or a fixed penalty;
- opening a vehicle door on a road (or causing or permitting it to be opened) and injuring or endangering any person (reg 105). Anyone in the vehicle can commit this offence, but if a child opens the door it is likely the driver would be deemed to have permitted the offence. The maximum penalty is £1,000 fine or a fixed penalty;

- driving a motor vehicle on a road if the driver is able to see directly, or by reflection, a TV or similar apparatus (reg 109). This does not apply to satnav apparatus or other apparatus used to display information about the state of the vehicle or to devices that help the driver to see the road adjacent to the vehicle;
- driving a motor vehicle on a road while using a hand-held phone or a similar device (reg 110).

16.8.7.1 Mobile phones and driving

The meaning of 'using' a mobile phone while driving was clarified in the case *DPP v Barreto* [2019] EWHC 2044 (Admin): it required there to be some form of electronic communication from or to the handset (such as data transmission); but this electronic communication did not have to continue throughout the use. However, this narrow interpretation of 'using' limited enforcement against this dangerous activity. This resulted in the government introducing, on 25 March 2022, the Road Vehicles (Construction and Use) (Amendment) (No 2) Regulations 2022 which amended reg 110 of the Road Vehicles (Construction and Use) Regulations 1986 relating to mobile phone use. The amended regulation broadens the offence criteria, so now the device must just be capable of transmitting or receiving data, whether or not the capability is activated. It adds the defence of using the device for making a contactless payment whilst the vehicle is stationary in addition to the previous exemption for calling the emergency services. It then broadens use to include these specific actions into reg 110(6)(c):

(i) illuminating the screen;
(ii) checking the time;
(iii) checking notifications;
(iv) unlocking the device;
(v) making, receiving, or rejecting a telephone or internet based call;
(vi) sending, receiving or uploading oral or written content;
(vii) sending, receiving or uploading a photo or video;
(viii) utilising camera, video, or sound recording functionality;
(ix) drafting any text;
(x) accessing any stored data such as documents, books, audio files, photos, videos, films, playlists, notes or messages;
(xi) accessing an application;
(xii) accessing the internet.

This redrafted regulation now encompasses all current functionality.

Communication by two-way radio, such as 'CB', is excluded from this offence, although obviously the general need for safe driving still applies. This offence can also be committed by a person supervising a learner driver. Where an employee commits an offence using a hand-held phone provided by their employer, the company can also be held liable if they have failed to prohibit the employee from using it while driving on company business. The penalty is an obligatory endorsement (six points), a discretionary disqualification, and a fine. Alternatively an FPN can be issued for six penalty points and £200.

TASK 3

1. What other offences might be considered for a person using a hand-held mobile telephone while driving, apart from the offence derived from reg 110 in the Road Vehicles (Construction and Use) Regulations 1986?
2. Driving while using a phone is clearly a significant distraction; what other circumstances or activities might adversely affect standards of driving?

16.8.8 Driving in places other than a road

The law surrounding 'off-road' driving is covered in s 34 of the Road Traffic Act 1988. This states that an offence is committed by a person who:

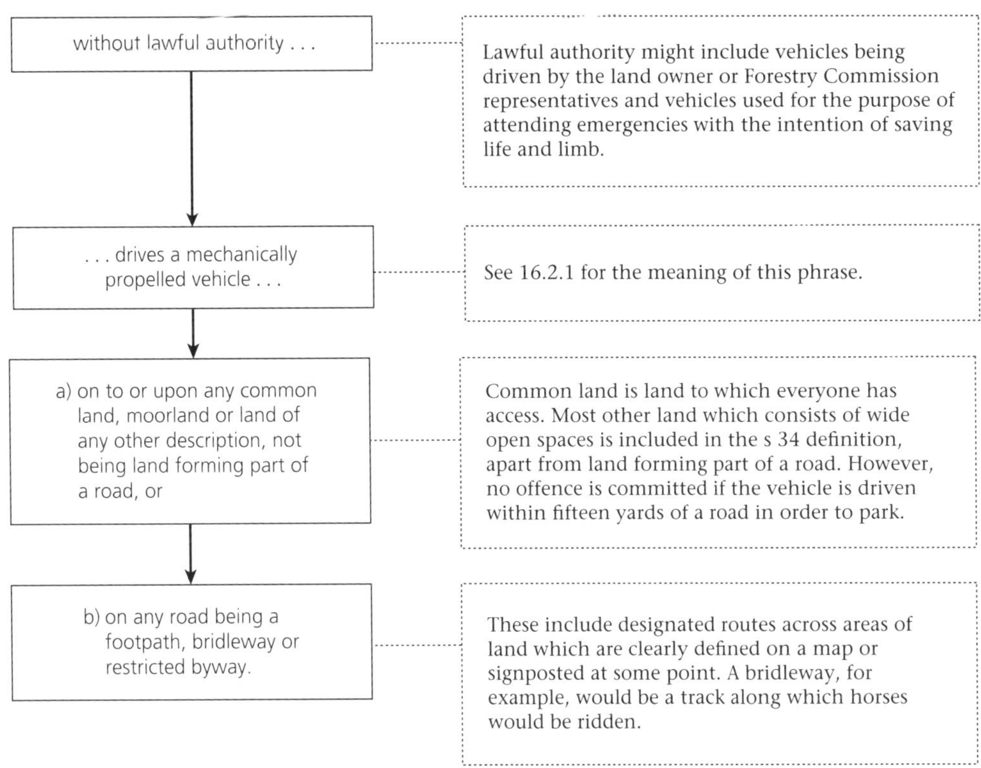

without lawful authority . . .
Lawful authority might include vehicles being driven by the land owner or Forestry Commission representatives and vehicles used for the purpose of attending emergencies with the intention of saving life and limb.
. . . drives a mechanically propelled vehicle . . .
See 16.2.1 for the meaning of this phrase.
a) on to or upon any common land, moorland or land of any other description, not being land forming part of a road, or
Common land is land to which everyone has access. Most other land which consists of wide open spaces is included in the s 34 definition, apart from land forming part of a road. However, no offence is committed if the vehicle is driven within fifteen yards of a road in order to park.
b) on any road being a footpath, bridleway or restricted byway.
These include designated routes across areas of land which are clearly defined on a map or signposted at some point. A bridleway, for example, would be a track along which horses would be ridden.

This is a summary offence and the penalty is a fine.

16.9 Drink- and Drug-driving

There are three driving offences relating to driving while under the influence of alcohol or other drugs, and these are all contained within the Road Traffic Act 1988:

- driving, or attempting to drive, or being in charge of a mechanically propelled vehicle whilst unfit to drive through drink or drugs (s 4);
- driving, or attempting to drive, or being in charge of a motor vehicle with alcohol (s 5) in excess of the prescribed limit; and
- driving, or attempting to drive, or being in charge of a motor vehicle with a specified drug (s 5A) in excess of the prescribed limit.

The s 4 offence is very different from s 5 and s 5A offences. For a s 4 offence, the prosecution has to prove that the suspect's ability to drive was actually impaired, whereas for a s 5 or 5A offence the only evidence required is a certain alcohol or drug concentration in the blood, breath, or urine (depending on the offence). They also involve different categories of vehicle.

Due to the complex nature of these offences and the numerous historical challenges to the procedures, the Department for Transport now issues standard forms (MGDD/A to MGDD/F, available online) to be used for investigating these offences. You should check that any hard copies at custody units are in fact the most up-to-date versions.

16.9.1 Key terms from the legislation

The notion of a person being 'in charge of a vehicle' only occurs within ss 4, 5, and 5A of the Road Traffic Act 1988 and there is no legal definition for this, but case law focuses on control of the vehicle and how likely it was for the person to drive. Therefore each set of circumstances is a matter of fact for a court to decide. The court would take into account whether a person had some control of the vehicle, had the keys, or was in or close to the vehicle. Being 'in charge' can also include supervising a provisional licence holder (see *Leach v Evans* [1952] 2 All ER 264 and *Haines v Roberts* [1953] 1 All ER 344).

Some defendants claim a defence in relation to being 'in charge'. For example, a person might attempt to prove that there was no likelihood of them driving the vehicle in the near future, but it has been held that simply stating there was no intention to drive is insufficient (see *CPS v Thompson* [2007] EWHC 1841 (Admin), [2008] RTR 70). A suitable defence could be that they had booked a hotel room for the night or that the vehicle had been wheel-clamped (see *Sheldrake v DPP* [2003] 2 All ER 497 and *Drake v DPP* [1994] RTR 411 respectively). If there is no witness evidence that a driver had been driving prior to a collision, the defence might also claim that they were too badly injured to drive or that the vehicle was too damaged, but the court can disregard such matters (see s 4(4) of the Road Traffic Act 1988 and *CPS v Thompson* [2008] RTR 70). This is a complex area and trainee officers should seek advice.

The term 'drug' has a different meaning depending on whether the offence is under s 4 or s 5A. For s 4 offences, a drug is any substance which can cause an intoxicating (psychoactive) effect. This includes all 'controlled drugs' and other psychoactive substances (see 21.5.1) For an offence under s 5A, the drug must be one of the 17 drugs listed in s 5A, and no other drugs or substances can be taken into account. A particular individual can be simultaneously investigated for a s 4 and s 5A offence so the difference in the meaning of the word 'drug' is important. The Department for Transport advises that if there is sufficient evidence, then officers should proceed with both a s 4 and s 5A process.

16.9.2 Unfit through drink or drugs

These offences are covered under s 4 of the Road Traffic Act 1988. The diagram shows this in detail (s 4(1)).

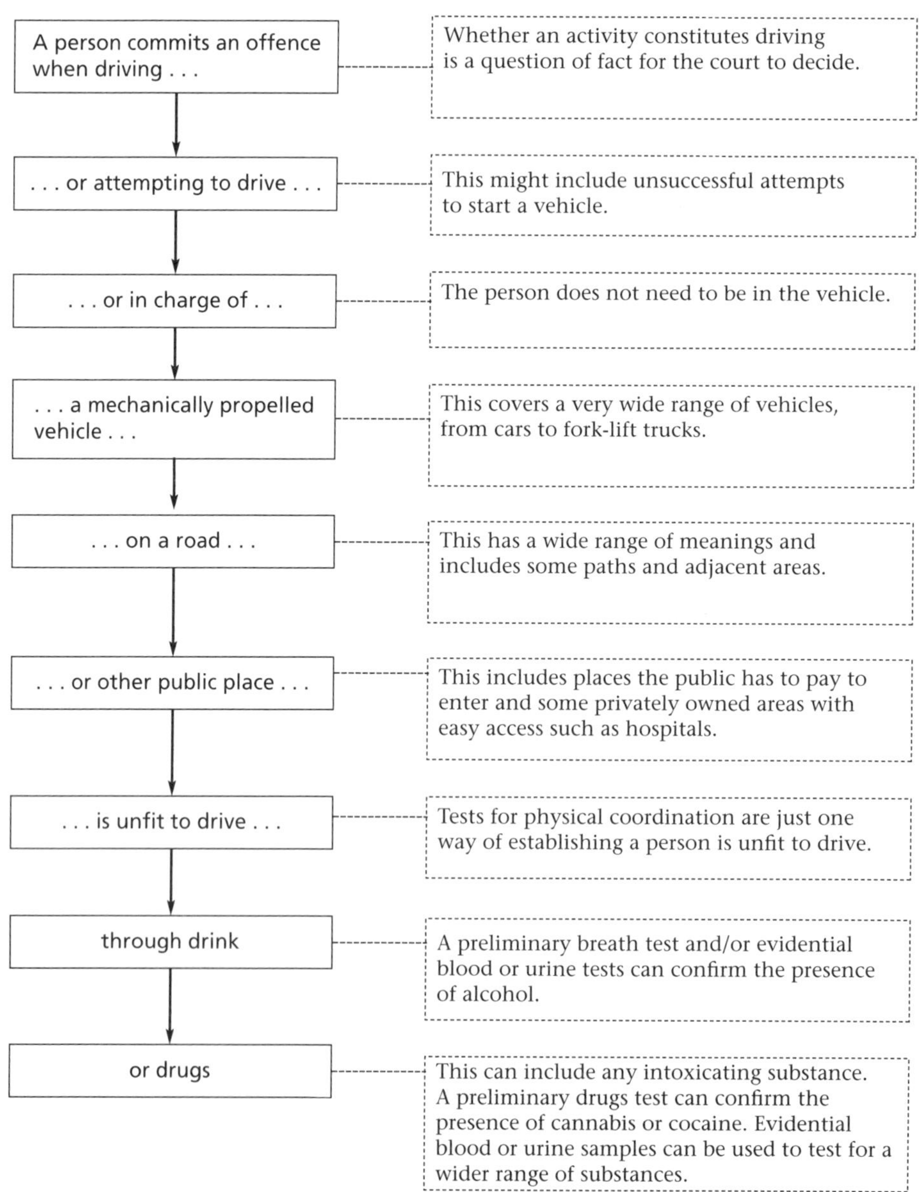

A person commits an offence when driving . . .
Whether an activity constitutes driving is a question of fact for the court to decide.
. . . or attempting to drive . . .
This might include unsuccessful attempts to start a vehicle.
. . . or in charge of . . .
The person does not need to be in the vehicle.
. . . a mechanically propelled vehicle . . .
This covers a very wide range of vehicles, from cars to fork-lift trucks.
. . . on a road . . .
This has a wide range of meanings and includes some paths and adjacent areas.
. . . or other public place . . .
This includes places the public has to pay to enter and some privately owned areas with easy access such as hospitals.
. . . is unfit to drive . . .
Tests for physical coordination are just one way of establishing a person is unfit to drive.
through drink
A preliminary breath test and/or evidential blood or urine tests can confirm the presence of alcohol.
or drugs
This can include any intoxicating substance. A preliminary drugs test can confirm the presence of cannabis or cocaine. Evidential blood or urine samples can be used to test for a wider range of substances.

There is no need to administer a preliminary test for alcohol or drug levels before arresting a driver for this offence, but an officer can choose to do so. A positive preliminary test result means that there is no need to arrange for medical confirmation that the person's condition is due to the presence of alcohol or a drug and the officers can immediately arrange for an evidential test (see 16.9.5). Remember that the result of a preliminary test for drugs will be negative if the intoxicant is not one of those covered by the test.

The suspect's level of impairment and ability to drive properly is assessed by the police officer through observations made during a preliminary impairment test (see 16.9.4.1). However, this would clearly not be required for a person who is so intoxicated that they fall out of the vehicle and are unable to stand.

If a preliminary test for alcohol or drugs had not been carried out or was negative, the doctor or health-care professional (custody nurse) at the police station will examine the person and judge if their condition is due to intoxication (with any substance). If the examination shows that the person's condition is due to intoxication, then an evidential test will be used (blood or urine) to prove the presence of alcohol or a drug in the body.

A suspect arrested for a s 4 offence can also be investigated for a s 5 or a s 5A offence. If there is sufficient evidence, a suspect should be charged with more than one offence and they will be dealt with independently. Section 4 can also be used if the driver is over the limit for alcohol or specified drugs but the vehicle involved is not a motor vehicle (assuming there is sufficient evidence of impairment).

The evidence presented to a court for a s 4 offence is likely to include:

- the style of driving before the accused was stopped;
- their demeanour at time of stop (speech, unsteadiness);
- the results of any preliminary tests;
- the report by a medical examiner whilst in custody (particularly if screening specimens are not obtained to prove the presence of alcohol or drugs in the body); and
- the results of evidential drug tests (using blood or urine samples).

Remember that it might be necessary to present evidence to counter an 'in charge' defence that the driver was not likely to drive.

An arrest for a s 4 offence would be under s 24 of the PACE Act 1984. (There is no power of arrest for a s 4 offence under the Road Traffic Act 1988.) A power of entry to arrest for a s 4 offence is available under s 17(1)(c)(iiia) of the PACE Act 1984 if there are reasonable grounds for believing that the suspect is on the premises.

Offences under s 4 of the Road Traffic Act 1988 are triable summarily and the penalties are:

- for driving and attempting to drive whilst unfit due to drink or drugs (s 4(1)), six months' imprisonment and/or a fine and obligatory disqualification; and
- for being in charge of a vehicle whilst unfit due to drink or drugs (s 4(2)), three months' imprisonment and/or a fine and discretionary disqualification.

16.9.3 Driving, attempting to drive or being in charge of a motor vehicle when over the prescribed limit

There are two prescribed limit offences, s 5 relates to alcohol and s 5A relates to 17 specified drugs. The offences under ss 5 and 5A only require evidence that the level of the substance in the suspect was over the prescribed limit and evidence that the person was driving, attempting to drive, or was in charge of a motor vehicle.

16.9.3.1 Alcohol in excess of the prescribed limit

This offence relates to having alcohol over the prescribed limit in blood, breath, or urine. The flowchart shows the wording for a s 5 offence; bold-edged boxes emphasize the features that distinguish a s 5 offence from a s 4 offence.

Section 5 states that it is an offence for a person to:

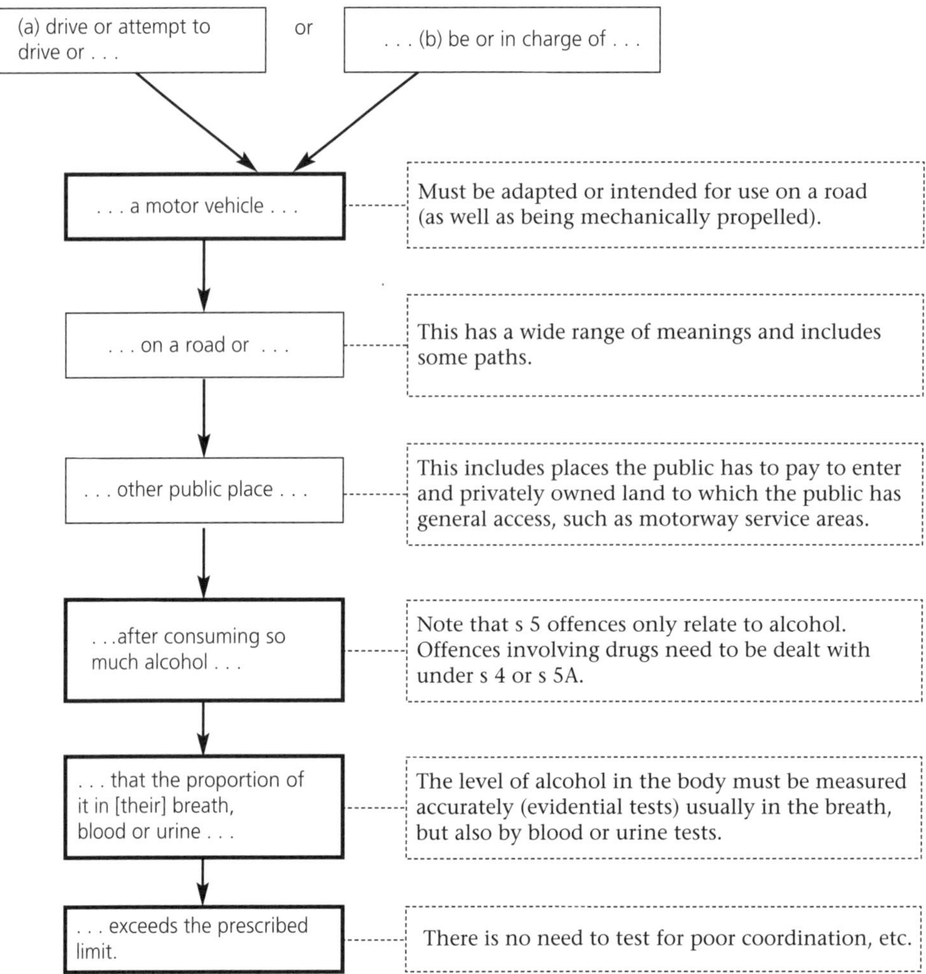
(a) drive or attempt to drive or . . .
or
. . . (b) be or in charge of . . .
. . . a motor vehicle . . .
Must be adapted or intended for use on a road (as well as being mechanically propelled).
. . . on a road or . . .
This has a wide range of meanings and includes some paths.
. . . other public place . . .
This includes places the public has to pay to enter and privately owned land to which the public has general access, such as motorway service areas.
. . .after consuming so much alcohol . . .
Note that s 5 offences only relate to alcohol. Offences involving drugs need to be dealt with under s 4 or s 5A.
. . . that the proportion of it in [their] breath, blood or urine . . .
The level of alcohol in the body must be measured accurately (evidential tests) usually in the breath, but also by blood or urine tests.
. . . exceeds the prescribed limit.
There is no need to test for poor coordination, etc.

The prescribed limits are shown in the table. Note the units: microgrammes (µg), milligrammes (mg), and millilitres (ml). A good way to help memorize these figures is to remember that the digits in each measurement add up to eight.

Type of sample	Amount of alcohol per 100 ml
Breath	35 µg
Blood	80 mg
Urine	107 mg

These offences are triable summarily and the penalties are:

- for driving or attempting to drive above the prescribed limit (s 5(1)(a)): six months' imprisonment and/or a fine and obligatory disqualification; and
- for being in charge of a vehicle above the prescribed limit (s 5(1)(b)): three months' imprisonment and/or a fine and discretionary disqualification.

16.9.3.2 Specified controlled drug in excess of the prescribed limit

Section 5A of the Road Traffic Act 1988 relates to driving with certain specified drugs over the legal limit in the blood. The drugs covered by s 5A and their legal limits are shown in the table.

Controlled drug	Limit (microgrammes (µg) per litre of blood)
Amphetamine	250
Benzoylecgonine	50
Clonazepam	50
Cocaine	10
Delta-9-Tetrahydrocannabinol (THC*)	2
Diazepam	550
Flunitrazepam	300
Ketamine	20
Lorazepam	100
Lysergic Acid Diethylamide (LSD)	1
Methadone	500
Methylamphetamine	10
Methylenedioxymethamphetamine	10
6-Monoacetylmorphine	5
Morphine	80
Oxazepam	300
Temazepam	1,000

* The active ingredient in cannabis.

Some of the drugs on the list are regularly prescribed by doctors to help patients with conditions such as anxiety. However, some people obtain these drugs by other means for recreational use often at much higher dosage levels. For these drugs, the legal limits have been set very high, much higher than medicinal dosage to avoid penalizing drivers who are taking them for medical reasons.

The wording and layout of s 5A is very similar to that of s 5; this was deliberate as the criminal justice system is very familiar with s 5 and how it is used. The flowchart for the s 5 offence can be applied for s 5A, replacing 'alcohol' with 'drugs', and 'breath, blood, or urine' with 'blood only'. The penalties for s 5A offences are the same as the penalties for the equivalent s 5 offences.

Defences are available if the suspect can show that the drug had been prescribed or supplied for medical or dental purposes (s 5A(3)(a)), had been taken in accordance with the instructions (s 5A(3)(b)), and that immediately before taking the drug its possession was not unlawful. These defences cannot be used if the suspect did not follow professional advice about the amount of time that should elapse between taking the drug and driving (s 5A(4)(a) and (b)). The advice could be from the person prescribing, supplying, manufacturing, or distributing the drug.

16.9.4 Preliminary tests

Preliminary tests are frequently referred to as roadside screening tests. There are two types of preliminary tests; preliminary impairment tests and tests for the presence of alcohol or certain drugs. Preliminary tests are covered in s 6A (breath), s 6B (impairment), and s 6C (drugs) of the Road Traffic Act 1988. A police officer does not need to be in uniform to require a person to take part in a preliminary test. However, the police officer actually administering a preliminary test must be in uniform (except after an accident). A Home Office statistical return form must be completed after administering a preliminary test. More recent equipment will do this automatically. Preliminary tests can also be used in police stations and hospitals.

The flowchart summarizes the circumstances for administering preliminary tests.

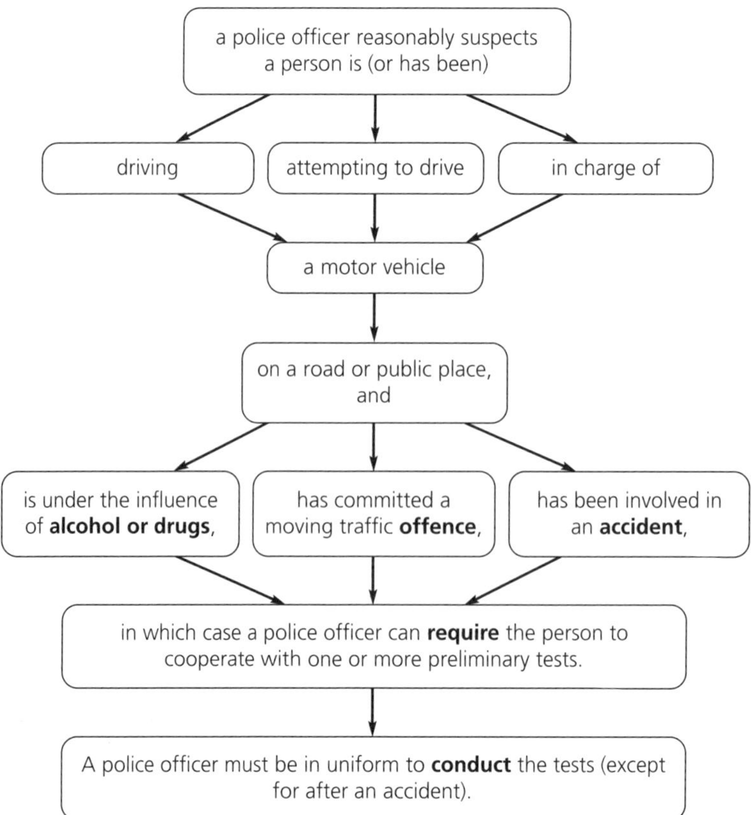
a police officer reasonably suspects a person is (or has been)
driving
attempting to drive
in charge of
a motor vehicle
on a road or public place, and
is under the influence of alcohol or drugs,
has committed a moving traffic offence,
has been involved in an accident,
in which case a police officer can require the person to cooperate with one or more preliminary tests.
A police officer must be in uniform to conduct the tests (except for after an accident).

There may be many individuals at a scene so it might not be clear who was driving. It should first be clarified who was in each vehicle at the time of the accident; witnesses may be able to help on this matter. However, remember that a police officer only has to 'reasonably believe' that a person was driving a vehicle at the time of the accident, so if no one admits to being the driver then more than one person from the vehicle can be tested. If a number of individuals were 'in charge' of the same vehicle, then all will be subject to testing.

The meaning of the term 'accident' has not been defined by statute and remains a question of fact for the courts to decide (see 16.7.2.1). When any such incident seems to be due at least in part to the presence of a motor vehicle on a road, it 'is a fair basis on which a police officer may request the provision of a specimen of breath' (Lord Widgery CJ in *R v Morris* [1972] RTR 201).

A power of entry is available in order to administer preliminary tests (s 6E of the Road Traffic Act 1988) but only after an accident which the police officer reasonably suspects has caused an injury. The power can be used for any place, using reasonable force if necessary.

Any refusal to cooperate with a preliminary test is an offence and the person can be arrested.

16.9.4.1 Preliminary impairment tests

The Field Impairment Test (FIT) is used as the preliminary impairment test for s 4 offences, and the officer carrying out the test must be suitably trained. The subject is asked to carry out a number of specific actions with their eyes closed, such as walking in a straight line or judging time. The tasks and subsequent recording of the observations are set out in the MGDD/F form. Failing the test provides the officer with grounds for arrest.

16.9.4.2 Preliminary breath tests for alcohol

Screening tests for alcohol are primarily used for s 5 offences but can also be used for s 4 offences. For s 5 offences, the preliminary test is used to find out if it is **likely** that there is sufficient alcohol in the subject's system to provide grounds for suspicion that an offence has been committed. If positive, it also allows the officer to consider arrest. For s 4 offences, the tests can confirm the presence of alcohol which avoids the need to arrange for a doctor or other health-care professional's opinion.

The preliminary breath-test devices sample air that has come from deep within the lungs and must be approved by the Secretary of State. Electronic devices include models such as the Lion Alcolmeter 500, the Alcosensor IV, the Draeger Alert, and the Draeger Alcotest 7410 or 6820. Non-electronic devices (such as Alcotest 80 and R80A and the Alcolyser) involve the inflation of a bag and are used less often.

For conducting the test, the police officer must make the requirement of the suspect in a form of words that complies with the legislation, including the implications of failing to comply. There is no prescribed format but officers will be advised on any locally agreed form of words during training and it may be specified in local police service policy.

The officer must also ask the person when they last drank alcohol or smoked as this can disrupt the test results if the test is taken within a certain time period. However, failing to ask these questions will not invalidate the test (*DPP v Kay* [1998] EWHC 258 (Admin)) nor will an innocent failure to follow the instructions render the arrest and subsequent evidential test unlawful (although the results may be considered as less reliable).

To carry out the test the driver should be asked to take a deep breath and to blow into the machine in one continuous breath until requested to stop. The person should be told the result of the test. A positive result justifies arrest because it provides the officer with the grounds to suspect that the proportion of alcohol in the person's breath or blood exceeds the prescribed limit. The reason for the arrest is the suspicion, not the positive result. The suspect must be told that they are under arrest and the reasons for the arrest (s 6D(1) of the Road Traffic Act 1988), and must be cautioned. An evidential test for alcohol should then be carried out.

A patient in a hospital must never be arrested (s 6D(3)). However, should such a wrongful arrest take place, a subsequent and lawfully obtained evidential specimen will not become unlawful (*DPP v Wilson* [2009] EWHC 1988 (Admin)).

16.9.4.3 Preliminary drug tests

Screening tests for drugs are used mainly for s 5A offences but can also be used for suspected s 4 offences. For s 5A offences, the preliminary test is used to provide grounds for suspecting that an offence has been committed and therefore arrest. For s 4 offences, the tests can confirm the presence of certain drugs. Once confirmed there will then be no need to arrange for a doctor or other healthcare professional to determine 'a condition due to ...' at the police station.

The test is carried out on a sample of saliva and currently identifies the presence of cocaine and cannabis (or more precisely its active ingredient THC). These feature on the s 5A list of drugs and are two of the most commonly used drugs. According to recent research, it seems they are likely to account for the vast majority of drivers under the influence of a drug (Department for Transport, 2013). The next drug proposed for inclusion in the saliva test is amphetamine.

There are currently two devices approved by the Home Office for roadside drugs screening; the Draeger DrugTest 5000 and the Suretec DrugWipe 3S. Both use the same technology to detect the drugs but display the results in different ways. A person may be under the influence of a drug that cannot be detected by the device. If an officer suspects this is the case and can justify an arrest due to the person's demeanour, the fact that it is not possible to screen for a particular drug is not relevant and is no bar to arrest.

16.9.4.4 What to do after a preliminary test

If the result of a preliminary alcohol or drugs test is positive, the person should be arrested so that evidential tests can be carried out. For a suspected s 5 or 5A offence (driving over the prescribed limit), the arrest power is provided under s 6D(1) of the Road Traffic Act 1988. For a suspected s 4 offence (driving while unfit), the arrest power is provided under s 24 of the PACE Act 1984. There is a power of entry in order to arrest a person who has been involved in an injury accident and provided a positive preliminary test (s 6 of the Road Traffic Act 1988).

If the result of a preliminary test is negative but it still seems that the driver is intoxicated, then the officer could:

- conduct a preliminary drugs or alcohol test (whichever has not already been done);
- conduct a preliminary impairment test (if they are qualified and have the apparatus available) and proceed as for a s 4 offence;
- arrest under s 5A if it seems likely the intoxication is caused by one of the other 15 specified drugs on the s 5A list; or
- arrest the driver under s 24 of the PACE Act 1984 on suspicion of driving whilst unfit (under s 4).

If the result of a preliminary test is negative and there is no evidence of impairment and no other offences have been committed, then the driver is free to leave.

16.9.4.5 Failing to cooperate with a preliminary test

If the driver does not take the test correctly, refuses to participate, or is unable to complete a preliminary test (eg due to a medical condition), this amounts to 'failure to provide'. The number of opportunities provided for completing a preliminary test will be determined locally.

If there is reasonable suspicion that the person is under the influence of alcohol or a drug, then they should be arrested and the relevant evidential tests carried out. If alcohol or drugs are not suspected, the person should instead be reported for the offence of failing to cooperate with the provision of a specimen for a preliminary test (s 6(6) of the Road Traffic Act 1988). The person's true identity will need to be ascertained through computer checks with Control and identity documents from the person. The address they give must be checked as genuine. The suspect should be interviewed under caution (all recorded in the officer's PNB) and then reported for the offence of failing to cooperate with a preliminary test and cautioned again. This offence is triable summarily and the penalty is obligatory endorsement (four points) and discretionary disqualification.

16.9.5 Evidential tests

The results of evidential tests for drugs and alcohol can be used as evidence in a court for an offence under s 3A, 4, 5, or 5A of the Road Traffic Act 1988. The specimens are usually provided at a police station or hospital but some types of tests can be conducted at the roadside. The requirement for any evidential test is usually made at a police station or hospital but the requirement for an evidential breath test can also be made at the roadside. It is usual to arrest a suspect before requiring an evidential test although this is not compulsory by law. Note that a suspect who is also a hospital patient cannot be arrested (s 6D(3) of the Road Traffic Act 1988).

If there is reasonable cause to believe that the suspect has a drug in their body (eg from a preliminary drug-test result or the medical examiner's opinion), a blood or urine specimen should be taken for a suspected s 4 offence and a blood specimen for a suspected s 5A offence. A single blood specimen can be used to investigate a s 4 and s 5A offence as long as there is sufficient quantity (the laboratory will need to be informed of this intention). For alcohol, an evidential breath test will always be used in preference to blood or urine tests (s 7(3) of the Road Traffic Act 1988) unless:

- there is reasonable cause to believe that a medical reason prevents the use of a breath test;
- the approved device is not available; and/or
- there is cause to believe the device gave an unreliable result.

A suspect at a police station cannot delay providing a specimen for an evidential test in order to obtain legal advice. There can only be a delay in exceptional circumstances and where a legal representative is available for immediate consultation (*Chalupa v CPS* [2009] EWHC 3082 (Admin)).

16.9.5.1 Evidential breath tests for alcohol

The test can be required and conducted at (or near) a place where a relevant preliminary breath test has been administered, at a police station, or in a hospital (s 7(2) of the Road Traffic Act 1988). For suspected offences of causing death by careless driving when under the influence of drink or drugs, or for being unfit to drive (ss 3A and 4 of the Road Traffic Act 1988 respectively), there is no need for a prior preliminary breath test.

Two samples of breath are required for the test and the process and period of time in which the two samples are collected is called a 'cycle'. The two samples must be obtained from the same cycle in order for the test to be valid. Only the sample containing the lower proportion of alcohol will be used as evidence and the other will be disregarded (s 8(1) of the Road Traffic Act 1988). The samples will be analysed by a device approved by the Secretary of State (currently the Camic Datamaster, the Lion Intoxilyzer 6000, or the Intoximeter EC/IR). The person operating the machine (often the custody officer) will have been trained to use it and will check that it is working properly. MGDD forms must be used to record the breath-test procedure and the completed forms will constitute the 'notes made at the time'.

As part of the requirement to provide specimens, the officer must say to the suspect 'I warn you that failure to provide either of these specimens will render you liable to prosecution' (para A12 in the MGDD/A and s 7(7) of the Road Traffic Act 1988).

Each organization will have its own policy on how many attempts can be allowed for the suspect to provide a sufficient volume of air in a proper manner (s 11(3) of the Road Traffic Act 1988). Note that regurgitation of stomach contents does not affect the accuracy of the measurements (see *McNeil v DPP* [2008] EWHC 1254 (Admin)).

The prescribed limit for alcohol in the breath is 35 µg of alcohol per 100 ml of breath (see 16.9.3), but the police do not proceed unless the level is above 40 µg (see MGDD/A, section A20). After the test, the MGDD forms are completed and if the result is above the prescribed limit the driver can be charged and bailed to court.

If the driver fails to provide two samples of breath, the offence of 'failing to provide a specimen of breath for an evidential breath test' (s 7(6)) has been committed. Refusing to provide suitable samples is equivalent to failure (s 11(2) of the Road Traffic Act 1988), including when not enough breath is provided (see *Rweikiza v DPP* [2008] EWHC 386 (Admin)). The suspect must be allowed sufficient time to provide the samples in each subsequent cycle; otherwise a subsequent prosecution may fail (see *Plackett v DPP* [2008] EWHC 1335 (Admin)). The suspect is not obliged to mention any medical condition which could account for failing to provide enough breath, but the court does not have to accept the excuse if they later claimed that this is the case (see *Piggott v DPP* [2008] WLR (D) 44). If the testing machine registers an error on the second sample in each of two cycles, then further breath samples can be required (eg at another police station or using another machine), and failing to comply is an offence (s 7(6)) even though previous samples were supplied (see *Hussain v DPP* [2008] EWHC 901 (Admin)). If the suspect does not speak English and a request for a specimen of breath is translated (by an accredited interpreter), a court can draw an inference (ie draw their own conclusions) on whether the suspect would have understood (see *Bielecki v DPP* [2011] EWHC 2245 (Admin)).

16.9.5.2 Blood and urine specimens

These may be required under s 7(3) of the Road Traffic Act 1988. For a suspected s 4 or s 5 offence, either type of specimen can be used, but for a s 5A offence it must be a blood sample. The requirement to provide a specimen of blood or urine can only be made at a police station or hospital. If the driver refuses (or is unable) to provide blood or urine samples, then they will have committed the offence of failing to provide samples for an evidential test (s 7(6) of the Road Traffic Act 1988).

Before a blood or urine sample is taken the driver must be told:

- for a suspected s 5 offence, the reason(s) why breath specimens cannot be taken (from the list under s 7(3) (see 16.9.5)); and
- that they are therefore required to give a sample of blood or urine; and
- that failing to provide the specimen could result in their prosecution.

Blood is the preferred medium. Apart from medical considerations, the driver cannot choose whether the sample will be blood or urine. Before proceeding with a blood test the driver should be asked if there are any medical reasons for not taking a blood sample. The sample must, of course, be taken by a medical examiner or health-care professional. After the sample has been obtained, the driver can be bailed to return to the police station when the results arrive back from the laboratory. Blood and urine samples are usually sent to the laboratory by post, although blood samples for a s 5A analysis must remain refrigerated and arrangements vary between police services.

16.9.5.3 Allowing for the delay between the offence and taking samples

As the human body continually breaks down alcohol it is assumed that the level of alcohol in a suspect's breath, blood, or urine at the time of an alleged offence will gradually decrease over time (if no more alcohol is consumed). It is a fact in law that a court will assume the level of intoxicants in the body at the time of the alleged offence was not less than the level measured in the evidential test (s 15(2) of the Road Traffic Offenders Act 1988).

However, the accused may claim they consumed alcohol or drugs after the offence but before the evidential sample was taken (eg that they ran off after a collision and went for a drink before the police arrived) or that they consumed intoxicants from a container (the proverbial (and sometimes actual) hip flask) in the vehicle after the preliminary test. This is formally referred to as 'post-incident drinking'. If they can prove this, the assumption under s 15(2) (see previous paragraph) cannot be made.

'Back calculations' can be used to establish that the driver was in excess of the legal limit when the incident occurred. These calculations are based on the time elapsed since the offence, the subsequent consumption of alcohol, and the estimated rate of elimination of alcohol from the human body. Evidence for back calculations should be recorded on Form MGDD/D at the police station. However, if this defence is not raised until later, the relevant laboratory should be provided with as much information as can be obtained from the case papers and the officer in charge of the case.

The following information is relevant:

- the type and quantity of alcohol consumed before the incident and, if possible, the times at which individual units of alcohol were consumed;
- the type and quantity of alcohol allegedly consumed after the incident but before the test;
- the driver's characteristics: weight, height, build, age, sex, and any medical conditions;
- details of any food consumed from six hours before the offence until the provision of a breath or laboratory specimen; and
- details of any medication taken regularly or within four hours prior to drinking.

16.9.6 Drink- and drug-driving, and admission to hospital

Some drivers need to be admitted to hospital after an accident. Investigations in these circumstances are covered under s 9 of the Road Traffic Act 1988, and an MGDD/C form is used. A hospital is defined by the Act as an institution which provides medical or surgical treatment for in-patients or out-patients. The term 'patient' is not defined and will be a question of fact for the court to decide, but generally speaking a patient is a person who is currently on hospital grounds receiving, or waiting to receive, medical treatment.

16.9.6.1 Obtaining samples from a hospital patient

The medical practitioner in immediate charge of the patient must be notified before a requirement is made or any test is carried out on the person (s 9(1) of the Road Traffic Act 1988). The procedures must be explained as the welfare of a patient is paramount. If the doctor does not object, the patient can be asked to cooperate with a preliminary test.

If the result is negative, the patient must be told that no further action will be taken regarding a drink- or drug-driving offence. If they do not cooperate and refuse to have the test, the patient should be reported for an offence under s 6(6) of the Road Traffic Act 1988. Remember a hospital patient cannot be arrested for failing to cooperate with a preliminary test (s 6D(3)).

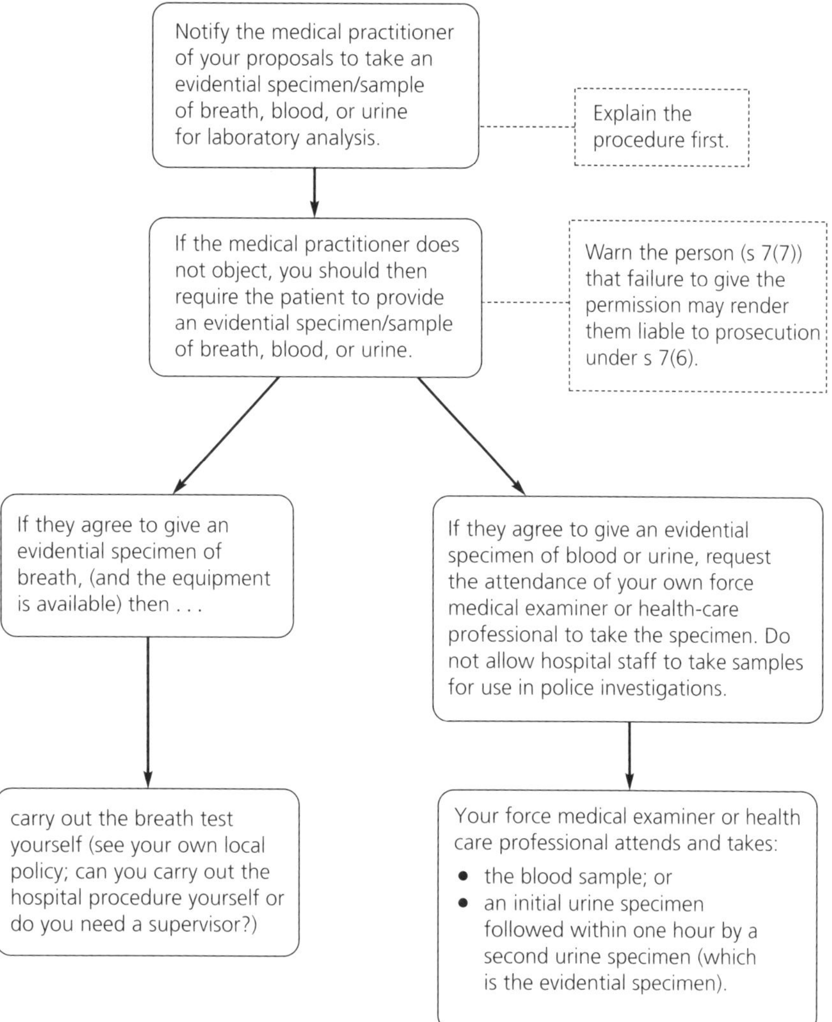

Notify the medical practitioner of your proposals to take an evidential specimen/sample of breath, blood, or urine for laboratory analysis.
Explain the procedure first.
If the medical practitioner does not object, you should then require the patient to provide an evidential specimen/sample of breath, blood, or urine.
Warn the person (s 7(7)) that failure to give the permission may render them liable to prosecution under s 7(6).
If they agree to give an evidential specimen of breath, (and the equipment is available) then . . .
If they agree to give an evidential specimen of blood or urine, request the attendance of your own force medical examiner or health-care professional to take the specimen. Do not allow hospital staff to take samples for use in police investigations.
carry out the breath test yourself (see your own local policy; can you carry out the hospital procedure yourself or do you need a supervisor?)
Your force medical examiner or health care professional attends and takes:
• the blood sample; or
• an initial urine specimen followed within one hour by a second urine specimen (which is the evidential specimen).

Evidential tests will be carried out if the result of the preliminary test is positive (or the patient fails to complete the test). The outline procedure is shown in the diagram above.

If a blood sample is required, it must be taken by a police medical practitioner or health-care professional. Very rarely, no such person is available and another medical practitioner who is not responsible for the clinical care of the patient should take it.

An unconscious patient (described as 'incapable of giving valid consent' on the MGDD/C) cannot take part in a breath test and so a blood sample will be required, and once again the relevant medical practitioner must be notified (see s 9(1A) of the Road Traffic Act 1988). However, the blood sample must not be analysed until the patient regains consciousness and can give permission (s 7A(4)). It is an offence to refuse permission (s 7A(6)).

TASK 4 A police officer attends the local hospital and makes a lawful requirement for a sample of breath, blood, or urine from a patient who was driving a vehicle at the time of a collision. Whilst waiting for the police medical practitioner to arrive, the patient is discharged from hospital and leaves. Does the obligation for the patient to provide that sample still stand? Refer to *Webber v DPP* [1998] RTR 111 for your answer.

16.10 Using Vehicles to Cause Alarm, Distress, and Annoyance

The police have a number of powers under s 59 of the Police Reform Act 2002 for situations where the anti-social use of motor vehicles (understood here under the wider meaning given in s 59(9)) is causing concern to other people in the area. The driving must amount to careless or inconsiderate driving, unlawful off-road driving, or unlicensed on-street racing. It must also cause, or be likely to cause, alarm, distress, or annoyance to other people. In such circumstances, a police officer, using reasonable force when required, has the power to:

- require a moving vehicle to stop (s 59(3)(a));
- seize and remove the vehicle, after warning the driver (s 59(3)(b)); and
- enter certain types of premises (this excludes private dwellings but does include any associated garage or land) in order to stop or seize a vehicle (s 59(3)(c) and s 59(9)).

Failing to stop is a summary offence under s 59(6) of the Police Reform Act 2002 and the penalty is a fine.

If the vehicle is to be seized under s 59(3)(b), there is no need for a warning if:

- it would be impracticable to do so;
- a warning has already been given on that occasion;
- there are reasonable grounds for believing that such a warning has been given on that occasion by someone else; or
- the officer has reasonable grounds for believing that the person has been given a warning (by any police officer, in respect of any vehicle being used in the same or a similar way) on a previous occasion in the previous 12 months.

The warning applies to both the driver and the particular vehicle they are driving when the police attend the call. The warning remains with the driver for a period of 12 months and applies regardless of the vehicle they are driving on future occasions. With the vehicle, however, the warning only remains valid for the duration of a single attendance of police to a location. The full duration of the single attendance of police at a location is described in the legislation as 'that occasion'. Therefore, any future police attendance involving the same vehicle but with a different driver will require a separate warning. The wording for a warning notice is not specified in the legislation so the wording can vary; pre-formatted forms may be available locally.

Core Aspects of Police Work

16.11 Road-related Anti-social Behaviour

Wilful obstruction is an offence under s 137 of the Highways Act 1980. It is an offence for a person:

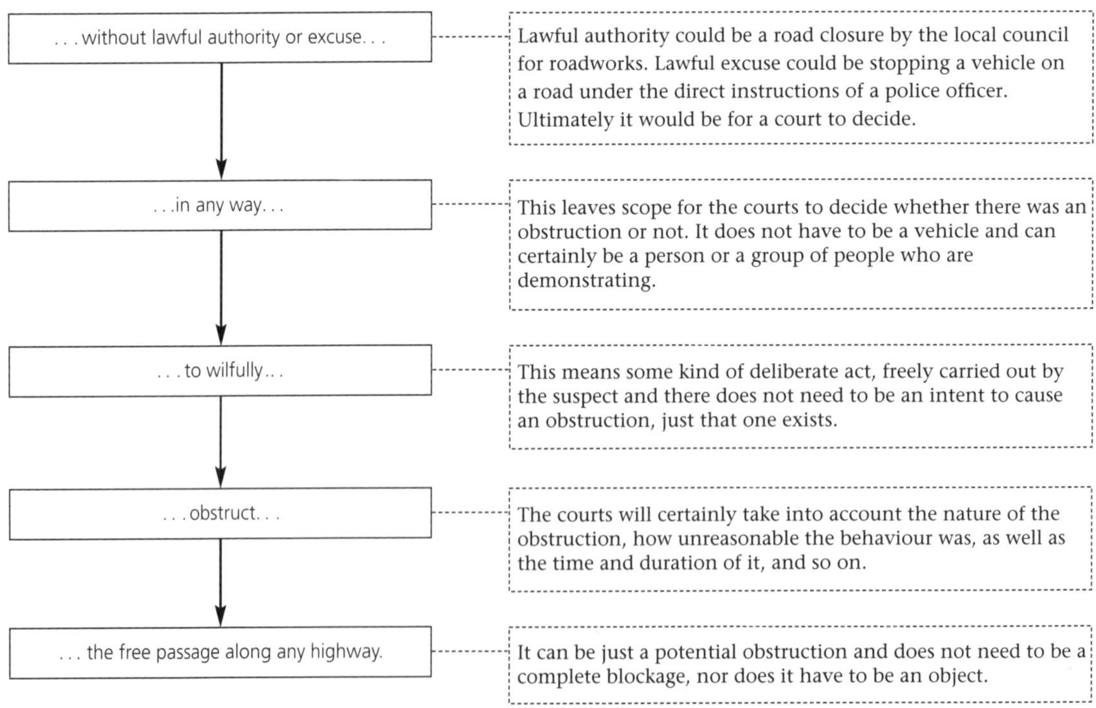

. . . without lawful authority or excuse. . .
Lawful authority could be a road closure by the local council for roadworks. Lawful excuse could be stopping a vehicle on a road under the direct instructions of a police officer. Ultimately it would be for a court to decide.
. . .in any way. . .
This leaves scope for the courts to decide whether there was an obstruction or not. It does not have to be a vehicle and can certainly be a person or a group of people who are demonstrating.
. . . to wilfully. . .
This means some kind of deliberate act, freely carried out by the suspect and there does not need to be an intent to cause an obstruction, just that one exists.
. . . obstruct. . .
The courts will certainly take into account the nature of the obstruction, how unreasonable the behaviour was, as well as the time and duration of it, and so on.
. . . the free passage along any highway.
It can be just a potential obstruction and does not need to be a complete blockage, nor does it have to be an object.

This offence is triable summarily and the penalty is a fine.

'Unauthorized campers' can be directed away from 'any land forming part of a highway, any other unoccupied property, or any occupied land without the consent of the owner' under s 77 of the Criminal Justice and Public Order Act 1994. This allows local authorities to direct people who are residing in vehicles in such locations to leave with the vehicles and any other property they have there.

Vehicles or trailers must not be left in a dangerous position on a road (s 22 of the Road Traffic Act 1988). It is an offence for a person in charge of a vehicle to cause or permit:

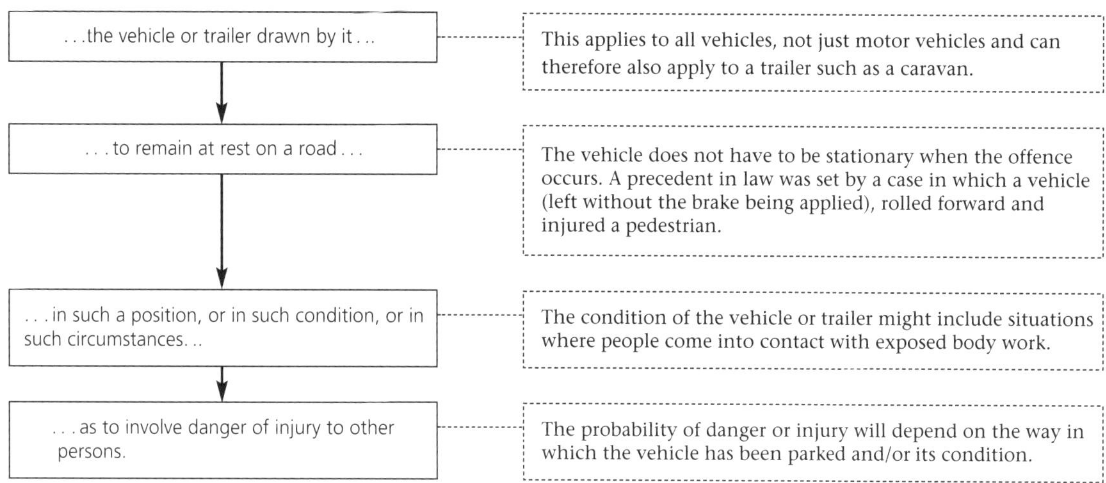

. . .the vehicle or trailer drawn by it . . .
This applies to all vehicles, not just motor vehicles and can therefore also apply to a trailer such as a caravan.
. . . to remain at rest on a road . . .
The vehicle does not have to be stationary when the offence occurs. A precedent in law was set by a case in which a vehicle (left without the brake being applied), rolled forward and injured a pedestrian.
. . . in such a position, or in such condition, or in such circumstances. . .
The condition of the vehicle or trailer might include situations where people come into contact with exposed body work.
. . . as to involve danger of injury to other persons.
The probability of danger or injury will depend on the way in which the vehicle has been parked and/or its condition.

This offence is triable summarily and the penalty is a fine.

Lighting fires or letting off firearms near a highway is an offence under s 161 of the Highways Act 1980. This prohibits any person (without lawful authority or excuse) from:

- depositing anything on a highway which leads to someone getting injured;
- lighting a fire on or over a carriageway; or
- discharging a firearm (or firework) within 50 feet of the centre of a highway if it could injure a user of the highway.

This offence is triable summarily and the penalty is a fine.

Interfering with road signs, other traffic equipment, or vehicles may put other road users at risk. Section 22A of the Road Traffic Act 1988 states that it is an offence to (intentionally and without lawful authority or reasonable cause) cause anything to be on or over a road, or interfere with a motor vehicle, trailer, cycle, or with traffic equipment (directly or indirectly) if this is likely to cause injury to a person or damage to property.

Traffic equipment is defined as:

- anything lawfully placed on or near a road by a highway authority;
- a traffic sign lawfully placed on or near a road by a person other than a highway authority; and
- any fence, barrier, or light lawfully placed on or near a road (eg to protect street works), or any item placed under the instructions of a chief officer of police.

This applies only if the activities would be regarded as obviously dangerous to a reasonable person or bystander. The reasonable person or bystander does not have to be a motorist (*DPP v D* [2006] EWHC 314 (Admin)). It is irrelevant that the suspect was unaware of the potential danger; this will be a question of fact for the court to decide given the circumstances. The offence is triable either way and the penalty is a fine or imprisonment (six months summarily and seven years on indictment).

Repairing vehicles in the street is a relatively common practice, but it may cause nuisance to other residents or environmental damage. Under s 4 of the Clean Neighbourhoods and Environment Act 2005, it is an offence in some circumstances to 'carry out restricted works on a motor vehicle on a road'. This includes the repair, maintenance, servicing, improvement, dismantling, installation, replacement, or renewal of a motor vehicle (or of any part of or accessory to a motor vehicle). However, a householder who repairs their own vehicle in the street and gives no reasonable cause for annoyance to persons in the vicinity does not commit this offence as the work is not for gain or reward or as part of a business. Nor is any offence committed if the work is required after an accident or breakdown and the repairs were necessary on the spot or carried out within 72 hours.

Skips placed on or near highways can present hazards. Permission must be given by a highways authority for placing a skip on a highway (s 139(1) of the Highways Act 1980) and conditions must be met in relation to its size, the way it is lit, and its position on the road (s 139(2)). An offence is committed if the skip is placed without permission (s 139(3)) or the conditions are not met (s 139(4)). These are summary offences and the penalty is a fine.

Holding or getting onto a motor vehicle (or an attached trailer) that is moving and on a road in order to be towed or carried is an offence (s 26(1) of the Road Traffic Act 1988). This is a summary offence and the penalty is a fine.

> **TASK 5** Several complaints have been made by residents in the neighbourhood of a club. At closing time they have seen people throwing rubbish bins and other items about the streets, tampering with traffic lights, and deflating vehicle tyres. What offences might have been committed?

16.12 Methods of Disposal for Motoring Offences

There are several ways of dealing with a suspect who has committed a road traffic offence, and the decision will be based upon a number of factors including local policy and the police officer's discretion. The methods of disposal for such offences include:

- a verbal warning;
- reporting a suspect for the purposes of issuing a written charge;
- the VDRS (Vehicle Defect Rectification Scheme);
- a TOR (Traffic Offence Report);
- an FPN (fixed penalty notice);
- arrest and charge.

The first flowchart summarizes the early stages of the investigative process for dealing with motoring offences. Note there may be some local variation about the use of police pocket notebooks (PNB in the flowchart) as well as matters relating to the issue of the HO/RT/1 form, FPNs, and the use of the VDRS. Officers should therefore follow local arrangements.

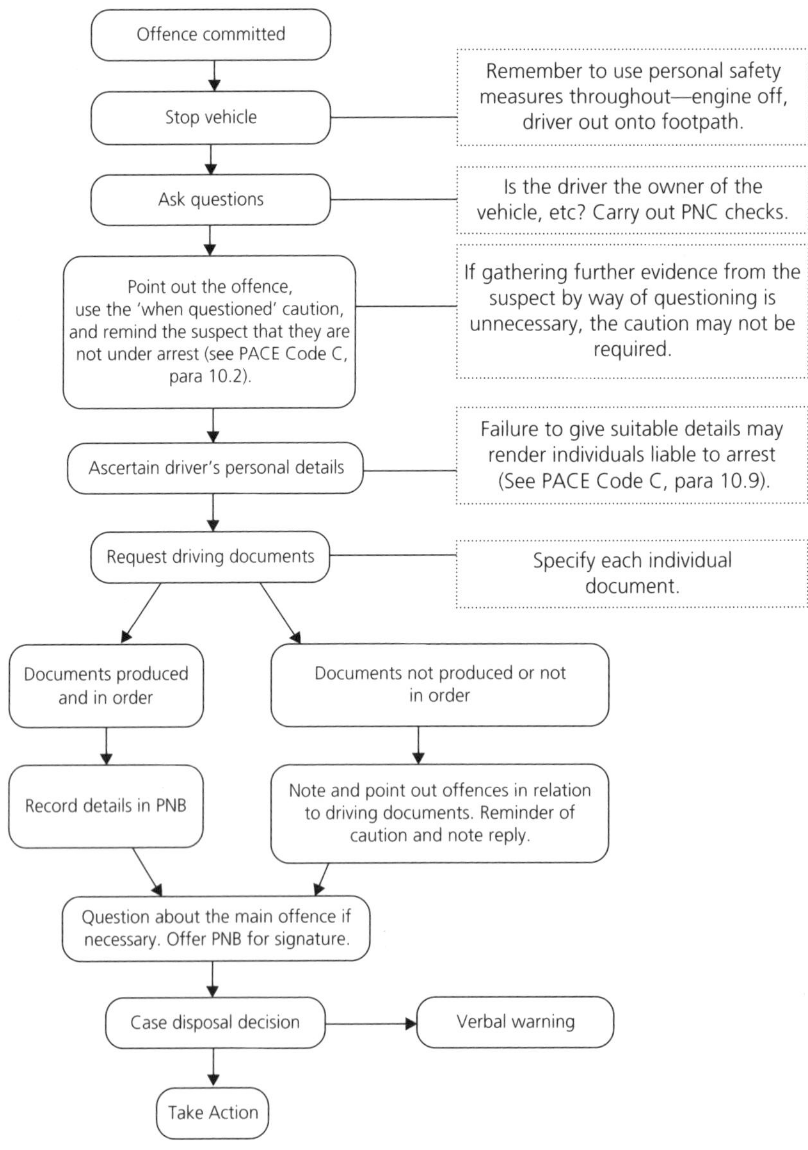

Offence committed
Stop vehicle
Remember to use personal safety measures throughout—engine off, driver out onto footpath.
Ask questions
Is the driver the owner of the vehicle, etc? Carry out PNC checks.
Point out the offence, use the 'when questioned' caution, and remind the suspect that they are not under arrest (see PACE Code C, para 10.2).
If gathering further evidence from the suspect by way of questioning is unnecessary, the caution may not be required.
Ascertain driver's personal details
Failure to give suitable details may render individuals liable to arrest (See PACE Code C, para 10.9).
Request driving documents
Specify each individual document.
Documents produced and in order
Documents not produced or not in order
Record details in PNB
Note and point out offences in relation to driving documents. Reminder of caution and note reply.
Question about the main offence if necessary. Offer PNB for signature.
Case disposal decision
Verbal warning
Take Action

Likewise, if a verbal warning is not appropriate the VDRS, a TOR, or an FPN can be used.

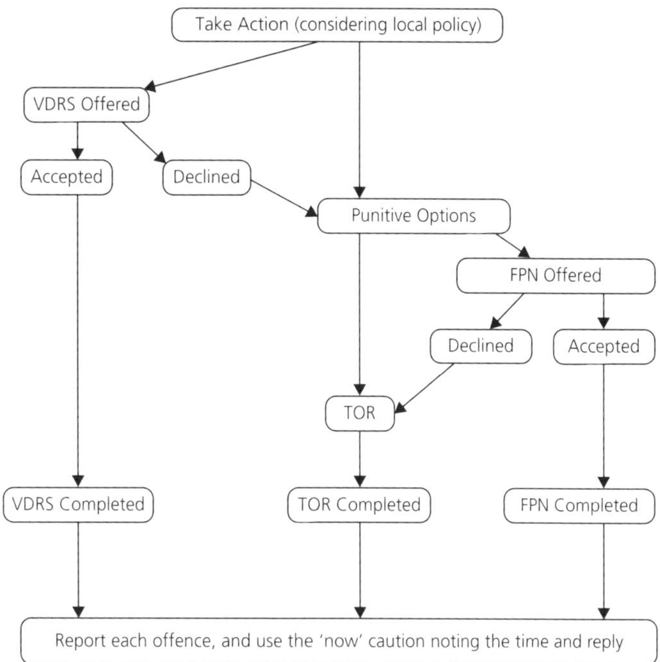

Note that criminals sought in connection with serious crimes often come to the attention of the police through committing minor road traffic offences. If a suspect has been arrested for the other offences, they can of course also be charged with the road traffic offences.

16.12.1 Reporting for the purposes of issuing a written charge

The suspect must be reported for the purposes of issuing a written charge (see 10.18.1.1) for all methods of disposal, apart from a verbal warning with no further action. The officer must ascertain the personal details of the suspect, including a suitable address for the issuing of a written charge (often referred to as suitable for 'the service of a summons') should that be necessary. The processes may vary, for example it is slightly different for completing a Traffic Offence Report compared with issuing an FPN. If a person refuses to provide this information, they may be liable to arrest and could then be charged with the traffic offences once in custody, as for any other offence. Sometimes the arrested person provides the required details just prior to being charged; local policies vary on how to proceed.

16.12.2 Vehicle Defect Rectification Scheme

Drivers of vehicles that are found to be in an unsuitable condition due to minor defects can be given the opportunity to use the Vehicle Defect Rectification Scheme (VDRS). This avoids the need to prosecute or issue an FPN. The use of the VDRS will be subject to local police service instructions and officers should be clear about when it can be used. Deciding whether to use the VDRS will also depend on the circumstances of the offence and the officer's discretion.

The advantages of the VDRS include:

- the defects are rectified, which contributes to road safety;
- the offender does not have to go to court; and
- improved police and public relations: many people will only come into contact with the police during the investigation of road traffic matters, and the VDRS is partly supportive, rather than wholly punitive.

When considering using the VDRS, the police officer must point out the offence to the person responsible for the vehicle and inform them that participation in the VDRS is voluntary and that no further action will be taken if they agree to participate in the scheme. If the driver declines the VDRS, they will normally be issued with a TOR or an FPN—follow local policy.

After receiving a VDRS notice, the driver must have the vehicle repaired within 14 days and submit it for examination at a Department for Transport approved MOT testing station where the VDRS form should be endorsed to confirm the fault is rectified. The driver must then send the completed form to the Central Ticket Office (or as guided by local policy). If the driver fails to return the form within the specified time, they could be prosecuted by way of written charge (as if the VDRS had not been used).

16.12.3 Traffic Offence Report (TOR)

In the majority of police services, most officers either offer advice for minor offences (where there has been no collision) or issue a Traffic Offence Report (TOR). Many police services are moving away from using FPNs in favour of TORs as they provide a range of disposal options, such as driver improvement courses, conditional offers with the same penalty as an FPN, or a written charge summoning the offender to court.

The procedures for issuing TORs vary so local policy should be followed. A TOR usually has at least two self-carbonating copies to record details of the driver, the offence, and the vehicle. Generally, the first copy is kept by the issuing officer (the reverse side is in effect an MG11 duty statement and should be completed according to local policy). The second copy is given to the driver. As the driver could eventually be prosecuted, the reporting procedures for issuing a written charge should be followed and recorded on the notice and the driver asked to sign the entry. The officer sends their copy of the completed TOR to the central processing department for a decision on disposal. The disposal options include issuing a Notice of Intended Prosecution, making a conditional offer, and referral to the National Driver Offender Retraining Scheme.

16.12.4 The fixed penalty system

The fixed penalty system for motoring offences (Part III of the Road Traffic Offenders Act 1988) provides offenders with the opportunity to pay a fixed fine instead of going to court (s 54 of the Road Traffic Offenders Act 1988). The FPN system is similar to the Penalty Notice for Disorder (PND) system for anti-social behaviour offences. Note that the use of FPNs is subject to local policy and that most parking offences have now been decriminalized (eg in London officers can only issue FPNs for unnecessary obstruction). There are two types of FPN:

- non-endorsable fixed penalty notices (NEFPN) for offences which do not add penalty points to an offender's driving licence (parking, seat belts, and vehicle lighting offences);
- endorsable fixed penalty notices (EFPN) for offences which add penalty points to an offender's driving licence (eg contravening a red traffic light, failing to stop at a stop sign, and driving a vehicle with defective tyres).

An FPN can only be issued to the person actually committing the offence or driving the vehicle involved; they cannot be used for people who cause or permit an offence (see 16.2.4). In some circumstances, an FPN can be issued by leaving the documents on the vehicle without the need for the driver to be present, such as a parking ticket affixed to a car's windscreen. An FPN can be issued to non-UK offenders and UK offenders, as well as those with no fixed abode, irrespective of whether the offence is endorsable. A financial penalty deposit can be requested from any offender who does not have a satisfactory address in the UK. If the FPN is not accepted, the driver will have to be reported. A fine for an FPN must be paid within 28 days (to the Central Ticket Office in the area) or it will be increased by 50 per cent, and can also be recovered by the courts.

For offences involving commercial vehicles such as breaches of drivers' hours rules and overloading of vehicles, the fixed penalty value can be increased, depending on the circumstances and the severity of the offence (see the VOSA *Guide to graduated fixed penalties and financial deposits*, available online).

16.12.4.1 Issuing a non-endorsable fixed penalty notice

When a police officer in uniform has reasonable grounds to believe that a person is committing or has committed a fixed penalty offence (and local policy indicates this is the suitable disposal option), an FPN can be issued. If the driver is present the police officer should:

1. point out the offence;
2. caution the driver using 'when questioned' and inform them that they are not under arrest (PACE Code C, para 10.2);
3. question the driver and allow them to ask questions (in relation to the offence(s));
4. if the driver fails to cooperate or answer any particular questions after being cautioned, they should be informed that failing to provide their name and address, for example, may make them liable to detention or arrest (PACE Code C, para 10.9);
5. check that the driver wishes to proceed with an FPN;
6. complete and issue the NEFPN;
7. report the driver or owner for the offence;
8. use the 'now' caution.

Certain parking-related NEFPNs can be attached to a stationary vehicle (s 62(1)) if the driver is absent, and it is an offence for any person other than the driver/owner to remove or interfere with the notice.

The flowchart summarizes the process.

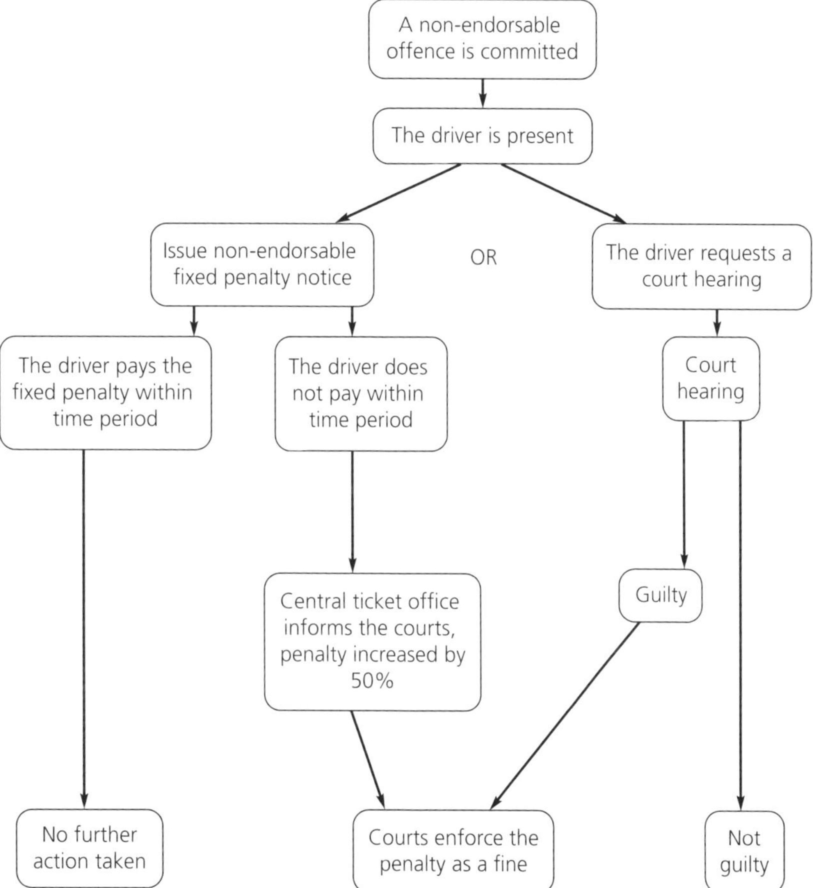

16.12.4.2 Endorsable fixed penalty notices

For some offences the penalty includes obligatory endorsement. An EFPN can be used if:

- the driver's file on the PNC can be checked to view the endorsement history;
- the total number of points including the new proposed points does not exceed 11; and
- the driver accepts an EFPN.

The procedure for issuing an EFPN is the same as that for a standard FPN, except for checking the driving licence status as set out earlier, and recording the driver number. If the proposed new points would take the total to 12 or more the driver will have to be reported for prosecution.

16.12.4.3 Conditional offer of fixed penalty

A conditional offer for a fixed penalty can be sent to the alleged offender if the FPN cannot be handed to a driver or attached to a vehicle (s 75 of the Road Traffic Offenders Act 1988). This could apply for speeding offences detected by automatic camera devices or when a police officer sees a driver disobeying a road sign but it is impossible to follow, or when a TOR has been issued and no suitable education course is available. The conditional offer will state the circumstances of the alleged offence and the relevant fixed penalty, and explain that no further proceedings will take place in relation to the offence for 28 days from the date of issue. If payment is made within that period, there will be no court proceedings. Police officers and staff at Central Ticket Offices can arrange for conditional offers to be sent.

16.12.4.4 Roadside deposit scheme

If a driver has been issued with an FPN or conditional offer but is unable to provide a satisfactory UK address at the time of an offence, the police officer can request a financial penalty deposit. The officer can prohibit the use of the vehicle and physically prevent its use (eg with a wheel clamp or a wire rope lock through the steering wheel) until the deposit is paid. Once paid, the driver can then choose whether to ultimately pay the FPN and allow the deposit to be used as part-payment or request a court hearing. If they are found not guilty in court, the deposit will be returned. Further information is available in the VOSA *Guide to graduated fixed penalties and financial deposits*, available online. This procedure will probably only be available to specialist roads policing units; officers should check which local arrangements apply.

16.12.5 Notice of Intended Prosecution

The rights of an individual suspected of committing certain road traffic offences are safeguarded under the Road Traffic Offenders Act 1988. They must be informed at the earliest opportunity of their suspected involvement in an offence, usually by means of a Notice of Intended Prosecution (NIP). This will specify the nature of the offence and the time and place where it is alleged to have been committed. It applies for offences listed in s 1(1) of the Road Traffic Offenders Act 1988, such as dangerous driving, dangerous cycling, careless and inconsiderate driving, careless and inconsiderate cycling, failing to conform with the indication of a police officer when directing traffic, failing to comply with a traffic sign, and speeding offences (see Sch 1 to the Road Traffic Offenders Act 1988 and gov.uk, 1988).

These offences are clearly serious matters but a person cannot be prosecuted for any of them (s 1(1)) unless they have been either:

- warned at the time of the offence of the possibility of prosecution (a verbal NIP, s 1(1)(a)), this is often described as the 'Warning Formula' and is reproduced in report books; or
- served with a written charge within 14 days of commission of the offence (s 1(1)(b)); or
- served with a NIP within 14 days of commission of the offence, setting out the possibility of prosecution (s 1(1)(c)).

It is advisable to provide the NIP as a document because the suspect may later claim not to have fully understood a verbal NIP and the prosecution would have to prove the contrary (see *Gibson v Dalton* [1980] RTR 410). The NIP can also be served by post when necessary, for example when a police officer observes a vehicle go through a red traffic light and it is too dangerous to follow. A PNC check on the vehicle's registration number should provide the name and address of the registered keeper. They must state who was driving the vehicle at the time of the incident (s 172(2) of the Road Traffic Act 1988); failing to comply is an offence (s 172(3)).

In *Whiteside v DPP* [2011] EWHC 3471 (Admin) it was decided that:

- a NIP has been lawfully served if it has been posted (even if the recipient does not receive it);
- the recipient does not have a defence simply because they have no knowledge of the NIP being sent, unless it can be proved that under the circumstances it was not reasonably practicable to have been made aware of it;
- the offence is committed even if a recipient of the NIP does not know that they are obliged to state who was driving.

A NIP is not required when the vehicle concerned has been involved in an accident (s 2(1)) unless the driver failed to stop, nor is it required if an FPN was issued at the time the offence was committed (s 2(2)). The final methods of disposal after a NIP has been served include a written charge or a conditional offer of a fixed penalty.

16.12.6 National Driver Offender Retraining Scheme

Another out-of-court disposal option for road traffic offences is the National Driver Offender Retraining Scheme (NDORS). Courses available include the National Driver Alertness Course and the National Speed Awareness Course (s 89(1) of the Road Traffic Regulation Act 1984). The driver must hold a current driving licence and their actions and the circumstances must be such that there would be a realistic prospect of convicting them for the offence. If they have previously attended an NDORS for the same offence, it must have been more than three years ago. For more information, see the *National Driver Offender Retraining Scheme (NDORS): Guidance on Eligibility Criteria for NDORS Courses*, available online.

16.13 Answers to Tasks

TASK 1 Defences to using a motor vehicle on a road without a test certificate are that the vehicle is:

- being driven to a pre-arranged MOT test;
- being driven from a failed MOT test to a garage for repairs by previous arrangement (reg 6(2)(a)(i) of the Motor Vehicle (Test) Regulations 1981); or
- being towed to a place to be broken up for scrap after failing an MOT (reg 6(2)(a)(iii)(B)).

Possible defences to not having a valid test certificate could be countered by asking the driver for the starting point, destination, and reason of their journey.

TASK 2

1. (a) Jerry is driving.
   (b) Maz is not driving.
   (c) Both Hari and Pat are driving.

TASK 3

1. Using a hand-held phone while driving could easily amount to failing to have proper control of the vehicle, or even dangerous driving (see 16.8.1).
2. Other 'careless driving' activities may include lighting a cigarette, turning round and looking at children, searching for a station on the radio, changing CDs, applying make-up, or any action that diverts attention from driving.

TASK 4 Yes, in such circumstances the required sample may then be taken at a police station, regardless of whether an appropriate breath-analysis machine is available. See *Webber v DPP* [1998] RTR 111.

TASK 5 Section 22A of the Road Traffic Act 1988 states that a person is guilty of an offence if they intentionally and without lawful authority or reasonable cause:

(a) cause anything to be on or over a road;
(b) interfere with a motor vehicle, trailer, or cycle; or
(c) interfere (directly or indirectly) with traffic equipment.

17 Criminology and Crime Prevention

17.1 Introduction

In this chapter we take a brief look at the nature of disorder, crime, and criminality in England and Wales. The subject matter covered here relates to the following parts of the National Policing Curriculum: 'Criminology and Crime Prevention', 'Evidence-based Policing', and 'Research Methods and Skills'. If you are undertaking the PCDA or DHEP, you will be expected to understand 'the causes, mitigations and prevention of crime and how this knowledge and understanding can influence and be applied to accountable decision-making in all operational policing environments'.

Social media, TV, radio, and newspapers often contain reports of disorder and crime. Numerous articles and research papers are devoted to understanding why people commit crimes and why certain crimes are more prevalent than others. Some of these topics are very complex; in this chapter we simplified these issues because this is not a handbook of criminology. However, it is important that you have a general awareness of these as, in a very real sense, you will be grappling with them throughout your police career.

Over the years, criminologists, social scientists, and ordinary members of the public have become increasingly interested in finding out more about policing and the police, and numerous texts concerning the organization, administration, governance, and general understanding of police work have been published (eg Newburn, 2011; Caless and Owens, 2016; Rowe, 2018; O'Neill, 2018; Bowling, Reiner, and Sheptycki, 2019; and Wood, 2020, to name but a few). More broadly, criminology has provided the police with important theories about the nature of crime and criminal behaviour; for example, the Neighbourhood Policing Model is supported by developments in criminological theories on crime prevention, the characteristics of victims, and the spatial movements of criminals, and also by evidence-based policing.

We will now provide a selection of ways in which criminology informs contemporary policing, which may encourage you to delve deeper into the growing body of criminological research on policing and crime. Your lecturers, trainers, and tutors will, no doubt, refer you to more in-depth texts that cover some of these. First, we will consider some fundamental questions, such as the definition of crime and its possible causes.

17.2 Definitions of Crime

What is crime? The answer may seem obvious, until we begin to think through the details and test our general ideas on it.

We might, for example, say that crime is what is forbidden by law, or that crime is an activity which society would like to eradicate or prevent. We can say that crime is a social construct, that it does not exist in itself, but is rather the product of decisions on what is and is not acceptable behaviour in a particular society, at a particular moment in time. Some authors and societies will relate crime to morality and religion. On the other hand, technically, an activity is a crime only if the law defines it as such; however, laws are created by people so, in the end, we are back to individuals and society.

TASK 1

1. List three crimes that would appear to be universal.
2. List three behaviours that are considered criminal in the UK today but were not 100 years ago.
3. List three behaviours that are considered criminal in other parts of the world but not in the UK.

One could say that without reference to contextualized notions of crime, there is nothing about an activity in itself that marks it out as a crime. Consider, for example, how some forms of sexual activity between consenting adult men were officially viewed as crimes in the recent past but are no longer treated as such. There are, in fact, only very few acts that have been consistently considered crimes throughout modern history (see Task 1). Definitions of crime often change as society and our attitudes change. For example, collecting birds' eggs or hunting foxes with dogs are now seen by many as unacceptable, and the laws have followed suit. Currently, there is debate around decriminalizing certain drugs such as cannabis and the law may be changed in response to changing societal views on what should be 'legal' or not. 'Upskirting' and 'revenge porn' recently became crimes, reflecting social attitudes towards these forms of behaviour and the evolving technology (see the Voyeurism Act 2019 and the Criminal Justice and Courts Act 2015, respectively).

Hate crime illustrates a particular case of subjectivity in law, as the perception of a victim can determine whether a crime has occurred. This is because the hate element in these incidents can be defined by the victim or a witness, irrespective of whether hate was present and/or intended.

Once again, the close relationship between the law, society, and individuals is a key factor in understanding crime.

17.2.1 Crime and deviance

It has been suggested that some types of deviant behaviour might have a role in promoting beneficial changes in society and that we should therefore be wary of too hastily classifying deviant behaviour as criminal. For example, John Stuart Mill (1806–73) believed it was important for the development of a healthy society that individuals should have as much freedom as possible, primarily because individuals who deviate from the norm can help society to advance. There are numerous examples throughout history of individuals, some of whom we now celebrate as heroes, who were regarded as a threat to society at an earlier time. In the UK, there are also examples of people and campaign groups willing to break the law, for example animal rights activists, anti-abortionists, and environmentalists such as Extinction Rebellion. These groups believe they are promoting values or demanding changes that will become widely accepted in the future, in the same way that those fighting at previous times in history for equal rights for women or the abolition of the slave trade eventually came to be recognized as heroic figures. However, there is no possible way to foresee which views that are currently deviations from the norm might become the accepted view in the future.

17.3 The Causes of Crime

There are different ways we can explain the causes of crime. Some are incompatible, others complement each other. For example, Blackburn (1995) made a distinction between crimes and criminality. He stated that people commit crimes as a rational response to the environment in which they find themselves and that criminality is a characteristic of an individual that emphasizes a propensity to commit crimes. This introduces us to an area of constant discussion and argument in criminological circles, namely the nature–nurture debate. Are criminals born as such, or do people become criminals due to the society they live in?

17.3.1 Criminal by nature?

The concept of criminality developed from what is referred to as the Positivist school of criminology, associated with Cesare Lombroso's *L'Uomo Delinquente* (*The Criminal Man*), published in 1876. Positivists believe that social life can be studied objectively and scientifically by employing methods comparable to those used in the natural sciences (Tierney, 2009). They suggest that criminals are pathological and distinct from non-criminals and, as such, criminality is determined by factors beyond their immediate control, rather than a product of their free will (Jones and Newburn, 1998, pp 101–2).

There are three main types of positivist theories:

- 'biological positivism' which suggests that some forms of criminality are due to a biological abnormality in the individual, such as a chemical imbalance in the brain, or unusual levels of certain hormones;
- 'psychological positivism' which suggests that some forms of criminality are linked to inter-related personality traits such as 'impulsivity'; and
- 'sociological positivism' which suggests that the social environment, such as the presence of anti-social subcultures, can lead to some forms of crime.

17.3.2 Criminal through nurture?

Some criminologists, however, propose that individuals are not (pre)determined to commit crimes, but rather that this is the result of a process. For example, rational choice theory (Cornish and Clarke, 1986) argues that criminals make a rational decision before committing a crime; they have thought through (at some level at least) their reasons for committing a criminal act, and rationalized the need to commit it. As such, a single parent with no money who steals nappies for their baby is certainly committing a crime, but we can see their actions as the result of a process of rationalization of circumstances and available options. However, we also know that not all parents in the same situation would resort to shoplifting. Irrespective of which moral position is adopted, this particular crime can be understood as a social response, rather than as an individual failing or compulsion to commit crime. This view is associated with what is referred to as classical criminology, which emerged in the late eighteenth century and informed the thinking of law reformers at the time (eg Bentham, Howard, Beccaria). This view of crime suggests that anyone could become a criminal given the right circumstances and that punishment is required to act as a deterrent to crime.

17.3.3 Nature and nurture

The relative effects of nature (how we are 'pre-wired') and nurture (the effect of our environment and upbringing) have been debated for centuries, but more recent research is beginning to clarify the relative contribution of each to our behaviour.

Nature refers to what we are born with or (such as our genetic make-up), and nurture relates to the environmental contexts in which we develop and includes everything from our schooling to how our parents and local community raised us.

The debates have frequently been polemical and exclusionary; that is, those favouring 'nature' explanations would dismiss 'nurture' as an influence and vice versa. However, the nature/nurture debate can often be oversimplified. Increasingly, today we recognize that both nature *and* nurture form part of the explanation and, indeed, that it is not always easy to distinguish one from the other, particularly as modern biology continues to uncover examples of genetic predispositions being either masked or revealed by various environmental factors.

17.3.4 Desistance

Most people reduce or stop their offending after an initial period of committing frequent crimes (and sometimes never commit any further offences). Stopping criminal activity is called 'desistance'. The reasons for this desistance are not clear and have only recently been subjected to rigorous academic enquiry (see Maruna, 2017 for example). It appears, perhaps unsurprisingly, that desistance is linked in part to the person's motivation and thinking, and that external threats (eg of punishment) will only have a limited effect. Personal relationships and the amount of social capital a person can access seem to be far more significant factors.

17.3.5 Criminological theories and policing

As already indicated above, some criminological approaches sought to explain crime by focusing on the free will of those committing crimes. This was countered by Positivist criminological accounts, which identify biological, psychological, and/or sociological characteristics that led to crime, making criminals distinct from the law-abiding population. There are numerous criminological theories that develop from these roots and are particularly important in policing. There is also a growing acknowledgement of the various ways in which individuals, groups, and communities are denied equal opportunities to live a successful life, which can lead to criminal alternatives. Policing, therefore, requires ever more awareness of the social contexts and a greater understanding of the links between the vulnerabilities imposed on people. On this last point, we are increasingly aware of the fact that criminals may also be victims of crime.

Some key criminological schools of thought and ensuing criminological theories include:

School	Example of theory	Brief description of theory	Possible application within policing
Classical or neo-classical	Rational Choice	Crime is a rational act that needs no special explanation; it results from a 'cost–benefits' analysis	Offering crime prevention advice after online fraud
	Routine Activity	Crime occurs when motivated offenders and attractive targets intersect in time and space, with no or ineffective capable guardianship	Policing of crime hotspots
	Control/General Theory of Crime	Crime is caused by a lack of effective controls (external, or within the individual)	Conducting 'visible' police patrol
Sociological	Social Disorganization	The breakdown of informal social controls allows the progressive dominance of criminal cultures (see also 'Broken Windows' theory)	Police provide support for members of the public, and workers such as bus drivers and park keepers
	Social Learning/ Differential Association/ Subcultures	Crime is a form of behaviour that is learned through association with criminals or people who tolerate crime	Police referring suspected 'gang members' to other agencies
Positivist	Strain (anomie)	Some individuals lack legitimate opportunities to achieve their goals (eg wealth, status, authority) and use illegal means instead to achieve them	Use of police discretion in case of suspected shoplifting by a child
	Labelling	Some individuals are 'labelled' as criminal or anti-social, and they unwittingly adopt the label (a form of self-fulfilling prophecy)	Adopting a professional approach when conducting 'stop and search'

17.4 Measuring Crime

There are various means of measuring crime, for example police and criminal justice statistical records, large-scale surveys (mostly government-sponsored), and small-scale academic studies. The government and criminal justice agencies use recorded crime figures from the police and crime surveys, such as the Crime Survey for England & Wales (CSEW), the Northern Ireland Crime Survey (NICS), and the Scottish Crime and Justice Survey (SCJS), as their key sources of information. In these crime surveys, thousands of households are randomly selected and interviews are conducted with the aim of measuring both recorded and unrecorded crime.

Various factors will tend to distort the accuracy of these measurements. Factors include the under-reporting of crime by the public, the under-recording of crime by the police, changes in recording practices, political interest, and intellectual bias. This distortion can also lead to difficulties in making meaningful comparisons between current crime levels and those in the past. Under-reporting and under-recording are particularly problematic for the police and have received considerable attention. Indeed, this led HMIC (2014c, p 49) to state that 'Victims of crime are being let down. The police are failing to record a large proportion of the crimes reported to them.'

Research practices can also contribute to a distorted picture of the true extent of crime. This can be due to weaknesses in the research design; for example, there may be inaccuracies due to small sample sizes, uneven access to research participants, ethical barriers, organizational limitations, and funding restrictions.

The CSEW and its predecessor (the British Crime Survey—BCS) are considered by many to be one of the most comprehensive crime surveys in the world, but even here there are limitations. For example, it was only in January 2009 that the BCS began including 10- to 15-year-olds in the survey, and it was not until 2016 that the CSEW first included questions to assess the extent of fraud and computer misuse offences. More recently, due to Covid-related restrictions, the CSEW had to be conducted by telephone only. It should also be noted that the wording of the questions in the survey has changed over the years and, because of this, year-on-year comparisons can be compromised. In addition, the wording of the questions has been shown to influence respondents' answers about 'fear of crime' (Farrall and Gadd, 2004).

Recognizing these limitations, researchers constantly review their methods to ensure that crime surveys are robust and as useful as possible. Establishing a more accurate picture of the extent of crime and ensuring that it is recorded properly are important aspects of modern policing.

17.4.1 Reported incidents and recorded crime

An important distinction needs to be made between *reported* crime (reports made by a member of the public to the police) and *recorded* crime. Imagine a person witnesses a heated argument in the street, perhaps with some pushing, shoving, and screaming. They phone the police and report it; the police will take note of the content of the call (it will be registered, or 'logged' in police jargon—see 13.5.1.1 for further discussion of police response to incoming calls). This registration of the incident is what most commentators mean when they refer to reported crime.

The police then must decide whether the incident should be recorded as an actual crime (a so-called 'notifiable offence'). They will first need to decide whether the circumstances as reported by the caller amount to an offence, based on their knowledge and the counting rules from the National Crime Recording Standard (NCRS) and Home Office Counting Rules (HOCR) which are currently under review. The police will also consider whether there is any credible evidence to the contrary. If on 'the balance of probability' the circumstances described in the report amount to an offence as defined by the law, then the incident should be recorded as a crime (Home Office, 2014e and 2018b).

As our incident illustrates, the decision is far from simple. In response to my call the police are required to make all reasonable enquiries to identify specific victims and secure any supporting evidence. Although pushing and shoving could technically be an offence of assault or battery (see 22.2) or a public order offence (see 3.8.3), this would depend on the circumstances, and these would probably not be clear from the account over the phone. More importantly, if a victim is unlikely to be identified, the basic recording rule of 'no victim, no crime' would be applied (although there are exceptions to this rule).

It has been acknowledged that there is a 'degree of subjective interpretation in making decisions about how to record crimes' (HMIC, 2013, p 3) and there are still major issues regarding how the police deal with incidents reported by the public. For example, an HMIC report (2014c, p 63) found that that only 81 per cent of the total crimes reported to the police were in fact recorded correctly, meaning that approximately 800,000 crimes per year, despite being reported to police, were not being recorded as such. Indeed, even more recently HMICFRS published a report regarding Greater Manchester Police's crime statistics which found that 'Over one in five of all crimes reported to Greater Manchester are not making it onto the books' (2020b, p 4).

The diagram shows some of the key decisions that are made after an incident is reported to the police.

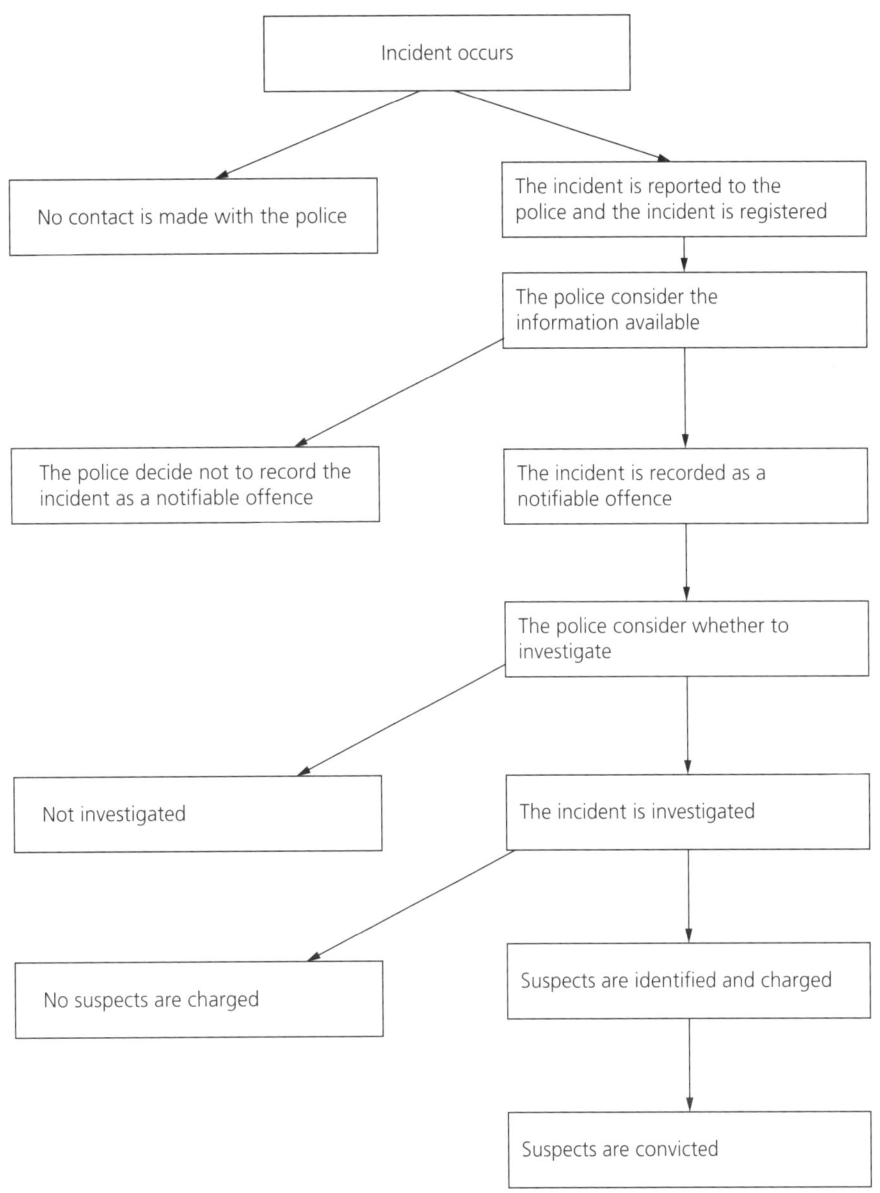
Incident occurs
No contact is made with the police
The incident is reported to the police and the incident is registered
The police consider the information available
The police decide not to record the incident as a notifiable offence
The incident is recorded as a notifiable offence
The police consider whether to investigate
Not investigated
The incident is investigated
No suspects are charged
Suspects are identified and charged
Suspects are convicted

17.4.1.1 National Crime Recording Standard and Home Office Counting Rules

The NCRS considers victims' reports to the police and applies legal definitions of crime to identify which crimes have been committed. It is used to ensure crimes are recorded in accordance with the law. The HOCR help to ensure that crimes are recorded consistently and accurately. It could be said that the HOCR are 'what must be done', the NCRS are 'why it must be done' (HMIC, 2014b). The College of Policing Code of Ethics emphasizes that complying with the NCRS is central to the HOCR.

Crime recording and counting methods were changed by the Home Office in 2013 and 2014, replacing the old system under which crimes were classed as either 'detected', 'undetected', or 'no crime'. There were then 21 possible outcomes for each recorded crime; for example, charge/summons, taking offences into consideration (TICs), community resolution, prosecution not in the public interest, and investigation complete—no suspect identified (for a full list see Heap, 2017, p 13).

The processes of reporting and recording crime are complex, and a review is again currently ongoing at the Home Office to revise the existing rules.

17.4.2 The perception of crime

The Covid-19 pandemic will have undoubtedly skewed crime levels in England and Wales due to the various lockdowns that have occurred. However, prior to this there was a general acceptance that the fear of crime and disorder has increased in recent years. For example, the CSEW ending March 2020 found that 82 per cent of adults believed that crime had risen nationally (ONS, 2020c). However, during this period most forms of recorded crime decreased, so it seems the year-on-year trends about perceptions in the survey might not be in line with recorded crimes (see 17.4 and Farrall and Gadd, 2004).

The survey also suggests that some sectors of the community are more likely to believe that crime has risen significantly, and to worry more about crime. For example, the CSEW ending March 2019 (ONS, 2020c) suggested that:

- women were more likely than men to believe that crime had risen in recent years, both nationally and locally;
- people aged 75 and over were most likely to believe that crime had risen nationally in recent years, while people in the 35–44 and the 45–54 age groups were more likely to believe that crime was increasing locally;
- individuals living in the most deprived areas perceived a larger rise in local and national crime in recent years (compared with people living in less deprived areas).

It is important to note that according to official statistics, those who feel most worried about crime or who perceive crime to be increasing are not necessarily the most likely to become victims of crime. Having said this, being fearful of crime is itself a form of harm to an individual, and the lifestyle implications can be profound. Therefore, an elderly person's statistically 'irrational' fears about crime still need to be taken into account. Another factor to consider is that even if the risk of an incident (such as a physical attack) may be low, the negative consequences of such an incident could be very high.

A key reason why many people overestimate the extent of crime and disorder is that people tend to base their judgements on the more obvious and visible local crimes or anti-social behaviour. Innes (2014) refers to these as 'signal crimes' or 'signal disorders', and believes they are perceived by residents as warning signals about the level of insecurity in their neighbourhood, even though they may be treated as less serious by the criminal justice agencies. Examples of signal crimes and disorder include:

- public drinking, swearing, and rowdy and uncivil behaviour;
- litter, graffiti, and other forms of damage and vandalism;
- evidence of drug taking and dealing, and prostitution;
- speeding;
- rubbish dumped in the street or outside houses; and
- abandoned or burnt-out vehicles.

Once spotted, these signals can give rise to a heightened sense of awareness, and individuals are more likely to notice other similar examples—a self-reinforcing feedback loop.

17.5 Modelling Crime and Criminality

Let us now move on from these general theories (often concerned with human nature and society) to examples of more detailed explanatory models, and suggest some possible responses for the police and others. A good account of criminological theories can be found in Roger Hopkins Burke's *An Introduction to Criminological Theory*, 5th edn (2019) and his more recent work (2021).

17.5.1 Opportunities for crime

Rational choice theory (Cornish and Clarke, 1986, see 17.3.2) assumes that criminals employ the same kind of thought processes as non-criminals when making everyday, non-criminal decisions (Wilson, 1996, p 312). Criminal activity results from an assessment of the circumstances and a choice to engage in certain behaviour. As a result, usually, crimes occur if they are easy to commit, and the results are sufficiently rewarding.

Routine-activity theory (Felson, 2002) is also predicated on the relationship between an individual's everyday experiences and their criminal behaviour. It suggests that crime occurs if there is: a motivated offender, a suitable target, and the absence of a guardian. The idea is that criminal opportunities arise when these three components coincide. For example, in a certain situation the number of offences might increase if there are few guardians and plenty of suitable targets, even if there is no increase in the number of motivated offenders. For example, schools are places where there are significant numbers of vulnerable children with mobile phones (suitable targets), and there are other largely unsupervised children who are keen to acquire them (motivated offenders and absence of guardians).

17.5.2 The 'hot' model

Some of the constituent elements of crime can be considered as being 'hot': that is, both frequently occurring and worthy of attention. The following owes much to Clarke (1999), although some terms such as 'hot offender' are of our own devising. Therefore, this section will discuss 'hot spots', 'hot offenders', and 'hot products'. It should be noted that the 'hot' model of crime might need to be adapted (or even abandoned) for cybercrime because it is difficult to determine the actual location for internet crimes; however, the notion of 'hot products' and repeat victimization are still relevant in cybercrime.

'Hot spots' are places that are particularly prone to crime, such as railway stations, shopping centres, high streets, particular shops and houses, post offices, or flats. These are related to the 'easy pickings' for people who are intent on theft, shoplifting, or mugging, for example. In addition, these may also be related to opportunity, for example in the vicinity of cash machines or racecourses, where people are more likely to be carrying large quantities of cash or other items of potential value. Hot spots create an uneven distribution of crime; in a city there will be some particular and relatively small geographical area that always, or nearly always, has a high crime rate (of all types), while other areas will be virtually crime free. Until some preventative action is taken, these hot spots will persist, and even if action is taken, they may still recur (see 17.6.2). However, Eck *et al* (2017, p 1) argue that the phenomenon of crime 'hot spots' is 'naturally occurring' and argue that 'the concentration of crime at places is unexceptional and should be treated as one manifestation of a general tendency of things to be concentrated'.

'Hot offenders' are defined as the relatively small number of people who are responsible for the majority of crime. A review by Marinez *et al* (2017, p 1) found that 'crime is highly concentrated in the population and across different types of offenders'. Furthermore, research, for example by Everson and Pease (2001), on repeat victimization (see 'hot victims') suggests that prolific offenders may be responsible for the bulk of these repeated crimes against the same person or target. However, opinion and research continue to differ over just how small a minority of criminals is responsible for just how large a majority of crimes.

'Hot products' are the items we know are more attractive to burglars or street robbers, and there is a logic to what they choose to steal. Clarke (1999) suggests a mnemonic for rating hot products: CRAVED.

C	Concealable
R	Removable
A	Available
V	Valuable
E	Enjoyable
D	Disposable

The CRAVED model can be used as a means of judging just how attractive an object may be for a thief. In the original work by Clarke (1999), disposability was considered to be one of the most important factors. Thieves prefer items which they can get rid of quickly and without fuss although they will probably receive only a small proportion of the retail value of the item (handling stolen goods is covered in 23.5). The average volume criminal will go for small items of value which are easily transportable and not easily traced. This is why cash (pre-eminently) and jewellery are popular targets for thieves. Cash, of course, is easily disposed of and generally untraceable, and most rings and watches are easily converted into money. Smartphones and laptops are also popular targets.

TASK 2 Estimate how CRAVED the following articles might be:

- an iPad;
- a laptop;
- £642.89 in coins;
- a 2012 mobile phone; and
- a manuscript copy of *The Lindisfarne Gospels*.

Processing Policing

Clearly, there are many possible interactions between hot spots, hot offenders, and hot products. Hot offenders are more likely to want hot products, and to target hot spots because, as we noted earlier, there are relatively easy opportunities for crime and relatively little chance of being caught. And, of course, the same offenders may return to burgle the same house again. It is hard to disentangle cause and effect, but the uneven distribution of crime cannot be ignored.

The concept of repeat victims, hotspots, and offenders forms part of the problem-oriented policing (POP) approach (see 11.3.2.2). This was ultimately linked to intelligence-led policing and the National Intelligence Model (see 12.6), a core element of Neighbourhood Policing Strategy in England and Wales.

17.5.3 Repeat victimization

Research into repeat victimization was initiated in the 1970s; however, it was the Kirkholt Burglary Prevention Project, which successfully targeted repeat burglaries for prevention (Seymore, 2001), that spurred other prevention efforts and a broader range of research into the extent and nature of repeat victimization from the late 1980s. The Home Office, in particular, supported a programme of research and development into repeat victimization with publications throughout the 1980s and 1990s.

It is important to note that 'victimization' in the academic literature (and to a lesser extent in policing circles) applies to more than people: it can include crime 'against' households, business premises, and vehicles and perhaps it would be better to use the word 'target'. Labelling someone as a 'victim' has been critiqued in the wider social science literature and sometimes the word 'survivor' is used instead.

One consequence of the increased interest in this phenomenon is the fact that it is now common for studies to incorporate a measure of repeat victimization. The previous practice of focusing on the number of crimes as 'the crime rate' was thought to be frequently misleading (Grove and Farrell, 2011).

The extent of repeat victimization in England and Wales is difficult to estimate for several reasons, including police recording systems. One study in 1998 found that approximately 2 per cent of the population experienced 44 per cent of property crime, and that 1 per cent of the population 'accounted for' 59 per cent of all personal crime (Pease, 1998).

An important distinction is between 'pure repeat' victims and 'near repeat' victims. Pure repeats are when the same person or household is victimized again and 'near repeat victimization' is when the crime is repeated nearby, but with a different victim. This distinction is important as the two types of victimization are thought to occur for somewhat different reasons (see Chainey, 2012).

In terms of cybercrime, repeat victimization is less well understood; however, a similar phenomenon to non-virtual victimization appears to be emerging: a minority of victims (people, websites) account for the majority of the crimes (such as online fraud, or Distributed Denial-of-Service (DDoS) attacks).

17.5.3.1 Pure repeat victimization

Pure repeats are when the same 'target', for example the same person or household, is repeatedly victimized. The repeat generally takes place quite soon after the original incident. Intuitively, it could be expected that old age, frailty, and naivety would make a person more vulnerable to 'pure repeat' victimization than the average person. There is, however, not much empirical evidence to support this, other than for distraction burglary (see the start of 23.4). The reasons for pure repeat victimization are not clearly understood, although research does suggest a number of possible factors (including combinations of factors). For example, the same household may be repeatedly burgled (sometimes by the same offender) and the reasons for this could be that:

- there is something inherently 'risky' about the location of the house or flat itself (it is close, but not too close, to the offender's 'anchor point'—see routine-activity theory);
- the perpetrator will be familiar with the layout of the dwelling;
- the perpetrator will be aware that stolen items may have been replaced with new items which can be taken on a subsequent burglary.

For interpersonal crimes (such as assault) there may be aspects of the victims' lifestyle that lead to an increased risk of pure repeat victimization, for example the kind of activities they undertake and their vulnerability or proximity to the offender in certain circumstances. A particularly important example of this kind of repeat victimization is domestic abuse (see 19.5).

If you are undertaking initial police training (via the Police Constable Degree Apprenticeship (PCDA) or Degree Holder Entry Programme (DHEP)), then you will probably receive inputs on the kind of crime prevention advice to provide for 'pure repeat' victims. Many constabularies will also have repeat victimization policies and procedures which will outline 'victim management' and reduction measures available to both the service and individual officers.

17.5.3.2 Near repeat victimization

Near repeats are, for example, when one household in a street has been burgled, and then nearby households are burgled soon after. The phenomenon is probably one of the causes of geographically located crime hotspots (see 17.5.2). As Farrell and Pease claimed, primarily high crime areas are high because of the numbers of repeat victimizations (2016). The modelling of near repeat victimization is often built into the algorithms for so-called 'predictive policing', but the success of this approach has been queried. For example, Chainey *et al* (2018, p 619) conducted research on data from New Zealand, and pointed out that the 'use of repeats and near repeats as a prediction and prevention framework is unlikely to yield consistent positive results'.

> **TASK 3** Does your local police constabulary use any 'predictive policing' algorithms? If so, how are they used to assist operational policing? How effective are they?

17.5.4 Social learning theory and differential association

One of the major criminological theories is 'social learning theory'. It was developed from Edwin Sutherland's differential association theory, and subsequently revised by others. According to social learning theory, crime is a learned behaviour and, in this sense, is essentially no different from other more socially acceptable learned behaviours, such as waiting in queues and taking turns. Individuals, particularly young people, learn through communicating and participating in groups, and for young children this is mainly the family. The child assimilates a general sense of what is 'normal' from personal experiences and what they see in day-to-day events. From adolescence onwards, other social groups become more influential, including peer groups. However, it is important to note that social learning theory is not the same as 'peer group pressure' but is instead a more subtle form of social learning. Social learning theory would predict that if a person associates mainly with groups that consider crime as normal and acceptable behaviour, and less frequently with those that consider criminal acts as unacceptable, the person is more likely to adopt the stance of the former than the latter. Hence, 'differential association' underpins the rationale for the theory.

Social learning theory would therefore seem to provide a persuasive explanation for at least some forms of crime. However, there are some general limitations for such theories, for example differential association offers no explanation for why people in superficially similar circumstances behave so differently or why do some choose to 'learn' deviant behaviour whilst others do not (Newburn, 2017). Also, like most 'general' theories of crime, it does not account for differences in offending between men and women. We would suggest that part of the explanation might be that a person is not merely a passive recipient of their environment; most people play an active role in creating and shaping their immediate environment, for instance when choosing friends and leisure activities.

17.6 Crime Reduction

We often hear the terms 'crime prevention', 'crime reduction', and 'community safety' used both within policing and more widely. Ekblom (2001) draws subtle distinctions between these concepts, whereas Pease (2002) suggests they are different expressions of the same thing. We will use the terms interchangeably.

Crime prevention is a long-standing but often neglected policing priority. Today we recognize that all police officers have a crime prevention responsibility, and that this is not simply the role of a designated 'Crime Prevention Officer' (as was the case in the recent past). The police now have a better understanding of how preventative measures can help to reduce crime, and that crime prevention is an integral aspect of a police officer's duties, alongside crime detection. Furthermore, crime prevention can be used in a targeted and directed manner to reduce crime and to thereby free more police resources. Given the apparent huge growth in online crime (see Chapter 14) and the current very low rates of detection for this form of criminal activity, crime prevention measures increasingly need to include public cyber-security awareness.

Crime can be reduced to some extent through detecting crimes and imprisoning (potential repeat) offenders. However, preventing crimes from happening in the first place represents a far more rational and economical approach, and provides clear benefits to society. The targeted use of crime prevention forms part of a problem-oriented approach to reducing crime (see 11.3.2.2). It is informed by routine-activity theory (see the start of 17.5.1) and the idea that there are three components of crime: the offender, the victim, and the location of a crime. Police officers should consider why a crime has occurred, as this can help to identify the appropriate preventative measures. The police response then becomes more proactive (as opposed to reactive).

The crime reduction agenda has also been bolstered by the move towards partnership approaches in policing and the increasing emphasis on crime prevention has altered the role of the police. Crime prevention requires good intelligence, and it is therefore important that police officers make the most of information provided by local intelligence officers. In turn, investigators also need to share information with the local intelligence officers (see 12.5 and 13.8.4). This joined-up approach was enshrined in the ten Principles of Neighbourhood Policing which were introduced by the National Centre for Policing Excellence in 2006 (NCPE/ACPO, 2006). The NCPE later merged with the National Police Improvement Agency and ultimately became part of the College of Policing. These form the core of the Neighbourhood Policing Guidelines which the College of Policing produced in 2018 (CoP, 2018c).

It is important that any intervention is properly evaluated. Policing in general (and crime reduction in particular) is increasingly subject to research and evaluation, and the results of this research will help to ensure that any claims used to justify preventative strategies are based on firm evidence (see eg Smith and Tilley, 2005).

The new emphasis on integrating crime prevention into everyday police work means that police officers must continually anticipate, recognize, and assess the risk of criminal activity. Measures can then be taken to reduce the risk. These measures could be straightforward, for example simply providing the public with crime prevention advice, but in some situations a more concerted effort is required.

17.6.1 Reducing the opportunities for crime

As an example, consider an unlit pathway which provides criminals with an appropriate location for committing crime. A police officer needs to be able to evaluate what short-term measures can be taken to reduce the criminal opportunity (eg increase the guardianship of the unlit pathway by increasing police patrols), but the police must also ensure that a longer term solution is provided (for example, by contacting the local council to ensure the lighting problem is addressed).

Routine-activity theory (RAT) and rational choice theory (RCT) are often used to explore the various causes of crime. Using these, it follows that preventative techniques could be organized under three headings: increasing the effort (eg target hardening), increasing the risks (eg CCTV), and reducing the rewards (eg marking property). Pease (2002) adds a fourth heading: 'reducing the excuses' or, in other words, making it harder for the offender to provide a valid or appropriate rationale for why they have carried out certain acts, and perhaps in the process causing them to feel guilty or ashamed. The relative significance of each of these strategies depends upon the particular crime in question: which strategy is most likely to have the greatest deterrent impact on the potential criminal?

TASK 4 Consider the following scenarios and identify whether increasing the effort, increasing the risk, or reducing the reward would be the most effective preventative measure. To some extent all three would be appropriate but try to identify the one that you think addresses the problem most directly.

1. There have been a number of valuable thefts from vehicles in a supermarket car park.
2. A shop is being repeatedly targeted at night by a group of known drug addicts.
3. Small amounts of money are being stolen by a member of staff from within a bank.

Routine-activity theory (Felson, 2002) suggests some other approaches that may be used in crime reduction: for example, ensuring that motivated offenders are not left unobserved where there are easy criminal targets, for example, goods that could be stolen. This theory suggests that the number of motivated offenders does not have to be reduced in order to reduce crime; they simply need to be monitored more closely. Goods could also be redesigned so that they are more difficult to sell on. To some extent routine-activity theory can also be applied to help to reduce the opportunities for online crime as well as the more 'well-established' crimes that involve physical locations. Online crime, however, does not have the relationship of proximity or distance between offenders and targets; here, the relevance of RAT is therefore more problematic (Leukfeldt and Var, 2016).

17.6.2 Environmental criminology

Environmental criminology (also known as socio-spatial criminology or sometimes the 'geography of crime') considers the spatial distribution of crime, criminality, and victimization. It should not be confused with Green Criminology or crimes against the environment. Environmental criminology is closely linked to 'situational crime prevention' (SCP), and also has links with routine-activity theory. SCP involves designing products, services, environments, or systems to reduce the likelihood of crime. Examples include traffic enforcement cameras for motoring offences, increased use of CCTV, designing better laid out housing estates to restrict vehicular access, and using metal detectors at airports.

Environmental criminology focuses less on criminality (eg the motivation of the offender as an individual, ie the 'why?') and more on crime events (the 'where?' and the 'when?').

Two 'principles' (essentially assumptions based on empirical research) underpin environmental criminology:

- the behaviour of offenders is significantly affected by the environment; and
- crime is non-randomly distributed in space and time (see hotspots in 17.5.2).

In practical terms, environmental criminology considers 'crime patterns', 'crime trends', 'distance of travel to crime', and how these relate to the physical environment. Understanding these patterns could help to reduce crime or even to identify an unknown offender. For example, some offenders will only commit certain offences beyond a certain distance from where they live (the 'anchor point'), but not too far away. Thus, a series of such crimes will take place within a broad ring (known in the US as the 'doughnut theory'). Beyond the crime-free zone around the offender's home location (the hole of the doughnut), the number of crimes committed by the offender decreases as the distance from the anchor point increases (a 'distance decay' effect), in a roughly mathematically predictable way. An application of environmental criminology would be to 'work backwards' from the crime location data to try to establish where an unknown serial offender is likely to live; this is an example of 'geographical profiling'.

17.6.3 The prevention of hot spots

The persistent presence of police officers, PCSOs, or local authority wardens would undoubtedly have a deterrent effect on hot spots, but this cannot be sustained for long due to its cost. Possible alternatives would be regular 10- to 15-minute patrols—the 'more but shorter' proposal. It has also been suggested that a more effective approach might be fewer visits of longer duration (Williams and Coupe, 2017). CCTV cameras are a possible short-term solution at a relatively lower cost, especially if coordinated with police action on the ground such as 'blitzes' on pickpockets, for example.

A longer-term and better solution is to 'design out' crime, for example by installing carefully designed walkways and better street lighting. Intelligence (see Chapter 12) is also likely to be an important part of any approach to dealing with hot spots. Analysts will consider the types of crime, the times when they occur, the sorts of people who commit those crimes, and the seasonal impact (if any) upon the nature of the crime. A detailed understanding and taking appropriate measures may lead to the cooling of a hot spot. Dealing with cybercrime hotspots on the internet normally involves a number of national agencies and private companies (such as ISPs).

17.6.4 Crime prevention advice

Crime prevention is the responsibility of all police officers, but a specialist Crime Prevention Officer (CPO) can provide further advice. The crime should be considered from the perspective of the victim, the offender, and the location. Pertinent questions can then be asked about why a crime has occurred, and this can help to provide the basis for practical solutions. The advice can be tailored to specific contexts, for example, regarding the most suitable locks, lighting, and other basic security measures in a home where a burglary has recently taken place. There is also a specific need to tailor crime prevention messages aimed at young people, children, and those at particular risk within online environments. The lessons learnt during the investigation of one particular crime incident should also be used to help to prevent future criminal activities.

Police officers can encourage communities as a whole to become involved in implementing effective crime prevention strategies, for example, Neighbourhood Watch schemes (see 3.3.3) and Street Watch. In addition, Neighbourhood Policing Teams (sometimes known as Safer Neighbourhood Teams (SNTs)), Crime Prevention Panels (CPPs), and Community Safety Partnerships (CSPs), all provide a local focus for crime prevention measures, alongside the national Crimestoppers Trust which works in collaboration with the police (see Chapter 11 on community policing).

17.6.5 Displacement

Crime prevention can lead to crime displacement, that is, crimes merely happening in other locations or at a later time (Johnson *et al*, 2014). Displaced crime may also occur through criminal innovation (see the following list). Displacement builds on the idea that those with a disposition to commit crimes will adapt and find different ways in which to realize their criminal intentions. The following types of displacement have been identified.

- **Temporal displacement:** the crime takes place at a later time. As an example, consider the depot that introduces a security guard overnight to counter a string of night-time burglaries, so the criminals choose a different time to commit the offence.
- **Spatial displacement:** the crime happens at another location. For example, a high police presence is introduced in Area 1 to address alleged incidents of anti-social behaviour from a group of young people, but some members of the group simply move to Area 2 and behave in the same way.
- **Displacement by type of crime:** the criminals turn to different crimes. Suppose that the local council introduces better street lighting on an estate prone to street robberies. The number of robberies falls but the number of burglaries increases in the area.
- **Displacement by innovation:** the criminals become better at what they do. An example is that people no longer carry large amounts of cash. As a result, some criminals turn to using stolen credit cards, thereby gaining access to sums of money in a different way.

Pease (1997) suggested that the extent of displacement is often exaggerated, and that the issue is raised on ideological rather than empirical grounds, as an excuse for taking no action. He also argues that displacement is never likely to be complete and illustrates ways in which displacement can be an advantage. For example, it might be beneficial to move a crime from one area to another to reduce its overall impact on society, or to change the type of crime committed. For instance, if sex-workers are soliciting on the street in a family residential area, it seems likely that a high police presence would move them on to another area. If they move to a non-residential area, it could reduce the concern that any children would be affected, but this needs to be balanced against a separate concern for the safety of the sex-workers. Some might innovate and use more discreet means of operating, while others might desist from sex-work. The effects of displacement can be predicted and then compared with the effect in practice. As Pease puts it, displacement is positive as long as 'the deflected crime causes less harm and misery than the original crime' (Pease, 1997, p 978).

17.6.6 Procedural justice

Procedural justice focuses on the way the police (and other legal authorities) interact with the public, particularly 'face to face', and how these interactions shape the public perception of the police. Claims have been made, particularly in the US, that 'if police treat citizens respectfully and make decisions in a fair way, then it can enhance public perceptions of police legitimacy' (Murphy, 2014, see also 3.2.7 on police legitimacy). This is thought to be true even if the outcome for a member of the public is a negative one, such as being arrested.

The concepts and research underpinning procedural justice are having a significant impact within both academic and professional policing spheres. For example, the College of Policing expects police officers to adopt a 'procedural justice approach' when conducting a stop and search (CoP, 2017b).

Procedural justice is based on some key principles: the police should treat people with dignity and respect, they must be neutral in their decision-making, and police actions must be seen to be fair and proportionate in the circumstances. It is important that policing is not seen as simply a rigid application of the law and associated police powers but also as acting fairly. A reasoned and principled use of professional discretion promotes police legitimacy, and procedural justice is likely to play a part in this. There is empirical evidence that the degree of procedural justice in a particular country is a good predictor of the level of state police legitimacy. It is also the case at the level of the individual that the way a police officer behaves and reacts to others has a bearing on the officer's personal authority.

However, simply applying procedural justice principles to everyday policing will not automatically lead to desirable outcomes. As Waddington *et al* (2017) observe, different people will interpret the same action of the police in a particular situation ('vignette') in different ways. A person's judgement about police authority and legitimacy may be rooted in experiences (their own, and the experiences of others) that predate any direct contact with the police.

17.7 Answers to Tasks

TASK 1 There are many possible answers, and we provide some suggestions here.

1. The answer is somewhat speculative, but they would seem likely to include theft, murder, and rape.
2. Activities that were not considered as crimes 100 years ago but are today include stalking and some types of outdoor night-time music and dancing events.
3. Activities that are not considered as crimes in the UK but are in some other countries include adultery (Nigeria), consuming alcohol (Saudi Arabia), and keeping African pygmy hedgehogs (some states of the US).

TASK 2 There is a difference between intrinsic value and 'CRAVED'. The thieves would probably leave the coins behind because they are bulky and heavy. The iPad would be easily pocketed for selling on. However, traffic in particular electronic goods is often short-lived as it is often the next-generation goods that the 'fences' demand; a 2012 mobile phone would yield no return and the laptop may be old and heavy. Apple Inc have introduced additional security measures in recent years to increase the difficulty of 'fencing' stolen iPads and iPhones. The manuscript would be very valuable but difficult to sell on. However, organized drugs importers and traffickers have used valuable art such as paintings or sculptures as 'cash' for their transactions—the more so since the Proceeds of Crime Act 2002 made depositing large amounts of cash in a bank account subject to scrutiny and investigation.

TASK 3 Kent Police started to use the commercial 'PredPol' predictive policing system in 2013, at a cost of around £100,000 per year (Chowdhury, 2018). However, in 2018 they cancelled their contract with the US firm concerned, explaining that it was 'challenging' to demonstrate whether the system had enabled police to reduce crime (BBC News, 2018).

When predictive policing algorithms were first marketed it was usually on the basis of their supposed ability to accurately and precisely 'predict' crime using 'scientific' (mathematical) algorithms performed using computing technology. However, as Ratcliffe (2014, p 5) noted, predictive policing is better thought of as the 'use of historical data to create a spatiotemporal forecast of areas of criminality or crime hot spots that will be the basis for police resource allocation decisions'. It is this coupling of operational decision-making with crime forecasting that forms the basis of any claim of novelty for 'predictive policing'.

There has also been some controversy, particularly in the US, around whether some of the algorithms involved lead to inadvertent and ongoing racial bias through a form of feedback loop.

TASK 4

1. Reducing the reward. The fact that the cars targeted have valuables on show suggests that the offenders are looking for easy rewards. The most cost-effective measure is likely to be encouraging people not to leave valuables in the car.
2. Increasing the effort. We can assume that these particular offenders are desperate and therefore unlikely to be concerned at either taking risks or being caught. Therefore, making it physically difficult to break in by installing metal bars and stronger locks is likely to be the most effective measure.
3. Increasing the risk. The rewards are already limited and making it more difficult to take the money is impractical because of the need for employees to handle money. Therefore, increasing the risk, for example by installing CCTV, is likely to have a deterrent effect because the employees have a lot to lose if they are caught.

18 Criminal Justice

18.1 Introduction

This chapter covers some of the key features of the criminal justice system (CJS) in England and Wales and provides you with key information relating to prosecution and court processes. It is important to note that the systems vary across the UK; whilst some areas are applicable to the whole of the UK (eg human rights), information noted here is predominantly based on the system in England and Wales unless otherwise stated.

We first start with the topic of the criminal justice system more widely—with an explanation of the law and the types of legislation, as well as principles of criminal liability. Then, we also provide a brief account of some of the legislation protecting the general rights of UK citizens, such as the Human Rights Act 1998 and the PACE Codes of Practice. Here we will concentrate on general legal aspects: how laws are made, some of the different branches of law, and the principles behind criminal law.

You will then be provided with an explanation of the court hierarchy and relevant processes which includes the role of the CPS and examination of aspects of the charging, prosecution, and court procedures. Prosecution, as all experienced police officers know, is often a lengthy and complex affair and many aspects are not solely in the control of the police. There are two forms of prosecution: written and criminal charge. Written charge is a relatively straightforward process (see 10.18.1.1). Here we cover the more complex process of criminal charge. The police may charge or take no further action on either evidential or public interest grounds in respect of any offence they have authority to charge. They have authority to charge any summary-only offence, any offence of retail theft (provided the magistrates have sufficient sentencing powers), and any either-way offence where a guilty plea is anticipated and the matter is suitable for sentence in the magistrates' court (see CPS, 2020a). The CPS make the charging decisions in respect of all other offences including all indictable offences and those cases involving complex or sensitive issues. Once a decision to charge has been made, the CPS will run the case to conclusion, working closely with the police officer in the case (OIC).

Both students on pre-join programmes and trainee police officers undertaking the PCDA or the DHEP will need to understand the different types of law and court procedures. The topics covered in this chapter are likely to contribute to the learning required for the National Policing Curriculum across many subject areas but specifically those of 'Understanding the Police Constable Role', 'Criminal Justice', and 'Valuing Difference and Inclusion'.

18.2 Aims and Structure of the Criminal Justice System

In the UK, the concept of the CJS refers to the law, law enforcement, and dealing with transgressions of the law. More recently, focus has also been placed on the role of criminal justice agencies in preventative work, such as preventing offending in the first place, through focus on vulnerability or trauma-informed practice through a public health lens (Christmas and Srivastava, 2019; Keay and Kirby, 2018). The CJS in England and Wales is overseen by: (a) the

Ministry of Justice, overseeing agencies such as the courts, youth justice board, or prison and probation services; (b) the Attorney General's Office, providing legal advice to the government and overseeing independent prosecuting departments, such as the Crown Prosecution Service (CPS); and (c) the Home Office, overseeing, among others, the police.

The system used by the criminal justice agencies in England and Wales is adversarial, whereas elsewhere in Europe the system is inquisitorial. There are a number of significant differences between the systems and without a formal Penal (or Criminal) Code, the way the system works is strongly guided by adversarial principles. Understandably, our CJS is constantly adapting and while we have, over time, borrowed some inquisitorial elements, our system remains mostly adversarial (Spencer, 2016). There are key differences between the systems in relation to the role of the judge, juries, precedence, police powers, or rights of victims and defendants. For example, in an inquisitorial system, the defendant is questioned by a judge during trial so the lawyers in court have a lower profile. From the policing perspective, this system often puts the 'truth finding' mission over the rights of the defendant. The adversarial model, in contrast, requires that two advocates representing their parties (the prosecution and the defence) present their cases to an impartial person or persons (a judge, jury, or magistrate) in order for the verdict to be determined. It also prioritizes the rights of the defendant which is why so much focus in this country is placed on police officers ensuring that they understand all relevant practices. Not doing so can have significant consequences for what can or cannot be presented in court. (For more details on the way the adversarial system manifests at the court level see 18.7.6.1).

A person who has been charged with an offence but has not yet appeared in court is known as the defendant. They are tried by a court (usually in open session) and the defendant's guilt must be proved beyond reasonable doubt. The prosecution (whether to progress a case or not) can be done in a number of ways but there are two main ones—(1) police-led prosecutions and (2) CPS prosecutions. For less complex crimes, police can normally lead on prosecutions (eg shoplifting of value of less than £200). The prosecution of more serious cases is conducted on behalf of the Crown, often referred to in written case law as 'R' (see 18.3.2 on the conventions for naming cases). This is to ensure objectivity of prosecutions as the CPS is independent of the police and the government. The Crown Prosecutors (CP) and Senior Crown Prosecutors (SCP) are lawyers employed by the CPS to review and, when appropriate, prosecute cases investigated by the police. Associate Prosecutors (legally trained but not lawyers) may also perform some of these functions at the level of the magistrates' courts. The CPS also employs Crown Advocates who deal almost exclusively with cases at Crown Court and Court of Appeal. The CPS also instructs barristers from the independent bar to conduct some prosecutions at court and to provide the CPS with advice on complex legal matters. The defendant is normally represented by a solicitor and in some circumstances by a barrister. They are known as 'defence counsel' or 'the defence' (see 18.7 for more details).

18.3 The Law in England and Wales

An understanding of the law in England and Wales is an important aspect of the police officer's epistemic authority (the authority that derives from having more knowledge than another person). You may have heard law referred to as: common law, statute law, case law, Acts of Parliament, Statutory Instruments, and by-laws. These all interrelate in a number of ways but there are also differences between them.

Common law (also known as 'judge-made law') can be traced back to the Norman invasion of Britain in the eleventh century. Local courts made decisions that were then passed by word of mouth to other courts. Over time, they were accepted by more courts throughout the country, creating a 'binding precedent'. Examples of common law offences include murder, manslaughter, perverting the course of justice, and escape from lawful custody. In the UK, new common law offences are no longer created but courts continue to interpret existing laws when setting precedents. Because common law is not set in statute (see below), it is more open to interpretation and misuse.

Statute law is the foundation of the current legal system in England and Wales. This primary source of law can be accessed electronically via the UK Statute Law Database at <https://www.legislation.gov.uk>. Bills or 'draft law' are needed to create new legislation or amend previous legislation; ministry officials write a proposal which must be approved by both Houses of Parliament. If accepted, it is given Royal Assent before becoming an Act of Parliament. For example, the Criminal Finances Bill was introduced in the House of Commons in October 2016 for discussion and it received Royal Assent in April 2017, becoming the Criminal Finances Act 2017 and thereby becoming statute law. A regularly revised list of Bills currently before Parliament for consideration is available at <http://services.parliament.uk/bills/>. Compared to common law, statute law is less open to interpretation and therefore more binding.

Case law helps to establish the precise meaning of legislation and sets precedents. Decisions made by higher courts about legislation are then accepted by lower courts throughout the country. This 'doctrine of precedent' sets out how the legislation should be used by a court in similar circumstances. It means that a court is *bound* by previous decisions made by a court equivalent or higher in the court hierarchy. It is only courts that are superior which have the ability to overrule (change) decisions taken by courts lower in the hierarchy. The use of precedents is also a key feature of adversarial justice. Although the specific circumstances of the case might change (referred to as *obiter dicta*), the court should use the same reasoning (or *ratio decidendi*) that was used by previous courts to reach a decision. An example of this would be any decisions made about identification evidence; this would follow the precedents set in the case *R v Turnbull* [1976] 3 All ER 549. When case law has been used, this is indicated as 'by way of case stated'.

Acts of Parliament are divided into sections containing, for example, definitions, offences, powers of arrest, exemptions, and interpretations of words used. An Act often includes technical details such as fines and penalties which may need frequent revision and updating. The updates are provided as Statutory Instruments such as Orders, Regulations, and Rules and are often left to government ministers, to reduce the pressure on parliamentary time.

Statutory Instruments (SIs) allow the details of an Act to be revised without using parliamentary procedures. They are as much part of the law of England and Wales as the main body of the Act of Parliament. SIs are given a number as well as a title, for example 'Criminal Justice (Electronic Monitoring) (Responsible Person) Order 2014' (SI 2014 No 163). The Home Secretary used this SI to enable private companies such as Capita and G4S to take responsibility for the electronic monitoring of people released on condition of bail or as part of a youth rehabilitation order, curfew, or community order.

By-laws are usually local laws which have been made by a local authority and approved by a Secretary of State of the government. They normally deal with local matters, for example dogs on leads in recreational areas. They can also refer to charters, which are documents created under a generic form of legislation to regulate certain activities within an organization. Examples of charters include trade union charters and the Department of Health Information Charter.

TASK 1 The Road Vehicles Lighting Regulations 1989 (SI 1989 No 1796) were introduced under s 43(3) of the Road Traffic Act 1988. Find out what regs 11–22 cover in relation to motor vehicles.

18.3.1 The naming system for legal cases

Each legal case in court has an official title, for example *R v Turnbull* [1976] 3 All ER 549. There is an official system for naming cases, for example 'R' stands for 'Regina' or 'Rex' (the queen or king respectively). The letter 'v' stands for versus and 'Turnbull' is the name of the defendant. The case was held in 1976 and can be found in Volume 3 of the 1976 All England Law Reports on page 549.

18.4 Principles of Criminal Liability

Most of the law relevant to a police officer's first few years of service is undoubtedly criminal rather than civil law. We therefore begin with the notion of 'criminal liability'—how do we *know* and then prove that a person has broken the law? There are two elements of criminal liability:

1. The *actus reus*—the action the defendant carried out, which must be proved beyond reasonable doubt, quite literally meaning 'guilty act'.
2. The *mens rea*—meaning a 'guilty mind', refers to the guilty mindset that the defendant had at the time the action was taken, which also must be proved; that is, that the defendant intended to commit the crime. However, there are some exceptions to this.

Both are set out within the relevant law, as explained in the previous section. Although the use of Latin can seem exclusionary, these terms are commonly used within the legal system and so are worth remembering (if you are unsure, you will find a number of internet sites that will help you to pronounce these two Latin phrases). We will now look at these two building blocks of criminal liability in more detail.

18.4.1 *Actus reus*

This is about a person's actions (including *a lack* of action). If a person is to be found guilty of a criminal offence, then it must be proved that they either:

- **acted criminally** in some way, for example the act of pulling a trigger which results in the crime of murder;
- **omitted to do an act**, and the omission brought about a criminal outcome, for example knowing that someone was going to commit a crime but doing nothing to stop it;
- **caused a state of affairs to happen**, for example knowingly drinking a lot of alcohol and then driving a car; or
- **failed to do an act which was required**, and which brought about a criminal outcome, for example failing to ensure that a vehicle was roadworthy when offering it for hire, thus leading to the criminal outcome of someone driving a car that was not in a safe condition to be driven.

18.4.2 *Mens rea*

This is about a person's thoughts or state of mind, and is about having guilty knowledge. The defendant's state of mind or *mens rea* is relevant to a number of offences, and to this end the legislation includes terms such as:

- 'dishonestly' such as for theft;
- 'wilfully' such as for neglect of children;
- 'recklessly' as in the offence of causing criminal damage; and
- 'with intent' as in burglary with intent to steal.

Such 'guilty knowledge' is not always straightforward and can be shown through various 'modes of culpability':

- direct intention—this is where there is clear foresight that an offence will be committed;
- oblique intention—meaning that while committing an offence is not absolutely certain, there is virtual certainty of it occurring;
- knowingly—where it is reasonably certain that an offence will be committed;
- recklessness—not caring whether there will or will not be consequences despite foreseeing that an offence may be committed;
- criminal negligence—where the actor (defendant) did not actually foresee consequences, but a reasonable person would have done so.

The level of intent is assessed by comparing the actions of the defendant with those of a hypothetical, average person under the circumstances of the alleged offence. For more serious situations (eg 'murder' and 'wounding or inflicting grievous bodily harm with intent'), the law requires that the suspect has a specific intent or *mens rea*. This would also include offences for which there is an ulterior purpose other than the main criminal act, for example when a defendant is charged with burglary with intent (see 23.4.1). Here, it would have to be proved that the defendant not only intended to enter a building as a trespasser, but also intended to inflict grievous bodily harm, cause damage, or steal. For other offences, such as common assault or battery, it is sufficient to prove basic intent. This requires that the defendant knew or at least closed their mind to the fact that their actions would result in harm being caused to the victim.

18.4.3 General defence

There are some circumstances where 'criminal defence' can be applied which may make a person not responsible for an offence. The defences vary across different offences. For example, for the crime of murder, only 'partial defence' or 'diminished responsibility' can be utilized, reducing the offence to manslaughter. Here are some examples of criminal defences:

- Mental disorder—you may have heard of this as the 'insanity defence'—you should not use such phrasing as it is outdated and does not actually encompass everything which this defence includes—it works within the realms of diagnosable conditions recognized by the law only and can be difficult to prove.
- Automatism—there are a number of reasons (eg epilepsy) which can cause our muscles to act beyond our control.
- Duress—this is where an individual may be compelled to commit a crime through threats.
- Necessity—similarly, this is where an individual may commit a crime for the purpose of avoiding serious injury to themselves or others.
- Self-defence—relates to when force (which has to be reasonable) is used when trying to defend oneself against another.

18.4.4 Strict liability offences

'Strict liability' offences are those for which only the guilty act (*actus reus*) needs to be proved. There is no need for a *mens rea* for a successful conviction (or a diminished *mens rea* may be sufficient). Two examples of strict liability offences are:

- paying for the sexual services of a sex worker who is being subjected to force by another (s 14 of the Policing and Crime Act 2009)—it is irrelevant whether the suspect knows about the use of force; and
- the sale of faulty goods (s 14 of the Sale of Goods Act 1979)—it is irrelevant whether the suspect knows the goods are faulty.

Strict liability offences are usually less serious and often correspond to statutory violations, but they can also include offences where the action itself is considered so socially unacceptable that there is no need to prove the offender's intention. However, it is not always clear whether a *mens rea* is required, and decisions concerning strict liability may be ultimately left to the courts.

18.4.5 Burden of proof

How do we prove that a person is guilty of a criminal offence? The law tells us that:

> throughout the web of the English criminal law one golden thread is always to be seen: that it is the duty of the prosecution to prove the prisoner's guilt. (*Woolmington v DPP* [1935] AC 462)

Therefore, in criminal proceedings the onus is on the prosecution to prove the guilt of the defendant, not on the defendant to prove their innocence. The degree of proof required for criminal cases is 'beyond reasonable doubt'. This was famously expressed by Geoffrey Lawrence (cited in Johnston and Hutton, 2005, p 133) in the following way:

> The possibility of guilt is not enough, suspicion is not enough, probability is not enough, likelihood is not enough. A criminal matter is not a question of balancing probabilities and deciding in favour of probability, a conviction must be formed beyond reasonable doubt that the accused is guilty, and this is done on the basis of the evidence provided in court.

The jury will therefore be directed by the judge that they should only return a guilty verdict if they are sure of the suspect's guilt, beyond any reasonable doubt. Magistrates will be aware of this responsibility from their training and may be reminded of it by their legal adviser.

18.5 Human Rights

The concept of human rights and the responsibilities of police officers in the preservation and maintenance of those rights runs throughout this Handbook. The police are expected to exercise their powers and procedures fairly and without bias, and in accordance with the Human Rights Act 1998, and PACE (the Police and Criminal Evidence Act 1984), as well as many other principles (see Chapter 7 for more information). You should see this as intertwined with the Code of Ethics, which police officers have to subscribe to and which must guide all their decisions. Human rights legislation stresses the entitlement of individuals to expect certain fundamental rights as part of their social contract with the state and other forms of authority.

18.5.1 The Human Rights Act 1998

There was much speculation about the future of the Human Rights Act 1998 (HRA) after Brexit—the UK's departure from the European Union (EU)—which was completed on 1 January 2021. However, the HRA found its background in the European Convention on Human Rights and Fundamental Freedoms created before the European Union even existed. Brexit does not impact on UK citizens' rights under the European Court of Human Rights, as the Court comes under the auspices of the Council of Europe, not the EU. The longer term impact of Brexit on our equality and human rights will depend on the laws that are passed after leaving the EU. The HRA continues to be at the cornerstone of criminal justice and lists a number of rights as shown in the table. Each right is considered as absolute (underlined), limited (L), or qualified (Q).

Article number	Article title
2	Right to life
3	Prohibition of torture
4	Prohibition of slavery and forced labour
5	Right to liberty and security (L)
6	Right to a fair trial (L)
7	No punishment without law
8	Right to respect for private and family life (Q)
9	Freedom of thought, conscience, and religion (Q)
10	Freedom of expression (Q)
11	Freedom of assembly and association (Q)
12	Right to marry (L)
14	Prohibition of discrimination (L)

The absolute rights of an individual cannot be restricted by the interests of the community as a whole.

Limited rights do not apply in all circumstances—for example, the right to liberty (part of Article 5) does not apply if the detention is lawful, such as after arrest. However, although the right to liberty may be limited, a lawfully arrested person would still have the right to security under Article 5. A further example of a limited right occurs within Article 6, under which both the public and the press have the right to access to any court hearing, but this right is subject to certain restrictions in the interests of morality, national security, or where the interests of young people under 18, or the privacy of the parties, require the exclusion of the press and public.

Qualified rights relate to matters where interference by the public authority is permissible if it is in the public interest and can be qualified, for example to prevent disorder or crime, for public safety, or for national security. However, a public authority (such as the police) may only interfere with a qualified right if the interference is:

- lawful and is part of existing common or statute law (see 18.3), such as the power to stop and search;
- made for one of the specifically listed permissible acts in the interests of the public, such as to prevent disorder for public safety; or
- necessary in a democratic society, where the wider interests of the community as a whole often have to be balanced against the rights of an individual (but it must still be proportionate).

All new statute law must be compatible with the HRA. An individual may take a public authority to a UK court (rather than directly to the European Court of Human Rights) if the authority has not acted in a manner compatible with the rights. UK courts are required to interpret all legislation in a way which is compatible with the Convention's rights, so far as is possible (s 3), and public authorities (eg government and the police) cannot act in a way which is incompatible with the Convention. Note, however, that there is no retrospective effect on existing law (*R v Lambert* [2001] 2 WLR 211).

18.5.2 Applying the Human Rights Act to everyday policing

A police officer should consider the following questions in relation to an individual or group before 'interfering' with another person's qualified rights:

1. Are my actions **lawful**? Is there common or statute law to support my interference with their rights?
2. Are my actions **permissible**? Am I permitted to interfere with their rights because it is in support of a duty, such as preventing crime?
3. Are my actions **necessary**? Do the needs of the many outweigh the needs of the few; in other words, must I take into account the interests of the community and balance one individual's rights against another's?
4. Are my actions **proportionate**? Having considered everything, will my actions be excessive or could I do something less intrusive and more in proportion to the outcome I need to achieve?

During initial police training, mnemonics may be used with regard to these questions, for example PLAN (Proportionality, Legality, Accountability, and Necessity) and JAPAN (Justification, Authorization, Proportionality, Auditable, and Necessary).

In addition to the above, it is also important to give consideration to issues relating to equality, diversity, and inclusion (see Chapter 7), as well as ethics in a wider sense. It is unlawful and unethical to discriminate on the grounds of certain 'protected characteristics' (the Equality Act 2010). These characteristics are: age, disability, race, religion or belief, sex, gender reassignment, sexual orientation, marriage and civil partnership, pregnancy, or maternity. As the Institute for Apprenticeships (2018b) explains, police constables:

> exercise wide-ranging powers to maintain the peace and uphold the law across complex and diverse communities. They must justify and personally account for their actions through differing legal frameworks including courts, while also under the close scrutiny of the public.

Processing Policing

18.6 The Police and Criminal Evidence Act 1984 (PACE)

The police have powers to arrest individuals, to search people and property, to enter buildings, and to seize objects. Many of these powers, and the restrictions on their use, are provided in the Police and Criminal Evidence Act 1984 (known as the PACE Act 1984 or simply as PACE), and some are considered in more detail later in this Handbook (in Chapters 4 and 10, for example).

The PACE Act 1984 contains key legislation in relation to:

- criminal investigation procedures in England and Wales;
- applying the principles of justice, honesty, and workability in the investigative process;
- protection of the rights of all individuals; and
- police powers for search and arrest.

The demonstration of knowledge of the PACE Act 1984 in practical policing contexts is an important element in both the knowledge and skills requirements of the PCDA and DHEP—for example, in relation to conducting searches (see 4.6 on searches).

18.6.1 PACE Codes of Practice

The PACE Codes of Practice provide guidelines on how investigative processes should be conducted. The Codes are divided into eight main sections and refer to contacts between the police and the public in the exercise of certain police powers.

Code	General areas covered	Last revised
A	Stop and search	2023
B	Search of premises	2013
C	Detention, treatment, and questioning of suspects	2019
D	Identification of suspects	2017
E	Audio-only recording of interviews	2018
F	Audio-visual recording of interviews	2018
G	Power of arrest	2012
H	Detention, treatment, and questioning of terrorist suspects	2022

A brief summary of each Code is provided here. The Codes are available as a smartphone app, and can also be downloaded in full from the Home Office website. It is key that you always work with the most up-to-date versions.

Code A covers the police statutory powers of stop and search, and the requirements for police officers and police staff to record public encounters. It provides guidelines on searching people who are not under arrest and covers the key principles a police officer needs to apply when deciding whether to use a power of search. In addition, the Code outlines what documentation must be completed at the end of such a search or encounter.

Code B covers searches of premises by police officers and the seizure of any property found (including property found on people present on the premises). It provides guidelines on how to protect a person's rights in relation to the conduct of the search, and the record to be made after the search. The Code covers pre-planned searches (with warrants issued by magistrates) as well as searches for the purposes of making an arrest or a search for stolen or unlawfully possessed property in premises.

Code C covers the detention, treatment, and questioning by police officers of suspects not related to terrorism and applies primarily to suspects under arrest. The Code outlines the procedure for protecting an arrested person's rights whilst in detention and the care they must be given while in custody at a police station. However, any person who is not under arrest but who is assisting with an investigation should be treated with 'no less' consideration (Note 1A). The Code emphasizes that discrimination against a detained person with 'protected characteristics' (listed under the Equality Act 2010) is unlawful and sets out how custody staff can exchange specified information with the detainee, using interpreters and written translations where necessary (see 10.15.4 for further details). Code C underlines the rights for detainees to communicate with other people, including legal representation, and describes how to protect those rights during questioning (a written notice of the rights is required). A detainee aged 10 to 17 years must have an appropriate adult present and a person responsible for their welfare must be informed. Particular requirements apply for 'vulnerable people' and the definition of 'vulnerable' has been recently updated (see para 1.13d). The Code also covers terrorism-related post-charge questioning and detention under Code H.

Code D covers the identification of persons by police officers. It protects the rights of a suspect regarding identification before and after arrest and refers to identification parade procedures, identification by body samples and fingerprints, and showing witnesses photographs of suspects.

Code E covers the audio recording of interviews with suspects (arrested or not) and safeguards the rights of an individual. It sets out that the recordings must be handled securely and in confidence and allows for breaks during interviews (see 13.8.2.10 for more details). Audio recording of voluntary interviews with suspects who have not been arrested is not automatically required for offences such as possession of cannabis or khat, shoplifting with a value up to £100, and criminal damage of up to a value of £300.

Code F covers audio-visually recorded interviews with suspects (arrested or not) and outlines the procedures to be followed. At the time of writing, there is no statutory requirement to visually record interviews, but the practice is becoming more common.

Code G covers the statutory power of arrest by police officers. It outlines the correct procedures for arresting a person in order that their right to liberty is considered at all times and that proper justification for the arrest is provided (see 10.11.2).

Code H covers suspects arrested on suspicion of being a terrorist under s 41 of the Terrorism Act 2000. Interpreters and written translations must be used where necessary and a written notice of rights and entitlements must be provided to each detainee (as for Code C). Code H ceases to apply once a terrorist suspect has been charged with an offence (Code C then applies), released without charge, or transferred to a prison.

A breach of any of the Codes could result in:

- disciplinary action for the police officer, depending on the circumstances ;
- evidence being deemed inadmissible or unfair by a court (s 78(1) of the PACE Act 1984); and/or
- liability for civil or criminal proceedings.

18.7 Prosecution and Court Procedures

Once an alleged crime has been reported, there will be an investigation at some level, usually by the police. If the investigation leads to a prosecution, it will usually be conducted by the police, or the CPS on behalf of the Crown (the state). The defendant will usually be represented by a solicitor or barrister but can choose to represent themselves.

18.7.1 The classification of criminal offences

Offences are classified as summary-only offences, indictment-only offences, and either-way offences.

Summary-only offences are less serious and are normally dealt with in the magistrates' court where they are governed by Part 37 of the Criminal Procedure Rules 2010. Examples of summary-only offences are common assault and being drunk and disorderly. The Crown Court may, however, deal with a summary offence in certain circumstances. For example, there are a small number of summary-only offences that can be added to the indictment (the formal document that sets out the offences to be heard in the Crown Court) along with connected indictable or either-way offences. These summary-only offences are listed under s 40 of the Criminal Justice Act 1988 and include common assault, taking a vehicle without consent, and driving while disqualified. Summary-only offences must be charged within six months of the offence having taken place.

Indictable-only offences are the most serious cases and can only be dealt with in a Crown Court. Examples include murder, causing death by dangerous driving, rape, aggravated burglary, and wounding with intent.

Either-way offences can be tried in a magistrates' court or a Crown Court. Examples of either-way offences include theft, obtaining property by deception, and assault occasioning actual bodily harm. Certain either-way offences can only be tried at a magistrates' court, for example criminal damage or aggravated vehicle taking with a cost below £5,000, and low-level shoplifting of goods worth less than £200 (ss 22–22A of the Magistrates' Courts Act 1980). At the first hearing for an either-way offence (in the magistrates' court), the defendant will be asked whether they wish to enter a plea. If the defendant enters a guilty plea, the magistrates will consider whether their sentencing powers are sufficient to deal with the matter. If not, they will commit the case to the Crown Court for sentence. If the defendant pleads 'not guilty' or 'withholds' their plea at the first hearing in the magistrates' court, there will be a 'mode of trial' hearing to decide where the trial should be held. The Crown Prosecutor will make representations, and the defence may object to an either-way offence going to a Crown Court. The magistrates make the final decision unless the defendant elects to be tried by judge and jury in a Crown Court, in which case the magistrates must comply.

The classification for each criminal offence and its mode of trial and penalty can be found either by reference to primary sources—that is, the legal texts themselves or secondary sources, such as Blackstone's Police Manuals. For example, the relevant legislation for handling stolen goods is in s 22 of the Theft Act 1968. This, in conjunction with Sch 1 and s 32 of the Magistrates' Courts Act 1980, states that handling stolen goods is triable either way, with a maximum penalty of 14 years' imprisonment on indictment or, if tried summarily, six months' imprisonment and/or a fine.

TASK 2 Use an appropriate textbook or the internet to determine for the offence of robbery:

- the relevant Act, including section;
- the mode of trial; and
- the maximum penalty for a person found guilty.

18.7.2 The courts

The structure of the courts system in England and Wales relates to the nature of the matters in hand and the seriousness of the cases handled by each category of court. The diagram shows some key elements in the relationships between the various types of court in England and Wales.

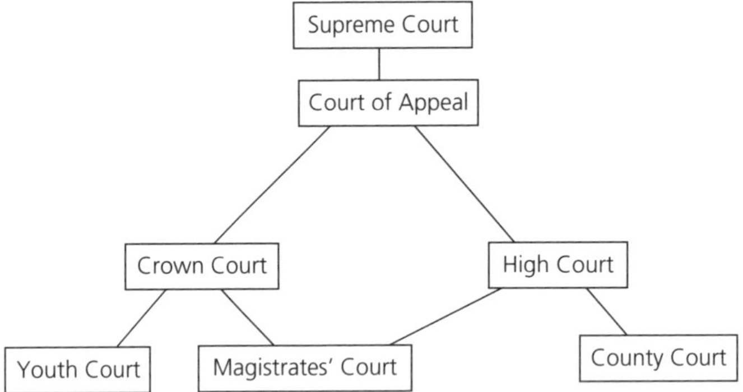

All of the courts shown here can deal with criminal cases, except for County Courts (which only deal with civil cases). The role of the courts that deal with criminal cases is our primary concern here, but police officers are occasionally required to give evidence in civil cases (eg an officer who attended a road traffic collision in which a pedestrian was seriously injured might be called as a witness in a civil court case in which claims for damages were in dispute).

The **magistrates' courts** are where all criminal cases start, regardless of classification. Around 95 per cent of all criminal cases are concluded in the magistrates' court. Summary matters stay in the magistrates' court along with less serious either-way offences. The more serious either-way offences tend to be sent straight to the Crown Court following the first hearing. Indictable-only offences will always be sent straight to the Crown Court from the magistrates' court. Magistrates deal with a variety of hearings, for example applications for bail, pleas, sentencing, trial management hearings, and trials. There are about 330 magistrates' courts across England and Wales. Hearings in magistrates' courts are presided over by a district judge (a qualified lawyer) or a bench of three magistrates (sometime referred to as the 'justices of the peace'). Magistrates are lay people drawn from the local community and not professional judges or lawyers, although they do receive training; they are advised on points of law by an adviser who is legally trained. Magistrates' courts also hear non-criminal cases, such as family law disputes. The Specialist Domestic Violence Courts are held in magistrates' courts.

There are limits to the penalties that can be imposed at a magistrates' court, as follows:

- a custodial sentence must be no longer than six months per individual offence, with a maximum of two consecutive six-month sentences (s 154 of the Criminal Justice Act 2003); and
- a fine at magistrates' courts cannot exceed £5,000;
- a community sentence (eg unpaid work);
- a ban (eg from driving);
- a combination of the above.

For either-way offences (see 18.7.1), the offender can be sent to the Crown Court for sentence if the magistrates believe that a more severe sentence is appropriate. If a defendant is dissatisfied with a verdict from the magistrates' courts, they may appeal to the Crown Court for matters of fact and law and to the High Court for matters of law only.

A **youth court** is normally used for defendants aged between 10 and 17 years (unless being charged jointly with an adult, or for the most serious cases such as murder or manslaughter in which case they are tried in the Crown Court). The procedures are very similar to those in a magistrates' court but are adapted to take account of the age of the defendant and are not usually open to the public. A particular courtroom within a magistrates' court is often formally designated as a youth court. Appeals from a youth court generally go to the Crown Court. There are different sentencing guidelines for those under 18 due to vulnerability through virtue of age and a greater focus on rehabilitation.

The **Crown Court** is a first instance court (ie not an appeal court) for more serious criminal cases, including indictable offences such as murder, rape, or robbery. There are 71 Crown Courts (as of March 2022) across England and Wales. They also try appeals from magistrates' courts, and 'either-way' cases referred by magistrates' courts. The trial takes place before a judge and a jury (if a guilty plea is not entered) and members of the public (unless exemption was granted, eg child abuse offences). Police officers and other relevant experts may give evidence as witnesses. On matters of fact and law, it is possible to appeal from the Crown Court to the Criminal Division of the Court of Appeal.

The **High Court** is, alongside the Crown Court and the Appeal Courts, part of the higher courts of justice in England and Wales. It hears cases at first instance and on appeal. The High Court consists of three divisions, the King's Bench Division, the Chancery Division, and the Family Division, and each hears different types of cases. Judges from the King's Bench Division hear the most important criminal cases at Crown Court.

The **Court of Appeal** considers appeals from the Crown Court (criminal cases) and the High Court (civil cases) but it also takes a few appeals from magistrates' and youth courts. It normally sits in up to 12 courts in the Royal Courts of Justice in London. Some hearings may now be recorded and broadcast (Crime and Courts Act 2013).

The **Supreme Court** is the highest court and the final instance of appeal on points of law and important legal disputes for criminal and civil cases in England and Wales. It is presided over by 12 appointed senior judges.

The following table gives a summary.

Courts	Type of cases	Features	Open to the public?	Appeals go to
Youth	Defendants aged 10 to 17 years	No jury	Not usually	Crown Court
Magistrates'	Offences triable summarily only, and either-way offences	No jury	Yes, usually	Crown Court or High Court
Crown	Offences triable only on indictment, and either-way offences referred from magistrates' courts. Appeals from magistrates' and youth courts	Judge and jury	Yes, usually	Court of Appeal (Criminal Division)
Appeal	Appeals from Crown Court	Judges only, no jury	Yes, usually	Supreme Court
Supreme	Appeals from Court of Appeal	Judges only, no jury	Yes, usually	Final point of appeal

The majority of courts are generally open to the public but a small number of cases are heard in private, for example particularly sensitive cases or where intimidation is of concern (s 25 of the Youth Justice and Criminal Evidence Act 1999).

18.7.3 The Crown Prosecution Service

The CPS was set up in 1986 under the Prosecution of Offences Act 1985 as an independent prosecuting authority for England and Wales. It is independent of the police and is therefore an important mechanism for maintaining fairness in the criminal justice system. CPS lawyers (Crown Prosecutors) are solicitors and barristers who are responsible for prosecuting criminal cases on behalf of the Crown.

Where a case is serious or complex, Senior Crown Prosecutors advise the police in the early stages of the investigation, sometimes about possible lines of investigation and always in terms of decisions about charging. These types of cases should not be charged by the police without the authority of a Senior Crown Prosecutor. Crown prosecutors prepare and then present cases in court. The CPS also provides information and guidance to victims and witnesses and will help to support them through the prosecution process.

The CPS is divided into 13 areas across England and Wales. Each area is headed up by a Chief Crown Prosecutor, who in turn is answerable to the Director of Public Prosecutions (DPP). The DPP is the head of the CPS and works under the superintendence of the Attorney General. The Attorney General oversees the work of the CPS and is accountable to the government in terms of its performance and conduct.

Crown prosecutors are governed by the *Code for Crown Prosecutors*. This is a public document and is available on the CPS website (CPS, 2018c). In short, it sets out that before pursuing a case, the Crown Prosecutor should be sure that there is sufficient evidence to provide a realistic prospect of conviction and that it is also in the public interest to pursue a prosecution. Only when both of these elements are met should a case be charged. The same standard applies in cases where the charging decision has been made by the police. There is one exception to this, and that is where a case is charged on the threshold test (see 18.7.4.2).

18.7.4 The charging process

As mentioned in the introduction to this chapter, the police are responsible for charging decisions in most cases involving straightforward summary offences and in lower level either-way offences that are likely to be dealt with in a magistrates' court (see 18.7.1 for discussion of summary and either-way offences). The charging decision should be referred to the CPS for indictable-only cases and for more serious or sensitive either-way offences likely to be heard at the Crown Court. Charging advice is normally provided to the police in one of three ways: CPS Direct, the direct submission of an electronic case file, or through a face-to-face or video conference meeting.

CPS Direct provides most of the charging advice given to the police. It consists of teams of Crown Prosecutors across England and Wales who are available 24 hours a day, seven days a week, 365 days of the year. The police contact CPS Direct by telephone and electronically transmit the evidence so that the advice may be provided straight away. At this point, a suspect could still be in custody and the police may be requesting charging advice on the threshold test, or the suspect may have been bailed pending a charging decision—in which case the charging advice is likely to be given in line with the full code test. Charging advice is requested on police MG3 forms (see 18.7.5.2) and the Crown Prosecutor sends the advice to the officer electronically on a CPS MG3 form.

For cases that are more complex and/or sensitive, an electronic file can be submitted directly to the CPS. A Crown Prosecutor will then review the file and provide charging advice to the police. Again, using MG3 forms.

Face-to-face meetings, or sometimes video-conference-style meetings, are held for large-scale, complex, sensitive, and serious cases. By their very nature, these cases will require more time and may involve the examination of large quantities of evidence.

18.7.4.1 The full code test

The majority of cases will be charged using the 'full code test'. This is set out in the *Code for Crown Prosecutors* (CPS, 2018c) but it also applies for cases where the charging decision is made by the police. There are two stages to the full code test. First, the prosecutor must be sure that there is sufficient evidence to provide a realistic prospect of conviction. A prosecutor does not need to be convinced of guilt beyond any reasonable doubt but must be sure that a properly directed and impartial jury, acting in accordance with the law, is more likely than not to find the defendant guilty. The prosecutor needs to be sure that the available evidence is credible and can be used in court. If there is insufficient evidence to provide a realistic prospect of conviction, then the case fails at this stage and the suspect should not be charged, no matter how serious the offence is. If the prosecutor decides there is sufficient evidence to provide a realistic prospect of conviction, the second stage of the test is applied.

The second stage of the full code test considers the public interest. If there is sufficient evidence, then a case will normally proceed unless there are significant public interest factors which suggest that the case should not go ahead. Public interest factors can include:

- the age of the suspect;
- the circumstances of, and the level of harm caused to, the victim;
- the impact on the community;
- whether there may be a source of information that requires protection; and
- whether a prosecution is a proportionate response or whether the suspect could be better dealt with by a method which diverts them from the court process, such as a caution.

There is no exhaustive list of public interest factors and there may well be factors unique to individual cases. If a case meets the full code test, then the appropriate charge(s) should be selected and the suspect charged as soon as practicable (CPS, 2018c).

18.7.4.2 The threshold test

The threshold test is used when there is a time limit and a decision has to be made on whether to charge, grant bail, or release under investigation. It applies in cases where further evidence still needs to be gathered but the suspect would pose a significant risk if released from custody. There are two questions that must be considered when applying the threshold test:

- Is there a reasonable suspicion, using the available evidence, that the suspect committed the offence?
- Is there further identifiable evidence to be gathered that could ultimately provide the prosecution with a realistic prospect of conviction?

If both factors are met, the Crown Prosecutor is likely to authorize a charge under the threshold test (CPS, 2018c). Once charged, the suspect must be placed in front of the next available court for the magistrates to decide whether to remand the defendant in custody or grant bail. The CPS, working together with the police, may apply for remand in custody but the court makes the actual decision.

When a case has been charged under the threshold test and the defendant has been detained on remand, the case must be kept under constant review to ensure that it is progressing as anticipated. As soon as practicable, the full code test must be applied and met in order for the case to continue. A defendant cannot be kept on remand indefinitely, and custody time limits (CTLs) apply. If a CTL expires before the case is concluded, then the suspect may be released. The CPS can make an application to extend a CTL, but the court will scrutinize this very carefully before agreeing to any such application. It is therefore very important that all efforts are made to ensure that cases where a defendant is remanded in custody are kept under constant review. The length of the CTL will depend on the type of case. A summary-only case carries a CTL of 56 days. An either-way case being dealt with in the magistrates' court carries a CTL of 70 days. Crown Court cases carry a CTL of 182 days.

18.7.4.3 Early consultation between the police and the CPS

In the case of very large-scale, complex, or sensitive cases, the police may decide to seek advice from the CPS at a very early stage in the investigation to ensure that the correct evidence is identified and gathered from the outset. This may involve a number of consultations and the CPS may also provide written advice setting out the case strategy and further reasonable lines of enquiry before charges are actually authorized. However, this additional effort ultimately saves the police from pursuing unnecessary lines of enquiry and ensures that the appropriate and required evidence is gathered as soon as practicable.

18.7.4.4 Selecting the correct charge

A CPS 'charging standard' can be used to determine the precise charge(s) made against an individual. For example, a suspected shoplifter might be charged with 'Theft contrary to sections 1(1) and 7 of the Theft Act 1968', in which case the charging standard would involve a consideration of the five elements of the offence of theft (see 23.2).

When selecting the charge, the Crown Prosecutor or police officer should make sure the charge fairly reflects the seriousness and the full extent of the offending. The charge selected should also give the court adequate sentencing power. Once charged, the 'suspect' becomes a 'defendant'.

18.7.5 Preparing and submitting case files

It is important that case files are completed accurately and with integrity for a prosecution to succeed. The case file will include a summary of the interview, the MG6 forms, charge sheets, and lists of exhibits (often forensic evidence).

18.7.5.1 The National File Standard

The National File Standard (NFS) is described by the CPS and the College of Policing as providing a 'staged and proportionate approach to the preparation of case files' (CoP, 2014c). The purpose is to provide the prosecutor, the defence, and the court with proportionate and relevant information throughout the case. The files submitted to the prosecution from the first hearing must contain the core information which the prosecutor will need to complete a Case Management Form. The required content for a case file depends on whether a guilty or not guilty plea is expected.

18.7.5.2 MG forms

The forms for case files are often referred to as 'MG forms' (see the Home Office document *Manual of guidance and MG forms Version 10.0*). Each MG form will show the suspect's details and the case file reference number (these will have been uploaded when the suspect was first presented to the custody officer upon arrest). The forms are numbered in the official lists, for example MG02, though the zero is often omitted in other written documents, and in conversation. Here we cover only the MG forms that a trainee police officer is likely to require for three different categories of case:

- straightforward cases where a guilty plea is entered (and there are no complications);
- contested cases ('not guilty' pleas); and
- Crown Court cases.

The forms required for straightforward and contested cases depend on whether the suspect has been charged. Charging decisions are usually based on the information received by the CPS in a pre-charge expedited case file. This will include forms MG3 and MG3A and any key evidence. Once the charge has been made, a post-charge expedited file is required so that an advanced disclosure pack can be built for the defence and the court. This pack should include a summary of the case and the interview (in the MG5), any available statements and exhibits, and a copy of the defendant's previous convictions.

If a 'not guilty' plea is entered, or if the case is to be heard in the Crown Court, upgrading to a Full File is required. If the case is disposed of at the first court appearance, then of course no upgrading is needed.

The forms required for each eventuality are shown in the table. A tick indicates that a particular form will almost certainly be needed and a question mark indicates that it might be needed.

Form	Description	straightforward		contested		full file
		pre-	post-	pre-	post-	
MG2	Special Measures Assessment				?	
MG3	Report to Crown Prosecutor	✓	✓	✓	✓	✓
MG3A	Further report to Crown Prosecutor	?	?	?	?	
MG4	Charge sheet		✓		✓	
MG4A	Conditional bail form		?		?	
MG4B	Request to vary police conditional bail		?		?	
MG4C	Surety/Security		?		?	
MG5	Police Report		✓		✓	✓
MG6	Case file evidence and information	?	?	?	?	
MG6B	Police officer/staff's disciplinary record					?
MG6C	Schedule of non-sensitive unused material					✓
MG6D	Schedule of sensitive material					✓
MG6E	Disclosure officer's report					✓

Form	Description	straightforward		contested		full file
		pre-	post-	pre-	post-	
MG7	Remand in custody application		?		?	?
MG8	Breach of bail conditions		?		?	
MG9	Witness list		✓		✓	✓
MG10	Witness non-availability		✓		✓	✓
MG11	Witness statements	?	?	?	?	?
MG12	Exhibits list					✓
MG15	Interview record: this could be an SDN, a ROTI, or a ROVI*		?		?	✓
MG16	Bad character/dangerous offenders				?	?
MG18	Offences taken into consideration		?		?	?
MG19	Compensation form (plus supporting documents)					✓
MG21/21A	Forensic submissions				?	✓
MGDD A/B	Driving under the influence of alcohol/ drugs forms	?	?	?	?	?
SDN	Short Descriptive Note; may be written on MG15, MG5, or officer's MG11		✓			✓
Phoenix print	Computer print-out of the suspect's previous convictions, cautions, etc	✓	✓	✓	✓	✓
PNC	Print-out of suspect and key prosecution witnesses' pre-convictions, including cautions, reprimands, final warnings, PNDs etc	✓	✓	✓	✓	✓
Copy of documentary exhibits/photos			✓	✓	✓	✓
Police racist incident form/crime report			?		?	?
Crime report and incident log				✓	✓	✓
Any unused material which might undermine the case		✓	✓	✓	✓	✓
Custody record						✓

* ROTI: Record of a Taped Interview; ROVI: Record of a Video-recorded Interview; both are written documents summarizing the content of the recordings.

18.7.6 In court

We will now concentrate on what happens at court, with particular emphasis on the likely role of a trainee officer. The course of events in both the magistrates' courts and the Crown Courts follows certain routines and patterns depending on the type of hearing. In the table you will find a description of the people who are most likely to be present in the magistrates' and the Crown Court.

Participants in the court room	Description of the role
The magistrate(s)	Unpaid, specially trained volunteers who hear cases in the magistrates' court. They are not legal professionals.
District Judge	A legal professional drawn from the rank of solicitor or barrister—hears cases in the magistrates' courts only
Court legal adviser	A legally trained professional who advises the lay magistrates on matters relating to the law
The defendant	The person who is charged with the offence with which the court is concerned
Representative for the prosecution	In the magistrates' court, this may be a solicitor, a barrister, or an associate prosecutor. (Associate prosecutors can review and present straightforward cases and with further training may present trials involving summary-only offences without the penalty of a custodial sentence.) In the Crown Court, the representative must be a barrister or a solicitor who has undertaken further training and obtained 'higher rights of audience'. They may be employed by the CPS or be a barrister from the independent bar who has been instructed by the CPS

Participants in the court room	Description of the role
Defence	A legal professional acting on behalf of the defendant. Again, this can be a solicitor or a barrister in the magistrates' court. In the Crown Court, it must be a barrister or a solicitor who has undertaken further training and obtained 'higher rights of audience'
The public	Courtrooms are open to the public and anyone may attend a hearing. There are certain exceptions to this, for example where the defendant is under 18
The judge	Crown Court judges are legally qualified professionals, normally drawn from the rank of solicitor and barrister who have held their qualification for a period of at least five years
The jury	The jury in the Crown Court consists of 12 members of the public who have been selected from a panel of people who have been 'summonsed' for jury service
Witnesses	People who have witnessed elements of the offence that need to be proved in court. The defence may wish to test a witness's evidence by cross-examination. Professional witnesses may also be called to give evidence in relation to particular evidence, for example a doctor may be asked to give evidence in relation to injuries they have examined
The media	Usually present at major trials, court reporters are sometimes also present at the magistrates' courts and are likely to report on cases of local interest
Probation Service	May be present during some types of hearing so that they are aware of the circumstances of a case, should a probation report be required in order to assist with sentencing. (The report would cover the offender's background, reasons for offending, levels of remorse, and appropriate sentences.)
Young Offender Service	Similar to the probation service but for young people under 18

Some courtrooms are still the traditional, imposing wood-panelled rooms, but many are now located in modern buildings. Wigs and gowns are not worn in the magistrates' courts where proceedings are generally less formal. There is no substitute for visiting a court and observing the procedures live, but remember that there are rules to follow when visiting court so make sure you look these up before visiting.

For a trainee police officer, giving evidence features as one of the PAC headings, a key aspect of qualifying to undertake Independent Patrol. However, after qualifying, a police officer might not attend court again for some time; indeed, to some extent the opportunities to experience court during training are specially arranged. A police officer is more likely to give evidence in court if they are a detective working on volume crime or are involved in a major police operation. Court appearances for police officers are less common now partly due to the increased proportion of early 'guilty' pleas. This increase is likely to be in some part attributable to advances in DNA evidence, the increased availability of discounted sentences in return for an early guilty plea, and the increased use of statutory fines and penalties (see 10.18.2.2). However, as court appearances by police officers now tend to relate to more serious offences and involve a substantial criminal trial, it is all the more important to get it right.

18.7.6.1 The adversarial justice system in court

In court, contested hearings are undertaken by two 'adversaries' or opponents, these being the representatives for the defence and the prosecution. Occasionally, a defendant elects to conduct their own defence but they will not always be permitted to cross-examine all witnesses (see 18.7.6.3.4 for details).

The defence and the prosecution must comply with certain rules concerning the evidence. The prosecution has a duty to ensure that all relevant evidence and unused material is disclosed under the CPIA (see 13.4). The Criminal Procedure Rules govern the process and these are regularly updated. Part 1 sets out the overriding objective that the court should be able to deal with cases justly. Dealing with a criminal case justly includes:

(a) acquitting the innocent and convicting the guilty;
(b) dealing with the prosecution and the defence fairly;
(c) recognizing the rights of a defendant, particularly those under Article 6 of the European Convention on Human Rights;

(d) respecting the interests of witnesses, victims, and jurors and keeping them informed of the progress of the case;
(e) dealing with the case efficiently and expeditiously;
(f) ensuring that appropriate information is available to the court when bail and sentence are considered; and
(g) dealing with the case in ways that take into account—
   (i) the gravity of the offence alleged,
   (ii) the complexity of what is in issue,
   (iii) the severity of the consequences for the defendant and others affected, and
   (iv) the needs of other cases.

In accordance with the overriding objective of fairness, the defence is unlikely to succeed if it seeks to ambush the prosecution with a piece of evidence or a point of law at a late stage in the proceedings (eg see *Gleeson* [2003] EWCA Crim 3357).

The defence occasionally challenges the prosecution's case and asks for the prosecution to cease. For example, the judge can be asked to dismiss the case at a Plea and Trial Preparation Hearing (PTPH) before the trial begins. The admissibility of critical evidence might be challenged and, if successful, the case for the prosecution may fail. Alternatively, in certain circumstances the challenge might come later on in the trial by way of a 'half time submission' by the defence once the prosecution has closed its case. A challenge is very likely to occur if a key witness fails to confirm (orally) the evidence in their written statements. The judge can also halt a trial for similar reasons and direct a jury to acquit, but this is rare.

By way of example, the defence could challenge the following issues:

- whether the alleged offence actually took place (eg when a point to prove has not been established in the evidence);
- whether the defendant carried out the relevant acts (perhaps they have an alibi);
- whether the defendant had the requisite intention (the act was unintentional or there were justifiable reasons for the act, such as self-defence); and/or
- whether the process which brought the defendant to court was at fault.

This last point can be used even if it seems very likely that the defendant clearly did commit the crime. The defence could claim, for example, that the relevant PACE Act 1984 and CPIA Codes of Practice had not been followed, and suggest that the trial is flawed and unfair, and the judge will be asked to dismiss the evidence and any related charges. Indeed, it is the role of the defence counsel to expose flaws in the prosecution case if that helps the defendant. Some people feel uncomfortable with these aspects of the defence counsel's role, believing such approaches to be morally ambiguous. This misses the point: the role of the defence is to do anything (within legal and ethical bounds) to act in the defendant's best interest. So the police have to get it absolutely right, every time. That is why we place so much emphasis here on getting the procedure correct.

18.7.6.2 A court as a public arena

Both the Crown Court and magistrates' courts have a public gallery and, with the exception of youth courts, anyone can watch any trial or hearing in progress. For some cases, however, special measures will apply (see 18.7.6.3.5) and the public will be excluded so that the trial can be held in private.

When associates of the defendant and the victim are present, public order problems may occasionally occur. If this seems likely, the ushers and security staff should be alerted. The judge or chairman of the bench may warn the public gallery about the possible consequences of disruptive behaviour, such as removal or arrest for contempt of court. Whilst efforts have been made to alter courtroom layouts, a member of a jury may still be intimidated by the defendant's circle of associates. In such circumstances the public gallery may be cleared, leaving the press bench to represent the public's interest. Communal corridors and external smoking areas also provide opportunities for the defendant's associates and the witnesses for the prosecution to meet. Separate rooms are available in most courts for witnesses to sit away from other people, and it may be possible for witnesses to enter the court building via a separate entrance. Intimidation of juries and witnesses is covered in Chapter 19.

Police officers are not immune from threats or intimidation and should identify and bring to the court's attention any person who seeks to threaten or intimidate an officer.

18.7.6.3 Court procedures

Evidence is largely presented in court in the form of the testimony of a witness. Witnesses give evidence of what they heard, saw, smelled, tasted, or felt. Sometimes an expert witness may be asked to give an opinion, such as a pathologist giving an opinion on the cause of death in a murder case, but ordinary witnesses (including police officers) will seldom be asked for an opinion. Witnesses who attend courts frequently (eg police officers) are known as professional witnesses, as distinct from expert witnesses.

On the basis of the given evidence, the bench or district judge (in a magistrates' court) or the jury (in the Crown Court) will decide whether the accused is guilty or not. In the case of the Crown Court, if the accused pleads guilty, there will be no need for a jury and the hearing will be much shorter.

18.7.6.3.1 The notification to attend court

At the outset, witnesses are 'warned for court'. For a magistrates' court, the notification to attend will be a simple letter or notice stating the date and time. For the Crown Court, there are two forms of witness warning—a 'conditional' and a 'full' warning. A conditional warning is used when the witness's evidence is not likely to be contested and so the witness may not be required to attend court. If nothing more is communicated then they can 'stand by' and are unlikely to have to give evidence (unless either side move to have the witness called). Note, however, that they still should not discuss the evidence with any third party. A witness receiving a full warning will certainly be called to attend but still might not be called to give evidence.

Waiting for a case to get to court can be a frustratingly long and drawn-out process. Delays can be caused by the sheer volume of cases the court has to deal with or difficulty finding a date when all witnesses and legal representatives can attend. Once in court, a case may still be put back, postponed, rescheduled, or otherwise not heard on that day for any number of procedural reasons.

18.7.6.3.2 The oath

Evidence must be given on oath by any witness or defendant at a statutory legal process, including a magistrates' court or the Crown Court. The Perjury Act 1911 and the Oaths Act 1978 require that a person must be sworn in the particular form or manner that is binding on their conscience. Those adhering to a religious belief touch or hold their respective holy books when giving the oath, and there may be other observances involved such as a ritual washing. Those who do not hold a particular religious belief may choose to affirm. The affirmation is a promise to tell the truth and was brought in under the Oaths Act 1978 (s 4(2)) to avoid the possibility of non-religious witnesses claiming their evidence to be invalid.

Perjury is when a person lies under oath. This is a serious criminal offence under the Perjury Act 1911. A person commits perjury when they wilfully make a material statement which they know to be false or do not believe to be true. This could be in a court or tribunal after the person has been sworn as a witness or as an interpreter (s 1(1) and (2)) or before any person legally empowered to hear and assess evidence. A court determines whether the statement was 'material' or not for the proceedings (s 1(6)). The false statement must have been made deliberately and not merely by mistake, and more than one witness must testify that the statement was false for a perjury conviction to succeed (s 13).

Perjury is an offence in criminal and civil proceedings, punishable on indictment with a maximum of seven years' imprisonment or a fine (CPS, 2017a), and the punishment must reflect the seriousness of the original offence (*R v Dunlop* [2001] 2 Cr App R (S) 27). Perjury in most cases will amount to perverting the course of justice but perjury specifically involves lying in court. Perverting the course of justice can occur in many different ways, such as arranging a false alibi, but lying about it in court would be perjury. A prosecution for perjury is appropriate when making a false statement in court is the principal act, but not if the false statement is part of a series of acts aimed at perverting the course of justice. Aiding, abetting, counselling, procuring, or suborning another person to commit perjury carries the same penalty as perjury itself (s 7(1)). Chapter 27 covers conspiracy and encouraging or assisting another to commit an offence.

18.7.6.3.3 Giving evidence

Oral evidence is the most common form of evidence presented to a court. A witness will say 'I saw them push the block over the bridge' or 'The drink tasted really bitter after I came back'. It is what has been directly experienced by someone on the spot at the time that the alleged offence was committed. A witness to an act must have perceived (seen, heard, felt, tasted, or smelled) that act directly, through their senses. Under s 9 of the Criminal Justice Act 1967, if both sides agree, a witness statement can be read out in court in the place of oral evidence from the witness (commonly referred to as a 'section 9 statement').

Real evidence is any article or thing which can be produced for the court, supported by testimony to link to the accused such as 'This is the iron bar I saw them holding'.

The evidential link to the accused generally has to made through supporting testimony, such as: 'These bloodstains were recovered from the clothing worn by the accused at the time of his arrest and match the blood type of the man found lying in the stairwell.' The significance of a piece of real evidence often has to be explained in court, especially if the relevant item is not within everyone's common experience, such as an explosive detonator for triggering a bomb. Large items, for example a lorry or a crash site, may be visited by a court if the evidence is vital for a case.

There must be an auditable trail for the article produced as real evidence, from the moment it was discovered or recovered until it is produced in court. This is referred to as 'continuity of evidence' or the 'chain of evidence' and is covered in more detail in Chapter 13.

Documentary evidence is a separate class of real evidence. The rules about the legal status of documents are complex but the general point is that the document should be produced in court by the person who created it and who can testify to its contents. This is not always possible (eg for a will) but a court can ask for a handwriting expert to testify that, within limitations, the author of one particular document is likely to be the author of another particular document.

Hearsay evidence is 'any statement not made in oral evidence in the proceedings' (s 114 of the Criminal Justice Act 2003 (CJA 2003)); it is one person's account of what another person said. There are concerns that hearsay evidence cannot be tested, contested, or verified in court because the originator of the evidence is not present. There have even been concerns that hearsay evidence might breach Article 6 of the ECHR (which establishes the right to a fair and public hearing) by not allowing the defence the opportunity, for example, to cross-examine an absent witness. The European Court of Human Rights found that this was unfounded and stated that the circumstances of each trial need to be taken into account (*Al-Khawaja & Tahery v UK* [2012] 2 Costs LO 139). So, while the term 'hearsay' or the 'hearsay rule' are commonly used to refer to the general inadmissibility of hearsay evidence within criminal proceedings, it is important to note that many exceptions to this general rule apply.

TASK 3 Are there exceptions you can think of that would allow for hearsay evidence to be used? The four 'gateways' to admissibility of hearsay evidence are:

1. The CJA 2003 or any other Act indicates that it may be used. (This will include, for instance, when a witness cannot attend court due to illness and statements from a person (eg a victim's friend) about what the victim had said about the incident (s 120 of the CJA 2003).)
2. Any of the common law exceptions preserved by the CJA 2003 (including confession evidence).
3. All parties to the proceedings agree to the evidence being given.
4. The court concludes that in the interests of justice the hearsay evidence should be admitted.

Gateway 4 is particularly useful for hearsay evidence that does not fit any of the recognized exceptions (it is sometimes referred to as the 'safety valve'). It was used when the Court of

Processing Policing

Appeal (Criminal Division) accepted hearsay evidence consisting of a police officer's record of a conversation with a 14-year-old witness. This contained details of the witness's relationship with the offender and was accepted on the grounds that it was useful to confirm evidence given by the witness earlier, despite it having been later denied (*Burton v R* [2011] EWCA Crim 1990).

Bad character evidence (BCE, see Chapter 13) can be used in court but the defence or the prosecution must first apply to the judge under s 100 of the CJA 2003. The main principle is to protect a witness or victim from having irrelevant aspects of their previous history brought up (see s 101(1) of the CJA 2003 for the full list). Where the defendant wishes to raise the previous sexual history of a complainant, this is likely to be excluded by virtue of s 41 of the Youth Justice and Criminal Evidence Act 1999 (YJCEA), unless it is relevant and admissible. Case law shows that judges are unlikely to allow BCE evidence to be introduced unless it is really significant and relevant (see *R v Bovell* [2005] 2 Cr App R 401).

Witness evidence is given from the witness box and the witness should face towards the judge or the bench when giving evidence. 'Evidence-in-chief' is the evidence given by the witness in response to the party that called them as a witness.

In most straightforward cases, oral evidence is given 'directly', which means providing a detailed and accurate chronology of events without any prompting. If there are logistical problems with a witness being able to attend court, evidence can be given via a live television link. In more complex cases, and always at the Crown Court, evidence is given in response to questions that seek to draw out detail from the witness, usually following the chronology of the events.

A police visual recording of an interview with a significant witness (see Chapter 13) may be shown to the court, particularly if there are inconsistencies between the oral evidence and the recorded evidence. A recording is not usually permitted as the sole source of evidence-in-chief, apart from when 'special measures' apply (see 18.7.6.3.5); this commonly happens in cases involving rape or sexual abuse and especially where the witness is a child. The court can exclude a recording if there is insufficient information about where it was made or if the recording contains serious violations of the rules of evidence.

18.7.6.3.4 Cross-examination

Cross-examination by opposing counsel takes place once the evidence has been given (either directly or in response to the counsel's questions). This may be quite stressful but there are a variety of 'special measures' available for vulnerable and intimidated witnesses and aggressive questioning is not normally tolerated. If the defendant is conducting their own defence, it will sometimes be inappropriate for them to cross-examine a particular witness, particularly in cases involving domestic violence, for example. In such circumstances, an application can be made by the prosecution for a legal representative to be appointed to act on the defendant's behalf, for cross-examination purposes only (s 36 of the YJCEA).

After the cross-examination, the counsel who called the witness has the right to ask further questions (re-examination), but this questioning is restricted solely to matters that arose in the cross-examination and is usually seeking clarification and removing ambiguity. And finally, the magistrates or judge may need to ask questions of a witness.

After a witness has finished giving evidence, the magistrate or judge gives permission for them to leave the witness box. There are two forms of 'permission to leave' and these are:

- to be stood down, which usually requires a witness to be available for recall; and
- to be discharged, which means the court does not expect them to be recalled so they may leave the court.

The witness can sit in the public gallery once they have been discharged.

18.7.6.3.5 Special measures in court

Special measures are available to assist some vulnerable and/or intimidated witnesses. Special measures are important in terms of witness well-being, which in turn impacts on the quality of the evidence they are able to give. All children and young people under the age of 18 are eligible for special measures. Vulnerable witnesses are eligible if the quality of their evidence is likely to be adversely affected due to their personal difficulties, as are intimidated witnesses whose quality of evidence is likely to be diminished by reason of fear or distress. An application is made to the court explaining what type(s) of special measure is being applied for and how and why this will assist the witness and improve the quality of their evidence. The application is made by the CPS based on information provided by the police.

The various types of special measure are set out in ss 23–30 of the YJCEA.

- screens are positioned around the witness (s 23). This is helpful in that the witness will not be able to see the defendant and vice versa;
- a TV live link is used so the witness gives evidence from another room within the court building or, sometimes, a different building altogether (s 24). Evidence is relayed live to the courtroom on large TV screens. This means that the witness does not have to go in to the same room as the defendant and it is possible to apply for the TV screens to be positioned in court such that the witness cannot be seen by the defendant;
- evidence is given in private—members of the public are excluded from the courtroom and only one nominated member of the press is permitted to stay for the proceedings (s 25). This is not used very often but can be employed in very sensitive cases or where intimidation is an issue;
- wigs and gowns (judges' and lawyers') are removed to create a less intimidating environment (s 26);
- video-recorded interviews can be used as 'evidence-in-chief' (s 27)—this allows the witness to give their account in a more relaxed environment, closer to the time of reporting the offence, hopefully resulting in a fuller more detailed account. The witness will, however, still be cross-examined by the defence;
- a pre-recorded cross-examination is used (s 28). This involves the witness being cross-examined in advance of the trial and is used in conjunction with s 27, negating the requirement for the witness to attend court;
- intermediaries (trained communication specialists) (s 29) may be instructed to help to facilitate communication between the witness and the court;
- communication aids (eg a computer) are used by the witness when giving evidence (s 30).

Each special measure may be used individually or in combination with others in order to ensure that the witness has the best possible opportunity to provide high-quality evidence. It should be noted that special measures are not guaranteed until the court has ruled on the application. Therefore, while it is a good idea to explain the available options to eligible witnesses at an early stage, premature promises should not be made.

18.7.6.3.6 Hostile witnesses

A lawyer can ask for a witness to be deemed 'hostile' by the judge. This is when a witness has made a statement previously but declines to confirm certain details in court, and is assumed to be deliberately not telling the truth. The judge will announce their decision to the court, often giving reasons. The witness can then be cross-examined and challenged about the change of evidence and the inconsistencies with previous statements will be explored.

18.7.6.4 Giving evidence as a police officer

Early on in their career, a police officer is most likely to give evidence in court as the 'officer in the case' (OIC). The officer's availability will be taken into consideration when the trial date is set.

This is the final phase of the investigation in a sense because it is the calling to account of the case against the accused and a consideration of the evidence. A police officer's role is to explain what they have done, heard, seen, or recorded, as concisely as possible. Any witness, including a police officer or an officer in training, should avoid discussing the case in detail with colleagues or associates before, and certainly during, the trial because recollections can be contaminated by verbally revisiting the circumstances.

18.7.6.4.1 Preparing for giving evidence as a police officer

After the case file has been prepared, further planning and preparation is needed for the actual process of giving evidence. As the OIC, you would have to:

- review the case, reread the case papers, and reread your PNB;
- ensure you have a copy of your duty statement to use as a reminder, if required, while giving evidence (permitted under s 139 of the CJA 2003);
- familiarize yourself with the rules of evidence (particularly on hearsay evidence and opinion);
- speak to the CPS lawyer who will be prosecuting;
- prepare for dealing with difficult questions from the defence, for example on certain points of evidence;
- check that everything in the case is administratively in order, including labelling the exhibits; and
- check the arrangements for witnesses, for example about any payment due to them and the holding areas where they will wait to be called, particularly if they feel vulnerable to intimidation.

You could also visit the court premises and sit through part of another case before checking the exact location of the courtroom for your case.

18.7.6.4.2 In the witness box as a police officer

It is becoming increasingly common, particularly in magistrates' court cases, for police officers to give their evidence via video link from their police station in order to save time. However this guidance applies equally to both scenarios. You will first take the oath or affirm and then introduce yourself by rank, police number, name, and the police station where you are based. When you are responding to questions, try to address your answers to the judge and jury or the magistrates. Speak clearly, do not rush your words, and try to keep to a steady pace as people will be taking notes of what you say.

If you want to refer to your PNB in court, you should ask for permission. The defence is entitled to object and may ask you to explain the manner and time of making your notes and whether your notes represent a 'contemporaneous account' (written at the time) or whether you wrote up your PNB afterwards. Any notes made reasonably soon after the event should be acceptable; however, if there is a significant time lag (two days or longer) the defence is likely to question this very closely. The court, prosecution, or defence may want to examine the entry itself so make sure that your grammar and spelling are always up to scratch and that your handwriting is at least legible! They might also examine it to look for any evidence of collusion with other officers (see 10.2.1.3). Heavy reliance on your PNB is not advised and it should not be thought of as a substitute for good preparation. If you ask to refer to it to answer simple questions, it will look as though you have no proper recollection of the case, which will reflect badly on your credibility as a witness. Referring to it for specific details, such as dates, or car registration plate numbers, is usually acceptable but do not expect to be allowed to use it as a script.

When giving evidence, you could be tempted to try to learn your evidence by heart but this is most inadvisable. Firstly, it will sound artificial. Secondly, the defence may try to put you off with questions so that you lose your thread and flounder and, finally, it suggests that maybe you do not have the confidence to rely on your recall of events. There is nothing wrong with referring to your PNB entries—after all, the lawyers and the judge constantly refer to their notes. However, you should not rely on your PNB exclusively as that will not create a good impression. It is much better to speak clearly and confidently, referring only now and then to your PNB to refresh your memory or to quote a particular detail. Always avoid hearsay or BCE unless it has been confirmed to you that it has been admitted. We discuss how to create a good impression in more detail in 18.7.6.4.4.

18.7.6.4.3 Cross-examination

As a witness, you can ask anyone to repeat a question which you did not hear or did not understand. This also gives you an extra moment to think. You should remain polite and courteous at all times and be prepared for the unexpected, for example the defence might begin by asking:

> PC Winn, what formal training have you had in interview techniques and did that training, if indeed you had it, cover the use of oppressive interrogation?

Here the defence is using a common tactic of double questioning as well as launching straight into querying the officer's qualifications. When faced with such a question, you might choose to reply as follows:

> [To the judge] I was accredited Tier 2 Investigative Interviewing, which means I am qualified by the police in investigative interviewing, which incorporates questioning styles. I did the training at the Police training centre in August last year. I routinely undertake interviews at this level and believe I have an understanding of the term 'oppressive' as it applies in the Police and Criminal Evidence Act 1984, section 76. [Turning back to the defence] Would you repeat the second part of your question, sir?

Note the politeness and refusal to be flustered by the defence's approach. In fact, replying in this way—the completeness of the first reply—would establish you as a professional and credible witness and the defence may seem merely querulous. If the defence persisted in making an innuendo in such a deliberately challenging tone, the judge might intervene to ask where it is leading and how it is relevant. You might also have noticed how in the example PC Winn 'collects' the question from the lawyer and delivers their answer directly to the judge, before politely asking the defence lawyer for the second part of the question. This emphasizes that they have been attentive and are not to be hurried into giving confused answers to complex questions.

The use of body language can certainly help to control pace and speed. It would be best to turn back to a person asking a question only when you think you have given a complete answer and you are ready for the next question. Some eye contact with the jury is always helpful as they are the people you would need to convince on issues of fact. You should avoid a one-to-one 'conversation' with either the defence or the prosecution counsel as this is likely to be irritating to the jury (they may feel distanced from the proceedings).

The defence may use a variety of approaches such as trailer questions, multiple questions, hypothetical questions, or out-of-sequence chronology. These should be dealt with one at a time. It is important to portray yourself to the jury as a competent professional.

The defence counsel will sometimes attempt to persuade juries that collusion has occurred between officers and that adjustments have been made to match their accounts. It is important that you limit yourself to recollections about matters that you have personal knowledge of, and can convey directly to the court, and do not adjust your evidence. Imagine if you truthfully recalled in your evidence to the jury that your memory is that the car you saw was green, and your colleague following you into the witness box had said it was red? Both of you are telling the truth, one possibly mistaken, but this would be far better than you 'changing your recall' to having seen a red car—when the car was in fact later proved to be green!

There will be occasions when your evidence as a police officer is favourable to the defendant and naturally enough the defence will want to make use of this.

You should expect to be questioned about how you conducted the investigation and the evidence you have already given, and asked for any additional facts which you have not already given. It is often not what you say that is fertile territory for the cross-examination—but rather what you did not say.

18.7.6.4.4 Creating the right impression

The impression a police officer creates in court, as noted earlier, will influence their credibility, particularly as some members of the jury might be subjective and 'go by feel' rather than by objective fact.

When giving evidence as a police officer, you should always watch your general attitude and remain calm and courteous at all times, even in the face of inflammatory questioning or an apparent attack on your integrity. Rising to the bait will only assist the defence. If in court you appear intolerant or impatient then your credibility as a police officer on oath or affirmation in court would be at risk. Police officers are subject to personal scrutiny (as any other witness can be); your record, your training, your job performance, and even your personal life may be closely investigated by the defence. Anything which can undermine your credibility or make the jury dubious about the reliability of your testimony may be exploited by a defence lawyer who will not hesitate to confront you with it during cross-examination. In the same way, any obvious bias demonstrated by a police officer against a defendant will be deeply unhelpful to the prosecution case and may in fact help the defence.

When giving evidence, you should speak clearly, keep your voice at an audible volume, and try not to talk too quickly. Clear, concise language should be used. No one would advise you to talk like a legal textbook but you should avoid using slang terms unless you are repeating something you have heard as part of your evidence, in which case you should say exactly what you heard, no matter how obscene the language. Another temptation is to say too much and to keep on talking, but you should keep your answers short and to the point.

For example:

> **Prosecutor**: Constable Winn, did you see the injuries?
> **PC Winn**: Yes, I did. This was at first during the initial interview, when Ms Bent showed me an extensive bruise to her left eye and cheekbone. She was then examined by the custody nurse for other injuries.
> **Prosecutor**: What did you do next?
> **PC Winn**: I arranged for the custody nurse to examine Ms Bent and prepare a body map of injuries, and arranged for them to be photographed.
> **Prosecutor**: With what result?
> **PC Winn**: We had the injuries photographed and listed. She was advised to attend A&E immediately after the interview, and I have obtained a doctor's report and statement.
> **Prosecutor**: Your Honour, I refer to the statement taken from Dr Salim Khan, A&E House Officer at Albright Hospital, in bundle 6, document 44A.

Notice that PC Winn gives clear answers but does not elaborate (knowing that the counsel will follow up with another question if more information is required). Note, too, that PC Winn does not try to give a medical opinion or to paraphrase Dr Khan's evidence or statement. This would be inappropriate because PC Winn has no medical qualifications and cannot speak with any authority. However, the court may allow PC Winn to comment on whether the apparent injuries were consistent with assault, based on their knowledge and experience as a police officer. The temptation to use someone else's evidence in your answers can be strong, but you must resist.

The use of acronyms (eg BCU, TIC, SIO) and overly technical words (eg 'lacerations' for cuts) should also be avoided as they may confuse the jury. You might appear to be trying too hard to impress if you say something like this (especially if your grasp of the meaning of words is a little shaky).

> I proceeded in a southerly direction towards the connurbative encompassment of commercial premises which is characterized by the soubriquet of 'shopping mall'. The chronological observation which was then essayed by myself was recorded contemporaneously as 13.45 hours, British Summer Time. It was at that juncture that I espied the trio of adult males engaging in what I deemed to be behaviour which warranted a sufficiency of explanation as to make my legitimated suspicions subside …

Perhaps all you needed to say was:

> I was on patrol in the shopping centre at 13.45 when I saw three men behaving suspiciously, so I challenged them.

Even this is fairly formal, but it has the great merit of being brief. Remember the impression you are creating as a concise, well-prepared professional.

You certainly need to be organized and to appear to be organized: 'Um … I will just check …' is not likely to impress the jury and you risk losing their attention. The statement 'May I please refer to document 24 in the bundle, your honour?' is far more professional and courteous. Using the correct terminology to address the court will certainly help create a good impression:

- 'Ma'am' or 'Sir' for the lawyers on either side;
- 'Your Honour', 'My Lady', or 'My Lord' for the judge in the Crown Court (depending on the status of the Crown Court);
- 'Your Worships' for the magistrates' court and 'Ma'am' or 'Sir' if addressing them individually; and
- 'Ma'am' or 'Sir' for a district judge in the magistrates' court.

It would be easy for us to ignore your appearance through some sense of respect for individual personal style, but non-verbal communication (see 8.8.3) is a powerful influence—you need to look as smart as you sound. A smart uniform, polished shoes, and neat hair can seem petty requirements but they help you to assert your authority and will boost your confidence in the witness box. Actions also convey attitudes; hands in pockets, fiddling with buttons or your glasses, and constantly shifting through documents creates a poor impression.

18.7.6.4.5 After giving evidence

You should wait in the witness box until the magistrate or judge gives you permission to leave. If you are in doubt about whether you are being 'stood down', you must speak to the CPS lawyer prosecuting the case at a convenient moment, and remain available within the court building.

If you wish to remain in court, you are entitled to do so and can sit in the public gallery. However, associates of the accused could be there so you might not feel particularly comfortable. You should also avoid making eye contact or nodding in agreement; this sort of action on your part might encourage the defence to question any influence you may be having on the jury or the magistrates and could easily lead to criticism of your conduct in open court.

You would also need to take care in relation to other witnesses who have not yet given evidence.

Imagine you travelled to court with a colleague and that you have given evidence and been discharged, but they are going to give evidence the following morning. You travelled together by car and intend to return home the same way; however, you would need to take care not to talk about the case. The following morning they may be asked about how they travelled to court, who with, and whether the case was discussed. The defence may look for forms of collusion or inconsistency between their written statement and the evidence they give orally, and suggest that any differences are an indication that they changed their account to suit yours. You will need to ensure that this type of situation does not arise.

18.7.6.4.6 Sentencing

If a court has found a defendant guilty, it has three primary sentencing options: community orders, fines, and custodial sentences. These may be used together or separately, depending on the offence and the offender's circumstances. Community orders (such as removing graffiti from buildings) combine rehabilitation with punishment and are supervised by the Probation Service. For the most serious offences, courts may opt for custodial sentences. The length of the sentence imposed depends on the maximum penalty (as defined in the legislation for that offence), the circumstances in which the offence was committed, and on the offender (eg whether they are a repeat offender).

The court may also make a conditional or an absolute discharge. For the former, the offender is discharged but with the condition of not committing any other offence for a certain time period (three years maximum). An offender who does then commit an offence within the time period will be convicted for breaching the conditional discharge and re-sentenced. For an absolute discharge, the person has either admitted to an offence or been found guilty, but is not penalized as the process of investigation and prosecution is deemed to be a sufficient response to the offence committed.

Sentences must be appropriate and proportionate, taking into consideration all of the circumstances. The Sentencing Council sets out sentencing guidelines to help magistrates and judges to decide on the appropriate sentence. There are different guidelines for those under the age of 18.

18.8 Answers to Tasks

TASK 1 You should have found that these Regulations (under Part II) cover issues such as the fitting and requirements of lights, lamps, reflectors, and rear markings on vehicles.

TASK 2 For the offence of robbery, you should have found:

- the Theft Act 1968, s 8(1);
- mode of trial: triable on indictment only;
- maximum penalty for a person found guilty: life imprisonment.

TASK 3 The exceptions usually agreed to be taken as evidence are declarations on the point of death and statements about confessions if the witness heard the confession themselves. Also see CPS (2019b) which provides four types of admissible hearsay evidence: (1) if it is identified as admissible within the Criminal Justice Act 2003 or other statutory legislation; (2) it is a common law exception; (3) all parties agree to it being admitted into proceedings; and (4) it can be established that justice is served by admitting the evidence.

19 Public Protection, Victims, and Witnesses

19.1 Introduction

In the police environment, the term 'public protection' has a broad meaning. Although it is often associated with the management of violent and sexual offenders, the term is also applied to protecting victims through investigating incidents involving sexual offences, violence, child abuse, vulnerable adult abuse, domestic and family violence, and coercive behaviour, harassment, stalking, human trafficking and modern slavery, hate crime honour-based crime, female genital mutilation (FGM), forced marriage, and missing persons.

The range of crimes covered by public protection are often serious and complex, affecting the most vulnerable in a community, and the police have a legal and moral duty to protect those adults and children who are at risk from harm. To do this effectively requires an awareness of the wider context in which an offence has taken place and appropriate management of the risk of harm. For example, it is suggested that the initial reporting of a domestic abuse incident may not be the first incident of abuse. There are contrasting views on this with HMIC (2014a) suggesting that a victim experiences harm on up to 50 prior occasions before contacting the police while Strang, Neyroud, and Sherman (2014) suggest these figures are a 'myth' that enjoy little evidential support. However, in the year ending March 2022, 2.4 million adults had experienced this type of harm (CSEW, 2022). A super complaint made by the Centre for Women's Justice in 2022 highlighted concerns regarding police failure to use existing legal protections for vulnerable people experiencing domestic abuse, sexual violence, harassment, and stalking, the majority of whom are women and girls. HMICFRS, the College of Policing, and the Independent Office for Police Conduct's (IOPC) joint investigation identified several areas of concern regarding the use of protected measures to keep victims safe (CWJ, 2019). This chapter will explain the available options for safeguarding victims.

In order to effectively tackle these complex crimes, the police do not, and cannot, operate in isolation. Multi-agency cooperation and effective information sharing is a critical feature of effective policing (Andrews, 2022). Therefore, this chapter will help you understand the role of other agencies while outlining initial police response to these situations and describe the procedures and available powers. Those victims who are vulnerable and/or suffering from mental ill health is covered extensively in Chapter 20 and under the Equality Act police have a duty to make reasonable adjustments to ensure individuals with protected characteristics are not discriminated against (see Chapter 7).

The effective policing of public protection related cases significantly relies on the management of risk and harm to victims and witnesses. In the second half of this chapter, we examine the law, policy, and guidance around supporting victims and witnesses who come into contact with the Criminal Justice System as a part of a police investigation. In addition to this, we will discuss the impact that victimization, and the witnessing of crime, can have on the mental wellbeing of a person, as well as how the needs of the victim and the acts of the investigating officer, play a significant role in the outcome of a case.

As police officers you are required to face multiple situations in which a criminal act has resulted in harm being caused to a member of society. The degree of harm caused can be varied. No two victim experiences are the same, and neither is the level of trauma experienced because of a crime.

The victims of crime may need support, and this needs to be done in an ethical, appropriate, and timely manner in adherence to the Victims' Code. Other persons present, at the time of an offence taking place, may also have been affected and may need just as much support. You need to consider the physical, psychological, and emotional impacts and adapt the support that you can offer accordingly.

The topics covered in this chapter are likely to contribute to the learning required for the National Policing Curriculum subject areas of 'the law, policy and guidance in the treatment of victims and witnesses' (including the Victims' Code of Practice), 'victim and witness care', 'appropriate behaviours and attitudes towards victims', 'initial assessment requirements', 'understanding judicial outcomes', and 'managing victims, pre and post judicial proceedings'.

As part of the PCDA, the police constable is expected to know and understand 'Key cross-cutting and inter-dependent areas of policing, including vulnerability, public protection and mental health and risk', so reading this chapter in conjunction with Chapter 20 is advised. If you are a trainee police officer, undertaking the PCDA or DHEP, then responding to a public protection incident as a 'first responder' may differ from other incidents to which you may be deployed. Chapter 9 provides information on how to manage violent and aggressive people. Responding to a domestic abuse incident is covered in detail below (see 19.4.2).

19.2 What Do We Mean by Public Protection?

The term 'public protection' represents a wide area of police work. While it is often misunderstood as relating to a few specific offences, in reality it refers to work around criminal and non-criminal matters impacting some of the most vulnerable victims, as well as most vulnerable but also dangerous offenders. Some of the issues public protection teams deal with include both child and adult victims, as well as crime and non-crime matters (each police service will have a department, or several, dedicated to public protection issues though they do not necessarily have to have this name). It is important to remember that it is not only criminal matters which are inherently complex and where risk assessment is of key importance, there are non-crime matters which need equal amounts of attention. Public protection matters can, and should be, seen through the 'wicked problems in policing' lens—in other words, these matters are of complex nature, highly interconnected, and every solution tends to uncover a number of new issues. This means that the area of public protection is constantly evolving, and officer inquisitiveness is very important. The current section provides you with a whistle stop tour of public protection matters to gain a better understanding of the breadth of the problem; later, we will go into more detail and legal definitions in relation to core areas and specific crimes.

19.2.1 The breadth of the problem

We will start with the area of intra-familiar matters (ie among family members in its widest sense, including between partners). This area includes a wide variety of different offences which tend to overlap. Domestic abuse incidents are specifically those where the victim and the perpetrator are over the age of 16 and include psychological, physical, sexual, financial, and emotional abuse. Through latest research guidelines, it has become apparent that as a police officer, you have to gain a good understanding of what domestic abuse looks like—it is not only the more stereotypical violent abuse scenario. It also includes a lot of controlling and coercive behaviours which make this a high-risk crime, because victims are often abused repeatedly over a long period of time. In domestic abuse relationships, we can see the development of a power imbalance between the victim and the perpetrator—this makes it incredibly difficult to engage in a policing response. Domestic abuse also impacts on any children in the household, making police response even more complex.

There are specific domestic abuse offences which need further consideration through an equality, diversity, and inclusion lens—cultural awareness is key when interacting with victims, their families and friends, as well as perpetrators. These are offences such as honour-based abuse and forced marriage. In these offences, the above notions of coercive and controlling behaviours very much stand. Forced marriage is one where the victim did not consent to marry and the perpetrator is aware of this. The crime of forced marriage is intrinsically interlinked with other offences often carried out with the view of committing the offence—eg harassment, grievous bodily harm, immigration offences, or fraud.

Whilst the above matters tend to exclusively happen *within* a familial context, there are those offences which span *inside* and *outside* the family context. These would include crimes relating to harassment and stalking. These crimes happen when someone causes the victim to feel scared, distressed, or threatened through the use of repeated behaviours over a period of time. Stalking and harassment are intrinsically intertwined with other offences such as coercive behaviours in intimate partnerships, and can make it difficult to effectively engage with a victim. Early risk assessment is key in this context as research highlights how they may be important predictors of homicide.

A specific area of public protection relates to child abuse; offences where a child is the victim are treated through specific processes where the safeguarding of children is the number one priority, above and beyond the investigative process alone. This is because children have an extra layer of vulnerability simply by virtue of their age. Children are often victim to multiple types of abuse at the same time (eg it can easily be argued that any form of physical abuse also causes psychological harm). Child witnesses to domestic abuse are also classed as victims and in any child abuse cases, further abuse within the family environment tends to occur. As a police officer, and hence a person in a position of authority, you should be very aware that some child abuse, and specifically child sexual abuse, can be attributed to perpetrators in a position of authority—there is a default power imbalance in this scenario—which might make it more difficult to report and engage with the justice system.

Female genital mutilation (FGM) can happen to women and girls alike though the more likely victims are girls. In such an instance where the victim is under the age of 18, it also constitutes child abuse (as above). This crime is especially personal to victims and easily hidden and you might need to act quickly as the victim may be trafficked to another country for the procedure. It is high likely that this offence is linked to others—including forced marriage or other forms of so called honour-based abuse. As with those, it is important to remember cultural sensitivity when dealing with victims and perpetrators.

There is a whole chapter in this book dedicated to sexual offences. Being a victim of a sexual offence means that a person is entitled to extra support. Anyone can be a victim and in fact, we are finding out more and more about the true number of male victims as their underreporting tends to be even more significant than that of female victims. Sexual offences include those where children are victims. As with child sexual abuse, many victims do not have high trust in the investigative process and there are many challenges they face when even deciding to report. You should appreciate that victims will be traumatized by what happened and be understanding of any trauma responses they may present with (eg describing what happened in extreme detail) (see 20.4.3 on trauma response).

Another area of public protection relates to modern slavery offences. Whereas the focus used to be on human trafficking alone, we are now appreciating the wide scope of modern slavery offences much more. As a police officer, you have to recognize that victims of modern slavery may be victims of multiple offences at the same time—this is what happens in the majority of cases. For example, a person may be trafficked into the country to engage in forced labour. You will likely be faced with further challenges—namely the need for an interpreter. It is important to be able to use non-verbal communication skills to ensure positive first interaction which can aid in further cooperation (see non-verbal communication in Chapter 8).

Serious hate crime offences also fall within the scope of public protection. Not all hate crime cases will be a public protection matter, however, in many instances, crime which includes the aggravated factor of being a hate crime will be more complex and can become a public protection matter—for example, what may seem like common assault to begin with might quickly be uncovered as being a case of harassment based on someone's religion. Further, many public protection offences can be hate motivated—for example, the rape of someone because of their race. In these cases you must show sensitivity to the victims/survivors, as they will come from populations where trust in the police is low, and experiences of the justice system are negative.

It is important to remember that it is not only criminal matters which are inherently complex and where risk assessment is of key importance, there are non-criminal matters which need equal amounts of attention. For example, going missing is related to a higher risk of sexual or criminal exploitation, there is significant risk of injury and the possibility of involvement in crime. Effective risk assessment is key as going missing is a frequently cited risk factor for a lot of criminal offences, including criminal or sexual exploitation, kidnapping, trafficking, and more.

A person may become a victim of poly-victimization or repeat victimization, in which they are targeted, more than once, and have a similar crime committed against them (Pease and Farrell, 2016). In its 2018 Crime Survey covering England and Wales, the Office of National Statistics (ONS, 2018b) found that 26 per cent of victims of violence were repeat victims within the previous 12 months. Of those, 12 per cent had been a victim of the same offence twice, and 7 per cent had been victims three or more times. Repeat victims of crime were most commonly those who had experienced domestic abuse at 34 per cent, in comparison to only 15 per cent of repeat victimization for stranger violence.

19.2.2 Victimization and victims

19.2.2.1 Poly-victimization

Poly-victimization is when a person suffers several types of victimization, such as bullying and physical violence. These forms of victimization are often inflicted intentionally by a variety of perpetrators at multiple time points and in multiple contexts. However, they can also arise as a result of neglect (particularly during formative developmental periods in the life of a growing child). Poly-victimization can include episodes of sexual, physical, and emotional maltreatment by caregivers or other adults; physical or sexual assault or bullying by peers or older youths; and witnessing violent and traumatic incidents in the home, school, and community. Poly-victims might also be disadvantaged through insufficient protection and limited social support, as this can buffer the adverse effects of other forms of traumatic stressors such as severe accidents, illnesses, disasters, and loss of loved ones.

Poly-victimization is associated with severe emotional, behavioural, and interpersonal problems throughout life, and often has a greater adverse impact than even the most traumatic single types of victimization (eg, sexual abuse or assault; catastrophic family or community violence). Therapeutic interventions for complex post-traumatic emotional and behavioural problems have shown promise in systematic empirical studies of the treatment of child/youth and adult poly-victims (Ford, 2017; Ford and Delker, 2017).

19.2.2.2 Repeat victimization

Repeat victimization is when the same victim suffers the same or similar form of victimization a number of times. A person who is a repeat victim of abuse is particularly vulnerable. Victims of crime frequently report experiencing a fear of re-victimization and heightened sensitivity to risk (Warr, 1987). Whilst there are a limited number of studies that explore a broad spectrum of crimes associated with re-victimization, those that do exist primarily relate to interpersonal violence. A recent meta-analysis of sexual revictimization revealed that 47.9 per cent of CSA survivors experienced re-victimization (Walker *et al*, 2019). For repeat victims of abuse, the level of victimization can increase to the point of serious harm being caused. The significance for organizations is that for policy purposes, and particularly crime prevention, a focus upon repeats can greatly increase the efficiency with which resources are used.

Police investigations can have a direct impact on the level of fear victims experience towards re-victimization.

19.2.2.3 Alpha Victims

An Alpha Victim is a person or persons who have been coerced, exploited, and or groomed to facilitate the exploitation of others (Anti-slavery Commission, 2020). In such cases, and despite their victim status, such individuals may experience a general improvement to their lifestyle conditions. Examples of Alpha Victims include those who become complicit in acts relating to human trafficking and modern slavery.

19.2.2.4 The 'Ideal Victim'

Obtaining the status of being a 'victim of crime' is regarded as being an important factor in receiving a greater level of treatment received during the criminal justice process (Inzunza, 2022). When victims are assigned a different status by police officers it directly affects the way in which the victim or witness is perceived, especially in relation to their level of credibility. Factors that influence the determined status of a victim or witness can be based on their level of attractiveness or even social status (Vrij and Firmin, 2001). Such factors also influence the way in which offenders and the level of harms that they have caused to their victims are perceived (Bradbury and Martellozzo, 2021). Such perceptions are a form of cognitive bias that officers must be mindful of during their investigations into allegations.

Men are more commonly perceived as being agents of harm rather than victims in comparison to women (Reynolds *et al*, 2020). This is also the case with children. Male students between the ages of 13 to 16 years, who sexually engage with their teachers, are viewed as being 'lucky' rather than as victims of child sexual abuse. This sentiment is amplified if the female perpetrator is young and attractive (Bradbury and Martellozzo, 2021).

There are also factors held by victims which can influence how they are perceived by others. These factors (Inzunza, 2022) include:

- Giving an impression of weakness
- Being a respectable member of society
- Not engaging in blameworthy behaviours
- Being the victim of a stronger person
- Having no ties to the offender

The concept of the ideal victim has developed with contemporary research but the ideal victim isn't solely based on background variables such as gender. There are characteristics that relate to what is now coined as *framing*—a form of stereotyping (Duggan, 2018). Models such as the Stereotype Content Model (SCM) suggest that the 'warmth' attributable to a victim directly correlates to the degree of sympathy awarded by others. For example, mothers and the elderly are viewed as being weaker or lower in competence therefore eliciting a greater degree of sympathy. In contrast to this, drug addicts elicit negative social responses, such as disgust, and what is coined as contemptuous prejudice (Bosma *et al*, 2018; Inzunza, 2022).

19.2.2.5 Coercive control and victimization

The government's offence for coercive controlling behaviour was created to target perpetrators of domestic abuse and bring them to justice for the psychological and emotional abuse of their victims. Coercive control does not involve a single incident against a victim. Rather a process of repeat victimization in which there is a purposeful pattern of controlling behaviours over an individual (Home Office, 2015d). Between April 2018 and March 2019, ONS reported there to have been 17,616 offences of coercive control recorded by the police in England and Wales. The survey revealed that 95 per cent of coercive control victims were women, and that 74 per cent of perpetrators were men (Women's Aid, 2020a). In a study specifically focusing on the most common controlling behaviours for this offence were technology (which included methods such as phone tracking, messaging, and content monitoring), sexual coercion, isolation, and financial abuse (Barlow *et al*, 2018).

19.2.2.6 Impact of childhood adversity and trauma on behaviours

You can read more about the topic of Adverse Childhood Experiences (ACEs) in Chapter 20. As a police officer, you need to be aware of the impact that adverse experiences in childhood, as well as trauma which can be experienced in adulthood, have on behaviours. This is with the view of ensuring that you understand the wide variety of behaviours you might experience specifically when dealing with public protection matters. We know that there are many risk factors which contribute to one's likelihood of both offending and victimization. These are varied and manifest themselves in different groupings based on the topic of interest. Through extensive research, it was identified that there are some factors which are most likely to contribute to lifelong negative outcomes including non-justice outcomes such as suicide or obesity. The factors include child maltreatment (verbal abuse, physical abuse, sexual abuse), and household issues (parental separation/divorce, witnessing domestic violence, mental illness, alcohol abuse, drug use, and incarceration). Even though these have been identified as key events, do not underestimate other risks relating to one's vulnerability (eg financial standing)—professional curiosity is key. Whilst much of the population is likely to experience at least one of these events, research tells us that those who experience four or more of these are at a higher risk. For example, a global ACE analysis uncovered that those with four + ACEs are 7.5 times more likely than the general population to experience victimization and 8.1 times more likely than the general population to perpetrate violence (Hughes *et al*, 2017). These events are prolonged and continuous exposure literally changes the child's brain functioning. This causes a toxic stress response to one's environment and the development of a *life preserving brain*—this brain can be disengaged, anxious, hyper vigilant and so on. Children often exhibit behaviours which make them seem mature for their age—this in fact does not have much to do with maturity, it is the sign of a brain used to toxic stress. Trauma experienced during adulthood, equally, has an enormous impact on the functioning of individuals. This is especially true in instances of repeat or poly victimization (see above). When one experiences trauma, the experience leaves a form of imprint on the brain—this is where the brain loops back when an individual finds themselves in a triggering situation. People might present as surprisingly happy, overly anxious, mute, graphically descriptive, and more, as a coping mechanism to such trauma. Your role as a police officer is to recognize vulnerability and not jump to conclusions relating to how you think one might react to a certain situation. You need to remain judgement free and follow trauma-informed policing practices in your day-to-day work. You should work with individuals to prevent future adversity.

Processing Policing

19.2.2.7 Families with multiple and complex needs

It is likely that when dealing with issues relating to both intra- and extra-familial crimes, including domestic and child abuse, that you will come across families with multiple and/or complex needs who need an extra level of support in regard to their vulnerability.

- There is no official definition for what constitutes a family with 'complex' needs; however, some things to look out for are: mental ill health, learning and/or physical disability, alcohol and drug misuse, cultural differences, poor housing, or financial situation. The more of these needs are present, the more complex working with a family can be (these factors are accumulative in their nature). Another factor to consider is trauma—this can be trauma brought forward from childhood (see previous section on Adverse Childhood Experiences) or trauma in adulthood. If you identify a 'complex' needs family, it is more likely that there will be domestic abuse and/or child abuse in the home, transferring into criminality outside of the home environment. These families are characterized by the need for intense intervention and so it is key that you identify this risk and engage with other agencies as soon as possible.

19.2.2.8 The position of women and girls within public protection

Many of the crimes noted here disproportionately impact on women and girls as the victims. Furthermore, reports have continuously highlighted police response failings when it comes to crimes involving women and girls. The most recent one, the Baroness Casey Review, is a necessary bit of reading for you, so that you can understand why organizational and cultural change in the police, which you can and should be a part of, is key (see Casey, 2023). The Review highlights failings among many fronts, but most relevant to this section, highlights misogyny and sexism, intertwined with other key issues such as racism. Please refer to Chapter 7 to better understand how the intersectionality of different protected characteristics (and others) impacts on victims, offenders, and police officers alike. Whilst the review focuses on the Metropolitan Police Service, these issues are talked about across the nation. You therefore need to be aware of the position women and girls find themselves in when interacting with the police—you need to put in extra effort, especially when it comes to public protection crimes, to ensure effective and satisfactory collaboration.

You should be thoroughly familiar with the Tackling Violence Against Women and Girls strategy (HM Government, 2021a) which provides an in-depth look into the unique challenges women and girls face within society and more specifically through the lens of policing. It highlights the impact crime has on them and the way police interactions truly matter. Alongside this, the strategy also pushes for better management of offenders and pursuing of perpetrators. Please also bear in mind that you will be dealing with many victims who are male and many offenders who are female. The focus on the treatment of women and girls as victims does not minimize others' experiences.

19.2.2.9 The police constable role in public protection matters

In this section, we have gone through a tour of the different offences and related issues which would fall within the remit of public protection. You should have noticed a few themes arising from the text. First, the interconnected nature between the offences—it is very likely that individuals you will be dealing with are either repeat or multiple victims. Second, the complexity of the issues public protection policing deals with. Third, the unique position that you hold as a police officer when dealing with highly vulnerable individuals. Therefore, here are some key points to remember about your role:

- Building resilience—there are a number of ways in which we can mediate adversity and trauma. Whilst your role is not that of a mental health professional, you can help victims build their resilience through effective signposting to different services, as well as ensuring that victims are kept up to date and have a single point of contact—we know that consistency is a key resilience building block.
- Empathy—in your role, you have certain priorities (eg gathering evidence) but the way you communicate with victims or offenders is important. No matter the circumstance, it is important to show empathy to victims—this means that you should be able to identify what the individual is going through and show your understanding of the hardship. It may be that an individual is unable to effectively communicate what happened or how they are feeling—being empathetic, compassionate and respectful can go a long way. As the first point of contact in many instances, showing empathy leaves a positive first impression.
- Cultural considerations—we talked about many crimes where cultural or religious considerations need to be implemented. Ensure that you are open-minded and do not treat people based on any pre-conceived prejudices. Individuals may have trouble communicating in English—remain patient and ask for an interpreter at your earliest convenience.
- Professional curiosity—in far too many instances of public protection matters, police did not show enough professional curiosity or inquisitiveness. The crimes you are dealing with are often well hidden (modern slavery) and/or professionals are being manipulated by offenders (child abuse). Ensure that you follow up on any concerns that you have and that you take note of everything you are told/you observe. Effective note taking can make or break a case.

19.3 Multi-agency Roles

As much as understanding the public protection offences and the unique position of its victims is key to police officers, it is equally important that you understand how the management of offenders plays a role in effectively policing these offences. The way offenders of these more serious and complex crimes are managed is largely reliant on multi-agency responses. You should be able to communicate effectively with agencies outside of the police and be aware of any strategies put into place for those individuals who are in the community whilst still being managed.

Multi-agency approaches are very important in preventing and addressing harm to vulnerable adults and children. Provision varies across the country but good practice often involves a Local Strategic Partnership (LSP) which brings together representatives from local authorities, public and private sectors, community and voluntary organizations. These organizations are supported with Information Sharing Agreements (ISA) that are informed by locally agreed protocols and national standards. They are required to share information in a way that is timely, proportionate, legal, and safe. This includes the courts, where sharing information with the family court system (through the Children and Family Court Advisory and Support Services (CAFCASS)) is also important, and police services should have protocols in place to this effect. The Domestic Abuse Act 2021 has placed a statutory requirement on the Secretary of State to issue guidance to police about the disclosure of police information for the purposes of preventing domestic abuse.

19.3.1 Multi-Agency Public Protection Arrangements—MAPPA

The Multi-Agency Public Protection Arrangements (MAPPA) are the key structure for the oversight of offenders in the community. They specifically deal with sexual and violent offenders and the two key bodies responsible for the arrangements are the police and HM Prison & Probation Service.

MAPPA are considered by many organizations as key to the successful management of violent and sexual offenders, especially their reintegration into society after a prison sentence. It is a mechanism rather than a statutory body. Its purpose is to help to reduce the re-offending behaviour of sexual and violent offenders in order to protect the public, including previous victims, from serious harm. You should note that offenders who are in the community can also exhibit trauma responses—from their own offending but mostly from their previous experiences (remember, ACEs are predictive of victimization as well as offending).

The police, probation, and the prison service in each area form a 'responsible authority' for MAPPA and work together with other agencies such as social services, electronic monitoring providers, registered social landlords, youth offending teams, children's services, local health services, local housing authorities, and Jobcentre Plus. MAPPA guidance identifies a framework with four core functions: identifying MAPPA offenders; ensuring relevant information is shared with appropriate agencies; assessing the risk of serious harm; and managing risk.

The guidance identifies three broad categories of offenders (with some overlap):

- Category 1—registered sexual offenders as defined in Part 2 of the Sexual Offences Act 2003;
- Category 2—violent offenders sentenced to 12 months or more imprisonment, sexual offenders not included in Category 1, and offenders disqualified from working with children; and
- Category 3—other dangerous offenders who are not included in the first two categories but are nonetheless still regarded by the responsible authority as presenting a serious risk to the public (eg they have a previous conviction or caution that indicates that they have the potential to cause serious harm to others).

There are three identified levels of risk management. Level 1 is for offenders who can be managed by one primary agency without necessarily involving other agencies. Level 2 management involves more than one agency but is not considered to be overly challenging or complex. Level 3 is used where managing the risk requires active conferencing and senior representation from the responsible authority and other agencies with a duty to cooperate.

On 31 March 2022, there were 89,438 offenders under MAPPA (74.6 per cent Category 1; 24.9 per cent Category 2; and 0.4 per cent Category 3) and 98 per cent of cases were managed at Level 1 (MoJ, 2022b).

In deciding what course of action to take, it is important that 'defensible decisions' are made. This is to ensure that the responsible authority has taken all reasonable steps and that the assessment methods utilized are reliable. A thorough evaluation of the collected information needs to be demonstrated and decisions need to have been recorded and acted upon. Throughout it is important to demonstrate that the appropriate policies and procedures have been followed and that a proactive approach has been adopted by the practitioners and managers. An important function of MAPPA is to ensure that public protection work is communicated to the public and all interested parties in a consistent manner. The MAPPA guidance was updated in 2023 and can be found here <https://www.gov.uk/government/publications/multi-agency-public-protection-arrangements-mappa-guidance>.

19.3.2 Multi-Agency Risk Assessment Conference—MARAC

MARACs (Multi-Agency Risk Assessment Conferences) receive referrals of and manage high risk domestic abuse cases and are often coordinated by local police services. The underlying principle of MARAC is that no single agency or individual understands the full picture but together they provide critical information to effectively safeguard the victim. They provide a forum for sharing information and developing a multi-agency risk management plan for each case. The police have a significant role in the work of a MARAC, particularly in detaining perpetrators and referring cases. APP advises that victims of domestic abuse should be referred to MARACs where they are identified as at high risk of harm, potential escalation, and/or repeat incidents (CoP, 2023i).

19.3.3 Multi-Agency Safeguarding Hubs—MASHs

MASHs enable the sharing of information between agencies in order to manage the risks to children. Services are co-located to facilitate communication in each area, mainly in relation to child protection.

19.3.4 Safeguarding Adult Boards—SABs

SABs manage the care and protection of vulnerable adults. They make decisions on whether and how to intervene when there is suspicion that an adult in the area has care and support needs, is experiencing (or is at risk of) abuse or neglect and is unable to protect themselves due to that lack of care and support.

19.3.5 Independent Domestic Violence Advisors (IDVAs)

IDVAs work with police officers to provide independent support, risk assessment, and safety planning for victims—they are important in helping the police to fast-track the investigation of domestic abuse incidents, can testify as expert witnesses, and should be kept informed of any changes in police practice and updated regularly on cases.

19.3.6 Specialist Domestic Violence Courts (SDVC)

SDVCs were set up to improve victim protection, increase offender accountability, and to promote multi-agency cooperation. They operate a coordinated approach with agencies such as police, prosecutors, court staff, probation, and specialist support for victims.

19.3.7 Domestic Homicide Reviews (DHRs)

DHRs are multi-agency reviews where a person aged 16 or above has died due to possible abuse, neglect, or violence in a domestic context.

19.3.8 Young People's Violence Advisors (YPVA)

YPVAs support domestic abuse victims aged 16–18 in a similar way to IDVAs' support for adult victims.

19.3.9 Independent Sexual Violence Advisors (ISVAs)

ISVAs provide targeted support to victims of sexual violence, irrespective of when the incident happened. Further information can be found here <https://sexualviolence.idas.org.uk/reporting-sexual-violence-and-abuse/what-is-an-isva-independent-sexual-violence-adviser/>.

19.3.10 Non-statutory agency support

The National Domestic Violence Helpline is run by Refuge and Women's Aid. It offers free and confidential 24-hour support on 0808 2000 247. The All-Wales Domestic Abuse and Sexual Violence Helpline is run by Welsh Women's Aid and is 0808 80 10 800.

19.3.11 Information about dangerous offenders: ViSOR

Information about dangerous offenders is stored in a central database called ViSOR (also known as the Dangerous Persons Database). The data can be accessed by the three responsible authority agencies (police, probation, prison service), and the cases are called nominals. When a case ceases to be an active MAPPA case, the information is archived and can be retrieved at a later stage if necessary. The police have a responsibility to create and maintain a ViSOR record for offenders in Categories 1 and 3 when this is not the responsibility of the Probation Trust. Nominal records will normally be removed at the 100th birthday of an individual after a review is conducted. As a police officer you may come across a potentially dangerous person in your routine duties. If someone has been identified as such an offender, they should have been assigned a MOSOVO officer for risk assessment and offender management. It is important that the MOSOVO officer is aware of **all relevant information** relating to the

Processing Policing

offender. It may be that information you come across appears a minor issue, but an intelligence report should always be created for the MOSOVO's attention as it could form a bigger picture requiring immediate action to safeguard the public.

19.4 Offender and Victim Behaviours

You can see through the preceding sections that victims of public protection offences are some of the most vulnerable people you will interact with. This is also often true for the offenders, though they are also likely to exhibit highly dangerous behaviours. The way people behave is based on a cumulation of personal, environmental, and social factors which create how people think and subsequently behave—this is the individual's social cognition. It is responsible for key public protection issues, such as reporting behaviours on the victim side or manipulation of authority on the perpetrator side. In this section, we take you through key offender characteristics, the reporting behaviours of victims, and the tactics offenders use to manipulate authority.

19.4.1 Offender characteristics

In the year ending March 2022 (ONS, 2022g), 91.5 per cent (48,663) of domestic abuse defendants were male and 8.4 per cent (4,445) of defendants were female. The risk of domestic abuse perpetration decreases with age. There are a number of factors which can be predictive of offending behaviour—many of these overlap with many types of offending (eg lower socio-economic status) but here we focus mainly on offenders involved in DA public protection matters. As we have noted, victimization in childhood is predictive of future physical abuse of others—this victimization can look like any form of child abuse and neglect (this links in with ACEs discussed earlier). Witnessing DA/experiencing abuse during childhood changes the individual's thought patterns and can cause anxiety, low self-esteem, social isolation, PTSD, as well as the internalization of aggression as a norm and a suitable outlet for difficult feelings.

Further childhood factors include those associated with the family home. Environmentally, living in a disadvantaged socio-economic state is a predictor. However, family dynamics are also important to understand—poor relationship with parents/guardians, growing up in a single parent household and witnessing domestic abuse are all predictive of future DA perpetration. Stepping into later life experiences, we know that the use of illicit substances increases the risk of becoming a perpetrator while poor social skills, such as an inability to maintain friendships, being unable to share feelings, and having trouble effectively problem-solving conflict situations are also risk factors. Continued living in lower socio-economic conditions in adulthood continues to be predictive of DA perpetration which is also linked with other factors, such as being unemployed or having lower levels of education. On a psychological level, on top of the above, perpetrators often hold inappropriate representations of the world around them—for example, they hold a view of superiority over another gender or over others in general. This type of thinking allows them to attribute blame to others, justifying their behaviours with ease. They also externalize blame which means they explain their behaviours through stress, anger, or indeed, their partner's behaviour. Some of the most serious offenders will show psychopathic traits where emotional responses to abuse, such as guilt or remorse, are non-existent.

There are unique elements in how offenders think and what tactics they use depending on the type of abusive relationship. For example, in heterosexual relationships where the male is the perpetrator, a frequent thinking is that the male is innately superior to the female. In contrast, much research notes that DA is less of a power phenomenon for female offenders who often seem to be reacting to ongoing abuse. In LGBT+ relationships, 'outing' someone is a common tactic not visible in other types of relationships—in other words, using the partner's sexuality against them. In some police services, you can find dedicated Lesbian and Gay Liaison Officers who are especially trained to build rapport with victims. For transgender victims, using derogatory terms, such as 'it', is an especially hurtful tactic which can be utilized. It is important that you appreciate how intersectionality of different risk factors can increase the likelihood of victimization.

As part of government strategy, addressing offending behaviours is a priority—data varies according to which statistics we investigate but when assessing *official* recidivism, research shows that between a fifth and a third of domestic abuse perpetrators commit another similar offence, most likely in the first six months (McCormick, Cohen, and Plecas, 2011). As a police officer, you will see that not all domestic abuse incidents follow along the criminal justice route. There are a variety of community programmes available to those perpetrators who are seeking change and domestic abuse charities can provide signposting to these.

19.4.2 Tactics to manipulate police officers and professionals

Domestic abuse offenders are often highly manipulative individuals. You will get more thorough information below about the controlling and coercive behaviours they use on their victims—but such behaviours extend into interactions with figures of authority—specifically for you, the police. Offenders use many different tactics to mask their behaviours. It is key that you are inquisitive and use your professional judgement and curiosity, alongside working with risk assessment tools which do not always allow for the whole context to be appreciated. Some of the manipulation tactics which can be used include:

- Taking charge when speaking to you and not allowing the victim to present their case—this can be through talking over the victim, not letting the victim talk at all, not allowing you to see the victim, or minimizing what the victim is saying
- Exploiting the victim's mental or physical health—using the victim's current mental or physical state to explain distress or injuries sustained. Offenders can make up a very believable story to minimize their involvement in the event
- It is also possible to purposefully involve you in further intimidating a victim—for example, wellness checks can be used to intimidate the survivor into thinking that the offender has control over the work of the police
- It is important that you gain as much information before attending the scene as you can or try to gain information as you are at the scene—this is because offenders are skilled in making an incident seem as isolated, and this might result in an officer not spotting a pattern of abusive behaviour over time
- Research found that officers were more likely to arrest if a perpetrator was exhibiting aggressive, violent, and anti-authority behaviours (Hoyle, 1998)—you should not be led by such behaviours alone—those most manipulative offenders will not act aggressively
- Similarly, you should consider the context of the incident—more recent research identified that police should record more than they do as they often accept the version of events presented to them—this means that no crime was recorded at that moment which can undermine any future prosecutions (Myhill, 2019)
- Always check what you were told about the incident via a call handler with what is being said to you on scene—offenders are good at using the time between the call and your arrival to manipulate the victim into minimizing what occurred and may then attempt to manipulate you into accepting the new version of events
- The current police culture which has been the topic of the latest Review by Baroness Casey combined with the perpetrator's manipulative tactics, can make an officer inclined to identify more with the perpetrator, especially if male (Myhill, 2018). If you see this happening, you should challenge the officer.

19.4.3 Victim reporting of domestic abuse incidents

The reporting of DA is minimal compared to the amount of DA experienced. Whilst data on self-reported victimization was not recorded by the Crime Survey for England and Wales during the pandemic (due to safety concerns as it was administered via telephone), information from the previous survey (year ending March 2020) uncovered that 10.3 per cent of respondents stated they were a victim of domestic violence (ONS, 2020d). In general, the reporting of domestic abuse has been increasing over the years, but we are still a long way from where we need to be. There are many reasons for this, and they relate to internal factors (within the DA context) and external factors (perception of the system).

- The internal factors relate to victim thought patterns relating to their abuse. Some victims internalize what is happening to them and accept it as normal behaviour—they learn to live with it and often do not recognize problems unless they are made aware of them. Many justify the perpetrator's actions and blame themselves for the abuse, thinking they deserve what is happening to them. Others feel that they are in a genuinely loving relationship and feel too connected to the abuser to report their behaviour—they think that the positives of what they are receiving from the relationship (eg perceived love) outweigh the abuse. The coercive and controlling nature of DA supports such thought patterns, entrapping victims in the abuse they are experiencing. Victims often become isolated and cannot see a way out as they do not feel they have the necessary support available to them to continue their life outside of the relationship. The victim might also be manipulated into feeling shame or embarrassment. There are further, more practical factors, preventing victims from reporting. Due to the nature of DA relationships, many victims do not have financial stability (eg partner is controlling finances, partner is not allowing victim to work) and in relationships where there are children involved, victims may feel a duty to keep a family unit intact and/or fear repercussions which could impact on the children. Victims often look to rectifying the situation themselves by accessing charity websites and managing their current situation.

- Externally, especially in this day and age, the public do not exhibit high levels of trust towards those in a position of authority. Victims tend to be sceptical about whether the police will believe them and if they do not, what the consequences of their reporting will be. The low prosecution rates associated with DA also do not fuel public trust. Male victims, as well as those in the LGBT+ population, face further challenges about not being believed and not being treated respectfully. Using inclusive language in these instances can go a long way (ie do not automatically assume 'he' is the perpetrator; ask about preferred pronouns).

19.5 Domestic Abuse and Controlling or Coercive Behaviour

Domestic abuse can affect anyone irrespective of age, disability, sex, sexual orientation, gender identity, gender reassignment, race, religion, or belief. However, it is women who are most frequently victims, CSEW data for the year ending March 2020 estimates that 1.6 million females and 757,000 males aged 16–74 experienced domestic abuse the previous year (ONS, 2020d). Statutory guidance defines domestic abuse related crimes as any incidence of threatening behaviour, violence, or abuse (psychological, physical, sexual, financial, or emotional) towards another 'personally connected' person, where it has been identified that an offence has taken place (Home Office, 2022f). This covers a variety of offences that can occur when some members of a family or social group seek to maintain control over other members of the group. This also includes 'honour'-based violence, female genital mutilation, and forced marriages; these issues have been addressed by governmental policy, particularly in terms of violence against women and girls (Home Office, 2016a), but see also the report from the National Police Chiefs' Council (NPCC, 2015b). Abuse within families can also include abuse of older people, child to parent abuse, and sibling abuse.

Managing incidents of violence in family settings presents unique difficulties. Some victims will have specific needs or characteristics that make them particularly vulnerable, such as age, gender, sexual orientation, cultural background, immigration status, or their profession (see Chapter 7). In the case of 'honour'-based violence (HBV) cooperation may be hampered by a lack of support from the extended family or the community. Officers should also be aware that when a victim has an insecure immigration status, the records of any police investigation may become part of their application to stay in the UK.

A new offence of controlling and coercive behaviour in an intimate or family relationship was introduced by the Serious Crime Act 2015. The offence is designed to address patterns of non-violent abuse which had proved difficult to prosecute under other legislation. The repetitive nature of the behaviour and its cumulative effect on the victim did not always meet the criteria for common assault or stalking and harassment offences. The new Domestic Abuse Act 2021 includes a legal definition of domestic abuse (see below) and consolidates some provisions contained in previous legislation. Please note, **sections of this act come into force between 2021 and 2024.** You will need to check with your constabulary and the commencement schedule to ensure you are legally implementing the legislation within your force area. Further information can be found here: <https://www.gov.uk/government/publications/domestic-abuse-act-2021-commencement-schedule/domestic-abuse-act-2021-commencement-schedule>.

Coercive and controlling behaviour falls within the scope of the new act by amending the definition of 'personally connected', as do some elements of stalking and harassment. This brings together the complexity of different offences that can overlap, requiring the attending officer to be cognisant of the broader context in which these offences occur. To note, although the act is accepted as a positive step by some charities and support services in this field (eg Women's Aid, 2020b), there is some concern regarding the suitability of responding to domestic abuse from a purely legal perspective (see Walklate, Fitz-Gibbon, and McCulloch, 2017).

19.5.1 The Domestic Abuse Act 2021

The new act defines the behaviour of a person (A) towards another person (B) as domestic abuse if:

- A and B are each **aged 16 or over**, and
- Are **personally connected** to each other, and
- The behaviour is **abusive**

Firstly, it **does not matter if the abusive behaviour is a single incident or course of conduct** and secondly, **A's behaviour may be considered as directed towards B, even if it is directed at another person** (for example, B's child). The behaviour can include:

- Physical or sexual abuse;
- Violent or threatening behaviour;
- Controlling or coercive behaviour;
- Economic abuse (any behaviour that has a substantial adverse effect on B's ability to acquire, use, or maintain money or other property, or obtain goods or services); and
- Psychological, emotional, or other abuse;

19.5.1.1 Physical or sexual abuse—non-fatal strangulation

Guidance on further detailed types of physical and sexual harm that fall within the remit of this act can be found within statutory guidance (Home Office, 2022j). However, it is important to note that Section 70 of the Domestic Abuse Act 2021 amends part 5 of the Serious Crime Act to create an offence of non-fatal strangulation, whether or not it arises in a sexual context. Here, a person (A) commits an offence if they:

> (A) Intentionally strangles another person (B) or does any other act to B that (i) affects B's ability to breath, and (ii) constitutes battery of B

It is a defence to an offence under this section for A to show that B consented to the strangulation or other act **BUT** this does **NOT** apply if B suffers serious harm as a result of the strangulation or other act and A either (i) intended to cause B serious harm, or (ii) was reckless as to whether B would suffer serious harm. (Serious harm includes grievous bodily harm, wounding, or actual bodily harm.)

19.5.1.2 Meaning of personally connected

The act amends the definition in s 76 of the Serious Crime Act 2015 and removes the 'living together' requirement. This means the offence will apply to ex partners, partners, or family members. For example, this legislates for situations when controlling or coercive behaviour is evident by an intimate partner post separation. Two people are considered personally connected to each other if they are or have been:

- **Married** to each other or **civil partners** of each other
- They have **agreed to marry** one another or enter into a civil partnership with each other (irrespective of whether this agreement has been terminated)
- They are, or have been, in an **intimate personal relationship** with each other
- They each have, or there has been a time when they each have had, a **parental relationship in relation to the same child**
  - o A person has a parental relationship to a child if the **person is a parent** of the child or the **person has parental responsibility** (for meaning see the Children Act, 1989 (s 3)) for the **child** (applies to under aged 18 years)
- They are relatives (as defined by s 63(1) of the Family Law Act 1996)

For further information on the new act, you can also read *Blackstone's Guide to the Domestic Abuse Act 2021* (Edwards, Malone, and Jones KC, 2021).

Processing Policing

19.5.1.3 Controlling/coercive behaviour in an intimate/family relationship

Section 76 of the Serious Crime Act 2015 ensured that the behaviour patterns in abusive relationships were addressed by criminalizing controlling and/or coercive behaviours. This recognized the complex nature of domestic abuse and the psychological and emotional harm on its victim. The initial police-led implementation of this legislation highlighted a challenge for officers in recognizing, recording, and proactively investigating this offence. This is particularly evident where there is a lack of physical evidence available and/or understanding of the impact of trauma (Bishop and Bettinson, 2018), however, trends demonstrate that recorded offences have generally increased. During development of the Domestic Abuse Act 2021, the Home Office undertook a rapid review of the CCB offence to assess its effectiveness and identified an increase in recorded offences from 4,246 in 2016/17 to 24,856 in 2019/20 and 37 per cent of the CCB offences recorded did not include any reports of physical violence (gov.uk, 2021).

Coercive or controlling behaviour is defined as:

The person (A) commits an offence if A repeatedly or continuously engages in behaviour towards another person that is controlling or coercive, at the time of that behaviour A and B are personally connected (as defined above), and the behaviour has a serious effect on B and A knows or ought to know that the behaviour will have a serious effect on B. It can include but is not limited to;

- controlling or monitoring the victim's daily activities and behaviour (eg dictating what they wear and where they may sleep)
- controlling the victim's access to finances, monitoring their accounts, and coercing them into sharing their passwords to bank accounts in order to facilitate economic abuse
- using children to control the victim (eg threatening to take them away)
- preventing the victim from learning a language or making friends outside of their ethnic or cultural background
- intimidation and threats of disclosure of sexual orientation and/or gender identity to family, friends, work colleagues, community

19.5.1.4 Children as victims of domestic abuse

The term victim is used in this Act to denote someone who has experienced domestic abuse. This also includes children who have seen, heard, or experienced the effects of domestic abuse, and are related to either the victim of the abusive behaviour, or the perpetrator.

19.5.1.5 National changes contained within in the Domestic Abuse Act 2021

The act establishes in law a new office of Domestic Abuse Commissioner and sets out the Commissioner's function and powers, supported by an advisory board and reporting to the Secretary of State. The Commissioner may request a specific public authority to cooperate in any way deemed necessary for the purpose of their function, this includes a chief officer of police, CPS, HMIC, BTP, a local policing body, CQC, NHS, the Parole board, and several others. These public authorities have a legal duty to respond to the Commissioner's recommendations.

19.5.1.6 Domestic Abuse Protection Notice (DAPN)

The new domestic abuse definition also applies to a DAPN, which is a notice that prohibits a person (P) from being abusive to a person **aged 16 or over** to whom P is **personally connected** (P cannot be under 18). A senior officer (Inspector and above) may give a DAPN to that P if;

(a) they have reasonable grounds for believing P has been abusive towards a person aged 16 or over to whom P is personally connected
(b) they have reasonable grounds for believing that it is necessary to give the notice to protect that person from domestic abuse, or the risk of domestic abuse, carried out by P.

It does not matter if the abusive behaviour took place in England or Wales or elsewhere and the DAPN has effect in all parts of the United Kingdom. The notice can stipulate various requirements of P to ensure safeguarding of the victim (for example, may not contact the person, may not come within a specified distance of a premises). **It must be served on P**

personally by a constable who should ask P for the address so that they may be given the notice of the hearing of the application for the domestic abuse protection order. It must also state:

(a) the grounds on which it has been given and
(b) that a constable may arrest P without warrant if the constable has reasonable grounds for believing that P is in breach of the notice
(c) that an application for a DAPO under s 28 will be heard by a magistrates' court within 48 hours of the time of giving the notices
(d) that the notice continues in effect until that application has been determined or withdrawn, and
(e) the provision that a magistrates' court may include in a domestic abuse protection order

There are particular requirements if P is serving with the armed forces. This includes that the officer must make reasonable efforts to inform P's commanding officer of the giving of the notice. The Domestic Violence Protection Order (not a notice) can also be applied for by the person for whose protection the order is sought. Please note that the above section on DAPNs is beginning to be trialled from Spring 2024; you need to ensure that you are using the right powers depending on whether you are in a trial area and/or whether the new notice and order are fully in place. Further information on civil responses to DA is available at 19.5.4.

The following changes have also been included in the Domestic Abuse Act 2021

- Places a duty on local authorities in England to prioritize all eligible homeless victims of DA. To support victims of domestic abuse and their children in refuges and other safe accommodation and appoint a domestic abuse local partnership board, made up of relevant multi-agency partners, to provide advice to the authority.
- Prohibits perpetrators of abuse from cross-examining their victims in person in the civil and family courts in England and Wales.
- Creates a statutory presumption that victims of domestic abuse are eligible for special measures in the criminal, civil, and family courts.
- Extends the extraterritorial jurisdiction of the criminal courts in England and Wales, Scotland, and Northern Ireland to further violent and sexual offences.
- Enables domestic abuse offenders to be subject to polygraph testing as a condition of their licence following their release from custody.
- Places the guidance supporting the Domestic Violence Disclosure Scheme ('Clare's Law') on a statutory footing. (Home Office, 2022g)
- Ensures that where a local authority, for reasons connected with domestic abuse, grants a new secure tenancy to a social tenant who had or has a secure lifetime or assured tenancy (other than an assured shorthold tenancy) this must be a secure lifetime tenancy.

Violence in the domestic context is prosecuted under the same legislation as any other violent crime (see Chapter 22). In terms of police action, the approach should be pro-arrest, and as much evidence as possible should be gathered. Detailed guidance on the investigation of domestic abuse is available in Authorised Professional Practice on Domestic Abuse updated by the College of Policing in March 2023. It emphasizes a multi-agency approach and the need for officers to take 'positive action'.

The Domestic Violence Disclosure Scheme ('Clare's Law') was introduced in 2014. It allows an individual to find out whether their partner has a history of violence. Members of the public have a 'right to ask' (similar to the Child Sex Offender Disclosure Scheme) and a 'right to know'. If the police receive relevant information, they can disclose it to the person at risk, after making the appropriate checks (Home Office, 2012d).

19.5.2 Reporting and responding to domestic abuse incidents

The following table will showcase to you the process through which a domestic abuse incident goes. Despite the commitments made by many police services, reviews of police responses to domestic violence suggest that while positive steps have been taken, many areas still need to be improved. These include how well police officers understand the nature of coercive and controlling behaviour, identify risk factors, and use positive action (eg arrest powers and charging perpetrators) (HMIC, 2014a; HMICFRS, 2017c). The previously mentioned Casey Review, as well as the current Strategy surrounding Tackling Violence against Women and Girls, further highlight the need for more improvement.

Part 1: Call handler

1. Provides initial response which includes gathering and recording information, as well as ensuring safety of the victim.
2. Things to note include victim's demeanour (and that of others present), background noise, any other contextual clues. You should note whether victims may call from unfamiliar locations or are in a fast-changing situation. Any records already existing should be checked. A victim may already have a safety code word for contacting the police after a previous interaction with the police (CoP, 2015e).
3. If a suspect is still on the scene, the call handler should keep the caller on the line—evidence should be gathered throughout this time and can be used in future prosecution.
4. If a suspect is no longer on the scene, support to the victim should be provided to keep safe (eg by locking doors and closing windows). A key word should be agreed on between the caller and the handler should the suspect return. Note that the suspect may still actually be present even if the caller said they are not.
5. A description of the suspect should be gained, and relevant checks performed (including ViSOR).
6. All information has to be effectively communicated forward and risk assessment completed to ensure officer safety.
7. An incident or crime report should be completed and the computer-aided dispatch (CAD) must remain open for domestic abuse incidents until a risk assessment has been carried out and the victim has been contacted (CoP, 2015e).

Part 2: Key considerations for initial attendance

1. The first priority is the safety of the victim, children, and officers present—risk assessment has to be dynamic in light of new information coming in. Refer to Chapter 10 for general procedures when attending a crime scene. After ascertaining the initial circumstances on arrival and having taken any immediate actions to prevent any further harm to individuals, you would conduct a risk assessment. When completing such an initial assessment, THRIVE is now often the preferred model adopted by police services, in conjunction with the National Decision Model (covered in 10.11.4.6).
2. The responding officer should try to build a rapport with the victim to provide reassurance; this will also help with the initial investigation and ensure a successful handover (CoP, 2015d). Do not forget about the importance of empathy, compassion, and respect.
3. If the suspect is no longer there, double check description and circulate.
4. In terms of evidence gathering, you should cross-check information given to the call handler and gather as much evidence as you can—all of which needs to be appropriately recorded.
5. You may be denied entry—you will need to consider why this is the case. If suspect is denying entry, do ask to speak to other members of the household. If the victim is denying entry, think about whether they are being coerced. There may be grounds to use the power of entry under s 17 of the PACE Act 1984 (to arrest for an indictable offence or to save life and limb). If this power is used, a full PNB record must be made, including the reason. Arrest for a breach of the peace (see Chapter 3) may also be considered.
6. When appropriate, you will gain a more thorough first account from the relevant parties. First accounts should be obtained from each individual as soon as possible after the events, especially any description of an absent suspect. Each person should be seen separately in a safe environment and video recording can be used. If the various accounts differ considerably, it can be difficult to establish who the victim is and who the assailant. An injured person could be the victim, but the aggressor can also be harmed when a victim acts in self-defence. The arrest of both parties should be avoided if at all possible. The apparent victim(s) should be offered immediate support.
7. If any children are present, a record should be made about each child's welfare, communication ability, demeanour, name, date of birth, sex, address, doctor, primary carer, and school. If no children are seen, officers should still be alert for signs of children as they may have been kept away from the immediate scene but still be on the premises. If children are deemed to be in danger, s 48 of the Children Act 1989 can be used (see also 19.9.2.1 on using police protection powers).
8. Evidence gathering is key for any further prosecution. You should be proactive (eg capture photographic evidence); ensure you are using body-worn video as this can enable better evidence gathering and context to offences (Owens, Mann, and McKenna, 2014); forensic evidence might be particularly useful to avoid over-reliance on victim statement (consider an early evidence kit if you suspect sexual assault).
9. Risk assessment must be carried out for all incidents involving domestic abuse as soon as possible (see earlier section in this chapter). Police officers are responsible for assessing the level of risk and must complete the process even if the victim refuses to answer questions. Note also that victims should not be asked to sign risk assessments. The degree of risk should be continuously reviewed to ensure the correct level of protection for victims. The primary risk assessment underpins the immediate safety planning and, if several risk factors are identified, it may be necessary to inform the victim and notify the relevant support services. In some police services, a secondary risk assessment is conducted by specially trained staff.

Part 3: Investigative strategy

- One of the challenges in prosecuting cases of domestic abuse is the often unwillingness of many complainants to give evidence (Pringle, 2022).
- The importance of following all reasonable lines of enquiry at the start and 'getting it right first time' will be the responsibility of officers attending the scene. The investigation needs to be thorough and should consider several lines of enquiry to identify all the relevant evidence. The NPCC and CPS have compiled a joint evidence check list that can be accessed here <https://www.cps.gov.uk/legal-guidance/domestic-abuse#a90>. This is a useful and comprehensive list to refer to when investigating a domestic abuse report. It asks you to consider if you have collected all available evidence (including material other than the complainants) and identified the wider pattern of behaviour, including its cumulative impact. For example:
  - 999 calls, body-worn video with current DASH, victim statement, photographs of scene/injuries (footwear if victim has been stamped on), admissions, medical evidence (signed consent form), statements from others such as children, others present or neighbours (following house to house enquiries), observations from the attending officer of injuries/disposition. Data/social media/ WIFI, bank records, CCTV, spyware technology (eg in cases of harassment) and evidence of any coercive and controlling behaviour, bank accounts and other financial information (the victim's earnings might be under the suspect's control), automatic number plate recognition (to identify the victim and suspect's whereabouts) and prison intelligence;
  - relevant information from Police Records. Such as, PND, ViSAR, risks of re offending, previous DASH or equivalent checklists and outcome, previous civil orders/child contact agreements (including disputes), previous allegations, use of firearms or firearm licences, consideration of Bail Amendment Act. Bad character evidence can also help a conviction (13.2.4.2);
  - information held by housing, social care, and probation services; evidence from professionals and staff from the emergency services who witnessed the abuse;
  - hearsay evidence—this may be acceptable, for example a witness's report of something said by a suspect or a child's account of events (see 18.7.6.3.3);
  - interviews (see Chapter 13) should explore details of the incident and possible existing evidence, for example details of witnesses; the victim's physical and emotional injuries; details of family members; the history of the relationship and any previous incidents or threats (including with other partners); whether children were present; whether the parties are separated; whether any civil action has been taken; whether any sexual offences have been disclosed; the points to prove; and the victim's perception of the future relationship in terms of the likelihood of further abuse. When interviewing a suspect, the victim's safety must be considered if the interviewer discloses information provided by the victim. The FAO should also be interviewed when relevant and the interview recorded.
- If a victim decides to withdraw from the investigation, the domestic abuse officer should take a comprehensive withdrawal statement to explain the witness's decision.
- The victim must be asked whether their original statement is true and whether they were put under pressure to withdraw, with whom they have discussed the matters, whether they are considering civil proceedings, and the perceived impact on the witness and any children were the prosecution to continue. This statement and a report from the officer for the case should then be sent to the CPS. The statement may be used as evidence in the prosecution of the current or other incidents. The risk assessment and safety plan for the victim should also be reviewed.
- All reports of domestic abuse must be recorded following the National Crime Recording Standards, particularly as domestic abuse may be associated with other crimes such as child abuse and harassment. All relevant information should be passed to police domestic abuse coordinators who will liaise with the Tasking and Co-ordination Group (see 12.6.1). The accuracy of the existing data can then be monitored, and further statistical information can be produced for sharing with partner agencies and other police personnel.

An evidence-led prosecution (ELP)

An ELP is considered a prosecution by the CPS and police that does not rely upon the victim supporting or giving evidence. The Criminal Justice Joint Inspection Team (HMCPSI and HMCFRS, 2020) when examining domestic abuse investigations around ELP criticized the CPS and police, claiming in many cases that the police did not investigate to the standards expected. Recommendations were made to the CPS to be more vigilant in seeking opportunities for ELP when the victim withdraws.

- An ELP strongly relies upon opportunities to gather evidence by means of *res gestae* or other forms of hearsay where a victim may make an oral or written statement of being assaulted but then later declines to support legal action. Types of evidence that may fall out of *res gestae* are:
  - CAD reports—computer records made of informant call to police;
  - WAV files—the audio recording of the call made to police;
  - PNB entry made by police of conversation with victim;
  - BWC—body-worn camera footage.

Part 4: Possible outcomes for suspects

- Police officers have a duty of positive action when responding to incidents of domestic abuse (CoP, 2018e). This often means arresting the suspect, but this is not always possible or the best solution. Alternatives to arrest include removing the suspect from the location to prevent breach of the peace and issuing a DVPN or other civil order (see 19.5.4).
- The decision to arrest a suspect should not be influenced by the victim's opinion or whether previous complaints have been withdrawn. However, it is important to show empathy to the victim and not disregard their voice. If the decision is not to arrest, the reasons need to be recorded. However, in some situations both parties have committed acts which could justify arrest, or it may be difficult to differentiate between the perpetrator and the victim. Dual arrests should be avoided, particularly if there are children involved. A thorough assessment of the situation and an understanding of the context of coercive and controlling behaviour are therefore necessary to establish the best course of action.
- Cautions are rarely appropriate in situations of domestic abuse (although they are sometimes used for a first incident where there is no intelligence of related incidents), and penalty notices for disorder are never appropriate (CoP, 2018e).When deciding whether to charge a suspect, the following CPS documents (available online) all provide guidance: The Director's Guidance On Charging 2020 (sixth edition), Domestic Abuse Guidelines for Prosecutors (updated December 2022), Domestic Abuse Charging Advice Sheet, and Code for Crown Prosecutors. The victim should be informed if the decision is against prosecution.
- Bail can be used for a suspect who has been detained but risk factors should be considered, and the victim consulted (see 10.18.3 on bail). Any attached conditions should ensure that the victim, children, and witnesses are protected. The conditions must be such that they can be policed effectively and not conflict with existing court orders. If the suspect is forbidden from contacting the victim, this includes indirect contact and contact through social media. It is important to be clear that the conditions of bail apply to the suspect's behaviour (not the victim's) and that breaches of bail will be treated seriously, even if the suspect and the victim become reconciled. Before a suspect is released from a police station, the victim should be informed where possible and the notification recorded. The suspect or the victim may need to remove their belongings from a joint residence and the police should help to arrange this, especially if the removal could otherwise lead to a breach of bail conditions. All control rooms and databases should be updated regarding the suspect's bail conditions.

19.5.3 Risk assessments

19.5.3.1 DASH: Domestic Abuse, Stalking and Harassment and honour-based violence checklist

The DASH risk assessment has been in use since 2009 and can be used with victims of domestic abuse, stalking and harassment, and 'honour'-based violence. It is used by police but also other agencies which support victims and are involved in investigations. It involves answering a number of questions; the version used by the police has 24 quick check-box questions to judge which risk factors may apply in a certain situation, as well as three consideration questions where you can include your professional judgement of the situation, as well as note any other areas you think are relevant. Relevant information often includes the frequency of repeat victimization, the seriousness of the injuries, any escalation of violence, and details of the victim and the suspect. All staff involved with the ongoing investigation, including the custody officer, should be encouraged to contribute information. You should note that the risk assessment can be completed without the victim's involvement—you will come across situations where a victim will refuse to discuss the situation any further—you should still complete the assessment to the best of your ability based on information available to you.

19.5.3.2 DARA: Domestic Abuse Risk Assessment

Following research and consultation, it was found that the DASH risk assessment was used inconsistently, was often not completed as fully as necessary, and patterns of behaviour (the controlling and coercive nature of DA) were not easy to identify. A new risk assessment was developed—DARA—which is the recommended primary assessment tool for first responders (CoP, 2022d). DARA includes 18 questions with more scope for professional judgement notes and does not include all the highly sensitive questions as DASH (eg it does not ask about previous sexual abuse as it may be difficult to disclose at that moment). However, the two risk assessments should work in unison. First responders should complete the faster and more consistent DARA assessment which can then be followed up by DASH by specialist domestic abuse officers, independent domestic violence advisors, and other relevant agencies. You need to ensure you are using your local police policy as it will state which risk assessment you should be using—some do not use the DARA risk assessment, yet.

19.5.4 Civil responses to domestic abuse

While criminal law is a formal criminal justice response aimed at preventing offending and reoffending, domestic abuse victims also have protections set out through civil law—this type of law is aimed at settling disputes between individuals (or organizations). The Family Law Act 1996 (FLA) provides opportunities under civil law to counter domestic violence and abuse. The FLA was modified by the Domestic Violence, Crime and Victims Act 2004 and provides the basis for most of the provisions covered here.

A non-molestation order is covered in s 42 and requires a person to refrain from molesting another named person who is associated with the respondent. It can be applied for directly or as part of other family proceedings where this action will be of benefit. It covers adults as well as children. Under s 42A of the FLA, it is a criminal offence to breach such an order without reasonable excuse (the person must, however, know of the existence of the order). If the CPS fails to act, the victim may be able to use contempt of court proceedings. The offence is triable either way and the penalty is a fine or a maximum of five years' imprisonment.

An occupation order allows an owner, tenant, spouse, or civil partner to seek the removal of an occupant from their home (s 33 of the FLA), and the recipient will be forbidden from entering the property (s 33(3)). A breach of the order is a civil offence but there is an associated power of arrest under s 47(1). These orders can be difficult to obtain, often because of the recipient's property rights (Herring, 2007, p 270). The lengthy procedures involved are an obvious disadvantage for applicants.

Domestic Violence Protection Orders (DVPOs) and Domestic Violence Protection Notices (DVPNs) were first introduced in the UK in 2014 to give victims more time to decide whether to leave the abuser or to apply for a non-molestation or occupation order. They are covered in the Crime and Security Act 2014 (ss 24–33). A DVPN is imposed by the police (and needs to be signed by someone of the rank of Superintendent or above) in the immediate aftermath of a domestic violence incident and prevents the abuser from having contact with the victim or returning to the victim's home for up to 48 hours. There is power of arrest associated with breaching the notice. During this time frame, an application needs to be made to a magistrates' court for a DVPO—a civil order under which there will be a further period of no contact for 14–28 days. *Please, note that the above section on DAPNs and DAPOs is beginning to be trialled from Spring 2024; you need to ensure that you are using the right powers depending on whether you are in a trial area and/or whether the new notice and order are fully in place.*

Prohibited Steps Orders (PSO) are used to prohibit someone with parental responsibility from exercising their parental responsibility. In this context, it is used specifically to prevent a suspect removing a child from the applicant (s 8 of the Children Act 1989). They can impose restrictions on certain activities unless prior permission is obtained from the court (eg taking the child abroad or out of the local area). Anyone with parental responsibility for the child can apply for a PSO (as described by Part 1 of the Children Act 1989, see 19.9.3). A breach of a PSO is a civil contempt of court; there is no associated power of arrest.

19.5.5 Further help for domestic abuse victims

There are many national and local not-for-profit organizations with dedicated team members to support victims of domestic abuse. You should find out, locally, which organizations operate in your area. It is likely there will be organizations providing specific services which you could direct individuals to (eg for male victims). Below, we provide some national forms of support.

The National Centre for Domestic Violence (NCDV) can help victims to apply for emergency injunctions and includes an electronic third-party injunction referral system. It also has a secure online ASSIST programme which allows police officers to access court papers related to non-molestation and occupation orders (NCDV, 2015a; 2015b).

The Bright Sky app provides information for victims about nearby services and also provides a dedicated system for recording particular incidents of abuse by text, images, or video. The victim can then share the recordings with the police and other support services (Vodafone, 2018; Hestia, 2018).

Helplines

Refuge run a free 24-hour national domestic abuse helpline. They provide effective signposting, as well as support. In instances where it is necessary, they also provide support to victims after potentially leaving the abusive environment through emergency accommodation and necessities. You should note that the website has a 'quick exit' button which victims should be directed to.

Respect Men's Advice line also run a 24-hour free national helpline but specifically for male victims. It also includes a 'quick exit' button.

19.6 Stalking and Harassment

This behaviour falls within the scope of the Domestic Abuse Act 2021, if at the time of occurring the perpetrator and victim are 16 years or over and personally connected. As a first responder differentiating between stalking or harassment can help you identify the most effective safeguarding measures to put in place. There is no formal definition of stalking, but the Stalking Protection Act 2019 defines it within the statutory guidance, as a pattern of unwanted, fixated, and obsessive behaviour which is intrusive. It can include harassment that amounts to stalking or stalking that causes fear of violence or serious alarm or distress to the victim. Harassment includes repeated attempts to impose unwanted communications and contact on a victim, in a manner that could be expected to cause distress or fear (Public Prosecutions Service, no date). Monckton-Smith, Szymanska, and Haile (2017) reviewed 358 homicides and found stalking behaviours evident prior to the murder in 94 per cent of cases. The importance of early identification and action in these cases cannot be underestimated. We will first look closer at the offence of harassment.

19.6.1 Protection from Harassment Act 1997

Sections 1–5 of the Protection from Harassment Act 1997 can be applied in a wide range of situations, including disputes between partners in a relationship, disputes between neighbours, stalking, and campaigning. The offences described in the Protection from Harassment Act 1997 are harassment without violence (s 2), stalking (s 2A), breaching an injunction (s 3(6)), putting people in fear of violence (s 4), stalking involving fear of violence or serious alarm or distress (s 4A), and breaching a restraining order (s 5(5)). The stalking offences are covered in 19.6.2.

The behaviour must be oppressive, unreasonable, and unacceptable, such as that displayed during an act of stalking (for which the offence was originally designed) and be of the sort that a reasonable person would find harassing (s 1(2) of the Protection from Harassment Act 1997). Harassing a person includes alarming the person or causing the person distress (s 7(2)). In legal terms, only a person can be harassed so an employee can be harassed but not a company or a corporate body (s 7(5) of the Protection from Harassment Act 1997).

For these offences (ss 1–5) the perpetrator must know or ought to know that their actions are likely to cause the relevant effect on the victim. The judgement on whether a suspect 'ought to know' is made by considering whether a reasonable person in possession of the same information would know that the actions would have these effects. The final decision on the likely effects of a particular behaviour is taken by the court.

Clearly, the Protection from Harassment Act 1997 is a potentially valuable piece of legislation that offers a number of options for providing support to victims of harassment. However, a considerable amount of evidence is required to secure a successful prosecution under this Act, and proving a course of conduct in particular can be difficult. Advice from the CPS should be sought at an early stage.

19.6.1.1 A course of conduct

Under s 1(1) of the Protection from Harassment Act 1997, a person must not pursue a 'course of conduct'. The conduct must be the sort of conduct that the perpetrator knows (or ought to know) amounts to harassment. In addition, it must occur on more than one occasion to be a course of conduct. A course of conduct exists when conduct is directed towards:

- an individual on at least two occasions (s 7(3)(a)); or
- two or more people, and in relation to each person on at least one occasion (s 7(3)(b)).

It is not just the number of incidents but whether those incidents are connected (*Lau v DPP* [2000] All ER (D) 224). It is, however, less likely that the court will accept that behaviour constitutes a course of conduct if there is a long period of time between the events.

The course of conduct does not have to comprise similar types of conduct: indeed, often it is not obvious that separate incidents are connected so be aware of this during any investigation. However, a number of irregular and unconnected incidents in a turbulent and unpredictable relationship in which all parties concerned play a part does not amount to a course of conduct (see *R v Curtis* [2010] EWCA Crim 123 and *R v David Roger Widdows* [2011] EWCA Crim 1500). A court may decide that there was a sequence of separate incidents instead (see (1) *Buckley* (2) *Smith v DPP* [2008] EWHC 136 (Admin)).

Conduct includes speech, letters, and emails so evidence will need to be gathered from a wide range of sources such as diary entries, emails, letters, photographs, and interviews with witnesses. A person might make an initial bona fide enquiry for example, but this could become harassing if it is followed up in a manner that is persistent (see *DPP v Hardy* [2008] All ER (D) 315 (Oct)).

The conduct can also involve more than one person. An example of where a group of people could be guilty of harassment would involve three people, X, Y, and Z, who stand along the route which H takes to work in order to give her a threatening letter. They give her the letter and later Z makes a threatening phone call to her. Provided that H feels alarmed or distressed, and X, Y, and Z knew (or ought to have known) that their actions were likely to be alarming or distressing, then X, Y, and Z would all be committing an offence (s 7(3A) of the Protection from Harassment Act 1997).

That a suspect did not initiate the contact on a particular occasion was held to be irrelevant: in *James v CPS* [2009] EWHC 2925 (Admin), a client who was receiving local authority care made repeated calls to the office but received no reply. The office worker returned the calls on a number of occasions and was verbally abused. Also, the offence of harassment does not have to include actually carrying out the conduct; mere planning or otherwise assisting with the course of conduct can amount to the offence.

19.6.1.2 Harassment without violence

It is an offence under s 2(1) of the Protection from Harassment Act 1997 for a person to pursue a course of conduct which involves harassment of one or more persons (s 1(1)(a) and (1A)(a)). Once initiated, a person continues to pursue a course of conduct even when they do not personally harass the victim but aid, abet, counsel, or procure another who carries it out instead (s 7(3A)). The suspect(s) must know (or ought to know) that the behaviour amounts to harassment (s 1(1A)(b)).

The course of conduct can be to persuade a person to carry out a particular act or to omit to carry out a particular act. The offender might try to persuade a person to do something that they are not under any obligation to do (s 1(1A)(c)(ii)). For example, an animal rights extremist might pressurize a person working with animals in research to supply information on work practices. This offence can also be committed when there is an intention to persuade a person to omit to do something that they are entitled or required to do (s 1(1A)(c)(i)). For example, an animal rights extremist might pressurize a person to stop working for a company that conducts research on animals.

The offence can also be committed when the course of conduct is intended to persuade any person to change their current routine (s 1(1A)(c)(i) and (ii)). This may form part of a wider campaign about political or social issues. It must be directed towards two or more person(s) in the first instance and occur on at least one occasion in relation to each of those persons.

As a possible defence to a s 2 offence, the suspect could try to show on the balance of probabilities that they acted either 'in reasonable circumstances' (this will be for the court to decide, probably using the 'reasonable person' test as in s 1(2)) or in the course of their work, for example as a police officer or court official. Full details of the defences are given in s 1(3) of the Protection from Harassment Act 1997.

This offence is triable summarily and the penalty is six months' imprisonment and/or a fine. It can also be racially or religiously aggravated (see 19.8).

19.6.1.3 Isolated events causing distress

If distress is caused only on one occasion, this does not constitute a course of conduct and can be dealt with under s 3(1) of the Protection from Harassment Act 1997. The result of a civil claim can be damages (a court order to pay money) and/or an injunction (a court order to impose sanctions on the offender). The injunction can be against a person or a company. If an injunction is breached, an offence is committed triable either way. The penalty is a fine or imprisonment (six months summarily and five years on indictment). There are no racially or religiously aggravated versions of the civil proceedings under s 3 of the Protection from Harassment Act 1997.

A 'First Incidence Harassment Warning' is another way of dealing with such a situation. This is an official written warning issued by the police which informs the perpetrator that any further incidents may form part of a 'course of conduct' that could then result in prosecution for harassment offences. The record of the warning provides evidence of the course of conduct and that the perpetrator 'knows or ought to know' that the conduct amounted to harassment. However, following the 2016/2017 HMICFRS inspection of police services nationally it was recommended that all police services cease the use of Harassment Warning letters. In 2020, MPS implemented a policy change to cease the use of harassment warning notices and letters. Therefore, please check on the relevant policy for your own constabulary.

19.6.1.4 Putting people in fear of violence

This offence is described in s 4 of the Protection of Harassment Act 1997 and involves more than sending insulting or abusive letters or emails. The conduct must be targeted at an individual and be calculated to cause fear of violence. It must also be oppressive and unreasonable (as identified in *Thomas v News Group Newspapers Ltd* [2001] EWCA Civ 1233, [2002] EMLR 78).

There are several key differences from the harassment (s 2) offence we described earlier. For s 4 offences:

- the victim must believe the violence will happen (as opposed to believing it might happen);
- the victim must fear the violence personally (and not on behalf of someone else, such as a family member) (*Caurti v DPP* [2002] Crim LR 131); and
- the fear of violence cannot be conveyed through a third party.

In most other ways, the conditions for this offence are similar to those for the offence of harassment (s 2) described; the court decides what is reasonable or unreasonable, it is an offence to pursue or assist the conduct and there must be a course of conduct amounting to harassment within the meaning of s 1 (see *Haque v R* [2011] EWCA Crim 1871). Other relevant case law includes *R v Curtis (James Daniel)* [2010] EWCA Crim 123, [2010] 1 WLR 2770 and *R v Widdows (David Roger)* [2011] EWCA Crim 1500, (2011) 175 JP 345. Stalking is covered in 19.6.2.

The defences to this offence are similar to those for s 2 but with one major addition: that the suspect's course of conduct was pursued reasonably for their own protection or for the protection of another or of property (belonging to them or another). This offence can be racially or religiously aggravated and is triable either way. The penalty is a fine or imprisonment (six months summarily and a maximum of ten years on indictment).

19.6.1.5 Restraining orders

A court can make a restraining order under s 5 of the Protection from Harassment Act 1997 against a person who has been convicted (s 5(1)) or acquitted (s 5A) of any offence, to protect a person from harassment. A restraining order will place restrictions on a person's future behaviour. It may last indefinitely or for a period stated by the court and it can be varied or discharged on application. The order will be recorded on the PNC, the police local intelligence database, and the PND. Breaching a restraining order is an offence (s 5(5)) and the penalty is a fine or imprisonment (six months summarily and five years on indictment).

19.6.1.6 Police response to harassment

When responding to complaints of harassment, the police priorities are to:

- investigate every report of harassment;
- preserve the safety and protect the lives of all victims;
- approach the harassment proactively;
- use a multi-agency approach when necessary;
- deal with offenders effectively, using any means within the criminal justice system.

Further information can be found in the College of Policing APP statement on Stalking or Harassment, available at <https://www.app.college.police.uk/app-content/major-investigation-and-public-protection/stalking-or-harassment/>.

TASK 1 Imagine you are a police officer requested to attend an address in your area where a complaint of harassment has been made. Write brief answers to the following questions:

1. What evidence would you need to collect to prove an offence under either s 2 or s 4 of the Protection from Harassment Act 1997?
2. What other methods could be used to stop the conduct?
3. How could future evidence be recorded?
4. What reason(s) would make an arrest necessary in these circumstances?

19.6.2 Stalking

The offence of stalking is covered under s 2A of the Protection from Harassment Act 1997. The suspect's acts (or omissions, although no examples are provided) must be associated with stalking. The acts include following the person, watching or spying on them, loitering in any place (whether public or private), contacting (or attempting to contact) them by any means, monitoring their use of electronic communications (eg social media or email), interfering with their property, and publishing any statement or other material relating to or originating from them (or purporting to). See 19.6.2.1 for stalking that causes fear of violence or serious alarm or distress.

Research into stalking by Knoll and Resnick (2007) reveals five known stalker types:

- Rejected stalkers—this is the most common type of stalker and can be the most dangerous. The victim is often a former intimate partner, and the perpetrator will often pursue the victim long after the relationship ends. They will have a complex and volatile mix of desire for reconciliation and revenge.
- Intimacy seeking stalkers—these want an intimate relationship with someone, believe that the victim is their 'true love' and project desirable romantic qualities onto the victim. Most perpetrators will have erotomanic (the uncommon delusion and strong belief that someone is in love with them despite evidence to the contrary). Some will have delusions and others have morbid infatuations with the victim. Legal sanctions are seen as a worthwhile price to pay for finding true love and are unlikely to stop their behaviour.
- Incompetent stalkers—they will probably know that the victim is not interested but will continue hoping that the stalking behaviour will somehow lead to a relationship. They can often be intellectually limited and have poor social skills which impedes meaningful social interactions. Unlike intimacy-seekers, they do not endow their victim with any unique qualities.
- Resentful stalkers—these types of stalkers intend to frighten their victim. Many have paranoid personalities or delusional disorders. They may pursue a vendetta against a specific victim or may just feel a general grievance and randomly pick a victim. They may also carry out stalking with an attitude of righteous indignation due to feeling persecuted by someone.
- Predatory stalkers—they will prepare for a sexual attack and use stalking to discover a victim's vulnerabilities. They do not often give any warning and the victim is often unaware of the danger. Predatory stalkers often suffer from paraphilias (abnormal sexual behaviours) and are likely to have previous convictions for sexual offences. They may also have a propensity for violence which can lead to a very violent sexual attack on their victim.

The stalker must pursue a course of conduct (as for s 2(1) offences) that involves harassment (s 2A(2)(a)), and it can be targeted at one or more persons (subsections (1)(a) and (1A) (a), respectively). The behaviour must be such that the suspect(s) must know (or ought to know) that it amounts to harassment (s 2A(2)(c)). A stalker who starts a course of conduct is regarded as continuing it even when the latter acts are carried out by someone else arranged by the suspect (s 7(3A)). This offence is triable summarily and the penalty is six months' imprisonment and/or a fine. It can be racially or religiously aggravated (see 19.8.2).

19.6.2.1 Stalking involving fear of violence or serious distress

These offences are covered under s 4A(1) of the Protection from Harassment Act 1997. Under s 4A(1)(a), the suspect's course of conduct must amount to stalking and also cause the victim:

- to fear on at least two occasions that violence will be used against them (s 4A(1)(b)(i)); or
- serious alarm or distress which has a substantial adverse effect on their usual day-to-day activities (s 4A(1)(b)(ii)).

For these offences, the behaviour must be such that the suspect must know (or ought to know) that their acts will have these effects on the victim (ss 4A(2) and 4A(3)). In *R v Qosja (Robert)* [2016] EWCA Crim 1543, it was held that to prove fear of violence, there must be evidence from the victim that they feared there would be violence directed at them (not just a possibility of violence).

The defences to this offence are given in s 4A(4) and are similar to the defences for s 4. The offence is triable either way and the penalty is a fine or imprisonment (12 months summarily and ten years maximum on indictment). A suspect found not guilty of this offence could instead be found guilty of an offence under s 2 or 2A (s 4A(7)). The s 4A offence can be racially or religiously aggravated (see 19.8.2).

19.6.2.2 The Stalking Protection Act 2019

The Stalking Protection Act 2019 came into force in January 2020. Its purpose is to close a gap in the existing framework for protective orders by creating the Stalking Protection Order (SPO) (Home Office, 2020d). Note that an SPO is not an alternative to prosecution for stalking offences under the Protection from Harassment Act 1997.

An SPO is a civil order granted in a magistrates' court and will be granted on the balance of probabilities. The criteria for applying for an SPO are set out in s 1(1) of the Stalking Protection Act 2019. The police should consider applying for an SPO if it seems that the suspect has carried out acts associated with stalking, poses a risk of stalking to a person, and there is reasonable cause for the proposed order being necessary to protect the other person from that risk (Home Office, 2020d). An SPO application can be made at the beginning of any investigation and will still apply even if a decision is made not to prosecute.

The person to be protected under the order does not need to have been a victim of the acts described above, but the police must have reasonable cause to believe that they may be at risk of such acts. The courts will make an assessment using the criteria set out in the House of Lords judgment in *R (McCann) v Crown Court at Manchester* [2003] 1 AC 787.

Interim SPOs are also available. These short-term temporary orders require a lower threshold of evidence and can be more quickly obtained. They are useful if immediate protection from harm is required.

Once an SPO is granted, it must be recorded on the PNC and include details such as the start and expiry dates and all the conditions imposed. Breaching an SPO or interim SPO without reasonable excuse is a criminal offence. The person should be arrested as soon as possible as a delay may result in a loss of victim confidence in the order and the suspect may cause further harm (Home Office, 2020d). This is an either-way offence, and the maximum penalty is 12 months' imprisonment, a fine, or both on summary conviction and five years' imprisonment, a fine, or both on indictment.

For full guidance on the Stalking Protection Act 2019 and SPOs, consult the Home Office guidance (Home Office, 2020d).

19.6.2.3 Sending nuisance communications

If the harassment involves communications such as telephone calls or letters, then alternative offences can be considered. This is particularly useful if a course of conduct is not evident.

19.6.2.4 Sending items to cause distress or anxiety

Under s 1 of the Malicious Communications Act 1988, it is an offence for a person to send, for the purpose of causing distress or anxiety, any item (including electronic communications) which contains:

- indecent or grossly offensive content (s 1(1)(a)(i));
- a threat (s 1(1)(a)(ii)) (unless it was made reasonably to reinforce a demand (s 2));
- information which is false and known or believed to be false (s 1(1)(a)(iii)); or
- any article which is entirely or partly indecent or grossly offensive (s 1(1)(b)).

This offence includes letters and parcels sent by post. It also includes electronic communication such as emails, text messages, and oral or other communication transmitted by means of a telecommunication system, for example landline or mobile telephone (s 2A(a) and (b)). For this offence, 'sending' includes delivering by hand, transmitting, and causing to be sent (s 3) by the sender but does not include the actions of the service provider.

19.6.2.5 Improper use of public communications network

It is an offence under s 127 of the Communications Act 2003 to send (or cause to be sent) a message by means of a public electronic communications network (eg mobile and landline telephones) which is grossly offensive, indecent, obscene, or menacing (s 127(1)), or false, or to persistently use the network for the purpose of causing annoyance, inconvenience, or needless anxiety to another (s 127(2)). These offences are triable summarily and the penalty is six months' imprisonment and/or a fine. A PND can be used for a s 127(2) offence (see 10.18.2.2).

19.7 Honour-based Crime

So-called honour-based crime is defined by the NPCC and CPS as 'an incident or crime involving violence, threats of violence, intimidation, coercion or abuse (including psychological, physical, sexual, financial or emotional abuse) which has or may have been committed to protect or defend the honour of an individual, family and/or community for alleged or perceived breaches of the family and/or community's code of behaviour' (CoP, 2023l). The abuse may present as a combination of these different harm behaviours, including forced marriage and female genital mutilation. In some cases, this may fall outside of the Domestic Abuse Act 2021 due to the requirement for a 'personal connection'. HBV typically involves attempts to maintain control in a family or social group to protect certain conceptions of honour and is likely to involve behaviours specified in the new act including violence, hence the term 'honour'-based violence (HBV). The perpetrators believe that an individual has brought shame to the family or community through their behaviour. We use inverted commas for the word 'honour' in this context because although the perpetrators may believe that they are defending a certain notion of honour (with some basis in cultural or religious beliefs), this is not accepted in the UK as an excuse for violence or oppression. It should be noted that an HMIC report criticized the police response to HBV, forced marriage, and female genital mutilation. It found that few police services correctly understood the issues or had adequate procedures in place to handle such cases (HMIC, 2015a, p 8).

It is very difficult to establish accurate numbers of honour-based crimes due to high levels of unreported cases and inconsistencies in police recordings of such crimes. Victims may fear authorities and/or reprisals from their family and great care must be taken to understand the victim's experience and concerns, while demonstrating an understanding of the unique circumstances of HBV domestic abuse. There have been some extremely violent and high-profile cases, which draw attention to the need to clearly identify cases as HBV so proper support can be provided for the victims. Although most victims of HBV are women (cases tend to occur in very male-dominated/highly patriarchal cultures), remember men can also be the targets of HBV, for example if they are homosexual or if they support victims of HBV.

It is important that cases of HBV are identified early on so that they are managed properly. Cases are prosecuted under the specific offence committed (eg assault, kidnap, rape, threats to kill, or murder) but should be flagged up as HBV in the case file. As the victim is often at risk from their own family and community, great care is needed when discussing the case with anyone else, for example translators from within the same community. In some cases, a person may be hired to kill a particular family member or distant relatives living in other areas of the country or abroad. Thus, a victim or a member of their extended family can be at risk even after leaving their community. Ensuring the victim's safety is a priority and the level of risk should not be underestimated. Information should be gathered not only about the victim but also about the alleged offender—they may be using younger members of the family to commit the criminal acts to deflect attention from themselves.

19.7.1 Forced marriage

Forcing a person to marry is a criminal offence (s 121 of the Anti-social Behaviour, Crime and Policing Act 2014) and the maximum custodial penalty is 12 months if tried summarily and seven years on indictment.

In 2020, the Forced Marriage Unit (FMU) changed their recording practices to exclude general enquiries, which has resulted in a reduction of the number of recorded cases. During 2021, only 337 advice and support cases of FM were recorded (down from 759 in 2020) and of these 316 related to forced marriage and 3 forced marriage and FGM, which predominantly affected female victims (74 per cent) (ONS, 2022g). Forced marriage is not limited to one country, religion, or culture and the FMU identified cases in 2021 relating to 32 'focus countries' that include: Pakistan (47 per cent), Bangladesh (9 per cent), Somalia (3 per cent), Kenya (2 per cent), Iraq (2 per cent), and Romania (2 per cent) (ONS, 2022g). Recent changes in the Marriage and Civil Partnership Act 2022 also increased the minimum age for marriage or civil partnership from 16 to 18 years, making it an offence under s 121 of the Anti-social Behaviour, Crime and Policing Act 2014 for a person to carry out any conduct for the purpose of causing a child to enter into a marriage before their eighteenth birthday.

It is very likely that many forced marriages remain unreported. The victim can be physically, emotionally, or psychologically pressured to marry by means of threats, physical or sexual violence, or other forms of coercion directed at the victim or a third person. If the victim lacks the capacity to consent under the Mental Capacity Act 2005 (see 20.5.4), any type of conduct can amount to the offence. Some victims are not coerced or threatened but are deceived into going abroad and are unaware that the purpose of the trip is a forced marriage (for a prosecution, it is not relevant whether the marriage took place). A forced marriage should be distinguished from an arranged marriage; the latter is a legal practice in which a third party arranges for two consenting people to marry. Government guidance for front line professionals on forced marriage can be found here: <https://www.gov.uk/government/publications/the-right-to-choose-government-guidance-on-forced-marriage>. Support services, such as Karma Nirvana are also available for those affected.

Possible cases of forced marriage must be identified and flagged up in the early stages so that appropriate management can be put in place. While some victims self-refer, around 64 per cent of referrals come from professionals such as specialized support agencies and NGOs (Home Office, 2020g, p 7). Information must be gathered about the alleged offender, the victim, and the community to ensure the case is managed appropriately.

19.7.2 Investigating and cultural considerations

In such investigations, there may be only one chance to speak to a victim (eg because travelling is imminent)—the 'one chance rule' (HM Government, 2014b, p 21). The attending police officer should therefore contact the designated person in their organization with expertise in forced marriages (often the same person leading the response in cases that involve the safeguarding of children, protection of vulnerable adults, or victims of domestic abuse). If access is not immediately possible, then information should be gathered to establish the facts and help with the referral.

The suspected victim must be seen in person, alone, and in a place where the conversation cannot be overheard, to try to avoid retaliation from other family members. They should be reassured of the confidentiality of the conversation. All the available options should be fully explained but their decision must be accepted.

A DASH risk assessment exercise should be performed (see 19.5.3.1) and any evidence of abuse or threats of abuse should be explored and documented. Any criminal offence committed in the context of a forced marriage (either before or after the marriage) will also be prosecuted (CPS, 2018d).

The case should be discussed with the Forced Marriage Unit and the victim referred to appropriate local and national support groups if they agree. The FMU have produced a number of support materials for professionals and those who are in (or at risk of) a forced marriage. These include leaflets, video clips, and a 'survivors' handbook', all available on the FMU section of the gov.uk website.

Police and social service records should be checked for previous referrals of family members, for example in relation to domestic abuse or missing persons. If relevant, a restricted entry in the force intelligence system should be created and a crime report submitted. Officers should reassure the victim about confidentiality, assess the need for immediate protection, and agree an effective method of contacting the victim discreetly in the future. If the person is under 18, a police protection referral should be made (see 19.9.2.1). Similarly, for adults with support needs, a referral should be made to the designated person responsible for safeguarding vulnerable adults and local safeguarding procedures should be activated.

Extensive guidance on best practice in responding to situations of forced marriage can be found in Multi-agency Practice Guidelines: Handling Cases of Forced Marriage here: <https://assets.publishing.service.gov.uk/government/uploads/system/uploads/attachment_data/file/1138703/Forced_marriage_guidance_0223.pdf>.

19.7.3 Forced Marriage Protection Orders

A Forced Marriage Protection Order (FMPO) can be issued by a civil court to a person who seems to be planning to implement a forced marriage. The victim, a relative or friend, voluntary worker or other official or any other person with the permission of the court can apply for a FMPO. Relevant documentation and guidance is available on the government website here: <https://www.gov.uk/apply-forced-marriage-protection-order/how-to-apply> and applications for a FMPO can be made at the same time as a police investigation or other criminal proceedings.

An FMPO has broad powers and sanctions for the recipient, which can be tailored to protect the victim. It can include requiring the recipient to hand over the passport of the person at risk or to reveal their whereabouts if missing. Breaking an FMPO is a criminal offence with a penalty of up to five years' imprisonment (s 120 of the Anti-social Behaviour, Crime and Policing Act 2014).

19.8 Hate Crime

Hate crime on its own is not an offence. Hate crime cases have an additional flag where another crime was committed (eg assault) and the police then gather evidence to show that the crime happened specifically because of one's race, religion, disability, sexual orientation or transgender identity. It is an aggravating factor to an offence. Please read Chapter 7 to find out more about these protected characteristics. These are only four out of ten protected characteristics—hatred on the grounds of any characteristic will amount to discrimination and you should still consider reports of such instances (especially as they may link into harassment or similar).

The police use the following definition of hate crime: 'Any criminal offence which is perceived by the victim or any other person, to be motivated by hostility or prejudice, based on a person's disability or perceived disability; race or perceived race; or religion or perceived religion; or sexual orientation or perceived sexual orientation or transgender identity or perceived transgender identity.' Whilst not all hate crime is necessarily of such nature that it becomes a public protection matter, hate-related behaviours are visible through a large majority of public protection issues—for example, using someone's sexual orientation to exploit them. We also know that the 'hate' element of a crime can cause a disproportionate impact on victims (usually this is psychological but it can be also physical; Home Office, 2018e).

19.8.1 Hate incidents

There will be instances when a hate incident may be recorded even though it is not a hate crime. Hate incidents have the potential to become critical incidents, especially when hate is being shown to groups of people—in such instances, appropriate reporting and responding to a hate incident is key, even if it is not a crime. For example, a hate incident may occur at a football event—due to its context, this can quickly escalate into a critical incident. You must apply the principle of proportionality when recording a non-crime incident. It has to be done through the least intrusive way (eg think about what actually needs to be recorded—do you need personal data?).

19.8.2 Hate crime offences

In order to prosecute crime as a hate crime, the offender either had to have:

- demonstrated hostility based on race, religion, disability, sexual orientation, or transgender identity **OR**
- been motivated by hostility based on race, religion, disability, sexual orientation, or transgender identity

You need to note that the victim does not actually have to be of the characteristic the offender perceives them to be—the offender might purely 'perceive' the characteristic (refer to concept of Discrimination by Perception).

Key pieces of legislation include:

- The Crime and Disorder Act 1998—specifically Part II referring to **racially and religiously aggravated crimes**
  - o s 28 Meaning of 'racially or religiously aggravated'
  - o s 29 racially or religiously aggravated assaults
  - o s 30 racially or religiously aggravated criminal damage
  - o s 31 racially or religiously aggravated public order offences
  - o s 32 racially or religiously aggravated harassment etc.
- The original Public Order Act 1986 was amended to address 'stirring up' (the phrase used in the legislation) or inciting hatred against a group of people on certain grounds.
  - o **racial hatred**, 'hatred against a group of persons defined by reference to colour, race, nationality (including citizenship), or ethnic or national origins' (s 17)
  - o **religious hatred**, hatred against a group of persons defined by reference to religious belief (eg Christianity or Islam) or to a lack of religious belief (eg atheists and humanists) (s 29).
  - o hatred on the grounds of **sexual orientation**, 'hatred against a group of persons defined by reference to sexual orientation whether towards persons of the same sex, the opposite sex or both' (s 29AB).
  - o Specific offences on the grounds of religious and/or sexual orientation hatred include: 'Use of words or behaviour or display of written material'; (ss 18 and 29B)—this relates to *inciting* hatred; 'Publishing or distributing written material' (ss 19 and 29C); 'Public performance of a play' (ss 20 and 29D); 'Distributing, showing or playing a recording' (ss 21 and 29E); 'Broadcasting or including programme in programme service' (ss 22 and 29F); 'Procession of inflammatory material' (ss 23 and 29G)
- The Sentencing Act 2020 (s 66)—whilst there are no specific offences relating to the other characteristics (eg disability or transgender orientation); it is a requirement to flag all crime where any of the characteristics form a part of the motivation for the offence—this can then be reflected in prosecution and sentencing.
- Hate incidents can happen offline as well as online—they should be taken with equal seriousness regardless of their location.

19.8.3 Responding to hate crime

Hate crime incidents are considered high priority. As a responding officer, it is likely you might want to seek advice from specialist departments/specialists who have more knowledge on how to effectively build rapport with those who hold the discussed protected characteristics.

After the call handler gathers relevant information and completes an initial risk assessment, your role as the responding officer is to ensure victim safety and the collection of relevant information and evidence. There is no specific risk assessment to be used but you should be guided by guidance on vulnerability-related risk. Here is what you need to remember as you enter the scene:

- Ensure you move the victim to a safe location and/or remove the suspect
- Whilst removing the suspect is often the right solution, in most hate crime cases, taking positive action with the suspect is the preference
- Evaluate what you need to effectively engage the victim—for example, do they need an interpreter? Is a disability preventing them from successfully engaging with you?
- Evaluate the victim's emotional state and their feelings surrounding the incident
- Collect any available evidence—you should also collect evidence to enable you to evidence hostility of the incident
- Check any previous records relating to the victim (ie to identify repeat or poly victimization)
- You should notify the local neighbourhood policing team
- If the case is very serious, you have the option to ask for a family liaison officer to be deployed but this should be done following a consultation
- You need to be emphatic and compassionate—you will work with populations who often perceive the justice system negatively and fear not being believed/understood or having their experiences minimized.

These offences are triable either way and the penalty is a fine or imprisonment (six months summarily and seven years on indictment).

19.9 Safeguarding Children

To start with, it is absolutely key to note that a child is anyone under the age of 18—it does not matter whether one is living independently, is of consent or criminal responsibility age, whether the individual is a suspect or an ex-offender, and so on. Safeguarding procedures concern all children. This was defined in the United Nations Convention on the Rights of the Child. The convention further highlights that the police have to keep the best interest of children in mind at all times, utilize maximum available resources, and promote children's self-worth. In English legislation, this translates to the 'Welfare principle' which is noted in the Children's Act 2004 as well as the Children and Young Person's Act 1993. The welfare of child victims tends to be at the forefront of much policy development, but the welfare of child suspects cannot be neglected. As per *R (M) v Chief Magistrate* [2010]—'The welfare of the child is an important and indeed fundamental consideration in determining how a child who has committed offences should be dealt with'.

The first significant piece of legislation relating to the safeguarding of children is the Children Act 1989. It covers any person under the age of 18 (s 105) but there are also references to children or young people of a particular age, for example 'under the age of 12'. The Children Act 1989 places great emphasis on encouraging multi-agency working and supporting children and families and reinforces approaches to child welfare that make children the primary concern. A number of high-profile cases had demonstrated that more was needed to protect children from harm. The inquiry into the death of Victoria Climbié in 2000, headed by Lord Laming, led to several key recommendations which help to ensure the thorough investigation of potential crimes, proper training for investigators, and appropriate and effective inter-agency working. In response, the government produced Every Child Matters, and eventually the Children Act 2004. These promote child welfare and inter-agency working, and place statutory obligations on local authorities to cooperate with other agencies. The role of Children's Commissioner was created, and Local Safeguarding Children Boards (now rebranded) were set up throughout the country to ensure that clear guidance and procedures were in place, and to provide multi-agency training.

The police have an obligation to safeguard children under s 11 of the Children Act 2004. The police should support other agencies when there are concerns for a child's well-being, even if no crime has been committed (Home Office, 2015c, p 34). The violent death of Peter Connelly (also known as Baby P) in 2007 (ie after the updated Children Act 2004) demonstrated that despite the recommendations, ongoing failures in child protection procedures had not been properly addressed. Lord Laming published a new report in 2009 (Laming, 2009) which highlighted the lack of appropriate action, both individually and collectively, from a number of the services involved. The death of Daniel Pelka in 2012, at the hands of his mother and her partner, further highlighted the need to improve the way vulnerable children are identified and the subsequent procedures for effective communication between organizations (Lock, 2013). Victoria Climbié, Peter Connelly, and Daniel Pelka had each been the subjects of contact with doctors, the police, social services, and schools, and these services had identified areas of potential neglect or abuse. They had, however, failed to take appropriate action to prevent the deaths of the children.

The centrality of protecting children's welfare and the importance of effective multi-agency work in this respect is clearly stated in the government's Children and Social Work Act 2017 and the 2018 Working Together to Safeguard Children policy (HM Government, 2018b). This policy was updated in 2022 to reflect changes through the introduction of the Domestic Abuse Act 2021 and the Health and Care Act 2022. The current multi-agency structure followed is through Safeguarding Children Multi-Agency Partnerships—these are composed of three statutory partners: local authorities, integrated care boards (previously clinical commissioning groups), and the police. These boards deal with guidance and consider some of the more serious cases. You can easily access the guidance online.

19.9.1 Child abuse

Child abuse is 'any form of maltreatment of a child. Somebody may abuse or neglect a child by inflicting harm on them, or by failing to act to prevent harm. Children may be abused in a family or in an institutional or community setting by those known to them or by others (eg, via the internet). They may be abused by an adult or adults, or by another child or children' (CoP, 2022f). You should note how wide this definition is—the term 'harm' for example refers to physical but also non-physical harm. The abuse can happen by anyone and in any setting. The Children Act 1989 (s 31(9)) states that harm can include:

1. ill-treatment or the impairment of health or development;
2. impairment suffered from seeing or hearing the ill-treatment of another;
3. sexual abuse; and
4. forms of ill-treatment which are not physical.

Child abuse is perceived differently to adult abuse. Whilst safeguarding in both scenarios is key, children present with multiple further vulnerabilities. Age is only one of them, but it impacts on the other reasons. For example, very young children will not be aware of abuse happening and/or will not be able to communicate about what is happening. Child abuse (other than child sexual exploitation) mostly occurs within the family environment or by someone known to the child—in this instance, the bond between the perpetrator and the victim is very strong and the child will be manipulated into not talking about what is happening to them. As children get older, they may also feel shame and fear. Child abuse is a significant adverse experience which changes children's brain chemistry, not only making it harder to report but also making it more difficult to be open about what happened to them. Child abuse and neglect have long-lasting effects on the victim of abuse, and different children will have their own response to the trauma.

The available evidence suggests that most child abuse occurs within the family. As children enter their teenage years, abuse outside of the family becomes more common (eg child sexual exploitation, abuse by a figure of authority). Child abuse is more prevalent than we like to think and based on findings from their telephone helpline referrals, the NSPCC (2022a) note that 62 children a day are referred to agencies due to suspicion of child abuse or neglect with two thirds of the cases being about children under the age of nine. However, the amount of abuse is probably much larger, and through self-report questions it is estimated that around half a million children suffer domestic abuse every year. The CSEW provides an estimate that 20 per cent of the adult population experienced some form of abuse before the age of 16.

There are many different types of child abuse cases, and they can be interlinked—repeat and polyvictimization is quite common. You should use your professional judgement when assessing whether something constitutes child abuse—for example, most people do not think of financial abuse as associated with children—however, withdrawing money for lunch, not using benefits to support a child and so on, are all present in child abuse cases.

- Child sexual abuse: based on the CSEW, 7.5 per cent of surveyed adults experienced sexual abuse before the age of 16. This type of abuse involves forcing or enticing a child to be involved in sexual activity. It includes penetrative contact crime (eg oral sex), non-penetrative contact crime (eg kissing, masturbation), but also non-contact crime (eg creating sexual images, watching sexual videos with children). Please note that the grooming of a child for the purposes of later abuse is also a child abuse activity. Most perpetrators are male, but females also commit this crime (their motivations are often different and they tend to co-offend with male perpetrators). Other children may also be perpetrators. Young children are often unaware anything is wrong as often force or violence is not used, and pain not always experienced (or is normalized from a young age).
- Emotional abuse—based on the CSEW, 9.2 per cent of surveyed adults experienced sexual abuse before the age of 16. This type of abuse involves behaviours and activities over a prolonged period of time which impact on the way a child develops—this can be physically or emotionally. Harsh parenting techniques, putting the child down, not giving the child a voice, overestimating what a child is capable of, limiting the child's exploration of their environment, or bullying are some behaviours visible in this type of crime.
- Child neglect/child cruelty—child neglect is encompassed within the child cruelty legislation (Children and Young Persons Act 1933). Child cruelty, specifically, refers to: 'if anyone who is 16 years or over wilfully assaults, ill-treats, whether physically or otherwise, neglects, abandons, or exposes a child, or procures a child to be assaulted, ill-treated, whether physically or otherwise, neglected, abandoned, or exposed, in a manner likely to cause unnecessary suffering or injury to health, whether the suffering or injury is of a physical or psychological nature, they are guilty of an offence'. Child neglect is when 'a parent or the legal guardian, or other person legally liable to maintain a child or young person has wilfully neglected the child in a manner likely to cause injury to health by failing to provide adequate food, clothing, medical aid or lodging or, if having been unable to provide such items, they fail to take steps to procure them'. You should note that with child neglect matters, there are often non-criminal justice responses which are preferred, such as parent/carer education as many acts of what appears to be child neglect are not actually wilful acts. The NSPCC (2021b) estimate based on their research that 1 in 10 children in the UK has been neglected.
- Physical abuse—based on the CSEW, 7.6 per cent of surveyed adults experienced sexual abuse before the age of 16. Physical abuse is any non-accidental infliction of physical force by one person on another, which may or may not result in physical injury. It can take many shapes, including shaking (especially during infanthood), kicking, pulling, choking, suffocating, burning, and many more. You should remember that offenders are likely to be careful about the injuries they cause so that they are not easy to see when the child is clothed.

A wide range of incidents may be associated with child abuse, such as: domestic abuse; missing children, including those truanting from school; children engaged in criminality, including bullying and abusing others; children abusing animals; children involved in sexual exploitation or prostitution; online and off-line sexual abuse, such as sexual grooming; parental drug or alcohol abuse. It is also key to note that abuse which is not addressed is predictive of future suspicious child deaths.

19.9.1.1 Child sexual offences

Sexual offences involving children are covered in Chapter 24 on sexual offending and are not included in this chapter. The following matters are covered there:

1. Child sexual abuse
2. Child sexual grooming
3. Child sexual exploitation
4. Sexual Harm Prevention Orders
5. Sexual Risk Orders
6. Sex Offender Disclosure Scheme
7. Police Officers and abuse of trust (see also Chapter 20)
8. Risk factors for vulnerability

19.9.1.2 Child non-sexual offences

Causing and allowing death or serious physical harm: This is considered in s 5 of the Domestic Violence, Crime and Victims Act 2004, amended by the same named 2012 amendment. The following events must be established in relation to the offence:

- a child or vulnerable adult ('V') has died or suffered serious physical harm;
- the death or serious physical harm was the result of an unlawful act, course of conduct, or omission of a person ('D') who was a member of the same household as V and who had frequent contact with V;
- there existed at the time of death a significant risk of serious physical harm being caused to V by the unlawful act of any member of that household and either:

  a. D was the person whose unlawful act caused V's death or serious physical harm; or
  b. D was, or ought to have been, aware of that risk and failed to take such steps as he or she could reasonably have been expected to take to protect V from that risk of serious physical harm; and
  c. The death or serious physical harm occurred in circumstances of the kind that D foresaw or ought to have foreseen.

You should read the 'Homicide: Manslaughter and Murder' guidance provided by the CPS for further considerations relating to this crime. The Police, Crime, Sentencing and Courts Act 2022 (s 123) raised the penalty for this offence from 14 years to life imprisonment for a death and from 10 years to 24 years for serious physical harm.

Child cruelty, neglect, and violence: this is considered in s 1(1) of the Children and Young Persons Act 1933 as amended by Part 5 s 66 of the Serious Crime Act. The following has to happen for this offence:

- a person who has attained the age of 16 years;
- who has responsibility for any child or young person under that age; wilfully
- assaults, ill-treats (whether physically or otherwise), neglects, abandons or exposes [them], or causes or procures [them] to be assaulted, ill-treated (whether physically or otherwise), neglected, abandoned, or exposed;
- in a manner likely to cause [them] unnecessary suffering or injury to health (whether the suffering or injury is of a physical or a psychological nature).

Section 1(2) of the Act refers to neglect likely to cause injury to health:

- Where a parent or person legally liable to maintain a child fails to provide adequate food, clothing, medical aid, or lodging for the child or having been unable to provide the above failed to take steps to procure it to be provided; or
- Where the cause of death for an infant under 3 years is suffocation (not being caused by disease or the presence of a foreign body in the throat or air passages) while the infant was in bed with some other person who has attained the age of 16 years and where that other person was under the influence of drink or a prohibited drug either when he went to bed or at any later time before the suffocation. Part 5 of the Serious Crime Act 2015 (s 66) defines a 'prohibited drug' for the purposes of s 1(2)(b); furthermore, it expands the reference to suffocation occurring in a bed, to include any kind of furniture or surface used for the purpose of sleeping.

Incidents should be assessed in terms of the history of acts and omissions to determine whether they constitute a criminal offence. Section 122 of the Police, Crime, Sentencing and Courts Act 2022 has increased the penalty for this offence from 10 years to 14 years.

Child abduction and kidnapping: This is considered in the Child Abduction Act 1984 as amended by the Children Act 1989.

- Section 1 states that abduction occurs when 'a person connected with a child (parent, guardian or anyone with custody) under the age of 16 takes or sends the child out of the UK without the appropriate consent'
- Section 2 of the Act refers to child abduction cases where the perpetrator is not someone connected with a child (unless they reasonably believed they were—this is a form of defence)
- Section 5 relates to child kidnapping cases of a child under the age of 16 by someone connected with a child (parent, guardian, or anyone with custody).

Child abduction warning notices: there are two types of warning notices available—one for all children under the age of 16 and one for children under the age of 18 who are under local authority care. The aim of the notices is to prevent incidents which can happen as a result of risks exhibited by children—eg spending time with much older associates. Their aims are as follows:

- To reduce repeat incidences of such children being missing from the care of those responsible for their welfare.
- To reduce the risk that such children are exposed to.
- To set out a clear, graduated, and proportionate response to such cases.
- To set out a clear procedure for the issue and audit of Child Abduction Warning Notices so that they are evidentially viable and sound in terms of potential prosecution.
- To adopt a problem-solving approach to reducing instances of children missing from home.

Whilst the notices are not set within any statutory or legislative provision, they are often used for case building and can be used as grounds for arrest (eg *Shepherd v CPS* [2017] EWHC 2566). And so, where a child is seen interacting with individuals where a notice was given, an arrest can be made on suspicion of having committed an offence.

Infanticide: The offence of infanticide is included under s 1 of the Infanticide Act 1938 and refers to where a woman causes the death of a child under 12 months in circumstances where her balance of mind was disturbed by reason of her not having recovered from the effects of giving birth to the child.

Assault offences: these are covered in this book in Chapter 22. These are mostly covered under the Offences Against the Person Act 1861.

Injuries to children from heating appliances: Carers have a responsibility to ensure that children are kept safe when heating appliances are in use. Under s 11 of the CYPA, a person over 16 commits an offence if a child under 12 is killed or suffers serious injury because the carer allowed 'the child to be in a room containing an open fire grate or any heating appliance'. The appliance must have been 'liable to cause injury to a person by contact with it' and 'not sufficiently protected to guard against the risk of being burnt or scalded without taking reasonable precautions against that risk'. The penalty for this summary offence is a fine.

Taking a child abroad to join a terrorist group: A more recent concern has been the involvement of children in terrorist acts. Local authorities are now obliged (under s 36 of the Counterterrorism and Security Act 2015) to establish 'Channel' panels to try to prevent children being drawn into terrorism. The panels (which include the local chief officer of the police) assess the likelihood of this and arrange for support to be provided (Home Office, 2015c, p 19). There are offences connected to this action which relate to child cruelty, neglect, and violence (s 1 CYPA 1933) and child abduction (s 1 Child Abduction Act 1984).

19.9.2 Investigating child abuse

It might be surprising to you that in instances of child abuse, the police are not necessarily the primary investigator. Safeguarding practices are set out by the Department of Education. You can find very good resources at the NSPCC website. A lot of child abuse is not reported directly to the police—rather, non-criminal justice processes take place whereby concern is reported to the local authority and social workers who then initiate proceedings. Local authorities can get referrals from schools, after school clubs, GPs, the police, or others. They need to acknowledge receipt of a report within 24 hours and complete a risk assessment to understand whether any immediate response is required.

In cases where there is risk that a child is suffering or may suffer significant harm, child protection procedures are engaged—ss 17 and 27 of the Children's Act 1989 not only focus on risk assessment but provide the police with powers to take any action necessary to safeguard a child. It is only a recent development that police are given powers such as the Power of Entry when child abuse is suspected. Further, s 47 of the Act introduced the concept of **significant harm**—it places a duty on a local authority to make enquiries where it is suspected a child is suffering harm or is likely to suffer harm.

All police services have a specialist Child Abuse Investigation Unit—this might be under a different name in your local area. Whilst there may be local and regional differences in the exact nature and scope of their work, these teams will usually be staffed by nationally trained investigators (trained in ICIDP or equivalent) and are likely to have successfully undertaken the College of Policing National Specialist Child Abuse Investigator Development Programme (SCAIDP). In some constabularies, such specialist officers are known as 'Child Abuse Investigators'. Officers involved in interviewing children in relation to abuse should also be trained to a very high standard in witness interviewing—undertaking high level Achieving Best Evidence training.

Once a referral is made to such a team, either from an internal notification or from an external agency (eg social services), the investigators will decide what type of investigation is required. These may often begin as joint agency investigations, but the police will take a lead role if criminal offences are suspected. According to s 47 of the Children Act 1989, the local authority has a duty to investigate where it believes that a child might be suffering significant harm. The police have certain powers under s 46 of the same Act in relation to police protection (see below), and the first consideration will be to secure the welfare of a child or children. Once this has been achieved, a thorough criminal investigation can take place, and other agencies will work to assure the current and future welfare of the child. You should note that instances of child abuse, especially those with a very serious injury outcome or where the perpetrator is someone in a position of authority, can be classed as a Critical Incident and you should then follow relevant guidelines.

The Child Abuse Investigation Units can help trainee officers (such as those undertaking the PCDA or DHEP) with decision-making where a child's welfare might be a concern. Further information is available from several online sources, including the College of Policing document *Risk and associated investigations*. There is also a College of Policing Professional Role profile for Child Abuse Investigators; this could also help trainee officers understand how such investigations are carried out.

Dealing with children who have been subjected to any form of abuse is a challenging and sensitive task. The NSPCC (2021a) provides some useful online resources on how to deal with difficult situations where the child might be distressed, confused, and worried about the consequences of police presence.

19.9.2.1 Police protection orders

The police have a statutory duty to safeguard the well-being of children (s 11 of the Children Act 2004). Police officers have a power to take children or young people under 18 into police protection if the child's safety seems to be at immediate risk if no action is taken (s 46 of the Children Act 1989). This power is only used in emergency situations and as a last resort and when absolutely necessary; any decision to remove a child/children from a parent or carer is usually made by a court by means of an Emergency Protection Order (Home Office, 2015c, pp 31, 58). Police protection is not a measure for circumventing the usual legal process; see the Safeguarding Hub document *Police Protection—A practical guide*, available online.

An Emergency Protection Order can be applied for by anyone, including the local authority or the police. The application is made to the Family Court. The requirements are:

- The court is satisfied that there is reasonable cause to believe that the child is likely to suffer significant harm if s/he is:
  - Not removed to accommodation provided by the applicant; or
  - Does not remain in the place in which the child is being accommodated; or
- If s 47 enquiries are being frustrated by unreasonable refusal of access to the child, and the local authority has reasonable cause to believe that access is needed as a matter of urgency.

Where possible, officers should speak with the child and the child's responses should be recorded word for word. Care should be taken to avoid 'contaminating' any future interviews. If a criminal investigation is initiated, the guidance set out in *Achieving Best Evidence in Criminal Proceedings: Guidance on interviewing victims and witnesses* (MoJ, 2022a), and guidance on using special measures should be followed. Once officers have secured the safety and well-being of the child, the case should be referred to the Specialist Child Abuse Investigation Unit or its equivalent. A child can be kept in police protection for up to 72 hours (s 46(6) of the Children Act 1989).

Police protection can involve moving the child to a safe place or preventing their removal from a safe place. Section 46(1) of the Children Act 1989 states that where a police officer 'has reasonable cause to believe that a child would otherwise be likely to suffer significant harm' they may:

- remove the child to suitable accommodation and keep them there; or
- take all reasonable steps to ensure that their removal from a hospital (or other place in which they are accommodated) is prevented.

There are two separate and distinct roles for the police in relation to police protection: the initiating officer who takes the key actions in relation to the child, and the designated officer who independently overviews the circumstances in which the child was taken into protection (Home Office Circular 17/2008). The designated officer will be at least the rank of inspector and cannot be the initiating officer for the same case.

Apart from in exceptional circumstances, no child should be taken into police protection until the initiating officer has seen the child and assessed the circumstances.

19.9.2.2 Role of initiating officer

The initiating officer takes the child into police protection, undertakes the initial enquiries, and completes a Police Protection Form as soon as possible. Under s 46(3) of the Children Act 1989, the initiating officer must as soon as is reasonably practicable also:

- inform the local authority where the child was found, and of the police protection steps that have been taken (and are proposed) concerning the child, and the reasons;
- tell the authority in which the child usually lives ('the appropriate authority') where they are now being accommodated;
- inform the child (if they appear capable of understanding) about the steps taken and the reasons, and about any further police protection steps that may be taken;
- try to establish the wishes and feelings of the child;
- ensure that a designated officer has been assigned for the case; and
- arrange for the child to be moved to local authority-provided accommodation if the child is not already in care.

In addition, as soon as is reasonably practicable, the initiating officer must contact the adults who have been caring for the child (s 46(4)). As well as the child's parents, this would include every person who has parental responsibility for the child and any other person with whom the child was living immediately before being taken into police protection. The adults who have most recently been caring for the child must be told about the police protection steps taken (or planned) concerning the child, and the reasons.

19.9.3 Meaning of parental responsibility

Parental responsibility in terms of the Children Act 1989, referred to and revised from the Children and Young Persons Act 1933, means 'all the rights, duties, powers, responsibilities and authority which by law a parent of a child has in relation to that child and [their] property'. It can be held by parents, step-parents, and by other people or administrative bodies such as a local authority. The question of who has parental responsibility is covered in ss 2 and 3 of the Children Act 1989. The key points are:

- If the father and mother were married to each other when the child was born, they will each have parental responsibility (s 2(1)). The father is no longer deemed the 'natural guardian' of a child (s 2(4)).
- If the biological parents were not married to each other when the child was born, the mother will have parental responsibility, and so will the father if the child was jointly registered after 1 December 2003 (s 2(2)).
- More than one person can have parental responsibility for the same child at the same time (s 2(5)), and each may act alone to meet that responsibility (s 2(7)).
- A person who has parental responsibility for a child does not cease to have the responsibility simply because another person acquires such responsibility for the child (s 2(6)).

The spirit of the legislation is that all the parties including the parents, the child, and the local authority must be kept informed and given reasons for any actions. The child's wishes must be listened to but not necessarily followed.

19.9.4 Suitable accommodation

Suitable accommodation will be local authority accommodation, a registered children's home, or foster care (see Home Office Circular 44/2003). Relatives or other appropriate carers can also be used if the designated officer and social services consider it appropriate. The child may also be taken to hospital if medical attention is required.

The circular also emphasizes that a child under police protection should not be taken to a police station unless there is absolutely no alternative, and under no circumstances should they be taken into the custody suite or cell area.

19.9.5 Specific considerations in child death cases

There is specific guidance provided to officers in cases of child deaths—this is the 2014 ACPO guidance on investigating child deaths. It is to be used in conjunction with the *Murder Investigation Manual*. Statutory multi-agency partnerships are responsible for a joint investigation of child death. There has been a sharp decrease in accidental child deaths following a number of campaigns related to preventable factors. This, however, means that a larger proportion of child death cases is likely to be suspicious/criminal in nature than before. Each child death needs to be thoroughly investigated to rule out homicide. An unexpected death can be understood as a death:

- Which was not anticipated as a significant possibility, for example, 24 hours before the death; or
- Where there was a similarly unexpected collapse or incident leading to or precipitating the events which led to the death.

As a first responder, your key role when attending to a child death is to approach a lead investigator at the earliest opportunity to take charge of the investigation. Understandably, this is alongside the usual five investigative building blocks. The following risk factors seem to be associated with suspicious deaths:

- History of violence to children;
- Inconsistent account;
- Mental health issues;
- Previous atypical hospital visits;
- History of alcohol abuse;
- Child over one year old;
- On child protection plan;
- Known to social services;
- History of drug abuse;
- History of domestic violence;
- Criminal record;
- Previous sibling dead;
- Presence of features of the RADI (rotational acceleration deceleration impact injuries sometimes referred to as the triad which is subdural haemorrhages, brain swelling, and retinal haemorrhages);
- Toxicological detection of drugs of abuse;
- Presence of fractures;
- Bruising at unusual sites, for example, torso;
- Post-mortem features indicating that the interval since death was significantly longer than stated by parents or carers.

TASK 2 A single parent is caring for a child who has been ill. There is no food in the house and they decide to go shopping while the child is fast asleep. The nearest open shop is a short drive away. During the journey, the car breaks down and the parent is left stranded by the roadside. While they are away, the child wakes up and becomes very upset. Having heard the screaming of a clearly distressed child, the neighbours call the police. All the doors and windows are shut and the child cannot open the door.

1. What power of entry, if any, is available?
2. How would you deal with the distressed child?
3. What offence might the parent have committed?

19.10 Female Genital Mutilation (FGM)

FGM occurs when part or all the external female genitalia are removed or injured for no medical reason (see WHO, 2023, for a typology of different forms of FGM). FGM may be referred to in several ways at community level (such as female circumcision, cutting, or being 'clean') and is usually performed before a girl starts puberty so is considered by the Government as a form of child abuse. However, this does affect some adult women before marriage or to ensure chastity. Although FGM is a deeply embedded social norm in certain cultures, it is not required by any religion. Perpetrators of FGM (sometimes known as cutters) often believe that they are protecting an important part of their cultural identity, and FGM may be presented as an occasion for celebration and a rite of passage. It may also be linked to ideas of family 'honour', in which sense it would be a form of 'honour'-based violence.

FGM is a violation of human rights, particularly the rights to health, security, and physical integrity, and the right to be free from torture and cruel, inhuman, or degrading treatment. It can also cause serious health problems and even death. As an under-reported offence, data sets for FGM have predominantly relied upon reporting via NHS trusts and GP practices where evidence of FGM is observed. These data trends have been increasing since 2015 and during a two-month period between July and September 2021, 1,530 women and girls were identified as affected (NHS Digital, 2021). Although FGM has been a crime under English law since the 1980s, the first prosecution was not made until 2014.

The College of Policing APP guidance on FGM pivots on prevention, protection, and prosecution (CoP, 2015c). Further information is available online in *A Protocol between the Police and the Crown Prosecution Service in the investigation and prosecution of allegations of FGM*. The document stresses the importance of early consultation between the police and the CPS. The NHS and the NSPCC websites provide further information and statistical data on FGM.

19.10.1 FGM offences

FGM offences are all listed in the Female Genital Mutilation Act 2003 (FGMA). The offences are:

- carrying out FGM (s 1);
- assisting a girl with carrying out FGM on herself (s 2);
- assisting a non-UK person outside the UK to perform FGM on a UK person (s 3); and
- failing to protect a girl from FGM (s 3A).

The offences under ss 1, 3, and 3A also apply for offences that take place outside the UK if the suspect is a UK citizen (s 4).

For a victim under 16 years of age, the persons responsible for her (such as a parent or someone assuming similar responsibility even if only temporarily) are committing an offence of failing to protect her, with a maximum penalty of seven years' imprisonment (s 3A).

FGM offences are punishable with a maximum of 14 years' imprisonment (FGMA, and ss 70–75 of the Serious Crime Act 2015).

19.10.2 Investigating and preventing FGM

Police officers if they suspect that FGM is likely to occur should consider the need to take immediate action to protect anyone at risk and inform a supervisor or specially trained officer. There may be indicators that suggest that FGM is being planned for a particular girl, for example, preparing for a trip, absence from school, and/or a special ceremony. The safety of the girl is paramount and an assessment of risk of significant harm should be conducted. It could be classed as a critical incident and the 'golden hour' principle applied (10.3.1.2). The girl could be taken into police protection for up to 72 hours (19.9.2.1).

A strategy meeting will be arranged (within a day at most) between the local authority children's social care department and health professionals. The parents will be informed of the law and the dangers of FGM but, if it seems that the girl is still at risk, the emergency protection powers and orders under the Children Act 1989 can be used.

A risk assessment should also be conducted for other female family members. If it is known that a particular woman has already undergone FGM, a multi-agency meeting must be convened, and a risk assessment carried out for any girls in her family.

Indicators that FGM has occurred include absences from school and noticeable changes in behaviour when the girl returns (such as difficulty sitting straight, complaining of pain, and being secretive). FGM is a crime and when carried out on girls it also amounts to child abuse, so a robust investigation must be conducted. Victims may not know that the events they experienced amounted to FGM and/or that it is illegal in the UK. They are often unwilling to report FGM and support a prosecution. Perpetrators may see the act as culturally justifiable and in the best interest of the child and might not know it is illegal. Other members of the family or the community may share these attitudes and beliefs or be reluctant to come forward for fear of being ostracized.

Police officers may also be reluctant to address cases of FGM for fear of being branded racist or culturally insensitive, but this should not deter them from exercising their duty of protection. A female police officer should conduct the interview and no member of the victim's family or community should be present. The language used should be sensitive and non-judgemental. An interpreter may sometimes be required, but if they have the same ethnic background as the victim this can inhibit the victim as she may fear a lack of confidentiality.

Officers rely heavily on information and support from other agencies to identify and address FGM. Covert tactics should also be considered and any opportunities for gathering intelligence should be maximized. The risk of FGM occurring to other female members of the same family should also be taken into account.

For suspected cases of FGM, local safeguarding procedures should be followed.

For known cases of FGM where the victim is under the age of 18 years, all registered health and social care professionals and teachers have a duty to report it to the police (s 5B of the FGMA). Failing to report a known case to the police is not a criminal offence but is treated as a serious disciplinary matter (CoP, 2015c). A case would be 'known' if the FGM has been verbally disclosed by the victim or visually identified by the professional involved. Medical evidence will be required for known cases of FGM.

The anonymity of the victim must be preserved for life so no information that could allow members of the public to identify her should be published. Any breach of this principle is punishable with a fine (s 4A of and Sch 1 to the FGMA).

19.10.3 FGM protection orders and emergency powers

FGM Protection Orders (FGMPO) can be issued to protect girls at risk of FGM (s 5A of and Sch 2 to the FGMA and the Serious Crime Act 2015). They can also be used for girls who have already undergone FGM as they may be threatened by other witnesses in an investigation into FGM. Note that although the term 'girl' is used, the legislation applies to females of any age.

Applications for an FGMPO can be made to the High Court or a family law court by the victim, local authorities, or a third party authorized by the court (such as the police, a healthcare professional, a teacher, a friend). The order provides flexibility for the courts in setting prohibitions and restrictions and can, for example, require the surrender of passports or travel documents to prevent FGM being arranged or carried out abroad. Breaching an FGMPO is an either-way offence (the penalty is up to 12 months' imprisonment if tried summarily and 5 years on indictment). A breach can also be treated as a civil matter, as contempt of court (see s 5A of and Sch 2, para 4(3) and (4) to the FGMA).

Emergency powers under the Children Act 1989 are also available when children are known to be at risk of FGM, for example under ss 44 and 46.

Section 70(1) of the Serious Crime Act 2015 ('the 2015 Act') amends s 4 of the 2003 Act so that the extra-territorial jurisdiction extends to prohibited acts done outside the UK by a UK national or a person who is resident in the UK. Consistent with that change, s 70(1) also amends s 3 of the 2003 Act (offence of assisting a non-UK person to mutilate a girl's genitalia overseas) so it extends to acts of FGM done to a UK national or a person who is resident in the UK.

19.11 Abuse of Vulnerable Adults

The Human Rights Act 1998 and the Care Act 2014 provide an important legal framework against which policies for the safeguarding of vulnerable adults have been developed. There is currently no single statutory framework for safeguarding adults equivalent to the Children Act 1989 which legislates for child protection.

Some adults are deemed to be vulnerable due to a mental, physical, or learning disability, age, or illness. Such a person may be unable to take care of, or protect themselves against, significant harm or exploitation. Vulnerability, including its definition, is discussed in detail in Chapter 20. There are two main types of incidents where adults may suffer abuse: those involving serious abuse, such as GBH or serious sexual assault, and those which involve a serious incident in a care or health-care environment (ACPO, 2012b). The Sexual Offences Act 2003 ss 38–44 stipulate specific offences for care workers who engage in sexual activity with a person with a mental disorder. This is in addition to those who are not care workers involved in sexual activity with a person with a mental disorder (found in ss 30–37 of the SOA 2003). Please see the relevant legislation for further detail.

The abuse can be physical, sexual, psychological, discriminatory, institutional, or financial, and can also include acts of omission and neglect. It can take place in a range of contexts, including day care, residential or nursing situations, as well as hospitals or indeed the person's own home. Offenders can include relatives, care workers, professional staff, volunteers, and strangers. Some perpetrate multiple offences against one person a number of times, while others abuse groups of people at the same time. A victim may be reluctant to report the abuse if the suspect is their primary carer as they might then be obliged to move into institutional residential care. Some victims may not even realize that the acts amount to abuse or be able to communicate about it.

19.11.1 The key responsibility of the FAO

As FAO you will be expected to protect the victim from further harm, to preserve evidence, and identify any criminal offences. According to the College of Policing (2021g) this should include:

- Care when communicating with a vulnerable victim (see 20.5.1 and 19.18). An officer should take into account the victim's level of comprehension, age, and preference being careful to avoid speaking to the adult in front of a potential suspect
- Using risk tools to identify vulnerabilities of an individual that may have contributed to them suffering or being at risk of harm (Judging the risk of harm is difficult, partly because the adult has the right to make their own decisions and choices and may not see themselves as vulnerable (see 20.9.1))
- Assessing the level of risks and determining whether immediate action is required to remove the risk of harm (high (immediate positive action required), medium, low risk)
- Consider suspects within the family or community that collude in the abuse (this is particularly important where potential shame or honour are culturally relevant)
- Consider the use of protective orders and/or other safeguarding activities to prevent against criminal targeting
- Consider referrals to other organizations for ongoing care and support (consent may be required)

For a vulnerable adult in custody, the PACE Codes of Practice provide a number of safeguards to protect their rights, including the appointment of a responsible adult (see 18.6.1).

A multi-agency approach to communication and decision-making may safeguard the victim and prevent further abuse by addressing the immediate protection needs of the victim at the earliest opportunity. This requires the FAO to have thoroughly recorded evidence from scene attendance, such as accommodation information, family/community networks, current and previous police involvement, victim's views, full circumstances of the referral etc. This list is not exhaustive, and all available evidence should be considered. Historically, failures to fully record and share information in previous high-profile cases has resulted in the relevant risks not being identified and/or effectively managed, leading to tragic outcomes.

Early investigations should be cognisant of the memorandum of understanding between the NPCC and the Care Quality Commission (CQC) for effective liaison and communication between the organizations and this is available on the CQC website. This determines the roles and responsibilities of the police and relevant organizations including a framework for investigation and sharing of information. CQC are the regulating body for several health care settings including care and nursing homes, hospitals (private and public), health and social care in secure settings, domiciliary care, GP and dental practices, and mental health services. Stipulated in the MOU is that since 1 April 2015, CQC has taken lead enforcement responsibility for health and safety incidents where patients have died or sustained avoidable harm or been exposed to a significant risk of avoidable harm as a result of a failure by the registered provider to meet the required standard.

Further information is available online in the College of Policing Guidance on Adults at Risk (2022) found here: <https://www.college.police.uk/app/major-investigation-and-public-protection/adults-risks>. The Care Act Statutory Guidance is currently under review following the Health and Care Act 2022 but will provide further guidance once complete. The Home Office Code of Practice for Victims of Crime (MoJ, 2020) can also be helpful in making decisions about how to best meet victims' rights and entitlements.

19.12 Modern Slavery and Human Trafficking

Whilst anyone can be a victim of modern slavery, victims often come from the poorer communities in their country of origin. Poverty places individuals at a greater risk of victimization, especially where there is a pressing need for money (such as a relative being ill). Any country with a relatively low socio-economic status is likely to be targeted for victims by human traffickers, and women are more likely to be victimized for two reasons: they usually have lower wages and greater difficulty in accessing education in their home country and, secondly, they may be more in demand in the country of destination (eg as female sex workers). The victims are recruited in a variety of ways, from advertisements for work, to abduction and kidnapping. Their travel documents may or may not be legitimate, for example a trafficker may arrange a new identity for a child and appoint themselves as a guardian, thus controlling almost every aspect of the child's life. Corruption in the country of origin (including by government officials) can impede the investigation and prevention of human trafficking. Victims are brought into the country through various points of entry.

Victims are highly vulnerable and also intimidated, making it difficult for them to report or cooperate with organizations. Its true prevalence is therefore also difficult to assess. Official referral statistics indicate over 10,000 potential victims (Home Office, 2021e) but this is not reflective of the actual number of victims. Initial indicators that a person may have been trafficked include: human rights breaches; threats or actual harm to family members; deprivation of food, water, and sleep; the withholding of medical care; being forced to perform sexual acts; having wages partly or totally withheld; debt-bondage; working excessive hours; not having access to identity documents such as a passport; or having restricted freedom of movement. Public authorities (including police authorities) have a statutory duty to notify the Secretary of State, or designated person, when there are reasonable grounds to suspect that a person may be a victim of slavery or human trafficking (s 52 of the MSA), and this should at least help to improve the accuracy of the data.

19.12.1 Modern slavery

Modern slavery is an umbrella term that includes human trafficking and slavery, servitude, and forced or compulsory labour. These crimes all involve exploitation. Slavery is where one or more persons seem to have ownership over another person(s) and can therefore exploit the victim. Human trafficking occurs when one or more persons make travel arrangements for a person to a destination where they become a victim of exploitation of one kind or another. This does not have to be across international borders.

Slavery is prohibited under the European Convention on Human Rights (Article 4). Slavery, servitude, and forced labour were first criminalized in 2010 and The Modern Slavery Act 2015 (MSA) consolidated these offences and explicitly addressed human trafficking. Slavery, servitude, and forced or compulsory labour are all offences under s 1 of the MSA. The Act also introduced an Independent Anti-Slavery Commissioner, with a UK-wide remit to improve the prevention, detection, investigation, and prosecution of modern slavery offences and identification of victims (Part 4 of the MSA).

19.12.2 Duty to report

Frontline police staff have a statutory duty to report cases of modern slavery to the Home Office (s 52 of the MSA). This is generally done through the National Referral Mechanism (NRM, see 19.12.6). The UK's strategy to address modern slavery is organized around four 'Ps' (HM Government, 2014a). These are:

- pursue (by prosecuting and disrupting offenders);
- prevent (individuals from offending);
- protect (vulnerable people from exploitation and raising awareness and resilience for modern slavery); and
- prepare (by improving victim identification and support).

19.12.3 Human trafficking

Human trafficking is often a complex phenomenon of significant national and international concern. Human trafficking is a modern-day form of slavery that involves the illegal trade of human beings for the purpose of some form of forced exploitation. The trafficking can be done internationally or nationally (eg county lines). The United Nations Protocol to Prevent, Suppress and Punish Trafficking Persons, also referred to as the Palermo Protocol, provides in Article 3 an internationally recognized definition:

> Trafficking in persons shall mean the recruitment, transportation, transfer, harbouring or receipt of persons, by means of the threat or use of force or other forms of coercion, of abduction, of fraud, of deception, of abuse of power or of a position of vulnerability or of the giving or receiving of payments or benefits to achieve the consent of a person having control of another person, for the purpose of exploitation. Exploitation shall include, at a minimum, the exploitation of the prostitution of others or other forms of sexual exploitation, forced labour or services, slavery or practices similar to slavery, servitude or removal of organs.

Section 2 of the MSA provides a legal definition of human trafficking:

> (1) A person commits an offence if the person arranges or facilitates the travel of another person ('V') with a view to V being exploited.
> (2) It is irrelevant whether V consents to the travel (whether V is an adult or a child).
> (3) A person may in particular arrange or facilitate V's travel by recruiting V, transporting or transferring V, harbouring or receiving V, or transferring or exchanging control over V.
> (4) A person arranges or facilitates V's travel with a view to V being exploited only if—
>   (a) the person intends to exploit V (in any part of the world) during or after the travel, or
>   (b) the person knows or ought to know that another person is likely to exploit V (in any part of the world) during or after the travel.
> (5) 'Travel' means—
>   (a) arriving in, or entering, any country,
>   (b) departing from any country,
>   (c) travelling within any country.
> (6) A person who is a UK national commits an offence under this section regardless of—
>   (a) where the arranging or facilitating takes place, or
>   (b) where the travel takes place.
> (7) A person who is not a UK national commits an offence under this section if—
>   (a) any part of the arranging or facilitating takes place in the United Kingdom, or
>   (b) the travel consists of arrival in or entry into, departure from, or travel within, the United Kingdom

You should note that human trafficking is not the same as smuggling. Smuggling involves bringing a person into a country illegally but on arrival the relationship between the parties ceases. In other words, there is no further exploitation by the smuggler (though individuals coming into a country illegally are vulnerable to victimization). Human trafficking and migrant smuggling are global crimes that use men, women, and children for profit. The organized networks or individuals behind these lucrative crimes take advantage of people who are vulnerable, desperate, or seeking a better life.

Being trafficked is by its very nature connected to organized crime networks. As a police constable and a first responder, it is not likely that you will be engaged with organized crime investigations; however, it is important to appreciate the level of intimidation and fear for themselves *and* for family/friends that victims feel. Therefore, appropriate victim care should be at the forefront of your decision making.

The victim can be of any age, and whether they consent to travelling is irrelevant, and the travelling can be to or from the UK or within the UK (s 2 of the MSA). Human trafficking impacts different areas of policing and incorporates a variety of offences, offenders, and forms of victimization. Police officers may come across trafficking victims whilst on patrol or when responding to incidents. Human trafficking does not always entail a sophisticated and complex operation; the exploitation of any one individual by another, for example with the promise of work in another part of the country, may also fall into this category.

19.12.3.1 Exploitation of trafficked persons

According to the UK Annual Report on Modern Slavery 2019, 6,985 individuals were identified as having been trafficked, an increase of 36 per cent compared to 2017. Of these cases, 45 per cent involved children, mainly of UK origin (Home Office, 2019b). Labour exploitation is the most common form of exploitation, followed by sexual exploitation (Home Office, 2019b, p 45). The circumstances under which a person is found can be used to help to determine whether they are being exploited, as can factors such as vulnerability due to age, familial relationship to the offender, or mental or physical illness. Section 3 of the MSA defines different forms of exploitation as necessary for a successful prosecution of the offence of human trafficking.

Sexual exploitation is more likely to affect women and girls. Some victims are forcibly taken from their homes, while others voluntarily travel to another destination unaware of the exploitation that will ensue. Some victims initially agree to travel to work in the sex industry but are unaware of the working conditions that will be imposed (eg number of clients and pay). Most of the offences relating to sexual exploitation following trafficking can be found in Part 1 of the Sexual Offences Act 2003; and s 1(1)(a) of the Protection of Children Act 1978 (indecent photographs of children).

Labour exploitation is when the victim is forced to work under unacceptable conditions, often in factory work, agriculture, construction, or hospitality. It often involves threats or physical harm, restrictions of movement, debt-bondage, retention of identity documents, and threats to reveal the illegal status of the worker to the authorities.

Servitude involves providing services through threat or coercion. For example, domestic servitude is when victims are forced to clean or cook in other people's homes. Unlike slavery, servitude does not involve 'ownership', but the victim will often have little chance of improving or changing their conditions and may also be the target of sexual abuse. Offenders may have attracted victims through the promise of employment or patronage (eg promising the parents of a child that they will provide them with an education). Most victims of servitude are from overseas.

Commercial organizations operating in the UK with an annual turnover over £36 million are now required to either disclose the steps they have taken to ensure their business does not involve modern slavery (including their supply chain) or to make a statement that they have taken no such action (s 54 of the MSA).

19.12.3.2 Child victims of trafficking

Human trafficking can take many different forms: sexual exploitation, trafficked for the removal of organs, for forced labour, forced marriage or for criminal activities (see <https://www.ilo.org/global/topics/forced-labour/lang--en/index.htm>). According to research conducted by the International Labour Organisation (ILO), it is estimated that there were as many as 40.3 million people in modern slavery in 2016. Over half of these people are exploited for labour services (24.9 million people), with 4.8 million people from that figure thought to be involved in sexual exploitation. Women and girls are disproportionally affected by forced labour, accounting for 99 per cent of victims in the commercial sex industry and 58 per cent in other sectors. Sadly, one in four victims of modern slavery is a child (International Labour Organisation, 2017). Child trafficking refers to the exploitation of girls and boys, primarily for forced labour and sexual exploitation. Save the Children states on its website that children account for 27 per cent of all the human trafficking victims worldwide, and two out of every three child victims are girls (see <https://www.savethechildren.org/us/charity-stories/child-trafficking-awareness>. Children are not deemed capable of consent, so any child who is transported to do work is a victim of trafficking; there is no need for any coercion, force, or deception. Some children may not be aware that they are being trafficked and others may deliberately conceal the fact. Trafficked children experience many types of abuse and neglect. Traffickers use physical, sexual, and emotional abuse as a form of control.

As a result of the subjected control, child victims may have particular characteristics such as unexpected possession of goods and money and may exhibit self-confidence and maturity beyond their years. Others may appear to have no money or have debts to pay but are in possession of goods that would suggest otherwise, such as an expensive mobile phone. A trafficked child may be unable to give details of a contact person or an address. For children trafficked within the UK, there may also be indications of physical abuse, sexual activity, substance abuse, self-harming behaviour, and homelessness. They may also have unexpected contacts or relationships (including online) with adults who are significantly older or outside their normal circle.

If cared for by adults, the carers may not be the child's parents, or they might have a difficult relationship with them or be one of several unrelated children living at an address. In addition, such children are unlikely to be registered with a GP or be enrolled at a school. Some children who are trafficked have gone missing from local authority care.

19.12.3.3 Police response

Police officers should ensure that suspected victims are safe and receive medical assistance as required and inform a supervisor and a senior detective officer of the situation. An intelligence report should be submitted and the NRM procedures should be followed (see 19.12.6).

It is important to be supportive and not to judge or stereotype possible victims, as their circumstances are often unique and difficult to understand for the outsider. The victim may not understand English, might have learning disabilities, or may have physical or mental ill health due to having suffered trauma. Some victims may have experienced long periods of isolation and may consequently feel dependent on their captor and therefore may not want to cooperate in bringing them to justice. Other victims might be fearful of reprisals from traffickers and fearful of any authority due to an insecure or illegal immigration status. Cultural or religious beliefs and shame and fear of dishonour can present additional difficulties. Forensic medical examination can be traumatic, especially for victims of sexual abuse.

Efforts must be made to communicate with them effectively and to reassure them of the role of the police and to explain any procedures that are required such as searches or medical examinations. Police officers should be mindful of their own conduct, gender, and appearance and the possible effects on victims. It is essential that adequate physical, psychological, and medical support is provided from the early stages of the investigation, for the well-being of the trafficked person but also to increase the chances of mounting a successful prosecution. Note that detailed information on interviewing is provided in Chapter 13.

Some individuals may be both perpetrators and victims of modern slavery, ie they may have been forced to exploit others. In these cases, a victim can use the statutory defence under s 45 of the MSA, but not for murder, kidnapping, and false imprisonment (see Sch 4 to the MSA). If a perpetrator is identified as a victim during the interviewing process, with their consent, they should be referred under the NRM.

19.12.3.4 Special considerations for child victims of trafficking

Child victims (ie those under 18) have additional vulnerabilities. Any victim suspected of being under 18 should be provided with immediate access to protection and support, as stipulated under s 51 of the MSA.

An officer who suspects that a child may be a trafficking victim has the power to remove the child to a safe place (or prevent the child's removal from a safe place) for a maximum of 72 hours (s 46 of the Children Act 1989). If there is a risk to life or likelihood of serious harm, the police can apply to a court for an Emergency Protection Order. The local authority children's social care service and police Child Abuse Investigation Unit should also be notified. Issues surrounding child abuse and the safeguarding of children are all considered in the previous section.

19.12.3.5 County lines

A fairly new public protection matter is that of county lines—this is where gangs from metropolitan areas exploit others to distribute drugs into more rural areas. Often, they will take over someone's house or flat (called cuckooing) for the purposes of establishing a distribution hub. These exploited individuals are usually children who tend to be between 16–18 years old but reports of children as young as eight have been made. The young people who are exploited, whilst taking part in criminal behaviour, should be seen as trafficked and exploited children—remember that the definition of Human Trafficking does not rely on it happening across national borders, transportation from any point A to any point B also falls within the scope.

19.12.3.6 Prevention of trafficking

To prevent a person from engaging in modern slavery, the police can apply for a Slavery and Trafficking Prevention Order (STPO) or a Slavery and Trafficking Risk Order (STRO). The application is made to a magistrates' court under s 2 of the MSA. An STPO (ss 14 and 15 of the MSA) lasts for at least five years and can be imposed following a conviction for a modern slavery offence or as a stand-alone order. An STRO (s 23 of the MSA) lasts for at least two years and is issued if there is evidence 'beyond reasonable doubt' that an individual poses a risk of harm. You can also apply for an interim Order if necessary.

Breaching an STPO or an STRO is a criminal offence, punishable with up to five years' imprisonment. The maximum custodial sentence for slavery including human trafficking is 12 months if tried as a summary offence and life imprisonment if tried under indictment (s 5 of the MSA).

19.12.4 Slavery, servitude, forced and compulsory labour

Not all modern slavery occurs alongside trafficking. Slavery and servitude are defined in legislation (s 1 of the MSA):

1. A person commits an offence if—
   (a) the person holds another person in slavery or servitude and the circumstances are such that the person knows or ought to know that the other person is held in slavery or servitude, or
   (b) the person requires another person to perform forced or compulsory labour and the circumstances are such that the person knows or ought to know that the other person is being required to perform forced or compulsory labour.
2. In subsection (1) the references to holding a person in slavery or servitude or requiring a person to perform forced or compulsory labour are to be construed in accordance with Article 4 ECHR.
3. In determining whether a person is being held in slavery or servitude or required to perform forced or compulsory labour, regard may be had to all the circumstances.
4. For example, regard may be had:
   (a) to any of the person's personal circumstances (such as the person being a child, the person's family relationships, and any mental or physical illness) which may make the person more vulnerable than other persons;
   (b) to any work or services provided by the person, including work or services provided in circumstances which constitute exploitation within s. 3(3) to (6) of the Act (see above)
5. The consent of a person (whether adult or child) to any of the acts alleged to constitute holding the person in slavery or servitude or requiring the person to perform forced or compulsory labour, does not preclude a determination that the person is being held in slavery or servitude or required to perform forced or compulsory labour

Note that there are exceptions to the offence, including work done during detention, military service, life-threatening situations, and work done within normal civic obligations.

19.12.5 Alternative offences

There are times when you are not able to satisfy all criteria of a certain offence. You could look at crimes which go beyond the Act—such as those relating to violence against the person, sexual offences, participating in an organized crime group, fraud/financial crime, or conspiracy to traffic.

19.12.6 NRM

The National Referral Mechanism (NRM) is the system for triggering the formal identification and provision of support for victims of modern slavery and human trafficking. It is a multi-agency provision ensuring the safeguarding of the victim. Police officers and other first responders such as ambulance staff, must refer potential victims to the 'Single Competent Authority' (SCA, see Home Office, 2019c). Specially trained 'case owners' will then determine whether the individual is a victim of modern slavery and, if so, the victim is entitled to state-funded support while further evidence is gathered.

A referral for an adult victim can only be done with the victim's consent. If the victim is a child, then you do not need to gain their consent and can submit a referral on their behalf. If you are making a referral, you should

- Explain the NRM in detail
- Complete the relevant form (available online but a printed version can be obtained if necessary)
- Contact the Salvation Army (0300 303 8151)
- Ensure victim safety via safeguarding and housing actions
- Record a modern slavery crime
- Provide updates to SCA

If the victim does not consent, there are still actions you can take

- Try to explain the aim of the referral again, reassuring the victim throughout
- Complete a 'Duty to Notify' form—this is a separate form from the NRM form
- Liaise with relevant partners who can enable successful safeguarding of the victim
- Record a modern slavery crime

Every report of modern slavery must be investigated as soon as possible, and the victim's safety and the types of exploitation must be considered. Many offences involve cross-national investigations, which add complexities (see also the College of Policing APP guidance on Major Investigation and Public Protection and Investigation).

19.13 Missing Persons

It is worth bearing in mind at the outset of this section that whilst a 'misper' is a relatively common and often routine matter for the police (the NCA's UK Missing Person's Unit 2021 data reported around 240,000 missing incidents recorded by the UK police services in 2020/2021), for the carers, families, and friends of the missing person it can be a highly traumatic and stressful few hours or days. Therefore, it is key that as a police officer you care about minimizing their distress and ensuring that you provide the same high level of service as in any other police matter. Further, going missing, even for a seemingly innocent reason, can make a vulnerable person a convenient target. For a very small number of people, an incident of a missing loved one may culminate in a tragedy. It is also the case that there are links between children and young people going missing and forms of serious criminality: for example, child sexual exploitation (where going missing can be both a cause and effect) and human trafficking. Further information can be found on the Missing People charity's website (<http://www.missingpeople.org.uk>). The agency overseeing all missing persons cases and the national, as well as the international point of contact, is the National Crime Agency.

Going missing is understood as not being able to establish a person's whereabouts at the time—it is not dependent on who the missing person is or how long they have been missing for—each report needs to be taken seriously. Adults, children, and young people can all go absent or missing and for a number of reasons:

- vulnerable adults, such as those with mental ill health, dementia, or other problems, who go missing as a result of confusion, despair;
- adults who deliberately absent themselves, often in an attempt to escape from problems in their home lives, such as a break up with a partner, domestic abuse, or financial problems;

- children or young people who run away from home or residential care, normally for one or two days (possibly because of neglect, abuse, unhappiness);
- children who are missing through abduction (by a non-custodial parent, a stranger, or through other means such as internet grooming (see 24.7.6));
- children and young people who are victims of Child Criminal Exploitation (CCE), for example 'county lines' (see 21.7);
- adults who have been abducted, for example for purposes of sexual assault or people trafficking;
- children who are missing through abduction (by a non-custodial parent, a stranger, or through other means such as internet grooming.

The vast majority of absent or missing persons are found quickly. For example, 80 per cent of children are found within 24 hours, 90 per cent of children are found within two days, only 2 per cent will be missing for longer than a week (Missing People, 2021). Unfortunately, a small number are found dead after many weeks and some are never found. Some individuals, particularly children in care, are reported missing repeatedly, and this might include when they leave a place of care without authorization or fail to return at the expected time. This may occur quite frequently but it is important to remember that on any occasion a person is reported as missing there may be a risk of harm, particularly if they are vulnerable.

A missing person is assigned one of four risk levels depending on their history and circumstances. A person will be categorized as the lowest risk level, 'absent' if there seems to be no apparent risk or they are simply not where expected (CoP, 2023). In these circumstances, the police are not likely to launch an investigation. However, 'absent' cases must be carefully monitored and the actions to locate the individual should be agreed early on, as should a review to reassess the level of risk. 'Going absent' must be considered as a possible indicator of something more serious, for example a child might go absent because they are being abused at home and, in such circumstances, the safe recovery of the child might be just the start of further investigations.

A person is 'missing' if their whereabouts cannot be established and the circumstances are out of character, or the context suggests they might be the subject of crime or at risk of harm to themselves or another. Missing person incidents sometimes become critical incidents (see 10.6), requiring the support of services other than the local constabulary. A search for a missing person can entail a considerable expenditure of resources and time, including rural and urban searches, dragging waterways, and exhaustive enquiries, particularly if the missing person is vulnerable. A police major crime unit (or equivalent) could be involved if there is a criminal aspect to the disappearance such as a suspicious death.

The National Crime Agency's UK's Missing Person's Unit (UKMPU) and the Missing Children's Team (MCT) are the UK's point of contact for cases of missing persons and unidentified bodies, both at national and international levels. They hold a national database and provide and facilitate the sharing of information with the aim of maximizing police resources. The database can be a valuable resource when investigating cases of missing persons (UK Missing Persons Unit, 2018).

19.13.1 Missing person enquiries

For all missing person reports, the minimum initial response should consist, broadly, of recording the incident, conducting a risk assessment, agreeing the first steps to trace the missing person with the informant (if applicable), and setting a timeline for reviewing decisions taken. Each case varies but there are standard considerations that always apply when the initial report is received by the call-taker, not least of which is to identify the likely level of risk for that person. The majority of missing person enquiries relate to children so a thorough knowledge of the procedures related to the disappearance of a child is vital.

It is also important to keep an open mind about why the person is missing. Officers should avoid making assumptions and should communicate with those who have more experience in cases of missing persons. The safety of the missing person should be the prime consideration of everyone involved in the investigation. Police services should consider how to provide the best support for the missing person's family as they are likely to be under considerable stress, but may also be required to provide detailed information on the disappearance.

If a person had left intentionally then certain items (eg credit cards and money) are likely to be missing. The missing person might be involved with crime or have employment or financial problems—there may be evidence of this. If there seems to have been a violent struggle, the person may have been abducted and the scene must be preserved for evidential and investigative purposes.

The main guidance is available online as follows:

- *Missing Persons* (CoP, 2023j);
- *Missing Children and Adults—A Cross Government Strategy* (Home Office, 2011); and
- UK Missing Persons Unit website.

19.13.2 Missing persons investigative processes

The first task in a 'misper' enquiry is to conduct a risk assessment. Information is required about the person and their circumstances prior to the disappearance, particularly any factors which indicate vulnerability (eg a child is on the Child Protection Register) and their lifestyle. The call handler, usually the first to receive a report, has to take down detailed information which enable them to assess risk: they will ask questions about the missing person's demographics, description, known risks, friends who the person might be in contact with, and any other relevant information.

No matter what the risk assessment, there are certain minimum actions to be undertaken:

- An official record has to be created and a risk assessment completed
- Immediate actions have to be agreed and a clear follow up schedule created
- The missing person should be circulated within the PNC network (not applicable to 'absent' cases unless a person remains missing)
- For cases where a child is missing, local children's services must be notified

As a responding officer, you will gain more context and establish what has happened so far. There is no official risk assessment tool for missing persons cases. You should be guided by the NDM, adopt an investigative approach and follow risk assessment principles set within the College of Policing's 'Risk Principles' guidelines and 'Missing Persons Decision Making guide'.

The police may ask those reporting someone as missing for a photograph of the missing person, details of their friends or relatives, details of the places the person often visits, whether the missing person has a medical condition (see Report or Find a Missing Person on the gov.uk website). They might also ask for a sample of the DNA of the missing person, for example from a toothbrush (ibid).

If relevant, forensic evidence should be collected as soon as possible before it is compromised or lost (within 24 hours for high-risk cases and within seven days for medium-risk cases). This will help to speed up the investigation by ruling out suspects and will also avoid the need for later requests to the person's family as this could cause them further distress (CoP, 2023j). Further to gaining information directly from the informant, you should also try to gather more information and intelligence by speaking to others who may provide more insight (eg associates, partner), look through previous missing persons reports and look through all available databases (eg PNC, PND, or others).

The levels of risk suggested by the College of Policing (2023j) are 'no apparent risk' (or, if the person is absent), 'low risk', 'medium risk', and 'high risk'.

- With 'absent' cases, you should set up actions to help locate the individual and/or gain more information, as well as agree on a review date when risk will be reassessed. These cases often do not require a first response—if the person remains missing and first response is required then risk has to be increased.
- With low-risk cases, it is assumed that potential harm to the person is minimal but still possible—therefore proportionate enquiries should be carried out—the first response here is a routine one.
- With medium-risk cases, it is assumed that harm to the person is likely but not serious—an active response is required in such cases—first response for such cases should be on the 'earliest available resource' basis. As soon as you are suspicious that a case might be high risk, you need to seek advice from a senior officer, it is key that you do not delay doing this—immediate deployment is required in these cases.

- With high-risk cases, it is assumed that risk of harm to the person or the public is very high—an immediate first response is required.

The particular actions needed for each level of risk are covered in police training but searching for the missing person is an obvious early step to take, assuming that carers, friends, or relatives have already tried to make contact with the missing person. For the relatives and friends of a missing person social media is a good tool for helping find them.

However, the search usually begins with the person's home (or last known address), garden, and any adjoining premises (bearing in mind that children can hide in very small spaces). At the same time, enquiries could be made concerning admissions to local hospitals. If there are concerns about the person's mental health, relevant services should be consulted.

The search could then be extended to include the surrounding area, concentrating on the person's 'habitual haunts' and then moving on to hazardous places such as pools, streams, caves, and empty buildings. In high-risk cases, and particular locations, searching might also be conducted by air. Preparation should be made to widen the search systematically, including making house-to-house enquiries. It may also be appropriate to request the services of a Police Search Advisor (PolSA) who can provide more specialist advice on planning searches and controlling search teams, including volunteers, who may assist in the search. This is usually done with cases classed as 'high risk'.

Workplace or school absence records can help to establish a person's recent movements and activities. Personal papers belonging to the missing person could be viewed (depending on the circumstances) and retained as possible evidence. Local and national police databases should also be interrogated. A list should be made of all relatives, friends, contacts, and work colleagues/fellow trainees in case these are needed, and recent photographs that are a good likeness should be obtained. It may seem an obvious idea to examine any digital devices known to belong to the missing person (smartphones, tablets, etc) and their online activities (such as any social network sites they might use), but there is no automatic legal right for the police to do so (the missing person has the right to privacy)—so be guided by local police policy. CCTV footage might also be examined. Depending on the assessed level of risk, the police may decide to enlist the help of the local media. If the person is still missing after 72 hours, the details have to be submitted to UKMPU.

The reliability of any person giving information should be considered. Ian Huntley, a caretaker at a school in Soham who murdered two young girls, provided false information to the police early in the investigation. Due to an inadequate system of recording and sharing information by Humberside Police and social services, Huntley's previous contacts with law enforcement were not identified. To avoid such omissions in the future, all police services now have to collate information on all absent and missing persons.

There are further considerations when it comes to some specific investigations—this includes when a child is identified as missing, when a person has dementia (more on both of these below), when a person goes missing from an emergency department, or with cross-border cases. It is important that you seek further advice when you come across these.

19.13.3 Missing People charity

Missing People is a national charity providing a variety of services and you should let the family/friends of a missing person know what they can do for them. Their services include family support, including a 24-hour confidential helpline, publicity, sightings helpline, 'TextSafe' service (a text sent to a missing person with information on how to reach confidential support), and child rescue alert.

19.13.4 Special considerations for missing children

All cases of missing children must be properly investigated and should never be considered as low risk. The safeguarding of children is a key requirement in these cases and guidance is provided by the Department of Education statutory guidance on children who run away or go missing from home or care, from 2014. The disappearance of a child (taken here to mean a person under the age of 18) is always medium or high risk, and concern would be even higher for a child on the Child Protection Plan or Register (despite the difference in terminology, plan and register are very similar). The Child Protection Register (CPR) is a confidential list of all children in the local area who have been identified as being at risk of significant harm. The register is useful in that it allows authorized individuals (including the police) to check if a child they are working with is known to be at risk. Missing children are particularly at risk of abuse. The Human Rights Act 1998 places a duty on public authorities to protect any person who may be at risk, therefore the police have a duty of positive action on the investigation of missing persons. The Children's Act 2004 makes safeguarding children a duty of the police and partner agencies.

Carers and parents are expected to help with finding a child whose whereabouts are not known (eg to make enquiries if a child is unexpectedly and significantly late returning home). They should, however, be provided with support if some level of risk has been identified, or the parents are highly distressed or unable to make enquiries. Looked-after children (children 'in care') make up a large proportion of cases of missing children and they often have other needs that compound their vulnerability. Carers may use the term 'unauthorized absence' but the police should avoid using it when recording a missing child as this might cause confusion. If a looked-after child is not where the carers expect, but their whereabouts are known or thought to be known (eg staying with a friend), it is the responsibility of the care staff to search and make enquiries. If the child is then reported to the police as missing, the police might want to consider searching the area.

Child Rescue Alert (CRA) procedures can be used if there is suspicion that a child may be at risk of serious harm. This involves seeking help from the public, for example through television, radio, text messages, and other social and digital media, as well as the charity Missing People (Missing People, 2023). Care should be exercised when using media in the case of children missing from care as their whereabouts may be deliberately being hidden from their birth parents.

19.13.5 Missing people with dementia—the Herbert Protocol

As Age UK explain, the 'Herbert Protocol' is a 'national scheme that encourages carers, family, and friends to provide and put together useful information, which can then be used in the event of a vulnerable person going missing' (Age UK, 2018). To date many, but not all, police services in England and Wales have adopted the protocol: the MPS were one of the first to do so.

Many people who go missing are vulnerable elderly adults with dementia and some will be residents at a care home. The Herbert Protocol includes the use of a form (completed before there is any likelihood of the person going missing) with a recent photograph and information about the person such as:

- 'background' information (first, last names, nicknames, mobile phone number, etc);
- 'physical description' (DoB, sex, build, ethnicity, hair colour, etc);
- whether they have been given a 'GPS tracker'—this potentially provides a very effective way of locating the person;
- 'medical history', including any communication and/or physical disabilities; and
- 'life history' (including hobbies, favourite places, which modes of transport they tend to prefer, favourite destinations when going out).

If the person goes missing, an additional form (or section of the initial form) is completed. This will include information such as the time and place they were last seen, the clothing they were wearing, what items might be in their possession.

The form(s) is passed to the police if the vulnerable person goes missing, and will be returned to the carer or care home when the person is located and safely returned.

19.13.6 Unidentified cases

It is possible to get a report of an unidentified person or an unidentified body—in all such instances, you have to submit a report to the UKMPU within 48 hours—it is possible that this can aid in a major investigation or bring closure to a family whose missing relative passed away. You have to inform UKMPU within 24 hours if the body/person is identified.

TASK 3 Why is the 'Herbert Protocol' so called? Has your local constabulary adopted the protocol?

19.14 Identifying Victims and Witnesses

It is important to understand how we identify victims and witnesses, and the different types of witnesses you may encounter, as they are critical component of the criminal justice system. It is also important to note that while we use the term 'victims' in this chapter some, particularly adult victims of child sexual abuse, prefer to self-identify as a survivor rather than victim as it has connotations of strength and an identity beyond their experiences of being victims to their abusers (NAPAC, 2019).

Victims and witnesses may not always be obvious to police or support agencies. They can either be identified at the scene or later through a various means which include police reports, other witness statements, first accounts, CCTV, house to house enquiries and media appeals. Understanding that the victim and/or witness might not identify themselves to police or even feel that they are a victim is important for police officers to understand. The earlier that they are identified, the more support, protection and guidance can be offered. Early considerations could have a huge psychological and emotional impact on the victim or witness and help the investigation process.

An early needs assessment is a requirement in the Victims' Code and, when identifying victims and witnesses, police officers should consider potential vulnerabilities, such as age, gender, mental health issues, physical disabilities, or cultural differences. Research suggests police underestimate how many of the people they deal with are in fact vulnerable (Burton *et al*, 2006). Vulnerability in this context may also include less obvious 'vulnerabilities' such as living near the offender.

19.14.1 Victims and complainants

During the investigation of a reported offence it is not always immediately clear whether a crime has been committed. Therefore, the term complainant is used as the legal term for an individual who has reported an offence but not had it proven in a court of law (CPS, no date).

The Victims' Code acknowledges both the terms complainant and victim as being persons who contact the police to report a criminal allegation. However, it defines a victim as being;

> *'A person who has suffered harm, including physical, mental or emotional harm or economic loss which was directly caused by a criminal offence.'* or *'Close relative (or a nominated family spokesperson) of a person whose death was directly caused by a criminal offence.'* (MoJ, 2020, p 3). Victims are also witnesses.

19.14.2 Types of witness

A witness of a crime is defined by Black's Law Dictionary as being '*one who sees, knows or vouches for something. One who gives testimony under oath or affirmation, in person, by oral or written deposition or by affidavit.*' A witness must be legally competent to testify (CoP, 2023k) and is a person, other than a defendant, who is likely to give evidence in court.

The success of any investigation depends largely on the accuracy and detail of the material obtained from witnesses. Investigators, whether tasked with a volume crime or major investigation, must recognize the individual needs and concerns of witnesses and treat them with dignity and respect. This can have a significant impact on how witnesses cooperate with the investigation and any subsequent prosecution (CoP, 2023k).

Significant witnesses, sometimes referred to as 'key' witnesses, are those who:

- have or claim to have witnessed, visually or otherwise, an indictable offence, part of such an offence or events closely connected with it (including any incriminating comments made by the suspected offender either before or after the offence) and/or
- have a particular relationship to the victim or have a central position in an investigation into an indictable offence

While significant witnesses are usually defined with reference to indictable-only offences, investigating officers may consider designating witnesses as significant in any other serious case where it might be helpful (CoP, 2023k). An interview with a significant witness may be visually recorded if it seems that this will contribute significantly to the investigation (see 13.8.3.1).

A defence witness is a person who the accused is going to call to give evidence at the trial in relation to an alibi or to other matters. The name, address, and date of birth of any such

Processing Policing

witness must be disclosed in advance to the prosecution (s 6 of the CPIA) as the police may wish to interview them. Prior to this, consultation with the CPS is advised and any interview with a defence witness has to comply with the relevant Code of Practice (under s 21A of the CPIA).

A vulnerable witness (s 16, Part II of the Youth Justice and Criminal Evidence Act 1999) is any person:

- under the age of 18 (as amended in s 98 of the Coroners and Justice Act 2009);
- with a 'mental disorder' (this is the phrase used in the Act);
- with significant impairment of intelligence and social functioning (eg a learning disability); or
- with a physical disability or a physical disorder.

An intimidated witness (s 17, Part II of the Youth Justice and Criminal Evidence Act 1999) is:

- any elderly and frail person;
- a witness experiencing fear or distress about testifying in the case;
- any witness who self-neglects or self-harms;
- any complainant in a sexual assault case;
- a victim of a domestic violence, a racially motivated crime, or repeat victimization; or
- a relative of the victim in a homicide case.

A reluctant witness is a witness who declines to cooperate or who makes a statement but then refuses to attend court; they might fear repercussions or reprisal or might simply not want to assist the police. If the police can establish that a reluctant witness has important evidence to offer, a witness summons can be issued to compel attendance in court (see Home Office Circular 35/2005). Some witnesses can offer opposing evidence against the party that called them, these are called hostile or adverse witnesses.

19.14.3 Expert witnesses

Expert witnesses are used by the court in order to provide an opinion which is both objective and unbiased. The definition of expert evidence and an expert witness is as follows;

> *Expert evidence is admissible to furnish the court with information which is likely to be outside the experience and the knowledge of a judge or jury* (Criminal Practice Direction V Evidence 19A Expert Evidence).
>
> *An expert witness can provide the court with a statement of opinion on any admissible matter calling for expertise by the witness if they are qualified to give such an opinion* (CPS, 2022b).

The duty of the expert witness overrides that of any side from which they are receiving instructions meaning that they do not represent a standpoint from either the prosecution or the defence. Expert witnesses can only provide evidence on matters that relate to their area of specialism. Whilst expert evidence can be extremely useful in criminal cases, there is a significant requirement for the prosecution to have knowledge and understanding of the evidence being given in order to effectively question and challenge it. Placing too much reliance upon expert testimony in weight of the other available pieces of evidence is dangerous as the Court of Appeal stresses that expert evidence should only be judged in consideration of the other evidence available in the case.

Section 30 of the Criminal Justice Act 1988 states that an expert's evidence report is admissible as evidence of fact and opinion, whether or not the expert attends court to give oral evidence. If it is not proposed to call the expert witness, the leave of the court must be obtained prior to introducing it.

An expert witness can be appointed at any stage during a case, from the initial point of an investigation to the trial. Before appointing an expert, it must be decided who will be financing the commission. This will fall to either the police or the CPS. For further information on expert witnesses see Chapter 13.

19.15 Legislation, Agencies, and Services for Supporting and Protecting Victims and Witnesses

It is vitally important to protect the rights and the ongoing wellbeing of both victims and witnesses for the criminal justice system to work effectively. Police officers and staff must be aware of the provisions set out in key parts of legislation to ensure a high standard of victim and witness care.

19.15.1 Legislation, Codes of Practice, guidance, and policies when dealing with victim and witnesses

The Human Rights Act 1998. This act has several sections that can be applied to victims and witnesses. The act sets out a right to respect for private and family life: this means that victims and witnesses have the right to privacy, and that their personal information and identities should be protected wherever possible. Another provision that is relevant is the prohibition of inhuman or degrading treatment. One of the most important provisions is the right to a fair trial. This means that victims and witnesses have the right to give their evidence in a fair and impartial court proceeding, and that they should have access to legal representation and other support to help them do so.

The Act has also been used to challenge aspects of the criminal justice system that are perceived as unfair or discriminatory towards victims and witnesses, such as the use of excessive force by police or the treatment of vulnerable witnesses in court. It has also been used to promote the rights of victims and witnesses, for example, by requiring courts to consider the harm caused to victims when sentencing offenders.

The Criminal Justice and Police Act 2001 covers the intimidation of witnesses in either civil proceedings (ss 39(1) and 40(1)) or criminal proceedings (ss 40(1)–(4), 40(7), and 40(8)).

Criminal Procedures Rules. This legislation focuses on the criminal court procedure and there are several provisions that are aimed particularly at victims and witnesses. These include communication and specific information about the trial process and their rights. They also require that the victims and witnesses are given appropriate support and assistance, including access to counselling and other forms of support. The rules provide for the use of victim impact statements also (see 10.16.2).

Achieving Best Evidence 2022. This was originally introduced in 2002 and sets out the principles of the interview process for witnesses and victims, especially those that are vulnerable. It ensures that that evidence is gathered in a sensitive and effective manner through a structured framework with trained interviewers. This is especially important to follow where the video recorded interview is used as a first account in court. The use of technology has been linked to enhanced efficiency of victims' testimony in court (Delagrange, 2018). The updated ABE also covers the pre-trial preparation process and support available.

The Youth Justice and Criminal Evidence Act 1999. This Act was introduced to help vulnerable and intimidated victims and witnesses give the best evidence they can. Some of the special measures include the ability to give evidence via video link. Giving evidence from a separate room or behind screens rather than having to be in the same room as the defendant, can help to reduce the anxiety and trauma experienced by witnesses, and can also help to improve the quality of their evidence. This can help to reduce the fear and intimidation that some witnesses may feel when giving evidence (Cooper and Roberts, 2005). Rather than having to face cross-examination in court the judge can also agree for pre-recorded cross-examination to occur in advance. Intermediaries, trained professionals who can help vulnerable victims and witnesses to communicate effectively in court, can also be utilized. Special measures are applied for by a police officer or staff to the court and it is up to the judge as to whether to grant these or not.

The Domestic Abuse Act 2021. This has also introduced new measures to protect victims of domestic abuse, including the criminalization of non-fatal strangulation and the creation of new offences, such as controlling or coercive behaviour. The Act also includes provisions to provide greater support and protection to victims of domestic abuse, including placing a duty on local authorities to provide support and accommodation to victims who are at risk of homelessness.

Victims can either self-refer or be referred to the National Centre for Domestic Violence. They can help victims apply for emergency civil injunctions such as a non-molestation order or occupation order.

Witness Charter. This document is important because it sets out the standards of care and support that witnesses in criminal cases should expect to receive to feel supported and protected throughout the criminal justice process. They should receive clear and timely information about the progress of the case and about the ongoing support and protection available to them. Witnesses should be able to communicate easily with police and other criminal justice agencies and receive appropriate protection and support. These include measures already mentioned above. Witnesses should be given the opportunity to participate fully and be kept informed about any decisions that affect them.

Victims' Code of Practice. On 1 April 2021, a new Victims' Code came into force (MoJ, 2020). The Code is structured around 12 overarching rights:

- To be able to understand and to be understood
- To have the details of the crime recorded without unjustified delay
- To be provided with information when reporting the crime
- To be referred to victim support services and have services and support tailored to your needs
- To be provided with information about compensation
- To be provided with information about the investigation and prosecution
- To make a Victim Personal Statement
- To be given information about the trial, trial process, and your role as a witness
- To be given information about the outcome of the case and any appeals
- To be paid expenses and have property returned
- To be given information about the offender following a conviction
- To make a complaint about rights not being met

The Code makes important considerations such as ensuring for example that victims of sexual violence are able to decide whether a female or a male officer should interview them (HM Government, 2021b). It also established the pre-recording of cross-examination exists for victims and witnesses deemed to be vulnerable due to age, mental disorders, or a physical impairment across all Crown Courts in England and Wales.

Victims' Right to Review. The Victims' Right to Review Scheme gives the victims a right to ask for a decision not to continue a criminal case to be reviewed to see if it was the wrong decision, but only when police have identified and interviewed a suspect and decided not to charge the suspect with any offences at all. If the criteria is met, a new officer reviews the case.

The CPS also have this scheme and this works for cases that they have decided not to charge or offered no evidence in. This scheme safeguards the criminal justice process and enables victims to have a transparent view of the criminal justice system.

19.15.1.1 Other measures available to protect victims and witnesses

Witness Care Units are predominantly police staffed units who provide information and support to victims and witnesses in cases progressing through the criminal justice system. They do not replace the responsibility placed upon police to keep the victims up to date with key decisions made as per the Victims' Code of Practice.

In more serious cases where there is a risk of harm or intimidation, witnesses may be provided with protection and anonymity orders. These orders prevent their identity being disclosed the public, including the media.

There are several measures specifically available to those that are victims of domestic abuse such as DVPN/DVPOs (see 19.5.4) and also:

- *Anonymity orders:* Anonymity orders can be used to protect the identity of the victim and/or witnesses
- *Disclosure orders:* A disclosure order can be issued by the court to require the disclosure of certain information, such as the abuser's previous convictions or details of any previous incidents of abuse.
- *Clare's Law,* named after Clare Wood who was murdered by her ex-partner in 2009, is a scheme where individuals can make a request to the police to check whether their partner has a history of domestic abuse or violence. If appropriate, the police will disclose information that may include details about the partner's previous convictions, cautions or warnings for domestic violence or abuse, and any other relevant information. However, police must consider the human rights of the person who is the subject of the request and disclosure

may only be made in certain circumstances such as a genuine concern for the safety of the individual making the request.

There are also specific measures to protect those who are the victim of stalking and harassment (see 19.6). Specialist stalking services exist such as the National Stalking Helpline and the Suzy Lamplugh Trust. These services provide advice, support, and advocacy for victims of stalking.

19.15.2 Involvement of multi-agency professionals

Officers should be sensitive to the needs of the victim or witness and recognize these needs can change several times during the case. Interventions will depend on the circumstances surrounding the nature of the offence. Officers should keep detailed records of their interactions with victims and witnesses, including any information provided, actions taken, and agreements made to ensure continuity of support.

Continuity of support will often include making referrals to victim services. Multi-agency partnerships are essential to minimize the risk of vulnerable persons slipping through the safeguarding system. In cases of domestic abuse this is of particular importance as the scope of victimization goes beyond that of a partner and abuser but also to the children living within the home. Multi-agency partnership working allows all of those involved in a case to see the whole picture by enabling:

- The early identification of risk
- Increased and improved information sharing
- Joint decision making
- Coordinated action to assess, manage, and mitigate risk

A key component of this risk management is information sharing. All constabularies should have a clear Information Sharing Agreement (ISA) in place with their partner agencies which is regularly reviewed in relation to outgoing and incoming requests.

Victims should be made aware that any information and evidence gathered during a police investigation may be used in the Family Court for hearings relating to child contact, care proceedings, and civil court hearings. This will relate to any information regarding instances of reported domestic abuse, 999 calls, withdrawal statements, interviews, photographs and medical reports, even in circumstances where no one was charged or prosecuted. In cases which are ongoing, the CPS will be included in the decision of whether to inform the Family Court as the disclosure of information could have an impact on an ongoing criminal case.

The information shared can assist safety planning for victims and their children, as well as assisting the courts in making any judgments. This requires police services to maintain information-sharing protocols with the Children and Family Court Advisory and Support Services (CAFCASS).

Domestic abuse specialist teams are required to take an active role in establishing strong multi-agency partnership links through:

- Local domestic abuse forums
- Specialist domestic violence courts (SDVC)
- Multi-agency risk assessment conferences (MARAC)
- Specific project or OP initiatives targeted at improving responses to domestic abuse

Domestic abuse forums should have representatives from voluntary sector groups who can assist with providing support through refuge, and advocacy. These forums are facilitated through policing domestic abuse coordinators/supervisors in their provision of service user consultation and any assistance must be under formal agreement. IDVAs are responsible for providing service user consultations. Policing domestic abuse teams, as well as IDVAs and any other frontline agency, are responsible for making risk assessments to determine whether a case meets the threshold for a referral to a local MARAC (see 19.3.2). The police should bring to the MARAC any information which highlights the risks to the victim and children and assist in devising an action plan to minimize those risks. The victim does not attend these meetings, but is represented by an IDVA who conveys any of their wishes, or concerns. MARACs provide highly effective responses to severe cases of domestic abuse, with 60 per cent of victims reporting no further incidences of violence after the intervention of a MARAC (Safe Lives, 2014).

19.15.3 The role of the Family Liaison Officer

The role of the Family Liaison Officer (FLO) is to act as an investigator by gathering information and evidence from the family for the investigation and to preserve the overall integrity of the case. The FLO is also a primary source of support for the families of victims after bereavement. Providing sensitive and compassionate care, securing their trust and confidence, and relaying information on the progress of a case. FLOs are not to be deployed as a solely supportive role, they are active investigators for the case. FLOs are required to be formally accredited with a continuous demonstration of competence against the required professional standards of the police service as well as continued professional development.The role of a FLO includes the following:

- Establish and maintain a supportive and ethical relationship with the family of the victim. Develop a mutual trust in line with local and national guidance to gathering information and evidence.
- Serve as the single point of contact between the family and the investigation team for cases relating to a mass disaster, homicide, suspicious death, or roads policing fatality. The purpose being to share information relating to the investigation.
- Collect best evidence to assist in the identification of a reported missing person (high risk of criminality/vulnerability) or assist in the identification of the deceased and consider potential future viewing requirements/post mortem(s) with the family to further the investigation.
- Provide information to the families about additional support services available for families, and explain both the Criminal Justice and Coronial procedures.
- Keep the families updated in a timely manner, regarding all relevant information concerning the police investigation, so that they are informed of progress and are in line with the strategy of the Senior Investigating Officer (SIO), Senior Identification Manager (SIM), or Lead Investigator.
- Obtain details regarding the victimology, as well as family personal statements and any other material to enable the gathering of evidence and to support the investigative process.
- Make formal records of any requests and/or complaints made by the family, which should be forwarded to the Senior Investigating Officer (SIO), Senior Identification Manager (SIM), or Lead Investigator for consideration.
- To keep a record of all contact with the family to ensure compliance with the Criminal Procedures and Investigations Act (CPIA) to maintain the integrity of the investigation.
- Liaise between families and the Coroner, Senior Investigating Officer (SIO), Senior Identification Manager (SIM), or Lead Investigator in relation to requirements under the Human Tissue Act 2004.

19.15.3.1 Creating an exit strategy for the FLO

Due to the nature of the FLO role it is often the case that bereaved families overcoming trauma can become over-reliant on the FLO and vice versa, which could result in there being long term negative wellbeing effects on both parties. To prevent such an occurrence, it is essential to formulate Exit Strategies that are both well timed and executed by the FLO and SIO to clarify the processes and procedures from that point onwards. At all times this transition must be carefully and sensitively executed. The Exit Strategy must be determined at a primary stage in the deployment of the FLO, with assistance of other multi-agency partnerships, such as victim support agencies, to ensure that the family continues to receive professional care, such as counselling, according to their needs and wishes.

19.16 Understanding Complexities of Victim/Witness Care

19.16.1 Relationships between victims and offenders

The willingness of victims and witnesses to come forward to report an offence to the police, or to continue with an investigation, can be significantly impacted by the relationship between the victim/witness and the offender (Knoth and Ruback, 2019). There are some offences which primarily occur between members of the same family or those in existing, or recently dissolved sexual relationships; such as domestic abuse, stalking, harassment, coercive control, neglect, and child sexual abuse. Additional factors, such as gender and ethnicity also play a significant role in the reporting of offences, specifically domestic abuse (Hine *et al*, 2020).

Men are less likely to report their experiences of domestic abuse than women as they minimize or fail to identify the seriousness of the abuse they receive (Machado *et al*, 2016); fear that they will not be believed or taken seriously (Drijber *et al*, 2013); or have their masculinity questioned (McCarrick *et al*, 2016). It is essential to consider such barriers to disclosure as in a survey conducted by the Office of National Statistics it was estimated that as many as one third of all domestic abuse victims are men (Home Office, 2020e). Research conducted by ManKind, a male domestic abuse advocacy service, revealed that there is a significant lack of support services for male victims, including clinical care (2021).

Victims who are in relationships with their abusers often do not leave as this can be highly dangerous (Women's Aid, 2020c). There is a significant increase in the likelihood of the level of violence increasing after victims separate from their abusers, with 41 per cent (37 out of 91) of female domestic abuse victims killed in 2018 dying after they had separated from partners. Of those 37 women, 11 were killed within the first month of leaving their partner, the remaining 24 were killed within the first year (Femicide Census, 2020).

19.16.2 Victim and witness intimidation

Victim and witness intimidation occurs when there is an attempt to persuade a victim or witness against giving evidence to either the police or during a trial or alternatively to give evidence that is in favour of the defendant (CPS, no date).

'Cultural intimidation' is a form of victim and witness intimidation conducted by the family and friends of the victim/witness in an attempt to dissuade them from engaging with the criminal justice system or giving evidence and can be caused by a fear of shame being brought on the family. Cultural intimidation also relates to beliefs in other methods of dealing with offending, methods that do not include agencies such as the police and criminal justice process (Caprioli and Crenshaw, 2017).

Section 51 of the Criminal Justice and Public Order Act 1994 creates two offences:

- s 51(1) creates an offence directed at acts against a person assisting in the investigation of an offence or who is a witness or potential witness or juror or potential juror whilst an investigation or trial is in progress; and
- s 51(2) creates an offence directed at acts against a person who assisted in an investigation of an offence or who was a witness or juror after an investigation or trial has been concluded.

The offences are triable either way. In the magistrates' court, the maximum penalty is six months' imprisonment and/or a fine to the statutory maximum. In the Crown Court, the maximum penalty is five years' imprisonment and/or a fine.

19.16.3 Offenders as witnesses for the prosecution

Under the Serious Organised Crime and Police Act 2005 (SOCPA), agreements can be reached with offenders (ss 71–72) who decide to assist with the police investigation or prosecution of offences committed by others (see 13.2.3.3).

19.16.4 Children as witnesses

Part 2, s 16 of the Youth Justice and Criminal Evidence Act 1999 as amended by the Coroners and Justice Act 2009 defines child witnesses as being under the age of 18.

Children can be significantly impacted by crime even if they are not witnesses or victims. An example of such an instance would be in cases of domestic abuse whereby a child may hear the incident from another room.

All child witnesses are defined as 'vulnerable' and as such are eligible for special measures by virtue of Part 2 YJCEA. Investigative interviews with child witnesses fall within the scope of *Achieving Best Evidence in Criminal Proceedings: Guidance on Interviewing Victims and Witnesses, and Using Special Measures* (MoJ, 2022a) (For further information on interviewing child witnesses and ABE see Chapter 13.)

It is important that officers understand that children are highly suggestible and this suggestibility can primarily come from inappropriate lines of questioning such as leading or repeated questions. Interviewers need to be mindful of interviewer influence, as research has shown that children's memory recall will be affected and they will alter their answers in an attempt to please an interviewer (Goodman and Quas, 2008). SIOs must be aware of factors relating to children's susceptibility during interview procedures.

19.16.5 Impact of proceedings on victims, witnesses, and their families

The severe potential impact of criminal proceedings on victims and witnesses should be considered by police officers from the early onset.

Trauma: Victims and witnesses may experience trauma because of the crime and the subsequent legal process. Reliving the details of the crime can be emotionally distressing, and may exacerbate feelings of anxiety and helplessness.

Disruption to daily life: The legal process can be time-consuming and may require victims and witnesses to take time off work or other responsibilities. This can disrupt their daily routine and cause additional stress.

Fear of retaliation: Victims and witnesses may fear retaliation from the perpetrator or their associates, particularly in cases of domestic violence or gang-related crimes.

Financial impact: The cost of legal proceedings, such as transportation, childcare, and legal representation, can be a burden on victims and witnesses, particularly if they are low-income or have limited resources.

Secondary victimization: Victims and witnesses may feel re-victimized by the legal process if they are not treated with respect and dignity by the criminal justice system. This can be particularly damaging for victims of sexual assault or other violent crimes.

Physical safety: Victims and witnesses may be at risk of physical harm during the legal process, particularly if the perpetrator is still at large or has access to weapons.

Privacy concerns: Victims and witnesses may be concerned about their privacy during the legal process, particularly if sensitive information is disclosed during the proceedings.

Overall, the impact of criminal proceedings on victims and witnesses can be significant and multifaceted. It is important for the criminal justice system to take steps to mitigate these impacts and support victims and witnesses throughout the legal process.

19.16.6 Psychological effects of crime on victim and witness behaviour

It is essential to understand and recognize the different ways that people can respond to trauma. Knowing that someone has deliberately caused harm against another person can be a difficult thing for people to process and understand and regardless of how serious the offence, victims and witnesses can be affected by their experiences for many years, and manifest in a variety of different physiological and psychological responses (Victim Support, 2023). Such responses can include, but are not limited to:

- **Post-Traumatic Stress Disorder (PTSD)**—This is a mental health condition that is brought on by experiencing or witnessing a traumatic incident causing an individual to undergo psychological stress (Andreasen, 2022). PTSD is frequently associated as an effect of experiencing wartime conflict, but is commonly experienced by victims of crime, and can be experienced by those witnessing a crime.
- **Flashbacks**—These are a symptom of PTSD and occur when victims or witnesses experience intense memory recall of an event to the extent that a person has all of the psychological and physiological responses of being back in the moment that the incident occurred. Flashbacks can be triggered by a variety of stimuli (PTSDUK, 2023).
- **Dissociation**—When victims experience traumatic events a psychological reaction can often be to dissociate oneself from the incident that is occurring. This method of self-preservation can be triggered in any stressful situation causing the victim to lose passages of time. It is a way of mentally switching off when a person is finding it difficult to cope. It can last for hours or days, even weeks or months (Mind, 2023).

- **Dissociative Amnesia**—When victims have an inability to recall instances in which they were a victim of a crime due to the extreme traumatic nature of the event (Loewenstein, 1996).
- **Shame and Guilt**—Victims can often blame themselves for the crimes that happen against them. This could include thoughts relating to their inability to protect themselves, for being deceived, and even their physiological responses to crimes such as sexual abuse. For example, victims of child sexual abuse (CSA) can feel shame and humiliation for the sexual acts that occurred. This has a significant effect on a victim's ability to disclose their history of CSA (Victim Support, 2020).

It is also important to understand that some victims may not be aware that they are victims. For example, children who are victims or sexual violence of physical abuse may not be aware that the abuse that they are experiencing is not a part of everyday life. They may love their abuser and fear that disclosing their abuse will result in their abuser being taken away from them, or their family breaking apart.

19.16.7 Impact of investigations on the investigator

Research conducted over the last few years has revealed that the nature of police investigations also has a considerable impact on police investigators. Investigator fatigue is a common consequence of the very nature of policing. The pressures exerted on police officers due to the unprecedented and extended working conditions innate to the role can have an impact on police performance (Kyriakidou *et al*, 2020). In addition to this, the continuous exposure to trauma can also have an effect on officer responses to victims of crime. The 'cost of caring', as coined by Charles Figley in 1995, can result in post-traumatic stress disorder and other symptoms of vicarious trauma including compassion fatigue (Figley, 1995; Foley and Massey, 2021).

Officers who frequently experience traumatic events, or are in specialist roles in which they engage with adult and child victims of violent crimes such as sexual violence, also experience an increased level of burnout, poor mental health, and compassion fatigue (Papazoglou *et al*, 2019). Compassion fatigue can also affect cognitive processes in the form of dissociation and poor concentration; emotional regulation; and behaviour. It can also have an impact on an officer's relationships with their family. Officers experiencing compassion fatigue can also experience an emotional numbness towards victims of crime (Papazoglou *et al*, 2020).

19.16.8 The police role in signposting victims and witnesses to specialist support

The Victims' Code sets out the minimum level of service and associated timeframes victims can expect from criminal justice agencies such as the police and courts, whether they choose to report the crime or not.

As part of the Victims' Code, police officers have the responsibility to continuously assess a victim's needs and ensure their rights to access support services. Police officers can refer victims to external services that can provide a high level of support throughout an investigation and beyond the outcome of a criminal case. Victims can require support in the following ways:

- Emotional support
- Finding a safe place to stay
- Counselling
- Specialist support for offences like domestic abuse or rape
- Financial aid

Victim and witness support provisions can assist from the point that a crime has taken place, regardless of whether an individual decides to proceed in supporting the investigation. There are many organizations to which police can refer victims for a range of support services, including Victim Support, which assigns support workers to victims (see 19.3). There are also advocates specifically trained to support children, and male victims (eg National Male Survivor Helpline). Such services provide further emotional and circumstantial care for victims of crime beyond that offered by the police within the Victims' Code. These services can explain the court process and undertake a detailed needs assessment if a victim or witness has to attend court to give evidence, update with relevant case specific information, for example; changes in court dates or bail conditions, discuss any concerns victims and witnesses may have about the process, offer help and support (Victim & Witness Care, 2022).

19.17 Behavioural and Communication Skills that can Provide Additional Support to Victims and Witnesses

Much of daily police work involves dealing with people in crisis. Police officers are often required to deliver difficult messages to victims and families of the bereaved and the attitude and actions of officers may have profound effects on those they come into contact with. It is important that all messages are accurate and complete. In cases of sudden death, relatives will likely ask if death was quick and without suffering, or whether the victim was aware, and whether anyone tried to save their life. It is essential that if you do not know the answers, you do not speculate with personal opinion.

When investigating a crime good communication skills on the part of the police are required to manage the individual's emotion and facilitate the disclosure of relevant investigative information. Officers with good communication skills can help a victim to move forward and gain control over their experience, whereas those with poor communication skills can inadvertently retraumatize and revictimize the victim. Communication skills are covered in Chapter 8 so here we provide a brief summary in relation to victims and witnesses specifically.

The goals of effective communication with crime victims are to:

- Identify victims' needs and attempt to meet them.
- Explain the justice process and the role of the victim service provider and allied professionals.
- Help victims to understand and exercise their statutory and constitutional rights in accordance with the law.
- Protect the safety of victims.
- Provide information.
- Obtain information.
- Be sensitive to special needs or concerns.

(Lewis and Jaramillo, 2008)

Non-verbal communication (NVC), or non-verbal behaviours, constitute the largest part of how we exchange information. When it comes to dealing with and supporting victims and witnesses, NVC can be vital to help put them at ease, increase their trust and encourage disclosure. However, NVC risks causing misunderstandings. On the victims and witnesses side, behaviours commonly exhibited by nervous and anxious individuals are often misunderstood as suspicious or not believable. Research suggests NVC also differs between people from different ethnic backgrounds (Vrij *et al*, 1992; Winkel and Vrij, 1990) and you should be conscious of this.

In the context of victims and witnesses you should adopt an active listening approach. An active listener is seen to be more concerned and caring which is important for reducing tension and hurt. It is very important that you take care not to use a tone that communicates disbelief, but one that shows interest, and that invites them to tell you more.

Working with victims and witnesses often involves having to manage and respond to their emotions. For that, emotional intelligence (EI) is required. EI is the capacity to recognize, assess, and manage emotions in oneself and others, name and acknowledge them, and handle them appropriately.

Related to this is the concept of empathy which is the action of communicating an understanding and appreciation of what another person is going through, and accepting their emotional response to that incident. Displaying empathy can aid in the gathering of information from interviewees and has the ability to enhance victims' trust not only in the police, but also in the entire judicial system (Kepinska Jakobsen, 2021). For example, rape victims have stated that they were more likely to take cases through to court and felt less likely to develop symptoms of post-traumatic stress disorder (PTSD) if they were interviewed with empathy (Maddox, 2011).

Rapport is essentially a mental and communicative connection between two people. Research has shown that if rapport is established and maintained well, it can decrease interviewees' level of suggestivity ie their ability to be influenced by misleading questions, it can increase the completeness of their account, and also heighten accuracy levels (Hershkowitz, 2011; Roberts *et al*, 2004; Wood *et al*, 1996). It has been found that feeling listened to and believed, might be even more important to a victim than whether the perpetrator actually gets punished (Powell and Cauchi, 2011).

By reporting a crime, a victim is gaining a sense of control over the narrative of what has occurred, therefore it is essential that all officers listen, support, and empathize with the victim's disclosure. The LEAPS Model is a good shorthand when thinking about effective communication.

- Listen—listen to the whole message and the feelings. Do not just take the content at face value, and try not to interrupt.
- Empathy—be open-minded about what is said, show understanding, and try not to judge.
- Ask—use effective questioning to establish or clarify the facts, seek opinions, and check understanding.
- Paraphrase—repeat back your understanding of what you have heard.
- Summarize—condense everything that has been said into a concise and simple statement, and check on any agreed actions.

(CoP, 2020d)

There are many occasions whilst on duty that an officer will be confronted with challenging, uncooperative and hostile individuals, and some of these may also be the victims of crime. All officers are trained to deal with such situations through personal safety training. Conflict management skills are discussed in Chapter 9.

19.18 Collecting and Understanding the Victim's Account

Whether a case is prosecuted and progresses or not is determined by the perceived strength of evidence, meaning perceptions of the victim's account are crucial. Poor prosecution outcomes are often due to the lack of quality, detail, and coherence in the statements obtained from both victims and suspects.

19.18.1 Taking initial accounts from victims and witnesses

An initial account is vital to establish whether there is a risk to life or property and whether an offence has occurred or not. An initial account is not meant to include vast amounts of detail but it is imperative that key details are taken (see 10.16). A comprehensive record of what the victim or witness says should be made or at least recorded on body-worn cameras. This may be used as evidence in court and therefore it is vital that the accuracy and completeness of the record is to the highest standard. Guidance on how to obtain a good initial account is available at <https://assets.college.police.uk/s3fs-public/2020-11/Initial_Accounts_Guidelines.pdf>.

Employing a narrative interview approach may help achieve complete and coherent accounts. This approach has been shown to lead to more charges in child abuse cases than the more typical question-and-short-answer-approach (Pipe, Orbach, Lamb, Abbott and Stewart, 2008). Interviewers encourage the person interviewed to give their account at their own pace, with next to no interruption, using non-directive, non-leading open questions that encourage details without any presumptions (Powell and Snow, 2007).

In certain crime types, most notably those of a domestic and sexual nature, which tend to take place behind closed doors and without witnesses, the victim's statement is often the only evidence that can be presented. Many such crimes are only reported long after they were committed, and there is often no corroborating independent evidence that can be offered. This one-word-against-the-other conundrum is one of the reasons why so few of these crimes are reported to police in the first place, and why the conviction rate is so low. It is crucial in this context to offer first-class victim support and highly-skilled interviewing, to enable the most detailed account to be captured, encapsulating the entire relationship between victim and offender, including capturing any earlier grooming or controlling behaviours that facilitated the later offending.

Once an initial statement has been taken it is important to communicate with the victim and/or witness exactly what is required of them and the next steps you are going to make as police officers. Conducting a thorough early assessment of needs and communicating effectively with the victim or witness enables a smooth passage through the criminal justice system for the parties involved.

Victim personal statements should also be discussed (see 10.16.2). These are not compulsory but provide extra information as to how the crime has affected the victim physically, emotionally, psychologically, financially, or in any other way. It should be taken into account by all criminal justice agencies involved in the case and it can play a key part in sentencing.

19.18.2 Legal concepts of reliability and credibility

At its most basic, 'credibility' involves the issue of whether the victim or witness appears to be telling the truth, or how believable they are. To be credible a witness must be competent—that is capable of giving evidence. Whether evidence is 'reliable' is a legal matter and concerns the inherent quality of evidence. Evidence is reliable if it is what it is purported to be, and reliability has to do with the accuracy of the witness's testimony. Accuracy engages consideration of the witness's ability to accurately observe and recount the events in issue. Even if a witness appears to be sincere, truthful, and honest, and even if the witness believes what he or she is saying, it does not necessarily follow that his or her evidence is reliable. Credibility alone, in this sense, is not enough.

For example, if a victim or witness identifies the person who committed the crime this may seem reliable and if the victim or witness seems to be an honest person, credible. However, if the witness could not positively identify the suspect until an officer suggested that a particular person was the perpetrator, the identification may not be what it purports to be, and thus is not reliable. This is not to say the person is not telling what they see to be the truth, but that the evidence is unreliable.

Credibility is a subjective concept, and there are many factors that influence how it is perceived. For example, it has been found that observers tend to perceive someone speaking their own native language as being more truthful than someone speaking a different language (Da Silva and Leach, 2013). Unconscious bias can be important as normal and genuine responses to victimization can be misunderstood, and certain stereotypical behaviours expected; for example, female victims who do not display clear emotions of being upset can be seen as less credible (Kaufmann *et al*, 2003).

Although seemingly more straightforward, reliability is not an objective assessment. There are different types of evidence that can be presented as part of an investigation, such as eyewitness testimony, CCTV footage, DNA, and fingerprints, for example. Even though these all belong to the overall category of evidence, they are not given equal weight in terms of how reliable they are perceived to be. A lot of research has shown that memory is malleable and has played a part in convicting innocent people through eyewitness misidentification (Wixted *et al*, 2018), accounting for 70 per cent of wrongful convictions that have since been exonerated through DNA evidence (Innocence Project, 2017). However, eyewitness memory is reliable, as long as it is not contaminated by investigative or other procedures. Just as DNA evidence can easily be contaminated, so too can memories (Wixted *et al*, 2018). It is worryingly easy to contaminate an interviewee's account of an incident through leading, biased, and/or mis-informed questions. As such the training and skill of a police interviewer is crucial when it comes to ensuring that witness evidence is as reliable as possible.

There are particular concerns regarding the reliability of the information that is obtained through police interviews with vulnerable people (Herrington and Roberts, 2012). There is also a level of disagreement on the topic of memories of traumatic events. Again, skilful interviewing is of utmost importance and a lack of detail or the presence of discrepancies and gaps in the account should not be mistaken as signs that the account is less credible, trustworthy, or reliable (Ellison and Munro, 2017).

19.18.3 Principles of victim consent and the right to privacy

During investigations of crime, victims are often requested to hand over varying degrees of personal items and information especially during cases relating to rapes and serious sexual offences (RASSO). Conviction for RASSO has been estimated as being as low as 3 per cent (Information Commissioner's Office, 2022), based on data retrieved from The House of Commons Home Affairs Committee report on rape prosecutions (2022) combined with data from the National Crime Survey conducted by the Office of National Statistics (2020d). In light of these findings the Victims' Commissioner's Office retrieved data from Rape Crisis England & Wales on the subject of why victims of RASSO withdraw complaints and they found that;

- One in five withdrew because of they had disclosure and privacy concerns
- Twenty-one percent had concerns that their digital material would be downloaded
- Concerns regarding their medical, school, and employment records being disclosed
- Concerns regarding media coverage

For many victims of RASSO, it was the scrutiny of their private lives that had the biggest impact on their decision not to report a crime. In the report (Victims' Commissioner, 2020) victims reported that the experience of giving over personal information was very traumatic. Only 33 per cent agreed that the police explained why access to mobile data was necessary, and only 22 per cent reported being told that only necessary data would be extracted.

The Data Protection Act 2018 contains specific principles for competent bodies, such as the police, in regards to obtaining and processing data. Police services must demonstrate that they are compliant by following the following principles:

- First principle: The processing must be lawful and fair.
- Second principle: The processing must be limited to a specified, explicit, and legitimate purpose, and it must not be processed in a manner that is incompatible with the purpose for which it was collected.
- Third principle: The data must be adequate, relevant, and not excessive in relation to the purpose for which it is processed.
- Fourth principle: The data must be accurate and, where necessary, kept up-to-date. Every reasonable step must be taken to ensure that personal data that is inaccurate, having regard to the law enforcement purpose for which it is processed, is erased or rectified without delay. In addition, as far as possible, a clear distinction must be made between different categories of people—those suspected of an offence, those convicted, witnesses, and complainants. Personal data based on fact must as far as possible be distinguished from personal data based on personal assessments.
- Fifth principle: Data should be stored for no longer than is necessary, and appropriate limits must be set for periodic review of the need for continued storage.
- Sixth principle: There must be adequate measures in place to ensure the appropriate security of data, including protection against unauthorized or unlawful processing and against accidental loss, destruction, or damage.

(Sections 35–40 of the DPA, 2018)

For law enforcement agencies the processing of a victim's data can be lawful only if and to the extent that it is based on law and either:

(a) the data subject has given consent (within the meaning of data processing law) to the processing for that purpose; or
(b) the processing is necessary for the performance of a task carried out for that purpose by a competent authority. (Section 35, DPA)

The definition of consent according to UK GDPR article 4(11) is:

> 'consent' of the data subject means any freely given, specific, informed and unambiguous indication of the data subject's wishes by which he or she, by a statement or by a clear affirmative action, signifies agreement to the processing of personal data relating to him or her.

The challenge with relying on the consent for data being used in lawful processing in criminal investigations lies in the validity of the consent given, due to factors such as:

- The limited capability of victims to give fully informed consent during a period of high trauma
- The power imbalance that exists between the police and the victim. The victim may fear that the refusal to give consent may have an impact on the viability of the case to proceed
- The absence of the ability to withdraw consent due to the legal requirements placed on the police and other legal authorities to retain material relevant to the criminal case.

Victims should be informed of how their data will be used throughout the investigation, including the likelihood of their personal information being disclosed to others such as the defendant.

In regards to 'Sensitive Data' processing this includes specific characteristic information on the following:

(a) the processing of personal data revealing racial or ethnic origin, political opinions, religious or philosophical beliefs, or trade union membership;
(b) the processing of genetic data, or of biometric data, for the purpose of uniquely identifying an individual;
(c) the processing of data concerning health;
(d) the processing of data concerning an individual's sex life or sexual orientation.
(Section 35(8) of the DPA)

When extracting sensitive data on the victim, there must be a demonstration of strict necessity. This is demonstrated if the police established consent as an appropriate condition sufficient to justify processing for law enforcement purposes. It is important to note that the protection of personal, sensitive, data is not an absolute right and is dependent on other fundamental rights that fall in accordance with the principle of proportionality (Information Commissioners Opinion, 2022).

Authorised Professional Practice (APP) guidelines on data protection has been written in order to assist police services to be compliant with the DPA (2018) and UK GDPR. It ensures effective policing by providing clear guidance to the structures, responsibilities, policies, and processes that must be in place to ensure consistency.

19.18.4 Data subject rights

Victims of crime, in data protection terminology, are also referred to as data subjects. All data subjects have rights that fall in line with the DPA and UK GDPR. These rights can be exercised both in written and verbal format so it is essential that officers can recognize these rights and relay them to the appropriate unit or department that is responsible for processing them.

The most commonly requested right, exercised by victims, is the request to access and erase personal data. In accordance with data regulations the police have one month in order to respond to any data subject's rights application. It is essential that any information and detail regarding the request is forwarded to the relevant department as soon as possible. It is the responsibility of all police officers and staff to ensure that they are familiar with their own constabulary's policies and procedures that relate to these rights and their applications.

Within the DPA and UK GDPR, there are exemptions which police services can consider prior to a request being processed. For example, personal data would not be released to a data subject under the right of access if doing so would prejudice law enforcement or the rights and freedoms of another person. Rights of access are also not the same as the right to request information under the Freedom of Information Act 2000. Rights of access are available to the data subject regarding their personal data, the latter relates to non-personal information.

19.19 The Different Justice Outcomes

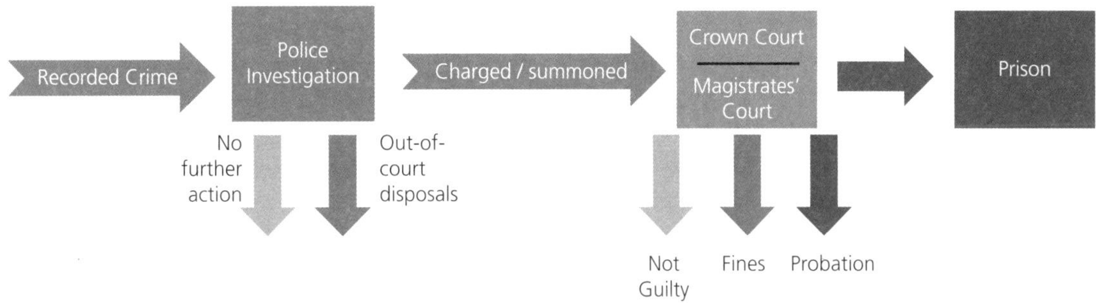

No further action—This can be the outcome if there is no evidence to support the investigation, for example if a complaint has been made maliciously or in error, or there is otherwise no prospect of locating any evidence to support the victim's account.

Out-of-court-disposal—This is an alternative to a formal charge and is less serious in nature. It can be applied when the offence has been proven to have been committed by the offender, and an admission of guilt may have been provided. Out-of-court-disposals are issued by the police, as they prevent the case from progressing to court. They include simple cautions, conditional cautions, penalty notices, or community resolutions.

Charge/summons—If the police (less serious cases) or the Crown Prosecution Service (more serious cases) decide that there is a realistic prospect of conviction, they will be charged by the police or summonsed to court by letter.

Crown Court—In more serious offences following a charge, the case will be heard in Crown Court by a judge and jury. Both the prosecution (the police, Crown Prosecution Service, and the victim) and the defence (the defendant and their legal counsel) will present their cases for a verdict to be reached.

Magistrates' Court—For less serious cases, a magistrate will preside over the hearing and make a decision.

The court will find the defendant not guilty if it cannot be proven beyond reasonable doubt that they have committed the offence in question. If they have been found guilty, depending on the severity of the offence and the defendant's prior criminal record, they may simply be issued a fine. Alternatively, they can be given probation as a sentence, where they will not be incarcerated as long as they adhere to the conditions that are part of their probationary sentence. If the offence has been proven and was more severe and/or the offender's criminal history is such that they cannot be given probation, they will go to prison.

19.19.1 Reasons why cases may not go to court

There can be a number of reasons why a case may not go to court:

Prosecution time limit expired—Occasionally, usually with summary only or low level offences, a suspect is identified but the time limit for prosecution expires. This is sometimes referred to as an offence's statutory time limit.

No realistic prospect of conviction—Either the police or the CPS may decide not to charge the suspect if there is no realistic prospect of conviction, in which case the suspect is released without charge.

Insufficient evidence—Either the police or the CPS may decide to drop the case before it reaches court after a suspect has been charged if insufficient evidence is submitted against the defendant.

Victim withdrawal—The victim may decide to no longer support a prosecution.

Not in the public interest—The case can be discontinued if it is not in the public interest to pursue the prosecution, for example if the defendant is terminally ill and did not have much longer to live.

The defendant cannot get a fair trial—If there is not enough evidence to suggest a realistic prospect of conviction or a prosecution is not in the public interest, ie the full-code test has not been met, the threshold test may be applied where the seriousness or circumstances of a case justify the making of an immediate charging decision, and there are substantial grounds to object to bail. The test must fulfil all five conditions in order to warrant immediate charging of the suspect: 1) There are reasonable grounds to suspect that the person to be charged has committed the offence; 2) Further evidence can be obtained to provide a realistic prospect of conviction; 3) The seriousness or the circumstances of the case justify the making of an immediate charging decision; 4) There are continuing substantial grounds to object to bail; and 5) It is in the public interest to charge the suspect. If any condition of the threshold test is not met, the threshold test cannot be applied and the suspect cannot be charged.

If there are no realistic ways of obtaining the necessary evidence, a case may not be able to be carried on any further. For example, a historic case where all relevant parties may have died, evidential documents have been destroyed and there are no other ways of obtaining the necessary information.

Remember victims and witnesses may need additional support if their case cannot be continued. On the one hand, they may be relieved that they will not have to appear at court.

However, they may feel that they have not had the opportunity to seek their own justice. Or they may worry the suspect feels vindicated or encouraged by the case being dropped and may feel vengeful for being publicly accused. It might be necessary to put additional support in place to safeguard the victim if this is the case.

19.19.2 Non-judicial outcomes

There are a range of disposals which the police can dispense to offenders with the purpose of securing effective outcomes as an alternative to the more formal line of criminal justice (CoP, 2022e). The two that most closely tie to victims and witnesses are restorative justice and community resolutions (see also Chapter 10).

Sometimes, it is not possible to secure all the information and evidence necessary in order to secure a charge within custody time limits and this may require an application to remand a suspect in custody, release them either with or without bail, in order for officers to continue with necessary enquiries in a timely manner (CoP, 2022e) (further information on this can be found in Chapter 10).

19.19.2.1 Restorative justice

The purpose of restorative justice is to bring together those who have been affected by crime with those responsible for causing that harm so that they can communicate and find a resolution (Restorative Justice Council, 2023).

Restorative justice meetings between victims and offenders can be direct or indirect sessions using an impartial mediator. It can include a focus of either restitution or reparation which is made in agreement between offenders and victims (CPS, 2023b).

The aims of restorative justice are:

- Victim satisfaction: Victims can feel a sense of justice through a feeling of having been 'paid back' for the impact that the crime has had on them. It can even reduce the fear experienced by the victim in their everyday lives.
- Engagement with the offender: It is an opportunity for the offender to understand how their actions have impacted victims and the wider community, make reparations, and determine a way of restoring the perpetrator back into the community.
- Creation of community capital: The purpose of this aim is to increase public confidence in the criminal justice system through a visible response to anti-social behaviour.

Restorative justice sessions provide victims with the opportunity to gain answers to questions that would not be possible to answer in court. Questions such as 'why have I been victimised?'. It is also an opportunity for a victim to receive an apology. The sessions are also positive for offenders as it provides an opportunity for them to face up to what they have done so that they can take responsibility and work towards repairing some of the harm that they have caused. Research into the benefits of restorative justice has shown there to be a positive psychological impact on victim wellbeing over a sustained period of time in comparison to those who actively chose not to engage with the offender (Nascimento *et al*, 2022).

Restorative justice can take place at any stage of the criminal justice process, even after the offender has been convicted. However, it is most commonly used prior to any case coming to court, for example, as part of a diversionary process (CPS, 2023b), and for consideration as a reparative condition as a part of a conditional caution.

Restorative justice processes are most commonly used in cases involving young offenders, and have been promoted as an ideal approach, by the Youth Justice Board since 2001 in their national standards for children in the youth justice system. It can be embedded in an order upon conviction such as a Youth Rehabilitation Order, or as part of a Youth Offending Team's rehabilitation programme after an individual has received a youth caution or conditional caution.

Restorative justice is available to all victims as stipulated in the Victims' Code of Practice. In cases where restorative justice is an option, it is the responsibility of the police to contact the victim (unless reasons indicate that this is not a suitable course of action) to determine whether they view reparation as an acceptable course of action that will become a stipulation in a caution. In addition to this, if an offender has already indicated that they are willing to engage in a process of restorative justice, then it must be determined whether the victim is willing to engage in either direct or indirect restorative justice sessions. Police officers must have a degree of sensitivity regarding the timing of proposing restorative justice as an outcome to victims of crime. If proposed too soon after an event then the victim may not have overcome the initial trauma of the event and will be unwilling or simply not ready to seek answers relating to their victimization. Likewise, if left too long, the victim may have psychologically moved on from the incident and no longer want to be drawn back to that time and place (CPS, 2023b).

If the victim chooses not to engage in any form of restorative justice then this must be noted in writing, by the investigating officer, within the case file and be taken into consideration when deciding on the conditions being applied. If the victim does not want to participate, the investigating officer should consider whether there is anyone from the wider community who would like to participate. If no one wants to participate, then it is still possible for a restorative approach to be used within the conditional caution whereby a one-to-one discussion with either an officer or facilitator (ideally also in the presence of family or partners) can be undertaken to discuss and consider the harm caused to others, and ways in which that harm can be rectified (CPS, 2023b).

19.19.2.2 Community resolutions

Community resolutions are a proportionate, low-level outcome that seeks to repair harm committed against communities by either adults or youths. Such resolutions can be offered when the offender accepts responsibility and the victim does not wish to proceed with more formal action (CoP, 2022e). The purpose of community resolutions is very much like that of restorative justice, to encourage an offender to face the harm that they have caused and make up to those that it has impacted with the goal of reducing further offending. Resolutions can include:

- Advice given to the offender on their behaviour
- Apologizing to those affected
- Writing a letter of apology to the victim/s
- Undertaking some form of reparations such as repair works to things that have been broken
- Paying for the damage caused

The following factors must be taken into consideration before applying a community resolution:

- Actual Offence—The circumstance around the offence must be in the public interest to warrant a community resolution
- Evidential standard—It must be clear that a crime has occurred and that there is reasonable suspicion that the offender committed the offence
- Admission of guilt—The offender must admit guilt regarding the offence in question
- Offender consent—The offender must consent, and be of mental capability of understanding, to their participation in a community resolution
- Offender history—There must be no offending history. If there is a prior history of offending then the investigating officer must refer the decision to a supervisor and all decisions must be recorded
- Victim check—all victims should be consulted and agreement sought. A community resolution can proceed without the agreement of the victims, but in such a case the decision must come from a supervisor and all decisions should be recorded
- Implications—A community resolution is not a part of a criminal record but can become known on a Disclosure and Barring Service check.

19.19.3 Victim views on what constitutes justice

Victims perceive more kinds of justice than simply the outcome of the case. For example, *informational* justice refers to how well victims are kept in the loop about the progress of their case; and *interpersonal* justice reflects victims' perceptions of representatives of the criminal justice system (Laxminarayan *et al*, 2012).

For some victims, the acknowledgement of the crime, feeling listened to, supported and believed, might be even more important than whether the perpetrator actually gets punished (Powell and Cauchi, 2011). Therefore, dealing with the victim with a high level of compassion, emotional intelligence, and empathy is vital. Research has found that victims often value an apology from the offender more than money or vengeance (Sherman *et al*, 2006). They frequently wish for the offender to understand the harm that was caused and how future offending can be prevented, rather than compensation (Strang *et al*, 2006).

Domestic abuse victims often remove their support for prosecution. Whilst this may be frustrating for police, there are often logical reasons for why victims do this. Abused people have been able to use the court system to their advantage in their relationships with the threat of prosecution as a deterrent, returning some sense of control to them and giving them bargaining power when dealing with their abusive partner. It is often this need for control and finding their voice again that motivates abused individuals to invoke the law, not necessarily the possibility of a complete prosecution.

19.19.4 Victim's decision not to proceed

It is not an uncommon occurrence for victims to report crimes to the police at points of high tempers and stress and then, once removed from the situation and into a calmer state, decide not to proceed with the complaint (Ellison, 2002). It is possible for the police to proceed without the support of the victim as the police do not need the victim's consent in order to make an arrest or place charges if an officer believes that there are reasonable grounds to suspect that, based on s 24 of PACE, an offence has taken place, is taking place or will take place; or that the arrest is necessary.

Regardless of this, the absence of evidence provided by the victim can lead to case complications for the CPS, especially if the victim proceeds to become what is known as a 'hostile witness'. A 'hostile witness' is a victim who, when required to attend court to give evidence, may answer questions posed by the prosecution that are detrimental to the CPS case.

There are often myriad complex reasons why victims decide no longer to support a police investigation including reconciliation with the accused, a fear of reprisal, concern for the safety of others such as children, financial consequences, fear of facing the perpetrator in court, fear of being cross-examined and having to relive the incident, and cultural factors.

The police and CPS have become increasingly aware of how such factors have an impact on successful investigations and therefore look to accumulate evidence from third parties, such as neighbours, support agencies, and family members. The availability of body-worn camera footage by the police provides a valuable source of observational evidence that can assist in an investigation, and lessen the pressure exerted on the victim.

In her 2021/22 report, Dame Vera Baird raised the question 'How have we got to the position where victims find their treatment by the criminal justice system to be worse than the crime itself' (Victims' Commissioner, 2022). Victims of crime want and need to be supported by a process of procedural justice. The criminal justice process, from the start of the investigation through to the courts, has a duty of care to acknowledge that how they engage with victims impacts upon their recovery. Victims can often appear reluctant to engage in criminal justice proceedings. This could be caused by previous experiences or fear of revictimization, to the extent that a victim would rather sacrifice their opportunity for justice than undergo any more pain and suffering. A high volume of victims disengage from the criminal justice system for this reason (MoJ, 2021a).

Some groups of victims are more disengaged and less satisfied with the criminal justice system than others, specifically, victims with disabilities and persons from Black and ethnic minority groups (MoJ, 2012). In a recent Victims' Survey conducted by the Victims' Commissioner (2021) the findings revealed that just 43 per cent of victims would report a crime again based on their experiences, and only 50 per cent would attend court again, a figure which is down from 67 per cent. Only 9 per cent of victims felt that their cases were dealt with promptly, but factors such as Covid-19 will have had an impact on these numbers as half of the survey's respondents had their cases investigated during this period.

A finding that is specifically significant for policing is that 48 per cent of respondents stated that the most important factor for them was the perception that the case was fully investigated. Of those, 38 per cent said that being treated fairly and with respect by the police was the second most important factor. When asked whether they had been treated as such by the police, only 42 per cent of victims believed that they had been, many commenting that they felt that their case had not been taken seriously, and there was a significant lack of action by the police.

19.20 Answers to Tasks

TASK 1

1. For either of these two offences to be proven, you would need evidence to prove a course of conduct: eg letters, photographs, or eyewitness accounts. If the harassment involved phone calls, seek police assistance to liaise with the service provider to obtain evidence of the calls. Clarify with the victim whether there had been any previous instances of harassment and any outcomes. Collect statements from colleagues who had previously seen the victim and any other witnesses, paperwork, letters, and photographs from the victim, and exhibit them in a statement. The case could be discussed with a CPS Evidence Review representative.
2. If the suspect was known but a course of conduct could not be proved and the victim had been harassed or put in fear of violence, you could warn the suspect. The warning would be recorded, preferably in the form of a First Incidence Harassment Warning or as a PNB entry, and you would also make sure it is recorded on the police database for future reference. This could be evidence towards proving a course of conduct in the future.
3. The victim should be advised to:
   - seek legal advice, as pursuing a civil remedy under s 3 of the Protection from Harassment Act 1997 could be appropriate;
   - contact Victim Support;
   - contact their phone service provider if the phone was being used to harass to arrange for a block to be placed on 'number withheld' incoming calls; and
   - keep a diary of events, retain physical evidence, and take photographs of any visible evidence.
4. If a course of conduct could be proved or suspected, the suspect could be arrested but only if there was a reason for the arrest being necessary. This could be to protect a child, to allow the prompt and effective investigation of the conduct of the person in question, or to prevent any prosecution for the offence being hindered by the disappearance of the person in question.

Processing Policing

TASK 2

1. Under s 17(1)(e) of the PACE Act 1984, an officer 'may enter and search any premises for the purposes of saving life or limb or preventing serious damage to property'. Evidence of a clearly distressed child and suspicion that the child is alone and cannot open the door justify the use of s 17 to save the life and limb of the child.
2. The child may be confused and distressed about the presence of the police and the missing parent. The NSPCC (<https://www.nspcc.org.uk/keeping-children-safe/reporting-abuse/what-if-suspect-abuse/>) provides useful guidelines for dealing with children who have suffered abuse and neglect.
3. It would appear that the parent has committed an offence under s 1 of the Children and Young Persons Act 1933. However although an offence has been committed, the child is no longer in immediate danger and arrangements could be made (perhaps with relatives) for the child's safety while the parent is absent. If there was any reason to believe the child was in immediate danger, the officer could consider taking them into police protection and arresting the parent. However, prosecution guidelines must be followed and the guidance of a CPS representative would be required. Whatever action is taken, it must be proportionate.

TASK 3

The 'Herbert Protocol' initiative for helping to locate vulnerable adults who go missing is named after George Herbert, a veteran of the 1944 D-Day landings in Normandy during the Second World War. As an elderly man, Mr Herbert developed dementia and was cared for in a residential home. He went missing in 2011 (apparently looking for his childhood home) but was found dead before he could be helped to return to his residential care. The Protocol was developed in response to this.

20 Vulnerability and Risk

20.1 Introduction

The aim of this chapter is to highlight the crucial role of the police when working with vulnerable people or with people at risk of being victimized. It also aims to equip officers with a better understanding of wider issues of victimization, including the impact that crime may have on victims and therefore the importance of effective response. The first interactions with victims are crucial as they will shape victims' responses, their views of the police, their likelihood of future reporting, and these can impact on their recovery. When the police or other authorities refer to a person as being 'vulnerable', they are normally making reference to those children, young people, or adults that are exposed to the possibility of being attacked, harmed, either physically, mentally, or emotionally, or exploited. The implication is that the person with a form of vulnerability is in need of special care, support, or protection, eg as the result of age or disability, to reduce the risk of being subjected to abuse or neglect, either now or in the future. In essence, the concept of vulnerability within policing 'encompasses the person and their circumstances' (NPCC, 2018b). The central argument here is that much of police work is about the relationship they establish with the public, so it is imperative that officers reflect on their practice.

You should note at the outset that there is no official (eg legal) and commonly held definition of 'vulnerability' in a law enforcement context. Whereas the statutory term 'vulnerable adult' (in s 59 of the Safeguarding Vulnerable Groups Act 2006) refers to individuals aged 18 or over for which there are specific safeguarding responsibilities (such as people receiving forms of health or social care) the NPCC, College of Policing, HMICFRS, and others use the term 'vulnerability' in a more inclusive but less precise way.

The topics covered in this chapter are likely to contribute to the learning required for the National Policing Curriculum subject area Vulnerability and Risk. There are also references to 'vulnerable' and 'vulnerability' throughout the pre-join, PCDA, and degree-entry curricula. A qualified police constable is expected to safely and lawfully be able to 'Provide leadership to protect the public, and empathetic and appropriate support to victims, witnesses and vulnerable people' and, when becoming 'emotionally astute' to 'value diversity and difference [...] and treat people with sensitivity, compassion and warmth' (Institute for Apprenticeships and Technical Education, 2018b). Many police services now have a 'vulnerability strategy' and an NPCC 'Vulnerability Delivery Plan'.

20.2 Defining Vulnerability

It is important to understand who may be considered to be 'vulnerable'. Just because someone is, for instance, older, or has a mental health condition or a learning disability, or has a physical disability, they are not necessarily 'vulnerable'. Indeed, they may take great offence if you were to consider them so. The clear absence of an evidence-based definition of vulnerability can come at a cost. Examples include the inability of some individuals or groups to gain access to varying support or health services, the amplification of multiple vulnerabilities, dual diagnoses by different organizations, and a communication breakdown between multi-agency partnerships (Enang *et al*, 2019).

Vulnerability, and some of the possible consequences, have been an increasing focus of attention in recent years. There have been a number of disturbing incidents such as the Rotherham child sexual abuse scandal, where between 1999 and 2013 approximately 1,400 children are believed to have been victims of child sexual exploitation (CSE). In 2014, the Alexis Jay *Independent Inquiry into CSE in Rotherham 1997–2013* proved to be a 'damning indictment of the failure of one local authority to protect children from organised sexual exploitation' (House of Commons Communities and Local Government Committee, 2014, p 5). The Inquiry found that although the Rotherham Safeguarding Children Board oversaw the development of good inter-agency policies and procedures applicable to CSE, members of the Safeguarding Board rarely checked whether these were being implemented or whether they were working. Further, Jay identified a number of professional barriers that impeded effective action against CSE, and a lack of understanding of the modus operandi used by the perpetrators such as grooming. A total of 15 recommendations were made relating to risk assessments, the management of looked-after children who are sexually exploited, accessibility of support services, joint teams to counter CSE, multi-agency working, working with and support for CSE victims, community engagement, and serious case reviews. Partly as a result of Rotherham and other child abuse scandals there is now a greater emphasis in the police service on identifying and managing the risks associated with vulnerability and responding to indicators of vulnerability. As Ford *et al* (2019, p 2) note, the majority of calls to police services in the UK are now related to vulnerability. Whilst there has been a visible decline in several reported crime categories there has been an increase in the number of calls received that relate to public safety and welfare (Keay and Hirby, 2018). A College of Policing (2015f) analysis of demand on the police service had already suggested that more attention should be paid to tackling vulnerability. The report highlighted the changing nature of crime and the ways in which police resources are deployed and concluded that whilst police recorded crime had generally been decreasing, the demand on policing had been increasing in other ways. In particular, the number of certain types of crimes seems to be increasing such as 'costly' crimes (for example in relation to complex crimes such as child sexual exploitation), and the number of incidents that police attend that involve people with mental health issues also seems to be on the up. This can be seen in the number of people detained under the Mental Health Act by the police. A 2022 report published by the Home Office revealed that there had been an 8 per cent increase in the number of people detained under s 136 of the Mental Health Act 1983 (Home Office, 2022h), in comparison to the previous year. In addition, the demands associated with protective statutory requirements also appear to be increasing. The regular Police Effectiveness, Efficiency and Legitimacy (PEEL) inspections by HMICFRS into police service effectiveness now place more emphasis on how vulnerability is addressed. One of the core indicators of overall effectiveness is the extent to which a police service is successful at identifying, protecting, and supporting those who are vulnerable. For example, annual inspection programmes now consider how a constabulary responds to domestic abuse victims and missing and absent children, and how well-prepared the service is to tackle child sexual exploitation.

20.2.1 The complex nature of vulnerability

As suggested earlier, although 'vulnerability' as a concept can be difficult to define, there is little doubt that it is the combination of the person and the circumstances that is important. Hence it makes more sense to talk about a 'person in a state of vulnerability' than it does a 'vulnerable person' although the latter is frequently used as a shorthand for the former. We will consider further some of the associations and possible causes of vulnerability, but we note here that officers need to be wary about simply labelling a person as 'vulnerable' (Schrems, 2014).

Some argue that vulnerability is a universal condition and state that is present in all of us when placed in danger of being threatened, experiencing psychological or physical health issues which render us requiring protection and support from others (Larkin, 2009). This suggests that anyone can become vulnerable during their lifetime (Enang *et al*, 2019). This brings challenges in developing protocols, strategies, and policies to support people in a state of vulnerability, and for some does not reflect the complexity of individual human experiences of being vulnerable (Wrigley and Dawson, 2016; Fineman, 2010).

By applying a label of vulnerability there is a risk of increasing stigma with connotations regarding a degree of intrinsic weakness of specific groups within society (Herring, 2016). The very act of labelling a person as vulnerable can also cause less obvious but potentially more serious problems; it can suggest that the person is partly responsible for the harm they experience at the hands of others. The attached label seems to 'locate the cause of abuse with the victim, rather than placing responsibility with the actions or omissions of others' (ADASS, 2005, p 4).

20.3 The Code of Practice for Victims of Crime

The Code of Practice for Victims of Crime in England and Wales (HM Government, 2021b) was developed to protect victims and witnesses of crime and is discussed in Chapter 19. It sets out some clear guidance for the identification and eligibility of vulnerable persons eligible for enhanced rights. A person meets the following criteria as a vulnerable victim or witness if:

- they are under 18 years of age at the time of the offence; or
- the quality of their evidence is likely to be affected because they:
- suffer from mental disorder within the meaning of the Mental Health Act 1983;
- otherwise have a significant impairment of intelligence and social functioning; or
- have a physical disability or are suffering from a physical disorder.

A victim or witness is also considered vulnerable if they are at risk of intimidation. Should a witness or victim be deemed vulnerable and their ability to provide accurate and reliable evidence then consideration should be made to their eligibility for support from a Registered Intermediary. A Registered Intermediary is a communication specialist who specifically supports individuals with communication difficulties to give their best evidence. Registered Intermediaries are often used for people with needs based on their age, with a learning or physical disability, or mental health disorder (MoJ, 2020).

It is important that the police correctly identify whether a victim or witnesses is vulnerable in the case files submitted to the CPS so that the following can be achieved:

- The court is aware of all circumstances around the case which can have a direct impact on factors such as sentencing decisions
- Any potential risks posed to victims or witnesses are identified by the court
- Victims and witnesses are enabled to provide their best evidence

It is essential that the police are able to recognize a victim or witness's vulnerability. Knowledge of a victim or witness's vulnerability can support an officer in their decision of whether to apply for Special Measures which are provisions, such as the method of giving evidence (eg televised from another location or the ability to give evidence by prior statement), to protect the victim or witness and enable them to give their best evidence. The application to the court for Special Measures to be put in place is reliant on the CPS Prosecutor making an application to the court based on the information regarding the needs of the vulnerable witnesses and victims identified by the police.

20.3.1 The influences of risk factors on vulnerability

In the context of vulnerability, a risk factor can be considered as any factor associated with the increased likelihood of a behaviour that usually has negative consequences (Hall and Lynskey, 2020). There are various ways of classifying risk factors for vulnerability, such as personal; situational; static; and dynamic. Similar terms are also used in assessing the likelihood of reoffending. There are also 'protective factors' that reduce the impact of a risk behaviour and help individuals to desist from engaging in potentially harmful behaviour, and/or promote an alternative pathway.

The factors that lead to a person becoming vulnerable and at risk are undoubtedly complex, and inter-relate with certain risks of encountering circumstances that could lead to harm. Much of the research that has been conducted has identified correlations between certain factors and risk, although a statistical correlation does not prove that a particular factor actually caused the harm. Further detailed work would be needed to establish any cause and effect.

In 2021 the College of Policing produced a paper entitled *Recognising and Responding to Vulnerability-related Risks* which refreshed an earlier paper *Vulnerability: A Review of Reviews* that summarized findings from research on factors associated with increased vulnerability (CoP, 2021h). Nineteen studies were included within the first review and related to a range of harms including becoming a victim of CSE, domestic violence, bullying, gang involvement, youth violence, and mental health crises (particularly suicidal behaviour).

The review established that certain personal and situational/environmental factors have a large individual impact on the risk or vulnerability of a person to harm, and that some risk factors appear to be common to a range of harms. However specific risk factors do not necessarily make a person vulnerable to particular types of harm. The degree of influence of particular factors also depends on context and the interaction with other factors, particularly the interaction between personal and situational factors. There is evidence that people with a high number of risk factors are likely to have a greatly increased vulnerability to harm.

It also seems that a person who has been a victim of certain types of harm becomes more vulnerable and, is then at increased risk of suffering other types of harm. For example, there is evidence that being a victim of child abuse increases the risk of becoming a victim of CSE, domestic abuse, and suicide. In some cases, it also seems that if a person has been a victim of certain types of harm this may increase the risk of him/her then becoming a perpetrator. It is difficult to disentangle these effects, and the mechanism by which this occurs is undoubtedly complex.

From the reviews it is clear that there are gaps in our understanding of how personal and situational factors contribute to an individual's vulnerability. For the frontline officer trying to identify vulnerability during an encounter, it would be ideal if there was some standard test or procedure that could be followed to identify the person's susceptibility to harm. However, this seems unlikely due to the wide range of risk factors, and the fact that many factors are difficult to identify during initial contact. It would be difficult to develop a high-quality risk assessment for vulnerability at initial contact that covers all situations.

To conclude, for effective assessments of risk of harm, police officers and staff need a good understanding of vulnerability, what evidences vulnerability, and good communications skills to elicit information. They also need the tools to support informed decision making.

20.4 Factors Associated with Vulnerability

The factors that may lead to a person becoming vulnerable can be classified as personal and situational factors (see Innes and Innes, 2013 who appear to have introduced this form of classification). Personal factors include age, disability, sexual orientation, religion, mental health, gender, and ethnicity. Many of these factors are not within the person's control. Situational factors include adverse family circumstances, adverse community circumstances, being under the coercive control of others, subject to grooming, having an illegal immigrant status, isolation, lack of support, language barriers, and poverty. Personal and situational factors both interact within and between themselves to increase or decrease the extent of risk.

20.4.1 Static and dynamic risk factors

Risk factors can also be classified as static or dynamic (Innes and Innes, 2013). Static risk factors (for example age, sex, offence history, health record) do not change over time. Dynamic factors are variable (for example drug use, employment status, traumatic events) and by definition could change with time, though many such factors might seem beyond the control of the individual. In terms of assessing future risks for an individual, the consideration of static factors alone has proved insufficient. This should be no surprise, given the interplay between personality, background, and current circumstances. A combination of static and dynamic factors must be used to increase the accuracy of predictions about risk. Examples of risk factors for children include:

- Previous abuse or neglect
- Parental substance misuse
- Domestic abuse
- Known or suspected sex offenders involved with the family

- Known or suspected violent offenders involved with the family
- Persons known or suspected of having seriously neglected children and young people previously
- Mental illness or serious mental health problems in caregivers
- Economic and social disadvantage
- Evidence of significant debt
- Young parents
- Parents and carers with physical disabilities
- Parents and carers who have unrealistic expectations of their child

It is important to understand that the relationship between the situational factors and a person's own characteristics and vulnerabilities may lead to harm and risk for an individual.

TASK 1 Consider the list of risk factors above. Identify three static risk factors and three dynamic risk factors from the list and apply them to the following scenario:

You are called to an address after a report of a disturbance made by neighbours. Upon your arrival Person A, who opened the door, appeared to be unharmed and calm in their demeanour, but there are signs of alcohol consumption. You enter the property and see a smashed coffee table in the living room. Person A informs officers that this occurred when their partner fell backwards during an argument and smashed the glass upon impact. The partner is located in the bathroom applying pressure to some injuries and attempting to stop the bleeding. You call for an ambulance to assist. The partner is unwilling to communicate with you and fellow officers despite your best efforts to enquire about the incident and the injuries sustained. You notice bruises on the partner's neck which are a mixture of new and old in their colouration. Upon further inspection of the house you find a seven-year-old child who is visibly upset in a bedroom. The child appears to be in physical good health. Yet the conditions in the room are far from adequate with the bed being a single mattress on the floor without bedsheets. This is not the first time the police have been called out to the address and records show that the family are supported by social workers from the MASH Team.

20.4.2 Personal characteristics and vulnerability

Personal characteristics are those that seem to be 'built-in' and part of our make-up, and include self-esteem, self-efficacy, mental well-being, and self-control. Many will be closely related to the personal and static categories of risk factors mentioned above, but some can be changed following medical treatment or therapy.

Intrinsic factors are very likely to impact our personality and our mental health. Intrinsic characteristics that may lead to a person to being harmed, or placed at risk of harm include:

- Low self-esteem
- Depression
- Anxiety
- Psychotic behaviour
- Being easily influenced
- Being unable to recognize risk
- Being isolated

It is important that when you attend incidents that you can recognize these characteristics in the people you encounter so that any additional help that they need can be identified.

The psychology of each individual is probably influenced by nature (our genetics), by nurture (the environment we have grown up in), and by the interaction between the two.

20.4.3 Childhood events and vulnerability

Children are particularly susceptible to adverse psychological effects from traumatic events, possibly because the brain is developing rapidly during childhood (Royal College of Psychiatrists, 2019). During traumatic experiences, the brain is in a heightened state of stress, and fear-related hormones are activated. Although stress is a normal part of life, when a child is exposed to chronic trauma such as abuse or neglect, the child's brain remains in this heightened pattern of response. This can change the child's emotional, behavioural, and cognitive functioning, in order to maintain survival. Thus, some experiences during childhood have been identified as having the potential to cause long-term psychological effects that could in turn affect the person's overall well-being (Sacks *et al*, 2018). These 'Adverse Childhood Experiences' (ACEs, see Chapman *et al*, 2004) are stressful events occurring in childhood, such as:

- witnessing domestic violence
- parental abandonment (eg, as a result of the separation of parents)
- having a parent or carer with a mental health condition
- being the victim of abuse (physical, sexual, and/or emotional)
- being the victim of neglect (physical and emotional)
- having a member of the household in prison
- growing up in a household in which there are adults with alcohol and drug abuse problems.

Witnessing domestic abuse has a tremendous impact on the lives of children. It can have an impact on mental health, well-being, and physical behaviour (Stanley *et al*, 2010), including experiences of PTSD (Royal College of Psychiatrists, 2019).

Children are not only vulnerable to abuse perpetrated by adults. Child-on-child abuse, formally peer-on-peer abuse, numbers are significantly rising, with the NSPCC receiving a 29 per cent increase in the number of calls received to their National Helpline between 2021 and 2022.

Child-on-child abuse includes, but is not limited to:

- Sexual abuse
- Sexual exploitation
- Physical abuse
- Emotional abuse
- Bullying (online and offline)
- Relationship abuse

Children are often used to groom other children for the purpose of exploitation by adults involved in criminal activity (OFSTED, 2019). This could be for offences relating to county lines and drugs and even sexual exploitation (Windle *et al*, 2020). One of the challenges in recognizing vulnerability, even in children, can relate to gender, despite the modern and progressive times in which we live. Society still maintains a degree of social scripts and schema that determine how we perceive harm and vulnerability. Research has shown that adults perceive sexual abuse committed against boys as being less harmful than sexual abuse committed against girls (Bradbury and Martellozzo, 2021; Denov, 2004). In addition to this, people perceive child abuse, perpetrated by women, as being less harmful than men, especially if the woman was attractive (Mackelprang and Becker, 2015; Bradbury and Martellozzo, 2021).

Processing Policing

20.4.4 Poverty

Poverty has been found to be a significant factor for maltreatment of children, and for children being placed on child protection plans (Bywaters *et al,* 2016), and also interacts with other factors in the parental background and family environments (Sidebotham and Heron, 2006). Another UK study followed a small group of children who had been identified before their first birthday as likely to suffer significant harm before reaching eight years age (Lumba-Brown *et al*, 2018). This study found that poverty, unemployment, poor housing, isolation, living in dangerous or hostile neighbourhoods, and parental physical and mental health problems all increased the stressors in families, and made the recurrence of factors associated with child maltreatment (eg, domestic violence, substance abuse) more likely.

20.4.5 Disability

As police officers, being at the frontline of the Criminal Justice System, the likelihood of interaction with individuals with a physical or intellectual disability is common (Gulati *et al*, 2020).

Research has shown that individuals who have a disability are more at risk of victimization than those who do not. The Office of National Statistics revealed in their 2022 Report, titled *Disability and Crime,* that this was indeed the case with those suffering from social and behavioural difficulties, Autism Spectrum Disorder (ASD) being the most commonly targeted for Antisocial Behaviour (59.8 per cent). Female and disabled people were more than twice as likely to experience domestic abuse and sexual assault than non-disabled persons of either gender.

When it comes to disabled children, they are significantly more likely to become victims of physical or emotional neglect (NSPCC, 2022b) with one in 10 experiencing some form of sexual violence (Fang *et al*, 2022).

Despite the high correlation between victimization and disability, such groups still encountered a significant number of challenges when engaging with the Criminal Justice System, especially during police investigations (Olsen *et al*, 2018; Åker and Johnson, 2020). This is often due to the nature of their impairments and the capability, or perception of their credibility, as reliable witnesses (Bull, 2010). In cases of sexual abuse, there is often very little physical evidence, only the account of the victim. The credibility and completeness of the account plays a significant determinant of the existence of evidence to uphold a complaint (Lumba-Brown *et al*, 2018).

20.5 Vulnerable People with Mental Ill Health

Some of the most vulnerable people police will encounter are people with mental ill health, learning disabilities, or a developmental condition (CoP, 2022b). Under PACE Code C, if an officer suspects that they are dealing with a person who may be 'vulnerable' they must be treated as such for the purposes of the Code (see Annex E for provisions), unless there is clear evidence to the contrary. 'Vulnerable' people under Code C include those who because of a 'mental health condition or mental disorder' may: have difficulty understanding or communicating effectively with police procedures; appear not to understand the questions asked or what they have been told; and appear prone to confusion, provide unreliable or incriminating evidence without meaning to, or readily agree to suggestions made to them without protest (see para 1.13(d) and Notes 1G and 1GB for these criteria and Dehaghani (2019) for a discussion about the concept of vulnerability).

Mental disorder under the Mental Health Act (MHA) 1983 is defined as 'any disorder or disability of the mind'. This can include a range of clinically recognized conditions including schizophrenia, bipolar disorder, personality and anxiety/stress-related disorders. For the clinically recognized conditions that fall within the meaning of mental disorder under Code C, para 1.13(d), see the MHA Code of Practice (Department of Health, 2015, p 26). Mental disorders should not be confused with learning disabilities, which cover a wide range of conditions with 'significant impairment of intelligence and social functioning' (s 1(4) of the MHA 1983).

Processing Policing

Vulnerable people may present in a variety of ways and it is important that you use your training to identify when someone needs further assessment or support. People with mental ill health may be difficult to identify because of a reluctance to share personal health information with the police. Some vulnerable people who 'present well' to the police have been found not to receive the support and protections they are entitled to (Dehaghani, 2019). The College of Policing APP provides comprehensive guidance on responding to people with mental health problems and/or learning disabilities (CoP, 2022b). Another good guidance document comes from MIND and Victim Support (2013).

Here, we will examine the relevant legislation, particularly the MHA 1983 (as amended by the MHA 2007 and the Policing and Crime Act (PCA) 2017) and the related Code of Practice (Department of Health, 2015), alongside the Mental Capacity Act (MCA) 2005 (as amended by the Mental Capacity (Amendment) Act 2019) and its related Code of Practice (Department for Constitutional Affairs, 2007). The MHA 1983 regulates the assessment, treatment, and rights of people with a mental disorder, while the MCA 2005 is used if a person is incapable of making a decision and requires care for any other reason, such as a medical condition. The scenario in 20.5.4 illustrates this further. Police training will include guidance on how to recognize the symptoms of mental ill health, and if you are undertaking the PCDA or DHEP further advice is provided through NCALT.

20.5.1 Interacting with people who may be vulnerable

As a police officer, you will encounter many people who have mental ill health or learning disabilities. These disabilities may sometimes mean that the person has difficulty in understanding or communicating effectively with police procedures. They may also find their experience of police contact more distressing and bewildering than those without mental ill health and/or learning disabilities (Marshall-Tate, 2019). Any contact with people in your role as a police officer therefore requires good communication (see Chapter 8).

As there is a range of clinically recognized mental health conditions, officers need to assess each situation on an individual basis to determine how best to intervene. Trainee police officers will be expected to learn how to deal with these situations effectively and maintain their own and others' safety.

Individuals with learning disabilities can be especially vulnerable and may have a limited understanding of the criminal justice system. Some may also have difficulty recalling events, understanding questions, and communicating effectively. Others may acquiesce to suggestions of events and actions in order to appease the interviewer. It is therefore very important that individuals with learning disabilities are identified when giving witness statements, and that this information is passed to the CPS. A doctor or a mental health practitioner can help to determine whether an individual has a learning disability.

When you are dealing with people with mental ill health or learning disabilities, the techniques you use may need to be adjusted. The College of Policing (2022b) advises that officers try to treat people in the least coercive manner, fairly and with respect, with compassion and patience, and to encourage their active participation so they feel they 'have a voice'. You should avoid any physical contact unless you are sure that it will not be perceived as threatening. Consider taking a step backwards to show that you are giving the person space, move slowly and as little as possible, but keep your hands visible. Make a visual check for weapons and remove anything dangerous from the individual's reach. You should maintain an adequate distance and may want to remove your headwear as this may be seen as threatening. You should explain what you are doing and repeat it to ensure that you are being understood. Use a calm, low-pitched tone, short sentences, and simple language and reassure the individual of what you are trying to achieve.

If you need to call for further assistance, ask for lights and sirens to be turned off. Ensure that only one officer talks at a time, do not whisper to your colleagues, and avoid using your radio where possible. Any onlookers should be removed from the scene. There are occasions when you may need to prevent a person experiencing mental ill health from engaging in harmful behaviour. You may need to use force to do this but make sure that it is only as a last resort and that it is absolutely necessary and proportionate in the circumstances. Before using any force, however, consideration should be given to the strategies described above to try and deescalate the situation.

The individual may carry a medical information card, a Crisis card (eg, if they find it difficult to express things clearly), or a Medic Alert bracelet. These could provide useful information and the individual should be asked about them. Other sources of information include the person who reported the incident, the call handler, any medical or support staff available at the scene, and CCTV footage. Family members and carers can also provide important information to establish the best way to engage with a person. However, police officers should not share information with these other people without prior consent from the person in question, unless not sharing would conflict with statutory duties to protect that person or others, hamper the prevention or investigation of a crime, or put a child at risk of significant harm or an adult at risk of serious harm.

You should familiarize yourself with any local policies and multi-agency protocols between the police and health services to ensure that you provide fair and adequate treatment of individuals experiencing mental ill health. It is important that you understand what services are available in your area for those who require more specialist support so that you can make appropriate decisions about how to respond. Liaison and Diversion (L&D) services, which may include services such as 'street triage', should now be available in all police areas.

Where a person is in police custody and appears to have a mental disorder and/or is vulnerable, an Appropriate Adult (AA) must be called (13.8.2.2). The aim of an AA is to help safeguard the rights of vulnerable people in police custody. AAs can be people known to the person in police detention but can also be a trained person from an organized AA scheme. To understand more about the AA role, see <https://www.appropriateadult.org.uk/>.

20.5.2 Responding to incidents relating to mental ill health

Many people suffer from mental ill health and cope well with their everyday lives. The police, however, may become involved if the person's immediate safety, or the safety of others, is in doubt. Under the MHA 1983, the police have powers to detain a person who is suspected of having a mental disorder and felt to be a possible risk to themselves or others in a place of safety. The procedure and the police powers depend on whether the person is located in a private dwelling. If the person is also suspected of committing an offence, there may be reasons that could justify an arrest, but this is not necessarily the most appropriate way of dealing with mental ill health.

A police officer can initially talk with the person to try to assess the situation and any issues relating to their mental health. If they seem to need help and are receptive, the police can explain the need for assessment and/or treatment and see if friends or relatives can be contacted. If there is a physical medical emergency, then treatment for this should be addressed first. Similarly, if a person is confused or starts to become aggressive due to an underlying medical condition (such as diabetes or a stroke), this should be treated as a medical emergency.

After talking with the person, the police officer might conclude that there are no significant issues relating to mental health but, if a breach of the peace seems likely, the person can be detained to prevent this. A person can be 'sectioned' for admission to hospital if they seem to need urgent mental health treatment but will not seek it voluntarily and present a danger to themselves or to others. A police officer may be asked to help to remove the person to hospital (see 20.5.3.1), by force if necessary (s 6 of the MHA 1983). A 'section application form' must be completed and signed prior to any such police involvement.

20.5.3 Powers relating to a place of safety

Sections 135 and 136 of the MHA 1983 (as amended by the PCA 2017) permit the police to detain a person who is suspected to have a mental disorder and is in need of immediate care or control, in a place of safety. Exercising place of safety powers should be used only as a final resort. Note that significant changes to place of safety powers under the MHA 1983 were introduced by the PCA 2017 and useful information about how to interpret these changes is set out in Department of Health (2017) guidance.

The police are sometimes called to a private residence to help a person with mental disorder. In the first instance, the officers should try and communicate with the person to reach some agreement on how to help. However, there may be occasions where the police need to use s 135 of the MHA 1983 to allow them to enter and search a premises in order to detain a person thought to have a mental disorder in a place of safety. A warrant issued by a magistrate is required and an Approved Mental Health Professional (AMHP) should be present. The police can also use force to enter premises if there is a breach of the peace, or if the entry is necessary to save life or limb, or to prevent serious damage to property.

If the person seems to need help but does not agree to it, an AMHP should coordinate the process of assessment and establish if detention under the MHA is appropriate. The police should remain until the AMHP has taken responsibility for carrying out an assessment (Code of Practice, para 14.41). Police officers have no obligation to stay for the assessment unless it is unsafe to leave (Code of Practice, para 16.34). The AMHP will arrange transport to hospital if required.

While s 135 powers require a warrant, s 136 powers do not. If the police suspect that a person, located anywhere other than in a private dwelling (and its associated buildings or grounds) (see s 136(1A) for specific definitions), has a mental disorder and requires immediate care and control, they can remove them to (or keep them at) a place of safety. This means that s 136 powers can be used in private spaces to which the public has access, such as railways, rooftops (of commercial premises), offices, schools, and hospitals. Where practicable, police officers should consult with one of the health professionals listed in s 136(1C) before exercising a s 136 power. The purpose of this consultation is to obtain information and advice relating to mental health which can be used to inform the officer's decision-making. Officers are not expected to canvass mental health services for advice but should familiarize themselves with the local arrangements in place. These may be part of street triage initiatives, through a control centre, or links to local mental health services. It is recognized that communication problems (ie, signal dead zones) might sometimes make consultation impracticable (Department of Health, 2017). Where consultation takes place, this should be recorded, and a note should be taken about the advice given and who gave it.

20.5.3.1 Removal to, and detention in, a place of safety

A person experiencing a mental health crisis should be kept at, or taken to, a place of safety that best meets their needs. A place of safety could include social services residential accommodation, a hospital, a police station, an independent hospital, or a care home. Under the PCA 2017, people can be kept at, as well as removed to, a place of safety (ie, a person at home can now be kept there for the purposes of assessment under s 135 rather than having to be removed). If a person needs to be transported to a place of safety, then hospital or ambulance transport should be used (as set out in agreed local policies) (MHA Code of Practice, para 14.48). Police transport should only be used in cases of extreme urgency or where there is a risk of violence (MHA Code of Practice, para 16.32).

The detention period under ss 135 and 136 must not exceed 36 hours from the time of arrival in the first place of safety. This is comprised of a maximum period of detention for 24 hours, with a possible extension for a further 12 hours, should the assessment of the detained person not have been possible, or is still ongoing, within the initial time period (ss 135(3ZA), 136(2A), and 136B).

20.5.3.2 A police station as a place of safety

Police station cells can only be used as a place of safety for adults in certain circumstances and in accordance with the Mental Health Act 1983 (Places of Safety) Regulations 2017. Police cells must never be used for a person under the age of 18 years. A person who is kept in a police cell as a place of safety for lack of a suitable alternative should not be detained there for more than 24 hours (MHA Code of Practice, para 16.40). Also note that if a detained person is excluded from a health-based place of safety and taken to a police station, the name of the person who made the exclusion decision (and the reasons for it) must be recorded (MHA Code of Practice, para 16.62).

Once in a place of safety, the MHA Code of Practice (para 14.67) recommends that a doctor (approved under s 12 of the MHA) and an AMHP should attend within three hours. Note also that when a person is taken to a police station as a place of safety under the MHA, then PACE Code C (with the exception of s 15) applies even if the person has not been arrested (MHA Code of Practice, para 16.66). That person would therefore have the same rights as a person who has been arrested and a police officer would have the power to search them under s 32 of the PACE Act 1984 (see para 16.68). If the person is also suspected of having committed an offence, they may be interviewed as part of an investigation. If this is the case, the police must ensure that an AA is arranged.

20.5.4 The Mental Capacity Act 2005

Consider the following scenario:

> Two police officers have been asked by a paramedic team to attend a bedsit in town. An extremely thin and naked individual is lying in bed with several open wounds on their body which look as if they could have been caused by hypodermic needles. They appear to be heavily intoxicated and are suspected of using controlled drugs. Blood-filled syringes are strewn all around the bed and the floor of the room and the person appears to be bleeding from body orifices. The police officers consider the health and safety of the people around them as a priority, so they and the paramedics don protective clothing and remove dangerous and contagious items to a toxic chemical receptacle and a 'sharps box'. The paramedics try to persuade the individual to go to hospital but every time they get close, the person mumbles and moves away violently. The police officers also try to communicate, but without success. They must now decide how to help this person, and under which legislation.

The Mental Capacity Act 2005 (MCA) provides a broad legal framework which aims to protect vulnerable people aged 16 years or over (s 2(5)) who do not have the capacity to make their own decisions. This could be through illness, unconsciousness, alcohol, drugs, or a severe learning disability that has been present since birth. The Act also empowers and offers protection to carers and others (such as police officers) who are involved in protecting people who may be vulnerable. The MCA may be necessary in emergency situations when the police come across someone who does not have mental capacity to make decisions and may be at significant risk if action is not taken on their behalf. Section 5 of the MCA provides the power to carry out acts related to the care or treatment (including restraint) of a person who lacks capacity. The MCA Code of Practice (Department for Constitutional Affairs, 2007) provides guidance on how the Act should be interpreted.

The Mental Capacity (Amendment) Act 2019 introduced the concept of Liberty Protection Safeguards (LPS) to replace the Deprivation of Liberty Safeguards scheme (DoLS). LPS aim to provide protection for those aged 16 and over who are, or need to be, deprived of their liberty in order to facilitate care or treatment and lack mental capacity to consent to such arrangements. This includes people who have a mental disorder, cannot make decisions for themselves regarding their care, and may put themselves in situations of harm (eg, due to an advanced state of dementia).

In the circumstance described in the scenario, s 136 powers under the MHA cannot be used because they do not apply to private dwellings, and also because the person is in need of immediate medical care. Although they might be suffering from a temporary mental disorder, the immediate concern is their apparent inability to make a decision about their medical care. The MCA 2005 can be used in these circumstances to facilitate making arrangements for transporting the person to hospital for medical treatment. Had the situation been less urgent, the officers could have either requested that an AHMP applied for a warrant to remove the individual to a place of safety under s 135 of the MHA 1983 or explored if it was appropriate for the AMHP to make an urgent application under s 4 of the MHA 1983 (CoP, 2022b).

20.5.4.1 General principles underlying the Mental Capacity Act 2005

Section 1(1) of the MCA provides some key principles, for example that a person:

- must be assumed to have capacity unless it can be established otherwise (s 1(2));
- must not be treated as unable to make a decision unless all practicable steps to help them to do so have been without success (s 1(3)); and
- must not be treated as if they are unable to make a decision merely because they have previously made a decision that is thought to be unwise (s 1(4)).

The Act also specifies that any decision or action that is taken must be in the person's best interests (s 1(5)) and must avoid (as far as possible) interfering with their rights and freedom (s 1(6)).

20.5.4.2 Judging a person's mental capacity

In this context, 'capacity' is the ability to take in information and use that information to make decisions. A lack of capacity could be caused by an impairment or disturbance in the functioning of the mind or brain (s 2(1) of the MCA), for example through a learning disability, dementia, brain damage, or acute confusion caused by drugs or another noxious substance. The lack of capacity could be permanent or temporary (s 2(2)). Any evaluation can only be made on the balance of probabilities.

The process of judging a person's capacity focuses on their ability to make decisions and is regulated by s 3 of the MCA 2005. In determining capacity, no reference can be made to the person's age or appearance, nor should any unjustified assumptions be made based solely on the person's condition or behaviour (s 2(3)). A functional test may be used to check, for example, if they are able to understand and retain any information relevant to a decision, use information to help make a decision, or inform another person of a decision (CoP, 2022b). The communication used by either party could include talking, writing or typed text, a sign language, or other gestures.

20.5.4.3 Acting on behalf of a person who lacks capacity

Under s 4 of the MCA, the decision made, and any subsequent action must be in the person's best interests. They must be encouraged to participate as fully as possible in any act or decision, and all reasonably practicable steps should be taken to achieve this. The likelihood of the person having the capacity to make the decision at some point in the future must be considered, and if there is no immediate need to make a particular decision and they are likely to regain the capacity to make the decision, then it should be delayed until they have sufficiently recovered.

If the person cannot make decisions and therefore lacks capacity, a decision might need to be made on their behalf. As far as possible, the person's wishes and feelings should be considered, especially their usual beliefs and values (if known). The views of the following people should also be taken into account:

- their carer;
- anyone else they would like to be consulted; and/or
- anyone with power of attorney or a deputy appointed by a court.

Actions carried out in connection with the care or treatment of a person do not incur any liability (s 5) if, prior to those acts, reasonable steps were taken to establish that the person lacked capacity and it was reasonably believed that the actions were in the person's best interests. If a decision relates to life-sustaining treatment, any consideration that it would be better if the person were allowed to die should be avoided.

If the actions are resisted (despite efforts to communicate and to encourage participation), then restraint may be needed. But there must be a reasonable belief that restraint has to be used to prevent harm to the person and the restraint must be proportional (s 6). Actions defined as restraint under s 6 include using force (or threatening to use it) in order to apply care or treatment and restricting a person's liberty of movement, whether or not they resist. It does not include depriving a person of their liberty (within the meaning of Article 5 of the European Convention on Human Rights) or contravening a decision made by a court or a person with a relevant power of attorney.

20.5.4.4 Applying the Mental Capacity Act 2005

In the illustrative scenario at the start of 20.5.4, all practicable steps to help this individual have been unsuccessful. The attending police officers and paramedics believe they need urgent treatment in hospital. On the balance of probabilities, the person is suffering from acute confusion which has caused an impairment or disturbance of mind or brain. The individual is therefore unlikely to have the capacity to make the decision to go to hospital and appears to be incapable of understanding the information relevant to the decision—ie, that they are seriously ill and need treatment. There is no information pertaining to family, friends, or carers, and no indication of how they might have wished to be treated when they had decision-making capacity. The police officers and paramedics have taken all reasonable steps required to establish that this individual lacks capacity and cannot make the relevant decision. Therefore, they need to make a decision on their behalf. The least restrictive action or decision to avoid interfering with any rights and freedom is to ensure they receive hospital treatment. They judge that the least restraint required under the circumstances is to help them onto a stretcher for transportation to hospital.

20.5.4.5 Ill-treatment or neglect of a person who lacks capacity

Some people have particular caring or legal responsibilities for an individual who lacks capacity and may also have a power of attorney. It is an offence under s 44 of the MCA for any such carer or responsible person to ill-treat or willfully neglect the person. This includes physical, psychological, financial, domestic, discriminatory, and sexual abuse.

The offence is triable either way and the penalty is a fine or imprisonment (summarily 12 months and five years on indictment).

TASK 2

What is your local police service policy on the use of s 136 MHA powers?

A police officer is called to the home of the parents of a young person (over 18) who seems to be suffering from a mental disorder. On arrival, the parents inform the officer that they are in a bedroom and holding the door handle to stop anyone opening the door. Using the minimum force necessary (and limiting your answers to the Mental Health Act 1983):

(a) how could the officer gain entrance for the parents, and
(b) what options are available should the officer decide the young person needs medical attention in relation to their apparent mental disorder?

20.6 Vulnerability and Abuse

If you are a trainee police officer then it is important that you are able to recognize the signs of abuse in adults and children when attending incidents, including those that, on first impression, may be unrelated to public protection.

The various types of abuse include:

- physical abuse;
- domestic violence;
- sexual abuse;
- psychological or emotional abuse (eg as used to coerce and control);
- financial and material abuse such as restricting sufficient access to money;
- modern slavery (eg as part of forced labour);
- discrimination (for example on grounds of sexual orientation);
- organizational/institutional abuse (eg in a care home for people with dementia); and
- neglect or acts of omission (eg of children).

Adults with care and support needs (due to age or disability for example) are more likely to be abused or neglected (Oktay and Tompkins, 2004). They may also be much less likely to identify their experiences as abuse, or to report it particularly if they have communication difficulties. Some victims may not even be aware that they are being abused, and this is especially likely if they have a cognitive impairment. Abusers may try to prevent police access to the victim, and signs of abuse can often be difficult to detect. The abuse of vulnerable adults is covered in 19.11 in more detail.

20.6.1 Who perpetrates abuse and why?

Potentially any person could cause harm to any other person, either someone known to the victim or a stranger. The abuser could be a child, young person or adult, and could be a family member, friend, or even a professional.

As you will learn when you study criminological theory, there is no one reason why people commit crime, and likewise there is no single reason why people are abusive towards others (Martellozzo, 2013). For example, when considering abuse where the victim is female and the offender is male, it is widely recognized that such abuse, whether it is physical, sexual, or emotional, is linked to the need for power and control over the victim, rather than being the result of a temporary loss of control by the offender (Roberts and Price, 2019). Emotional and psychological abuse may be used to establish control, whilst physical and sexual abuse can further establish and then reinforce it (Rakovec-Felser, 2014).

While it is important to note that women commit abuse against men, other women, and children, violence committed by men against women is the probably the most common form of abusive behaviour and is certainly the most reported. While debates concerning the causes of abuse by men against women are beyond the scope of this book, some explanations suggest that societal structures could underly this, for example patriarchy (the social structure where men are more powerful and receive disproportionate benefits).

Factors such as culture, age, ethnicity, gender, disability and/or sexuality of the victim and offender, and other components of a person's identity also contribute to our understanding of why the abuse has happened and how it has impacted the victim and those around them.

Regrettably and possibly inevitably, some police officers will commit abuse; constabularies across England and Wales received 436 allegations of abuse of power for a sexual purpose by police personnel over a two-year period (Herald Scotland, 2017). The complaints were made against 306 police officers, 20 PCSOs, and eight staff members, but the HMICFRS inspectors believed the problem is far greater. If you are a trainee police officer, you will be expected to understand the importance of appropriate professional conduct when encountering individuals who are, or may be, vulnerable. If you have any concerns about a colleague in relation to this you are obliged under the Code of Ethics to report it by contacting your Professional Standards Department, or through the confidential reporting system via your constabulary intranet home page. One of the behaviours expected of a trainee officer undertaking the PCDA is also to 'maintain the highest standards of professionalism [. . .] including challenging others where appropriate' (Institute for Apprenticeships and Technical Education, 2018b).

20.6.2 People in positions of authority and power who abuse

A person in a position of authority is anyone who has a job or title that puts a person in control of other people. The abuse may take place within the workplace, or outside. Some examples of common positions of authority are:

- a teacher
- a public figure (actors, musicians, royals)
- a religious figure
- a manager, CEO
- a political leader
- a military leader
- a doctor
- a police officer

Please note that in child protection, 'position of trust' is a legal term that refers to certain roles and settings where an adult has regular and direct contact with children. Examples of positions of trust include:

- teachers
- care workers
- youth justice workers
- social workers
- doctors

In England, Wales, and Northern Ireland changes to the law under the Police, Crime, Sentencing and Courts Act 2022 extend the definition to include:

- faith group leaders
- sports coaches

Abusive people gain and maintain power over their victim with controlling or coercive behaviour, and proceed to subject that person to psychological, physical, sexual, or financial abuse. If abuse is not reported and stopped, it can continue for years, and may be encouraged by those surrounding the abuser. Not taking action to stop the abuse is a form of abuse itself.

Although most police officers are law-abiding citizens and work hard to keep the community safe, there have been an unfortunate number of cases where there have been abuses of power.

A key area of focus in the national framework is responding unequivocally to allegations of police-perpetrated abuse and addressing sexism and misogyny within policing.

Data released in 2023, as part of the performance assessment, shows that during the period 1 October 2021 to 31 March 2022, 653 conduct cases against 672 individuals were flagged as relating to violence against women and girls by police services in England and Wales as well as the British Transport Police (BTP). In the same period, 524 public complaint cases against 867 individuals were recorded. In total this equates to 0.7 per cent of the police workforce employed in March 2022.

Police officers are expected to demonstrate the highest standards of personal and professional conduct. When officers break the law and abuse their position for their own benefit, they undermine public confidence in policing and the justice system.

20.7 Impact of Abuse on Victims

Independent of who the abuser might be, the impact that abuse has on victims is enormous and long term. There is a significant volume of research available which describes the experiences and the impact of different types of abuse on victims, according to gender, culture, ethnicity, and age. It is important that you bear in mind that every experience of abuse is different, and the long-term impact will therefore vary from person to person. The effects will depend on the nature of the individual victim, circumstances, and the type of abuse. For example, research by Chandan *et al* (2019) found that women who have been abused by a partner are more likely to experience mental health issues, and Maniglio (2009) found that survivors of child sexual abuse are significantly at risk of a wide range of medical, psychological, behavioural, and sexual disorders in later life. Further details about the impact of child abuse offences and other sexual offences such as rape can be found in Chapter 19.

The psychological consequences and impact of victimization on crime victims can be numerous. For instance, interpersonal crimes like violence and sexual assaults have been found to cause more emotional disturbances such as sleep and eating disorders, feelings of insecurity and fear, and low self-esteem. The table below summarizes some of the psychological, behavioural, and affective consequences of criminal victimization.

Type of consequence	Effects
Psychological	Cognitive meaning shattered (cannot make sense of things; becomes distrusting and withdrawn) Low self-esteem (feeling disempowered; loss of confidence) Self-blame
Emotional	Fear Anger Poor/problematic coping (eg hiding feelings)
Behavioural	Changes in lifestyle Withdrawal from social settings
Physical	Injury from offence Self-harm Suicide
Financial	Loss of earnings Costs of replacing items Excesses

Source: Adapted from Spalek (2006)

Spalek (2006) contends that the potential impact of victimization is mediated by three factors:

- **pre-victimization factors**—static or changeable variables such as age, marital status, employment, education, or sexuality;
- **victimization factors**—the situational context of victimization; for example, if an offence occurs in an environment considered safe, such as at home or while in someone's care, the effect is greater;
- **post-victimization factors**—support, intervention, and so on can help victims cope.

One of the greatest challenges to identifying vulnerable children who are or who have been victims of child abuse lies in the barriers to disclosure. Research led by the Royal Commission into Institutional Responses to Child Sexual Abuse (Royal Commission, 2017) revealed that two-thirds of children never disclose their abuse during their childhood, of which only 25 per cent go on to disclose as adults. The reasons why children do not disclose their abuse may include reasons such as:

- Fear of not being believed, often as a result of manipulation by the abuser
- Fear of reprisal from the abuser
- Having no one to disclose to as they are isolated—eg institutional abuse
- Feelings of embarrassment, shame, and guilt (includes grooming)
- Being unaware that they are experiencing abuse as it has been normalized in their lives
- Having no one listen on previous attempts to disclose
- Fear of being separated from family
- Inhibition due to the shock and trauma of the abuse experienced
- Fear of any disclosure affecting any future care placement

It is important to understand and acknowledge that no two experiences of trauma related to child abuse are the same. There are many ways in which trauma, experienced as a consequence of child abuse, can have an impact on a person as an adult. Trauma is the consequence of experiencing frightening, upsetting, and stressful events (Rivas *et al*, 2020). It can result in Post-Traumatic Stress Disorder (PTSD) and this can be exhibited in many ways which include but are not limited to:

- Difficulty maintaining relationships
- Low self-esteem and self-worth

- Anxiety and depression
- Self harm
- Substance abuse
- Anger
- Dissociative Identity Disorder
- Flashbacks
- Dissociative Amnesia

These factors make survivors of child abuse vulnerable as adults to repeat victimizations of sexual abuse. The Office of National Statistics reported that 31 per cent of adults who experienced child sexual abuse reported experiencing sexual abuse as an adult (ONS, 2017), in comparison to only 7 per cent of adults who had had no childhood experience of abuse. The same data collection also revealed that women who experience child abuse are more vulnerable to sexual abuse as an adult than male survivors, at a rate of 43 per cent for women and 11 per cent for men.

Male victims of physical and sexual abuse have many of the same effects as women, but there are also some different challenges that they may face based on gender stereotyping and labelling. Some of their feelings of shame may be caused by the belief that they should be strong or that they have been emasculated by their inability to fight off their abuser (Sivagurunathan *et al*, 2019). This sense of shame can also be compounded by the physiological responses that they may have received during the abuse. Male victims have reported that other factors, such as being viewed as homosexual or concerns that they might become abusers themselves, significantly impacted on their willingness to come forward and disclose abuse (Alaggia *et al*, 2017). See Chapter 19 for discussion of poly- and repeat victimization.

20.8 Vulnerability and Anti-Social Behaviour (ASB)

There is evidence that some people and communities are more likely to being targets of anti-social behaviour, and suffer particularly negative effects. Innes and Innes (2013) carried out a large study on the impacts of ASB upon victims, and the police response to such incidents. The researchers assessed the vulnerability and the associated risks for around ten thousand incidents, and the results suggested that people and communities with lower social, economic, and psychological resilience are affected more than others and also found it more difficult to deal with the effects of being targeted.

Some individuals are more vulnerable and at risk than others. The ability to contact the correct person within an organization and being able to communicate clearly, for example, will also vary from person to person; some people will find this very daunting, and others may not think it worth even trying. In the Innes and Innes study, 45 per cent of the most acute category of repeat and vulnerable ASB victims viewed their call to police as having made 'no difference' while only 35 per cent of victims who were neither repeat victims nor vulnerable felt that way. Whilst the needs of repeat or vulnerable victims may often be well met by police, they are still more likely to fall through the net.

20.8.1 Vulnerability and offending

Some types of vulnerability can make a person more susceptible to manipulation or intimidation (psychologically or physically). They may be targeted by criminals and extremists for involvement in acts of crime, or to support criminal activity. Some individuals may not even be aware of having been 'recruited' in this way, due to their particular vulnerability, so it is important to recognize their potential vulnerabilities and the risk of exploitation and radicalization. The types of crime can range from encouraging a person with learning difficulties to commit theft such as shoplifting to order, through to utilizing vulnerable people to become involved in county lines and cuckooing, child sexual exploitation, people trafficking, and radicalizing individuals to commit acts of terrorism (Home Office, 2018f). County lines are covered in 21.7, CSE in 24.7.6 and trafficking in 19.12.

Vulnerable persons at risk of radicalization can be either adults or children. They are defined as being those individuals who have characteristics that make them more susceptible to being radicalized and exposed to extremist ideologies and environments that enable them

(Clemmow *et al*, 2021). Factors that can increase a person's vulnerability to radicalization are similar to those that make a person vulnerable to crime in general, but with a greater emphasis on isolation and displacement from society. Such factors include:

- Experiencing racism and or discrimination
- Being a victim of a traumatic incident
- Family difficulties
- Low self-esteem
- Struggling with a sense of identity
- Lacking a sense of belonging in a society
- Poor cognitive awareness—impact of actions and empathy

There are also broader external factors that relate to social, political, and environmental conditions that can increase a person's vulnerability to radicalization, such as war or community tensions (Clemmow *et al*, 2021). Terrorist groups deliberately target vulnerable persons in order to promote their narratives therefore it is paramount that multi-agency partnerships work together identify and safeguard those at risk. The CONTEST strategy reflects all aspects of counter-terrorism and within this it is the PREVENT strand which specifically focuses on the prevention of vulnerable people to radicalization (see also Chapter 15).

20.9 Policing and Vulnerability

Police services have been effective at decreasing the recorded levels of so-called traditional volume crime, such as residential burglary, but it is now widely recognized that more needs to be done to protect the vulnerable (Rudd, 2016). Significant changes are occurring to try to ensure that those with particular needs receive the appropriate assistance. For example, a national framework for police, healthcare, and social care professionals (the Serious and Organised Crime Strategy (HM Government, 2018a)) is being put in place to help protect vulnerable adults who go missing from care. The framework provides clear guidance on the responsibilities of each agency, and on what information should be shared in order to carry out the most effective enquiries. There are also plans to introduce a 'licence to practice' for professionals working with vulnerable people, and the 'prevention of vulnerability related crime' has also received attention; the National Police Crime Prevention Strategy includes two intended outcomes that are particularly relevant to vulnerability:

- reduce the threat, harm, and demands associated with crime, anti-social behaviour and other preventable demand; and
- tackle drivers and vulnerabilities associated with victimization

It could be argued that for any police service to be effective in safeguarding the vulnerable, retaining public confidence is crucial. This is rooted in the principles of policing by consent (see 3.2.6). If a victim or witness perceives a lack of support from the police there could be negative consequences for the police and victims/witnesses, and to wider society as well.

When the police attend incidents in circumstances where a person might be vulnerable, they will need to assess the risk, and adapt their communication style as required. If you are undertaking the PCDA or the DHEP then you will be required to demonstrate your ability to safely and lawfully 'communicate effectively, in accordance with the varied needs of differing situations, individuals, groups and communities' (Institute for Apprenticeships and Technical Education, 2018b). We also provide a brief list of some of the legislation and policies that support and guide the police in responding where vulnerability may be a factor at the end of this chapter (see 20.10).

If a person is deemed as being immediately vulnerable and at risk, the extent of the risk must be assessed. Remember that a person may be vulnerable due to many factors such as age, disability, or financial circumstances but these factors in isolation do *not* automatically make a person vulnerable.

It is also important to understand the differences between increased risk and actual vulnerability. If an officer does not understand the difference, they won't be able to make an accurate assessment about the level of risk to a person. In this context, risk is commonly taken to be a function of threats and vulnerability, where a person's vulnerabilities are exploited in order to cause them harm. Thus, threats may exist, but if there are no vulnerabilities and relevant circumstances then there is potentially a lesser risk. Similarly, a person could be vulnerable in one or more of the many ways we have previously identified, but if there is no threat, then there is less or even no risk. Accurately identifying and assessing threats, establishing if a person is vulnerable, and then making an assessment of the level of risk are key to the process.

However, the police service is not the only organization that encounters and deals with persons who are vulnerable (or are at risk of becoming vulnerable). Many other organizations such as health and social services will also be involved, and each will have their own definitions of vulnerability, to help them identify and manage risk. Other agencies are better equipped to deal with certain types of incidents, although the police will often assist (see 20.5). Irrespective of the agencies involved, it is important that individuals are treated fairly and do not suffer discrimination due to vulnerabilities. This is an obligation under s 149 of the Equality Act 2010.

20.9.1 The 'THRIVE' risk management tool applied to vulnerability

The THRIVE risk management tool can be used in many situations and ensures that all relevant considerations are made. As you might expect, THRIVE is an acronym with each letter representing a part of the risk assessment tool. Each part is explained in the table below.

THRIVE	Meaning	Further explanation
Threat	Something (person, object) that is able to cause injury, damage, loss or danger	What is the nature of the overall threat, not only to the victim, but to the immediate family, children, community, and location?
Harm	The form of injury, damage, or danger (physical or psychological)	What is the potential impact of the threat? Consider not just the victim or witnesses, but also the community impact.
Risk	The likely level of risk (eg low, medium, or high)	What risks are obvious, or yet to be determined? What resources and specialist assets are needed to safeguard the victim or community?
Investigation	Is a police investigation needed?	What is the legality, necessity, proportionality of the actions needed in relation to the offence/incident being reported?
Vulnerability	The vulnerability of the people involved	What are the individual or community vulnerabilities? Identify how police partners best safeguard against harm.
Engagement	Determining the rapidity (eg, immediate) and depth (eg, phone investigation) of police response required	What is the best means of engagement in terms of victim safety, and being most effective?

Source: Table based in part on Kent Police, 2017.

Processing Policing

Many police services (eg the West Midlands Police) now use 'THRIVE' (sometimes 'THRIVE+'). This approach to managing risk is derived from the work of Wolpert *et al* (2015) and was originally devised to support professionals responsible for supporting children and young people with mental health problems. Many constabularies now usefully identify THRIVE as part of a policy to become more victim centred in their approach to policing. In some areas THRIVE is used in a range of contexts, such as at the scene of an incident to help an officer assess risk during incidents.

Knowing the elements of THRIVE and how to apply them will assist you in recognizing a person's vulnerabilities. You will then be able to take decisions and actions to reduce the risk of harm (see also the National Decision Model). In this way you are more likely to be able to work in partnership, through taking a problem-solving approach in addressing vulnerability.

20.9.2 Limitations of risk assessments

Before an officer begins any risk assessment of vulnerability it is vitally important that they are familiar with the APP *Identifying, Assessing and Managing Risk* (CoP, 2017e). This provides the official basis for conducting risk assessment and management. However, the possible problems of undertaking risk assessments also need to be considered.

Conducting a risk assessment is a human activity and as such there are a number of possible limitations, such as the person making the assessment:

- does not have full knowledge of the situation (for example the complainant may not have been completely honest)
- will inevitably have their own personal biases
- may have only limited experience and expertise in conducting risk assessments in similar contexts

Risk assessment is therefore an inherently uncertain process, and there may also be conflicting results from different research studies about the significance of particular factors. It is also important to remember that just because certain risk factors exist, it doesn't mean abuse (or other harms) has necessarily taken place. Officers must be aware of these limitations and proceed with caution, with the best available information.

20.9.3 Interacting with a person who may be vulnerable

Policing policies and processes and the consequent interactions with members of the public can have a significant impact on a person, both short and long term. Police officers need to be able to engage and interact effectively with all types of people with all types of vulnerabilities. If the interactions are successful, then ultimately future policing demand could fall due to a reduction in the number of victims and offenders. This is because the impression a person has of the police can influence whether he/she decides to call for help in the future or support an investigation.

Most members of the public will remember any interaction they have with the police, and it will leave a certain impression. Officers should therefore ensure that they:

- communicate a positive attitude towards the person
- really listen to what the person says
- demonstrate respect for the person's opinions (even if the person and the officer disagree!)
- look out for any opportunities to help the person access any support they need

It can sometimes seem that a person has or continues to make the wrong choices in life, but that person might be doing their best under very difficult circumstances. It is difficult for an outsider to judge properly. For a particular person with vulnerabilities, talking to their friends, family, or acquaintances can throw light on the situation, and professional curiosity can also help reveal a fuller picture. As a police officer, you are likely to encounter the most unexpected and unimaginable situations, some of which may be difficult to accept (see Chapter 6 on coping with stress).

People with mental ill-health, learning disabilities, or substance misuse problems need effective help from the police and partner agencies with the relevant responsibilities. Home Office guidance on this (Home Office, 2015e) provides a strategic overview of the range of suitable approaches for police services in England and Wales and partner agencies including the voluntary and community sector. The guidance could apply in a wide range of contexts and help shape appropriate local responses to others who may be deemed vulnerable.

20.9.4 Responding to incidents involving vulnerability—a case study

Here we will examine and explain some of the practicalities surrounding police interaction with people experiencing a vulnerability, using a 'what works' approach.

We will examine a particular scenario:

> Imagine you are a police officer and you have been sent to the home of a person who has complained of receiving numerous letters, cards, and gifts from a co-worker. On the way to the incident, you receive information from your control room that the caller is known to the police as they have made numerous calls about this in the past. These incidents have been closed and finalized with no further action. There are no markers on the caller or on the address. You arrive at the address and notice it is a bungalow with support handrails. When you knock on the door, it is answered by a middle-aged person with a crutch.

With the knowledge that you have so far you must establish your first considerations in relation to the possible vulnerability of the complainant. These considerations will include:

- Is the complainant a 'victim'?
- Are they vulnerable?
- If so, in what way? Consider their care and support needs, and the type of offence.
- What can the property tell us about any vulnerabilities?
- What may the use of a crutch suggest to you about any vulnerabilities?
- Do you need to consider the information provided by the control room of previous police contact?

The person introduces themselves to you as Sam and the person who called the police. They seem a little agitated about the situation and say, 'Oh great, another officer I have to explain things to, and another person who won't believe me just because I have a limp'. Sam goes on to let you know that they have ulcers on their leg and a nurse attends every couple of days to change the dressing. Sam invites you to sit down in a sitting room which is quite small and cramped. Sam sits opposite you in an armchair.

You would need to use your communication skills to help provide support as Sam may be vulnerable. You would want to build rapport with them and try and reduce the tension and conflict between Sam and yourself as 'the police' (see Chapter 8 on communication skills).

You should employ an empathetic approach that allows Sam to be open about these experiences. This will involve using active listening and behaving in a way that conveys you believe Sam. You might also consider a conversational approach rather than asking a set of routine and disjointed questions (see Chapter 13 on interviewing), as this can really help build a rapport. Empathy can be created through what you say, but also through the way you say it (tone of voice, and the sort of words you choose). Body language is also important in creating an empathetic atmosphere. You might feel that you do not particularly warm to Sam, but you must still deal with an individual without being unduly judgmental and in a manner appropriate to their needs.

It seems that you have gained trust through good communication skills, as Sam agrees to explain the full situation to you, from the very start—three months ago. You decide that the best route forward is to make notes, and eventually take a statement, covering everything that has happened over the past few months so it can be investigated together as a whole.

When taking this account, you must consider:

- Applying the investigative mind set (see Chapter 13).
- Using your professional curiosity to build an understanding of the situation and history (see Chapter 13).
- Investigating robustly if the person may not be able to explain the situation due to communication issues or the impact another person may have on them (such as an abusive person exerting coercive control)
- Using different question styles such as 'open' and specific 'closed' questioning (see Chapter 13).

Sam tells you that over the last three months they have received 30 letters and 10 cards from a colleague with whom they had a 'one-night stand' about six months ago. Three months ago, Sam developed an ulcer on one leg and has since been off work. As soon as Sam went off work the cards and letters began to arrive, which Sam was unhappy about. They have also received unwanted flowers and food gifts. Despite feeling upset about it Sam has kept all the correspondence in a box, kept a list of the flowers and food. The actual flowers and food are in a bin bag in Sam's shed. Sam recently moved (due to the leg problems) to this current property, but the person found out the new address.

Sam is getting more concerned and has been reading up about the behaviour of the co-worker. Sam believes this is stalking and is starting to feel unsafe, mainly due to the issues with the leg and the fact that Sam's mobility is compromised.

As a police officer it is your duty to share some of the responsibility for Sam's safety. You must consider:

- Immediate safeguarding considerations in respect of Sam, or others who may be at risk through association
- Are alarms needed at the property?
- Flagging the property on the command-and-control system as needing an immediate response
- Does Sam need advice regarding civil orders?
- Should the alleged suspect be arrested?

A referral to another agency might also be applicable, such as to adult/social services for further support, to a stalking adviser or clinic, or to a domestic abuse advisor. A multi-agency referral might be needed.

In this scenario Sam is a vulnerable adult and safeguarding them differs from safeguarding a child. Adults have the right to make their own decisions and choices about their safety, and may not consider themselves at risk, so this can make it harder to provide safeguarding.

> You discuss safeguarding with Sam, and Sam accepts some personal attack alarms from you, and referrals to some stalking and domestic abuse support services. After completing a full statement, Sam is very thankful to you for listening and for taking this further as a possible criminal incident (with the information so far available). You will continue to investigate this further as a possible case of harassment.
>
> You seize the cards and letters and the list of perishable items as evidence and take photos of the rotting flowers and food items in the binbag.

When you are dealing with an incident involving a vulnerable person, as in this scenario, you will need to use your professional judgement to identify and assess the risks posed to a vulnerable person. The THRIVE mnemonic will help guide your assessment (20.9.1).

20.9.5 Hard empathy

If you are a trainee police officer, you need will often need to employ good communication skills when dealing with people at incidents, and empathy is a large part of this, alongside good leadership. However, you have to be practical and realistic, so the empathy needs to be tailored to help resolve the situation. Hard empathy (also known as tough empathy) has been described as 'giving people what they need and not what they want' and also 'balances respect for the individual and for the task at hand' (Goffee and Jones, 2000, p 5).

Good leaders act in a straightforward manner towards people, and this approach should be used by you as a police officer when dealing with people, especially those who may be vulnerable. These can sometimes be difficult conversations. Gaj (2018) suggests it is similar to a parent trying to persuade a child to abandon a bad decision and make a wiser move instead, and that this is an example of effective leadership.

Let us take the previous stalking and harassment scenario as an example. Sam probably wants certain things to happen, they want the colleague arrested and dealt with in the courts, and Sam wants this to happen straight away. You need to make sure, however, that the proper processes are followed within the investigation and that it complies fully with PACE 1984. At this stage Sam is still a complainant, not necessarily a victim; the allegations against the co-worker have not been proved. During your conversation with Sam, you would need to emphasize that you understand what they want to happen and that you empathize. But you would also need to explain in appropriate terms that certain processes need to be followed within an investigation. Depending on how Sam reacts you might even hint that they will need to be patient and possibly adjust their expectations. See also Chapter 19 for discussion of dealing with victims.

20.10 Legislation and Policies Relevant to Vulnerability

The police and other partner services are bound by several pieces of legislation that outline responsibilities towards vulnerable people, and how investigations are conducted. Below we list several pieces of relevant legislation and policies and provide a summary of the key points. Child protection and the relevant legislation is covered in 19.9.2. Full versions of the legislation can be accessed via <www.legislation.gov.uk>.

The Serious Crime Act 2015 introduced measures to enhance the protection of vulnerable children and others. It extended the definition of child cruelty to incorporate abuse, neglect, and psychological damage, and also covered sexual communication with children and child sexual exploitation (ss 67 and 68 respectively). It strengthened the law to tackle female genital mutilation (ss 70–75). The Act also created the offence of 'Controlling or coercive behaviour in an intimate family relationship' (s 76), extending the extant domestic abuse legislation.

The Mental Capacity Act 2005 applies to everyone involved in the care, treatment, and support of people living in England and Wales aged 16 and over, and who are unable to make all or some decisions for themselves. The Act is designed to protect and restore power to people who lack capacity.

The Mental Health Act 1983 sets out the rights of people with mental health problems regarding assessment and treatment in hospital, treatment in the community, and the various civil and criminal pathways leading to hospitalization. It also provides the police and other relevant partners with powers to enter premises and detain people with mental health issues (see 20.5 and the relevant College of Policing APP).

The Code of Practice for the Mental Health Act 1983 explains the rights and responsibilities of patients and service providers. It helps patients treated under the Mental Health Act 1983 to receive the most appropriate treatment, care, and support. The Code of Practice is also relevant for the families and friends of people with mental health problems, hospital managers, the police, and ambulance staff. The Code was revised in 2015.

The Care Act 2014 sets out a clear legal framework for how local authorities and other parts of the system should protect adults at risk of abuse or neglect. It introduced safeguarding duties for local authorities; they must:

- lead a multi-agency local adult safeguarding system that seeks to prevent abuse and neglect, and stop it quickly when it happens;
- make enquiries, or request others to make them, when they think an adult with care and support needs may be at risk of abuse or neglect, to establish what action may be needed;
- establish 'Safeguarding Adults Boards' (including the local authority, the NHS, and police) which will develop, share, and implement a joint safeguarding strategy;
- carry out 'Safeguarding Adults Reviews' when someone with care and support needs dies as a result of neglect or abuse, and there is a concern that the local authority or its partners could have done more to protect the person;
- arrange for an independent advocate to represent and support a person who is the subject of a safeguarding enquiry or review, if required.

The government guidance **Information sharing: Advice for Practitioners Providing Safeguarding Services to Children, Young People, Parents and Carers 2018** helps practitioners and senior managers with decisions on when and how to share personal information legally and professionally. It might also be helpful for practitioners working with adults who are responsible for children who may be in need (HM Government, 2018c). This advice has been recently updated to ensure that it is 'GDPR compliant'.

The **Code of Practice for Victims of Crime 2015 and 2020** (the Victims' Code) sets out the minimum levels of service which victims can expect (MoJ, 2015; 2020). Victims are entitled to receive services under the Code if they have made an allegation to the police that they have directly experienced criminal conduct, or had an allegation made on their behalf. It also applies for some relatives of victims; see Chapter 20 for more details.

Achieving Best Evidence in Criminal Proceedings is about how to interview victims and witnesses who may be vulnerable (see 13.8.3.2). It also gives guidance on how to provide 'special measures' to enable them to give evidence in court (see 18.7.6.3.5) (MoJ, 2022a).

20.11 Answers to Tasks

TASK 1 It is possible, in this scenario, for multiple factors to be considered and applied. Factors such as:

- Static: previous abuse or neglect, economic and social disadvantage, young parents
- Dynamic: mental illness or serious mental health problems in caregivers, parental substance misuse, domestic abuse

You may be considering whether some of the dynamic factors are genuinely dynamic. Can they be changed? This would depend of course on the situation and the level of support available from social and medical services.

TASK 2

1. There are likely to be policy agreements and local arrangements with health-care services in your area.
2. Advice to the police officer would be as follows:
   (a) A dynamic risk assessment of the situation should be made first. Can the officer safely enter the room or should they seek the assistance of other officers with appropriate personal safety equipment? Entrance can be gained by seeking the permission of the parents/owners of the property to unscrew the door handle and withdrawing the bar a little, so the handle on the other side no longer works. Then the officer could turn the handle themselves to open the door.
   (b) The officer needs to find out if the young person will voluntarily go to hospital. If not, an AMHP should be called to see if they can be taken into hospital under the MHA.

21 Alcohol, Drugs, and Substance Use

21.1 Introduction

Many incidents encountered by police officers will be alcohol- or drug-related, particularly on late shifts. The health and safety of all persons present must be considered, as there is potential for injury. Alcohol or drugs was recorded as an 'impact factor' in 68 per cent of the 608,164 recorded incidents where a police officer had to use force in the year ending March 2022 (Home Office, 2022i).

Alcohol and drug consumption is not only confined to adults. According to a 2021 survey involving 9,289 pupils aged 11–15, around 40 per cent had consumed alcohol at some time, generally provided in their own homes at weekends by parents or guardians (NHS Digital, 2022b). In the same survey, 18 per cent of pupils reported that they had taken drugs. In terms of illegal use of drugs and other substances, the 2021/22 Crime Survey for England and Wales (ONS, 2022h) found that 9.2 per cent of adults (aged 16–59) had taken a drug controlled by the Misuse of Drugs Act 1971 in the previous year. This amounts to around 3 million people, slightly lower than when the survey was last conducted in 2019/20. In terms of Class A drug use, 2.7 per cent of adults (aged 16–59) and 4.7 per cent of young people (aged 16–24) reported use in the last year which was a significant decrease from the year ending March 2020. There were also significant decreases in the use of ecstasy and nitrous oxide (ie, laughing gas). These decreases in the use of Class A drugs, ecstasy, and nitrous oxide may be the result of the restrictions on social contact imposed by the Covid-19 pandemic (ONS, 2022h). Around 0.4 per cent of adults aged 16–59 had used a new psychoactive substance (ie substances such as mephedrone or spice that mimic the effect of drugs such as cannabis and powder cocaine) which showed no change compared to the year ending March 2020 (ONS, 2022h).

Although this chapter is mainly concerned with the application of the law surrounding alcohol- and drug-related incidents, the PCDA, DHEP, and pre-join programmes also provide an introduction to the wider issues surrounding substance use. In recent years, 'county lines' have become a problem in many constabularies which often involves exploitation of vulnerable people. We cover this complex topic in 21.7. Drink- and drug-driving is covered separately in 16.9.

The topics covered in this chapter are likely to contribute to the learning required for the National Policing Curriculum subject areas of 'Understanding the Police Constable Role', 'Policing the Roads', 'Vulnerability and Risk', and 'Managing Conflict'.

21.2 Alcohol-related Offences and Powers

There is no doubt that alcohol causes problematic behaviour for a minority of users. In the year 2019/20, there were an estimated 280,000 admissions to hospital in England attributable to alcohol, which was 2 per cent higher than the previous year (NHS Digital, 2022b). In the year ending March 2018, 39 per cent of victims of violent incidents believed their assailants to be under the influence of alcohol (latest available data from ONS, 2019b), and the police recorded that 14 per cent of violence against the person offences were alcohol-related, with the offence of 'assault without injury on a constable' being the most common at 32 per cent.

Here we explore the legislation and powers available to a police officer to deal with people who have drunk alcohol to excess, and to help to prevent the consumption of alcohol by young people. The word 'alcohol' is used in some legislation; it is defined in s 191(1) of the Licensing Act 2003 as spirits, wine, beer, cider, or any other fermented, distilled, or spirituous liquor (in any state).

21.2.1 Drunkenness as an offence

Drunkenness is an offence in certain circumstances (s 12 of the Licensing Act 1872, and see diagram).

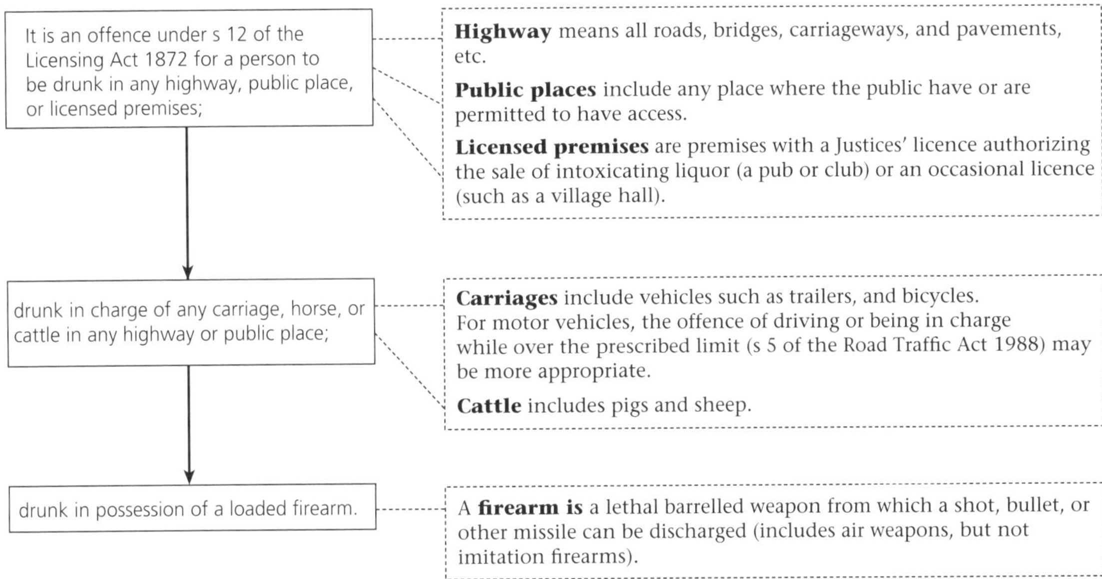

It is an offence under s 12 of the Licensing Act 1872 for a person to be drunk in any highway, public place, or licensed premises;
Highway means all roads, bridges, carriageways, and pavements, etc.
Public places include any place where the public have or are permitted to have access.
Licensed premises are premises with a Justices' licence authorizing the sale of intoxicating liquor (a pub or club) or an occasional licence (such as a village hall).
drunk in charge of any carriage, horse, or cattle in any highway or public place;
Carriages include vehicles such as trailers, and bicycles. For motor vehicles, the offence of driving or being in charge while over the prescribed limit (s 5 of the Road Traffic Act 1988) may be more appropriate.
Cattle includes pigs and sheep.
drunk in possession of a loaded firearm.
A **firearm is** a lethal barrelled weapon from which a shot, bullet, or other missile can be discharged (includes air weapons, but not imitation firearms).

Note that it is irrelevant whether the person is on the highway or in the public place of their own volition or recently ejected from nearby premises (*Winzar v Chief Constable of Kent* (1983) The Times, 28 March).

The terms 'drunk' and 'drunkenness' are not defined in law, but the case of *R v Tagg* [2002] 1 Cr App R 2 determined that the everyday meaning of 'drunk' should be used as a precedent. The *Oxford English Dictionary* defines drunk as 'having drunk intoxicating liquor to an extent which affects steady self-control' (*Shorter Oxford English Dictionary*, 2002, although the 1933 edition was cited in the case). The Court of Appeal also accepted that the *Collins Dictionary* definition (used by the judge in the original case under appeal) and the *Shorter Oxford English Dictionary* definitions were essentially the same and were helpful in determining the existence of a state of drunkenness.

The court itself must decide whether or not a suspect was drunk. Generally, the opinion of a witness is inadmissible as evidence, but for drunkenness a 'competent witness' may give evidence that, in their opinion, a person was drunk (*R v Davies* [1962] 1 WLR 1111). A competent witness is defined as a person who understands questions and can respond coherently, and would of course include a police officer. The witness should also provide facts to support the opinion, for example that the person was unsteady on their feet or that their breath smelt of intoxicating liquor. This offence is triable summarily and the penalty is one month's imprisonment or a fine (s 1 of the Penalties for Drunkenness Act 1962). A Penalty Notice for Disorder (ss 1–11 of the Criminal Justice and Police Act 2001) can also be used.

During your studies, you might hear this offence referred to as 'drunk and incapable', which is not strictly correct as the word 'incapable' is not used in the current legislation. The term 'incapable' probably came into use after it appeared in s 1 of the Licensing Act 1902 which provided any person with the power to apprehend any other person found drunk, if they appeared 'to be incapable of taking care of himself' (sic). This legislation was repealed by the Serious Organised Crime and Police Act 2005. Note, the power for a police officer to arrest a person for drunkenness under s 12 of the Licensing Act 1872 is now provided by s 24 of the PACE Act 1984 (see 10.11).

Whilst the word 'incapable' does not need to be proved for the offence to be committed, you might find it useful to consider how the notion of 'being incapable' might apply in relation to vulnerable people; one such scenario is presented here:

> Two police officers are deployed to a local hospital at the request of NHS staff who have refused admission to an elderly patient who is apparently drunk. On arrival the patient appears to be uninjured and capable of walking unaided but is a little unsteady on their feet. It becomes clear to the officers that the person's breath smells of intoxicating liquor. The patient refuses to communicate and their breathing rate appears to be increasing. The individual then starts shouting, pointing a finger at the NHS staff member and demanding treatment. The officers take these signs as an indication that behaviour may be escalating towards physical violence.

They know the patient may be suspected of committing the offence of being drunk but also know they are vulnerable due to age and intoxication. Rather than taking the person into custody, they request the hospital staff to admit them for treatment. Their continued presence calms the patient down while reassuring the hospital staff of their safety while appropriate treatment is given.

21.2.2 Drunk and disorderly behaviour

It is a summary offence for any drunken person to display 'disorderly behaviour' in any highway, public place, or licensed premises (s 91(1) of the Criminal Justice Act 1967). This is a very common problem, indeed in the year ending June 2022, 47 per cent of all Penalty Notices for Disorder were issued for this offence (MoJ, 2022c). The precise meaning of 'disorderly behaviour' is not defined by statute but its everyday meaning is 'unruly or offensive behaviour'. The penalty is a fine, a Penalty Notice for Disorder, or one month's imprisonment.

It is widely accepted that excess alcohol may cause aggression in some people and in some circumstances (Parrott and Eckhardt, 2018) and the link between alcohol use and certain forms of anti-social behaviour and violence has been examined (Ostrowsky, 2014). Such violence can inevitably lead to conflict, so you might find it useful to consider how police officers can deal with such situations in practice.

> Two police officers are deployed to a reported incident of anti-social behaviour outside a house. On arrival, the police officers see a number of people in the street outside a house where loud music is being played. The officers inform them that their actions are disturbing the neighbours and ask them to go back inside. A teenager is slumped against the wall of the house. The person appears to be aged around 15 years and is very unsteady on their feet. Eyes are glazed and breath smells of intoxicating liquor. The teenager is also sweating profusely even though the air temperature is quite cool. The group playing music in the street, who also seem to have been drinking, say they will look after the teenager. The officers knock on the door of the house where the teen is but get no response. The group in the street begin to get agitated by the continued police presence.

A situation such as this is not always easy to control, there is little time to make an assessment and prepare a response. Medical professionals often find themselves in similar situations and Harwood (2017) promotes prevention and de-escalation as an initial response. Good communication is key and a consideration of transactional analysis (Berne, 1968) could be useful in this situation. If the police officers are friendly, polite, and show respect this might help the situation. General conversation using everyday language may help to build a rapport, and the officers should communicate in a calm and non-threatening way. The potential aggressor might remain in a heightened state of anxiety, so humiliation and contradiction should be avoided at all costs.

Should the situation escalate to violence, officers will need to be proactive and employ rapid initial restraint, using, for example, rigid handcuffs or incapacitant spray. Some officers may also have been trained in the use of a Taser, or a Taser-trained officer could be summoned if necessary.

It would clearly be an advantage to know about any known medical conditions or about warning signs and risk factors for physical violence, but it is unlikely that such information will be available in this type of situation. However, general principles apply in relation to restraint; to reduce the chances of positional asphyxia, a person who is initially restrained lying face down, should as soon as possible be sat up, placed on their side, or put in a kneeling or standing position (see 9.7 for further details).

21.2.3 Drunk in charge of children

Under s 2 of the Licensing Act 1902, it is an offence for a person to be drunk while 'having charge' of a child under the age of seven years in any highway, public place, or licensed premises. The precise meaning of 'having charge' is not defined by statute but probably means some sort of care or control over the child(ren); the suspect must be the only person with the child or alternatively everyone in a group with the child must be drunk. This is a summary offence and the penalty is one month's imprisonment or a fine.

21.2.4 Controlled drinking zones

Under s 235 of the Local Government Act 1972, a local authority can designate an area as a 'controlled drinking zone' (CDZ) to help to control anti-social behaviour. It is not an offence to drink alcohol in a CDZ, but it is an offence to fail to comply with a request to surrender alcohol or to cease drinking. However, note that Home Office advice is 'it is not appropriate to challenge an individual consuming alcohol where that individual is not causing a problem' (Home Office, 2009). Local policies determine how to dispose of confiscated alcohol. Public Space Protection Orders (PSPO) introduced under the Anti-social Behaviour, Crime and Policing Act 2014 introduced new tools to address anti-social and alcohol-related nuisance behaviour (Local Government Association, 2018). The offence of failing to comply is triable summarily and the penalty is a fine, imposed through a fixed penalty notice (see 10.18.2.2).

> **TASK 1** Imagine you are a trainee police officer undertaking the PCDA. You often see someone who drinks large quantities and then becomes abusive to passing members of the public. How would you approach them in terms of their vulnerability and what long-term solution could improve the situation? Look at s 34(1) of the Criminal Justice Act 1972 to help to determine a suitable course of action.

21.3 Alcohol and Young People

Alcohol is a problem for a significant minority of young people. In the year 2019/20, around four in ten young people in substance use treatment (41 per cent) said they had problems with alcohol (Office for Health Improvement and Disparities, 2022a). Certain legislation is available to help to limit their alcohol consumption in public places, while other legislation relates to young people on licensed premises. On a more general note, if an officer encounters a 'child' carrying unopened cans of alcohol, then they should at least consider how the cans were acquired and take action accordingly. This applies even if there are no grounds to reasonably believe that the child has been consuming alcohol or is about to consume it.

21.3.1 Confiscation of alcohol from young people

A police officer (in or out of uniform) or a suitably designated PCSO may confiscate alcohol from a young person in a 'relevant place' (s 1(1) of the Confiscation of Alcohol (Young Persons) Act 1997). A relevant place includes:

- any public place, for example streets, parks, and shopping centres (but not licensed premises such as pubs); and
- a place to which the person has unlawfully gained access.

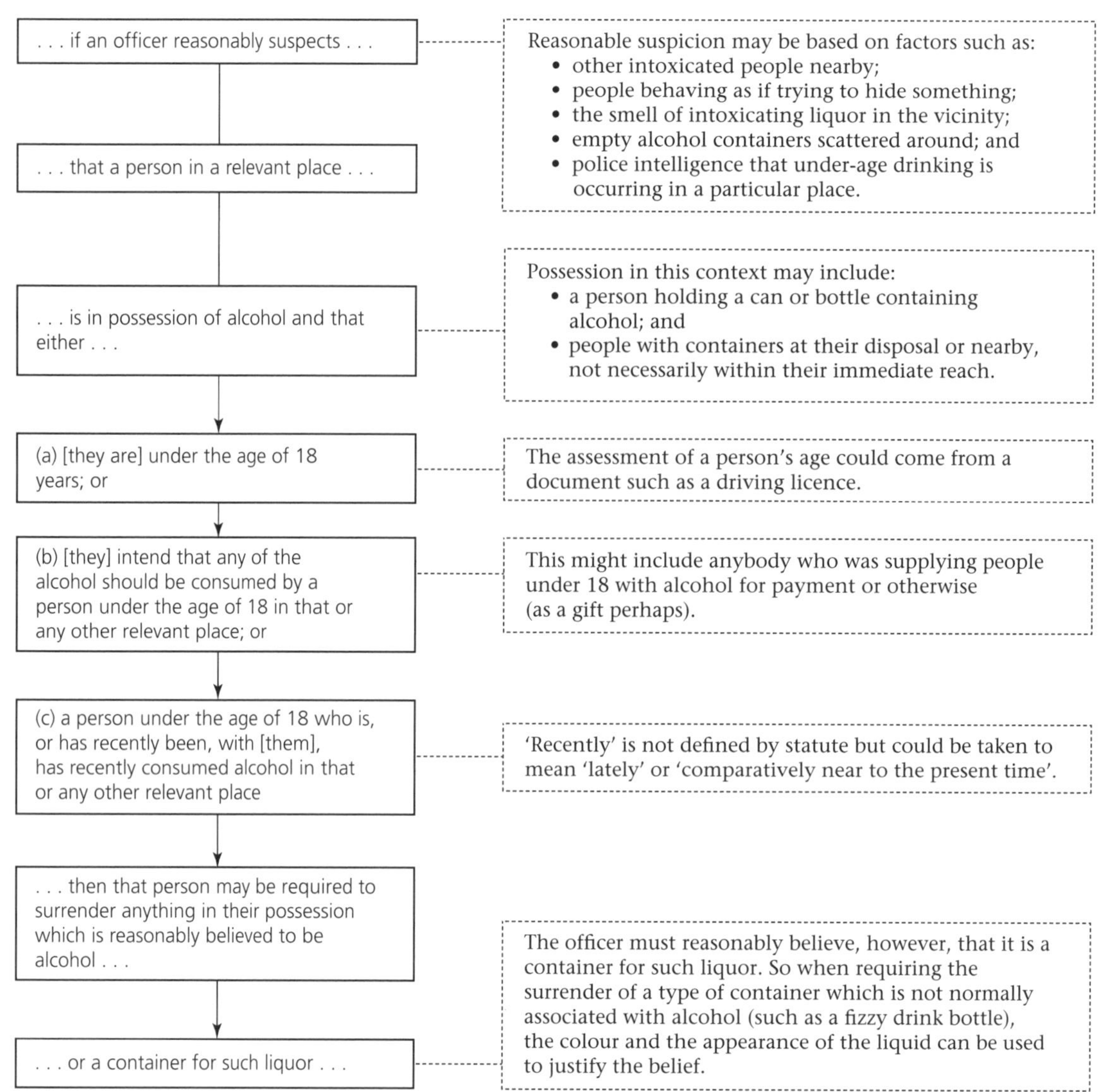

. . . if an officer reasonably suspects . . .
Reasonable suspicion may be based on factors such as:
• other intoxicated people nearby;
• people behaving as if trying to hide something;
• the smell of intoxicating liquor in the vicinity;
• empty alcohol containers scattered around; and
• police intelligence that under-age drinking is occurring in a particular place.
. . . that a person in a relevant place . . .
. . . is in possession of alcohol and that either . . .
Possession in this context may include:
• a person holding a can or bottle containing alcohol; and
• people with containers at their disposal or nearby, not necessarily within their immediate reach.
(a) [they are] under the age of 18 years; or
The assessment of a person's age could come from a document such as a driving licence.
(b) [they] intend that any of the alcohol should be consumed by a person under the age of 18 in that or any other relevant place; or
This might include anybody who was supplying people under 18 with alcohol for payment or otherwise (as a gift perhaps).
(c) a person under the age of 18 who is, or has recently been, with [them], has recently consumed alcohol in that or any other relevant place
'Recently' is not defined by statute but could be taken to mean 'lately' or 'comparatively near to the present time'.
. . . then that person may be required to surrender anything in their possession which is reasonably believed to be alcohol . . .
. . . or a container for such liquor . . .
The officer must reasonably believe, however, that it is a container for such liquor. So when requiring the surrender of a type of container which is not normally associated with alcohol (such as a fizzy drink bottle), the colour and the appearance of the liquid can be used to justify the belief.

The officer must inform the person of their suspicion under s 1(1) (s 1(4) of the Confiscation of Alcohol (Young Persons) Act 1997). The young person can also be required to state their name and address (s 1AA), and if suspected to be under 16 can be removed to their place of residence or a place of safety (s 1AB) (see 19.9.2.1). Failing to comply without reasonable excuse with a requirement under s 1(1) or (1AA) is an offence, and the young person must be informed of this. The offence is triable summarily and the penalty is a fine.

21.3.2 Persistently possessing alcohol in a public place

It is an offence for a person under 18 to be in possession of alcohol without reasonable excuse in any relevant place on three or more occasions within a year (s 30 of the Policing and Crime Act 2009). The offence is triable summarily and the penalty is a fine.

TASK 2 Imagine you see a young person assumed to be under the age of 18 at a bus station drinking alcohol. What requirements can you make? Write down a list of things you would have to say for the requirements to be lawful.

21.4 Premises Licensing Legislation

The Licensing Act 2003 includes legislation to address drunkenness in 'relevant premises'. Relevant premises in this context are premises where alcohol can be sold by retail eg a pub or a shop, club premises like a working men's club, but also any premises with 'permitted temporary activity' such as a village hall hired out.

Staff working in places where alcohol is served have a legal responsibility to try to prevent drunkenness and disorder. People with these responsibilities are listed in s 140(1) of the Licensing Act 2003 and are referred to here as 'responsible staff' (a term of our own invention, not a legal term). They include:

- the holder of a premises licence;
- the designated supervisor of a licensed premises;
- any person who works at the premises in a capacity which authorizes them to prevent disorderly conduct;
- any member or officer of a club (with a club premises certificate) who has the capacity to prevent disorderly behaviour; and
- the user of a premises with permitted temporary activity, at the permitted time.

21.4.1 Disorderly conduct on licensed premises

An offence is committed by responsible staff who knowingly allow disorderly conduct on licensed premises (s 140(1) of the Licensing Act 2003). This offence is triable summarily and the penalty is a fine.

A drunk or disorderly person commits a summary offence under s 143(1) of the Licensing Act 2003 if without reasonable excuse they:

- fail to leave relevant premises (when requested to do so by a police officer or a responsible staff member); or
- enter (or attempt to enter) relevant premises having been requested not to enter.

A police officer must respond to requests from responsible staff to help expel or refuse entry to a drunken person (s 143(4) of the Licensing Act 2003). Reasonable force may be used to encourage the person to comply (see *Semple v Luton and South Bedfordshire Magistrates' Court* [2009] EWHC 3241 (Admin)).

21.4.2 Providing a drunk person with intoxicating liquor

Responsible staff who knowingly sell alcohol to a person who is drunk on relevant premises commit an offence under s 141(1) of the Licensing Act 2003. It is also an offence for anyone to obtain or attempt to obtain alcohol for a drunken person on relevant premises (s 142(1)). These offences are triable summarily and the penalty is a fine; a PND can also be used.

21.4.3 Powers of entry

There is a power of entry to any place if there is reason to believe that an offence under the Licensing Act 2003 is being committed or is about to be committed (s 180(1) of the Licensing Act 2003). Reasonable force can be used (s 180(2)). The term 'any place' is defined in s 193; it includes vehicles, vessels, or moveable structures, licensed or not.

For premises (or any other place) with a club premises certificate, there is a similar power of entry (also under the Licensing Act 2003), if there is reasonable cause to believe that:

- a breach of the peace may occur (s 97(1)(b)); or
- an offence relating to supplying a controlled drug has been committed (see 21.6.2), or is about to be, or is being committed at that moment (s 97(1)(a)).

Reasonable force may be used when exercising this power (s 97(2)).

For premises with permitted temporary activities, a police officer may enter the premises at any reasonable time to assess the effect of the event in relation to prevention of crime, public safety, the prevention of public nuisance, and the protection of children from harm (s 108(1) of the Licensing Act 2003). There is no specific offence of obstructing a police officer under s 108, but an offence under the Police Act 1996 could be considered (obstruction in the lawful execution of police duties).

21.4.4 Selling alcohol to children and young people

Alcohol cannot legally be sold to a person under the age of 18 years. It is an offence to:

- sell alcohol to a person under 18 in any place (s 146(1) of the Licensing Act 2003)—this is a penalty offence (see 10.18.2.2); or
- knowingly allow the sale of alcohol on relevant premises to an individual aged under 18 (s 147(1) of the Licensing Act 2003).

A further, more serious, offence is committed if on two or more occasions (within three consecutive months) alcohol is unlawfully sold on the same licensed premises to a young person under 18 (s 147A of the Licensing Act 2003). These offences are triable summarily and the penalty is a fine.

21.5 Controlled Drugs and Psychoactive Substances

Police officers will frequently encounter people who have been using controlled drugs or psychoactive substances. According to police recorded crime in the year ending March 2020, victims of violent incidents believed their assailants to be under the influence of drugs in 29 per cent of cases (Allen and Tunnicliffe, 2021). Personal safety equipment may be required as the consequences of contamination from bodily fluids or equipment used by a person who injects drugs can be very serious. A virus-contaminated sharp article could cause a life-threatening infection, such as hepatitis C or HIV. Understanding of appropriate health and safety measures is included in the PCDA/DHEP knowledge requirement.

21.5.1 Definitions of controlled drugs and psychoactive substances

A controlled drug is a drug that is subject to legal control under the Misuse of Drugs Act 1971 and Misuse of Drugs Regulations 2001. New substances are added to the Home Office list as they come to the attention of the authorities. However, any alteration to the chemical structure of a controlled drug makes it a different substance and the new substance will not be subject to the existing controlled drugs legislation. Any such altered substance that has a psychoactive effect and is classed as a 'psychoactive substance' would, however, be covered by the Psychoactive Substances Act (PSA) 2016.

21.5.1.1 The definition of a controlled drug

Controlled drugs contain one or more defined chemical compounds with recognized effects, and are classed as Class A, B, or C (Misuse of Drugs Act 1971) according to the potential for harm they are thought to present.

Class A	eg Ecstasy, heroin, cocaine, crack cocaine, 'magic mushrooms' (containing psilocin or psilocybin), 'crystal meth' (methamphetamine), and LSD
Class B	eg cannabis leaves, cannabis resin, 'Spice' (a synthetic cannabinoid), mephedrone, amphetamines (but not methamphetamine), and barbiturates
Class C	eg khat, tranquillizers (such as Temazepam), anabolic steroids, and some painkillers

A full list of controlled drugs can be found on the Home Office website: <https://www.gov.uk/government/publications/controlled-drugs-list--2#full-publication-update-history>. Note that medicinal cannabis is now available on prescription.

The illegal use of controlled drugs often involves particular equipment and some examples of this equipment are shown here:

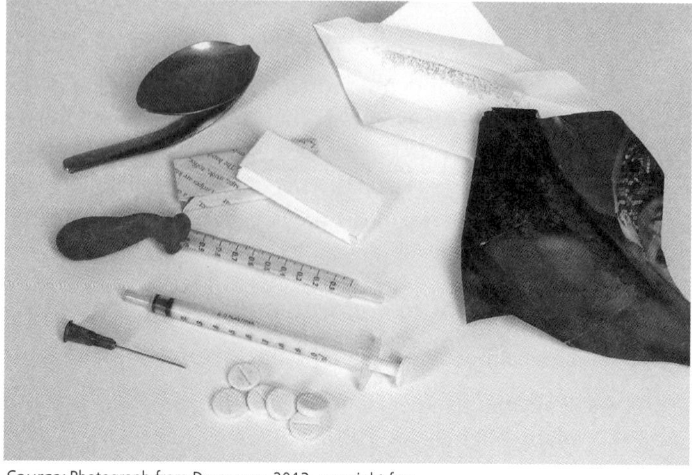

Source: Photograph from Drugscope 2013, copyright free.

Recognizing controlled drugs is difficult as there are many different shapes and sizes including pills, tablets, liquids, and powders. Therefore, a police officer who finds such a substance without pharmaceutical company packaging should not try to identify it, but should act on the suspicion that it is a controlled drug. The excellent encyclopaedia resource available on the DrugWise website will be helpful: <https://www.drugwise.org.uk/drugsearch-encyclopedia/>.

In the year ending March 2021, there were 223,106 seizures of Class A, B, and C drugs, with around 71 per cent being for cannabis (herbal, plant, and resin) (Home Office, 2022j). The table shows further information on drug seizures.

Class of drug	A	B	C
Number of seizures in the year ending March 2021	43,586	168,332	9001
Change in seizures compared with previous year	+17%	+21%	+55%
Most commonly seized drugs	cocaine	cannabis	other Class C drugs (eg Tramadol, Zoplicone, khat)

TASK 3 If you are a trainee police officer undertaking the PCDA or DHEP, find out the common street names and prices for the most common Class A, B, and C drugs in your policing area.

21.5.1.2 The definition of a psychoactive substance

In the legislation, a 'psychoactive substance' is any substance (other than controlled drugs, alcohol, or tobacco) which is capable of producing a psychoactive effect in a person who consumes it (s 2(1)(a) of the Psychoactive Substances Act 2016).

In recent years, many new psychoactive substances (sometimes referred to as NPS) have been manufactured. These substances are often referred to as legal highs and include 'Spice' (a synthetic cannabinoid), 'GBL' (gamma butyrolacetone), and 'GHB' (gamma hydroxybutyrate). The PSA 2016 was drafted to counter production and supply of such substances. In 2020/21, there were 3,289 NPS seizures—an increase of 18 per cent on the previous year. The most commonly seized type of NPS was synthetic cannabinoids (Home Office, 2022b).

It is not an offence to possess an NPS (except in a custodial institution (s 9 of the PSA 2016), but there are dedicated police powers to stop and search for such substances (see 4.5.1 for further details) and there are offences of production and supply (see 21.6). The Crime Surveys for England and Wales now include references to new psychoactive substances, and a New Psychoactive Substances Resource Pack is available on the gov.uk website. The DrugWise website also provides 'evidence-based information' on NPS.

Some everyday retail items also contain psychoactive substances including solvent-based glues, correction fluids, marker pens, aerosols, anti-freeze, nail varnish, and whipped cream canisters. Where substances are sold by a retailer for their intended use, the sale will not be an offence unless the cashier suspects or believes the product is likely to be consumed for its psychoactive effect.

21.5.2 Unlawful possession of a controlled drug

The most frequently encountered drugs offence is unlawful possession. In order to commit this offence (s 5(2) of the Misuse of Drugs Act 1971), 'it shall not be lawful for a person to have a controlled drug in [their] possession'.

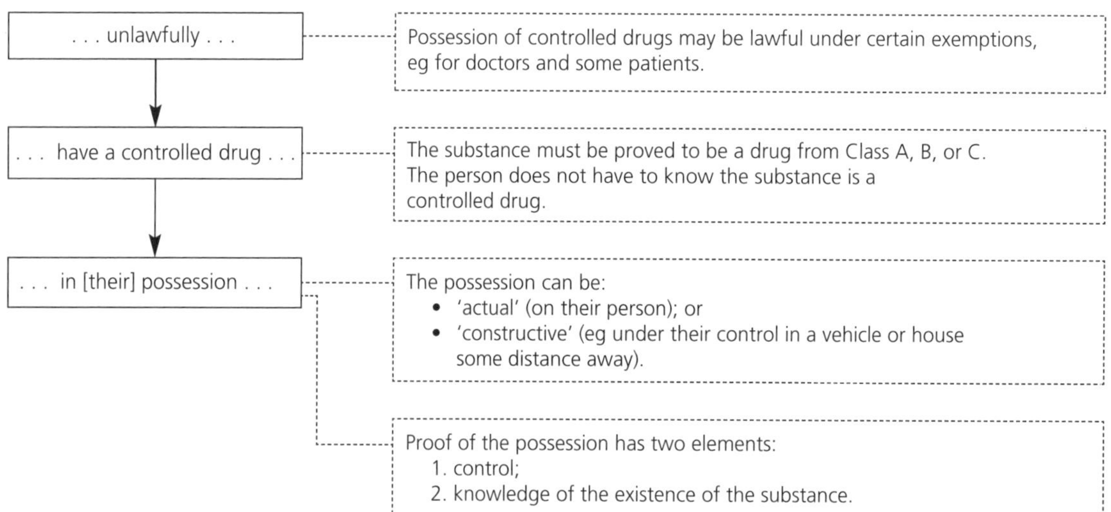

. . . unlawfully . . .
Possession of controlled drugs may be lawful under certain exemptions, eg for doctors and some patients.
. . . have a controlled drug . . .
The substance must be proved to be a drug from Class A, B, or C. The person does not have to know the substance is a controlled drug.
. . . in [their] possession . . .
The possession can be:
• 'actual' (on their person); or
• 'constructive' (eg under their control in a vehicle or house some distance away).
Proof of the possession has two elements:
1. control;
2. knowledge of the existence of the substance.

Control of a substance is indicated by the rights the person has over the substance and generally amounts to ownership. It would include:

- 'actual possession', items found on a person (eg in the pocket of a jacket they are wearing);
- 'constructive possession', items under their control in a vehicle or house some distance away.

Having control would also include having custody of an item when a person knows they have temporary or partial responsibility for an item, with the owner's consent or knowledge.

Knowledge of the existence of a substance is also required. If someone has something in their pocket, they must know it is there. If the substance is inside a container, it must be proved that they both knew the container was in their pocket and that it contained a substance.

As an example, imagine that someone is searched using the powers under s 23 of the Misuse of Drugs Act 1971. The police officer finds some kitchen foil with traces of brown powder on it tucked into the top of the person's sock which is identified as heroin. To prove the offence of possession, it must be shown that:

- the foil with the powder was in the sock;
- the person knew the foil and powder were there (it does not matter whether or not they knew the substance was a controlled drug);
- the powder was heroin; and
- they were not lawfully entitled to possess heroin.

In relation to stop and search, s 23(2) of the Misuse of Drugs Act 1971 has its own power of search (see 4.5.2).

21.5.2.1 Exemptions permitting lawful possession of a controlled drug

Possession of a controlled drug is lawful for some workers as part of their job, for example as suppliers to the pharmaceutical trade or as doctors (note that proper prescribing records must be kept). Such exemptions are provided under the Misuse of Drugs Regulations 2001 and made by the Home Secretary under s 7 of the Misuse of Drugs Act 1971. Patients who have been prescribed controlled drugs are also provided for under the exemptions (see 21.5.3.4). Regulation 6 allows police officers, police support employees, customs officers, and postal workers to possess drugs whilst acting in the course of their duties.

21.5.3 Unlawful possession of cannabis and khat

Cannabis is a Class B drug and khat (a herbal stimulant which is usually chewed) is a Class C drug. The majority of cannabis available illegally in the UK is 'skunk', which generally contains higher concentrations of psychoactive compounds compared with other forms of cannabis (Potter *et al*, 2018).

21.5.3.1 Intervention model for the unlawful possession of cannabis and khat

The intervention model helps to provide a justifiable and proportionate response, and the intention is to send out the message that cannabis and khat are harmful and illegal. There are three levels of intervention (see the diagram) but the guidance emphasizes that arrest remains the first presumption, although discretion can be used at all times. Cannabis and khat warnings are covered in more detail in 21.5.3.2.

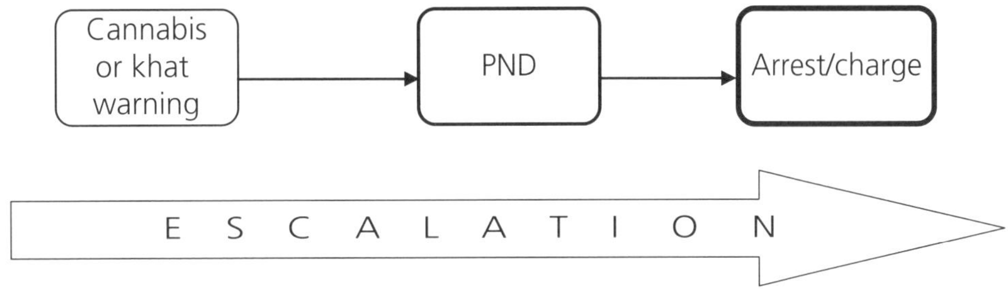

Under the intervention model, PNDs and cannabis and khat warnings can only be used if the person:

- is aged 18 years or over and has verifiable personal details (name, date of birth, and address);
- is not vulnerable;
- is competent enough to grasp the meaning of the officer's questions and can reply to questions coherently;
- is not under the influence of alcohol or drugs at the time the warning or PND is issued;
- possesses an amount of cannabis or khat only suitable for personal use (in the officer's judgement);
- is not in possession of any other drug; and
- admits the possession of cannabis or khat (this only applies for warnings and not for PNDs) (Sentencing Council, 2022).

Aggravating factors must be taken into consideration when deciding which option to take in the intervention model, for example the location where the person is found to be in possession. This could be a previously identified 'hot-spot' for anti-social behaviour or any place young people are more likely to be such as a playground or youth club. Other possible aggravating factors include smoking cannabis or chewing khat in a public place or in the view of the public, being a repeat offender (including other criminal offences) or someone who continually engages in anti-social behaviour, and appears to fail to recognize the seriousness of the situation. If there are one or more aggravating factors, then professional discretion (see Chapter 4) should be used to decide whether to issue a PND or make an arrest. If there are no aggravating factors, then a warning is the likely outcome.

The PNC can be used to find out whether the suspect has received a relevant warning or a PND, as these cannot be used more than once. Professional police discretion should be applied, but there is no need to employ each stage of the model in sequence: arrest can be used even if the suspect has never received a relevant warning or a PND. When a suspect does not admit the unlawful possession, a PND can only be used if there is sufficient evidence (see 21.5.2) to prove the offence. For suspects aged under 18, a youth caution can be used as an alternative (see 10.18.2.4).

The large flowchart with the shaded boxes shows the main factors to take into account when dealing with suspects in possession of cannabis or khat. The use of discretion means that the diagram can only provide an indication of the more usual outcomes, and does not cover every eventuality. The shaded boxes relate to the intervention model.

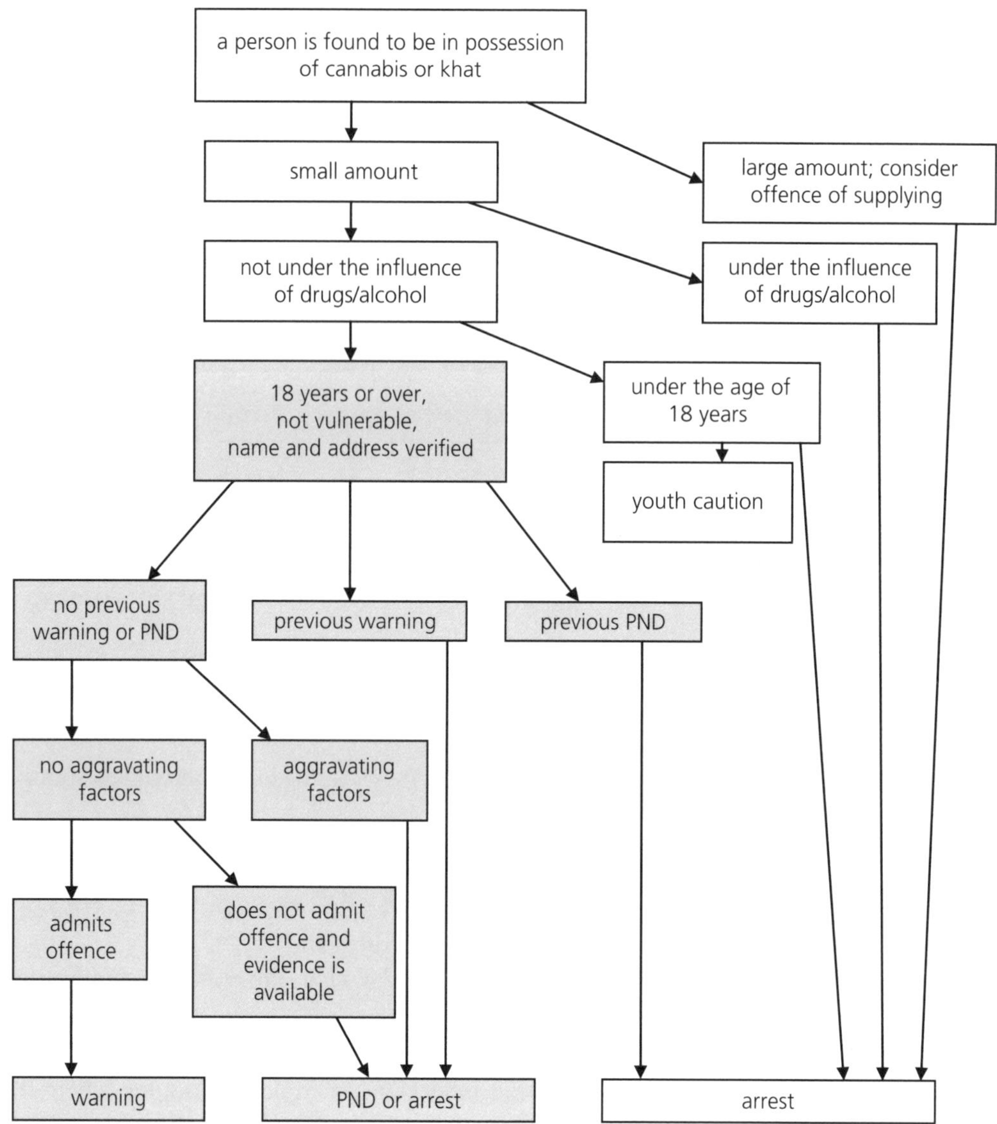

21.5.3.2 Cannabis and khat warnings

These warnings can only be issued when there are no aggravating factors (see 21.5.3.1) and when the person is compliant with the procedure, admits to the offence, and has no previous records of relevant warnings, PNDs, or convictions. The current guidance is that no more than one warning should be issued to an individual. However, under the previous guidance two warnings were allowed, so warnings issued before 26 January 2009 should not be taken into account except as part of the general previous offending history.

There is no formal group of words for a cannabis or khat warning, but the terms 'cannabis warning' or 'khat warning' should be used (rather than 'street warning'). The officer should tell the suspect that the warning will not amount to a criminal record or conviction but will:

- be recorded and added to local police databases for future reference;
- produce a record of a detected crime for the purposes of statistics as a recordable crime; and
- lead to the issuing of a PND or arrest if they are found in unlawful possession of cannabis or khat in the future.

Further guidance on cases involving khat can be found in the document *National Policing Guidelines on KHAT Possession for Personal Use Intervention Framework* available online (CoP, 2014d).

21.5.3.3 Possession of small amounts of cannabis or khat: practical aspects

For suspects in possession of small amounts of cannabis or khat, a police officer should investigate the suspected unlawful possession, remembering to follow the PACE Codes of Practice to protect the rights of the individual (see 10.9.1 on cautions). The officer should try to establish whether there is any lawful excuse for possession or if there is any evidence of a more serious offence such as intent to supply (see 21.6.2 and 21.6.3). The drugs should be seized and secured according to local policy. The incident should be recorded at the time as a PNB entry and stop and search forms will need to be completed (see 4.3.1.5). Intelligence reports and crime reports can be completed later.

Any arrest must be 'necessary' (see 10.11.4). For details on issuing a PND for possessing cannabis or khat, see para 3.2 of the Home Office operational guidance available at <http://www.justice.gov.uk/downloads/oocd/pnd-guidance-oocd.pdf>.

21.5.3.4 Medical prescription of cannabis-based products

Cannabis-based products can now be prescribed by doctors for medicinal use (Misuse of Drugs (Amendments) (Cannabis and Licence Fees) (England, Wales and Scotland) Regulations 2018). The drug is often prescribed in the form of a mouth spray, for example Sativex. Note that the 2018 Regulations still prohibit the smoking of cannabis and cannabis-based products for medicinal use.

You might find it useful to consider here how the new regulations might apply in practice in relation to valuing difference and inclusion within the community

A police officer has been deployed to managed accommodation for senior citizens. The manager reports that a 70-year-old resident has not been seen for a couple of days and there is cause for concern. Once inside the flat, the officer can clearly make out an earthy, herbal aroma and asks the pensioner what they are smoking. They reply that they have been prescribed cannabis and show the officer a small Sativex container, a quarter ounce bag of cannabis resin, some rolling tobacco, cigarette papers, and a repeat prescription form in their name. The senior citizen appears to be in unlawful possession of the cannabis resin and the officer is obliged to take action. The intervention model described in 21.5.3.1 can be used here and taking into account the elderly person's circumstances, the officer decides to simply issue a warning (after seizing the cannabis resin and checking all the criteria for a warning have been met).

21.5.4 Defence and penalties for unlawful possession of a controlled drug

In addition to the possession being lawful (see 21.5.2.1), a number of other circumstances can provide a defence (s 5(4) of the Misuse of Drugs Act 1971). Preventing unlawful possession under s 5 of the Misuse of Drugs Act 1971 is defined as:

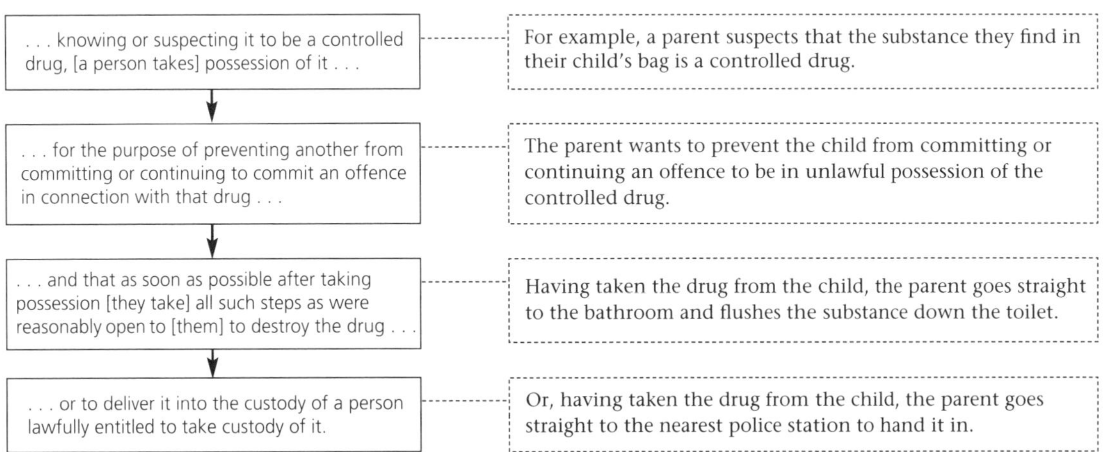

. . . knowing or suspecting it to be a controlled drug, [a person takes] possession of it . . .
For example, a parent suspects that the substance they find in their child's bag is a controlled drug.
. . . for the purpose of preventing another from committing or continuing to commit an offence in connection with that drug . . .
The parent wants to prevent the child from committing or continuing an offence to be in unlawful possession of the controlled drug.
. . . and that as soon as possible after taking possession [they take] all such steps as were reasonably open to [them] to destroy the drug . . .
Having taken the drug from the child, the parent goes straight to the bathroom and flushes the substance down the toilet.
. . . or to deliver it into the custody of a person lawfully entitled to take custody of it.
Or, having taken the drug from the child, the parent goes straight to the nearest police station to hand it in.

Other defences are available under s 28 of the Misuse of Drugs Act 1971. These relate to two main issues: whether the suspect knew or believed the substance was a controlled drug, and

whether they were entitled to possess that particular drug (s 28(3)(b)(i) and (ii) respectively). The onus is on the suspect to prove that they did not know some relevant point of fact alleged by the prosecution. Trainee police officers are unlikely to be involved in this process.

Possession offences involving Class A, B, or C drugs are triable either way and depending on the quantity, the penalty can be imprisonment, community order, and/or a fine. The maximum lengths of prison sentences are shown in the table. Unlawful possession of cannabis can also be dealt with by issuing a PND for £90.

Possession of a controlled drug (Misuse of Drugs Act 1971, s 5(2))—triable either way:

Class A
Maximum: 7 years' custody
Offence range: fine—51 weeks' custody

Class B
Maximum: 5 years' custody
Offence range: discharge—26 weeks' custody

Class C
Maximum: 2 years' custody
Offence range: discharge—medium community order

Source: Sentencing Council (2023a), Sentencing Guidelines: 'Possession of a Controlled Drug'.

TASK 4 Establishing whether someone is in unlawful possession of controlled drugs is not always straightforward. Identifying a substance as a controlled drug is relatively straightforward but proving possession is more complicated. Consider the following scenarios and try to decide whether possession has been established in each case.

1. Before going out to a party one night, an individual puts some cannabis into a wallet. They get very drunk and can't remember the night's events. They return home the next day and put the coat containing the wallet back into the wardrobe. Some days later, the person puts the coat on again forgetting it contains the wallet with the cannabis. They are subsequently stopped and searched by the police and the cannabis is found. Is the person guilty of unlawful possession?
2. Someone is entertaining visitors when a search warrant under s 23(3) of the Misuse of Drugs Act 1971 is executed. A small quantity of heroin is found on the sofa inbetween two guests and the host tells the police officers present that they are the owner. When formally interviewed, the person names the individual they claim is the true owner. They also state that one of the visitors probably had drugs in their possession in the flat and that another had been preparing to take heroin before the search took place. Are the circumstances sufficient for the host to have been in control of the drugs?

21.6 Production and Supply Offences

Drugs legislation has been carefully worded so that it is not only the illegal end user who is subject to prosecution, but also (and perhaps more importantly) the people involved in the supply chain. The legislation relating to the illegal production and supply of controlled drugs is in ss 4–6 of the Misuse of Drugs Act 1971. Defences to production and supply offences relate to proving possession and whether the substance in question actually is a controlled drug. For psychoactive substances, production and supply offences are covered in ss 4–7 of the PSA 2016. As for controlled drugs, certain activities, such as approved scientific research or work carried out by health-care professionals, are exempted for the purposes of this Act (s 11).

The supply of drugs to smaller towns often occurs through 'county lines'. Investigating such matters often involves a number of constabularies working together which creates additional challenges (Spicer, 2021).

21.6.1 Production of controlled drugs/cultivation of a cannabis plant

It is an offence to produce a controlled drug or be concerned in the production without a licence from the Secretary of State (s 4(2) of the Misuse of Drugs Act 1971). Growing plants and carrying out chemical processes are included under the term 'producing', while 'being concerned in the production' would include delivering chemicals, providing premises, or providing finance.

For production of cannabis plants, the Home Office recommends charging under s 4(2) as the charge of 'cultivation of cannabis' (s 6(2)) does not allow for confiscation proceedings (Circular 82/1980). The defences outlined in s 28 of the Misuse of Drugs Act 1971 apply to both these offences.

Offences involving production of controlled drugs are triable either way and the penalty is imprisonment, community order, and/or a fine. The maximum lengths of prison sentences are shown in the table and depend on the role performed by the defendant, ie 'leading role', significant role, 'lesser role'.

Production of controlled drugs/cultivation of cannabis plant (Misuse of Drugs Act 1971, s 4(2)(a) or (b), Misuse of Drugs Act 1971, s 6(2)):

Class A
Maximum: life imprisonment
Offence range: high level community order—16 years' custody

Class B
Maximum: 14 years' custody and/or unlimited fine
Offence range: Band B fine—10 years' custody

Class C
Maximum: 14 years' custody and/or unlimited fine
Offence range: discharge—8 years' custody

Cultivation of a cannabis plant
Maximum: 14 years' custody
Offence range: Band A fine—8 years' custody

Source: Sentencing Council (2023b), Sentencing Guidelines 'Production of a controlled drug/ Cultivation of cannabis plant'.

Section 4(2) offences for a Class A drug are 'trigger' offences under s 63B of the PACE Act 1984: this means a sample can be demanded from a person in police custody (see Chapter 13).

The intentional production of a psychoactive substance is an offence under s 4(1) of the PSA 2016. The person must know or suspect that the substance is a psychoactive substance and also:

- intend to consume it for its psychoactive effects; or
- know (or be reckless as to whether) it will be consumed by another person for its psychoactive effects.

This offence is triable either way and the penalty is a fine and/or imprisonment (12 months if tried summarily and up to seven years' imprisonment on indictment).

21.6.2 Supply offences

These offences (including offering to supply) are covered under s 4 of the Misuse of Drugs Act 1971 for controlled drugs and under s 4 of the PSA 2016 for psychoactive substances. A court must treat a supply offence more seriously if it was committed in or near to a school or if the suspect used a courier under the age of 18 (Sentencing Council, 2022c).

For controlled drugs, supply offences are covered under s 4(3) of the Misuse of Drugs Act 1971 as shown in the diagram.

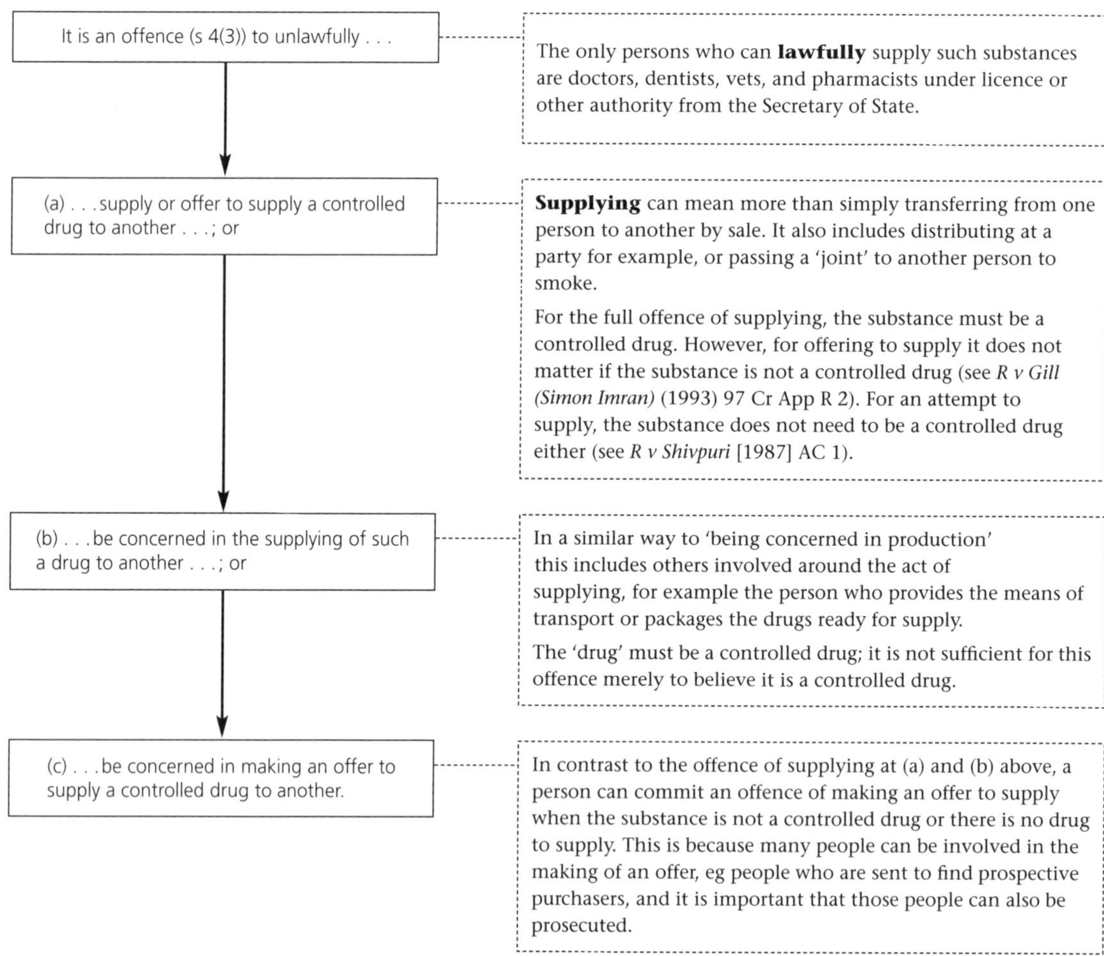

It is an offence (s 4(3)) to unlawfully . . .
The only persons who can **lawfully** supply such substances are doctors, dentists, vets, and pharmacists under licence or other authority from the Secretary of State.
(a) . . . supply or offer to supply a controlled drug to another . . .; or
Supplying can mean more than simply transferring from one person to another by sale. It also includes distributing at a party for example, or passing a 'joint' to another person to smoke.
For the full offence of supplying, the substance must be a controlled drug. However, for offering to supply it does not matter if the substance is not a controlled drug (see *R v Gill (Simon Imran)* (1993) 97 Cr App R 2). For an attempt to supply, the substance does not need to be a controlled drug either (see *R v Shivpuri* [1987] AC 1).
(b) . . . be concerned in the supplying of such a drug to another . . .; or
In a similar way to 'being concerned in production' this includes others involved around the act of supplying, for example the person who provides the means of transport or packages the drugs ready for supply.
The 'drug' must be a controlled drug; it is not sufficient for this offence merely to believe it is a controlled drug.
(c) . . . be concerned in making an offer to supply a controlled drug to another.
In contrast to the offence of supplying at (a) and (b) above, a person can commit an offence of making an offer to supply when the substance is not a controlled drug or there is no drug to supply. This is because many people can be involved in the making of an offer, eg people who are sent to find prospective purchasers, and it is important that those people can also be prosecuted.

The defences outlined in 21.5.4 also apply here. The penalties are the same as for the production of a controlled drug. The offence is a trigger offence: a police officer can demand a sample from a suspect in police custody.

For psychoactive substances, it is an offence to intentionally supply such a substance to another person (s 5(1) of the PSA 2016), but this only applies if the suspect:

- knows or suspects (or ought to) that the substance is psychoactive; and
- knows or suspects (or ought to) or is reckless as to whether another person is likely to consume it for its psychoactive effects.

The parallel offences concerning an offer to supply are covered under s 5(2) of the PSA 2016. These offences are all triable either way and the penalty is a fine and/or imprisonment (12 months if tried summarily and up to seven years' imprisonment on indictment).

21.6.3 Possession with intent to supply

Possession of a controlled drug with intent to supply is an offence under s 5(3) of the Misuse of Drugs Act 1971. The substance in question must be a controlled drug (unlike the s 4(3) supplying offence), but need not be the drug the suspect believes it to be, so a suspect who believed the drug was heroin can still be guilty even if it is found to be cocaine. It is not relevant whether the possession is lawful so a chemist in lawful possession could commit this offence if they intended to unlawfully supply the drug. The defences outlined in s 28 of the Misuse of Drugs Act 1971 also apply to s 5(3). The penalties are the same as for the production of a controlled drug and the s 5(3) offence is a trigger offence: a police officer can demand a sample from a suspect held in police custody.

For psychoactive substances, possession with intent to supply is covered under s 7(1)(a) of the PSA 2016. The suspect must know (or suspect) that the substance is psychoactive (s 7(1)(b)) and intend to supply it to another person for consumption (by any person) for its psychoactive effects. Offences under s 7 are triable either way and the penalty is a fine and/or imprisonment (12 months if tried summarily and up to seven years' imprisonment on indictment).

21.6.4 Occupier or manager of premises used for controlled drug offences

The offence of occupier or manager of premises used for controlled drug offences (s 8 of the Misuse of Drugs Act 1971) concerns persons who occupy or are involved in the management of a premises and who 'knowingly permit or suffer' any of the following activities to take place there:

(a) producing or attempting to produce a controlled drug;
(b) supplying, attempting to supply, or offering to supply a controlled drug to another;
(c) preparing opium for smoking;
(d) smoking cannabis, cannabis resin, or prepared opium.

There must be evidence that one of these activities has actually occurred (see *R v Auguste* [2003] EWCA Crim 3329). For example, in relation to (b) above, there must be evidence of a controlled drug actually being supplied on the premises: the simple existence of sufficient quantities and equipment for supplying controlled drugs is insufficient to prove the offence (see *R v McGee* [2012] EWCA Crim 613). The suspect does not need to know what type of controlled drug is involved.

To be an 'occupier', the person does not have to be a tenant or owner but needs to have sufficient control over the premises such that they could prevent drug-related activities. A student who pays for a room on campus would be regarded as an occupier. A person 'concerned in the management' does not have to have a legal interest in the premises and would include a trespassing squatter (see *R v Tao* [1976] 3 All ER 65). A cleaner would be neither an occupier nor concerned in the management. To 'knowingly permit or suffer' would include the occupier or manager of the premises having suspicions but choosing to take no action, and also trying to stop the activity but without success. Powers are available to close premises that are being used for controlled drug offences.

Offences under s 8 are triable either way. If tried summarily, the penalty is a fine and/or imprisonment (six months for Class A and B and three months for Class C). On indictment, the penalty is a fine and/or up to 14 years' imprisonment.

21.6.5 Import and export of controlled drugs or psychoactive substances

The legal import and export of controlled drugs requires a licence and is covered under s 3(1) of the Misuse of Drugs Act 1971. Without a relevant licence, it is an offence under s 170 of the Customs and Excise Management Act 1979 to knowingly acquire possession or be concerned in transporting, storing, or concealing such drugs or be concerned in any fraudulent evasion or attempted evasion of such a restriction. These offences are triable either way. The penalty for a Class A or B drug is imprisonment (life and 14 years, respectively), and for Class C on summary conviction three months' imprisonment and/or a fine and, on indictment, five years' imprisonment.

For psychoactive substances, it is an offence to intentionally import or export such a substance (s 8(1) and (2) of the PSA 2016, respectively). The person must know or suspect (or ought to know or suspect in the circumstances) that the substance is psychoactive. They must also either intend to consume it for its effects, or know or be reckless as to whether, the substance is likely to be consumed by another person for its effects. Offences under s 7 are triable either way and the penalty is a fine and/or imprisonment (12 months if tried summarily and up to seven years' imprisonment on indictment).

21.7 'County Lines'

Under the NPCC definition, a 'county line' is the term used to describe gangs and organized criminal networks involved in exporting illegal drugs into one or more importing areas within the UK, using dedicated mobile phone lines (NCA, 2021). County lines have become more evident since around 2013. Coomber and Moyle (2018, p 1338) suggest that county lines are 'a new insidious drug-dealing model, fast permeating provincial drug markets in the United Kingdom'. In January 2019, the NCA estimated that there were at least a thousand county lines in the UK, with approximately 300 originating in the Greater London area (NCA, 2019, p 2). It is likely, therefore, that county lines are in almost all police service areas across the UK.

Criminal groups create a network between an urban hub, such as areas within London or Liverpool, and county locations, typically towns in counties such as Kent, to supply recreational and other types of illegal drugs. There is some evidence that county lines developed because drug suppliers needed to establish new markets owing to 'market saturation' in city locations (Robinson *et al*, 2019, p 695) and also to avoid police attention (Stone, 2018, p 286).

There are a number of informal terms associated with county lines which student police officers might find useful, as shown in the table.

Term	Explanation
'Trap house'	A building in the county location which is used as a base from which drugs are sold. Occupants include drug users. Examples include homes of those 'cuckooed' but also short-term lets and cheap hotel accommodation.
'Cuckooing'	The term is a reference to the nesting behaviour of cuckoos—they take over the nests of other birds. A county lines group will take over the home of a vulnerable person (eg those experiencing drug dependency, mental health problems, financial insecurity) using acts of intimidation and violence. The group will then use the property as their trap house.
'Going country' (or 'out there', 'OT')	This has different meanings such as: county lines activity in general, an individual becoming involved in county lines, or the act of travelling to another area, city, or town to deliver drugs or money.
'Trapping'	Either the selling of illegal drugs via a county line or the moving of drugs from the urban hub to the county location.
'Deal line'	The branded mobile phone number operated by the county line group and used to communicate (primarily to take orders for drugs) with possibly hundreds of drug users.
'Taxing'	Use of violence to exercise control over a county lines member (eg marking or injuring).

A dedicated 'branded' mobile phone line is set up to take supply orders from local illegal drug users, usually operated by a 'third party'. The urban hubs are often also the locations for the storage of imported drugs. Drugs are supplied according to the orders taken on the 'branded' phone and the payments are collected by locally recruited couriers. The NCA reports that vulnerable children, such as those experiencing family breakdown or developmental disorders, are frequently targeted by county line offenders (NCA, 2019, p 3) to work as couriers. As the NCA (2019) notes, the groups involved in running county lines will often employ coercion and violence. Sexual exploitation, modern-day slavery, and human trafficking can also be present as part of the functioning of a county line. The Home Office has published guidance aimed at helping to counter the criminal exploitation of children and vulnerable adults (Home Office, 2020f).

A recent example of a law enforcement initiative against a county line was the Devon and Cornwall Police 'Ligament' operation to take down the 'Billy Line', which had been running a drugs supply network from London to Cornwall. In July 2018, local police visited a house in Newquay after reports from members of the public concerning apparent drug dealing. A 16-year-old boy was found in possession of a large quantity of drugs and enquiries showed that the boy had been reported as missing. It emerged that the boy had been moved by a county line group to the flat of a 56-year-old heroin addict in Bodmin after failure to meet a debt (*The Guardian*, 2019). The boy had found himself caught up in a county line supplying over 90 drug users in that part of Cornwall. The group had used hire cars to transport drugs from their north London hub to Cornwall; a total of 18 vehicles were hired and 65 return journeys made between January and December 2018 (Cornwall Live, 2019). Five different mobile phones were used to operate the 'Billy Line'. The whole scheme was run by a prisoner from his cell in Wandsworth Prison (BBC, 2019b).

21.7.1 Offences associated with county lines

The offences associated with county lines include:

- Illegal drugs supply offences—the illegal distribution and dealing in potentially dangerous drugs from town to town, eg s 4(3) of the Misuse of Drugs Act 1971 (see 21.6.2).
- Use of firearms, offensive weapons, and bladed objects—the Firearms Act 1968, the Prevention of Crime Act 1953, and the Criminal Justice Act 1988 are relevant here (see Chapter 25).
- Violence—gangs use violence to intimidate children and young people in order to recruit them. Offences to be considered include those offences set out in the Offences Against the Person Act 1861; and attempted murder.
- Abuse and exploitation—young people and children are exploited to move drugs and money. Both young girls and boys may be coerced into relationships and made to perform sex acts. Women who have entered into relationships with county line members are often controlled, coerced, and subject to sexual abuse and exploitation; relevant legislation will include the Sexual Offences Act 2003 (see Chapter 24) and the Modern Slavery Act 2015 (see 19.12).

There are sometimes complex issues for police and CPS about whether some of those involved in committing offences with a county line were also at the same time victims of trafficking and/or exploitation (particularly children and young people, and in some cases female partners of county line members). In principle, s 45 of the Modern Slavery Act 2015 provides a statutory defence for victims of trafficking. The Crown Prosecution Service has published guidance on the approach to be adopted in these circumstances (CPS, 2022c).

21.7.2 Detailed characteristics of county lines

Research is ongoing concerning the structures and MOs typically employed by county lines and, in any event, these are likely to change over time. There are also likely to be significant local and regional variations. What follows is a summary of current thinking but if you are a trainee police officer, your local police service training is likely to provide greater detail and local contextualization.

A county line group will be based in an urban location. It is likely to have an informal structure but may include some sort of hierarchy with 'teenies, runners, youngers, links, baby mamas, baes/wifeys, gangster girls, elders and faces/olders' (Williams and Finlay, 2018, p 730). Many county line operations will operate over 50 to 75 miles, but some may span several hundred miles. Locations experiencing economic problems with plentiful availability of cheap accommodation and higher concentrations of at-risk individuals seem to have been targets. However, houses in more affluent towns and locations such as rooms at university halls of residence with a strong local market in 'recreational' illegal drugs, have also been subject to county lines 'takeovers'.

County lines groups often use public transport or hire cars to move illegal drugs and other commodities from the urban hub to the county locations. Runners from hubs sometimes stop short of the final destination in order to avoid detection by law enforcement or complete the journey by a different means. Runners are often young people, particularly young women, and the illegal drugs might be 'plugged' within the body of the runner, typically in the rectum and/or vagina.

To promote and organize the selling of illegal drugs, the county line will probably use a 'branded' mobile phone number to create a brand that drug users can associate with. The number is then marketed in the area, for example through social media, business cards, and free cigarette lighters (Wigmore, 2018, p 6). These numbers have value and so are maintained and protected. However, there are some signs that offenders may now be moving to more 'secure' forms of communication that use end-to-end forms of encryption, such as WhatsApp.

At the end of the line are the county line drug distribution centres (the 'trap houses', some of which have been 'cuckooed'). County line gang members will probably 'assess what such a base could offer (proximity to the town centre, nearby alleyways, the absence of CCTV etc.)' (Jaensch and South, 2018, p 8). The trap house is a local base for the county line and will be the centre for providing illegal drugs for not only the town but for surrounding estates and other nearby towns as well. Drug orders made through the branded line are collected from the trap house by the purchaser or delivered by locally recruited runners. The runners are often children and young people and 'clean skins' are preferred, ie those without previous convictions. Forms of 'recruitment' include not only financial inducements (cash, designer clothes) but also coercion, grooming, deception (eg apparent friendship and status), intimidation and threats, and forms of 'debt bondage' (services provided to the county line in lieu of repayment of debts). There is some evidence that county lines groups deliberately target vulnerable children and young people, such as those excluded from school, living in care homes, or those with learning difficulties (Children's Society, 2020).

21.7.3 Law enforcement response

Given the complex nature of county lines and their geographical spread, a multi-agency approach (see 19.3.1) is usually adopted to detect or disrupt their activities. This will include the police services affected working in collaboration with other agencies (such as Local Authority Social Services) and with their Regional Organised Crime Unit (ROCU). A ROCU covers many police services over a large area—the North-West ROCU, for example, covers Cumbria, Cheshire, Lancashire, Greater Manchester, Merseyside, and North Wales (National Crime Security Centre, 2022). The police will need to agree on how to utilize intelligence on county lines operating in their areas, and then select the best disruptive measures in the particular context and make arrangements for joint investigation.

In 2018, the NCA and NPCC launched the National County Lines Coordination Centre (NCLCC). The NCLCC is responsible for mapping out the threat from county lines nationally and prioritizing action against the most significant perpetrators' and also provides support for frontline police officers. National county line intensification weeks (IW) are established to significantly disrupt country lines drugs markets. The safeguarding issues for children, young people, and other vulnerable individuals (such as those with mental health problems) will necessitate a multi-agency response. Where the local police service has reason to believe that a child is involved in a county lines network, they are expected (without delay) to make a safeguarding referral using a locally agreed 'pathway' process. If there are reasonable grounds to suspect that a child is suffering or is likely to suffer significant harm, a s 47 enquiry (Children Act 1989) is initiated (see 19.9.2).

The police can also use orders and injunctions in addition to prosecutions for offences, or where such prosecutions might be difficult to mount including:

- Slavery and Trafficking Risk Orders (STRO);
- Drug Dealing Telecommunications Restriction Orders Regulations 2017 (under the Digital Economy Act 2017), though these are unlikely to cause long-term disruption to county lines communications as the operators are likely to keep separate records of customers' contact details to transfer to a replacement phone (it is easy in the UK for anyone (including drug dealers) to anonymously buy a replacement 'burner' mobile phone and number through 'pay as you go' services);
- injunctions under the Policing and Crime Act 2009 to prevent gang-related violence and gang-related drug dealing activity to be sought against an individual;
- 'closure of premises' powers under the Anti-social Behaviour, Crime and Policing Act 2014 can be used to close down 'trap houses'; and
- Criminal Behaviour Orders are available for people convicted of offences associated with county lines.

Student police officers should be aware of the local recruitment strategies employed by county line offenders, including through social media. Increasing your knowledge of the street-level slang language associated with drug dealing and county lines is also useful. You should also pass on any intelligence using the NIM approach adopted by your constabulary. Relevant intelligence could include:

- changes in drug supply patterns;
- unusual hire car use;
- the names of any local branded lines (a weakness of a county line set up is that their 'business' model depends on promoting the existence of the semi-permanent branded line);
- changes in 'ownership' of the line (it is not unknown for these to be traded or sold between groups);
- signs and symptoms of cuckooing at local properties;
- signs of targeting of vulnerable children and adults.

In particular, where children go missing or absent, even if only for a few hours or overnight, consideration should be given to a possible connection with a county line (see the Safeguarding Hub, 2020).

21.8 Answers to Tasks

TASK 1 Look at s 34(1) of the Criminal Justice Act 1972 to help with the answer.

- The health and safety of the individual is paramount—are they injured in any way and how drunk are they?
- What offence has been committed? Are they just drunk, or 'drunk and disorderly'?
- Is arrest necessary to prevent them from causing physical injury (to themselves or others) or could the matter be dealt with in another way?
- What other agencies could be contacted? If there is an approved treatment centre for alcoholism in the area, the officer could treat the person as being in lawful custody for the purposes of the journey (s 34(1) of the Criminal Justice Act 1972).

TASK 2

- Introduce yourself.
- Explain that you suspect they are under 18 years of age.
- Tell them that they are in a public place.
- Make clear that you wish them to surrender any intoxicating liquor in their possession and to give their name and address, and that failure without reasonable excuse to comply is an offence.

TASK 3 Some common unlawfully used controlled drugs are:

- **amphetamines** (speed, whizz, w, billy, uppers, phet, amph, wizz, white, sulphate).
- **cocaine** (coke, crack, charlie, sniff, white, ching, snow white, snuff, rock, nose candy, okey cokey, fairy dust).
- **heroin** (smack, crack, brown, gear, shit, jack, henry, horse, needles).
- **cannabis** (weed, skunk, pot, dope, bud, green, blow, hash, ganja, grass, puff, gange, herb, blow, soap, blunt).

(Source: <https://www.drugwise.org.uk/drugsearch-encyclopedia/>)

TASK 4

1. Yes. In *R v Martindale* (1986) 84 Cr App R 31 (CA), Lord Lane stated that:

   > Possession does not depend upon the alleged possessor's powers of memory. Nor does possession come and go as memory revives or fails. If it were to do so, a man with a poor memory would be acquitted, he with a good memory would be convicted.

2. No, the host cannot be said to be in control of the drug. There is insufficient actual or physical control of the heroin in this situation (see *Adams v DPP* [2002] All ER (D) 125 (Mar)).

22 Unlawful Violence Against Persons and Premises

22.1 Introduction

Unlawful personal violence is a common occurrence and police officers are called to investigate such incidents with alarming frequency. Police recorded violence against the person increased by 21 per cent to over 2.1 million offences from pre-Covid levels in March 2020 to the year ending September 2022 (ONS, 2023b).

During incidents involving unlawful violence, the health and safety of the public and police officer(s) is paramount, as these incidents can be difficult to control. Often there is little time to assess a situation and plan a response because the events can be spontaneous.

On receipt of a call requesting police assistance at a violent incident, call-handlers will obtain as much detail as possible and relay it to the attending officers (see Chapter 13). If the identity of the suspect is known, they can be checked on the Police National Computer (PNC) or local constabulary databases which will help officers attending the scene with risk assessment prior to arrival. The deployed officers will carry out a further risk assessment based on the information from the initial report.

Once at the scene, a reassessment of victim and officer safety should be made, including the immediate risk posed by the possible use of weapons. The need for first aid or other medical assistance for anyone present will need to be assessed. In a domestic setting, the individuals involved should be separated, especially if children are present (see 9.5.2). The National Decision Model (see 4.2.1) should be applied to ensure priorities such as safety of victims and the preservation of evidence (see 10.3) are met.

At any assault, early investigative actions will be crucial for there to be any chance of a successful prosecution; accurate records must be kept of anything said by the suspect (see 10.2) and evidence might need to be recorded, for example by taking photographs or using body-worn video. If the alleged offender has left the scene, their identity and description should be obtained from the people still present and broadcast to other police patrols in the area (see 10.10) in order to locate the suspect. If the identity of the offender is known, then further searches on any violent history might be obtained through the local police service as well as national databases such as the ViSOR (see 19.3.11), the PNC for warning markers, or the PND, which could hold intelligence on historic out-of-area incidents.

The general provisions of criminal law apply equally to violence and abuse in domestic settings; the only additional offence that relates specifically to domestic violence is coercive or controlling behaviour (s 76 of the Serious Crime Act 2015). This latter offence recognizes the extreme psychological and emotional abuse that some victims may experience (see 19.5).

Before going into the details about the offences of unlawful violence, the various meanings of the word 'assault' must be considered. There is no legal definition of assault. In *R v Brown* [1993] 2 All ER 75, Lord Templeman referred to the definition of assault as that adopted by the

Law Commission in their Consultation Paper No 122, *Legislating the Criminal Code: Offences against the Person and General Principles* (1992), para 9.1. This stated:

> in common law an assault is an act by which a person intentionally or recklessly causes another to apprehend immediate and unlawful personal violence and a battery is an act by which a person intentionally or recklessly inflicts personal violence upon another.

Clearly, there is a distinction between a victim experiencing the application of force by battery and apprehending the threat of an application of force, although both can amount to an assault (*R v Rolfe* (1952) 36 Cr App R 4). Hence, whenever the word assault is used, the intended meaning for that particular context must be considered.

The topics covered in this chapter are likely to contribute to the learning required for the National Policing Curriculum subject areas of 'Understanding the Police Constable Role' and 'Managing Conflict'. If you are undertaking the PCDA or DHEP, you will also be expected to know how to 'interpret and apply the letter and essence of all relevant law, as it relates to any encountered policing situation, incident or context'.

22.2 Common Assault and Occasioning Actual Bodily Harm

Historically, the Offences Against the Person Act 1861 provided magistrates with the opportunity to imprison or fine anyone committing the common law offences of assault or battery. The same statute provided the offences of assault occasioning actual bodily harm, GBH, and GBH with intent. Assault and battery remained as common law offences until they became summary offences by virtue of s 39 of the Criminal Justice Act 1988.

The CPS advises prosecutors and the police to consider both the level of injuries and the likely sentence that a court would apply when deciding how to charge a case of assault. They should take into account the *Sentencing Council's Definitive Guideline on Assault* (published in March 2011). In general, if there are no serious injuries, then the offence should be charged as common assault. The police can make the charging decision on common assault as it is a summary offence (CPS, 2020a). If the injury is serious, the charge should be ABH but if it is really serious the charge should be GBH. There may be instances where it is necessary to deviate from this general principle (Sentencing Council, 2012b). If the prosecutors are considering changing the charge from ABH to common assault, the statutory time limit must be taken into account (as common assault is only a summary offence so must be laid before the court within six months of the offence (*Dougall v Crown Prosecution Service* [2018] EWHC 1367 (Admin)).

22.2.1 Common assault

Under s 39 of the Criminal Justice Act 1988, there are two possible offences:

- common assault as a threat; and
- common assault by battery.

The naming of common assault offences is widely acknowledged to be confusing but the two forms of common assault are mutually exclusive alternatives and should never be charged together (see *DPP v Little* [1992] 1 All ER 299). They are both triable summarily only and the penalty is six months' imprisonment. (Note that if the assault is against an emergency worker, the maximum sentence is two years' custody (see 22.4.2.1); if the assault is racially or religiously aggravated, the maximum sentence is also two years' custody, see 19.8.2).

22.2.1.1 Common assault (threat)

Common assault as a threat can take a number of forms but does not include any physical contact or physical force on the victim:

- common assault (threat)—any act which makes a victim understand they are going to be immediately subjected to some personal violence. This includes when there is no means to carry out the threat, such as holding a replica gun against a person and threatening to shoot them, if the victim believes there is a threat of violence (see *Logdon v DPP* [1976] Crim LR 121, DC);

- conditional threat (or conditional assault) conveys a threat on condition of another event, for example 'Get out the car or I'll cut you.' It is reasonable for the victim to expect that bodily harm will be likely to follow any refusal. If the victim gets out of the car and the suspect takes no further action, the suspect would still be guilty of assault.

Non-conditional threat is not considered an assault, for example one person says to another, 'Get me some water.' The person refuses and the other says, 'If your friends weren't here, I'd thump you.' The wording of the threat shows that the first individual is not going to assault the second and therefore there is no immediate threat.

In the context of common assault, a threat is:

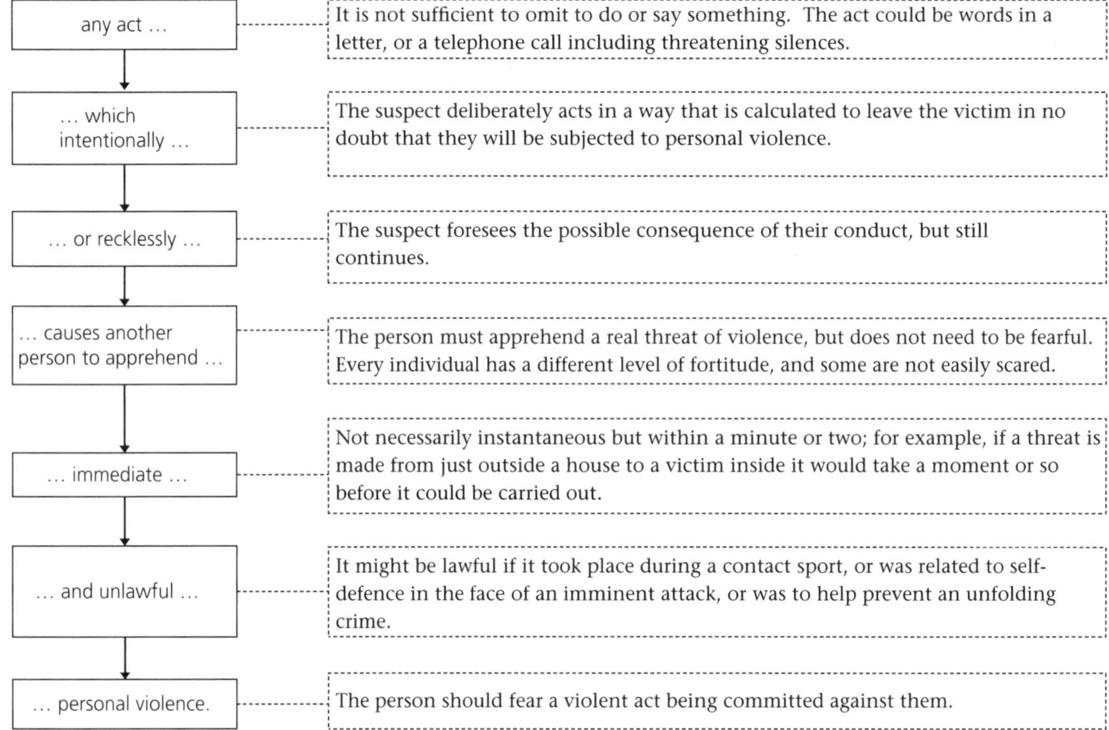

any act …
It is not sufficient to omit to do or say something. The act could be words in a letter, or a telephone call including threatening silences.
… which intentionally …
The suspect deliberately acts in a way that is calculated to leave the victim in no doubt that they will be subjected to personal violence.
… or recklessly …
The suspect foresees the possible consequence of their conduct, but still continues.
… causes another person to apprehend …
The person must apprehend a real threat of violence, but does not need to be fearful. Every individual has a different level of fortitude, and some are not easily scared.
… immediate …
Not necessarily instantaneous but within a minute or two; for example, if a threat is made from just outside a house to a victim inside it would take a moment or so before it could be carried out.
… and unlawful …
It might be lawful if it took place during a contact sport, or was related to self-defence in the face of an imminent attack, or was to help prevent an unfolding crime.
… personal violence.
The person should fear a violent act being committed against them.

22.2.1.2 Common assault (battery)

Common assault by battery (beating) involves the actual use of force by an assailant on a victim but only results in very minor or no perceivable injury. It is the intentional or reckless application of force on another and is dependent on how much harm is done and the injury received. It can also include spitting in a person's face (although this would not be recognized as assault in terms of witness intimidation legislation (*Normanton* 1997 WL 1103134)). Note that the Police, Crime, Sentencing and Courts Act 2022 has disapplied the time limit for bringing a prosecution for cases of common assault where the alleged behaviour of the accused amounts to domestic abuse. It was six months from the time of the offence and it is now six months from the reporting of the offence to police.

> **TASK 1** Two people have been arguing. One has pushed and shoved the other but the victim is uninjured. Is the offence common assault or common assault by beating?

22.2.2 Actual Bodily Harm

This offence is covered under s 47 of the Offences Against the Person Act 1861. The main factor which distinguishes common assault by beating from ABH is the degree of injury. *R v Donovan* [1934] 2 KB 498 at 509, [1934] All ER Rep 207 suggested that 'bodily harm has its ordinary meaning' and includes 'any hurt or injury calculated to interfere with the health or comfort of the prosecutor. Such hurt or injury need not be permanent, but must, no doubt, be more than merely transient and trifling'.

The injury must therefore be real and it should be capable of being seen or felt by the victim. It also includes psychiatric injury/illness or psychological damage (*R v Ireland* [1998] AC 147 (HL)). All of these latter 'injuries to the mind' must be more than transient emotions such as fear, distress or panic and must be supported by medical evidence (see *R v Chan Fook* [1994] 2 All ER 552, [1994] 1 WLR 689).

The term 'harm' can have a broad meaning, for example in one case the victim visited their ex-partner who then cut off their ponytail. Such an act was held to amount to ABH (see *DPP v Smith (Michael Ross)* [2006] EWHC 94 (Admin), [2006] 2 All ER 16).

The aspects of intention or recklessness are the same for ABH as they are for common assault by beating; it only needs to be proved that the assault was intended or that it was carried out recklessly. There is no need to prove that the accused intended to cause injuries amounting to ABH (or was reckless as to whether injuries amounting to ABH would be caused).

This offence is triable either way and the penalty if tried summarily is six months' imprisonment and/or a fine and five years' imprisonment on indictment. Note that if the assault is racially or religiously aggravated, the maximum sentence is seven years' custody (see 19.8).

22.3 Unlawful and Malicious Wounding or Inflicting Grievous Bodily Harm

Section 20 of the Offences Against the Person Act 1861 states that it is an offence to 'unlawfully and maliciously ... wound another person' or to 'inflict grievous bodily harm [upon another person]'. The suspect must know that the actions would result in some kind of injury but does not necessarily have to foresee the degree of injury. The injuries can be caused either with or without a weapon.

To understand this offence, careful consideration needs to be given first to the meaning of certain words. 'Grievous' should be taken to mean 'really serious' (*DPP v Smith* [1961] AC 290). 'Unlawfully' means 'without lawful justification' (as opposed to cases of lawfully inflicted injury, eg self-defence). 'Maliciously' means there is:

- an actual intention to do that particular kind of harm; or
- recklessness (unreasonably persisting in taking that risk) as to whether such harmful consequences will occur as a result of the actions taken. For example, in the possible transmission of a sexually transmitted infection by sexual activity, it would be reckless for the suspect to take that risk (*R v Dica* [2004] 3 All ER 593 (CA)).

Note that although malice must be present, it does not have to be towards the victim personally.

22.3.1 The extent of the injury

The injury must amount to either wounding or grievous ('really serious') bodily harm. Wounding is defined as breaking all the layers of the skin ranging from a minor cut to a deep incision. It does not have to be caused with a weapon. If any of the layers of skin are still intact, this would not be considered a wound even if a bone is broken (*R v Wood and M'Mahon* (1830) 1 Mood CC 278) although a broken bone could still amount to GBH.

GBH is not defined in the Act but case law has established that it should be given its ordinary meaning, which is 'really serious bodily harm' (*DPP v Smith* [1960] 3 All ER 161), but the results do not necessarily have to be permanent. Note that in law there is no distinction between 'serious' and 'really serious'.

The CPS suggests the following as examples of GBH (CPS, 2017b):

- injury resulting in some permanent disability;
- visible disfigurement;
- broken or displaced bones;
- injuries with substantial blood loss, usually requiring blood transfusion;
- injuries resulting in lengthy treatment or incapacity;
- psychiatric injury (expert evidence is required).

GBH does not have to include an assault or a battery. For example, a person infecting their partner knowingly with the HIV virus while concealing the infection from the partner is committing the offence of GBH. There have been at least ten convictions for GBH based on the reckless transmission of HIV in England and Wales. Telephone calls that would result in serious psychiatric injury to the victim can also amount to GBH.

This offence is triable either way and the penalty if tried summarily is six months' imprisonment and/or a fine and up to seven years' imprisonment on indictment. Note that if the assault is racially or religiously aggravated, the maximum sentence is seven years' imprisonment (see 19.8.3).

22.3.2 GBH with intent

Section 18 of the Offences Against the Person Act 1861 states that the offence is 'wounding or causing grievous bodily harm with intent to do grievous bodily harm or to resist or prevent arrest'. The main difference between simple GBH and this offence is the element of intent. Inevitably, it can be difficult to prove intent, although there will be some obvious examples, for instance if a weapon is used. It is important to note that it is not possible to attempt to commit simple GBH as any attempt clearly has the intent to cause serious harm, therefore it would be charged as an attempted s 18. GBH with intent can also be committed by someone resisting or preventing the lawful apprehension of any person.

The offences are triable on indictment only and the maximum penalty is life imprisonment. There was no perceived need to create a racially or religiously aggravated offence for this offence as the maximum sentence is already life imprisonment.

22.4 Police Officers and the Use of Force

In the course of their work, police officers sometimes have to use force to control a situation or to carry out their duties. When a police officer suspects that they might need to use force, a systematic approach is essential to ensure that it is absolutely necessary.

Members of the public sometimes use force against police officers and data from the Office for National Statistics (ONS, 2022i) shows there were over 41,000 assaults on police officers in England and Wales (in the year ending March 2022).

Section 2 of the Police, Crime, Sentencing and Courts Act 2022 has increased the maximum custodial sentence for battery against emergency workers from 12 months to two years, as well as it becoming an aggravating factor meriting an increased sentence (the maximum available) for other assault offences (see 22.4.2).

22.4.1 The use of force by police officers

Force should only be used by police officers when justified and must be applied proportionately to protect the officer(s) or others from harm or when detaining a person after arrest or for the purpose of a search. However, it is important that the police officer is always acting in the line of duty otherwise their actions could be unlawful and even amount to an assault.

If violence seems likely to occur, the officer should first ascertain whether their mere presence could be sufficient to calm the situation. If this has no impact, then they will use communication skills to ask if assistance is required, and use active listening skills to try to calm the situation down. If there is an escalation and the officer perceives the use of force on a person to be required, then primary control skills will be used, ie pushing away with open hands and using restraining techniques such as arm locks. If the officer struggles to take control and is overpowered, they may need to use incapacitant sprays, baton strikes, and 'takedowns'. Increasingly, officers are now being trained and issued with Tasers for use in extreme situations. In a life-threatening situation, authorized firearms officers (AFOs) can attend.

Officers will assess the risk by profiling a subject's behaviour on a scale ranging from compliant to serious/aggravated resistance, and also consider if there is any prior information on the subject, for example from intelligence. The number of persons present at the scene, the location, and whether any potential weapons are present will also be taken into account. The National Decision Making Model (see 4.2.1) can be used to help ensure that the decisions made and the actions taken are reasoned and justified, and will hold up in any subsequent court case.

22.4.1.1 Reasonable use of force by police officers

The use of force must be reasonable (see 22.5 for a general discussion on the reasonable use of force). For police officers particular considerations apply, for example if a police officer restrains a person without intending to arrest them, this can amount to an assault (as in common assault by beating, ABH, or GBH) and applies even if an arrest could have been justified (see *Fraser Wood v DPP* [2008] EWHC 1056 (Admin)). In another case, it was decided that a police officer who fired a taser twice was not using unreasonable force as the officer genuinely believed that he and others close by were under the threat of immediate attack (*Chief Constable of Merseyside Police v McCarthy* [2016] EWCA Civ 1257).

22.4.2 Assaults on Emergency Workers (Offences) Act 2018

Some people deliberately assault officers or emergency workers, and others may resist police actions. This legislation covers the offence of common assault, or battery, when committed against an emergency worker acting in the exercise of functions as such a worker (including when an emergency worker is not at work but is carrying out the same activities as they would at work). Section 3 of the Act provides a definition of the term 'emergency worker' and includes, for example, a police constable (and any person who has the powers of a constable or is otherwise employed for police purposes or is engaged to provide services for police purposes), fire and rescue service staff, and ambulance staff (and some other health workers). It is immaterial whether the employment or engagement is paid or unpaid and the word 'function' is used (rather than duty) in the Act to encompass a wide range of emergency workers.

Section 1 of the Act creates two new offences:

- common assault of an emergency worker; and
- assault by beating of an emergency worker.

Both these offences are triable either way and the penalty is a fine or imprisonment for up to two years. Section 2 of the Act also refers to more serious assaults and offences where an emergency worker is a victim; this is now an aggravating factor meriting an increased sentence (the maximum available) and includes the following offences:

- threats to kill (see 22.6);
- wounding with intent to cause GBH (see 22.3.2);
- assault occasioning ABH (see 22.2.2);
- sexual assault under s 3 of the Sexual Offences Act 2003 (see 24.6.5).

Section 3 of the Police, Crime, Sentencing and Courts Act (2022) now also states that there is a required life sentence for the manslaughter of an emergency worker. This is known as 'Harper's Law'.

22.4.2.1 Assaulting, resisting, or wilfully obstructing a police officer

This offence (under s 89 of the Police Act 1996) can be committed against police officers acting in the lawful execution of their duties and against anyone assisting a police officer in the lawful execution of such duties. Note, however, that assault to resist arrest is a separate offence and is covered by s 38 of the Offences Against the Person Act 1861.

Under s 89 of the Police Act 1996, it is an offence for any person:

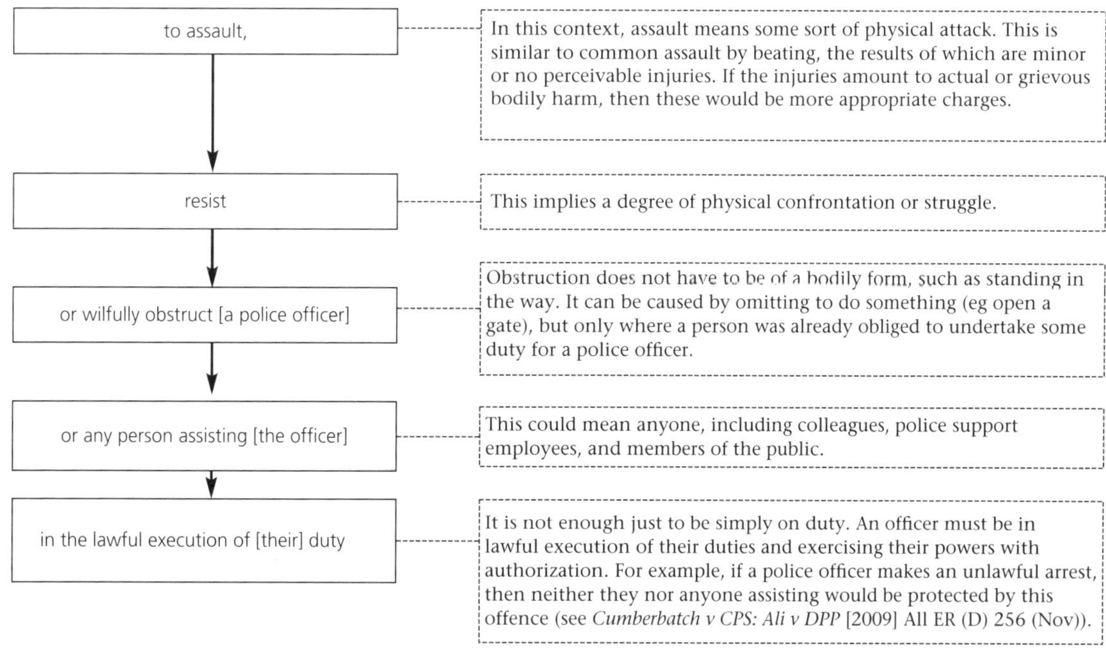

to assault,
In this context, assault means some sort of physical attack. This is similar to common assault by beating, the results of which are minor or no perceivable injuries. If the injuries amount to actual or grievous bodily harm, then these would be more appropriate charges.
resist
This implies a degree of physical confrontation or struggle.
or wilfully obstruct [a police officer]
Obstruction does not have to be of a bodily form, such as standing in the way. It can be caused by omitting to do something (eg open a gate), but only where a person was already obliged to undertake some duty for a police officer.
or any person assisting [the officer]
This could mean anyone, including colleagues, police support employees, and members of the public.
in the lawful execution of [their] duty
It is not enough just to be simply on duty. An officer must be in lawful execution of their duties and exercising their powers with authorization. For example, if a police officer makes an unlawful arrest, then neither they nor anyone assisting would be protected by this offence (see *Cumberbatch v CPS: Ali v DPP* [2009] All ER (D) 256 (Nov)).

The police sometimes need to enter and search a premises without the consent of the occupier to save life or limb, including the prevention of self-harm. If the occupier is present and resists, this offence may be committed. If a police officer receives injuries consistent with common assault, then s 1 of the Assault on Emergency Workers (Offences) Act 2018 would now be the preferred charge.

The s 89 offences are triable summarily and the penalties are a fine or imprisonment (maximum six months for a s 89(1) offence and one month for a s 89(2) offence).

22.5 General Defences to the Use of Violence

There are a great many defences to the application of force, for example self-defence which is also known as 'common law self-defence'. Self-defence is not, however, defined by statute and the courts decide whether a particular act amounts to self-defence. In *Dewar v DPP* [2010] EWHC 1050 (Admin), it was reaffirmed that there is a two-part test to self-defence:

- that the individual believes that they were acting in self-defence; and
- that the force used was reasonable in the circumstances.

There is no need to consider which person was the initial aggressor (see *Marsh v DPP* [2015] EWHC 1022 (Admin)). The timing of the use of force can also vary, for example in the case of *R v Bird* ([1985] 1 WLR 816), the defendant poured wine on the victim before being slapped and pinned against the wall. The defendant then punched the victim forgetting a glass was in their hand. The appeal upheld that they had used self-defence. The definition of reasonable force is examined in more detail below.

'Reasonable chastisement' of a child by their parent can be a defence but this does not apply if it involves assault occasioning ABH, unlawfully inflicting GBH, causing GBH with intent, or cruelty to a child (s 58 of the Children Act 2004). The Education Act 1996 removed the right of schools to use corporal punishment.

That consent had been given for the use of force can be a defence, for example in some sports although the level of force used must be appropriate and in keeping with the rules of the game (see *R v Barnes* [2004] EWCA Crim 3246 and *R v Coney* (1882) 8 QBD 534). Consent can also be used as a defence in a medical context, eg that the act was a necessary part of medical treatment, and for piercings or tattoos. It might also be used where there has been horseplay where there is no intention to cause injury (*R v Jones (Terence)* [1986] Crim LR 123). The defence of consent cannot, however, be relied on in offences under ss 47 and 20 of the Offences Against the Person Act 1861 where the injuries resulted from sadomasochist activities (*R v Brown* [1993] 2 All ER 75 (HL)).

Intoxication can only be used as a defence for crimes of specific intent, such as offences under s 18 (maliciously inflicting GBH with intent), as the defence can argue that the level of intoxication prevents the person from forming the necessary *mens rea*. The other more common types of assault (common, causing ABH, assault of a police officer) require no specific intent and therefore this defence cannot apply. Involuntary intoxication, eg due to spiked drinks, could be considered as a defence for offences of basic intent such as common assault or ABH.

22.5.1 The meaning of 'reasonable force'

The use of reasonable force for self-defence, defence of property, and law enforcement is defined in law, for example its use for certain powers of arrest and entry provided under s 117 of the PACE Act 1984 (see 10.13.1.2). Defences that include the notion of 'reasonable force' include:

- self-defence (a common law defence, see s 76(2)(a) of the Criminal Justice and Immigration Act 2008);
- defence of property (a common law defence, see s 76(2)(aa) of the Criminal Justice and Immigration Act 2008); and
- the use of force in the course of prevention of crime or in making an arrest (s 3(1) of the Criminal Law Act 1967.

For these defences, the person must have an honest belief that it was necessary to use force *and* the force used was not disproportionate (see *Palmer v R* [1971] AC 814). The person's perceptions of the circumstances at the time will be taken into account, as well as the reality of the situation. If the defendant had a mistaken belief as to the circumstances but this misunderstanding is considered to have been reasonable, then a jury could find the defendant not guilty (*R v Williams (Gladstone)* [1987] 3 All ER 411, 78 Cr App R 276). Also, it is not reasonable to expect all defendants in the heat of the moment to be able to judge the precise degree of force required. Therefore, a person who uses the force honestly and instinctively thinking that it was necessary will be provided with some leeway.

22.5.2 Defending against intruders in a dwelling

Where a person is defending themselves or others from intruders in their home, it might still be reasonable to use a degree of force that might be considered disproportionate in other circumstances.

Amendments to s 76(5)(a) of the Criminal Justice and Immigration Act 2008 introduced the idea of disproportionate force, but also the idea that the force used by an individual must always be reasonable in the circumstances as they believed them to be. The question as to whether the degree of force used was reasonable in the circumstances is to be decided by reference to the circumstances as they were believed to be. For example, a burglar breaks into a home and the resident goes downstairs where a struggle ensues. The resident punches the burglar, knocking them out. This might be considered disproportionate but is reasonable taking the circumstances into account. However, if the resident then started beating the unconscious burglar, this would be considered grossly disproportionate and therefore unlawful. A resident who shot indiscriminately at burglars with a gun (*R v Martin* [2002] 2 WLR 1) was held to have used grossly disproportionate force.

The degree of force used will be considered lawful if the resident is acting in self-defence or to protect other people in their home, and the force used was disproportionate but not grossly disproportionate.

Protecting property by using disproportionate force, however, is still unlawful. Further information regarding the defence of property is available in the Parliament briefing paper 'Householders and the criminal law of self-defence' available online.

22.6 Threats to Kill

Section 16 of the Offences Against the Person Act 1861 (as amended by Sch 12 to the Criminal Law Act 1977) is about making threats to kill and can be committed in two main ways. The simplest form of this offence is when A threatens to kill B and intends that B will believe the threat.

This offence can also be committed in a slightly more complicated way: person A communicates a threat to kill and intends that B should believe the threat. But the threat is not about killing B, it is about killing another person C. It is irrelevant whether C knows about the threats.

To prove this offence, it is not necessary for A to intend to kill anyone, but it must be proved that A intends that B should fear that this will be carried out. The threats made by A can be premeditated or spontaneous and can be communicated by any means including digitally. There does not have to be the sense that the killing will be carried out immediately. The offence could be useful where an assault has been prevented, yet the victim B was in fear that it would be carried out.

Threats to kill are relatively common and it is difficult to prove an offence has occurred because it is often one person's word against another. The onus is on the prosecution to prove that there was no lawful excuse for making such a threat. (A lawful excuse could be that the defendant honestly believed that it was necessary in self-defence.) The threat to kill should be plain to see for the jury (*R v Solanke* [1970] 1 WLR 1). If it is not obvious, then perhaps a charge under s 4 of the Public Order Act 1986 or a charge of affray would be more appropriate.

This offence is triable either way and the penalty if tried summarily is six months' imprisonment and/or a fine and on indictment ten years' imprisonment. Section 156 of the Police,

Crime, Sentencing and Courts Act creates a new s 68A to the Sentencing Act 2020 so that an assault or threat to kill is aggravated if it is on an individual who is providing a public service.

> **TASK 2** Using the information given here, decide what offences may have been committed in relation to the injuries sustained by the victims.
>
> Someone is holding a baby and arguing with a second person. The second person loses their temper and pushes the shoulder of the first person causing them to drop the baby. As a result, the baby sustains a minor fracture to its right arm.
>
> After months of alleged harassment by local youngsters in the street outside their house, the occupant comes out and slaps one of the youngsters, leaving a large red mark on their cheek.

22.7 The Use of Violence to Enter Premises

It is an offence to use violence to gain entry to premises occupied by any person opposing the entry (s 6 of the Criminal Law Act 1977). Convictions for this offence are usually in the context of domestic disputes, a person trying to force their way into their own flat is committing an offence if their live-in partner is inside and does not want them to come in.

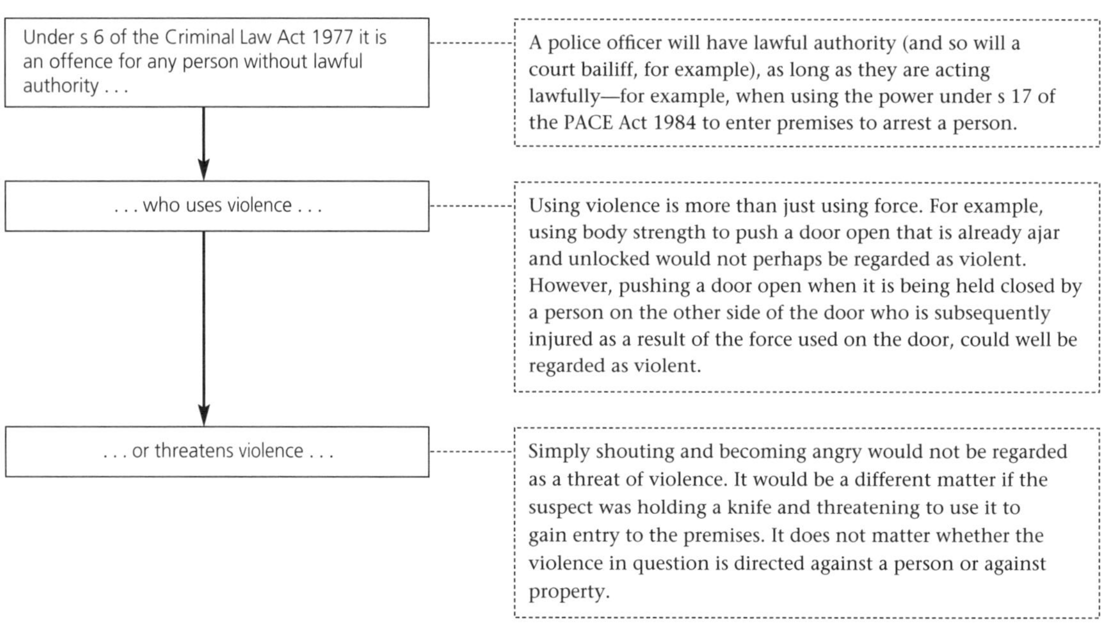

Under s 6 of the Criminal Law Act 1977 it is an offence for any person without lawful authority . . .
A police officer will have lawful authority (and so will a court bailiff, for example), as long as they are acting lawfully—for example, when using the power under s 17 of the PACE Act 1984 to enter premises to arrest a person.
. . . who uses violence . . .
Using violence is more than just using force. For example, using body strength to push a door open that is already ajar and unlocked would not perhaps be regarded as violent. However, pushing a door open when it is being held closed by a person on the other side of the door who is subsequently injured as a result of the force used on the door, could well be regarded as violent.
. . . or threatens violence . . .
Simply shouting and becoming angry would not be regarded as a threat of violence. It would be a different matter if the suspect was holding a knife and threatening to use it to gain entry to the premises. It does not matter whether the violence in question is directed against a person or against property.

So, for this offence the suspect must have no lawful authority to enter and must either use violence or threaten to use violence.

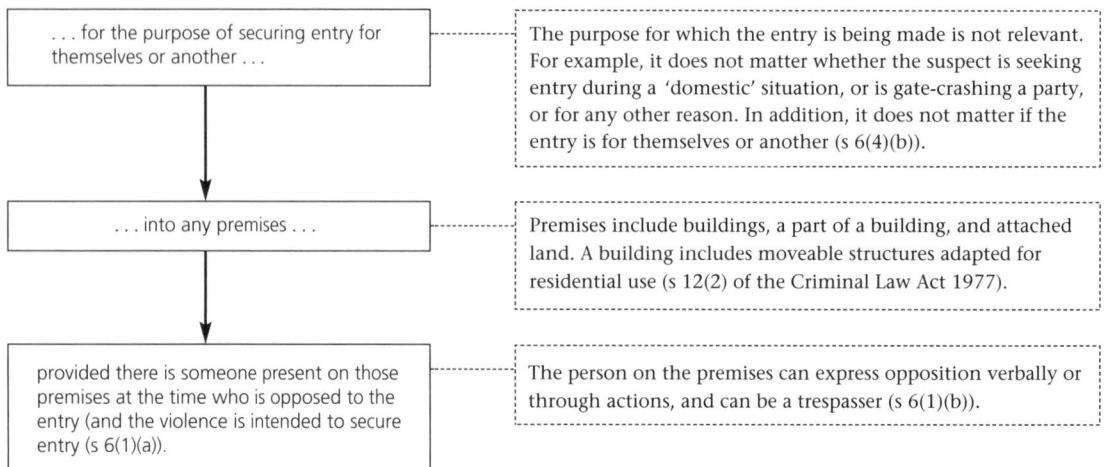

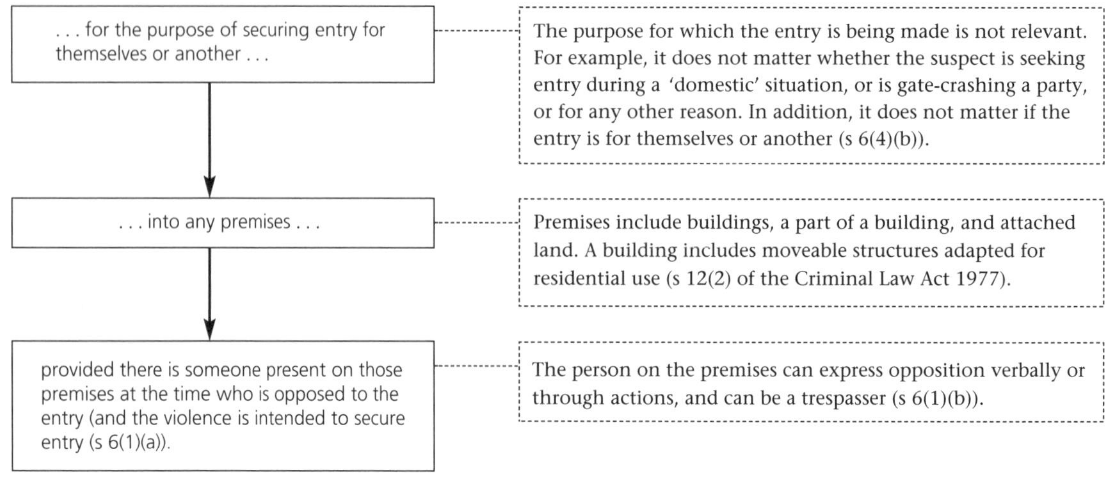

Premises include buildings, a part of a building, and attached land. A building includes moveable structures adapted for residential use (s 12(2) of the Criminal Law Act 1977).

The person on the premises can express opposition verbally or through actions, and can be a trespasser (s 6(1)(b)).

This offence does not apply for a home-owner, tenant, or legally intended occupier who comes home and finds a trespasser(s) in their property; they can legally use or threaten violence to enter the property. The exemption does not include using or threatening violence towards the trespasser; the trespasser can be asked to leave and it is an offence under s 7 of the Criminal Law Act 1977 if they refuse to do so.

The offence of using violence to gain entry is triable summarily and the penalty is six months' imprisonment and/or a fine. There is a power of entry to arrest under s 17 of the PACE Act 1984 for this offence (see 10.13.1.2).

TASK 3 The police are called to a house at night where a young person is banging on the front door with their fists. The police speak to an older person inside the house. It emerges that the two people live together in the house and are joint owners. The young person had arrived home in the early hours, very drunk, to find the front door would not open with the key. The neighbours report hearing the individual inside the house shouting 'Go away!' In relation to s 6(1) of the Criminal Law Act 1977, has the youngster committed an offence by banging on the door?

22.8 Answers to Tasks

TASK 1 Common assault by beating (battery): only the very slightest degree of force is required to constitute a battery and little or no injury is necessary to prove the offence.

TASK 2 Based entirely on the limited information available to you, the following are the possible offences that could be considered:

An assault can be committed directly or indirectly. So, when one individual pushes the person with the baby they cause a direct common assault against the baby holder. As a result of this reckless behaviour, they have also committed a s 20 GBH offence on the baby (see 22.3).

A large red mark may have interfered with the health and comfort of the youngster, therefore ABH could be considered. Alternatively, the red mark could be considered as a hardly perceivable injury so this might be a common assault by beating (s 39 of the Criminal Justice Act 1988).

TASK 3 Section 6(1) of the Criminal Law Act 1977 states that any person who, without lawful authority, uses or threatens violence for the purpose of securing entry into any premises for themselves or for any other person is guilty of an offence provided that:

- 'a person is present on those premises, and they are opposed to the entry which the violence is intended to secure'; and
- 'the person using violence or threatening the violence knows that that is the case'.

It appears that the person is only hammering on the door and therefore these actions fall short of the violence required for this offence. If their actions escalate to the likelihood of damage being caused, or threats or use of violence, then the offence would be committed (provided they knew their partner was on the premises and opposed the entry).

23 Theft, Fraud, and Related Offences

23.1 Introduction

This chapter examines the law and procedure concerned with a number of criminal offences associated with theft and fraud. It presents the basic knowledge of the criminal law required for approved pre-join professional policing degrees, the PCDA, and the DHEP. This Handbook will provide the essence of the most relevant law and interpretations (both academic and from case law or precedent).

Student officers are likely to be involved in most stages of the investigation of theft and simple types of fraud, from reporting to investigation and possibly prosecution. Student officers are less likely to become involved in complex fraud investigations which, by their very nature, require protracted enquiries and specialist training. This is particularly the case for large-scale fraud where complex decisions need to be made concerning the 'screening' of reported offences to decide which should be the subject of a secondary investigation (see Chapter 13) and with reference to the National Intelligence Model (NIM) (see 12.6). The investigation is likely to be conducted by a specialist unit, which may also investigate cybercrime (see Chapter 14).

Officers should consider the most appropriate way of dealing with certain low-level or low impact offences (e.g. shoplifting items with a value below £200) and exercise their police powers accordingly. Theft is considered a volume crime and is managed via the Volume Crime Management Model (VCMM). The investigative response must fall within the directions of your police service policy and you should always check with a workplace tutor and/or supervisor for guidance. Options include out-of-court disposals such as Community Remedies described by the Anti-social Behaviour, Crime and Policing Act 2014; Anti-social Behaviour Statutory guidance for frontline professionals (Home Office, 2022k), and Community Resolutions as described by the Sentencing Council (2023c). These options can reduce the pressures on the criminal justice system and divert individuals, particularly juveniles, from the criminal justice system.

The topics covered in this chapter support the learning outcomes required by the National Policing Curriculum subject area of 'Understanding the Police Constable Role'.

23.2 Theft

Of the dishonesty criminal offences police officers deal with early in their careers, theft will probably be the most common.

Theft includes shoplifting and stealing from an employer as well as several other similar crimes. The primary source of legislation relating to theft is to be found in ss 1–6 of the Theft Act 1968. Sections 1–6 form the basis of the definition of the offence of theft, and its component parts are required to prove an offence of theft. The point to note is that the definition of theft is not a singular definition but rather consists of several strands distinguished through ss 1–6. Taken together, they form the basis of theft contrary to s 1(1) of the Theft Act 1968.

There are many legal complexities surrounding theft and this chapter will examine the basic principles involved.

A person is guilty of theft (s 1(1) of the Theft Act 1968) if they 'dishonestly [appropriate] property belonging to another with the intention of permanently depriving the other of it'. A thief is a person who commits a theft. There are five key concepts relating to the definition of theft:

- dishonesty;
- appropriation;
- property;
- belonging; and
- the intention to permanently deprive.

We will examine each of these in turn, however it is important to stress that you *must* have each of these facets in order for the offence of theft to be considered 'complete'. This does not mean a crime has not been committed, under s 1 of the Criminal Attempts Act 1981 or some other legislation, only that *theft* has not been committed. This applies to the points to prove for any offence but as you will note, in some of the examples described below, there is a lot of context to consider around each of these points to prove.

23.2.1 Dishonesty

The Theft Act 1968 does not define dishonesty, but it does state that dishonesty can include where a person would have been willing to pay for property they took (s 2(2)). The Theft Act 1968 defines where a person should not be treated as dishonest (s 2(1)). The person is not acting dishonestly if they believe that:

- they had the lawful right to take the item (eg a man sees a woman leaving with their bag and decides to take it back from them);
- they would have had the owner's consent if the owner had known the circumstances (eg your neighbour is on holiday and you are looking after their garden but your lawnmower breaks down so you take your neighbour's from their shed to cut your grass); or
- the owner cannot be discovered by taking reasonable steps (eg a person finds cash in the street).

Following the 2017 ruling (see *Ivey v Genting Casinos (UK) Ltd* [2017] UKSC 67), the courts must decide what it was that the defendant believed, and then decide whether the defendant's actions were dishonest against the standards of an everyday, honest person.

Besides *Ivey v Genting Casinos (UK) Ltd* [2017] UKSC 67, the complex case law for these tests is to be found in Lord Nicholls in *Royal Airlines Sdn Bhd v Tan* [1995] 2 AC 378 and Lord Hoffmann in *Barlow Clowes International Ltd (in liquidation) v Eurotrust International Ltd* [2005] UKPC 37.

23.2.2 Appropriation

Appropriation (s 3(1) of the Theft Act 1968) is assuming the rights of an owner of property by keeping it or controlling its movements. This would include a person who borrows something from a friend and chooses to keep it hoping the friend forgets about it.

A person can agree to the appropriation, but the consent may be in doubt if the person:

- has been deceived about the nature of the circumstances;
- is not of sound mind (including having serious learning difficulties) (see *R v Hinks* [2000] 4 All ER 833); or
- cannot understand the language being spoken (*R v Lawrence* [1972] AC 262).

If a person buys an item in good faith but later finds out it is stolen property, the purchase can amount to theft, including if the person tries to sell it, destroy it, dispose of it, or keep it.

23.2.3 Property

Property within the Theft Act 1968 (s 4) has its common meaning of a moveable object (such as items for sale in a shop, money, and physical items) or being an individual's personal property (which includes a wide variety of things such as purses, illegal drugs, pets). However, it also includes other things such as ideas, and intangible items.

'Things in action' are also taken to be property under the Act. By 'things in action' the law is referring to rights rather than tangible objects; for example, the right to sue. For the student police officer, considering property as a 'thing in action' is most likely to occur in connection with alleged crime involving bank or building society accounts; for example, when a person entrusted by an organization makes a cheque payable to themselves. When we deposit funds in a bank account, the ownership of the money passes to the bank but, in turn, we gain the right to 'sue' the bank, in law, for this amount to be refunded—this right to sue is the 'thing in action'. If someone tries to dishonestly debit an account holder's bank balance by transferring money to their own account, they are attempting to steal our right to sue for the money, not the money itself.

23.2.3.1 Land and buildings as property

The legal term for this is 'real property'. Land itself generally cannot be stolen so if, for example, someone goes on holiday and their neighbour moves the fence over a little to increase the size of their own garden this would not be regarded as theft. That would be a matter for a civil court.

However, if a trustee in charge of an estate or a person with a power of attorney choses to sell another's land for profit, this could amount to theft. Turf, topsoil, and cultivated trees and shrubs on land are sometimes removed without permission, as are parts of buildings such as roof tiles, fireplaces, and fixtures and fittings. These items are all regarded as 'real property' so taking such items could amount to theft. Whole buildings, however, cannot be stolen as such.

23.2.3.2 Wild plants and animals on land

The taking of wild plants, fruit, flowers, and fungi only amounts to theft if taken for sale, reward, or a commercial purpose, or taken in such a manner that the plant or fungus cannot grow back (eg the plants have been uprooted).

The taking of wild animals from land can be regarded as theft but only if:

- the animal had been tamed and was being kept in captivity such as in a zoo or a home; or
- the animal had been killed there without the landowner's permission and taken.

Note, however, that other legislation such as the Wildlife and Countryside Act 1981 might prohibit the taking of certain wild animals and plants in a wider range of circumstances.

23.2.4 Belonging to a person

When something belongs to a person, under s 5 of the Theft Act 1968 this means that the person is either the owner or they have:

- a proprietary right or interest, for example the owner of a car takes it to a garage for repairs. The mechanic spends time and money on parts repairing and servicing the car. The mechanic would now have a proprietary right of interest in the car as they have put an investment into it and now have part ownership until the debt is settled. If the owner takes the car without settling the debt this might be theft (see *R v Turner (No 2)* [1971] 1 WLR 901);
- possession, for example, whoever has the vehicle in their possession. Whether that possession is lawful depends on the circumstances and the timing. If the owner of the car took it without having paid then their possession might not be lawful; or
- control, for example the mechanic who carries out the repairs on the car.

23.2.5 The intention to permanently deprive

This is shown by a person treating another person's property as if it were their own and is described in s 6(1) of the Theft Act 1968. It could include:

- borrowing and lending over an extended time scale (eg borrowing and then lending on to someone else); or
- pawning an item that belongs to another person

It has been held to include a person stealing a car and then offering it back to the owner in the same condition for money (*R v Raphael* [2008] EWCA Crim 1014).

23.2.6 Mode of trial and penalties for theft

The offence of theft is triable either way, depending on the value of the goods in question. For retail property worth £100 (inclusive of VAT) or less, a PND can be used (see 10.18.2.2). The offence is tried summarily if the value of the property stolen is less than £5,000 (s 22A of the Magistrates' Courts Act 1980) and the penalty is six months' imprisonment and/or a fine. The penalty when tried on indictment is up to seven years' imprisonment.

The police powers for entry and search provided under the PACE Act 1984 for indictable offences (see 10.13.5) apply for all suspected thefts (s 176 of the Anti-social Behaviour, Crime and Policing Act 2014).

23.3 Robbery and Blackmail

Robbery and blackmail are two separate offences under the Theft Act 1968, but there are some similarities. Robbery (s 8 of the Theft Act 1968) is theft involving the use of physical force (or the threat) to appropriate property belonging to another person.

For blackmail (s 21(1) of the Theft Act 1968), a demand is made of the victim with the aim of causing them a loss. These demands could be expressed, implied, written, spoken, or through conduct. However, for blackmail no property needs to have been taken and no physical force needs to be involved for the offence to be proved.

23.3.1 Robbery

Robbery is the act of stealing from a person whilst using or threatening violence (s 8 of the Theft Act 1968). It is an aggravated form of the primary offence of theft and therefore, for robbery to be proved, theft must be proved first. Force or a threat of force must be used immediately before, at the time of the theft, and in order to carry out the theft.

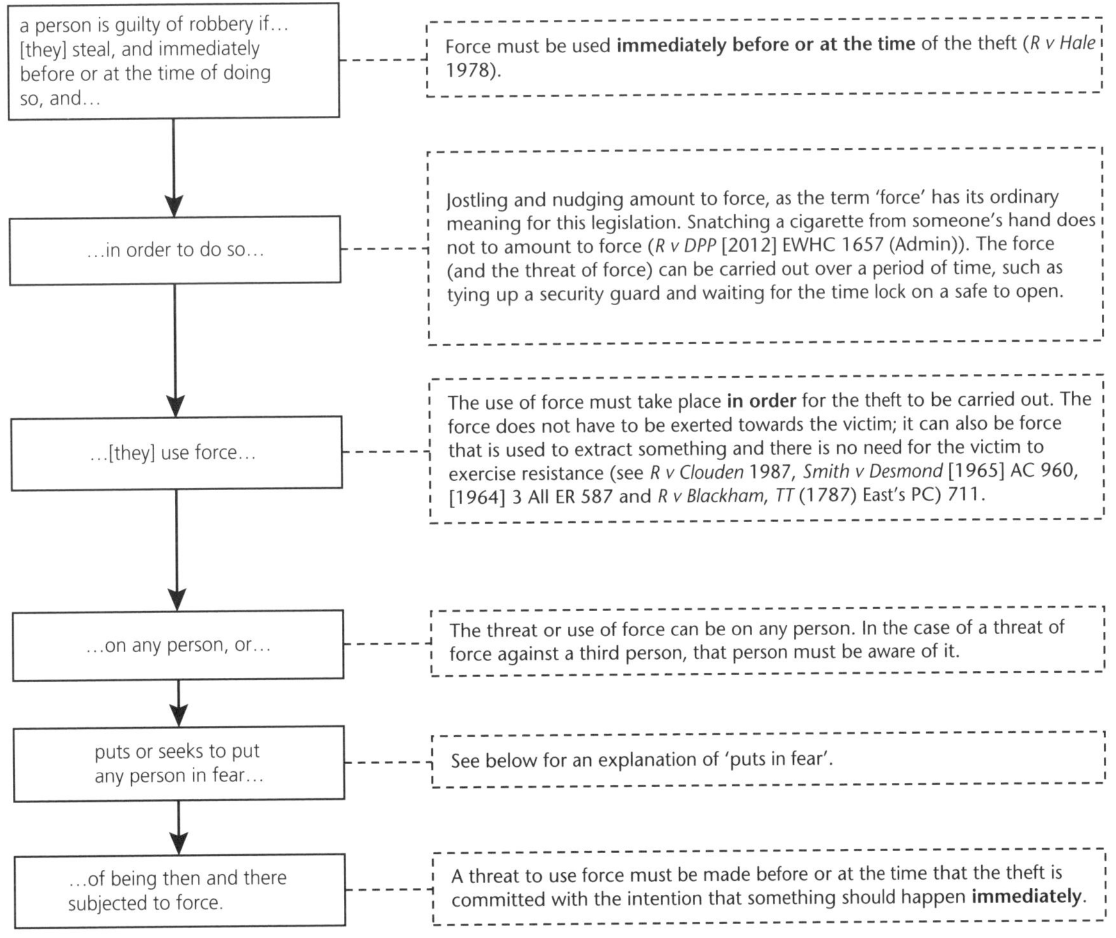

a person is guilty of robbery if... [they] steal, and immediately before or at the time of doing so, and...
Force must be used **immediately before or at the time** of the theft (*R v Hale* 1978).
...in order to do so...
Jostling and nudging amount to force, as the term 'force' has its ordinary meaning for this legislation. Snatching a cigarette from someone's hand does not to amount to force (*R v DPP* [2012] EWHC 1657 (Admin)). The force (and the threat of force) can be carried out over a period of time, such as tying up a security guard and waiting for the time lock on a safe to open.
...[they] use force...
The use of force must take place **in order** for the theft to be carried out. The force does not have to be exerted towards the victim; it can also be force that is used to extract something and there is no need for the victim to exercise resistance (see *R v Clouden* 1987, *Smith v Desmond* [1965] AC 960, [1964] 3 All ER 587 and *R v Blackham, TT* (1787) East's PC) 711.
...on any person, or...
The threat or use of force can be on any person. In the case of a threat of force against a third person, that person must be aware of it.
puts or seeks to put any person in fear...
See below for an explanation of 'puts in fear'.
...of being then and there subjected to force.
A threat to use force must be made before or at the time that the theft is committed with the intention that something should happen **immediately**.

There are two main ways the 'puts in fear' element of the offence could be established:

- the victim's statement could show that they were put in fear—the degree of fear is not important because the fortitude shown by different people will inevitably vary (see *R v DPP; B v DPP* [2007] EWHC 739 (Admin), 171 JP 404); or
- the state of mind of the suspect (intending to make a person fear that force will be used) could be evidenced from the suspect's statement, evidence from other witnesses, or circumstantial evidence, such as the suspect had been holding an offensive weapon.

When force is threatened but the force is to be used against a third person, they must know about it; they must 'apprehend' the force. For example, suppose a person goes into a bank and passes a note to the bank teller to hand over cash or they will stab the person behind them in the queue. The person in the queue does not know the threat has been made so even if the teller hands over the money this would not be robbery (although it might be blackmail, see 23.3.2).

If a suspect says, 'Give me your mobile now, or I'll stab you', and the mobile is handed over it would be robbery. If a suspect says , 'If you don't give me your mobile tonight, I'll stab you', it is not robbery as the threat of force is for the future (although it might be blackmail). If force is used after the theft, it would not be robbery, but the two separate offences of theft and assault could be considered. An example of this could be a person snatching a mobile phone from someone's hand without force and then pushing that person.

Note that all five elements of theft must be proven (see 23.2) to have applied at the time of the robbery. For example, in *R v Zerei* [2012] EWCA Crim 1114, where a car had been taken by violence and abandoned shortly afterwards, a conviction for robbery was held to be unsafe as the intention to permanently deprive was not proved.

The offence of robbery is triable on indictment only and the maximum penalty is life imprisonment.

23.3.2 Blackmail

A person commits the offence of blackmail if they make any unwarranted demand with menaces with a view to making a gain (for themselves or any other person) or with intent to cause a loss to any other person (s 21(1) of the Theft Act 1968).

The term demand is not defined by the Theft Act 1968; however, it is understood here to be made implicitly as well as expressly and therefore may appear as a simple request. What is important is that it is clear that the requester is making such a demand even if the person tries to disguise it as something different. A demand must be unwarranted and unreasonable (some demands may be considered reasonable, eg in relation to repaying a debt). The communication can be made by phone, text, or letter and will be considered to be made the moment a text is sent, or letter posted, not upon receipt (*Treacy v DPP* [1971] 1 All ER 110). Spoken or written demands do not need to be received by the victim; they will be considered 'made' for the purposes of establishing this element of the offence as soon as they are addressed to the victim, whether received or not.

The offence of blackmail is triable on indictment only and the maximum penalty is 14 years' imprisonment.

23.4 Burglary and Trespassing

Burglary is a 'volume' and 'acquisitive' crime. Student police officers will undoubtedly encounter crimes of burglary whilst on Supervised and Independent Patrol. It is a serious offence; aggravated burglary carries a maximum sentence of life imprisonment. Research suggests that an increasing number of burglaries are committed with the main aim of obtaining vehicle keys to steal vehicles (Chapman *et al*, 2012; Allcock *et al*, 2011).

There is also the phenomenon of distraction burglary (in some police services called 'artifice' burglary), where entry is gained to the home of a person by an offender pretending to be an official. An important case in establishing this type of offence was *R v Boyle* [1954] 2 QB 292,

[1954] 2 All ER 721. Boyle was charged with burglary as he had falsely represented himself as being employed by the BBC to locate radio disturbances. He gained admittance to the person's home and stole a handbag. On appeal against conviction, it was held that the use of deception to gain entry meant he was a trespasser. Artifice burglars usually commit a series of similar crimes within a short period of time ('spree offences').

The legislation concerning burglary is to be found in ss 9–10 of the Theft Act 1968. We look separately at the basic offence of burglary, then at aggravated burglary, and finally at various aspects of trespass associated with this type of crime.

23.4.1 The basic offence of burglary

The basic offence of burglary is set out in s 9 of the Theft Act 1968. There are two subsections (s 9(1)(a) and (b)) which describe the main ways the offence can be committed, as shown in the diagram.

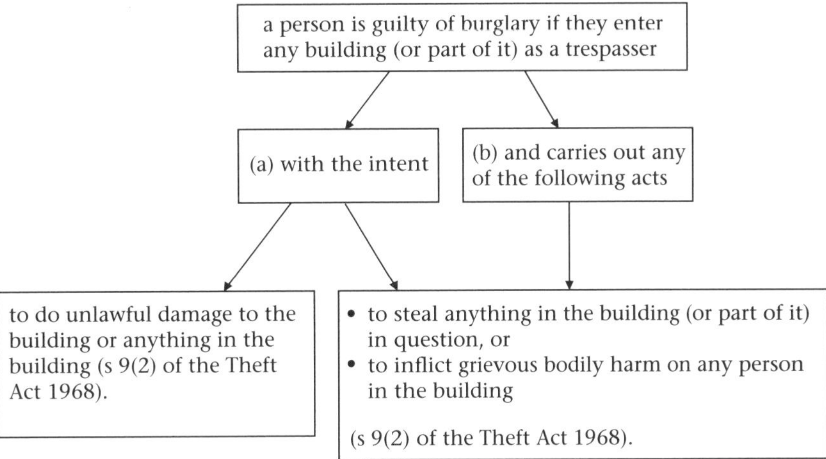

Certain terms, such as 'entry', 'trespasser', and 'building' and 'dwelling' need to be carefully defined to fully appreciate the range of activities that might count as burglary under s 9(1) of the Theft Act 1968.

Entry can be gained in a number of clearly defined ways:

- In person, by walking or climbing into a building, either completely or by inserting a body part (eg an arm or a leg) through a window or letter box. However, there must be more than minimal insertion; sliding a hand between a window and frame from the outside of a building to release the catch would be insufficient.
- Using a tool or article as an extension of the human body to carry out one of the relevant offences. In these circumstances, no part of the body needs to be inserted, only the article that is being used to gain entry. The article must be used for more than just gaining entry; using a crowbar just to prise open a door would not qualify as the full offence but a length of garden cane pushed through the letter box of a shop to hook a scarf from a display would qualify as the full offence.
- Using a blameless accomplice in a similar way to using an article as an extension of the suspect's body. For example, a child under ten years of age could be lifted through a small window to obtain property from inside. Note that if the child only prepared an entry point the offence has only been attempted.

Trespass involves a person entering a building or part of a building (for the purpose of committing burglary) in one of the following ways:

- entering a building for a purpose other than the intended purpose of that building, for example going into a shop with the intention to steal (rather than an intent to browse or buy);
- entering by some kind of deception, for example pretending to represent a utility company for the purpose of reading a meter and being invited into the building;
- crossing over a demarcation line of some kind, unlawfully and without invitation or permission;

- exceeding a general consent to enter premises, such as entering your parent's house at night to take something (see *R v Jones; R v Smith* [1976] 3 All ER 54, [1976] 1 WLR 672).

The person must have guilty knowledge (*mens rea*: see 18.4.2) that what they are doing amounts to trespass or, alternatively, not care about whether they are trespassing. The trespass must also be voluntary.

Burglary involves entering a building as a trespasser. **Building** is not comprehensively defined in the statute, although s 9(4) provides that it includes any **inhabited** vehicle or vessel. It is implicit in the wording of the subsection that uninhabited vehicles and vessels will not be 'buildings' for the purposes of the 1968 Act (CPS, 2019c).

The meaning of 'a building' is reasonably well established through case law:

- 'building is an ordinary word, which is a matter of fact' (*Brutus v Cozens* [1973] AC 854, 861);
- a building is 'a structure of considerable size and intended to be permanent or at least to endure for a considerable time' (*Stevens v Gourley* (1859) 7 CBNS 99); and
- 'a building need not necessarily be a completed structure; it is sufficient that it should be a connected and entire structure' (Lush J in *R v Manning & Rogers* (1871) LR 1 CCR 338). A house under construction becomes a building when it has all its walls and a roof.

Examples of buildings include garages, bandstands, and garden sheds. However, telephone kiosks, bus shelters, and lorry trailers have been ruled not to be buildings in this context. Similarly, a motor home or caravan inhabited during a holiday is a building but not when it is parked and empty during the winter.

Localized police policy and procedures may vary with regard to burglary from different types of building.

23.4.1.1 Dwelling

The Theft Act 1968 uses the term 'dwelling'. What a 'dwelling' is will be a question of fact in each case. There is no statutory definition within the 1968 Act, and no entirely definitive case law that assists, although s 9(4) does provide for an inhabited vehicle or vessel to be a dwelling for the purposes of the section. Examples would include an inhabited building or a vehicle or vessel which is inhabited at the time of the offence (the occupier need not be present at the time of the burglary). An inhabited houseboat moored at a riverbank is regarded as a building for the purposes of the Theft Act 1968. However, a tent would not be included since it is not a semi-permanent structure.

Gross LJ delivering the judgment of the Administrative Court in *R v Hudson* [2017] EWHC 841 (Admin), said: 'In broad terms, the more habitable a building as a matter of fact, the more, other things being equal, it is likely to be a "dwelling" within s.9(3)(a) of the Act. Beyond that I would not go.'

The Court of Appeal said that burglary of a hotel room with theft of the guest's personal possessions was 'much more akin' to burglary of domestic premises than it was to burglary of a small shop or business. It did not say that burglary of an occupied hotel room was in fact a burglary of domestic premises (see *R v Massey* [2001] EWCA Crim 531).

A common-sense approach to what is a 'dwelling' should be applied and each case treated on its own facts using the normal and natural meaning of the word.

The question of what constituted a dwelling under s 9 of the Theft Act 1968 was specifically considered by the Court of Appeal in the case of *R v Rodmell* (1994) (unreported, 24 November). This was a case that involved the burglary of a garden shed and the theft of power tools. The shed stood in three and a quarter acre of grounds of a house and some 60 yards from the house (CPS, 2019c).

Further information on the definitions of premises and locations can be found in 4.3.1.1

This legislation also covers part of a building, and when a person is lawfully within a building but enters a part of it that they are not meant to enter (eg if a customer in a shop goes behind the counter to take money out of the till). It will be a matter for the jury to decide whether the area in question amounts to 'part of a building' from which the general public are excluded (see *R v Walkington* [1979] 2 All ER 716, [1979] 1 WLR 1169).

Source: Image © Zoe Lawton-Barrett.

23.4.1.2 Section 9(1)(a) and (b)

Section 9(1)(a) relates to intent only, while s 9(1)(b) relates to actually carrying out the acts (as shown in the diagram at the start of 23.4.1).

For an offence under s 9(1)(a) of the Theft Act 1968, the suspect must enter a building (or part of a building) as a trespasser and intend to commit a further act as follows:

- steal something from the building;
- inflict grievous bodily harm on anyone in the building; or
- unlawfully damage the building or anything inside it.

However, the further acts do not have to be committed, only intended. The intent can be proved in a number of ways (or in combination), such as the suspect admitting to having guilty knowledge or criminal intent to commit the offence. Alternatively, other suspects (who admit to involvement in committing the offence) might name the suspect as an accomplice.

Circumstantial evidence can also help to prove intent, such as finding the suspect in the building in possession of property that is known to originate from the premises. Witness statements and the arresting officer's observations on the suspect's proximity to the crime scene when they were arrested could also be used. Fingerprint evidence could also indicate the suspect had been at the location.

If the offence relates to an intent to inflict GBH then the entry must have been made with that in mind. Consequently, in relation to proving the offence, the same degree of evidence of intent will be required as would be needed to prove intent under s 18 of the Offences Against the Person Act 1861 (see 22.3.2).

Under s 9(1)(b) of the Theft Act 1968, burglary involves trespassing and committing acts which amount to:

- theft (or attempted theft); or
- inflicting GBH (or attempting to inflict GBH).

(Note that subsection (b) does not include inflicting unlawful damage.)

In relation to inflicting GBH, the meaning of 'inflict' includes situations where force is applied indirectly (*R v Wilson* [1983] 3 All ER 448). For example, it would include a situation where a person in their home is frightened by a burglar and as a result falls down the stairs and breaks their leg; harm has been inflicted by the suspect even though there has been no application of force. For further information on judging whether the acts amount to an attempt, see 27.2.

An offence under either subsection is triable either way and the penalty if tried summarily is six months' imprisonment and/or a fine. If tried on indictment, the maximum penalty is ten years' imprisonment (14 years if the building or part of the building was a dwelling), and at least three years for a third or subsequent domestic burglary.

23.4.2 Aggravated burglary

Aggravated burglary (s 10 of the Theft Act 1968) involves the use of weapons or explosives to commit burglary. The following elements need to be established to prove the offence of aggravated burglary:

- that the defendant had the offensive weapon with them;
- that the defendant had it at the time of the burglary.

The types of weapon or explosive (articles) covered by this legislation are shown in the table, and can be recalled by the mnemonic WIFE.

Article	Details	Theft Act 1968
Weapon of offence	Any article made or adapted for use for causing injury or incapacitation to a person, or intended for such use (see 25.2.1 on offensive weapons)	s 10(1)(b)
Imitation firearm	Anything which has the appearance of being a firearm, whether capable of being discharged or not (see 25.7)	s 10(1)(a)
Firearm	Includes air weapons (see 25.3) and 'component parts' of a firearm (ie parts essential to discharging the weapon) but not 'additions' (see 25.3.1.1)	s 10(1)(b)
Explosive	Any article manufactured for the purpose of producing a practical effect by explosion (excluding fireworks or matches) or intended for that purpose by the person who has it	s 10(1)(c)

The phrase 'has with them' means 'constructive possession', ie the person is carrying the item, including carrying it in a bag. (The meaning is therefore not the same as under the Firearms Act 1968 where the item can be at a short distance away.) Anyone else who is present and knows about the constructive possession is also regarded as having constructive possession.

The point in time when the offence is committed depends upon the subsection and the type of burglary:

- for a s 9(1)(a) burglary, the offence is committed the moment a person enters a building with intent (and has in their possession one of the WIFE articles);
- for a s 9(1)(b) burglary, the offence is committed when the person commits the theft or grievous bodily harm (and has in their possession one of the WIFE articles).

This offence is triable by indictment only and the penalty is life imprisonment.

23.4.3 Trespass offences related to burglary

A trespass or vagrancy offence may be committed if an offender enters a premises, but their actions do not amount to burglary.

Trespassing with a weapon of offence is committed when a person is on any premises as a trespasser and has a weapon of offence in their possession without lawful authority or reasonable excuse (s 8 of the Criminal Law Act 1977). It is different from burglary under s 9(1)(a) because there is no intent to commit theft, GBH, or damage. The offence is triable summarily and the penalty is three months' imprisonment and/or a fine.

Trespassing with an intent to commit a sexual offence is covered under s 63 of the Sexual Offences Act 2003. The offender must be on premises or land without the owner's or the occupier's consent and know that they are trespassing or be reckless as to whether they are trespassing. There must also be an intent to commit a sexual offence while there, and this could be proved from statements from the offender or intended victim or items seized from the offender at the scene such as a knife. The intent can be formed at any time, for example before entering the premises or only later while on the premises. It is immaterial whether any sexual offence is actually committed. The s 63 offence is triable either way, and the penalty if tried summarily is six months' imprisonment and/or a fine not exceeding the statutory maximum and ten years' imprisonment on indictment. As part of the Police, Crime, Sentencing and Courts Act 2022, the 1824 Vagrancy Act, which had often been used as a way of dealing with trespass for an unlawful purpose, was repealed. However, the 2022 Act also created a new offence of trespass with intent to search for or to pursue hares with dogs (s 63).

TASK 1 Someone enters a house as a trespasser with intent to steal jewellery. While they are on the premises, they take a screwdriver from a cupboard under the stairs and continue the search. Twenty minutes later, the occupier returns, and the intruder stabs them, causing serious injury. Has the intruder committed burglary?

23.5 Stolen Goods and the Proceeds of Crime

Stolen goods include 'money and every other description of property, except land, and includes things severed from the land by stealing' (s 34(2)(b) of the Theft Act 1968). For this offence, goods are 'stolen goods' if they have been obtained through theft, blackmail, or fraud (ss 1 and 21 of the Theft Act 1968 and s 1 of the Fraud Act 2006, respectively).

Stolen goods also include any gain or return from the disposal of the original stolen items such as money or other items which have been received in exchange (s 24(2) of the Theft Act 1968). These are known as notionally stolen goods. After the original theft, there is often a whole chain of handlers commiting the offence of handling stolen goods, if each has guilty knowledge (*mens rea*) that the goods were originally acquired by a theft. The chain will only be broken when a person receiving the goods is unaware of their origins.

It is not always possible for a criminal to benefit from a crime if stolen items remain in their original state. In the majority of cases, the profits have to be realized, exchanged, or hidden to be of any worth, for example through money laundering. Such activities consequent to a theft are covered by the Proceeds of Crime Act 2002.

23.5.1 Handling stolen goods

This offence is described in s 22 of the Theft Act 1968 and is committed when a person handles goods that they know or believe to have been stolen. The person can receive the items or agree to or assist with their retention, removal, disposal, or realization by another person. This could be for the benefit of another person. It is also an offence to make arrangements for any of these acts.

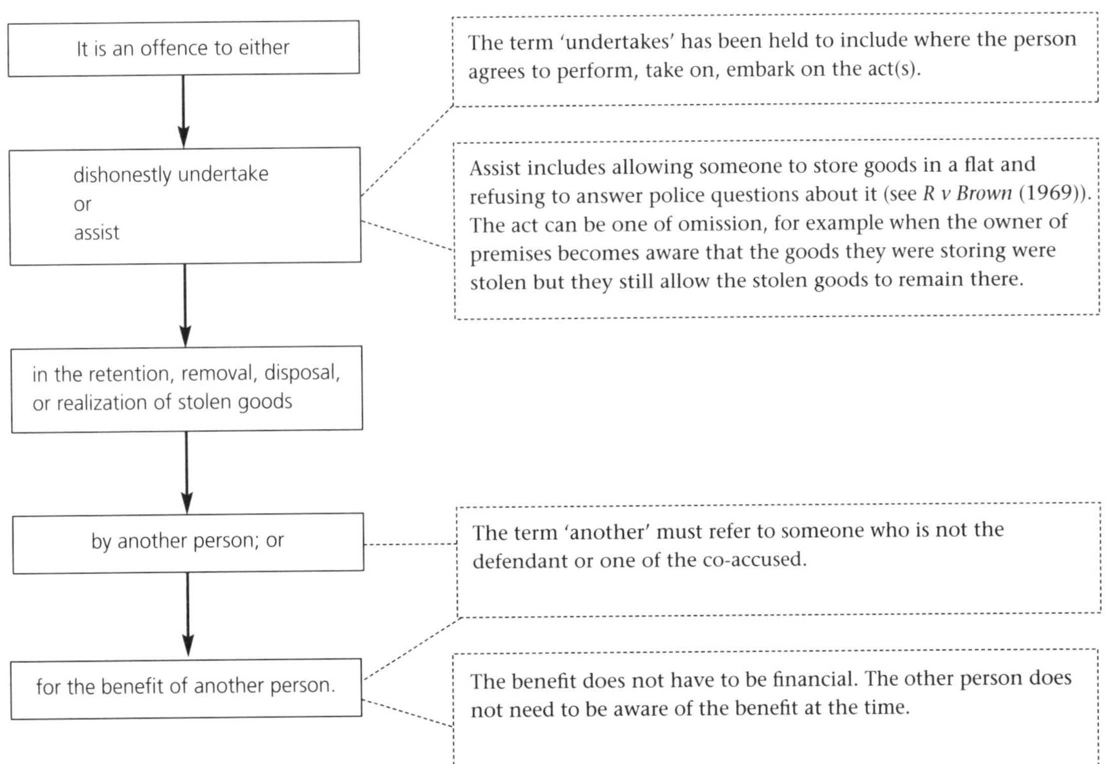

It is an offence to either
dishonestly undertake
or
assist
in the retention, removal, disposal, or realization of stolen goods
by another person; or
for the benefit of another person.
The term 'undertakes' has been held to include where the person agrees to perform, take on, embark on the act(s).
Assist includes allowing someone to store goods in a flat and refusing to answer police questions about it (see R v Brown (1969)). The act can be one of omission, for example when the owner of premises becomes aware that the goods they were storing were stolen but they still allow the stolen goods to remain there.
The term 'another' must refer to someone who is not the defendant or one of the co-accused.
The benefit does not have to be financial. The other person does not need to be aware of the benefit at the time.

The meaning of receiving has been established through case law as 'gaining possession or control' and would obviously include carrying or holding the goods. It also includes having control over goods which is when a person has remote possession; the goods could be kept in storage in a garage or lock-up, for example. The receiver does not need to gain in any way from handling the goods, but they must know that the goods are stolen at the time of their receipt, and there must be proof that the goods were actually received.

If the receiver is still negotiating the receipt of the goods, then such an act might be construed as 'arranging' so this would also constitute handling. The suspect would have been given an opportunity at interview to explain how they had acquired the stolen property. If the jury viewed the explanation as reasonable then the defendant might be acquitted. If no explanation is given then the judge might direct the jury to the fact the defendant had been found with stolen property and did not account for this (see *R v Schama; R v Abramovitch* (1914) 11 Cr App R 45, 79 JP 184).

The offence of handling stolen goods can also be committed by a person who is involved in the retention, removal, disposal, or realization of the goods, where:

- retention means continuing to possess something (especially when someone else wants it);
- removal means taking something away from the place where it was;
- disposal means passing on, getting rid of, giving away;
- realization means obtaining money or profit by selling something.

The offence of handling stolen goods is triable either way. The penalty if tried summarily is six months' imprisonment and/or a fine and on indictment up to 14 years' imprisonment. Note that all five elements of theft must be proven (see 23.2) to have applied at the time of the incident.

23.5.1.1 Knowing or believing that items are 'stolen goods'

The handler must know or believe that items have been stolen for their actions to be dishonest; suspicion would not be enough. A suspect would know that the goods were stolen if they had been told so by the thief or someone with first-hand knowledge or might believe that they were stolen if there was no other likely explanation in the circumstances (see *R v Hall* [1985] 1 QB 496).

The court must decide what is dishonest by everyday standards and whether the suspect was aware that they were dishonest by those standards. The suspect may claim to have a right to the property in law, to have the owner's consent, or that the owner cannot be traced, but none of these is relevant. It would also be perfectly correct to direct a jury to use common sense, such as when a person chooses to become deliberately blind to the circumstances of goods being stolen (see *R v Griffiths* (1974) 60 Cr App R 14). In the case of *R v Hall* (1985) 81 Cr App R 260, two men carried out a burglary and took the stolen property. The following morning, police observed the two men meeting Hall at Hall's flat and raided it ten minutes later. The property was recovered. All three men were arrested. Hall was convicted of receiving stolen goods. He appealed, arguing that he did not know or believe the goods to be stolen but this was dismissed on the grounds that there could be no other reasonable explanation.

23.5.1.2 The distinction between 'handling' and 'theft'

It is important to distinguish clearly between 'handling' and 'theft'. The court will take several key factors into account such as whether the theft was complete, whether there was a break in the proceedings, and whether the suspected handler became involved only after the theft had occurred.

For example, Person A visits a large out-of-town electrical store. They take two smart speakers from a shelf and hide them in a waste bin outside the store. Person B then takes them away. The table presents a number of different scenarios to illustrate some differences between handling and theft.

Offences committed by the second person:

Person B's actions …	Offence committed by Person B
Waiting by pre-arrangement and takes the radios away	Theft
Arrives half an hour later by pre-arrangement and takes the radios away	Theft, particularly if the proceeds are to be shared out between Person A and Person B. However, handling may be considered if Person B subsequently pays Person A for the goods
Told where the radios are but only after they have been stolen. Then collects the radios	Handling

A thief can become a handler of the property that they originally stole, but only if they lose control of the property and later decide to have dealings with the property once again (whilst the goods can still be referred to as stolen goods).

When an individual is caught with items very recently reported as stolen, they owe an explanation as to how they came by the property. An item that has recently been stolen is 'hot property' and local criminals are likely to know about it, so it is unreasonable for a person to claim they did not know it was stolen property. However, if a period of months extended between the original crime and the handling it would be harder to prove that the person knew the goods were stolen unless it was a particularly unusual item. In the case of *R v Cash* [1985] QB 801, [1985] 2 All ER 128, nine days was considered a reasonable period of time for the possession to be 'recent' and the so-called 'doctrine of recent possession' could apply.

23.5.2 Proceeds of crime offences

It is an offence under the Proceeds of Crime Act 2002 (POCA) to benefit from any kind of proceeds of crime. Criminals will often try to convert the proceeds of crime into assets in order to make its origin appear legitimate; this is often referred to as money laundering.

The legislation makes reference to the proceeds of crime as 'criminal property', defining it as any property which the suspect knows or suspects to be, or represent, the benefit from any criminal conduct (s 340(3)) in the UK (s 340(2)). Criminal property is defined in s 340(9) and includes:

- money (including cryptocurrencies);
- property (real, personal, inherited, and moveable);
- things in action such as patents, copyrights, and trademarks; and
- other intangible or incorporeal property such as property rights, leases, or mortgages.

The definition of criminal property under POCA is very similar to the definition of property in s 4 of the Theft Act 1968 (see 23.2.3). Real property is land and things forming part of the land, such as plants and buildings; moveable property is not attached to the land (eg furniture, art, books). Although you cannot generally steal land, it can be seized if it has been gained through criminal activity.

There are three main offences under POCA and these cover most eventualities in benefiting from the proceeds of crime:

- **Concealing, converting, or transferring criminal property** (s 327(1)). A person commits an offence if they conceal, disguise, convert, transfer, or remove any criminal property from the UK. For example, a person knows that their partner brings back large quantities of tobacco from cross-Channel ferry trips to sell on to local people. The person hides the money in their house. The person is guilty of concealing criminal property. Lodging, receiving, retaining, or withdrawing can amount to converting (*R v Fazal* [2009] EWCA Crim 1697).
- **Involvement in arrangements for criminal property** (s 328(1)). A person commits an offence if they enter into (or become concerned in) an arrangement which they know (or suspect) will help with the acquisition, retention, use, or control of criminal property by (or on behalf of) another person. The suspect must know or believe it was criminal property when the arrangement was made (see *R v Geary* [2010] WLR (D) 228). For example, a person derives a considerable income from targeting vulnerable householders to carry out unnecessary repairs for cash. The person's partner knows how the money is obtained and has opened several bank accounts for depositing the profits and has therefore been concerned in an arrangement that will help in the retention or control of criminal property.
- **Acquisition, use, and possession of criminal property** (s 329(1)). For example, a drug dealer gives some of their profits to their sibling. The sibling knows where the money comes from and uses it to buy food; and has 'used' criminal property.

There is a power of search for premises (s 289(1) of POCA): if a police officer has reasonable grounds for suspecting the presence of cash obtained through unlawful conduct (s 304(1)), or intended to be used by any person for an unlawful purpose, the officer may also search a suspect and any article they possess at that time (s 289(2) and (3)). The officer's presence must be lawful and they must comply with s 2 of the PACE Act 1984 and the PACE Codes of Practice (see 4.6).

23.5.2.1 Defences and penalties

Three defences are available for offences under ss 327(1), 328(1), and 329(1) of POCA:

- the suspect makes or intends to make (with reasonable excuse) an 'authorized disclosure' to a police, border force, or nominated officer, concerning their actions;
- the suspect knows (or reasonably believes) that the criminal conduct took place outside the UK and that it was not unlawful in that other country (s 327(2) and (2A)); and
- law enforcement authorities (such as the police) have a defence if they convert or transfer seized criminal property, for example they place seized money in an interest-earning account.

An additional defence is available for s 329(1) where a person acquires, uses, or has possession of the criminal property for 'adequate consideration'. A shopkeeper could claim this defence if they sell goods to a customer and the customer pays with money that comes from crime. Solicitors or accountants who receive money for costs also have this defence.

The ss 327, 328, and 329 offences are all triable either way and the penalty is a fine or imprisonment (six months summarily or up to 14 years on indictment).

> **TASK 2** A police officer carries out a lawful s 1 PACE Act 1984 stop and search on a young person and complies with the PACE Codes of Practice throughout the process. The 18-year-old is a persistent offender and prolific shoplifter whose favoured MO is to steal items from shops, to sell on quickly and cheaply. Local intelligence has indicated that they have an extremely modest lifestyle but that they have recently become a courier for local drug suppliers. During the search, £10,000 is found concealed in various locations in their clothing. The young person cannot account for this money and there is no evidence of its origin. Assess the likelihood of a successful prosecution for acquiring, retaining, using, or controlling the criminal property under s 328(1) of POCA. Refer to the cases of *R v NW, SW, RC & CC* [2008] EWCA Crim 2 and the conjoined cases of *R v Allpress; R v Symeou; R v Casal; R v Morris; R v Martin* [2009] EWCA Crim 8 for your answer.

23.6 Going Equipped

The offence of going equipped for theft can be a serious allegation linked to accusations of burglary or theft. Going equipped is an offence defined by s 25 of the Theft Act 1968.

A wide range of articles are used to carry out thefts, such as equipment for removing security tags from clothes or for gaining entry to vehicles or buildings (including keys). The offence is not committed by simple possession of the articles alone. The suspect must also be on their way to carry out a theft (see *R v Ellames* [1974] 3 All ER 130). A direct connection to a specific burglary or theft does not need to be established but it must be possible to prove that the article is intended to be used to commit crime (by the suspect or another person). The offence cannot be committed when coming away from the crime.

In terms of possession of the article, the phrase used in the legislation is 'has with [them]' which includes having it ready to hand, such as in a nearby bush a few feet away or in a car parked outside the address they intend to break into. Note that the meaning of 'has with [them]' here is not the same as for aggravated burglary (for which constructive possession is required (see 23.4.2)).

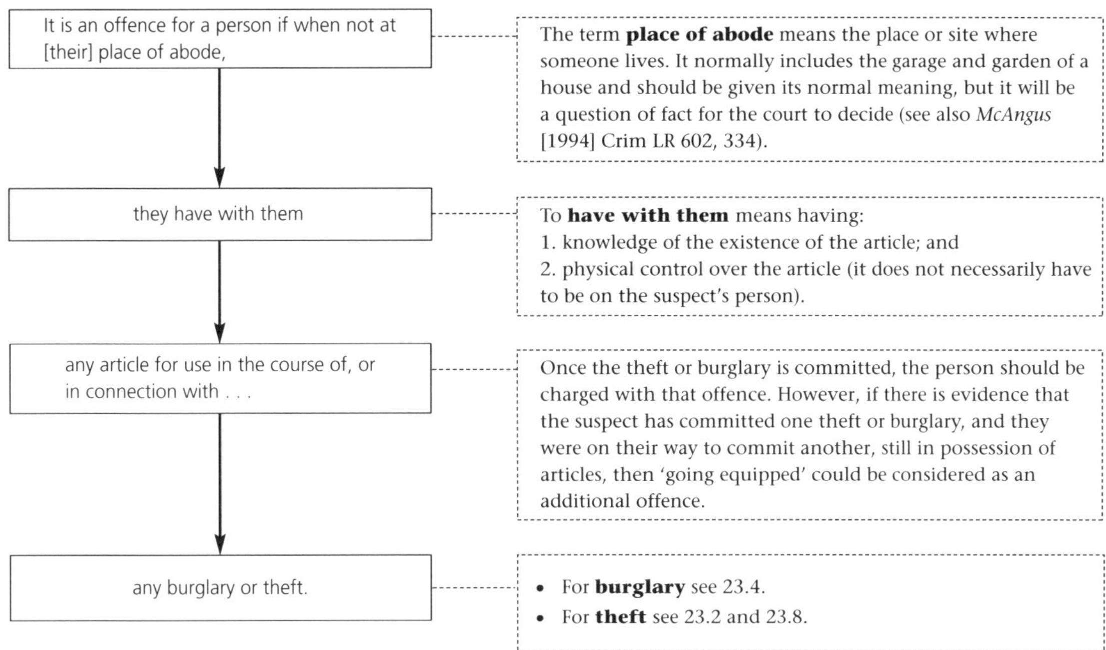

To **have with them** means having:

• For **theft** see 23.2 and 23.8.

This offence is triable either way and the penalty is six months' imprisonment and/or a fine if tried summarily and up to three years' imprisonment on indictment.

23.7 Abstracting Electricity

Electricity does not fall within the definition of property in the Theft Act 1968 and therefore it cannot be stolen, in legal terms. Instead, s 13 of the 1968 Act creates the offence of dishonestly using electricity without authority or dishonestly causing electricity to be wasted or diverted.

Here, the term 'abstracting' means illegally taking and using without due authority, such as a householder reconnecting the supply after it has been cut off (see *Boggeln v Williams* [1978] 2 All ER 1061). The abstracted electricity could be from the mains or from a battery in a caravan for example. As electricity is not property within the Theft Act 1968, entering premises with the sole intention of abstracting electricity does not amount to burglary.

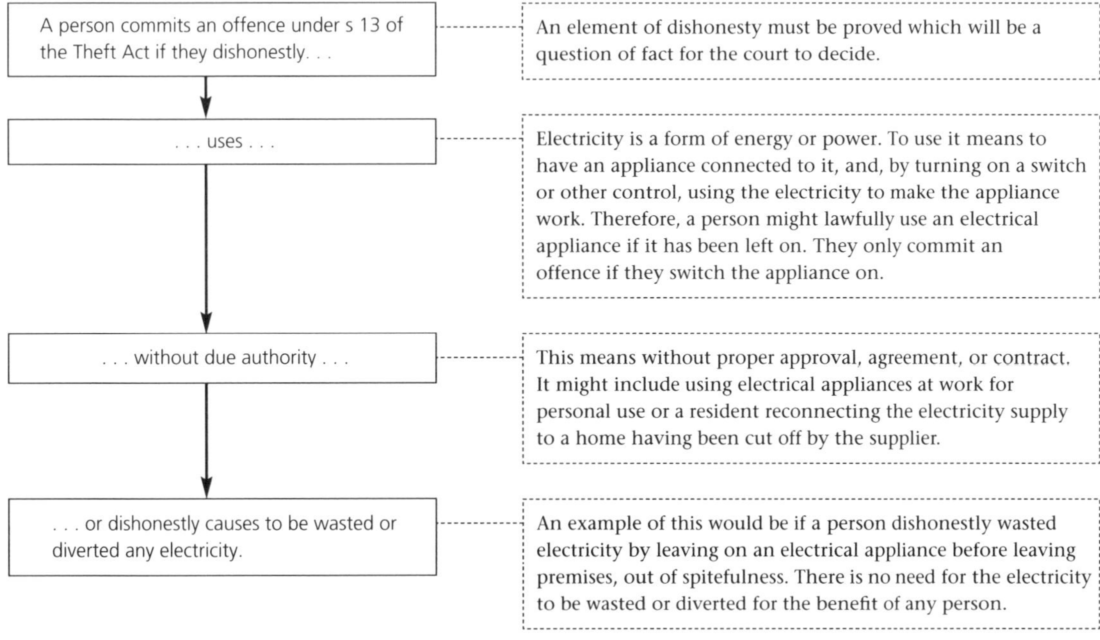

A person commits an offence under s 13 of the Theft Act if they dishonestly. . .
An element of dishonesty must be proved which will be a question of fact for the court to decide.
. . . uses . . .
Electricity is a form of energy or power. To use it means to have an appliance connected to it, and, by turning on a switch or other control, using the electricity to make the appliance work. Therefore, a person might lawfully use an electrical appliance if it has been left on. They only commit an offence if they switch the appliance on.
. . . without due authority . . .
This means without proper approval, agreement, or contract. It might include using electrical appliances at work for personal use or a resident reconnecting the electricity supply to a home having been cut off by the supplier.
. . . or dishonestly causes to be wasted or diverted any electricity.
An example of this would be if a person dishonestly wasted electricity by leaving on an electrical appliance before leaving premises, out of spitefulness. There is no need for the electricity to be wasted or diverted for the benefit of any person.

This offence is triable either way and the penalty is six months' imprisonment and/or a fine if tried summarily and up to five years' imprisonment on indictment.

TASK 3 In the early hours of the morning, Alex walks through an industrial estate where there are several storage warehouses. One of them has an open door and they decide to go in to shelter from the rain. Inside the warehouse they notice a separate office and force open the door, damaging the lock. Alex switches on an electric fire to keep warm and falls asleep to be woken by a security guard patrolling the industrial estate. Has Alex committed burglary?

23.8 Theft of Vehicles and Related Offences

Every year thousands of cars are stolen in England and Wales. This section examines some of the legal aspects and police procedures surrounding a number of vehicle crimes, particularly stolen vehicles.

The police will receive reports of vehicles being stolen by telephone, through online crime reporting systems, and occasionally personally whilst on patrol. The Police National Computer (PNC) (see also 12.8.1) will be updated, and if the registration number of the stolen vehicle is spotted by a police officer or an automatic number plate reader system (ANPR), action will be taken. If a stolen vehicle is found by the police, they will usually arrange for an approved recovery operator to take it to a secure location (reg 4 of the Removal and Disposal of Vehicles Regulations 1986). It may be examined by a crime scene investigator, depending on local policy. The owner of the vehicle or their insurance company must pay the recovery and storage fees (Removal, Storage and Disposal of Vehicles (Prescribed Sums and Charges) Regulations 2008).

Some vehicles are stolen for resale and their origin will often be disguised when sold on. Other vehicles may be broken down for parts while the cost of vehicle repairs motivates some owners to arrange (or claim) that the vehicle has been stolen so that they can claim the insurance.

Other vehicles are taken for 'joyriding'. This is not theft because there is no intention to permanently deprive the owner of the vehicle. The offence of TWOC (taking a conveyance without consent, see 23.8.2) was created to cover these circumstances. TWOC may also result in damage and injury so we also describe 'aggravated vehicle taking'. We also cover 'interference' and 'tampering' with motor vehicles along with the theft of pedal cycles.

As vehicles become 'smarter' cyber-security considerations will loom larger. A 2017 government document highlighted the key cyber-security principles for connected and automated vehicles (gov.uk, 2017) to help vehicle industry designers and suppliers to promote security. This area is likely to require ongoing research to inform future investigations and to provide drivers with suitable advice on reducing the opportunities for hacking.

23.8.1 Detection of stolen vehicles

There are a number of ways of establishing whether or not a particular vehicle is a stolen vehicle. The registration plates provide clues; for example, do the plates look as though they have been replaced or have new plates been affixed over the old plates? Do the plates seem different from the rest of the car—for example, is the car clean and the plates old and dirty or are the plates plain with no reference to a vehicle dealership? To investigate further, a police officer will need to establish the specific identifying features of a vehicle (see Chapter 16).

23.8.1.1 Disguising stolen vehicles

When a vehicle is reported as stolen, it is recorded on police and other databases using the VICE identifying features (see 16.2.1.1). So, if it is to be sold or used long term it would need to have a new 'identity' to evade detection.

Criminal gangs will often produce desirable vehicles with new identities to sell. The perpetrator first obtains an in-demand but damaged vehicle. It must have a V23, the form sent to the DVLA either by an insurance company whenever a total loss payment is made on a vehicle or by a police officer when reporting a vehicle that has been 'written off' in an accident. (It is legal to repair such a vehicle and use it on the roads.) The criminal then steals a very similar vehicle in good condition—the colour and make must be the same as the damaged vehicle. The identifying features from the damaged vehicle are then transferred to the stolen vehicle which will then be sold to an innocent purchaser. Some vehicles are exported as their resale value may be higher in other countries.

Thus, police officers must be alert to vehicles with identifying features that do not exactly match the database records as such a vehicle may have been stolen and provided with a new identity. Also, any vehicle on the roads which has had a V23 should show evidence of extensive repairs; if these are not noticeable then further investigation may be required.

23.8.1.2 Procedure for checking vehicle VICE details

The recommended procedure is outlined in the diagram. If the vehicle needs further examination, a local police service vehicle examiner can carry this out.

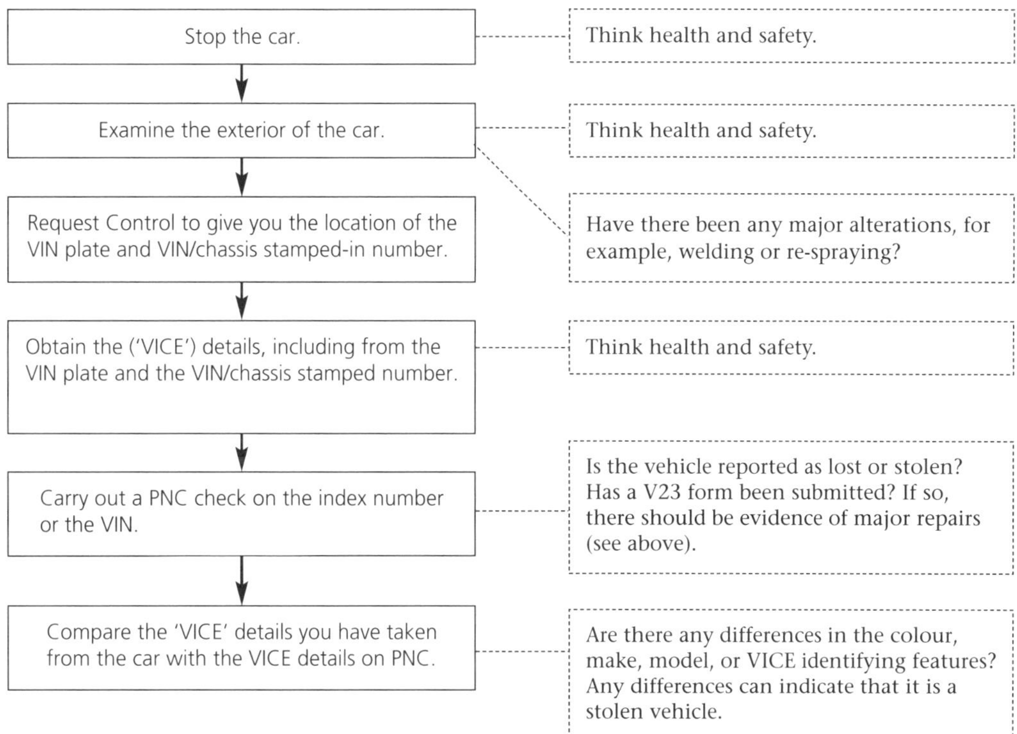

Stop the car.
Think health and safety.
Examine the exterior of the car.
Think health and safety.
Request Control to give you the location of the VIN plate and VIN/chassis stamped-in number.
Have there been any major alterations, for example, welding or re-spraying?
Obtain the ('VICE') details, including from the VIN plate and the VIN/chassis stamped number.
Think health and safety.
Carry out a PNC check on the index number or the VIN.
Is the vehicle reported as lost or stolen? Has a V23 form been submitted? If so, there should be evidence of major repairs (see above).
Compare the 'VICE' details you have taken from the car with the VICE details on PNC.
Are there any differences in the colour, make, model, or VICE identifying features? Any differences can indicate that it is a stolen vehicle.

23.8.2 Taking a Conveyance without the Owner's Consent or Authority (TWOC)

This offence (TWOC) is described in s 12 of the Theft Act 1968. 'Taking a conveyance' is a very common offence in England and Wales and, unfortunately, modern technology has failed to deter criminals from this activity.

A conveyance is any equipment constructed or adapted for the carriage of a person or persons whether by land, water, or air. In this context, a conveyance does not include anything constructed or adapted for carrying items other than people, such as the pedestrian-controlled trolleys used by postal workers to transport mail. Pedal cycles are not included under this legislation either; taking a cycle is covered by another subsection.

The term 'taking' has its ordinary meaning and can include loading a conveyance onto a trailer (see *R v Pearce* [1973] Crim LR 321).

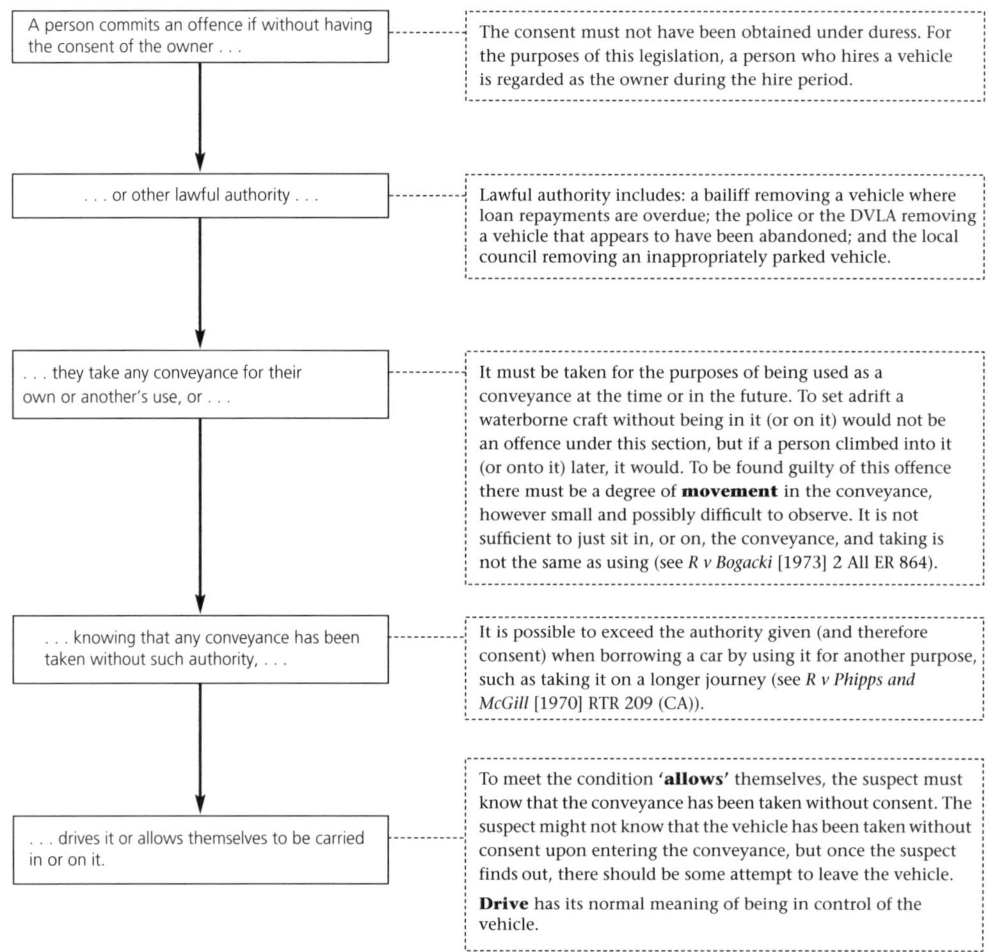

A person commits an offence if without having the consent of the owner . . .
The consent must not have been obtained under duress. For the purposes of this legislation, a person who hires a vehicle is regarded as the owner during the hire period.
. . . or other lawful authority . . .
Lawful authority includes: a bailiff removing a vehicle where loan repayments are overdue; the police or the DVLA removing a vehicle that appears to have been abandoned; and the local council removing an inappropriately parked vehicle.
. . . they take any conveyance for their own or another's use, or . . .
It must be taken for the purposes of being used as a conveyance at the time or in the future. To set adrift a waterborne craft without being in it (or on it) would not be an offence under this section, but if a person climbed into it (or onto it) later, it would. To be found guilty of this offence there must be a degree of **movement** in the conveyance, however small and possibly difficult to observe. It is not sufficient to just sit in, or on, the conveyance, and taking is not the same as using (see *R v Bogacki* [1973] 2 All ER 864).
. . . knowing that any conveyance has been taken without such authority, . . .
It is possible to exceed the authority given (and therefore consent) when borrowing a car by using it for another purpose, such as taking it on a longer journey (see *R v Phipps and McGill* [1970] RTR 209 (CA)).
. . . drives it or allows themselves to be carried in or on it.
To meet the condition **'allows'** themselves, the suspect must know that the conveyance has been taken without consent. The suspect might not know that the vehicle has been taken without consent upon entering the conveyance, but once the suspect finds out, there should be some attempt to leave the vehicle.
Drive has its normal meaning of being in control of the vehicle.

Case law provides a number of clarifications in relation to this offence. For a floating conveyance, the movement can be caused by a sail but cannot 'be natural movement' created by waves or water currents (see *R v Miller* [1976] Crim LR 147). A conveyance must be taken for the purpose of being used as such (including future use) and not just for 'mischief' (see *R v Stokes* [1982] Crim LR 695). A vehicle ceases to be 'taken' once it has been recovered by the victim, police, or insurance company, but this would probably not include simply receiving a report from a member of the public reporting its location.

A defence (s 12(6) of the Theft Act 1968) is that the person believes that they have the consent of the owner or had other lawful authority. This offence is triable summarily and the penalty is six months' imprisonment and/or a fine.

In law, the basic offence of taking a conveyance cannot be attempted (see 27.2 on criminal attempts) as the offence is not indictable. If some form of attempt has taken place, the offence of vehicle interference or tampering with a motor vehicle could be used (see 23.8.2.2) or an attempted offence of theft (as theft is an indictable offence).

23.8.2.1 Aggravated vehicle-taking

When a vehicle is taken without consent, an aggravated offence can be committed (s 12A of the Theft Act 1968). The aggravating circumstances for this offence are that after it was taken without consent:

- the vehicle was driven dangerously on a road or other public place (see 16.8.1 on dangerous driving; and for definitions of 'road' see 16.2.2 and for 'public place' see 4.3.1.1);
- an accident occurred (due to the driving of the vehicle) which caused injury to a person or damage to property other than the vehicle. The court can take into account what an ordinary person would consider to be an accident (see *R v Morris* [1972] RTR 201). Injuries include shock, and damage includes any damage caused during the whole incident and does not have to be deliberately inflicted.

The aggravating events must occur after the vehicle has been taken without consent and before it is recovered by its owner, the police, or the insurance company. The person who is driving at the time of the aggravating events commits the s 12A offence. They need not be the same person who first took the vehicle without consent (the s 12 offence). Defences include that the dangerous driving, damage, or accident had occurred before the suspect took the vehicle or that they were not in or on the vehicle or in its 'immediate vicinity' when the dangerous driving, accident, or damage occurred (s 12A(3)). Immediate vicinity is a question of fact for the court to decide. If the suspect can disprove aggravating factors, they can still be found guilty of the basic offence (s 12A(5)).

This offence is triable either way, being tried summarily if the value of the property damaged or destroyed is less than £5,000 (s 22 of the Magistrates' Courts Act 1980). The penalty is a fine (no upper limit) or imprisonment (six months summarily or two years on indictment). If the accident caused death, the penalty is up to 14 years' imprisonment.

23.8.2.2 Interference and tampering with motor vehicles

When a suspect takes a conveyance without the consent of the owner, in many cases they will go through a process of selecting a vehicle, gaining entry either forcibly or by trying door handles, overcoming anti-theft devices such as alarms and steering locks, and then applying a technique such as 'hot wiring', starting the engine by bypassing the ignition system. This process inevitably takes time and sometimes the suspect can be apprehended before the vehicle is taken. However, TWOC is a summary offence and therefore cannot be attempted under s 1(1) of the Criminal Attempts Act 1981 (see 27.2). So, the offences of interfering with and tampering with motor vehicles were created to cover situations where TWOC appears to have been attempted.

Section 9(1) of the Criminal Attempts Act 1981 states that it is an offence for a person to interfere with a motor vehicle or trailer or with anything carried in or on a motor vehicle or trailer with the intention of committing:

- 'theft of the motor vehicle or part of it';
- 'theft of anything carried in or on the motor vehicle or trailer'; or
- the offence of taking a conveyance.

However, proving intent is difficult. Earlier in the Handbook, we discussed the two main building blocks to a criminal act: *actus reus* (the act itself) and *mens rea* (an intention to commit an act). In this case, the act cannot simply be preparation but needs to go further than this. Unfortunately, case law provides us with little guidance on what interference means in practice. Nonetheless, it must be proved that the suspect had at least one of the three intentions, but it is not necessary to prove which one. This is a summary-only offence, and the penalty is three months' imprisonment and/or a fine.

Tampering as an activity is more readily understood than interference and the legislation (s 25(1) of the Road Traffic Act 1988) refers specifically to vehicle brakes. It is an offence for a person without lawful authority or reasonable cause to tamper with the brake or any other part of its mechanism, or to get on or into the vehicle. This applies to motor vehicles on a road or in a local authority parking place. It is a summary offence only and the penalty is a fine or imprisonment for up to three months.

TASK 4 Which of the following would constitute an offence of interfering with a motor vehicle?

1. Trying to remove a horse box from the tow bar of a vehicle in order to steal the horse box.
2. Attempting to remove a go-kart from the garden of a house in order to steal it.
3. Opening the unlocked front driver's door of a car to steal a satnav fixed to the dashboard.

23.8.3 Taking a pedal cycle

Taking a pedal cycle is an offence under s 12(5) of the Theft Act 1968 and is not a TWOC offence (because a pedal cycle is not a conveyance for the purposes of s 12(1) of the Theft Act 1968). The offence would include riding a pedal cycle knowing it to have been taken by another person without consent or lawful authority. The penalty is six months' imprisonment and/or a fine.

23.9 Fraud and Bribery Offences

The continual evolution of technology opens new ways for fraud to be committed via computer misuse offences or cybercrime. The annual UK losses due to fraud are estimated to be around £110 billion (Copper-Ind, 2018). Many frauds relate to procurement and involve the use of fake invoices but others involve tax, housing, and benefit fraud. In terms of individual susceptibility to fraud, people aged 35–44 years are most likely to be the victims of fraud (ONS, 2018a). The National Fraud Initiative tackles public sector fraud by cross-matching data from all public sectors to identify fraud and overpayments and resulted in annual savings of nearly £200 million (Experian, 2018). This might sound significant, but it is in fact only a tiny proportion of the losses; for every £100 of public sector losses, only 54p was saved. It is believed that many businesses could reduce fraud by simply improving identity checks (Experian, 2018).

Much of the law surrounding the crime of fraud is now encapsulated in the Fraud Act 2006. Section 1 states that the offence of fraud can be committed in one or more of three distinctive ways:

1. by false representation, for example presenting a stolen credit card to pay for goods at a till thereby implying it is yours to use (s 2);
2. by failing to disclose information, for example omitting important information when applying for a job or for health insurance (s 3); and
3. through abuse of position, for example demanding fares from local residents whilst driving a local authority minibus that is intended as a free service (s 4).

For all these offences, there is the same intent; the same dishonesty, for the perpetrator to make a gain for themselves or another, to cause a loss to another, or to expose another to a risk of loss. The gain or loss can be temporary or permanent and could involve 'personal' property, 'real' property, things in action, and other intangible property, such as the name of a company or the copyright to a product. This is similar to the definitions of property under the Theft Act 1968.

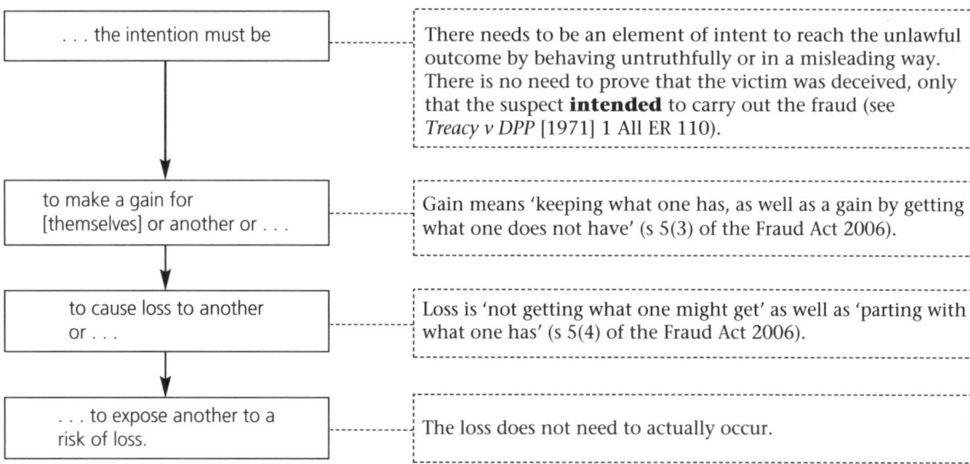

. . . the intention must be
There needs to be an element of intent to reach the unlawful outcome by behaving untruthfully or in a misleading way. There is no need to prove that the victim was deceived, only that the suspect **intended** to carry out the fraud (see *Treacy v DPP* [1971] 1 All ER 110).
to make a gain for [themselves] or another or . . .
Gain means 'keeping what one has, as well as a gain by getting what one does not have' (s 5(3) of the Fraud Act 2006).
to cause loss to another or . . .
Loss is 'not getting what one might get' as well as 'parting with what one has' (s 5(4) of the Fraud Act 2006).
. . . to expose another to a risk of loss.
The loss does not need to actually occur.

The fact that a person has created a risk is analogous to a bullet that has been fired from a gun; once it has left the chamber, it cannot be taken back.

The offences are all triable either way and the penalty is a fine or imprisonment (12 months summarily or up to ten years on indictment).

From a practical policing perspective, the majority of fraud reports, those classified as volume crimes, are submitted to *Action Fraud* (<https://www.actionfraud.police.uk/reporting-fraud-and-cyber-crime>), an organization attached to City of London Police and the National Fraud Intelligence Bureau (NFIB). The NFIB's role is to collate and analyse reports of fraud but contrary to popular myth, they do not investigate fraud offences (Action Fraud, 2018). Offences with reasonable lines of enquiry are screened back into owning police service/law enforcement agency for further investigation. The NFIB look to connect the dots between similar incidents to provide a wider national picture.

In some cases, police will need to act outside of this process, to accommodate urgent incoming intelligence. The College of Policing provides Authorised Professional Practice (CoP, 2022g) around fraud investigation. Police should still step in if a fraud incident is:

Happening imminently or within set time parameters
Has just occurred or been witnessed or is likely to re-occur
There is risk of harm
Failure to act could be detrimental to the police force

23.9.1 False representation

Section 2 of the Fraud Act 2006 states that a person commits an offence if that person 'dishonestly makes a false representation and intends ... to make a gain for [themselves] or another, or to cause loss to another or to expose another to a risk of loss'. The suspect must intend that the false representation will cause a gain or loss (*R v Gilbert* [2012] EWCA Crim 2392). The meaning of the term 'dishonesty' is covered in 23.2.1. This would include a person who advertises a fake brand item for sale. Even if no one responds, the person has still risked causing somebody a loss—the offence is committed the moment the item is offered. False representation means misleading or lying about a fact or law, for example a roofer who knowingly presents a grossly inflated estimate to a customer (see *R v Silverman* [1987] 86 Cr App R 213). The representation can be made verbally, in writing (including online), or through actions. A false representation can also be made to a device or machine which is designed to receive, convey, or respond to communication; for example, using forged coins at a coin-operated snack dispenser (s 2(5)).

23.9.2 Failure to disclose information

Section 3 of the Fraud Act 2006 states that a person commits an offence if that person 'dishonestly fails to disclose to another person information which [that person] is under a legal duty to disclose, and intends, by failing to disclose the information to make a gain for [themselves] or another, or to cause loss to another or to expose another to a risk of loss'.

The failure to disclose can be made by an oral or written omission. The legal duty to disclose (and some examples of a failure to disclose) derives from:

- statute, for example where a company must publish yearly accounts under company law but fails to do so;
- assumed good faith, such as failing to disclose a serious illness in order to reduce health insurance premiums;
- the express or implied terms of a contract, from the custom of a particular trade or market, such as an estate agent failing to reveal to a client all the bids she received for a property;
- the existence of a fiduciary relationship (where a person is entrusted with another person's financial arrangements), for example where a solicitor does not tell their client there is another beneficiary to a contract.

To provide evidence for this offence, it is often simplest to show that there was a failure to notify information to the victim. They will then have a legitimate claim for seeking damages for non-disclosure and will also be able to clarify their position regarding future consent.

23.9.3 Abuse of position

This offence (s 4) can be committed by a person who occupies a position in which they are expected to safeguard (or not to act against) the financial interests of another. The offence is committed if they dishonestly abuse that position intending to make a gain for themselves or another, or to cause loss to another or to expose another to a risk of loss.

The offence could apply for anyone who has relied upon or has knowledge of another person's financial affairs, such as between an employer and an employee, between a trustee and a beneficiary. The meaning of the term 'abuse' in this context is not defined in law but is held to have its normal everyday meaning and includes a failure to act (s 4(2)). Examples might include a person who has access to their elderly relative's bank account and takes money for their own use. The abuse must take place at the time the suspect occupies the position of trust, and not later. For example, a person might leave a company but still have the contact details of clients on their laptop and they then decide to sell the information to another company. As the person was not in post at the time they formed the intent, the s 4 offence is not committed (although they might have committed an offence of possessing an article for committing fraud).

23.9.4 Possession, making, or supplying of articles for committing fraud

A person can commit an offence by 'going equipped' (see 23.6) to carry out a fraud rather than actually having committed the fraud itself. In this context, going equipped means being in possession or control of articles for use in a fraud (s 6 of the Fraud Act 2006) or making or supplying such articles (s 7).

The articles can include clothing to imitate company representatives, mechanisms to slow down electricity meters, false identity cards, credit cards, cheque books, shopping bags, till receipts, passports, and driving licences. It also includes a computer program or data held in electronic form (see 14.2).

Section 6 of the Fraud Act 2006 covers possession or having the article under their control. For possession, the person must have immediate physical control over the article and know that it is there. Having control would include having physical control at a distance (eg having the key to a cupboard where the item is kept) and knowing that the article is there. If one person is shown to be in possession of an article, then any other person present who is also aware of the possession is also guilty of possession. Unlike most other statutory preventative measures this offence can be committed anywhere, including when the articles are in the suspect's home.

Section 7 of the Fraud Act 2006 states that a person commits an offence if they make, adapt, supply (or offer to supply) any article, knowing that it is designed or adapted for use in the course of or in connection with fraud (or intending it to be used to commit or assist with the commission of fraud). An example of this could be offering to make a false ID card for someone when it's known they are going to use it to pose as a charity collector. Under s 1 of the PACE Act 1984, a police officer has the power to search for articles made or adapted for use in fraud.

The offences are triable either way and the penalty is a fine or imprisonment (12 months summarily, five years on indictment for a s 6 offence, and ten years on indictment for a s 7 offence).

23.9.5 Dishonest obtaining of services

Section 11 of the Fraud Act 2006 deals with obtaining a service by dishonest means. The services must be of a type for which payment is generally required and would include transport rides, haircuts, a stay in a hotel room, dry-cleaning, admission to a sports event. The service must be obtained through a dishonest act (not an omission), such as using a false credit card, giving false personal details, and making false promises or agreements of payment in full or part with no intention of meeting them (see 23.2.1 on dishonesty). The offence is triable either way and the penalty is a fine or imprisonment (12 months summarily or five years on indictment). This is satisfied upon the successful obtainment of any service. Neither obtain nor service is given further definition in the Act and thus must be taken at the ordinary and natural meanings of the words (Law Teacher, 2018).

23.9.6 Making off without payment ('bilking')

If a person makes off without paying but made no dishonest representation and had every intention to pay for goods before the property was obtained, this is an offence under s 3 of the Theft Act 1978 (rather than fraud under s 1 of the Fraud Act 2006). The s 3(1) offence of making off without payment covers cases where the debtor makes off from the place where they obtained the property and where payment for the property was due and, in seeking to avoid the debt, removes themselves from the place where the liability to pay was incurred. Section 3 does not require the prosecution to prove the property involved actually belonged to another or that any false representation was made (Law Teacher, 2019).

For example, a person might fill up with petrol with every intention of paying for the petrol, but seeing the staff otherwise engaged decides to drive off without paying. Note that this offence only applies if payment on the spot is the norm in that particular situation, such as collecting goods on which work has been done (eg shoe repairs) or paying for a service which has been provided (eg a haircut). It does not apply if a customer has a credit arrangement with the service provider. The offence is triable either way and the penalty is a fine or imprisonment (six months summarily or two years on indictment).

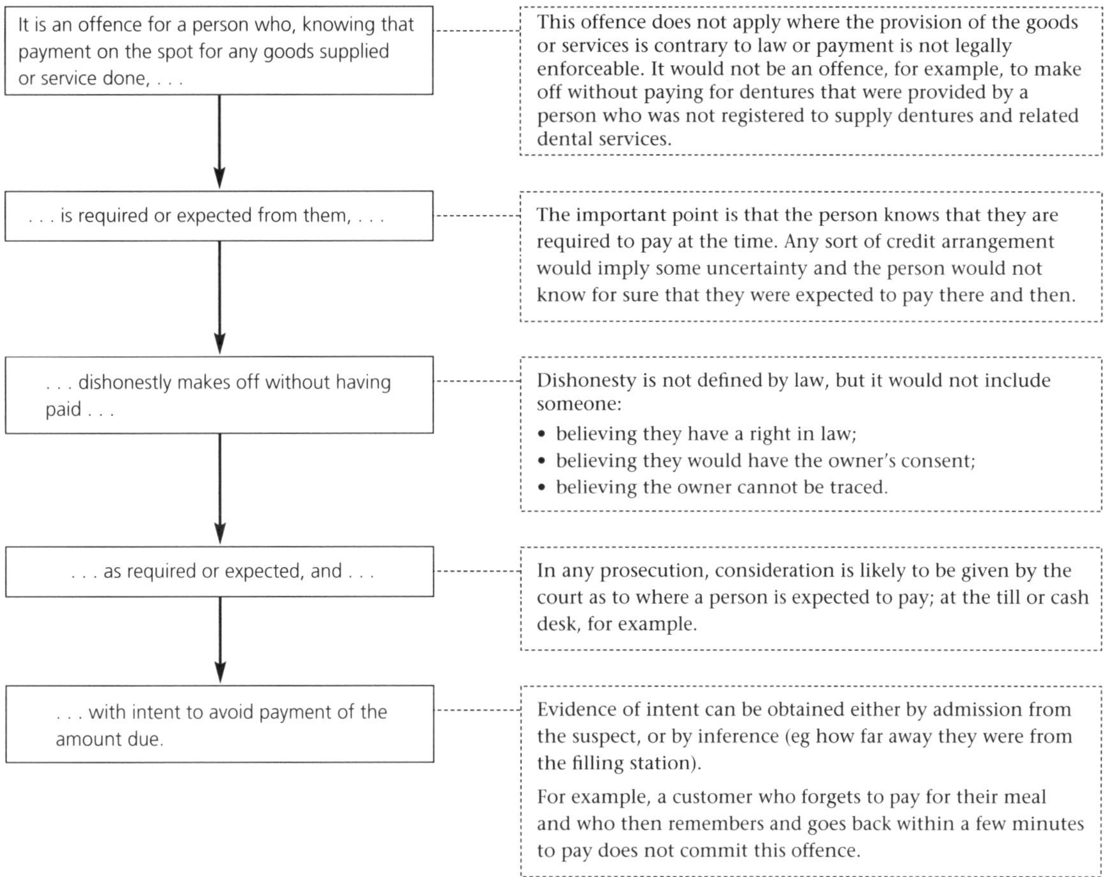

It is an offence for a person who, knowing that payment on the spot for any goods supplied or service done, . . .
This offence does not apply where the provision of the goods or services is contrary to law or payment is not legally enforceable. It would not be an offence, for example, to make off without paying for dentures that were provided by a person who was not registered to supply dentures and related dental services.
. . . is required or expected from them, . . .
The important point is that the person knows that they are required to pay at the time. Any sort of credit arrangement would imply some uncertainty and the person would not know for sure that they were expected to pay there and then.
. . . dishonestly makes off without having paid . . .
Dishonesty is not defined by law, but it would not include someone:
• believing they have a right in law;
• believing they would have the owner's consent;
• believing the owner cannot be traced.
. . . as required or expected, and . . .
In any prosecution, consideration is likely to be given by the court as to where a person is expected to pay; at the till or cash desk, for example.
. . . with intent to avoid payment of the amount due.
Evidence of intent can be obtained either by admission from the suspect, or by inference (eg how far away they were from the filling station).
For example, a customer who forgets to pay for their meal and who then remembers and goes back within a few minutes to pay does not commit this offence.

TASK 5 Diners at a restaurant can sometimes fail to pay for a meal and this could be a criminal offence under s 1 or s 11 of the Fraud Act 2006, or under s 3 of the Theft Act 1978, depending on the sequence of events. Complete the following table: the case of *DPP v Ray* [1974] AC 370 may assist.

Scenario	Possible offence
People order a meal in a restaurant, even though they know they cannot pay for it. They leave before it is served.	
A person orders a meal and it is served to their table. The person claims it is inedible and leaves without paying.	
Two colleagues finish their meals. Then they decide not to pay and quickly leave the restaurant.	

23.9.7 False identification documents

A false identity document is:

- a genuine and unadulterated document being used by a different person;
- a genuine document that has been altered; or
- a fake document (a copy of a genuine document or a form of ID that does not exist).

The Home Office has published *Guidance on Examining Identity Documents*, which gives details of some of the documents that might be used, such as passports, driving licences, and national identity cards.

In licensed premises, some customers may present false identity documents during age-verification checks (required by the Licensing Act 2003 (Mandatory Licensing Conditions)). Such documents can also be used by a fraudster to present false personal information about themselves or to induce another to ascertain personal information about the person named on the document (s 4(2) of the Identity Documents Act 2010). Possession of a false identity document which the person intends to use in this way is an offence under s 4(1). The offence is triable on indictment only and the maximum penalty is ten years' imprisonment, a fine, or both.

Possession without reasonable excuse of a false identity document is an offence under s 6(1) of the Identity Documents Act 2010, triable either way. The penalty is a fine or imprisonment (six months summarily or two years on indictment).

23.9.8 Bribery

The Bribery Act 2010 provides an effective legal framework to combat bribery in the public and private sectors. It also includes offences relating to bribery of foreign officials and to commercial organizations that allow their agents to commit bribery. An organization will have a defence if it provides evidence of having policies and practices in place that prohibit bribery.

The offences relate to bribing another person and to accepting a bribe. Two particular terms used within the legislation have specific meanings:

- 'improper performance' means failing to perform a function or activity with good faith or impartially (s 4); and
- 'relevant function or activity' includes all functions of a public nature, for example those carried out by public authorities (such as the police) and all activities connected with a business, trade, or profession (s 3).

The offences are triable either way and the penalties are a fine or imprisonment (one year if tried summarily and 12 years on indictment).

23.9.8.1 Bribing or attempting to bribe another person

Under s 1(1) of the Bribery Act 2010, it is an offence for a person to offer, promise, or give a financial or other advantage to another person in order to:

- bring about an improper performance by any person of a relevant function or activity; or
- reward any person for such improper performance (s 1(2)).

It is sufficient for the perpetrator to intend to induce or reward the misconduct; the actual outcome of their actions is irrelevant. It is also sufficient for them to know or believe that the acceptance of the advantage constitutes the improper performance of a function or activity (s 1(3)). The advantage can be offered, promised, or given by the perpetrator or through a third party (s 1(5)).

23.9.8.2 Requesting, accepting, or benefiting from a bribe

Under s 2(1) of the Bribery Act 2010, a person commits an offence if they request, agree to receive, or accept an advantage if:

- they intend improper performance (by anyone) to follow as a consequence (s 2(2));
- their request (in itself), agreement, or acceptance amounts to improper performance (s 2(3));
- they accept the reward for anyone's subsequent improper performance (s 2(4)).

It is irrelevant whether the perpetrator receives any advantage. The meaning of 'advantage' is a question of fact for the court to decide.

23.10 Answers to Tasks

TASK 1 The following offences are likely to have been committed:

- burglary with intent to steal (s 9(1)(a) of the Theft Act 1968), since the person entered as a trespasser with the necessary intent;
- burglary (s 9(1)(b) of the Theft Act 1968) has been committed since the individual, having entered as a trespasser, inflicts grievous bodily harm on the occupier; and
- aggravated burglary (s 10 of the Theft Act 1968) has taken place because, whilst committing the s 9(1)(b) burglary, the intruder was armed with a weapon of offence at the time of the search for something to steal.

TASK 2

Without identifying the specific criminal conduct a successful prosecution is unlikely. The case of *R v NW, SW, RC & CC* [2008] EWCA Crim 2 was important with respect to the interpretation of POCA. The Court of Appeal ruled that the CPS could not just focus on inexplicable affluence. Unless there is evidence that the person had the necessary knowledge or suspicion that the property represented a benefit from criminal conduct, a successful prosecution under s 328(1) of POCA would not be possible. Even if it could have been proved that the money was from the unlawful supply of controlled drugs, if their only role was as a courier for the money, the money did not amount to property that could be confiscated from them under POCA (see *R v Allpress; R v Symeou; R v Casal; R v Morris; R v Martin* [2009] EWCA Crim 8). For a successful prosecution under s 328(1), it would be necessary to prove that they had benefited, for example by receiving payments for passing on the money

TASK 3 No burglary has been committed. Although Alex entered the storage warehouse as a trespasser, she had no intention to commit theft, criminal damage, or GBH (the offences specified in s 9(1)(a) of the Theft Act 1968). Once inside the warehouse, Alex damaged the door (which is property) and also abstracted electricity by using the fire, but neither damage to property nor abstraction of electricity are relevant to s 9(1)(b) of the Theft Act 1968 (see 23.4.1.1).

TASK 4

1. This would be interference (a horse box is a trailer).
2. No, because a go-kart is not a motor vehicle adapted or intended for use on the road.
3. Yes, there is an intention to commit theft of an item which is 'carried in or on the motor vehicle' so this counts as interference.

TASK 5

Scenario	Offence that is likely to have been committed
People order a meal in a restaurant, even though they know they cannot pay for it. They leave before it is served.	This is 'false representation', an offence under s 1 of the Fraud Act 2006. This is because the 'dishonest representation' took place before the property was obtained. By entering a restaurant people imply that they have the means and intention to pay for goods they order.
A person orders a meal and it is served to their table. The person claims it is inedible and leaves without paying.	The person intended to pay for their meal but changed their mind when it was served. The person has received service, which is part of the charge for the meal. The person implied that they were an ordinary customer by accepting the service so an offence of 'obtaining services dishonestly' may have been committed (s 11 of the Fraud Act). The dishonesty has occurred after obtaining the property, so this cannot be a s 1 offence.
Two colleagues finish their meal. Then they decide not to pay and quickly leave the restaurant.	The dishonesty takes place after obtaining the property and therefore the offence is more likely to be s 3 of the Theft Act 1978.

24 Sexual Offences

24.1 Introduction

The incidence of sexual offences in England and Wales is notoriously difficult to determine, beset as it is by issues of under-reporting and lack of definitional clarity. These difficulties have been further exacerbated by the measures and restrictions to public life following the outbreak of the Covid-19 pandemic. The most recent data from the Office for National Statistics (ONS, 2023b) reports that the police recorded 199,021 sexual offences during the year ending September 2022. This can be broken down into rape offences (70,633), and other sexual offences (128,388). The overall statistics represents a 22 per cent increase from year ending March 2020, and also a significant increase since April 2021 (ONS, 2023b), a trend that the ONS suggests may be related to numerous factors including higher reporting post-lockdown, police willingness to record and investigate such crimes, as well as high-profile events that serve to highlight the need to report offences. The kidnap, rape, and murder of Sarah Everard occurred in March 2021 and could be one potential reason for the surge in reported cases. In July 2021, the government also produced a Tackling Violence Against Women and Girls strategy, citing tragedies in murder cases such as Sarah Everard, Julia James, Bibaa Henry, and Nicole Smallman as high-profile examples of a deeper problem of persistent violence against women and girls in society. The strategy pledges to tackle crime against women and girls (HM Government, 2021a).

There has been persistent criticism that the criminal justice system fails to bring offenders to justice. In a recent end-to-end rape review (HM Government, 2021c, p i), ministers identified consistently poor criminal justice responses to rapes in particular:

> In the last five years, there has been a significant decline in the number of charges and prosecutions for rape cases and, as a result, fewer convictions. Over the same period, there has been little change in the overall prevalence of rape and sexual violence crimes. The vast majority of victims do not see the crime against them charged and reach a court: one in two victims withdraw from rape investigations.

In the report, it was noted that whilst recorded cases have increased, prosecutions have decreased markedly since 2015/16. The government set out its intention to improve the situation and at least return to 2015/16 prosecution successes and set out an action plan to improve the way the whole system deals with cases of this gravity. This ambition to return to 2016 successes arguably lacks ambition and is somewhat controversial. The Law Commission is also set to review evidence and sexual offences (Law Commission, 2022).

There have been several pervasive beliefs surrounding sexual offences including 'rape myths' which assumes rape only happens to certain types of women or that women in some way provoke the offence (Croall, 2011, p 267). Another myth is that a rape is usually committed by a stranger whereas around 90 per cent of female victims of the most serious sexual offences know their attacker. Rape is also not restricted to female victims. However, so pervasive are some of these myths, particularly in relation to the expected behaviour of victims, that in 2015 the CPS and the Metropolitan Police developed a joint action plan on rape that aimed to address some of these misconceptions (CPS and MPS, 2015a). Because police officers are members of our society where rape myths are prevalent, it is reasonable to assume that some may also believe them. Such myths could affect the quality and depth of investigations into rape cases, hence why education and training are important broadly in society and more specifically inside policing. Recent investigations into the attitudes and behaviours of MPS officers at Charing Cross police station attest to some misogynistic attitudes and behaviours, although the extent of the problem within UK policing is currently unknown (IOPC, 2022b).

Recent revelations about a police officer in Gwent Police, and the criminal conduct of serving police officers Wayne Couzens and David Carrick also fuel serious concerns about the attitudes of police officers to certain crimes and their criminal behaviours.

Establishing that the victim did not consent to a sexual act is another problematic aspect of this type of offence. The Sexual Offences Act 2003 defines consent and presumptions about consent (ss 74–76). It is also presumed that there is no consent if the victim is under 16. In relation to marriage, it has never been the case that by marrying a man, a woman irrevocably consents to sexual intercourse with her husband (*R v R* [1992] 1 AC 599 (HL)). A man was convicted of raping his wife on a number of occasions from 1970 onwards, and this case credited the *R v R* decision as exploding the myth that it was ever acceptable (*R v C* [2004] EWCA Crim 292). More generally, however, consent has at times been assumed rather than actively given, for example when a victim has consumed large amounts of alcohol or drugs, or a change of mind not respected when engaging in sexual activity.

More recently, there has been increasing concern about the sexual abuse of children, and particularly the use of online means to facilitate grooming of victims and to share images of child abuse. The possession and sharing of illicit images of children will be covered in more detail in 24.4.2. Individuals concerned with the safety of children can raise concerns with the police, who in certain circumstances will be able to disclose information in order to protect children, under the Child Sex Offender Disclosure Scheme (see 24.8.3).

The police tend to define policy in terms of 'serious' sexual offences and 'other' sexual offences. There is no collective official definition of 'serious' and in a sense every sexual offence is a serious one. For example, 'flashing' (see 24.2) is not normally included within the category of serious sexual offences but its impact on victims might well be serious, and it has been suggested that this type of sexual crime, alongside voyeurism and image-related offences, may be precursors to more serious offending. However, the police consider that a distinction between 'other' and 'serious' is needed for a number of reasons, including the pragmatic necessity to make decisions on the deployment of resources and the development of policy. Many police services will make reference to the use of the word 'serious' in the context of the Sexual Offences Acts 1956 and 2003 and derive seriousness in this way. In broad terms, the following are normally considered serious sexual offences when committed against adults (including attempts to commit these offences):

- rape (vaginal, anal, and oral);
- sexual assault by penetration;
- sexual assault where the assault is particularly serious (or is aggravated, for example by the involvement of a person with a mental disorder); and
- causing a person to engage in sexual activity without consent.

Where the offences relate to children, they will always be treated as serious because by their very nature they relate to issues of safeguarding and whether other abuse may have occurred. From a police perspective, where a more serious crime is identified, the required level of PIP-qualified investigator is correspondingly higher. For example, all of the above examples are likely to require a qualified officer of at least PIP Level 2 to investigate. PIP 2 relates to 'serious and complex' crime.

Reports of sexual offences to the police will arise from a variety of circumstances and in a number of forms and there may also be referrals from a Sexual Assault Referral Centre (SARC). Reports can range from a very recent sexual assault, to a rape that took place decades ago. Because most laws are not retrospective, when a sexual offence is reported many years after the event, the law that applied at the time of the offence still applies (as illustrated in the convictions of high-profile celebrities such as Rolf Harris, Gary Glitter, and Stuart Hall). Even though the range of sexual offences currently on the statute books appears to cover many eventualities, it may not cover historical reports. For instance, rape law prior to the 1990s would only encompass vaginal penetration and not anal or oral penetration. The latter form of penetration was added to the definition of rape in the Sexual Offences Act 2003. Therefore, the date when an offence was committed focuses the investigation towards relevant legislation and case law. For example, although non-consensual oral penetration was not considered rape in the 1990s, it constituted an offence of indecent assault within the Sexual Offences Act 1956. The difference is that indecent assault carried a maximum sentence of ten years' imprisonment upon conviction, whereas since 2003, oral rape carries a potential maximum sentence of life imprisonment in line with penetration of other orifices.

The investigation of sexual offences has been a problematic area for the police, although the situation has improved markedly since the documentary made by Roger Graef in Thames Valley in 1982. This showed the bullying and unsympathetic police interrogation of a woman who had reported rape. Moreover, the woman suffered mental health problems, and these vulnerabilities seem to have increased the officers' suspicions and concerns over the truthfulness and accuracy of her account. Given the particular controversies surrounding the police investigation of rape in the past, it is perhaps not surprising that detailed information on best practice is now available. The guidance from ACPO (the predecessor of the NPCC) is a key document; access to the full version is restricted but the abridged version can be viewed online (ACPO, 2010). This is, however, over ten years old, so more guidance may be found on the College of Policing website.

There is undoubtedly an increased emphasis within the police service on improving both the rate of reporting of sexual crimes and the proportion that are brought to a successful prosecution or outcome (Angiolini, 2015). That said, it has been powerfully argued that rape investigations, and the treatment of victims in these cases, is a measure of women's equality in society (Hohl and Stanko, 2015), and consistent failings and poor conviction rates do little to allay concerns in this regard. Recent high-profile cases where charges have been dropped at court due to poor police investigations and a lack of disclosure do not serve to enhance the credibility of the police. Former Lord Chief Justice, Lord Judge, suggests that juries could even find suspects *not* guilty at trial for fear that they have not been provided with all relevant material (Polianskaya, 2018). Controversies over the suggested early release of serial rapist John Worboys are unlikely to encourage victims to report rape either, especially given the large number of reports against him that were not pursued by the CPS and the apparent lack of notification to survivors that he could be released. Worboys was initially granted parole in 2018 but this decision was successfully challenged by survivors. He has since been prosecuted for a number of further attacks. The problem for the police is that high-profile 'exceptional' case failures seem to arise all too regularly, despite reviews, government papers, guidance, and significant developments in practice (Jordan, 2011).

The topics covered in this chapter are likely to contribute to the learning required for the National Policing Curriculum subject areas of 'Understanding the Police Constable Role', 'Public Protection', 'Vulnerability and Risk', and 'Response Policing'.

24.2 Acts of a Sexual Nature in Public Places

Exposure is covered by s 66(1) of the Sexual Offences Act 2003. It is commonly referred to as 'flashing'. A person commits an offence if they expose their genitals and intend that someone will see this and be caused alarm or distress. It is not necessary for a person to actually have seen the exposed genitals or to have been distressed as a result; the offence is still committed. It can be committed in a private or public place (see 4.3.1.1 for definitions of places).

The important points to prove would be the double intention—an intent that someone will see and an intention to cause alarm or distress. Therefore, a 'streaker' planning to cause amusement by intending others to see their exposed genitals, does not commit this offence because they had no intent to cause alarm or distress.

This offence is triable either way and the penalty is imprisonment (summarily, six months and two years on indictment).

Outraging public decency is covered by common law which states that it is an offence:

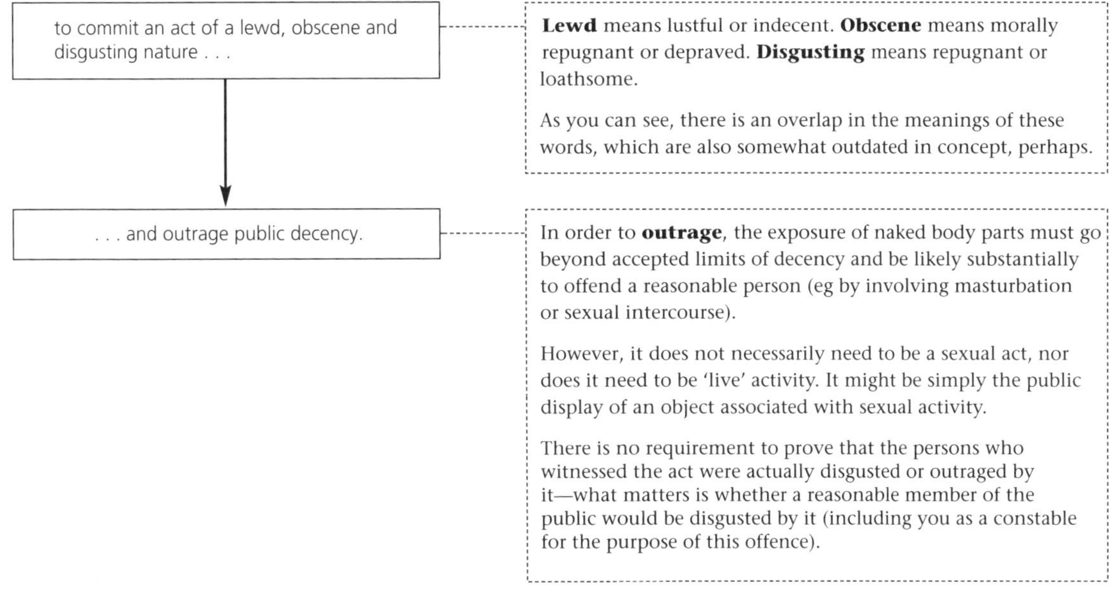

to commit an act of a lewd, obscene and disgusting nature . . .
Lewd means lustful or indecent. **Obscene** means morally repugnant or depraved. **Disgusting** means repugnant or loathsome.
As you can see, there is an overlap in the meanings of these words, which are also somewhat outdated in concept, perhaps.
. . . and outrage public decency.
In order to **outrage**, the exposure of naked body parts must go beyond accepted limits of decency and be likely substantially to offend a reasonable person (eg by involving masturbation or sexual intercourse).
However, it does not necessarily need to be a sexual act, nor does it need to be 'live' activity. It might be simply the public display of an object associated with sexual activity.
There is no requirement to prove that the persons who witnessed the act were actually disgusted or outraged by it—what matters is whether a reasonable member of the public would be disgusted by it (including you as a constable for the purpose of this offence).

The public must have access to (whether they have a right to such access or not), or be able to see the relevant location, such as a private balcony in public view (*R v Walker* [1996] 1 Cr App R 111; *Smith v Hughes* [1960] All ER 859). It must also have been possible for more than one person to witness the act.

This offence is triable either way and the penalty is imprisonment (summarily, six months and unlimited on indictment).

Sexual activity in a public lavatory is an offence under s 71 of the Sexual Offences Act 2003. There is no need for any person to witness the activity and, if there are witnesses, they do not have to be in any way outraged or distressed. The activity must be such that a reasonable person would regard it as sexual in nature. This offence is triable summarily only and the penalty is six months' imprisonment and/or a fine.

24.3 Voyeurism

Voyeurism is an offence under s 67(1) of the Sexual Offences Act 2003 whereby a suspect secretly observes another person undressing or having sexual intercourse, a 'private act', for the purposes of the suspect's own sexual gratification.

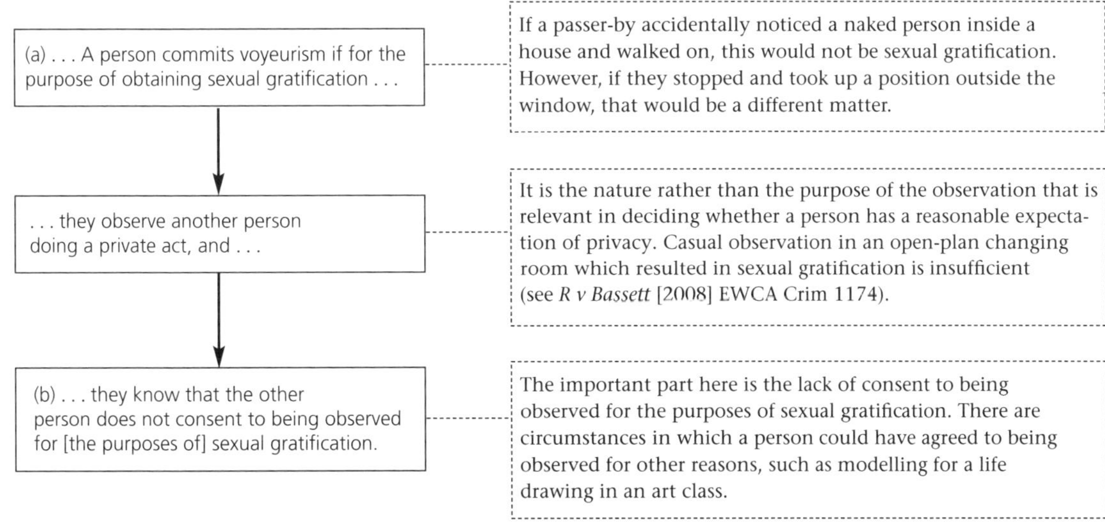

(a) . . . A person commits voyeurism if for the purpose of obtaining sexual gratification . . .
If a passer-by accidentally noticed a naked person inside a house and walked on, this would not be sexual gratification. However, if they stopped and took up a position outside the window, that would be a different matter.
. . . they observe another person doing a private act, and . . .
It is the nature rather than the purpose of the observation that is relevant in deciding whether a person has a reasonable expectation of privacy. Casual observation in an open-plan changing room which resulted in sexual gratification is insufficient (see *R v Bassett* [2008] EWCA Crim 1174).
(b) . . . they know that the other person does not consent to being observed for [the purposes of] sexual gratification.
The important part here is the lack of consent to being observed for the purposes of sexual gratification. There are circumstances in which a person could have agreed to being observed for other reasons, such as modelling for a life drawing in an art class.

Section 68(1) of the Sexual Offences Act 2003 explains that for the purposes of s 67 a person undertakes a private act if they are in a place which would reasonably be expected to provide privacy, such as in a home or hotel but not on a beach or in an open-plan changing room, and at least one of the following conditions is met:

- their genitals, buttocks, or female breasts are exposed or covered only with underwear (see *R v Bassett* [2008] EWCA Crim 1174);
- they are using a lavatory; or
- they are participating in 'a sexual act that is not of a kind ordinarily done in public' such as sexual intercourse, masturbation, or oral sex.

There is a form of voyeurism linked to 'dogging' which refers to outdoor sexual activities; however, if the 'doggers' encourage people to watch, the offence of voyeurism is not committed because consent has been given. Other offences may have been committed, however, depending on the particular circumstances. Aggravating factors for voyeurism include threatening the victim to dissuade them from reporting the offence (CPS, 2017d).

24.3.1 Facilitating voyeurism and the use of equipment

Voyeurism using live link equipment is covered by s 67(2) of the Sexual Offences Act 2003. Person A commits an offence if they operate equipment with the intention of enabling another person B to observe, for sexual gratification, a third person C doing a private act. Person A must know that C has not consented to this. For example, a landlord commits an offence if they operate a webcam so that people on the internet can gain sexual gratification from viewing their tenant having sex. The landlord must know that the tenant did not agree to this. There is no need to prove that the landlord personally gained sexual gratification.

The recording of images in relation to voyeurism is covered by s 67(3) of the Sexual Offences Act 2003. It is similar to the legislation under s 67(2), except that the acts are recorded and not just transmitted. The Sentencing Council (2014a and 2014e) has published guidelines identifying case characteristics that raise both harm and culpability, such as the availability of recordings to be viewed by others and whether recordings took place in their own home (harm) and whether there was a breach of trust, significant planning, or commercial motivations (culpability). The more aggravating the features, the higher the recommended sentence.

In a recent case, the defendant was alleged to have secretly filmed his consensual sexual activity with sex workers and argued that there was no case to answer under s 67(3) because he himself was a participant in the sexual activity. The Court of Appeal made clear that participants in sexual activity are entitled to expect privacy, and not to be secretly filmed by either a non-participating observer or any other participant (*R v Richards* [2020] EWCA Crim 95).

Installing equipment and adapting structures for voyeurism is covered by s 67(4) of the Sexual Offences Act 2003. The offence is committed even if the installation or adaptation is never used. A 'structure' can include a tent, vehicle, or some other temporary structure.

These offences are triable either way and the penalty is imprisonment (summarily, six months and two years on indictment).

Note that the Police, Crime, Sentencing and Courts Act 2022 has created a new offence of voyeurism concerning recording while a person is breastfeeding (s 48).

24.3.2 Upskirting

The term 'upskirting' is used to describe practices where an individual photographs or films from below under another person's clothing (without consent) with the intention of viewing the victim's genitals or buttocks. The victims are usually female and the offence can be committed even if the area is concealed or partly concealed by a garment such as underwear. There had been a tendency to minimize the intrusive effects of such conduct but one victim, Gina Martin, finding that the activity was not illegal, initiated a campaign to make it a criminal offence (*Telegraph*, 2019). From 12 April 2019, two specific offences were added to the existing voyeurism legislation under s 67A of the Sexual Offences Act 2003. The new offences relate to operating equipment without consent, and the recording of images without consent. It must be proven that the offences were committed for sexual gratification or for humiliating, alarming, or distressing the victim. The offences carry a maximum sentence of two years' imprisonment on indictment and six months if tried summarily.

TASK 1 Consider the following scenarios and what offences might have been committed:

1. Members of a rugby club have taken to celebrating by exposing their naked buttocks ('mooning') at the rear window of the team bus. A police officer is asked to deal with the most recent incident that occurred in the busy main high street. What offence might have been committed?

Specific Aspects of Police Work

2. Person A is visiting a friend's house. Everyone is having a meal when Person A decides to go to the toilet. When Person A reaches the toilet, they realize that their friend's child (aged 17) is using the lavatory with the door ajar. Rather than retreat, Person A is aroused and stays on the landing watching them. Could Person A be guilty of voyeurism? Does the child's age matter?

24.4 Sexual Images Offences

Many aspects of adult pornography are completely legitimate, but if it involves 'extreme images' or indecent images of children, it will be illegal.

24.4.1 Possession of extreme pornographic images

This offence is covered by s 63(1) of the Criminal Justice and Immigration Act 2008. It is an offence to be in possession of an 'extreme pornographic image' (s 63(2)). An image includes moving images and electronic data that can be converted into an image and/or stored on mobile phones or a computer drive, for example (s 63(8)). An image is said to be pornographic if it appears to have been produced solely or principally for the purpose of sexual arousal (s 63(3)), and it must be explicit and realistic. An image is regarded as 'extreme' (see s 63(7)) if it depicts (or appears to depict) activities which:

- threaten a person's life;
- depict rape or non-consensual sexual penetration (this was added by the Criminal Justice and Courts Act 2015, and therefore does not apply to material held prior to 13 April 2015);
- result in (or are likely to result in) serious injury to a person's anus, breasts, or genitals (including surgical reconstructions);
- involve sexual interference with a human corpse (necrophilia); or
- involve a person having intercourse or oral sex with an animal (bestiality), and the act, person, or animal depicted in the image is real or appears to be real.

The offence of possession of an extreme pornographic image does not apply for 'excluded images' as defined below (s 64(2)). Defences for possessing extreme images (s 65 of the Criminal Justice and Immigration Act 2008) include that the person: had a legitimate reason for possessing it; had not seen it and did not know (nor had any cause to suspect) it was an extreme pornographic image; or had received it without requesting it and did not keep it for an unreasonable time.

The offence cannot be prosecuted without the consent of the DPP. It is triable either way and the penalty is 12 months' imprisonment and/or a fine if tried summarily. For trials on indictment, the penalty is imprisonment (three years for images which depict life-threatening acts or involve serious injury, and two years for images which involve necrophilia or bestiality).

The Ministry of Justice has issued guidance for dealing with the offence of possession of extreme pornographic images, available on the CPS website. The Internet Watch Foundation operates an internet hotline for the public and IT professionals to report potentially illegal websites.

24.4.1.1 Excluded images

These images are excluded in the sense that they would not be of concern for the offences under s 63(1) of the Criminal Justice and Immigration Act 2008 or s 62(1) of the Coroners and Justice Act 2009 (for child sex abuse imagery, see 24.4.2). For material to be regarded as an excluded image, it must be part of a full-length mainstream or documentary film classified by the British Board of Film Classification (BBFC) and will not be considered as pornographic if shown as part of the complete film. However, if parts of the classified work have been extracted solely or principally for the purpose of sexual arousal, they will no longer count as 'excluded' (s 63(3)). Such cases will be a question of fact for the court to decide, for example part of a film could have been unintentionally recorded or reproduced for a purpose other than pornography.

24.4.2 Images of children and pornography

Sexualized images of children are used by sex offenders as masturbatory fantasy material, and for some this usage can also produce sexual disinhibition, making the actual abuse of children more likely. To help to protect children from harm and exploitation additional legislation applies in relation to images of children. Early legislation only applied to photographs and pseudo-photographs but new legislation specific to drawings and other fantasy-style images was introduced in 2009. For the purpose of legislation relating to child sexual abuse imagery any person under the age of 18 is a child, except where defences of marriage apply.

Some photographs of children may appear indecent but are not indecent in terms of the legislation (s 1 of the Protection of Children Act 1978). Exception 1A is that the photograph was of a person aged 16 or over and that at the time of the alleged offence the person and the suspect were married or lived together as partners in an enduring family relationship. Exception 1B is that the photograph is for use in criminal investigation or proceedings, in any part of the world.

24.4.2.1 Possession of an indecent photograph of a child

Section 160(1) of the Criminal Justice Act 1988 states that it is an offence for a person to have in their possession any indecent photograph or pseudo-photograph of a child. A pseudo-photograph of a child could, for instance, involve a child's naked body with an adult's face added to it. The law does not define 'indecent'. According to *R v Stamford* [1972] 2 QB 391, it is up to a jury to decide whether or not an image is indecent based on 'recognized standards of propriety' (not necessarily their personal views—see also *R v Neil* [2011] EWCA Crim 461). Possession relates to knowledge of relevant digital files which a person knows they have the capacity to access, and whether they actually opened, scrutinized, or accessed the material is irrelevant to the basic offence. These issues may be determined with reference to the defences that a defendant may argue (*Okoro (Cyprian) (No 3)* [2018] EWCA Crim 1929.

Defences (s 160(2)) include having a legitimate reason for possessing the image, having not seen the image nor having cause to suspect what it was, and receiving the image without requesting it and not keeping it for an unreasonable time. The offence is triable either way and the penalty is a fine or imprisonment (six months if tried summarily and five years on indictment).

24.4.2.2 Producing and distributing indecent photographs of children

This offence is covered in s 1 of the Protection of Children Act 1978 and is explained in more detail in the flowchart.

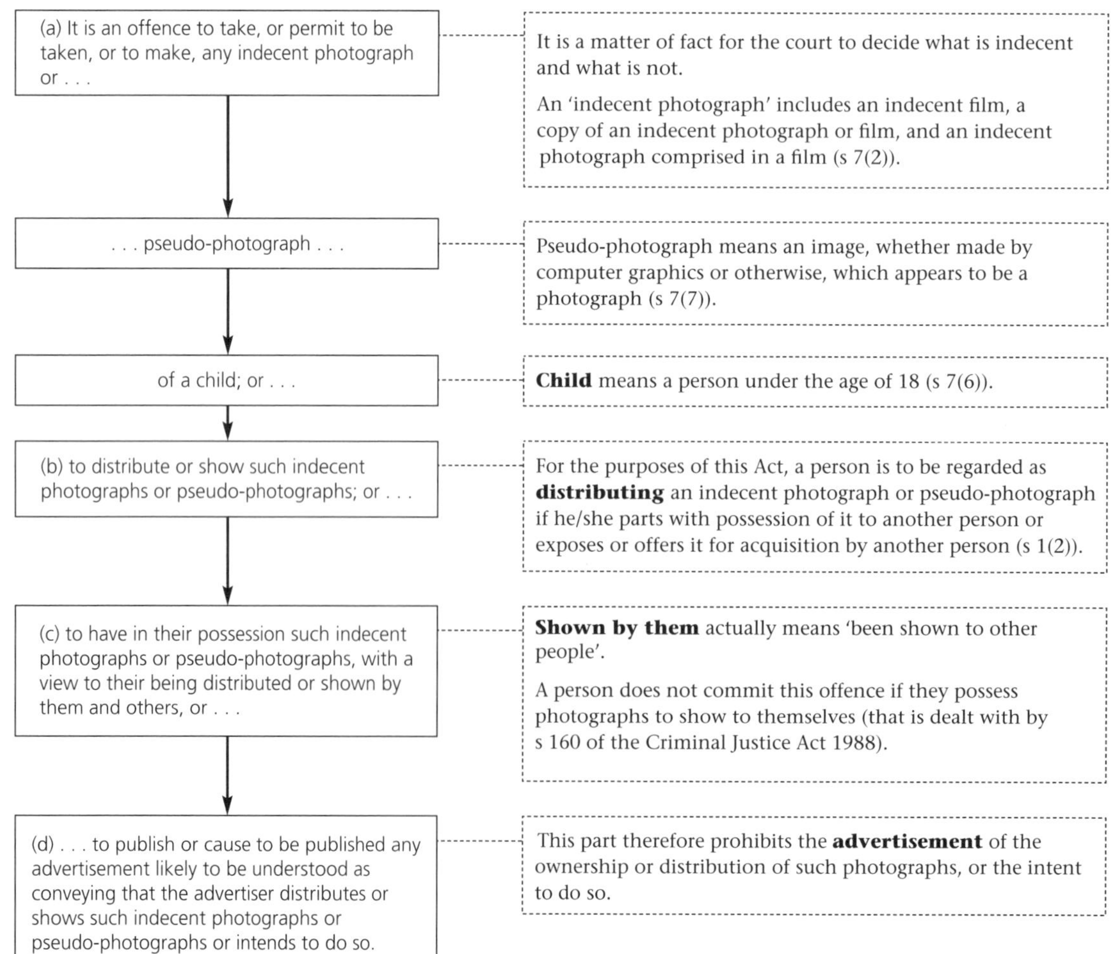

(a) It is an offence to take, or permit to be taken, or to make, any indecent photograph or . . .
It is a matter of fact for the court to decide what is indecent and what is not.
An 'indecent photograph' includes an indecent film, a copy of an indecent photograph or film, and an indecent photograph comprised in a film (s 7(2)).
. . . pseudo-photograph . . .
Pseudo-photograph means an image, whether made by computer graphics or otherwise, which appears to be a photograph (s 7(7)).
of a child; or . . .
Child means a person under the age of 18 (s 7(6)).
(b) to distribute or show such indecent photographs or pseudo-photographs; or . . .
For the purposes of this Act, a person is to be regarded as **distributing** an indecent photograph or pseudo-photograph if he/she parts with possession of it to another person or exposes or offers it for acquisition by another person (s 1(2)).
(c) to have in their possession such indecent photographs or pseudo-photographs, with a view to their being distributed or shown by them and others, or . . .
Shown by them actually means 'been shown to other people'.
A person does not commit this offence if they possess photographs to show to themselves (that is dealt with by s 160 of the Criminal Justice Act 1988).
(d) . . . to publish or cause to be published any advertisement likely to be understood as conveying that the advertiser distributes or shows such indecent photographs or pseudo-photographs or intends to do so.
This part therefore prohibits the **advertisement** of the ownership or distribution of such photographs, or the intent to do so.

Two defences to this offence are listed in s 1(4) of the Protection of Children Act 1978:

- the defendant had a legitimate reason for distributing, showing, or having possession of the photographs or pseudo-photographs; and
- the defendant did not see the photographs or pseudo-photographs, or saw them and did not know they were indecent or have any cause to suspect them to be indecent.

The offence is triable either way. If tried summarily, the penalty is six months' imprisonment and/or a fine, and on indictment the penalty is ten years' imprisonment.

24.4.2.3 Possession of a prohibited image of a child

Under s 62(1) of the Coroners and Justice Act 2009, it is an offence to be in possession of a prohibited image of a child (under 18 years of age). The image can be moving, still, or in data form and is said to be prohibited if it is either:

- pornographic (produced for the purpose of sexual arousal); or
- 'grossly offensive, disgusting or otherwise of an obscene character'.

The image must either focus solely or principally on a child's genitals or anal region, or portray a child as a witness or participant for sexual intercourse or oral sex with a person or an animal (the animal can be dead, alive, or imaginary), masturbation, or penetration of the anus or vagina.

Defences for possession of a prohibited image of a child (s 64) are similar to those for possessing an indecent photograph of a child (see 24.4.2.1). The offence is triable either way and the penalty is a fine or imprisonment (12 months if tried summarily and three years on indictment).

24.4.3 Disclosing private sexual images with intent to cause distress

Revenge pornography is when private sexual images, usually of a former partner, are made available to the public as a form of revenge against that other person. It is now an offence to disseminate to the public (or a section of the public) films or photographs of a sexual nature without the consent of the portrayed person and with the intent of causing them distress (s 33(1) of the Criminal Justice and Courts Act 2015). It is not an offence to disclose the images to the portrayed person. Images that have been altered are also included in the remit of this offence (eg using software that enables the manipulation of photographs), but not if the unaltered images were non-sexual and only became sexual due to the alteration(s).

Defences include that the disclosure is necessary to prevent, detect, or investigate a crime (s 33(3)) or relates to preparation or publication of journalistic material which is in the public interest (s 33(4)). A further defence is that there was reasonable belief that the images had already been released for reward and there was no reason to doubt the portrayed person had not consented to the release, for example as commercial pornography (s 33(5)).

The offence is triable either way, with a penalty of a fine and/or 12 months' imprisonment if convicted summarily and a fine and/or a maximum of two years' imprisonment if convicted on indictment. One of the first people to be convicted was sentenced to six months' imprisonment (suspended for 18 months), ordered to undertake unpaid work, fined costs, and became subject to a restraining order. This relatively robust approach is intended to act as a deterrent to what is judged by the authorities to be an increasingly common phenomenon. Many campaigners argued that the offence did not cover situations where a perpetrator *threatened* to disclose private sexual images, and that existing laws also may not have always covered every eventuality (ie coercive control, harassment, and stalking, each of which has specific points to prove). The government agreed, particularly because of the perceived gap in the law in this area. Accordingly, s 69 of the Domestic Abuse Act 2021 amends s 33(1) of the Criminal Justice and Courts Act 2015 to make *threats* to disclose private sexual images a separate criminal offence carrying the same maximum penalty as the disclosure offence. A new section is added making clear that the prosecution does not need to prove the existence of a particular image for the threat offence to be made out, nor does it need to demonstrate that the image threatened to be disclosed was a private sexual image. This offence commenced from 29 June 2021 (other Domestic Abuse Act 2021 changes commence gradually over time).

24.5 Prostitution

A prostitute is defined as 'a person ... who, on at least one occasion and whether or not compelled to do so, offers or provides sexual services to another person in return for payment or a promise of payment to [them] or a third person' (s 51(2) of the Sexual Offences Act 2003). Almost all public manifestations of prostitution are illegal. So, for example, it is an offence for a sex worker (a less judgemental term) to be clearly waiting for potential customers in a public place or for a person to be seen to actively seek the services of a sex worker in a public place.

The strong association between street sex work and drug dependence, and between off-street sex work and organized crime, was recognized by ACPO in its 2011 *Strategy & Supporting Operational Guidance for Policing Prostitution and Sexual Exploitation* (available online via NPCC website). Drug dependence, violence, and intimidation may play a large part in explaining sex work but low self-esteem and having been abused as a child are also significant factors. Some victims of trafficking are also forced into sex work. It is therefore important to determine whether an offence was committed, whether the sex worker needs any kind of assistance, and which support organizations could help.

24.5.1 Soliciting in a public place

Some of the activities relating to prostitution are described in s 1(1) of the Street Offences Act 1959. This states that it is an offence for a person to:

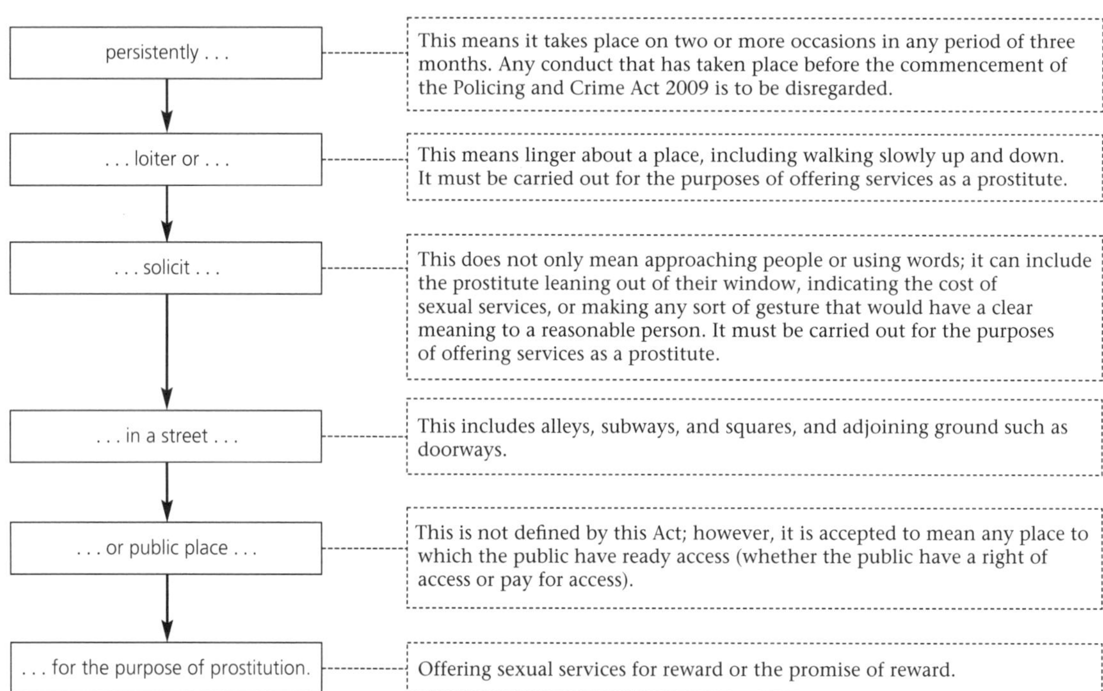

persistently . . .
This means it takes place on two or more occasions in any period of three months. Any conduct that has taken place before the commencement of the Policing and Crime Act 2009 is to be disregarded.
. . . loiter or . . .
This means linger about a place, including walking slowly up and down. It must be carried out for the purposes of offering services as a prostitute.
. . . solicit . . .
This does not only mean approaching people or using words; it can include the prostitute leaning out of their window, indicating the cost of sexual services, or making any sort of gesture that would have a clear meaning to a reasonable person. It must be carried out for the purposes of offering services as a prostitute.
. . . in a street . . .
This includes alleys, subways, and squares, and adjoining ground such as doorways.
. . . or public place . . .
This is not defined by this Act; however, it is accepted to mean any place to which the public have ready access (whether the public have a right of access or pay for access).
. . . for the purpose of prostitution.
Offering sexual services for reward or the promise of reward.

This offence is triable summarily and the penalty is a fine or a court order requiring the offender to attend three meetings with a 'suitable person' (specified in the order).

24.5.2 Procuring the services of a prostitute

It is an offence for a person to solicit the services of a prostitute in a public place (s 51A of the Sexual Offences Act 2003). This is known as *kerb crawling* when carried out from a vehicle. The offence is triable summarily and the penalty is a fine.

The penalties are more severe in relation to paying or offering to pay for the services of an 'exploited prostitute'. This is when a third person motivated by gain (for themselves or another) has used exploitative conduct to induce or encourage provision of the sexual services anywhere in the world (s 53A of the Sexual Offences Act 2003). The conduct can include the use of force, threats (not necessarily violent), coercion, and deception. It is irrelevant whether the services are actually provided or whether the 'client' is aware of the exploitative context. ACPO emphasized that anyone exploited through sex work needs help and support, most often in the form of access to health and welfare services (ACPO, 2011, p 4). This offence is triable summarily and the penalty is a fine.

24.5.3 Sex for rent

In recent years, there has been an increase in the number of reports of 'sex for rent' scandals, where a landlord takes advantage of financially vulnerable individuals to secure agreement to waive or lower rent in exchange for sexual favours. Whilst there is considerable debate about the actual criminality of these arrangements, the CPS (2019d) have issued amended legal guidance which suggests the practice may amount to an offence under ss 52–54 of the Sexual Offences Act 2003.

Section 52 concerns causing or inciting prostitution for gain and states that a person commits an offence if they:

(a) intentionally cause or incite another person to become a prostitute in any part of the world; and
(b) do so for or in the expectation of gain (for themselves or a third person).

Section 54(1) defines gain as being wider than purely financial advantage and includes the provision of sexual services whether gratuitously or at a discount. The wording of the offence thus appears to cover these kinds of arrangements.

The guidance on these offences observes that they may be difficult to prove. It also specifies some circumstances where the s 52 offence might not apply, such as where the tenant proposed the arrangement. In this type of case, the CPS suggests s 53 as a possible alternative offence (controlling prostitution for gain). The offences under ss 52 and 53 both carry a maximum sentence of seven years' imprisonment on indictment.

It is hoped that these penalties will act as a deterrent to would-be perpetrators. That said, it will be interesting to see whether prosecutions for these offences in such situations will succeed.

TASK 2

1. Two police officers are on uniformed patrol and notice a young person standing in the car park. As they approach, the youngster walks away towards the town centre but returns a few minutes later. Later, the officers see two cars stop next to the young person. Each time the occupants of the cars talk to the youngster and then drive off. What could the officers do?
2. A person offering a professional body-piercing service passes round a mobile phone amongst a group of strangers. It shows images of genitals into which sharp metal objects of various shapes and sizes have been inserted. In relation to the possession of extreme pornographic images, have any offences been committed?

24.6 Sexual Assault, Rape, and Other Sexual Offences

This part of the chapter covers the following offences within the Sexual Offences Act 2003:

- rape (s 1);
- assault by penetration (s 2);
- sexual assault (touching) (s 3); and
- causing another person to engage in sexual activity without consent (s 4).

In law, the offender must be aged ten or over and the victim can be of any age. Remember that the question of consent is of paramount importance when considering whether a sexual act relevant to these sections amounts to an offence.

The term 'sexual' now appears in ss 2, 3, and 4 as well as many of the child sex offences. An activity will be sexual if a reasonable person would consider it is obviously sexual (s 78 of the Sexual Offences Act 2003). This would cover, for example, masturbation, which most people would consider to be sexual.

Paragraph (b) of s 78 covers more ambiguous activities which may or may not be sexual, depending on the circumstances or the intentions of the perpetrator (or both). A two-stage test may be applied:

1. Would a reasonable person consider the general nature of the act to be potentially sexual in nature?

2. What are the specific circumstances of the person carrying out the potential sexual act? For example, if the penetration was carried out by a GP as part of a necessary medical examination, it would be unlikely to be considered as sexual.

If a person has a hidden sexual motive to an apparently innocent activity, this will not be considered sexual for the purpose of the Act; the general opinion is that the definition under s 78 excludes obscure sexual fetishes.

Whatever the situation, the term 'sexual' is defined so as to make it clear that not every potentially sexual activity will automatically be considered to be sexual under s 78. However, a number of observers have pointed to the possible tautological problems with s 78 definitions of sexual (it defines sexual in terms of itself) and you might consider researching this further. A case that discusses the meaning of 'sexual' and the *mens rea* required for sexual touching is *Attorney General's Reference (No 1 of 2020)* [2020] EWCA Crim 1665. It was considered necessary to prove intentional sexual touching, without consent or a reasonable belief in consent, but not necessary to prove an intention that the touching be sexual. This would be determined by the tests in s 78 and no *extra* proof was required.

24.6.1 Initial police response to sexual crime

All reports of serious sexual assault made by complainants should be taken seriously, although there has been considerable debate recently as to whether all complaints should automatically be assumed to be true. Certainly, an investigation should be initiated. As noted earlier, the historical context to rape complaints was the poor response from the police. Victims felt that they were being subjected to investigation and this practice arguably continued into modern times despite police advice to officers to be more sensitive and professional toward complainants. To redress this balance, it then became police practice to treat victims as if they were always telling the truth. There has been disagreement about the true nature of this advice: whether it was meant to apply only to the recording of a report or throughout an investigation, but more recently the approach was criticized because of the negative affect it might have on investigations, particularly anyone suspected to be the perpetrator. By simply believing the complainant, the police effectively reverse the burden of proof against a suspect and label the suspect as guilty at the outset of an investigation (Henriques, 2016). An independent review of 'Operation Midland' (the MPS investigation into historic sexual offence allegations against prominent people) was critical of this practice.

Interestingly, Henriques (2016) also suggested that even the use of the term 'victim' was value-laden. Whilst this observation was disputed by some quarters within the police service, Henriques suggested that people who report alleged crimes to the police should be regarded as 'complainants' as they only become 'victims' in the truest sense once a court has decided guilt. However for our purposes, the words 'victim' and 'complainant' will be used synonymously, with no value judgements attached to either term. Whatever terminology is ultimately used within policing circles, there is little doubt that an objective investigation is the only appropriate approach, consistent with the values of the criminal justice system. Clearly, a person reporting such an incident is entitled to the full services offered by both the police and other supportive agencies, whatever label is assigned to them.

The initial investigation into an alleged serious sexual offence will be conducted by response officers and detectives allocated to investigate the crime. Guidance for first responders attending the report of rape or sexual assault has been produced by the College of Policing (2018f), available online. Some police services have specialist units dedicated to investigating rape and serious sexual assault (eg the MPS Sapphire Teams). If the victim is a child (under 16) then other specialist police staff may also be involved. An officer of at least detective sergeant rank will be appointed to lead the investigation and will review its progress on a regular basis. ACPO's *Guidance for the Investigation and Prosecution of Rape* (ACPO, 2010) remains applicable to other types of 'serious' sexual offences. It promotes the use of a multi-agency approach to the investigation of rape.

Some police services (eg Kent Police) also provide extra training to uniformed response officers to ensure that appropriate levels of investigation and support are provided at the initial investigation stage. Most services also have specially trained 'SOIT' officers (Sexual Offences Investigation Trained officer). The SOIT training is at PIP Level 2. A SOIT will become the single point of contact (SPOC) between the victim and the investigative team, and also provide early support to the victim. In theory, the same officer will support the victim throughout the investigative process through to court, and sometimes beyond. In practice, this role is shared with Independent Sexual Violence Advisors and other volunteer agencies.

24.6.1.1 Information from the complainant

A rape or serious sexual assault is often reported to the police by the complainant but often some time after the event. It may also initially be reported as domestic abuse, perhaps due to mistrust in the justice system, fear of not being believed, or fear for their personal safety (or that of their children). Maintaining the complainant's anonymity is therefore an important part of investigating sexual offences.

A victim of rape or other serious sexual offences may be reluctant to disclose events of a traumatic and intimate nature. They could also suffer from 'post-traumatic stress disorder' which can take on a variety of expressions. There may also be severe disorientation before they can begin to readapt to 'normal' life where the incident no longer takes a central role (Mason and Lodrick, 2013).

A trainee officer is unlikely to be involved much beyond the initial stages of investigation into an alleged serious sexual offence. As for other incidents, the priority of the first attending officer (FAO) will be the protection of the victim and any other individuals at risk (see 10.3.1). An initial report should be taken (location, identity, times, description of suspect, etc) and accurate and relevant entries made in the PNB, followed by rapid referral to line managers and the SOITs. A trainee officer would not be expected to take a detailed account from the victim (this would be the SOIT's responsibility if one is deployed), but they would need to be mindful that this could be the first stage of a prolonged investigation. The FAO should remain the single point of contact with the victim until a SOIT is appointed. The College of Policing APP (2018f) specifies the minimum response at initial attendance of a report of rape or serious sexual assault.

Report-takers should display active listening (see 8.8.2) and concern for the victim when taking the statement. It is important to establish a relationship of trust with the victim early on as this will encourage them to provide as much detailed information as possible at a later stage. The focus should be on assessing the immediate safety of the victim and be sufficient for briefing of the officers investigating the events.

Certain questions must be addressed during the initial stages. These depend on the urgency of the report and include, amongst other things, asking the identity of the person making the report (and for phone calls, their location), the location and time of the incident, whether the person making the report is the victim or a third party (and if the latter, in what capacity), the nature of the incident, the location and identity of the suspect, and details of any known injuries (ACPO, 2010, pp 24–5). As courts can hear evidence from others a victim has told of the crime in certain circumstances (under s 120 of the Criminal Justice Act 2003), it would be advisable for police officers to ask who else they have told so that such evidence can be obtained by the investigation team. Any decision to arrest the offender (or involve them in any other way in the investigation) should consider the risk that this may present to the victim.

Forensic requirements must be considered (see 10.3), including the use of evidence-recovery methods if appropriate (see Chapter 13). Sexual assault victims should not smoke, eat, drink, wash, or go to the toilet (unless absolutely necessary) until they have been forensically examined as the preservation of physical evidence is essential. An Early Evidence Kit (EEK) can be used during the initial response to secure relevant forensic evidence. The kit usually includes a plastic container to collect urine samples, sheets of toilet paper, a mouth swab, and a mouth rinse.

Following recent controversies regarding failure to investigate and disclose relevant exonerating material to the defence in rape and serious sexual assault investigations (MPS and CPS, 2018), it had become police practice to routinely ask victims for their mobile phones. This has now been clarified by the Court of Appeal (*CB; Mohammed (Sultan)* [2020] EWCA Crim 790) where the court stressed that there was no obligation to review material on mobile phones without good cause, and phones should not be routinely obtained by police from witnesses. The court stressed that the defence would have an opportunity to demonstrate good cause in interview under caution and/or with a defence statement provided to the prosecution.

24.6.1.2 Information from others

Reports may be made by third parties, in which case the report-taker should try to establish in which capacity the third party is acting. The third party should be provided with the contact details of an investigating officer (IO) so that any further information can be provided later if necessary. Direct police contact with the victim should usually be avoided without the knowledge of the third party. This does not mean, however, that contact with the victim should be avoided altogether; a risk assessment should be made under the supervision of an IO, who should consider using a SOIT to take matters forward. If the third party identifies an offender, the IO should consider further investigation and arrest if there is reasonable suspicion of the offence having taken place. If the third party making the report is from another agency, the recording and investigation should follow the pre-agreed information-sharing protocols. The information should be auditable and can be used, for example, to analyse trends and patterns of offending. Specialist sexual violence services should be made aware of any anonymous reports. The IO will need to decide whether there is enough evidence to justify reasonable suspicion and a subsequent arrest.

24.6.2 Consent

In many sexual offence prosecutions, particularly those relating to ss 1–4 of the Sexual Offences Act, the court will focus on the issue of consent. A defence is available if the suspect believes that consent was given but the suspect will need to demonstrate that their belief was reasonable. The court will decide whether the belief was reasonable after considering the circumstances and the steps that the suspect took to obtain consent (s 1(2) of the Sexual Offences Act 2003). In general terms, the court will seek to establish whether the suspect made a conscious effort to initially establish consent and then monitor the consent—the other person might change their mind and withdraw consent, indicated by a change of physical expression or voice tone, for example.

The Sexual Offences Act 2003 introduced two sets of presumptions which courts can make in relation to the guilty knowledge of the defendant about consent: 'conclusive presumptions' and 'evidential presumptions' (see below). These set out certain situations where it is clear that consent cannot truly have been given.

If evidential and conclusive presumptions about consent do not apply (and these only apply exceptionally), then establishing lack of consent is more difficult and arguments relate to the more general definition of consent provided in s 74 of the Sexual Offences Act 2003. In order to address this difficulty and to ensure that officers steer away from the myths surrounding rape, in 2015 the CPS and the Commissioner of the Metropolitan Police issued a joint action plan. This encourages the police to look more closely at the behaviour of the accused when trying to establish whether or not consent was granted rather than focusing solely on the complainant (CPS and MPS, 2015a). The action plan includes an aide-memoire with information on consent that summarizes relevant legislation and dispels some of the myths associated with rape. Before considering s 74 further, we say more about s 76 and s 75 as understanding the reasoning underpinning each section of the Act in this way is more straightforward.

24.6.2.1 Conclusive presumptions about consent

Conclusive presumptions about consent are covered by s 76 of the Sexual Offences Act 2003. This outlines specific circumstances where a victim has been deceived and has engaged in sexual activity as a consequence. It must be proved that the defendant intentionally:

- deceived the complainant about the nature or purpose of the relevant act; or
- impersonated an individual personally known to the victim, with whom the victim would have consented to such activity.

The presumption about consent (ie the lack of consent and lack of a reasonable belief in consent) is conclusive and final: if the victim has been deceived in any of these ways, no amount of evidence can prove that consent had been given.

24.6.2.2 Consent and s 75 of the Sexual Offences Act 2003

Section 75 of the Sexual Offences Act 2003 covers evidential presumptions about consent.

Under s 75 the court will presume that the victim did not consent (and that there was no reasonable belief in consent) if evidence presented in court proves that the circumstances involved any of the following:

- use of or fear of immediate violence against that or another person;
- any kind of unlawful detention of the victim (and not the offender);
- being asleep or unconscious;
- inability to communicate due to physical disability; and/or
- substances that are capable of stupefying or overpowering (such as drugs) that were non-consensually administered.

It also has to be proved that the defendant knew of these circumstances and carried out the act in question, except in the last example, where the section does not require it to be the person who administered to be the person taking advantage of the situation.

The defence may provide evidence to prevent any of the s 75 presumptions being applied. The defence will need to convince the judge on the balance of probabilities that there is a definite issue about consent and then produce relevant evidence from the defendant, a witness, or the victim. The defendant's belief (that consent had been granted) and their reasoning cannot be merely 'fanciful or speculative' (*R v Ciccarelli* [2011] EWCA Crim 2665).

24.6.2.3 Consent and s 74 of the Sexual Offences Act 2003

Section 74 of the Sexual Offences Act 2003 states that a person consents if they agree by choice and have the freedom and capacity to make that choice. Whilst ss 75 and 76 appear clearer cut because they list specific circumstances that demonstrate a lack of consent, s 74 plays an important role in providing the general definition of consent.

A choice has not been made freely if the person has, for instance, taken part under duress, through being blackmailed, or if deceived into thinking negative consequences might follow non-compliance. Capacity to agree means the ability to decide either way, and to be able to communicate the decision. If a person is 'unable to refuse', through intoxication (see *R v Bree* [2007] EWCA Crim 256) for example, then they do not have the capacity to make the choice.

The general definition of consent under s 74 of the Act is wide enough to encompass circumstances where the victim has been deceived into giving consent. For example, in *R v Jheeta* [2007] EWCA Crim 1699 the victim felt compelled to have sex after being deceived into believing that she would otherwise be fined by the police. Because of the deception, it could not be said that she legally gave consent. This case is a good example where the presumption in s 76 did **not** apply because the person deceiving the victim was a fictitious police officer not a real person. However, the courts made it clear that other kinds of deception are capable of being considered under the general definition of consent provided in s 74.

Case law has established a number of other situations where the victim has been deceived and consent is negated under s 74 (rather than ss 75 and 76). This includes deceptions concerning the gender of the perpetrator (*R v McNally* [2013] EWCA Crim 1051), whether a condom will be used (*R (on the application of F) v DPP & A (interested party)* [2013] EWHC 945 (Admin); *Assange v Swedish Prosecution Authority* [2011] EWHC 2849 (Admin)) and blackmail (*R v B* [2013] EWCA Crim 823).

There is, however, considerable debate on the limits of s 74, for example an old case, *R v Linekar* ((1995) 2 Cr App R 49), suggested that a man lying to a prostitute that he would pay for her services did not constitute deceptive conduct sufficient to negate consent. Consideration has also been given to deceptions such as: 'I will marry you'; 'I am a millionaire' and so on, that have been used to secure sexual activity. Such deceptions are undoubtedly morally questionable behaviour, but are unlikely to negate consent under s 74, mainly because they are deemed too remote from deceptions closely linked to the nature or purpose of the sexual act (unlike *Jheeta*, *McNally*, *F*, and *Assange*).

The limits of s 74 were further considered in a case relating to sexual activity between a male undercover police officer and a female environmental activist. The whole relationship was based on the activist being deceived and she said that had she known his true identity she would never have consented to sexual activity. The CPS declined to prosecute, deciding that the facts did not constitute rape. The activist challenged this decision, but the Divisional Court rejected the challenge after reviewing the ambit of consent in older offences (eg of rape and procuring sexual activity by deceptive conduct (now repealed) under the Sexual Offences Act 1956), and the more recent definition of consent provided in s 74 of the Sexual Offences Act 2003. The court suggested that it was inappropriate to introduce a subjective element into the law to considerations of consent, as the victim would need to show that the fraud/deception was regarded by them as fundamental or critical to their decision-making (*R (on the application of Monica) v DPP* [2018] EWHC 3508 (Admin). This decision appears to be in line with the authorities above.

In a very important recent case, a man successfully appealed his conviction for rape where he had reportedly lied to the victim about having had a vasectomy. The court considered that this deception was insufficient to negate consent (*R v Lawrance* [2020] EWCA Crim 971). The court went on to consider the developing law in terms of consent. It made clear that some deceptions can mean that there is no true consent but that the deceptions had to be 'closely connected' to the performance of the sexual act. It also stressed that 'close connection' would be narrowly interpreted by the courts. Accordingly, it highlighted that the deception must relate to the physical performance of the act rather than the circumstances surrounding it. It specifically discussed the condom cases and suggested that these illustrate closeness because the wearing of a condom physically changes the nature of the act. In contrast, it clarified that lying about fertility does not. It went on to point out that the way a deception is communicated is also irrelevant as the key test is close connection to the sexual act. This might help to explain why cases like *Lawrance*, *Monica*, and the old case of *Linekar* fail that test. The following will now deal with the separate non-consensual offences in ss 1–4 of the Sexual Offences Act 2003. The issue of consent is relevant to all of them. In addition, each of these sections begins with the word 'intentional'. An essential element of proof therefore required is that the defendant intentionally penetrated, intentionally touched, or intentionally caused the victim to engage in sexual activity. In *R v Heard* [2007] EWCA Crim 125, the Court of Appeal decided that the s 3 offence (and by implication ss 1, 2, and 4) is a crime of basic intent, meaning that any claim of intoxication to deny *mens rea* will fail.

24.6.3 Rape

This is detailed in s 1 of the Sexual Offences Act 2003 and can only be committed by a man, but the victim can be male or female.

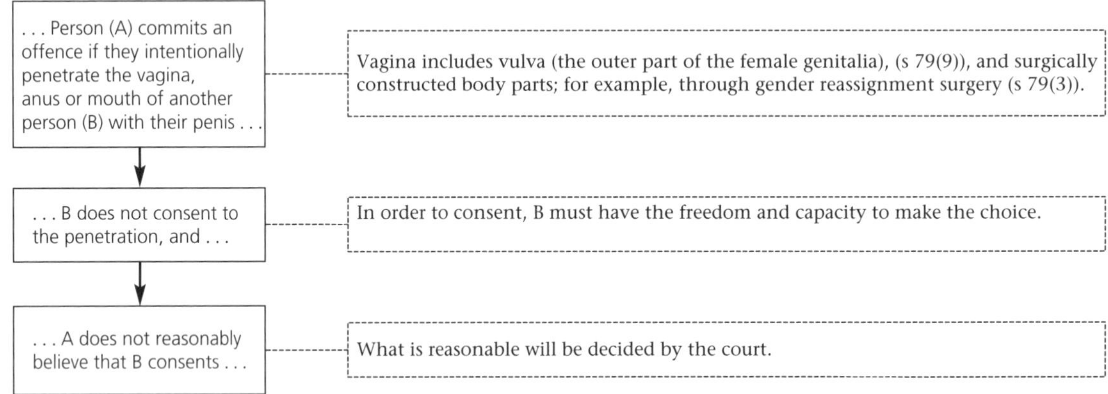

. . . Person (A) commits an offence if they intentionally penetrate the vagina, anus or mouth of another person (B) with their penis . . .
Vagina includes vulva (the outer part of the female genitalia), (s 79(9)), and surgically constructed body parts; for example, through gender reassignment surgery (s 79(3)).
. . . B does not consent to the penetration, and . . .
In order to consent, B must have the freedom and capacity to make the choice.
. . . A does not reasonably believe that B consents . . .
What is reasonable will be decided by the court.

There are some important points to consider about penetration, which also apply for other sexual assaults:

- the very slightest degree of penetration is still penetration (*R v Hughes*, (1841) 9 C & P 752);
- penetration is a continuing act from entry to withdrawal (s 79(2)); person (A) may have penetrated person (B) with B's consent, but B then changes their mind (quite legitimately) and makes this clear. If A does not withdraw, this amounts to a continuing penetration (and potentially rape);
- references to a part of the body also include surgically constructed parts (in particular through gender reassignment surgery) (s 79(3)). This leaves open the possibility that the offence can be committed by a person who was not born a man but who has a surgically constructed penis.

The offence of rape is triable on indictment only and the maximum penalty is life imprisonment.

Specific Aspects of Police Work

24.6.4 Assault by penetration

This is an offence under s 2 of the Sexual Offences Act 2003; person A commits an offence if they intentionally penetrate (with a part of their body or anything else) B's vagina or anus without B's consent. Person A must be sexually motivated and not have a reasonable belief that B consents. Penetration is a continuing act from entry to withdrawal, and references to body parts include surgically constructed parts (see 24.6.3). The issue of consent can be considered by looking at the general definition under s 74 or any of the evidential or conclusive presumptions in s 75 or 76. Rather than seeing this offence as a form of rape (because it involves the act of penetration), it is perhaps more appropriate to see it as an aggravated form of sexual assault. It is now (since the Sexual Offences Act 2003) a separate offence with higher penalties than previously. The penalty for penetrative sexual assault offence can be life imprisonment, whereas prior to 2003 the maximum sentence was only ten years. The offence of assault by penetration is triable on indictment only.

24.6.5 Sexual assault

This is covered under s 3 of the Sexual Offences Act 2003 and the details are shown in the flowchart.

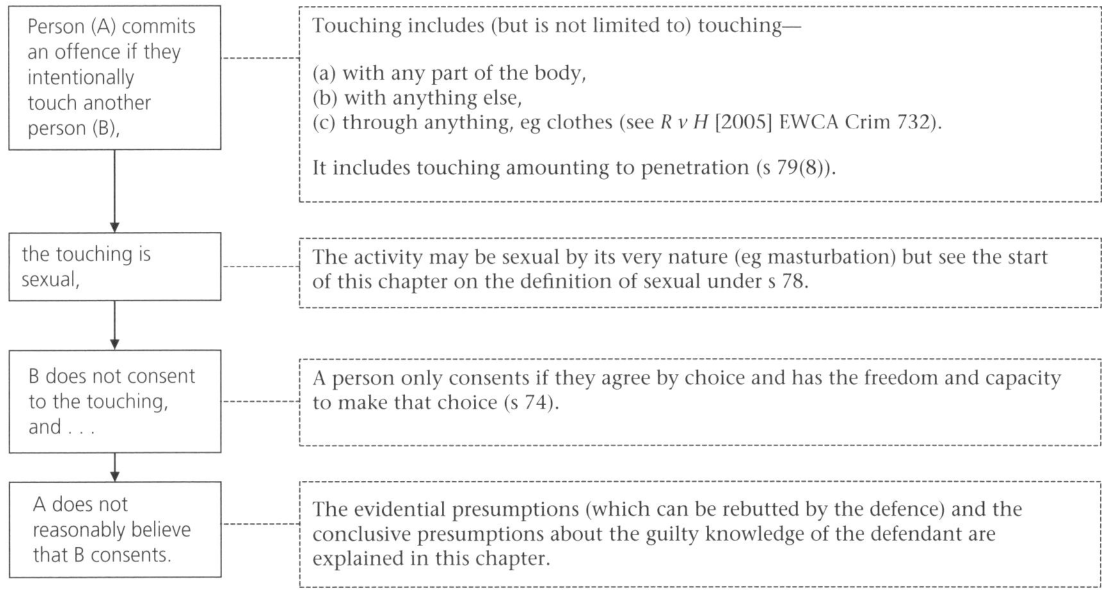

Person (A) commits an offence if they intentionally touch another person (B),
Touching includes (but is not limited to) touching—
(a) with any part of the body,
(b) with anything else,
(c) through anything, eg clothes (see *R v H* [2005] EWCA Crim 732).
It includes touching amounting to penetration (s 79(8)).
the touching is sexual,
The activity may be sexual by its very nature (eg masturbation) but see the start of this chapter on the definition of sexual under s 78.
B does not consent to the touching, and . . .
A person only consents if they agree by choice and has the freedom and capacity to make that choice (s 74).
A does not reasonably believe that B consents.
The evidential presumptions (which can be rebutted by the defence) and the conclusive presumptions about the guilty knowledge of the defendant are explained in this chapter.

Unlike the old offence of indecent assault, the s 3 offence requires an intentional touching of the person (along with the other relevant points to prove) before an offence is complete. Note the very broad definition of 'touching' provided in the flowchart. In circumstances where the suspect has only tried to touch in a sexual manner, but failed to touch the person targeted, this could be an attempted offence (see Chapter 27).

Unlawful sexual touching is triable either way. The maximum penalties are six months' imprisonment and/or a fine if tried summarily and ten years' imprisonment on indictment. In a recent case, the Court of Appeal clarified that the prosecution does not need to prove that the defendant intended the touching to be sexual. What was required was proof the touching was intentional, and that the touching was sexual (*Attorney General's Reference (No 1 of 2020)* [2020] EWCA Crim 1665).

24.6.6 Causing another person to engage in sexual activity without consent

It is an offence to intentionally cause another person to engage in sexual activity if they do not consent and the perpetrator does not reasonably believe that consent has been given (s 4(1) of the Sexual Offences Act 2003). An example of this type of offence is where a man threatens to stab a woman with a knife if she does not perform a sexual act in front of him. She performs the sexual act for fear of being assaulted. He has caused her to engage in sexual activity although there was no contact between the two of them. It would also need to be proven that there was no consent and no reasonable belief in consent. The difficulty for police investigators in these types of cases is that these offences are often committed in private with no witnesses present. A thorough investigation will be needed as other elements of proof might be uncovered, for example evidence from the suspect's phone. Aggravating factors include a large age difference between offender and victim, general vulnerability of the victim, and the use of weapons to commit the offence. The penalty is six months' imprisonment and/or a fine if tried summarily and ten years' imprisonment on indictment.

If the sexual activity involves penetration, the offence is more serious. Under s 4(4), the perpetrator (A) can cause penetration involving person B in a number of different ways. It can be:

(a) penetration of B's anus or vagina by anything;
(b) penile penetration of B's mouth (with person A's penis or any other man's penis);
(c) penetration of any person's anus or vagina by B, using part of B's body, or any item; or
(d) penetration of person A's or any other person's mouth with B's penis (if B is a male).

This would cover situations where groups of people cause others to engage in penetrative sexual activity with other people in the group. Some of the group may facilitate the offences by restraining the victim whilst others engage in the penetrative activity. The participants could, of course, be prosecuted for rape or conspiracy to rape but this has often proved difficult when groups of people have been involved. However, the s 4(1) offence can be used to cover the conduct of all persons involved and is classed as a serious sexual offence. Therefore, any of the people involved who were found guilty could be placed on the Violent and Sex Offenders Register (ViSOR) not just those who actually penetrated the victim.

The penetrative elements to s 4 are triable on indictment only and the maximum penalty is life imprisonment.

TASK 3 Many victims of rape will be concerned about their identity becoming known during the investigation and any subsequent court case. What legislation is available to provide anonymity in relation to complaints of rape and restrictions on evidence at trials for rape? Is there any anonymity afforded to a defendant in these cases?

24.6.7 Sexual activity with an animal or a human corpse

Sexual intercourse with an animal is covered under s 69 of the Sexual Offences Act 2003. It involves penile penetration of animals by humans and of humans by animals. The animals and the human participants must be alive and the penetration can be of the vagina or the anus. This activity is also known as bestiality. The offence can also be committed by allowing or causing such an act. (Note that penetration of an animal with an object does not come under this legislation but could be pursued through legislation for prevention of cruelty to animals.)

Penetration of a human corpse is covered under s 70 of the Sexual Offences Act 2003 and can be committed by men or women. Any part of the body or any object can be used to perform the penetration and any part of the corpse may be penetrated. The offender must have some kind of sexual motivation and must know or be reckless about whether they are penetrating a corpse.

These offences are triable either way. The penalty if tried summarily is six months' imprisonment and/or a fine not exceeding the statutory maximum and two years' imprisonment on indictment.

24.7 Children, Young People, and Sexual Offences

Sexual activity between an adult and a child under the age of 16 is unlawful. Here we cover some of the sexual offences legislation that applies specifically to offences involving younger victims. (The offences listed in 24.6 can also be considered where the child did not consent.) For a victim under 13 years of age, the law considers that they cannot give consent in any sense, so the offences are of strict liability.

Sexual contact may take place between an adult (aged 18 or over) and a child under 16, or between children both of whom are aged under 16. Whilst all of these activities might be sexual offences, some of the activities will attract criminal sanction whilst others might not.

First, where a person aged ten or over engages in sexual activity with another child, and the activities are clearly non-consensual, the prosecutor could employ any of the offences in ss 1–4 of the Sexual Offences Act 2003.

Secondly, where an adult engages in sexual conduct with a child under the age of 13, there are offences of rape, assault by penetration, sexual assault, and causing or inciting sexual activity that do not rely upon proof of lack of consent (ss 5–8 of the Sexual Offences Act 2003). In essence, these offences are of strict liability due to the age of the child. In many ways, the offences covered by ss 5–8 effectively mirror the offences under ss 1–4 of the Sexual Offences Act, apart from the requirement to prove the age of the child, the irrelevance of consent, and the addition of the term 'incitement' in s 8 to criminalize conduct aimed at encouraging children under 13 to engage in sexual activity. In all other respects, the requirements of proof are the same. Note that the Police, Crime, Sentencing and Courts Act 2022 has widened the number of offences to which the charge of 'arranging or commissioning a child sex offence' can be applied to include ss 5–8 of the Sexual Offences Act 2003.

Thirdly, where an adult (aged 18 or over) engages in sexual activity with a child between the ages of 13 and under 16, where lack of consent does not feature, the Sexual Offences Act 2003 creates a series of further offences designed to criminalize such conduct (ss 9–12 of the Sexual Offences Act 2003). Again, there is no need to prove that consent was not given, although consent may be relevant to mitigation and/or sentence if a person is convicted. In these cases, the adult might be able to use a defence of reasonable belief that the child was 16 or over but this would be dependent upon the circumstances of the case.

Finally, there may be circumstances where both parties engaging in sexual activity are under the age of 16. Section 13 of the Sexual Offences Act 2003 makes it possible for those under the age of 16 to be guilty of sexual offences under ss 9–12. However, provided there is true agreement, a prosecution is not always considered to be in the public interest. Further details on this are given in the Rape and Sexual Offences Guidance on the CPS website. Under s 13 of the Sexual Offences Act 2003, children charged with any of these offences would be subject to a lower maximum sentence of five years' imprisonment.

Grooming and child sexual exploitation have received particular attention in the political and law enforcement fields in recent years, particularly due to a number of high-profile cases involving individuals, groups of individuals, and gangs that sexually exploited children. We consider some of the measures to tackle these problems in 24.7.6 and 24.8.

24.7.1 Child rape

Rape of a child under the age of 13 is an offence under s 5 of the Sexual Offences Act 2003. It can only be committed by a man but the victim can be male or female. For this offence, the victim's anus, vagina, or mouth must be penetrated by the offender's penis. The sexual organs can have been constructed through surgery (as with s 1 rape: see 24.6.3) and penetration is a continuous act from entry to withdrawal (s 79(2)).

Whether the victim appears to consent or otherwise agree to the activity is of absolutely no relevance, nor can the defendant contend that he thought the victim was aged 16 or over. Proof that the victim was under the age of 13 must be provided for a prosecution. This offence is triable on indictment only and the maximum penalty is life imprisonment.

For a victim aged 13–15 years, there is no specific offence so the offence will need to fit the general definitions for rape under s 1, and lack of consent would need to be proven. Where lack of consent is difficult to prove, or the circumstances reveal willing participation, then offences between ss 9–12 could be considered (see 24.7.3, for example).

24.7.2 Sexual assault of a child

Sexual assault by penetration of a child under the age of 13 years is an offence under s 6 of the Sexual Offences Act 2003. The penetration can be carried out using any part of the body (such as a finger) or a separate object and can be committed by a male or a female. The child does not need to be aware of the nature of the penetrating object. As for other offences, penetration is a continuous act from entry to withdrawal (s 79(2)). This offence is triable on indictment only and the maximum penalty is life imprisonment.

Sexual assault on a child under the age of 13 without penetration is covered by s 7(1) of the Sexual Offences Act 2003. It involves intentionally touching a child under the age of 13 in a sexual manner (see 24.6.5 for more detail on the meaning of 'touching' and 'sexual'), and can be committed by a male or a female. This offence is triable either way and the penalty is six months' imprisonment and/or a fine if tried summarily and 14 years' imprisonment on indictment.

For these offences (s 6 and s 7) the victim must be under 13 years old and proof of this must be provided for a prosecution. Whether the victim appears to consent or otherwise agree to the activity is irrelevant. Nor would it be possible for a defendant to contend that they thought the victim was aged 16 or over.

For a victim aged 13–15 years old with non-consensual activity, offences under ss 1–4 can apply. If, however, the activities seem to have been consensual, a prosecution under s 9 or 10 could be considered.

24.7.3 Sexual activity with a child

It is an offence under s 9 of the Sexual Offences Act 2003 for a person (male or female) to intentionally touch a child in a sexual manner. Where the child is less than 13 years old, it is more likely that the suspect would be prosecuted under s 6 or 7 for such activities, but the prosecutor will decide which is the most appropriate.

For a s 9 offence, the child victim has to be under 16 and proof of age is required. The accused will have a defence if they reasonably believed the victim was aged 16 or over, so the investigation should seek evidence that could justify the suspect's belief. Prior to 2003, only young men under the age of 23 were able to use this defence but any person charged with child sex offences can now use it. Where a child is aged under 13 years, the defence is not available.

The s 9(1) offence (assault with no penetration) is triable either way and the penalty is six months' imprisonment and/or a fine if tried summarily and 14 years' imprisonment on indictment. If the sexual activity involves penetration, then a more serious form of the offence is committed, under s 9(2). (Such an activity where the victim is under 13 would be prosecuted under s 6.) Section 9(2) describes the acts carried out by the suspect (person A) that can constitute this more serious offence:

(a) they penetrate the child's anus or vagina (with a part of A's body or anything else);
(b) person A is a man and uses his penis to penetrate the child's mouth;
(c) they cause a part of the child's body (eg a finger) to penetrate A's anus or vagina; or
(d) person A forces a boy to put his penis in A's mouth.

This offence is triable by indictment only and the penalty is up to 14 years' imprisonment.

24.7.4 Causing or inciting a child to engage in sexual activity

These offences (under ss 8 and 10 of the Sexual Offences Act 2003) can be committed by a man or a woman and can involve the child acting alone or with another person. The offender might not be physically involved and no sexual activity actually has to occur; incitement alone can amount to the offence.

Causing or inciting a child under 13 years old to engage in sexual activity is covered by s 8 of the Sexual Offences Act 2003. If the sexual activity caused or incited involves no penetration, the offence is committed under s 8(1), and under s 8(2) if penetration is involved. Section 8 therefore creates four separate offences: causing non-penetrative sexual activity, causing penetrative sexual activity, inciting non-penetrative sexual activity, and inciting penetrative sexual activity. Proof of age is once again required, consent is irrelevant, and the defendant will not be able to use the defence that they thought the child was older.

Section 8(1) offences (no penetration is caused or incited) are triable either way. The penalty is six months' imprisonment and/or a fine if tried summarily and 14 years' imprisonment on indictment. Section 8(2) offences (penetration is caused or incited) are triable on indictment only and the maximum penalty is life imprisonment.

For a victim under 16 years of age, these activities are covered by s 10 of the Sexual Offences Act 2003. Non-penetrative sexual activity is covered under s 10(1) and penetrative sexual activity under s 10(2). Reasonable belief that the child was aged 16 or over is available as a defence for this offence. The s 10(1) offence is triable either way. Consent is again irrelevant to the offence but might be relevant to mitigation and sentence. The penalty is six months' imprisonment and/or a fine if tried summarily and 14 years' imprisonment on indictment. An offence under s 10(2) is triable on indictment only and the penalty is imprisonment for up to 14 years.

24.7.5 Causing a child to witness sexual acts

There are two offences under the Sexual Offences Act 2003 where the offender causes a child to witness sexual acts: where the offender commits the sexual acts themselves (s 11) and where other people commit the acts (s 12).

For the s 11 offence, the offender must know or believe that the child will be aware of the sexual acts in some way and gain some sexual gratification from the child's presumed awareness. However, the victim does not actually have to be aware of the activity (eg if the child does not notice). For the s 12 offence, the offender must gain sexual gratification from causing a child to watch a third party involved in sexual activity (live or recorded). The child need not be coerced to watch and may even agree to watch; this is irrelevant to whether the offence has been committed. In the case of *R v Abdullahi (Osmund) Mohammed* [2006] EWCA Crim 2060, the Court of Appeal made it clear that the showing of material and the sexual gratification did not have to occur at the same time. It was possible therefore to show a child sexualized videos with the intention to gain sexual gratification some hours later.

These offences are both triable either way. The penalty is six months' imprisonment and/or a fine if tried summarily and ten years' imprisonment on indictment.

TASK 4 Imagine you are a trainee officer and you are asked to attend the home of a 15-year-old. They allege that a family friend has been visiting the house on a regular basis and has sometimes touched the 15-year-old's genitals. If the allegations are substantiated, could the family friend have a defence to any possible charge? Would it make a difference if the victim was 12 years old?

24.7.6 Countering grooming and organized child sexual exploitation

Grooming and child sexual exploitation have gained considerable attention in the political and law enforcement fields in recent years, particularly due to a number of high-profile cases concerning groups of individuals that have sexually exploited children. Grooming is now addressed under several offences and measures are being put in place to counter child sexual exploitation.

24.7.6.1 Sexual grooming

There are two main offences associated with sexual grooming under the Sexual Offences Act 2003:

- person A meeting or travelling to meet with a child (B) following sexual grooming or B travels to meet A following sexual grooming (s 15); and
- communicating with a child for the purpose of sexual gratification for the sender (s 15A).

For both offences, the perpetrator must be over 18 years of age and the victim must be under 16 years of age. However, if the perpetrator reasonably believed the victim was 16 or over this can be a defence. The s 15A offence was introduced in 2017 to fill a perceived gap in the law where sexualized communication with a child with no intention of meeting up was not previously a criminal offence.

Under s 15 of the Sexual Offences Act 2003, it is an offence to meet with or travel to meet a child following sexual grooming (s 15 of the Sexual Offences Act 2003). The overall aim of this legislation is to criminalize behaviour where an adult contacts a child on one or more occasions and meets (or intends to meet) the child in order to commit any offence under Part 1 of the Sexual Offences Act 2003 against them.

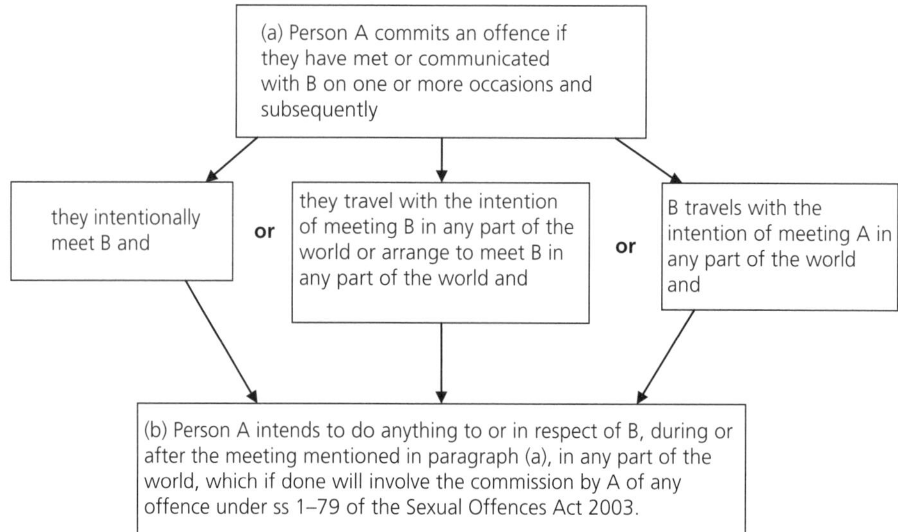
(a) Person A commits an offence if they have met or communicated with B on one or more occasions and subsequently
they intentionally meet B and
or
they travel with the intention of meeting B in any part of the world or arrange to meet B in any part of the world and
or
B travels with the intention of meeting A in any part of the world and
(b) Person A intends to do anything to or in respect of B, during or after the meeting mentioned in paragraph (a), in any part of the world, which if done will involve the commission by A of any offence under ss 1–79 of the Sexual Offences Act 2003.

The communication between the two need not be sexualized, for example it could seem to be about attending a sporting event. The contact can be by any means and includes meeting up, an email, messages on a social networking site, and SMS texts. Bearing in mind the rapid growth in the use of the internet and social media by young people, it would seem likely that some 16- or 17-year-olds commit such acts, but surprisingly the s 15 offences cannot be committed by a person under 18 years old (see s 13 of the Sexual Offences Act 2003 which makes clear that 18-year-olds can commit child sex offences committed between s 9 and s 12 and sets out a five-year sentence ceiling if they do so. It is silent on s 15).

A Sexual Risk Order (SRO) can be used to try to prevent online sexual approaches to children under 16 if it is feared that the person intends to meet a child and commit sexual abuse (see 24.8.2).

Section 15A of the Sexual Offences Act 2003 makes it an offence for a person aged 18 years or over to communicate with a person under the age of 16 years if the communication is for the purpose of sexual gratification for the sender. The communication must either be sexual or be made with the intention of encouraging the recipient to make a sexual communication. The maximum penalty on indictment is two years' imprisonment.

24.7.6.2 Child sexual exploitation

Child sexual exploitation (CSE) occurs whenever a child under 18 years of age engages in sexual acts for a reward such as drugs, alcohol, accommodation, gifts, or even simply some attention from a particular person. The reward can also be to a third person, in which case it is more likely to be money or drugs. For this offence, the sexual act can be carried out by the young person on another person or by another person on the young person. The exploitation can involve technology (eg asking the child to send sexual images on a mobile phone). People who sexually exploit children generally have power over them, usually as a result of being older and having more disposable income. Instances of violence, coercion, and intimidation are not uncommon and usually occur because the child has no means of escape.

Child sexual exploitation can be difficult to identify. Common indicators of abuse have been covered in 19.9.1 and include the most obvious signs of physical violence to the child having expensive possessions that cannot be explained. Such children may also have health problems, including sexually transmitted diseases, and can also display a range of behavioural problems such as going missing for periods of time, skipping school or being disruptive in class, mood swings, using drugs and alcohol, and inappropriately sexualized behaviour (NHS, 2013).

Any child can suffer sexual exploitation, including those from stable and loving families, but risk factors include being homeless or in care, having had a recent bereavement, experiencing low self-esteem, or caring for a family member with an illness (NHS, 2013). (See 20.4 for more on vulnerability risk factors.) A history of domestic violence in the family, living in a chaotic environment, having parents with a history of substance abuse, and experiencing social exclusion are added risk factors. Girls are more likely to be sexually abused than boys (although it is likely that victimization of boys is underestimated) and there is a higher rate of victimization amongst black and ethnic minority children when compared to their proportion in the overall population (Office of the Children's Commissioner, 2012, p 14). Other factors that may place a child at risk of sexual abuse are unsupervised use of social networking websites, having learning difficulties, suffering from mental ill health, being unsure about their sexual orientation, having a history of substance abuse, having friends who are sexually abused, being excluded from mainstream education, being bullied, and belonging to a gang or living in an area with gang associations (CoP, 2014e). Sexual exploitation can have a devastating impact on children, with many suffering from health problems (such as drug and alcohol abuse, self-harming, and mental health problems), going missing, or offending as part or as a result of their exploitation (Office of the Children's Commissioner, 2012, pp 49, 50).

'Hotel Notices' can be used to help to investigate organized groups involved in child sexual exploitation. Under the Anti-social Behaviour, Crime and Policing Act 2014, the police can require the owner, operator, or manager of a hotel or B&B (or similar) to provide information about their guests (including name, address, and age). Failure to comply with the notice without a reasonable excuse, or giving information without taking reasonable steps to verify it, or knowing that it is incorrect, are criminal offences under s 118 of the Anti-social Behaviour, Crime and Policing Act 2014, punishable with a fine of up to £2,500.

24.8 Protecting the Public from Sexual Harm

Records of sexual offenders are kept by the police on what is commonly called the 'sex offenders register' (part of ViSOR, see 19.3.11). Part 2 of the Sexual Offences Act 2003 determines that offenders convicted for certain sexual offences, for example rape and certain child sex offences committed by adults, are required to notify the police of personal information such as their name and address (s 80) and this information is stored on the register. The requirements were extended in 2012 to include other offender information such as bank and credit card details, and if they are living in a household with a child (s 83(5A)(h)). Notification requirements are imposed for a fixed or indefinite period, depending on the sentence received, and offenders have three days to notify the police of any relevant changes. The offender can appeal against the notification requirements and these can be revised (s 82). Failure to comply with a notification order is an either-way offence under s 91, with punishment ranging from a fine to five years' imprisonment.

24.8.1 Sexual Harm Prevention Orders

A Sexual Harm Prevention Order (SHPO) is applicable to anyone convicted or cautioned for a sexual or violent offence. It can be issued by a court upon conviction, or the police or the National Crime Agency (NCA) can apply to a magistrates' court. The order is issued if it is deemed necessary to protect the public or a specific member of the public (in the UK or overseas) from sexual harm. The offender must have committed any of the acts in Sch 3 or 5 to the Sexual Offences Act 2003, and been convicted as a result, either in the UK or abroad. SHPOs have a fixed term of not less than five years and can prohibit an individual from travelling overseas. Individuals with an SHPO are subject to the same notification requirements as registered sex offenders and must notify the police of their name and address within three days of the order being served. The breach of an SHPO is an offence, triable either way. The punishment is up to six months' imprisonment or a fine if tried summarily and a maximum of five years' imprisonment if tried on indictment.

24.8.2 Sexual Risk Orders

A Sexual Risk Order (SRO) is a preventative order applicable to an individual who seems likely to present a risk of sexual harm to the public as a result of having committed an act of a sexual nature. Unlike an SHPO, the individual does not need to have been convicted or cautioned for committing this act (s 122A of the Sexual Offences Act 2003). The order prohibits the individual from committing specified actions, which can include travelling overseas. It also requires the recipient to provide their name and address to the police within three days of the order being served. The police or NCA apply to a magistrates' court for an SRO and must have a reasonable belief that it is necessary to protect the public or specific members of the public in the UK or overseas from sexual harm. SROs have a fixed term of at least two years, except for those with international travel prohibitions which must last for at least five years. Breaching an SRO is a criminal offence with a maximum penalty of five years' imprisonment.

24.8.3 The Child Sex Offender Disclosure Scheme

Under this scheme (CSODS), a member of the public can ask the police about a particular person who has access to children to find out whether they have a record for child sexual offences. This is sometimes referred to as 'Sarah's law' in memory of Sarah Payne who was killed by a convicted sex offender. The police will confidentially disclose any relevant information to the people who are deemed most capable of protecting the children at risk (usually parents, guardians, and carers), but only if the police believe it is in the child's interests. The information will not necessarily be disclosed to the person who actually made the original request. Information on convicted sexual offenders is not immediately disclosed to the public to avoid any public backlash and to ensure that registered sex offenders engage with the system rather than going underground.

The CSODS request can be made in person, by telephone, or email. Individuals making the request in person should be allowed to do so privately, and will be informed about how the process will be conducted and the associated timescales. Within 24 hours, there should be an initial risk assessment and minimum standard checks using PNC, ViSOR, and other local intelligence systems. Immediate action must be taken if it seems there is an imminent risk to a child; the procedures for safeguarding children are followed (see 19.9.2.1). There are five further stages for the CSODS (see the Home Office's *Child Sex Offender Disclosure Scheme Guidance*, available online).

24.8.4 Police officers and abuse of trust

Over the last few years, attention has been drawn to a form of police corruption which involves police officers and staff abusing their positions to enter into sexual relationships with members of the public. Abuse of position is defined by the NPCC (2017, p 6) as:

> Any behaviour by a police officer or police staff member, whether on or off duty, that takes advantage of their position as a member of the police service to misuse their position, authority or powers in order to pursue a sexual or improper relationship with any member of the public.

Some individuals encountering the police are clearly vulnerable and there is an imbalance of power between the parties (see, for instance, IPCC and ACPO, 2012; HMIC, 2017b). In such circumstances, a completely professional approach is required to protect the vulnerable.

The NPCC has issued a national strategy (NPCC, 2017) to address the problem and emphasized the importance of having mechanisms in place to receive reports of such conduct, investigate appropriately, and ensure that cases are also referred to the Independent Office of Police Conduct (IOPC).

24.9 Answers to Tasks

TASK 1

1. Section 66 of the Sexual Offences Act only applies to exposure of a person's genitals, not the buttocks. And in any case the suspects might claim that their intention was to entertain not to distress. In the common law offence of Outraging Public Decency, there must be a deliberate act that is lewd, obscene, or disgusting. In *R v Rowley* [1991] 4 All ER 649, Lord Simon decided that outraging public decency goes considerably beyond offending the sensibilities of 'reasonable' people. Therefore, the CPS should be asked whether the common law offence might be committed by members of the rugby team. The public order offences could also be considered, for example s 5 of the Public Order Act—non-intentional harassment, alarm, or distress.
2. Section 67(1) of the Sexual Offences Act 2003 appears to have been committed in these circumstances. The voyeurism offence can be committed within private premises. The host's child is engaged in a private act and Person A is observing them under conditions where it is reasonable for them to expect privacy. It is clear from the circumstances that Person A did not seek consent and it is unlikely that it would have been given in these circumstances.

The age is irrelevant in these circumstances. The trickiest element in the case would be to prove that Person A's observations were for the purpose of sexual gratification, although it is likely that this would be left to a court to determine.

TASK 2

1. The person could be investigated under s 1(1) of the Street Offences Act 1959 as 'persistently loitering or soliciting in a street or public place for the purposes of prostitution'. There must be evidence of the behaviour on two or more occasions in any period of three months. The police officers should speak to the person and check whether they have any record of soliciting in the last three months. If they are a persistent offender, they may need to consider further action. Otherwise they could warn the person about the possible consequences of continuing this behaviour. This will provide evidence that they have already been acting in this way to any police officer who may need to check in the future. Each police officer should record the incident in their PNB.
2. This offence can certainly be committed by the possession of extreme images stored on a mobile telephone. However, body piercing is unlikely to result in serious injury to a person's genitals. If the owner of the mobile was a professional piercer trying to get business, they could claim the images were for advertising and is likely to have a defence.

TASK 3 Section 1 of the Sexual Offences (Amendment) Act 1992 (previously covered by s 7 of the Sexual Offences (Amendment) Act 1976) provides anonymity for victims of rape. The anonymity can be waived by a victim at any time (eg the late Jill Saward who was sexually assaulted in an Ealing vicarage in 1986). Anonymity for defendants in rape cases was removed by s 158 of the Criminal Justice Act 1988. Celebrities such as Sir Cliff Richard and Paul Gambaccini, have campaigned for a change in the law to provide anonymity for those accused of sexual offences.

TASK 4 For the offence of sexual activity with a child (s 9(1) of the Sexual Offences Act 2003), there is a defence available if the child is at least 13 years old and the perpetrator reasonably believed that they were aged 16 or over. There would be no defence if the child was younger than 13 years, assuming proof of the behaviour.

25 Weapons Offences

25.1 Introduction

In this chapter we outline the legislation that covers the use and ownership of weapons, including firearms, and which prohibits possession of weapons in certain circumstances.

Many of the policies aimed at reducing the number of offensive weapons being carried in public are part of a multi-agency approach. For example, in some schools there are walk-through scanners for detecting weapons and staff can search pupils; both measures are allowed under the Violent Crime Reduction Act 2006 (VCRA). In addition, Part 7 of the Education and Inspections Act 2006 allows for the use of reasonable force by school staff and describes the circumstances in which confiscation from pupils would be lawful. In most cases, school policies on searching and seizing of offensive weapons will have been agreed with the local police.

Health and safety should, of course, be of primary concern for the police constable when weapons are suspected to be present. The topics covered in this chapter are likely to contribute to the learning required for the National Policing Curriculum subject areas of 'Understanding the Police Constable Role', 'Policing Communities', and 'Response Policing'.

25.2 Weapons Offences

Firearms, knives, clubs, crossbows, batons, and swords are all clearly weapons but so is a simple length of rope in the wrong hands. Firearms are covered under separate firearms legislation. Note that some items are easily and legally obtained abroad and then brought into the UK, where they become subject to UK legal restrictions.

In some cases, individuals found in possession of weapons fear attack from others. Whatever the circumstances, police officers have a duty to attempt to prevent criminal use of these weapons and, if at all possible, locate and remove such items before they can be used.

25.2.1 Offensive, dangerous, and specified weapons

An offensive weapon for the purposes of the Prevention of Crime Act 1953 is any article made, adapted, or intended for causing injury (s 1(4)). A made article is something that has been made or manufactured for the purposes of causing injury to people, for example a flick knife or telescopic baton. The courts need no proof of its intended use.

An adapted article is something which has been modified in some way for the purposes of causing injury, for example a broken bottle with sharp edges. A jury would need to decide whether or not articles have been specifically adapted to be offensive weapons. For example, in the case of *Prosecution right of appeal (No 23 of 2007), sub nom R v R* [2007] EWCA Crim 3312 it was decided that gloves filled with sand should be regarded as offensive weapons because the prosecution had produced evidence that similar gloves had been advertised for sale on a website as self-defence gloves. The jury would also need to be convinced that the defendant had no reasonable excuse for possessing the item(s).

An intended article is any item in the suspect's possession with which they intend to cause injury. The precise nature of the article is not important: a pillow can be an offensive weapon if it can be proved that the suspect intended to use it to cause injury, eg to a frail person. Once again, gathering evidence through interview is important because it must first be proved that the suspect intended to cause injury with the article. Only then would any reasonable excuse for the possession be considered (see *R v Sundas* [2011] EWCA Crim 985).

25.2.1.1 Dangerous weapons

Some offensive weapons are classified as dangerous weapons under s 28 of the Violent Crime Reduction Act 2006, because they are listed as specified weapons under s 141 of the Criminal Justice Act 1988. Examples include: knuckleduster, stealth knife, telescopic truncheon, hand claw, and blow pipe.

25.2.2 Possessing an offensive weapon in a public place

Section 1(1) of the Prevention of Crime Act 1953 states that: 'Any person who without lawful authority or reasonable excuse, the proof whereof shall lie on him, has with him in any public place any offensive weapon shall be guilty of an offence.'

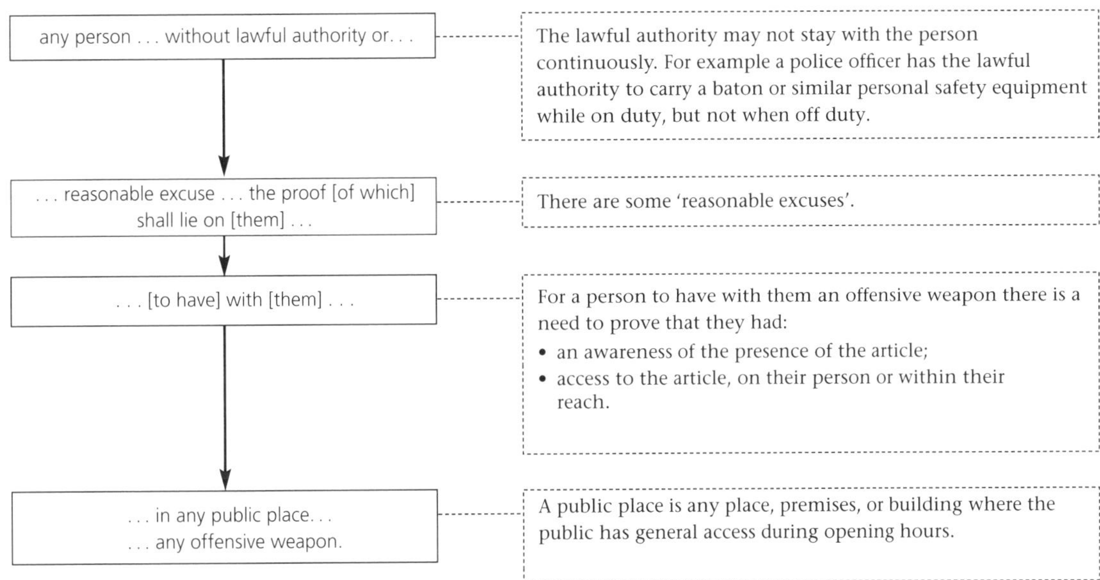

any person . . . without lawful authority or. . .
The lawful authority may not stay with the person continuously. For example a police officer has the lawful authority to carry a baton or similar personal safety equipment while on duty, but not when off duty.
. . . reasonable excuse . . . the proof [of which] shall lie on [them] . . .
There are some 'reasonable excuses'.
. . . [to have] with [them] . . .
For a person to have with them an offensive weapon there is a need to prove that they had:
• an awareness of the presence of the article;
• access to the article, on their person or within their reach.
. . . in any public place. . .
. . . any offensive weapon.
A public place is any place, premises, or building where the public has general access during opening hours.

A police officer has the power to search for offensive weapons under s 1 of the PACE Act 1984. Possessing an offensive weapon in a public place is an either-way offence and the penalty is a fine or imprisonment (six months if tried summarily and four years if tried on indictment).

25.2.2.1 Reasonable excuses

A person may have a reasonable excuse for possession of an offensive weapon in a public place if they fear for their safety: for example, a person who feels they are about to be assaulted and cannot escape, picks up a chair to defend themselves. Other reasonable excuses include having an innocent reason such as a chef carrying kitchen knives to work.

Unreasonable excuses include:

- Forgetfulness—for example, a person forgetting they have a cosh in the glove compartment of their car (see eg *R v McCalla* (1988) 87 Cr App R 372). However, when the forgetfulness is combined with other circumstances, eg relating to the original acquisition of the article, there might be a reasonable excuse, but it will be for the court to decide (see *R v Vasil Tsap* [2008] EWCA Crim 2679). An example might be when a weapon is left by a passenger in a taxi and the driver moves it to the front seat foot-well intending to dispose of it later. If the taxi is later stopped by the police, the driver may claim to have forgotten that the weapon was there (see *R v Glidewell* (1999) LTL 19/5/99, The Times, 14 May).
- Ignorance—not knowing the true identity of the item, for example believing that a truncheon is an umbrella.

- General self-defence—having a weapon just in case when there is no reason to fear an attack; this would be for a court to decide.

The burden of proving a reasonable excuse for possession of an offensive weapon lies with the defendant. Therefore, officers should gather as much evidence as possible about any reasonable excuse the defendant might put forward.

25.2.3 Possessing a bladed or sharply pointed article in a public place

The Criminal Justice Act 1988 (CJA 1988) created the offence of having a bladed or sharply pointed article in a public place (s 139(1)) in an attempt to prevent serious crimes involving the use of such items. Historically, under the Prevention of Crime Act 1953, if the defendant had been in possession of a kitchen knife, pair of scissors, or large pocket knife, they would not be found guilty if the court could be persuaded on the balance of probabilities that they had had a reasonable excuse. The CJA 1988 makes this less likely. We define some key terms as follows:

- 'Bladed' includes any kind of bladed article, for example a kitchen knife, a retractable blade knife, scissors, or any article which has been given a cutting edge or blade. Pocket knives with a blade 7.62 cm (3 inches) long or less which cannot be locked in the open position, are exempt from this legislation.
- 'Sharply pointed' includes any kind of sharply pointed article, for example a needle, geometry compasses, or any article which has been given a sharp point.

A court must decide whether an article has a blade or is sharply pointed, so the onus is on the prosecution to prove that the article fits the relevant description. For example, in *R v Davis* [1998] Crim LR 564 the suspect was carrying a screwdriver which the court was asked to consider as a bladed article capable of causing injury. The court decided that it was more important to determine whether the screwdriver had a cutting edge or point than to consider whether it was capable of causing injury. Therefore, unless a screwdriver has a pointed end or has been sharpened to make a blade, it is not an article for the purposes of this Act. A power to search for bladed or sharply pointed articles is provided under s 1 of the PACE Act 1984.

The table shows some possible defences but self-defence, ignorance, or forgetfulness are not accepted as defences.

Defence	Example
Lawful authority	The lawful authority may not stay with the person continuously. A police officer would have lawful authority to have a bladed or sharply pointed article after seizure and before placing it into a property store. Members of the armed services will also have lawful authority to carry articles such as bayonets whilst on duty but may be liable for prosecution if such an article is carried off duty
For use at work	A joiner uses wood chisels with very sharp cutting edges and may need to carry them in a bag in the street while moving between jobs. The work can be casual and the bladed article does not have to be used on a regular basis (see *Chahal v DPP* [2010] EWHC 439 (Admin)). This would not be a valid claim if they had a chisel in a nightclub.
Religious reasons	Followers of the Sikh religion may carry kirpans (a small rigid knife) for religious reasons
Part of any national costume	Whilst wearing national costume, some Scots carry a skean dhu (a small dagger). However, this defence could not be used if the person was carrying the knife but not wearing national costume

The offence is triable either way and the penalty is a fine or imprisonment (six months if tried summarily and four years on indictment).

> **TASK 1** A police officer stops a vehicle and notices two bayonets in their scabbards in the foot-well of the passenger seat. What should the officer consider and what actions may be needed?

25.2.3.1 Tackling knife crime

Knife crime is widespread so police services are under great pressure to take the lead in initiatives to reduce this threat. The use of knives and other sharp instruments across a range of sexual and violent offences are recorded by police and pressure from the public, media, and police service bodies to introduce preventive measures, resulted in the enactment of the Offensive Weapons Act (OWA) 2019. The measures in the OWA are one aspect of wider action the Government is taking to address the increase in serious violence (see Home Office, 2018g and CPS and NPCC, 2022).

The OWA 2019 makes it illegal to possess dangerous weapons in private. This will help to prevent knives being bought online and sent to residential addresses; the seller must not send such an item unless they have made arrangements with the delivery company to ensure that it is not delivered to a person under 18. The Act also creates Knife Crime Prevention Orders (KCPOs) to help the police to target those most at risk of being drawn into knife crime and to help set them on a more positive path. Knife crime prevention orders are civil orders that can be imposed on people who the courts believe pose a threat to the public through the use of a bladed weapon. KCPOs allow for restraints to be placed on suspects, such as limiting their social media activity to prevent gang rivalries escalating online. In addition s 165 of the Police, Crime, Sentencing and Courts Act 2022 introduced Serious Violence Reduction Orders (SVROs)—a civil order made in respect of an offender convicted of an offence involving a bladed article or offensive weapon. The order provides the police with the power to search a person subject to a SVRO, to ascertain if they have a bladed article or offensive weapon with them and to detain them for the purpose of carrying out that search, provided that person is in a public place.

To support this knife crime legislation, in November 2022 the police in England and Wales once again conducted Operation Sceptre, a week-long initiative to tackle knife crime, which focused on engagement, prevention, and enforcement in a bid to find the root cause of this phenomenon and facilitate early intervention. The main message of this campaign is that there are no positives to carrying a knife. Supporting the ongoing campaign, the College of Policing and NPCC issued a problem-solving guide (CoP, 2021i).

25.2.4 Weapons in schools

Section 139A of the Criminal Justice Act (CJA) 1988 prohibits certain weapons on school premises (s 139A(1) for bladed or sharply pointed articles and s 139A(2) for other offensive weapons). Here a school is an educational institution providing primary and secondary education (s 14(5) of the Further and Higher Education Act 1992), and school premises include land used for the purposes of a school such as playing fields and playgrounds (s 139A(6) of the CJA 1988).

The classification of these offences and powers of search are the same as for possessing an offensive weapon in a public place. For searching a person, the officer does not need to have grounds to suspect that the particular person is in possession of a weapon, but the decision should still be based on objective factors connected with the reason for searching the premises (PACE Code A, para 2.29). The officer does not have to be in uniform to enter school premises if they suspect a s 139A offence, and reasonable force can be used to secure entry. If offensive weapons, or bladed or sharply pointed articles, are found, they can be seized (s 139B of the CJA 1988).

Defences for s 139A offences include that the article or weapon was for use at work, educational purposes, religious reasons, or as part of a national costume. The offence is triable either way with a penalty of a fine or imprisonment (six months if tried summarily and four years on indictment).

25.2.5 Threatening with a weapon in a public place or school

It is an offence to threaten a person in a public place or on school premises with:

- an offensive weapon (s 1A of the Prevention of Crime Act 1953); or
- a bladed or sharply pointed article (s 139AA of the CJA 1988).

The threat must be intentional and unlawful and create an immediate risk of serious physical harm meaning harm that amounts to grievous bodily harm. Due to the location, these offences are aggravated versions of the basic possession offences. The offences are triable either way with the penalty of a fine or imprisonment (one year if tried summarily and four years on indictment). If the suspect is found not guilty of the aggravated offence, they can still be found guilty of one of the relevant basic possession offences (s 10 of the Prevention of Crime Act 1953 and s 12 of the CJA 1988).

25.2.6 Possession of a weapon in a private place

The offences we have discussed so far relate to the possession of weapons in public places or schools. For similar incidents on private property, s 64 of the Offences Against the Person Act 1861 could be considered. For this, it is an offence to possess, make, or manufacture any item with intent to commit, or enable any other person to commit, any other offence within the Act. The items include explosive substances, machines, and any other dangerous or noxious thing. The penalty is imprisonment for up to two years.

25.2.7 Manufacture, import, sale, or hire etc. of offensive weapons

For certain types of weapon, it is an offence for a person to manufacture, sell, or hire such an item. This includes offering such an item for sale or hire, or exposing it or possessing it for the purpose of selling, hiring, lending, or giving it to another person.

If the weapon in question is a specified weapon, the offence is committed under s 141 of the CJA 1988. For a flick knife, which opens automatically by hand pressure, or a gravity knife, which opens by the force of gravity or by centrifugal force, the offence is committed under s 1 of the Restriction of Offensive Weapons Act 1959.

These are both summary offences with a penalty of six months' imprisonment and/or a fine.

25.2.7.1 Selling bladed or pointed items to young people

Selling a knife, a knife blade, a razor blade, or an axe to a young person under 18 is an offence (s 141A(1) of the CJA 1988). This offence also applies for any other bladed or sharply pointed article which is made or adapted for causing injury to a person. The offence is triable summarily with a penalty of six months' imprisonment and/or a fine.

25.2.8 Arranging the minding of a dangerous weapon

It is an offence to make arrangements for another person to look after, hide, or transport a dangerous weapon to help to make it available for an unlawful purpose (s 28 of the Violent Crime Reduction Act 2006). These weapons include the sharp and bladed articles referred to above, and firearms excluding air weapons.

The arrangements must help to make the weapon available for the offender to use at a particular time and place, and possession of the weapon must either constitute an offence in itself or be likely to lead to the commission of an offence. The minder would not be committing a s 28 offence but might be committing a weapons possession offence. The s 28 offence is triable either way.

TASK 2 A 17-year-old carries a knife for their own personal protection. They are under threat from others and have good grounds to fear for their safety. Putting aside any discussion of whether they have a reasonable excuse, what factors should be taken into account when deciding what action, if any, to take?

25.3 Firearms

Any police officer could find themselves unexpectedly at the scene of a firearms incident or may come across a firearm during a search. Officers may also be called to investigate incidents where air weapons have been used or to establish where there is doubt that a firearm is legally owned. For these reasons, it is important for all police officers to have a basic knowledge of firearms, particularly with regard to safety.

The injuries caused by firearms are almost always catastrophic. Therefore, when handling or being in the vicinity of firearms remember that:

- all bullet wounds are serious—so anyone who has suffered such an injury must receive professional medical care as soon as possible;
- the entry wound is usually small and the exit wound is often much larger;
- body armour struck by a bullet can cause blunt trauma injuries such as broken bones, internal bleeding, and organ damage.

When a firearm is found at an incident, there are particular procedures to be followed. The most important consideration is safety; the safety of the evidence but more importantly the physical safety of anyone who will come into contact with the firearm.

The type of firearm, the numbers encountered, and any percentage variation are recorded by the Office for National Statistics and released on an annual basis.

25.3.1 Definition of a firearm

Section 57(1) of the Firearms Act 1968 provides a definition of a firearm as shown in the flowchart.

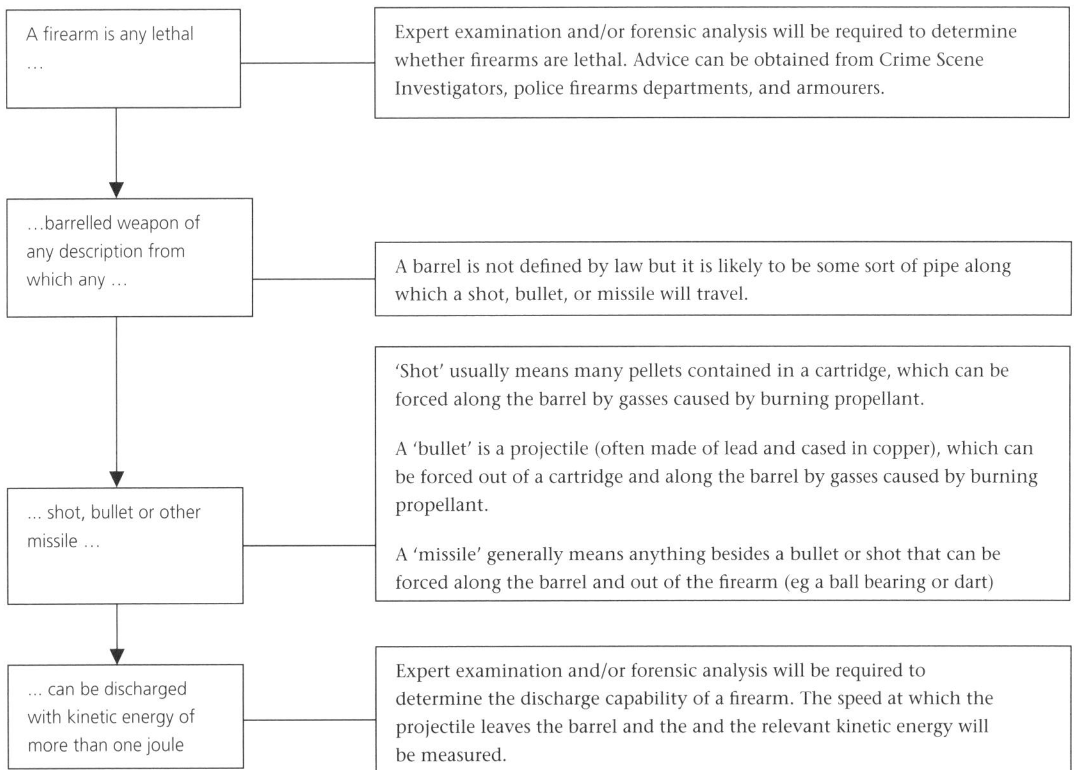

A firearm is any lethal …
Expert examination and/or forensic analysis will be required to determine whether firearms are lethal. Advice can be obtained from Crime Scene Investigators, police firearms departments, and armourers.
…barrelled weapon of any description from which any …
A barrel is not defined by law but it is likely to be some sort of pipe along which a shot, bullet, or missile will travel.
… shot, bullet or other missile …
'Shot' usually means many pellets contained in a cartridge, which can be forced along the barrel by gasses caused by burning propellant.
A 'bullet' is a projectile (often made of lead and cased in copper), which can be forced out of a cartridge and along the barrel by gasses caused by burning propellant.
A 'missile' generally means anything besides a bullet or shot that can be forced along the barrel and out of the firearm (eg a ball bearing or dart)
… can be discharged with kinetic energy of more than one joule
Expert examination and/or forensic analysis will be required to determine the discharge capability of a firearm. The speed at which the projectile leaves the barrel and the and the relevant kinetic energy will be measured.

There are many different types of firearm such as revolvers, pistols, and rifles. Firearms are loosely grouped into four categories under the Act: Section 1 firearms (covered under s 1 of the Firearms Act 1968), shotguns, air weapons, and prohibited weapons. The legislation relating to imitation firearms was significantly changed in the Violent Crime Reduction Act 2006, in particular.

25.3.1.1 The parts of a firearm

A firearm consists of 'component parts' which are essential for it to work and 'additions' such as magazines, sights, torches, trigger guards, grips, sound moderators, and flash eliminators also known as accessories. Component parts are vital to the functioning of a firearm and some of these are, therefore, legally controlled so that they cannot be acquired separately and then assembled to make an uncertificated firearm. However, the Firearms Act does not list all component parts and case law should be considered, for example *R v Ashton* [2007] EWCA Crim 234, where it was held that 'Component part for present purposes must as a matter of reasonable interpretation, mean a part that is manufactured to the purpose …'

The photograph shows a self-loading pistol (SLP) with the main parts of a firearm identified. Note that this particular SLP would be classed as a prohibited weapon due to its short barrel (see 25.8).

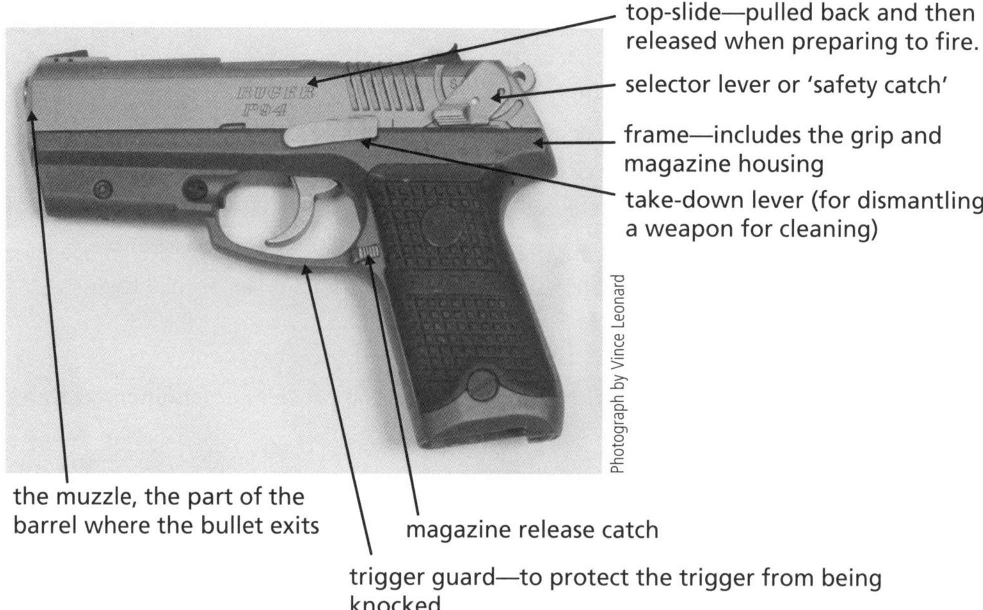

The ammunition is stored in a 'magazine' which is located in the frame. Pulling and releasing the top-slide moves a round of ammunition from the magazine into the breech end of the barrel, and also 'cocks' the action. The safety catch prevents the weapon from firing unless it is in the 'fire' position.

The second photograph shows another SLP which is also a prohibited weapon and which has been partly disassembled to reveal some of the internal mechanism.

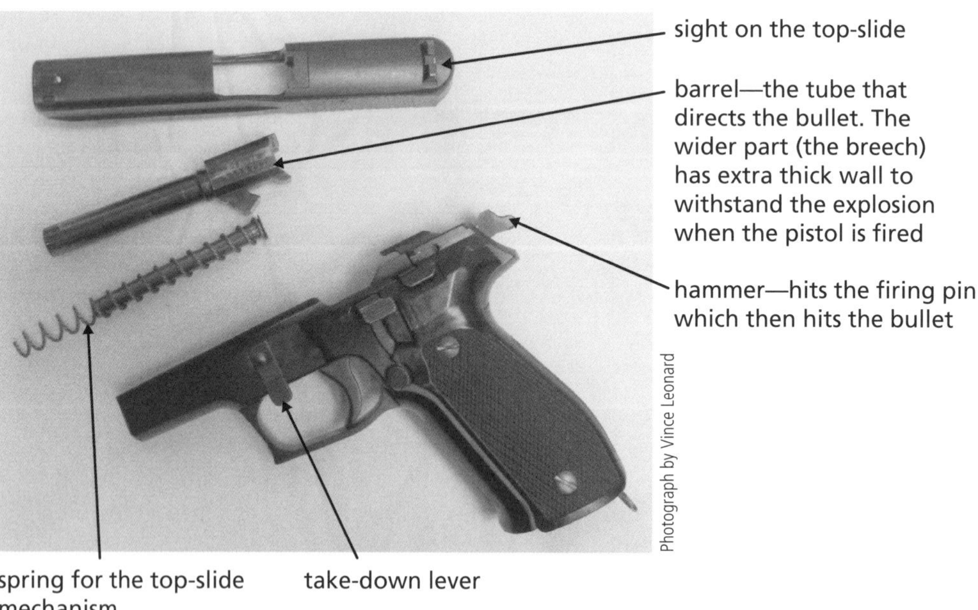

Pulling the trigger fires the weapon—the propellant powder ignites and produces hot gases that force the bullet down the barrel. It also pushes the top-slide backwards which releases the empty cartridge case. The mechanism is self-loading in that it also feeds the next round of ammunition from the magazine into the breech end of the barrel. The trigger can then be pulled again to fire another round, and the whole process can be repeated until the magazine is empty. This is different from an automatic firearm for which simply maintaining pressure on the trigger will cause it to fire repeatedly.

The barrel of a firearm can be smooth or rifled. Smooth-bore weapons enable the easy passage of shot and, although normally associated with lead shot as used in sport shooting, these weapons can also fire a single or several larger lead slugs. Generally, smooth-bore weapons have a limited range, are less accurate than rifled firearms, and produce a spread of shot. They are often used to commit crimes, partly due to their greater availability to criminals but also because the spread of shot means that accuracy is not required. Rifled-bore weapons are, historically, a more recent development, with the inside of the barrel being grooved or rifled in a helical pattern. There are between two and 16 curved grooves which cause the bullet to spin. This imparts stability to the round and increases both firing accuracy and range.

Calibre is the measurement of the diameter of the barrel. In rifled weapons, the calibre is normally expressed in metric or imperial figures (eg 7.62 mm, 9 mm, .38 inch, .357 inch). For smooth-bore weapons, the calibre is not stated as the diameter of the barrel because it was difficult for engineers in the past to make such accurate measurements. Instead, the calibre is stated in terms of the mass of the largest lead sphere that would just fit into the barrel, the mass being stated as a fraction of a pound. For example, the barrel of a 12-bore (UK) or 12-gauge (US) weapon would just accommodate a lead ball that weighs one-twelfth of a pound, approximately 37g. In May 2022, the UK's Health & Safety Executive began a six-month public consultation on proposals to ban most lead bullets and lead pellets for outdoor target shooting and hunting, plus a ban on the sale and use of lead shot. The consultation closed in November 2022 and is yet to report.

Sound moderators, also known as *silencers*, are designed to reduce the noise or flash of a firearm. A flash eliminator reduces the flash from the round exiting the barrel and thereby aids the firer's vision, especially when firing in low light. Detachable sound moderators are generally subject to certificate control but integral sound moderators, and those for air weapons, are not. It will be for a court to decide whether a particular sound moderator or flash eliminator could be used with the firearm in question, and whether the suspect had it for that purpose.

25.3.1.2 Ammunition

A conventional round of modern ammunition for a handgun, rifle, or carbine consists of a cartridge and a bullet.

The base of the cartridge has a 'primer' which will ignite when struck by the firing pin. This sends a flame through a 'flash-hole' to the main body of the cartridge, which ignites the propellant powder. The propellant burns and creates expanding gases which force the bullet out of the cartridge, and along and out of the barrel.

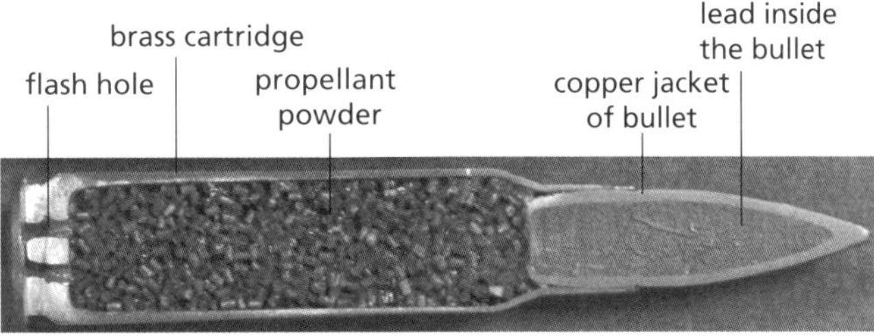

Photograph by Vince Leonard

Shotgun cartridges work on the same basic principle, but the outer covering is plastic or cardboard, and they contain a number of shot rather than a single bullet.

25.3.1.3 Different types of firearm

Firearms have many different features such as the barrel length, the loading mechanism for ammunition, and the kinetic energy of the projectiles fired. These features affect how dangerous a particular weapon could be and are used in classifying firearms under the Firearms Act 1968.

Firearms can also be classed in terms of their design, for example:

- a revolver is a hand-held firearm with a cylinder that revolves as it is fired, to align a new round of ammunition with the breech of the weapon. There are usually spaces for six rounds, hence the 'six gun' of the American cowboy. A revolver with a short barrel would be a prohibited weapon.

- a pistol is a hand-held firearm, often fed by a removable magazine. A pistol with a short or rifled barrel will be a prohibited weapon, as would any self-loading pistol, often mistakenly referred to as an automatic pistol.
- a rifle has a long rifled barrel and is designed to be an intrinsically accurate long-distance weapon; many have a large sight mounted on the top. The ammunition is usually fed from a magazine but each round has to be manually fed into the breech by operating a bolt.

Some types of firearm can fire in automatic mode, ie pulling and holding the trigger will cause a continuous discharge of rounds until the magazine is empty; all such weapons are classified as prohibited under the Firearms Act 1968.

25.3.2 Firearms certificates

A certificate is needed for s 1 firearms, shotguns, some types of ammunition, and any component parts of a firearm (see 25.3.1.1). The Firearms (Amendment) Rules 2021 introduced changes made under the Firearms Rules 1998 to allow for the recording of the 'unique identifying mark' on the firearm or shotgun or its component parts to be recorded on the prescribed forms for firearm and shotgun certificates and, clarification of the obligation to inform the chief officer of police of the theft, loss, or destruction in Great Britain of a firearm or shotgun certificate, or of any firearm or shotgun or ammunition to which the certificate relates.

From 1 April 2016, information sharing processes between GPs and police were introduced to ensure that people licensed to possess firearm and shotgun certificates are medically fit. The Home Office guide on firearms licensing law (Home Office, 2012g; 2022l) contains a section on medical information, and the British Medical Association (BMA 2022b) has issued guidance for GPs about firearms licencing.

Other categories of firearm such as air weapons in England and Wales, and some imitation firearms do not require certificates. Air guns, air rifles, and air pistols are exempt from the certification requirement if they are not of a type declared specially dangerous by the Firearms (Dangerous Air Weapons) Rules 1969 (SI 1969/47) (as amended). These Rules provide that any air weapon is 'specially dangerous' if it is capable of discharging a missile so that the missile has, when discharged, a kinetic energy in excess, in the case of an air pistol, of 6 foot-pounds or, in the case of an air weapon other than an air pistol, 12 foot-pounds. An air rifle with a muzzle energy in excess of 12 foot-pounds must be held on a firearm certificate. Any short air weapons, which either have a barrel less than 30cm in length or are less than 60cm in length overall, with a muzzle energy in excess of 6 foot-pounds, are prohibited firearms.

It is an offence to have a s 1 firearm or a shotgun without the requisite certificate.

A police officer has the power to demand the production of a firearm certificate from any person whom they believe to be in possession of any firearm(s) or ammunition requiring a firearms certificate (s 48(1) of the Firearms Act 1968). The interpretation of the term 'demand' varies between services; for some, it means the certificate should be produced on the spot, while for others it could be produced at some specified time in the future. A police officer can also require such a person to give their name and address.

If the person does not produce the certificate and permit a police officer to read it, or otherwise show that they are entitled to have the items in their possession, then the firearm or ammunition may be seized and retained (s 48(2)).

25.3.3 Other offences relating to possession of firearms

Apart from not having the relevant certificate for a firearm there are other offences related to possession of a firearm. For example, under s 19 of the Firearms Act 1968 it is an offence to have certain types of firearm and ammunition in a public place without lawful authority or reasonable excuse. This applies to the following, whether loaded or not—air weapons, any s 1 firearm, prohibited weapons—and also loaded shotguns, imitation firearms, and ammunition suitable for use in a s 1 firearm. This offence is triable either way, except for air weapons where the offence is triable summarily. The penalty is six months' imprisonment and/or a fine.

Possessing a firearm with the intention that a person will cause any other person to fear that violence will be used is also an offence (s 16A of the Firearms Act 1968). This offence can be committed in a public or a private place; for example, by a farmer brandishing a shotgun and shouting 'Get off my land!' at a rambler. The offence is triable on indictment only and the penalty is ten years' imprisonment and/or a fine.

It is also an offence to be in possession of a firearm or an imitation firearm at the time of arrest, for example if a person is arrested for shoplifting and is found to have a firearm in their pocket (s 17(2)).

25.3.4 Requesting a person to hand over a firearm or ammunition

Health and safety always come first. A police officer can require any person to hand over a firearm and/or ammunition for examination (s 47(1) of the Firearms Act 1968). The officer must have reasonable cause to suspect that the person is in possession of a firearm, with or without ammunition, in a public place or is committing or is about to commit a relevant offence. Here, a relevant offence would include other offences from the Firearms Act 1968, such as carrying a firearm with criminal intent (s 18), trespassing in a building with a firearm (s 20(1)), or trespassing on land with a firearm (s 20(2)). It is a summary offence to fail to hand over a firearm or ammunition when required to do so (s 47(2)) and the penalty is three months' imprisonment and/or a fine.

25.3.5 The power to stop and search for firearms

This is provided by s 47 of the Firearms Act 1968 (s 47(3) for a person and s 47(4) for a vehicle). It applies if a firearms offence has been committed or is about to be committed. A power of entry (s 47(5)) is available to search for firearms. For such a search, s 2 of the PACE Act 1984 and the associated Codes of Practice must be followed.

25.3.6 Young people and access to firearms

For all types of firearms, including imitations and ammunition, it is a summary offence under the Firearms Act 1968 to sell or hire such an item to a person under 18 (s 24(1)) and for a young person under 18 to purchase such an item (s 22(1)). It is also an offence to give, lend, or otherwise part with a s 1 firearm or ammunition to a person under 14 (s 24(2)). A defence is available for the s 24 offences if it can be shown that there were reasonable grounds for believing that the young person was older than the relevant age limit (s 24(5)).

Other legislation applies to specific types of firearms and this is covered where the various categories of firearm are described separately.

25.3.7 Trading in firearms

Any person who trades or carries out any business with firearms, including air weapons, without being registered as a firearms dealer commits an offence (s 3(1) of the Firearms Act 1968). This includes manufacturing, exposing for sale, repairing and testing firearms. These offences are triable either way and the penalty is six months' imprisonment and/or a fine if tried summarily and five years' imprisonment on indictment.

25.4 Section 1 Firearms

Section 1 firearms are defined in s 1 of the Firearms Act 1968. They include any firearm that is not a shotgun, a legal air weapon, a prohibited weapon, or an imitation firearm. A sawn-off shotgun, however is classed as a s 1 firearm. The photograph shows a rifle that would be classed as a s 1 firearm.

Photograph by Nathan van der Nest

25.4.1 Legislation relating to s 1 firearms

It is an offence to have a s 1 firearm without the appropriate certificate (s 1), as shown in the flowchart.

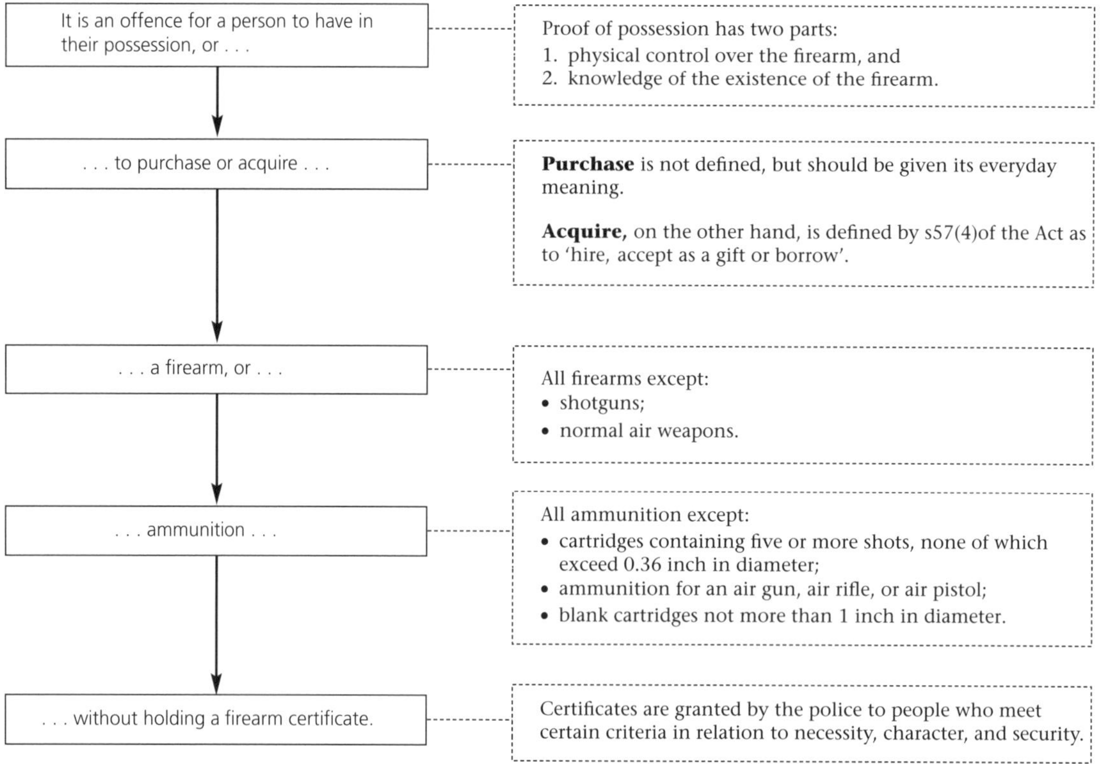

It is an offence for a person to have in their possession, or . . .
Proof of possession has two parts:
1. physical control over the firearm, and
2. knowledge of the existence of the firearm.
. . . to purchase or acquire . . .
Purchase is not defined, but should be given its everyday meaning.
Acquire, on the other hand, is defined by s57(4)of the Act as to 'hire, accept as a gift or borrow'.
. . . a firearm, or . . .
All firearms except:
• shotguns;
• normal air weapons.
. . . ammunition . . .
All ammunition except:
• cartridges containing five or more shots, none of which exceed 0.36 inch in diameter;
• ammunition for an air gun, air rifle, or air pistol;
• blank cartridges not more than 1 inch in diameter.
. . . without holding a firearm certificate.
Certificates are granted by the police to people who meet certain criteria in relation to necessity, character, and security.

This offence is triable either way and the penalty is a fine or imprisonment (six months if tried summarily but, if on indictment five years and seven for a 'sawn-off' shotgun).

In some circumstances, a s 1 firearm might not require a certificate. This may apply for handguns for killing animals and for antique firearms. However, some firearms that were previously regarded as antique and exempt from control, no longer qualify as such and must be licensed. See HO Circulars 001/2021 (Home Office 2021f) and 008/2021 Antique Firearms (Home Office 2021g). Previously, the Firearms Act 1968 did not define 'antique firearm' but s 126 of the Policing and Crime Act 2017 created a statutory definition of 'antique firearm' by inserting new subsections (2A) to (2H) into s 58, which define an antique firearm by reference to its date of manufacture, the type of cartridge it was designed to use, and by reference to its propulsion system.

Various people are excluded from the requirement to hold a firearms certificate, provided the firearms are used in connection with their occupations or relevant activities eg:

- Firearms dealers and their servants
- Minature rifle ranges
- Police and Crown Servants (including Cadet Corps)
- Visiting Forces
- Visitors to GB
- Museums
- Ship, signaling, and bird-scaring equipment
- Auctioneers
- Licensed Slaughtermen
- Theatre, film, and TV productions.

A member of an approved club may temporarily possess a firearm solely in connection with target shooting on the club's range, or other ranges which it may use. However, a person cannot possess a firearm under this exemption if it is a class of firearm for which the club is not approved. It should also be noted that s 15(1) of the 1988 Act, as amended, does not apply to the use of long barrelled pistols or s 1 shot guns used for target shooting, as it only allows possession of rifles or muzzle-loading pistols by members of suitably approved clubs. Accordingly, club approval cannot be extended to cover the use of these firearms. Members may not purchase or acquire firearms or ammunition unless they have been granted firearm certificates and the exemption does not cover the use of firearms for purposes other than target shooting. The case of *R v Maxim Wilson* (1989) held that possession of firearms and ammunition must only be in connection with the club's activities, and does not give members a wider authority.

The age restrictions for s 1 firearms are shown in the table. Note that a person of any age can carry a s 1 firearm for a person over 18 during a sporting activity.

The person may	Under 14	Age 14\+	Age 15\+	Age 17\+	Age 18\+
Hold a firearm certificate	*	✓	✓	✓	✓
Carry a firearm for a person over 18 during a sporting activity	✓	✓	✓	✓	✓
Receive a s 1 firearm as a gift	–	✓	✓	✓	✓
Purchase or hire a s 1 firearm	–	–	–	–	✓

* A parent can be granted a certificate (or have an existing certificate varied) that includes a child under 14, if for example the child is to participate in competitive target shooting.
It is possible to make a firearm using a 3D printed process. However, the manufacture, purchase, sale, and possession of 3D printed firearms, ammunition, or their component parts is fully captured by the provisions in section 57(1) of the Firearms Act 1968.

25.5 Shotguns

The definition of a shotgun is provided in s 1(3)(a) of the Firearms Act 1968, as shown in the flowchart.

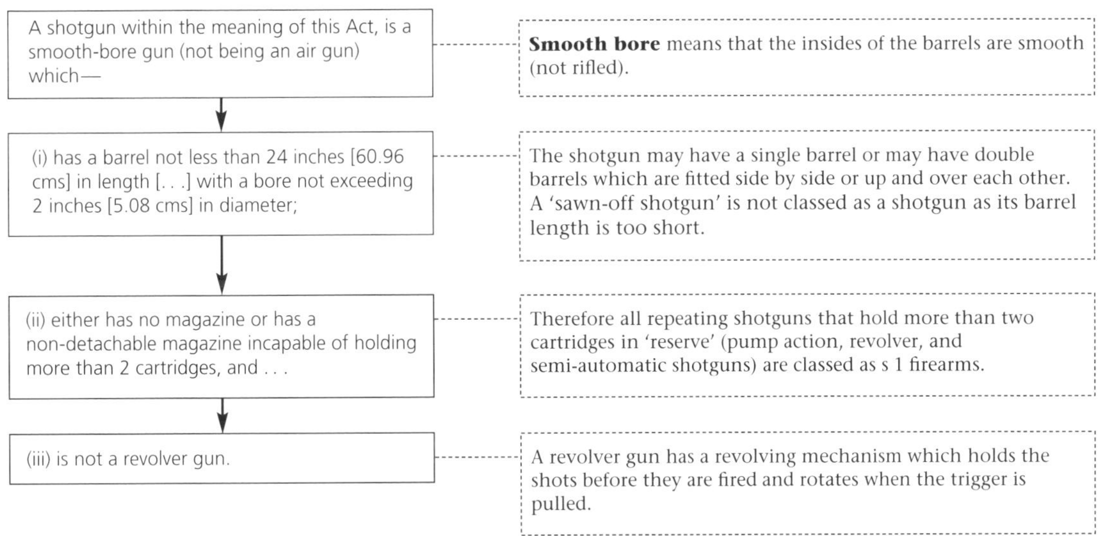

A shotgun within the meaning of this Act, is a smooth-bore gun (not being an air gun) which—
Smooth bore means that the insides of the barrels are smooth (not rifled).
(i) has a barrel not less than 24 inches [60.96 cms] in length [. . .] with a bore not exceeding 2 inches [5.08 cms] in diameter;
The shotgun may have a single barrel or may have double barrels which are fitted side by side or up and over each other. A 'sawn-off shotgun' is not classed as a shotgun as its barrel length is too short.
(ii) either has no magazine or has a non-detachable magazine incapable of holding more than 2 cartridges, and . . .
Therefore all repeating shotguns that hold more than two cartridges in 'reserve' (pump action, revolver, and semi-automatic shotguns) are classed as s 1 firearms.
(iii) is not a revolver gun.
A revolver gun has a revolving mechanism which holds the shots before they are fired and rotates when the trigger is pulled.

A typical shotgun cartridge consists of a plastic or cardboard tube containing shot and protective wadding, with a brass battery cup at the base containing the primer. The photograph shows a cartridge with part of the casing cut away.

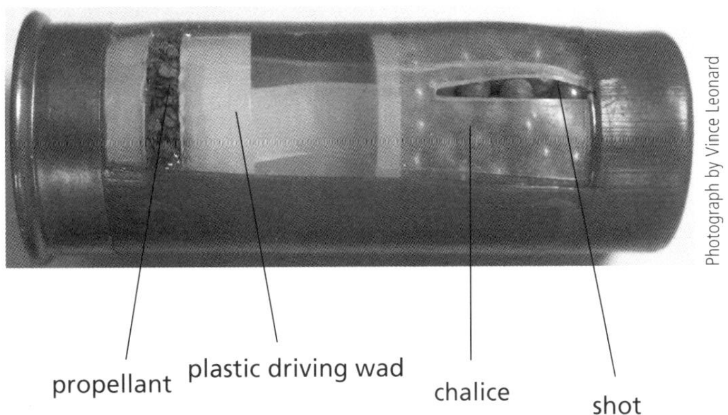

Photograph by Vince Leonard

The propellant is contained in the cartridge directly adjacent to the primer and separated from the shot by a driving wad—a circular piece of plastic or compressed fibrous material. In modern shotgun ammunition, this wad is usually integral to a chalice which holds the shot. When the shotgun is fired, the propellant ignites and forces all the shot and wadding out through the barrel.

There are different designs of shotguns with different loading systems. The most commonly owned and used type of shotgun is double-barrelled, either side-by-side or over-and-under, and has no magazine. The double barrel allows for two shots before reloading is required. The cartridges are individually loaded into each barrel by breaking the weapon to allow access to the rear part of the barrel.

Pump-action shotguns have a single barrel and a magazine for cartridges. After firing, the empty cartridge is extracted by sliding the fore-end backwards, and the next one loaded by sliding it forwards. The non-detachable magazine should be incapable of holding more than two cartridges. Such a shotgun becomes a prohibited weapon if it either has a barrel less than 24 inches in length or is less than 40 inches in length overall (Firearms Act 1968, s 5(1)).

Photograph by Vince Leonard

A self-loading shotgun, often referred to as a semi-automatic, has a magazine from which the cartridges are loaded into the breech and then discharged in a similar manner to a self-loading pistol. The loading and ejection mechanism is operated by the gas created when a cartridge is discharged. This allows the weapon to be fired as fast as the trigger can be pulled. Again, such a weapon should have a non-detachable magazine incapable of holding more than two cartridges and becomes prohibited if it either has a barrel less than 24 inches in length or is less than 40 inches in length overall (Firearms Act 1968, s 5(1)).

25.5.1 Shotgun certificates and age restrictions

A shotgun certificate, also referred to as a licence, is granted by the chief police officer of the constabulary where the applicant lives. Shotguns are frequently used for sporting purposes and unless there is a specific reason to refuse an application it will normally be granted, in marked contrast to the issue of certificates for s 1 firearms. Possessing, purchasing, or acquiring a shotgun without holding the relevant certificate is an either-way offence under s 2(1) of the Firearms Act 1968. The penalty is a fine or imprisonment (six months if tried summarily and five years on indictment).

A number of conditions are placed upon the holder of a shotgun certificate, for example that the shotgun(s) will be kept secure when not in use. It is a summary offence for a person to fail to comply with a condition relating to a shotgun certificate (s 2(2)) and the penalty is six months' imprisonment and/or a fine.

In certain circumstances, a person may have a shotgun without a shotgun certificate, such as when borrowing a shotgun from a person who holds a certificate and then using it on that person's land in their presence. Nor is a certificate required for possession of shotgun cartridges with many small pellets, that is five or more shot pellets in a cartridge with pellets not more than 0.36 inches in diameter.

The age restrictions specifically for shotguns are shown in the table. Note that there is no age limit to having a shotgun certificate and that any person of any age can have an assembled shotgun in their possession if supervised by a person aged at least 21 years with a certificate.

The person may	Under 14	Age 14\+	Age 15\+	Age 17\+	Age 18\+
Hold a shotgun certificate	✓	✓	✓	✓	✓
Possess an assembled shotgun if supervised by a person aged 21 or over with a certificate	✓	✓	✓	✓	✓

The person may	Under 14	Age 14\+	Age 15\+	Age 17\+	Age 18\+
Receive a shotgun as a gift	–	–	✓	✓	✓
Have an uncovered/unsecured shotgun	–	–	✓	✓	✓
Purchase or hire a shotgun	–	–	–	–	✓

It is an offence to gift a shotgun or ammunition to a young person under 15 (s 24(3)). A defence is available if it can be shown that there were reasonable grounds to believe the young person was 15 or over (s 24(5)).

25.6 Pellet Firearms

There are various types of firearm that fire small pellets. They are usually less dangerous than other firearms because the pellets are discharged from the barrel relatively slowly and have a relatively small mass. Pellet weapons include air weapons such as air rifles, BB guns, and airsoft weapons.

25.6.1 Air weapons

Air weapons include air pistols, air guns, and air rifles. The velocity of the projectiles is low because the pellets are propelled by a spring or compressed gas or air, rather than by an explosive charge. However, air weapons can still cause serious injury and fatalities, particularly involving children, are not unknown. Air weapon offences make up approximately one-third of all recorded firearms offences and it is clear that they should be taken very seriously.

The photograph shows an air pistol that uses a sliding mechanism to generate the air pressure to cock the spring so that it is ready to fire.

Photograph by Vince Leonard

The pressure in an air-weapon can also be generated by folding the barrel into the broken position; this system is used for air rifles, as shown in the photograph.

Photograph by Vince Leonard

There are many different types of design of air weapons, so unless you know how to safely handle firearms you should always ask someone who knows about firearms to assist you in their safe handling and storage.

An air weapon does not require a certificate under s 1 of the Firearms Act 1968 unless it exceeds the authorized kinetic energy. The kinetic energy can be measured by a forensic laboratory.

Any air weapon that uses self-contained gas cartridges, those containing compressed gas and a pellet, is automatically classed as a prohibited weapon. For further information, see the Firearms (Dangerous Air Weapons) Rules 1969 (gov.uk, 1969).

25.6.1.1 Age limits for possessing and firing air weapons

The age restrictions that apply to all firearms including air weapons are covered in 25.3.6.

For a person under the age of 18, it is an offence to have with them an air weapon or ammunition for an air weapon anywhere and at any time (s 22(4)) unless:

- they are a member at an air rifle club and firing at targets; or
- the weapon does not exceed .23 calibre and is being fired at a gallery (s 23(2)).

On private land with the landowner's permission, a young person under 18 years can use an air weapon, but under-14s must be supervised by a person of 21 years or over. It is an offence if the pellets go beyond the premises, unless the owner of the adjoining property gave permission (s 23(1) and (1A) and s 21A(1) and (2)).

For other locations, a young person aged 14–17 years can use an air weapon anywhere if supervised by a person aged over 21 (s 23(1)). This includes a public place, provided the young person and supervisor have a lawful authority or reasonable excuse, for example if employed in the authorized and licensed destruction of pests.

25.6.1.2 Young people and access to air weapons

The legislation already described helps to prevent young people having access to firearms in general, including air weapons, but other legislation applies specifically to air weapons. Subject to the exemptions for supervisors of young people outlined previously, it is an offence:

- to make a gift or to otherwise part with any air weapon or ammunition to a young person under 18 (s 24(4));
- for a person in possession of an air weapon to fail to take reasonable precautions to prevent a young person under 18 from having an air weapon (s 24(ZA)(1)).

A defence is available if it can be shown that there were reasonable grounds to believe the young person was aged 18 or over (s 24(5)). These offences are triable summarily and the penalty is a fine.

TASK 3

A 16-year-old has been firing an air rifle from their parents' bedroom window at drink cans on top of their garden wall and some of the pellets have clearly gone into the neighbour's garden. What offence has the teenager committed?

25.6.2 BB guns

BB guns fire small, round, plastic or aluminium balls which resemble ball bearings, hence the term. They were originally manufactured for recreational target practice and for shooting vermin, so they have some capacity to injure. More recently, some BB guns are manufactured to look like real firearms so may also be 'realistic imitations' (see 25.7.1).

The force to fire the projectiles from a BB gun is derived from a spring, batteries, or from gas in an external aerosol canister. However, if the gun appears to be more powerful than a typical BB gun or has large projectiles, it may need to be assessed by a forensic laboratory because it might be sufficiently powerful to be classified as an air weapon or a 's 1 firearm'. Any air weapon with a self-contained cartridge resembling a bullet and casing, and using gas to propel the projectiles, will be classed as a prohibited weapon.

25.6.3 Airsoft guns

Airsoft guns fire plastic pellets or marking projectiles not exceeding 8 mm in diameter, and are generally less powerful than BB guns or standard air weapons (see s 57A(2) of the Firearms Act 1968 (as amended by the Policing and Crime Act 2017) for a fuller definition). They are generally used in leisure activities. The UK Airsoft Retailers Association (UKARA) holds a database of registered skirmishers.

Some airsoft weapons appear identical to real firearms, as shown in the photograph, and are therefore classed as 'realistic imitation firearms'.

Photograph by Vince Leonard

Other airsoft weapons are brightly coloured so they do not resemble real firearms. The restrictions on the sale of airsoft weapons depend on whether the weapon is classed as an imitation or a realistic imitation.

25.7 Imitation Firearms and Blank-firers

Police officers are likely to encounter objects which resemble firearms and these imitations can cause considerable fear and alarm. Firearms that can fire lethal projectiles will not be regarded as imitations. They will be subject to the Firearms Act 1968 and all the relevant legislation will apply, including any requirements for certificates or licences.

The terms replica firearm, imitation firearm, and realistic imitation firearm can appear to mean the same thing but there are important differences. We cover the key points here, but the full details are provided in the Violent Crime Reduction Act 2006 (VCRA). Note that imitating possession of a firearm by putting a hand with extended fingers inside clothing to look like a gun does not amount to possession of an imitation (*R v Bentham* [2005] UKHL 18).

The sale of all imitation firearms is restricted to adults, those aged 18 or over, and additional restrictions apply for realistic imitations.

25.7.1 Realistic imitation firearms

Any item that looks like a modern real firearm but does not meet the definition of a firearm under the Firearms Act 1968 is now classed as a realistic imitation firearm (s 36 of the VCRA). Realistic imitation firearms (RIFs) do not have to be capable of firing projectiles, although many are.

Realistic imitations of the types of firearms made before 1870 are not subject to this legislation so can still be sold by anyone over the age of 18 years. Prior to 2006, RIFs were known as replica firearms and could be owned, bought, sold, and imported with very few restrictions. The photograph shows a RIF which is also a cigarette lighter.

Photograph by Vince Leonard

RIFs are easy to mistake for conventional firearms and can cause alarm and distress to others if seen in public places; this can cause significant problems for the police.

25.7.1.1 Restrictions on realistic imitation firearms

The sale of RIFs is restricted to adults, those aged 18 or over, and under s 37 of the VCRA the seller must be certain that the purchaser will use the weapon for:

- the purposes of a museum or gallery;
- the purposes of theatrical productions, films, and television programmes;
- historical re-enactments under regulations set by the Secretary of State;
- duties concerned with service as a Crown servant; or
- skirmishing at a registered site. See also airsoft weapons.

The carrying of RIFs in a public place is also restricted to the above purposes. In any other circumstances, carrying any imitation firearm in a public place is a summary offence under s 19 of the Firearms Act 1968 and the penalty is a fine or six months' imprisonment.

25.7.2 Imitation firearms (non-realistic)

These imitations do not look like real firearms due to their colour or size. The principal colour must be mainly bright red, orange, pink, yellow, green, blue, or purple, or they must be formed from transparent materials (s 38(3) of the VCRA). In terms of size, for an imitation of normal colour, ie dark or metallic, to be classed as a non–realistic, it must be small, no more than 38 mm in height or 70 mm in length.

Their use is subject to fewer restrictions than for realistic imitations as they are more clearly identifiable as imitations. However, it is important to note that some customized and fully functional firearms are also manufactured in bright colours and designs, so police officers should carefully examine such an item to determine its true nature. If there is any uncertainty, the officer should seize it for examination at a specialist laboratory.

25.7.3 Readily convertible imitation firearms

Some imitation firearms (including realistic imitations) can be converted into a functional firearm of a type requiring a certificate under s 1 of the Firearms Act 1968 or even fall into the category of a prohibited weapon. If the conversion process is simple and does not require special skills or special tools (s 1(6)), the firearm is regarded as being readily convertible. Here, a special tool is a tool which would not generally be used in the home for construction and maintenance, so, for example, if the conversion can be carried out with a normal screwdriver, the weapon would be regarded as readily convertible.

Any object will be regarded as a firearm under s 1(1) and (2) of the Firearms Act 1968 if it:

- has the appearance of a firearm;
- can be readily converted into a weapon from which a shot, bullet, or other missile can be discharged; and
- when converted, would fall under s 1 of the Firearms Act 1968.

Possession of a readily convertible imitation firearm without a certificate is an offence as it would be regarded as a functioning firearm. Ultimately, only a court can decide whether a particular article requires a certificate, and testing at a forensic laboratory would usually be required before commencing any prosecution. There might be a defence if it can be shown that the owner did not know, and had no reason to suspect, that the item was readily convertible (s 1(5) of the Firearms Act 1982). Possession of a tool or article with the intention of using it to convert an imitation firearm into a working firearm is an offence (s 127 of the Policing and Crime Act 2017). It is also an offence to unlawfully supply, or offer to supply, a defectively deactivated weapon to another person in the UK or in a member state of the EU (s 128 of the Policing and Crime Act 2017). This would cover a firearm that could relatively easily be re-activated, eg by re-drilling a blocked barrel.

The Firearms Regulations 2019 require the notification to the Home Office, as the relevant national authority, of possession of a deactivated firearm and their transfer—but only when the transfer is for a period of more than 14 days. Regardless of when they were acquired, the firearm must meet current deactivation standards before being transferred. See Home Office Circular 010/2019 for detail (Home Office, 2019d).

25.7.4 Blank-firing firearms

A blank-firing firearm is one that cannot discharge a projectile. Blank cartridges contain powder or propellant but no bullet. For a blank-firer to comply with the VCRA and the Firearms Act 1968, it must discharge gas from the top of the weapon and have a solid, blocked barrel. Blank-firers sold in Europe and the US are often manufactured to fire out of the muzzle, and are therefore not legal in the UK. In terms of their appearance, blank-firing firearms can be imitation or realistic imitation firearms.

It is legal for an adult at least 18 years old to buy, sell, and own a blank-firing imitation or realistic imitation firearm without a certificate. However, these items may not be carried in public and may only be used on private land or property with the landowner's permission. Further details on the buying, selling, and importing of blank-firers are provided in the VCRA.

25.8 Prohibited Weapons

Parliament decided that the general public have no reasonable need to possess certain types of potentially highly dangerous weapon such as many types of handgun, machine guns, PAVA (an incapacitating pepper spray), or CS spray.

The two canisters on the left are examples of CS Spray and those on the right, pepper spray. All are examples of s 5 prohibited weapons.

Under s 5 of the Firearms Act 1968, it is an offence to possess or make such items without special authority. The table shows some features which cause a weapon to fall into the prohibited category, along with some examples. There are some exceptions to these prohibitions as shown in the final column of the table (information derived from the CPS website).

Prohibited feature	Example of a prohibited firearm	Permitted exceptions
Short barrel (less than 30 cm) or short overall (less than 60 cm)	short handguns and short revolvers or designed as signalling apparatus	any air weapon, muzzle-loading gun
Can discharge a noxious substance (liquid, gas, or other thing)	stun guns (including a 'Taser') and aerosol incapacitant sprays	
Two or more missiles can be successively discharged without repeated pressure on the trigger	any machine gun	
Self-loading or pump-action with a rifled barrel	short-barrelled rifles	if chambered for .22 inch rim-fire cartridges
Self-loading or pump-action with a short smooth-bore barrel (barrel less than 24 inches, or overall length less than 40 inches)	short self-loading shotguns	if it is an air weapon, or is chambered for .22 inch rim-fire cartridges
Smooth-bore revolver gun	'Dragon'	if it is either a muzzle-loading gun, or is designed for 9 mm rim-fire cartridges
Can project a stabilized missile	rocket launcher	if designed for line-throwing, pyrotechnics, or as signalling apparatus
Has a self-contained gas cartridge system	Brococks	
Ammunition designed to explode on or just before impact, or containing a noxious substance		
Any firearm disguised as another object	pen guns, key fob guns, and phone guns	a rifle which is chambered for .22 rim-fire cartridges
Any rifle with a chamber from which empty cartridge cases are extracted using: (i) energy from propellant gas, or (ii) energy imparted to a spring or other energy storage device by propellant gas, other than a rifle which is chambered for .22 rim-fire cartridges	VZ 58 Manually Actuated Release System (MARS) rifle and the Southern Gun Company SGC lever release rifle	
Any device (commonly known as a bump stock) which is designed or adapted so that: (i) it is capable of forming part of or being added to a self-loading lethal barrelled weapon (as defined in section 57(1B) and (2A)), and (ii) if it forms part of or is added to such a weapon, it increases the rate of fire of the weapon by using the recoil from the weapon to generate repeated pressure on the trigger (section 5(1)(ba)); Section 5(1)(ba) covers bump stocks, which significantly increase the rate of fire of self-loading rifle		

This revolver is a prohibited weapon as its barrel is less than 30 cm in length.

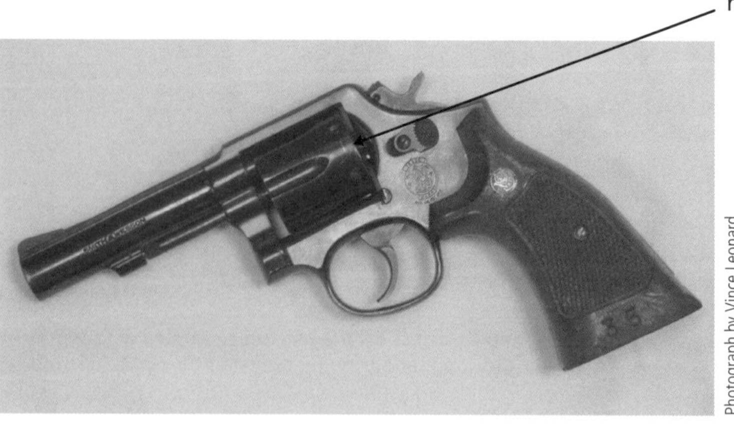

Photograph by Vince Leonard

The rifle shown in the second photograph is a prohibited weapon because it can be converted so it can discharge two or more rounds successively.

The third photograph shows a carbine, a type of rifle with a short barrel. It is a prohibited weapon due to the barrel, the barrel is rifled, shorter than 30 cm, and the calibre is more than .22 inch.

It is an offence to possess, purchase, acquire, manufacture, sell, or transfer a prohibited weapon or ammunition (s 5(1) of the Firearms Act 1968) without written authority from the Defence Council, which comprises the Secretary of State for Defence, other MoD ministers, the Chiefs of Staff, and senior civil servants. This offence is triable either way and the penalty is a fine or imprisonment (six months if tried summarily and ten years on indictment).

25.8.1 Police use of prohibited weapons

Tasers are in widespread use by police services across the UK and most taser-trained officers are not firearms officers. Tasers are a conducted energy device (CED) and classed as a prohibited weapon. The cartridge is fired from the main part of the weapon but remains attached by fine wires that conduct electricity, so delivering a series of electrical shocks to the target.

The only Home Office approved devices at the time of writing are the Taser X2, at the top of the photograph, with its cartridge on the right, and below the Taser X26e, marked X26, with its cartridge on the left, and the Taser 7, which was approved for use by UK police services in August 2020.

Photograph by Vince Leonard

These less-lethal weapons bridge the gap between a baton and a firearm and are designed to temporarily incapacitate a person, rather than be lethal. However, the use of such weapons can have fatal consequences, for example if the subject was soaked in flammable liquids or was fitted with a pacemaker. Most injuries caused will be due to the way in which the person falls. A full explanation of the rules and procedures governing the issue and use of these devices can be found on the College of Policing website.

TASK 4 Sixteen pupils and one teacher were killed in a firearms incident at Dunblane in Scotland in 1996. Consider the report by the Hon Lord Cullen *The Public Inquiry into the Shootings at Dunblane Primary School on 13 March 1996*, and the subsequent Firearms (Amendment) Act 1997 and the Firearms (Amendment) (No 2) Act 1997. What changes were introduced by this legislation and why was this thought to be necessary?

25.9 Answers to Tasks

TASK 1 Consider the following:

- Does the driver have a reasonable excuse for the presence of the items?
- Who do the items belong to?
- Has an offence been committed? And if so can the person be arrested?
- You could explain the law, including how a display of such weapons could be misinterpreted and cause fear and alarm.

TASK 2 You probably considered the following:

- Is the person above the age of criminal responsibility?
- What type of knife is it and has it been made, adapted, or intended to cause injury?
- Will they hand it over?

TASK 3

It is generally an offence for a person under the age of 18 to have an air weapon or ammunition for an air weapon, but there are exceptions. For example, it is not an offence for a person aged 14 years or over to possess the air weapon on private premises with the consent of the occupier, and they do not have to be supervised. However, it is an offence to use an air weapon to fire a missile beyond those premises (s 21A of the Firearms Act 1968).

TASK 4

The private ownership of handguns was completely banned. Cullen recommended a cautious approach, for example storing firearms at clubs or police stations, and although this was considered to be unworkable by shooters, the restrictions had public backing. The first new Act banned the higher calibre handguns, classing them as prohibited weapons, and the second new Act added .22 calibre firearms to the prohibited list. These changes introduced some of the world's toughest gun control laws. However, a new market for realistic imitation firearms developed, along with new criminal supply routes and an upsurge in the re-activation of firearms.

The 2015 HMIC report *Targeting the Risk* recommended tough new licensing conditions for the owners of shotguns and other firearms, including improving the process of checking applicants' medical fitness to own such weapons. These recommendations were enacted in the Policing and Crime Act 2017.

26 Damage to Buildings and Other Property

26.1 Introduction

This chapter will examine the law surrounding damage to property, much of which stems from the Criminal Damage Act 1971. We also look at legislation to help to protect ancient monuments and heritage sites in the UK. An understanding of these aspects of the law will help a student officer undertaking the PCDA or DHEP to achieve the requirement to 'conduct diligent and efficient … high volume investigations'. It is also relevant to the National Policing Curriculum requirements regarding knowledge of legislation and procedures (part of 'Understanding the Police Constable Role').

Criminal damage is both one of the most common crimes in England Wales and often one of the most visible; it is an example of one of the so-called *signal crimes* described in 17.4.2. It often comes to the notice of the police through reports from the public however, intelligence might also feature, particularly in terms of identifying and taking action for *taggers*, individuals who spray graffiti on buildings or trains or other objects. Likewise, the tags themselves might also provide useful information about the activities of a local criminal gang (see 12.6).

The investigation of criminal damage, arson, and heritage crime provides good examples of the multi-agency approach to crime reduction. Detection of criminal damage might well involve PCSOs and local authorities while investigations into suspected arson are often carried out by specialist fire investigation teams, subject to local agreements. Cultural crime detection might well involve the police working in partnership with, for example, Historic England.

Police officers have a power of entry to search premises in order to prevent serious damage to property (s 17(1)(e) of the PACE Act 1984).

26.2 Criminal Damage

In terms of criminal damage, an officer is most likely to encounter graffiti and minor damage to fences, cars, and bus shelters. To help reduce the prevalence of grafitti the sale of containers of aerosol paint to a young person under the age of 16 is a summary offence (s 54(1) of the Anti-Social Behaviour Act 2003).

Section 1(1) of the Criminal Damage Act 1971 describes the offence of criminal damage. It states that an offence is committed by a person who without lawful excuse:

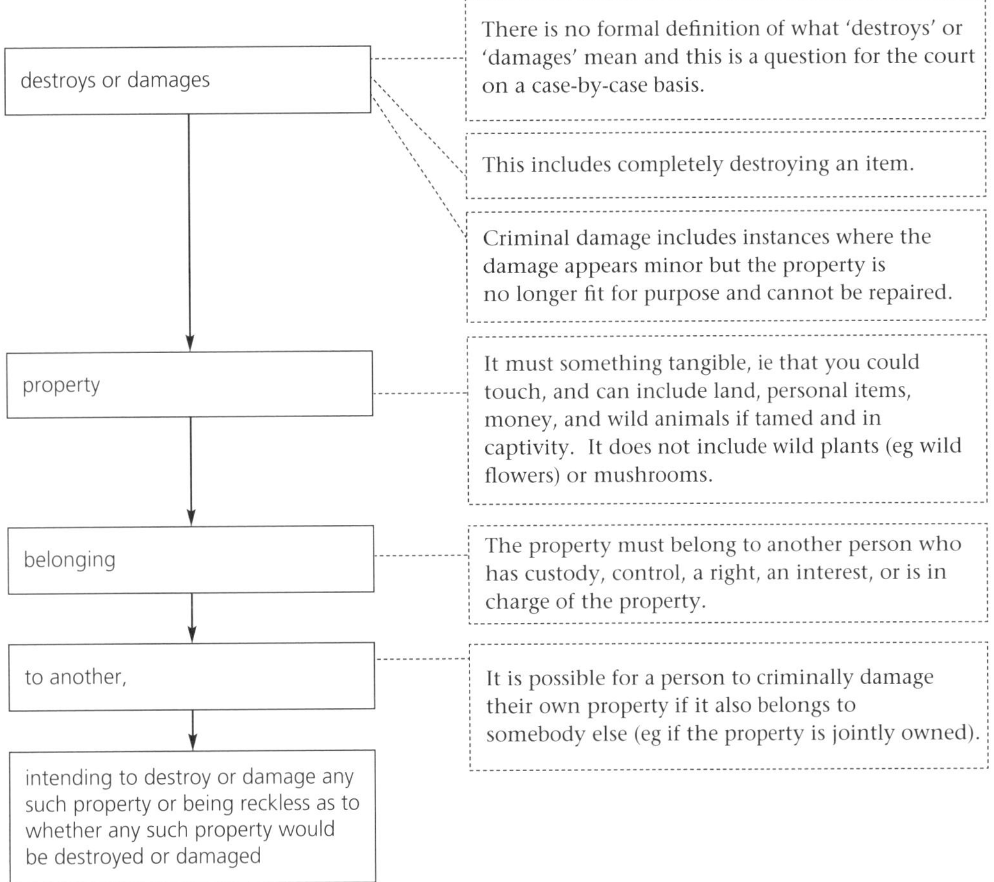

destroys or damages
There is no formal definition of what 'destroys' or 'damages' mean and this is a question for the court on a case-by-case basis.
This includes completely destroying an item.
Criminal damage includes instances where the damage appears minor but the property is no longer fit for purpose and cannot be repaired.
property
It must something tangible, ie that you could touch, and can include land, personal items, money, and wild animals if tamed and in captivity. It does not include wild plants (eg wild flowers) or mushrooms.
belonging
The property must belong to another person who has custody, control, a right, an interest, or is in charge of the property.
to another,
It is possible for a person to criminally damage their own property if it also belongs to somebody else (eg if the property is jointly owned).
intending to destroy or damage any such property or being reckless as to whether any such property would be destroyed or damaged

There are some circumstances where a person could have a lawful excuse for causing the damage. This requires that they would have an honestly held belief that:

- they had permission from the owner of the property (or an appropriate person) to carry out the relevant acts; or
- their own or another's property was in immediate need of protection by reasonable means.

There may even be occasions where an incorrect belief could still constitute an honestly held belief and would therefore negate liability for a criminal act. For example, if a vehicle owner is unconscious in hospital after a car accident, the recovery operator might honestly believe that the owner would give permission for the car to be moved.

The person carrying out the offence must either intend to cause the damage or be reckless as to whether the property will be damaged. The appropriate test of recklessness for criminal damage is:

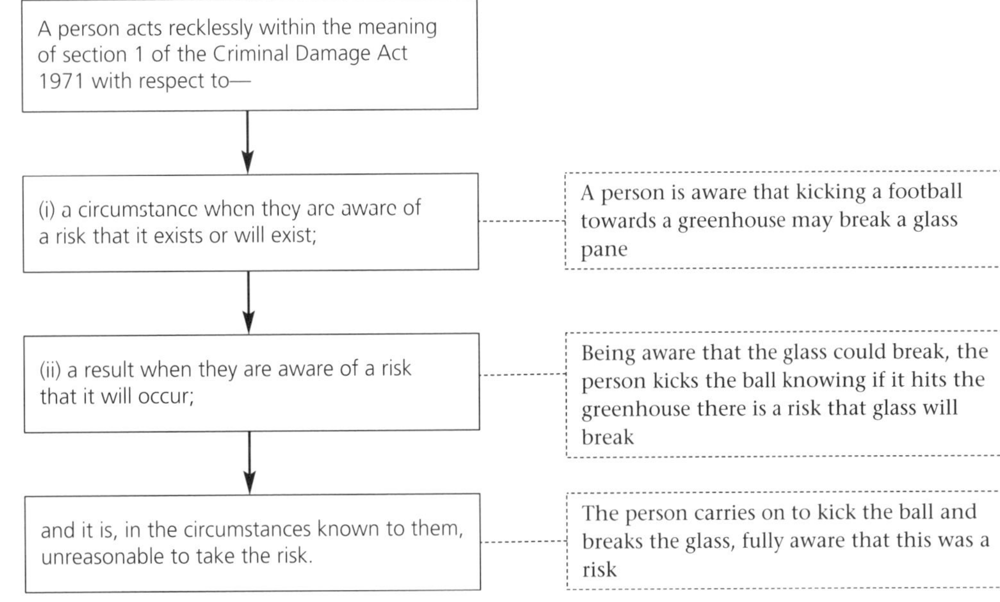

A person acts recklessly within the meaning of section 1 of the Criminal Damage Act 1971 with respect to—
(i) a circumstance when they are aware of a risk that it exists or will exist;
A person is aware that kicking a football towards a greenhouse may break a glass pane
(ii) a result when they are aware of a risk that it will occur;
Being aware that the glass could break, the person kicks the ball knowing if it hits the greenhouse there is a risk that glass will break
and it is, in the circumstances known to them, unreasonable to take the risk.
The person carries on to kick the ball and breaks the glass, fully aware that this was a risk

The person who takes the risk must be fully aware of it. The risk may be obvious to others but, as we can see in the case of *R v G* [2003] UKHL 50, it might not always be obvious to the defendant(s). In this case, two children, aged 11 and 12, set a fire under a wheelie bin in the back yard of a shop and then left, assuming that the fire would soon go out on the concrete floor. However, it continued to burn and resulted in damage of around £1 million. They were convicted of arson but this was overturned by the House of Lords because although the risk seemed obvious to most adults, it was not to the children. This will be decided by the court on a case-by-case basis.

The offence of criminal damage is triable either way and will be tried summarily if the value of the property damaged or destroyed is less than £5,000 (s 22 of the Magistrates' Courts Act 1980). The penalty is six months' imprisonment and/or a fine if tried summarily and ten years' imprisonment on indictment. If the damage is aggravated by religious or racial hatred, then the maximum penalty on indictment is increased to 14 years (s 30(1) of the Crime and Disorder Act 1998). Cases relating to Criminal Damage are not always straightforward; during a *Black Lives Matter* protest, a statue of Edward Colston was pulled down and thrown into Bristol Harbour. Four anti-racist protestors, who admitted being involved in the toppling of the statue, were nonetheless found not guilty of criminal damage.

TASK 1 After being arrested for being drunk and disorderly, an individual smears their own excrement on the walls of the police station cell. Discuss whether this constitutes criminal damage.

26.2.1 Aggravated criminal damage (endangering life)

The offence of 'criminal damage, life endangered' (s 1(2) of the Criminal Damage Act 1971) is committed by a person who destroys or damages property intending, or being reckless as, to endanger life. To prove the offence, there is no requirement for the offender to try to kill someone or for any actual injury or harm to occur. There is only a necessity to prove that the damage was caused intentionally or recklessly and that there was potential for another to be harmed as a result of that damage being caused. In the case of *R v Sangha* [1988] 2 All ER 385 (CA), the defendant lit a fire on a mattress in an empty flat. The flat was in a block which had been constructed to prevent the spread of fire from one flat to another. The court held that it was irrelevant that no lives were actually endangered by the defendant's actions; the fact that the circumstances could be considered to endanger life was sufficient.

For this offence, the property can belong to another person or to the offender, in contrast with the basic offence of criminal damage where the property must belong, at least in part, to another. For example, someone deliberately damages the brakes of their own car knowing that their partner will be driving it later that day and intending their life to be endangered. The damage caused must also be the cause of the danger; for example, shooting at someone in a room through a window both endangers life and damages the window, but it is the bullet that endangers the life rather than the damage from the broken window, so this would not be criminal damage life endangered.

This offence is triable by indictment only and the penalty is life imprisonment.

26.3 Arson

Arson is destroying or damaging property by fire. It is covered under s 1(3) of the Criminal Damage Act 1971. For a person to be found guilty of this offence, at least some of the damage must have been caused by fire excluding smoke damage. For the offence to be proved, there must be an intent or an element of recklessness in relation to the use of fire.

If no life is endangered, then arson is triable either way with a penalty of six months' imprisonment and/or a fine if tried summarily and up to life imprisonment on indictment. If life is endangered, this offence must be tried on indictment.

TASK 2 For what reasons might the crime of arson be committed?

26.4 Threats to Damage

This offence is covered in s 2 of the Criminal Damage Act 1971 and there are two points to prove in relation to such a threat:

- the conduct that is threatened must refer to damage; and
- the extent of the threatened damage must constitute an offence under s 1 of the Criminal Damage Act 1971. This can include acts of simple damage under s 1(1), as well as criminal damage where life is endangered (s 1(2)).

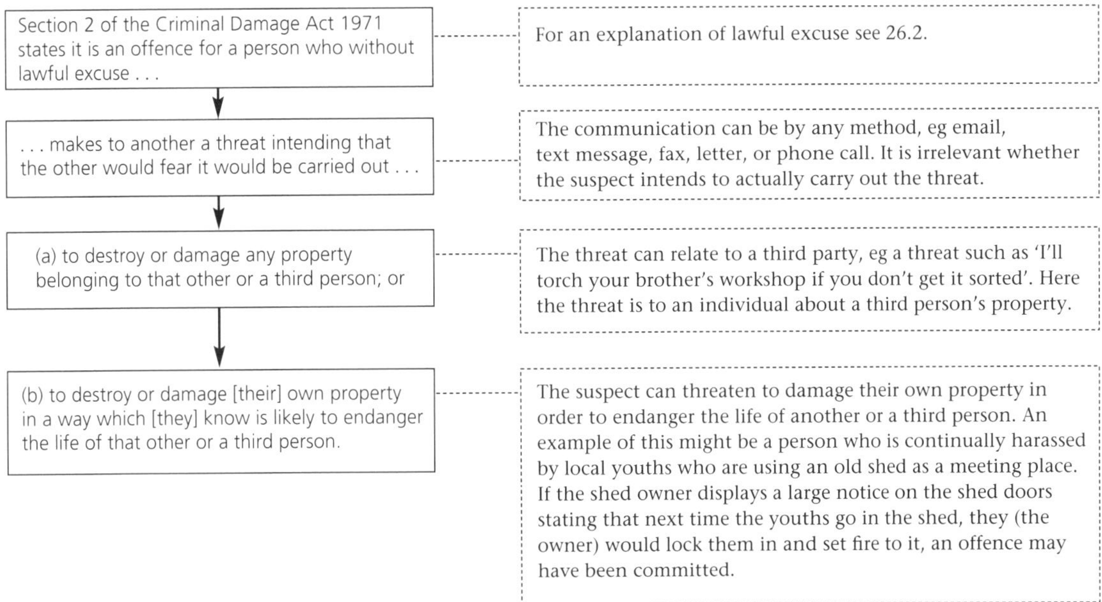

Section 2 of the Criminal Damage Act 1971 states it is an offence for a person who without lawful excuse . . .
For an explanation of lawful excuse see 26.2.
. . . makes to another a threat intending that the other would fear it would be carried out . . .
The communication can be by any method, eg email, text message, fax, letter, or phone call. It is irrelevant whether the suspect intends to actually carry out the threat.
(a) to destroy or damage any property belonging to that other or a third person; or
The threat can relate to a third party, eg a threat such as 'I'll torch your brother's workshop if you don't get it sorted'. Here the threat is to an individual about a third person's property.
(b) to destroy or damage [their] own property in a way which [they] know is likely to endanger the life of that other or a third person.
The suspect can threaten to damage their own property in order to endanger the life of another or a third person. An example of this might be a person who is continually harassed by local youths who are using an old shed as a meeting place. If the shed owner displays a large notice on the shed doors stating that next time the youths go in the shed, they (the owner) would lock them in and set fire to it, an offence may have been committed.

The person who makes the threat must intend that the recipient will believe that the threat will be carried out. It is for the court to decide whether what was communicated had enough substance to constitute a threat. In some circumstances, it might be more appropriate to consider an offence under s 4 of the Public Order Act 1986.

The offence of making threats to damage cannot be committed if the threat involves an element of recklessness as to whether the property will actually be destroyed or damaged. For example, an angry neighbour shouts, 'If your kid keeps throwing stones over my wall, I'll start chucking them back, and no, I don't care what it does.' They are reckless as to whether damage is caused or not so would not have committed the offence of 'threats to damage'. Note that the feelings of the person receiving the threat are not relevant for this offence.

This offence is triable either way and the penalty is six months' imprisonment and/or a fine if tried summarily and ten years' imprisonment on indictment.

26.5 Possessing an Article with Intent to Cause Criminal Damage

This offence is covered in s 3 of the Criminal Damage Act 1971.

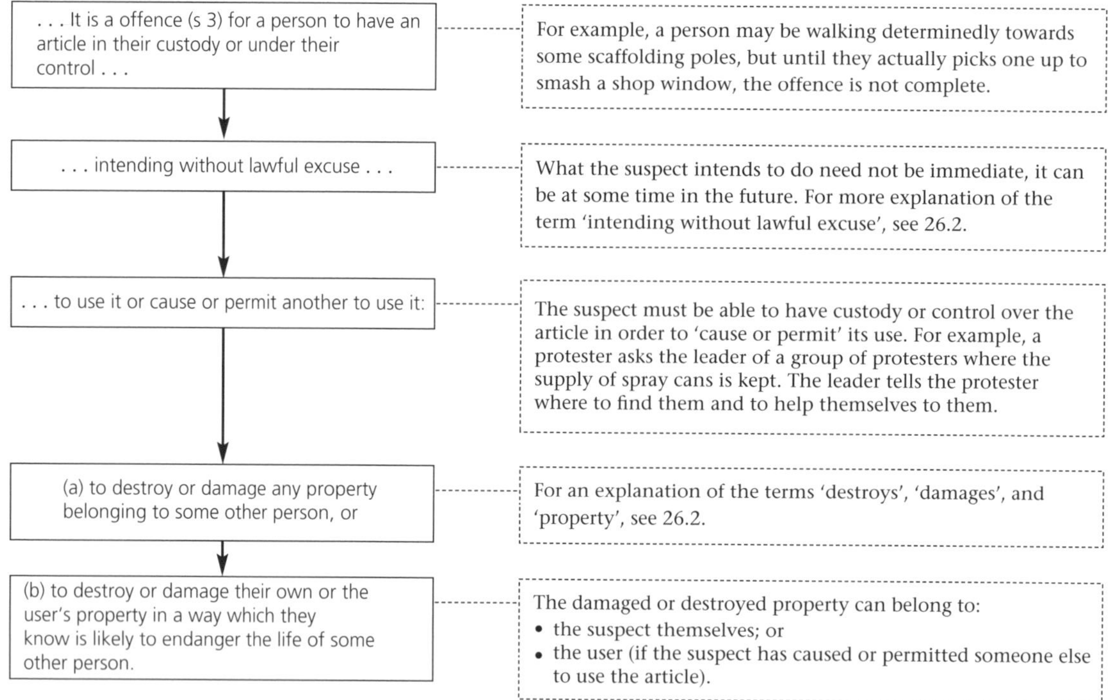

. . . It is a offence (s 3) for a person to have an article in their custody or under their control . . .
For example, a person may be walking determinedly towards some scaffolding poles, but until they actually picks one up to smash a shop window, the offence is not complete.
. . . intending without lawful excuse . . .
What the suspect intends to do need not be immediate, it can be at some time in the future. For more explanation of the term 'intending without lawful excuse', see 26.2.
. . . to use it or cause or permit another to use it:
The suspect must be able to have custody or control over the article in order to 'cause or permit' its use. For example, a protester asks the leader of a group of protesters where the supply of spray cans is kept. The leader tells the protester where to find them and to help themselves to them.
(a) to destroy or damage any property belonging to some other person, or
For an explanation of the terms 'destroys', 'damages', and 'property', see 26.2.
(b) to destroy or damage their own or the user's property in a way which they know is likely to endanger the life of some other person.
The damaged or destroyed property can belong to:
• the suspect themselves; or
• the user (if the suspect has caused or permitted someone else to use the article).

The type of article involved here can be anything tangible. The Law Commission, which advised on the Act, explained that:

> The essential feature of the proposed offence is to be found, not so much in the nature of the thing, as in the intention with which it is held. (Law Commission No 29, para 59)

This offence is triable either way. The penalty is six months' imprisonment and/or a fine not exceeding the statutory maximum if tried summarily and ten years' imprisonment on indictment.

A power to search for articles made or adapted for use in the course of or in connection with an offence under s 1 of the Criminal Damage Act 1971 is provided under s 1(2)(a) of the PACE Act 1984. Any person or vehicle, and anything in or on a vehicle, can be searched and detained for the purpose of such a search. Section 2 of the PACE Act 1984 and its Codes of Practice must be followed, including providing the person with the GO WISELY information listed in para 3.8 of Code A (see Chapter 4 on stop and search procedures).

26.6 Causing Damage to Heritage Sites

Buildings and sites of historic interest have had some form of legal protection in the UK since 1882. Over the years further specific legislation has been introduced and this provides protection to many types of historic site such as:

- scheduled monuments (an archaeological site or building that is of national importance, eg Dover Castle);
- listed buildings (over 500,000 in England alone);
- protected marine wreck sites (53 in English coastal waters);
- protected military remains of aircraft and vessels of historic interest (includes losses during peacetime);
- conservation areas (local authority designated areas; around 9,000 in the UK);
- registered parks and gardens (gardens of stately homes, public parks, and cemeteries on a national register; over 1,600 in the UK);
- registered battlefields (46 in the UK); and
- World Heritage Sites (25 in the UK, eg Hadrian's Wall).

26.6.1 Legislation to protect heritage sites

A number of bodies (local authorities, the police, and Historic England) share the responsibility to enforce legislation designed to protect heritage sites. Partnership-working plays a fundamental role in tackling heritage crime. However, this is a challenging task due to the relative rarity of incidents and the lack of expertise and understanding of the nature of the possible harm. Despite the challenges, there have been some successful prosecutions.

Historic England Case (2020)

In 2019, the Mac family were fined a total of £160,000 for causing irreversible damage to Withybrook mediaeval village. The site is located on land owned by the Mac family, who bulldozed a road across the site and installed pipes and fencing. Historic England were consistently refused access to the site, a scheduled monument, and issued repeated warnings that the work was not permitted. Historic England then instigated court proceedings but the work had already caused significant damage.

Importantly, s 50 of the Police, Crime, Sentencing and Courts Act 2022 amends the Magistrates' Courts Act 1980 to remove the monetary level of £5,000 worth of damage which was necessary before a case could be heard in the Crown Court. Memorials are now exempt from this minimum monetary value of damage so these cases can also be heard in the Crown Court with its fuller sentencing powers.

26.6.1.1 The Ancient Monuments and Archaeological Areas Act 1979

It is an offence under s 28 of the Act to damage or destroy without lawful excuse a 'protected monument' (defined in s 28, and includes a scheduled monument). The suspect must know that it is a protected monument and intend to destroy or damage it, or be reckless as to whether it will be destroyed or damaged. The offence is triable either way and the penalty is a fine and/or imprisonment (six months if tried summarily and two years on indictment).

Other sections of this Act may also be relevant to the trainee police officer, for example:

- s 42 under which it is a summary offence to use a metal detector in a 'protected place' without the written consent of English Heritage, and an either-way offence to remove an object in such circumstances;
- s 9 under which it is an either-way offence to damage, demolish, or alter a listed building.

26.6.1.2 The protection of wrecks and military remains

The Protection of Wrecks Act 1973 can be used to designate an area containing a 'protected wreck'. All retrieved wreck material, eg coins, cannon, and wreck timbers, must be reported to the Receiver at the Maritime and Coastguard Agency.

The Protection of Military Remains Act 1986 makes it an offence to interfere, without a licence, with the wreckage of any crashed, sunken, or stranded military aircraft or designated vessel. The Act provides two levels of protection depending on whether the site is designated as a 'protected place' or a 'controlled site'. Greater restrictions are placed upon activities at the latter. Investigations under this Act usually relate to diving and are undertaken by the Ministry of Defence supported by the police and Historic England. Most of the offences in relation to this Act are triable either way.

26.6.2 Offences relating to cultural objects and treasure

Legislation is available to help to regulate the trade in cultural objects and treasure found at archaeological or other heritage sites.

A 'cultural object' is defined here as an object of historical, architectural, or archaeological interest. It is 'tainted' if a person illegally excavates an object from its original position in the ground or removes it from a building, structure, or monument of historical, architectural, or archaeological interest in the UK or elsewhere. Dishonest dealing of a tainted cultural object while knowing or believing it is tainted is an either-way offence (s 1 of the Dealing in Cultural Objects (Offences) Act 2003).

'Treasure' here includes old coins, collections of prehistoric metalwork, and objects found with such coins or metalwork (s 1 of the Treasure Act 1996). Such finds must be reported through the Portable Antiquities Scheme. It is a summary offence to fail to notify the district coroner within 14 days of finding 'treasure' (s 8(3) of the Treasure Act 1996).

26.7 Answers to Tasks

TASK 1 The excrement will not have destroyed the walls of the police cell but the walls will need to be cleaned and have therefore been damaged. The cost of the damage will be equal to the cost of the cleaning operation. The suspect will need to be interviewed decide whether they intended to damage the walls or were reckless as to the damage. One of these must be proved for the offence to have been committed. If the drunken state was self-induced, this will not be an acceptable defence (*DPP v Majewski* [1977] UKHL 2).

TASK 2 In 2007, a Home Office analysis of incidents identified particular motives for arson in the UK.

Form of arson	Motive	Proportion of all arson (year 2000 data)	
		Property	Vehicles
Youth disorder and nuisance	Vandalism and boredom	36%	39%
Malicious	Revenge, racism, clashes of beliefs/rivalries, or personal animosities	25%	3%
Psychological	Mental illness or suicide	26%	13%
Criminal	Financial gain and fraud, or the concealment of other crimes (theft, murder, etc)	13%	45%

However, there are alternative but complementary ways of understanding the causes of arson. For example, Canter and Fritzon (1998) identified two main categories; person-orientated arson and object-orientated arson. A further distinction is possible of being either expressive (eg to express some form of emotion or psychological need) or instrumental (eg to serve as a means of achieving another goal). This gives rise to a fourfold typology:

	Person-orientated	Object-orientated
Expressive	Directed inwards (towards the offender) possibly as the result of anxiety, depression, or suicidal tendencies	Directed at an object (eg building) but for symbolic or emotional needs of the offender
Instrumental	Directed outwards (to others), possibly as revenge for perceived wrongdoing	Directed at an object (eg building), but where arson is a consequence of another motive, for example to hide evidence of a burglary

Source: Based on Canter and Fritzon, 1998 and Fineman, 1995.

Canter and Fritzon (1998) found that there were statistically significant associations between each of the four motive categories and the offender's social and psychological background. For example, repeat arsonists tended to fall into the expressive/object-orientated category, whereas an expressive/person-orientated arson was more likely to be committed by a person with a history of psychiatric problems.

27 Attempts, Conspiracy, and Encouraging or Assisting Crime

27.1 Introduction

In this chapter we discuss legislation designed to deal with suspects or offenders who stop just short of committing indictable offences but can nonetheless be prosecuted for attempting to commit the full offence, or for conspiracy. Additionally, those accomplices who are not the actual perpetrators of an offence but who encourage or assist in the commission of a crime are also considered. This relatively new legislation has a slighter wider scope than the common law offence of incitement that it replaces. These kinds of offences are referred to as *inchoate*—meaning anticipatory or preparatory. Those accused of the offences described in this chapter are also sometimes loosely or informally described as *accessories* to a crime.

The maximum sentence for inchoate offences is usually the same as for the actual offence. It is fair to say, though, that charges for inchoate offences are much rarer than those for the full offence.

Whilst inchoate offences can often be revealed, the CPS generally reserves prosecuting for these kinds of crimes for quite serious cases only. The CPS and the police will always look first for the substantive offence(s) as this usually provides a clearer and more convincing base for securing a conviction.

27.2 Criminal Attempts

A person who is planning or preparing a criminal offence might not actually go on to commit the full offence. Occasionally, the police learn of such criminal intentions and will covertly observe the suspect's activities—such evidence can sometimes be used to support a charge for an inchoate offence. This often applies in very serious cases like terrorism where it is clearly in the public interest that the harmful intent of terrorists is thwarted before the full offence can be committed or in serious assaults where sometimes an attempted murder charge might be appropriate.

Let us first look at attempts. This offence is described under s 1(1) of the Criminal Attempts Act 1981:

> If with intent to commit the offence to which this section applies, a person does an act which is more than merely *preparatory* to the commission of the offence, [they are] guilty of attempting to commit the offence.

The attempted offence must be an indictable offence, however, see 27.2.3 for certain indictable offences which cannot be attempted. Summary offences cannot be attempted in terms of the Criminal Attempts Act 1981.

The mode of trial is the same as for the main offence. For either-way offences, the penalty is the same maximum penalty as the substantive offence when tried summarily. For an indictable-only offence, the maximum penalty is the same as for the substantive offence.

27.2.1 Attempts and criminal intent

The suspect must have formed criminal intent, *mens rea*, in all of these areas: the intent to commit the full offence, have taken part in a series of acts which will lead to a final outcome of committing the full offence, and have carried out all the elements of the offence.

For a person to be found guilty of an attempt to commit an offence, the suspect must have more than an intention to do it (*R v Campbell* [1991] Crim LR 268). The suspect must demonstrate a guilty intent by carrying out the type of acts which amount to *more* than merely preparing to commit the full offence. For example, it would not be enough for a suspect to have some rags and a container of petrol in a bag and to take them to their rival's house; these actions might still be considered as preparatory and we must seek evidence that went ***beyond*** this. If, on the other hand, they went to their rival's front door and pushed petrol-soaked rags through the letter box, and then used a match to try to set the rags alight, this would show a clear intent to carry out arson. These acts would almost certainly be considered as more than merely preparatory and could therefore constitute an attempt under the Criminal Attempts Act 1981.

The final act carried out by the accused must be in combination with all the other preparatory acts and have no purpose other than to complete the full offence. For example, imagine a group of people arrive in a van at a yard containing copper scrap one night. They cut a large hole in the fence, big enough for a person to pass through, but then spot a security guard and quickly leave. When they are stopped, one of the group has some wire cutters in their pocket and another is seen to quietly drop some bolt croppers on the ground next to the van. Their actions amount to more than preparations to steal; they have committed an attempt under s 1(1) of the Criminal Attempts Act 1981 (see *Davey v Lee* (1967) 51 Cr App R 303).

It is sometimes difficult to identify between on the one side preparatory acts, and on the other attempts. However, this decision is primarily the jury's to make, based on common sense.

To help to make that decision, the following needs to be clarified: does the available evidence demonstrate that the defendant has performed an action which shows that they tried to commit the offence in question? Or did they merely put themselves in a position, or equip themselves, to do so (*R v Geddes* (1996) 160 JP 697)?

With regard to theft, the law introduced the specific offence of going equipped to steal (s 25 of the Theft Act 1968, see 23.6). It states that a person is guilty of this offence if, 'when not at [their] place of abode, [they have] with [them] any article for use in the course of or in connection with any burglary or theft'. One can see here how the law seeks to cover all eventualities of criminal endeavour—walking down the street with implements to steal a car would **not** amount to an attempt but would amount to the offence of going equipped to steal.

For an attempt, if the person **believes** that they are committing an offence but does not actually commit it, they will still be regarded as having attempted it, even if it is proved later that it would not have been possible to commit the full offence (s 1(3)(b)). For example, a person is paid money to travel from another country to the UK with a suitcase that they believe contains heroin. On arrival in the UK, their suitcase is searched and they admit to importing heroin into the UK. However, tests on the substance in the suitcase reveal it to be harmless vegetable matter and not drugs. The offence of importing controlled drugs has not been committed but they have still attempted to commit the crime (*R v Shivpuri* [1987] AC 1).

The case of *L v CPS* [2013] EWHC 4127 (Admin) demonstrates that the prosecution needs to prove more than the person's mere presence at the scene of a robbery to convict them of involvement in attempted robbery. In this case, a group of youths were accused of acting together to attempt to rob young children of their phones. All were convicted but an appeal was allowed in the case of individual L as there was insufficient evidence to demonstrate that they encouraged the attempted robbery at any stage.

27.2.2 Thorough planning and practical preparation

Section 1(2) of the Criminal Attempts Act 1981 states that there must be evidence that the person actually planned to personally carry out the act rather than just planning it, in which case someone else could have carried it out: 'the person does an act which is more than merely preparatory to the commission of the offence'. If there is something else to be done before the completion of the offence, it does not amount to an attempt.

As has been alluded to, it does not matter for the offence of criminal attempt whether the attempted offence would actually have been impossible to carry out (s 1(2)). This example amply demonstrates this:

- A person tries to steal property from another person's coat. They insert their hand into the pocket of the person's coat but find nothing because the pocket is empty. Even though the full offence of theft is impossible, there has still been an attempt to commit the offence of theft.

27.2.3 Offences that cannot be criminally attempted

Section 1(4) of the Criminal Attempts Act 1981 lists several categories of offence that cannot be 'attempted', such as summary offences. There are also a number of indictable offences that **cannot** be attempted. These include:

- conspiracy to commit an indictable offence: that is, an agreement between people to commit an offence;
- aiding, abetting, counselling, procuring, or suborning the commission of an indictable offence: for example, a person knew all the circumstances concerning a particular murder and did everything apart from deliver the fatal kick to the head; and
- assisting offenders: for example, knowingly helping offenders to avoid arrest or concealing information.

The reason these particular offences cannot be attempted is because they are, of themselves, preparatory criminal conduct. In other words, one cannot attempt an attempt.

However, some summary offences amount to attempts in themselves, for example attempting to drive whilst unfit through drink or drugs (see 16.9.2) and interfering with vehicles (see 23.8.2.2).

TASK 1 The following case relating to an attempt subsequently went to appeal. Predict the result of the appeal and explain your reasoning:

A person was seen by a teacher in the lavatory block at a school. Their rucksack, containing a large kitchen knife, some rope, and a roll of masking tape, was found in some nearby bushes. They were charged and convicted of attempted child abduction, the prosecution putting forward the argument that they had been hiding in the lavatories to abduct a child. The person appealed on the grounds that they had not attempted to commit the offence (*R v Geddes* [1996] Crim LR 894).

27.3 Conspiracy

The word *conspiracy* is usually employed to describe a plan made in secret by a group of people to do something unlawful. If the full offence is not apparent and neither is an attempt, then what other legal provisions exist to deal with criminals who are apparently engaged in planning to commit offences? The answer lies in the law's provisions for the offence of conspiracy. Conspiracy to commit an offence is described in the Criminal Law Act 1977, but it is worth mentioning that under common law there are non-statutory conspiracies, such as conspiracy to defraud and conspiracy to corrupt public morals or outrage public decency. Further information on these is available on the CPS website.

Conspiracy (s 1 of the Criminal Law Act 1977) is seen as an incomplete offence as are attempts to commit crime. This is because it is committed as soon as the parties agree to carry out a course of conduct that will involve committing the main offence (known as the substantive offence). The conspirator does not have to commit the substantive offence to commit conspiracy. Note that, like attempts, a person can still be found guilty of conspiracy even if the commission of the substantive offence is impossible due to the existence of particular circumstances (subsection (b)). Thus, if two individuals agree a course of conduct to kill an associate, it does not matter if (unknown to the individuals) the associate is already dead.

For there to be a conspiracy, at least **two people** must make the agreement. There can be no criminal conspiracy where a person acts alone, and mere negotiation does not constitute an agreement (*DPP v Nock* [1978] AC 979). However, if a person enters into an agreement and then withdraws, this still amounts to a conspiracy and the withdrawal would be regarded only as mitigation (*R v Gortat and Pirog* [1973] Crim LR 648). In addition, there are certain classes of people who cannot be guilty of a conspiracy. First, the intended victim of a crime cannot be guilty and, unsurprisingly, a conspiracy cannot be said to exist when a child under ten is the only other person in an agreement to commit crime (s 2 of the Criminal Law Act 1977). Finally, a husband and wife cannot be guilty of conspiracy to commit crime if they are the only people in the agreement. This relates to the traditional notion that when two people are married they become one, in the eyes of the law. If, however, they both entered into a conspiracy with a third party then they could all be guilty of the offence.

Evidence for conspiracy can be difficult to obtain because such agreements are usually made in secret with no other parties present. However, it can be proved by demonstrating the parties' pursuit of a common purpose ie through text messages and emails showing plans to commit a crime. In serious investigations, the police will often use surveillance to obtain evidence of a conspiracy (see 12.4.2 on covert surveillance). Charges for conspiracy are quite rare and are usually reserved for very serious crimes such as terrorism or organized crime gangs. The police use the offence of conspiracy to arrest such offenders—as a pre-emptive action that ensures the commission of the main or substantive offence never takes place.

The sentence for conspiracy is exactly the same as for the substantive offence planned. Conspiracies are indictable-only offences, and thus can only be tried at a Crown Court. The CPS supports charges for conspiracy when it is in the public interest. If substantive offences have been committed, the CPS is much more likely to charge for these rather than a conspiracy, unless many people have been involved only at the conspiracy stage or the crime that was planned was very serious. Where parties conspire to commit other offences abroad, in some circumstances the convictions can be pursued in England and Wales (s 1A of the Criminal Law Act 1977).

27.4 Encouraging or Assisting Crime

The commission of a crime often involves two or more accomplices, but they may not all actually carry out the offence. Some accomplices are at the crime scene but merely offer encouragement, while others might assist in the commission of a crime from a distance, providing information, transport, or financial support.

A person who encourages or assists in a crime, but does not perpetrate the main offence, may believe or claim that they were not a true accomplice. However, under the Serious Crime Act 2007 there are three criminal offences which involve encouraging or assisting another person to commit an offence. Together they replace the common law offence of incitement, now abolished, and also provide additional scope for prosecution in cases where the crime has not yet taken place; previously, there was no criminal liability for assisting the commission of an offence unless the offence had been committed or attempted. The legislation providing for these offences came into force on 1 October 2008 and does not apply retrospectively.

Note that a person cannot be convicted of encouraging or assisting a crime for which they are the intended victim. For instance, a 16-year-old schoolchild cannot be convicted of encouraging or assisting their teacher to engage in sexual activity with them. The teacher would commit the sexual offence of breach of a position of trust but the young person could not be convicted of encouraging or assisting as they are the person protected by that particular piece of legislation (s 51 of the Serious Crime Act 2007).

Like conspiracy offences, prosecutions for encouraging and assisting offences are quite rare. This is partly due to the difficulties in obtaining the required evidence but also because the police and the CPS will generally search for substantive offences wherever possible., Similarly, charges for encouraging or assisting in a crime are usually reserved for offenders involved in helping to facilitate very serious crimes such as murder or terrorism. The maximum penalties for an offence under s 44, 45, or 46 of the Serious Crime Act 2007 will be the same as the maximum for the relevant main offence.

27.4.1 Intentionally encouraging or assisting an offence

This is covered by s 44 of the Serious Crime Act 2007 which states that an offence is committed by a person who:

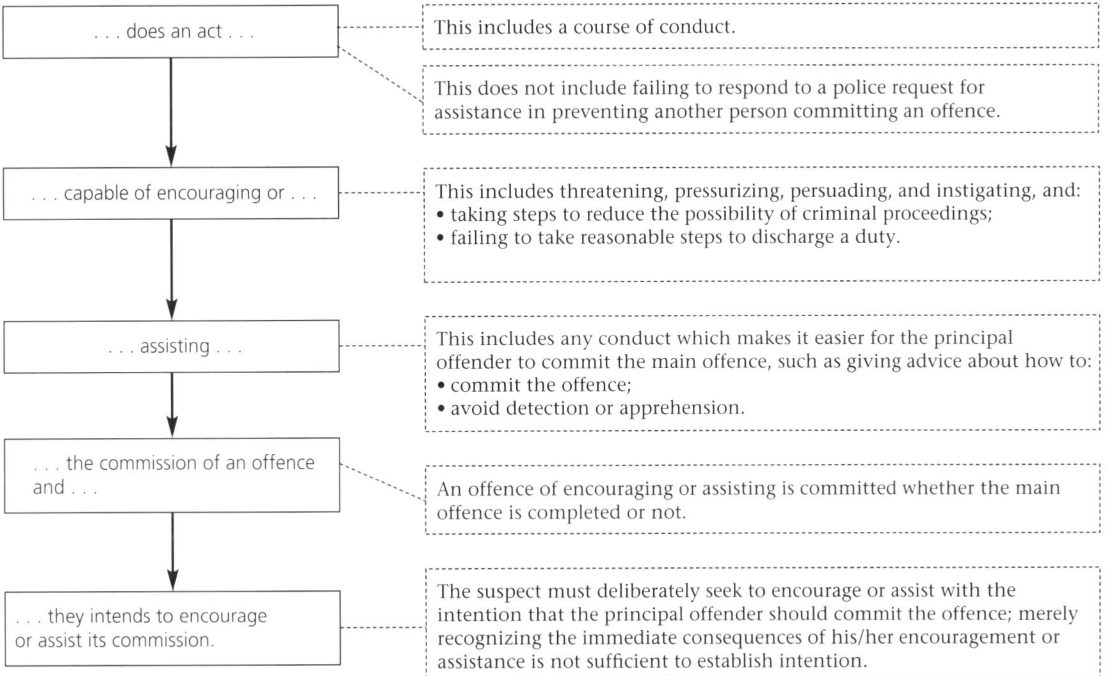

. . . does an act . . .
This includes a course of conduct.
This does not include failing to respond to a police request for assistance in preventing another person committing an offence.
. . . capable of encouraging or . . .
This includes threatening, pressurizing, persuading, and instigating, and:
• taking steps to reduce the possibility of criminal proceedings;
• failing to take reasonable steps to discharge a duty.
. . . assisting . . .
This includes any conduct which makes it easier for the principal offender to commit the main offence, such as giving advice about how to:
• commit the offence;
• avoid detection or apprehension.
. . . the commission of an offence and . . .
An offence of encouraging or assisting is committed whether the main offence is completed or not.
. . . they intends to encourage or assist its commission.
The suspect must deliberately seek to encourage or assist with the intention that the principal offender should commit the offence; merely recognizing the immediate consequences of his/her encouragement or assistance is not sufficient to establish intention.

We provide a few examples to illustrate some key points:

- Frankie lends a baseball bat to a neighbour who is scared that someone might possibly break into their house to steal antiques. Frankie knows that a baseball bat is sometimes used as a weapon to injure people but gives it to their neighbour with the sole purpose of helping them to feel more confident. Subsequently, an intruder is seriously injured by the neighbour using the baseball bat. For Frankie, this would probably not amount to assistance or encouragement to cause grievous bodily harm.
- Brown works for a double-glazing firm. In return for payment, they provide Mal with a spare key from a recently installed door, knowing that Mal is likely to use the key to burgle the house. Three days later, Mal enters the house and steals cash and jewellery. Brown has intentionally assisted in the commission of burglary (for burglary, see 23.4).

27.4.2 Believing one or more offences will be committed

Offences under ss 45 and 46 of the Serious Crime Act 2007 relate to belief rather than intent.

An offence is committed under s 45 of the Serious Crime Act 2007 when a person 'does an act capable of encouraging or assisting the commission of an offence' (the main offence). They must believe that the main offence will be committed and that their act will encourage or assist its commission. The following example is likely to constitute a s 45 offence.

A car salesperson makes a copy of a key of the most expensive car on the forecourt. They give that spare key to a friend knowing they will probably steal the car in the near future. The next day that friend is arrested during a burglary and is found in possession of the spare key. At interview, they outline their reasons for possessing the spare key, including the salesperson's involvement. The salesperson has committed the s 45 offence because, although they did not intend that their friend should commit theft, the salesperson still believed that the friend would commit the offence. It is irrelevant that the car was not in fact stolen.

The s 46 offence is very similar to the s 45 offence but applies in circumstances where there are a number of possible main offences planned by person B, rather than just one, and person A who is providing the encouragement or assistance does not know which of the offence(s)

B is going to commit. No main offence needs to actually be completed. Examples of offences under s 46 include:

- a gun shop owner providing guns to a criminal gang knowing they will use them in criminal enterprises such as robbery, but not knowing where or when;
- providing cutting agents to drug dealers being unaware of what class of drugs the dealers may be supplying and to whom (*R v Omar Saddique* [2013] EWCA Crim 1150).

27.4.3 Possible defences to encouraging or assisting offences

If the defendant can prove that it was reasonable for them to act the way they did, in the circumstances they were aware of or believed existed, this may be a defence (s 50) to an offence under s 44, 45, or 46. When determining what was reasonable, the seriousness of the anticipated main offence, the purpose of the act of encouragement or assistance, and the authority under which the person was acting will all be considered:

- With regard to the seriousness of the anticipated main offence, it might be reasonable to encourage or assist in the commission of a minor offence in order to prevent a more serious offence being committed. For example, Peta infiltrates a gang who are conspiring to commit an armed robbery and tells one of the other members of the gang to steal a car for the gang to use as a getaway from the robbery. Peta's intention is to look credible in front of the other gang members so Peta can achieve their main objective of preventing the robbery from taking place. Therefore, Peta may have a 'reasonable' defence.
- When considering the purpose of the act of encouragement or assistance, it might be reasonable to encourage or assist in the commission of a minor offence in order to prevent more serious harm from being inflicted. For example, imagine two members of a gang who initially plan to stab the leader of a rival gang. However, one of the members does not want to stab anyone and succeeds in persuading the other to smash the windows of the rival's car instead. That first gang member is charged with encouraging the perpetrator to commit criminal damage but may have a 'reasonable' defence that their actions were to prevent a more serious offence.
- The authority under which they were acting should also be taken into account as it might be reasonable to encourage or assist in the commission of an offence if it was done for the benefit of collecting evidence during an investigation by law enforcement agencies. For example, a 15-year-old is tasked by a local authority trading standards department with going into a local shop and purchasing a lottery ticket.

The defendant may be able to plead impossibility as a defence. This is because a person can only be convicted if their acts are genuinely capable of encouraging or assisting a crime, which cannot apply if it is impossible for the main offence to be committed. However, a person could still be convicted of a criminal attempt as an alternative (see 27.2.2). Remember also that a person cannot be convicted of encouraging or assisting a crime for which they are the intended victim (see the introduction to 27.3).

27.5 Answer to Task

TASK 1 The suspect had never had any communication or made any other contact with any of the pupils. As a result, the Court of Appeal concluded that the acts of the suspect were merely preparatory and that the suspect had not attempted to abduct a child or children.

Bibliography and References

Abanonu, R (2018), 'De-escalating police-citizen encounters', *Southern California Review of Law and Social Justice* 27, 239–269.

Abdel-Fattah, H M M (2020), 'Emotional intelligence and emotional stability in crises', *Journal of Psychiatry and Psychiatric Disorders* 4, 56–62.

ACPO (2006), *Murder Investigation Manual*, 3rd edn (Wyboston: National Centre for Policing Excellence).

ACPO (2010), *Guidance on Investigating and Prosecuting Rape*, abridged edn, available at <https://library.college.police.uk/docs/acpo/Guidance-Investigating-Prosecuting-Rape-(Abridged-Edition)-2010.pdf> (accessed 2 March 2023).

ACPO (2011), *Strategy & Supporting Operational Guidance for Policing Prostitution and Sexual Exploitation* available at <http://www.npcc.police.uk/documents/crime/2011/20111102%20CBA%20Policing%20Prostitution%20and%20%20Sexual%20Exploitation%20Strategy_Website_October%202011.pdf> (accessed 1 May 2023).

ACPO (2012a), *ACPO Good Practice Guide for Digital Evidence March 2012* available at <http://library.college.police.uk/docs/acpo/digital-evidence-2012.pdf> (accessed 1 May 2023).

ACPO (2012b), *Guidance on Safeguarding and Investigating the Abuse of Vulnerable Adults* available at <http://library.college.police.uk/docs/acpo/vulnerable-adults-2012.pdf> (accessed 2 March 2023).

ACPO Centrex (2005), *Practice Advice on Core Investigative Doctrine* (Camborne: National Centre for Policing Excellence).

Action Fraud (2018), *What is the National Fraud Intelligence Bureau?* <https://www.actionfraud.police.uk/what-is-national-fraud-intelligence-bureau> (accessed 30 March 2023).

ADASS (2005), *Safeguarding Adults: A National Framework of Standards for good practice and outcomes in adult protection work* available at <https://www.adass.org.uk/AdassMedia/stories/Publications/Guidance/safeguarding.pdf> (accessed 1 May 2023).

Age UK (2018), *The Herbert Protocol* available at <https://www.ageuk.org.uk/bournemouthpooleeastdorset/about-us/latest-news/articles/2020/the-herbert-protocol/> (accessed 30 March 2023).

Aked, J, Marks, N, Cordon, C, Thompson, S (n.d.), *Five Ways to Wellbeing*, New Economics Foundation available at <https://neweconomics.org/uploads/files/five-ways-to-wellbeing-1.pdf> (accessed 17 April 2023).

Åker, T H and Johnson, M S (2020), 'Sexual abuse and violence against people with intellectual disability and physical impairments: Characteristics of police-investigated cases in a Norwegian national sample', *Journal of Applied Research in Intellectual Disabilities* 33(2), 139–145.

Alaggia, R and Wang, S (2020), '"I never told anyone until the #metoo movement": What can we learn from sexual abuse and sexual assault disclosures made through social media?', *Child Abuse and Neglect* 103, 104312.

Alderson, J (1998), *Principled Policing: Protecting the Public with Integrity* (Winchester: Waterside Press).

Alison, E and Alison, L (2020), *Rapport: The Four Ways to Read People*. (United Kingdom: Ebury Publishing).

Allcock, E, Bond, J W, and Smith, L L (2011), 'An investigation into the crime scene characteristics that differentiate a car key burglary from a regular domestic burglary', *International Journal of Police Science and Management* 13(4), 1–11.

Allen, G and Tunnicliffe, R (2021), *Drug Crime: Statistics for England and Wales*, House of Commons Library Research Briefing, 23 December 2021, available at <https://researchbriefings.files.parliament.uk/documents/CBP-9039/CBP-9039.pdf> (accessed 8 February 2023).

Allen, G and Zayed, Y (2022), *Hate Crime Statistics*, House of Commons Library, 2 November 2022, available at <https://researchbriefings.files.parliament.uk/documents/CBP-8537/CBP-8537.pdf> (accessed 18 April 2023).

Allport, G (1954), *The Nature of Prejudice*. (Boston, USA: Addison-Wesley).

Anderson, D (2017), *Attacks in London and Manchester between March and June 2017* available at <https://assets.publishing.service.gov.uk/government/uploads/system/uploads/attachment_data/file/664682/Attacks_in_London_and_Manchester_Open_Report.pdf> (accessed 18 April 2023).

Anderson, D (2019), *2017 Terrorist Attacks M15 and CTP Reviews Implementation Stock-take* available at <https://assets.publishing.service.gov.uk/government/uploads/system/uploads/attachment_data/file/807911/2017_terrorist_attacks_reviews_implementation_stock_take.pdf> (accessed 18 April 2023).

Anderson, J (2008), 'Developing active listening skills', *IDEA Fitness Journal* 5(5), 85–87 available at <https://search.ebscohost.com/login.aspx?direct=true&db=s3h&AN=31972292&site=eds-live> (accessed 20 April 2023).

Andreasen, N (2022), 'What is post-traumatic stress disorder?', *Dialogues in Clinical Neuroscience* 13(3), 240–243.

Andrews, T (2022), 'Co-operation or unification: Is the future of police multi-agency working simply to become one agency?' *The Police Journal: Theory, Practice and Principles* [Preprint] 96(3) available at <https://doi.org/10.1177/0032258x221094494> (accessed 20 April 2023).

Angiolini, E (2015), *Report of the independent review into the investigation and prosecution of rape in London* available at <https://www.cps.gov.uk/sites/default/files/documents/publications/dame_elish_angiolini_rape_review_2015.pdf> (accessed 1 March 2023).

Anti-Slavery Commission (2020), *Training Framework: Identification, Care and Support of Victims and Survivors of Modern Slavery and Human Trafficking* available at <https://www.antislaverycommissioner.co.uk/media/

1468/training-framework-identification-care-and-support-of-victims-and-survivors-of-modern-slavery-and-human-trafficking.pdf> (accessed 14 March 2023).

Anti-Torture Initiative (2021), *Principles on Effective Interviewing for Investigations and Information Gathering* available at <www.interviewingprinciples.com> (accessed 8 March 2023).

Antonakis, J (2011), 'Predictors of leadership: The usual suspects and the suspect traits' in A Bryman, D Collinson, K Grint, B Z Jackson, and M Uhl-Bien (eds), *The Sage Handbook of Leadership* (London: Sage), pp 269–285.

Antrobus, E, Thompson, I, and Ariel, B (2019), 'Procedural justice training for police recruits: results of a randomized controlled trial' *Journal of Experimental Criminology* 15, 29–53.

Ary, D, Jacobs, L C, and Sorensen, C K (2010). *Introduction to research in education*, 8th edn (Wadsworth).

Badshah, N and Carroll, R (2023), 'Off-duty police officer in "critical but stable" condition after Omagh shooting' in *The Guardian* (22 February 2023) available at <https://www.theguardian.com/uk-news/2023/feb/22/off-duty-police-officer-shot-in-omagh-report> (accessed 23 February 2023).

Baldwin, J (1992), 'Video Taping of Police Interviews with Suspects—An Evaluation', *Police Research Series* Paper 1 (London: Home Office).

Barclay, D (2009), 'Using forensic science in major crime inquiries', in F Fraser and R Williams (eds), *Handbook of Forensic Science* (Cullompton: Willan), pp 337–358.

Barlow, C, Walklate, S, Johnson, K, Humphreys, L, and Kirby, S (2018), 'Police responses to coercive control', Commissioned report, Lancaster University, Published Online 8, 76.

BBC (2017), 'Police pay out at least £22m to informants in five years' available at <http://www.bbc.co.uk/news/uk-38902480> (accessed 1 March 2023).

BBC (2018), 'Kent Police stop using crime predicting software' available at <https://www.bbc.co.uk/news/uk-england-kent-46345717> (accessed 16 March 2023).

BBC (2019a), 'BBC News launches "dark web" Tor mirror' available at <https://www.bbc.co.uk/news/technology-50150981> (accessed 2 April 2023).

BBC (2019b), 'London to Cornwall county lines drugs conspiracy "run from prison" ' available at <https://www.bbc.co.uk/news/uk-england-cornwall-49335302> (accessed 16 March 2023).

BBC (2022), 'Pitch invasions: Offenders to receive automatic club ban under new Premier League & EFL measures' available at <https://www.bbc.co.uk/sport/football/62293635> (accessed 5 May 2023).

BBC (2023) 'Met officer dismissed for discriminatory behaviour' available at <https://www.bbc.co.uk/news/uk-england-london-65045539> (accessed 25 March 2023).

Bellanca, F (2020), *The Social Identity Theory*, The Team Building Company available at <https://www.teambuilding.co.uk/thseory/social-identity-theory.html> (accessed 16 April 2023).

Berne, E (1968), *Games People Play: The psychology of human relationships* (Harmondsworth: Penguin).

Bichard, Sir M (2004), *Return to an Address of the Honourable the House of Commons dated 22nd June 2004 for the Bichard Inquiry*, Report HC 653 (London: TSO).

Bishop, C and Bettinson, V (2018), 'Evidencing domestic violence*, including behaviour that falls under the new offence of "controlling or coercive behaviour" ', *The International Journal of Evidence and Proof* 22(1), 3–29, available at <https://doi.org/10.1177/1365712717725535> (accessed 2 May 2023).

Blackburn, R (1995), *The Psychology of Criminal Conduct: Theory, research and practice* (Chichester: Wiley & Sons).

Boag-Munroe, F (2019), 'Career Progression Expectations and Aspirations of Female Police Officers in England and Wales', *Policing: A Journal of Policy and Practice* 13(4).

Bosma, A, Mulder, E, and Pemberton, A (2018), 'The ideal victim through other(s') eyes' in M Duggan (ed), *Revisiting the 'Ideal Victim'* (Bristol: Policy Press) pp 27–42.

Bottoms, A and Tankebe, J (2012), 'Beyond procedural justice: A dialogic approach to legitimacy in criminal justice', *Journal of Criminal Law and Criminology* 102(1), 119–170.

Bowcott, O (2018), 'Solicitor for student in rape case criticises police and CPS', *The Guardian* (30 January 2018) available at <https://www.theguardian.com/uk-news/2018/jan/30/metpolice-and-cps-apologise-to-man-after-collapse-of-case> (accessed 8 March 2023).

Bowers, K J, Johnson, SD, and Pease, K (2004), 'Prospective hot-spotting: The future of crime mapping?', *British Journal of Criminology* 44(5), 641–658.

Bowling, B and Sheptycki, J (2012), *Global Policing* (London: Sage).

Bowling, B, Reiner, R, and Sheptycki, J (2019), *The Politics of the Police*, 5th edn (Oxford: Oxford University Press).

Bowman, T (2019), 'Ireland: Rebellion and counter-insurgency, 1848–1867' in M Lawrence (ed), *Small Wars & Insurgencies* (London: Taylor and Francis), pp 895–912.

Brabban, A and Turkington, D (2002), 'The Search for Meaning: detecting congruence between life events, underlying schema and psychotic symptoms' in A P Morrison (ed), *A Casebook of Cognitive Therapy for Psychosis* (New York: Brunner-Routledge), pp 59–75.

Bradbury, P and Martellozzo, E (2021), ' "Lucky Boy!" Public perceptions of child sexual offending committed by women' *Journal of Victimology and Victim Justice* 4(2), 160–178.

Bradford, B, Jackson, J, and Stanko, E (2009), 'Public encounters with the police: On the use of public opinion surveys to improve contact and confidence', *Policing and Society* 19(1), 20–46.

Braga, AA, Turchan, BS, Papachristos, AV, and Hureau, DM (2019), 'Hot spots policing and crime reduction: an update of an ongoing systematic review and meta-analysis', *Journal of Experimental Criminology* 15(3), 289–311.

Braun, V and Clarke, V (2006), 'Using thematic analysis in psychology', *Qualitative Research in Psychology* (3)2, 77–101.

British Medical Association (2022a), *Vicarious trauma: signs and strategies for coping* available at <https://www.bma.org.uk/advice-and-support/your-wellbeing/vicarious-trauma/vicarious-trauma-signs-and-strategies-for-coping> (accessed 17 April 2023).

British Medical Association (2022b), *The Firearms Licensing Process* available at <https://www.bma.org.uk/advice-and-support/gp-practices/gp-service-provision/the-firearms-licensing-process> (accessed 2 February 2023).

Brook, R and Servatka, M (2016), 'The anticipatory effect of nonverbal communication', *Economic Letters* 144, 45–48.

Brown, J (2021), 'Police powers: An introduction', House of Commons Library Briefing Paper 8637 (21 October), available at <https://researchbriefings.files.parliament.uk/documents/CBP-8637/CBP-8637.pdf> (accessed 14 March 2023).

Brown, R (2010), *Prejudice: Its social psychology*. (Chichester: John Wiley & Sons).

Brown University (2021), *The Cost of War Project*, Watson Institute of Public Affairs available at <https://watson.brown.edu/costsofwar/> (accessed 18 April 2023).

Bruce-Smith, R, Middleton, E, Moreton, K, Smith, J, and Quinton, P (2023), *Ethical decision-making in policing. A rapid evidence assessment*, College of Policing, (March 2023) available from <https://assets.college.police.uk/s3fs-public/2023-03/Rapid-evidence-assessment-ethical-decision-making-in-policing.pdf> (accessed 9 May 2023).

Bryant, R (2019), 'Innate Reasoning and Critical Incident Decision-Making' in M Roycroft and J Roach (eds), *Decision Making in Police Enquiries and Critical Incidents* (London: Palgrave Macmillan), pp 47–67.

Bryant, R and Bryant, S (2014), *Policing Digital Crime* (Farnham: Ashgate).

Bryant, R H (2021), *Contemporary Criminological Theory: Crime and Criminal Behaviour in the Age of Moral Uncertainty* (Abingdon: Routledge).

Bryman, A (2016), *Social Research Methods*, 5th edn (Oxford: Oxford University Press).

Bull, R (2010), 'The investigative interviewing of children and other vulnerable witnesses: Psychological research and working/professional practice', *Legal and Criminological Psychology* 15(1), 5–2.

Bullock, K and Tilley, N (2003), *Crime Reduction and Problem-oriented Policing* (Cullompton: Willan).

Burke, J (2007), *Al Qaeda* (London: Penguin).

Burke, M (1994), 'Homosexuality as deviance: the case of the gay police officer', *British Journal of Criminology* 34(2), 192–203.

Burke, R H (2019), *An Introduction to Criminological Theory*, 5th edn (Abingdon: Routledge).

Burton, M, Evans, R, and Sanders, A (2006), *Are special measures for vulnerable and intimidated witnesses working*? Evidence from the Criminal Justice Agencies. On-line Report 01/06 (Home Office: London).

Butler, L D, Morland, L A, and Leskin, G A (2007), 'Psychological Resilience in the Face of Terrorism' in B Bongar, L M Brown, L E Beutler, J N Breckenridge, and P G Zimbardo (eds), *Psychology of Terrorism*, (Oxford: Oxford University Press), pp 400–417.

Bywaters, P, Bunting, L, Davidson, G, Hanratty, J, Mason, W, McCartan, C, and Steils, N (2016), *The relationship between poverty, child abuse and neglect: An evidence review* (York: Joseph Rowntree Foundation).

Cabinet Office (2022), *National Cyber Strategy 2022* (updated 7 February 2022), available at <https://www.gov.uk/government/publications/national-cyber-strategy-2022/national-cyber-security-strategy-2022> (accessed 2 April 2023).

Caless, B and Owens, J (2016), *Police and Crime Commissioners: The Transformation of Police Accountability* (Bristol: Policy Press).

Caluori, J, Corlett, M, and Stott, J (2020), *County Lines and Looked After Children*, Social Care Institute for Excellence/Crest Advisory available at <https://b9cf6cd4-6aad-4419-a368-724e7d1352b9.usrfiles.com/ugd/b9cf6c_83c53411e21d4d40a79a6e0966ad7ea5.pdf> (accessed 27 April 2023).

Canter, D and Alison, L (2000), *Precursors to Investigative Psychology: Criminal Detection and the Psychology of Crime* (Aldershot: Ashgate).

Canter, D and Fritzon, K (1998), 'Differentiating arsonists: A model of firesetting actions and characteristics', *Legal and Criminological Psychology* 3, 73–96.

Cape, E (2015), 'Transposing the EU Directive on the right to information: a firecracker or a damp squib?', *Criminal Law Review* 1, 48–67.

Caprioli, S and Crenshaw, D A (2017), 'The culture of silencing child victims of sexual abuse: Implications for child witnesses in court', *Journal of Humanistic Psychology* 57(2), 190–209.

Carroll, R (2022), 'Lyra McKee: man jailed for possessing gun used to kill journalist' *The Guardian* (14 September 2022) available at <https://www.theguardian.com/news/2022/sep/14/lyra-mckee-niall-sheerin-jailed-for-possessing-gun-used-to-kill-journalist> (accessed 18 April 2023).

Cartright, A and Roach, J (2020), 'The wellbeing of UK Police: A study of recorded absences from work of UK police employees due to psychological illness and stress using Freedom of Information Act data', *Policing: A Journal of Policy and Practice* 15(2), 1326–1338.

Casey, L (2023), *Final Report, An independent review into the standards of behaviour and internal culture of the Metropolitan Police Service, Baroness Casey of Blackstock DBE CB. March 2023* available at <https://www.met.police.uk/SysSiteAssets/media/downloads/met/about-us/baroness-casey-review/update-march-2023/baroness-casey-review-march-2023.pdf> (accessed 4 April 2023).

CEBCP (2018a), *Evidence-Based Policing Matrix* available at <https://cebcp.org/evidence-based-policing/the-matrix/> (accessed 12 April 2023).

CEBCP (2018b), *MatrixAllStudiesNov2017.xlsx* available at <https://cebcp.org/wp-content/evidence-based-policing/the-matrix/MatrixAllStudiesNov2017.xlsx> (accessed 12 April 2023).

Centerstone, (no date), *Healthy Vs. Unhealthy Coping Mechanisms* International Investment (21 May 2018) available at <https://centerstone.org/our-resources/health-wellness/substance-use-disorder-healthy-vs-unhealthy-coping-mechanisms/> (accessed 17 April 2023).

Centre for Social Justice (2020), *Ethnicity and Disadvantage in Britain*, available at <https://www.centreforsocialjustice.org.uk/wp-content/uploads/2020/11/CSJJ8513-Ethnicity-Poverty-Report-FINAL.pdf> (accessed 27 April 2023).

Centre for Women's Justice (2019), *CWJ Launch Super-Complaint: Police Failure To Use Protective Measures In Cases Involving Violence Against Women And Girls* available at <https://www.centreforwomensjustice.org.uk/news/2019/3/20/cwj-launch-super-complaint-police-failure-to-use-protective-measures-in-cases-involving-violence-against-women-and-girls> (accessed 20 April 2023).

CEOP (2013), 'Welcome to CEOP's thinkuknow website' available at <http://www.thinkuknow.co.uk/> (accessed 23 March 2023).

Chainey, S (2012), *Repeat Victimisation*, JDI Briefs (London: UCL Jill Dando Institute of Security and Crime Science).

Chandan, J S, Thomas, T, Gokhale, K M, Bandyopadhyay, S, Taylor, J, and Nirantharakumar, K (2019), 'The burden of mental ill health associated with childhood maltreatment in the UK, using The Health Improvement Network database: a population-based retrospective cohort study', *The Lancet Psychiatry* 6(11), 926–934.

Chapman, B (2019), 'Body-worn Cameras: What the evidence tells us', *NIJ Journal* 280, available at <https://www.ojp.gov/pdffiles1/nij/252035.pdf> (accessed 19 January 2023).

Chapman, D, Whitfield C, Felitti V, Dube S, Edwards V, and Anda R (2004), 'Adverse childhood experiences and the risk of depressive disorders in adulthood', *Journal of Affective Disorders* 82(2), 217–225.

Chapman, R, Smith, L L, and Bond, J W (2012), 'An investigation into the differentiating characteristics between car key burglars and regular burglars', *Journal of Forensic Science* 57(4), 939–945.

Charman, S (2020), 'Making sense of policing identities: the "deserving" and the "undeserving" in policing accounts of victimisation', *Policing and Society* 30:1, 81–97, available at <DOI: 10.1080/10439463.2019.1601721> (accessed 1 May 2023).

Chenery, S, Henshaw C, and Pease, K (1999), 'Illegal Parking in Disabled Bays: A means of offender targeting', Police and Reducing Crime Briefing Note 1/99 (London: Home Office).

Children's Society (2020), 'What is county lines?' available at <https://www.childrenssociety.org.uk/what-is-county-lines> (accessed 16 March 2023).

Chowdhury, H (2018), 'Kent Police stop using crime predicting software', *The Telegraph* (27 November 2018) available at <https://www.telegraph.co.uk/technology/2018/11/27/kent-police-stop-using-crime-predicting-software/> (accessed 16 March 2023).

Christmas, H and Srivastava, J (2019), *Public Health Approaches in Policing* available at <https://cleph.com.au/application/files/7615/5917/9047/Public_Health_Approaches_in_Policing_2019_England.pdf> (accessed 30 March 2023).

Clarke, C and Milne, R (2001), *A National Evaluation of the PEACE Investigative Interviewing Course*, Home Office Report PRAS/149 (London: Home Office).

Clarke, C, Milne, R, and Bull, R (2011), 'Interviewing suspects of crime: The impact of PEACE training, supervision and the presence of a legal advisor', *Journal of Investigative Psychology and Offender Profiling* 8(2), 149–162.

Clarke, R V (1999), 'Hot Products: Understanding, anticipating and reducing demand for stolen goods', Police Research Series Paper 112 (London: Home Office).

Clemmow, C, Bouhana, N, Marchment, Z, and Gill, P (2022), 'Vulnerability to radicalisation in a general population: a psychometric network approach', *Psychology, Crime & Law* 29(4), 1–29.

Cohen, L and Felson, M (1979), 'Social change and crime rate trends: a routine activity approach', *American Sociological Review* 44(4), 588–608.

College of Policing (2013a), *Risk* available at <https://www.college.police.uk/app/risk/risk> (accessed 27 April 2023).

College of Policing (2013b), *Operational Review* available at <http://www.app.college.police.uk/app-content/operations/operational-review/#officers-conferring> (accessed 1 April 2023).

College of Policing (2013c), *Intelligence collection, development and dissemination* available at <https://www.app.college.police.uk/app-content/intelligence-management/intelligence-cycle/#prison-intelligence> (accessed 6 March 2023).

College of Policing (2014a), *Code of Ethics: A Code of Practice for the Principles and Standards of Professional Behaviour for the Policing Profession of England and Wales* available at <http://www.college.police.uk/What-we-do/Ethics/Documents/Code_of_Ethics.pdf> (accessed 6 March 2023).

College of Policing (2014b) *Forensics and Evidence Gathering: Search powers, procedures and stop and search* available at <https://www.whatdotheyknow.com/request/328410/response/856745/attach/5/20160518%203%20of%203%2004%20Search%20Powers%20Procedures%20and%20Stop%20and%20Search%20v2%2001.pdf?cookie_passthrough=1> (accessed 7 April 2023).

College of Policing (2014c), *Prosecution and Case Management* available at <http://www.app.college.police.uk/app-content/prosecution-and-case-management/charging-and-case-preparation/#summonsing> (accessed 18 March 2023).

College of Policing (2014d), *National Policing Guidelines on KHAT possession for personal use Intervention Framework* available at <https://www.college.police.uk/app/investigation/policing-drugs> (accessed 30 March 2023).

College of Policing (2014e), *Major investigation and public protection responding to child sexual exploitation, risk factors* available at <http://www.app.college.police.uk/app-content/major-investigation-and-public-protection/child-sexual-exploitation/#warning-signs> (accessed 2 March 2023).

College of Policing (2015a), *Leadership Review, Recommendations for delivering leadership at all levels* available at <https://assets.college.police.uk/s3fs-public/2021-03/cop-leadership-review-2015.pdf> (accessed 13 February 2023).

College of Policing (2015b), *Possible justice outcomes following investigation* available at <http://www.app.college.police.uk/app-content/prosecution-and-case-management/justice-outcomes/> (accessed 6 April 2023).

College of Policing (2015c), *Female genital mutilation* available at <https://www.app.college.police.uk/app-content/major-investigation-and-public-protection/female-genital-mutilation/> (accessed 28 April 2023).

College of Policing (2015d), *First response* available at <https://www.app.college.police.uk/app-content/major-investigation-and-public-protection/domestic-abuse/first-response/> (accessed 26 April 2023).

College of Policing (2015e), *Call handler and front counter staff response to a domestic abuse incident* available at <https://www.app.college.police.uk/app-content/major-investigation-and-public-protection/domestic-abuse/call-handler-and-front-counter-staff-response/> (accessed 26 April 2023).

College of Policing (2015f), *College of Policing analysis:Estimating demand on the police service* available at <https://assets.college.police.uk/s3fs-public/2021-03/demand-on-policing-report.pdf> (accessed 1 May 2023).

College of Policing (2016a), *Police Action in Response to Youth Produced Sexual Imagery 'Sexting'* available at <https://www.westsussexscp.org.uk/wp-content/uploads/Police-Action-in-Response-to-youth-produced-sexual-imagerySexting.pdf> (accessed 7 April 2023).

College of Policing (2016b), *Module F6: Police Liaison Team Trainers Guide (version 2.2)* (Coventry: College of Policing).

College of Policing (2017a), *Vetting Code of Practice* available at <https://library.college.police.uk/docs/college-of-policing/Vetting-Code-of-Practice-2017.pdf> (accessed 12 May 2023).

College of Policing (2017b), *Stop and Search* available at <https://www.college.police.uk/app/stop-and-search/stop-and-search> (accessed 16 March 2023).

College of Policing (2017c), *Personal safety manual: Modules 1–15* available at: <https://library.college.police.uk/HeritageScripts/Hapi.dll/search2?searchterm=%22personal%20safety%20manual%22&Fields=%40&Media=PDF&Bool=AND> (accessed 5 March 2023).

College of Policing (2017d), *Civil emergencies* available at <https://www.college.police.uk/app/civil-emergencies> (accessed 5 April 2023).

College of Policing (2017e), *Authorised Professional Practice: Identifying, Assessing and Managing Risk* available at <https://www.college.police.uk/app/major-investigation-and-public-protection/managing-sexual-offenders-and-violent-offenders/identifying-assessing-and-managing-risk> (accessed 11 May 2023).

College of Policing (2018a), *College of Policing published research* available at <https://www.college.police.uk/research/what-works-centre-crime-reduction> (accessed 12 April 2023).

College of Policing (2018b), *Impact Evidence for Engaging Communities* available at <https://assets.college.police.uk/s3fs-public/2021-02/np_rea_summary.pdf.> (accessed 16 March 2023).

College of Policing (2018c), *Neighbourhood Policing Guidelines* available at <https://www.college.police.uk/guidance/neighbourhood-policing> (accessed 17 March 2023).

College of Policing (2018d), *Intelligence Management: Intelligence report* available at <https://www.app.college.police.uk/app-content/intelligence-management/intelligence-report/> (accessed 6 March 2023).

College of Policing (2018e), *Arrest and Other Positive Approaches* available at <https://www.college.police.uk/app/major-investigation-and-public-protection/domesticabuse/arrest-and-other-positive-approaches> (accessed 18 May 2023).

College of Policing (2018f), *Briefing note: For police first responders to a report of rape or sexual assault* available at <http://library.college.police.uk/docs/appref/C909E0418-First-Responders-Brief.pdf> (accessed 2 March 2023).

College of Policing (2019), *Management of police information* available at <https://www.college.police.uk/app/information-management/management-police-information> (accessed 3 May 2023).

College of Policing (2020a), *College of Policing Limited Annual Report and Accounts for the year ended 31 March 2019* available at <https://assets.publishing.service.gov.uk/government/uploads/system/uploads/attachment_data/file/860261/CoP-Annual-Report-and-Accounts-2018-2019-web.pdf> (accessed 4 April 2023).

College of Policing (2020b), *Resources for Reflective Practice* available at <https://whatworks.college.police.uk/About/Pages/What-is-EBP.aspx> (accessed 13 May 2023).

College of Policing (2020c), *Authorised Professional Practice: Conflict Management* available at <https://www.college.police.uk/guidance/conflict-management/conflict-management-skills> (accessed 21 April 2023).

College of Policing (2020d), *Conflict Management Skills* available at <https://www.college.police.uk/guidance/conflict-management/conflict-management-skills#example-model-five-step-appeal-personal-safety-manual> (accessed 22 April 2023).

College of Policing (2020e), *Community engagement and tension* available at <https://www.app.college.police.uk/app-content/major-investigation-and-public-protection/hate-crime/community-engagement-and-tension/> (accessed 6 March 2023).

College of Policing (2020f), *Key trends and implications out to 2040* available at <https://assets.college.police.uk/s3fs-public/2020-08/Future-Operating-Environment-2040-Part1-Trends.pdf> (accessed 6 March 2023).

College of Policing (2021a), *APP on Vetting* available at <https://assets.college.police.uk/s3fs-public/Vetting-APP-2021.pdf> (accessed 12 May 2023).

College of Policing (2021b), *Policing education qualifications framework (PEQF)* available at <https://www.college.police.uk/career-learning/learning/PEQF> (accessed 28 April 2023).

College of Policing (2021c), *College of Policing Limited Annual Report and Accounts for the year ended 31 March 2021* available at <https://assets.college.police.uk/s3fs-public/2021-12/Annual-Report-and-Accounts-2021.pdf> (accessed 30 May 2023).

College of Policing (2021d), *Job-related fitness standards* available at <https://www.college.police.uk/support-forces/health-safety-welfare/job-related-fitness-standards> (accessed 17 April 2023).

College of Policing (2021e), *Discovery report into workplace adjustments 2021* available at <https://assets.college.police.uk/s3fs-public/2021-08/discovery-report-workplace-adjustments.pdf> (accessed 17 April 2023).

College of Policing (2021f), *Development resources for leaders across policing* available at <https://www.college.police.uk/article/development-resources-leaders-across-policing#:~:text=Everyone%20in%20policing%20has%20a,a%20large%20team%20or%20department> (accessed 4 April 2023).

College of Policing (2021g), *Briefing note for adults at risk: initial response and safeguarding* available at <https://library.college.police.uk/docs/college-of-policing/Briefing-note-adults-at-risk-initial-response-2021.pdf> (accessed 3 May 2023).

College of Policing (2021h) *Recognising and Responding to Vulnerability-related Risks* available at <https://assets.college.police.uk/s3fs-public/2021-11/Report-on-refresh-vulnerability-review-of-reviews.pdf> (accessed 11 May 2023).

College of Policing (2021i), *Knife crime: A problem solving guide* available at <https://assets.college.police.uk/s3fs-public/2021-11/Knife-crime-a-problem-solving-guide.pdf> (accessed 7 March 2023).

College of Policing (2022a), *Fundamental review of the College of Policing: Full report* available at <https://assets.college.police.uk/s3fs-public/2022-02/Fundamental-review-of-the-College-of-Policing-full-report.pdf> (accessed 4 April 2023).

College of Policing (2022b), *Mental health* available at <https://www.app.college.police.uk/app-content/mental-health/> (accessed 19 April 2023).

College of Policing (2022c), *Police Covenant published to support policing community* available at <https://www.college.police.uk/article/police-covenant-published-support-policing-community> (accessed 17 April 2023).

College of Policing (2022d), *Domestic Abuse Risk Assessment* (*DARA*) available at <https://library.college.police.uk/docs/college-of-policing/Domestic-Abuse-Risk-Assessment-2022.pdf> (accessed 2 May 2023).

College of Policing (2022e), *Possible justice outcomes following investigation* available at <https://www.college.police.uk/app/prosecution-and-case-management/possible-justice-outcomes-following-investigation> (accessed 1 April 2023).

College of Policing (2022f), *Investigating child abuse and safeguarding children* available at <https://www.college.police.uk/app/major-investigation-and-public-protection/investigating-child-abuse-and-safeguarding-children> (accessed 3 May 2023).

College of Policing (2022g), *Investigating Fraud* available at <https://www.college.police.uk/app/investigation/investigating-fraud> (accessed 25 March 2023).

College of Policing (2023a), *Barred List*, available at <https://www.college.police.uk/ethics/barred-list> (accessed 16 March 2023).

College of Policing (2023b), *National Decision Model*, available at <https://www.college.police.uk/app/national-decision-model/national-decision-model#reviewing-decision-making> (accessed 6 April 2023).

College of Policing (2023c), *Leadership Expectations*, available at <https://www.college.police.uk/guidance/leadership-expectations> (accessed 12 April 2023).

College of Policing (2023d), *National Level of Policing*, available at <https://profdev.college.police.uk/professional-profiles/profiles/national-level-policing/> (accessed 13 April 2023).

College of Policing (2023e), *Tutor/Tutor Constable*, available at <https://profdev.college.police.uk/professional-profile/tutor-tutor-constable/> (accessed 13 April 2023).

College of Policing (2023f), *Wellbeing* available at <https://www.college.police.uk/support forces/health-safety-welfare/wellbeing> (accessed 22 April 2023).

College of Policing (2023g), *Code of Ethics – Have Your Say* available at <https://www.college.police.uk/article/code-ethics-have-your-say> (accessed 12 Apri 2023).

College of Policing (2023h), *Competency and Values Framework: We are emotionally aware* available at <https://profdev.college.police.uk/competency-values/we-are-emotionally-aware/#why-is-it-important> (accessed 21 April 2023).

College of Policing (2023i), *Partnership working and multi-agency responses/mechanisms* available at <https://www.college.police.uk/app/major-investigation-and-public-protection/domestic-abuse/partnership-working-and-multi-agency-responsesmechanisms> (accessed 20 April 2023).

College of Policing (2023j), *Missing Persons* available at <https://www.college.police.uk/app/major-investigation-and-public-protection/missing-persons/missing-persons> (accessed 3 May 2023).

College of Policing (2023k), *Working with victims and witnesses* available at <https://www.college.police.uk/app/investigation/working-victims-and-witnesses#:~:text=A%20witness%20is%20a%20person,website%20in%20the%20same%20tab> (accessed 14 March 2023).

College of Policing (2023l), *Forced Marriage and Honour-based Abuse* available at <https://www.college.police.uk/app/major-investigation-and-public-protection/forced-marriage-and-honour-based-abuse> (accessed 18 May 2023).

Connell, NM, Miggans, K, and McGloin, JM (2008), 'Can a community policing initiative reduce serious crime? A local evaluation', *Police Quarterly* 11(2), 127–150.

Coomber, R and Moyle, I (2018), 'The Changing Shape of Street-level heroin and crack supply in England: Commuting, Holidaying and Cuckooing Drug Dealers across "County Lines"', *British Journal of Criminology* 58, 1323–1342.

Cooper, D and Roberts, P (2005), *Special measures for vulnerable and intimidated witnesses: An analysis of crown prosecution service monitoring data* (London: CPS).

Cope, N, Fielding, N, and Innes, M (2005), 'The appliance of science? The theory and practice of crime intelligence analysis', *British Journal of Criminology* 45(1), 39–55.

Copley, S (2011), *Reflective Practice for Policing Students* (London: SAGE Publications Limited).

Copper-Ind, C (2018), *Fraud epidemic costs the UK £110bn annually* available at <https://www.internationalinvestment.net/internationalinvestment/news/3500818/fraud-epidemic-costs-uk-gbp110bn-annually-report> (accessed 16 March 2023).

Cornish, D B and Clarke, R V (1986), *The Reasoning Criminal: Rational Choice Perspectives on Offending* (New York: Springer-Verlag).

Cornwall Live (2019), 'The full story of how a gang flooded Cornwall with heroin and crack from London' (13 September 2019) available at <https://www.cornwalllive.com/news/cornwall-news/full-story-how-gang-flooded-3275472> (accessed 16 March 2023).

Cosgrove, F and Ramshaw, P (2015), 'It is what you do as well as the way that you do it: the value and deployment of PCSOs in achieving public engagement', *Policing and Society* 25(1), 77–96.

Cottrell, S (2019), *The Study Skills Handbook* (Macmillan Study Skills) (London: Red Globe Press).

Council of Europe (2001), *Convention on Cybercrime*, Budapest, 23.XI.2001, European Treaty Series, ETA 185, available at <https://www.europarl.europa.eu/meetdocs/2014_2019/documents/libe/dv/7_conv_budapest_/7_conv_budapest_en.pdf> (accessed 6 May 2023).

Council of Europe (2022), *Enhanced co-operation and disclosure of electronic evidence: new countries join additional Protocol to Cybercrime Convention* available at <https://www.coe.int/en/web/portal/-/enhanced-co-operation-and-disclosure-of-electronic-evidence-new-countries-join-additional-protocol-to-cybercrime-convention> (accessed 26 February 2023).

Cox, LJ (2012), *Preliminary ruling R v Halliwell* (9 May, Bristol Crown Court), Judiciary of England and Wales media briefing report (February and May 2012) available at <https://www.judiciary.gov.uk/wp-content/uploads/JCO/Documents/Judgments/halliwell-ruling.pdf> (accessed 27 April 2023).

CPS (2017a), *Perjury* available at <https://www.cps.gov.uk/legal-guidance/public-justice-offences-incorporating-charging-standard> (accessed 19 March 2023).

CPS (2017b), *Offences Against the Person, Incorporating Charging Standard* available at <https://www.cps.gov.uk/legal-guidance/offences-against-person-incorporating-charging-standard> (accessed 20 March 2023).

CPS (2018a), *Disclosure Manual* available at <https://www.cps.gov.uk/legal-guidance/disclosure-manual> (accessed 29 April 2023).

CPS (2018b), *Joint Review Disclosure Plan* available at <https://www.cps.gov.uk/publication/joint-review-disclosure-process-case-r-v-allan> (accessed 16 March 2023).

CPS (2018c), *The Code for Crown Prosecutors* available at <http://www.cps.gov.uk/publication/code-crown-prosecutors> (accessed 16 March 2023).

CPS (2018d), *Honour-Based Violence and Forced Marriage* available at <https https://www.cps.gov.uk/legal-guidance/so-called-honour-based-abuse-and-forced-marriage-guidance-identifying-an> (accessed 12 April 2023).

CPS (2019a), *Cybercrime – prosecution guidance* (updated 26 September 2019), available at <https://www.cps.gov.uk/legal-guidance/cybercrime-prosecution-guidance> (accessed 31 March 2023)

CPS (2019b), *CPS legal guidance on Hearsay* (updated 3 September 2019), available at <https://www.cps.gov.uk/legal-guidance/hearsay> (accessed 12 March 2023).

CPS (2019c), *CPS legal guidance on Theft Act Offences* (updated 25 November 2019), available at <https://www.cps.gov.uk/legal-guidance/theft-act-offences> (accessed 14 March 2023).

CPS (2019d), *CPS legal guidance on Prostitution and Exploitation of Prostitution* (updated 4 January 2019), available at <https://www.cps.gov.uk/legal-guidance/prostitution-and-exploitation-prostitution> (accessed 2 March 2023).

CPS (2020a), *Charging, (the Director's Guidance)*, 6th edn (December 2020), available at <https://www.cps.gov.uk/legal-guidance/charging-directors-guidance-sixth-edition-december-2020> (accessed 14 March 2023).

CPS (2022a), *National Disclosure Improvement Plan (NDIP) Report on Phase Two - March 2021*, available at <https://www.cps.gov.uk/publication/national-disclosure-improvement-plan-ndip-report-phase-two-march-2021> (accessed 13 January 2023).

CPS (2022b), *Expert Evidence* available at <https://www.cps.gov.uk/legal-guidance/expert-evidence> (accessed 3 May 2023).

CPS (2022c), *County Lines Offending, Legal Guidance, Drug Offences* available at <https://www.cps.gov.uk/legal-guidance/county-lines-offending> (accessed 20 January 2023).

CPS (2023a), *Terrorism* available at <https:www.cps.gov.uk/crime-info/terrorism> (accessed 23 March 2023).

CPS (2023b), *Restorative Justice* available at <https://www.cps.gov.uk/legal-guidance/restorative-justice> (accessed 6 May 2023).

CPS (no date), *A guide for victims: What happens when a case comes to the CPS* available at <https://www.cps.gov.uk/sites/default/files/documents/publications/A-guide-for-victims-what-happens-when-a-case-comes-to-the-CPS-English.pdf> (accessed 14 March 2023).

CPS (no date), *Witness Intimidation* available at <https://www.cps.gov.uk/cps-page/witness-intimidation> (accessed 3 May 2023).

CPS and MPS (2015a), *Joint CPS and Police Action Plan on Rape* available at <https://www.cps.gov.uk/sites/default/files/documents/publications/rape_action_plan_april_2015.pdf> (accessed 2 March 2023).

CPS and MPS (2015b), *What is Consent?* available at <https://www.cps.gov.uk/sites/default/files/documents/publications/what_is_consent_v2.pdf> (accessed 1 May 2023).

CPS and NPCC (2022), *CPS legal guidance on Offensive Weapons and Knife Crime* available at <https://www.cps.gov.uk/legal-guidance/offensive-weapons-knife-crime-practical-guidance> (accessed 2 February 2023).

Crawshaw, R, Devlin, B, and Williamson, T (1998), *Human Rights and Policing: Standards for good behaviour and a strategy for change* (The Hague: Kluwer Law International).

Crelinsten, R and Ozkut, I (2000), 'Counterterrorism Policy in Fortress Europe: Implications for Human Rights' in F Reinares (ed), *European Democracies Against Terrorism: Governmental Policies and Intergovernmental Cooperation* (Aldershot, UK: Aldgate), pp 245–271.

Crelinsten, R (2002), 'Analysing terrorism and counter-terrorism: A communication model', *Terrorism and Political Violence* 14(2), 77–122.

—— (2009), *Counterterrorism* (Cambridge: Polity).

Crenshaw, K W (1989), 'Demarginalizing the Intersection of Race and Sex: A Black Feminist Critique of Antidiscrimination Doctrine, Feminist Theory, and Antiracist Politics', *University of Chicago Legal Forum* 1989(1), 139–167.

Creswell, J W (2018), *Educational Research: Planning, Conducting, and Evaluating Quantitative and Qualitative Research*, 6th edn (Cambridge: Pearson).

Croall, H (2011), *Crime and Society in Britain*, 2nd edn (Harlow: Pearson Education).

CSEW (2022), *Crime in England and Wales: year ending March 2022* available at <https://www.ons.gov.uk/peoplepopulationandcommunity/crimeandjustice/articles/domesticabuseprevalenceandtrendsenglandandwales/yearendingmarch2022> (accessed 20 April 2023).

CSIS (2022), *Significant Cyber Incidents*, available at <https://www.csis.org/programs/strategic-technologies-program/significant-cyber-incidents> (accessed 2 April 2023).

Cuff, B M P, Brown, S, Taylor, L, and Howat, D J (2016), 'Empathy: A Review of the Concept' *Emotion Review* 8(2), 144–153.

Dalfonzo, V A and Deitrick, M L (2015), 'An Evaluation Tool for Crisis Negotiators', *Law Enforcement Bulletin* available at <https://leb.fbi.gov/articles/focus/focus-on-training-an-evaluation-tool-for-crisis-negotiators> (accessed 21 April 2023).

Daly, M (2003), 'My Life as a secret policeman' BBC (21 October 2003) available at <http://news.bbc.co.uk/1/hi/magazine/3210614.stm> (accessed 6 April 2023).

Da Silva, C and Leach, A M (2013), 'Detecting deception in second-language speakers', *Legal and Criminological Psychology* 18, 115–127.

Davies, L E, Brooks, M, and Braithwaite, E C (2022), 'Compassion fatigue, compassion satisfaction, and burnout, and their associations with anxiety and depression in UK police officers: A mixed method analysis', *The Police Journal* 0(0) 1–21 available at <https://doi.org/10.1177/0032258X221106107> (accessed 17 April 2023).

Davis, M (2014), 'Professional Ethics without Moral Theory: A Pratical Guide for the Perplexed Non-Philosopher', *Journal of Applied Ethics and Philosophy* 6, 1–9.

Dawda, S, Janjeva, A, and Moiseienko, A (2021), 'The UK's Response to Cyber Fraud. A Strategic Vision', *RUSI Occasional Paper* (London: Royal United Services Institute for Defence and Security Studies), available at <https://www.rusi.org/explore-our-research/publications/occasional-papers/uks-response-cyber-fraud-strategic-vision> (accessed 8 May 2023).

Dawson, P A and Williams, E (2009), 'Reflections from a police research Unit—An Inside Job', *Policing—an International Journal of Police Strategies & Management* 3, 373–380.

Dearden, L (2020), 'Teenage neo-Nazi "obsessed" with mass shootings jailed for preparing acts of terrorism' *The Independent* (2 October 2020) available at <https://www.independent.co.uk/news/uk/crime/neo-nazis-uk-rugby-teenager-paul-dunleavy-feuerkrieg-division-jailed-b1647248.html> (accessed 15 February 2023).

Dehagani, R (2019), *Vulnerability in Police Custody. Police decision-making and the appropriate adult safeguard* (Abingdon: Routledge).

Delagrange, M (2018), 'The Path Towards Greater Efficiency and Effectiveness in the Victim Application Processes of the International Criminal Court', *International Criminal Law Review* 18(3), 540–562.

Delattre, E J (2004) 'Justice, Safety and the Limits to the Tolerable', in P Villiers and R Adlam (eds), *Policing a Safe, Just and Tolerant Society: An International Model for Policing*. (Winchester: Waterside Press), pp 24–35.

Delattre, E J (2011), *Character and Cops. Ethics and Policing*, 6th edn (Lanham, Maryland: Rowman & Littlefield).

Denov, M S (2004), 'The Long-Term Effects of Child Sexual Abuse by Female Perpetrators: A Qualitative Study of Male and Female Victims', *Journal of Interpersonal Violence* 19(10), 1137–1156.

Department for Constitutional Affairs (2007), *Mental Capacity Act 2005. Code of Practice* (London: TSO).

Department for Transport (2011), *Instructions for the Completion of Road Accident Reports from non-CRASH Sources: STATS20* available at <https://assets.publishing.service.gov.uk/government/uploads/system/uploads/attachment_data/file/995423/stats20-2011.pdf> (accessed 22 March 2023).

Department for Transport (2013), *Driving under the influence of drugs: Report from the Expert Panel on Drug Driving* available at <https://www.gov.uk/government/uploads/system/uploads/attachment_data/file/167971/drug-driving-expert-panel-report.pdf> (accessed 26 March 2023).

Department for Transport (2020), *Reported road casualties in Great Britain: main results 2019* available at <https://www.gov.uk/government/statistics/reported-road-casualties-great-britain-annual-report-2020/reported-road-casualties-great-britain-annual-report-2020> (accessed 23 March 2023).

Department for Transport (2021a), *Reported road casualties in Great Britain: main results 2020* available at <https://www.gov.uk/government/statistics/reported-road-casualties-great-britain-annual-report-2020/reported-road-casualties-great-britain-annual-report-2020> (accessed 16 March 2023).

Department for Transport (2021b), *Guide to severity adjustments for reported road casualties Great Britain* available at <https://www.gov.uk/government/publications/guide-to-severity-adjustments-for-reported-road-casualty-statistics/guide-to-severity-adjustments-for-reported-road-casualties-great-britain> (accessed 7 February 2023).

Department for Transport (2022a), *Average value of prevention per reported casualty and per reported road collision: Great Britain (RAS4001)* available at <https://assets.publishing.service.gov.uk/government/uploads/system/uploads/attachment_data/file/1106330/ras4001.ods> (accessed 7 February 2023).

Department for Transport (2022b), *Factors contributing to collisions and casualties: Collisions, casualties and road user type (RAS0701)* available at <https://assets.publishing.service.gov.uk/government/uploads/system/uploads/attachment_data/file/1106324/ras0701.ods> (accessed 7 February 2023).

Department for Transport (2022c), *Reported road casualties Great Britain, annual report 2021* available at <https://www.gov.uk/government/statistics/reported-road-casualties-great-britain-annual-report-2021/reported-road-casualties-great-britain-annual-report-2021> (accessed 7 February 2023).

Department of Health (2015), *Mental Health Act 1983 Code of Practice* available at <https://www.gov.uk/government/news/new-mental-health-act-code-of-practice> (accessed 19 April 2023).

Department of Health (2017), *Guidance for the implementation of changes to police powers and places of safety provisions in the Mental Health Act 1983* available at <https://www.gov.uk/government/uploads/system/uploads/attachment_data/file/656025/Guidance_on_Police_Powers.PDF> (accessed 7 February 2023).

Disabled Police Association (no date), 'Welcome to the Disabled Police Association' available at <http://www.disabledpolice.info/> (accessed 17 April 2023).

Dobby, J, Anscombe, J, and Tuffin, R (2004), 'Police leadership: expectations and impact', Home Office Online Report 20/04 available at: <https://citeseerx.ist.psu.edu/document?repid=rep1&type=pdf&doi=4d926359637557561ca063e54cd63e67c7605c8d> (accessed 16 March 2023).

Dodd, V (2017), 'Met police deny systemic failure in rape case disclosures', *The Guardian* (20 December 2017), available at <https://www.theguardian.com/uk-news/2017/dec/20/met-police-deny-systemic-failure-in-case-disclosures> (accessed 16 February 2023).

Dovidio, J F, Hewstone, M, Glick, P, and Esses, V M (2010), *The Sage Handbook of Prejudice, Stereotyping and Discrimination*. (London: Sage Publications Ltd).

Doyle, J (2008), 'Barriers and facilitators of multidisciplinary team working: a review', *Paediatric Nursing* 20(2), 26–29.

Drijber, B C, Reijnders, U J L, and Ceelen, M (2013), 'Male victims of domestic violence', *Journal of Family Violence* 28, 173–178.

Drollinger, T and Comer, L B (2013), 'Salesperson's listening ability as an antecedent to relationship selling', *Journal of Business & Industrial Marketing* 28(1), 50–59.

Duggan, M (2018), (ed) *Revisiting the 'ideal victim': Developments in Critical Victimology* (Bristol: Policy Press).

Durkee, A (2022), 'Attacks On Abortion Providers Surged In 2021, Report Finds As Supreme Court Overturns Roe V. Wade', *Forbes* (24 June 2022) available at <https://www.forbes.com/sites/alisondurkee/2022/06/24/attacks-on-abortion-providers-surged-in-2021-report-finds-ahead-of-roe-v-wade-ruling/> (accessed 31 March 2023).

Eck, J E, Lee, Y J, O, S H, and Martinez, N (2017), 'Compared to what? Estimating the relative concentration of crime at places using systematic and other reviews', *Crime Science: An Interdisciplinary Journal* 6(8), available at <https://crimesciencejournal.springeropen.com/articles/10.1186/s40163-017-0070-4> (accessed 15 March 2023).

ECPAT International (2016), *Terminology Guidelines for the Protection of Children from Sexual Exploitation and Sexual Abuse*, available at <https://www.ecpat.org.uk/Handlers/Download.ashx?IDMF=767a10a9-bd87-4531-b901-ae86dbb3e795> (accessed 31 March 2023).

Eddlestone, J (2012), *Blind Justice: Miscarriages of Justice in 20th Century Britain*, e-book (London: Bibliofile Publishers).

Ede, R and Shepherd, E (2000), *Active Defence: Lawyer's guide to police and defence investigation and prosecution and defence disclosure in criminal cases* (London: Law Society Publishing).

Ekblom, P (2001), *The Conjunction of Criminal Opportunity: A framework for crime reduction toolkits* (UK National Crime Reduction website) available at <http://webarchive.nationalarchives.gov.uk/20100413151441/crimereduction.homeoffice.gov.uk/learningzone/cco.htm> (accessed 15 March 2023).

Ellison, L (2002), 'Prosecuting domestic violence without victim participation', *The Modern Law Review* 65(6), 834–858.

Ellison, L and Munro, V E (2017), 'Taking trauma seriously: Critical reflections on the criminal justice process', *The International Journal of Evidence & Proof* 21(3), 183–208.

Emsley, C (1991), *The English Police: A Political and Social History* (Harlow: Pearson Education).

Enang, I, Murray, J, Dougall, N, Wooff, A, Heyman, I, and Aston, E (2019), 'Defining and assessing vulnerability within law enforcement and public health organisations: a scoping review', *Health & Justice* 7(1), 1–13.

Equality and Human Rights Commission (2010), *Stop and Think: A Critical Review of the Use of Stop and Search Powers in England and Wales* (London: EHRC).

Europol (2021), 'World's most dangerous malware EMOTET disrupted through global action' (updated 21 January 2021), available at <https://www.europol.europa.eu/media-press/newsroom/news/world%E2%80%99s-most-dangerous-malware-emotet-disrupted-through-global-action> (accessed 31 March 2023).

Everson, S and Pease, K (2001), 'Crime against the same person and place: Detection opportunity and offender targeting' in G Farrell and K Pease (eds), *Crime Prevention Studies*, vol 12 (Monsey, NY: CRC Press).

Experian (2018), 'New Experian research shows online fraud continues to be a top concern across the globe' (24 January 2018) available at <https://www.experianplc.com/media/news/2018/84-of-businesses-could-reduce-fraud-risk-if-certain-about-customers-identity/> (accessed 12 March 2023).

Fang, Z, Cerna-Turoff, I, Zhang, C, Lu, M, Lachman, J M, and Barlow, J (2022), 'Global estimates of violence against children with disabilities: an updated systematic review and meta-analysis', *The Lancet Child & Adolescent Health* (6)5, 313–323.

Farrall, S and Gadd, D (2004), 'Evaluating crime fears: A research note on a pilot study to improve the measurement of the "Fear of Crime" as a performance indicator', *Evaluation* 10(4), 493–502.

Felson, M (2002), *Crime and Everyday Life*, 3rd edn (Thousand Oaks, CA: Sage Publications).

Femicide Census (2020), *Femicide Census* available at <https://www.femicidecensus.org/wp-content/uploads/2022/02/010998-2020-Femicide-Report_V2.pdf> (accessed 9 April 2023).

Fenton, S (2018), *The Good Friday Agreement* (London: Biteback Publishing).

Ferris, C (2020), *Behind the Enigma: The Authorised History of GCHQ, Britain's Secret Cyber Intelligence Agency* (London: Bloomsbury Publishing).

Fetzek, S and Mazo, J (2014), 'Climate, Scarcity and Conflict, Survival' *Global Politics and Strategy* 56(5), 143–170.

Fielding, N (1999), 'Policing's Dark Secret: The Career Paths of Ethnic Minority Officers' *Sociological Research Online* 4(1), 129–136.

Figley, C R (1995), 'Compassion fatigue: Toward a new understanding of the costs of caring' in B H Stamm (ed), *Secondary traumatic stress: Self-care issues for clinicians, researchers, and educators* (Derwood MD: The Sidran Press), pp 3–28.

Filley, A C (1982), 'Problem Definition and Conflict Management' in G B J Bomers and R B Peterson (eds), *Conflict Management and Industrial Relations* (Dordrecht: Springer) available at <https://doi.org/10.1007/978-94-017-1132-6_4> (accessed 18 April 2023).

Fineman, K (1995), 'A model for the qualitative analysis of child and adult fire deviant behaviour', *American Journal of Forensic Psychology* 13, 31–60.

Fineman, M A (2010), 'The vulnerable subject and the responsive state' *Emory University School of Law LJ* 60, 251.

Fisher, B A (1970), 'Decision emergence: Phases in group decision-making', *Speech Monographs* 37:1, 53–66,

Foley, J and Massey, K L D (2021), 'The "cost" of caring in policing: From burnout to PTSD in police officers in England and Wales', *The Police Journal* 94(3), 298–315.

Ford, J (2017), 'Complex trauma and developmental trauma disorder in adolescence', *Adolescent Psychiatry* 7(4), 220–235.

Ford, J and Delker, B (2017), (eds) *Polyvictimization: Adverse Impacts in Childhood and Across the Lifespan* (London: Routledge).

Ford, K, Newbury, A, Meredith, Z, Evans, J, Hughes, K, Roderick, J, Davies, A, and Bellis, M (2019), 'Understanding the outcome of police safeguarding notifications to social services in South Wales', *The Police Journal* 93(2), 1–22.

Forensic Science Regulator (2021), *Codes of Practice and Conduct for forensic science providers and practitioners in the Criminal Justice System*, Issue 7 (Updated March 2021), available at <https://www.gov.uk/government/publications/forensic-science-providers-codes-of-practice-and-conduct-2021> (accessed 30 March 2023).

Foster, G (2015), *The Irish Civil War and Society (* New York: Palgrave Macmillan).

Fridin, M, Barliya, A, Schechtman, E, de Gelder, B, and Flash, T (2009), 'Computational model and human perception of emotional body language (EBL)'. In Proceeding of the Symposium on Mental States, Emotions and their Embodiment. Edinburgh, Scotland available at <https://www.academia.edu/64940583/Computational_model_and_the_human_perception_of_emotional_body_language_EBL_> (accessed 5 March 2023).

Furlong, G T (2020), *The Conflict Resolution Toolbox: Models and Maps for Analyzing, Diagnosing, and Resolving Conflict* (Chichester: John Wiley & Sons).

Gaj, M (2018), 'Selected leadership qualities', *Scientific Journal of the Military University of Land Forces* 50(4), 140–151.

Gander, S (2023), *The Essential Police Constable Degree Apprenticeship EPA Handbook* (St Albans: Critical Publishing).

Gechkova, T and Kaleeva, T (2021), Protection of the Critical Infrastructure – Behavioural Analysis, KNOWLEDGE – *International Journal* 48(1), 205–208.

Gibbs, G (1988), *Learning by doing: A guide to teaching and learning methods* (Oxford: Oxford Further Education Unit).

Goffee, R and Jones, G (2000), 'Why should anyone be led by you?' (eds), *Communication, Relationships and Care: A Reader*, pp 354–360.

Goodman, G S and Quas, J A (2008), 'Repeated interviews and children's memory: It's more than just how many', *Current Directions in Psychological Science* 17(6), 386–390.

Gill, C, Weisburd, D, Telep, CW, Vitter, Z, and Bennett, T (2014), 'Community-oriented policing to reduce crime, disorder and fear and increase satisfaction and legitimacy among citizens: A systematic review', *Journal of Experimental Criminology* 10(4), 399–428.

Gill, P and Phythian, M (2012), *Intelligence in an Insecure World*, 2nd edn (Cambridge: Polity).

Given, L M (ed) (2008), *The Sage Encyclopaedia of Qualitative Research Methods*. (London: Sage Publications).

Glasl, F (1982), 'The Process of Conflict Escalation and Roles of Third Parties' in G B J Bomers and R B Petersons (eds), *Conflict Management and Industrial Relations* (Dordrecht: Springer Netherlands), pp 119–140.

GMC (2012), *Continuing professional Development Guidance for all doctors* available at <https://www.gmc-uk.org/-/media/documents/cpd-guidance-for-all-doctors-0316_pdf-56438625.pdf> (accessed 4 April 2023).

Goldstein, H (1990), *Problem-orientated Policing* (New York: McGraw Hill).

Goleman, D (1995), *Emotional intelligence* (Bantam Books).

Goodall, K (2022), 'Trauma Informed Policing', Centre for Research and Evidence on Security Threats available at <https://crestresearch.ac.uk/comment/trauma-informed-policing/> (accessed 17 April 2023).

gov.uk (1351), *Treason Act*, (c.2). Edw. III. available from <https://www.legislation.gov.uk/aep/Edw3Stat5/25/2> (accessed 30 January 2023).

gov.uk (1969), *The Firearms (Dangerous Air Weapons) Rules*, available at <https://www.legislation.gov.uk/uksi/1969/47/made> (accessed 3 April 2023).

gov.uk (1974), *Prevention of Terrorism (Temporary Provisions) Act 1974* (c.56) available at <https://www.legislation.gov.uk/ukpga/1974/56/enacted#:~:text=1974%20CHAPTER%2056,terrorism%2C%20and%20for%20connected%20purposes> (accessed 20 February 2023).

gov.uk (1984), *Road Traffic Regulation Act* available at <https://www.legislation.gov.uk/ukpga/1984/27/contents> (accessed 20 May 2023).

gov.uk (1986), *The Road Vehicles (Construction and Use) Regulations 1986* available at <https://www.legislation.gov.uk/uksi/1986/1078/contents/made> (accessed 20 May 2023).

gov.uk (1988), *Road Traffic Offenders Act 1988* available at <https://www.legislation.gov.uk/ukpga/1988/53/contents> (accessed 20 May 2023).

gov.uk (1989a), *Security Services Act 1989* (c.5) [Online] available at <https://www.legislation.gov.uk/ukpga/1989/5/contents> (accessed 30 January 2023).

gov.uk (1989b), *Road Vehicles Lighting Regulations 1989* available at <https://www.legislation.gov.uk/uksi/1989/1796/contents/made> (accessed 20 May 2023).

gov.uk (1994), *Intelligence Services Act 1994*. (c.13). [Online] available at <https://www.legislation.gov.uk/ukpga/1994/13/section/1> (accessed 30 January 2023).

gov.uk (1997), *Zebra, Pelican and Puffin Pedestrian Crossings Regulations 1997* available at <https://www.legislation.gov.uk/uksi/1997/2400/contents/made> (accessed 24 May 2023).

gov.uk (2000), *Terrorism Act 2000*, (c.11) [Online] available at <https://www.legislation.gov.uk/ukpga/2000/11/contents> (accessed 30 January 2023).

gov.uk (2010), *Equality Act 2010* available at <https://www.legislation.gov.uk/ukpga/2010/15/contents> (accessed 22 April 2023).

gov.uk (2015), *Counter-Terrorism and Border Security Act 2015*, available at <https://www.gov.uk/government/collections/counter-terrorism-and-security-bill> (accessed 18 April 2023).

gov.uk (2016), *GD8 – Youth Produced Sexual Imagery - Guidance for Disclosure [Online]* available at <https://assets.publishing.service.gov.uk/government/uploads/system/uploads/attachment_data/file/578979/GD8_-_Sexting_Guidance.pdf> (accessed 7 April 2023).

gov.uk (2017), *The key principles of vehicle cyber security for connected and automated vehicles* available at <https://www.gov.uk/government/publications/principles-of-cyber-security-for-connected-and-automated-vehicles> (accessed 16 March 2023).

gov.uk (2018a), *Data Protection Act*, available at <https://www.legislation.gov.uk/ukpga/2018/12/contents/enacted> (accessed 5 May 2023).

gov.uk (2018b), *Counter Terrorism Strategy*, available at <https://www.gov.uk/government/publications/counter-terrorism-strategy-contest-2018> (accessed 18 April 2023).

gov.uk (2019), *About the Emergency Services Network* available at <https://www.gov.uk/government/publications/the-emergency-services-mobile-communications-programme/emergency-services-network> (accessed 16 March 2023).

gov.uk (2021), *Review of the controlling or coercive behaviour offence (2021) GOV.UK* available at <https://www.gov.uk/government/publications/review-of-the-controlling-or-coercive-behaviour-offence/review-of-the-controlling-or-coercive-behaviour-offence> (accessed 21 March 2023).

gov.uk (2022), *Police, Crime, Sentencing and Courts Act 2022* available at <https://www.legislation.gov.uk/ukpga/2022/32/contents/enacted> (accessed 25 May 2023).

Grimshaw, A D (ed) (1990), *Conflict talk: Sociolinguistic investigations of arguments in conversations*. (Cambridge: CUP Archive).

Grint, K (2010), *Leadership: A very short introduction* (Oxford: OUP).

Grove, LE and Farrell, G (2011), *Repeat victimization*, OxfordBibliographies Online (Criminology), edited by R Rosenfeld (www.oxfordbibliographiesonline.com) (1) (PDF) Preventing Repeat Victimization: A Systematic Review available at <https://www.researchgate.net/publication/274312621_Preventing_Repeat_Victimization_A_Systematic_Review> (accessed 13 March 2023).

Guardian, The (2019), ' "I agreed because I was scared": boy, 16, on county lines ordeal' (3 September 2019) available at <https://www.theguardian.com/uk-news/2019/sep/03/boy-x-county-lines-ordeal-cornwall> (accessed 16 March 2023).

Gulati, G, Kelly, B D , Cusack, A, Kilcommins, S, and Dunne, C P (2020), 'The experience of law enforcement officers interfacing with suspects who have an intellectual disability–A systematic review', *International Journal of Law and Psychiatry* 72, 101614.

Hall, J A, Roter, D L R, and C S (1981), 'Communication of affect between patient and physician', *Journal of Health Social Behaviour* 22(1), 18–30.

Hall, J and Knapp, M (2013) *Nonverbal Communication* (Berlin: Gruyter).

Hall, W and Lynskey, M (2020), 'Assessing the public health impacts of legalizing recreational cannabis use: the US experience', *World Psychiatry* 19(2), 179–186.

Hamilton, F (2023), 'Baroness Casey review: Met Police has lost public faith: Met found to be riddled with misogyny, bias and bullying' *The Times* (21 March 2023) available at <https://www.thetimes.co.uk/article/casey-review-met-police-report-released 2023-689ttwf9h> (accessed 20 April 2023).

Harfield, C and Harfield, K (2005), *Covert Investigation* (Oxford: Oxford University Press).

Harfield, C and Harfield, K (2008), *Intelligence: Investigation, Community, and Partnership* (Oxford: Oxford University Press).

Harris, Lord (2022), *London Prepared: A City-Wide Endeavour* MOPAC Publications available at <https://www.london.gov.uk/mopac-publications-0/london-prepared-city-wide-endeavour> (accessed 18 April 2023).

Harwood, RH (2017), 'How to deal with violent and aggressive patients in acute medical settings', *Journal of the Royal College of Physicians Edinburgh* 47, 94–101.

Heap, D (ed) (2017), *Crime Outcomes in England and Wales: Year Ending March 2017*, 2nd edn (London: Home Office).

Henriques, R, Sir (2016), *An Independent review of the Metropolitan Police Service's handling of non-recent sexual offence investigations alleged against persons of public prominence* HMICFRS available at <https://www.met.police.uk/SysSiteAssets/foi-media/metropolitan-police/other_information/corporate/mps-publication-chapters-1---3-sir-richard-henriques-report.pdf> (accessed 2 March 2023).

Herald Scotland (2016), 'Hundreds of police accused of abusing power to sexually exploit people, Her Majesty's Inspectorate of Constabulary reveals', (8 December 2016) available at <https://www.heraldscotland.com/news/14953947.hundreds-police-accused-abusing-power-sexually-exploit-people-majestys-inspectorate-constabulary-reveals/> (accessed 11 May 2023).

Herbert, N The Rt Hon (2011), 'Restorative justice, policing and the Big Society', Speech given before the Restorative Justice Council, Manchester, 22 February.

Herring, J (2007), *Family Law*, 3rd edn (Cambridge: Pearson).

Herring, J (2016), *Vulnerable Adults and the Law* (Oxford: Oxford University Press).

Herrington, V and Roberts, K (2012), 'Addressing psychological vulnerability in the police suspect interview' *Policing: A Journal of Policy and Practice* 6(2), 177–186.

Hershkowitz, I (2011), 'Rapport building in investigative interviewers of children' in M E Lamb, D J La Rooy, L C Malloy, and C Katz (eds), *Children's Testimony: A Handbook of Psychological Research and Forensic Practice* (Malden, MA: J Wiley), pp 109–129.

Hesketh, I, Cooper, C, and Ivy, J (2019), 'Leading the asset: Resilience training efficacy in UK policing', *The Police Journal* 92(1), 56–71 available at <https://journals.sagepub.com/doi/full/10.1177/0032258X18763101> (accessed 12 April 2023).

Hestia (2018), 'Bright Sky' (webpage) available at <https://www.hestia.org/brightsky> (accessed 12 April 2023).

Higgins, A (2018), *Modernising neighbourhood policing guidelines: big cogs turning* available at <http://www.police-foundation.org.uk/2018/07/modernising-neighbourhood-policing-guidelines-big-cogs-turning/> (accessed 6 March 2023).

Hillyard, P (1993), *Suspect community: People's experiences of the prevention of terrorism acts in Britain*. (London: Pluto Press).

Hine, B, Bates, E A, and Wallace, S (2022), 'I have guys call me and say "I can't be the victim of domestic abuse" Exploring the experiences of telephone support providers for male victims of domestic violence and abuse', *Journal of Interpersonal Violence* 37(7–8), NP5594–NP5625.

Historic England (2020), 'Costly Convictions for Family Guilty of Seriously Damaging Historic Site in Warwickshire' (3 February 2020) available at <https://historicengland.org.uk/whats-new/news/costly-convictions-for-damaging-historic-site-in-warwickshire/> (accessed 16 March 2023).

HMCPSI (2017), *Living in fear – the police and CPS response to harassment and stalking* available at <https://www.justiceinspectorates.gov.uk/hmcpsi/living-in-fear-harassment-and-stalking-joint-report/> (accessed 29 April 2023).

HMCPSI and HMCFRS (2020), *Evidence Led Domestic Abuse Prosecutions*, Criminal Justice Joint Inspection (London: HMCPSI) available at <https://www.justiceinspectorates.gov.uk/cjji/wp-content/uploads/sites/2/2020/01/Joint-Inspection-Evidence-Led-Domestic-Abuse-Jan19-rpt.pdf> (accessed 28 April 2023).

HM Government (1988), *Belfast Agreement* available at <https://www.gov.uk/government/publications/the-belfast-agreement> (accessed 22 April 2023).

HM Government (2014a), *Modern Slavery Strategy* available at <https://www.gov.uk/government/uploads/system/uploads/attachment_data/file/383764/Modern_Slavery_Strategy_FINAL_DEC2015.pdf> (accessed 23 April 2023).

HM Government (2014b), *Multi-agency practice guidelines: Handling cases of Forced Marriage* available at <https://assets.publishing.service.gov.uk/government/uploads/system/uploads/attachment_data/file/322307/HMG_MULTI_AGENCY_PRACTICE_GUIDELINES_v1_180614_FINAL.pdf> (accessed 7 April 2023).

HM Government (2015), *Counter Extremism Strategy* available at <https://assets.publishing.service.gov.uk/government/uploads/system/uploads/attachment_data/file/470088/51859_Cm9148_Accessible.pdf> (accessed 18 April 2023).

HM Government (2018a), *Serious and Organised Crime Strategy* available at <https://assets.publishing.service.gov.uk/government/uploads/system/uploads/attachment_data/file/752850/SOC-2018-web.pdf> (accessed 9 February 2023).

HM Government (2018b), *Working Together to Safeguard Children 2018* available at <https://assets.publishing.service.gov.uk/government/uploads/system/uploads/attachment_data/file/729914/Working_Together_to_Safeguard_Children-2018.pdf> (accessed 28 April 2023).

HM Government (2018c), *Information sharing Advice for practitioners providing safeguarding services to children, young people, parents and carers* available at <https://assets.publishing.service.gov.uk/government/uploads/system/uploads/attachment_data/file/1062969/Information_sharing_advice_practitioners_safeguarding_services.pdf> (accessed 20 April 2023).

HM Government (2021a), *Tackling Violence against women and girls* available at <https://assets.publishing.service.gov.uk/government/uploads/system/uploads/attachment_data/file/1033934/Tackling_Violence_Against_Women_and_Girls_Strategy_-_July_2021.pdf> (accessed 3 April 2023).

HM Government (2021b), *New Victims' Code* comes into force available at <https://www.gov.uk/government/news/new-victims-code-comes-into-force> (accessed 18 March 2023).

HM Government (2021c), *The end-to-end rape review report on findings and actions* available at <https://assets.publishing.service.gov.uk/government/uploads/system/uploads/attachment_data/file/1001417/end-to-end-rape-review-report-with-correction-slip.pdf> (accessed 29 March 2023).

HM Government (2022), *Consultation on Proposed Changes to the Mental Capacity Act 2005 Code of Practice and implementation of the Liberty Protection Safeguards. Including the Liberty Protection Safeguards Secondary Legislation* (London: HM Government) available at <https://assets.publishing.service.gov.uk/government/uploads/system/uploads/attachment_data/file/1061441/changes-to-the-MCA-code-and-implementation-of-the-LPS-consultation-document.pdf> (accessed 19 April 2023).

HMIC (2012), *A Review of National Police Units which Provide Intelligence on Criminality Associated with Protest* available at <https://www.justiceinspectorates.gov.uk/hmicfrs/publications/review-of-national-police-units-which-provide-intelligence-on-criminality-associated-with-protest-20120202/> (accessed 6 March 2023).

HMIC (2013), *Crime Recording in Kent: A report commissioned by the Police and Crime Commissioner for Kent* available at <https://www.justiceinspectorates.gov.uk/hmicfrs/media/crime-recording-in-kent-130617.pdf> (accessed 11 March 2023).

HMIC (2014a), *Everyone's business: Improving the police response to domestic abuse* available at <http://www.justiceinspectorates.gov.uk/hmic/wp-content/uploads/2014/04/improving-the-police-response-to-domestic-abuse.pdf> (accessed 20 April 2023).

HMIC (2014b), *Crime Recording: A matter of fact. An interim report of the inspection of crime date integrity in police forces in England and Wales* available at <https://www.justiceinspectorates.gov.uk/hmicfrs/wp-content/uploads/2014/05/crime-data-integrity-interim-report.pdf> (accessed 15 March 2023).

HMIC (2014c), *Crime-recording: Making the victim count. The final report of an inspection of crime data integrity in police forces in England and Wales* available at <https://www.justiceinspectorates.gov.uk/hmicfrs/wp-content/uploads/crime-recording-making-the-victim-count.pdf> (accessed 15 March 2023).

HMIC (2015), *The depths of dishonour: Hidden voices and shameful crimes, An inspection of the police response to honour-based violence, forced marriage and female genital mutilation* available at <https://www.justiceinspectorates.gov.uk/hmic/wp-content/uploads/the-depths-of-dishonour.pdf> (accessed 4 May 2023).

HMIC (2017a), *PEEL: Police legitimacy 2016* available at <https://www.justiceinspectorates.gov.uk/hmicfrs/wp-content/uploads/peel-police-legitimacy-2016.pdf> (accessed 6 March 2023).

HMIC (2017b), *The State of Policing: The Annual Assessment of Policing in England and Wales 2016* available at <https://www.justiceinspectorates.gov.uk/hmicfrs/wp-content/uploads/state-of-policing-2016.pdf> (accessed 2 March 2023).

HMICFRS (2017a), Peel: Police efficiency 2017 available at <https://www.justiceinspectorates.gov.uk/hmicfrs/wp-content/uploads/peel-police-efficiency-2017.pdf> (accessed 19 February 2023).

HMICFRS (2017b), *Making it Fair: The Disclosure of Unused Material in Volume Crown Court Cases* available at <https://www.justiceinspectorates.gov.uk/cjji/wp-content/uploads/sites/2/2017/07/CJJI_DSC_thm_July17_rpt.pdf> (accessed 16 March 2023).

HMICFRS (2017c), *A progress report on the police response to domestic abuse* available at <https://www.justiceinspectorates.gov.uk/hmicfrs/wp-content/uploads/progress-report-on-the-police-response-to-domestic-abuse.pdf> (accessed 12 April 2023).

HMICFRS (2018a), *Understanding the difference: The initial police response to hate crime* available at <https://www.justiceinspectorates.gov.uk/hmicfrs/wp-content/uploads/understanding-the-difference-the-initial-police-response-to-hate-crime.pdf> (accessed 12 April 2023).

HMICFRS (2018b), *Peel: Police Leadership 2017 - A national Overview* available at <https://www.justiceinspectorates.gov.uk/hmicfrs/wp-content/uploads/peel-police-leadership-2017.pdf> (accessed 13 April 2023).

HMICFRS (2019), *Leading Lights: An Inspection of the Police Service's Arrangements for the Selection and Development of Chief Officers* available at <https://www.justiceinspectorates.gov.uk/hmicfrs/publications/leading-lights-an-inspection-of-the-police-services-arrangements-for-the-selection-and-development-of-chief-officers/> (accessed 27 April 2023).

HMICFRS (2020a), *Roads Policing: Not optional—An inspection of roads policing in England and Wales* available at <https://www.justiceinspectorates.gov.uk/hmicfrs/wp-content/uploads/roads-policing-not-optional-an-inspection-of-roads-policing-in-england-and-wales.pdf> (accessed 19 March 2023).

HMICFRS (2020b), *Greater Manchester Police: An inspection of the service provided to victims of crime by Greater Manchester Police* available at <https://www.justiceinspectorates.gov.uk/hmicfrs/wp-content/uploads/an-inspection-of-the-service-provided-to-victims-of-crime-by-greater-manchester-police.pdf> (accessed 11 May 2023).

HMICFRS (2021), *Disproportionate use of police powers: A spotlight on stop and search and the use of force* available at <https://www.justiceinspectorates.gov.uk/hmicfrs/wp-content/uploads/disproportionate-use-of-police-powers-spotlight-on-stop-search-and-use-of-force.pdf> (accessed 6 April 2023).

HMICFRS (2022), *The State of Policing: The Annual Assessment of Policing in England and Wales 2021* available at <https://www.justiceinspectorates.gov.uk/hmicfrs/publications/state-of-policing-the-annual-assessment-of-policing-in-england-and-wales-2021/> (accessed 6 March 2023).

HMIP (2021), *Neurodiversity in the Criminal Justice System: A Review of Evidence* (London: TSO).

Hoey, P (2019), 'Dissident and dissenting republicanism: From the Good Friday/Belfast Agreement to Brexit', *Capital and Class* 43(1), 73–87.

Hohl, K and Stanko, EA (2015), 'Complaints of rape and the criminal justice system: Fresh evidence on the attrition problem in England and Wales', *European Journal of Criminology* 12(3), 324–341.

Holdaway, S (1996), *The Racialisation of British Policing* (Basingstoke: Macmillan).

Holdaway, S and Parker, S K (1998), 'Policing Women Police: Uniform Patrol, Promotion and Representation in the CID', *The British Journal of Criminology* 38(1), 40–60.

Holdaway, S (2013), 'Police race relations in the big society: continuity and change', *Criminology and Criminal Justice* 13(2), 215–230.

Home Affairs Select Committee (2022), *Investigation and prosecution of rape – Report Summary* available at <https://publications.parliament.uk/pa/cm5802/cmselect/cmhaff/193/summary.html> (accessed 18 May 2023).

Home Office (2001), *Policing a New Century: A blueprint for reform*, Cm 5326 (London: Home Office).

Home Office (2009), *Designated Public Place Orders Guidance* available at <https://www.gov.uk/government/publications/designated-public-place-orders-guidance> (accessed 29 May 2023).

Home Office (2010), *Policing in the 21st Century: Reconnecting police and the people* available at <http://www.homeoffice.gov.uk/publications/consultations/policing-21st-century/> (accessed 6 March 2023).

Home Office (2011), *Missing Children and Adults* available at <https://www.gov.uk/government/uploads/system/uploads/attachment_data/file/117793/missing-persons-strategy.pdf> (accessed 11 April 2023).

Home Office (2012a), *Definition of policing by consent* available at <https://www.gov.uk/government/publications/policing-by-consent/definition-of-policing-by-consent> (accessed 08 March 2023).

Home Office (2012b), *Ending Gang and Youth Violence: one year on* available at <http://www.official-documents.gov.uk/document/cm84/8493/8493.pdf> (accessed 10 May 2023).

Home Office (2012c), *Police community support officer powers* available at <https://www.gov.uk/government/publications/police-community-support-officer-powers> (accessed 1 May 2023).

Home Office (2012d), *Domestic Violence Disclosure Scheme Pilot: Guidance* available at <http://www.homeoffice.gov.uk/publications/crime/dvds-interim-guidance?view=Binary> (accessed 21 April 2023).

Home Office (2013a), *Penalty Notices for Disorder (PNDs)* available at <http://www.justice.gov.uk/downloads/oocd/pnd-guidance-oocd.pdf> (accessed 30 March 2023).

Home Office (2013b), *Surveillance Camera Code of Practice* available at <https://www.gov.uk/government/uploads/system/uploads/attachment_data/file/204775/Surveillance_Camera_Code_of_Practice_WEB.pdf> (accessed 6 March 2023).

Home Office (2013c), *The Regulation of Investigatory Powers (Covert Human Intelligence Sources: Relevant Sources) Order 2013* available at <https://www.legislation.gov.uk/uksi/2013/2788/pdfs/uksi_20132788_en.pdf> (accessed 6 March 2023).

Home Office (2014a), *Anti-social Behaviour, Crime and Policing Act 2014: Reform of anti-social behaviour powers: Statutory guidance for frontline professionals: July 2014* available at <https://www.gov.uk/government/publications/anti-social-behaviour-crime-and-policing-bill-anti-social-behaviour> (accessed 1 May 2023).

Home Office (2014b), *Home Secretary outlines reforms to the Police Federation* available at <https://www. gov.uk/government/news/home-secretary-outlines-reforms-to-the-police-federation> (accessed 26 March 2023).

Home Office (2014c), *Best Use of Stop and Search Scheme* available at <https://www.gov.uk/government/uploads/system/uploads/attachment_data/file/346922/Best_Use_of_Stop_and_Search_Scheme_v3.0_v2.pdf> (accessed 7 April 2023).

Home Office (2014d), *Operational briefings and planning* available at <https://www.gov.uk/government/uploads/system/uploads/attachment_data/file/488513/Operational_briefings_and_planning_v3.0EXT_clean.pdf> (accessed 8 April 2023).

Home Office (2014e), *Home Office Counting Rules for Recorded Crime* (London: Home Office).

Home Office (2015a), *Statutory Guidance Injunctions to Prevent Gang-Related Violence and Gang-Related Drug Dealing* available at <https://www.gov.uk/government/uploads/system/uploads/attachment_data/file/432805/Injunctions_to_Prevent_Gang-Related_Violence_web.pdf> (accessed 11 May 2023).

Home Office (2015b), *Initial Operational Response to a CBRN incident* available at <http://www.jesip.org.uk/uploads/media/pdf/CBRN%20JOPs/IOR_Guidance_V2_July_2015.pdf> (accessed 8 April 2023).

Home Office (2015c), *Working together to safeguard children. A guide to inter-agency working to safeguard and promote the welfare of children* available at <https://www.gov.uk/government/publications/working-together-to-safeguard-children--2> (accessed 23 April 2023).

Home Office (2015d), *Coercive or controlling behaviour now a crime* available at <https://www.gov.uk/government/news/coercive-or-controlling-behaviour-now-a-crime> (accessed 14 March 2023).

Home Office (2015e), *Supporting vulnerable people who encounter the police: A strategic guide for police forces and their partners* available at <https://assets.publishing.service.gov.uk/government/uploads/system/uploads/attachment_data/file/405397/6.379_Supporting_guidance_web_doc_v3.pdf> (accessed 11 May 2023).

Home Office (2016a), *Ending Violence Against Women and Girls Strategy 2016–2020* available at <https://www.gov.uk/government/uploads/system/uploads/attachment_data/file/522166/VAWG_Strategy_FINAL_PUBLICATION_MASTER_vRB.PDF> (accessed 23 April 2023).

Home Office (2018a), *Home Office Guidance: Police Officer Misconduct, Unsatisfactory Performance and Attendance Management Procedures* available at <https://assets.publishing.service.gov.uk/government/uploads/system/uploads/attachment_data/file/732466/Home_Office_Guidance_on_Police_Misconduct.pdf> (accessed 6 March 2023).

Home Office (2018b), Counting rules for recorded crime available at <https://www.gov.uk/government/publications/counting-rules-for-recorded-crime> (accessed 4 April 2023).

Home Office (2018c), *The Data Retention and Acquisition Regulations* available at <https://www.legislation.gov.uk/ukdsi/2018/9780111170809> (accessed 6 March 2023).

Home Office (2018d), *The Communications Data Code of Practice, 2018* available at <https://assets.publishing.service.gov.uk/government/uploads/system/uploads/attachment_data/file/757850/Communications_Data_Code_of_Practice.pdf> (accessed 6 March 2023).

Home Office (2018e), Hate Crime, England and Wales available at <https://www.gov.uk/government/statistics/hate-crime-england-and-wales-2017-to-2018> (accessed 5 March 2019).

Home Office (2018f), *Criminal Exploitation of Children and Vulnerable Adults: County Lines guidance* available at <https://assets.publishing.service.gov.uk/government/uploads/system/uploads/attachment_data/file/741194/HOCountyLinesGuidanceSept2018.pdf> (accessed 18 April 2023).

Home Office (2018g), *Serious Violence Strategy* available at <https://assets.publishing.service.gov.uk/government/uploads/system/uploads/attachment_data/file/698009/serious-violence-strategy.pdf> (accessed 2 February 2023)

Home Office (2019a), 'Police Workforce, England and Wales, 31 March 2019', 2nd edn, Statistical Bulletin 11/19 available at <https://assets.publishing.service.gov.uk/government/uploads/system/uploads/attachment_data/file/831726/police-workforce-mar19-hosb1119.pdf> (accessed 6 March 2023).

Home Office (2019b), *2019 UK Annual Report on Modern Slavery* available at <https://assets.publishing.service.gov.uk/government/uploads/system/uploads/attachment_data/file/840059/Modern_Slavery_Report_2019.pdf> (accessed 23 April 2023).

Home Office (2019c), *Independent Review of the Modern Slavery Act 2015: Final Report* available at <https://assets.publishing.service.gov.uk/government/uploads/system/uploads/attachment_data/file/803406/Independent_review_of_the_Modern_Slavery_Act_-_final_report.pdf> (accessed 24 April 2023).

Home Office (2019d), *Circular 010/2019, Firearms Regulations 2019 and the Firearms (Amendment) (No.2) Rules 2019* available at <https://www.gov.uk/government/publications/circular-0102019-firearms-regulations-2019-and-the-firearms-amendment-no2-rules-2019/0102019-firearms-regulations-2019-and-the-firearms-amendment-no2-rules-2019> (accessed 3 April 2023).

Home Office (2020a), *Home Office Guidance: Conduct, Efficiency and Effectiveness: Statutory Guidance on Professional Standards, Performance and Integrity in Policing* available at <https://assets.publishing.service.gov.uk/government/uploads/system/uploads/attachment_data/file/863820/Home_Office_Statutory_Guidance_0502.pdf> (accessed 7 May 2023).

Home Office (2020b), *Hate Crime, England and Wales, 2019/20* available at <https://www.report-it.org.uk/files/hate-crime-1920-hosb2920.pdf> (accessed 12 April 2023).

Home Office (2020c), *Crime Outcomes in England and Wales 2019 to 2020* available at <https://assets.publishing.service.gov.uk/government/uploads/system/uploads/attachment_data/file/901028/crime-outcomes-1920-hosb1720.pdf> (accessed 11 April 2023).

Home Office (2020d), *Stalking Protection Orders: Statutory guidance for the police* (London: Home Office).

Home Office (2020e), *Forced Marriage Unit Statistics 2019, 25 June 2020* available at <https://assets.publishing.service.gov.uk/government/uploads/system/uploads/attachment_data/file/894428/Forced_Marriage_Unit_statistics_2019.pdf> (accessed 3 May 2023).

Home Office (2020f), *Criminal Exploitation of Children and Vulnerable Adults: County Lines* available at <https://www.gov.uk/government/publications/criminal-exploitation-of-children-and-vulnerable-adults-county-lines/criminal-exploitation-of-children-and-vulnerable-adults-county-lines> (accessed 15 March 2023).

Home Office (2021a), *Review into the role of police and crime commissioners: letter from Kit Malthouse MP to PCCs* available at <https://www.gov.uk/government/publications/part-2-of-the-police-and-crime-commissioner-review/review-into-the-role-of-police-and-crime-commissioners-letter-from-kit-malthouse-mp-to-pccs-accessible> (accessed 6 April 2023).

Home Office (2021b), *Police powers and procedures: Stop and search and arrests, England and Wales, year ending 31 March 2021* available at <https://www.gov.uk/government/statistics/police-powers-and-procedures-stop-and-search-and-arrests-england-and-wales-year-ending-31-march-2021> (accessed 6 April 2023).

Home Office (2021c), *Beating Crime Plan* available at <https://www.gov.uk/government/publications/beating-crime-plan/beating-crime-plan> (accessed 6 April 2023).

Home Office (2021d), 'Police, Crime, Sentencing and Courts Act 2022: pre-charge bail factsheet', Policy Paper, 9 March 2021 (updated 20 August 2022) available at <https://www.gov.uk/government/publications/police-crime-sentencing-and-courts-bill-2021-factsheets> (accessed 11 April 2023).

Home Office (2021e), *2021 Annual Report on Modern Slavery* available at <https://www.gov.uk/government/publications/2021-uk-annual-report-on-modern-slavery/2021-uk-annual-report-on-modern-slavery-accessible-version#annex-a-uk-annual-report-on-modern-slavery--data-tables> (accessed 3 May 2023).

Home Office (2021f), *Antique Firearms Regulations* available at <https://www.gov.uk/government/publications/circular-0012021-antique-firearms/circular-0012021-antique-firearms-regulations-2021-and-the-policing-and-crime-act-2017-commencement-no11-and-transitional-provisions-regulations> (accessed 3 April 2023).

Home Office (2021g), *Amendments to the Antique Firearms Regulations 2021* available at <https://www.gov.uk/government/publications/circular-0082021-antique-firearms/circular-0082021-amendments-to-the-antique-firearms-amendment-regulations-2021> (accessed 3 April 2023).

Home Office (2022a), *New police powers to crack down on unauthorised encampments come into force* available at <https://www.gov.uk/government/news/new-police-powers-to-crack-down-on-unauthorised-encampments-come-into-force> (accessed 5 May 2023).

Home Office (2022b), *Statutory Guidance for Police on Unauthorised Encampments a summary of available powers* available at <https://assets.publishing.service.gov.uk/government/uploads/system/uploads/attachment_data/file/1086073/E02764577_Unauthorised_Encampments.pdf> (accessed 5 May 2023).

Home Office (2022c), *Hate crime, England and Wales, 2021 to 2022* available at <https://www.gov.uk/government/statistics/hate-crime-england-and-wales-2021-to-2022/hate-crime-england-and-wales-2021-to-2022> (accessed 11 April 2023).

Home Office (2022d), *The Covert Human Intelligence Sources Revised Code of Practice, December 2022* available at <https://www.gov.uk/government/publications/covert-human-intelligence-sources-code-of-practice-2022> (accessed 6 March 2023).

Home Office (2022e), *Extraction of Information from electronic devices: Code of Practice, updated October 2022* available at <https://assets.publishing.service.gov.uk/government/uploads/system/uploads/attachment_data/file/1110883/E02802691_Electronic_Devices_Code_of_Practice_WEB.pdf> (accessed 26 February 2023).

Home Office (2022f), *Domestic Abuse Act statutory guidance* available at <https://www.gov.uk/government/consultations/domestic-abuse-act-statutory-guidance> (accessed 22 March 2023).

Home Office (2022g), *Domestic Violence Disclosure Scheme Guidance* available at <https://www.gov.uk/government/consultations/domestic-violence-disclosure-scheme-guidance> (accessed 21 March 2023).

Home Office (2022h), *Police powers and procedures: Other PACE powers, England and Wales, year ending 31 March 2022* available at <https://www.gov.uk/government/statistics/police-powers-and-procedures-other-pace-powers-england-and-wales-year-ending-31-march-2022/police-powers-and-procedures-other-pace-powers-england-and-wales-year-ending-31-march-2022> (accessed 13 April 2023).

Home Office (2022i), *Police use of force statistics, England and Wales: April 2021–March 2022* available at <https://www.gov.uk/government/statistics/police-use-of-force-statistics-england-and-wales-april-2021-to-march-2022/police-use-of-force-statistics-england-and-wales-april-2021-to-march-2022> (accessed 19 January 2023).

Home Office (2022j), *Seizures of drugs in England and Wales, financial year ending 2021* available at <https://www.gov.uk/government/statistics/seizures-of-drugs-in-england-and-wales-financial-year-ending-2021/seizures-of-drugs-in-england-and-wales-financial-year-ending-2021> (accessed 8 February 2023).

Home Office (2022k), *Anti-social Behaviour Statutory Guidance*, Revised 2022 available at <https://assets.publishing.service.gov.uk/government/uploads/system/uploads/attachment_data/file/1088750/2022_Updated_ASB_Statutory_Guidance-_FINAL.pdf> (accessed 16 March 2023).

Home Office (2022l), *Home Office Guidance on Firearms Licensing 2022* available at <https://assets.publishing.service.gov.uk/government/uploads/system/uploads/attachment_data/file/1116230/Firearms_guide_November_2022.pdf> (accessed 13 February 2023).

Home Office (2023a) *Police workforce, England and Wales: 30 September 2022* available at <https://www.gov.uk/government/statistics/police-workforce-england-and-wales-30-september-2022/police-workforce-england-and-wales-30-september-2022> (accessed 8 March 2023).

Home Office (2023b), *The Strategic Policing Requirement* available at <https://assets.publishing.service.gov.uk/government/uploads/system/uploads/attachment_data/file/1138740/20230223_Strategic_Policing_Requirement__V1.2__-_OS.pdf> (accessed 15 March 2023).

Hoppe, M H (2014), *Active Listening: Improve Your Ability to Listen and Lead, First Edition: Improve Your Ability to Listen and Lead*. Center for Creative Leadership.

Horner, M (1997), 'Leadership theory: past, present and future', *Team Performance Management: An International Journal* 3(4), 270–287.

Horsman G (2017), 'Can we continue to effectively police digital crime?', *Science and Justice* 57(6), 448–454 available at <https://doi.org/10.1016/j.scijus.2017.06.001> (accessed 24 May 2023).

House of Commons Communities and Local Government Committee (2014), *Child Sexual Exploitation in Rotherham: some issues for local government* available at <https://publications.parliament.uk/pa/cm201415/cmselect/cmcomloc/648/648.pdf#:~:text=Professor%20Alexis%20Jay%E2%80%99s%20Independent%20Inquiry%20into%20Child%20Sexual,Rotherham%2C%20to%20protect%20children%20from%20organised%20sexual%20exploitation> (accessed 1 May 2023).

Hoyle, C (1998), *Negotiating domestic violence: police, criminal justice and victims* (Oxford: Oxford University Press).

Hoyle, C, Bellis M A, Hardcastle K A, et al (2017), 'The effect of multiple adverse childhood experiences on health: a systematic review and meta-analysis', *Lancet Public Health* 2(8), e356–e366.

Iganski, P and Lagou, S (2015), 'Hate crimes hurt some more than others: Implications for the just sentencing of offenders', *Journal of Interpersonal Violence* 30(10), 1696–1718.

ICO (2017), *In the picture: A data protection code of practice for surveillance cameras and personal information* available at <https://webarchive.nationalarchives.gov.uk/ukgwa/20170319145051/https://ico.org.uk/media/for-organisations/documents/1542/cctv-code-of-practice.pdf> (accessed 6 March 2023).

Information Commissioner's Opinion (2022), *Who's Under Investigation? The processing of victims' personal data in rape and serious sexual offence investigations* available at <https://ico.org.uk/media/4020539/commissioners-opinion-whos-under-investigation-20220531.pdf> (accessed 1 April 2023).

Inman, K and Rudin, R (2002), 'The origin of evidence', *Forensic Science International* 126, 11–16.

Innes, M (2014), *Signal Crimes: Social Reactions to Crime, Disorder and Control* (Oxford: Oxford University Press).

——, and Innes, H (2013), *Personal, Situational and Incidental Vulnerabilities to ASB Harm: a follow up study* available at <https://orca.cardiff.ac.uk/id/eprint/52681/1/personal-situational-and-incidental-vulnerabilities-to-anti-social-behaviour-harm-a-follow-up-study.pdf> (accessed 19 April 2023).

Innocence Project (2017), *Eyewitness misidentification* available at <https://www.innocenceproject.org/causes/eyewitness-misidentification/> (accessed 5 May 2023).

Institute for Apprenticeships & Technical Education (2018a), *End Point Assessment Plan for Police Constable Integrated Degree Apprenticeship at Level 6* available at <https://www.instituteforapprenticeships.org/apprenticeship-standards/police-constable-degree/> (accessed 12 March 2023).

Institute for Apprenticeships & Technical Education (2018b), *Police Constable (Degree)* available at <https://www.instituteforapprenticeships.org/apprenticeship-standards/police-constable-degree/> (accessed 18 March 2023).

International Labour Organization (2017), *Global Estimates of Modern Slavery* available at <https://www.ilo.org/wcmsp5/groups/public/---dgreports/---dcomm/documents/publication/wcms_575479.pdf> (accessed 3 May 2023).

Inzunza, M, Brown, G T L, Stenlund, T, and Wikström, C (2022), 'The relationship between subconstructs of empathy and general cognitive ability in the context of policing', *Frontiers in Psychology* 13, 907610.

IOPC (2017a), *Information for police officers and staff* available at <https://policeconduct.gov.uk/complaints-and-appeals/information-police-officers-and-staff> (accessed 31 March 2023).

IOPC (2020), *Statutory guidance on the police complaints system* available at <https://policeconduct.gov.uk/sites/default/files/Documents/statutoryguidance/2020_statutory_guidance_english.pdf> (accessed 17 February 2023).

IOPC (2021), *Metropolitan Police Service officer sacked for racist remark in WhatsApp message* available at <https://www.policeconduct.gov.uk/news/metropolitan-police-service-officer-sacked-racist-remark-whatsapp-message> (accessed 12 April 2023).

IOPC (2022a), *National Stop and Search Learning Report, April 2022* available at <https://www.policeconduct.gov.uk/national-stop-and-search-learning-report-april-2022> (accessed 6 April 2023).

IOPC (2022b), *Operation Hotton: Learning report* available at <https://www.policeconduct.gov.uk/sites/default/files/Operation%20Hotton%20Learning%20report%20-%20January%202022.pdf> (accessed 6 March 2023).

IOPC (2022c), *IOPC Public Perceptions Tracker Summary Report, Waves 5.1–5.3*. available at <https://www.policeconduct.gov.uk/sites/default/files/Documents/statistics/IOPC_Yonder_Public_Perceptions_Tracker_Annual_Summary_Report_2021_22_Final.pdf> (accessed 8 April 2023).

IOPC (2023a), *Police response to locate a missing man – Northamptonshire Police, October 2021* available at <https://www.policeconduct.gov.uk/recommendations/police-response-locate-missing-man-%E2%80%93-northamptonshire-police-october-2021> (accessed 20 April 2023).

IOPC (2023b), *Recommendation - Sussex Police, March 2023* available at <https://www.policeconduct.gov.uk/recommendations/recommendation-sussexpolice march-2023> (accessed 22 April 2023).

IPCC and ACPO (2012), *The abuse of police powers to perpetrate sexual violence* available at <https://www.policeconduct.gov.uk/sites/default/files/Documents/research-learning/abuse_of_police_powers_to_perpetrate_sexual_violence.pdf> (accessed 2 March 2023).

Ishoy, G A (2016), 'The Theory of Planned Behavior and Policing: How Attitudes about Behavior, Subjective Norms, and Perceived Behavioral Control Affect the Discretionary Enforcement Decisions of Police Officers', *Criminal Justice Studies: A Critical Journal of Crime, Law and Society* 29(4), 345–362.

Jackson, J (2012), 'Why do people comply with the law? Legitimacy and the influence of legal institutions', *British Journal of Criminology* 52(6), 1051–1071.

Jackson, J, Bradford, B, Stanko, B, and Hohl, K (2013), *Just Authority? Trust in the police in England and Wales* (London: Routledge).

Jacques, P (2023a), 'Officer dismissed for "discriminatory behaviour" towards black colleagues' *Police Professional* available at <https://www.policeprofessional.com/news/officer-dismissed-for-discriminatory-behaviour-towards-black-colleagues/> (accessed 25 March 2023).

Jacques, P (2023b) 'Review highlights "serious failures of culture and leadership" at MPS, says Home Secretary' *Police Professional* available at <https://www.policeprofessional.com/news/review-highlights-serious-failures-of-culture-and-leadership-at-mps-says-home-secretary/> (accessed 4 April 2023).

Jacques, P (2023c), 'Revised Code of Ethics to promote "professional culture" in policing' *Police Professional* available at: <https://www.policeprofessional.com/news/revised-code-of-ethics-to-promote-professional-culture-in-policing/> (accessed 12 April 2023).

Jaensch, J and South, N (2018), 'Drug Gang Activity and Policing Responses in an English Seaside Town: "County Lines", "Cuckooing" and Community Impacts', *Revija za kriminalistiko in kriminologijo/Ljubljana* 69/2018/4, 269–278, available at <https://www.policija.si/images/stories/Publikacije/RKK/PDF/2018/04/RKK2018-04_JessicaJaensch_DrugGangActivityAndPolicingResponses.pdf> (accessed 16 March 2023).

JESIP (2017), *IIMARCH template* available at <http://www.jesip.org.uk/IIMARCH-template> (accessed 8 April 2023).

JESIP (2021), *Joint Doctrine: The Interoperability Framework* available at <https://www.jesip.org.uk/uploads/media/pdf/Joint%20Doctrine/JESIP_Joint_Doctrine_Guide_OCT21.pdf> (accessed 7 April 2023).

Johnson, N N and Johnson, T (2019), 'Microaggressions: An Introduction' in U Thomas (ed), *Navigating Micro-Aggressions Toward Women in Higher Education* (Hershey, Philadelphia: IGI Global), pp 1–22.

Johnson, S D, Guerette, R T, and Bowers, K (2014), 'Crime displacement: what we know, what we don't know, and what it means for crime reduction', *Journal of Experimental Criminology* 10(4), 549–571.

Johnston, D and Hutton, G (2005), *Blackstone's Police Manual, Volume 2: Evidence and Procedure* (Oxford: Oxford University Press).

Jones, M and Williams, M (2013), 'Twenty years on: lesbian, gay and bisexual police officers' experiences of workplace discrimination in England and Wales', *Policing & Society* 25(2), 188–211.

Jones, M (2015), 'Who Forgot Lesbian, Gay, and Bisexual Police Officers? Findings from a National Survey', *Policing* 9(1), 65–76.

Jones, O (2023), 'Scrapping the Met isn't enough. There are radical – and proven – alternatives', in *The Guardian*, (23 March 2023) available at <https://www.theguardian.com/commentisfree/2023/mar/23/met-police-uk-radical-alternatives-policing> (accessed 28 April 2023).

Jones, T and Newburn, T (1998), *Private Security and Public Policing* (Oxford: Clarendon Press).

Jordan, J (2011), 'Here we go round the review-go-round: Rape investigation and prosecution—are things getting worse not better?', *Journal of Sexual Aggression* 17(3), 234–249.

Judd, C M and Park, B (1993), 'Definition and Assessment of Accuracy in Social Stereotypes', *Psychological Review* 100(1), 109–128. Available at <https://psycnet.apa.org/doiLanding?doi=10.1037%2F0033-295X.100.1.109> (accessed 28 May 2023).

Junger, M, West, R, and Timman, R (2001), 'Crime and risk behaviour in traffic', *Journal of Research in Crime & Delinquency* 38(4), 439–459.

Kappeler, V E (2017), 'Community Policing' in A Brisman, E Carrabine and N South (eds), *The Routledge Companion to Criminological Theory and Concepts* (London: Routledge), pp 435–438.

Kaspersky (2019), *The State of Stalkerware 2019, Coalition Against Stalkerware* available at <https://media.kasperskydaily.com/wp-content/uploads/sites/92/2019/11/18053214/Kaspersky_Coalition_The-state-of-stalkerware-in-2019_ENG_fin.pdf> updated online 16 April 2020 at <https://securelist.com/the-state-of-stalkerware-in-2019/93634/> (accessed 2 April 2023).

Kaspersky (2021), *Stalkerware in 2020 is still a burning issue* (updated 19 March 2021), available at <https://www.kaspersky.co.uk/blog/stalkerware-in-2020/22465/> (accessed 2 April 2023).

Katzenbach, J R and Smith, D K (1992), 'Why teams matter', *The McKinsey Quarterly* (3), McKinsey & Company, Inc.

Kaufmann, G, Drevland, G C B, Wessel, E, Overskeid, G, and Magnussen, S (2003), 'The importance of being earnest: Displayed emotions and witness credibility', *Applied Cognitive Psychology* 17, 21–34.

Keay, S and Hirby, S (2018), 'Defining Vulnerability: From Conceptual to the Organisational', *Policing: A Journal of Policy and Practice* 12(4), 428–438.

Kemmis, S and McTaggart, R (2005), 'Participatory action research: Communicative action and the public sphere' in N K Denzin and Y S Lincoln (eds), *The Sage Handbook of Qualitative Research*, 3rd edn. (London: Sage), pp 559–603.

Kennedy-Pipe, C (2014), *The Origins of the Present Troubles in Northern Ireland* (London: Routledge).

Kent PCC (2022), *Making Kent Safer* available at <https://www.kent-pcc.gov.uk/SysSiteAssets/media/downloads/plan-annualreports-hmic/making-kent-safer-spring-2022.pdf> (accessed 24 March 2023).

Kent Police (2017), *Force Control Room* available at <https://democracy.gravesham.gov.uk/documents/s38698/THRIVE%20-%2012102017.pdf> (accessed 20 April 2023).

Kenyon, J, Binder, J and Baker-Beall, C (2022), 'The Internet and radicalisation pathways: technological advances, relevance of mental health and role of attackers', *Ministry of Justice Analytical Series 2022*, HM Prison and Probation Service.

Kepinska Jakobsen, K (2021), 'Empathy in investigative interviews of victims: How to understand it, how to measure it, and how to do it?', *Police practice and research* 22(2), 1155–1170 available at <https://doi.org/10.1080/15614263.2019.1668789> (accessed 5 May 2023).

Kerslake, R (2017), *The Kerslake Report. An independent review into the preparedness for, and emergency response to, the Manchester Arena attack on 22nd May 2017* available at <https://www.jesip.org.uk/uploads/media/Documents%20Products/Kerslake_Report_Manchester_Are.pdf> (accessed 7 April 2023).

Khan, K K and Mohsin Reza, M (2022), 'Social Research: Definitions, Types, Nature, and Characteristics in Islam' in M R Islam, N A Khan, and R Baikady (eds), *Principles of Social Research Methodology* (Singapore: Springer), pp 29–41.

Kilby, B (2015), *Why Scaring Kids Out of Committing Crimes Doesn't Work* available at <https://www.vice.com/en_us/article/kwxxba/why-scaring-kids-out-of-committing-crimes-doesnt-work-1105> (accessed 12 April 2023).

Kilmann, R H and Thomas, K W (1977), 'Developing a Forced-Choice Measure of Conflict-Handling Behavior: The "Mode" Instrument', *Educational and Psychological Measurement* 37(2), 309–325. Available at: <https://doi.org/10.1177/001316447703700204> (accessed 18 April 2023).

Kim, S, Alison, L, and Christiansen, P (2020), 'Observing rapport-based interpersonal techniques to gather information from victims', *Psychology, Public Policy, and Law* 26(2), 166–175 available at <https://doi.org/10.1037/law0000222> (accessed 21 April 2023).

Kirk, P (1963), 'The Ontogeny of Criminalistics', *Journal of Criminal Law, Criminology and Police Science* 54(2), 235–238.

Knight, R (2015), 'How to handle difficult conversations at work', *Harvard Business Review* available at <https://hbr.org/2015/01/how-to-handle-difficult-conversations-at-work> (accessed 5 May 2023).

Knoll, J L and Resnick, P J (2007), 'Stalking Intervention: Know the 5 Stalker Types, Safety Strategies for Victims', *Current Psychiatry* 6(5).

Knoth, L K and Ruback, R B (2019), 'Reporting crimes to the police depends on relationship networks: Effects of ties among victims, advisors, and offenders', *Journal of Interpersonal Violence* 34(13), 2749–2773.

Kohlberg, L (1969), 'Stage and sequence: The cognitive-development approach to socialization' in D A Goslin (ed), *Handbook of Socialization Theory and Research* (Chicago: Rand McNally), pp 347–480.

Kolb, D (1984), *Experiential Learning: Experience as the source of learning and development* (Upper Saddle River, NJ: Prentice Hall).

Kotter, J (2012), *Leading Change* (Boston, Massachusetts: Harvard Business Review Press).

Kyriakidou, M, Blades, M, Cherryman, J, Christophorou, S, and Kamberis, A (2020), 'The impact of interviewer working hours on police interviews with children', *Journal of Police and Criminal Psychology*, 1–10.

LaFree, G and Hendrickson, J (2007), 'Build a criminal justice policy for terrorism', *Criminology and Public Policy* 6(4), 781–790.

Laming, Lord (2009), *The Protection of Children in England: A Progress Report* available at <https://www.gov.uk/government/uploads/system/uploads/attachment_data/file/328117/The_Protection_of_Children_in_England.pdf> (accessed 7 April 2023).

Lammy, D (2017), *The Lammy Review. An independent review into the treatment of, and outcomes for, Black, Asian and Minority Ethnic individuals in the Criminal Justice System*, available at <https://www.gov.uk/government/publications/lammy-review-final-report> (accessed 12 April 2023).

Lapakko, D (1997), 'Three cheers for language: A closer examination of a widely cite study of nonverbal communication', *Communication Education* 46(1), 63–67.

Larkin, M (2009), *Vulnerable Groups in Health and Social Care* (London: Sage Publications).

Law Commission (2022), *Review of Evidence in Sexual Offences: A Background Paper* available at <https://s3-eu-west-2.amazonaws.com/lawcom-prod-storage-11jsxou24uy7q/uploads/2022/02/Evidence-in-sexual-offences-background-paper.pdf> (accessed 29 March 2023).

Law Teacher (2018), 'Fraud Lecture', Law Teacher Free Law Study Resources, available at <https://www.lawteacher.net/lectures/criminal-law/fraud/?vref=1> (accessed 16 March 2023).

Law Teacher (2019), 'Theft Act 1968', Law Teacher Free Law Study Resources, available at <https://www.lawteacher.net/acts/theft-act-1978.php?vref=1> (accessed 16 March 2023).

Laxminarayan, M, Henrichs, J, and Pemberton, A (2012), 'Procedural and interactional justice: a comparative study of victims in the Netherlands and New South Wales', *European Journal of Criminology* 9(3), 260–275.

Leishman, F and Mason, P (2003), *Policing and the Media: Facts, fictions and factions* (Cullompton: Willan).

Lentz, S and Chaires, R (2007), 'The Invention of Peel's Principles: A Study of Policing "Textbook" History', *Journal of Criminal Justice* 35, 69–79.

Leonardo, N (2020), *Active Listening Techniques: 30 Practical Tools to Hone Your Communication Skills*. (United States: Rockridge Press).

Leukfeldt, E and Var, M (2016), 'Applying Routine Activity Theory to Cybercrime: A Theoretical and Empirical Analysis', *Deviant Behaviour* 37(3), 263–280.

Lewis, N and Jaramillo, A (2008), 'Communication with Victims and Survivors', National Victim Assistance Academy, available at <https://ce4less.com/Tests/Materials/E055Materials.pdf> (accessed 5 May 2023).

Lewis, H (2012), *Body Language: A Guide for Professionals*, 3rd edn. (New Delhi: Sage Publications Pvt. Ltd).

Lippmann, W (1922) *Public Opinion* (New York: Harcourt Brace & Co).

Lister, S, Adams, B, and Phillips, S (2015), *Evaluation of police-community engagement practices* (Swindon: Economic and Social Research Council).

Local Government Association (2018), *Public Spaces Protection Orders: Guidance for Councils. UK: Local Government Association* available at <https://www.local.gov.uk/sites/default/files/documents/10.21%20PSPO%20guidance_06_1.pdf> (accessed 2 March 2023).

Lock, R (2013), *Final Overview Report of Serious Case Review re Daniel Pelka—September 2013*, Coventry Child Safeguarding Board available at <https://edemocracy.coventry.gov.uk/documents/s13038/Daniel%20Pelka%20Serious%20Case%20Review%20SCR.pdf> (accessed 20 April 2023).

Loewenstein, R J (1996), 'Dissociative amnesia and dissociative fugue', *Handbook of dissociation: Theoretical, empirical, and clinical perspectives,* pp 307–336.

London Evening Standard (2020), 'Streatham terror attack: London Ambulance Service defends response time after claims paramedics took 30 minutes to arrive' (3 February 2020) available at <https://www.standard.co.uk/news/health/streatham-terror-attack-london-ambulance-service-response-time-a4351816.html> (accessed 26 May 2023).

Lumba-Brown, A, Yeates, K O, Sarmiento, K, Breiding, M J, Haegerich, T M, Gioia, G A, Turner, M, Benzel, E C, Suskauer, S J, Giza, C C, and Joseph, M (2018), 'Centers for Disease Control and Prevention guideline on the diagnosis and management of mild traumatic brain injury among children', *JAMA Pediatrics* 172(11), e182853–e182853.

Macdonald, S and Cosgrove, F (2019), Dyslexia and policing: Understanding the impact that dyslexia has in the police service in England and Wales, *Equality, Diversity and Inclusion* 38(6), 634 651.

Machado, A, Hines, D A, and Matos, M (2016), 'Help-seeking and needs of male victims of intimate partner violence in Portugal', *Psychology of Men and Masculinity* 17, 255–264.

MacIntyre, A (1985), *After Virtue*, 2nd edn (London: Duckworth).

Mackelprang, E and Becker, J (2015), 'Beauty and the Eye of the Beholder: Gender and Attractiveness Affect Judgments in Teacher Sex Offense Cases', *Sexual Abuse* 29(4), 375–395 available at <https://doi.org/10.1177/1079063215597646> (accessed 18 May 2023).

Macpherson, Sir W (1999), *The Stephen Lawrence Inquiry* available at <https://www.gov.uk/government/publications/the-stephen-lawrence-inquiry> (accessed 4 April 2023).

MacVean, A and Neyroud, P (2012) *Police Ethics and Values* (London: Learning Matters).

Maddox, L (2011), 'Police empathy and victim PTSD as potential factors in rape case attrition', *Journal of Police and Criminal Psychology* 26(2), 112–117

Majid, S, Liming, Z, Tong, S, Raihana, S (2012), 'Importance of Soft Skills for Education and Career Success', *International Journal for Cross-Disciplinary Subjects in Education (IJCDSE)*, Special Issue Volume 2 Issue 2.

Maniglio, R (2009). 'The impact of child sexual abuse on health: A systematic review of reviews', *Clinical Psychology Review* 29(7), 647–657.

Mankind Initiative (2021), 'Statistics on Male Victims of domestic abuse' available at <https://www.mankind.org.uk/statistics/statistics-on-male-victims-of-domestic-abuse/> (accessed 3 May 2023).

Marinez, N N, Lee, Y J, Eck, J E, and O, S H (2017), *Ravenous wolves revisited: A systematic review of offending concentration*, *Crime Scene Journal* 6(10) available at <https://crimesciencejournal.springeropen.com/articles/10.1186/s40163-017-0072-2> (accessed 15 March 2023).

Marshall-Tate, K (2019), 'Learning disabilities: supporting people in the criminal justice system', *Nursing Times* 115(7), 22–26, available at <https://www.nursingtimes.net/roles/learning-disability-nurses/learning-disabilities-supporting-people-in-the-criminal-justice-system-17-06-2019/> (accessed 13 April 2023).

Martellozzo, E (2013), *Online child sexual abuse: Grooming, policing and child protection in a multi-media world* (Abingdon: Routledge).

Maruna, S (2017), 'Desistance as a Social Movement', *Irish Probation Journal* 14, 5–20.

Mason, F and Lodrick, Z (2013), 'Psychological consequences of sexual assault', *Best Practice and Research Clinical Obstetrics and Gynaecology* 27, 27–37.

Massey, M E (1979), *The People Puzzle: Understanding Yourself and Others* (Michigan: Reston Publishing Company).

Mayer, A (2015), 'Is there a Link between Climate Change and Terrorism?' CBC News (26 May 2015), available at <https://www.cbc.ca/news/science/is-there-a-link-between-climate-change-and-terrorism-1.3088380> (accessed 13 April 2023).

Mayor of London (2023), 'Stop and search based on the smell of cannabis (2)' [Online] London Assembly Mayoral Question Time available at <https://www.london.gov.uk/who-we-are/what-london-assembly-does/questions-mayor/find-an-answer/stop-and-search-based-smell-cannabis-2#:~:text=Metropolitan%20Police%20policy%20has%20been,reasonable%20grounds%20for%20a%20search> (accessed 7 April 2023).

McCarrick, J, Davis-McCabe, C, and Hirst-Winthrop, S (2016), 'Men's experiences of the criminal justice system following female perpetrated intimate partner violence', *Journal of Family Violence* 31, 203–213 available at <https://doi.org/10.1007/s10896-015-9749-z> (accessed 3 May 2023).

McCarthy, M T (2002), 'USA Patriot Act Recent Developments', *Harvard Journal on Legislation* 39, 435–455, available at <https://heinonline.org/HOL/Page?handle=hein.journals/hjl39&id=1&collection=journals&index=> (accessed 10 April 2023).

McCauley C and Moskalenko S (2017), 'Understanding political radicalization: The two-pyramids model', *The American Psychologist* 72(3), 205–216.

McCormick, AV, Cohen, I M, and Plecas, D (2011), *Reducing recidivism in domestic violence cases*. Centre for Public Safety and Criminal Justice Research, University of the Fraser Valley available at <https://ufv.ca/media/assets/ccjr/reports-and-publications/Reducing_Recidivism_in_Domestic_Violence_2011.pdf> (accessed 3 May 2023).

McEwen, K (2011), *Building resilience at work* (Australian Academic Press).

McGuire, M and Dowling, S (2013), 'Cyber crime: A review of the evidence', Research Report 75 (London: Home Office).

McLean, R, Robinson, G, and Densley, J A (2019), *County lines: Criminal networks and evolving drug markets in Britain* (ebook Springer Briefs in Criminology).

McNaughton, D, Hamlin, D, McCarthy, J, Head-Reeves, D, and Schreiner, M (2007), 'Learning to Listen: Teaching an Active Listening Strategy to Preservice Education Professionals', *Topics in Early Childhood Special Education* 27(4), 223–231.

Mehrabian, A and Feris, S R (1967), 'Inference of attitudes from nonverbal communication in two channels', *Journal of Consulting Psychology* 31(3), 248–252 available at <https://doi.org/10.1037/h0024648> (accessed 21 April 2023).

MI5 (2022), 'MI5 Director General Ken McCallum gives annual threat update' available at <https://www.mi5.gov.uk/news/director-general-ken-mccallum-gives-annual-threat-update#sthash.VcW4UkUq.dpuf> (accessed 27 March 2023).

MI5 (2023a), 'People and Organisation' available at <https://www.mi5.gov.uk/people-and-organisation> (accessed 24 May 2023).

MI5 (2023b), 'Home Page' available at <https://www.mi5.gov.uk/> (accessed 20 February 2023).

MI5 (2023c), 'Threat Levels' available at <https://www.mi5.gov.uk/threat-levels> (accessed 24 May 2023).

MI5 (2023d), 'Introduction to Joint Terrorism Analysis Centre (JTAC)' available at <https://www.mi5.gov.uk/joint-terrorism-analysis-centre> (accessed 20 February 2023).

Millar, A, Devaney, J, and Butler, M (2019), 'Emotional Intelligence: Challenging the Perceptions and Efficacy of "Soft Skills" in Policing Incidents of Domestic Abuse Involving Children', *Journal of Family Violence* 34, 577–588 available at <https://doi.org/10.1007/s10896-018-0018-9> (accessed 21 April 2023).

Mills, J (2021), 'Employee resource groups: Leading the way to greater disability inclusion in policing', *Policing Insight,* available at <https://policinginsight.com/features/opinion/employee-resource-groups-leading-the-way-to-greater-disability-inclusion-in-policing/> (accessed 17 April 2023).

Milne, R and Bull, R (1999), *Investigative Interviewing: Psychology and practice* (Chichester: John Wiley & Sons).

Mind (2022), 'Stress' available at <https://www.mind.org.uk/information-support/types-of-mental-health-problems/stress/signs-and-symptoms-of-stress/> (accessed 17 April 2023).

Mind (2023), 'Dissociation and dissociative disorders' available at <https://www.mind.org.uk/information-support/types-of-mental-health-problems/dissociation-and-dissociative-disorders/about-dissociation/> (accessed 3 May 2023).

Mind and Victim Support (2013), *Police and mental health, How to get it right locally* available at <https://www.mind.org.uk/media-a/2116/2013-12-03-mind_police_final_web.pdf> (accessed 19 April 2023).

Minhas R and Walsh, D (2018), 'Influence of racial stereotypes on investigative decision-making in criminal investigations: A qualitative comparative analysis', *Cogent Social Sciences* [Online] 4(1).

Ministry of Justice (2011), *Achieving Best Evidence* available at <https://www.justice.gov.uk/downloads/legislation/bills-acts/circulars/achieving-best-evidence-circular-2011-03.pdf> (accessed 3 May 2023).

Ministry of Justice (2012), *Getting it right for victims and witnesses* available at <https://consult.justice.gov.uk/digital-communications/victims-witnesses/supporting_documents/gettingitrightforvictimsandwitnesses.pdf> (accessed 1 April 2023).

Ministry of Justice (2015), *Code of Practice for Victims of Crime* available at <https://www.gov.uk/government/uploads/system/uploads/attachment_data/file/470212/code-of-practice-for-victims-of-crime.PDF> (accessed 18 May 2023).

Ministry of Justice (2020), *Code of Practice for Victims of Crime in England and Wales* available at <https://assets.publishing.service.gov.uk/government/uploads/system/uploads/attachment_data/file/974376/victims-code-2020.pdf> (accessed 29 April 2023).

Ministry of Justice (2021), *Delivering Justice for Victims A consultation on improving victims' experiences of the justice system* available at <https://assets.publishing.service.gov.uk/government/uploads/system/uploads/attachment_data/file/1039431/delivering-justice-fo-victims-consultation.pdf> (accessed 1 April 2023).

Ministry of Justice (2022a), *Achieving Best Evidence in Criminal Proceedings* available at <https://assets.publishing.service.gov.uk/government/uploads/system/uploads/attachment_data/file/1051269/achieving-best-evidence-criminal-proceedings.pdf> (accessed 8 March 2023).

Ministry of Justice (2022b), *Multi-agency Public Protection Arrangements (MAPPA) Annual: 2021 to 2022*, available at <https://www.gov.uk/government/statistics/multi-agency-public-protection-arrangements-mappa-annual-2021-to-2022> (accessed 17 March 2023).

Ministry of Justice (2022c), *Criminal Justice Statistics Quarterly, England and Wales, year ending June 2022* available at <https://assets.publishing.service.gov.uk/government/uploads/system/uploads/attachment_data/file/1118309/criminal-justice-statistics-june-2022.pdf> (accessed 19 January 2023).

Ministry of Justice and Youth Justice Board (2015), *Youth Out-of-Court Disposals Guide for Police and Youth Offending Service* available at <https://www.gov.uk/government/uploads/system/uploads/attachment_data/file/438139/out-court-disposal-guide.pdf> (accessed 6 April 2023).

Mirea, M, Wang, V, and Jung, J (2019), 'The not so dark side of the darknet: a qualitative study', *Security Journal* 32(2), 102–118.

Mishra, D S (2017), *Handbook of research methodology: A Compendium for scholars & researchers*. (New Delhi: Educreation Publishing).

Missing People (2021), 'Key Information' available at <https://www.missingpeople.org.uk/for-professionals/policy-and-research/information-and-research/key-information> (accessed 3 May 2023).

Missing People (2023), 'How Can We Help You?' available at <https://www.missingpeople.org.uk/about-the-charity/how-we-help> (accessed 3 May 2023).

Mitchell, R J (2022), *Twenty-one mental models that can change policing: a framework for using data and research for overcoming cognitive bias* (London: Routledge).

Monckton-Smith, J, Szymanska, K, and Haile, S (2017), *Exploring the relationship between stalking and homicide,* Research Repository. University of Gloucestershire in association with Suzy Lamplugh Trust available at <https://eprints.glos.ac.uk/4553/> (accessed 22 March 2023).

Morita, P P and Burns, C M (2014), 'Trust tokens in team development' *Team Performance Management* 20 (1/2), 39–64 available at <https://www.emerald.com/insight/content/doi/10.1108/TPM-03-2013-0006/full/html> (accessed 16 April 2023).

Motor Insurers Bureau (2020), 'Police seize the UK's 2 millionth uninsured vehicle' available at <https://www.mib.org.uk/media-centre/news/2020/february/police-seize-the-uk-s-2-millionth-uninsured-vehicle/> (accessed 22 March 2023).

MPS and CPS (2018), *Joint review of the disclosure process in the case of R v Allan* available at <https://www.cps.gov.uk/sites/default/files/documents/publications/joint-review-disclosure-Allan.pdf> (accessed 14 March 2021).

Muir, R, Higgins, A, Halkon, R, and Walcott, S (2022), *The Final Report of the Strategic Review of Policing in England and Wales. A new mode of protection. Redesigning policing and public safety for the 21st century* The Police Foundation, available at <https://www.policingreview.org.uk/wp-content/uploads/srpew_final_report.pdf> (accessed 16 March 2023).

Munton, J (2021), 'Prejudice as the misattribution of salience', *Analytic Philosophy* 64(1), 1–19 available at <https://onlinelibrary.wiley.com/doi/10.1111/phib.12250> (accessed 22 April 2023).

Muro, Diego (2016), 'What does Radicalisation Look Like? Four Visualisations of Socialisation into Violent Extremism', CIDOB available at <https://www.cidob.org/en/articulos/monografias/resilient_cities/what_does_radicalisation_look_like_four_visualisations_of_socialisation_into_violent_extremism> (accessed 30 May 2023).

Murphy, K (2014), 'Procedural Justice, Legitimacy, and Policing' in G Bruinsma and D Weisburd (eds), *Encyclopedia of Criminology and Criminal Justice* (New York: Springer), available at <https://doi.org/10.1007/978-1-4614-5690-2_65> (accessed 24 May 2023).

Myhill, A (2018), *The police response to domestic violence: Risk, discretion, and the context of coercive control* (Doctoral dissertation, City, University of London).

Myhill, A (2019), 'Renegotiating domestic violence: Police attitudes and decisions concerning arrest', *Policing and Society* 29(1), 52–68.

Nascimento, A M, Andrade, J, and de Castro Rodrigues, A (2022), 'The psychological impact of restorative justice practices on victims of crimes—a systematic review', *Trauma, Violence, & Abuse* available at <https://journals.sagepub.com/doi/10.1177/15248380221082085> (accessed 6 May 2023).

National Audit Office (2016), *Upgrading emergency service communications: the Emergency Services Network* available at <https://www.nao.org.uk/report/upgrading-emergency-service-communications-the-emergency-services-network/> (accessed 4 April 2023).

National Crime Security Centre (2022), *Regional Organised Crime Units* available at <https://www.ncsc.gov.uk/information/regional-organised-crime-units-rocus> (accessed 16 March 2023).

National Police Autism Association, (no date), 'Our Aims' available at <https://www.npaa.org.uk/aims/> (accessed 17 April 2023).

NAPAC (2019), *Survivors?* available at <https://napac.org.uk/wp-content/uploads/2019/10/1_Survivors_A5_web.pdf> (accessed 14 March 2023).

NCA (2017), *National Strategic Assessment of Serious and Organised Crime* available at <https://www.nationalcrimeagency.gov.uk/who-we-are/publications/32-national-strategic-assessment-of-serious-and-organised-crime-2017/file> (accessed 2 April 2023).

NCA (2019), *Intelligence Assessment County Lines Drug Supply, Vulnerability and Harm 2018* available at <https://www.nationalcrimeagency.gov.uk/who-we-are/publications/257-county-lines-drug-supply-vulnerability-and-harm-2018/file> (accessed 15 March 2023).

NCA (2021), 'County Lines' available at <https://www.nationalcrimeagency.gov.uk/what-we-do/crime-threats/drug-trafficking/county-lines> (accessed 15 March 2023).

NCDV (2015a), *ASSIST* available at <https://www.assist.uk.net> (accessed 26 April 2023).

NCDV (2015b), 'Third Party Injunction Referral' available at <http://www.ncdv.org.uk/information-for-police-agencies/third-party-injunction-referral/> (accessed 26 April 2023).

NCPE/ACPO (2006), *Practice advice on professionalising the business of Neighbourhood Policing* available at <http://library.college.police.uk/docs/acpo/Professionalising-NeighbourhoodPolicing.pdf> (accessed 15 March 2023).

Neighbourhood Watch (2020), 'Our Values' available at <https://www.ourwatch.org.uk/about-us/who-we-are/our-values> (accessed 4 April 2023).

Neuman, W L and Robson, K (2018), *Basics of Social Research: Qualitative and Quantitative Approaches*, 4th edn (Ontario: Pearson Canada Inc).

Newburn, T (ed) (2011), *Handbook of Policing*, 2nd edn (Abingdon: Routledge).

Newburn, T (2017), *Criminology*, 3rd edn (Abingdon: Routledge).

Newson, N (2023), *Police and crime panels: Structure, purpose and powers*, House of Lords Library available at <https://lordslibrary.parliament.uk/police-and-crime-panels-structure-purpose-and-powers/> (accessed 24 March 2023).

Newton, S (2017), 'Knife, Gun and Gang Crime and Crime Prevention' available at <https://www.gov.uk/government/news/government-announces-further-funding-to-tackle-gang-related-violence> (accessed 8 May 2023).

New York Times (2022), 'The New York Times is Now Available as a Tor Onion Service' (27 October 2017) available at <https://open.nytimes.com/https-open-nytimes-com-the-new-york-times-as-a-tor-onion-service-e0d0b67b7482> (accessed 2 April 2023).

NHS (2013), 'How to Spot Child Sexual Exploitation' available at <http://www.nhs.uk/livewell/abuse/pages/child-sexual-exploitation-signs.aspx> (accessed 2 March 2023).

NHS Digital (2021), *Female Genital Mutilation July 2021–September 2021* available at <https://digital.nhs.uk/data-and-information/publications/statistical/female-genital-mutilation/july-2021-to-september-2021> (accessed 3 May 2023).

NHS Digital (2022a), 'Stress Busters', available at <https://www.nhs.uk/mental-health/self-help/guides-tools-and-activities/tips-to-reduce-stress/> (accessed 28 May 2023).

NHS Digital (2022b), 'Smoking, Drinking and Drug Use among Young People in England, 2021', available at <https://digital.nhs.uk/data-and-information/areas-of-interest/public-health/smoking-drinking-and-drug-use-among-young-people-in-england> (accessed on 19 January 2023).

Nicholls, M (1991), *Investigating Gunpowder Plot* (Manchester: Manchester University).

Nickolls, L and Allen, G (2022), 'Police powers: Strip Searching' Research Briefing, 8 August 2022, Number CBP 9593, *House of Commons Library Online* available at <https://researchbriefings.files.parliament.uk/documents/CBP-9593/CBP-9593.pdf> (accessed 4 May 2023).

Noon, M (2018), 'Pointless Diversity Training: Unconscious Bias, New Racism and New Agency', *Work, Employment and Society* 32(1), 198–209 available at <https://www.jstor.org/stable/26969786> (accessed 28 May 2023).

Norman, J and Williams, E (2017), 'Putting learning into practice: Self reflections from cops', *European Law Enforcement Research Bulletin* 3, 197–203, available at <https://bulletin.cepol.europa.eu/index.php/bulletin/article/view/294> (accessed 13 May 2023).

NPCC (no date), 'Structure and Membership' available at <https://www.npcc.police.uk/About-Us/structure-and-membership/structure/> (accessed 6 May 2023).

NPCC (2015a), *Advice on the structure of visually recorded witness interviews*, 3rd edn, available at <http://library.college.police.uk/docs/appref/NPCC-(2015)-Guidance-Visually-Recorded-Interviews%203rd%20Edition.pdf> (accessed 10 March 2023).

NPCC (2015b), *Honour based Abuse, Forced Marriage and Female Genital Mutilation* available at <http://library.college.police.uk/docs/appref/Final%20NPCC%20HBA%20strategy%202015%202018December%202015.pdf> (accessed 8 April 2023).

NPCC (2016), *Policing Vision 2025* available at <https://www.npcc.police.uk/SysSiteAssets/media/downloads/publications/policing-vision/policing-vision-2025.pdf> (accessed 6 March 2023).

NPCC (2017), *National Strategy to address the issue of police officers and staff who abuse their position for a sexual purpose* available at <https://npcc.police.uk/documents/Abuse%20of%20position%20for%20sexual%20purpose%20National%20Strategy.pdf> (accessed 2 March 2023).

NPCC (2018a), *NPCC Diversity, Equality and Inclusion Strategy*, available at <https://www.derbyshire-pcc.gov.uk/Document-Library/Transparency/Policy-and-Procedures/NPCC-Diversity-Equality-Inclusion-Strategy-May-2018.pdf> (accessed 27 April 2023).

NPCC (2018b), *National Vulnerability Action Plan 2018–2021* available at <https://npcc.police.uk/documents/crime/2018/National%20Vulnerability%20Action%20Plan_18_21.pdf> (accessed 16 April 2023).

NPCC (2022), *National Roads Policing Strategy 2022–2025* available at <https://library.college.police.uk/docs/NPCC/Roads_Policing_Strategy_2022.25.pdf> (accessed 7 February 2023).

NPIA (2009), 'National Investigative Interviewing Strategy', Briefing Paper, available at <https://zakon.co.uk/admin/resources/downloads/bp-nat-investigative-interviewing-strategy-2009.pdf> (accessed 10 April 2023).

NPIA (2011), *Practice Advice on Critical Incident Management*, National Police Improvement Agency, 2nd edn, available at <http://library.college.police.uk/docs/NPIA/Practice-Advice-on-CIM-Jul2011.pdf> (accessed 8 April 2023).

NPIA and ACPO (2009), *Practice Advice on the Management of Priority and Volume Crime (The Volume Crime Management Model)*, National Police Improvement Agency, 2nd edn, available at <https://staging.profdev.college.police.uk/professional-profile/1474/> (accessed 1 May 2023).

NSPCC (2021a), 'What to do if you suspect child abuse' available at <https://www.nspcc.org.uk/keeping-children-safe/reporting-abuse/what-if-suspect-abuse/> (accessed 3 May 2023).

NSPCC (2021b), *Child Neglect Statistics Briefing* available at <https://learning.nspcc.org.uk/research-resources/statistics-briefings/child-neglect> (accessed 18 May 2023).

NSPCC (2022a), *Half a million children suffer abuse in the UK every year* available at <https://www.nspcc.org.uk/about-us/news-opinion/2022/childhood-day/> (accessed 3 May 2023).

NSPCC (2022b), *Safeguarding d/Deaf and disabled children and young people* available at <https://learning.nspcc.org.uk/safeguarding-child-protection/deaf-and-disabled-children> (accessed 12 May 2023).

Nunn, J (2018), 'The Criminal Histories of Drug-Drive Offenders', *Policing: A Journal of Policy and Practice* 14(2) 456–568 available at <https://academic.oup.com/policing/advance-article/doi/10.1093/police/pay026/4967630> (accessed 21 March 2023).

Nutley, S M, Davies, H T O, and Walter, I (2002), *Evidence based policy and practice: cross sector lessons from the UK*, ESRC UK Centre for Evidence Based Policy and Practice: Working Paper 9.

Oberai, H and Anand, I M (2018), 'Unconscious bias: thinking without thinking.' *Human Resource Management International Digest* 26(6), 14–17.

Office for Health Improvement and Disparities (2022a), *Substance misuse treatment for young people: statistics 2020 to 2021* available at <https://www.gov.uk/government/statistics/substance-misuse-treatment-for-young-people-statistics-2020-to-2021/young-peoples-substance-misuse-treatment-statistics-2020-to-2021-report> (accessed on 19 January 2023).

Office for Health Improvement and Disparities (2022b), *Health disparities and health inequalities: applying All Our Health*, available at <https://www.gov.uk/government/publications/health-disparities-and-health-inequalities-applying-all-our-health/health-disparities-and-health-inequalities-applying-all-our-health> (accessed 27 April 2023).

Office of the Children's Commissioner (2012), *I thought I was the only one. The only one in the world* available at <https://www.childrenscommissioner.gov.uk/report/i-thought-i-was-the-only-one-in-the-world/> (accessed 3 March 2023).

OFSTED (2019), 'What is peer-on-peer abuse?' available at <https://educationinspection.blog.gov.uk/2019/10/04/what-is-peer-on-peer-abuse/> (accessed 20 February 2023).

Oktay, J S and Tompkins, C J (2004), 'Personal assistance providers' mistreatment of disabled adults' *Health & Social Work* 29(3), 177–188.

Olsen-Franchino, H, Silverstein, H A, Kahn, N F, and Martin, S L (2022) 'Physical disabilities and low cognitive ability increase odds of minor sex exchange among adolescent males in the United States', *Journal of Child Sexual Abuse* 31(8), 967–986.

O'Neill, M (2018), *Key Challenges in Criminal Investigation* (Bristol: Policy Press).

ONS (2017), *People who were abused as children are more likely to be abused as an adult,* available at <https://www.ons.gov.uk/peoplepopulationandcommunity/crimeandjustice/articles/peoplewhowereabusedaschildrenaremorelikelytobeabusedasanadult/2017-09-27> (accessed 2 May 2023).

ONS (2018a), *Overview of fraud and computer misuse statistics for England and Wales* available at <https://www.ons.gov.uk/peoplepopulationandcommunity/crimeandjustice/articles/overviewoffraudandcomputermisusestatisticsforenglandandwales/2018-01-25> (accessed 12 March 2023).

ONS (2018b), *Crime in England and Wales: year ending March 2018* available at <https://www.ons.gov.uk/releases/crimeinenglandandwalesyearendingmarch2018> (accessed 2 May 2023).

ONS (2019a), *Population estimates for the UK, England and Wales, Scotland and Northern Ireland: mid-2018* available at <https://www.ons.gov.uk/file?uri=%2Fpeoplepopulationandcommunity%2Fpopulationandmigration%2Fpopulationestimates%2Fdatasets%2Fpopulationestimatesforukenglandandwalesscotlandandnorthernireland%2Fmid20182019laboundaries/ukmidyearestimates20182019ladcodes.xls> (accessed 26 March 2023).

ONS (2019b), *The Nature of Violent Crime in England and Wales: year ending March 2018* available at <https://www.ons.gov.uk/peoplepopulationandcommunity/crimeandjustice/articles/thenatureofviolentcrimeinenglandandwales/yearendingmarch2018> (accessed 16 March 2020).

ONS (2020a), *Ethnicity Pay Gap 2019* available at <https://www.ons.gov.uk/employmentandlabourmarket/peopleinwork/earningsandworkinghours/articles/ethnicitypaygapsingreatbritain/2019> (accessed 27 April 2023).

ONS (2020b), *Deaths registered in England and Wales: 2019* available at <https://www.ons.gov.uk/releases/deathsregisteredinenglandandwales2019> (accessed 22 March 2023).

ONS (2020c), *Crime in England and Wales: Annual supplementary tables* available at <https://www.ons.gov.uk/peoplepopulationandcommunity/crimeandjustice/datasets/crimeinenglandandwalesannusalsupplementarytables> (accessed 13 March 2023).

ONS (2020d), *Domestic abuse prevalence and trends, England and Wales: year ending March 2020* available at: <https://www.ons.gov.uk/peoplepopulationandcommunity/crimeandjustice/articles/domesticabuseprevalenceandtrendsenglandandwales/yearendingmarch2020> (accessed 2 May 2023).

ONS (2021a), *Crime in England and Wales: year ending September 2020*, ONS Statistical Bulletin (3 February 2021), available at <https://www.ons.gov.uk/peoplepopulationandcommunity/crimeandjustice/bulletins/crimeinenglandandwales/yearendingseptember2020> (accessed 31 March 2023).

ONS (2022b), *Homicide in England and Wales* available at <https://www.ons.gov.uk/peoplepopulationandcommunity/crimeandjustice/articles/homicideinenglandandwales/yearendingmarch2021> (accessed 14 March 2023).

ONS (2022c), *Ethnic Group, England and Wales, Census 2021* available at <https://www.ons.gov.uk/peoplepopulationandcommunity/culturalidentity/ethnicity/bulletins/ethnicgroupenglandandwales/census2021> (accessed 28 May 2023).

ONS (2022d), *Police workforce, England and Wales: 31 March 2022* available at <https://www.gov.uk/government/statistics/police-workforce-england-and-wales-31-march-2022/police-workforce-england-and-wales-31-march-2022> (accessed 18 April 2023).

ONS (2022e), *Gender Pay Gap in the UK 2022* available at <https://www.ons.gov.uk/employmentandlabourmarket/peopleinwork/earningsandworkinghours/bulletins/genderpaygapintheuk/2022> (acessed 27 April 2023).

ONS (2022f), *Disability Pay Gap in the UK 2021* available at <https://www.ons.gov.uk/peoplepopulationandcommunity/healthandsocialcare/disability/articles/disabilitypaygapsintheuk/2021> (accessed 27 April 2023).

ONS (2022g), *Domestic abuse and the criminal justice system* available at <https://www.ons.gov.uk/peoplepopulationandcommunity/crimeandjustice/datasets/domesticabuseandthecriminaljusticesystemappendixtables> (accessed 20 April 2023).

ONS (2022h), *Drug misuse in England and Wales: Year ending June 2022* available at <https://www.ons.gov.uk/peoplepopulationandcommunity/crimeandjustice/articles/drugmisuseinenglandandwales/yearendingjune2022> (accessed on 19 January 2023).

ONS (2022i), *Annex: Statistics on the number of police officers assaulted in the year ending March 2022, England and Wales* available at <https://www.gov.uk/government/statistics/police-workforce-england-and-wales-31-march-2022/annex-statistics-on-the-number-of-police-officers-assaulted-in-the-year-ending-march-2022-england-and-wales> (accessed 20 March 2023).

ONS (2023a), *Disability, England and Wales: Census 2021* available at <https://www.ons.gov.uk/peoplepopulationandcommunity/healthandsocialcare/healthandwellbeing/bulletins/disabilityenglandandwales/census2021> (accessed 27 April 2023).

ONS (2023b), *Crime in England and Wales: year ending September 2022, ONS Statistical Bulletin*, available at <https://www.ons.gov.uk/peoplepopulationandcommunity/crimeandjustice/bulletins/crimeinenglandandwales/latest> (accessed 2 March 2023).

Onursal, R and Kirkpatrick, D (2019), 'Is Extremism the "New" Terrorism? The Convergence of "Extremism" and "Terrorism" in British Parliamentary Discourse', *Terrorism and Political Violence* 33(5), 1094–1116

Ostrowsky, M K (2014), 'The Social Psychology of Alcohol Use and Violent Behavior Among Sports Spectators', *Aggression and Violent Behavior* 19(4), 303–310.

Owens, C, Mann, D, and McKenna, R (2014), *The Essex Body Worn Video Trial*, Bureau of Justice Assistance available at <https://bja.ojp.gov/sites/g/files/xyckuh186/files/bwc/pdfs/bwv_reportesstrial.pdf> (accessed 1 May 2023).

Papazoglou, K, Weerasinghe, A, Tuttle, B M, and Blumberg, D M (2019), 'Police Compassion Fatigue and Compassion Satisfaction', *Crisis, Stress, and Human Resilience: An International Journal* 1(2), 2–20.

Papazoglou, K, Marans, S, Keesee, T, and Chopko, B (2020), 'Police compassion fatigue', *FBI Law Enforcement Bulletin* (Online article 9 April 2020) available at <https://leb.fbi.gov/articles/featured-articles/police-compassion-fatigue> (accessed 17 April 2023).

Parrott, DJ and Eckhardt, CI (2018), 'Effects of alcohol on human aggression', *Current Opinion in Psychology* 19, 1–5.

Patel, P (2022), 'Police and Crime Commissioner Review: Part 2' Hansard House of Commons written statements, 7 March, available at <https://hansard.parliament.uk/Commons/2022-03-07/debates/22030711000009/PoliceAndCrimeCommissionerReviewPart2> (accessed 24 March 2023).

PDS and NPTC (2020), *National Policing Digital Strategy 2020–2030: Digital, Data and Technology Strategy. Co-authored by the Police Digital Service and the National Police Technology Council*, Co-published by the Police Digital Service and the National Police Technology Council available at <https://pds.police.uk/national-policing-digital-strategy-2020/> (accessed 6 May 2023).

Pearson-Goff, M and Herrington, V (2014), 'Police leadership: A systematic review of the literature', *Policing: A Journal of Policy and Practice* 8(1), 14–26.

Pease, K and Barr, R (1990), 'Crime Placement, Displacement and Deflection' in *Crime and Justice: A Review of Research* Vol 12 (Chicago: Chicago University Press).

Pease, K (1998), *Repeat Victimisation: Taking Stock* (London: Police Research Group, Home Office).

Pease, K (2002), 'Crime reduction' in M Maguire, R Morgan, and R Reiner (eds), *The Oxford Handbook of Criminology*, 3rd edn (Oxford: Oxford University Press), pp 947–979.

Pease, K and Farrell, G (2016), 'Repeat Victimisation' in R Wortley and M Townsley (eds), *Environmental Criminology and Crime Analysis*, 2nd edn (London: Routledge), pp 199–217.

Pepper, I K and McGrath, R (2020), *Introduction to Professional Policing: Examining the Evidence Base*. (Abingdon: Routledge).

Pickles, J (2020), 'Policing hate and bridging communities: a qualitative evaluation of relations between LGBT+ people and the police within the North East of England', *Policing and Society* (30)7, 741–759.

Pipe, M E, Orbach, Y, Lamb, M, Abbott, C B, and Stewart, H (2008), 'Do best practice interviews with child abuse victims influence case processing?' Final unpublished report submitted to the U.S. Department of Justice.

Polianskaya, A (2018), 'Former Lord Chief Justice warns rapists may now go free after string of prosecutions collapse', *The Independent* (20 January), available at <http://www.independent.co.uk/news/uk/rape-trial-lord-chief-justice-oliver-mears-samson-makele-snaresbrook-crown-court-disclosure-a8169661.html> (accessed 8 May 2023).

Police Foundation (2015), *Neighbourhood Policing, Past, Present and Future* available at <https://www.researchgate.net/profile/John_Chapman6/publication/277018498_Neighbourhood_policing_Past_present_and_future_-_A_review_of_the_literature/links/555f3bd208ae9963a117f164.pdf> (accessed 6 March 2023).

Police Foundation (2022), *The Final Report of the Strategic Review of Policing in England and Wales* available at <https://www.policingreview.org.uk/wp-content/uploads/srpew_final_report.pdf> (accessed 6 March 2023).

Porter, B (1987), *The Origins of the Vigilant State: The London Metropolitan Police Special before the First World War* (Woodbridge: The Boydell Press).

Potter, D J, Hammond, K, Tuffnell, S, Walker, C, and Di Forti, M (2018), 'Potency of Δ9 -tetrahydrocannabinol and other cannabinoids in cannabis in England in 2016: Implications for public health and pharmacology', *Drug Test Analysis* Apr 10(4), 628–635.

Powell, M B and Snow, P C (2007), 'Guide to questioning children during the free narrative phase of an investigative interview', *Australian Psychologist* 42, 57–65.

Powell, M B and Cauchi, R (2011), 'Victims' perceptions of a new model of sexual assault investigation adopted by Victoria Police', *Police Practice and Research: An International Journal* (online first) 14(3), 228–241, available at <10.1080/15614263.2011.641376> (accessed 5 May 2023).

Pringle, K (2022), *Applying & resisting res gestae: Domestic assault*, Exchange Chambers available at <https://www.exchangechambers.co.uk/victimless-prosecution-applying-and-resisting-res-gestae/> (accessed 24 March 2023).

PTSDUK (2023), *Understanding PTSD flashbacks and triggers* available at <https://www.ptsduk.org/what-is-ptsd/understanding-ptsd-flashbacks-and-triggers/?gclid=Cj0KCQjw2cWgBhDYARIsALggUhqLBLtDBB3_JX2dvM7_YbppYkQNDpyVkEtheu6ARb2Spev94ejawwEaAkqAEALw_wcB> (accessed 15 March 2023).

Public Health England (2020), '*No child left behind: Understanding and quantifying vulnerability*' available at <https://assets.publishing.service.gov.uk/government/uploads/system/uploads/attachment_data/file/913974/Understanding_and_quantifying_vulnerability_in_childhood.pdf> (accessed 27 April 2023).

Public Prosecution Service (no date), *Stalking and domestic abuse, cyberstalking and overlap of offences* available at <https://www.ppsni.gov.uk/stalking-and-domestic-abuse-cyberstalking-and-overlap-offences> (accessed 9 May 2023).

Quinton, P (2019), 'Officer strategies for managing interactions during police stops', *Policing and Society* 30(1), 11–27. Routledge, Taylor and Francis Group.

Race Disparity Unit (2021), *Final Report on Progress to Address Covid 19 Health Inequalities*, available at <https://www.gov.uk/government/publications/final-report-on-progress-to-address-covid-19-health-inequalities/final-report-on-progress-to-address-covid-19-health-inequalities> (accessed 27 April 2023).

Rakovec-Felser, Z (2014). 'Domestic violence and abuse in intimate relationship from public health perspective', *Health Psychology Research*, 2(3), 1821.

Ratcliffe, J H (2008), *Intelligence-Led Policing* (Cullompton: Willan).

Rawlings, P J (2002), *Policing: A Short History* (Cullompton: Willan).

Reiner, R (2000), *The Politics of the Police*, 3rd edn (Oxford: Oxford University Press).

Reis, H T (2017), 'The interpersonal process model of intimacy: Maintaining intimacy through self-disclosure and responsiveness' in J Fitzgerald (ed), *Foundations for Couples' Therapy*, pp 216–225. (Abingdon: Routledge).

Restorative Justice Council (2023), 'What is Restorative Justice?' Available at <https://restorativejustice.org.uk/what-restorative-justice> (accessed 1 April 2023).

Reynolds, T, Howard, C, Sjåstad, H, Zhu, L, Okimoto, T G, Baumeister, R F, Aquino, K, and Kim, J (2020), 'Man up and take it: Gender bias in moral typecasting' in *Organizational Behavior and Human Decision Processes* 161, 120–141.

Richards, A (2013), 'Conceptualizing Terrorism', *Studies in Conflict and Terrorism* 37(3), 213–236 (accessed 30 January 2023).

Rickards, T and Moger, S (2000), 'Creative Leadership Processes in Project Team Development: An Alternative to Tuckman's Stage Model', *British Journal of Management* 11(4), 273–284.

Rigg, G, Hill, M, Drew, J, and Gulvin, A (2018), *Our Approach to Ending the Criminal Exploitation of Vulnerable Children and Adults by Gangs, Kent and Medway Gangs Strategy* available at <https://democracy.kent.gov.uk/documents/s90178/Kent%20and%20Medway%20Gangs%20Strategy%202018-21.pdf> (accessed 12 May 2023).

Rivas, E, Bonilla, E, and Vázquez, J J (2020), 'Consequences of the exposure to abuse in the family of origin among victims of intimate partner violence in Nicaragua', *American Journal of Orthopsychiatry* 90(1), 1.

Roach, J (2017), 'Self-selection Policing and the Disqualified Driver', *Policing: A Journal of Policy and Practice* 13(3) 300–311 available at <https://academic.oup.com/policing/article-lookup/doi/10.1093/police/paw056> (accessed 21 March 2023).

Roberts, K P, Lamb, M E, and Sternberg, K J (2004), 'The effects of rapport-building style on children's reports of a staged event', *Applied Cognitive Psychology* 18, 189–202.

Roberts, K, Herrington, V, Jones, W, White, J, and Day, D (2016), 'Police leadership in 2045: The value of education in developing leadership', *Policing: A Journal of Policy and Practice* 10(1), 26–33.

Roberts, N and Price, D (2019), 'Gendered Perceptions of Domestic Violence: how young females are more likely than young males to know controlling domestic violence behaviours' Working Paper, CASS, University of Sunderland available at <https://sure.sunderland.ac.uk/id/eprint/10722/1/CASS%20working%20paper%20No5.pdf> (accessed 11 May 2023).

Robinson, G, McLean, R, and Densley, J (2019), 'Working County Lines: Child Criminal Exploitation and Illicit Drug Dealing in Glasgow and Merseyside', *International Journal of Offender Therapy and Comparative Criminology* 63(5), 694–711.

Robson, C (2011), *Real World Research: A Resource for Social Scientists and Practitioner Researchers*, 3rd edn (Oxford: Blackwell).

Rocci, A and Saussure, L D (eds) (2016), *Verbal communication* (Berlin: De Gruyter, Inc.)

Rose, G (2000), 'The criminal histories of serious traffic offenders', HORS 206 (London: Home Office).

Ross, A (2018), 'Police officer sacked after looking up partners on force database', *Express & Star*, available at <https://www.expressandstar.com/news/crime/2018/05/22/police-officer-sacked-over-misuse-of-database/> (accessed 3 May 2023).

Rowe, M (2008), *Introduction to Policing*, 2nd edn (London: Sage Publications).

Rowe, M (2018), *Introduction to Policing*, 3rd edn (London: Sage Publications).

Royal College of Psychiatrists (2019), 'Domestic violence and abuse for parents and carers' available at <https://www.rcpsych.ac.uk/mental-health/parents-and-young-people/information-for-parents-and-carers/domestic-violence-and-abuse-for-parents> (accessed 20 February 2023).

Royal Commission (2017), *Royal Commission into Institutional Responses to Child Sexual Abuse* available at <https://www.childabuseroyalcommission.gov.au/final-report> (accessed 19 April 2023).

Royal United Services Institute (RUSI) (2015), *A Democratic License to Operate: Report of the Independent Surveillance Review* available at <https://rusi.org/explore-our-research/publications/whitehall-reports/a-democratic-licence-to-operate-report-of-the-independent-surveillance-review> (accessed 20 March 2023).

Rudd, A (2016), 'Home Secretary's College of Policing speech on vulnerability', College of Policing Annual Conference on Vulnerability, 30 November 2016, available at <https://www.gov.uk/government/speeches/home-secretarys-college-of-policing-speech-on-vulnerability> (accessed 11 May 2023).

Ruggeri, K, Garcia-Garzon, E, Maguire, A, Matz, S, and Huppert, FA (2020), 'Well-being is more than happiness and life satisfaction: a multidimensional analysis of 21 countries', *Health and Quality of Life Outcomes* 18(192), 1–16 available at <https://hqlo.biomedcentral.com/articles/10.1186/s12955-020-01423-y> (accessed 17 April 2023).

Sacks, V and Murphey, D (2018), *The prevalence of adverse childhood experiences, nationally, by state, and by race or ethnicity*, Child Trends available at <https://www.childtrends.org/publications/prevalence-adverse-childhood-experiences-nationally-state-race-ethnicity> (accessed 11 May 2023).

Safeguarding Hub (2020), *County Lines—Get a step ahead by improving your knowledge* available at <https://safeguardinghub.co.uk/county-lines-get-a-step-ahead-by-improving-your-knowledge/> (accessed 16 March 2023).

Safe Lives (2014), *Multi-Agency Risk Assessment Conferences* available at <https://safelives.org.uk/sites/default/files/resources/MARAC%20FAQs%20General%20FINAL.pdf> (accessed 1 April 2023).

Sampson, F (2021), *Annual Report 2019: Commissioner for the Retention and use of Biometric Material* available at <https://assets.publishing.service.gov.uk/government/uploads/system/uploads/attachment_data/file/1036487/E02669527_Biometrics_Commissioner_ARA_2020_Text_Elay.pdf> (accessed 12 March 2023).

Sarantakos, S (2013), *Social Research*, 4th edn (London: Palgrave Macmillan).

Saunders, M, Lewis, P, and Thornhill, A (2009). *Research methods for business students*. (London: Pearson Education).

Scarman, Lord (1981), *Report into the Brixton Disorders*, Cmnd 8427 (London: HMSO).

Scarman, L G (1982), *The Scarman Report: The Brixton Disorders 10-12 April 1981 Report of an inquiry by the Rt Hon The Lord Scarman*. (Harmondsworth: Penguin).

Schaubhut, N A (2007), 'Technical Brief for the Thomas-Kilmann Conflict Mode Instrument', CPP Research Department available at <https://kilmanndiagnostics.com/wp-content/uploads/2018/04/TKI_Technical_Brief.pdf> (accessed 18 April 2023).

Schmid, A (2004), 'Terrorism—The Definitional Problem', *Case Western Reserve Journal of International Law* 36(2), 375–419.

Schön, D (1983), *The Reflective Practitioner: How Professionals Think in Action* (New York: Basic Books).

Schrems, B M (2014), 'Informed consent, vulnerability and the risks of group-specific attribution' *Nursing Ethics* 21(7), 829–843.

Scientific Advisory Group for Emergencies (2022), *COVID-19 Ethnicity subgroup: Interpreting differential health outcomes among minority ethnic groups in wave 1 and 2, 24 March 2021* available at <https://www.gov.uk/government/publications/covid-19-ethnicity-subgroup-interpreting-differential-health-outcomes-among-minority-ethnic-groups-in-wave-1-and-2-24-march-2021/covid-19-ethnicity-subgroup-interpreting-diffe

rential-health-outcomes-among-minority-ethnic-groups-in-wave-1-and-2-24-march-2021> (accessed 27 April 2023).

Scorer, C (1980), 'The United Kingdom Prevention of Terrorism Acts, 1974 and 1976', Human Rights in the Northern Ireland Conflict: 1968-80, *The International Journal of Politics* 10(1), 105–111.

Scottish Government (2021), *Homicide in Scotland 2020–2021: statistics* available at <https://www.gov.scot/publications/homicide-scotland-2020-2021/> (accessed 14 March 2023).

Sebire, J (2020), 'Why gender equality in policing is important for achieving United Nations Sustainable Development Goals 5 and 16', *International Journal for Crime, Justice and Social Democracy* 9(1), 80–85.

Seidler, P and Adderley, R (2013), 'Criminal Network Analysis inside Law Enforcement Agencies: A Data-Mining System Approach under the National Intelligence Model', *International Journal of Police Science & Management* 15(4), 323–337 available at <https://doi.org/10.1350/ijps.2013.15.4.321> (accessed 12 April 2023).

Sentencing Council (2012a), *Offences taken into consideration and totality—definitive guideline* available at <https://www.sentencingcouncil.org.uk/publications/item/offences-taken-into-consideration-and-totality-definitive-guideline/> (accessed 1 May 2023).

Sentencing Council (2012b), *Assault: Definitive Guideline* available at <https://www.sentencingcouncil.org.uk/publications/item/assault-definitive-guideline/> (accessed 20 March 2023).

Sentencing Council (2014a), *Sexual assault. Sentencing Council Guidance* available at <https://www.sentencingcouncil.org.uk/offences/magistrates-court/item/sexual-assault/> (accessed 2 March 2023).

Sentencing Council (2014b), *Offences at Magistrates Court: Voyeurism. Sentencing Council Guidance* available at <https://www.sentencingcouncil.org.uk/offences/magistrates-court/item/voyeurism/> (accessed 2 March 2023).

Sentencing Council (2022), *Out of Court Disposals* available at <https://www.sentencingcouncil.org.uk/explanatory-material/magistrates-court/item/out-of-court-disposals/> (accessed 1 March 2023).

Sentencing Council (2023a), *Sentencing Guidelines, Possession of a Controlled Drug* available at <https://www.sentencingcouncil.org.uk/offences/crown-court/item/possession-of-a-controlled-drug-2/> (accessed 20 January 2023).

Sentencing Council (2023b), *Sentencing Guidelines, Production of a controlled drug/Cultivation of a cannabis plant* available at <https://www.sentencingcouncil.org.uk/offences/crown-court/item/production-of-a-controlled-drug-cultivation-of-cannabis-plant-2/> (accessed 20 January 2023).

Sentencing Council (2023c), *Explanatory Material, Out of Court Disposals/Community Resolution* available at <https://www.sentencingcouncil.org.uk/explanatory-material/magistrates-court/item/out-of-court-disposals/6-community-resolution/> (accessed 16 March 2023).

Seymore, A (2001), 'Kirkholt Burglary Prevention Project' in *Crime Victims Report* 5(1), 3, 10, 12.

Sharp, D and Atherton, S (2007), 'To Serve and Protect?: The Experiences of Policing in the Community of Young People from Black and Other Ethnic Minority Groups', *The British Journal of Criminology* 47(5), 746–763.

Shawcross, W (2023), *Independent Review of Prevent*, available at <https://assets.publishing.service.gov.uk/government/uploads/system/uploads/attachment_data/file/1134986/Independent_Review_of_Prevent.pdf> (accessed 18 April 2023).

Shepherd, E (2008), *SE3R: A Resource Book*, 4th edn (East Hendred: Forensic Solutions).

—— and Griffiths, A (2021), *Investigative Interviewing: The Conversation Management Approach*, 3rd edn (Oxford: Oxford University Press).

Sherman, L W (1998), 'Ideas in American Policing: Evidence Based Policing', Police Foundation lecture series available at <<https://www.cebma.org/wp-content/uploads/Sherman-Evidence-Based-Policing.pdf> (accessed 10 April 2023).

Sherman, L W, Gartin, P R and Buerger, M E (1989), 'Hot Spots of Predatory Crime: Routine Activities and the Criminology of Place', *Criminology* 27, 27–56.

Sherman, L W, Strang, H, Barnes, G C, and Woods D J (2006), 'Race and Restorative Justice', Paper presented to the American Society of Criminology, Los Angeles, November.

Signal A I (2019), 'Lessons from Christchurch: How the media finally acknowledged far-right terrorism', Signal AI blogpost, available at <https://www.signal-ai.com/blog/lessons-from-christchurch-how-the-media-finally-acknowledged-far-right-terrorism> (accessed 11 April 2023).

Silva, S C, Silva, R M, Pinto, R C, and Salles, R M (2013), 'Botnets: A survey', *Computer Networks* 57(2), 378–403.

Silvestri, M (2006), '"Doing Time": Becoming a Police Leader', *International Journal of Police Science & Management* 8(4), 266–281.

Sivagurunathan, M, Orchard, T, MacDermid, J C, and Evans, M (2019), 'Barriers and facilitators affecting self-disclosure among male survivors of child sexual abuse: The service providers' perspective', *Child Abuse & Neglect* 88, 455–465.

Skogan, W G (2006), 'Asymmetry in the Impact of Encounters with Police', *Policing and Society* 16(2), 99–126 available at <DOI: 10.1080/10439460600662098> (accessed 21 April 2023).

Skogan, W G and Steiner, L (2004), *Community Policing in Chicago, year ten* (Chicago, IL: Illinois Criminal Justice Information Authority).

Smith, G (2018), 'The proposed changes to the UK Investigatory Powers Act', *Privacy and Data Protection* 18(3), 16–17.

Smith, G, Hagger Johnson, H, and Roberts, C (2012), 'Disproportionality in police professional standards' [online]. Greater Manchester Police available at <https://www.escholar.manchester.ac.uk/api/datastream?publicationPid=uk-ac-man-scw:170650&datastreamId=FULL-TEXT.PDF> (accessed 7 April 2023).

Smith, G, Hagger Johnson, H, and Roberts, C (2015), 'Ethnic minority police officers and disproportionality in misconduct proceedings', *Policing and Society* 25(6), 561–578.

Smith, M J and Tilley, N (2005), *Crime Science: New approaches to preventing and detecting crimes* (Cullompton: Willan).

Spalek, B (2006), *Crime Victims: Theory, Policy and Practice* (Basingstoke: Palgrave-Macmillan).

Spencer, J (2016), *Evidence of Bad Character*, 3rd edn (Oxford: Hart Publishing).

Spencer, J R (2016), 'Adversarial vs inquisitorial systems: is there still such a difference?', *International Journal of Human Rights* 20(5), 601–660.

Spicer, J (2021), *Policing County Lines: Responses to Evolving Provincial Drug Markets* (Basingstoke: Palgrave Macmillan).

Squires, P (2017), 'Anti-social behaviour' in A Brisman, E Carrabine, and N South (eds), *The Routledge Companion to Criminological Theory and Concepts* (London: Routledge), pp 427–430.

Stangor, C (2000), *Stereotypes and Prejudices: Key Readings in Social Psychology*. (Philapelphia, USA: Taylor & Francis).

Stanley, N, Miller, P, Richardson Foster, H, and Thomson, G (2010), *Children and families experiencing domestic violence: police and children's social services' responses*, University of Central Lancashire online store available at <http://clok.uclan.ac.uk/2947/1/children_experiencing_domestic_violence_report_wdf70355.pdf> (accessed 11 May 2023).

Sternberg, R J and Soriano, L J (1984), 'Styles of Conflict Resolution', *Journal of Personality and Social Psychology*, 47, 115–126.

Stone, D N, Heen, S, and Patton, B (2010), *Difficult conversations: How to discuss what matters most* (Harmondsworth: Penguin Books).

Stone, N (2018), 'Child Criminal Exploitation: "County Lines", Trafficking and Cuckooing', *Youth Justice* 18(3), 285–293.

Stonewall (2018a), 'LGBT in Britain, Health Report', available at <https://www.stonewall.org.uk/system/files/lgbt_in_britain_health.pdf> (accessed 27 April 2023).

Stonewall (2018b), 'LGBT in Britain, Home and Communities', available at <https://www.stonewall.org.uk/sites/default/files/lgbt_in_britain_home_and_communities.pdf> (accessed 27 April 2023).

Stonewall (2018c), 'LGBT in Britain, Work Report', available at <https://www.stonewall.org.uk/system/files/lgbt_in_britain_work_report.pdf> (accessed 27 April 2023).

Stonewall (2022), 'Rainbow Britain', available at <https://www.stonewall.org.uk/system/files/rainbow_britain_report.pdf> (accessed 27 April 2023).

Strang, H, Neyroud, P, and Sherman, L (2014), 'Tracking the evidence for a "mythical number": Do UK domestic abuse victims suffer an average of 35 assaults before someone calls the police?', *Policing* 8(2), 222–228. Available at <HMIC> (accessed 19 April 2023).

Strang, H, Sherman, L, Angel, C M, Woods, D J, Bennett, S, Newbury-Birch, D, and Inkpen, N (2006), 'Victim Evaluations of Face-to-Face Restorative Justice Conferences: A Quasi-Experimental Analysis', *Journal of Social Issues* 62(2), 281–306.

Tajfel, H (ed) (1978), *Differentiation Between Social Groups: Studies in the Social Psychology of Intergroup Relations* (London: Academic Press).

Taylor, K (1986), 'Learning for self-direction in the classroom: The pattern of a transition process', *Studies in Higher Education* 11(1), 55–72.

Telegraph (2019), 'Gina Martin: how I got the law changed and made upskirting illegal', *The Telegraph* available at <https://www.telegraph.co.uk/women/life/gina-martin-got-law-changed-made-upskirting-illegal/> (accessed 2 March 2023).

Teng, E, Zhang, L, and Lou, M (2020), 'I Am Talking but Are You Listening? The Effects of Challenge and Hindrance Stressors on Effective Communication', *Human Performance* 33(4), 241–257.

Thames Valley Police (2018), 'Thames Valley Police Sharing Thames Valley Police research and practice' in *TVP Journal* 1(1) available at <https://www.thamesvalley.police.uk/SysSiteAssets/foi-media/thames-valley-police/other_information/tvp-journal---volume-1---first-edition---april-2018.pdf> (accessed 12 April 2023).

The Brain Charity, (no date), 'Neurodivergent, neurodiversity and neurotypical: a guide to the terms' available at <https://www.thebraincharity.org.uk/neurodivergent-neurodiversity-neurotypical-explained/#:~:text=While%20some%20individuals%20do%20refer,both%20neurodivergent%20and%20neurotypical%20individuals> (accessed 17 April 2023).

Tierney, J (2009), *Key Perspectives in Criminology* (Maidenhead: Open University Press).

Tilley, N (2008a), *The Development of Community Policing in England: Networks, Knowledge and Neighbourhoods* (Chichester, UK: John Wiley & Sons, Ltd.), pp 95–116.

Tilley, N (2008b), 'Modern Approaches to Policing: Community, problem-orientated and intelligence-led' in T Newburn (ed), *Handbook of Policing* (Cullompton: Willan), pp 373–403.

Tilley, N (2016), 'EMMIE and engineering: What works as evidence to improve decisions?', *Evaluation* 22(3), 304–322.

Tjosvold, D, Wong, A S, and Feng Chen, N Y (2014), 'Constructively managing conflicts in organizations', *Annual Review of Organizational Psychology and Organizational Behavior* 1, 545–568.

Tong, S (2008), 'Interagency Approaches to Policing' in T Newburn and P Neyroud (eds), *Dictionary of Policing* (Cullompton: Willan), pp 148–149.

Tor (2016), 'Tor' available at <https://www.torproject.org/> (accessed 15 March 2023).

Tuckman, B W (1964), 'Personality structure, group composition, and group functioning', *Sociometry* 27(4), 469–487.

Tuckman, B W and Jensen, M A (1977), 'Stages of small-group development revisited', *Group and Organization Studies* 2(4), 419–427.

Tuffin, R, Morris, J, and Poole, A (2006), *An Evaluation of the Impact of the National Reassurance Policing Programme* (London: Home Office).

Tyler, T R (1990), *Why people obey the Law* (New Haven, CT: Yale University Press).

Tyler, T R (2003), 'Procedural justice, legitimacy, and the effective rule of law' in M Tonry (ed), *Crime and Justice: A Review of Research*, Vol 30 (Chicago, IL: Chicago University Press), pp 431–505.

UK Missing Persons Unit (2018), 'Who We Are' available at <http://missingpersons.police.uk/en-gb/about-mpu/who-we-are> (accessed 8 April 2023).

UK Missing Persons Unit (2021) *Missing Persons Data Report 2020/21* National Crime Agency available at <https://missingpersons.police.uk/en-gb/resources/downloads/missing-persons-statistical-bulletins> (accessed 3 March 2023).

UK Trauma Council. (No date), 'Trauma', available at <https://uktraumacouncil.org/trauma/trauma> (accessed 17 April 2023).

United Nations (2001), Resolution 1368 *Threats to international peace and security caused by terrorist acts* available at <http://unscr.com/en/resolutions/1368> (accessed 10 April 2023).

Vallano, J P and Schreiber Compo, N (2015), 'Rapport-building with cooperative witnesses and criminal suspects: A theoretical and empirical review', *Psychology, Public Policy, and Law* 21(1), 85–99.

Van Dongen, T (2010), 'Mapping Counterterrorism: A Categorization of Policies and the Promise of Empirically Based, Systematic Comparisons', *Critical Studies on Terrorism* 3(2), 227–241.

Vasanthakumari, S (2019), 'Soft skills and its application in work place', *World Journal of Advanced Research and Reviews* 3(2), 66–72.

Victim & Witness Care Unit (2022), 'Attending Court' available at <https://victimandwitnesscare.org.uk/court.php> (accessed 1 April 2023).

Victims' Commissioner (2020), Rape Survivors and the criminal justice system available at <https://victimscommissioner.org.uk/document/rape-survivors-and-the-criminal-justice-system/> (accessed 1 April 2023).

Victims' Commissioner (2021), *New survey reveals low victim confidence, as Victims' Commissioner warns victims remain an 'afterthought'* available at <https://victimscommissioner.org.uk/news/2021-victim-survey/> (accessed 1 April 2023).

—— (2022*), 2021/22 Annual Report Dame Vera Baird QC Victims' Commissioner for England and Wales* available at <https://s3-eu-west-2.amazonaws.com/jotwpublic-prod-storage-1cxo1dnrmkg14/uploads/sites/6/2022/06/MOJ7216_Victims-commisioner-Annual-report_AW-WEB.pdf> (accessed 1 April 2023).

Victim Support (2020), *Understanding shame and guilt* available at <https://www.victimsupport.org.uk/wp-content/uploads/2020/11/P2661CSA-survivors-shame.pdf> (accessed 15 March 2023).

—— (2023), 'How crime can affect you' available at <https://www.victimsupport.org.uk/help-and-support/coping-crime/how-can-crime-affect-you/> (accessed 14 March 2023).

Vodafone (2018), *Vodafone Foundation and Hestia launch the UK's first app to provide nationwide domestic abuse support* available at <https://www.vodafone.co.uk/newscentre/press-release/bright-sky-launches/> (accessed 12 April 2023).

Vrij, A, Dragt, A, and Koppelaar, L (1992), 'Interviews with ethnic interviewees: non-verbal communication errors in impression formation', *Journal of Community & Applied Social Psychology* 2(3), 199–208.

Vrij, A and Firmin, H R (2001), 'Beautiful thus innocent? The impact of defendants' and victims' physical attractiveness and participants' rape beliefs on impression formation in alleged rape cases', *International Review of Victimology* 8(3), 245–255.

Waddington, P A J (1999), *Policing Citizens* (London: UCL Press).

Waddington, P A J (2013), 'Introduction' in P A J Waddington, J Kleinig, and M Wright (eds), *Professional Police Practice. Scenarios and Dilemmas*. (Oxford: Oxford University Press), pp 3–24.

Waddington, P A J, Wright, M, Williams, K, and Newburn, T (2017), *How People Judge Policing* (Oxford: Oxford University Press).

Walker, H E, Freud, J S, Ellis, R A, Fraine, S M, and Wilson, L C (2019). 'The prevalence of sexual revictimization: A meta-analytic review', *Trauma, Violence, & Abuse* 20(1), 67–80.

Walker, R (2019), 'Deeds, Not Words: The Suffragettes and Early Terrorism in the City of London', *The London Journal* 45(1), 53–64.

Walklate, S, Fitz-Gibbon, K, and McCulloch, J (2017), 'Is more law the answer? Seeking justice for victims of intimate partner violence through the reform of legal categories', *Criminology and Criminal Justice* 23(11), 1–17. Available at <https://journals.sagepub.com/doi/pdf/10.1177/1748895817728561> (accessed 9 May 2023).

Walsh, D and Milne, R (2008), 'Keeping the PEACE? A study of investigative interviewing practices in the public sector', *Legal and Criminological Psychology* 13(1), 395–397.

Warr, M (1987), 'Fear of victimization and sensitivity to risk', *Journal of Quantitative Criminology* 3, 29–46.

Weaver, M (2010), 'Animal rights activists jailed for terrorising suppliers to Huntingdon Life Sciences', *The Guardian* available at: <https://www.theguardian.com/science/2010/oct/25/animal-research-animal-welfare#:~:text=Sarah%20Whitehead%2C%2053%2C%20Nicole%20Vosper,years%20at%20Winchester%20crown%20court> (accessed 31 March 2023).

Wedlock, E and Tapley, J (2016), *What Works in Supporting Victims of Crime,* Victims' Commissioner available at <https://victimscommissioner.org.uk/published-reviews/what-works-in-supporting-victims-of-crime-a-rapid-evidence-assessment/> (accessed 12 April 2023).

Weir, J (2007), [2007] NICC 49, The Queen v Sean Hoey (Belfast: Lady Chief Justice Office) available at <https://www.judiciaryni.uk/sites/judiciary/files/decisions/Queen%20v%20Sean%20Hoey.pdf> (accessed 13 April 2023).

Weisburd, D (2015), 'Small worlds of crime and criminal justice interventions: discovering crime hot spots' in MD Maltz and SK Rice (eds), *Envisioning Criminology* (New York: Springer), pp 261–267.

Weisburd, D, Telep, CW, Hinkle, JC, and Eck, JE (2010), 'Is problem-oriented policing effective in reducing crime and disorder?', *Criminology and Public Policy* 9(1), 139–172.

What Works (2015), *Restorative Justice (RJ) Conferencing*, College of Policing available at <http://whatworks.college.police.uk/toolkit/Pages/Intervention.aspx?InterventionID=24> (accessed 6 April 2023).

Whelehan, N (2012), *The Dynamiters: Irish Nationalism and Political Violence in the Wider World, 1867-1900* (Cambridge University Press: Cambridge).

WHO (2020), *Burnout an 'occupational phenomenon': International Classification of Diseases* available at <https://www.who.int/news/item/28-05-2019-burn-out-an-occupational-phenomenon-international-classification-of-diseases> (accessed 17 April 2023).

WHO (2023), *Classification of Female Genital Mutilation* available at <https://www.who.int/news-room/fact-sheets/detail/female-genital-mutilation> (accessed 1 May 2023).

Wicks, J, Nakisher, S, and Grimm, L (2023), 'Emotional Intelligence'. *Salem Press Encyclopedia of Health* (Cambridge Massachusetts: Harvard) available at <https://search.ebscohost.com/login.aspx?direct=true&db=ers&AN=93871908&site=eds-live> (accessed 20 April 2023).

Wigmore, J (2018), *Recognising & acting on signs of 'county lines' child exploitation: A case study*, NHS available at <https://www.england.nhs.uk/wp-content/uploads/2018/11/recognising-acting-on-signs-of-county-lines.pdf> (accessed 16 March 2023).

Williams, A and Finlay, F (2018), 'County lines: how gang crime is affecting our young people', *Archives of Disease in Childhood* 104, 730–732.

Williams, S and Coupe, T (2017), 'Frequency Vs. Length of Hot Spots Patrols: a Randomised Controlled Trial', *Cambridge Journal of Evidence-Based Policing* 1(1), 5–21.

Wilson, JQ (1996), 'On deterrence' in J Muncie, E McLaughlin, and M Langan (eds), *Criminological Perspectives: A reader* (London: Sage Publications).

Wilson, JQ and Kelling, G (1982), 'Broken windows', *Atlantic Monthly*, March, 29–38.

Wilson, R and Adams, I (2015), *Special Branch: A History: 1883–2006* (London: Biteback Publishing).

Windle, J, Moyle, L, and Coomber, R (2020), 'Vulnerable kids going country: children and young people's involvement in county lines drug dealing', *Youth Justice* 20(1-2), 64–78.

Winkel, F and Vrij, A (1990), 'Interaction and impression formation in a cross-cultural dyad: frequency and meaning of culturally determined gaze behavior in a police interview setting', *Social Behavior* 5(5), 335–350.

Wixted, J T, Mickes, L, and Fisher, R P (2018), 'Rethinking the reliability of eyewitness memory', *Perspectives on Psychological Science* 13(3), 324.

Wolpert, M, Harris, R, Hodges, S, Fuggle, P, James, R, Wiener, A, McKenna, C, Law, D, York, A, Jones, M, and Fonagy, P (2015), *THRIVE elaborated*, CAHMS Press available at <https://www.annafreud.org/media/3214/thrive-elaborated-2nd-edition29042016.pdf> (accessed 11 May 2023).

Women's Aid (2020a), 'What is Coercive Control?' available at <https://www.womensaid.org.uk/information-support/what-is-domestic-abuse/coercive-control/#1510155261553-02d2b1d3-af67> (accessed 14 March 2023).

Women's Aid (2020b), *Women's Aid statement on the Royal Assent of the domestic abuse bill* available at <https://www.womensaid.org.uk/womens-aid-statement-on-the-royal-assent-of-the-domestic-abuse-bill/#:~:text=%E2%80%9CFour%20years%20after%20the%20domestic%20abuse%20bill%20was,organisations%20who%20have%20made%20this%20new%20law%20possible.> (accessed 2 May 2023).

Women's Aid (2020c), 'Why don't women leave abusive relationships?' available at <https://www.womensaid.org.uk/information-support/what-is-domestic-abuse/women-leave/> (accessed 3 May 2023).

Wong, K and Christmann, K (2016), 'Increasing hate crime reporting: Narrowing the gap between policy aspiration, victim inclination and agency capability', *British Journal of Community Justice* 14(3), 5–23.

Wood, D A (2016), 'The importance of liberal values within policing: police and crime commissioners, police independence and the spectre of illiberal democracy', *Policing and Society: An International Journal of Research and Policy* 26(2), 148–164.

Wood, D A (2020), *Towards ethical policing* (Bristol: Bristol University Press).

Wood, D A, Cockcroft, T, Tong, S, and Bryant, R (2017), 'The importance of context and cognitive agency in developing police knowledge: going beyond the police science discourse', *The Police Journal* 91(2), 173–187.

Wood, J M, McClure, K A, and Birch, R A (1996), 'Suggestions for improving interviews in child protection agencies', *Child Maltreatment* 1, 223– 230.

Wright, J E and Headley, A M (2021), 'Can technology work for policing? Citizen perceptions of police-body worn cameras', *The American Review of Public Administration* 51(1), 17–27.

Wright, K L, Etchells, M J, and Watson, N (2018), 'Meeting in the Middle: Eight Strategies for Conflict Mediation in Your Classroom', *Kappa Delta Pi Record* 54(1), 30–35.

Wrigley, A and Dawson, A, (2016), 'Vulnerability and marginalized populations' in D H Barrett, L W Ortmann, A Dawson, C Saenz, A Reis, and G Bolan (eds), *Public Health Ethics: Cases Spanning the Globe* (Cham: Springer Nature), pp 203–240.

Zaccaro, S, Kemp, C, and Bader, P (2004), 'Leader traits and attributes', *The Nature of Leadership* 101, 124.

Zhang, J, Chang, J P, Danescu-Niculescu-Mizil, C, Dixon, L, Hua, Y, Thain, N, and Taraborelli, D (2018), *Conversations Gone Awry: Detecting Early Signs of Conversational Failure*, (New York: Cornell University Press).

Ziemer, J (2016), 'Rethinking Radicalism' LSEblog (27 October 2016) available at <https://blogs.lse.ac.uk/polis/2016/10/27/rethinking-radicalism/> (accessed 18 April 2023).

Zvi, L (2022), 'Police Perceptions of Sex-worker Rape Victims and Their Offenders: A Vignette Study', *Journal of Interpersonal Violence* 37(15–16), NP14189–NP14214.

Index

Tables are indicated by *t* following the page number

D

E

F

J

K

L

S

W

Y

Z